March 29–April 1, 2015
Atlanta, Georgia, USA

Association for
Computing Machinery

Advancing Computing as a Science & Profession

IUI'15

Proceedings of the 20th ACM International Conference on
Intelligent User Interfaces

Sponsored by:

ACM SIGAI and ACM SIGCHI

Supported by:

Google, Microsoft Research, Yahoo Labs, eBay, HPCC Systems, and Symantec

Association for
Computing Machinery

Advancing Computing as a Science & Profession

The Association for Computing Machinery
2 Penn Plaza, Suite 701
New York, New York 10121-0701

Notice to Past Authors of ACM-Published Articles
ACM intends to create a complete electronic archive of all articles and/or other material previously published by ACM. If you have written a work that has been previously published by ACM in any journal or conference proceedings prior to 1978, or any SIG Newsletter at any time, and you do NOT want this work to appear in the ACM Digital Library, please inform permissions@acm.org, stating the title of the work, the author(s), and where and when published.

ISBN: 978-1-4503-3306-1 (Digital)

ISBN: 978-1-4503-3768-7 (Print)

Additional copies may be ordered prepaid from:

ACM Order Department
PO Box 30777
New York, NY 10087-0777, USA

Phone: 1-800-342-6626 (USA and Canada)
+1-212-626-0500 (Global)
Fax: +1-212-944-1318
E-mail: acmhelp@acm.org
Hours of Operation: 8:30 am – 4:30 pm ET

Printed in the USA

Welcome

It is with great pleasure that we welcome you to the 2015 ACM International Conference on Intelligent User Interfaces – ACM IUI 2015 in Atlanta, Georgia, USA. Starting in 1993, ACM IUI is now in its 20th edition and serves as a premier international forum for reporting outstanding research and development on intelligent user interfaces. ACM IUI is where the Human-Computer Interaction (HCI) community meets the Artificial Intelligence (AI) community. We are also very interested in contributions from related fields, such as psychology, behavioral science, cognitive science, computer graphics, design, the arts, etc.

At ACM IUI, we focus on the interaction between machine intelligence and human intelligence. While other conferences focus on one side or the other, we address the complex interaction between the two. We welcome research that explores how to make the interaction between computers and people smarter, which may leverage solutions from data mining, knowledge representation, novel interaction paradigms, and emerging technologies.

For the 20th edition of the conference, the call for papers attracted a record number of 205 long and short paper submissions, 41 poster paper submissions, 18 demo paper submissions, and 24 student consortium submissions. The final program of the conference includes 3 keynotes, 47 long and short papers (22.9% acceptance rate), 17 posters, 8 demos, 4 workshops, 3 tutorials, and 12 student consortium papers. The program opens with a keynote by Professor Dan Weld on "Intelligent Control of Crowdsourcing", continues with a keynote by Ed Chi on "Blurring of the Boundary Between Interactive Search and Recommendation" on the second day, and ends with a keynote by Rosalind Picard on "Recognizing Stress, Engagement, and Positive Emotion". Four workshops (Personalized Access to Cultural Heritage, Intelligent Digital Games for Empowerment and Inclusion, Interacting with Smart Objects, and Visual Text Analytics) and three tutorials (Speech-based Interaction, Personalization for Behavior Change, and User Affect and Sentiment Modeling) complement the main conference program.

The conference could not be organized without the help of a large number of individuals who volunteered a lot of their own time and enthusiasm. Their names can be found on the following pages. The organization committee has worked very hard and a big thank you goes to all people who helped overcome all sorts of problems. We must also thank our senior program committee for coordinating the review process and all the members of the program committee for providing high quality reviews. And, most important, we must thank the authors for providing the content for a never seen number of submissions, and also those whose papers could not be included in the 22.9% selected for the program. Finally, we must thank our sponsors, ACM, SIGCHI and SIGART, AAAI, as well as our generous corporate supporters (found on the following pages).

We hope you will find the program interesting and thought-provoking. We also hope the conference will provide you with a valuable opportunity to share ideas with other researchers and practitioners from around the world, leading to further advancements in the field of intelligent user interfaces.

Oliver Brdiczka, Polo Chau
ACM IUI 2015 General Co-Chairs

Giuseppe Carenini, Shimei Pan, Per Ola Kristensson
ACM IUI 2015 Program Co-Chairs

Table of Contents

Interactive Machine Learning / Decision Making / Topic Modeling / Robotics

Recommenders / Web

Personalization / Adaptation / Recommendation / Sentiment

Visualization / Video / Augmented Reality

Affect / Health

Tutorials

Workshops

ACM IUI 2015 International Conference on Intelligent User Interfaces — Organization

General Chairs: Oliver Brdiczka *(Vectra Networks, Inc.)*
Polo Chau *(Georgia Tech)*

Program Chairs: Giuseppe Carenini *(University of British Columbia)*
Shimei Pan *(University of Maryland)*
Per Ola Kristensson *(University of Cambridge)*

Treasurer: Jalal Mahmud *(IBM Research)*

Sponsorship Chair: Sumit Basu *(Microsoft Research)*

Workshop and Tutorial Chairs: Ben Steichen *(University of British Columbia)*
Nava Tintarev *(University of Aberdeen)*

Poster and Demo Chairs: Sven Kratz *(FXPAL)*
Eelco Herder *(L3S)*

Student Consortium Chairs: Wai-Tat Fu *(University of Illinois at Urbana-Champaign)*
Brent Hecht *(University of Minnesota)*

Publicity Chairs: Matthijs van Leeuwen *(KU Leuven)*
Jilles Vreeken *(Max Planck Institute of Informatics)*
Alan Said *(Recorded Future)*
Ali Jahanian *(Purdue University)*

Senior Program Committee:

Gregory Abowd
Elisabeth Andre
Liliana Ardissono
Sumit Basu
Shlomo Berkovsky
Pradipta Biswas
Fang Chen
Ashok Goel
Joaquim Jorge
Matthijs van Leeuwen
Henry Lieberman
Christian Mueller
Petteri Nurmi
Nuria Oliver
Cecile Paris
Fabio Paterno
Catherine Pelachaud
Chris Schmandt
Amanda Stent
Simone Stumpf
Manas Tungare
Keith Vertanen
Jilles Vreeken
Chen Yu

Program Committee:

Safurah Abdul Jalil
Fadel Adib
Aaron Adler
Ana Afonso
Elena Agapie
Imtiaj Ahmed
Dzmitry Aliakseyeu
Bilal Alsallakh
Florian Alt
Saleema Amershi
Anima Anandkumar
Fraser Anderson
Salvatore Andolina
Michelle Annett
Craig Anslow

Lisa Anthony
Cláudia Antunes
Bruno Araujo
Kamyar Ardekani
Ahmed Arif
Kenneth Arnold
Kumaripaba Athukorala
Oscar Kin-Chung Au
Ignacio Avellino
Myroslav Bachynskyi
Sriram Karthik Badam
Zhen Bai
Tyler Baldwin
Rafael Ballagas
Tadas Baltrusaitis
Betul Batun
Patrick Baudisch
Joerg Baus
Christian Becker-Asano
Roman Bednarik
Steve Benford
Goran Bergqvist
Sven Bertel
F.J. Bex
Ganesh Bhutkar
Nadia Bianchi-Berthouze
Rafael Bidarra
Gautam Biswas
Alan Blackwell
Rachel Blagojevic
Marco Blumendorf
Francesca Bonin
Sebastian Boring
Nis Bornoe
Paolo Bottoni
Matt-Mouley Bouamrane
François Bouchet
Judy Bowen
Jay Bradley
Joel Brandt
Michael Brock
A.J. Brush
Peter Brusilovsky
George Buchanan
Andreas Bulling
Andrea Bunt
Margaret Burnett
Jim Burton
Heloisa Candello
Angelo Cafaro
Pável Calado
Gaelle Calvary
Pedro Campos
Jose Campos
Karina Caro
Juan Pablo Carrascal
Luis Carriço
Mark Cartwright
Jessica Cauchard
Marc Cavazza
Federica Cena
Daniel Cernea
Pablo Cesar
Allison Chaney
Samir Chatterjee
Debaleena Chattopadhyay
Ge Chen
Xiang 'Anthony' Chen
Zhenyu Chen
Alex Qiang Chen
Jingyuan Cheng
Keith Cheverst
Jun Dong Cho
Mathieu Chollet
Ming Ki Chong
Jason Chuang
Dahee Chung
Karen Church
José Coelho
Nathalie Colineau
Ashley Colley
Kay Connelly
Amelie Cordier
Mark Cottman-Fields
Michael Crabb
Sally Jo Cunningham
Franco Curmi
Aba-Sah Dadzie
Florian Daiber
Ionut Damian
Andreea Danielescu
Sauvik Das
Scott Davidoff
Nadja De Carolis
Luigi De Russis
Aidan Delaney
Nicola Dell
Alexandre Demeure
Carrie Demmans Epp
Sarah Diefenbach
Stefan Diewald
Shalaka Dighe
Karthik Dinakar
Anke Dittmar
Divya Bansal Divya Bansal
Paul Dourish
Fan Du
Sumit Gulwani
Carlos Duarte
Andrew Duchowski
Henry Duh
Cody Dunne
Varun Dutt
James Eagan
David England
Barrett Ens
Irfan Essa
Bernd Ewert
Myriam Frejus
Robert Farrell
Andrew Faulring
Karla Felix Navarro
Tom Feltwell
Jennifer Ferreira
Denzil Ferreira
Francesco Ferrise
Bruce Ferwerda
Rebecca Fiebrink
Leah Findlater

Daniel Fitton
David Flatla
Scott Fleming
Eelke Folmer
Manuel Fonseca
Angus Forbes
Andrew Fowler
Jill Freyne
Christopher Fry
Chi-Wing Fu
Jochen Huber
Steve Funke
Susanne Furman
Krzysztof Gajos
William Gaver
Patrick Gebhard
Sven Gehring
Gretchen Gelke
Hans Gellersen
Cristina Gena
Werner Geyer
Giuseppe Ghiani
Marco Gillies
Romain Giot
Patrick Girard
Elena Glassman
Mayank Goel
Jennifer Golbeck
Steven Gomez
David Gotz
Liang Gou
Visda Goudarzi
Sten Govaerts
Anna Goy
Nitesh Goyal
Saul Greenberg
Tobias Grosse-Puppendahl
Paul Groth
Jens Grubert
Dan Gruen
Tiago Guerreiro
Jan Gugenheimer
Enkelejda Kasneci
Philip Guo
Rongkai Guo
Anhong Guo
Sidhant Gupta
Eben Haber
Jonna Hakkila
Scott Hale
Martin Halvey
William Hamilton
Tracy Hammond
Kotaro Hara
Marian Harbach
Erik Harpstead
Daniel Harrison
Chris Harrison
Kirstie Hawkey
Brent Hecht
Elliott Hedman
Christin Henzen
Eelco Herder
Thomas Hermann
Ken Hinckley
Liangjie Hong
Sungsoo (Ray) Hong
Enamul Hoque
Eva Hornecker
Steven Houben
Pei-Yun Hsueh
Mengdie Hu
Mao Huang
Andrew Kun
Pei-Yi Kuo
Shah Rukh Humayoun
Axel Hösl
Kori Inkpen
Stephen Intille
Shamsi Iqbal
Tobias Isenberg
Jason Jacques
Javier Jaen
Mohit Jain
Dietmar Jannach
Caroline Jay
Sampath Jayarathna
Haiyan Jia
Jiepu Jiang
Priscilla Jimenez Pazmino
Bonnie John
Michael Johnston
Brian Jones
Park Joongsin
Tejinder Judge
Hyunggu Jung
Marko Jurmu
Antti Jylhä
Pradyot K biswas
Gerrit Kahl
Sanjay Kairam
Santosh Kalwar
Alexandros Karatzoglou
Sarvnaz Karimi
Kostas Karpouzis
Pedro Lopes
Pasquale Lops
Konstantinos Kazakos
Rubaiat Habib Kazi
Simeon Keates
Kerstin Keil
Caitlin Kelleher
Maryam Khademi
Mohammadreza Khalilbeigi
Peter Kiefer
Jeeeun Kim
HyungSeok Kim
Reuben Kirkham
Felix Kistler
Styliani Kleanthous
Mark Klein
Franziska Klügl
Peter Knees
Søren Knudsen
Andrew Ko
Christian Koehler
Boriana Koleva
Oleg Komogortsev
Matthias Kranz

Kyriakos Kritikos
Jan-Peter Krämer
Antonio Krüger
Thomas Kubitza
Tsvi Kuflik
Todd Kulesza
Arun Kulshreshth
Vikas Kumar
Alex Mitchell
Monika Mitrevska
Darya Kurilova
Sandeep Kaur Kuttal
Bum Chul Kwon
Andol LI
Thomas LaToza
Shyong Lam
Patrick Langdon
Walter Lasecki
Neal Lathia
Yann Laurillau
Sungjin Lee
Uichin Lee
Chaiwoo Lee
Jong-Seok Lee
Luis A. Leiva
Catherine Letondal
Margot Lhommet
Jane Li
Shuowei Li
Thomas Lieber
Henry A. Lieberman
James Lin
Jimmy Lin
Rhema Linder
Lars Lischke
Meizhu Liu
Ying Hsang Liu
Tomek Loboda
Ronan Longergan
Ricardo Lopes
Zhihan Lv
Alex Olwal
Tihomir Orehovacki

Pilar Orero
Zhihan Lu
Jie Lu
Bernd Ludwig
Christopher Lueg
Kurt Luther
Kris Luyten
Markus Löchtefeld
Lindsay MacDonald
Blair MacIntyre
Allan MacLean
Haley MacLeod
Sylvain Malacria
Marco Manca
Jennifer Mankoff
Jennifer Marlow
Diogo Marques
William Marsh
Roberto Martinez Maldonado
Mikhil Masli
Cindy Mason
Masood Masoodian
Tara Matthews
Michael Mauderer
Christopher Mayer
David McGee
Daniel Mendes
Xiaojun Meng
Rafał Michalski
Robert Miller
Fatemeh Rajabiyazdi
Ramesh Raju
Raf Ramakers
Manas Mittal
Leonel Morales Diaz
Fabio Morreale
Ahmed E. Mostafa
Christos Mousas
Adiyan Mujibiya
Cosmin Munteanu
Emerson Murphy-Hill
Mirco Musolesi
Bilge Mutlu

Frank Nack
Hideyuki Nakanishi
Yukiko Nakano
Kim Nam Wook
N. Hari Narayanan
Fedelucio Narducci
Majid Nasirinejad
Michael Nebeling
Surya Nepal
Grace Ngai
Tien Nguyen
Karin Niemantsverdriet
Onyinyechukwu Nnadi (chigbo)
Pedro Nogueira
Diana Nowacka
Nuno Nunes
John O'Donovan
Timo Ojala
Thomas Olsson
Arvind Satyanarayan
Christopher Scaffidi
Florian Schaub
Jason Orlosky
Lucas Paletta
Ye Pan
Aasish Pappu
Alexandros Paramythis
Deokgun Park
Souneil Park
Aman Parnami
Paul Parsons
Evan Peck
Ruggero Pensa
Lucas Pereira
Giovanna Petrone
Tamara Peyton
Martin Pielot
Thomas Pietrzak
Laura Pina
Till Plumbaum
Scott Pobiner
Benjamin Poppinga

Christopher Power
Rui Prada
María Prato
Felix Putze
Yin Qu
Pernilla Qvarfordt
Frederic Raber
Emilee Rader
Erin Solovey
Yale Song
Daniel Sonntag
Danny Soroker
Martin Raubal
Khasfariyati Razikin
Janet Read
Sofia Reis
Steven Reiss
Norbert Reithinger
Yosra Rekik
Christian Remy
Kui Ren
Philippe Renevier Gonin
Peter Robinson
Simon Robinson
Michael Rohs
Elizabeth Rosenzweig
Thijs Roumen
Rebekah Rousi
Paulami Roy Choudhury
Spencer Rugaber
Nicolas Sabouret
Ramik Sadana
Alireza Sahami Shirazi
Alan Said
André Salgado
Jose San Pedro
Carmen Santoro
Olga Santos
Sanat Sarangi
Sayan Sarcar
Ha Trinh
Frank Trollmann
Hien Truong
Huawei Tu
Michael Schellenbach
Stefan Scherer
Gianluca Schiavo
Albrecht Schmidt
Dominik Schmidt
Martin Schmitz
Oliver Schneider
Stacey Scott
Kenneth Scott-Brown
Michael Sedlmair
Hasti Seifi
Ted Selker
Jonghoon Seo
Jinwook Seo
Teddy Seyed
Metin Sezgin
Orit Shaer
S. Andrew Sheppard
Roy Shilkrot
Frank Shipman
Sajad Shirali-Shahreza
Mark Shovman
Paula Alexandra Silva
Aneesha Singh
Pushpendra Singh
R. Singh
Laurianne Sitbon
Jan Smeddinck
Mathias Wilhelm
Jason D Williams
John Williamson
Maria Wolters
Caleb Southern
Lucio Davide Spano
Lucio Davide Spano
Lübomira Spassova
Rob Speer
Robert St. Amant
Richard Stallman
Chad Steed
Ben Steichen
Svetlana Stoyanchev
Yuta Sugiura
Bongwon Suh
Shamik Sural
Craig Sutherland
Federico Tajariol
Peter Thomas
Edison Thomaz
Feng Tian
Nava Tintarev
Marko Tkalcic
Kashyap Todi
Kashyap Todi
Dereck Toker
Mercan Topkara
Thomas Torsney-weir
Takumi Toyama
Scott Trent
Vlad Trifa
Victor de Boer
Lilian de Greef
Alwin de Rooij
Anuradha Uduwage
Heli Väätäjä
Haley Vaigneur
Dimitar Valkov
Max Van Kleek
Herwin van Welbergen
Jean Vander Donckt
Keith Vander Linden
Radu-Daniel Vatavu
Swaroop Vattam
Ansh Verma
Jo Vermeulen
Emanuel von Zezschwitz
Romain Vuillemot
Erin Walker
James Wallace
Wen Wang
Tao Wang
Na Wang
Ji Wang
Jingtao Wang
William Yang Wang

Morten Warncke-Wang
Gloria Washington
Rainer Wasinger
Daryl Weir
Justin Weisz
Komminist Weldemariam
Weng-Keen Wong
Kanit Wongsuphasawat
Liming Xu
Anbang Xu
Qianli Xu
Yi Yang
Svetlana Yarosh
Yina Ye
Sang Ho Yoon
Neil Yorke-Smith
James Young
Kun Yu
Chen-Hsiang Yu
John Zaientz
Massimo Zancanaro
Cheng Zhang
Bo Zhang
Kunpeng Zhang
Tong Zhang
Dejin Zhao
Yu Zhong
Jianlong Zhou
Kening Zhu
Roshanak Zilouchian-Moghaddam
John Zimmerman
Arkaitz Zubiaga

Poster & Demo Reviewers:

Ragaad Al Tarawneh
Michelle Annett
Liliana Ardissono
Bo Begole
Shlomo Berkovsky
Federico Botella
Gaelle Calvary
Michael Crabb
Luigi De Russis
Vania Dimitrova
Fan Du
Carlos Duarte
Guihuan Feng
Bruce Ferwerda
Chris Frisina
Steve Funke
Leman Gul
Tracy Hammond
Michael Heidt
Christin Henzen
Eelco Herder
Shah Rukh Humayoun
Germaine Irwin
Dhiraj Joshi
Jeeeun Kim
Styliani Kleanthous
Bart Knijnenburg
Soren Knudsen
Birgitta Koenig-Ries
Sven Kratz
Tsvi Kuflik
Rodrigo Laiola Guimaraes
Shyong Lam
Samantha LeVan
Agnes Lisowska Masson
Ying Hsang Liu
Chulhong Min
Toni-Jan Keith Monserrat
Frank Nack
Petteri Nurmi
Jason Orlosky
Sameer Patil
Celeste Paul
Pernilla Qvarfordt
Fatemeh Rajabiyazdi
Raf Ramakers
Christian Remy
Philippe Renevier Gonin
Michael Rohs
Thijs Roumen
Alan Said
Yann Savoye
Ben Steichen
Carlo Strapparava
Simone Stumpf
Wu-Chen Su
Zachary Toups
Christoph Trattner
Nikos Tsourakis
Ilyas Uyanik
Emanuel von Zezschwitz
Romain Vuillemot
Yulin Wang
Pawel Wozniak
Huichuan Xia
Guo Yu
Xiaojun Yuan
Lv Zhihan
Kening Zhu
Arkaitz Zubiaga

Student Consortium Mentors:

Elizabeth Andre
Joyce Chai
Krzysztof Gajos
Yolanda Gil
Anthony Jameson
Henry Lieberman
Robert St. Amant
Michelle Zhou

ACM IUI 2015 Sponsors & Supporters

Sponsors:

Silver Supporters:

Bronze Supporters:

Lanyard:

Intelligent Control of Crowdsourcing

Daniel S. Weld
Department of Computer Science & Engineering
University of Washington
Seattle, Washington 98195, USA
weld@cs.washington.edu

Abstract

Crowd-sourcing labor markets (e.g., Amazon Mechanical Turk) are booming, because they enable rapid construction of complex workflows that seamlessly mix human computation with computer automation. Example applications range from photo tagging to audio-visual transcription and interlingual translation. Similarly, workflows on citizen science sites (e.g. GalaxyZoo) have allowed ordinary people to pool their effort and make interesting discoveries. Unfortunately, constructing a good workflow is difficult, because the quality of the work performed by humans is highly variable. Typically, a task designer will experiment with several alternative workflows to accomplish a task, varying the amount of redundant labor, until she devises a control strategy that delivers acceptable performance.

Fortunately, this control challenge can often be formulated as an automated planning problem ripe for algorithms from the probabilistic planning and reinforcement learning literature. I describe our recent work on the decision-theoretic control of crowd sourcing and suggest open problems for future research. In particular, I discuss:

- The use of partially-observable Markov decision Processes (POMDPs) to control voting on binary-choice questions and iterative improvement workflows [3].
- Decision-theoretic methods that dynamically switch between alternative workflows in a way that improves on traditional (static) A-B testing [4].
- A novel workflow for crowdsourcing the construction of a taxonomy — a challenging problem since it demands a global perspective of the input data when no one worker sees more than a tiny fraction [2, 1].
- Methods for optimizing the acquisition of labeled training data for use in machine learning applications; this an important special case, since data annotation is often crowd- sourced [5].

Author Keywords: crowdsourcing; planning; adaptive interfaces

IUI 2015, March 29–April 1, 2015, Atlanta, GA, USA.
ACM 978-1-4503-3306-1/15/03.
http://dx.doi.org/10.1145/2678025.2700997

Short Bio

Daniel S. Weld is Thomas J. Cable / WRF Professor of Computer Science & Engineering at the University of Washington and an Entrepreneurial Faculty Fellow. After formative education at Phillips Academy, he received bachelor's degrees in both CS and Biochemistry at Yale University in 1982. He landed a Ph.D. from the MIT Artificial Intelligence Lab in 1988, received a Presidential Young Investigator's award in 1989, an Office of Naval Research Young Investigator's award in 1990, was named AAAI Fellow in 1999 and deemed ACM Fellow in 2005. Dan was a founding editor for the Journal of AI Research, was area editor for the Journal of the ACM, guest editor for Computational Intelligence and Artificial Intelligence, and was Program Chair for AAAI-96. Dan has published two books and scads of technical papers.

Dan is an active entrepreneur with several patents and technology licenses. He co-founded Netbot Incorporated, creator of Jango Shopping Search (acquired by Excite), AdRelevance, a monitoring service for internet advertising, (acquired by Media Metrix), Nimble Technology, a data integration company (acquired by Actuate). Dan is a Venture Partner at the Madrona Venture Group, and a member of the Technical Advisory Boards for the Allen Institute for Artificial Intelligence, Context Relevant, Spare5, and Madrona.

References

1. Bragg, J., Mausam, and Weld, D. S. Crowdsourcing multi-label classification for taxonomy creation. In HCOMP (2013).
2. Chilton, L., Little, G., Edge, D., Weld, D., and Landay, J. Cascade: Crowdsourcing taxonomy creation. In CHI '13, ACM Press (New York, NY, USA, 2013).
3. Dai, P., Lin, C., Mausam, and Weld, Daniel, J. S. POMDP-based control of workflows for crowdsourcing. *Artificial Intelligence* 202 (2013), 52–85.
4. Lin, C. H., Mausam, and Weld, D. S. Dynamically switching between synergistic workflows for crowd-sourcing. In AAAI (2012).
5. Lin, C. H., Mausam, and Weld, D. S. To Re(label), or not to Re(label). In HCOMP (2014).

Blurring of the Boundary Between Interactive Search and Recommendation

Ed H. Chi
Google, Inc.
Mountain View, California, USA
chi@acm.org

Abstract

Search and recommendation engines are increasingly more intelligent. They have become more personalized and social as well as more interactive. No longer just offering ten blue links, search engines have increasingly been integrated with task and item recommenders directly, for example, to offer news, movie, music, and dining suggestions. Vice versa, recommendation systems have increasingly became more search-like by offering capabilities that enable users to tune and direct recommendation results instantly.

As the two technologies evolve toward each other, there is increasingly a blurring of the boundary between these two approaches to interactive information seeking. On the search side, this is driven by the merging of question answering capabilities with search, led by systems like Google Now and Apple Siri that move search toward intelligent personal assistants. On the recommendation side, there has been a merging of techniques from not just keyword search but also faceted search, along with user-based and item-based collaborative filtering techniques and other more proactive recommenders.

This blurring has resulted in both critical re-thinking about not just how to architect the systems by merging and sharing backend components common to both types of systems, but also how to structure the user interactions and experiences.

ACM Classification

H.3.5. On-line Information Services; H.1.2 User/Machine Systems: Human information processing.

Author Keywords: Search Engine; Recommendation; Interaction.

Short Bio

Ed H. Chi is a Staff Research Scientist at Google, leading a team in social computing and recommender research. With over 30 patents and over 90 publications, he is known for research in Web and online social sites, and the effects of social signals on user behavior, as well as past research on web data mining and user modeling, information visualization, and crowdsourcing. Previous to Google, he was the Area Manager and a Principal Scientist at Palo Alto Research Center's Augmented Social Cognition Area. He completed three degrees (B.S., M.S., and Ph.D.) in 6.5 years from University of Minnesota. He was recently recognized as an ACM Distinguished Scientist. In his spare time, Ed is an avid photographer and snowboarder.

IUI 2015, March 29–April 1, 2015, Atlanta, GA, USA.
ACM 978-1-4503-3306-1/15/03.
http://dx.doi.org/10.1145/2678025.2700997

Recognizing Stress, Engagement, and Positive Emotion

Rosalind W. Picard
MIT Media Lab, picard@media.mit.edu
Empatica Inc, rp@empatica.com
http://affect.media.mit.edu/publications.php

Abstract
An intelligent interaction should not typically call attention to emotion. However, it almost always involves emotion: For example, it should engage, not inflict undesirable stress and frustration, and perhaps elicit positive emotions such as joy or delight. How would the system sense or recognize if it was succeeding in these elements of intelligent interaction? This keynote talk will address some ways that our work at the MIT Media Lab has advanced solutions for recognizing user emotion during everyday experiences.

ACM Classification
A.0 General: Biographies, I.5 Pattern Recognition, J.3 Life and Medical Sciences, Health

Author Keywords: Affective computing; wearable sensors; emotion recognition; autonomic nervous system

Biography

Professor Rosalind W. Picard, Sc.D. is founder and director of the Affective Computing Research Group at the Massachusetts Institute of Technology (MIT) Media Lab where she also leads the MIT Media Lab's Advancing Wellbeing initiative. Picard has co-founded two businesses, Empatica, Inc. creating wearable sensors and analytics to improve health, and Affectiva, Inc. delivering software to help measure and communicate emotion, especially through facial expression analysis.

Picard holds a bachelor's degree in electrical engineering with highest honors from the Georgia Institute of Technology, and masters and doctorate degrees, both in electrical engineering and computer science, from MIT. She started her career as a member of the technical staff at AT&T Bell Laboratories, where she designed VLSI chips and algorithms for image compression.

IUI 2015, March 29–April 1, 2015, Atlanta, GA, USA.
ACM 978-1-4503-3306-1/15/03.
http://dx.doi.org/10.1145/2678025.2700999

In 1991 she joined the MIT faculty where she became internationally known for constructing mathematical texture models for content-based retrieval of images and for pioneering methods of automated search and annotation in digital video including creation of the Photobook system.

In 1996 she wrote and published the book Affective Computing, which envisioned a new area of research and became instrumental in starting a new field by that name. Today that field has its own journal, international conference, and professional society. Picard was also a founding member of the IEEE Technical Committee on Wearable Information Systems in 1998, helping launch the field of wearable computing.

Picard has authored or co-authored over two hundred scientific articles and chapters spanning computer vision, pattern recognition, machine learning, human-computer interaction, wearable sensors and affective computing. She is a recipient of several best paper prizes, including work on machine learning with multiple models (with Minka, 1998), a best theory paper prize for affect in human learning (with Kort and Reilly, 2001) a best paper prize for work with facial expressions (with McDuff, Kaliouby and Demirdjian, 2013) and the best UBICOMP paper for an automated conversation coach (with Hoque et al, 2013). Her paper (with Healey, 2005) showing how to measure driver stress won best paper of the decade 2000-2009 for IEEE Intelligent Transportation Systems.

Picard is an active inventor with patents including wearable and non-contact sensors, algorithms, and systems for sensing, recognizing, and responding respectfully to human affective information. Her inventions have applications in autism, epilepsy, sleep, stress, autonomic nervous system disorders, depression, human and machine learning, health behavior change, market research, customer service, and human-computer interaction and usability research. In 2005 she was named a Fellow of the IEEE for contributions to image and video analysis and affective computing. Picard has been honored with dozens of distinguished and named lectureships and other international awards. She has given over 100 keynote talks.

Picard has served on numerous international and national science and engineering program committees, editorial boards, and review panels, including the Advisory Committee for the National Science Foundation's (NSF's) division of Computers in Science and Engineering (CISE), and the Advisory Board for the Georgia Tech College of Computing. Picard has also served on non-profit boards, including a school for children with special needs, and a pro-life organization to help women with crisis pregnancies.

Picard interacts regularly with industry and has consulted for companies including Apple, AT&T, BT, HP, i.Robot, Merck, Motorola, and Samsung. Her group's achievements have been featured in forums for the general public such as The New York Times, The London Independent, National Public Radio, Scientific American Frontiers, ABC's Nightline and World News Tonight, Time, Vogue, Wired, Voice of America Radio, New Scientist, and BBC programs such as "Hard Talk" and BBC Horizon with Michael Mosley. Picard lives in Newton, Massachusetts with her amazing husband and three energetic sons.

REFERENCES

[1] Healey, J., Picard, R.W. "Detecting Stress During Real-World Driving Tasks Using Physiological Sensors," *IEEE Trans. on Intelligent Transportation Systems*, Volume 6, No. 2, June 2005, pp. 156-166

[2] Picard, R.W. (2009), "Future Affective Technology for Autism and Emotion Communication," *Philosophical Transactions of the Royal Society B: Biological Sciences*, doi: 10.1098/rstb.2009.0143 Phil. Trans. R. Soc. B 12 December 2009 vol. 364 no. 1535 3575-3584.

[3] Poh, M-Z, Swenson, N-C, Picard R.W. (2010), "A Wearable Sensor for Unobtrusive, Long-term Assessment of Electrodermal Activity," *IEEE Transactions on Biomedical Engineering*, Volume 57, Number 5, pp. 1243-1252. May 2010. doi: 10.1109/TBME.2009.2038487.

[4] Picard, R.W. (2010), "Emotion research by the people, for the people," *Emotion Review,* Volume 2, Issue 3, July 2010.

[5] Poh, M.Z., Loddenkemper, T., Reinsberger, C., Swenson, N.C., Goyal, S., Madsen, J.R., Picard, R.W. (2012) "Autonomic Changes with Seizures Correlate with Postictal EEG Suppression," *Neurology*, Volume 78, Number 23, 1868-1876, June 5, 2012.

[6] Hoque, M.E., McDuff, D.J., Picard, R.W. (2012), "Exploring Temporal Patterns in Classifying Frustrated and Delighted Smiles," *IEEE Transactions on Affective Computing*, Volume 3, Issue 3, September 2012.

[7] Dinakar, K., Jones, B., Havasi, C., Lieberman, H., Picard, R.W. (2012) "Common Sense Reasoning for Detection, Prevention, and Mitigation of Cyber bullying." *ACM Transactions on Interactive Intelligent Systems,* archive, Volume 2 Issue 3, September 2012, Article No. 18. doi>10.1145/2362394.2362400.

[8] Sano A., Picard R.W., "Recognition of Sleep Dependent Memory Consolidation with Multi-modal Sensor Data", *The 10th Annual Body Sensor Networks Conference 2013*, Cambridge, MA, May 2013.

[9] McDuff D., Kaliouby R., Senechal T., Amr M., Cohn J., Picard R.W., "AMFED Facial Expression Dataset: Naturalistic and Spontaneous Facial Expressions Collected In-the-Wild", *The 2013 IEEE Computer Society Conference on Computer Vision and Pattern Recognition Workshops (CVPRW'10),* Portland, OR, USA, June 2013.

[10] Hoque, M. E., Courgeon, M., Martin, J.-C., Mutlu, B., Picard, R. W., "MACH: My Automated Conversation coacH", 15th International Conference on Ubiquitous Computing (Ubicomp), September 8-12, 2013.

[11] McDuff, D., Gontarek, S. & Picard, R. W., "Improvements in Remote Cardio-Pulmonary Measurement Using a Five Band Digital Camera." *Transactions on Biomedical Engineering*, (To Appear).

[12] Picard, R. W., Fedor, S., & Ayzenberg Y., "Multiple Arousal Theory and Daily-Life Electrodermal Activity Asymmetry" *Emotion Review*, (To Appear).

[13] Hernandez, J.*, Hoque, M. E.*, Drevo, W., Picard, R.W., "Mood Meter: Counting Smiles in the Wild", Proceedings of International Conference on Ubiquitous Computing (Ubicomp), Pittsburgh, PA, September 5-8, 2012. (*equal contribution)

Improving Inquiry-Driven Modeling in Science Education through Interaction with Intelligent Tutoring Agents

David A. Joyner
Design & Intelligence Lab.
Georgia Institute of Technology
85 5th Street NW
Atlanta, GA 30332
david.joyner@gatech.edu

Ashok K. Goel
Design & Intelligence Lab.
Georgia Institute of Technology
85 5th Street NW
Atlanta, GA 30332
goel@cc.gatech.edu

ABSTRACT
This paper presents the design and evaluation of a set of intelligent tutoring agents constructed to teach teams of students an authentic process of inquiry-driven modeling. The paper first presents the theoretical grounding for inquiry-driven modeling as both a teaching strategy and a learning goal, and then presents the need for guided instruction to improve learning of this skill. However, guided instruction is difficulty to provide in a one-to-many classroom environment, and thus, this paper makes the case that interaction with a metacognitive tutoring system can help students acquire the skill. The paper then describes the design of an exploratory learning environment, the Modeling and Inquiry Learning Application (MILA), and an accompanying set of metacognitive tutors (MILA–T). These tools were used in a controlled experiment with 84 teams (237 total students) in which some teams received and interacted with the tutoring system while other teams did not. The effect of this experiment on teams' demonstration of inquiry-driven modeling are presented.

Author Keywords
Metacognitive tutoring; scientific discovery; scientific inquiry; discovery-based learning; inquiry-based learning; constructionism; guided instruction.

ACM Classification Keywords
K.3.1: Computer Uses in Education (Computer-Assisted Instruction); I.2.11: Distributed Artificial Intelligence (Intelligent Agents); J.3 Life and Medical Sciences.

INTRODUCTION
Constructionism has been one of the dominant theories of modern instructional design for several decades. Originating from the theories of Jean Piaget [38] and Seymour Papert [37], constructionist learning approaches advocate learning in open-ended environments where the learner plays a significant role in driving the learning goals and outcomes. Constructionist learning approaches come in various forms, such as discovery-based learning [19], problem-based learning [14], project-based learning [5], experiential learning [29], and inquiry-based learning [13].

IUI 2015, March 29–April 1, 2015, Atlanta, GA, USA.
Copyright 2015 © ACM 978-1-4503-3306-1/15/03...$15.00.
http://dx.doi.org/10.1145/2678025.2701398.

An inquiry-oriented approach to science education has two valuable effects. First, the literature on discovery-based learning points to improvements to student engagement and learning through participation with such a pedagogical approach [42, 46, 48]. Second, inquiry and discovery are valuable in and of themselves because they are authentic representations of participation in real scientific research. One goal of early science education is to stoke students' mastery of science and interest in science careers [43]; toward this end, participation in an authentic exercise is a valuable learning experience on its own [21].

However, these constructionist learning approaches are not without valid criticisms. Kirchner, Sweller, & Clark argue, from both theoretical and empirical viewpoints, that purely unguided or minimally-guided instructional approaches are insufficient [27]. Rather, they suggest that guided instruction is critical early in the learning process. Guided instruction, they argue, provides the learner with the foundational knowledge and skills necessary to begin to drive their own discovery and learning. Other studies have similarly corroborated the weakness of discovery-oriented approaches in certain settings and domains [28, 32].

The work presented here addresses this need for guided instruction in the context of scientific inquiry, modeling, and discovery. The objective of this research is to teach students the metacognitive process of inquiry-driven modeling through interaction with a set of intelligent agents embedded in a software environment. We have developed a series of exploratory learning environments that enable students to investigate complex ecological phenomena [23, 50] which leverage inquiry-driven teaching. Students demonstrated significant improvement in deep understanding after using these environments [17], but we also observed the kinds of weaknesses noted above. Learners often exhibited subpar investigative processes, and while their deep understanding of the systems improved, the actual process of inquiry and modeling did not.

Informed by these experiences, we have augmented our most recent exploratory learning environment, the Modeling & Inquiry Learning Application (MILA), with an extension to provide guided instruction directly in the context of a modeling and inquiry activity. This extension, MILA–Tutoring (MILA–T), supplies five distinct intelligent agents, each mimicking a particular functional role that a teacher traditionally plays in a classroom. In this paper, we first present the design of five pedagogical agents, the ways in which they track student behavior over time, the feedback that they provide, and the way in which they interact with teams during the inquiry-driven modeling process. We then present the design and results of an experiment with 238 middle school science students working in groups of two or three to investigate and construct a model of an ecological phenomenon. We present the differences in behavior seen based on interaction with the tutoring system and deeper analysis of the role that these tutoring agents played in the inquiry-driven modeling process.

RELATED WORK

This research builds on prior research in a variety of communities, including intelligent tutoring systems, exploratory learning environments, artificial intelligent in education, intelligent user interfaces, and learning sciences. Most prominently, however, this work represents the union of two communities: modeling and inquiry in science education and metacognitive tutoring.

Modeling and Inquiry in Education

Significant attention has been devoted to developing approaches to science education that encourage participation in authentic scientific practice. This kind of teaching strategy leverages the appeal of constructionist learning approaches described previously as well as exposes students to the authentic way in which science is performed in the real world. Such directions have been encouraged by both policy makers [33] and researchers [12, 30, 42]. Generally speaking, scientific models are representations of the system and are used to make predictions about the system for further analysis [34]. Models come in many different forms, including descriptive, prescriptive, conceptual, simulative, causal, dynamic, mechanistic, explanatory, visual, and more [8, 18]. For this research, we focus on models that are explanatory and mechanistic [17].

Scientific inquiry is tightly connected with scientific modeling. Inquiry is the process by which scientists or learners examine the domain or phenomenon that they are investigating, find useful observations or data, and use that data to test and expand their understanding of the system [43]. A scientific model, in this sense, serves as the destination for newly-unveiled data, as well as an organizing tool for determining future areas of inquiry [34]. Scientists use models to make predictions for what observations they would expect if the model is accurate; they then gather that data as part of the inquiry process and use it to corroborate the model's predictive power or elaborate on the model's mechanistic explanations [52].

Educational approaches that unite modeling and inquiry have been used extensively in science education [24, 43, 52]. However, these discovery-based approaches are subject to the same challenges noted previously [27, 28, 32]. Implementing guided instruction in these types of interventions presents a pragmatic difficulty: it is difficult for a single teacher to monitor and guide the open-ended inquiry and discovery of multiple students or groups of students at once. This difficulty is exacerbated in inquiry and modeling by the more general difficulties with teaching metacognitive skills, which have previously been identified by the metacognitive tutoring community.

Metacognitive Tutoring

Metacognitive tutoring is an extension of cognitive or intelligent tutoring. Whereas intelligent tutoring systems typically address cognitive skills [e.g. 49, 53], metacognitive tutoring initiatives attempt to construct intelligent agents that teach students metacognitive skills like self-regulated learning [2], self-explanation [9] and help-seeking [1]. These kinds of metacognitive skills have been identified as one of the most crucial learning goals of early education [3, 6, 11]. However, teaching metacognition has a number of unique challenges. Roll et al. 2007 provides an overview of many of these unique challenges [40]. Metacognitive skills tend to be domain-independent, but must be taught within a specific domain. Students have a natural tendency to emphasize the domain-specific learning rather than the metacognitive skills. Metacognitive skills are also difficult to teach explicitly. Because metacognition occurs within the mind of the reasoner, there is no inherent externally observable behavior or skill from which to learn. In the following section, the nature of inquiry and modeling as metacognitive skills is presented; however, we may also see the connection between inquiry, modeling, and metacognition by the shared difficulties both present. Like other metacognitive skills, inquiry and modeling are difficult to teach because they exist largely in the mind of the learner or scientist and because there is a tendency to focus on the domain knowledge rather than the metacognitive skill.

INQUIRY-DRIVEN MODELING

This research aims to teach students the process of inquiry-driven modeling within an authentic activity in ecological investigation. We define 'inquiry-driven modeling' as a particular type of the modeling and inquiry process in which the modeling process is driven by the results and data uncovered during inquiry activities; in turn, the resultant model helps structure and direct the continued inquiry activities. Other initiatives have taught inquiry [26, 48] and modeling [4, 47] separately, but this work teaches them together as directed by the literature on inquiry and modeling in authentic scientific research [34].

The case for inquiry-driven modeling as a metacognitive skill is derived from three connections. First, inquiry-driven modeling meets the definition of a metacognitive skill. Metacognition, as defined by Weinert 1987, is "cognition about cognition; that is, it refers to second-order cognitions: thoughts about thoughts, knowledge about knowledge or reflections about actions" [51]. The target of an inquiry-driven modeling task is one's own knowledge or understanding, aligning with the definition of a metacognitive skill. Second, inquiry-driven modeling is in many ways a local instantiation of the broader self-regulated learning process. Inquiry-driven modeling takes the general principles of self-regulated learning [2, 7, 11, 36], such as planning, self-monitoring, strategizing, and self-assessment, and deploys them in a particular domain with an additional set of rules, standards, and practices. Third, prior research has articulated the nature of inquiry and modeling as metacognitive skills. Most notably, White & Frederiksen explored this issue by initially using metacognition as a way of creating educational interventions grounded in inquiry and modeling [41, 52]. This work develops the idea of "metamodeling" knowledge, which is an understanding not simply of the process of modeling, but also to the role, function, and need for modeling in scientific inquiry. Metacognitive tutoring has also been applied previously to the inquiry phase of the process [16].

Process of Inquiry-Driven Modeling

The objective of this research is to teach students the metacognitive process of inquiry-driven modeling. In order to do so, we must first articulate a desirable process of inquiry-driven modeling. Based on significant existing research on inquiry and modeling in both education [39, 43, 44, 52] and science [10, 34], and supported by our own experience with inquiry and modeling in our exploratory learning environments in the past [17, 23, 50], we have developed a model of the process of inquiry-driven modeling, as shown in Figure 1. In this process, the learner (whether a student learning about ecology in a classroom or a scientist learning about the world in an authentic research setting) starts off by observing and describing some phenomenon to investigate. They then propose one or more hypotheses that could explain this phenomenon (although some researchers suggest scientists gather information

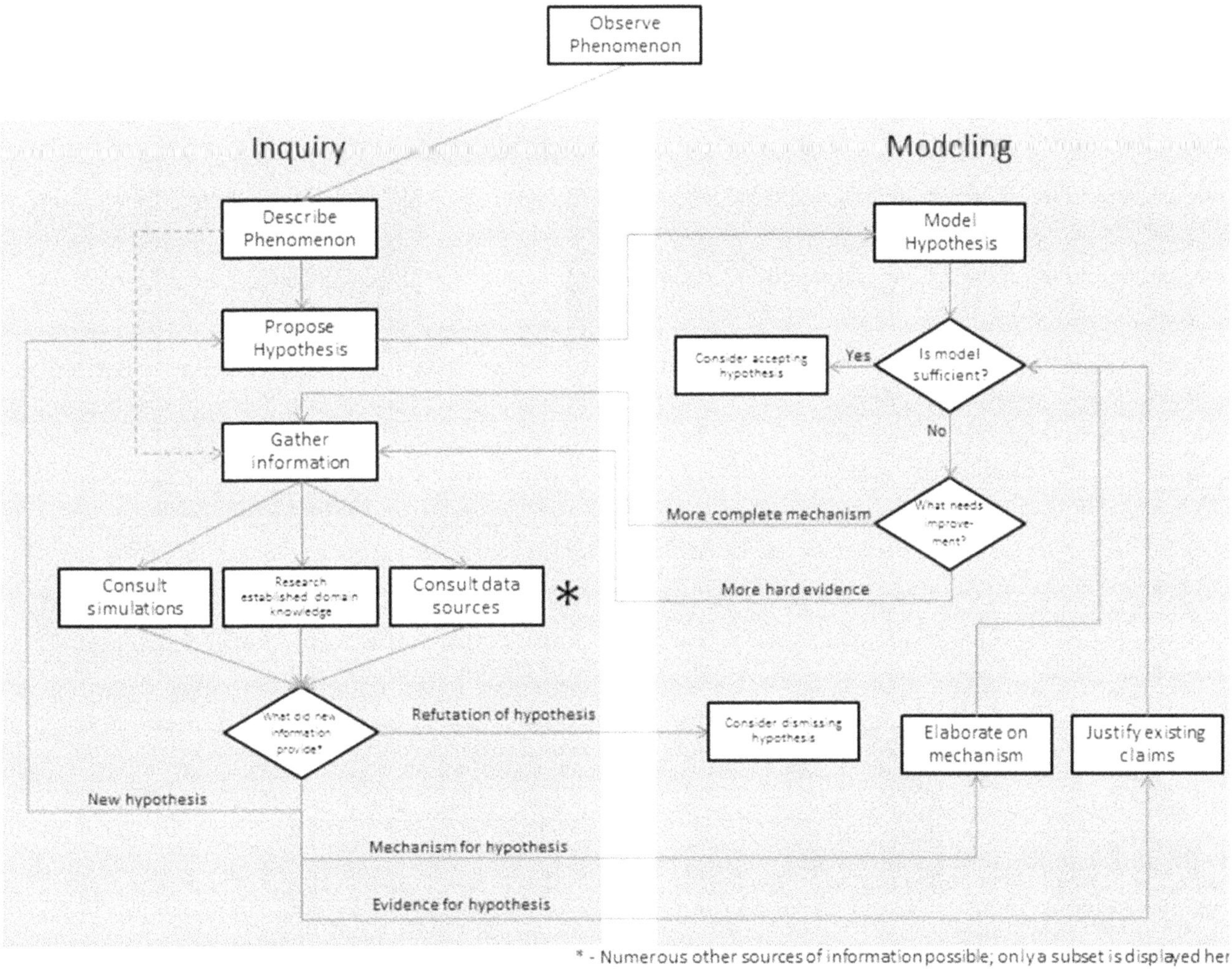

Figure 1: A model of a desirable process of inquiry-driven modeling.

before developing hypotheses [35], which is also supported by this model). These hypotheses then become preliminary models of the phenomenon. Using these models, the learner determines what is needed to confirm or expand the model. This leads to information-gathering in the world, which brings new information back to the model. Based on this new information, the model is altered, either dismissing it if the new information contradicts the model, expanding it if the new information provides mechanistic information, or strengthening it if the new information confirms predictions that the model had previously made. This process then continues to further elaborate and strengthen the model. It is important to note that the model presented in Figure 1 is not suggested as an ideal representation of the process, but rather just one faithful formalization of the literature on the inquiry and modeling process.

This model of a desirable inquiry-driven modeling process connects to the advice given in the metacognitive tutoring community that learning goals must be made explicit and explicitly communicated to the learners [40]. However, this process presents many of the learning challenges noted in the existing literature on modeling and inquiry in education and on metacognitive tutoring, as referenced in the Related Work section above. In a traditional classroom, all these difficulties are exacerbated even further by the need for a single teacher to provide guidance and instruction to multiple students or groups of students at once. This process is inherently explorational but demands guided instruction for productive learning [27], and a single teacher often will not be able to guide multiple groups exploring in different directions simultaneously. For these reasons, this research uses a metacognitive tutoring system to provide targeted, guided instruction to groups of students directly in the discovery context.

MODELING AND INQUIRY LEARNING APPLICATION

The inquiry-driven modeling in this research takes place in an exploratory learning environment called the Modeling & Inquiry Learning Application (MILA). In order to understand the nature of the tutoring and inquiry-driven modeling that takes place in this environment, it is first necessary to understand the nature of the models that students construct within this environment.

Figure 2 shows the main MILA window. In the top left, teams write their description of the phenomenon that they are trying to describe. Teams then propose one or more hypotheses; each of these hypotheses then becomes a model of how that hypothesis could lead to the phenomenon. Teams may also use the left sidebar to launch simulations, take notes, and dismiss models they no longer wish to consider. Within the model, teams construct explanations comprised of nodes and edges. Each node features three parameters: the physical component of the system in the

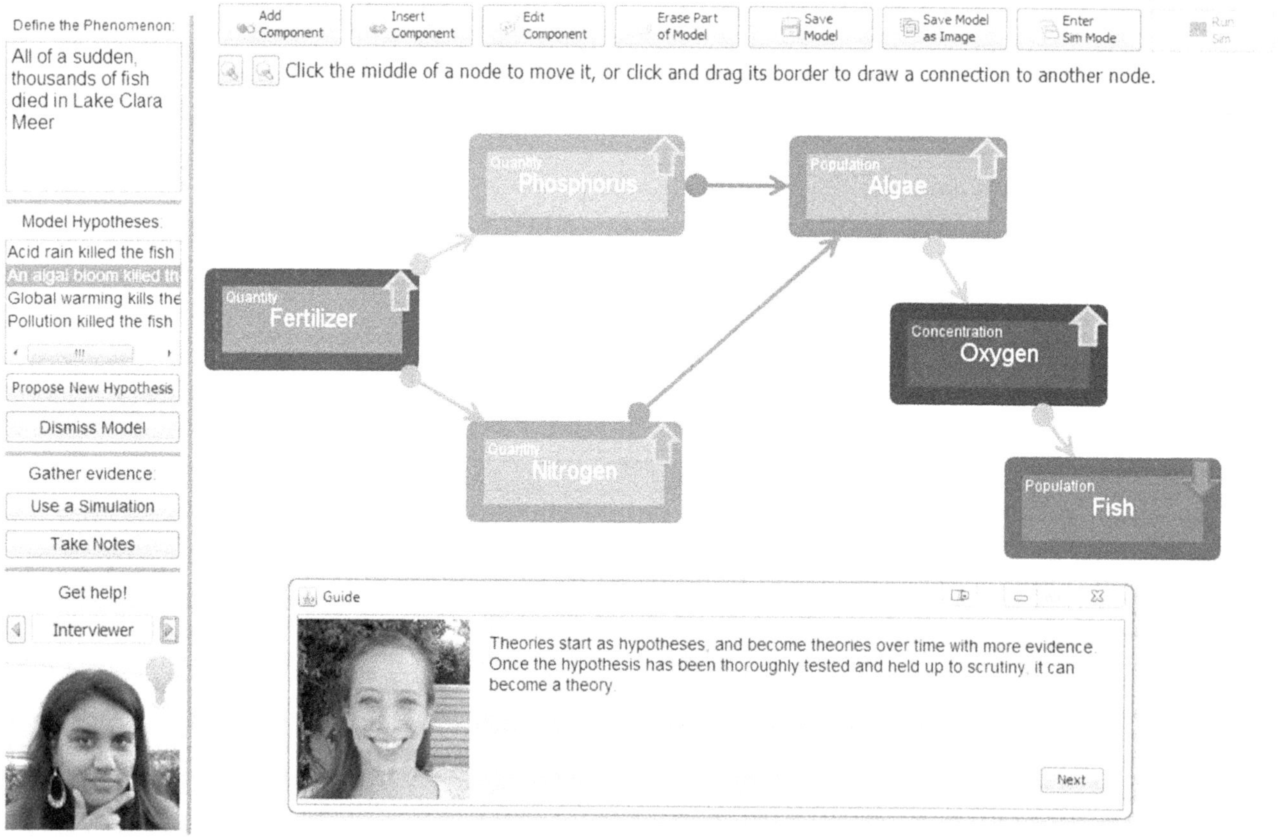

Figure 2: The Modeling & Inquiry Learning Application being used to model a sudden, massive fish kill. MILA-T is shown in the bottom left, and pop-up feedback from the Guide is shown in the bottom middle.

center (such as Fish or Phosphorus), the variable of the component in the top left (such as Population or Quantity), and the direction of change in the top right. Edges between nodes are causal; each trend causes the next one. For example, in this model, an increase in the quantity of fertilizer in a system causes an increased in the quantity of phosphorus and nitrogen. Students provide evidence for their models on the edges between nodes. On these edges, teams can write their explanation for why they believe a given connection is true and code it according to one of several categories of evidence, such as Logical Explanations and Similar System Observations. Based on the evidence provided, the color of the edge changes from red to orange to green; red signifies no evidence while green signifies ample evidence.

MILA–TUTORING

In this research, MILA is augmented with a tutoring extension called MILA–Tutoring (MILA–T). MILA–T is comprised of five distinct pedagogical agents that monitor and respond to students' behavior within the software. The goal of these agents is to help the process of inquiry-driven modeling in which students participate converge more closely to the process presented in Figure 1. To do so, these agents specifically monitor for successful demonstration of the process, as well as for the errors described previously.

During engagement with MILA, the tutoring system is available in the bottom left corner of the window, as shown in Figure 2. Four tutors are visible: a Guide, a Critic, a Mentor, and an Interviewer. Each tutor plays a different functional role with regard to interaction with the team of students, but all are structured to teach the process of inquiry-driven modeling. A fifth tutor, the Observer, is invisible to students but operates in the background to provide information to the other tutors. Two of the tutors, the Guide and the Critic, will not provide feedback until it is solicited by the team, while the Mentor, Interviewer, and Observer are constantly monitoring the team's behavior and interrupting accordingly. When the Mentor and Interviewer wish to provide feedback to the team, they illuminate a light bulb icon on their avatar in the corner of the screen, as seen in Figure 2. Each agent follows a unique decision routine to intelligently select feedback to provide. The Guide and Critic run their routines whenever they are prompted for feedback by the team. The Mentor, Interviewer, and Observer run their decision routines after every action that the team takes, with a threshold constraining how often they will provide feedback to the team.

The Observer

The Observer constantly monitors the activity of the team and constructs three different assessments of the team's ability: a modeling assessment, an inquiry assessment, and an ecology assessment. Each model reflects a different aspect of the desired inquiry-driven modeling process. To construct the modeling assessment, the Observer watches the pattern of teams' construction and revision activities over time, checking for a willingness to rescind earlier conjectures, dismiss earlier hypotheses, and propose new explanations. To construct the inquiry assessment, the Observer monitors the quality and quantity of evidence teams provide in support of their explanation, including the degree to which articulating evidence is embedded in the model construction process. To construct the ecology assessment, the Observer checks for the presence of certain desired components and relationships, such as the team's ability to include invisible components in their model like chemicals and microscopic organisms. Each assessment is constructed of a number of lower-level criteria, such as a measure of the tendency of a team to rely on weak forms of evidence or the willingness of a team to remove or revise past portions of their explanation. These criteria are then used to establish an overall level of ability with the target skill for the other tutors to check (although the other tutors may also check the individual criteria). One example of a rule that the Observer uses to construct its assessment of the team's ability is:

> **IF:** Students have just added a new connection to their model; AND: That new piece connection establishes a model demonstrating the complexity of parallel chains of causation.
>
> **THEN:** Increment the Parallel Causation criteria of the Modeling assessment.

These models are provided to the other tutors to help them establish the team's ability and provide the proper feedback. The Observer also has a rudimentary model describing the team's interaction with the various tutors themselves so that the other tutors may provide feedback praising teams' willingness to seek help or encouraging them to use the tutoring system.

The Guide

The Guide's functional role is to anticipate the questions that the team may want to ask and provide answers to those questions on demand. To accomplish this, the Guide constructs a list of questions that the team may want to ask, with answers (or a list of follow-up questions) prepared for each question. To do so, she iterates through a list of rules each containing a set of percepts. These percepts examine several sources: the Observer's current model of the team's ability across all three dimensions, the current classroom context, and the current status of the team's models. Each rule maps a particular set of percepts to a question or set of questions the Guide may offer to the team; offering the question to the team is thus the action that the rule selects in response to the particular set of percepts. One example of a rule that the Guide uses to choose a question is:

> **IF:** Students have begun to add evidential justifications to their models; OR: (Students have reached a point in the curriculum when evidence has been introduced; AND: Students have not yet reached efficacy with evidential justifications according to the

Observer's model); OR: The students' current model is very large but lacks any evidential justifications.

THEN: Add to question list, "What does evidence mean?"; AND: Add to question list, "What are the different types of evidence?"; AND: Add to question list, "How should evidence be used in a model?"; AND: Add to question list, "What is the importance of evidence in science?".

As she checks her rules, the Guide compiles a list of questions to offer. Once this compilation is done, the Guide offers the questions to the team, and they may select a question to which to receive an answer. Figure 2 shows the Guide providing an answer to a team's question about the difference between a hypothesis and a theory.

The Guide is equipped with dozens of questions to offer to teams. These questions range from novice-oriented questions such as simple information on interacting with the software to expert-oriented questions on evaluating explanations and establishing scientific theories. The Guide is also equipped with targeted questions that identify and address specific actions or features of the team's model; for example, if the team constructs a model reliant on logical explanations, the Guide offers a question about how one might gather data to test such explanations.

The Critic

The Critic's functional role is to provide teams with feedback on the current quality of their model. Teams are encouraged to consult with the Critic when they are unsure of how to proceed or believe their explanation is sufficient. Like the Guide, the Critic is equipped with a set of rules that determine what feedback he selects and provides. The rules are ordered from basic feedback to advanced feedback. When called upon, the Critic iterates over each rule and checks the percepts associated with the rule; if the percepts trigger a match to the current state of the team's models or the Observer's assessment of the team's ability, the feedback associated with the rule is added to a pool of potential feedback to provide. Once an adequate selection of feedback is attained (~5 different suggestions), the Critic randomly selects one and displays it to the team. In this way, if the team asks for feedback multiple times, they receive different suggestions and can proceed even if the Critic provides a piece of feedback they cannot currently address. One example of a rule the Critic uses to select a piece of feedback is:

IF: Students have not yet written a phenomenon definition; AND: Students have already begun creating models.

THEN: Add to the advice selection pool, "You've created some models, but you have not yet written a description of your phenomenon. Remember, it is very important to have a strong idea of what you are trying to explain before you start explaining it!"

Like the Guide, the Critic's feedback is based partially on the Observer's model of the team's ability and partially on the current state of the model that the team is currently constructing. For example, if a team has previously demonstrated an understanding of desirable forms of evidence (as seen in the Observer's assessment of the team's ability), the Critic will skip to more advanced feedback even if the current model retains some more basic weaknesses. In this instance, the Critic infers that the team is aware of this weakness because they have demonstrated an understanding of it in the past (although the Critic will still default to this feedback if it cannot find any more advanced feedback).

The Mentor

The Mentor similarly monitors for weaknesses in the team's modeling and evidence, but unlike the Critic, the Mentor will intervene and provide the team with unsolicited feedback. Thus, the Mentor plays the functional role of providing teams with feedback even when they are not soliciting help. The Mentor is comprised of a list of rules that he checks every time the team performs an action in the software. If the Mentor identifies a piece of feedback that he has not previously provided to the team, and if he has waited a certain period of time since the previous piece of feedback was provided, he interrupts the team to provide the feedback. If no such piece of feedback is identified, the Mentor remains dormant. One example of a rule used by the Mentor to identify feedback for the team is:

IF: The student has recently dismissed one of their models; AND: The student had not yet demonstrated proficiency with proposing and dismissing models according to the Observer's model of the student; AND: The student has not yet received positive feedback on dismissing models.

THEN: Make feedback available, "I see you've dismissed one of your initial hypotheses. Well done! Proposing and then ruling out hypotheses is an important part of science. It's crucial to reflect on your ideas and understand when you have disproven an earlier hypothesis."

The Mentor is primarily comprised of pairs of rules each targeting certain portions of the Observer's assessment of the team's ability. If the team demonstrates a certain desired skill, the Mentor will praise the team's ability; if the team has not demonstrated that skill within a certain period of time, the Mentor will describe the skill and its value to the team.

The Interviewer

The Interviewer's function is to ask the team questions that they ought to learn to ask themselves. Every time the team performs an action, she checks if the action and other present information match the percepts for one of her rules. If so, she provides the question to the team, along with a text box to use to answer the question. An example of a rule used by the Interviewer to select a question is:

IF: Students have just dismissed a hypothesis; AND: (It is relatively early in the lesson; OR: The dismissed model was relatively simple.)

THEN: Ask, "What prompted you to dismiss that hypothesis so quickly?", followed by, "Sometimes hypotheses don't go anywhere at all and can be dismissed pretty quickly, but remember to always have a reason to dismiss an earlier hypothesis!"

The Interviewer checks every action that the team performs and intervenes at critical junctures to ask the team to explain its reasoning. In this way, the Interviewer aims to encourage reflective learning by explicitly asking the team to reflect on their reasoning at critical junctures of the inquiry-driven modeling process. When prompted to reflect by the Interviewer, she provides the team with a text box in which to write their answer; this information is stored for subsequent analysis.

Interactions Among Tutors

The tutors are also symbiotic in that they also reference one another during their interactions with the teams. The Critic, for example, suggests the team consult the Guide if they are unclear about why he is emphasizing strong pieces of evidence or more elaborate mechanisms. The Guide encourages teams to pay attention to the feedback from the Mentor in order to discern whether they are successfully executing the inquiry-driven modeling process. The Mentor promotes heavy use of the Critic when teams appear to stagnate in development of their explanations as a way of discerning areas for improvement. Both the Guide and the Mentor also help frame the Interviewer's questions as reflective exercises rather than summative assessments. This symbiotic relationship may also explain the observation that interaction with the tutoring system most often spawns further interaction with the tutoring system. As noted below, 56.34% of all interactions with one of the tutors were followed by another interaction with the tutoring system.

EXPERIMENTAL DESIGN

MILA and MILA–T were deployed in two-week unit in 7th grade life science classrooms. During this unit, students were broken into teams of two or three and completed two projects. The first project (the "Learning" project) was given four 50-minute periods; in this project, students were asked to explain a sudden, massive fish kill in Lake Clara Meer. The second project (the "Transfer" project) was given one 50-minute period; in this project, students were asked to explain Atlanta's record-high temperatures over the past 20 years. In addition to these five periods, students spent two periods gathering data and completing lab exercises without MILA and two periods completing assessments.

Two teachers participated in the intervention, each with five classes. For each teacher, two classes were assigned to a control group and three classes were assigned to an experimental group. In the control group, 34 teams of students (99 total students) used MILA without MILA–T. In the experimental group, 50 teams of students (138 total students) used MILA with MILA–T during the Learning project and MILA without MILA–T during the Transfer project (only 47 experimental teams completed the Transfer project). This design enables identification of how teams interact differently while receiving feedback from the tutoring system and how teams' behavior changes in future projects based on prior interaction with a tutoring system.

We collected several types of data during this intervention. For this analysis, the most significant data are the interaction logs taken from each team. At the conclusion of the intervention, these logs were gathered together and separated by group (control or experimental) and project (Learning or Transfer). These logs then became the primary data source for the analysis outlined below.

ANALYSIS

We conducted two analyses on these interaction logs. First, we compared the interaction logs between the control and experimental students to see how interaction with MILA–T altered students' modeling and inquiry process, both during interaction with MILA–T (the Learning project) and after MILA–T was disabled (the Transfer project). Then, we analyzed the way in which the tutoring system was used by the experimental group during the Learning project. In order to perform both these analyses, the raw interaction logs were processed into Markov Chains mapping the software interactions into phases of the inquiry-driven modeling process described in Figure 1.

Markov Chains

To analyze the log data, we developed Markov chains describing the patterns of interaction in which teams engaged. Markov chains are mathematical systems that summarize transitions amongst a number of distinct states in a state space [25]. Markov chains are characterized as memoryless; it is inferred that next state chosen in the state space is determined by a probability function taking only the current state as an argument [31]. Although we would infer that a longer history of interactions likely helps determine the next state in a sequence in our analysis, for the purpose of this analysis Markov chains provide a useful device for examining differences based on the presence of the metacognitive tutoring system. Markov chains differ from hidden Markov models in that Markov chains allow the states themselves to be identified separately from the data; hidden Markov models derive the states from patterns in the data [15]. Markov chains were chosen rather than hidden Markov models to allow for more direct mapping to the inquiry-driven modeling process described earlier.

Part of one of these Markov chains is shown in Figure 3. Given the complexity of these Markov chains (twelve states with almost 100 notable edges), the chain is presented here as a table rather than a more traditional set of nodes and

	Number of Instances	Constructing Evidence	Constructing Model	Consulting Tutor	Dismissing Model	Proposing Hypothesis	Reconsidering Model	Revising Evidence	Revising Model	Taking Notes	Using Simulation	Writin
Constructing Evidence	866	51.96%	3.35%	23.09%	1.62%			7.39%	8.31%	1.62%	2.08%	
Constructing Model	1520	5.07%	55.59%	11.91%		2.30%			23.16%		0.53%	
Consulting Tutor	1821	8.68%	11.20%	56.34%	2.20%	2.25%	0.55%	2.14%	7.80%	2.31%	4.01%	2.53%
Dismissing Model	167	1.20%	5.39%	32.34%	21.56%	5.99%	23.95%	1.80%	4.79%	1.80%	0.60%	0.60%
Proposing Hypothesis	194		41.24%	24.23%	8.76%	19.59%			2.58%	1.03%	0.52%	2.06%
Reconsidering Model	54		5.56%	27.78%	51.85%	5.56%	1.85%		3.70%		3.70%	
Revising Evidence	229	27.51%	2.62%	17.03%				41.48%	7.86%	1.75%		
Revising Model	2100	4.90%	15.24%	5.86%	0.76%	0.62%		1.10%	70.62%			
Start	50			30.00%		8.00%						62.00%
Taking Notes	102	8.82%	5.88%	36.27%	3.92%			0.98%	2.94%	37.25%	2.94%	0.98%
Using Simulation	242	2.89%	4.13%	26.03%	2.07%	2.48%			6.61%	2.48%	52.48%	
Writing Problem Definition	110	1.82%	7.27%	33.64%		38.18%			2.73%	0.91%	0.91%	14.55%

Figure 3: One of the Markov models used to analyze teams' patterns of interaction with MILA and MILA-T. Due to the number of activities, the chain is shown as a table.

edges. Along the left and along the top, the twelve activities in which students engage during the inquiry-driven modeling process are shown; these activities summarize lower-level software interactions and map those interactions to the inquiry-driven modeling process presented in Figure 1. Differentiating construction and revision of evidence is done to capture modifications to prior ideas instead of merely ongoing additions to the model. Consulting Tutor is not a part of the inquiry-driven modeling process, but rather is a general activity to be performed whenever students are stuck, believe they are finished, or otherwise receive input. The rows represent the "previous" activity a team completed and the columns represent the "next" activity a team completed (except the "Number of Instances" column, which shows the number of observed instances of the activity for that row). In this way, each cell of the table represents the number of times teams followed the activity on the left with the activity on top. For example, at the intersection of the Constructing Model row and Constructing Evidence column is the number 5.07%; this means that 5.07% of the time that teams performed an action in the Constructing Model activity, they followed it with a Constructing Evidence activity. Similarly, the intersection between the Consulting Tutor row and the Consulting Tutor column shows the number 56.34%: this means that 56.35% of interactions with the tutoring system were followed by another interaction with the tutoring system.

These Markov chains are useful tools for analysis because they summarize the overall pattern of interaction performed by each group. Aggregating together the interaction logs from all teams in the control and experimental groups gives us expansive Markov chains summarizing thousands of activities, allowing us to compare the patterns of interaction between teams interacting with the tutoring system and those without it. However, merely comparing the patterns of interaction is of limited usefulness; the goal of interaction with the intelligent tutoring agents is to improve the team's inquiry-driven modeling. Toward that end, it is necessary to articulate what "improved" inquiry-driven modeling would look like in these models.

Desired Improvements

The objective of this research is to teach students the metacognitive process of inquiry-driven modeling. As described previously, MILA–T gives students feedback on the modeling process, and the desire is to see students respond to this feedback by improving their inquiry-driven modeling process. In order to identify improvement, however, it is first necessary to operationalize what improvement would look like in terms of these Markov models. Based on the research and our prior experience in developing and deploying exploratory learning environments, we derived nine behaviors that would be indicative of improved inquiry-driven modeling that are captured by these Markov chains. For the purposes of describing the operationalization of these desired improvements, 'Using Simulation' and 'Taking Notes' are combined under the broader activity of 'Data Gathering Activities'. The nine differences we monitor for in the Markov chains are:

- Greater incidence of articulating the problem prior to modeling and inquiry. This is operationalized by a greater prevalence of a transition between Start and Writing Problem Definition (found at the intersection of the Start row and Writing Problem Definition column in the Markov chain in Figure 3).
- Greater incidence of using the results of data-gathering activities to construct new evidential justifications. This is operationalized as a greater prevalence of a transition between Data-Gathering Activities and Constructing Evidence.

- Greater incidence of using the results of data-gathering activities to revise previous evidential justifications. This is operationalized as a greater prevalence of a transition between Data-Gathering Activities and Revising Evidence.
- Greater incidence of using the results of data-gathering activities to refute previous hypotheses. This is operationalized as a greater prevalence of a transition between Data-Gathering Activities and Dismissing Model.
- Greater incidence of using the results of data-gathering activities to propose new hypotheses. This is operationalized as a greater prevalence of a transition between Data-Gathering Activities and Proposing Hypothesis.
- Greater incidence of revising the problem definition throughout the process. This is operationalized as a greater overall prevalence of the Writing Problem Definition activity (the percentage of all actions that fall into the Writing Problem Definition activity, not shown in the model in Figure 3).
- Greater incidence model revision. This is operationalized as a greater overall prevalence of the Revising Model activity (the percentage of all actions that fall into the Revising Model activity, not shown in the model in Figure 3).
- Greater incidence of model construction activities spawning further information-gathering activities. This is operationalized as a greater prevalence of a transition between Model Construction and Data-Gathering Activities.
- Greater incidence of note-taking. This is operationalized as a greater overall prevalence of Taking Notes from data-gathering outside MILA (the percentage of all actions that fall into the Taking Notes activity, not shown in the model in Figure 3).

These nine criteria are regarded as indicators that one team's metacognition is superior to another's. Even in the absence of acceptance of these criteria as indicative of improved metacognition, however, these nine criteria represent desirable improvements in the inquiry-driven modeling process.

Comparison of Markov Chains

This research hypothesizes that interaction with the metacognitive tutoring system will improve teams' inquiry-driven modeling process compared to teams that do not interact with the metacognitive tutoring system. For this analysis, improvement is operationalized as greater incidence of the nine desirable behaviors outlined previously. Thus, the goal of this analysis is to identify whether teams in the experimental group exhibited greater incidence of any of these nine desired behaviors compared to teams in the control group. To determine whether the experimental group was superior in any of these nine comparisons, we performed a two-tailed Z-test on each pair of numbers derived from the Markov chains. For example, in order to test whether the experimental group demonstrated a great incidence writing problem definitions prior to performing any modeling and inquiry activities during the Learning project, we performed a two-tailed Z-test comparing the value at the intersection of the Start row and Writing Problem Definition column in the experimental group's Markov chain (in this case, 90.00%) with the corresponding value in the control group's Markov chain (in this case, 88.24%).

This repeated Z-test approach raises the odds of a Type I (false positive) error. To account for this, we used $\alpha = 0.01$ as the threshold for accepting the results of any one of the Z-tests. We then performed a Bernoulli (or binomial) trial to determine the number of expected false positives with nine trials and $p = 0.01$. This Bernoulli trial revealed a 91.4% chance of no false positives, an 8.3% chance of one false positive, and a 0.3% chance of more than one false positive. Thus, we may infer that no more than one significant difference in the repeated Z-test is a false positive (given that $p < 0.01$ that more than one false positive would occur).

During the Learning project, three of the nine criteria showed statistically significant differences between the control and experimental groups. Teams in the experimental group demonstrated an increased propensity to revise their problem definitions over time ($p < 0.001$, $Z = 4.102$) and to revise their models over time more generally ($p < 0.01$, $Z = 2.647$). The control group demonstrated an increased propensity to take notes ($p < 0.01$, $Z = -2.89$). Based on the aforementioned Bernoulli trial, we can conclude that no more than one of these differences was a false positive, and therefore there did exist statistically significant improvements by the experimental group in their propensity to revise either problem definitions or models over time. Given that one of the three differences presented improved performance by the control group, we must stop short of claiming that the experimental group was more generally superior. Nonetheless, we may conclude that the experimental group was superior in at least one dimension.

During the Transfer project, three of the nine criteria showed statistically significant differences between the control and experimental groups. Teams in the experimental group demonstrated an increased propensity to revise their models over time ($p < 0.01$, $Z = 2.716$) and to take notes ($p < 0.0001$, $Z = 3.593$). Teams in the control group demonstrated a significantly increased propensity to revise their problem definitions over time ($p < 0.01$, $Z = -3.511$). Interestingly, the control and experimental groups alternated areas of superiority between the two projects. Considering the Bernoulli trial described, we can conclude that a minimum of two of these observed differences were not false positives. The experimental group was superior to the control group in either their propensity to revise their models over time or their propensity to take notes. Although we again must stop short of claiming that the experimental group was more generally superior, we can conclude that the experimental group was superior in at least one dimension.

The results of the Bernoulli trials show that given three successes, two must not be false positives; thus, for each project, either the experimental group was superior in two dimensions or the control and experimental groups were each superior in one dimension. Given that either possibility features the superiority of the experimental group in at least one dimension, we may conclude that the experimental group was superior in at least one dimension during both the Learning and Transfer projects.

Examination of Tutor Usage Patterns

Following the previous analysis of the difference in inquiry-driven modeling processes between control and experimental groups, we conducted a follow-up analysis more narrowly on the role that MILA–T played in the experimental group during the Learning project. The goal of this analysis is to determine the nature of teams' interaction with the tutoring system and to construct a case for how the tutoring system impacts the teams' inquiry-driven modeling process, with the hypothesis that interaction improves their execution of the process. Using an additional Markov chain of the transitions amongst the activities including each tutor individually, we identified a number of patterns to the usage of MILA–T among experimental teams. These observations are qualitative given the lack of an alternate pattern of engagement with the tutors against which to test these values.

The first observation is that interaction with MILA–T was deeply embedded in experimental teams' interactions with MILA during the Learning project. 24.64% of all interactions during the Learning project fell into the Consulting Tutor activity, with 1769 total individual instances of teams consulting the tutoring system. Each of these instances represent the team receiving feedback from a tutor or giving an answer to one of the Interviewer's questions. The second observation is that tutor interaction most often begets further tutor interaction. 56.34% of tutor interactions are followed by an additional tutor interaction, suggesting that teams of students seek multiple pieces of feedback. This most often was seen in interactions with the Critic as students requested different feedback.

The third significant observation is that after exiting a loop of tutor interactions, teams most often transition to either model construction or evidence construction. This mirrors the feedback teams most often receive from the tutoring system. Much of the tutoring system's targeted feedback attempts to support teams in transitioning toward mature modeling and inquiry behaviors characterized by varied and strong evidence in support of their models and thorough mechanisms explaining the chain of events leading from their hypotheses to the phenomenon. In both these cases, the solution is to construct additional portions of the model by either providing more evidence or elaborating on the mechanism. The tutors most often ground this feedback in the teams' current explanations, pointing out when they are relying too heavily on simple logical explanations and observations. In these instances, though, removing prior evidence is not encouraged; instead, teams are encouraged to corroborate their logical explanations with stronger evidence. These observations are corroborated by other Markov chains at the level of the specific tutor. The Mentor's feedback is most often followed by model construction (15.45%) and model revision (10.30%), while the Critic's feedback is most often addressed by evidence construction (15.63%) and evidence revision (2.95%).

CONCLUSIONS

This paper presents a set of intelligent tutoring agents that teach students an authentic metacognitive process of inquiry-driven modeling. Based on the results seen here, we see evidence that engagement with a metacognitive tutoring system during an inquiry-driven modeling activity improved students' participation in the process in certain specific ways. Although the Bernoulli trial leaves open the possibility that certain improvements may be false positives, the repeated improvement in propensity to revise models over time in the Learning and Transfer projects suggests that teams both acted on and internalized the feedback received from the tutoring system. The qualitative analysis of interaction with the tutoring system, which showed tutor interactions were most often followed by construction and revision activities, further supports that interaction with the tutors encouraged further construction and revision. This suggests more frequent iteration through the inquiry-driven modeling process, which may be interpreted as decreased propensity to accept an explanation of the phenomenon too early. Further analysis is required to validate these ideas; the data presented here merely shows that teams receiving feedback from the tutoring system show an increased propensity to revise their models over time rather than adhere to their initial conjectures.

This analysis provides one perspective on the results of this intervention. We have also found that engagement with MILA–T improves students' dispositional orientation toward science and science careers [21], and improves the final explanations of the target phenomena that teams generate [20]. We are also exploring the impact of other features of MILA, such as MILA–S, a system for generating simulations from the conceptual models developed within MILA [22].

ACKNOWLEDGMENTS

We are grateful to Lara Catall, Vickie Bates, and Kristina Strickland for teaching in this intervention and to Nicolas Papin and Rochelle Lobo for their support in developing MILA, MILA–T, and MILA–S.

REFERENCES

1. Aleven, V., McLaren, B., Roll, I., & Koedinger, K. (2006). Toward metacognitive tutoring: a model of help seeking with a cognitive tutor. *International Journal of Artificial Intelligence and Education 16*(2), 101-128.
2. Azevedo, R., Witherspoon, A., Chauncey, A., Burkett, C., & Fike, A. (2009). MetaTutor: A MetaCognitive tool for enhancing self-regulated learning. In R. Pirrone, R. Azevedo, & G. Biswas (Eds.), *Proceedings of the AAAI Fall Symposium on Cognitive and Metacognitive Educational Systems*. 14-19.
3. Baker, L., & Brown, A. L. (1984). Metacognitive skills and reading. *Handbook of reading research, 1*, 353-394.
4. Biswas, G., Leelawong, K., Schwartz, D., & Vye, N. (2005). Learning By Teaching: A New Agent Paradigm For Educational Software. *Applied Artificial Intelligence 19*(3-4). 363-392.
5. Blumenfeld, P. C., Soloway, E., Marx, R. W., Krajcik, J. S., Guzdial, M., & Palincsar, A. (1991). Motivating project-based learning: Sustaining the doing, supporting the learning. *Educational psychologist, 26*(3-4), 369-398.
6. Bransford, J., Brown, A., & Cocking, R. (2000). *How people learn: Brain, mind, experience, and school*. Washington, D.C.: National Academy Press.
7. Butler, D. L., & Winne, P. H. (1995). Feedback and self-regulated learning: A theoretical synthesis. *Review of educational research*, *65*(3), 245-281.
8. Clement, J. (2008). *Creative Model Construction in Scientists and Students: The Role of Imagery, Analogy, and Mental Simulation*. Dordrecht: Springer.
9. Conati, C., & Vanlehn, K. (2000). Toward computer-based support of meta-cognitive skills: A computational framework to coach self-explanation. *International Journal of Artificial Intelligence in Education, 11*, 389-415.
10. Crawford, S., & Stucki, L. (1990). Peer review and the changing research record. *Journal of the American Society for Information Science, 41*(3), 223-228.
11. Dweck, C. (2000). *Self-theories: Their role in motivation, personality, and development*. Philadelphia, PA: Psychology Press.
12. Edelson, D. (1997). Realizing authentic scientific learning through the adaptation of scientific practice. In K. Tobin & B. Fraser (Eds.), *International Handbook of Science Education*. Dordrecht, NL: Kluwer.
13. Edelson, D. C., Gordin, D. N., & Pea, R. D. (1999). Addressing the challenges of inquiry-based learning through technology and curriculum design. *Journal of the Learning Sciences, 8*(3-4), 391-450.
14. Gallagher, S. A. (1997). Problem-based learning. Journal for the Education of the Gifted, 20(4), 332-62.
15. Ghahramani, Z. (2001). An introduction to hidden Markov models and Bayesian networks. *International Journal of Pattern Recognition and Artificial Intelligence*, *15*(01), 9-42.
16. Gobert, J., Sao Pedro, M., Toto, E., Montalvo, O., & Baker, R. (2011). Science ASSISTments: Assessing and scaffolding students' inquiry skills in real time. Paper presented at The Annual Meeting of the American Educational Research Association, April, 2011, New Orleans, LA.
17. Goel, A., Rugaber, S., Joyner, D. A., Vattam, S., Hmelo-Silver, C., Jordan, R., Sinha, S., Honwad, S., & Eberbach, C. (2013). Learning Functional Models of Complex Systems: A Reflection on the ACT project on Ecosystem Learning In Middle School Science. In R. Azevedo & V. Aleven (Eds.) *International Handbook on Meta-Cognition and Self-Regulated Learning.*
18. Griffith, T., Nersessian, N., & Goel, A. (2000). Function-follows-Form: Generative Modeling in Scientific Reasoning. In *Proceeds of the 22nd Cognitive Science Conference*.
19. Jacobs, G. (1992). Hypermedia and discovery-based learning: a historical perspective. British Journal of Educational Technology, 23(2), 113-121.
20. Joyner, D. (2015). *Metacognitive Tutoring for Inquiry-Driven Modeling* (Doctoral dissertation). Georgia Institute of Technology, Atlanta, GA.
21. Joyner, D. A. & Goel, A. (2014). Attitudinal Gains from Engagement with Metacognitive Tutors in an Exploratory Learning Environment. In *Proceedings of the 12th International Conference on Intelligent Tutoring Systems*. Honolulu, Hawaii.
22. Joyner, D. A., Goel, A., & Papin, N. (2014). MILA–S: Generation of agent-based simulations from conceptual models. In *Proceedings of the 19th International Conference on Intelligent User Interfaces*. Haifa, Israel. 289-298.
23. Joyner, D. A., Goel, A., Rugaber, S., Hmelo-Silver, C., & Jordan, R. (2012). Evolution of an Integrated Technology for Supporting Learning about Complex Systems: Looking Back, Looking Ahead. In *Proc. Of 11th International Conference on Advanced Learning Technologies*, Athens, GA.
24. Kaberman, Z., & Dori, Y. J. (2009). Question posing, inquiry, and modeling skills of chemistry students in the case-based computerized laboratory environment. *International Journal of Science and Mathematics Education, 7*(3), 597-625.
25. Kemeny, J. G., & Snell, J. L. (1960). *Finite markov chains* (Vol. 356). Princeton, NJ: van Nostrand.
26. Ketelhut, D. J. (2007). The impact of student self-efficacy on scientific inquiry skills: An exploratory investigation in River City, a multi-user virtual environment. *Journal of Science Education and Technology*, *16*(1), 99-111.
27. Kirschner, P. A., Sweller, J., & Clark, R. E. (2006). Why minimal guidance during instruction does not work: An analysis of the failure of constructivist, discovery, problem-based, experiential, and inquiry-based teaching. *Educational psychologist*, *41*(2), 75-86.

28. Klahr, D., & Nigam, M. (2004). The equivalence of learning paths in early science instruction effects of direct instruction and discovery learning. *Psychological Science, 15*(10), 661-667.
29. Kolb, D. A. (1984). *Experiential learning: Experience as the source of learning and development.* Englewood Cliffs, NJ: Prentice-Hall.
30. Lajoie, S., Lavigne, N., Guerrera, C., & Munsie, S. (2001). Constructing knowledge in the context of Bio World. *Instructional Science, 29*, 155-186.
31. López, G. G. I., Hermanns, H., & Katoen, J. P. (2001). Beyond memoryless distributions: Model checking semi-Markov chains. In *Process Algebra and Probabilistic Methods. Performance Modelling and Verification* (pp. 57-70). Springer Berlin Heidelberg.
32. Mayer, R. E. (2004). Should there be a three-strikes rule against pure discovery learning?. *American Psychologist, 59*(1), 14.
33. National Research Council. (1996). *National science education standards.* Washington, DC: National Academy Press.
34. Nersessian, N. (1999). Model-based reasoning in conceptual change. In L. Magnani, N. Nersessian, & P. Thagard (Eds.), *Model-based reasoning in scientific discovery.* New York: Kluwer/Plenum Publishers.
35. Nersessian, N. (2008). *Creating Scientific Concepts.* Cambridge, MA: MIT Press.
36. Palinscar, A. S., & Brown, A. L. (1984). Reciprocal teaching of comprehension-fostering and comprehension-monitoring activities. *Cognition and instruction, 1*(2), 117-175.
37. Papert, S. (1980). Mindstorms: Children, computers, and powerful ideas. New York: Basic Books.
38. Piaget, J. (1950). The Psychology of Intelligence. New York: Routledge.
39. Razzouk, R. & Shute, V. J. (2012). What is design thinking and why is it important? *Review of Educational Research, 82*(3), 330-348.
40. Roll, I., Aleven, V., McLaren, B., & Koedinger, K. (2007). Designing for metacognition—applying cognitive tutor principles to the tutoring of help seeking. *Metacognition in Learning 2*(2).
41. Roll, I., Aleven, V., & Koedinger, K. R. (2010). The invention lab: Using a hybrid of model tracing and constraint-based modeling to offer intelligent support in inquiry environments. In V. Aleven, J. Kay, & J. Mostow (Eds.), In *Proceedings of the international conference on intelligent tutoring systems.* 115-24. Berlin: Springer Verlag.
42. Schmidt, H. G. (1998). Problem-based learning: Does it prepare medical students to become better doctors? *The Medical Journal of Australia 168.* 429-430.
43. Schwarz, C. V., & White, B. Y. (2005). Metamodeling knowledge: Developing students' understanding of scientific modeling. *Cognition and Instruction, 23*(2), 165-205.
44. Schwarz, C. V., Reiser, B. J., Davis, E. A., Kenyon, L., Achér, A., Fortus, D., ... & Krajcik, J. (2009). Developing a learning progression for scientific modeling: Making scientific modeling accessible and meaningful for learners. *Journal of Research in Science Teaching, 46*(6), 632-654.
45. Schweingruber, H. A., Duschl, R. A., & Shouse, A. W. (Eds.). (2007). *Taking Science to School:: Learning and Teaching Science in Grades K-8.* National Academies Press.
46. Soloway, E., Pryor, A. Z., Krajcik, J. S., Jackson, S., Stratford, S. J., Wisnudel, M., & Klein, J. T. (1997). ScienceWare's Model-It: Technology to Support Authentic Science Inquiry. *Technological Horizons in Education, 25*(3), 54-56.
47. Ting, C. Y., Zadeh, M. R. B., & Chong, Y. K. (2006, January). A decision-theoretic approach to scientific inquiry exploratory learning environment. In *Intelligent Tutoring Systems* (pp. 85-94). Springer Berlin Heidelberg.
48. van Joolingen, W. R., de Jong, T., Lazonder, A. W., Savelsbergh, E. R., & Manlove, S. (2005). Co-Lab: Research and development of an online learning environment for collaborative scientific discovery learning. *Computers in Human Behaviors 21.* 671-688.
49. VanLehn, K., Siler, S., Murray, C., Yamauchi, T., & Baggett, W. B. (2003). Why do only some events cause learning during human tutoring? *Cognition and Instruction, 21*(3), 209-249.
50. Vattam, S., Goel, A. K., Rugaber, S., Hmelo-Silver, C., Jordan, R., Gray, S., & Sinha, S. (2011). Understanding Complex Natural Systems by Articulating Structure-Behavior-Function Models. *Educational Technology & Society, Special Issue on Creative Design, 14*(1), 66-81.
51. Weinert, F. E. (1987). Introduction and overview: Metacognition and motivation as determinants of effective learning and understanding. *Metacognition, motivation, and understanding.* 1-16.
52. White, B. & Frederiksen, J. (1998). Inquiry, modeling, and metacognition: Making science accessible to all students. *Cognition and Instruction, 16*(1). 3–118.
53. Woolf, B. P. (2010). *Building intelligent interactive tutors: Student-centered strategies for revolutionizing e-learning.* Morgan Kaufmann.

Automated Social Skills Trainer

Hiroki Tanaka[1], Sakriani Sakti[1], Graham Neubig[1], Tomoki Toda[1], Hideki Negoro[2], Hidemi Iwasaka[2], Satoshi Nakamura[1]
[1]Nara Institute of Science and Technology, Japan, [2]Nara University of Education, Japan
[1]{hiroki-tan,ssakti,neubig,tomoki,s-nakamura}@is.naist.jp, [2]{gorosan,hiwasaka}@nara-edu.ac.jp

ABSTRACT
Social skills training is a well-established method to decrease human anxiety and discomfort in social interaction, and acquire social skills. In this paper, we attempt to automate the process of social skills training by developing a dialogue system named "automated social skills trainer," which provides social skills training through human-computer interaction. The system includes a virtual avatar that recognizes user speech and language information and gives feedback to users to improve their social skills. Its design is based on conventional social skills training performed by human participants, including defining target skills, modeling, role-play, feedback, reinforcement, and homework. An experimental evaluation measuring the relationship between social skill and speech and language features shows that these features have a relationship with autistic traits. Additional experiments measuring the effect of performing social skills training with the proposed application show that most participants improve their skill by using the system for 50 minutes.

Author Keywords
Social skills training (SST); behavior detection; dialogue system; embodied conversational avatar; computer-based training.

ACM Classification Keywords
H.5.2. Information Interfaces and Presentation: User Interfaces – User-centered design; K.3.1. Computing Milieux: Computers and Education – Computer-assisted instruction (CAI)

INTRODUCTION
Many people have difficulties or are anxious in social interactions such as presentations and job interviews. The extreme example of people with these difficulties are those with autism spectrum disorders (ASD) [1]. Persistent social skill deficits impede those afflicted with them from forming relationships or succeeding in social situations.

IUI'15, March 29–April 01, 2015, Atlanta, GA, USA.

http://dx.doi.org/10.1145/2678025.2701368

Figure 1. SST with the automated social skills trainer.

Social skills training (SST) is a general cognitive behavior therapy to train these social skills for people who have difficulties in social interaction, and is widely used by teachers, therapists, and trainers [4]. However, SST requires well-trained teachers, so the number of participants joining SST program is restricted and applications are competitive.

On the other hand, if part or all of the SST process could be automated, it would become easier for those requiring SST to receive it anywhere and anytime. In addition, it may be easier for those with social difficulties to use computers than interact directly. Donna Williams, who has autism, wrote a book entitled "Nobody nowhere" (1992), in which she stated

> *"The comprehension of words works as a progression, depending on the amount of stress caused from fear and the stress of relating directly. At best, words are understood with meaning, as with the indirect teaching of facts by a teacher or, better still, a record, television, or book. In my first three years in the special class at primary school, the teacher often left the room and the pupils responded to the lessons broadcast through an overhead speaker. I remember responding to it without the distraction of coping with the teacher. In this sense, computers would probably be beneficial for autistic children once they had the skills to use one."*

We propose a novel tool that tries to replicate conventional SST using a systematic and computer-based design. We develop a dialogue system named "automated social skills trainer," which is an application including video modeling of human behavior and real-time behavior detection as well as data visualization to help people improve their social skills (Figure 1). We investigate whether it is possible to help people who have difficulties in social interaction improve their social skills using an automated system which can be used anywhere, anytime.

RELATED WORK

The design of an automated social skills trainer for social-skills training brings together several fields, including research into computers in education, intelligent virtual agents, and affective computing. The following paragraphs briefly outline work in these areas.

The use of computers in SST is motivated by the fact that while individuals with social impairments have difficulty in social interaction, they also show good and sometimes even superior skills in "systemizing" [2]. Systemizing is the drive to analyze or build systems, and to understand and predict behaviour in terms of underlying rules and regularities. The use of systematic computer-based training for people who need to train social skills can take advantage of the following: 1) they favor the computerized environments because they are predictable, consistent, and free from social demands, 2) they can work at their own speed and level of understanding, 3) training can be repeated over and over again until the goal is achieved, 4) interest and motivation can be maintained through computerized rewards [5, 17, 18].

There has been one previous work on automated conversational coaches [15], which are dialogue systems aimed to train people for improving interview skills through real-time feature detection and feedback. They achieved 1) a realistic task involving training real users, 2) formative affective feedback that provides the user with useful feedback on the behaviors that need improvement, and 3) the interpretation or recognition of user utterances to drive the selection of backchannels or formative feedback. While this work is an excellent first step, it did not faithfully follow the traditional SST framework, omitting steps such as modeling of human behavior [9].

As conventional SST is a well-established method to improve human behavior and has clear goals and definitions for each module in the framework, our motivation is to follow the traditional SST framework as closely as possible. This paper presents the system design, modeling, and evaluation of the automated social skills trainer. Two experimental evaluations show that social skill is related to automatically extracted features and has a relationship to autistic traits, and that some participants improve in social skill using the automated social skills trainer.

SOCIAL SKILLS TRAINING

Conventional SST is an established method developed by Liberman for schizophrenics to reduce their anxiety and discomfort in social interaction [25]. SST is often performed with multiple sessions, and each session focuses on the training of one target skill for one or two hours. It is well known that SST can be used to effectively improve social skills for people with social disorders and ASD [4].

SST can be classified into individual (one to one training) and group (one to many or many to many training) settings. One

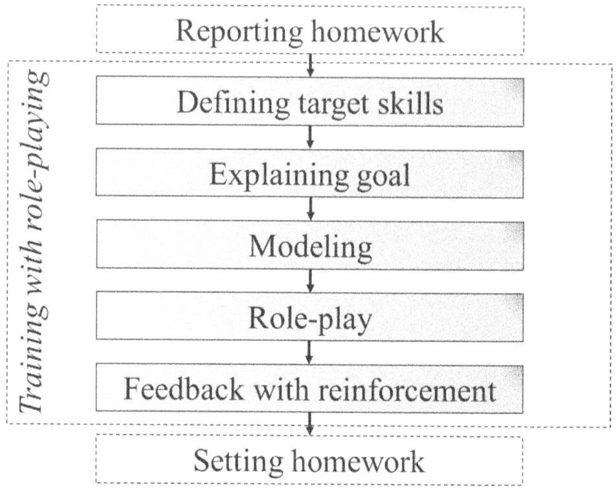

Figure 2. Human-to-human SST framework.

advantage of group SST is that it enables participants to observe other participants' behaviour and also receive feedback from others. On the other hand, the advantage of individual SST is that the training can be relaxed and comfortable for participants, and that lessons can be tailored to the individual's needs.

As shown in Figure 2, SST is generally based on the following steps: defining target skills, modeling, role-play, feedback, reinforcement, and homework. We briefly describe these steps as follows:

- **Defining target skills:** The major social problem is identified, and the skills to be trained are decided based on this problem. In order to figure out the major problems, the participants and trainers work together through discussion or trainers decide the target skills. Once the target skills are decided the trainers decide the goal after intervention. In this step, trainers sometimes use related books to help participants understand target skills and the goal of SST. Examples of target skills include presentation skills, job interview skills, self-introduction skills, or skills regarding how to decline another's offer or request.

- **Modeling:** Before participants are asked to perform an interaction, trainers act as a model, demonstrating the skill that the participants are focusing on so that participants can see what they need to do before attempting to do it themselves. For example, trainers may show a good story telling example using appropriate verbal and non-verbal cues.

- **Role-play:** Participants are asked to role-play. For example, participants tell their experience to the trainer. This allows the participants to practice their own skills in the target situation. Trainers observe participants' social skills subjectively, but mainly focus on voice quality, amplitude, facial expression, eye-gaze and other factors. This practice is a very important aspect of SST.

- **Feedback:** Trainers provide feedback at the end of role-playing (in the case of group SST, participants also receive feedback from other participants). This feedback helps participants to identify their strengths and weaknesses. For example, trainers may tell the participant that the role-play was very good because he/she used appropriate voice amplitude.

- **Reinforcement:** Trainers give positive reinforcement, praising the participant about their achievement of targeted behaviors, in addition to feedback. This is a very important aspect of the SST, because the participants often do not have confidence in social interaction, and tend to have low self-esteem. Therefore, positive encouragement helps build confidence in social environments.

- **Homework:** Trainers set little homework challenges that participants are required to do in their own time throughout the week. For example, trainers may ask the participant to tell their story to friends or family, and let the trainer know about the result.

By performing this training, participants can learn better social skills in a number of different ways, a core aspect contributing to the effectiveness of training. However, it should be noted that the human trainer plays a very involved role in the majority of these steps. As a consequence, SST requires professional or at least well-trained trainers satisfying the above abilities (e.g. being able to perform modeling and give appropriate feedback comments). The number of skilled trainers is small, and thus the number of participants joining SST program is restricted and applications are competitive.

AUTOMATED SOCIAL SKILLS TRAINING

In this section, we describe our proposed automated social skills trainer following the conventional individual SST framework. We replicate human-to-human individual SST by using a spoken dialogue system. While one disadvantage of individual SST is that there is no chance to see other participants' behaviour, we can provide a surrogate by playing video of others on the computer screen.

Table 1 shows the correspondence between conventional SST and our proposed method. In the following few pages, we describe each proposed module corresponding to a step in conventional SST.

Table 1. Correspondence of conventional SST and our proposed method.

Conventional SST	Proposed Method
Defining target skills	Story telling/narrative
Modeling	Recorded model video
Role-play	Conversation with an avatar
Feedback	Generation of visual feedback
Reinforcement	Generation of positive comments
Homework	Spoken instructions

- **Defining target skills:** Ideally, we would define specific target skills for each user through an initial interaction with the system. We plan to tackle this in future work, but for the time being we focused on a single target skill that has been shown to be widely applicable: story-telling or narrative ability. Story telling/narrative is a task of telling memorable stories, and is related to social interaction skills such as presentations and job interviews [8]. It has also been shown useful to distinguish children with ASD and children with typical development [22]. In the step of defining this goal, the system tells users that "This application will help you learn to tell stories well, and after training you will have more fun telling stories."

Figure 3. An example of video modeling.

- **Modeling:** Users can watch a recorded model video (Figure 3) before the role-playing. The recorded models are people who have relatively good narrative skills according to subjective evaluation. Users can watch and imitate the good examples.

- **Role-play:** The main part of the proposed system is the role-playing, which is performed through interaction with an avatar. When the user says "start role-playing," the system says "Please tell me your recent memorable story" The role-playing starts after the avatar's question, and continues for one minute. During this time, the avatar nods its head, and the system detects and analyzes language and speech features automatically. In this work, we focus on features that could differentiate between people with and without ASD as described in [22]: F0 variation, amplitude, voice quality, pauses, words per minute, words more than 6 letters, and fillers. We show a list of these features as follows:

  F0 variation: F0 indicates fundamental frequency, or pitch of voice. F0 variation therefore corresponds to the amount of variety in pitch, with less variety corresponding to a more monotone voice. We use these features because it has been widely noted that people with ASD have prosody that differs from that of their peers [12, 16, 6, 13, 23]. For instance, Kiss *et al.,* [14] found several differences in the fundamental frequency characteristics of people with ASD.

  Amplitude: In human-to-human SST, trainers often focus on volume of voice because both overly small and loud voices are not appropriate for many social situations. A previous study investigating the amplitude (power) of people with ASD [22] confirmed the importance of amplitude to identify children with ASD.

  Voice quality: People with ASD often exhibit abnormal voice quality, often described as more clear than their peers. Bonneh *et al.,* [7] quantified speech abnormalities in terms of the properties of the voice quality

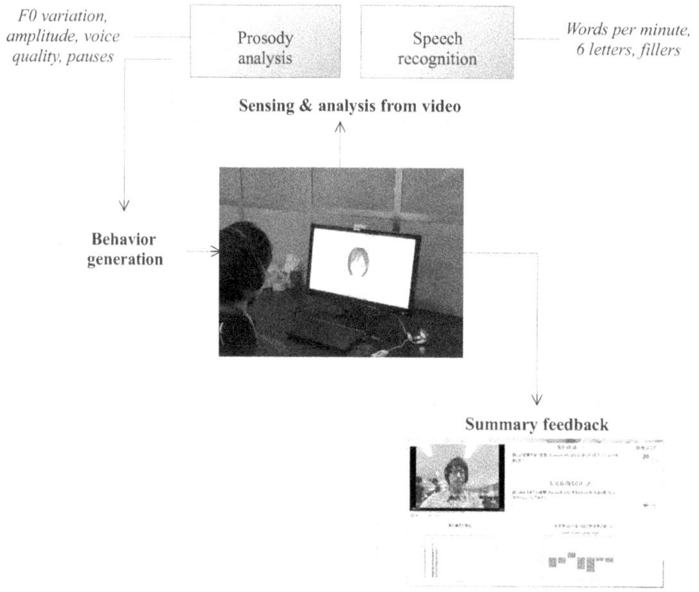

Figure 4. The automated social skills trainer framework.

and was able to identify children with ASD with more than 80% accuracy.

Pauses: There are reports finding that children with ASD tend to delay responses to their parent more than children with typical development in natural conversation [11].

Words per minute (WPM): There is a report that speaking rate was strongly correlated to interview skills [15]. WPM is related to frequency of speech.

Words more than 6 letters: Children with ASD use more complicated or unexpected words than typically developing children, and deficits of ASD affect inappropriate usage of words [21]. Words more than six letters may be related to complicated words [19].

Fillers: The frequency of filler usage is important in story telling or presentation. Too frequent use of fillers disturbs listener focus on the contents of speech.

- **Feedback:** The system displays summary feedback according to detected features. The feedback includes comments, the user's video, the parameters compared to model speaker, and the overall narrative score. The user can objectively confirm their strengths and weaknesses.
- **Reinforcement:** In addition to simply listing scores, the system also chooses good parts of the interaction, and gives positive feedback encouraging the targeted behavior.
- **Homework:** The system tells users to "Please tell your story to others throughout the week, and let me know about it." However, it should be noted that we did not evaluate SST across sessions in this work, though we plan to do so in the future.

Through this framework, we can replicate to some extent conventional individual SST with the spoken dialogue system replicating each module in the framework.

IMPLEMENTATION DETAILS

The automated social skills trainer system works on a regular laptop, which processes the audio input in role-playing. The processed data is used to generate the behaviors of an avatar that interacts with and provides feedback to users.

The role-playing, feedback, and reinforcement consist of three modules: behavior generation, sensing & analysis from video, and summary feedback as shown in Figure 4. The following subsections describe the modules in detail. It should be noted that the target language of our system is Japanese, and all data creation and experiments are performed with native Japanese speakers.

Data creation and subjective evaluation

As a first step towards building our system, we collected model data of people with relatively high levels of social skills. This video data is used both in the modeling module and for predicting scores in the feedback module. We collected data from a total of 19 people. Using this data, we assigned each dialogue an overall narrative skill score based on subjective evaluation, and the top five people were selected as models. Subjective evaluation was performed by having two

Figure 5. The avatar used in the automated social skills training system.

raters watch the recorded participants' narrative and answer a questionnaire. This process is described in more detail in the following Experiment 1.

Dialogue agent

The automated social skills trainer was developed using MMDAgent[1], which is a Japanese spoken dialogue system integrating speech recognition, dialogue management, text-to-speech, and behavior generation. MMDAgent works as a Windows application. We selected a character who is similar to an actual human, as we hope that this will make it easier for the user to generalize learned skills in a real situation. The avatar is displayed from the front, and there are no distractions in background (Figure 5). The user can operate and interact with the avatar by using speech throughout the training. All dialogue system utterances were created using templates written by the first author.

In addition, the system performs a number of behaviors to keep the user engaged. It blinks its eyes once every three seconds, and reacts to users during the role-playing. When the system recognizes an utterance, after a few seconds the system nods its head. The blinking and nodding behaviour motions were created by MikuMikuDance[2].

Sensing and analysis from video

To calculate the linguistic features, we performed automatic speech recognition (ASR) using the Julius dictation kit[3]. We used Mecab[4] for part-of-speech tagging in Japanese utterances. For speech feature extraction, we used the Snack sound toolkit[5].

The implementation of features is as follows: 1) F0 variation: We used the coefficient of variation for fundamental frequency with a minimum pitch of 100 Hz. We did not use mean, maximum and minimum values because there are individual and gender differences in terms of these features, 2) Amplitude: We used the mean value of amplitude, 3) Voice quality: We extracted the spectral tilt by calculating the difference between the first harmonic and the third formant "h1a3" as a feature expressing voice quality [10], 4) Pauses: We calculated values of pauses before new turns as time between the end of the avatar's utterance and the start of the user's utterance, 5) WPM: In the automated social skills trainer, the narrative continues for one minute, and we counted the number of words in one narrative, 6) Words more than 6 letters: We extracted percentage of words more than 6 letters as a feature, 7) Fillers: We calculated percentage of fillers such as "umm," or "eh" in Japanese. This feature automatically extracted by using output of the Mecab.

[1]http://www.mmdagent.jp/
[2]http://www.geocities.jp/higuchuu4/
[3]http://julius.sourceforge.jp/index.php
[4]https://code.google.com/p/mecab/
[5]http://www.speech.kth.se/snack

Summary feedback

Based on the calculated features, we provide feedback to the users about their social skills (Figure 6). Our goal was to design visualizations so that it would be easy for users to understand and interpret their narrative skill. The summary feedback provides following information.

- **User video:** Participants can watch the recorded video and audio in the narrative. In doing so, the user can confirm their speech contents, facial expression, posture and so on [15], which are not analyzed automatically in the current version of the automated social trainer.
- **Overall score:** People with ASD prefer to check their improvement quantitatively [2]. The system displays the predicted overall score, which motivates the user to practice more and improve their score. We predict the overall score using the multiple regression method on a scale of 0 to 100.
- **Pitch variation:** Participants can see their pitch movement corresponding to the time. This also shows a visualization of how frequently they spoke.
- **Comparison with models:** The system visualizes the comparison of extracted features between the user's current narrative and model persons' narratives in terms of z-score, which is a statistical measurement of a score's relationship to the mean in a group of scores. The users are informed that they should attempt to emulate the model in all aspects.
- **Good points:** The system generates positive comments that reinforce the user's motivation with encouraging words [4]. The comments are generated based on the features that have values close to those of the models.
- **Points to be improved:** The system generates comments about points to be improved for next trial. The comments are generated based on the features that have values far from the models.
- **Screenshot:** Participants can save the feedback by clicking a button, and this is used for checking improvements over the course of training.

EXPERIMENT 1: DEFINING MODEL PERSONS

To evaluate the effectiveness of the proposed automated social skills trainer, we performed two experiments. In the first experiment, we sought to answer the following questions:

1) Does narrative skill relate to linguistic, acoustic, and other information?

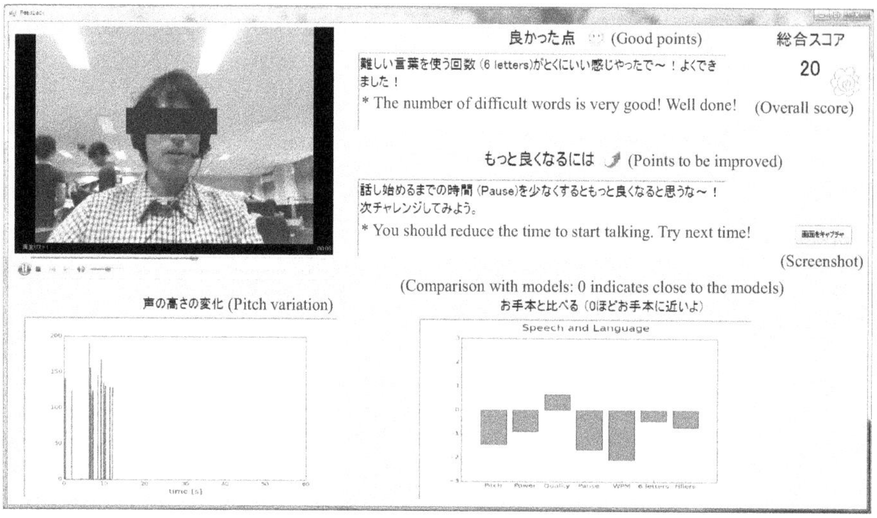

Figure 6. The summary feedback provided by the automated social skills trainer.

2) Is there a difference between talking to humans (human-human interaction: HHI) and talking to avatars (human-computer interaction: HCI) in terms of narrative?

3) Does narrative skill relate to autistic traits?

4) Are the extracted features effective for identifying narrative skill?

The result of the first experiment is used in data collection and summary feedback of the automated social skills trainer.

Procedure

We recruited 19 graduate students (16 males and 3 females), all of whom were native Japanese speakers[6]. All subjects used the proposed system and were told that their speech and video would be recorded. A webcam (ELECOM UCAM-DLY300TA) placed on top of the laptop and headset (ELECM HS-HP168K) recorded the video and audio of participants. We recorded not only HCI but also an HHI setting in which the first author listened to the speaker's story and nodded his head according to the speaker's utterances. The same 19 participants participate in the HCI and HHI. For HCI, participants interact with the same avatar.

To get a grasp of each subject's social skills independent of the proposed system, or the narrative setting in general, we also administered a social skills test for each subject. Specifically, we measured the sum of subarea scores for communication and social skills of Japanese version of the Autism-spectrum quotient (AQ) [3, 24] which is a standard tool to measure autistic traits with a total of 50 questions including 5 subareas.

Next, we had raters watch the interactions of each participant and rate their narrative skill. Although it would be ideal for raters to be professional social skills trainers, they are few and far between, so it is difficult to recruit them for the experiment. Thus, as a proxy, we selected raters from members of the general population. Because raters are required to have good social skills to recognize users' non-verbal expressiveness, we selected two people (male and female) with good social skills as annotators. Specifically, the annotators were selected to have low sums of the AQ subarea scores for communication and social skills (where lower indicates better social skills). The sums of both areas were 1 and 4, which is lower than the mean value of 7.6 for Japanese students [24]. The raters did not participate in the experiments as subjects. The raters did not know the recorded participants, and were trained by rating several examples prior to the evaluation. Two raters watched recorded participants' narrative for both HHI and HCI, and answered a questionnaire[7], which is based on [15]. The questionnaire included the following items related to the participant's overall narrative performance and use of non-verbal cues such as intonation, amplitude, and lexicon usage, rated on a scale of 1 (not good, not appropriate, or small (few)) to 7 (good, appropriate, or large (frequent)).

Q1. Overall narrative skill

Q2. Concentration

Q3. Friendliness

Q4. Attractiveness

Q5. Speaking rate

Q6. Usage of fillers

Q7. Intonation

Q8. Voice quality

Q9. Amplitude

Q10. Usage of easy words

[6]Note that the Research Ethic Committee of our institution has reviewed and approved both this and the following experiments. Written informed consent was obtained from all subjects before the experiments.

[7]https://docs.google.com/forms/d/1AQRc1sAQQooEt7zY89H7aJQzKFf8zqGH4u-nCCVwnGs/viewform?c=0&w=1&usp=mail_form_link

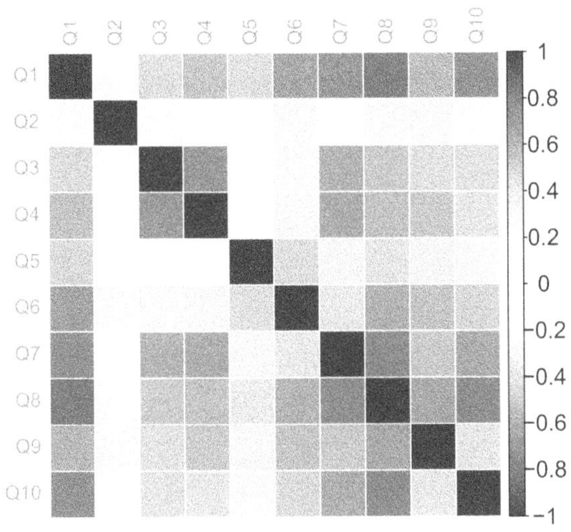

Figure 7. Pearson's r correlations between various questions. Color indicates the strength of statistically significant correlations, and white indicates zero. Rows and columns represent the questions in the same order, so the diagonal is self-correlation.

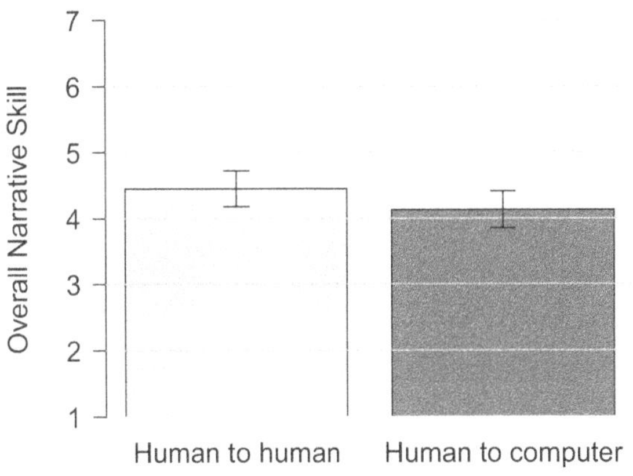

Figure 8. The difference of raters' scores between HHI and HCI. Error bars indicate standard error.

Agreement

The agreement of the two raters was measured by Cohen's kappa-coefficient, which calculates agreement beyond chance by distinguishing the observed agreement (A_{obs}) from the agreement by chance (A_{ch}), as follows:

$$\kappa = (A_{obs} - A_{ch}) / (1 - A_{ch}) . \quad (1)$$

The two raters answered the ten questions for each speaker's narrative. We analyzed agreement for the question of overall narrative skills. For each rater, each subject was assigned a class of being either above or below the average score for the rater, and agreement between the classes was used to calculate the coefficient. The Kappa coefficient of two classes for two raters was 0.580, which corresponds to moderate agreement according to the scale proposed by [20].

Correlation between questions

Figure 7 shows the correlation matrix of each question. For Q6, because usage of fillers can be assumed to be inversely proportional to social skill, we inverted the ratings before measuring correlation. The result showed that questions especially asking about the speech and language features were significantly related to overall narrative skill. On the other hand, questions asking about concentration were not related to overall skills and other features. We can also see that questions related to speech and language features, excluding Q5, were correlated each other.

Differences between human and computer interaction

To examine the difference between HHI and HCI, we show averaged rater scores for HHI and HCI in Figure 8. We can see that there were differences between HHI and HCI, and raters' scores of narrative skill in HHI were slightly higher than HCI. However, we did not find a statistical difference ($p > .05$) by Student's t-test. It is likely that if differences exist between interaction with our proposed system and interaction with an actual human in terms of overall narrative skills, they are small.

Model people and autistic traits

Based on the raters' scores, we determined the top 5 of 19 subjects to be our models for additional experiments including the modeling step of SST. As shown in Figure 9, the median value of the AQ was 1 in the case of model persons, and 13 in the case of the others. This indicates that there is also a strong relationship between the raters' assessment of narrative skill and the subjects' answers on the AQ test.

Regression

We calculated the statistical differences of the automatically extracted features between model persons and others using Student's t-test. We found that WPM, words of more than 6 letters, and amplitude were significantly different between the groups ($p < .05$), and other features were not significantly different ($p > .05$). Thus we used these three features to predict overall narrative skill using the multiple regression method. Finally we found that the correlation between the predicted value and actual value was 0.51 ($p < .05$). This regression model was integrated into the system as the feedback module's overall score.

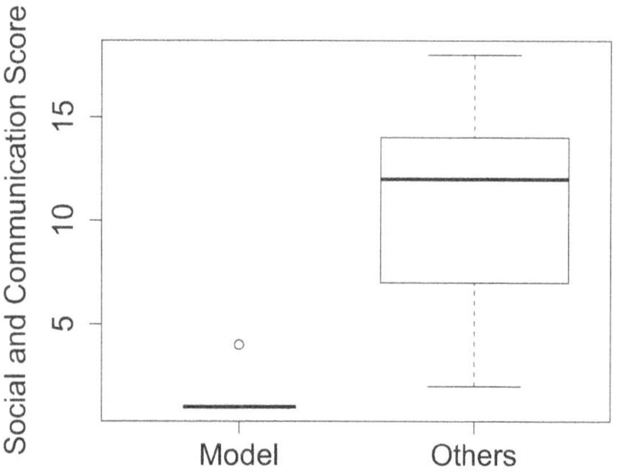

Figure 9. The ranges of the AQ for model persons and others. Zero indicates high social and communication skills, and 20 indicates low social and communication skills.

EXPERIMENT 2: SOCIAL SKILLS TRAINING

In the second experiment, we examined whether the automated social skills trainer is effective to train social skills, specifically:

1) How effective is the automated social skills trainer in helping users improve their narrative skills?

2) Do users find the automated social skills trainer easy to use and helpful?

Procedure

We recruited a total of 30 graduate students (22 males and 8 females) all of whom were native Japanese speakers, different from those who participated in the first experiment. Participants first entered the experiment room, and were given instructions by the first author. All subjects were told that their speech and video would be recorded. The webcam (ELECOM UCAM-DLY300TA) placed on top of the laptop and headset (ELECM HS-HP168K) recorded the video and audio of participants.

We separated participants into 3 groups: the reading book group (10 males), the video modeling group (6 males and 4 females), and the feedback group (6 males and 4 females). The reading book group, which serves as a control, read two types of social skills books which were related to story telling/narrative skills. The book titles were "Social skills training: collection of cases" and "The easiest guide to presentations" (in Japanese). The video modeling group and the feedback group used the automated social skills trainer for their training. The video modeling group only watched the model videos, while the feedback group performed role-play and received automated feedback. The feedback group can also watch the model videos. As shown in Figure 10, all subjects spoke their narratives to the agent (pre), received training for 50 minutes, and spoke their narratives to the agent again (post).

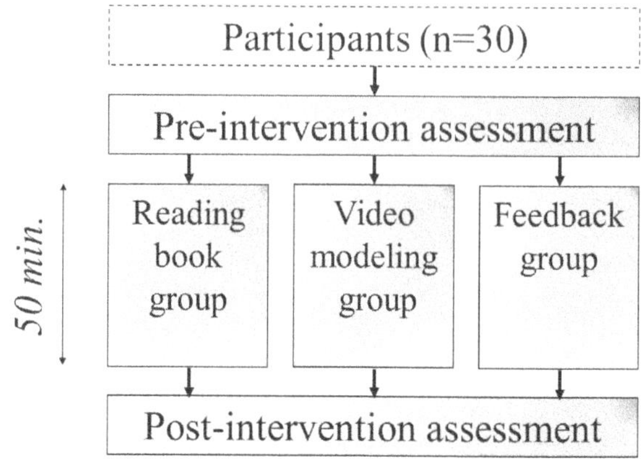

Figure 10. Study design and participant assignment to experimental groups in the second experiment.

The same two raters from the first experiment evaluated the subjects' narrative skill by answering overall narrative skill (Q1 of the first experiment) rated on a scale of 1 to 7. Raters did not know subjects, and the order of the pre- and post-training narratives was randomized to prevent bias. We averaged the two raters' scores and calculated improvement in score (post - pre) for each group[8]. Note that the initial scores of each group were not significantly different ($F[2,25]=0.90$, $p > .05$).

The effect of intervention type was analyzed using one-way analysis of variance (ANOVA). Post-hoc comparisons between the feedback group and the reading book group, and the feedback group and the video modeling group involved Bonferoni's method.

After using the automated social skills trainer, the feedback group answered a questionnaire to evaluate usability and effectiveness of the system[9]. The questionnaire included the following items related to the system usability and training effect, rated on a scale of 1 (disagree) to 7 (agree). The users were also asked to provide comments about each question.

Q1. The system was easy to use.

Q2. I would like to use this system frequently.

Q3. The trainer looks like a human.

Q4. Watching my own video and feedback were useful.

Q5. Watching model video was useful.

Agreement

We calculated agreement according to the same procedure described in the previous section. The Kappa coefficient of two classes for two raters was 0.638, which indicates good agreement based on [20]. The agreement of the two raters was almost the same as the first experiment.

[8] Among the 30 participants, one subject each in the reading book and feedback group did not have sufficient time to train for 50 min, so we omitted these subjects.

[9] https://docs.google.com/forms/d/1Qhe1UvXrZlHvOfY5YewQD1d2pwue5APhrNiLHl3lasc/viewform?c=0&w=1

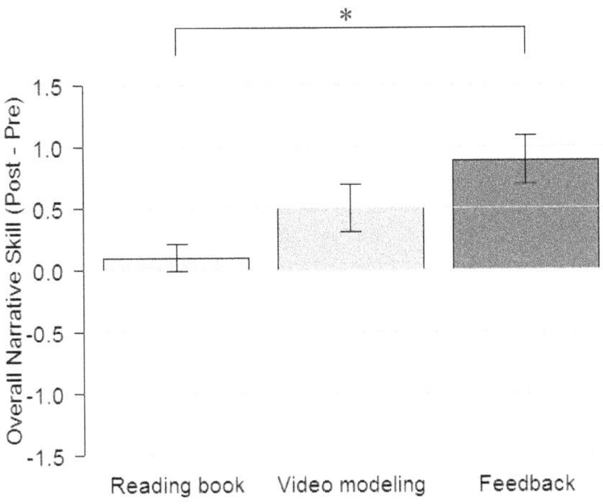

Figure 11. The overall narrative score of each group. Error bars indicate standard error (*: p < .05).

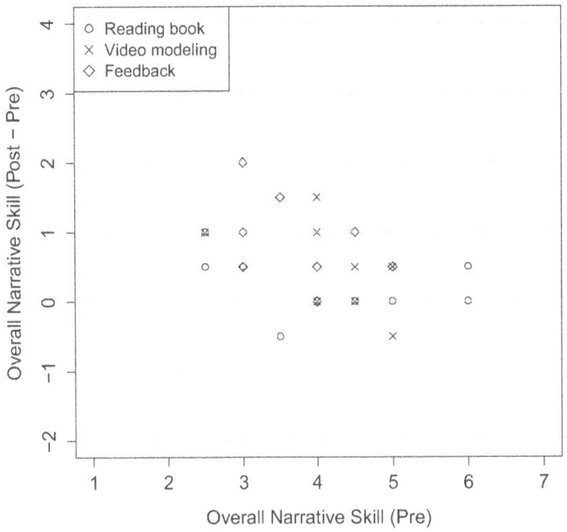

Figure 12. The relationship between initial and improvement in scores.

Training effect

Figure 11 shows the improvement of overall narrative skills in each group. These results show that intervention type significantly affected the change in raters' scores (F[2,25]=4.67, $p < .05$) with $\eta^2 = .26$ according to ANOVA. Comparisons showed that the change in raters' scores of participants in the feedback group who used the automated social skills trainer was significantly higher than the reading book group ($p < .05$). The difference between the video modeling group and the feedback group, and the video modeling group and the reading book group was not judged as statistically significant ($p > .05$).

Figure 12 shows the improvement of overall narrative skills and initial scores in each group. The correlation coefficient between overall narrative skills prior to training and improvement was -0.438 ($p < .05$) showing a weak negative correlation. This is a natural result, because people who have difficulties in social interaction have more space to improve.

Subjective evaluations

The paragraphs below describe findings from the participants' subjective evaluations of the automated social skills trainer and their feedback on their experience. We analyzed qualitative and quantitative results to represent user experience and system usability.

- **The system was easy to use:** The usability of the automated social skills trainer was rated an average of 5.4 (SD = 0.9). Most participants found the system is easy to use.

  "It is easy to operate the system using only speech. My voice was recognized and I felt comfortable."

  "The content of training was separated according to purpose (e.g. modeling, feedback, and homework), and it was easy for me."

- **I would like to use this system frequently:** The question regarding whether the user would like to use the system again was rated an average of 5.0 (SD = 0.7). Most participants would like to use the system frequently.

  "I would like to talk to system with more variation. I want to use this system every day, and also record a life log."

  "It is interesting to watch my score with helpful comments."

- **The avatar looks like a human:** The question about whether the avatar looks like a human was rated an average of 4.8 (SD = 0.4). Some participants thought the character looks like a human.

  "I thought avatar's behavior is natural, and I did not feel unnaturalness in interaction."

  "I felt like I spoke to real human."

  However, some participants thought the avatar did not seem like a human specifically in terms of speech synthesis.

  "I felt the synthesized speech is robot-like, the intonation was unnatural."

- **Watching my own video and feedback were useful:** According to the participant's responses to the questionnaire, the feedback and watching the user's own video was rated an average of 5.6 (SD = 1.1). Most participants thought the feedback and video were useful.

  "It was easy to train my skill because the system indicated the points to be improved."

  "I was happy to be encouraged."

  "Conversation is abstract, but the system displayed the concrete values. It is very interesting and helpful."

- **Watching model video was useful:** Overall, participants rated their preference toward watching the models' video an average of 5.2 (SD=1.5), suggesting the usefulness of model video.

  "After watching the role model, I easily started to talk because of the good reference."

  "I was interested in the variation of the good examples."

  However, the result also showed the SD value was large. Some participants did not say that model video was helpful.

  "I think I already had good skill so the modeling is not useful for me."

  "I would like to see the good points of the model persons."

DISCUSSION

In this paper, we developed a dialogue system named "automated social skills trainer" which provides social skills training in the context of human-computer interaction. The automated social skills trainer is based on conventional SST including defining target skills, modeling, role-play, feedback, reinforcement, and homework. We focus on story telling/narrative skill as a target skill. The system includes several modules: behaviour generation, sensing & analysis from recorded video, and summary feedback. In this study, our focus was to assess the effectiveness of an automated social skills trainer that follows human-to-human SST as closely as possible. To evaluate effectiveness of the automated social skills trainer, we performed two experiments.

In our first experiment, we confirmed the relationship between overall narrative skills and speech and language information, confirmed that there was no significant difference between HHI and HCI, set model persons according to the evaluation of two raters, and found a relationship between observed narrative ability and AQ. Baron-Cohen and their colleagues reported that the AQ value was widely distributed among members of the general population and that it is related to autistic traits [3]. Our result showing a relationship between AQ and overall narrative skills is consistent with the above report.

In our second experiment, we confirmed a training effect particularly for participants in the case of the feedback group rather than the reading book group. It showed that the system could help people who have difficulties in social interaction improve their social skills. The video modeling group also improved in their scores, which is consistent to the previous work [9]. The video modeling of others was also helpful in social skills training. In this experiment, we did not set a group that watched their own video and did not watch the feedback. There is previous work reporting that subjects dislike looking at their own video during interview skill training and the skills did not change [15], so we plan to investigate these elements separately in the future. We also confirmed a weak negative correlation between initial narrative skills and improvements in scores. This shows that training effects are found more strongly in people who have difficulties in social interaction than others. In subjective evaluation, we confirmed most participants of the feedback group were satisfied with the system in terms of usability and the feedback.

For future directions, we would like to confirm the training effect over a longer period, and recruit special-need populations such as people with ASD. We also plan to add other target social skills in the automated social skills trainer, and compare with human-to-human SST. In order to do so, we will more thoroughly examine SST from the viewpoint of HHI and HCI including types of agent (e.g. the effect of human-like avatars). Multi-modal feature analysis is also important. For example, we plan to incorporate visual image processing and eye-gaze analysis into the automated social skills trainer.

ACKNOWLEDGMENTS

We would like to thank Kazuyo Iida for her helpful comments regarding the system. This study is supported by JSPS KAKEN 26540117 and Foundation for Nara Institute of Science and Technology.

REFERENCES

1. American Psychiatric Association. *Diagnostic and statistical manual of mental disorders* (5th ed.). Washington, DC, (2013).
2. Baron-Cohen, S., Richler, J., Bisarya, D., Gurunathan, N., Wheelwright, S. The systemizing quotient: an investigation of adults with Asperger syndrome or high-functioning autism, and normal sex differences. *Philosophical Trans. the Royal Society of London Series B: Biological Sciences 358*, 361-374 (2003).
3. Baron-Cohen, S., Wheelwright, S., Skinner, R., Martin, J., Clubley, E. The Autism-Spectrum Quotient (AQ): evidence from Asperger syndrome/high-functioning autism, males and females, scientists and mathematicians. *J. Autism and Developmental Disorders 31*, 5-17 (2001).
4. Bauminger, N. The facilitation of social-emotional understanding and social interaction in high-functioning children with autism: Intervention outcomes. *J. Autism and Developmental Disorders 32*, 283-298 (2002).
5. Bishop, J. The Internet for educating individuals with social impairments. *J. of Computer Assisted Learning 19*, 546-556 (2003).
6. Bone, D., Black, P., Lee, C., Williams, E., Levitt, P., Lee, S., Narayanan, S. Spontaneous-Speech Acoustic-Prosodic Features of Children with Autism and the Interacting Psychologist. *Proc. Interspeech*, (2002).
7. Bonneh, Y., Levanon, Y., Dean Pardo, O., Lossos, L., Adini, Y. Abnormal speech spectrum and increased pitch variability in young autistic children. *Frontiers in Human Neuroscience 4*, (2011)
8. Davis, M., Dautenhahn, K., Nehaniv, C., Powell, S. Towards an Interactive System Facilitating Therapeutic Narrative Elicitation. *Proc. 3rd Conf. on NILE*, (2004).

9. Essau, C. A., Olaya, B., Sasagawa, S., Pithia, J., Bray, D., Ollendick, T. H. Integrating video-feedback and cognitive preparation, social skills training and behavioural activation in a cognitive behavioural therapy in the treatment of childhood anxiety. *J. Affect Disorders 167*, 261-267 (2014).

10. Hanson, M. H. Glottal characteristics of female speakers. *Harvard University, Ph. D. dissertation*, (1995).

11. Heeman, P. A., Lunsford, R., Selfridge, E., Black, L., Van Santen, J. Autism and interactional aspects of dialogue. *Proc. 11th SIGDIAL*, 249-252 (2010).

12. Kanner, L. Autistic disturbances of affective contact. *Nervous Child 2*, 217-250 (1943).

13. Kiss, G., Van Santen, H. Estimating Speaker-Specific Intonation Patterns Using the Linear Alignment Model. *Proc. Interspeech*, 354-358 (2013).

14. Kiss, G., Van Santen, H., Prud'hommeaux, T., Black, M. Quantitative Analysis of Pitch in Speech of Children with Neurodevelopmental Disorders. *Proc. Interspeech*, (2012).

15. Hoque, E., Courgeon, M., Mutlu, B., Martin, C., Picard W. MACH: my automated conversation coach. *Proc. 15th Conf. on UbiComp*, 697-706 (2013).

16. McCann, J., Sue, P. Prosody in autism spectrum disorders: a critical review. *International J Language & Communication Disorders 38*, 325-350 (2003).

17. Moore, D., Mcgrath, P., Thorpe, J. Computer-aided learning for people with autism - a framework for research and development. *Innovations in Education and Teaching International 37*, 218-228 (2000).

18. Parsons, S., Mitchell, P. The potential of virtual reality in social skills training for people with autistic spectrum disorders. *J. Intellectual Disability Research 46*, 430-443 (2002).

19. Pennebaker, W., Martha, F., Roger, B. Linguistic inquiry and word count (LIWC). LIWC [Computer software], (2005).

20. Rietveld, T., Van Hout, R. Statistical techniques for the study of language behaviour. *Mouton de Gruyter*, (1993).

21. Rouhizadeh, M., Prud'hommeaux, E., Roark, B., Van Santen, H. Distributional semantic models for the evaluation of disordered language. *Proc. NAACL-HLT*, 709-714 (2013).

22. Tanaka, H., Sakriani, S., Neubig, G., Toda, T., Nakamura, S. Linguistic and Acoustic Features for Automatic Identification of Autism Spectrum Disorders in Children's Narrative. *ACL2014 Workshop on Computational Linguistics and Clinical Psychology*, 88-96 (2014).

23. Van Santen, H., Richard, S., Alison, H. Quantifying repetitive speech in autism spectrum disorders and language impairment. *Autism Research 6*, 372-383 (2013).

24. Wakabayashi, A. Baron-Cohen, S., Wheelwright, S., Tojo, Y. The Autism-Spectrum Quotient (AQ) in Japan: a cross-cultural comparison. *J. Autism and Developmental Disorders 36*, 263-270 (2006).

25. Wallace, C. J., Nelson, C. J., Liberman, R. P., Aitchison, R. A., Lukoff, D., Elder, J. P., Ferris, C. A review and critique of social skills training with schizophrenic patients. *Schizophr Bull 6*, 42-63 (1980).

Evaluating Subjective Accuracy in Time Series Pattern-Matching Using Human-Annotated Rankings

Philipp Eichmann
peichmann@cs.brown.edu

Emanuel Zgraggen
ez@cs.brown.edu

Brown University
Department of Computer Science
Providence RI, United States

ABSTRACT
Finding patterns is a common task in time series analysis which has gained a lot of attention across many fields. A multitude of similarity measures have been introduced to perform pattern searches. The accuracy of such measures is often evaluated objectively using a one nearest neighbor classification (1NN) on labeled time series or through clustering. Prior work often disregards the subjective similarity of time series which can be pivotal in systems where a user specified pattern is used as input and a similarity-based ranking is expected as output (query-by-example). In this paper, we describe how a human-annotated ranking based on real-world queries and datasets can be created using simple crowdsourcing tasks and use this ranking as ground-truth to evaluate the perceived accuracy of existing time series similarity measures. Furthermore, we show how different sampling strategies and time series representations of pen-drawn queries effect the precision of these similarity measures and provide a publicly available dataset which can be used to optimize existing and future similarity search algorithms.

Author Keywords
Time series; crowd sourcing; result ranking; sketching; information retrieval; sampling; pen & touch.

ACM Classification Keywords
H.3.3. Information Storage and Retrieval: Query formulation; H.5.m. Information Interfaces and Presentation (e.g. HCI): Miscellaneous

INTRODUCTION
Data in the form of time series can be found in any domain. Stock prices, medical data, trajectories of objects, crime statistics, "Quantified Self" data, temperatures or sales figures can all be represented as data streams over time and even higher dimensional data are straightforward to visualize using two-dimensional line graphs. Such visualizations enable humans to interpret and compare time series data.

IUI'15, March 29 - April 01 2015, Atlanta, GA, USA.

ACM 978-1-4503-3306-1/15/03 $15.00
http://dx.doi.org/10.1145/2678025.2701379

However, visually identifying patterns within large time series or across multiple time series is a tedious and error prone task. Since traditional query languages (e.g. SQL) are often not well suited for this type of temporal pattern search, researchers have published an abundance of papers introducing pattern-matching algorithms.

Modern hardware, which supports pen and/or touch input allows users to swiftly sketch query patterns for time series data. Consider a medical researcher who wants to find patients with a specific disease who have a decreasing platelet count or a stock-trader who wants to find stocks following a certain trend. While such queries are cumbersome to specify through standard UI controls, drawing an upward or downward line on a tablet through a pen-stroke or a touch-gesture is simple and intuitive. These hand-drawn patterns, however, are not exact and therefore, the retrieved results should be displayed as similarity-based rankings, where the first item is the time series most similar to the input sketch.

Figure 1 shows a screenshot of TimeSketch, a pen and touch-based application that allows users to query time series through such hand-drawn patterns and displays results as similarity-based rankings. We implemented this prototype to test and experiment with different time series pattern-matching algorithms and sampling strategies. Through an informal user evaluation of TimeSketch, we realized that algorithms oftentimes produce perceivably inaccurate results, as depicted in the screenshot.

The accuracy of many existing pattern-matching algorithms have been evaluated through nearest neighbor classification (1NN) with much less attention given to how humans gauge the results of such similarity searches. This does not come as a surprise; label prediction with no further distinction within a label group can be sufficient to compare the overall performance of different techniques. However, in cases where the expected output of a search is a similarity-based ranking, a more detailed comparison is required. These rankings also need to align with human intuition and a user's perceived similarity. "Good" matches, as defined by a distance metric of an algorithm, might not coincide with the subjective similarity. This is especially important for the top k matches, whereas dissecting time series which are dissimilar to the query pattern is more difficult and arguably less important to a user. Due to the lack of datasets that contain hand-drawn patterns and human-annotated similarity rankings based on those patterns, it is currently hard to understand the type of patterns

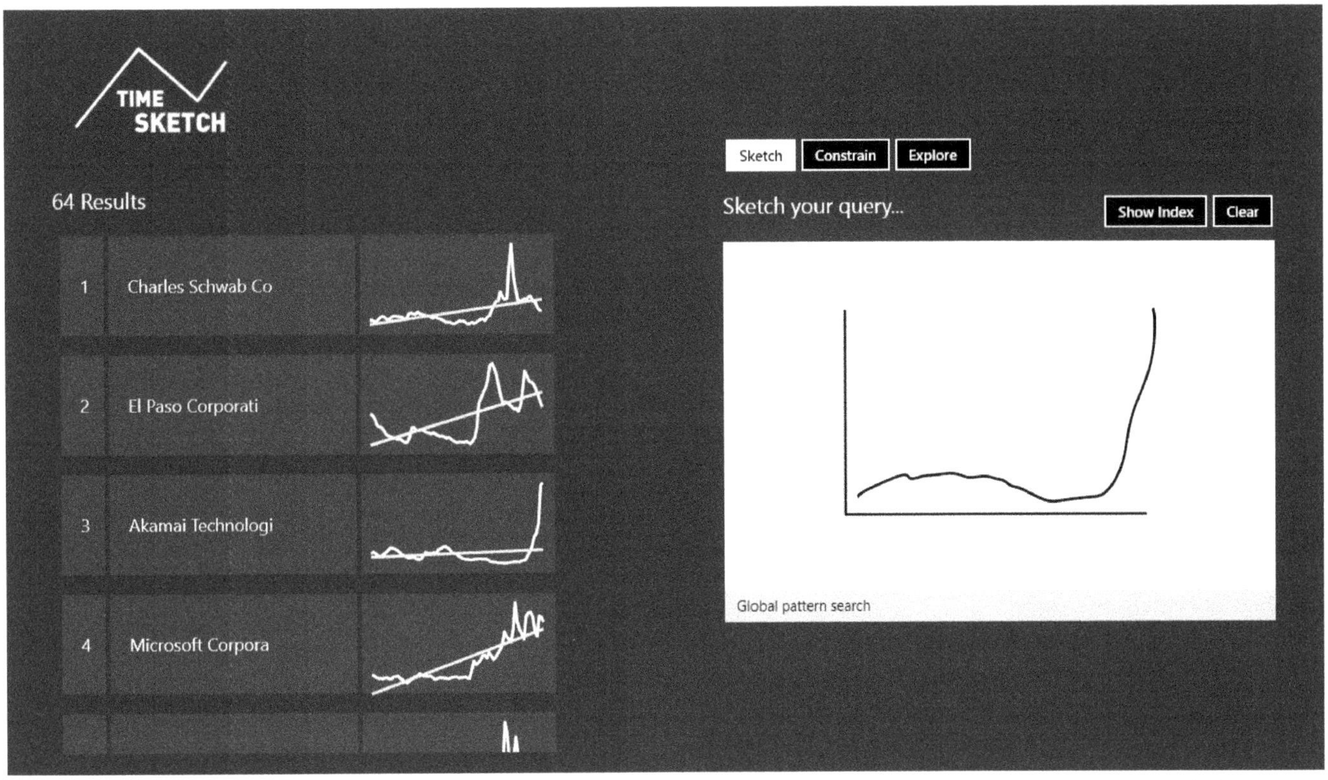

Figure 1. Screenshot of TimeSketch, a pen and touch-based application which allows users to query time series through pen or touch-drawn query patterns. Different combinations of sampling strategies and similarity measures (uniform linear downsampling to 80 points and SpADe similarity measure, in this case) sometimes return a perceivably incorrect ranking of the search results. Result number 3, for instance, should be clearly ranked first.

users draw as well as to measure the subjective accuracy of existing algorithms for such use-cases.

In this paper, we present a methodology to create human-annotated rankings of time series based on the perceived distance to a hand-drawn reference pattern. We then use these rankings to evaluate the accuracy of existing time series similarity measures, across different sampling strategies and with varying time series representations. Furthermore, we provide some analysis of our collected hand-drawn patterns and our evaluation that provide insights for possible future research efforts.

PRELIMINARIES AND RELATED WORK

In this section, we give an overview of research efforts in the areas of query-by-example for time series data, time series representations, and similarity measures. In addition, we introduce definitions that we will refer to throughout this paper. We refer the reader to [6] and [20] for a more comprehensive summary of time series representations and similarity measures.

Definitions and Notations

In the upcoming sections will use similar definitions as in [21] and [6]:

Time Series: A time series T is an ordered list $T = t_1, t_2, ..., t_n$ where each t_i is a data point in a $d-$dimensional space.

Subsequence: A subsequence $T_{i,k}$ of time series T where i is the starting index in T and $k = |T_{i,k}|$ is the length of the subsequence in number of data points.

Query Pattern: A Query Pattern Q is a subsequence used as input for similarity search whose data points correspond to either a subsequence of an existing time series or to one defined by other means (e.g. mouse/pen/touch-sketch).

Time Series Representations

An unmodified time series is called a *raw representation* [6] and its length depends on both, the time-span of the recorded data and the sampling rate. Typically, before a similarity search is executed, the two time series are converted to a different representation. This has the advantage of reducing (or sometimes also increasing) the number of data-points i.e. the dimensionality for reasons of space and search efficiency, noise reduction or simply scaling both sequences to an equal length. The GEMINI framework [8], for instance, proposes to find candidate matches by downsampling the time series to a dimension that works well with index structures. Once all candidate matches are found, their full-resolution time series is read from disk and compared with the query sequence using a distance metric such as the Euclidean Distance. This greatly speeds up the pattern-matching process as opposed to having to sequentially scan all time series.

Time series representations can be categorized as follows: data-adaptive, non-adaptive, model-based and data-dictated

[22]. An overview and description of many representations can be found in [6, 17]. In previous publications, time series representations have been solely compared to each other in terms of indexing performance using a metric called *Tightness of lower the bound (TLB)*. This is the ratio of the estimated distance between two sequences under that representation, over the true distance between the same two sequences [13]. Interestingly, it has been found that there is very little difference between different representations in terms of indexing speed [19, 6]. Moreover, it was claimed that a representation should not be chosen based on its approximation fidelity, but rather on other features such as the visual appearance. In this paper, we exploit this fact to choose a suitable segmentation technique in order to project a query pattern defined by a pen stroke to a time series using different representations. Specifically, we use variants of Perceptually Important Points (PIP) [9] and Piecewise Linear Segmentation (PLS) [14] among two other approaches which we describe in the Method section.

Similarity Measures

Similarity measures are used to compute a distance between two time series. [6] distinguishes between *lock-step*, *elastic*, *threshold-based* and *pattern-based* measures.

The simplest similarity measures are lock-step measures, which compute the distance between two time series in a one-to-one fashion, where each data point in one time series is only compared to its direct counterpart in the other. Typically, the *Euclidean Distance* is used because it penalizes larger distances more, but other Lp-norms such as the Manhattan Distance fall into this category. One of the biggest shortcomings of lock-step measures is that they are sensitive to local time shifting [4], such that even two time series that are perceived to be similar could be separated by a large distance. This makes the Euclidean Distance unsuitable for our application, as hand-drawn queries should be invariant to local time shifting and scaling. Nonetheless, we use this measure in our experiments in order to draw a comparison to other methods.

Elastic measures support shifts and scaling in time-dimension. Most notably Dynamic Time Warping (DTW), which was recently claimed to be the best measure in terms of speed and accuracy [21]. It tries to find the optimal alignment between two time series by allowing for local warping within a certain window. DTW uses the Euclidean Distance as distance measure between two points. Thus, the Euclidean Distance is essentially a special case of DTW, where the warping window size is equal to 1. Other edit distance based measures include Longest Common SubSequence (LCSS) [1, 24], Edit Sequence on Real Sequence (EDR) [23], Swale [18], Edit Distance with Real Penalty (ERP) [3]. Elastic measures are especially important for human-drawn queries as the query patterns are never exact. Due to its popularity and recent research efforts, we use DTW in our experiments.

SpADe (Spatial Assembly Distance) is a pattern-based measure that promises to handle time/amplitude- shifting and scaling and noise [4]. It works by computing features over short subsequences of two time series, called *local patterns*, finding similar patterns called *local pattern matches* in both time series and eventually calculating the shortest distance between all found matches from the start of the time series to the end. As we consider time and amplitude invariance important characteristics of similarity measures for human-drawn queries, we also employ SpADe in our experiments.

Pattern-Matching Invariance

Some similarity measures reduce variance in pattern-matching by making the measure flexible to time-shifting/scaling and amplitude-shifting/scaling, which is important in applications where the query pattern is defined by hand. Based on [2], we give a brief overview on how these and other types of invariance can be implemented.

Even though many subsequences in a dataset may look similar to a query pattern, they may be defined at different amplitude ranges or they are located at different offsets. *Amplitude invariance* can be achieved by normalizing the time series which are compared to each other. It is known that a *z-score normalization* follows the original shape of the data-points more closely than a *min/max normalization* [17]. Elastic similarity measures handle *local scaling* in time-dimension. To fix *global scaling*, on the other hand, we have to either test all possible window sizes or define a time range for a query pattern to eliminate the problem entirely. To tackle *phase invariance*, we have to test all possible alignments in time. Moreover, [2] suggests that *occlusion invariance*, the case where we want to ignore one or multiple subsequences in a pattern, can be achieve by simply ignoring the distance on those time intervals.

Defining Query Patterns

The idea of specifying time series queries in a query-by-example fashion has been around for over a decade. Typically, the goal of a similarity search is to perform a k-NN-search i.e. to return the k nearest neighbors given an input [25]. Similar to our prototype TimeSketch, QuerySketch lets users define arbitrary queries by sketching onto an empty graph, where the time scale can be adjusted by using a zoom function [26]. The Euclidean Distance between the query pattern and the time series in the dataset is used as similarity measure and each result is labeled with the distance to the query.

TimeSearcher uses the concept of timeboxes, rectangular regions that can be drawn over a time series, and uses the containing subsequences as query patterns [11]. Since timeboxes define value-ranges rather than fix-valued data points, the similarity of the specified query and the time series in a dataset is determined by an orthogonal range tree algorithm [5]. Counters are used as degree of similarity by measuring how many data points lie in the specified amplitude and time range. Even though the bulk of this paper focuses on query patterns rather then range-queries, TimeSearcher provides inspiration for further research (see Discussion and Future Work).

[10] presents TimeSearcher: Shape Search Edition (SSE), an extension of TimeSearcher where query patterns can be defined by shapes such as spikes, sinks, rises, drops, lines, plateaus, valleys and gaps. The authors describe attributes of

these shapes by which they can be identified, compared and ranked. The similarity measures we used in our evaluation are purely mathematical. However, as we note in the Discussion and Future Work section, a combination of high and low level similarity measures is a promising research direction.

Methods to evaluate time series similarity

Keogh et al. propose two ways to measure the true similarity of two time series [13], subjective evaluation and objective evaluation. The latter can be carried out by using a 1NN classification to predict a label for a time series from its nearest neighbor in a training dataset, where the classifier's distance measure is the similarity measure in question. A major drawback of this approach when evaluating similarity is that both, the training and test data must be labeled. Even though there are publicly available labeled datasets, new and unlabeled datasets cannot be tested. Furthermore, this method only measures how often the prediction of a label failed or succeeded but fails to provide a distance of how well it actually matched a query pattern, which is inevitable to create rankings. Also, it is often unclear who created the labels and based on which decisions.

Subjective evaluation relies on human judgment. A trivial way to evaluate the perceived accuracy of time series is to simply visualize matching results of different similarity measures and let people assess the quality of the algorithm. Another commonly used approach is to create a dendrogram of multiple time series using the single linkage method and let humans determine, if similar time series are reasonably linked. The authors of [15] and [14] note that the "correct" distance measure depends on user preference and the data domain. They describe an approach to adjust the similarity metric by using feedback from users. More specifically, they propose the time series to be represented as piecewise linear segments (PLS) and a weight vector to describe the relative importance of each segment. The weights are dynamically updated based on the user's relevance feedback, which allows for a custom weighting scheme for each user and domain.

METHOD

While existing time series datasets, such as [16], are suitable to benchmark classification and clustering accuracy, there are currently no datasets that provide a distance-based ranking or other means to fine-tune a similarity search algorithm which returns an ordered list of results, based on a given input sequence. The subjective accuracy of a similarity search algorithms depends on the data-domain and user preference [15, 14]. Therefore, when creating a system similar to TimeSketch, it is important to evaluate the perceived accuracy on a case-by-case basis. In this section, we show how human-annotated rankings can be created for any type of time series data based on [12] and using simple crowdsourcing tasks. Using the help of the crowd is especially advantagous in the absence of expert annotators or when annontating large amounts of time series data becomes unfeasible.

In Computer Vision, for instance, the human-perceived accuracy of image classification systems can be determined by testing the classifier against a human-annotated set of images (ground-truth). Borrowing this idea, we describe how a ground-truth for selected subsequences in a given dataset can be created using a crowdsourcing platform and use this ground-truth to compute a similarity-based ranking over all subsequences.

Creating Human-Annotated Rankings

In order to create a human-annotated ranking for a specific query, we first generate all possible subsequences in a dataset that match the length of a query pattern. We then create a set of all unordered pairs of subsequences and use a pairwise comparison between each of the subsequences to build a global ranking, according to their similarity to the query pattern.

More formally, for a given query pattern q and a dataset d, we generate a set S_q comprising all subsequences in d of the same length as q, where S_q is the set of all subsequences that will be part of the similarity ranking. Let U_{Sq} be the set of all unordered pairs in S_q. For each pair of subsequences $\langle a, b\rangle$ in U_{Sq}, we create a task on a crowdsourcing platform, where the workers' task is to decide, which of the two subsequences resembles the query pattern more (binary classification). We let the same task be answered by n distinct workers, in our case $n = 9$. The degree of agreement among all workers i.e. the probability of one subsequence being more similar to the query pattern than the other, can then be used to compute a global score of similarity. To obtain such a score for any subsequence $a \in S_q$, we can sum up the probabilities of a being more similar to q then all other subsequences in S_q.

$$\mathit{score}(a) = \sum_{b \in S_q} p(\langle a, b\rangle) \tag{1}$$

Where p in Equation 1 is a function that returns the probability of a being more similar to q than to the other subsequence b of a pair, according to the number of received votes in the binary classification task. To create the ranking, S_q can be sorted by the score of its elements.

Comparing Rankings

Computing a ranking from the distances provided by a similarity measure is as simple as ordering all subsequences based on their distance in ascending order. Once all rankings for all similarity measures and query pattern representations have been established for a particular query, they can be compared to the human-annotated ranking to see how well both rankings align. Given a human-annotated ranking R_H and any similarity-measure based ranking R_S, we compute the Spearman's rank correlation coefficient

$$\rho = 1 - \frac{6 \sum d_i^2}{n(n^2 - 1)} \tag{2}$$

where d_i is the difference of the ith ranking in R_S and R_H respectively and n is the total number of ranks. A Spearman coefficient of 1 or -1 indicates that the two ranking correlation perfectly (positively or negatively) which means the produced ranking is identical to the human created one. We use this correlation coefficient as a measure of how well two

ID	Dataset	Length
1	Daily reported crimes in Chicago	4,748
2	Microsoft Stock Values	5,036
3	NBA Player Scores	930
4	City Temperatures	2,920

Table 1. List of all datasets used in survey

Dataset	Question
1	Crime rate which fluctuates periodically for a couple of months
1	A period of a year, where the crime rate increased steadily
2	Find the 2008 stock market crash
2	A situation where the stock value dropped and remained low for a while
3	Find a player who started off really well at the beginning of his career, but had decreasing scores over his entire career
3	Find a period where a player consistently scored more than 20 points per game
4	Find a place in the United States where it is warmer in Winter than in Summer
4	Find places with hot months in 2013

Table 2. Example questions users tried to answer with a pen/touch-based interface.

rankings align because the distance between two ranks are squared. Thus small differences in ranks (i.e., transpositions) are less penalized than larger ones.

EVALUATION AND ANALYSIS

Using the method described in the previous section, we created 8 different human-annotated rankings through Amazon Mechanical Turk, using 8 pen-drawn query patterns over 4 different datasets and compared the accuracy of 3 different similarity measures in conjunction with 4 distinct sampling strategies.

Datasets

To avoid bias in queries towards a certain domain, we created 4 different datasets with varying lengths and context, as shown in Table 1. Dataset 1 contains daily reported crime incidents in the city of Chicago from 2001 to 2013. In the second dataset, we listed the Microsoft stock closing values of all trading days over a period of 10 years (1994-2013). Dataset 3 contains the number of points former NBA player Michael Jordan scored per game for all season games he had played. Finally, dataset 4 comprises maximum daily temperatures of 8 different cities in the United States.

Collecting Query Patterns

Instead of merely using a subsequence of a time series as query pattern, we asked 6 users to draw queries using a pen/touch-based application, which records all strokes and pen-related meta-data. Before recording a query pattern, we instructed the participants on how to use the tool and which dataset their queries should target. For instance, a user was requested to draw an arbitrary number of queries for a dataset comprising the maximum daily temperature of 8 different

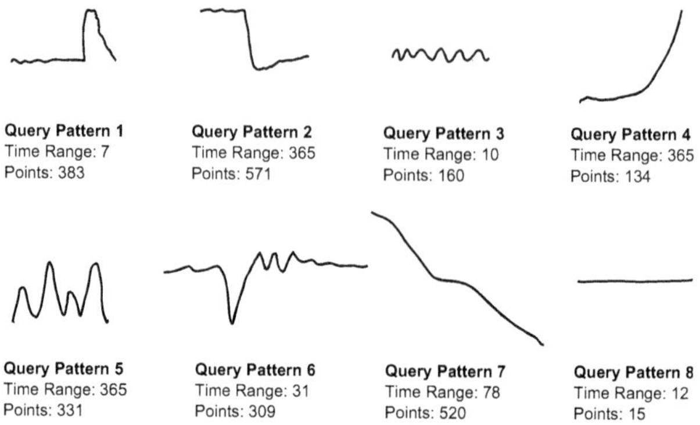

Figure 2. Eight hand-picked query patterns used to create human-annotated rankings.

cities in the United States. The user was then asked to define a pattern length in terms of number of data points (e.g. 30 days) and optionally instructed the application to draw guide lines, which some users found helpful to define their queries more precisely. Also, the participants were able to choose whether or not they wish to ignore the given minimum and maximum amplitude in their query and to change the size of the drawing area.

We recorded a total number of 112 pen-drawn queries (shown in Figure 8 at the end of this paper) over the 4 different datasets. The participants of our survey were all graduates students with no prior experience in time series analysis. For each pattern, we recorded what question the user wants to answer with her/his query, some of which can be found in Table 2.

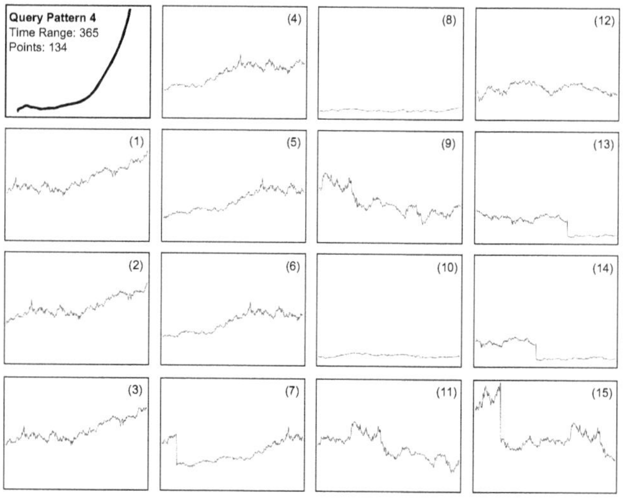

Figure 3. Example of a human-annotated ranking created through crowd-sourcing tasks.

Creating a Human-Annotated Ranking

After collecting sketches, we proceeded to creating human-annotated rankings based on our method outlined earlier in the paper. Since the number of required pairwise comparisons becomes very large for a large number of subsequences, we followed the following procedure: from the set of all recorded

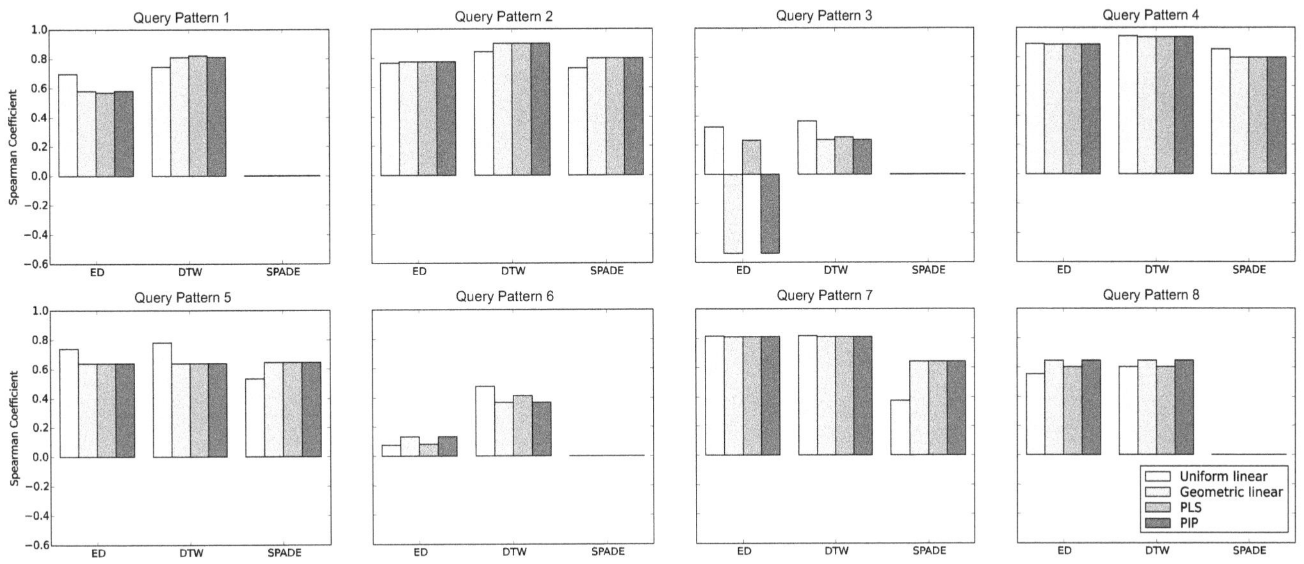

Figure 4. Spearman correlation coefficients of different algorithms and sampling methods when compared to human-annotated rankings (1 indicating perfect positive correlation, -1 perfect negative correlation).

query patterns, we hand-picked eight (two for each dataset) to assure coverage of the most distinct types of user-drawn queries. Using a window of the size of the pattern length, we then generated all possible subsequences with step size 1. Next, we assigned each retrieved subsequence to one of 25 clusters using k-means clustering and randomly picked 4 from each cluster. This left us with 100 subsequences to be compared with the query pattern. Since this would still require us to do 44,550 pairwise comparisons ($9 \cdot \binom{100}{2}$), we used a two-task crowdsourcing strategy. In a first task, we displayed the query pattern and a plot of one of the 100 subsequences. The workers' task was to judge the similarity of two graphs by selecting a value from 1 to 10. We let each comparison between the query pattern and every subsequence be answered 5 times and then selected the 15 subsequences that resemble the query pattern most, according to the workers' median answer. Using these steps, we were able to reduce the number of required pairwise comparisons for each query pattern to 105. In a second crowdsourcing task, we employed our method of creating a human-annotated ranking. We created a set of all unordered pairs of the 15 subsequences and built a binary classification task where the query pattern is displayed along with the two subsequences of a pair. The workers' task was then to select the one subsequence of a pair which resembled the query pattern more. We let each task be answered 9 times and then computed the score of each subsequence using Equation 1.

Evaluating Similarity Search Accuracy

In order to create a similarity measure based ranking for the query pattern, we first need to transform the sketch into an evenly spaced time series. This is a delicate task, as the strokes provided by pen/touch hardware consist of a varying number of non-uniformly distributed 2D-points, whereas the time series in our datasets are evenly spaced. To conduct this transformation, we first order all points by their time stamp. We then remove all points that are not monotonically spaced in time. Next, we sample the points to match the length of the query pattern with one of the following algorithms:

Uniform Linear: A uniform linear sampling stores the values of all points in an array and performs up/down-sampling using a linear smoothing kernel. It is naive in the sense that it distorts the shape of the originally drawn pattern by directly converting an unevenly spaced time series to an evenly spaced one.

Geometric Linear: A geometric linear sampling maps each point of the resulting time series to a location between two 2D-points of the input stroke. The value at that location is computed using linear interpolation.

PLS: PLS sampling performs a piecewise linear segmentation on the input stroke as described in [14]. The value is then retrieved in the same manner as in the Geometric Linear approach.

PIP: PIP sampling applies the PIP-algorithm on the input stroke as described in [9]. As in PLS, the value is then retrieved in the same manner as in the Geometric Linear approach.

Once the query pattern is converted to a time series, we can z-normalize both the pattern and subsequences and use a similarity measure to compute the distance between them. We employ three different algorithms in our experiments: Euclidean Distance, DTW and SpADe. To avoid implementation bias, we use the original implementation from [21, 4] respectively. The results of our comparisons can be seen in Figure 4. DTW produces rankings that are closest to the human-annotated rankings. For short query patterns (1, 3,

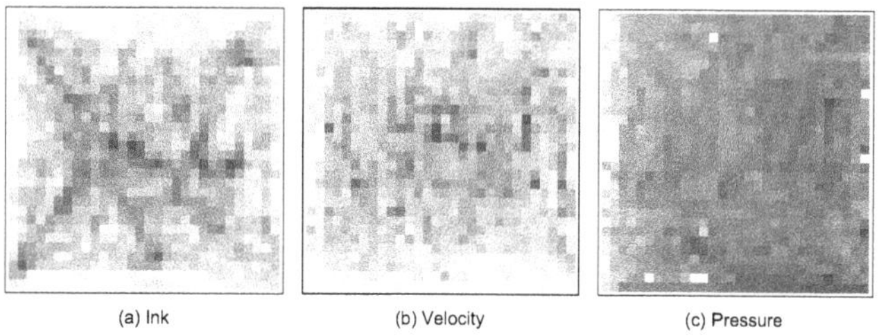

Figure 5. Heat-maps visualizing different properties across all query patterns over the normalized sketching area. Dark-red indicates a higher value.

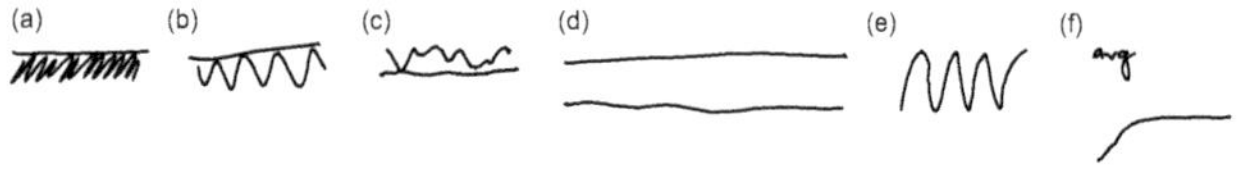

Figure 6. More involved multi-stroke query patterns that are not supported by tested time series pattern-matching algorithms.

6 in Figure 3), SpADe was unable to output meaningful distances. We verified this fact with the author, who confirmed that SpADe does not work well for very short time series. For larger time series it yields competitive results (query patterns 2, 4 and 5). The Euclidean Distance expectedly performed worse than DTW or equally well in some cases. Interestingly, it performed very badly in combination with Geometric Linear and PIP sampling in some cases (query pattern 3 and 6). We found that, especially for short time range queries, Geometric Linear and PIP sampling significantly distort the original sketch, which can lead to a comparitively large Euclidean Distance. DTW, however, manages to remedy a poorly sampled sketch to a certain extend. The naive uniform linear sampling did surprisingly well. One plausible reason for its good performance is that even though there are changes in velocity across the drawing area, as can be seen in Figure 5, the smoothing kernel makes up for the non-uniformly distributed points.

Overall, different sampling strategies do not seem to impact the accuracy of algorithms drastically. In fact, Geometric Linear, PLS and PIP actually often yield roughly the same results due to their identical interpolation method and only differ in the way the points are chosen during down-sampling.

Query Patterns

In order to get a better understanding of the types of questions users try to answer with the patterns they draw, we analyzed various properties of the sketches. Figure 5 shows some results of that analysis. (a) depicts the average ink distribution of all queries over a normalized sketching area (note that users were able to adjust the size of the sketching area). Users tend to focus on patterns that either target some extrema (corners) or align their patterns within the center region. We also recorded pen-speed as well as pen-pressure for each pattern. On average, velocity is highest within the center of the sketching area (b). We explain this through the ease-in/ease-out style that users tend to draw their patterns with. (c) suggests that there is no clear trend for pen-pressure as it appears to be uniform across the drawing area.

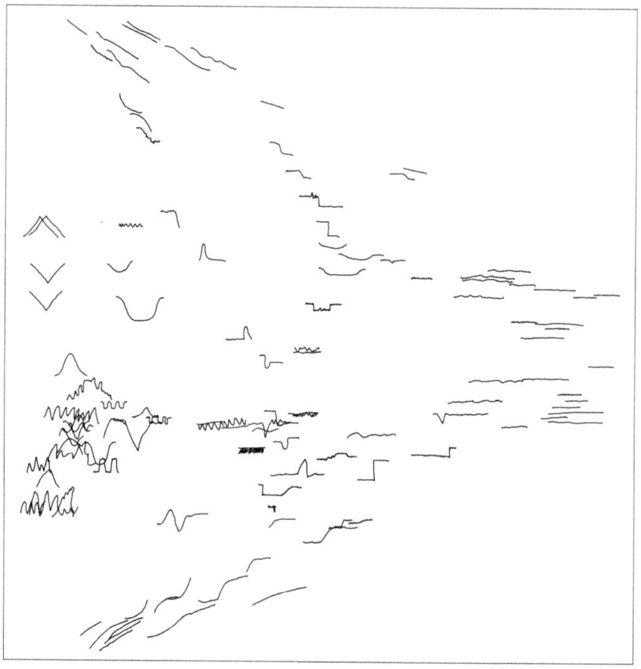

Figure 7. Automatic layout of all query sketches generated by applying PCA to the feature histograms of individual sketches.

While most of our 112 pen-drawn query patterns were simple single stroke patterns that were intended to find subsequences which followed a specific trend, some of our users wanted to search for more complex relations in the data. Questions like "Find a period where a player consistently scored more than 20 points per game" were usually drawn with multi-stroke sketches by our users. Figure 6 shows some queries with these characteristics. The sketches in (a), (b) and (c) are instances where users wanted to search for inequalities (e.g., "find everything above / below X"), while (d) depicts a range query (e.g., "find everything within X and Y"). Query (e) is an example where a user wanted to find time series which shows periodic fluctuations over a specific time period ("find all inconsistent basketball players") . However, our user did not intend to find time series that were close in shape to her sketch. (f) is a case, where a user annotated the sketch to provide some more information to the system. It is important to note that current state of the art time series pattern-matching algorithms, such as the ones we tested, do not support such queries directly. In a future effort, we aim to collect more hand-drawn sketches and try to extract a common sketching language that could be used to express other relations such as inequalities, ranges, fuzziness or fluctuations.

DISCUSSION AND FUTURE WORK

To get an intuition of the quality of the produced human-annotated rankings we inspected them visually. Although we agreed on most of the decisions made by the crowd, there were cases where we felt that a pair of subsequences should have been swapped. It is important to note that apart from a qualification test, the workers' answers were not validated or filtered using sentinel tasks or any other noise reduction technique. Also, with only 9 votes per pairwise comparison, chances are relatively high that some subsequences receive the same score. Increasing the number of required votes could help reducing ambiguities in generated rankings. Alternatively, multiple 9-round tasks could be averaged.

The analysis of the sampling methods used in our evaluation suggests that there are more suitable sampling methods than the ones used in our experiments. Sampling between two points artificially distorts the resulting time series. This is especially the case for short-length query pattern with high complexity. An adaptive sampling method, where the perceivably important points are aligned with the resulting time series could potentially lead to better results.

To further understand the different types of queries that users draw, we wanted to see if there are certain categories of patterns that occur across users and across datasets. Just by visually inspecting Figure 8, we can identify that for example straight-line or upward/downward trend patterns are drawn frequently. We obtain automatic clusters of such sketch categories by applying a similar approach as discussed in [7]. Each sketch is rendered as an image which we then represent by using a normalized feature histogram that is computed through a bag-of-words model over densely sampled local features. Figure 7 shows an automatic layout generated by applying dimensionality reduction (PCA) over these feature histograms. This initial experiment hints at the possibility of creating an accurate classifier to assign category labels to input sketches. Such labels could in turn be used to detect different pattern types, such as inequalities, range queries, etc. or to optimize algorithms through fast-rejection techniques.

We are planning to conduct a more rigorous study on what type of time series queries users are interested in. The results of the study could be used to define a visual vocabulary i.e. sketching-language which supports common types of queries. Because our approach of evaluating the subjective accuracy in time series pattern-matching can be extended to an entire conceptual query space, algorithms supporting these kind of queries could then be evaluated using the method proposed in this paper. Other possible areas for future research include finding better sampling/alignment methods for hand-drawn queries (possibly using weighted strokes) and combining high and low-level similarity measures to improve the perceived accuracy of pattern-searches. For instance, DTW could be used to retrieve the top n matches while shape attributes described in [10] could be used to generate a ranking over the n matches.

Our comparison of algorithms and sampling strategies through our 8 collected human-annotated rankings offers anecdotal evidence that human-rankings can differ drastically from rankings generated by algorithms. For a better understanding of the different approaches, rigorous statistical analysis is needed. Such an analysis should cover a wide range of time series from different domains and queries drawn by experts in these domains. Our method to create human-annotated rankings can be used to create datasets for different domains that would, over time, allow for such an extensive analysis.

CONCLUSION

In this paper, we showed why currently available datasets are not suitable for testing the subjective accuracy of similarity measures and demonstrated how human-annotated rankings can be created using crowdsourcing tasks. We published a freely available dataset comprising 8 different human-annotated rankings including the query pattern and 15 subsequences per query. This dataset can be used to optimize new and existing algorithms and serves as starting point for further research in this area. Furthermore, we collected 112 different query patterns from different users, analyzed their meaning and characteristics and proposed future ideas for a visual vocabulary for time series queries.

All queries and human-annotated rankings are available on `http://cs.brown.edu/~peichmann/timeseries/`

ACKNOWLEDGMENTS

The authors wish to thank Bob Zeleznik, Joseph La Viola and Andries van Dam for their comments and suggestions, Yueguo Chen and Eamon Keogh for the source code as well all our participants and Mechanical Turk workers for their time and their invaluable feedback.

REFERENCES

1. André-Jönsson, H., and Badal, D. Z. Using signature files for querying time-series data. In *Principles of Data Mining and Knowledge Discovery*. Springer, 1997, 211–220.
2. Batista, G. E., Wang, X., and Keogh, E. J. A complexity-invariant distance measure for time series.
3. Chen, L., Özsu, M. T., and Oria, V. Robust and fast similarity search for moving object trajectories. In *Proceedings of the 2005 ACM SIGMOD international conference on Management of data*, ACM (2005), 491–502.
4. Chen, Y., Nascimento, M. A., Ooi, B. C., and Tung, A. Spade: On shape-based pattern detection in streaming time series. In *Data Engineering, 2007. ICDE 2007. IEEE 23rd International Conference on*, IEEE (2007), 786–795.
5. De Berg, M., Van Kreveld, M., Overmars, M., and Schwarzkopf, O. C. *Computational geometry*. Springer, 2000.
6. Ding, H., Trajcevski, G., Scheuermann, P., Wang, X., and Keogh, E. Querying and mining of time series data: experimental comparison of representations and distance measures. *Proceedings of the VLDB Endowment 1*, 2 (2008), 1542–1552.
7. Eitz, M., Hays, J., and Alexa, M. How do humans sketch objects? *ACM Trans. Graph. 31*, 4 (2012), 44.
8. Faloutsos, C., Ranganathan, M., and Manolopoulos, Y. *Fast subsequence matching in time-series databases*, vol. 23. ACM, 1994.
9. Fu, T.-c., Chung, F.-l., Luk, R., and Ng, C.-m. Stock time series pattern matching: Template-based vs.

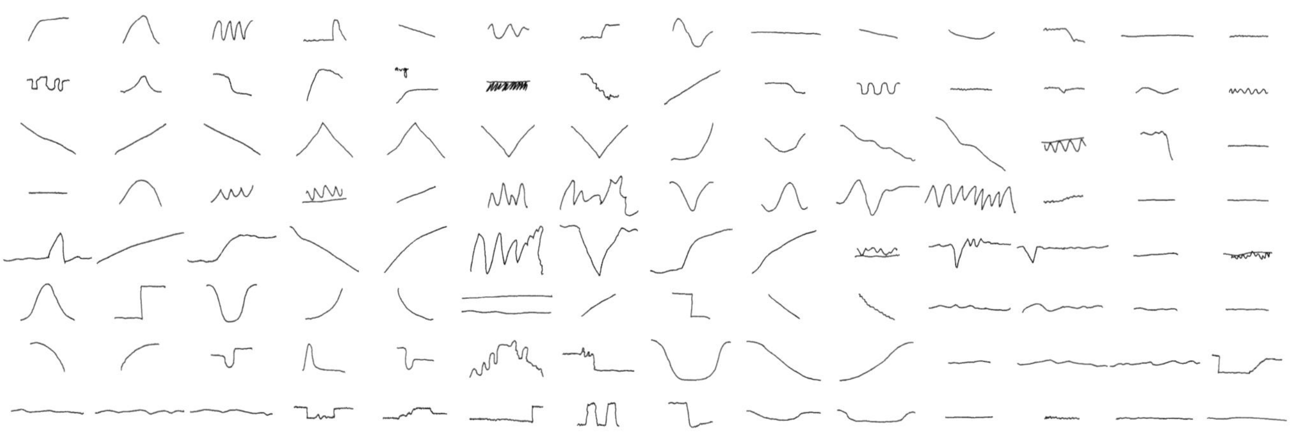

Figure 8. 112 Pen-drawn query patterns collected from 6 different users.

rule-based approaches. *Engineering Applications of Artificial Intelligence 20*, 3 (2007), 347–364.

10. Gregory, M., and Shneiderman, B. Shape identification in temporal data sets. 305–321.

11. Hochheiser, H., and Shneiderman, B. Dynamic query tools for time series data sets: timebox widgets for interactive exploration. *Information Visualization 3*, 1 (2004), 1–18.

12. Hüllermeier, E., Fürnkranz, J., Cheng, W., and Brinker, K. Label ranking by learning pairwise preferences. *Artificial Intelligence 172*, 16 (2008), 1897–1916.

13. Keogh, E., and Kasetty, S. On the need for time series data mining benchmarks: a survey and empirical demonstration. *Data Mining and knowledge discovery 7*, 4 (2003), 349–371.

14. Keogh, E. J., and Pazzani, M. J. An enhanced representation of time series which allows fast and accurate classification, clustering and relevance feedback. In *KDD*, vol. 98 (1998), 239–243.

15. Keogh, E. J., and Pazzani, M. J. Relevance feedback retrieval of time series data. In *Proceedings of the 22nd annual international ACM SIGIR conference on Research and development in information retrieval*, ACM (1999), 183–190.

16. Keogh, E., Z. Q. H. B. H. Y. X. X. W. L. . R. *The UCR Time Series Classification/Clustering Homepage*, 2011. `www.cs.ucr.edu/~eamonn/time_series_data/`.

17. Mitsa, T. *Temporal data mining*. CRC Press, 2010.

18. Morse, M. D., and Patel, J. M. An efficient and accurate method for evaluating time series similarity. In *Proceedings of the 2007 ACM SIGMOD international conference on Management of data*, ACM (2007), 569–580.

19. Palpanas, T., Vlachos, M., Keogh, E., Gunopulos, D., and Truppel, W. Online amnesic approximation of streaming time series. In *Data Engineering, 2004. Proceedings. 20th International Conference on*, 339–349.

20. Papapetrou, P., Athitsos, V., Potamias, M., Kollios, G., and Gunopulos, D. Embedding-based subsequence matching in time-series databases. *ACM Transactions on Database Systems (TODS) 36*, 3 (2011), 17.

21. Rakthanmanon, T., Campana, B., Mueen, A., Batista, G., Westover, B., Zhu, Q., Zakaria, J., and Keogh, E. Searching and mining trillions of time series subsequences under dynamic time warping. In *Proceedings of the 18th ACM SIGKDD international conference on Knowledge discovery and data mining*, ACM (2012), 262–270.

22. Ratanamahatana, C., Keogh, E., Bagnall, A. J., and Lonardi, S. A novel bit level time series representation with implication of similarity search and clustering. In *Advances in Knowledge Discovery and Data Mining*. Springer, 2005, 771–777.

23. Vlachos, M., Hadjieleftheriou, M., Gunopulos, D., and Keogh, E. Indexing multidimensional time-series. *The VLDB JournalThe International Journal on Very Large Data Bases 15*, 1 (2006), 1–20.

24. Vlachos, M., Kollios, G., and Gunopulos, D. Discovering similar multidimensional trajectories. In *Data Engineering, 2002. Proceedings. 18th International Conference on*, IEEE (2002), 673–684.

25. Wan, X., Yang, J., and Xiao, J. Towards a unified approach to document similarity search using manifold-ranking of blocks. *Information Processing & Management 44*, 3 (2008), 1032–1048.

26. Wattenberg, M. Sketching a graph to query a time-series database. In *CHI'01 Extended Abstracts on Human factors in Computing Systems*, ACM (2001), 381–382.

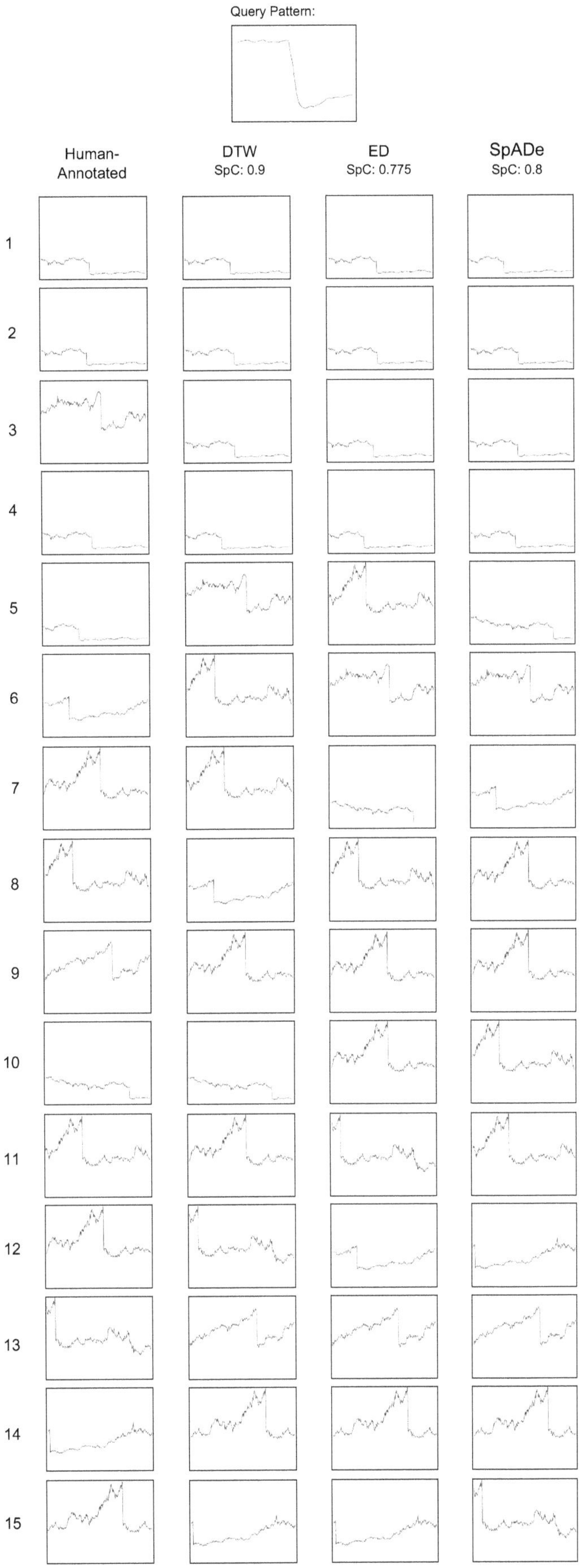

Figure 9. A human-annotated ranking for query pattern 2 and three different rankings produced by DTW, ED, and SpAde similarity measure using PIP sampling. The algorithms produce reasonable results according to the Spearman coefficient (SpC). Note that even the crowd sometimes fails to agree upon a most similiar shape (see rank 3 in the human-annotated ranking).

Cohort Comparison of Event Sequences with Balanced Integration of Visual Analytics and Statistics

Sana Malik, Fan Du, Megan Monroe*
University of Maryland
College Park, MD 20740
{maliks, fan, madeyjay}@cs.umd.edu

Eberechukwu Onukwugha
University of Maryland
Baltimore, MD 21201
eonukwug@rx.umaryland.edu

Catherine Plaisant, Ben Shneiderman
University of Maryland
College Park, MD 20740
{plaisant, ben}@cs.umd.edu

ABSTRACT
Finding the differences and similarities between two datasets is a common analytics task. With temporal event sequence data, this task is complex because of the many ways single events and event sequences can differ between the two datasets (or cohorts) of records: the structure of the event sequences (e.g., event order, co-occurring events, or event frequencies), the attributes of events and records (e.g., patient gender), or metrics about the timestamps themselves (e.g., event duration). In exploratory analyses, running statistical tests to cover all cases is time-consuming and determining which results are significant becomes cumbersome. Current analytics tools for comparing groups of event sequences emphasize a purely statistical or purely visual approach for comparison. This paper presents a taxonomy of metrics for comparing cohorts of temporal event sequences, showing that the problem-space is bounded. We also present a visual analytics tool, CoCo (for "Cohort Comparison"), which implements balanced integration of automated statistics with an intelligent user interface to guide users to significant, distinguishing features between the cohorts. Lastly, we describe two early case studies: the first with a research team studying medical team performance in the emergency department and the second with pharmacy researchers.

Author Keywords
temporal data; cohort comparison; visual analytics

INTRODUCTION
Sequences of timestamped events are currently being generated across nearly every domain of data analytics. Consider a typical e-commerce site tracking each of its users through a series of search results and product pages until a purchase is made. Or consider a database of electronic health records containing the symptoms, medications, and outcomes of each patient who is treated. Every day, this data type is reviewed by humans who apply statistical tests, hoping to learn everything they can about how these processes work, why they break, and how they can be improved upon.

Human eyes and statistical tests, however, reveal very different things. Statistical tests show metrics, uncertainty, and statistical significance. Human eyes see context, accountability, and most notably, things that they may not have even been looking for.

Visualization tools strive to capitalize on these latter, human strengths. For example, the EventFlow visualization tool [39] supports exploratory, visual analyses over large datasets of temporal event sequences. This support for open-ended exploration, however, comes at a cost. The more that a visual analytics tool is designed around open-ended questions and flexible data exploration, the less it is able to effectively integrate automated, statistical analysis. Automated statistics can provide answers, but only when the questions are known.

The opportunity to combine these two approaches lies in the middle ground. By all accounts, the goal of open-ended questions is to generate more concrete ones. As these questions come into focus, so too does the ability to automatically generate the answers. This paper introduces CoCo (for "Cohort Comparison", Figure 1), a visual analytics tool that is designed to capitalize on one such scenario.

Consider again the information that is tracked on an e-commerce site. From a business perspective, the users of the site fall into one of two groups: people who bought something and people who did not. If the goal is to convert more of the latter into the former, it is critical to understand how these two groups, or cohorts, are different. Did one group look at more product pages? Or spend more time on the site? Or have some clear demographic identifier such as gender, race, or age? Similar questions arise in the medical domain as well. Which patients responded well to a given medication? How are did their treatment patterns differ the patients who didn't?

Although comparing two groups of data is a common task, with temporal event sequence data in particular, the task of running many statistical tests becomes complex because of the variety of ways the cohorts, sequences (entire records), subsequences (a subset of events in a record), and events can differ. In addition to the structure of the event sequences (e.g., order, co-occurrences, or frequencies of events), the attributes about the events and records (e.g., gender of a patient), and

*Current Address: IBM T. J. Watson Research Center, Cambridge, MA 02142

IUI 2015, March 29–April 1, 2015, Atlanta, GA, USA.

http://dx.doi.org/10.1145/2678025.2701407

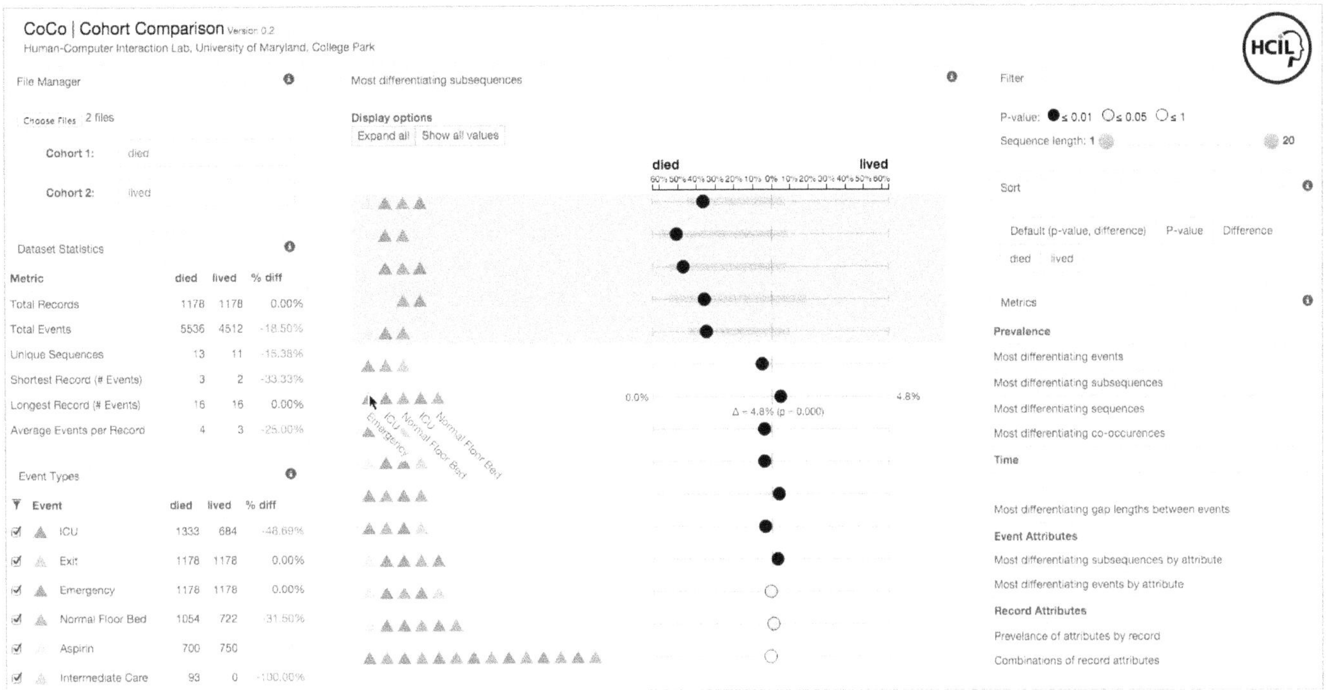

Figure 1. CoCo combines automated statistical analysis with an intelligent user interface to enable insights, hypothesis generation, and data exploration when comparing two groups of temporal event sequences. Users are provided with pre-defined metrics (bottom right) as a starting point for their exploration and they are able to parse results with a visualization and interactions such as sorting and filtering. In this example, we have two groups of patients as they are transferred throughout a hospital: those who lived and those who died. The selected metric is the most differentiating subsequences. We can see that being transferred from the emergency room (purple) directly to the normal floor bed (blue) appears statistically significantly more in the group of patients who died ($p \leq 0.01$).

the timestamps themselves (e.g., an event's duration) can be distinguishing features between the cohorts. For this reason, running statistical tests to cover all these cases and determining which results are significant becomes cumbersome. Additionally, the factor on which the cohorts are formed may call for different types of questions to be asked about the data. For example, in a set of medical records split by date (e.g., last month's trials vs. this month's), a research may be interested in how outcomes for the patients differ between the cohorts, whereas a dataset split by the patient's outcome (e.g., patients who die vs. those who live) would ignore such a metric.

Current tools for cohort comparison of temporal event data (described in the next section) emphasize one of two strategies: 1) purely visual comparisons between groups, with no integrated statistics, or 2) purely statistical comparisons over one or more features of the dataset. By contrast, CoCo is designed to provide a more balanced integration of both human-driven and automated strategies. We begin by showing that the task of cohort comparison is specific enough to support automatic computation against a bounded set of potential questions and objectives. From this starting point, we demonstrate that the diversity of these objectives, both across and within different domains, as well as the inherent complexities of real world datasets, still require human involvement to determine meaningful insights. Through case studies, we look at how CoCo can support the task of cohort comparison more specifically than previous visualization efforts.

The direct contributions of this paper are:

1. A taxonomy of metrics for comparing groups of temporal event sequences.
2. A visual analytics tool which demonstrates balanced integration of automated analysis and user-guided analysis with an intelligent user interface.
3. Case studies that illustrate the benefits of CoCo's utility while suggesting further refinements.

On a broader level, the goal of this paper is to highlight the relationship between task specificity and the ideal balance between humans and statistical analysis, so that future efforts can better leverage the strengths of both approaches.

RELATED WORKS

Visualizing Groups of Sequential Data

Work on visualization of sequential data is described here in two parts: visualizations of a single group of event sequences and visualizations comparing two or more sequences.

Single Groups

EventFlow [39] (Figure 2) and OutFlow [56] create simplified visualizations of collections of event and interval sequences. Both tools aggregate a single cohort and the complete sequences of records, with EventFlow allowing users to view details about individual records as well. While they only support visualizing a single group of records, comparison of multiple cohorts can be facilitated by using multiple instances

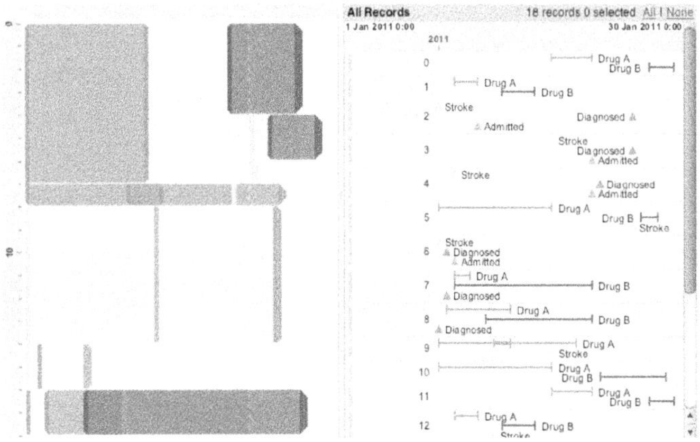

Figure 2. EventFlow visualizes event sequences in an aggregated, tree-like overview and as individual records in a timeline.

of the visualization and visual inspection by the user. These tools do not provide statistical information about the differences. CoCo borrows some event icon motifs from EventFlow (such as triangles for point events and T-shaped markers for interval events).

Event Sequence Comparison

Solutions for comparing sequential data have been explored in many different fields, including comparative genomics, text mining, and tree comparison. They are discussed here in the context of event history data and discrete-time models [3].

We draw first on methods to compare collections of general sequences without the notion of time, most notably the fields of comparative genomics and text mining, where the data is ordered with respect to some index [32].

Genome browsers [13, 21, 29, 52, 55, 12] visualize genome sequences. They compare genomes by visualizing the position of each nucleotide and consider a genome as a long and linear sequence of nucleotides. Scientists also compare genomes at the gene level. However, most existing tools are able to compare either only the similarities or only the differences of collections of gene sequences. For example, MizBee [37] measures the similarity between genomes by visualizing the regions of shared sequences, while Variant View [20], cBio [11] and MuSiC [17] only support displaying sequence variants. Further, genome sequences are often compared as a sequence of linear *positions*, which does not lend itself to distinctions between point and interval events.

Texts are often compared by extraction of frequent n-grams [9]. FeatureLens by Don et al. [18] define an n-gram as a contiguous sequence of words and use a visualization approach to compare the co-occurrences of frequent n-grams in texts. However, it only supports locating n-grams with specific features but does not find which n-grams are the most differentiating. Jankowska et al. [28] proposed the conversion of documents into vectors of frequent character n-grams and designed a relative n-gram signature to encode the distance between n-gram vectors. Viégas et al. presented history flow [54] to visually compare between versions of a document, which assumes that the later version of a document is developed based on the earlier one, which is not applicable to event history data.

Most of the techniques mentioned above (in both genomics and text mining) only provide a visual comparison between single long sequences, whereas event history data consists of large numbers of independent transactional sequences.

Temporal event sequences are often represented as trees. While many comparison techniques exist for trees, many do not take into account values or attributes of nodes and none are specifically designed for temporal data. Munzner presented the TreeJuxtaposer [42] system to help biologists explore structural details of phylogenetics, but focuses only on structural differences in the trees and not any attributes about the nodes (such as timestamps). Bremm [8] studied the comparison of phylogenetic trees in a more statistical way by extending the algorithms of TreeJuxtaposer to compare more than two trees and considers "edge length" which could be generalized to durations of gaps between sequential events. Holten [27] presented an interactive visualization method to compare different versions of hierarchically organized software systems. He proposed two methods of tree comparison: icicle plot and hierarchical sorting, but does not propose any statistical comparison technique, and focuses more on "leaf-to-leaf" matching, which considers whole paths (or sequences) only. TreeVersity2 [24] compares by tree structure and the node values. Though TreeVersity2 is general to all trees, it leaves out temporal-specific analysis such as duration of or between interval events. TreeVersity2 compares two datasets over time, but assumes these time periods are disjoint. TreeVersity2 also includes a textual reporting tool that highlights outliers in the data.

Many of these comparison techniques also lack statistical tests for the comparisons. In our work, the balanced integration supports both visual and statistical approaches.

Statistics for Comparing Cohorts

In medical cohort studies, the most prevalent approach for comparison is survival analysis, where survival time is defined as the time from a defined point to the occurrence of a given event [7]. The Kaplan-Meier method is often used to analyze the survival time of patients on different treatments and to compare their risks of death [14, 19, 23]. Based on the Kaplan-Meier estimate, survival time of two groups of patients can be visualized and compared with survival curves, which plot the cumulative proportion surviving against the survival times [7]. Also, the log-rank test is often used to statistically compare two survival curves by testing the null hypothesis. Compared with survival analysis, the event sequences data used in our work is much more complicated, and requires a more advanced analysis model.

Currently tools that combine visualization and statistics for medical cohort analysis focus on single cohorts. CAVA [57] is a visualization tool for interactively refining cohorts and performing statistics on a single group. Recently, Oracle published a visualization tool for cohort study [45]. Based on patients' clinical data, it supports interactive data exploration and provides statistics as well as visualization functionalities.

These tools similarly focus on combining visualization with automated statistics and providing an interactive interface for selecting cohorts; however, both tools aim at grouping and identifying patient cohorts for further characterization, while our work focuses on comparing two existing cohorts based on their event histories.

Temporal Data Mining

Previous work studying temporal data mining has mostly focused on discovering frequent temporal patterns [4, 6, 15, 43, 33, 22, 2, 36, 46] and computing temporal abstractions [30, 41, 5] of time-oriented data.

Pattern discovery is an open-ended problem which aims to unearth all patterns of interest [32]. Much of the literature is concerned with developing efficient algorithms to automatically discover frequent temporal patterns and extract temporal association rules [4, 6, 15, 33, 22, 2, 36]. To constrain the search procedure, some algorithms [4, 15] allow users to provide initial knowledge and rules. To show the results, Norén et al. [43] used a graphical approach to visualize temporal associations. This work can be extended to address unique temporal constraints, such as dealing with concurrent events, which Cule et al. address in the context of pattern mining [16] and association rule mining [50].

Temporal abstraction focuses on obtaining a succinct and meaningful description of a time series [41]. Various approaches have been proposed. Klimov et al. [30] developed VISITORS to visualize patient records by grouping the event attribute values at different temporal granularities. Moskovitch et al. [41] aggregated values of point data by state and trend, to obtain its interval representation. Batal et al. [5] converted time series data into vectors of frequent patterns, which can be used with standard vector-based algorithms. However, most of the work in this topic only focused on the time and changes in an event's value (a concept), which is considered as event attributes in our work. Tatti and Vreekan [51] introduce a novel algorithm for summarizing a set of a sequences by providing a descriptive and non-redundant set of sequences, accounting for long gaps.

METRICS FOR COMPARING COHORTS

Metrics for comparing cohorts are numerous and can be grouped into five main categories: summary metrics, time metrics, event sequence (both whole record sequences and subsequences thereof) metrics, event attribute metrics, and record attribute metrics. These metrics are a direct result of observing EventFlow users as they analyzed cohorts of event sequences in seven case studies performed over three years [38]. Five case studies were in the health care domain (with pharmacists and epidemiologists), one in sports analytics (basketball), and one in transportation.

Summary Metrics

Summary statistics deal with the cohorts as a whole and provide a high-level overview of the datasets.

Number of records Total number of records in each cohort.

Number of events Total number of events in each cohort.

Number of unique records Total number of unique records in each cohort based on the sequence of events (absolute times are not considered).

Number of each event Total number of occurrences for each event type per cohort.

Minimum, Maximum, and Average length of records The length of a record is considered as the number of events per that record.

Event Sequence Metrics

Event sequence metrics deal with the order and structure of event sequences. Sequences are differentiated by whether they occur as an entire *sequence* in a record or a *subsequence* of a record. Each of the following metrics can be presented as the percent of records containing the event or sequence or as the percent of all events or sequences that it occurs. The former method provides a sense of how many individual records had this sequence occur, whereas the latter method provides a sense of how events or sequences might repeat themselves within one record.

Prevalence of an event The percent of records or total number of events that a particular event occurs in.

Prevalence of a subsequence The percent of records in which the subsequence appears. For example, patients who lived are given aspirin before going to the emergency room more often than the patients who died.

Prevalence of a whole sequence Percent of records with a given sequence.

Order of sequential events in a subsequence The percent of records containing event A directly preceding event B versus B preceding A. For example, perhaps patient who go to the ICU before the floor are more likely to live than patients who have these events in the reverse order.

Commonly Co-occurring (non-consecutive) events The percent of records containing both events A and B (in any order, with any number of events between them).

Prevalence of Outcomes If a single event is prevalent as an "outcome" (i.e., the last event in the sequence). This metric in particular applies only to cohorts that are not already split on an outcome event.

Time Metrics

Time metrics deal with the timestamps at both the event and sequence levels – relative and absolute.

Absolute time of an event Prevalence of a particular timestamp of an event or multiple events (e.g., if all events in one cohort occurred on the same day).

Duration of interval events The duration of particular interval event. For example, this can be the length of exposure to a treatment or the duration of a prescription.

Duration between sequential events The time between the end of one event and the beginning of the next. For example, the average length of time between hospital patients entering the emergency room and being transferred to the ICU is under two hours in patients who lived and over two hours in those who died.

Duration between co-occurring (non-sequential) events The length of time between non-sequential events (two events with some number of other events occurring between them).

Duration of a subsequence The length of time from the beginning of the first event in a subsequence to the end of the last event in the subsequence.

Duration from a fixed point in time The length of time from a user-specified, fixed point – aligned by either a selected event or absolute date-time.

Duration of overlap in interval events The overlap (or lack thereof) of interval events. For example, the overlap of Drug A and Drug B could be more common in the cohort of patients who lived versus those who died.

Cyclic events and sequences The duration between cyclic events and sequences.

Survivor analysis How an event or sequence occurs or diminishes over time.

Statistics for each of these metrics include the minimum, maximum, and average durations or values and the distributions of the values between the cohorts.

Event Attribute Metrics

Any of the above metrics can be applied over values of an attribute of the events instead of the event type itself. This can be done by swapping an event type by the values of a particular attribute. For example, in a medical dataset, we might be interested in seeing how a particular emergency room doctor might be related to the outcome of a patient. We would then switch all events of type "Emergency" with the value of its "doctor" attribute. If there are three doctors, this would create 3 new pseudo-event types. We can use the metrics from above to see the difference in event sequences, times, or prevalence of each doctor in either cohort.

Record Attribute Metrics

Record level attributes (such as patient gender or age) compare the cohorts as population statistics. General statistics across the entire dataset is a problem already tackled by analytics tools such as Spotfire [53] or Tableau [1], however these tools look at a single attribute. For example, they might compare the number of males versus females or patients on Wednesday versus Thursday. There may be implications about the *combinations* of record attributes (e.g., the women on Wednesday versus the women on Thursday versus the men on Wednesday versus the men on Thursday). In clinical trials, it is important that all patient attributes are balanced and currently no tools exist for visually confirming that all attribute combinations are balanced.

Combining Metrics

The number of metrics is further multiplied because any combination of the above metrics is a new metric. For example, a sports analytics researcher may be interested in how a particular player (as an attribute of an event) performs within two minutes (time) after halftime (event order).

BALANCING AUTOMATION WITH HUMAN INTERACTION

Purely statistical methods of comparison would benefit from user intervention. With the sheer number of metrics, it would be computationally time consuming to run every metric ahead of time, especially when not every metric may be required for analysis. Users with domain knowledge about the datasets would ideally be able to select from the metrics and easily eliminate unnecessary metrics. Further, questions asked during cohort comparison may vary based on how the cohorts were divided. If the cohorts were divided by outcome (e.g., patients who lived versus patients who died), the sequence of events leading up to them becomes more important. Analysis might revolve around determining what factors (time or attributes) or events lead to the outcome by determining how the metrics differ between the groups. Conversely, if the cohorts were split based on an event type, questions may revolve around finding distinguishing outcomes (e.g., patients who took Drug A may result in more strokes than patients who took Drug B). Exploration of cohorts that are split by time (e.g., the same patients over two different months) may be more open-ended and require all metrics. The cohorts can be distinguished by time factors, event attributes, or events themselves (sequences of events or outcomes).

Our contribution is to enable researchers to be far more flexible in examining cohorts and facilitate human intervention where it can save time and effort. Because of the pre-defined problem space of comparing temporal event sequences, we can save users time by having answers to common questions readily available and giving them a starting point for their exploration.

Purely visual tools for temporal event sequences are a good starting point for developing analysis tools for cohort studies, but can be improved by the inclusion of the statistical tests used in automated approaches. For example, EventFlow assumes that each patient record consists of time-stamped point events (e.g. heart attack, vaccination, first occurrence of symptom), temporal interval events (e.g. medication episode, dietary regime, exercise plan), and patient attributes (e.g. gender, age, weight, ethnic background, etc.). In multiple case studies with EventFlow, the researchers repeatedly observed users visually comparing event patterns in one group of records with those in another group. In simple terms the question was: what are the sequences of events that differentiate one group from the other? A common aspiration is to find clues that lead to new hypotheses about the series of events that lead to particular outcomes, but many other simple questions also involved comparisons. Epidemiologists analyzing the patterns of drug prescriptions [40] tried to compare the patterns of different classes of drugs. Hospital administrators looking at patient journeys through the hospital compared the data of one month with the previous month. Researchers analyzing task performance during trauma resuscitation [10] wanted to compare performance between cases where the response team was alerted of the upcoming arrival of the patient or not alerted. Transportation analysts looking at highway incident responses [25] wanted to compare how an agency handled its incidents differently from another. Their observations suggest that some broad insights can be gained by visually comparing pairs of EventFlow displays (e.g., users could see if the patterns were very similar overall between one month and the next) or very different (e.g., a lot more red or the most common patterns were different) but users repeatedly expressed the desire for more systematic ways to compare cohorts of records.

COHORT COMPARISON WITH COCO

Though CoCo can be used in a variety of fields, the synthetic dataset used as an example for the remainder of the paper consists of records of patients admitted to the emergency room and follows their movement through their stay at the hospital: being administered aspirin, being admitted into the hospital room, transferring between a normal floor bed, intermediate care, and the intensive care unit (ICU), and ultimately being discharged either dead or alive. The dataset is split into two cohorts: patients who died and patients who lived.

Design

Based on the case studies which shaped the taxonomy, our three design goals for balanced integration were:

G1. Automatic, efficient computation of metrics.

G2. Guided process for reading results.

G3. Visualization and interaction techniques for parsing and sorting results.

We used an iterative design process based on feedback from on-going case study partners and a user study [35]. We now describe the first operational CoCo prototype, organized by those three goals.

G1: Computation of Metrics

In automatically applying the metrics to the datasets, we must consider (1) what are the appropriate statistical tests for each metrics, and (2) how to compute the results quickly for the user.

Towards the first goal, the user should be involved in selecting appropriate significant tests for the metrics. Currently, CoCo implements only non-parametric tests and thus does not provide methods for selecting parametric tests. Percent prevalence and attribute significances are calculated by Chi-squared and the time significance metrics use a Wilcoxon sum-rank test across the distribution of values.

To date, we implemented two methods for automatically computing these metrics on a large set of data. The first was to apply every metric after the datasets are loaded, in order to rank the metrics from potentially most meaningful to least. However, this resulted in a long wait time for users. The current implementation computes a metric as the user selects it. However, this offers less guidance than if the metrics were pre-computed. Our future goal is to minimize wait time, but give prompt feedback on which metrics might be meaningful to look at immediately, in accordance with Stolper et al.'s design guidelines for progressive visual analytics [49].

G2: Interface

To guide users to most meaningful results, we organize results by first providing high-level dataset statistics followed by specific metrics grouped by type.

CoCo consists of a file manager pane, a dataset statistics pane, an event legend, a list of available metrics, the CoCo visualization, and options for filtering and sorting the results (Figure 1).

The summary statistics panel includes high-level statistics about both datasets, including the total number of records and events in each record. Users are then shown the Event Type pane, which serves as the legend (pairing each event type with a marker and color) and filter control. When an event is checked or unchecked, it displays or hides rows containing that event from the analysis. Frequencies of each event in the two cohorts are also shown, as the raw number of occurrences of that event type.

The right panel consists of filtering and sorting mechanisms and a list of metrics. The metrics panel contains the list of metrics is organized according to the taxonomy. We found that many users started with metrics dealing with prevalence to understand how events and sequence occur within the datasets before moving onto metrics dealing with time. Similarly, within each group, the metrics are organized from simplest to more complex: singular event metrics, subsequence metrics, then finally whole record metrics.

The filtering and sorting panels provide ways for users to parse the results of their selected metric. Users may filter by p-value or sequence length. The default sorting behavior for the results is first by p-value group, then by magnitude of difference. Users may also choose to sort by only p-value, only absolute difference, or by most differentiating in cohort α or by β.

Preliminary versions of CoCo introduce each panel one-by-one, so users could click-through as they finished analyzing each section. However, feedback from users suggested this was more cumbersome than helpful and we opted to display all panels at once.

G3: CoCo Visualization

The visualization needs to convey the differences themselves (e.g., proportion of records in each cohort containing a sequence), but also the result of the statistical test. Since the meaning of the results differ between results (e.g., some metrics refer to a percentage of records while others refer to a time duration), it was also important to visualize the results in a way that supports both types of results. Because users are more focused on the *difference* of a value between two cohorts, we chose to use a back-to-back bar chart in order to emphasize the magnitude and direction of the difference, so users can more easily scan across multiple rows for results they are interested in.

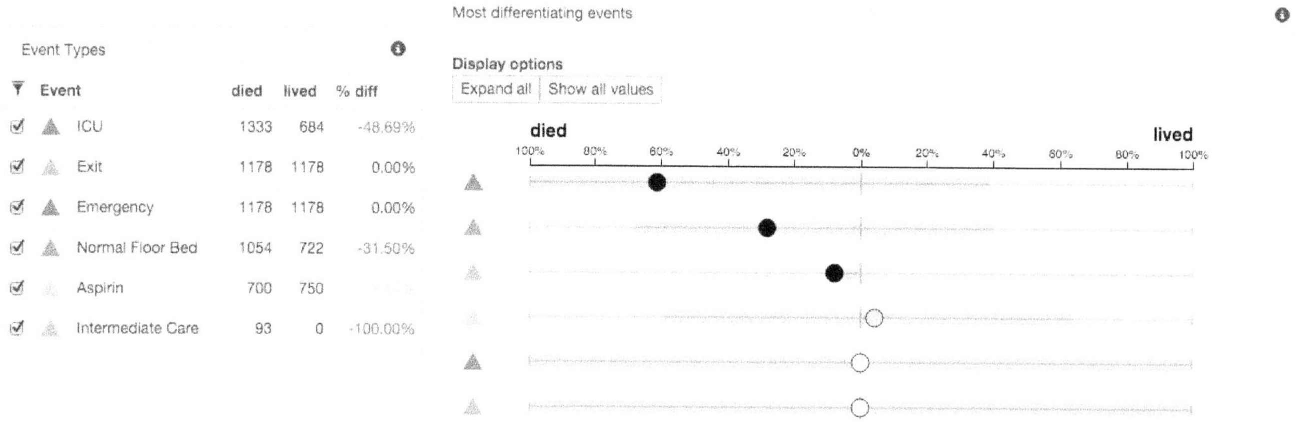

Figure 3. The CoCo visualization shown with the event legend. In this example, we see that ICU, Normal Floor Bed, and Intermediate Care events occur significantly more frequently in the "died" cohort than in the "lived." Because of the nature of the dataset, 100% of records in both cohorts contain the "Emergency" and "Exit" events, so there is no significant difference and the circle marker is placed in the middle.

The CoCo visualization (Figure 3) displays the results of significance tests in a unified form. For each event or sequence of events, CoCo displays the value of the metric in each cohort (e.g., percent of prevalence, gap duration), the difference between the two values, and the significance value of the difference.

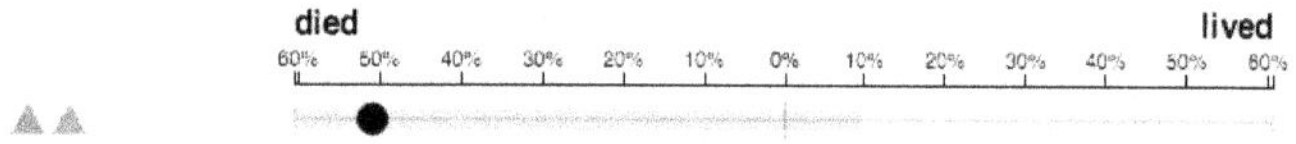

Figure 4. The sequence "Emergency" followed by a "Normal Floor Bed" event occurs in about 60% of records in "died" and only 10% of records in "lived" for a statistically significant difference of 50% ($p \leq 0.01$)

Each row (Figure 4) consists of a horizontal axis, where the left is cohort α and the right is cohort β (the labels can be renamed by users). A semi-transparent bar grows from the middle towards each direction in the respective cohort to show the value of the metric for that particular event or sequence. The axis is scaled by the maximum value for all sequences (e.g., if the maximum percentage is 60%, the maximum value on the axis will also be 60%). The axis works for both percentage and time. The circle marker is placed horizontally based on the difference between the values, in the direction of whichever cohort's value is higher. The circle marker is filled corresponding to the significance of the difference: black is used for p-values with a significance of less than or equal to 0.01, grey for less than or equal to 0.05 but higher than 0.01, and white for values over 0.05 up to 1.

Rows are ranked first by their p-value group (with records with the most significant p-value appearing first), and within each of the three significance groups, rows are ordered by the absolute percent difference between the two groups. Users can filter out records by p-values in a certain group with the legend on the top right of the visualization.

Hovering over any sequence displays an informational tooltip (Figure 5), which gives the event names for each event marker, the corresponding value in each cohort, the values' difference, and the exact p-value. Users can choose to always

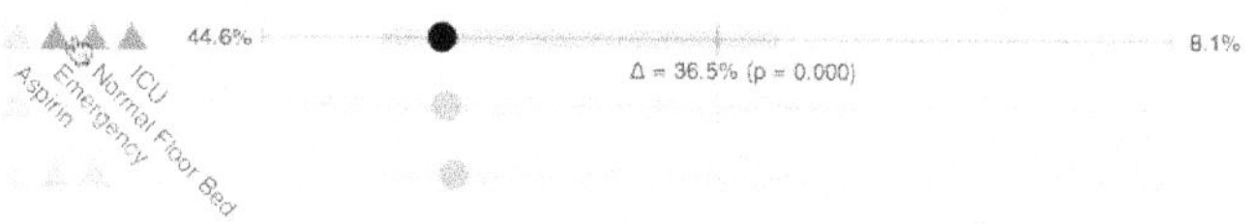

Figure 5. Exact values for each row are shown in the hover tooltip. The sequence "Aspirin," "Emergency," "Normal Bed Floor," then "ICU" appears in 44.6% of records in "died" and 8.1% of records in "lived."

display these values in the display options in the top left of the visualization (Figure 3).

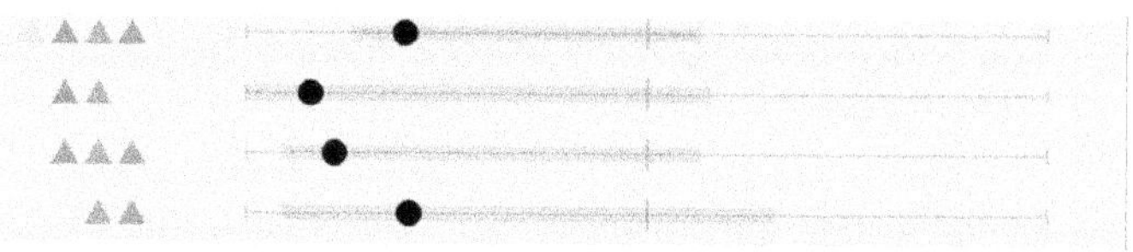

Figure 6. Rows whose sequence are a subsequence of another row are aggregated together and only the longest sequence is shown. The nested records are expanded on click and are visually grouped with the rest of the aggregated rows in the group on a dark background.

With rows that are sequences of events, there are sometimes shorter subsequences of that sequence that have a similar significance value. In these cases, CoCo aggregates rows when a sequence is a subsequence of another row and both event sequences fall within the same significance category. An aggregated row is indicated with a "+" indicator to the right of the sequence markers (Figure 5) and is expanded on when the top-level (nested) row is clicked. Nested subsequences of the row are aligned with the marker and displayed on a darker background color with the top-level record (Figure 6). Users can expand or collapse all nested records at once in the display options to the top left of the visualization (Figure 3).

In metrics dealing with attributes, users can select a particular attribute from a drop-down under the display options in the visualization. Events that contain a value with the selected attribute are outline with a black border and the value of the attribute is shown on hover as the value appended to the event type with a pipe ("|") separator (Figure 7).

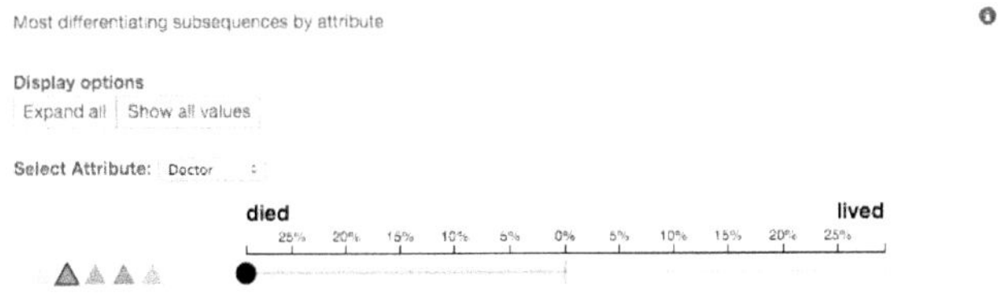

Figure 7. Users can select an attribute from the drop-down in the display options. Events containing an attribute value are outlined in black and its value is shown in the hover tooltip. In this example, the attribute selected is the doctor that is on call in the emergency room (purple). The event containing the attribute is highlighted in black.

G3: Interactions for Parsing Results

Though CoCo initially sorts the results based on the significance and magnitude of difference in the results, in preliminary sessions with case study partners, it became clear that researchers might have more specific questions that require displaying the results differently. CoCo allows users to sort and filter the results based on their needs. Specifically, the sorting method may be changed based on:

- Magnitude of difference and p-value group (default)
- P-value only
- Magnitude of difference only
- Most differentiating towards the alpha group
- Most differentiating towards the beta group

To further filter out potentially noisy data, we added controls for filtering by p-value or sequence length. For example, if users are interested in a particular subset of events, they can use the event type legend to uncheck events that they are not interested in. Then, only sequences containing the checked event types will appear.

PRELIMINARY CASE STUDIES

Case Study: Exploring Adherence to Advanced Trauma Life Support Protocol

To investigate the strengths and limitations of CoCo as an automated cohort comparison tool, we conducted a case study following the procedure of a Multi-Dimensional, Long-term In-depth case study (MILC) [48]. We worked with medical researchers at Children's National Medical Center who were investigating trauma teams' adherence to the Advanced Trauma Life Support (ATLS) protocol and possible reasons for deviations. In a previous study [10], they found that about 50% of resuscitations did not follow the ATLS protocol. As a follow-up, the researchers collected additional data about the resuscitation process after implementation of an ATLS compliance checklist to re-evaluate the attributes associated with protocol deviations. Specifically, the researchers' questions were:

1. What percent of patients are treated in adherence to protocol?
2. Are there distinguishing attributes (e.g., time of day, patient gender, team lead) between protocol adherence and non-adherence?
3. What are the most common deviations from the protocol?

After an initial training session and interviews to understand the researchers' goals and questions, we observed the researchers as they conducted a 3-hour session of data exploration and analysis.

The dataset consisted of 181 patient records, with event types for the five steps in the ATLS protocol: airway evaluation, listening for breath sounds, assessment of circulation, evaluation of neurological status disability, and temperature control. Patient attributes included injury severity score (ISS), the day of week, length of hospital stay, time between notification and arrival at the hospital, and if the patient was admitted to the hospital.

The dataset was stored as a single file. They used EventFlow's "group by attribute" feature to split the dataset into separate cohorts based on attributes and adherence to the protocol. Over the course of the 3 hours, the researchers split the dataset in six ways to load six different pairs of cohorts in Coco as they explored different hypotheses:

1. Patients treated in adherence to the ATLS protocol versus those that showed any deviation.
2. Patients admitted to the floor versus ICU (with discharged patients removed).
3. Patients who arrived with at least five minutes warning before arrival at the trauma bay versus those who arrived with no warning ("now" patients).
4. Patients with a high (above 25) versus low ISS.
5. Patients treated on the weekend versus on a weekday.
6. Patients treated during the day versus at night.

In every comparison group, the analysts began by looking at the prevalence of single events, to determine how often they occurred. The analysts then looked at the most differentiating *entire record* sequences, because the subsequences were less informative about how the protocol was followed. They would then make their way down the provided metrics list, in the order that they appeared: most differentiating time gaps and then prevalence of record attributes. They did not look at the prevalence of record attribute combinations for any of the datasets.

For this dataset, they expected to see that all records contained every event. This finding was not observed for two of the comparisons: correctly treated patients versus those with deviations and day versus night patients, with the latter of both groups receiving the airway check significantly less that daytime patients. In the day versus night group, the analyst also found that the "most differentiating sequence" was the *correct* order, meaning that the nighttime patients were treated in the correct order significantly less than daytime patients. Additionally, patients treated at night had more variance in the procedure, with 26 unique sequences in the 83 patients versus 20 unique sequences in the 101 daytime patients. A possible reason for this finding is that during the day, nurse practitioners perform these procedures, but at night, less experienced junior residents are on-call instead.

At times, the researchers saw that certain groups occurred only rarely in the cohorts (under 20 times), so the researchers decided not to consider the comparisons. For example, among patients admitted to the ICU or floor, only about 80 patients remained, making the sample sizes too small to run many of the significance metrics about event types. As one analyst worked to confirm her expectations and check several hypotheses, she found a surprising and potentially important result: about 25% more patients who were admitted to the floor were "now" patients ($p < 0.05$), which led to splitting the cohort into the third group: now versus not now patients.

In the closing interview, one analyst said, *"We don't need to solve everything with EventFlow and CoCo. These tools let us explore the data and narrow our hypothesis."* From these results, the analysts submitted abstracts about and presented these findings at an internal symposium on trauma care.

Additional case studies and targeted controlled studies will be necessary to characterize the effectiveness of CoCo, but this first case study suggests that CoCo can be effective for exploratory analysis and hypothesis generation.

On-going Case Study: Comparing Algorithms for Distinguishing Types of Radiation to the Bone

We are currently working with our partners at the Department of Pharmaceutical Health Services Research at the University of Maryland School of Pharmacy in Baltimore. In previous work, the researchers were interested in developing an algorithm using claims data to differentiate between radiation delivered to the bone versus radiation delivered to the prostate gland, because billing codes available in claims data do not distinguish the site of radiation. Reliable measures for identifying the receipt of radiation to the bone are important in order to avoid bias in estimating the prevalence and/or mortality impact of skeletal-related events, including radiation to the bone.

Studies using healthcare claims employ various claims-based algorithms to identify radiation to the bone and mostly condition on prior claims with a bone metastasis diagnosis (billing) code [47, 44, 31]. They developed three classification algorithms that were compared using CoCo and EventFlow to investigate the timing of possible radiation to the bone among patients diagnosed with incident metastatic and nonmetastatic prostate cancer. One algorithm was based on prior literature while the other two were based on insights gained from data visualization software. Based on clinical input regarding the duration of palliative [26, 34] versus curative radiation, the researchers investigated the length of radiation episodes and found differences between cohorts in terms of the length of radiation. As expected, patients diagnosed with metastatic disease received shorter course radiation than patients diagnosed with nonmetastatic disease.

The feedback on CoCo was positive and the team valued the opportunity to visually compare cohorts of patients using summary statistics that pertained to the timing and frequency of events. The graphical results were shared with clinicians on the research team in order to determine whether the patterns were consistent with their expectations. The researchers felt the meaning of metrics could be explained more clearly; it was sometimes unclear what the x-axis represented and what statistical tests were used. They also suggested always showing the event labels, particularly for single-event metrics, to make understanding the icons a bit easier. The researchers expressed a need to be able to sort the rows of results with different factors, including by raw percentage of values in each cohort. We implemented this feature before the formal case study.

We are also starting to work on case studies in other application domains such as transportation. For example, we started a project with the Baltimore Metropolitan Council and are currently preparing and cleaning data with EventFlow so that their analysts can then use CoCo to compare how different jurisdictions are managing highway incidents or how their incident management has changed over the years.

CONCLUSIONS AND FUTURE WORK

CoCo is a novel visual analytics tool with balanced integration of visual analytics and statistics. CoCo's benefits include: better collaboration among colleagues, easier intermediate results discussion, and meaningful outcome presentations. Though CoCo was initially designed for expert users, primarily in healthcare, the taxonomy can be extended and refined for other specific domains, and our approach for the interface and visualizations would allow extensions in many ways. First, the metrics implemented are already proving valuable, but many more metrics are possible. Our current focus has been identifying sequential, contiguous subsequences in the datasets, but generalizing to identify any co-occurring, non-contiguous events is a natural next step (e.g., did patients have more than three aspirins at any time during their treatment) which would require more research. The comments by our colleagues in the usability study and the way they compared the cohorts motivate CoCo design improvements including new visualizations. Additional data mining and statistical techniques could be added to improve insight discovery, such as anomaly detection to find unusual records or clustering find similar records between the datasets. As we continue developing CoCo, we will conduct controlled experiment to understand its strength and weaknesses, as well as long-term case studies with domain experts to demonstrate value with realistic problems and to guide our development.

We recognize that there are limitations to CoCo in terms of the complexity of datasets, current emphasis on two cohorts, and the need for more user control on which events to study. On the other hand, the fresh possibilities for statistical comparisons, supported by visual presentations and an intelligent user interface, opens many doors for further research. While we are encouraged by our initial feedback, we see a huge set of possible features to add, which will empower medical and other researchers as they conduct exploratory data analysis on temporal event sequences.

ACKNOWLEDGEMENTS

The authors wish to thank Chris Imbriano and Seth Powsner for their input during the development of CoCo. We also thank our partners James Gardner at the School of Pharmacy at University of Maryland, Baltimore and Randall Burd and Rachel Webman at Children's National Medical Center in Washington, DC. This work is supported in part by Oracle. We gratefully acknowledge funding provided by The University of Maryland/Mpowering the State through the Center for Health-related Informatics and Bioimaging.

REFERENCES

1. Tableau software. `http://www.tableausoftware.com/`, Mar 2014.
2. Agrawal, R., and Srikant, R. Mining sequential patterns. In *Proc. 11th International Conference on Data Engineering*, IEEE Comput. Soc. Press (1995), 3–14.
3. Allison, P. D. Discrete-time methods for the analysis of event histories. *Sociological Methodology 13*, 1 (1982), 61–98.
4. Álvarez, M. R., Félix, P., and Cariñena, P. Discovering metric temporal constraint networks on temporal databases. *Artificial Intelligence in Medicine 58*, 3 (July 2013), 139–54.
5. Batal, I., Sacchi, L., Bellazzi, R., and Hauskrecht, M. A temporal abstraction framework for classifying clinical temporal data. *Proc. AMIA Annual Symposium 2009* (Jan. 2009), 29–33.
6. Bellazzi, R., Sacchi, L., and Concaro, S. Methods and tools for mining multivariate temporal data in clinical and biomedical applications. *Proc. Annual International Conference of the IEEE Engineering in Medicine and Biology Society. 2009* (Jan. 2009), 5629–32.
7. Bewick, V., Cheek, L., and Ball, J. Statistics review 12: survival analysis. *Critical Care (London, England) 8*, 5 (Oct. 2004), 389–94.
8. Bremm, S., von Landesberger, T., Hess, M., Schreck, T., Weil, P., and Hamacherk, K. Interactive visual comparison of multiple trees. In *Proc. 2011 IEEE Conference on Visual Analytics Science and Technology (VAST)* (2011), 31–40.
9. Brown, P. F., DeSouza, P. V., Mercer, R. L., Pietra, V. J. D., and Lai, J. C. Class-based n-gram models of natural language. *Computational Linguistics 18*, 4 (Dec. 1992), 467–479.
10. Carter, E., Burd, R., Monroe, M., Plaisant, C., and Shneiderman, B. Using eventflow to analyze task performance during trauma resuscitation. *Proceedings of the Workshop on Interactive Systems in Healthcare (WISH 2013)* (2013).
11. Cerami, E., Gao, J., Dogrusoz, U., Gross, B. E., Sumer, S. O., Aksoy, B. A., Jacobsen, A., Byrne, C. J., Heuer, M. L., Larsson, E., Antipin, Y., Reva, B., Goldberg, A. P., Sander, C., and Schultz, N. The cBio cancer genomics portal: an open platform for exploring multidimensional cancer genomics data. *Cancer Discovery 2*, 5 (May 2012), 401–4.
12. Chelaru, F., Smith, L., Goldstein, N., and Bravo, H. C. Epiviz: interactive visual analytics for functional genomics data. *Nat Meth 11*, 9 (Sept. 2014), 938–940.
13. Chen, Y., Cunningham, F., Rios, D., McLaren, W. M., Smith, J., Pritchard, B., Spudich, G. M., Brent, S., Kulesha, E., Marin-Garcia, P., Smedley, D., Birney, E., and Flicek, P. Ensembl variation resources. *BMC genomics 11*, 1 (Jan. 2010), 293.
14. Collett, D. *Modelling survival data in medical research*. CRC press, 2003.
15. Concaro, S., Sacchi, L., Cerra, C., Fratino, P., and Bellazzi, R. Mining health care administrative data with temporal association rules on hybrid events. *Methods of Information in Medicine 50*, 2 (Jan. 2011), 166–79.
16. Cule, B., Tatti, N., and Goethals, B. Marbles: Mining association rules buried in long event sequences. *Statistical Analysis and Data Mining 7*, 2 (2014), 93–110.
17. Dees, N. D., Zhang, Q., Kandoth, C., Wendl, M. C., Schierding, W., Koboldt, D. C., Mooney, T. B., Callaway, M. B., Dooling, D., Mardis, E. R., Wilson, R. K., and Ding, L. MuSiC: identifying mutational significance in cancer genomes. *Genome Research 22*, 8 (Aug. 2012), 1589–98.
18. Don, A., Zheleva, E., Gregory, M., Tarkan, S., Auvil, L., Clement, T., Shneiderman, B., and Plaisant, C. Discovering interesting usage patterns in text collections. In *Proc. 16th ACM Conference on Conference on Information and Knowledge Management - CIKM '07*, ACM Press (New York, USA, Nov. 2007), 213.
19. Dupont, M., Gacouin, A., Lena, H., Lavoué, S., Brinchault, G., Delaval, P., and Thomas, R. Survival of patients with bronchiectasis after the first ICU stay for respiratory failure. *Chest 125*, 5 (May 2004), 1815–20.
20. Ferstay, J. A., Nielsen, C. B., and Munzner, T. Variant view: visualizing sequence variants in their gene context. *IEEE Transactions on Visualization and Computer Graphics 19*, 12 (Dec. 2013), 2546–55.
21. Fiume, M., Williams, V., Brook, A., and Brudno, M. Savant: genome browser for high-throughput sequencing data. *Bioinformatics (Oxford, England) 26*, 16 (Aug. 2010), 1938–44.
22. Fournier-Viger, P., Faghihi, U., Nkambou, R., and Nguifo, E. M. CMRules: Mining sequential rules common to several sequences. *Knowledge-Based Systems 25*, 1 (Feb. 2012), 63–76.
23. Goel, M. K., Khanna, P., and Kishore, J. Understanding survival analysis: Kaplan-Meier estimate. *International Journal of Ayurveda Research 1*, 4 (Oct. 2010), 274–8.

24. Guerra-gómez, J. A., Pack, M. L., Plaisant, C., and Shneiderman, B. Visualizing changes over time in datasets using dynamic hierarchies. *IEEE Transactions on Visualization and Computer Graphics 19*, 12 (2013), 2566–2575.

25. Guerra-gómez, J. A., Wongsuphasawat, K., Wang, T. D., Pack, M. L., and Plaisant, C. Analyzing incident management event sequences with interactive visualization. *Proceedings of the Transportation Research Board 90th annual meeting* (2011).

26. Hartsell, W. F., Scott, C. B., Bruner, D. W., Scarantino, C. W., Ivker, R. A., Roach, M., Suh, J. H., Demas, W. F., Movsas, B., Petersen, I. A., Konski, A. A., Cleeland, C. S., Janjan, N. A., and DeSilvio, M. Randomized trial of short- versus long-course radiotherapy for palliation of painful bone metastases. *Journal of the National Cancer Institute 97*, 11 (2005), 798–804.

27. Holten, D., and van Wijk, J. J. Visual Comparison of Hierarchically Organized Data. *Computer Graphics Forum 27*, 3 (May 2008), 759–766.

28. Jankowska, M., Keselj, V., and Milios, E. Relative N-gram signatures: Document visualization at the level of character N-grams. In *2012 IEEE Conference on Visual Analytics Science and Technology (VAST)*, IEEE (Oct. 2012), 103–112.

29. Kent, W. J., Sugnet, C. W., Furey, T. S., Roskin, K. M., Pringle, T. H., Zahler, A. M., and Haussler, a. D. The Human Genome Browser at UCSC. *Genome Research 12*, 6 (May 2002), 996–1006.

30. Klimov, D., Shahar, Y., and Taieb-Maimon, M. Intelligent visualization and exploration of time-oriented data of multiple patients. *Artificial Intelligence in Medicine 49*, 1 (May 2010), 11–31.

31. Lage, M., Barber, B. L., Harrison, D. J., , and Jun, S. The Cost of Treating Skeletal-Related Events in Patients With Prostate Cancer. *Am J Manag Care 14*, 5 (2008), 317–322.

32. Laxman, S., and Sastry, P. S. A survey of temporal data mining. *Sadhana 31*, 2 (Apr. 2006), 173–198.

33. Lee, Y. J., Lee, J. W., Chai, D. J., Hwang, B. H., and Ryu, K. H. Mining temporal interval relational rules from temporal data. *Journal of Systems and Software 82*, 1 (2009), 155–167.

34. Lutz, S. T., Jones, J., and Chow, E. Role of radiation therapy in palliative care of the patient with cancer. *Journal of Clinical Oncology* (2014).

35. Malik, S., Du, F., Monroe, M., Onukwugha, E., Plaisant, C., and Shneiderman, B. An evaluation of visual analytics approaches to comparing cohorts of event sequences. In *EHRVis Workshop on Visualizing Electronic Health Record Data at VIS '14* (2014).

36. Mannila, H., Toivonen, H., and Verkamo, A. I. Discovery of Frequent Episodes in Event Sequences. *Data Mining and Knowledge Discovery 1*, 3 (Sept. 1997), 259–289.

37. Meyer, M., Munzner, T., and Pfister, H. MizBee: a multiscale synteny browser. *IEEE Transactions on Visualization and Computer Graphics 15*, 6 (Jan. 2009), 897–904.

38. Monroe, M. *Interactive Event Sequence Query and Transformation*. PhD thesis, University of Maryland, "2014".

39. Monroe, M., Lan, R., Lee, H., Plaisant, C., and Shneiderman, B. Temporal event sequence simplification. *Visualization and Computer Graphics, IEEE Transactions on 19*, 12 (Dec 2013), 2227–2236.

40. Monroe, M., Meyer, T. E., Plaisant, C., Lan, R., Wongsuphasawat, K., Coster, T. S., Gold, S., Millstein, J., and Shneiderman, B. Visualizing patterns of drug prescriptions with eventflow: A pilot study of asthma medications in the military health system. *Proceedings of Workshop on Visual Analytics in Healthcare (VAHC 2013)* (2013).

41. Moskovitch, R., and Shahar, Y. Medical temporal-knowledge discovery via temporal abstraction. *Proc. AMIA Annual Symposium 2009* (Jan. 2009), 452–6.

42. Munzner, T., Guimbretière, F., Tasiran, S., Zhang, L., and Zhou, Y. TreeJuxtaposer: Scalable Tree Comparison using Focus+Context with Guaranteed Visibility. In *ACM SIGGRAPH 2003*, no. 1, ACM Press (New York, USA, 2003), 453.

43. Norén, G. N., Hopstadius, J., Bate, A., Star, K., and Edwards, I. R. Temporal pattern discovery in longitudinal electronic patient records. *Data Mining and Knowledge Discovery 20*, 3 (Nov. 2009), 361–387.

44. Nørgaard, M., Jensen, A. Ø., Jacobsen, J., Cetin, K., Fryzek, J., and Sørensen, H. Skeletal related events, bone metastasis and survival of prostate cancer: a population based cohort study in Denmark (1999 to 2007). *J Urol. 184*, 1 (2010), 162–167.

45. Oracle. Oracle Health Sciences Cohort Explorer User's Guide. Tech. rep., Oracle, 2011.

46. Perer, A., and Wang, F. Frequence: Interactive mining and visualization of temporal frequent event sequences. In *Proceedings of the 19th International Conference on Intelligent User Interfaces*, IUI '14, ACM (New York, USA, 2014), 153–162.

47. Sathiakumar, N., Delzell, E., Morrisey, M., Falkson, C., Yong, M., Chia, V., Blackburn, J., Arora, T., and Kilgore, M. Mortality following bone metastasis and skeletal-related events among patients 65 years and above with lung cancer: A population-based analysis of U.S. Medicare beneficiaries, 1999-2006. *Lung India 30*, 1 (2013), 20–26.

48. Shneiderman, B., and Plaisant, C. Strategies for evaluating information visualization tools: Multi-dimensional in-depth long-term case studies. In *Proceedings of the 2006 AVI Workshop on BEyond Time*

and Errors: Novel Evaluation Methods for Information Visualization, BELIV '06, ACM (New York, NY, USA, 2006), 1–7.

49. Stolper, C., Perer, A., and Gotz, D. Progressive visual analytics. In *To appear in IEEE Transactions on Visualization and Computer Graphics*, TVCG (2014).

50. Tatti, N., and Cule, B. Mining closed episodes with simultaneous events. In *Proceedings of the 17th ACM SIGKDD International Conference on Knowledge Discovery and Data Mining*, KDD '11, ACM (New York, NY, USA, 2011), 1172–1180.

51. Tatti, N., and Vreeken, J. The long and the short of it: Summarising event sequences with serial episodes. In *Proceedings of the 18th ACM SIGKDD International Conference on Knowledge Discovery and Data Mining*, KDD '12, ACM (New York, NY, USA, 2012), 462–470.

52. Thorvaldsdóttir, H., Robinson, J. T., and Mesirov, J. P. Integrative Genomics Viewer (IGV): high-performance genomics data visualization and exploration. *Briefings in Bioinformatics 14*, 2 (Mar. 2013), 178–92.

53. TIBCO. Spotfire. `http://spotfire.tibco.com/`, Mar 2014.

54. Viégas, F. B., Wattenberg, M., and Dave, K. Studying cooperation and conflict between authors with history flow visualizations. In *Proc. 2004 Conference on Human Factors in Computing Systems - CHI '04*, ACM Press (New York, USA, Apr. 2004), 575–582.

55. Wang, J., Kong, L., Gao, G., and Luo, J. A brief introduction to web-based genome browsers. *Briefings in Bioinformatics 14*, 2 (Mar. 2013), 131–43.

56. Wongsuphasawat, K., and Gotz, D. Exploring flow, factors, and outcomes of temporal event sequences with the outflow visualization. *IEEE Transactions on Visualization and Computer Graphics 18*, 12 (2012), 2659–2668.

57. Zhang, Z., Gotz, D., and Perer, A. Interactive Cohort Analysis and Exploration. *Journal of Information Visualization (IVS), to appear.* (2014).

Real-Time Community Question Answering: Exploring Content Recommendation and User Notification Strategies

Qiaoling Liu Tomasz Jurczyk Jinho D. Choi Eugene Agichtein
Mathematics and Computer Science Department, Emory University, USA
{qiaoling.liu, tomasz.jurczyk, jinho.choi, eugene.agichtein}@emory.edu

ABSTRACT
Community-based Question Answering (CQA) services allow users to find and share information by interacting with others. A key to the success of CQA services is the quality and timeliness of the responses that users get. With the increasing use of mobile devices, searchers increasingly expect to find more local and time-sensitive information, such as the current special at a cafe around the corner. Yet, few services provide such hyper-local and time-aware question answering. This requires intelligent content recommendation and careful use of notifications (e.g., recommending questions to only selected users). To explore these issues, we developed *RealQA*, a real-time CQA system with a mobile interface, and performed two user studies: a formative pilot study with the initial system design, and a more extensive study with the revised UI and algorithms. The research design combined qualitative survey analysis and quantitative behavior analysis under different conditions. We report our findings of the prevalent information needs and types of responses users provided, and of the effectiveness of the recommendation and notification strategies on user experience and satisfaction. Our system and findings offer insights and implications for designing real-time CQA systems, and provide a valuable platform for future research.

Author Keywords
Real-time; community; question answering; recommendation; mobile notification;

INTRODUCTION
Community-based Question Answering (CQA) services such as Yahoo! Answers [11] and Quora [8] provide an increasingly effective way of finding and sharing information online. Users turn to community help for various reasons, e.g., unsuccessful web searches or a need for answers from real humans. A key to the success of CQA services is the quality and timeliness of the responses that the users get. To reduce the response latency between questions and answers, several real-time question-answering systems have been introduced [18, 30, 36]. To improve the response quality, question recommendation has been explored [15, 34]. At the same time, as the use of mobile devices has increased, the information needs related to the content near the user's location have also become more prevalent [35]. To satisfy such location-related needs, location-based CQA systems have been introduced [4, 5, 27].

Although both real-time and location-based aspects are important, we are not aware of CQA systems that support both aspects. To investigate the interplay of relevance, location, and timeliness in real-time CQA, we built a research system called *RealQA*, utilizing a mobile application supporting instant notification and location detection, and a server backend handling recommendation and notification strategies. Our system supports common CQA functions such as asking and answering questions, voting for questions and answers, and retrieving a list of questions to answer. We also investigate novel features specifically designed for real-time receiving recommendation notifications of newly posted questions, and receiving new answers for subscribed questions. User locations are recorded while they interact with the system, which are later used for real-time question recommendation.

Our system was developed iteratively, incorporating insights from the analysis of two user studies - the pilot study and the main study, conducted with students at Emory University. We focused on evaluating the overall functionality of our system during the pilot study, and on comparing different recommendation algorithms during the main study. Specifically, we investigated: 1) the types of questions asked and quality of answers; 2) user preference for question recommendation strategies: letting users pull a list of questions from the main page vs. pushing questions to the users via notifications; 3) the effectiveness of question-ranking and user-ranking algorithms for different recommendation strategies; 4) the effectiveness of automated question tag recommendation algorithms.

The specific contributions of our work include:

- A novel, location-aware real-time CQA system named RealQA as a research platform (Section 3).
- Two user studies with two versions of the system, showing improvements with both qualitative survey analysis and quantitative behavior analysis (Section 4).
- Comparison of different algorithms for question ranking, user ranking, and tag ranking (Section 4).
- Insights, data, and code (`http://ir.mathcs.emory.edu/projects/realqa/`) for future studies (Section 5).

IUI 2015, March 29–April 1, 2015, Atlanta, GA, USA.

http://dx.doi.org/10.1145/2678025.2701392

RELATED WORK

Real-time question answering

Real-time question answering (QA) systems have been designed to shorten the time for a question to be answered. These systems typically use synchronous communication channels for asking and answering questions. For examples, Aardvark automatically routes a question to people in the asker's extended social network who are most likely to answer [18]. The user ranking algorithm considers user's expertise in the question topic, connectedness to the asker, and availability to respond. IM-an-Expert provides an instant message service deployed in an organization to find experts for a question and automatically create dialog sessions for the asker [30, 36]. The expert ranking algorithm is based on matching question text with user profiles using TF-IDF, an established method in information retrieval. Mimir, a market-based real-time QA system, broadcasts a question to all other users [19].

Some systems allow users to locate potential responders for new questions.For example, the Quora service called "Online Now" enables an asker to find a list of experts who are currently online, to choose whom to ask [9]. [26] proposed a system which can find a set of Twitter friends for a query based on availability, willingness, and knowledge. [24] presented methods to locate targeted strangers on Twitter for information solicitations.

Our work is most relevant to Aardvark. Table 1 compares the statistics reported in [18] and the statistics collected in our main study, although the comparison is not quite fair due to different deployment settings and participation incentives. We found that the nature of questions collected by our system is more subjective and local-intent. Moreover, the proportion of users answered any questions (or recommended questions) is higher in our case. The main difference between the two systems is that Aardvark focuses more on social network while our system focuses more on location proximity when exploring recommendation and notification strategies.

	Aardvark	RealQA
% of subjective questions	64.7%	71%
% of questions with local intent	10%	77%
% of questions answered	87.7%	89.3%
% of users received rec. questions	86.7%	66%
% of users clicked rec. questions	70%	74%
% of users answered rec. questions	38%	48%
% of users answered any questions	50.0%	74.3%

Table 1: Comparative statistics for Aardvark and our system (RealQA).

Location-based question answering

Location-based QA systems have been designed to facilitate the information seeking and knowledge sharing about some geographic locations [4, 5, 27]. Typically, these systems allow users to post questions to users around a specific geographic location. Our system provides similar features, i.e., when posting a question, users can select "asking people around a specific location". Then, the question recommendation algorithm uses this location information to recommend the question to users who are not only interested in answering but also close to that location.

Mobile-based question answering

Asking and answering questions from mobile devices have become increasingly popular [20, 28]. Most web QA services also provide mobile-friendly websites or mobile apps such as Yahoo! Answers [11], Quora [8], and Stack Overflow [10].

The portability of mobile devices also makes accurate location detection and real-time interaction with users easier. This motivates our system to support real-time and location-aware question answering services based on a mobile app. Recently, [29] studied the effect of mobile phone notifications on the daily lives of mobile users, and showed that an increasing number of notifications correlated with negative emotions. From our study, we found that carefully sending notifications to users and let users have control resulted in better system performance and user satisfaction. [29] also found that silent notifications were not viewed slower than non-silent ones, which supports our design decision to send silent notifications for recommendations.

Question recommendation

There are two ways for users to retrieve questions: proactively request questions from QA services (PULL), or let the system push questions to them (PUSH). Accordingly, question recommendation can be done using two strategies. The PULL strategy computes a list of questions for a user to answer, e.g., by considering question content signals and user social signals [15], and question relevance, diversity, and freshness [34]. The PUSH strategy computes a list of users to route a question for getting answers, e.g., by considering user interests [17], authority [22], availability [21], and compatibility [14]. Real-time QA systems often use this strategy [18, 36]. A detailed survey of the question recommendation methods can be found in [16].

To the best of our knowledge, the only work supporting both the PULL and PUSH strategies in a single system is Aardvark [18]. In their study, more users answered via PUSH because users were willing to answer questions to help friends in their social networks. However, in our studies, PULL is preferred, when a closely knit social network may not exist.

Tag recommendation

A question in a CQA service may span multiple topics or be interesting to different users. Tags have become a de-facto standard way to organize such content in a meaningful way, but are not always provided by the users. Automatic tag recommendation has been studied for a variety of content (e.g., blogs [32], micro-blogs [23, 37], discussion forums [33]), and social recommender systems have been introduced [31]. We adapted and compared several methods in our system, including a method similar to the one in [37] in order to automatically suggest tags for users' questions.

SYSTEM OVERVIEW

Our system consists of two parts: a front-end mobile application and a back-end server system. Users can post, upvote, and downvote questions and answers using the mobile app. From the main page of the mobile app, users can browse questions recommended by our server system. Users may also get questions recommended via mobile notifications. Moreover, users can subscribe to questions they want to get notifications about when new answers are posted for the questions.

Our system was developed iteratively, incorporating insights from the analysis of two user studies. In both studies, we analyzed users' interactions with our system and their survey responses. From the pilot study, we received user feedback and improved our system for both the front-end mobile application and the back-end sever system based on their feedback. We also collected feedback from users from the main study, which will be used for future improvement. Table 2 shows main functions and comparisons between systems used for the pilot and the main studies.

Front-end: mobile application

Our mobile application has been designed and built for smart phones using an Android OS (version 4.0 or higher, occupying 87.9% of the whole Android device market). Our application is distributed through the official Android distribution platform, Google Play (`http://play.google.com`).

Registration, login, and navigation

During the registration process, each user is asked to enter a username, a password, and tags of interests. After registration, the user is logged into the system, and directed to the main page. The *navigation drawer* is used to view different pages in the application, and can be prompted when the user presses the application icon in the top-left corner (Figure 1a).

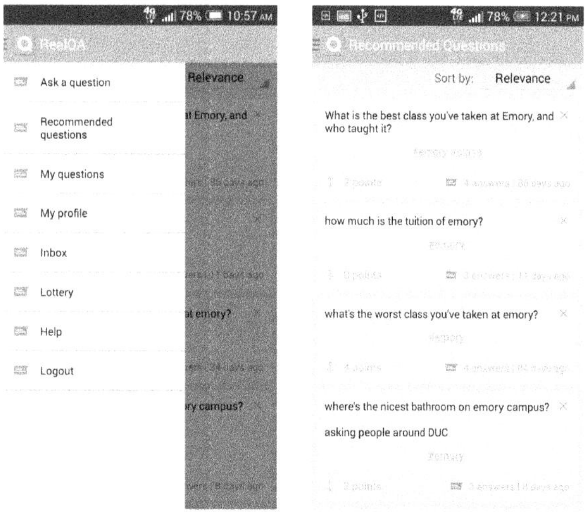

(a) Navigation drawer. (b) Recommended questions.

Figure 1: The main page of our mobile application.

Application main page

By default, the application main page shows a list of questions recommended to this user (Figure 1b). Each row consists of a question body, tags related to the question, the score of the question, the number of answers to the question, and the time since question is posted. The cross icon in the upper right corner of each question item can be used to dismiss this question.

By clicking the choice box in the upper right corner, users can choose different question ranking algorithms (see the 'server' section for more details about the algorithms). It also gives an option of retrieving all questions. Any click on either the question body or the number of answers displays the *question thread*, consisting of the question and all answers that have been posted for the question (Figure 2a). Additionally, two buttons are placed in the upper right corner; the left button lets the user subscribe to this question, and the right button lets the user post an answer to this question.

Posting a question

A key aspect of our system is the ability to post a new question in real-time (Figure 2b). When the user enters a question body, the system shows 3 recommended tags and an option to retrieve 10 recommended tags based on the question body (see the 'server' section for more details about the recommended tags).

Another important aspect is that our system allows the user to post a question to only people around a specific location. By default, each question is asked to people in all locations with no specific location annotated. If the user chooses "my current location", the question is annotated with the user's current location (using latitude and longitude). Other locations can be also chosen, including 21 popular locations on campus such as food courts or residence halls, in which case, the question is annotated with this particular location.

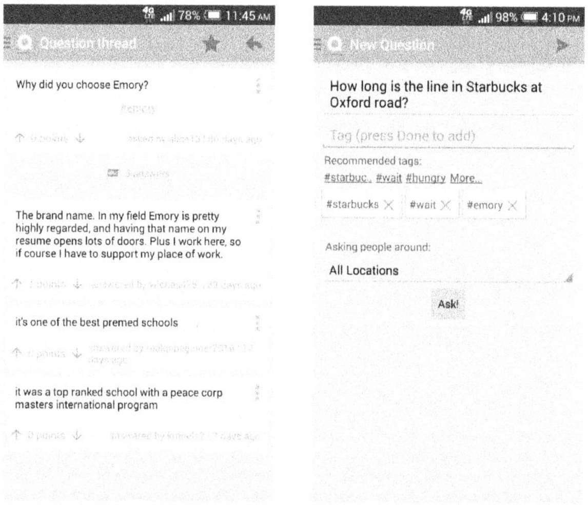

(a) Question thread. (b) Question post.

Figure 2: Question thread and question post.

By clicking on either the *Ask* button or the right upper corner icon, the question gets posted. The author is automatically subscribed to this question, and receives a notification whenever a new answer is posted for this question.

	Pilot Study	Main Study
User related		
· Getting notifications (e.g., question recommendations, answer updates)	2 recommendation algorithms with sound & vibration	3 recommendation algorithms silent notifications
· Updating user's tags of interest	Y	Y
· Turning off notifications	Y	Y
· Setting maximum # of recommendations per day	**N**	**Y**
· Managing user's notifications in the inbox	**N**	**Y**
· Participating in the weekly lottery	**N**	**Y**
Question related		
· Browsing recommended questions in the main page	1 assigned ranking algorithm	5 selectable algorithms
· Browsing all questions in the system	via navigation menu	via ranking options in main page
· Subscribing questions automatically	for asked/answered questions	for asked questions only
· Subscribing questions manually	Y	Y
· Browsing user's asked/answered/subscribed questions	Y	Y
· Asking questions (optionally, annotating locations)	Y	Y
· Answering questions	Y	Y
· Voting for questions and answers	Y	Y
· Getting recommended tags based on question text	**N**	**Y**
· Dismissing questions from the main page	**N**	**Y**

Table 2: Functions in our systems used for the pilot and the main studies.

User profile and notification inbox

Users can update their profiles from the *user profile* tab consisting of user statistics, notification settings, and tags settings (Figure 3a). From the notification settings, users can control whether to receive subscription notifications (when a subscribed question receives a new answer) and recommendation notifications (when a newly-posted question is recommended for the user to answer), as well as the number of maximum recommendations that users receive per day (the default is 5).

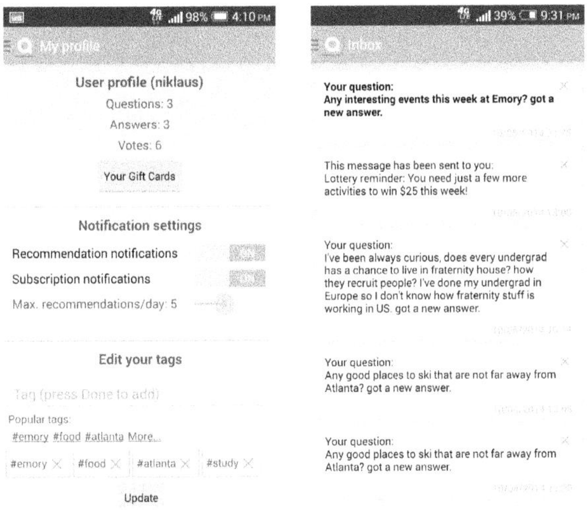

(a) User profile. (b) Notification inbox.

Figure 3: User profile and notification inbox.

The *notification inbox* tab contains notifications that have been sent to the user (Figure 3b). The user can view the associated question by clicking on any notification. Notifications that have not been clicked are shown in bold.

Miscellaneous

The *my questions* tab is similar to the *recommended questions* in Figure 1b, except that the dismissal icon is not present and the right upper choice box include options: asked, answered, subscribed. The *lottery* tab provides information about the status of weekly lotteries. The *help* tab lets users see the terms of service, run the tutorial, or report bugs.

Back-end: server system

For the implementation of the server system, we adapted the Django REST framework [1] and extended the Django models from the Open Source Q&A system (OSQA [7]).

Search component

We adapted Haystack [3] and Elasticsearch [2] for implementing our search component: Haystack provides modular search for Django and Elasticsearch provides scalable real-time indexing and search. Adapting these tools allows our system to create indices for questions, users, and tags dynamically, as well as to search them in real time. Each document in our index contains two fields: a question text field and a tag field. Detailed content of each type of documents is provided in Table 3. We used field level boosting to weigh the tag field twice more than the question text field. We also applied decapitalization, stop word removal, and stemming to the texts in documents and queries.

Document Type	Question Text Field and Tag Field
question	· Question body · Tags of this question
user	· Question bodies answered by this user. · Tags of questions answered by this user, and tags pre-entered in user's profile.
tag	· Question bodies with this tag. · The name of this tag.

Table 3: Index structure for questions, users, and tags.

Our system uses a vector space model for measuring the relevance between documents and queries. All documents and queries are represented in a multi-dimensional vector space, where each dimension stands for a unique term. The relevance between a document and a query is measured by Lucene's practical scoring function [6]: $score(q, d) = \sum_{t \in q}(tf(t, d) \cdot$

$idf(t)^2 \cdot norm(t,d)) \cdot queryNorm(q) \cdot coord(q,d)$, where $queryNorm(q)$ is the query normalization factor, $coord(q,d)$ is a score factor based on how many of the query terms are found in document d, $tf(t \in d)$ is the term frequency for term t in document d, $idf(t)$ is the inverse document frequency for term t, $norm(t,d)$ is the field length norm, combined with the index-time field-level boost.

Question ranking

Our system offers 5 different options for ranking questions when a pull (of questions) is requested by a user:

- **Relevance** - questions that are more relevant to the user's interests are ranked higher. To find relevant questions, search queries are extended with contents in both question text field and tag field of user document, which provide information about the user's interests. This is the default option.
- **Freshness** - more recent questions are ranked higher.
- **Location** - if questions are annotated with locations, ones closer to the user's current location are ranked higher.
- **Popularity** - questions viewed by more unique users are ranked higher.
- **Answer count** - questions with a fewer number of answers are ranked higher.

Previous studies have shown that factors such as relevance and freshness are important for question recommendation [34]. During the pilot study, our system assigned a random ranking algorithm to each user; however, it lets the users choose the ranking algorithm during the main study, which is an improvement made from the analysis of our pilot study.

User ranking

Given a newly posted question, our system randomly assigns one of the following algorithms for ranking users to send recommendation notifications for answering this question:

- **Matching questions** - This algorithm first finds the top 20 questions in the history that are similar to the new question using our search component, then ranks the answerers of these questions. The score of each answerer is measured by the sum of similarity scores between the new question and questions previously answered by the user [17].
- **Matching users** - This algorithm uses the new question as a query against the user documents, and returns the top ranked users using our search component [17, 36].
- **Location proximity** - This algorithm computes the distance between user's and the question locations, and returns the users with closest distances. This algorithm is used for only questions that are annotated with a specific location.

The top 5 ranked users will be sent recommendation notifications for the question. Our system during the pilot study always used the location proximity strategy for questions annotated with specific locations, and the matching users strategy for the rest. During the main study, random algorithms are assigned to new questions to evaluate the differences between these strategies.

Tag recommendation ranking

When the user moves onto the tag input field after completing a new question, a list of recommended tags is displayed. The following algorithms are used for ranking these tags:

- **Matching questions** - This algorithm is similar to the user ranking one, except the score of each tag is measured by the sum of similarity scores between the new question and questions annotated with this tag [37].
- **Matching tags** - This algorithm uses the new question as a query against the tag documents, and returns the top ranked tags using our search component.
- **Tag popularity** - This algorithm ranks the tags based on their use frequencies. A tag is ranked higher if more questions are annotated with this tag.

When a new question is entered, the user is randomly assigned one of the first two ranking algorithms, which returns the top 10 ranked tags. If the number of ranked tags is smaller than 10, then the third algorithm is used to fill in the rest.

USER STUDIES

To evaluate our system for real-time question answering, we conducted two user studies. During the pilot study, we focused on evaluating the overall functionality of the system, while we focused on comparing different recommendation algorithms during the main study. The key aspects of our studies are:

- Types of questions and quality of answers.
- Preference of question recommendation strategies: letting users pull a list of questions in main page (PULL) vs. pushing questions to users via notifications (PUSH).
- Effectiveness of question ranking algorithms for PULL.
- Effectiveness of user ranking algorithms for PUSH.
- Effectiveness of tag recommendation algorithms.

Statistics	Pilot	Main
# of registered users	27	35
# of qualified users	14	16
# of all questions	120	56
# of questions annotated with locations	5	6
% of answered questions	83%	89%
# of all answers	244	238
# of upvotes for questions	76	76
# of upvotes for answers	134	155
# of downvotes for questions	15	5
# of downvotes for answers	33	26
Avg. # of tags in user profiles	3.6	4.5
Avg. # of tags for a question	1.9	2.3

Table 4: Statistics of the data collected from our user studies.

Any student with an Android phone was eligible to participate in these studies. Each participant was asked to install and use our mobile app for a limited period of time. The runtime, minimum required activities, compensation, and initial database were different between two studies. The pilot study was run for a week in July, 2014. In this study, participants received $10 gift cards if they met the following requirements: 1) posted at least 5 questions, 10 answers, 10 votes; 2) performed 1 activity (ask, answer, or vote) per day for 5 days; 3) completed the survey. The initial database included 7 questions posted by the authors of this paper.

The main study was run for 3 weeks in Sep. 2014. In this study, participants received $5 gift cards if they met the following requirements: 1) posted at least 1 question, 5 answers, 5 votes; 2) performed at least 1 activity per day for 3 days; 3) completed the survey. Moreover, we encouraged users to keep using our system for winning lotteries even after they received the gift cards; participants who completed the minimum required activities in a week were eligible to play the lottery held at the end of that week, and each winner received a $25 gift card. The initial database included most questions, answers, tags, votes from the pilot study (some noisy data were discarded).

Statistics and survey responses

In both studies, we analyzed users' interactions with the systems and their survey responses. Table 4 shows statistics from our studies. Qualified users are the ones who finished the minimum required activities. The percentage of qualified users is lower in the main study; one reason is that the pilot study was conducted during the summer when students had more free time, whereas the main study was conducted during the regular school year. The difference in the number of all questions is most likely due to the different minimum required activities in each study. The percentages of answered questions are both high and comparable to the one provided by Aardvark (Table 1). The number of upvotes is much higher than of downvotes for both studies, similar as in Stack Overflow [13]. Users in the main study tended to utilize tags more, as they are generally younger than the ones in the pilot study.

Table 5 shows the survey questions and the responses from users collected during our studies. The average ratings for all questions increased from the pilot study to the main study. In fact, all the negative average ratings had turned to positive. This shows that the overall user satisfaction with our system in the main study had improved from the pilot study. From users' feedback from the pilot study, we found that being able to ask a question to the local community was most important, and pushing the notifications about new answers to their questions was also important. Moreover, we found that too many notifications, irrelevantly recommended questions, and the lack of options to sort recommended questions could annoy users. Based on the feedback, we improved both the mobile application and the server system as described in Table 2 (e.g., sending silent notifications, allowing users to set the maximum number of recommendation notifications per day, managing notification inbox, providing ranking options in the main page, sending answer updates to only askers, and using better recommendation algorithms).

From users' feedback from the main study, we found that the most significant issue was having not enough participants. Some users mentioned improving the quality of recommended questions, improving robustness of tag recommendation, as well as supporting discussion forums for answers.

Question types and answer quality

Types of questions

To understand what types of questions had been asked, we manually categorized all questions, shown in Table 6, based on the question types discussed in [18, 25]. Many questions were with local intent, and meanwhile more subjective questions (recommendation, conversational, opinion) were found than objective ones (factual). The main topics of the questions were about food, study, and relaxing activities. Some example questions and answers from the study participants are shown in Table 7. Such characteristics of the questions were related to the deployment of our system within a campus setting. Compared to Aardvark, the percentages of subjective questions are similar; however, the percentage of questions with local intent is much higher in our study (Table 1).

From the analysis of the question types, we found that many questions were with local intent; however, only 5 and 6 questions were annotated with specific locations in the pilot and main studies, respectively. One reason is that such local intents are often at the university or city level, while the locations provided by our system are at a finer granularity of the building or part-of-campus level. Therefore, users prefer to ask questions to people around all locations in the system, which is the default option. We plan to automatically detect the local intent based on the question text and tags, and dynamically suggest locations with various granularity in the future. As shown in Table 5 (Question 10), users found the function of "asking people around a specific location" somewhat useful in both studies (0.57 → 0.63). This aspect can be improved if users have more freedom to select locations or areas.

Types	Pilot	Main
Local-intent	63.3%	76.8%
Time-sensitive	12.5%	14.3%
Recommendation	26.7%	50.0%
Conversational	48.3%	14.3%
Opinion	10.0%	7.1%
Factual	15.0%	28.6%
Food	10.8%	26.8%
Study	14.2%	14.3%
Entertainment	20.8%	19.6%
Annotated with locations	4.2%	10.7%

Table 6: Types of questions asked and their proportions.

Q1: my mom is coming into town and I need to entertain her for the weekend. where do people bring their parents for fun things to do? #hungry #music #parents A1: I would definitely take her to the botanic garden, the aquarium, and walking around emory. Make it a walking weekend with a focus on being active!
Q2: are there any upcoming food festivals in or around ATL? #food #atlanta #festival A2: Taste of Atlanta! it's next month. great event.
Q3: Where can I get the most food at Emory (for a meal) for the best value? #food #emory #hungry A3: the DUC is unlimited (all you can eat) for a meal swipe or dooley dollars. If you're tired of the DUC, try the Woodrec in Woodruff hall. you get up to 4 items for a meal swipe or dooley dollars. it's pretty filling, but not all you can eat.
Q4: is there free parking anywhere on campus? #broke A4: the parking lots on campus open at different times. I know peavine opens at 4, but then fishbourne doesn't open till later 6. and don't risk parking overnight. I've seen people in the morning get tickets
Q5: What class do you recommend for any major to take? #emory #class #professors A5: Astronomy with the physics department. No prior knowledge needed and lots of fun and pretty easy. Chaucer with Professor Morey was also excellent.

Table 7: Example questions and answers from our studies.

	Survey questions	Pilot	Main
1.	How satisfied are you with the answers?	0.71	1.13*
2.	How would you rate the timeliness of receiving your answers?	0.57	0.94
3.	How satisfied are you with the questions recommended via notification?	−0.86	0.75*
4.	How satisfied are you with the questions recommended via main page?	−0.36	0.50*
5.	Which do you prefer, question recommendation via notification or main page?	21%, 71%, 8%	25%, 56%, 19%
6.	Which do you prefer for ranking recommended questions in main page?	–	relevant, fresh, popular
7.	How satisfied are you with the tags recommended when asking a question?	–	0.75
8.	How useful are the notifications about answer updates?	0.57	1.19
9.	How useful are the notifications about question recommendations?	−0.43	0.81*
10.	How useful is the "ask people around some place" feature?	0.57	0.63
11.	What did you like (like best) about the system?	...	...
12.	What did you dislike (dislike most) about the system?	...	...
13.	Comments/Suggestions.	...	...

Table 5: Survey responses. Ratings are scaled in {2, 1, 0, -1, -2}. Tuples in Question 5 represent percentages of notification, main page, and no preference. * indicates statistically significant difference according to the Mann-Whitney test at $p = 0.05$.

Response latency

For the analysis of the response latency, we measured the duration between questions and their first answers being posted. The median of this duration is 3.2 hours and 36 minutes in the pilot and the main studies, respectively. One reason for the faster latency in the main study can be found from the more active use of recommendation notifications (Table 9; 11% → 24%). Mobile notifications are usually checked within minutes [29], which largely shortens the time for a user to see and answer a newly posted question. The proportion of questions being answered within the first 10 minutes is 34% in our main study, which is lower than 57.2% as reported by Aardvark [18]. This number could be increased if we had a larger user base. The improvement on timeliness of receiving answers in the main study over the pilot study is also supported by the survey responses shown in Table 5 (Question 2; 0.57 → 0.94).

Quality of answers

From the survey responses in Table 5 (Question 1), we see that users are mostly satisfied with the answer quality in both studies, and the satisfaction had increased in the main study (0.71 → 1.13). Since the answer length is an important feature for predicting answer quality [12], we measured the average answer length in each study and found that the average answer length in the main study was longer (Table 8; 10.8 → 12.4). Compared to Aardvark (median answer length: 22.2 as reported in [18]), the answer length tends to be shorter in our main study (median answer length: 7). One reason is that the input device is limited to mobile devices in our study while users in Aardvark could also use desktop computers.

Measurements	Pilot	Main
Avg # of words in answers	10.8	12.4
Avg # of words in answers (score>0)	13.5	16.6
Avg time editing an answer	52s	40s
Avg time editing an answer (score>0)	66s	46s
% of answers with score>0	39%	31%

Table 8: Statistics related to the answer quality.

Another good indicator for the answer quality is the answer score, which is measured by subtracting the number of downvotes from the number of upvotes. We found that answers with positive scores tended to be longer in both studies (13.5 vs. 10.8, 16.6 vs. 12.4), and users spent more time for editing them (66s vs. 52s, 46s vs. 40s). An interesting observation is that users in the main study tend to type faster, probably because they are generally younger than users in the pilot study.

Question recommendation strategies: PULL vs. PUSH

Which leads to more answers? Which is preferred by users?

Table 9 shows which way the qualified users used the most to find questions they wanted. We consider only behavior of qualified users here because behavior of unqualified users is too sparse and unreliable to be analyzed. For both studies, users answer more questions from the main page than from notifications (39% vs. 11%, 61% vs. 24%). Besides, we see the percentage of answers from recommendation notifications increased in the main study (11% → 24%), implying the improvement of notification recommendation. On the other hand, the percentage of answers from subscription notification decreased (6% → 3%). In addition, the percentage of answers from all questions list also decreased (44% → 12%), as in the main study we removed the "all questions" choice from the navigation menu, but added it to the ranking options in the main page.

Source of answers	Pilot	Main
all questions	90 (44%)	25 (12%)
main page	80 (39%)	133 (61%)
recommendation notification	23 (11%)	51 (24%)
subscription notification	13 (6%)	7 (3%)
total	206 (100%)	216 (100%)

Table 9: Sources of answers (considering only qualified users).

The preference result is also supported by the survey responses (Table 5, Question 5), i.e., the majority of users prefer main page rather than notification for question recommendation (71% vs. 21%, 56% vs. 25%). Meanwhile, more users express no preference between the two recommendation strategies in the main study (8% → 19%), with the improvement made on these strategies.

We are aware that the interpretation of these results highly depends on how PULL and PUSH are performed. Yet, the implication here is that it is important to allow users to pull questions, even in a real-time QA system. This is also mentioned in Aardvark [18] that 16.9% of all users have proactively tried answering questions. However, in Aardvark more users answered via notification than via pulling questions. The explanation was that users were willing to answer questions to help their friends or connected people, but not everyone does so proactively. In our system, the users were not as connected. This might be one important reason for the different preference of PULL and PUSH in our system compared to Aardvark.

Recommendation from the main page: question ranking

Which ranking is viewed more and leads to more answers?

How satisfied are users with main page recommendations?

Which ranking is preferred by users?

Table 10 shows the results from different ranking algorithms. Users mostly viewed questions ranked by relevance, partially because it is the default option. When considering the likelihood of answering, ranking by relevance and freshness are among the best. This is consistent with the observation in [34] that freshness is an important factor besides relevance for question recommendation.

Ranking	Views	Answers	Answers per view
Relevance	336	87	0.259
Freshness	163	38	0.233
Popularity	21	4	0.190
Location	14	2	0.143
Answer count	8	2	0.250
all questions	114	25	0.219

Table 10: Question ranking in the main study.

From the survey responses (Table 5; Question 4), users are somewhat satisfied with the main page recommendations in the main study (0.50), better than in the pilot study (-0.36). One important reason is that in the pilot study, each user was randomly assigned a single question ranking algorithm, whereas users chose the ranking algorithm by themselves in the main study, which was more preferred by the users. From survey responses in the main study (Table 5; Question 6), ranking questions by relevance (31%), freshness (31%), and popularity (31%) are among the best. An interesting observation is that although users claimed to be interested in popular questions, they were less likely to answer these questions.

Recommendation via notification: user ranking

How many recommendation notifications are sent? How many are clicked and answered? How satisfied are users with this?

Table 11 shows the statistics about recommendation notifications. The average number of recommendations sent per question to qualified users in the main study is higher than in the pilot study (3.0 $\rightarrow$ 4.3). This implies that a larger proportion of recommendations was sent to unqualified users during the pilot study. Looking at the recommendation notifications sent to qualified users, the likelihood of users clicking on them and the likelihood of users answering the recommended questions had increased (0.40 $\rightarrow$ 0.52, 0.15 $\rightarrow$ 0.28).[1] This shows that our system performed better in notification recommendations during the main study, thanks to several improvements (i.e., managing notification inbox, setting max recommendation notifications per day, and the recommendation algorithm). First, as notification inbox was not supported in the pilot study, users could only see the latest one, and miss some previous ones since their last check of mobile notifications. This would affect clicks and answers. Second, we noticed that active users received more and more notifications per day in the pilot study. One reason is that the user ranking algorithm had a bias towards active users. Another reason is that we did not limit max recommendations per day in the pilot study in the first 3 days. To avoid the unbalance of user workloads getting worse, we set limitation to 5 in the last 4 days. Users were not aware of this number. However, in the main study users were allowed to reset this number at any time of the study.

	Pilot	Main
recommendations	356	239
avg rec. per question	3.0	4.3
clicks	142	124
click rate	0.40	0.52
answers	54	66
answer rate	0.15	0.28

Table 11: Statistics of question recommendation notifications.

The improvement of the system regarding notification recommendations is also supported by survey responses. As shown in Table 5 (Question 3), users' satisfaction with notification recommendations increased in the main study compared to the pilot study (-0.86 $\rightarrow$ 0.75).

Which algorithm is better for user ranking?

To evaluate the three algorithms used in our user ranking component, we use both click related metrics (considering users who clicked on a given question as the ground truth) and answer related metrics (considering users who answered a given question as the ground truth). Specifically, average precision, recall, and F1 scores are computed across all questions using both click and answer based ground truths.

Table 12 shows the results of comparing the three algorithms. When looking at questions that are not annotated with a specific location, the algorithm based on matching users performed better in both click and answer related metrics. First, this algorithm has a bias towards active users, because the document of an active user contains more answered questions and corresponding tags, which makes it more likely to match a new question. Meanwhile, active users are more likely to respond to recommended questions, e.g., by clicking on the question and answering it. The workload balance is handled using the maximum number of recommendations per day set by each user, therefore active users will not get over-annoyed. This is however different from the observation in [17] that matching questions is more effective than matching users for finding potential answerers for a question. First, questions in their setting, i.e., from Yahoo! Answers, is much more diverse in terms of topics than in our setting, i.e., posted by university students, where the main topics are food, study, and entertainment. Therefore, active users are able to answer a larger

[1] Note that all the questions recommended to a user that got answered by him/her are counted here. A user might have not clicked on the recommendation notification but answered it from the main page.

percentage of questions. Second, our results come from live user studies while their results are based on offline simulation experiments. Therefore, it is hard to predict how the results would change from offline simulation to online application.

When looking at questions that are annotated with a specific location, the algorithm based on location proximity showed better performance. This indicates that location proximity is an important factor other than relevance for ranking questions related to specific locations. Yet, more data is needed to do more meaningful analysis regarding the algorithms.

Tag ranking

Which algorithm is more effective for tag recommendation?

To evaluate the algorithms used in our tag ranking component, we use the actual tags entered by the asker as the ground truth, and compute the average precision, recall and F1 scores across all the questions for top 10 and top 3 results of each algorithm.

Table 13 shows the results of comparing the algorithms. For both top 3 and top 10 results, the live system combining the three algorithms achieved the best results on all metrics. The algorithm based on matching questions performed better than matching tags, as matching questions and then summing scores of questions for a tag would better filter out noisy tags in top results while matching tags directly are more likely to return noisy tags because their documents might well match the given question text. Our algorithm based on matching questions is similar to the SimilarityRank approach [37], with the distinction that we sum the scores of similar questions for a tag as its score while their approach chose the max score of similar questions for a tag as its score. Our precision and recall are comparable to the ones in [37].

As shown in Table 5 (Question 7), users are somewhat satisfied with tag recommendations (0.75). This may be improved by applying more state-of-the-art tag recommendation algorithms [23], which will be our future work.

Notification Settings

How many users changed their default notification settings?

How annoying are the notifications?

In the pilot study, three users turned off recommendation notifications. In the main study, one user turned it off, and three users reset the number of max recommendation notifications per day (from 5 to 10, 3, 3 respectively). One user in the pilot study and no user in the main study turned off subscription notifications. This improvement is mainly because we were more careful about sending notifications in the main study, e.g., notifications being sent in silent mode, answerers not getting answer updates on their answered questions, at most 5 recommendation notifications per day and allowing users to reset it, and the improvement of the recommendation algorithms.

From survey responses, we also observe improved user experience about notifications. As shown in Table 5 (Question 9), in the pilot study users rated recommendation notifications somewhat annoying (-0.43), but in the main study users rated them useful (0.81). Meanwhile, in the main study users rated notifications about answer updates more useful (Question 8; $0.57 \rightarrow 1.19$).

DISCUSSION AND IMPLICATIONS

By analyzing the types of questions posted in our studies, we found a large proportion of questions asked are with local intent, subjective, and about food, study, and relaxing activities. Previous research on question recommendation focused more on matching questions and potential answerers based on user interest, expertise and availability [16], while less effort was made on question recommendation considering question types, e.g., questions with local intent. Our preliminary study results indicate that location proximity is an important factor for finding potential answerers to answer such questions besides relevance. More investigation on how to integrate location proximity with relevance and other factors for question recommendation in such cases is needed.

From our studies, we learned that the majority of users prefer pulling questions to answer rather than being pushed questions to answer. However, there are some users who really like to receive notifications, for example, one user commented in survey that "I like the notifications. it's a good way to get people to look at questions without having to browse the app." Therefore, question recommendation systems would achieve better performance if such personal preferences are detected and supported. One solution is to ask users during registration about their preferred settings of recommendation strategies, and then learn based on user behavior to suggest change of the settings or even perform automatic change.

When users do a pull of questions to answer, we found that overall ranking questions by relevance and freshness leads to higher answer rate, which is consistent with the observation in [34]. However, users express different preferences of relevance, freshness, and popularity for ranking the questions for this purpose. Therefore, question recommendation systems need to consider the different importance of factors for ranking questions for different users in the pulling mode. We also found that the question dismissal function was not actively used (75% of the qualified users never dismissed any question from their pulled questions). A potential improvement is to consider users' feedback of dismissing a question in question ranking algorithms, and meanwhile inform users of the benefit.

For deciding which users to push a new question, we found that ranking users by matching user profiles leads to better performance than by matching questions, which differs from the observations in [17], due to the differences in user base (university students vs. Yahoo! Answers users) and in experiment type (live user studies vs. offline simulation experiment). We found that this better performing algorithm has a bias towards active users, who are more likely to answer questions. Therefore, question recommendation systems could rely on active users to contribute more answers, and will benefit from predicting active users before they actually behave actively. Yet, control is needed to avoid over-annoy active users.

Regarding interface design for asking a question, we learned that careful design of location annotation for questions is needed. We found a large gap between the number of questions with local intent and the number of questions that are annotated with a specific location by the asker, partially because the granularity of the predefined locations in our system

	Algorithm	Click based ground truth Prec@5	Rec@5	F1@5	Answer based ground truth Prec@5	Rec@5	F1@5
location not annotated	matching questions	0.49	0.30	0.35	0.20	0.36	0.24
	matching users	**0.60**	**0.37**	**0.44***	**0.29**	**0.38**	**0.32**
location annotated	matching questions	0.53	0.27	0.35	0.15	0.44	0.21
	location proximity	**0.55**	**0.32**	**0.39**	**0.2**	**0.58**	**0.29**

Table 12: Comparing algorithms for ranking users to send recommendations for a newly posted question. * indicates statistically significant difference according to the Mann-Whitney test at $p = 0.05$.

Algorithm	Prec@3	Rec@3	F1@3	Prec@10	Rec@10	F1@10
matching questions	0.283	0.358	0.300	0.102	0.419	0.158
matching tags	0.220*	0.301*	0.240*	0.092*	0.401*	0.145*
tag popularity	0.289	0.376	0.309	0.111	0.453	0.173
combined live system	**0.294***	**0.400***	**0.319***	**0.116***	**0.485***	**0.180***

Table 13: Comparing algorithms for tag recommendation. * indicates statistically significant difference according to the Wilcoxon signed-rank test at $p = 0.05$.

is not so useful. Meanwhile, Letting askers make manual annotation of locations is annoying, which takes extra effort of askers, especially to select diverse granularity of locations using a complex interface. Therefore, location-aware question answering systems might have user experience improved if they can automatically detect the local intent based the question text and tags, and dynamically suggest locations with various granularity to be annotated with the question.

Our system was designed to be highly scalable. The Django REST framework [1] and Open Source QA models [7] used have proven their success to build scalable server systems. The recommendation algorithms are based on query evaluation using Elasticsearch [2], a scalable distributed real-time search software. The system could be used for multiple communities as well after extending the current limited location choices to cover more places using a map.

The presented studies have a few limitations. First, the data collected is from 27 users in 7 days and 35 users in 3 weeks in the pilot and the main studies, respectively. This limited user base and study period makes it hard to draw definitive conclusions from the data. Further, since users were mainly university students, observations in our studies may not generalize to other populations. Second, we are aware that the two studies have similar but different settings, e.g., the pilot study was conducted in summer with more graduate students joined, while the main study was conducted in fall with more undergraduate students joined. Third, we used rewards as participation incentives. However, given that participants were rewarded for total activity, they could freely choose how to allocate their effort and time. Also, we found that qualified users performed more activities than the required minimum, not just being perfunctory for rewards. Therefore, comparing recommendation strategies and ranking algorithms in this setting is still meaningful. Thus, the findings and results would still be likely to apply in more realistic settings.

CONCLUSION

This paper presented RealQA, a real-time community based question answering system with a mobile interface. Our system provided two strategies for users to get recommended questions to answer: users doing a pull of questions in the main page or being pushed questions via mobile notifications. Two live user studies were conducted to test the effectiveness of the system. Based on user feedback from the first study, we improved both the front-end interface and back-end algorithms of the system. Both users' self-reported satisfaction and behavior related metrics were improved in the main study compared to the pilot one. Different algorithms for question ranking, user ranking, and tag ranking were adapted and compared. Our system is useful for conducting further research on location-aware real-time question answering, and is publicly available to other researchers.

To sum up, our main findings were: 1) a large portion of questions asked were with local intent, subjective, and about food, study, and relaxing activities; both answer quality and timeliness of receiving an answer were reported good by users; 2) the majority of users prefer pulling questions to answer rather than being pushed questions to answer in our setting, though some users like to receive notifications more; 3) for the pulling strategy, ranking questions by relevance and freshness leads to higher answer rate, which is consistent with the observation in [34]; 4) for the pushing strategy, ranking users by matching users leads to better performance than by matching questions, which is different from the observation in [17], due to differences in user base and experiment type; 5) for tag recommendation, the algorithm combining both relevance and popularity performed best.

In future, we plan to improve our system towards asking and answering questions with local intent, and to investigate more personalized question recommendation strategies. We are also building an iOS version of the mobile front end and a web front end for our system.

ACKNOWLEDGMENTS

This work was supported by the National Science Foundation grant IIS-1018321 (EA, QL) and the Yahoo! Faculty Research and Engagement Program grants (QL, EA).

REFERENCES

1. Django rest framework. http://www.django-rest-framework.org/. Accessed: 2014-10-05.
2. Elasticsearch. http://www.elasticsearch.org/. Accessed: 2014-10-05.
3. Haystack. http://haystacksearch.org/. Accessed: 2014-10-05.
4. Localmind. http://www.localmind.com/. Accessed: 2014-08-28.
5. LOCQL. http://www.locql.com/. Accessed: 2014-08-28.
6. Lucene's practical scoring function. https://lucene.apache.org/core/4_0_0/core/org/apache/lucene/search/similarities/TFIDFSimilarity.html. Accessed: 2014-10-05.
7. Osqa. http://www.osqa.net/. Accessed: 2014-08-28.
8. Quora. http://www.quora.com/. Accessed: 2014-08-28.
9. Quora online now. http://blog.quora.com/Getting-Answers-Faster. Accessed: 2014-08-28.
10. Stackoverflow. http://stackoverflow.com/. Accessed: 2014-08-28.
11. Yahoo! answers. https://answers.yahoo.com/. Accessed: 2014-08-28.
12. Agichtein, E., Castillo, C., Donato, D., Gionis, A., and Mishne, G. Finding high-quality content in social media. In *Proceedings of the 2008 International Conference on Web Search and Data Mining*, WSDM '08, ACM (New York, NY, USA, 2008), 183–194.
13. Anderson, A., Huttenlocher, D., Kleinberg, J., and Leskovec, J. Discovering value from community activity on focused question answering sites: A case study of stack overflow. In *Proceedings of the 18th ACM SIGKDD International Conference on Knowledge Discovery and Data Mining*, KDD '12, ACM (New York, NY, USA, 2012), 850–858.
14. Chang, S., and Pal, A. Routing questions for collaborative answering in community question answering. In *Proceedings of the 2013 IEEE/ACM International Conference on Advances in Social Networks Analysis and Mining*, ASONAM '13, ACM (New York, NY, USA, 2013), 494–501.
15. Dror, G., Koren, Y., Maarek, Y., and Szpektor, I. I want to answer; who has a question?: Yahoo! answers recommender system. In *Proceedings of the 17th ACM SIGKDD International Conference on Knowledge Discovery and Data Mining*, KDD '11, ACM (New York, NY, USA, 2011), 1109–1117.
16. Furlan, B., Nikolic, B., and Milutinovic, V. A survey and evaluation of state-of-the-art intelligent question routing systems. *International Journal of Intelligent Systems 28*, 7 (2013), 686–708.
17. Guo, J., Xu, S., Bao, S., and Yu, Y. Tapping on the potential of q&a community by recommending answer providers. In *Proceedings of the 17th ACM Conference on Information and Knowledge Management*, CIKM '08, ACM (New York, NY, USA, 2008), 921–930.
18. Horowitz, D., and Kamvar, S. D. The anatomy of a large-scale social search engine. In *Proceedings of the 19th International Conference on World Wide Web*, WWW '10, ACM (New York, NY, USA, 2010), 431–440.
19. Hsieh, G., and Counts, S. Mimir: A market-based real-time question and answer service. In *Proceedings of the SIGCHI Conference on Human Factors in Computing Systems*, CHI '09, ACM (New York, NY, USA, 2009), 769–778.
20. Lee, U., Kang, H., Yi, E., Yi, M., and Kantola, J. Understanding mobile q&a usage: An exploratory study. In *Proceedings of the SIGCHI Conference on Human Factors in Computing Systems*, CHI '12, ACM (New York, NY, USA, 2012), 3215–3224.
21. Li, B., and King, I. Routing questions to appropriate answerers in community question answering services. In *Proceedings of the 19th ACM International Conference on Information and Knowledge Management*, CIKM '10, ACM (New York, NY, USA, 2010), 1585–1588.
22. Liu, M., Liu, Y., and Yang, Q. Predicting best answerers for new questions in community question answering. In *Proceedings of the 11th International Conference on Web-age Information Management*, WAIM'10, Springer-Verlag (Berlin, Heidelberg, 2010), 127–138.
23. Ma, Z., Sun, A., Yuan, Q., and Cong, G. Tagging your tweets: A probabilistic modeling of hashtag annotation in twitter. In *Proceedings of the 23rd ACM International Conference on Conference on Information and Knowledge Management*, CIKM '14, ACM (New York, NY, USA, 2014), 999–1008.
24. Mahmud, J., Zhou, M. X., Megiddo, N., Nichols, J., and Drews, C. Recommending targeted strangers from whom to solicit information on social media. In *Proceedings of the 2013 International Conference on Intelligent User Interfaces*, IUI '13, ACM (New York, NY, USA, 2013), 37–48.
25. Morris, M. R., Teevan, J., and Panovich, K. What do people ask their social networks, and why?: A survey study of status message q&a behavior. In *Proceedings of the SIGCHI Conference on Human Factors in Computing Systems*, CHI '10, ACM (New York, NY, USA, 2010), 1739–1748.
26. Nandi, A., Paparizos, S., Shafer, J. C., and Agrawal, R. With a little help from my friends. In *ICDE* (2013), 1288–1291.

27. Park, S., Kim, Y., Lee, U., and Ackerman, M. Understanding localness of knowledge sharing: A study of naver kin 'here'. In *Proceedings of the 16th International Conference on Human-computer Interaction with Mobile Devices & Services*, MobileHCI '14, ACM (New York, NY, USA, 2014), 13–22.

28. Pelleg, D., Savenkov, D., and Agichtein, E. Touch screens for touchy issues: Analysis of accessing sensitive information from mobile devices. In *Proceedings of the Seventh International Conference on Weblogs and Social Media, ICWSM 2013, Cambridge, Massachusetts, USA, July 8-11, 2013.* (2013).

29. Pielot, M., Church, K., and de Oliveira, R. An in-situ study of mobile phone notifications. In *Proceedings of the 16th International Conference on Human-computer Interaction with Mobile Devices & Services*, MobileHCI '14, ACM (New York, NY, USA, 2014), 233–242.

30. Richardson, M., and White, R. W. Supporting synchronous social q&a throughout the question lifecycle. In *Proceedings of the 20th International Conference on World Wide Web*, WWW '11, ACM (New York, NY, USA, 2011), 755–764.

31. Song, Y., Zhang, L., and Giles, C. L. Automatic tag recommendation algorithms for social recommender systems. *ACM Trans. Web 5*, 1 (Feb. 2011), 4:1–4:31.

32. Sood, S., Owsley, S., Hammond, K. J., and Birnbaum, L. Tagassist: Automatic tag suggestion for blog posts. In *Proceedings of the First International Conference on Weblogs and Social Media, ICWSM 2007, Boulder, Colorado, USA, March 26-28, 2007* (2007).

33. Stanley, C., and Byrne, M. D. Predicting tags for stackoverflow posts. In *Proceedings of the the 12th International Conference on Cognitive Modelling ICCM 2013* (2013).

34. Szpektor, I., Maarek, Y., and Pelleg, D. When relevance is not enough: Promoting diversity and freshness in personalized question recommendation. In *Proceedings of the 22Nd International Conference on World Wide Web*, WWW '13, International World Wide Web Conferences Steering Committee (Republic and Canton of Geneva, Switzerland, 2013), 1249–1260.

35. Teevan, J., Karlson, A., Amini, S., Brush, A. J. B., and Krumm, J. Understanding the importance of location, time, and people in mobile local search behavior. In *Proceedings of the 13th International Conference on Human Computer Interaction with Mobile Devices and Services*, MobileHCI '11, ACM (New York, NY, USA, 2011), 77–80.

36. White, R. W., Richardson, M., and Liu, Y. Effects of community size and contact rate in synchronous social q&a. In *Proceedings of the SIGCHI Conference on Human Factors in Computing Systems*, CHI '11, ACM (New York, NY, USA, 2011), 2837–2846.

37. Zangerle, E., Gassler, W., and Specht, G. Recommending #-tags in twitter. In *Proceedings of the Workshop on Semantic Adaptive Social Web (SASWeb 2011). CEUR Workshop Proceedings*, vol. 730 (2011), 67–78.

Seeing the Big Picture from Microblogs: Harnessing Social Signals for Visual Event Summarization

Jiejun Xu
HRL Laboratories, LLC
Malibu, CA, USA
jxu@hrl.com

Tsai-Ching Lu
HRL Laboratories, LLC
Malibu, CA, USA
tlu@hrl.com

ABSTRACT
We propose an approach to automatically select a set of representative images to generate a concise visual summary of a real-world event from the Tumblr microblogging platform. Central to our approach is a unified graph model with heterogeneous nodes and edges to capture the interrelationship among various entities (e.g., users, posts, images, and tags) in online social media. With the graph representation, we then cast the summarization problem as a graph-based ranking problem by identifying the most representative images regarding to an event. The intuition behind our work is that not only can we crowdsource social media users as sensors to capture and share data, but we can also use them as filters to identify the most useful information through analyzing their interaction in the microblogging network. In addition, we propose a greedy algorithm to encourage diversity among top ranked results for the generation of temporal highlights of targeted events. Our approach is flexible to support different query tasks and is adaptable to additional graph entities and relationships.

Author Keywords
Visual Event Summarization, Tumblr, Online Social Network, Crowdsourcing

ACM Classification Keywords
H.3.4 Online Information Services: Web-based services; H.4 Information Systems Applications: Miscellaneous

INTRODUCTION
Microblogging platforms such as Twitter and Tumblr have emerged as major hubs for information diffusion, through which a massive volume of data relating to real-world events are generated and shared on a daily basis. As a result, a large body of research work has been devoted to extracting knowledge of specific events from these platforms. For instance, [6, 17] proposed novel methods to analyze and forecast civil unrest events using social media data from Twitter and Tumblr. [5] demonstrated the benefits of utilizing social media and microblogging services for disaster monitoring and relief. [14] proposed different mechanisms to extract tweets related to influenza-like illness from the Twitter stream for epidemic tracking and prediction. Essentially these works are different forms of crowdsourcing applications in which microblogging users serve as low-level sensors to provide timely information regarding specific events. However, this sensor information is usually massive and inherently noisy. It is very challenging, if not impossible, to obtain a full picture of an event by sifting through individual posts manually. In this work, we propose an algorithm to automatically generate a concise and representative summary of a targeted event by extracting the most relevant information from microblogging platforms. Specifically, we focus on visual event summarization, as multimedia contents such as images and videos are becoming prevalent in online platforms. These visual contents complement text and provide vivid descriptions of different aspects of an event. We continue to explore the potential of crowdsourcing for this application. However, instead of explicitly delegating high-level tasks to social media users, such as the ones in [8], we take an implicit crowdsourcing approach to extract and summarize the most useful information by analyzing the interrelationship among users. Specifically, we focus on the Tumblr microblogging platform. According to the recent study of [16], close to 80% of the Tumblr posts are image-based. In addition, many of the posts are related to real-word events [17]. These aspects make it an ideal platform to study visual event summarization. To our knowledge, our work is the first attempt to conduct real-world event summarization by utilizing the community generated data on Tumblr.

IUI'15, March 29 – April 01, 2015, Atlanta, GA, USA.

http://dx.doi.org/10.1145/2678025.2701385

RELATED WORK
Microblog summarization: There are a few existing works on event summarization using the Twitter microblogging platform. For example in [13], a Phrase Reinforcement algorithm was proposed to identify the best tweet that matches a given phrase, such as trending keywords. Note that only a single representative tweet is identified as the summary. In [3], an approach was introduced to summarize the most relevant tweets based on learning an underlying hidden state representation of an event for real-time summaries from tweets. The authors showed superior results for some highly structured and recurring events, such as sports. In [10], an alternative approach was proposed to generate journalistic summaries for sport events using Twitter status updates. Simple temporal cues, such as spikes in the volume of status updates, are used to determine the important moments within an event. Then a phrase graph [13] is used to extract the longest relevant sentences from the corpus of status updates to describe each important moment

within the event. In [15], a multimedia system was presented to analyze and explore events from microblogging platforms. The system includes a bi-lateral correspondence topic model to extract representative content and meaningful facets about events over time. In [4], a tweet summarization framework with a Decay Topic Models was proposed to leverage the temporal correlation that exists among tweets written around the same time. This framework extracts meaningful topics that capture different aspects of the underlying event effectively. Other related work on microblog summarization can be found in [9, 18, 19]. In contrast to the aforementioned text-based event summarization works, we focus on generating a visual summary to cover various highlights of an event.

Visual summarization: Many existing visual summarization methods focus on finding canonical or representative images that are related to particular landmarks. For example, [7] proposed a two-step method to identify canonical photos of landmarks from Flickr. First a location-driven approach is used to generate region-specific tags for different areas in the world. Then a vision algorithm is applied to images with the corresponding tags to discover representative photos. Methods with similar steps have been proposed in [2, 11] for location recommendation for tourists. More recently in [12], a heterogeneous graph-based ranking approach was proposed to generate visual summaries for geographic areas using community-contributed images. In contrast to existing visual summarization approaches, our method does not explicitly utilize visual similarity for image selection. Instead, we "crowdsource" the image selection process by exploiting the implicit user interactions.

SUMMARIZATION FOR THE SOCIAL WEB

The intuition behind the proposed summarization method is to generate temporal highlights of a targeted event through fine-grained analysis of user interactions and activities. Inspired by the success of graph-based ranking algorithms, we proposed to abstract the social entities and their interactions on a microblogging platform with a unified graph model.

Graph Construction

Let $G = (V, E)$ be an undirected graph with the set of nodes V and the set of edges E. The nodes correspond to common object entities in the Tumblr microblogging platform, namely *users*, *posts*, *tags*, and *images*. There are two types of edges in the graph, attribute links and temporal links, which signify the relationship among different object entities. The relationship among objects are modeled by the structure given in Figure 1. Note that nodes and edges can be appended to the graph incrementally as time progresses, and the graph can grow over time. For simplicity, we focus on a portion of the time-evolving graph with a fixed time window centered around a targeted event. The proposed unified graph is symmetric and consists of the following set of nodes:

Post nodes $P = p_1, p_2, ..., p_N$: For each N Tumblr posts collected for a particular event, a post node is introduced. P consists of original post only, and does not include *reblogs*[1].

[1] *reblogs* are similar to *retweet* in Twitter.

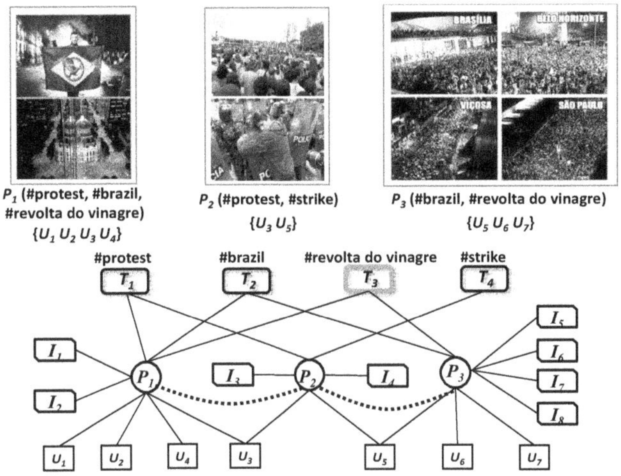

Figure 1. Three sample posts with images from Tumblr related to a protest event. Tags and associated users are listed below each sample post. A graph with heterogeneous nodes and edges are constructed. The red rectangle corresponds to the tag representing the targeted event.

Tag nodes $T = t_1, t_2, ..., t_{N_t}$: A tag node is added for each N_t tags used within the collected Tumblr posts.

User nodes $U = u_1, u_2, ..., u_{N_u}$: A user node is introduced for each N_u users who has interacted with any Tumblr posts collected for an event. The interaction we consider includes: *uploads*, *reblogs* and *likes*.

Image nodes $I = i_1, i_2, ..., i_{N_i}$: An image node is added for each image attached to any of the collected Tumblr posts. An image node only links to its parent post. In addition, we do not introduce additional links among images according to their visual similarities as done in many existing methods [2, 12]. The reason is that image similarity does not play a central role in event summarization, and unreliable links could introduce unnecessary bias and noise to the graph-based ranking algorithm. For instance, images could appear radically different from each other and yet still very much related to an targeted event (see Figure 4).

The final set of nodes V in the graph G is the union of the aforementioned nodes as:

$$V = P \cup T \cup U \cup I. \tag{1}$$

There are two types of edges in the proposed unified graph-based model as follows.

Attribute edges: Multiple social interactions and activities are captured through edges added between Tumblr posts and their surrounding attribute objects (i.e., users, tags, and images). For instance, a user can *reblog* posts from others, a tag can be associated to multiple posts, and a post can be *liked* by many users. These edges are marked with solid lines as in Figure 1. We denote the attribute relationship between object entities with adjacency matrices W_{PU}, W_{PT} and W_{PI}. Uniform weight (e.g., 1) is used for all edges in these matrices.

Temporal edges: Edges are introduced among post nodes when they are published within a close temporal proximity. Formally, the adjacency matrix for posts is defined as:

$$W_{PP}(i,j) = \mathbf{U}(th_e - |\tau(i) - \tau(j)|), \quad (2)$$

where $\mathbf{U}$ is a step function which returns 1 if its input is greater than zero, and return 0 otherwise. $\tau(i)$ and $\tau(j)$ correspond to the times at which two posts are published; th_e is a constant threshold controlling the temporal proximity of two posts (fixed at 1800s in this work). These edges are marked with dotted lines as in Figure 1.

Subsequently, the proposed unified graph can be represented with the adjacency matrix $\mathbf{W}$ with 0s everywhere, but except for the aforementioned submatrices as

$$\mathbf{W} = \begin{bmatrix} W_{PP} & W_{PT} & W_{PU} & W_{PI} \\ W_{TP} & & & \\ W_{UP} & & & \\ W_{IP} & & & \end{bmatrix}. \quad (3)$$

Query for Representative Images

Given the constructed graph and a tag corresponding to an event, graph-based ranking is a natural choice to select the representative images for the targeted event. Here we adopt the well-known manifold ranking [20] for the task. Essentially the algorithm computes a relevance score for each nodes with respect to the query tag node based on the intrinsic graph structure. Let $f \in R^{|V| \times 1}$ be the vector containing the final ranking scores of all graph nodes. The solution can be obtained with the following closed-form

$$f = (\mathbf{I} + \frac{1}{\mu}\mathbf{L})^{-1} y, \quad (4)$$

where $\mathbf{L} = D^{-1/2}(D - \mathbf{W})D^{-1/2}$, which is commonly known as the *normalized graph Laplacian*; D is a diagonal matrix whose (i,i)-entry equals to the sum of the i-th row of $\mathbf{W}$; μ is a constant coefficient set to 0.1; $y \in R^{N \times 1}$ is a zero vector only with 1 at the node corresponding to the query tag. Subsequently by keeping only image nodes among f, we can obtain a ranked list of candidate images for visual summarization.

Diversification

Manifold ranking takes into account relevance and importance of the data, but it does not consider diversity. For example, if a node is very close to a high ranked node, it will share a similar high rank. However, diversity is important to our task, as we want to cover different aspects of an event. Specifically, we would like to deliver a diverse set of temporal highlights. To address this problem, we develop a greedy algorithm which explicitly penalizes redundancies and promotes diversity (see Algorithm 1). The central idea of the diversification algorithm is to decrease the overall ranking scores of nodes which have information already conveyed by the more informative ones in nearby temporal proximity. After this step, image nodes with the highest overall scores will be selected for visual summarization of the query event.

EXPERIMENT

We provide an initial demonstration of the proposed method by showing visual summaries of four real-world events. The

Algorithm 1 Diversification

Input: Set $A = \{x_i | i = 1, 2, ..., N_i\}$ containing the list of image nodes, and each element is associated with a score computed from manifold ranking, i.e., $Score(x_i) = f_i^*, i = 1, 2, ..., N_i$.

Output: Set B containing the nodes with updated ranks

1: Initialization $B = \emptyset$
2: Sort the images in A by their current overall ranking scores in descending order
3: Identify the images with the highest ranked value, i.e. first element in the sorted list. Suppose image x_i is the highest, first move it from set A to B, and then a penalty is imposed to all other images whose parent posts are linked with the post of x_i. For each image x_j satisfy the criteria, we update its score as follows: $Score(x_j) = Score(x_j) - \omega S'_{\rho(i),\rho(j)} f_i^*$, where $\rho(i)$ and $\rho(j)$ are the corresponding posts of image i and j; ω is a constant penalty coefficient (fixed at 1 in this work); $S' = D_{PP}^{-1/2} W_{PP} D_{PP}^{-1/2}$ is the normalized matrix of W_{PP}
4: Repeat from step 2 again until $A = \emptyset$ or the pre-defined iteration count has been reached

selected event tags are: "Boston Marathon" (bombing tragedy, 2013), "Coachella" (music and art festival, 2014), "Salvador Allende" (anniversary of Chilean coup d'etat, 2013), and "V de Vinagre" (protest in Brazil, 2013). For each event, we focus on a 5-day window starting from the first day of the event. We obtained the complete Tumblr data coverage through GNIP [1] firehose for each targeted time frame. To construct the proposed entity network, we first scan through the Tumblr corpus to collect posts which are annotated by the specific event tag. Then a unified graph is constructed for each event based on the entity interaction derived from the collected posts. In our experiment, we filtered out posts which attracted less than 5 users (for *reblogs* and *likes*). Similarly, we filtered out tags which occurred less than 5 times in the data corpus to reduce noise. Figure 2 shows the summary of the final numbers of entities in each constructed graph.

	# Posts	# Photos	# Users	# Tags
Boston Marathon	320	674	61108	2317
Coachella	733	1803	63404	3022
Salvador Allende	305	523	952	120
V de Vinagre	613	842	11466	547

Figure 2. Summary of the collected Tumblr dataset.

Unlike traditional image retrieval, evaluation of visual summarization on the social web is inherently difficult due to the absence of groundtruth. On the other hand, it involves collective human judgment. Here we assess the summarization quality based on subjective evaluations on the visual summaries with the top-20 images returned by the proposed algorithm. Specifically, we are interested in the following questions:

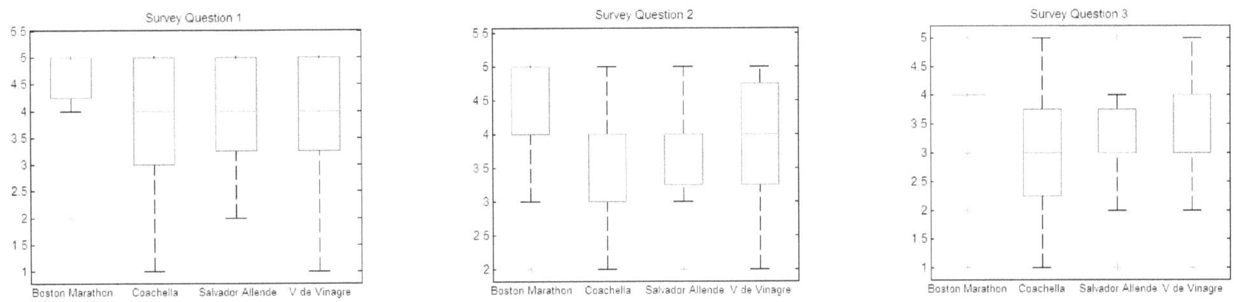

Figure 3. Subjective evaluation of visual event summarization by users.

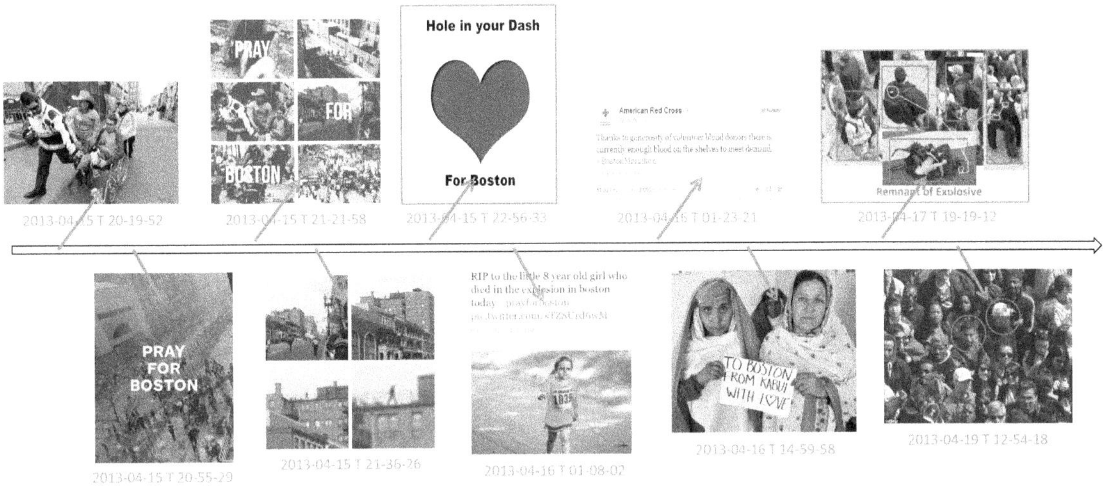

Figure 4. Visual summary of the "Boston Marathon" tragedy in 2013.

1) *Does the generated visual summary provide any indication on the nature of the event?*

2) *Do you agree that these images cover different (diverse) aspects of the targeted event?*

3) *Do you think the visual summary help you understand the temporal highlights of the target event effectively?*

A group of 15 users participated in the evaluation and provided their feedback from a scale of 1 (worst) to 5 (best). Figure 3 shows the box plots of the human user responses. Overall ratings show that the median answer to all questions are on or above 3 which is quite satisfactory. Figure 4 show an example of visual summary of the 2013 tragedy "Boston Marathon". As can be seen, the summary starts with the images after the bombing on the date of the tragic event, followed by images representing immediate responses of the general public, and then images signifying early investigation of the event. Note the graph representation is flexible to different query tasks. For instance, the same ranking framework can be applied to identified a set of "influential" users or a set of emerging tags with respect to a targeted event. Additional heuristics such as user geo-locations and interests can also be taken into account by introducing addition linkages to the graph among object entities. Furthermore, the graph-based algorithm is quite scalable as Eq. 4 can be computed efficiently using an iterative sparse matrix multiplication approach.

DISCUSSION AND CONCLUSION

In this work, we proposed a unified graph framework to capture the social activities and interactions on the Tumblr microblogging platform for visual event summarization. We proposed a combination of manifold ranking and greedy diversification to increase the probability that a relevant yet diverse set of visual results are obtained for visual summary of the targeted event. We believe our work has direct impact on designing intelligent visualization tool to present community-generated content harvested from the crowd.

Although not explicitly shown in the experiment, the proposed algorithm has substantial advantage over basic count-based ranking techniques (e.g., view counts, likes counts). This is because the latter is heavily bias on the most popular posts, and is unable to deliver a diverse event highlights. For instance, the most viewed images of "Boston Marathon" are concentrated on the day of the tragedy.

In our followup work, we would like to develop an efficient and principled method to determine the criteria for introducing temporal linkages. This is because different events should be summarized at different temporal granularity. For instance, the hour-long Oscar versus the month-long World Cup should be summarized rather differently. In addition, we are interested in leveraging existing computer vision techniques such as near-duplicate detection and canonical image selection for enhanced visual summarization.

REFERENCES

1. Tumblr Data - Gnip. `https://gnip.com/sources/tumblr/`, 2014.
2. Cao, L., Luo, J., Gallagher, A. C., Jin, X., Han, J., and Huang, T. S. A worldwide tourism recommendation system based on geotaggedweb photos. In *ICASSP* (2010), 2274–2277.
3. Chakrabarti, D., and Punera, K. Event summarization using tweets. In *ICWSM* (2011).
4. Chua, F. C. T., and Asur, S. Automatic summarization of events from social media. In *ICWSM* (2013).
5. Gao, H., Barbier, G., and Goolsby, R. Harnessing the crowdsourcing power of social media for disaster relief. *IEEE Intelligent Systems 26*, 3 (May 2011), 10–14.
6. Hua, T., Lu, C.-T., Ramakrishnan, N., Chen, F., Arredondo, J., Mares, D., and Summers, K. M. Analyzing civil unrest through social media. *IEEE Computer 46*, 12 (2013), 80–84.
7. Kennedy, L., Naaman, M., Ahern, S., Nair, R., and Rattenbury, T. How flickr helps us make sense of the world: context and content in community-contributed media collections. In *ACM Multimedia* (2007).
8. Lee, J. H. Crowdsourcing music similarity judgments using mechanical turk. In *ISMIR* (2010), 183–188.
9. Meng, X., Wei, F., Liu, X., Zhou, M., Li, S., and Wang, H. Entity-centric topic-oriented opinion summarization in twitter. In *KDD*, ACM (2012), 379–387.
10. Nichols, J., Mahmud, J., and Drews, C. Summarizing sporting events using twitter. In *IUI*, ACM (2012), 189–198.
11. Pang, Y., Hao, Q., Yuan, Y., Hu, T., Cai, R., and Zhang, L. Summarizing tourist destinations by mining user-generated travelogues and photos. *Computer Vision and Image Understanding 115*, 3 (2011), 352–363.
12. Rudinac, S., Hanjalic, A., and Larson, M. Finding representative and diverse community contributed images to create visual summaries of geographic areas. In *ACM Multimedia* (2011).
13. Sharifi, B., Hutton, M.-A., and Kalita, J. Summarizing microblogs automatically. HLT '10, Association for Computational Linguistics (2010), 685–688.
14. Signorini, A., Segre, A. M., and Polgreen, P. M. The use of twitter to track levels of disease activity and public concern in the u.s. during the influenza a h1n1 pandemic. *PLoS ONE 6*, 5 (05 2011), e19467.
15. Wang, Z., Cui, P., Xie, L., Chen, H., Zhu, W., and Yang, S. Analyzing social media via event facets. In *Proceedings of the 20th ACM International Conference on Multimedia*, MM '12, ACM (New York, NY, USA, 2012), 1359–1360.
16. Xu, J., Compton, R., Lu, T.-C., and Allen, D. Rolling through tumblr: Characterizing behavioral patterns of the microblogging platform. In *ACM Web Science* (2014).
17. Xu, J., Lu, T.-C., Compton, R., and Allen, D. Civil unrest prediction: A tumblr-based exploration. In *SBP* (2014).
18. Yang, X., Ghoting, A., Ruan, Y., and Parthasarathy, S. A framework for summarizing and analyzing twitter feeds. In *KDD*, ACM (2012), 370–378.
19. Yin, W., Mei, T., and Chen, C. W. Automatic generation of social media snippets for mobile browsing. In *ACM Multimedia* (New York, NY, USA, 2013).
20. Zhou, D., Weston, J., Gretton, A., Bousquet, O., and Schölkopf, B. Ranking on data manifolds. In *Neural Information Processing Systems (NIPS)* (2003).

BeyondTouch: Extending the Input Language with Built-in Sensors on Commodity Smartphones

Cheng Zhang, Anhong Guo, Dingtian Zhang, Caleb Southern, Rosa Arriaga, Gregory Abowd
Georgia Institute of Technology
85 Fifth Street NW, Atlanta GA 30332, USA
{chengzhang, guoanhong, dingtianzhang, caleb.southern, abowd}@gatech.edu, arriaga@cc.gatech.edu

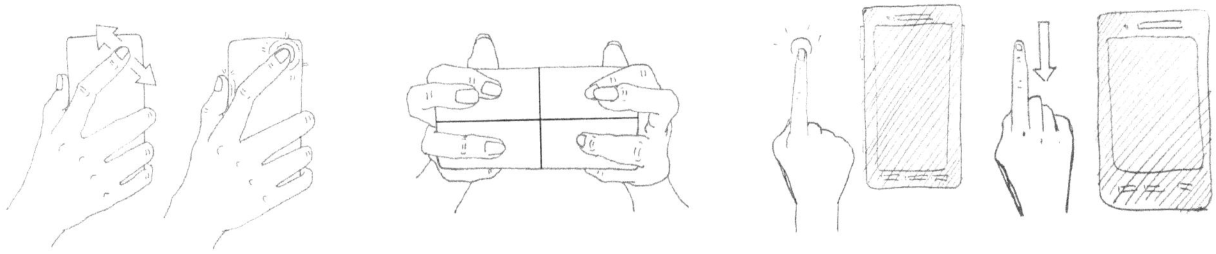

Figure 1: BeyondTouch interaction techniques.

ABSTRACT
While most smartphones today have a rich set of sensors that could be used to infer input (*e.g.*, accelerometer, gyroscope, microphone), the primary mode of interaction is still limited to the front-facing touchscreen and several physical buttons on the case. To investigate the potential opportunities for interactions supported by built-in sensors, we present the implementation and evaluation of BeyondTouch, a family of interactions to extend and enrich the input experience of a smartphone. Using only existing sensing capabilities on a commodity smartphone, we offer the user a wide variety of additional tapping and sliding inputs on the case of and the surface adjacent to the smartphone. We outline the implementation of these interaction techniques and demonstrate empirical evidence of their effectiveness and usability. We also discuss the practicality of BeyondTouch for a variety of application scenarios.

Author Keywords
Mobile interactions; smartphones; inertial sensors; acoustic sensors.

ACM Classification Keywords
H.5.2. Information Interfaces and Presentation: User interfaces; Input devices and strategies.

IUI 2015, March 29–April 1, 2015, Atlanta, GA, USA.
Copyright 2015 ACM 978-1-4503-3306-1/15/03…$15.00.
http://dx.doi.org/10.1145/2678025.2701374

INTRODUCTION
Currently, the primary mode of interaction with a smartphone is limited to the front-facing touchscreen and a small number of physical buttons along the sides. However, there are various scenarios when it is not convenient to touch the screen or the buttons, such as when the phone is on the table and the user's hands are dirty or wet, when touching the screen occludes the display, or when the user is holding the phone in one hand while the other hand is occupied with another task. To address these limitations, we implemented and evaluated a family of interaction techniques, called BeyondTouch, that allow a user to perform additional inputs *one-handed*, *two-handed* and *on-table*, extending the input language of a smartphone in several interesting ways (see Figure 1).

Contributions and Overview of Paper
While it is possible to accommodate many of these interaction scenarios by adding capabilities to the smartphone through external sensors (*e.g.*, a capacitive touchscreen on the back of the phone [11, 22]), it is also possible to augment the input language of a commodity smartphone through proper leverage of its existing sensing platform. Current smartphones are equipped with an increasing number of sensors, specifically accelerometers, gyroscopes and microphones, all of which can be exploited to support a wider variety of software-detected input events without the need for additional hardware.

While previous work has suggested the possibility of sensing a small set of input events, BeyondTouch is distinguished by the breadth of input events enabled and the discussion on practical issues about applying machine learning on mobile interactions (*e.g.*, personalization on models) and challenges deploying them in real applications.

BeyondTouch (Figure 1) extends the input language of a smartphone by offering:

- On-case interactions (one-handed and two-handed), to avoid occluding the limited screen area with the fingers;
- Indirect interaction, by touching the surface (*e.g.*, a table) on which the phone is placed.

We will provide a review of related work next. We then describe the technical approach behind the implementation of BeyondTouch, the machine learning approach to recognize the various input events. We provide an empirical evaluation of the performance of BeyondTouch and discuss the implication of these results for practical use. Our results suggest a hybrid machine learning approach for some scenarios in which a little bit of personalized training data improves performance for some users.

RELATED WORK

We review past work on using sensors to enable novel interaction techniques, and position our contribution of providing a broad range of interactions for a smartphone without having to add any new sensing capabilities to the device.

Some of the earliest demonstrations of broadening interactions with mobile devices were presented by Hinckley et al., who instrumented a PDA with a variety of extra sensing capabilities to demonstrate a wide variety of interactions that could augment the user experience [9]. This work inspired much of the related research we have reviewed. While most of the above work has taken the same approach of adding sensors to the device to demonstrate interactions that can be supported, contemporary smartphone platforms include increasingly sophisticated sensors, and there is an opportunity to produce many discrete interactions without adding sensors.

On-case Interactions

One of the main problems with touchscreens is that users' fingers occlude the screen. Several researchers have experimented with shifting the interaction away from the touchscreen to the side and back of devices in order to eliminate occlusion or increase efficiency and accessibility of the device. This can be accomplished by adding additional hardware, such as a keypad [11,14], a touchpad [1,24,25,26,30] or through computer vision [23,29].

Other research has explored the potential gestures supported by the built-in sensing capabilities on the phones. Hinckley et al. explored techniques using only inertial sensors and touch input for hand-held devices that leverage the multimodal combination of touch and motion, providing touch-enhanced motion and motion-enhanced touch gestures as well as the detection of tap events [10]. Tap events have been further investigated by recognizing side taps [15], detecting taps on the back case of a phone using the microphone as a sensor relying on off-device computation to process the input [20] or distinguishing between a single gentle or firm tap on the case [8]. Besides using tap gestures while holding the phone, there are often situations in which a simple tap directed to some location on the device is an easy and often preferred eyes-free way to interact [21], such as interacting with the phone while it is inside a pocket. Taking the phone out for interactions demands a high level of attention, both cognitively and visually, and is often socially disruptive. Whack Gestures explored quick access to a device in a pocket through striking its case forcefully with the palm or heel of the hand [12]. Goel et al. demonstrated the possibility of inferring hand postures while holding the phone using only built-in sensors, but requiring a somewhat undesirable constant vibration source [5].

Off-the-phone Interaction

In some contexts, it is desirable to interact with the phone without directly touching it. The space around the phone can be used to interact with the phone. Airlink exploits the Doppler effect to detect the gestures above the phone [3]. Others have explored off-the-phone interactions while a phone is placed on a flat surface (*e.g.*, table), requiring customized pickups attached on the surface to capture the acoustic signals on the surface, such as a modified stethoscope [6] or contact piezoelectric sensors [19]. Goel et al. used both the customized sensors on the surface as well as the phone sensors (*e.g.*, inertial sensors) to support a wider set of around-phone gestures [4]. However, what kind of off-the-phone gestures can be detected without using any additional hardware other than the built-in sensors is still unclear. In addition, we introduce the use of dual microphones available in most modern smartphones for recognizing gestures. Although previous work has explored recognizing gestures by differentiating sounds generated by gestures [7], the on-table interaction in BeyondTouch can detect both sliding and tapping gestures with only built-in sensors.

Snooping Users Input on Smartphones

Interestingly, several researchers outside the HCI community have explored nefarious uses of sensing mobile device interaction, uncovering information security risks afforded by easy access to smartphone sensors such as the accelerometer to detect users input on touchscreen [2,16,18,31]. However, most of these techniques rely on off-line inference; it is unclear how they will work for real-time interaction tasks.

MOTIVATION AND APPLICATIONS

BeyondTouch was motivated by many common smartphone usage scenarios, where the touchscreen or on-case buttons limit convenient interactions. For example, when the user is cooking, he may need to clean or dry his hands before using the touchscreen. In other scenarios, such as gaming, the user's fingers occlude the already limited viewing area of the touchscreen. To address these limitations, we implemented three classes of interaction scenarios: one-handed, two-handed, and on-table.

One-Handed
When the user is interacting with the phone with a single hand, it is not easy to move the thumb across the entire touchscreen area, especially as screen sizes increase. In addition, the other hand may be occupied doing something else. BeyondTouch allows the user to tap on the side of the phone with the thumb, and to tap or slide on the back of the phone with the index finger (Figure 1a).

The one-handed tapping interactions can be used for applications such as browsing through images and webpages. They can also be used for camera functions, like taking selfies, zooming in and out, and so forth. Other applications include accessing functions with coarse input gestures. For example, the user can simply turn on and off the flashlight by tapping on the back of the phone. The one-handed sliding interactions are naturally matched with applications that require scrolling operations, such as proceeding to the next/previous voicemail, or song on a playlist.

Two-Handed
The two-handed interactions address usage scenarios where the touchscreen is available, but the users' hands may occlude the small screen area of the phone while holding it in two hands. We implemented the two-handed interaction to address this problem, employing a similar user experience to a traditional game controller on a laptop or a game console. The user can hold the phone in landscape orientation with two hands and tap on soft buttons on the back of the case (Figure 1b).

In the current implementation, we offer six soft buttons on the back and side of the case. Applications include games and navigation, with the advantage of exposing the entire screen area because the fingers are touching the back case rather than covering the touchscreen.

On-Table
On-table interaction explores possible interactions around the phone by using only built-in sensors on commodity smartphones. When the user is cooking and a phone call comes in, his phone is on a table and his hands may be dirty or wet. How would he answer the phone call without polluting the screen by touching it? BeyondTouch allows the user to tap and slide on the table around the phone to interact with the device indirectly (Figure 1c). Furthermore, the on-table interactions can be extended for many applications that demand straightforward interactions, such as responding to a phone call or controlling the music player.

IMPLEMENTION OF BEYONDTOUCH

Table 1 describes the complete set of input events and related sensors that BeyondTouch supports. We implemented the BeyondTouch interactions on commodity smartphones by interpreting data from a combination of three common built-in sensors: the accelerometer, gyroscope, and microphones. We applied machine-learning techniques in order to identify the characteristic signature of each input event. The machine learning techniques were implemented using Weka [27], a publicly available tool that provides implementations of various machine-learning algorithms that can be run in real-time on a smartphone.

Table 1: Interaction techniques.

Scenario	Interaction	Input Events	Sensors
One-Handed	Tap	back-single-tap, back-double-tap, side-tap	Gyroscope, accelerometer, the microphone at bottom
	Tap-Slide	back-single-tap, back-double-tap, back-slide-up, back-slide-down	Gyroscope, accelerometer, the microphone at bottom
Two-Handed	6-point-tap	up-left, up-right, top-left, top-right, bottom-left, bottom-right	Gyroscope, accelerometer, the microphone at bottom
On-Table	Slide, Tap	Slide, tap on the surface around a phone	Gyroscope, accelerometer, two microphones

Choice of Detection Technique

In the early exploration of this project, we applied a rule-based method to recognize the four corner taps for on-case interactions. Based on our observation, the rotation of the phone case presents distinct quantitative signatures when tapping on each of the four corners of the phone case. We implemented a straightforward rule-based solution to detect the four corners, which worked well. The advantages of the rule-based approach are: 1) a lightweight software implementation (given the limited processing power of a smartphone); 2) ease of implementation; and 3) no requirement for training and personalization. However, machine learning, by contrast, is appropriate for interactions that are more complex, where the difference between input events are not obvious from observation of the sensor input streams. Therefore, we decided to employ machine-learning based methods to explore other interactions potentially supported by the built-in sensors on a smartphone.

Choice of Built-in Sensors

In our initial investigation, we examined data from the accelerometer to determine if a tap occurred anywhere on the case of a phone, inspired by work such as Whack Gestures [12]. In order to detect where the user tapped on the case, we then added the gyroscope, which better reflects the difference on the tapping events on four corners.

In pilot testing we observed that when the user held the phone with a tight grip, these two motion sensors often failed to detect the tap event, even with a strong tap on the back case. To address this problem, we added the microphones as a third input stream. We only consider loudness from the microphone buffer, measured in decibels (dB). To calculate the decibel level, we first normalize each audio sample and calculate the average root mean square

(P_{rms}) of the samples in the buffer. We then calculate the decibel value (Equation 1), where P_{ref} is equal to the standard reference sound pressure level of 20 micropascals.

$$L_P = 20 \times log_{10}\left(\frac{P_{rms}}{P_{ref}}\right)\ dB \quad (1)$$

In addition, a sensor fusion of microphone and inertial sensors are complementary to filter out most of the noise, which works well.

Implementation of On-case Interactions

We implemented the *one-handed* (Tap, Tap-Slide) interactions and *two-handed* interactions using a combination of rule-based (segmentation) and machine learning approaches (classification).

We use a traditional sliding window method, with a window size of 0.64 seconds. Since a tap or slide event usually last 0.5 seconds, we round it up to 0.64 seconds for the convenience of computation in the Fourier transform. Since the sample rate of gyroscope and accelerometer in the phones we used are 100 Hz, each frame contains 64 samples with 50% overlap with adjacent frames. For each frame, the system will extract features to determine whether an event happens (segmentation) and which event it is (classification).

To detect the occurrence of an input event, we use a rule-based approach to detect whether an input event (either tap or slide) has occurred by examining the combination of thresholds for sensors, including the difference between the maximum and minimum value from x-axis/z-axis of the accelerometer and y-axis/z-axis of gyroscope.

For classification, we extract three sets of features for each 0.64-second length buffer from data of three axes of gyroscope and accelerometer. The features we selected were based on our observation and understanding of the data and gestures, which are also common statistical features used in related works. We plotted out the data in both time and frequency domains and decided on which features to use and estimated the time each gesture took and chose the appropriate window size. The first set is the time-domain features. For each axis of the data from gyroscope and accelerometer, we calculated the seven features over each frame, including root-mean-square, the derivative of root-mean-square, maximum and minimum value, mean, variance, and median. We also calculate the ratio between maximum and minimum for the three axes of the gyroscope and the total energy for both the gyroscope and accelerometer, which indicates the magnitude of the whole event. In addition, the maximum decibel value and the derivative of neighboring decibel values are also computed as features. Therefore, we have $7\times6+3+2+2 = 49$ features related to amplitude.

The second set of the features includes frequency and energy, which are calculated for each axis of both the accelerometer and gyroscope. We compute the Fast Fourier Transform (FFT) using JTransform [13] to calculate the frequency energy on each frequency band. We build 31 bins over the frequency 100 Hz for each axis as well as the standard deviation of frequency energy over 31 bins, since we observe that our input events are equally distributed in terms of energy over frequencies. In total, we have $31\times6+6 = 192$ features.

As a result, we compute 241 features for each frame to detect the one-handed and two-handed interaction gestures. We pass these features to a support vector machine (SVM), provided by the Weka machine-learning library [27], and then use this model to classify gestures.

Implementation of On-table Interaction

The on-table interaction is also implemented using a combination of rule-based and machine learning approach.

In the segmentation stage of our implementation, we use a rule-based approach to detect whether an input event (either tap or slide) has occurred by examining the combination of thresholds for the three sensors, including the loudness level of bottom microphone and the maximum and minimum value from z-axis of the accelerometer or y-axis of the gyroscope.

To classify the input event, we extract features from microphones, the gyroscope, and the accelerometer. To capture the full duration of a slide event, we used a sliding window of one second. Then we divide the one-second window into ten frames. For each frame, we extract the following basic time-domain features for all sensors: 1) level; 2) derivative of level[1]; 3) maximum and minimum level; and 4) energy[2]. A feature vector of each window is the combination of the feature vector of the ten frames. We put the feature vector of a window into the pre-trained model for classification.

We compared the performance of different machine learning algorithms on our collected training data using ten-fold-cross validation provided by Weka. Both SVM and K Nearest Neighbor (KNN) provided above 97.5% for precision and recall. We elected to use KNN in our implementation.

Building Training Model

Usually, a trained machine-learning model can be categorized based on whether it is session-dependent or user-dependent. A session-dependent model requires recollecting training data before using the model each time. A user-dependent model demands collecting training data from each user. Both of them would increase the barrier of applying them in real-world usage. Therefore, we adopted a

[1] We approximate the derivative of sensor data as the change in value divided by the change in time.

[2] Energy is the square root of the sum of squares for all samples in the frame.

user-independent model in our implementation, which applies a pre-collected training data set and does not require any data collection from each user. Based on our pilot study result, we found that the performance of one-handed and two-handed interactions were dependent on how the user holds the phone and performs the gestures. However, the phone's position was not changed when performing gestures for on-table interaction. Therefore, we collected a larger set of data for building the model for one-handed and two-handed interactions.

For on-table interaction, we first conducted a small pilot study with the authors. A classifier was trained with the training samples only from one author. We tested that model with other authors and the accuracy was very high. We thought that was because the gestures for on-table interaction did not require any direct contact with the phone, which greatly reduced the variance between gestures. As a result, we collected training data from only one of the researchers, who performed approximately 600 gestures for each slide event and the tap event on a table. We varied the tapping position and strength in order to approximate the behavior of different users.

To build the training set for two-handed and one-handed interactions, we collected training data from 10 users, including two authors. Four of them provided examples for both two interactions, while others provided examples for only one of the interaction. As a result, each interaction has 10 trainers and approximately 1000 instance for each input event. During the training process, we asked each user to repeat each input event 100 times on a Galaxy S3, with approximately a one-second gap between each gesture. The data collection program did not provide any feedback to users. Therefore, the users performed the input gestures in the manner most comfortable and natural to them.

After collecting all the data, we manually labeled each input event in the training set. If the researcher was not sure about the label of an instance, we discarded it to avoid polluting the training set. Around 85% of the gestures ended up in the training set.

EVALUATION METHOD

We evaluated the accuracy and usability of BeyondTouch for the interactions listed in Table 1. We presented users with a series of stimuli for the interactions, and recorded the responses interpreted by the pre-trained machine-learning models. All interactions were performed in a lab environment.

Participants and Apparatus

We recruited 12 participants (1 female) for two-handed and one-handed interaction using a Samsung Galaxy S3 phone, and another 11 participants (6 female) for on-table interaction using a Samsung Galaxy S3 (7 participants) and a Samsung Nexus phone (4 participants).

Study Procedure

In the practice phase of the study, we first explained the interactions to the participants and allowed them to practice the gestures, receive feedback after performing each gesture, and ask questions. Then each participant performed practice sessions, responding to stimuli for each gesture in the assigned interaction technique ten times in a row.

In the evaluation phase, we presented the participant with blue-colored visual stimuli on the smartphone screen indicating which gesture to make. The user also received visual feedback after responding to the stimuli. When classification result matched the stimuli, the feedback was given in green, otherwise red. Each participant responded to 40 stimuli (2 sessions × 20 stimuli) for each gesture with random order in one-handed and two-handed interactions. For the on-table interaction, each participant responded to 90 stimuli (3 sessions × 30 stimuli), randomly chosen between tap and slide gestures. For each interaction, we asked the users to report any self-made errors in this phase. It took less than one hour for each participant in the user study, and there was no compensation.

RESULTS

We report accuracy for each interaction as the percentage of responses where the gesture classification matched the stimulus, and the user impressions of each interaction based on a questionnaire administered at the end of the evaluation phase.

Accuracy

For one-handed and two-handed interactions, there were 480 examples (20×2×12) for each gesture, and 990 inputs (30×3×11) for on-table interaction. Table 2 presents the overall accuracy and standard deviation for each interaction.

Table 2: Accuracy of each interaction technique.

Interaction	Two-Handed	One-Handed-Tap	One-Handed-Tap-Slide	On-Table
Accuracy	71.28% (SD=12.89%)	88.47% (SD=3.55%)	72.92% (SD=6.53%)	93.74% (SD=4.64%)

One-handed Interaction

For one-handed-Tap interaction, the overall accuracy is 88.47%. The confusion matrix is reported in Table 3. Side-tap was the most accurate (98.54%), and double-tap was the least accurate (73.96%). There is a lot of confusion between double-tap and back-tap, due to the variation of strength and interval of taps between different users.

Table 3: One-handed-Tap confusion matrix.

User Input	Classification		
	BackSingleTap	BackDoubleTap	SideTap
BackSingleTap	92.92%	4.79%	2.29%
BackDoubleTap	24.17%	73.96%	1.88%
SideTap	0.83%	0.63%	98.54%

If we collapse back-tap and double-tap into one gesture, higher accuracy can be achieved (97.92%) (Table 4).

Table 4: One-handed-Tap (back tap combined + side) confusion matrix.

User Input	Classification	
	BackTap(Combined)	SideTap
BackTap(Combined)	97.92%	2.08%
SideTap	1.46%	98.54%

For one-handed-tap-slide interaction, the overall accuracy is 72.92%. The confusion matrix is reported in Table 5. Back-slide-up was the most accurate (92.08%), and back-slide-down was the least accurate (41.25%). There is a lot of confusion from back-slide-down to back-slide-up. There is also a lot of confusion from double-tap to back-tap.

Table 5: One-handed-Tap-Slide confusion matrix.

User Input	Classification			
	BackSingleTap	BackDoubleTap	BackSlideDown	BackSlideUp
BackSingleTap	84.38%	4.38%	2.71%	8.54%
BackDoubleTap	20.00%	73.96%	0.63%	5.42%
BackSlideDown	4.58%	0.21%	41.25%	53.96%
BackSlideUp	2.50%	0%	5.42%	92.08%

Collapsing back-tap and double-tap into one gesture, and back-slide-down and back-slide-up into another gesture, improves accuracy to 91.35% for taps and 96.35% for slides (Table 6).

Table 6: One-handed-Tap-Slide (backtap combined) and slide (combined) confusion matrix.

User Input	Classification	
	BackTap(Combined)	Slide(Combined)
BackTap(Combined)	91.35%	8.65%
Slide(Combined)	3.65%	96.35%

Two-handed Interaction

For two-handed interaction, the overall accuracy is 71.28%. The confusion matrix is reported in Table 7. The up-right corner was the most accurate (83.33%), and the bottom-right corner was the least accurate (50.83%).

Some users reported that up and top points are much easier to perform than bottom points. Some users also reported that the test sessions were so long (240 taps in two sessions), making them feel tired. This also led to 12 user self-made errors.

Table 7: Two-handed-6-point confusion matrix.

User Input	Classification					
	UpLeft	UpRight	TopLeft	TopRight	BottomLeft	BottomRight
UpLeft	77.92%	14.58%	3.96%	2.92%	0%	0.63%
UpRight	5.63%	83.33%	3.13%	6.46%	0%	1.46%
TopLeft	2.50%	8.75%	70.83%	15.42%	1.04%	1.46%
TopRight	0%	10.21%	8.75%	79.17%	0%	1.88%
BottomLeft	0%	7.29%	21.46%	2.92%	65.63%	2.71%
BottomRight	0.21%	17.29%	9.38%	19.38%	2.92%	50.83%

On-Table Interaction

For the on-table interaction, eleven participants averaged 93.74% accuracy (S.D. = 4.64%) over 990 input events total. Tap gestures were recognized with 95.68% accuracy, and slide gestures were recognized with 91.11% accuracy.

DISCUSSIONS

Like any recognition technique, BeyondTouch is not perfect. Here we discuss the results to uncover a better understanding of how and when BeyondTouch is suitable.

Accuracy and User Impressions

Some users reported that tapping continuously for so long (tap and slide for over 500 times) made them feel less natural and comfortable. While the experimental procedure allowed us to gather much data under different situations, we recognize that it put unrealistic demands on the users that would not be the case in everyday life.

Similar to real applications, we provided real-time feedback while participants were testing our technique. But we observed some users adjusted their gestures according to the feedback given by the system, especially if they saw misclassified instances. We take this as a self-learning process and may potentially have positive influence in the user study result.

We discuss other observations for each scenario that impacted results.

One-handed Interaction

When the users tried to perform back-slide-down, they would first wave their index fingers up. Although there is no contact with the phone, the shake of the phone is very similar to back-slide-up, resulting in many false classifications.

Two-handed Interaction

We observed that the variations in the way users hold the phone, the positions they tap, and the strengths of the taps affected individual results a lot. When the users adjust hands positions while holding the phone, some false-positives were introduced.

On-table Interaction

Both slide and tap gestures in on-table interaction required the user to touch the surface around the phone. Since we used microphones to recognize the gestures, if users did not generate loud enough sound it would increase the difficulty of detecting the occurrence of an event. From our observation, most users can learn very fast during the practice to use their fingertips and nails together to perform the gestures, which were well recognized by the system. However, user fatigue resulted in false negatives in the latter stages of the experiment.

Personalization

In the user study, the one-handed and two-handed machine learning based interactions showed an obvious drop in terms of accuracies compared with the result we computed on the training data set using 10-fold cross validation and leave-one-participant-out method. This gap is mostly caused by individual differences, such as a user's finger length, tap position, and strength of tap. Recall that there were 16 total trainers and we collected training data for each scenario from a different subset of 10 of the overall 16. We further tried to encourage each trainer to perform the input events in whatever way he or she felt most comfortable, thus introducing lots of opportunities for these individual differences to be revealed in the models generated. A personalization procedure, should improve the results of the machine-learning model for any given user.

Our approach to personalization is a revision on the leave-one-participant-out method. Instead of leaving one trainer's [3] complete training set out, we methodically incorporated a stratified and randomly selected subset of that person's training data into the model that was then used to test the remainder of that trainer's input data. We refer to this as "leave-one-participant-partially-out", to reflect that some of an individual's data is incorporated into the learned model that is used for classification.

Specifically, for one-handed and two-handed interactions, we have collected approximately 100 training instances for each event from 10 different trainers. Instead of using 9 trainers' data to build the model to evaluate the 10th trainer's data, we gradually added a portion of instances from the 10th trainer's data into the training set to build a new model. Then we used this new model to evaluate the rest of the 10th trainer's data set. To avoid bias, we ran the sample selection process 10 times, then built and evaluated the model for each of them. Then we averaged results from the 10 sample runs and report those below. Note that though the ratio of test data to training data changes based on the amount of training events extracted from the 10th trainer, the difference in those ratios is negligible for purposes of comparison.

To evaluate this method, we compare the accuracy results for different sizes of the trainers' input set (randomly selected subsets of size 10, 20, 30, 40, 50 of the approximately 100 overall events) against the baseline of using none of that person's training set to build the model (*i.e.*, using 0 of the overall events).

In Figure 2, we show the personalization results for the three usage scenarios. For each graph, the red/bolder line represents the averaged result for the "leave-one-participant-partially-out" method across all trainers in our training set. The x-axis indicates how many of the trainer's input events were added to build the personalized ML model. For example, the one-handed-tap interaction scenario provides three input events: back-tap, back-double-tap, and side-tap. Each user provided around 100 instances for each input event. An x-axis value of 10 represents random selection of 10 instances for each input event from the 10th user's data set. Since the one-handed-tap-slide scenario has three distinct input events, a total of 10×3=30 instances were incorporated into the personalized training set.

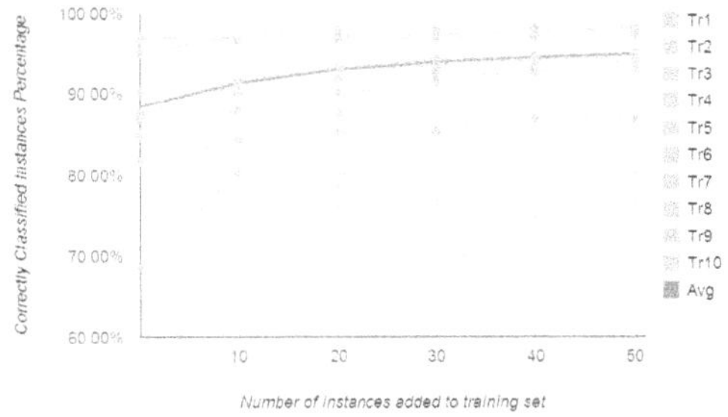

a. One-handed-Tap

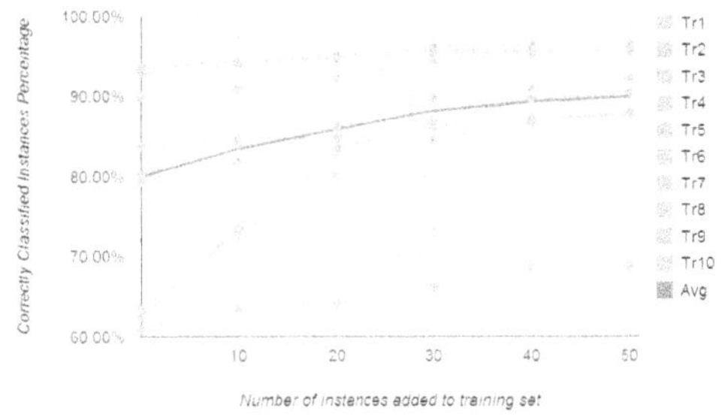

b. One-handed-Tap-Slide

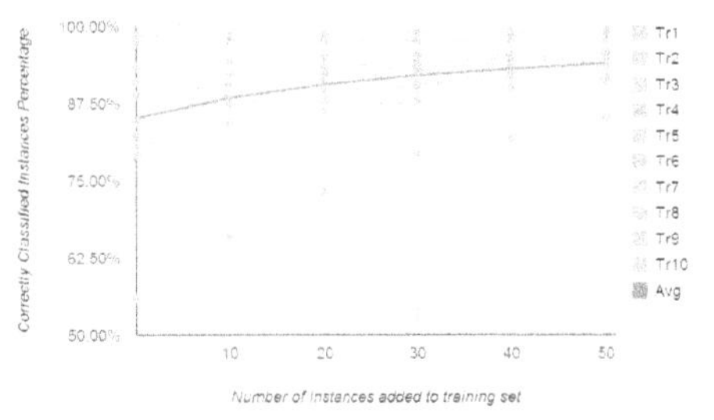

c. Two-handed-6-point

Figure 2: Personalization results

Figure 2 reveals an interesting insight. There is a pretty significant spread of accuracy results across the trainers, with each scenario having at least one trainer whose classification accuracy is much poorer than the rest of the trainers with no personalization (x-axis value of 0). That

[3] We refer to these individuals as "trainers" in the following discussion, distinct from user study participants.

classification gap decreases when personalization is introduced. Without personalization, the average accuracy across all 10 trainers is 80.00% (one-handed-tap-slide), 88.42% (one-handed-tap), and 85.06% (two-handed) with standard deviations of 0.13, 0.08, and 0.12, respectively. Using 30 personal training events (per input type), the average accuracies increase to 88.17%, 93.89%, and 92.06% while the standard deviations decrease to 0.09, 0.04, and 0.06. Figure 2 demonstrates these positive trends for all three of the machine learning scenarios.

Furthermore, beyond using 30 examples of each event from the trainer's, there is no appreciable improvement of the personalization. This is also good, as it means we need collect only a small set of an individual BeyondTouch user training data to sufficiently personalize that user's model.

A closer examination of the results in Figure 2 shows that what personalization is doing is more about improving the classification for the poorest performers in the "leave-one-participant-out" results. The better performing trainer's do not improve that much. This suggests that it might be worthwhile in practice determining on the fly how well classification accuracy is for a given user. If that accuracy is below some acceptable threshold, BeyondTouch can recommend additional training from that user to personalize and improve his results.

For example, it may be possible to infer incorrect real-time classifications by BeyondTouch by sensing the user repeating an interaction or developing some other situation-specific heuristic. A running count of these errors can help determine if a threshold of error tolerance is met. If so, training can be suggested to the user. With this approach, BeyondTouch could be used "out of the box" and, for a smaller percentage of users, and only after having some experience with BeyondTouch, a user could decide whether it would be worthwhile to improve accuracy by taking some time out to give personalized training data.

Challenges for Practical Deployment

There are a number of issues beyond recognition rates that impact the practical utility of BeyondTouch.

Calibration on Different Phones

Smartphones vary in terms of form factor and sensor capabilities, which calls into question how our results work across devices. In our user study, we did not test our technique on a large variety of phones. However, since the sensors we used are most common ones and we applied machine learning technique in the implementation, calibration across phones is a matter of collecting enough training data prior to installation on a given phone, and then allowing for personalization as described above. While this data collection may be time-consuming, it does not directly impact the user of the device, until and unless personalization is warranted.

Rule-based Methods vs. Machine-learning Methods

BeyondTouch employed a combination rule-based (segmentation) and machine learning (classification) techniques for detecting input events. However, in our early exploration, we found that rule-based techniques are also appropriate for classifying less complex input gestures with easy implementation (*e.g.*, tap events on the four corners). Machine-learning methods can recognize more complicated gestures at the price of collecting training data and personalization as well as a higher requirement for computation. A potential mixture between these two methods can be an effective practical method.

Usage of Multiple Microphones

Most smartphones now have more than one microphone. Usually, the manufacturer positions one of the microphones at the bottom to receive the user's voice input and the other at the top to detect the ambient sound (to improve the call quality by reducing the environment noise). These two microphones can also be leveraged for interaction purposes, as demonstrated in our on-table interaction. According to basic physical principles, if the distances between a sound source and two audio receivers are different, the loudness level of the audio received by the two receivers should be different. We found that to be true when the physical touch event was close to or on the phone case. We imagine richer potential interaction events can be detected by combing the data from multiple microphones and inertial sensors.

Interactions by Contexts

In practice, many of the interactions we developed are designed to work in specific contexts. For example, the one-handed interaction is designed for the scenario when the user prefers to hold and interact with the phone in one hand, while two-handed interaction is tuned for a user holding the phone in two hands. If the phone runs two-handed interaction while holding it in one hand, would increase the false-positives and false-negatives. Hence, an automatic detection of context about the position and orientation of the phone [28] is a necessary step for applying BeyondTouch in real life.

Energy Consumption

BeyondTouch interactions are largely dependent on sensors. However, recent released smartphones (*e.g.*, Moto X, iPhone 5S/6) are beginning to feature a low-power, always-on coprocessor for managing the sensors. With this kind of new hardware, we expect the energy consumption of the sensor usage will be greatly reduced going forward and would not be a concern while using these sensor-based techniques.

CRITIQUE OF APPLICATIONS OF BEYONDTOUCH

In addition to the applications we proposed in the introduction, the study participants also suggested interesting usage scenarios for BeyondTouch. In this section, we will discuss how we can apply our techniques to these scenarios by exploring the limitations of

BeyondTouch and the opportunities to address these constraints in future work.

One-handed

One-handed interactions can support up to five input events. In our evaluation, some gestures were detected with high accuracy while others were confused with other gestures. However, not all the applications require all of the five events. As reported in the results, we can achieve higher accuracy by combining the single and double back taps into a single gesture, and by combining the up and down swipes into a single gesture. However, how would new combination of input events influence the usability still needs to be further evaluated.

Applications

While a user is holding the phone in one hand on a phone call, a common task is to mute the microphone. Instead of moving the phone from the ear and finding the mute button on the screen, the user can directly use the index/thumb to tap on the phone to activate the mute function. Vibration feedback can be provided for this eyes-free interaction. Participants suggested many other applications which only need a single input event from one-handed gestures, such as taking selfies with the front-camera, playing flappy bird (requires high speed), quick check of the time, and so forth.

The most common scenarios for one-handed interaction with phones are reading websites/books/emails or playing videos. These usually require two or three input gestures, such as forward/backward. From the evaluation, we can see there is little confusion between tap and slide events or tap on back and tap on side events. Therefore, we can map these pairs to backward/forward functions (*e.g.*, map tap with forward and slide with backward). Unfortunately, this mapping is arbitrary and unnatural [17]. The natural mapping should be slide up and down, which exhibited some confusion of classification in the evaluation and may require personalization in actual application. These simple tap events can also be used as shortcut to certain functions/menus, for example, mapping tap events to open the task managers, and then using the slide up/down or side tap for switching applications.

Limitations

One limitation of one-handed interaction is the potential for false positives while users are adjusting their hands. Based on our observation, even if a user performs gestures while walking around, as long as he is holding the phone steadily, there will be a lower chance of triggering false-positives. But if a user shakes the phone and generate sound noise at the same time (*e.g.*, scratching the case), there will be a higher chance of triggering false-positives.

Future work

We are mostly using rule-based method for segmentation now. However, a machine learning plus rule-based method can be built to provide much better results to minimize false-positive errors. One way is to systematically collect noise input from various users and add them into the machine learning classifier. Another possible way is to apply more signal processing method and look at the frequency domain of the data. For example, when the user is moving the hands, the relative sound is different from a tap event, which can be separated by a band-pass filter. In addition, we can explore a higher resolution of input events, such as which position of the back case is tapped, and sliding up/down on the side case. Our preliminary investigation indicates a high likelihood of detecting these events for one-handed gestures. However, considering the dexterity of fingers while holding a phone in one hand, too many input events may be unnatural and unnecessary. Therefore, identifying a natural mapping is prudent before applying these gestures to any applications.

Two-handed

With the two-handed interaction techniques, even one or two input events on the back of the phone can be useful. For example, we may hold the phone in two hands to take a picture in landscape orientation. With BeyondTouch, the user can tap the side case with the thumb (up-left/right gesture) to take a picture, which is a very natural mapping.

The two-handed interactions may also support other common scenarios where users hold the phone in two hands, such as gaming, watching videos, browsing websites, or reading books. For example, it is very natural to map the top-left and top-right event to backward/forward events to navigate a video or website, mapping the remaining events to other functions like stop/start. One of the most common two-handed usage scenarios is gaming, such as playing car-racing games or Whac-a-mole. For car racing, we can map top-left to brake and top-right to gas, and up-left/right for directions, which avoids the fingers occluding the screen.

Limitations

One limitation of the two-handed interaction is the input detection speed, as one input event usually lasts more than 0.5 seconds. Any event that occurs too fast may influence the classification result. Another limitation is similar to the one-handed one, that is, the user's additional hand movement may introduce false positives.

Future work

The solutions to the false-positive problems are similar to what we propose for the one-handed interactions: collecting more noise data and applying other signal processing method. The variance of user's tap positions requires personalization. And another possible solution is to add simple physical tactile feedback on the back of phone (*e.g.*, a plastic button), such that each user can tap on the same position.

On-table

The on-table interaction can help with many scenarios that require simple and quick response without touching the phone, when the phone is placed on a surface.

Applications

Because on-table only recognizes two-input events (slide and tap), it is best suited for applications using simple input events. The best applications are the one where a user has to interact with the phone without touching it, such as controlling a music player or a phone call. One motivation of the on-table interaction is to provide interaction gestures, which can be performed when your hands are dirty (*e.g.*, while cooking). Applying on-table to a music player, we can use the tap events to play/pause a song and the slide event to switch to another song. This is also a very natural mapping between on-table gestures and the touchscreen gestures. Similarly, we can map the tap and slide event to answer or reject a phone call.

Limitations

In the study, if the nail of the participants' finger were too long, they felt uncomfortable to use their fingers and nails to conduct the slide gesture. Also some users spent longer time to learn how to perform these gestures, especially if their initial tap gestures were light. In the study, the surface below the phone was either wood or plastic, making detection simpler. Although we have not tested yet, we expect the on-table interaction may not work well on other surfaces that do not conduct sound well. Another limitation for the current implementation of on-table is that the classifier may be influenced when there is a significant noise source nearby.

Future work

To address the ambient noise issue, one obvious next step is to introduce frequency-domain features in order to distinguish different sound sources. We can apply a band-pass filter in the segmentation part to filter out noise. The system must also be tuned for the varying sound propagation properties of different surface materials. In addition, by utilizing the frequency difference of the sound generated from performing gestures, we expect to further increase the variety of input events [7].

CONCLUSION

We presented the implementation and evaluation of BeyondTouch, a family of interaction techniques that extend the input language to areas off the touchscreen of a smartphone while using only built-in sensors. BeyondTouch can be used in contexts when the touchscreen is not readily available, such as when touching the screen occludes the display, when the user is holding the phone in one hand and performing another task with the other hand, or when the user's hand is dirty or wet. Our evaluation shows that user-independent recognition results for various events range from just over 70% to over 90%, with significant improvements possible with extra personalization. We explored the space of practical applications of BeyondTouch, given its current recognition rates, which we plan to review in the future.

ACKOWLEDGEMENT

We would like to thank Thomas Ploetz, Agata Rozga and the Ubicomp Lab at Georgia Institute of Technology for their feedback. We also want to thank all reviewers for their suggestions and the user study participants. This material is based in part upon work supported by the National Science Foundation Graduate Research Fellowship under Grant No. DGE-1148903.

REFERENCES

1. Baudisch, P., & Chu, G. (2009, April). Back-of-device interaction allows creating very small touch devices. In *Proceedings of the SIGCHI Conference on Human Factors in Computing Systems* (pp. 1923-1932). ACM.
2. Cai, L., & Chen, H. (2011, August). TouchLogger: Inferring Keystrokes on Touch Screen from Smartphone Motion. In *HotSec*.
3. Chen, K. Y., Ashbrook, D., Goel, M., Lee, S. H., & Patel, S. (2014, September). AirLink: sharing files between multiple devices using in-air gestures. In *Proceedings of the 2014 ACM International Joint Conference on Pervasive and Ubiquitous Computing* (pp. 565-569). ACM.
4. Goel, M., Lee, B., Islam Aumi, M. T., Patel, S., Borriello, G., Hibino, S., & Begole, B. (2014, April). SurfaceLink: using inertial and acoustic sensing to enable multi-device interaction on a surface. In *Proceedings of the 32nd annual ACM conference on Human factors in computing systems* (pp. 1387-1396). ACM.
5. Goel, M., Wobbrock, J., & Patel, S. (2012, October). GripSense: using built-in sensors to detect hand posture and pressure on commodity mobile phones. In *Proceedings of the 25th annual ACM symposium on User interface software and technology* (pp. 545-554). ACM.
6. Harrison, C., & Hudson, S. E. (2008, October). Scratch input: creating large, inexpensive, unpowered and mobile finger input surfaces. In *Proceedings of the 21st annual ACM symposium on User interface software and technology* (pp. 205-208). ACM.
7. Harrison, C., Schwarz, J., & Hudson, S. E. (2011, October). TapSense: enhancing finger interaction on touch surfaces. In *Proceedings of the 24th annual ACM symposium on User interface software and technology* (pp. 627-636). ACM.
8. Heo, S., & Lee, G. (2011, August). Forcetap: extending the input vocabulary of mobile touch screens by adding tap gestures. In *Proceedings of the 13th International Conference on Human Computer Interaction with Mobile Devices and Services* (pp. 113-122). ACM.
9. Hinckley, K., Pierce, J., Sinclair, M., & Horvitz, E. (2000, November). Sensing techniques for mobile interaction. In *Proceedings of the 13th annual ACM*

symposium on User interface software and technology (pp. 91-100). ACM.

10. Hinckley, K., & Song, H. (2011, May). Sensor synaesthesia: touch in motion, and motion in touch. In *Proceedings of the SIGCHI Conference on Human Factors in Computing Systems* (pp. 801-810). ACM.
11. Hiraoka, S., Miyamoto, I., & Tomimatsu, K. (2003). Behind Touch, a Text Input Method for Mobile Phones by The Back and Tactile Sense Interface.*Information Processing Society of Japan, Interaction 2003*, 131-138.
12. Hudson, S. E., Harrison, C., Harrison, B. L., & LaMarca, A. (2010, January). Whack gestures: inexact and inattentive interaction with mobile devices. In *Proceedings of the fourth international conference on Tangible, embedded, and embodied interaction* (pp. 109-112). ACM.
13. JTransform:https://sites.google.com/site/piotrwendykier/software/jtransforms
14. Li, K. A., Baudisch, P., & Hinckley, K. (2008, April). Blindsight: eyes-free access to mobile phones. In *Proceedings of the SIGCHI Conference on Human Factors in Computing Systems* (pp. 1389-1398). ACM.
15. McGrath, W., & Li, Y. (2014, October). Detecting tapping motion on the side of mobile devices by probabilistically combining hand postures. In *Proceedings of the 27th annual ACM symposium on User interface software and technology*(pp. 215-219). ACM.
16. Miluzzo, E., Varshavsky, A., Balakrishnan, S., & Choudhury, R. R. (2012, June). Tapprints: your finger taps have fingerprints. In *Proceedings of the 10th international conference on Mobile systems, applications, and services* (pp. 323-336). ACM.
17. Norman, D. A. (2002). *The design of everyday things*. Basic books.
18. Owusu, E., Han, J., Das, S., Perrig, A., & Zhang, J. (2012, February). Accessory: password inference using accelerometers on smartphones. In *Proceedings of the Twelfth Workshop on Mobile Computing Systems & Applications* (p. 9). ACM.
19. Paradiso, J. A., Leo, C. K., Checka, N., & Hsiao, K. (2002, April). Passive acoustic knock tracking for interactive windows. In *CHI'02 Extended Abstracts on Human Factors in Computing Systems* (pp. 732-733). ACM.
20. Robinson, S., Rajput, N., Jones, M., Jain, A., Sahay, S., & Nanavati, A. (2011, May). TapBack: towards richer mobile interfaces in impoverished contexts. In *Proceedings of the SIGCHI Conference on Human Factors in Computing Systems* (pp. 2733-2736). ACM.
21. Ronkainen, S., Häkkilä, J., Kaleva, S., Colley, A., & Linjama, J. (2007, February). Tap input as an embedded interaction method for mobile devices. In *Proceedings of the 1st international conference on Tangible and embedded interaction* (pp. 263-270). ACM.
22. Saponas, T. S., Harrison, C., & Benko, H. (2011, October). PocketTouch: through-fabric capacitive touch input. In *Proceedings of the 24th annual ACM symposium on User interface software and technology* (pp. 303-308). ACM.
23. Schmieder, P., Hosking, J., Luxton-Reilly, A., & Plimmer, B. (2013). Thumbs Up: 3D Gesture Input on Mobile Phones Using the Front Facing Camera. InHuman-Computer Interaction–INTERACT 2013 (pp. 318-336). Springer Berlin Heidelberg.
24. Schwesig, C., Poupyrev, I., & Mori, E. (2004, April). Gummi: a bendable computer. In *Proceedings of the SIGCHI conference on Human factors in computing systems* (pp. 263-270). ACM.
25. Scott, J., Izadi, S., Rezai, L. S., Ruszkowski, D., Bi, X., & Balakrishnan, R. (2010, September). RearType: text entry using keys on the back of a device. In *Proceedings of the 12th international conference on Human computer interaction with mobile devices and services* (pp. 171-180). ACM.
26. Sugimoto, M., & Hiroki, K. (2006, September). HybridTouch: an intuitive manipulation technique for PDAs using their front and rear surfaces. In *Proceedings of the 8th conference on Human-computer interaction with mobile devices and services* (pp. 137-140). ACM.
27. Weka. DOI: http://www.cs.waikato.ac.nz/ml/weka/
28. Wiese, J., Saponas, T. S., & Brush, A. J. (2013, April). Phoneprioception: enabling mobile phones to infer where they are kept. In *Proceedings of the SIGCHI Conference on Human Factors in Computing Systems* (pp. 2157-2166). ACM.
29. Wigdor, D., Forlines, C., Baudisch, P., Barnwell, J., & Shen, C. (2007, October). Lucid touch: a see-through mobile device. In *Proceedings of the 20th annual ACM symposium on User interface software and technology* (pp. 269-278). ACM.
30. Wobbrock, J. O., Myers, B. A., & Kembel, J. A. (2003, November). EdgeWrite: a stylus-based text entry method designed for high accuracy and stability of motion. In *Proceedings of the 16th annual ACM symposium on User interface software and technology* (pp. 61-70). ACM.
31. Xu, Z., Bai, K., & Zhu, S. (2012, April). Taplogger: Inferring user inputs on smartphone touchscreens using on-board motion sensors. In *Proceedings of the fifth ACM conference on Security and Privacy in Wireless and Mobile Networks* (pp. 113-124). ACM.

Hairware: The Conscious Use of Unconscious Auto-contact Behaviors

Katia Vega
Pontifical Catholic University of Rio de Janeiro
Rua Marquês de São Vicente 225 - Gávea, Rio de Janeiro - RJ, Brazil
kvega@inf.puc-rio.br

Marcio Cunha
Pontifical Catholic University of Rio de Janeiro
Rua Marquês de São Vicente 225 - Gávea, Rio de Janeiro - RJ, Brazil
mcunha@inf.puc-rio.br

Hugo Fuks
Pontifical Catholic University of Rio de Janeiro
Rua Marquês de São Vicente 225 - Gávea, Rio de Janeiro - RJ, Brazil
hugo@inf.puc-rio.br

ABSTRACT
Beauty Technology is a wearable computing paradigm that uses the body's surface as an interactive platform by integrating technology into beauty products applied directly to one's skin, fingernails and hair. Hairware is a Beauty Technology Prototype that connects chemically metalized hair extensions to a microcontroller turning it into an input device for triggering different objects. Hairware acts as a capacitive touch sensor that detects touch variations on hair and uses machine learning algorithms in order to recognize user's intention. Normally, while someone touches her own hair, unconsciously she is bringing comfort to herself and at the same time is emitting a non-verbal message decodable by an observer. However, when she replays that touch on Hairware, she is not just emitting a message to an observer, because touching her hair would trigger an object, creating in this way, a concealed interface to different devices. Therefore, Hairware brings the opportunity to make conscious use of an unconscious auto-contact behavior. We present Hairware's hardware and software implementation.

Author Keywords
Hairware; Conductive Hair; Beauty Technology; Wearable Computers; gesture recognition.

ACM Classification Keywords
H.5.2 Information interfaces and presentation: User Interfaces; Haptic I/O.

IUI 2015, March 29 - April 1, 2015, Atlanta, GA, USA.

ACM 978-1-4503-3306-1/15/03…$15.00.
http://dx.doi.org/10.1145/2678025.2701404

INTRODUCTION
Given today's wearables revolution, the human body will become a new design standpoint. Thus, the next logical step in wearable computers seems to be the use of the body's roughly two square meters of skin as a canvas for applying sensors and attaching other computing devices in ways that enhance human experience. The body surface, i.e., the skin, nails and hair, plays crucial roles as a protective barrier, sensory monitor, heat and moisture regulator, and an integral part of the body's immune system. Nevertheless, humanity, since its inception, has used beauty products to adorn the body for a variety of reasons. Nowadays, beauty products have become quite sophisticated with advances in chemistry but have remained mostly aesthetically oriented. Even though the $382 billion global beauty business market is mostly supported by women and 4 in 5 women wear makeup [10], beauty products still have not been thoroughly explored in relation to their possible use as wearable computers. Beauty Technology [23,24,25] disrupts this frontier by placing technology directly on the body surface and allowing women to use beauty products to control their environment through technology in a personal, seamless and fashionable way.

When embedding technology into everyday life objects, Weiser envisioned it functioning in an invisible and unobtrusively way [27]. For that reason, minimizing awareness while interacting with technology, continue to be an important guideline in Ubiquitous Computing. Our concern with this vision is that users are not consciously aware that these pieces of technology are gathering data and processing it for them. In contrast, we propose interactions that the user is consciously aware of and intends to generate them, though in a concealed way, by enacting auto-contact behaviors. Thus, the invisibility of the interaction is not hidden to the user but it is hidden to the observer.

It is worth to remember that there are two interactions taking place. One with the observer as a result of the auto-contact behavior and another, concealed from the observer, with the object. According to the literature [12], auto-contact behavior is to bring comfort to oneself: Does the concealed interaction increase one's own comfort?

The hair is public as everyone could see it, personal as it is a body part, and malleable as it suits cultural and personal preferences [7]. It has for centuries been a vital decorative organ but also it is a powerful source of communication, often being employed as an additional gender signal that differentiates males than females, and as a badge of age and status [12]. In addition to the way it looks, the way it is touched expresses a whole set of non-verbal messages. A woman with longish hair that throws the hair backward attempts to make herself more visible to the opposite sex, but this can also be done in a rather aggressive manner, such as during an argument for making her looks a little larger to her opponent [6]. Straightening the hair over and over again like when a woman tucks her hair behind her ear continuously, is often a sign that indicates anxiety [6]. Twirling the hair around a finger is a gesture that mimics the innocence of childhood and is often used as a flirtation device and as something that a person does when she's bored or trying to settle herself down [6]. Those self-intimacies are movements that provide comfort because they are unconsciously mimed acts of being touched [12]. Conversely, this work aims to recognize conscious touches on hair using those conventional self-intimacies. The wearer touches her Hairware and only she would know what device is being triggered.

This work proposes the use of Hairware as a novel electronic device to be used in wearable computing. We used a chemical platting technique that makes the artificial hair extensions to be conductive but, at the same time, remains looking like regular human hair. This paper introduces Hairware, a capacitive touch sensor that detects a variety of touches for the triggering of different devices. Section 2 identifies previous work on body technologies as input devices. Section 3 presents the hardware and software implementation to detect touch on Hairware. Section 4 shows the model used for learning and recognizing touches on hair. Section 5 presents the evaluation results and reviews the lessons learned using Hairware. Conclusion and future work are shown in the last section.

RELATED WORK

Wearable Computing changed the way individuals interact with computers, intertwining natural capabilities of the human body with processing apparatus [27]. Most of this technology has been designed just for clothing or accessories. However, some works place technology on the body's surface. Thus, the skin and its regenerative appendages (i.e. hair and nails) not just play the crucial role in human beings but also embedded electronics to act as input devices. For example, Skinput [8] uses a bioacoustics microphone to sense the vibration that occurs when the body is tapped. Another example is Senskin [15], a wearable device that uses multiple IR reflective sensors implanted in an armband to allow the skin to be used as a soft input interface by comparing the actual force and the sensor values using an elastic model of the human skin. Touché [18] is a sensing technology that proposes a Swept Frequency Capacitive Sensing technique by using bracelets that detects touches on different parts of the body by sensing the impedance variability between electrodes. Thus, the user could put the phone into silent mode by making a "shh" gesture bringing her index finger to the lips.

In previous Beauty Technology prototypes, Conductive Makeup [23,24,25] was presented as an interface for detecting voluntary blinking. Conductive Makeup includes conductive eyeliner and chemically metalized fake eyelashes that act as blinking switches. While conductive eyeliners (Figure 1a) connect sensors and actuators by using conductive materials that stick to the skin, replacing conventional eyeliners, conductive fake eyelashes (Figure 1b) sense blinking. In order to prove the feasibility of the prototype as a conductive component, some applications were developed. Blinklifier [25] uses blinking for switching LEDs on and off on an artistic headdress. Arcana [23] uses blinking for changing music tracks and images visualizations. Superhero [24] is another artistic application that makes use of Conductive Makeup for triggering a remote control to levitate an object (Figure 1c).

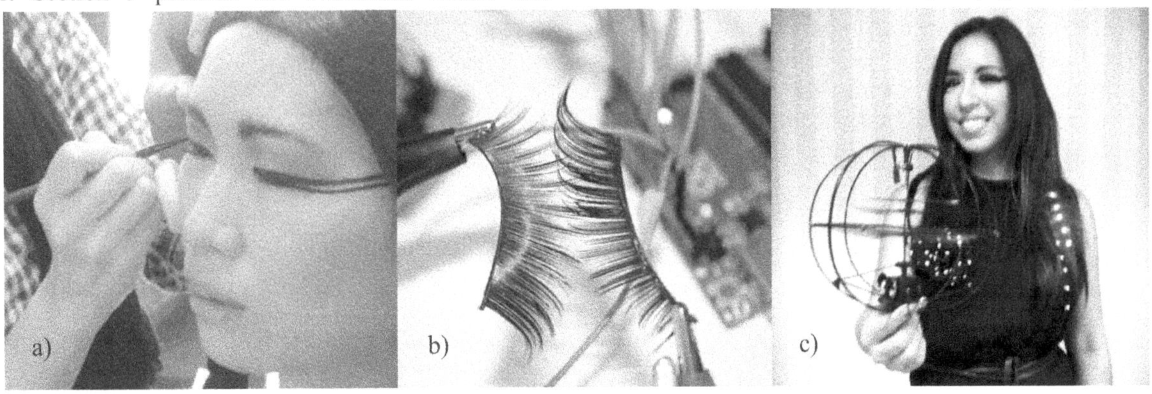

Figure 1. Beauty Technology: Conductive Makeup [23]. (a) Conductive eyeliner that connects the eyelashes to the circuit; (b) Chemically metalized fake eyelashes; (c) Application that makes use of Conductive Makeup for flying a drone by blinking.

Figure 2: Interaction through wearables (a) Google Glass [5]; (b) Talk to the hand [14]; (c) Sixthsense [11] .

Wigs could be used as to enhance someone's appearance and also to follow cultural and religious traditions. SmartWig [22] is a wearable device that uses a wig for hiding electronics that communicates wirelessly with other external devices. SmartWig suggests applications that could fulfill a number of functions, from acting as a health care device that monitors users' vital signs to helping blind people navigate roads, or changes slides in a presentation by tapping their sideburns, under which buttons are hidden. A further potential improvement of the wig may use ultrasound waves to detect objects around a user. Hair accessories that vary from clips to corsages, designed to give every look a final flourish, could also be used for creating discreet and fashionable gadgets attached to the hair. First Sign Hair Clip [20] is an electronic hair clip that communicates with a mobile application to automatically call for help and collect evidence when the user is in danger. By using accelerometers and gyroscopes, it detects head impacts associated with violent crimes, automatically triggering an alarm, while evidence is collected by a microphone.

CONCEALED INTERACTION

Weiser [27] envisioned a ubiquitous computing paradigm where technology is integrated into everyday experiences in a way that computers vanish into background. In this way, the major challenge of the Disappearing Computer paradigm [21] is the development of new invisible technologies that fit the task so well that the tool becomes a part of the task [13]. This approach converges in the use of implicit interactions where the user concentrates on her prime goal or targeted activity—tool use is intended, but the user isn't actually aware of the interaction with the computer system. In contrast, we propose using explicit interactions meaning that a user operates a system aiming to achieve a certain goal—that is, the user is fully aware of the tool that she is using.

Mainstream research focuses more in creating technologies that users get so used to them that the task becomes invisible rather than investing on the invisibility of the device. Currently, the human body is becoming an important topic in the field of human-computer interaction due to the proximity of wearables to the body combined with the aim of processing user's data in everyday objects. However, there is no doubt that current wearable technologies are nevertheless very distinguishable. On the other hand, recently there have been some efforts in making technology disappear, as is the case with Ringly [16], a jewelry device that connects to smartphones and gives the user notifications. Ralph Lauren's Polo Tech shirt [9] is another example of seamless fashionable technology that contains conductive silver threads and sensors designed to measure user's performance looking like a classic sport shirt. Moreover, instead of using clothing and accessories, Beauty Technology [23] uses beauty products to hide technology and place them straight on the body surface.

Interactions through gestures and body movements are clearly visible to any user's observers. Figure 2 shows some examples of wearable's interactions through gestures that by touching them in a certain way (Google Glass [5] in Figure 2a), simulates a known gesture (Talk to the Hand Project [14] in Figure 2b) and also creates new gestures (Sixthsense Project [11] in Figure 2c). There has being previous exploration using clothes and accessories such as PocketTouch detects finger-strokes through fabric [17], CheekyWear that mimics a flirting gesture for triggering actions [2] and Cord Input that detects grasping, pulled and twisted gestures on a cord [19]. In contrast, we are proposing an interface that uses the own body surface where the non-verbal communication is not straightforwardly decoded. Non-verbal communication modalities might include body motion or kinesics behavior such as facial expression and posture; paralanguage such as laughing and yawning; proxemics; olfaction; skin sensitivity; and the use of objects such as a dress and cosmetics [3]. In this way, most wearable gadgets use body motion for sensing gestures. Body motions comprise four types of cues that convey information about the nature and the intensity of an emotion: body acts (clear movements), body positions (non movement of a body part), facial expressions, and head orientations. [4]. In this research, we used auto-contact behaviors [12], a body act that takes place whenever we touch, stroke or hug ourselves in order to provide comfort and sometimes suggests anxiety or sexual invitation. For example, this kind of act could also be classified as an adaptor [3] that is triggered by an unconscious feeling that the person rarely intends to communicate and the observer is typically not aware of. In this way, we conceal the interaction with the wearable device, creating a concealed interface (Figure 4). For example, in a social meeting, a Hairware user touches the tip of Hairware to make her phone rings, touches the middle to put her phone in mute mode and touch the top to send a pre-customized message to a colleague. In this way, she will continue her activity at the meeting and, at the same time, not straightforwardly noticed, she will be interacting with her phone.

IMPLEMENTATION APPROACH

Our implementation comprises the hardware and software development of the prototype. The hardware connects the conductive hair extensions to a circuit. While touching, the software detects on it and identifies the user's intention.

Hardware

Hairware is artificial hair extensions that were chemically metalized for acquiring electrical conductivity and also keeping a natural coloration. The chemical process is carried out in two phases: Activation and Electrolysis. During the first phase, artificial hair extensions, being plastic non-conducting surfaces, require some kind of activation to enable them to be submitted to an electrochemical process. For the first activation, hydrogen and tin (II) chloride are used (Figure 3a). Then, a silver nitrate solution is added for the second activation, where the extensions are set up to catalyze electron transfer reactions, making them ready for metalizing. Next, electrolysis is used for platting them. Copper is electrochemically deposited for making them electrically conductive (Figure 3b and 3c) while "black nickel" gives the natural black effect (Fugure 3d). We used a Hairware strand of approximate 1.5 by 25cm and with a surface resistivity of less than 5 ohm/sq. We could dismiss the step of black nickel electrolysis but we added it for getting dark hair coloration. However other reagent could be used instead of it for getting a different color.

Hairware is connected to a circuit to work as a capacitor sensor. This circuit creates a delay in the pulse that is the time the capacitor takes to charge and discharge. In this way, Hairware is used as a conductive surface that detects when another conductive surface approximates to it. Therefore, as the human body is conductive, the average internal resistance of a human trunk is ~100 □ [26], touching Hairware will affect capacitance and result in a different charging time.

We use hair clips for attaching the circuit to the hair extensions in order to be easily removable and replaceable. Also this makes it possible to put the circuit in different accessory such as a hairclip, headband, brooch and the top of the hair extensions.

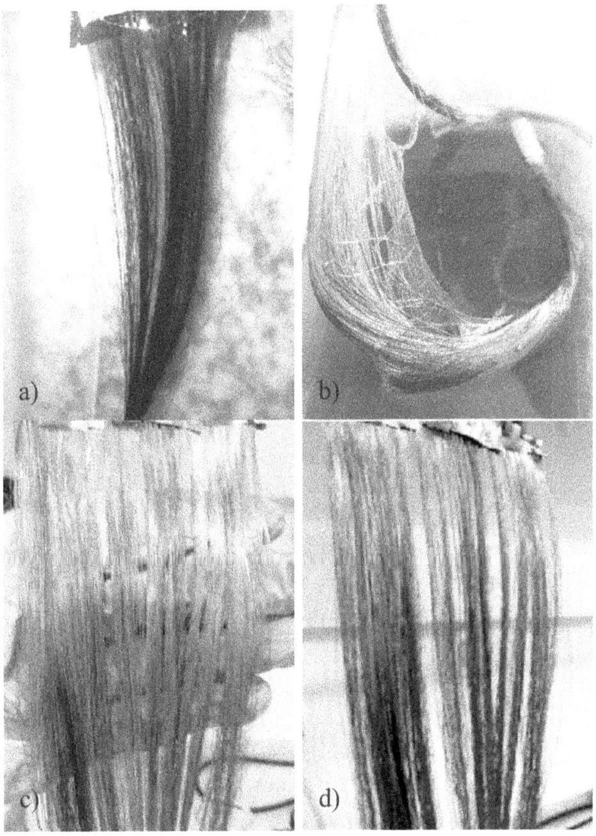

Figure 3 - Hair Extensions during the chemical process: (a) After activation 2, (b) copper electrolysis, (c) Copper Acid, (d) Black nickel electrolysis.

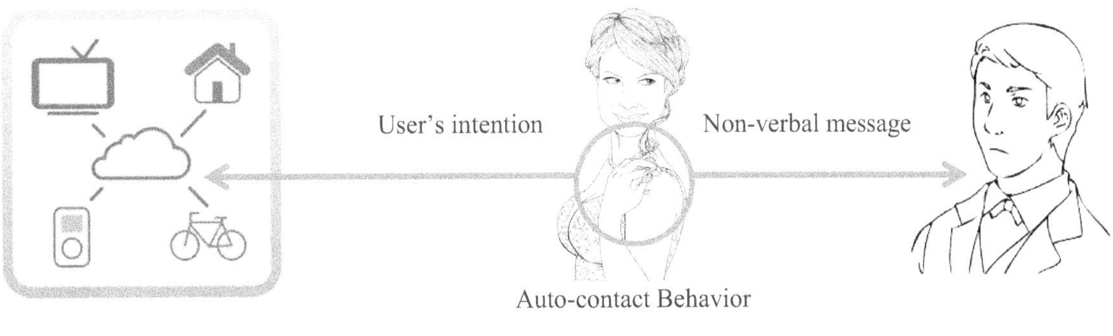

Figure 4: Concealed Interaction through Hairware.

Figure 5 shows 3 layers of non- conductive hair extensions that are added for isolating the hair from the skin. Also, these layers improved the capacitor sensor values. Each time the user touch the top, middle or tip, the capacitor sensor differentiates these values. The circuit compares an output that transmits the pulse and an input, which receives the pulse. When a finger touches Hairware, it creates a delay in the pulse, and this delay is recalculated by the Arduino microcontroller. The circuit diagram (Figure 6) is also composed with four 1MΩ resistors and one 100pF capacitor. The resistors selects the sensitivity, bigger the resistor, the farther away it detects a human. With 4MΩ resistor between the output and input pins the circuit is tuned to start to respond one inch away, just the sufficient to overcome the non-conductive hair layer. The small capacitor (100 pF) placed from sensor pin to ground improves stability and repeatability. Some LEDs were added to the system to give feedback to the user whenever a touch is detected (Figure 7).

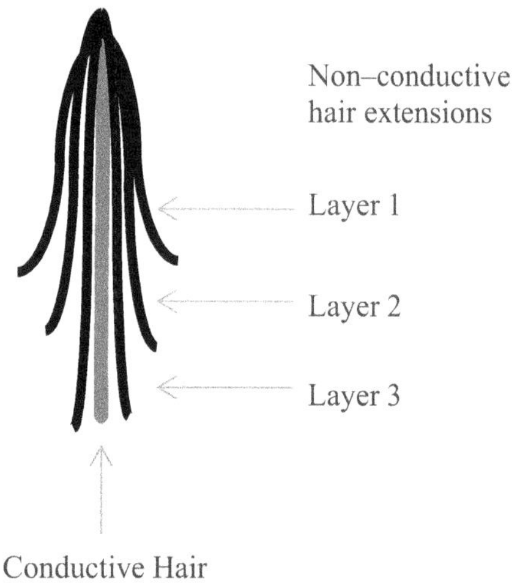

Figure 5 – Changing the capacitance of Hairware by non-conductive artificial hair extensions

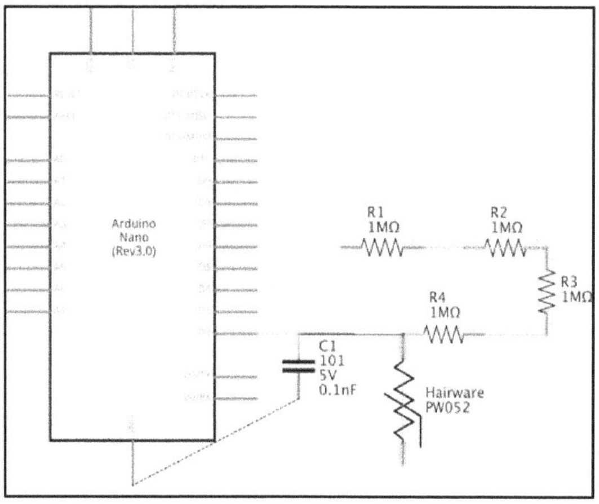

Figure 6- Hairware Circuit using Arduino

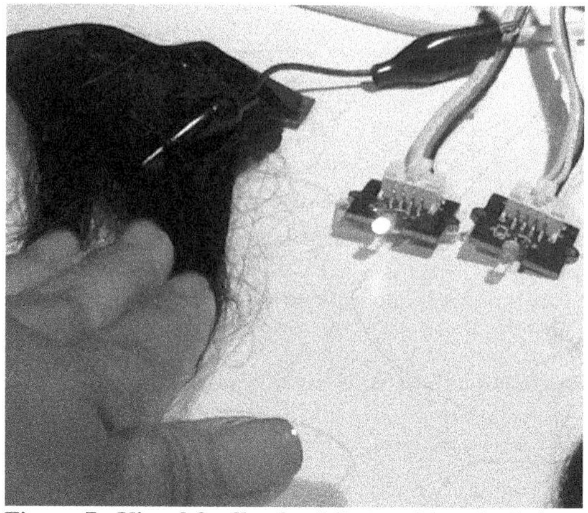

Figure 7 –Visual feedback while touching the hair

Software

For classification, we use a decision tree implementation provided by BigML [1]. Each transmission from the sensor contains a capacitive charging time in milliseconds, from which we extract for classification. Currently, we can classify five touches interaction in the Hairware: no touch, touch on the top, touch on the middle, touch on tip and straightening.

When trained, the decision tree build an actionable model (Figure 8) that we use as an Arduino function to classify the interaction in real time. Each node represents the confidence action from the read value. The key feature to recognize touch on the hair is not to detect the touch itself, but the circuit must be fined tune to detect small capacitance charge variation along the hair.

Figure 9 shows data collected from the five interactions used to classification evaluation. The charts plotted from this data set show the charging time difference from each interaction. As expected the touch on the tip has the higher value due to that layer of non-conductive hair is thinner (layer 3). The charging value will decrease when the interaction gets near the top where there are more non-conductive hair layers acting as a filter. The straightening actions have the lowest values due to its speed and skin contact time with the sensor. The "No Touch" graph ranges from zero to 60 because the hair gets in contact with the human skin without configuring a touch, (no other touch got these low results.) "Touch in Top" moves to 1000, "Middle" to 1500, "Tip" to 2200 and "Straightening" to 750. That is because the Hairware layers' design sets apart touch from the conductive material, by making the top of the hair having a lower capacitance (because it is more covered) and the tip of the hair more expose (the capacitance is higher.) Noise appeared on the readings given that the hair was in direct contact with the skin. However, our algorithm recognizes it as noise and obtains 92% accuracy on the five trained touch gestures.

EVALUATION

For our evaluation, we aim to identify the exposure of the technology in Hairware and also we measure the accuracy in replaying the hair straightening, top, middle, and tip touch. We recruited 5 female participants, ranging in age from 28 to 35. We made our evaluation with female participants because most of them use or had used long hair, they are more knowledgeable about hair care and its looks and they are the ones who do auto-contact behaviors with their hair. The study took approximately 30 minutes per each participant and included a gratuity. Given that Hairware is a proof of concept of the technology, evaluations were taken in the same laboratory under the same conditions (temperature, humidity and pressure). We acknowledge that geotemporal factors will affect the results and a calibration method is required. At the beginning, we conducted pre-questionnaires to identify the participants' profiles. All participants were right handed. They do not own any wearable technologies but everyday they use other electronic devices like smartphones and tablets. None used before a hair extension but they knew what was it and they saw them applied in other person. All of them expressed that they touch their hair when they feel anxious, thoughtful and nervous. Three of them noticed them using their hair as a flirting tool.

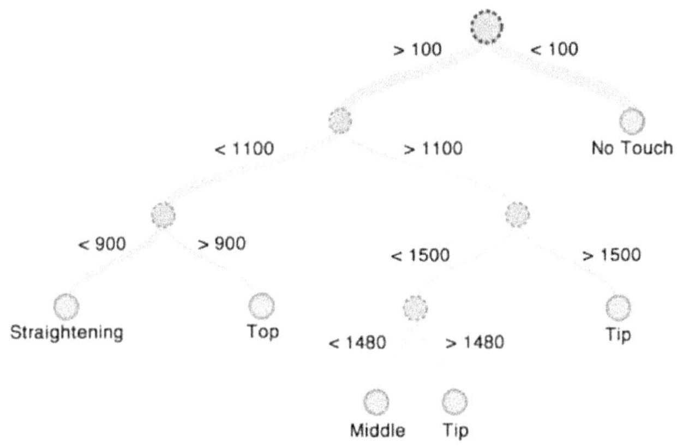

Figure 8 - Confidence from the decision tree

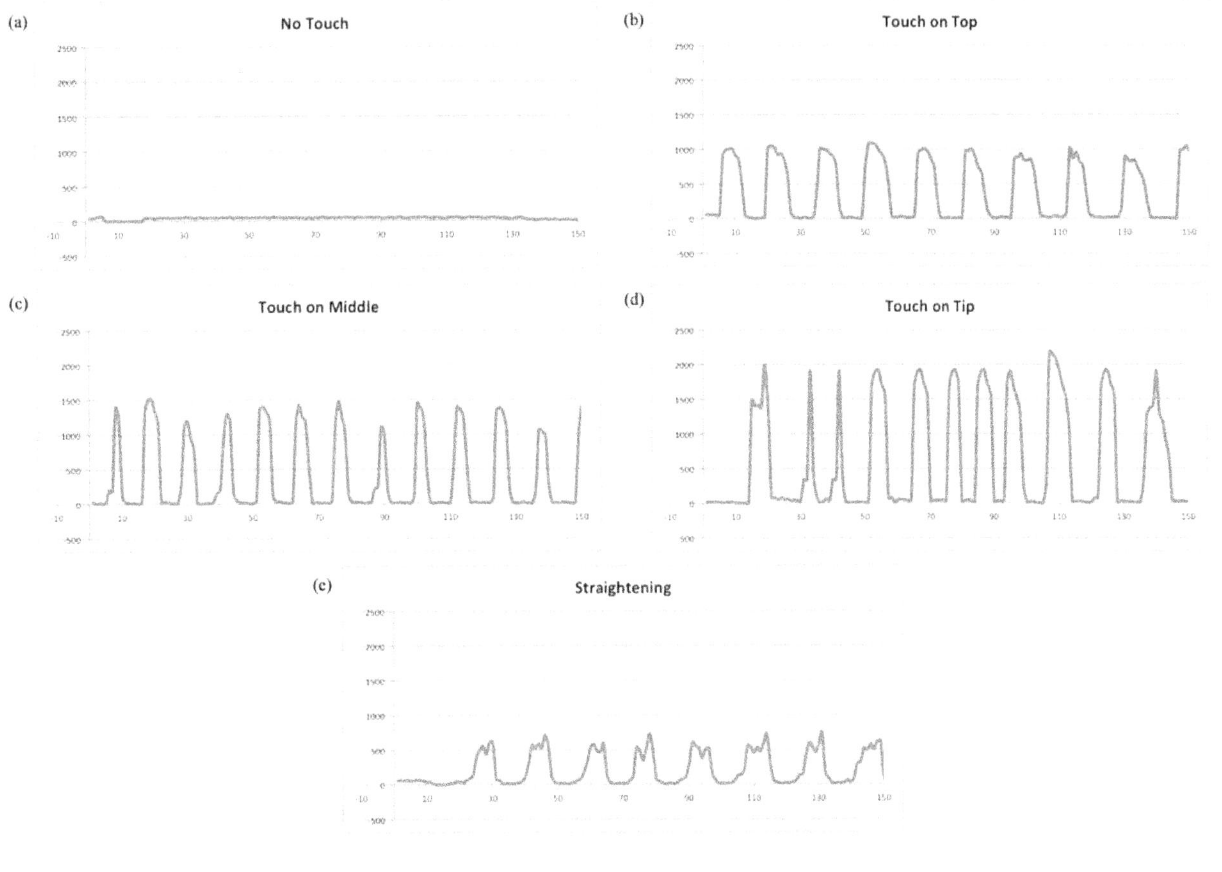

Figure 9: Capacitor Sensor Values in the different touches (a) No Touch; (b) Touch on the Top; (c) Touch on the Middle; (d) Touch on the Tip; (e) Straightening

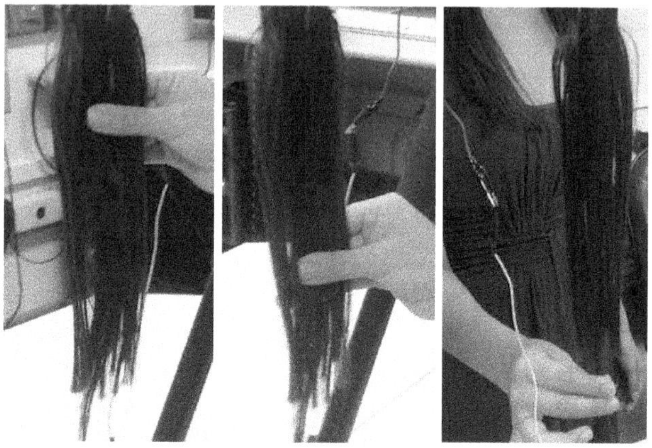

Figure 10 – Participant testing different touch on Hairware

We interview the participants before they observe and use the wearable device. We asked them questions related to Hairware visibility and their use of hair extensions. While showing Hairware, we asked them about their impressions about it, if they could identify a difference between this hair extensions, and normal or artificial hair. Then we showed a non-conductive artificial hair extension and asked about the differences they could detect between them and Hairware.

After 2 minutes of training on the different tasks, we asked them to reply the different 5 touches. They made each touch 10 times. Figure 10 shows the participant touching the top, middle and bottom part of Hairware during the test. Finally an interview asking for recommendations and future uses was conducted.

RESULTS AND DISCUSSION

After listening the answers of the first interview, we identified that, at first sight, Hairware wasn't noticed as a technological device and they weren't aware of its conductivity. Most of the participants thought it was natural hair extensions and when compared it with the artificial hair, they noticed that the artificial hair extension is more shining and with a smoother texture. They also expressed that, when Hairware would be attached to someone's hair, the difference between it and natural hair wouldn't be noticeable.

During the tests, we observed that, even that each touch was perceptible by our algorithm, a previous calibration must be done for each user. Differences in skin capacitance and hand position whenever are doing the touches could make the capacitor sensor identify different values for each user. We also notice that other feedback must be designed. LEDs won't be notice if the user is wearing Hairware. We will replace this feedback by vibration motors.

After using Hairware, they expressed that it was easy to use and adding the layers of non-conductive artificial hair extensions, gave the device a shinny look and it was smooth to touch. They expressed that, if the circuit is hidden into the hair or into a accessory, an external observer wouldn't notice the device. Future versions of Hairware will also add the touches that the participants exposed that they usually perform: twirling their hair and passing the fingers through the head.

During the final interview, participants expressed that they would use Hairware for specific purposes. Most of them recommended using it as a security device. That is, when they feel in danger or are located in a risky area, they would like to send a message to the police or to someone they trust without anyone around noticing that she is doing it. Another suggestion was to use it as an input device for triggering house appliances. Thus, they could turn on and off from anywhere. Another suggestion was to use it as an alarm each time she is making continuously her nervous tick. Also, it would be used as a therapy for relaxing when the device noticed she is stressed.

Our approach is to use Hairware as an input device that senses human touch on hair that are not noticeable by an external observer. In this way, depending on the way Hairware is used, there are some concerns related to privacy that could be controversial. For example, a Hairware user could start recording a conversation without authorization of the observer.

Due to the skin resistance, Hairware must be placed on any non-conductive material for isolating it from the skin like a shirt. Also other conductive materials like jewelry could affect the way it operates. Our design covers it with layers of non-conductive hair extensions. Future works will include a new step in our chemical process that isolates all conductive hair extensions but preserving its capacitance sensitivity.

CONCLUSION AND FUTURE WORK

The main contribution of this work is the design of novel interfaces that are hidden, i.e. no one knows that the user is wearing such device; that make it possible concealed interactions, i.e. no one knows that the user is triggering an event; and that the body surface is being used as a novel wearable interface by transforming materials into devices that look like body parts. Thus, we add new functionalities to hair extensions, turning them into a seamless device that recognizes auto-contact behaviors concealed to outside observers. Hairware was designed using artificial hair extensions that are chemically metalized to maintain a natural coloration and when connected to a microcontroller could be used as an input device. Thus, not just the technology is seamless but also the action of touching her hair that trigger devices are hardly noticed by an external observer. Touching her hair is an unconscious action that woman do for getting more comfort. This action rarely intends to communicate and the observer is typically not aware of, making it less noticeable than other gestures like winking or waving hands. Using Hairware, they will replay this act on her hair but she is not just emitting a message to an observer, she would be triggering an object, creating a concealed interface to different devices. In this way,

Hairware brings the opportunity to make conscious use of an unconscious auto-contact behavior.

This paper explained our processes in designing the interface, creating the hardware and implementing the algorithm for detecting a touch on the top, middle, tip, straightening the hair and no touch. A study case was conducted with 5 participants to identify if the technology is noticeable by an observer and for testing our gesture recognition system. We used 80% of the data of each different touch to train our model and 20% for testing its accuracy. Then, again, we tested the model with the users to verify whether the touches were being interpreted correctly. The prototype achieved 92% accuracy on five touch gestures. The prototype was tested in the laboratory under the same conditions. Non-intended gestures and other factors could affect the results and a calibration method would be required. Future works will include an activation gesture such as pressing Hairware for a few seconds.

We used Hairware as an input device that consciously used unconscious auto-contact behaviors to trigger different devices such as a TV, Home appliances and Smartphones. We envision the use of Hairware in situations whenever the interaction is intended to be hidden such as in certain meetings, fir secret agents and for magicians. However, Hairware could explore the different meanings of hair in terms of culture and emotions. A new study case that senses the unconscious auto-contact behaviors in order to understand the levels of stress and anxiety when the user touches her hair could be conducted. Also, as hair is generally a focus of women, Hairware could be used as a tool for protection against risky situations. In this way, it could be used as an alarm device that send messages with the user's location but also it could embed an RFID and other sensors in order to provide more evidence to the law court and the police.

Future works will include the use of Hairware not just as hair extensions but also as other hair replacements as beard. Other sensors, such as accelerometers and gyroscopes will be integrated on the hair extensions to make combinations of movements and hair touch.

ACKNOWLEDGMENTS

Marcio Cunha (grant 163066/2013-2) and Hugo Fuks (Project 302230/2008-4) are recipients of grants awarded by the National Research Council (CNPq). This work was partially financed by Research Support Foundation of the State of Rio de Janeiro-FAPERJ/INCT (E-26/170028/2008) and CNPq/INCT (557.128/2009-9). Katia Vega is a postdoctoral fellow with grant funding from PNPD/CAPES Portaria 086/2013.

REFERENCES

1. BigML. BigML. https://bigml.com/.
2. Charlesworth, J. Wearables as "relationship tools." *Ai & Society 22*, 1 (2007), 63–84.
3. Duncan Jr, S. Nonverbal communication. *Psychological Bulletin 72*, 2 (1969), 118.
4. Ekman, P. and Friesen, W. V. The repertoire of nonverbal behavior: Categories, origins, usage, and coding. *Nonverbal communication, interaction, and gesture*, (1981), 57–106.
5. Google. Google Glass. http://www.google.com.br/glass/start/.
6. Hagen, S. *The Everything Body Language Book: Succeed in work, love, and life-all without saying a word!* Adams Media, 2011.
7. Hallpike, C.R. Social hair. *Man*, (1969), 256–264.
8. Harrison, C., Tan, D., and Morris, D. Skinput: appropriating the body as an input surface. *Proceedings of the SIGCHI Conference on Human Factors in Computing Systems*, (2010), 453–462.
9. Lauren, R. Polo Tech Shirt - RalphLauren.com. http://www.ralphlauren.com/shop/index.jsp?categoryId=46285296.
10. Mint. Beauty or Bust. Obsessed with cosmetics. https://www.mint.com/blog/consumer-iq/splurge-vs-save-which-beauty-products-are-worth-the-extra-cost-0413/?display=wide.
11. Mistry, P. SixthSense. http://www.pranavmistry.com/projects/sixthsense/.
12. Morris, D. and Desebrock, G. *Manwatching: A field guide to human behaviour.* HN Abrams New York, 1977.
13. Norman, D.A. *The invisible computer: why good products can fail, the personal computer is so complex, and information appliances are the solution.* MIT press, 1998.
14. O2. Talk to the hand - O2 upcycle. http://news.o2.co.uk/?press-release=talk-to-the-hand-o2-upcycle#.
15. Ogata, M., Sugiura, Y., Makino, Y., Inami, M., and Imai, M. Senskin: adapting skin as a soft interface. *Proceedings of the 26th annual ACM symposium on User interface software and technology*, (2013), 539–544.
16. Ringly. RINGLY. https://ringly.com/.
17. Saponas, T.S., Harrison, C., and Benko, H. PocketTouch: through-fabric capacitive touch input. *Proceedings of the 24th annual ACM symposium on User interface software and technology*, (2011), 303–308.
18. Sato, M., Poupyrev, I., and Harrison, C. Touch{é}: enhancing touch interaction on humans, screens, liquids, and everyday objects. *Proceedings of the SIGCHI Conference on Human Factors in Computing Systems*, (2012), 483–492.
19. Schwarz, J., Harrison, C., Hudson, S., and Mankoff, J. Cord input: an intuitive, high-accuracy, multi-degree-of-freedom input method for mobile devices. *Proceedings of the SIGCHI Conference on Human Factors in Computing Systems*, (2010), 1657–1660.

20. Sign, F. Products - First Sign. 2014. http://www.firstsign.us/products/.
21. Streitz, N., Kameas, A., and Mavrommati, I. *The disappearing computer: interaction design, system infrastructures and applications for smart environments.* Springer-Verlag, 2007.
22. Tobita, H. and Kuzi, T. SmartWig: wig-based wearable computing device for communication and entertainment. *Proceedings of the International Working Conference on Advanced Visual Interfaces*, (2012), 299–302.
23. Vega, K. and Fuks, H. Beauty Technology: Body Surface Computing. *Computer 47*, 4 (2014), 71–75.
24. Vega, K. and Fuks, H. Beauty Technology As an Interactive Computing Platform. *Proceedings of the 2013 ACM International Conference on Interactive Tabletops and Surfaces*, ACM (2013), 357–360.
25. Vega, K. and Fuks, H. Empowering Electronic Divas through Beauty Technology. *Lecture Notes in Computer Science*, Springer (2013), 237–245.
26. Webster, J.G. Medical instrumentation. *Application and Design, Houghton Mifflin Company, Boston. 197& g*, (1973).
27. Weiser, M. The computer for the 21st century. *Scientific american 265*, 3 (1991), 94–104.

Math Boxes: A Pen-Based User Interface for Writing Difficult Mathematical Expressions

Eugene M. Taranta II
University of Central Florida
Orlando, FL 32816 USA
etaranta@gmail.com

Joseph J. LaViola Jr.
University of Central Florida
Orlando, FL 32816 USA
jjl@eecs.ucf.edu

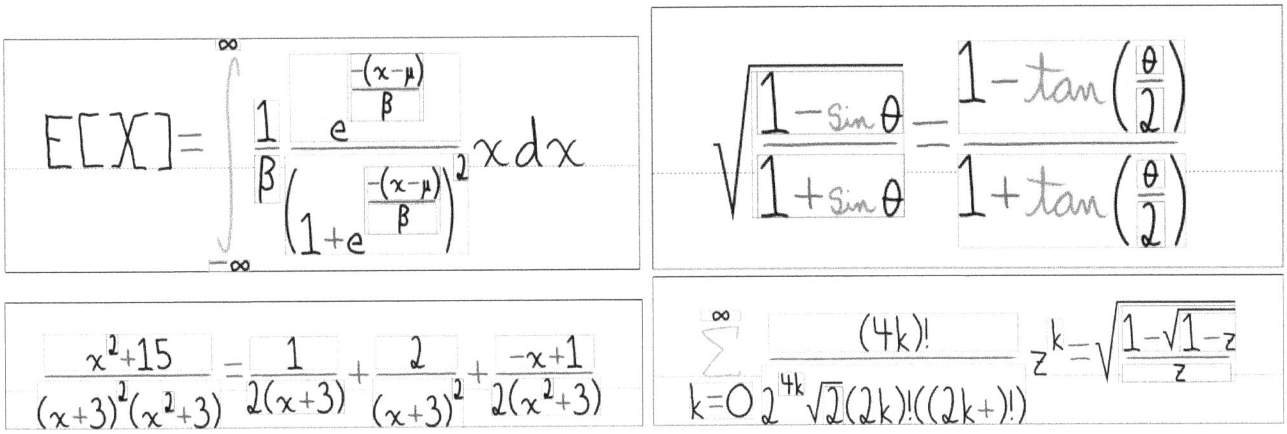

Figure 1: Four examples equations utilizing math boxes. Subexpressions, according to their spatial relationship with neighboring terms, are entirely contained in a hierarchy of boxes. A math box and its parent boxes are dynamically resized when the user hovers over a box's boundary so that the associated subexpression can be easily extended.

ABSTRACT

We present *math boxes*, a novel pen-based user interface for simplifying the task of hand writing difficult mathematical expressions. Visible bounding boxes around certain subexpressions are automatically generated as the system detects specific relationships including superscripts, subscripts, and fractions. Subexpressions contained in a box can then be extended by adding new terms directly into its given bounds. Upon accepting new characters, box boundaries are dynamically resized and neighboring terms are translated to make room for the larger box. Feedback on structural recognition is given via the boxes themselves. We also provide feedback on character recognition by morphing the user's individual characters into a cleaner version stored in our ink database.

To evaluate the usefulness of our proposed method, we conducted a user study in which participants write a variety of equations ranging in complexity from a simple polynomial to the more difficult expected value of the logistic distribution. The math boxes interface is compared against the commonly used *offset typeset (small)* method, where recognized expressions are typeset in a system font near the user's unmodified ink. In our initial study, we find that the fluidness of the offset method is preferred for simple expressions but as difficulty increases, our math boxes method is overwhelmingly preferred.

Author Keywords

Sketch-based User Interfaces; Sketch Recognition; Mathematical Sketching; Handwritten Mathematics

ACM Classification Keywords

H.5.2 Information Interfaces and Presentation: User Interfaces - Graphical user interfaces.

General Terms

Human Factors; Design; Measurement.

IUI 2015, March 29–April 1, 2015, Atlanta, GA, USA.

http://dx.doi.org/10.1145/2678025.2701400

Introduction

Recognition of handwritten mathematics has a long history [2] and is a critical component of numerous pen-based software interfaces for physics [7, 9], geometric theorem proving [4], Boolean logic visualization and manipulation [5], and algebraic intelligent tutoring systems (ITS) [1] among others. Users of these systems demand high accuracy. For instance, Anthony et al. [1] estimate that 91—97% recognition accuracy is required for acceptance in a mathematics oriented ITS system. However, based on results from the fourth international Competition on Recognition of Online Handwritten Mathematical Expressions (CROHME) [11], expression level recognition rates are still well below this threshold. Complementary to mathematical expression parsing and recognition, user interface (UI) design can play a crucial role in usability and can potentially assist individuals in writing difficult expressions as well as help simplify error correction. That is, a well designed UI can go a long way towards improving a user's experience and acceptance of such systems.

To this end, our work is motivated by two observations. First, without in-depth technical knowledge of the algorithms and architecture employed by the mathematical parser, it can be difficult to determine the source of a parsing error (or set of errors) and consequently, equally difficult to correct the underlying issue. Second, we observe that even when an expression is available to a user beforehand, he or she will not ration sufficient space in advance to write out the full expression. For example, parenthesis are often too small for large inner expressions; fractions bars are too short for long numerators or denominators; and superscripts are initiated too low when they contain fractions. Worse still is that when these issues do occur, moving symbols around into their desired positions or rewriting subexpressions may not be enough to ameliorate any or all errors. With *math boxes*, we aim to address both of these issues.

Math boxes relies on simple structural parsing only to be able to detect superscripts, subscripts, and fraction bars. Once a particular relationship has been determined to exist between two symbols, one in which they do not share the same baseline of math, then boxes are created to contain symbols as is appropriate for the specific relationship; see Figure 1 for a few examples. Math boxes are visible to the user and can be easily extended. Hovering over a box with a stylus or writing into a box causes its boundaries to grow, and neighboring ink that overlaps with the box is translated aside, to make room for the expanded box and possibly new symbols. This eliminates the need for complex structural parsing and helps to ensure that users will always have enough room to continue writing long expressions. As a consequence of this approach, error correction is simplified because an expression's structure is tied directly to the math boxes interface, which therefore does not require a guess as to why the underlying recognizer went astray when an error occurs, or trial and error correction.

Based on these ideas, a prototype system utilizing math boxes was developed and subsequently evaluated and compared against the currently best known and highly rated user interface design *offset typeset (small)* [8, 22]. After asking participants to write a range of equations varying in complexity, we find that participants prefer using math boxes for difficult equations and further, accuracy and time to completion improves as expressions become more complex, as compared to the offset typeset (small) interface.

RELATED WORK

Recognition of handwritten mathematics has been an active area of research for many years, with most effort focusing on techniques for parsing characters and structure [16, 19], though less attention has been given to UI techniques for providing recognition feedback and editing features. Zanibbi et al [20] introduced the concept of style preserving morphs to provide instant feedback on the system's interpretation of an expression's structure. Individual characters are resized and translated into their correct structural position, however, this technique does not indicate what symbol was actually recognized nor does it help to prevent errors. Further, by moving characters into their correct structural position, users may not have enough space to extend a subexpression.

Smithies et al.'s Freehand Formula Entry System (FFES) [14, 15] is a pen-based interface for editing equations. The system supports four modes of operation: draw, modify stroke groups, modify characters, and select and move (for equation level error editing). FFES, therefore, does not provide a seamless integration between recognition and editing. Labahn et al.'s MathBrush [6] is designed specifically to work with a computer based algebra system. One interesting feature of their UI is that users have the ability to circle subexpressions and work with them separately. Although this was designed for algebraic manipulation, it is a potentially useful UI technique that is slightly related to math boxes in that boxes help to isolate subexpressions.

Unlike most previous work that focuses on the construction of equations, Zeleznik et al.[22] focused specifically on UI design for feedback of recognition results. To the best of our knowledge, this work represents the state of the art. In their work they describe several variations of typesetting. These include replacing recognized characters with system font characters or prerecorded ink characters, and typesetting the recognized equation underneath the user's ink in a system font of varying size. They also experiment with ink color as well as techniques for dealing with allographs. All of these variations were thoroughly evaluated by LaViola et al. [8] who found that *offset typeset (small)* was the preferred choice of recognition feedback, which is described in the next section. Zeleznik et al.[21] introduced Hands-On Math, a pen and touch bimanual interface that makes computer algebra systems accessible to users through virtual pages. They developed a rich set of interaction techniques to manipulate algebraic expressions and manage virtual pages. However, the error correction and space issues discussed previously that are handled by math boxes are not addressed in their work.

Non pen-based interfaces also exist that supports structural mechanisms akin to math boxes. For instance, BrEdiMa [12] is a web-based tool for editing mathematical expressions where each math object contains its own rectangular region, though actual structural changes still requires various WIMP interactions. We are unaware of any other pen-based UI technique that structures mathematical expressions utilizing interactive and dynamic boxes as we describe.

OFFSET TYPESET (SMALL) USER INTERFACE

Zeleznik et al.'s offset typeset (small) user interface [22], or just offset hereon, is a well studied interface and is the preferred feedback interface for recognition of handwritten mathematics [8]. Their design provides recognition feedback in a number of ways. Most notably, results from the math recognizer are displayed in a typeset system font underneath the user's ink. In this way a writer is not distracted by recognition feedback (such as by character morphing) and he or she can

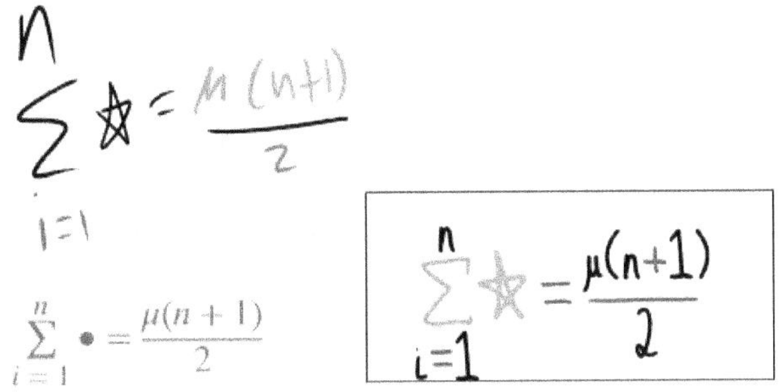

(a) Offset UI (b) Boxes UI

Figure 3: Side by side comparison of various aspects of the the offset (a) and math boxes (b) user interfaces. Specifically, differences in how unrecognized characters are handled, how ink is colored, how each system typesets mathematics, and how much space is required is shown.

verify recognition correctness as is convenient. Further, the user's ink is colored according to the recognized structure of the expression. This allows for quick validation of alignment and various parsing results. An example of the offset interface is shown in Figure 3(a).

To edit an expression, offset provides two techniques. First, scribble-erase allows a user to scribble over previously penned ink, thus erasing those strokes that overlap with the convex hull of the scribble stroke. Second, ink is translated by using the lasso-drag gesture. Targeted strokes are circled and subsequently dragged into the new position. Note that the system continues to parse ink as it is being dragged around, allowing for instant feedback so that the user can stop dragging when he or she is satisfied with the result.

A major disadvantage of the offset interface is that user feedback does not provide enough information as to what errors have occurred when the typeset equation does not match the user's expectation. Therefore users have to guess as to which strokes or arrangements may have caused their error. This violates Wais et al.'s [18] guidance that recognition errors must be predictable and/or understandable. Wais et al. also report that users generally prefer to correct errors when they are done drawing, which may further exacerbate the problem. In mathematical sketch recognition, delayed error correction can potentially make the task of understanding and correcting an underlying error more difficult.

MATH BOXES USER INTERFACE

Math boxes are dynamic containment units for subexpression symbols that share a common spatial relationship. For instance, consider the expression:

$$x^{2+ab} + \frac{y^3}{z} + w^5. \qquad (1)$$

In this equation, the symbols x, $+$, w, and the fraction bar share a common baseline of math and consequently, a common math box. Symbols of the subexpression $2 + ab$ are offset from the previous math box, being a superscript of x, and therefore also share their own math box. Note, however, that even though 5 is offset in the same manner, it is a superscript of a different symbol and so will reside in its own math box. For similar reasons the numerator, denominator and 3 superscript all reside within their own math boxes. In total, the expression of Equation 1 is comprised of six unique math boxes.

For reference throughout the remainder of this section, the flowchart diagrams in Figure 4 show how changes in the stylus hover state and how new strokes are handled. Most notably, math boxes are created on-the-fly as new symbols are added to an expression. Since the boxes are visible to the user, they also convey useful information about the recognized spatial relationship between the various symbols. For example, a user can be certain that a new symbol is recognized as a superscript because the new symbol is instantly wrapped inside of a new math box.

Recall that one goal of this work is to eliminate space planning issues for when a user does not leave his or herself enough room to write a large expression. To accomplish this goal, each math box dynamically resizes itself as symbols are added into a math box's boundary. However, as boxes are resized, they may expand into and overlap with other already existing symbols. This clutter and confusion is avoided by translating neighboring ink out of the way, to make room for an expanded math box as is depicted in Figure 5.

Superscripts and Subscripts

New strokes that are determined to exist in the superscript or subscript space of the left adjacent symbol will cause an associated math box to be created. The subexpression of either the superscript or base can then be extended by writing into the appropriate math box. If a user pens what he or she expects to be a subscript or superscript and a math box does not appear, then the user instantly knows the stroke was not parsed correctly. If this goes uncorrected, then the symbol will be brought down to the baseline at a later point in time (when the expression is typeset).

Only certain symbols can contain superscripts or subscripts. Alphabetic characters can have both whereas numbers can only have superscripts. Left brackets (rounded, curly, or squared) cannot have either and closing brackets can have only superscripts. These restrictions are not only reasonable, supporting most mathematical notation requirements, but also help to eliminate various parsing errors.

Fraction Bars

Fractions generate two math boxes, one for the numerator and another for the denominator. If a horizontal line is drawn and there are no symbols above or below the line, then the stroke is assumed be a negation or minus sign operator. On the other hand, when a character is written above or below the line, then both math boxes are created and the new character is added to the appropriate math box. Another way to work with fractions is to first write one or more symbols of the numerator or denominator and then draw the fraction bar. Any symbols that overlap with the projection of the fraction bar onto the horizontal axis are automatically added into the appropriate

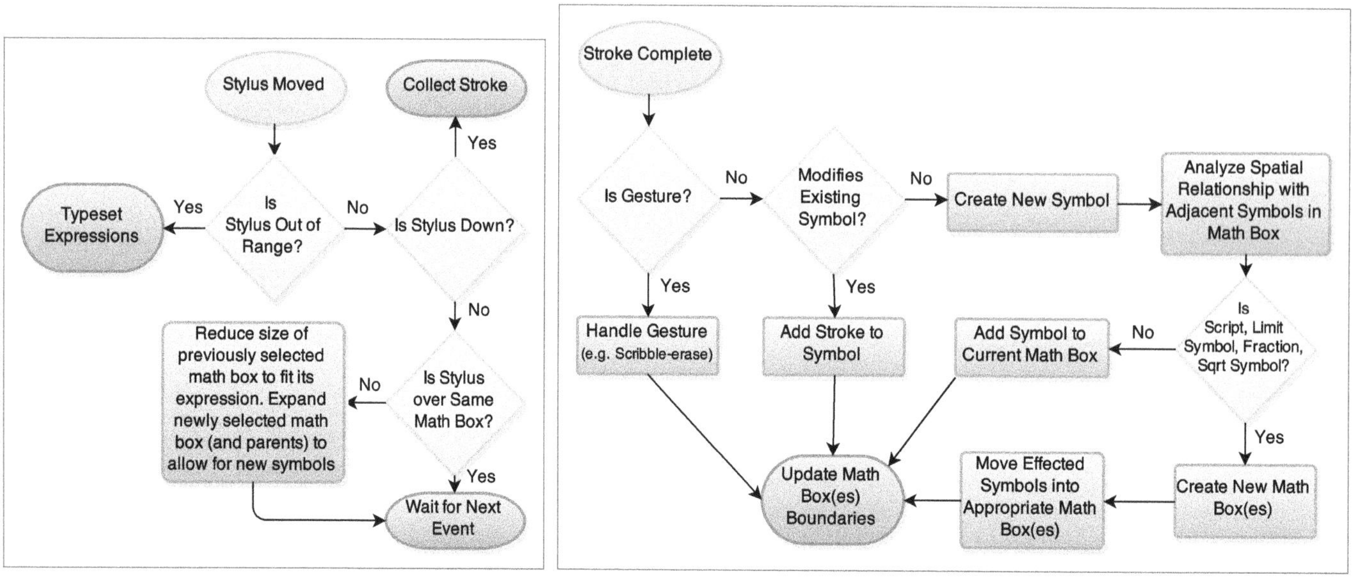

(a) Hovering stylus. (b) New stroke collected.

Figure 4: Flowchart for stylus events when (a) the stylus is hovering and when (b) a new stroke is collected. Details of the system are discussed throughout math boxes user interface section.

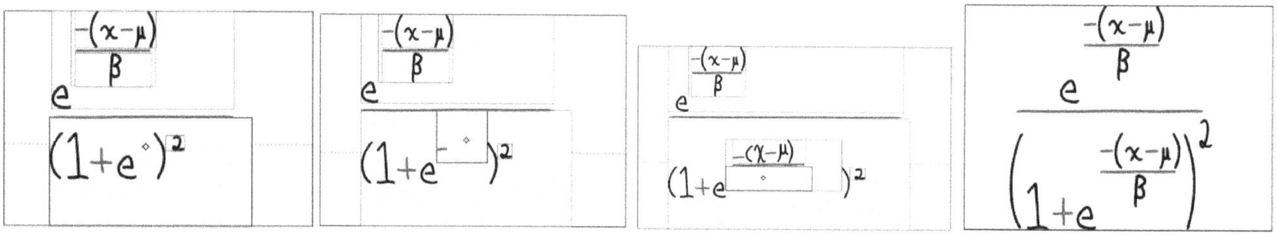

(a) (b) (c) (d)

Figure 5: An example of writing a complex expression. A typical scenario (a) occurs when the user fails to reserve enough space for the denominator $(1 + \exp(-(x - \mu)/\beta))^2$. In (b), once the minus sign is recognized in e's superscript space, a superscript box is generated, providing enough additional space so that the subexpression can be further extended if desired. After the fraction bar is drawn (c), terms above the line are moved into a numerator box. Similarly, a denominator box is supplied as surrounding ink is simultaneously pushed aside. Finally in (d), by moving the stylus out of range, our system typesets the expression.

math box. Further, the fraction bar automatically resizes as the numerator or denominator grows so that users can be certain of and confident in the relationship between the math boxes.

Limits

Limit boxes are automatically created for sigma and integral symbols. These symbols have to be drawn first, before any limits are written. If the limits are written first, then we assume these symbols were intended to be part of the math box's baseline of math. However, this is something we intend to address in future versions of the prototype system.

Symbol Morphing

Many users in fact do not prefer to see their handwriting changed [8], but without typesetting the equation separately (and thus wasting space in user interface), we are unaware of a better method to provide feedback concerning character recognition correctness. Therefore we choose to morph the user's symbols into cleaner versions of the recognized characters stored in our database of prerecorded examples. This differs from style preserving morphs [20] since recognized characters are not only rescaled and translated, but they are also reshaped. To avoid annoyances with rapidly replacing the original character, the morph is instead animated. Dynamic timing warping [17] is utilized to determine which points from the original ink best aligns with the replacement ink characters points, to make the transition as smooth as possible.

Typesetting

When the stylus is taken out of range of the tablet PC, then any modified expression is typeset. All symbols are properly aligned according to their 2D spatial relationships and spacing between symbols is corrected. Because users do not write uniformly with proper variation between offsets (e.g., from the baseline to the superscript space), most symbols also have to be resized. To minimize the amount of change to each character, we utilize the golden section search [13] such that the change in character height is the error to minimize. Consequently, the baseline capital letter height is selected to be the value that minimizes the height change of all symbols. We tried similar techniques for determining the baseline and left offset but found through iterative design that utilizing the initial character's original position for the baseline and left offset worked best. Otherwise an expression's change in position could be too distracting, even if this minimizes the total overall movement of each symbol.

As part of typesetting an expression, parentheses and integral symbols are resized to match the subexpression associated with the operator or group. In both cases however, resizing only occurs when the expression is typeset, not as the user is inking new symbols. As already mentioned above though, this contrasts with fraction bars, which are dynamically resized as new math is added into either math box. Finally, parentheses resizing also only occurs if the group set is complete (i.e., a subexpression with an open left parenthesis will be resized if their is a matching closing right parenthesis).

Typesetting an expression removes excess space between symbols created by the math boxes, but this is not a problem however. If the user thereafter wishes to extend a subexpression, hovering over the associated math box will cause the box to expand again, so that the subexpression can be further modified.

Editing

The same scribble-erase gesture that is supported by the offset interface is also supported by math boxes. However, the lasso-drag gesture is not directly applicable. As an alternative, if a user needs to make room for additional symbols in-between two preexisting characters, he or she can hover-drag a character horizontally to create the necessary space. That is, a user single-taps a symbol he or she wishes to move. The convex hull of the symbol is highlighted yellow and then the symbol is dragged horizontally while hovering over the display. A final single tap releases the symbol into its new position. At the same time, terms left or right of the symbol (depending on the direction of displacement) are also translated and the associated math box expands to accommodate the new configuration. Math boxes also provide a mechanism for easily expansion. If a user feels constrained and requires additional space, he or she can simply tap in an empty region of the math box to inflate the box's boundaries.

EVALUATION

StarPad[1] (stylized starPad) is an open source SDK for the recognition of handwritten mathematics developed for Microsoft's .NET framework and is based on [10, 22, 23]. The SDK comes with an example application that implements the offset user interface described in [8, 22], therefore we utilized this system in our evaluation. Further, to ensure a fair comparison between user interfaces, we developed a math boxes implementation around the same underlying character recognizer.

[1] `http://pen.cs.brown.edu/starpad.html`

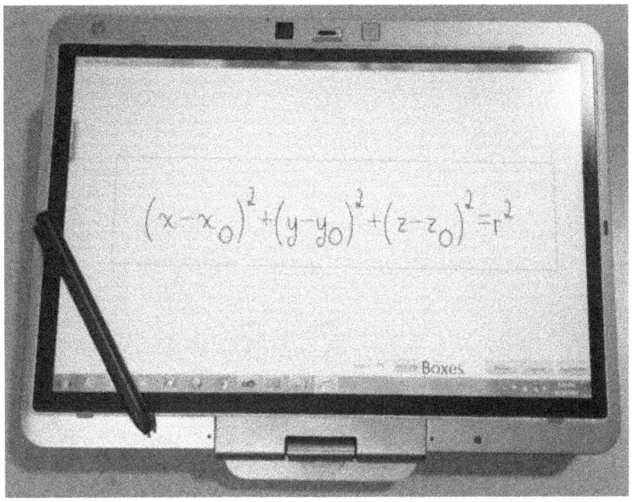

Figure 6: Apparatus utilized for user study with Eq 4 in Table 1 shown.

We conducted a user study to evaluate the effectiveness of math boxes. From the University of Central Florida, we recruited 12 participants, ranging in age from 18—53 (mean=24.67). Nine participants were male and three were female, two left handed and ten right. The participants' backgrounds included communication sciences and disorders (1), health information management (1), computer science (7), electrical engineering (1), statistics (1), and physics (1). Six participants had some prior experience with handwriting recognition systems (mostly for note taking on tablet devices). Each participant took between 90—120 minutes to complete the study and were compensated $20.

The evaluation was conducted on a Hewlett Packard HP EliteBook 2760p Tablet PC with an Intel® Core™ i5-2410M CPU (2.3GHz) having four gigabytes of memory, running Microsoft Windows 7 Professional. The touch interface was disabled so that participants would write naturally without having to worry about interfering with the interface. The tablet PC was rested upon a table and pitched at an adjustable incline so that participants could sit and work comfortably.

Experimental Design and Procedure

We conducted a within-subjects experiment to evaluate user performance and perception of the math boxes interface compared to the offset interface. The independent variable was the interface used to write a set of equations, and the dependent variables were the time to completions, accuracies, and post-questionnaires. Participants first filled out a short pre-questionnaire in order to collect demographic information and prior experience with handwritten mathematics on a stylus or touch device. Subsequently, each participant was then introduced to both user interfaces via two practice problems per method. In this training phase, complex expressions are constructed incrementally through a number of stages that let users become familiar with each system and their editing features. For the offset method, this included explanations on and practice with the scribble-erase and lasso gestures. For the

Eq 1	$(a+b)^2 = a^2 + 2ab + b^2$
Eq 2	$\sum_{i=1}^{n} = \frac{n(n+1)}{2}$
Eq 3	$f(x) = ax^3 + bx^2 + cx^1 + dx^0$
Eq 4	$(x-x_0)^2 + (y-y_0)^2 + (z-z_0)^2 = r^2$
Eq 5	$\int \frac{e^{ax}}{b+ce^a x}\mathrm{d}x = \frac{1}{ac}\log(b+ce^{ax})$
Eq 6	$\sqrt{\frac{1-\sin\theta}{1+\sin\theta}} = \frac{1-\tan\left(\frac{\theta}{2}\right)}{1+\tan\left(\frac{\theta}{2}\right)}$
Eq 7	$\frac{x^2+15}{(x+3)^2\,(x^2+3)} = \frac{1}{2(x+3)} + \frac{2}{(x+3)^2} + \frac{-x+1}{2\,(x^2+3)}$
Eq 8	$\int_{-\infty}^{\infty} \frac{1}{\sigma\sqrt{2\pi}} e^{\frac{(x-\mu)^2}{2\sigma^2}}\mathrm{d}x = 1$
Eq 9	$\sum_{x=0}^{\infty} \frac{(4x)!}{2^{4x}\sqrt{2}(2x)!((2x+1)!)} z^x = \sqrt{\frac{1-\sqrt{1-z}}{z}}$
Eq 10	$E[X] = \int_{-\infty}^{\infty} \frac{1}{\beta} \frac{e^{\frac{-(x-\mu)}{\beta}}}{\left(1+e^{\frac{-(x-\mu)}{\beta}}\right)^2} x\mathrm{d}x$

Table 1: Equations used in the evaluation, ordered from shortest to longest in average time taken to write the equation using the offset method. Note that the equations are labeled to match Figure 7 and Figure 9.

math boxes method, scribble-erase was similarly demonstrated and practiced, but also the hover-drag gesture was introduced. In addition to allowing participants to become familiar with the interface, we also provided guidance on best practices to ensure characters are correctly recognized and how to fix commonly occurring errors. Training lasted between twenty minutes to one half hour.

After having completed training and once the participant was ready to continue, he or she was asked to write ten unique equations twice, once for each method. These equations are shown in Table 1 and vary in complexity but are roughly ordered from easiest to hardest in the evaluation. To ensure that the participant's focus was not drawn away from the screen, the equation under consideration was typeset in a system font and displayed in the upper left corner of the display; the participant was free to write anywhere else on the display. The order of which method was used first for each equation was constant throughout the training and evaluation, however, this order alternated between participants so that half started with offset

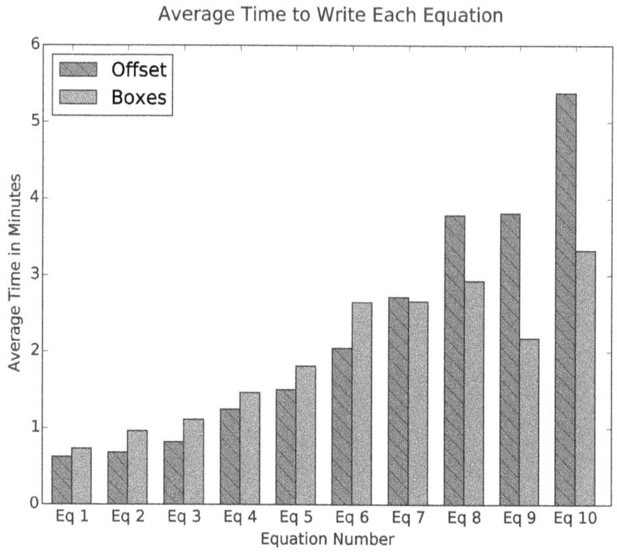

Eqs 1—5	t_{11}-values	1.956	2.085	2.920	1.641	1.343
	p-values	0.076	0.061	<0.05	0.129	0.206
Eqs 6—10	t_{11}-values	1.761	-0.184	-1.659	-2.112	-3.655
	p-values	0.106	0.858	0.125	0.058	<0.05

Figure 7: Average time in minutes taken to write each equation using both methods and the T-test results for each equation. The equations are given in Table 1 and are roughly in order of difficultly.

and half started with math boxes. Throughout the evaluation and only on occasion, if the user struggled to correct an error (usually while using the offset method), we would provide suggestions on how to correct the error. Further, because the tablet PC exhibited sluggishness in certain situations (see the discussion section), we would occasionally have to remind the participant to write slower and wait for the dynamic resizing and rendering of the boxes to complete before penning new characters. Once the participant completed writing an equation using the second method, he or she was then asked to provide feedback on a 7-point Likert scale concerning the difficulty of each method.

Data Collected

During the evaluation, the time to completion (TTC) for each equation was recorded. We also recorded each modification so that the entire sequence of events could be replayed if necessary. The number of modifications is also used to calculate the error rate as discussed in the results section. For each equation we also collected immediate ease of use feedback for each interface. Finally, in a post-questionnaire we collected information on general/overall impressions.

Results

Quantitative Results

For each equation we recorded time to completion (TTC) and total modifications required to complete the equation. Figure 7 gives the average TTC results in increasing order by offset TTC as well as the T-test results for each equations. For simple and moderately simple equations, the TTC results

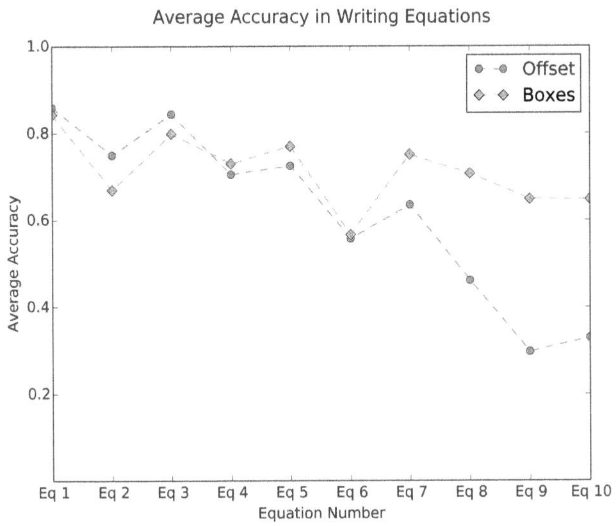

Eqs 1—5	t_{11}-values	1.412	0.789	-0.471	-0.493	-0.136
	p-values	0.816	0.188	0.448	0.648	0.632
Eqs 6—10	t_{11}-values	-0.136	-2.007	-3.007	-2.720	-5.175
	p-values	0.895	0.073	<0.05	<0.05	<0.05

Figure 8: Average accuracy for each equation and the T-test results for each equation. Accuracy is calculated as the minimum number of required strokes to complete an equation over the total number of modifications.

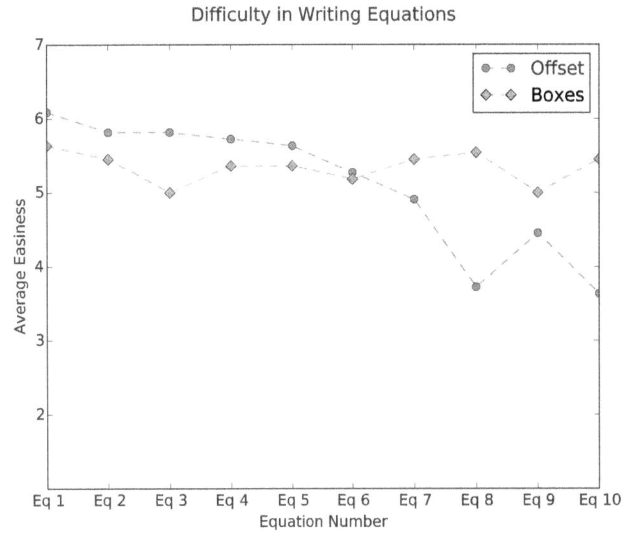

Eqs 1—5	z-values	10.500	7.000	10.000	25.000	18.000
	p-values	0.281	0.206	0.130	0.449	0.584
Eqs 6—10	z-values	9.000	9.000	2.000	10.500	0.000
	p-values	0.739	0.196	<0.05	0.286	<0.05

Figure 9: Perceived difficulty of writing each equation for both methods where 1 is very hard and 7 is very easy, and the Wilcoxon signed-rank test results. Notice that the offset method trends downward as the equations become more complex whereas boxes remains consistent.

are similar even though math boxes is slightly slower (reasons for this are outlined in the discussion). In general, for the more complex set of equations, there is a noticeable difference in TTC rates where math boxes outperforms offset. Even though we only observed statistical significance for equation 10 ($t_1 1 = -3.655, p < 0.05$), we believe this result is representative of the true distribution. There were also two instances where a participant gave up on an equation, in both cases the offset method was under consideration and in both cases the same equation was completed using the math boxes interface.

There are a number of approaches to calculating accuracy [3]. Since we are concerned with reducing difficulty in writing complex expressions, we utilize an accuracy measure that relates to the total amount of work a participant needs to do to write an equation and therefore, we rely on modification counts. A modification is any action that results in an invocation of the parser, such as when a user pens new characters, erases previous ink, or repositions symbols via the lasso-drag gesture. To calculate accuracy we first determined the minimum number of strokes required to complete an equation, which is equivalently the minimum number of modifications needed to complete the equation. The minimum is then divided by the total number of modifications observed so that accuracy is in terms of effort. Using this metric, accuracy results from the evaluation are shown in Figure 8. For simpler equations, where structural parsing errors are less likely, the accuracy of both methods are approximately equivalent. However, as the equations become more difficult, accuracy diverges such that math boxes is significantly more accurate. Also notice that offset continues on a downward trend as the complexity increases which contrasts with math boxes that is moderately consistent across all equations. One exception, however, is Eq 6 which was especially subject to the issues covered in the discussion section.

Qualitative Results

In addition to TTC and accuracy, we asked each participant to rate how easy each user interface was to use for each equation, where 1 is very hard and 7 is very easy. These results are shown in Figure 9. The outcome here matches the quantitative data in that for simpler and moderately similar equations, there is little difference. Offset has a slight advantage with higher scores, but the difference is not statistically significant. This is consistent with our expectations as we would not anticipate math boxes to be significantly harder to use for these equation types. For complex equations, however, using the Wilcoxon signed-rank test, math boxes is reported to have an advantage over offset with two of the complex equations—they have statistical significance ($Z = 2.0, p < .05$) and ($Z = 0.0, p < 0.05$ for Eq 8 and Eq 10 respectively). As before, offset's ease of use trends downward from approximately 6 to below 4 as complexity increases, which contrasts with math boxes that remains fairly level with some fluctuation around 5.5.

Participants were asked via a post-questionnaire to rate their overall impressions of both systems, for specific features and in terms of ease of use. The results of this questionnaire are shown in Table 2. All questions have a value range of 1—7, where 7 is generally more favorable. The offset method

Overall (1=hard, 7=easy)	Offset	Boxes	Z	p
Ease of use	4.417	5.5	5.5	<0.05
Ease in identifying errors	5.50	5.667	15.5	0.723
Ease in correcting errors	3.583	5.5	0.0	<0.05

Preference (1=offset, 7=boxes)	Offset	Boxes	Std. dev.
For simple equations	1.545	–	0.988
For complex equations	–	6.364	1.494

Typesetting (1=disliked, 7=liked)	Offset	Boxes	Z	p
Typesetting System	5.5	5.167	4.0	0.336

Math boxes features (1=disagree, 7=agree)	Boxes	Std. dev.
Liked character morphing	5.08	1.61
Boxes were comfortable	5.33	1.49
Boxes were not distracting	5.25	1.64
Boxes were helpful	6.000	0.912

Table 2: Results of post-questionnaire. Each question has a value range of 1–7 for which the meaning (given in the table) varies per question. The mean is shown for question and where applicable, the Wilcoxon signed-rank test (Z), otherwise, the standard deviation.

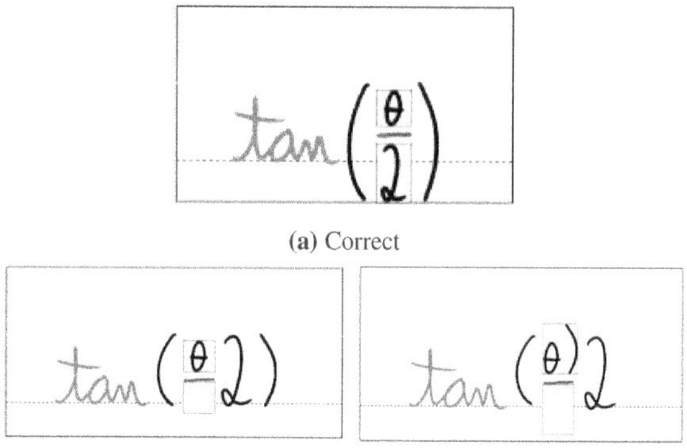

(a) Correct

(b) Error 1

(c) Error 2

Figure 11: Example errors that occurred using the math boxes method. The correct form is shown in (a). In (b) and (c) the 2 is drawn faster than the fraction bar can be registered, before the denominator box is rendered. This results in the 2 being accepted as part of the top level white box, as a character inserted after "$\tan(\frac{\theta}{-}$". In (c), the numerator box containing θ is registered but not yet rendered as the user begins writing the closing parenthesis. Because the stylus lands in the numerator box's bounds, the closing parenthesis is accepted into the numerator box despite not being visible.

received a moderate score of 4.417 in overall ease of use, whereas math boxes achieved a more enthusiastic response, scoring 5.50 with statistical significance between interfaces using the Wilcoxon signed-rank test ($Z = 5.5, p < 0.05$). This is despite similar ease of use ratings, completion times, and accuracy for most equations. While ease in identifying errors were positive for both systems (5.5 and 5.667 for offset and math boxes respectively with $Z = 15.5, p = 0.723$), there was a much greater contrast for ease in correcting errors. With high significance ($Z = 0.0, p < .05$), offset received a moderately negative score at 3.583 and math boxes achieved 5.50. This may directly relate to why math boxes is considered easier to use overall. For equations that are considered simple as defined by the participant's intuition, offset is preferred over math boxes unanimously and the converse is similarly true. Math boxes, as equations become complex, is strongly preferred by all participants.

With respect to each interface's typesetting approach, offset averaging 5.5 and math boxes closely trailing at 5.167 ($Z = 4.0, p = 0.336$), there seems only small (without significance) preference towards offset. This difference, with offset having a slightly higher average, is consistent with LaViola et al.'s findings [8], where users report offset-variant interfaces to be less distracting and less frustrating than ink modifying interfaces.

A subset of post-questionnaire questions focused on specific features of the math boxes interface. Participants gave a moderately positive response to symbol morphing, 5.08 with $\sigma = 1.605$. Note that one issue identified in symbol morphing was that participants would rather see characters morphed into their own handwriting. Overall, participants found that working in and with boxes was very helpful (scoring 6, $\sigma = 0.91$) and that, despite their dynamic resizing, the boxes were not too distracting (5.25, $\sigma = 1.64$). Though the features and interface provided by math boxes gained positive reviews, there were still a number of issues that caused confusion and frustration, that kept math boxes from earning higher scores. The discussion section goes into detail on these issues.

DISCUSSION

Math boxes was designed to address space constraint issues that arise naturally in writing long expressions and to simplify error correction, so that having intimate knowledge of the the underlying parser is not necessary to fix even trivial errors. The unanimous conclusion based on participant feedback is that math boxes accomplishes its goal. This is also reflected in the time to completion results, in the accuracy results, and in the per equation ease of use surveys for complex equations. In discussions following the evaluation, many participants stated that the structure provided by math boxes was helpful, especially when the expression contains multiple levels of subexpressions. Math boxes is not a perfect system however.

The offset method was said to be considerably more fluid and was preferred by all participants for writing simple equations, a result that is reflected in both the quantitative and psychometric data. Many also felt that a hybrid system might offer a better alternative, so that one can write fast in normal circumstances but be able to utilize a yet unspecified gestural type of mechanism to create math boxes when needed.

Observations, Feedback, and Suggestions

The system that we used in our evaluation may have been the cause of a number of errors and difficulties that occurred during the evaluation of math boxes. Some of these issues are depicted in Figure 11. Namely, the primary issues were due to sluggishness in the system. With the collection and processing of each new stroke, the associated boxes have to be dynamically resized. In many cases, to make room for larger boxes, surrounding ink also needs to be translated (so that the boxes do not overlap with other characters). When new boxes have to be created, in some of the worst case scenarios, the entire process of handling a new stroke can take as long as 600–1000ms to complete. Because users are not accustomed to having to wait for the system to catch up to write new characters, participants would often get ahead of the process and wind up writing into blank areas that would normally have a box (such as in a denominator space), but before the box actually exists. In another common scenario and for similar reasons, a box expansion would be in progress with the final boundaries already defined. However, the box would not yet be fully rendered and so the user, believing he or she was in the outer box, would add a character to the canvas that was actually accumulated into the inner box not yet visible. We believe that if such updates had occurred in real-time, then the overall times for the math boxes method would be faster and less errors would have occurred. We found through instrumentation that the majority of the latency came from interacting with ink points (.NET WPF components). In other words, the time it takes to calculate the new position of each ink point when typesetting, morphing, expanding, and so forth is negligible.

Another issue that occasionally caused frustration occurred when a user accidentally drew his or her fraction bar imprecisely, so that characters left or right of the targeted subexpression were unintentionally accumulated into the numerator or denominator box. Presently, the only way to correct this error is to scribble-erase the character and rewrite it into the correct position. To help with this issue and those previously discussed, and based on discussions with the participants, having an easy to use gesture to simply move symbols between adjacent boxes would have likely improved the overall user experience.

The math boxes system was designed so that characters could be modified by writing over previous characters. Therefore when a new stroke overlaps with previously written ink, the new stroke is accumulated into the character space and the previous character is either modified (if the additional stroke results in a valid character) or completely overwritten. In this regard, our system is too rigid as this sometimes results in accidents where users unintentionally overwrite neighboring characters.

A final issue that caused frustration and sometimes errors was due to the automatic and frequent typesetting. Users would periodically raise the stylus out of range of the tablet, causing the system to typeset their equation, and then bring the stylus back down to continue writing. Because symbols and their associated boxes had been moved around, the participant would land the stylus in the wrong position. Usually this was quickly noticed and corrected with a scribble-erase. However, a separate gesture or delayed typesetting timer mechanism could easily resolve this issue and, again, further improve the user experience.

Despite these issues and limitations, participants still preferred working with math boxes as equations became more complex. This response is reflected not only in the post-questionnaire results, but also in the accuracy and TTC results. Participants stated that math boxes's dynamic resizing and ink transformations greatly simplified situations involving multiple levels of subexpressions such as when a term in the denominator of a fraction possesses a superscript.

Future Work

In addition to addressing those issues aforementioned discovered during the user study, we wish to explore techniques that increase the acceptance of morphing recognized symbols into an alternate form for the purpose of recognition feedback. We are also interested in methods of typesetting parts of the equation that are not being modified in realtime without causing frustration or distraction, which we believe is an important part of space management, readability, and thus of the user interface. Last, the current design requires the interface to track an input device while it is hovering over the display. Many systems do have this support such as most mobile devices. Therefore, a math boxes interface that does not require hovering is another important avenue of research.

CONCLUSION

We have presented math boxes, a UI design for handwritten mathematics to make identifying and correcting errors easier and to assist users with writing difficult equations. In a user evaluation, we discovered that we did indeed make significant progress towards our goals but we also discovered several ways to improve the interface. While all users preferred to use our math boxes interface for complex equations, they still preferred the fluidness of the traditional offset method for simpler equations. We believe with further work and some refinement, that math boxes will be the preferred option for expressions of every complexity.

ACKNOWLEDGMENTS

This work is supported in part by NSF CAREER award IIS-0845921 and NSF award CCF-1012056. We also would like to thank the members of ISUE lab for their support and the anonymous reviewers for their useful comments and feedback.

REFERENCES

1. Anthony, L., Yang, J., and Koedinger, K. R. A paradigm for handwriting-based intelligent tutors. *Int. J. Hum.-Comput. Stud. 70*, 11 (Nov. 2012), 866–887.
2. Blackwell, F. W., and Anderson, R. H. An on-line symbolic mathematics system using hand-printed two-dimensional notation. In *Proceedings of the 1969 24th National Conference*, ACM '69, ACM (New York, NY, USA, 1969), 551–557.
3. Bott, J. N., Gabriele, D., and LaViola, Jr., J. J. Now or later: An initial exploration into user perception of mathematical expression recognition feedback. In *Proceedings of the Eighth Eurographics Symposium on Sketch-Based Interfaces and Modeling*, SBIM '11, ACM (New York, NY, USA, 2011), 125–132.
4. Jiang, Y., Tian, F., Wang, H., Zhang, X., Wang, X., and Dai, G. Intelligent understanding of handwritten geometry theorem proving. In *Proceedings of the 15th International Conference on Intelligent User Interfaces*, IUI '10, ACM (New York, NY, USA, 2010), 119–128.

5. Kang, B., and LaViola, J. Logicpad: A pen-based application for visualization and verification of boolean algebra. In *Proceedings of the 2012 ACM International Conference on Intelligent User Interfaces*, IUI '12, ACM (New York, NY, USA, 2012), 265–268.

6. Labahn, G., Lank, E., Marzouk, M., Bunt, A., MacLean, S., and Tausky, D. Mathbrush: A case study for pen-based interactive mathematics. In *Proceedings of the Fifth Eurographics conference on Sketch-Based Interfaces and Modeling*, Eurographics Association (2008), 143–150.

7. LaViola, Jr., J. J., and Zeleznik, R. C. Mathpad2: A system for the creation and exploration of mathematical sketches. *ACM Trans. Graph. 23*, 3 (Aug. 2004), 432–440.

8. LaViola Jr, J. J., Leal, A., Miller, T. S., and Zeleznik, R. C. Evaluation of techniques for visualizing mathematical expression recognition results. In *Proceedings of graphics interface 2008*, Canadian Information Processing Society (2008), 131–138.

9. Lee, W., de Silva, R., Peterson, E. J., Calfee, R. C., and Stahovich, T. F. Newton's pen: A pen-based tutoring system for statics. In *Proceedings of the 4th Eurographics Workshop on Sketch-based Interfaces and Modeling*, SBIM '07, ACM (New York, NY, USA, 2007), 59–66.

10. Li, C., Zeleznik, R., Miller, T., and LaViola, J. J. Online recognition of handwritten mathematical expressions with support for matrices. In *Pattern Recognition, 2008. ICPR 2008. 19th International Conference on*, IEEE (2008), 1–4.

11. Mouchère, H., Viard-Gaudin, C., Zanibbi, R., Garain, U., et al. Icfhr 2014 competition on recognition of on-line handwritten mathematical expressions (crohme 2014). In *Proceedings of International Conference on Frontiers in Handwriting Recognition* (2014).

12. Nakano, Y., and Murao, H. Bredima: Yet another web-browser tool for editing mathematical expressions. In *Proceedings of MathUI* (2006).

13. Press, W. H., Teukolsky, S. A., Vetterling, W. T., and Flannery, B. P. *Numerical Recipes in C (2Nd Ed.): The Art of Scientific Computing*. Cambridge University Press, New York, NY, USA, 1992.

14. Smithies, S., Novins, K., and Arvo, J. A handwriting-based equation editor. In *Graphics Interface*, vol. 99 (1999), 84–91.

15. Smithies, S., Novins, K., and Arvo, J. Equation entry and editing via handwriting and gesture recognition. *Behaviour & information technology 20*, 1 (2001), 53–67.

16. Tapia, E., and Rojas, R. A survey on recognition of on-line handwritten mathematical notation. *Freie Universitat Berlin, Institut fur Informatik, Germany* (2007).

17. Vintsyuk, T. Speech discrimination by dynamic programming. *Cybernetics and Systems Analysis 4*, 1 (1968), 52–57.

18. Wais, P., Wolin, A., and Alvarado, C. Designing a sketch recognition front-end: User perception of interface elements. In *Proceedings of the 4th Eurographics Workshop on Sketch-based Interfaces and Modeling*, SBIM '07, ACM (New York, NY, USA, 2007), 99–106.

19. Zanibbi, R., and Blostein, D. Recognition and retrieval of mathematical expressions. *International Journal on Document Analysis and Recognition (IJDAR) 15*, 4 (2012), 331–357.

20. Zanibbi, R., Novins, K., Arvo, J., and Zanibbi, K. Aiding manipulation of handwritten mathematical expressions through style-preserving morphs. In *Proceedings of Graphics Interface 2001*, GI '01, Canadian Information Processing Society (Toronto, Ont., Canada, Canada, 2001), 127–134.

21. Zeleznik, R., Bragdon, A., Adeputra, F., and Ko, H.-S. Hands-on math: A page-based multi-touch and pen desktop for technical work and problem solving. In *Proceedings of the 23Nd Annual ACM Symposium on User Interface Software and Technology*, UIST '10, ACM (New York, NY, USA, 2010), 17–26.

22. Zeleznik, R., Miller, T., and Li, C. Designing ui techniques for handwritten mathematics. In *Proceedings of the 4th Eurographics workshop on Sketch-based interfaces and modeling*, ACM (2007), 91–98.

23. Zeleznik, R., Miller, T., Li, C., and Laviola Jr, J. J. Mathpaper: Mathematical sketching with fluid support for interactive computation. In *Smart Graphics*, Springer (2008), 20–32.

Predicting Task Execution Time on Natural User Interfaces based on Touchless Hand Gestures

Orlando Erazo[1,2], José A. Pino[1]

[1] Department of Computer Science
University of Chile
{oerazo, jpino}@dcc.uchile.cl

[2] Escuela de Informática
Universidad Técnica Estatal de Quevedo, Ecuador
oerazo@uteq.edu.ec

ABSTRACT

Model-based evaluation has been widely used in HCI. However, current predictive models are insufficient to evaluate Natural User Interfaces based on touchless hand gestures. The purpose of this paper is to present a model based on KLM to predict performance time for doing tasks using this interface type. The required model operators were defined considering the temporal structure of hand gestures (i.e. using *gesture units*) and performing a systematic bibliographic review. The times for these operators were estimated by a user study consisting of various parts. Finally, the model empirical evaluation gave acceptable results (root-mean-square error = 10%, R^2 = 0.936) when compared to similar models developed for other interaction styles. Thus, the proposed model should be helpful to software designers to carry out usability assessments by predicting performance time without user participation.

Author Keywords

Natural user interfaces; touchless gestures; mid-air gestures; predictive model.

ACM Classification Keywords

H.5.2. [Information interfaces and presentation]: User Interfaces.

INTRODUCTION

The availability of new body-tracking devices—such as Microsoft Kinect, Leap Motion and Myo—has contributed significantly to the development of Natural User Interfaces (NUI) based on touchless hand gestures (THG), but using them in systems generates new problems and challenges to software designers [28]. These interfaces may appear "natural" to users [38], but designers must conduct usability assessments in any case. One way of doing them is by analyzing human performance, particularly the concerning time (how long a user takes to accomplish a set of tasks [7]). In this sense, predictive models can contribute meaningfully. However, this approach is not currently available since a comprehensive model for touchless interaction does not exist. Of course, designers would appreciate to have available a model that could be used without undertaking time-consuming and resource-intensive ad-hoc experiments. Thus, an evaluation model for NUIs based on THG would be very useful for designers to be able to develop good software products.

Models have been widely used to analyze interaction problems in HCI [22] particularly by estimating performance time. The Keystroke-Level Model (KLM) [7] is one of the most widely used models for quantitative evaluation of user interfaces. Although it is based on keystrokes, it has been extended or adapted for assessing other interface types [12, 20] including touch-sensitive mobile user interfaces [34]. Nevertheless, the original KLM and its variants are not adequate to assess touchless interaction because they do not have operators for these gesture types. Other options are CLC [6] and Isokoski's [13] model, although they were built to predict production times of pen stroke gestures and unistroke writing time respectively. Thus, these models must be adapted, improved and validated to evaluate NUIs.

Various studies have been carried out to evaluate NUIs using predictive models. Several of these studies can be used to identify usability issues, but they are focused on other factors like quality [4] or difficulty for performing THG [9]. Likewise, Fitts' Law [10], which is a well-known validated model, has been applied to touchless interaction evaluation. It has been used to compare various interface types and input devices [29, 31, 39, 30]; to evaluate methods of pointing and selecting in the air using hand gestures and Kinect [32], etc. These works show that Fitts' law is a well-studied model, and it may be successfully used to estimate performance time on NUIs. However, Fitts' Law usefulness is constrained mainly to point and select tasks. Therefore, new models are needed to predict performance time on NUIs based on THG.

Accordingly, the purpose of this research was to build a model to predict performance time in doing tasks on NUIs based on THG. For this goal, we decided to analyze gestures considering their temporal characteristics and to follow the KLM assumptions. Also, as a first step, it was assumed that gestures are performed by young adults

IUI'15, March 29 - April 01 2015, Atlanta, GA, USA
Copyright 2015 ACM 978-1-4503-3306-1/15/03...$15.00
http://dx.doi.org/10.1145/2678025.2701394

(maybe teenagers as well) in normal health conditions with basic or no experience in touchless interaction and using the dominant hand (fingers are not considered). Additionally, we had to make some simplifications. The resulting model obtained acceptable performance as shown below. Consequently, we expect this model will become a useful tool for software designers to carry out usability assessments, improve interface designs, and develop better software applications using NUIs and THG.

BACKGROUND

Model-based Evaluation

There are several models for evaluating user interfaces in the Human-Computer Interaction area. Models are useful for designing, evaluating, or providing a basis for understanding interfaces [21], especially as a preliminary step or when it is difficult to do tests with users. Models can be descriptive or predictive. Descriptive models give designers a framework to describe and reflect on problems [21]. Predictive models are based on mathematical expressions that allow forecasting users' task performance. Although models may be useful in evaluating interfaces, there is no way of knowing whether these predictions are accurate before systems are tested with users.

Over the years, many models have been proposed to predict users' performance time, such as Model Human Processor (MHP) [8] and GOMS [8]. On the one hand, MHP is based on the idea that the human mind is an information processing system. MHP is described by a set of processors (perceptual, cognitive, and motor), memories (working memory and long-term memory), and principles of operation [8]. Each processor has a cycle time (derived from the literature) to calculate the time to perform tasks. On the other hand, GOMS allows analyzing user behavior with interactive systems. This behavior is modeled in terms of Goals, Operators, Methods and Selection rules [8]. GOMS is a rather generic term used to refer to a family of models. The simplest variant of GOMS is KLM.

KLM [7] is a well-known and validated model that predicts the time to execute a task by expert users. The main idea is that the *execution part*[1] of a task can be described in terms of operators. Operators are actions—such as pressing keys, moving the mouse, pressing a button, etc.—that a person should follow to carry out a task. Also, most operators are assumed to take a constant time. Then, the times required by such actions are added up to estimate the total task time. Given the method, this time can be predicted within about 21% of error [7]. However, the method must be specified in detail at the level of keystrokes and the performance must be error-free.

[1] A unit task has two parts: acquisition and execution of the task [7]. Acquisition time is beyond the scope of this research.

Another well-known model is Fitts' Law [10]. It allows estimating the time it takes to point at a target, based on the object size and distance. Formally, the time required to move the cursor to a target grows logarithmically with distance and decreases with target size. This model allows predicting the time it takes to use an input device—such as a mouse—to click on objects on a screen.

Natural User Interfaces

A NUI is a user interface designed to reuse existing skills [5, 36] to interact appropriately with content and becomes invisible with successive interactions [36]. A NUI allows interacting with an application without using intermediate input devices such as mice or keyboards. Users can control an application through body movements or gestures of everyday life. Gestures are performed in the air using hands, fingers or whole body. However, NUIs can also include more than touchless gestures, e.g., speech recognition, facial expressions or multitouch (all beyond the scope of this paper). In any case, interfaces of this type have been developed to make users act and feel naturally [38].

Gesture-units

A good way to analyze gestures is to look at their temporal structure which can be described in terms of *gesture units* (*g-units*) and *gesture phrases* (*g-phrases*) [23, 14, 16]. McNeill defines a g-unit as "the period of time between successive rest of the limbs; a g-unit begins the moment the limb begins to move and ends when it has reached a rest position again" [23]. A g-unit may contain one or more g-phrases (a **whole gesture**), and a g-phrase in turn consists of one or more *phases*. In the first phase, *preparation*, the hand moves away from its rest position to the initial position of the *stroke*. The meaning of the gesture is expressed in the stroke phase, which is the only obligatory phase. Preceding or following a stroke there may be two phases called *pre-stroke hold* and *post-stroke hold* [16] respectively. At the end, there may be a *retraction* when the hand relaxes and returns to its original or rest position, but this phase is not part of any gesture phrase. Additionally, some gestures have a single meaningful still phase, which is called *independent hold* [16], for static gestures (or *hold gestures* [27]) instead of a stroke. As a result, we distinguish two phrases types, *stroke-phrase* (*S-phrase*) and *hold-phrase* (*H-phrase*). These concepts are illustrated in Figure 1.

G-unit = {G-phrases} + [Retraction]
G-phrase = S-phrase | H-phrase
S-phrase = [preparation] + [pre-stroke hold] + **Stroke** + [post-stroke hold]
H-phrase = [preparation] + **Hold**

Figure 1. G-units and g-phrases (based on [23, 14, 16]).

THE TOUCHLESS HAND GESTURE LEVEL MODEL (THGLM)

The THGLM allows estimating the required time to perform a task using a NUI based on THG in a relatively easy way. The model is inspired on KLM [7] and based on g-units [23, 14]. Like KLM, the method for performing a task must be known and executed without errors. Also, various operators are defined and most of them are assumed to take constant time. However, gestures are more complex than keystrokes, and it is necessary to analyze them in a different way. That is why we decided to use gesture units.

Model Description

The model asserts that the execution part of a task can be described by means of g-units. A task may have one or more g-units depending on its complexity and the system design. A g-unit must be counted every time the user's hand begins to depart from a position of relaxation until the moment when it finally returns to one. For instance, the period of time when a user raises the hand toward a region of space, performs some swipes, and returns to a relaxing position, is equivalent to a gesture unit. For computing the execution time of a task, each g-unit time is added up (equation 1).

$$T_{execute} = \sum_{i=1}^{m} T_{\mathrm{Gunit}_i} \qquad (1)$$

Likewise, g-units can have different lengths (i.e. one or more g-phrases) depending on tasks and system design. For example, a drag and drop task could consist of one g-unit with three g-phrases: select, move and release an object. Besides, a g-unit may have a retraction phase (optional). Thus, a g-unit time is equal to the sum of all g-phrase times plus an optional retraction time (equation 2).

$$T_{\mathrm{Gunit}} = \left(\sum_{j=1}^{n} T_{\mathrm{Gphrase}_j} \right) + [T_r] \qquad (2)$$

Although we have distinguished two types of g-phrases (Figure 1), the method for computing the time of each one is similar (equation 3), i.e. to add an optional preparation time with hold time or stroke time as appropriate. The method to calculate hold time is explained later. For stroke phase, the time may be calculated in various ways. However, we propose to compute stroke time in a way similar to KLM [7] (equation 4). The used operators are defined in the following section. Additionally, we have not taken into account pre-stroke hold and post-stroke hold phases in this model version, although we have not discarded to perform further analysis on both phases.

$$T_{\mathrm{Gphrase}} = [T_p] + \{T_{stroke} \mid T_{hold}\} \qquad (3)$$

$$T_{\mathrm{stroke}} = \sum_{op \in OP} n * op \qquad (4)$$

where OP is the set of gestures that must be defined, and n is the number of occurrences of each operator.

Model Parameters

Given the description made in the previous section, we distinguish three groups of operators: movement operators, expressive operators and general operators. The operators corresponding to each group are described below. Keep in mind that preparation, retraction and hold phases have been included as operators.

Movement Operators

*(1) Preparation (**Pr**)*: ***Pr*** is the average time a user needs to move his/her hand from a position of rest or relaxation to the position where a stroke begins. Although we propose to use a constant time, preparation time could be estimated in another way (e.g. use a different time depending on the initial location of the hand, with higher values at the top and lower values at the bottom of interaction space.) It is necessary to remember this physical preparation phase is optional and different than mental preparation. Therefore, the ***Pr*** operator should be used each time the user must physically prepare his/her hand to perform a gesture.

*(2) Retraction (**Re**)*: The ***Re*** operator is used each time a g-unit finishes. The value of ***Re*** is the average time to move the hand from the position where a stroke or hold finishes to a resting position. Similar to ***Pr***, ***Re*** may be omitted and estimated in alternative ways.

*(3) Pointing (**P**)*: The ***P*** operator may be defined in a way similar to KLM [7] and according to Fitts' Law [10, 22]. However, pointing tasks in a NUI are different than in other interface types. For instance, designers may use different methods for reaching a target (e.g. hand [32, 31] or cross-shaped [29] cursors) and diverse strokes for selecting it [32]. Therefore, it is necessary to consider other aspects (e.g. [26, 29, 39, 32]) generating even modified versions of Fitts' Law. In addition, it is necessary to consider that some R^2 values reported are lower than usual values for Fitts' tasks. Beyond this, the ***P*** operator should be used just to estimate the time to point a target. This operator does not include the stroke that follows to select such target [7], and another operator is used for this sub-action (i.e. a proper S-phrase operator). Finally, we suggest care when placing the ***P*** and ***Pr*** operators together to avoid redundancy.

Expressive Operators

(1) H-phrase Operators: Remembering that an H-phrase has an optional preparation and a hold phases (Figure 1), we defined the ***H*** operator (*Holding*) for the second one (***Pr*** was defined above). The ***H*** operator is used when a user must perform static gestures or hold a hand on a target, position, or pose, a pre-set time. This operator has two parts. The first one is the time users have to hold a hand for considering the action valid. This time is established by designers and called *feedback time* (or *feedback delay time* according to [25]). The second one is the time a user's hand remains in the same position or pose after feedback

time is completed and the hand is moved away. This usually happens when the user receives a confirmation about the recognition of the stroke. It is called *exit time* [25]. Consequently, the total time for this operator is the sum of feedback time and exit time [25] (equation 5).

$$H = feedback\_time + exit\_time \qquad (5)$$

(2) S-phrase Operators: There are many operators that we could use as part of S-phrase since interface designers may want to use different gestures. Although there are several gestures which are "universally" used, we do not know a standard concerning gestures to be used in NUIs. Therefore, it is necessary to choose gestures that would be considered as operators for the stroke phase somehow (except ***Pr*** which was defined before).

With the aim of defining the S-phrase operators, a systematic literature review was performed [17]. We followed a protocol trying to answer the question "Which are the most used (and/or suitable to use) gestures in NUIs based on THG or touchless interaction?" The search was carried out in four bibliographic databases: ACM, IEEE, Springer and ScienceDirect. There were nine search terms used (Table 1). Afterwards, a search filter was applied: the publication year of the papers (since 2011). As expected, the database search returned many results; we had to discard many of them because they were not applicable (e.g. use the whole body, multi-touch interaction, etc.)

Three inclusion and exclusion criteria for the papers were used. (1) The study participants are young adults in normal health conditions, with experience using computers, and basic or no experience in THG. (2) The interaction is based on uni-manual gestures. Moreover, if a study also comprises gestures performed with two hands and/or including fingers for creating different hand shapes (except for closing and opening the hand), it was included but these gestures were not counted. (3) The used gestures are explicitly mentioned[2]. Initially, these criteria were applied by reading the title, keywords and abstract of each search result. This allowed eliminating repetitions and papers that clearly were irrelevant. After that, every pre-selected paper was further analyzed looking for sections in which the authors give details on the aforementioned criteria.

The database search returned a total of 1353 results, but applying the selection criteria, we selected 38 studies[3]. The results were divided in two groups. The first one ("Group 1" in Figure 2) contains 22 studies, which describe software based on THG for specific applications. The second group comprises papers (the remaining ones) in which a specific gesture or a set of gestures, for general or specific purposes, are studied.

Search terms	No. papers returned	No. papers selected*
'"natural user interfaces" AND NOT (multi-touch)'	753	21
touchless+hand+gestures	222	13
"touchless interaction"	77	6
"freehand gestures"	71	6
"mid-air gestures"	66	3
"mid-air interaction"	56	3
"freehand interaction"	52	3
"In-Air Gestures"	43	4
"Touchless User Interfaces"	13	1

Table 1. Search terms. (*) Including repeated papers.

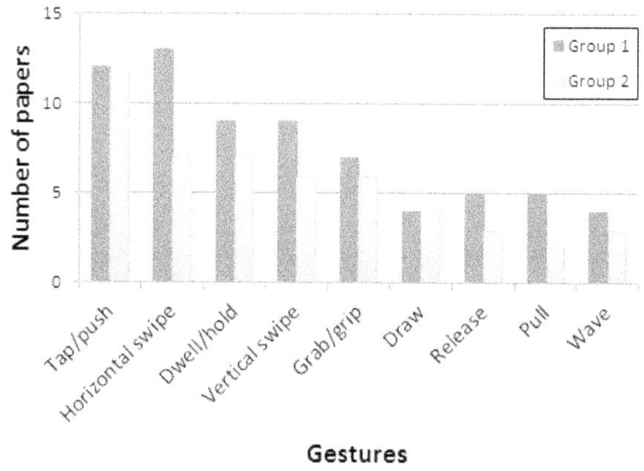

Figure 2. Literature review results. Gestures are ordered by the total number of occurrences in both groups. See the text for explanation about Group 1 and 2.

In addition, backward and forward search [37] was carried out for complementing the database search. For each paper, the bibliographic section was analyzed for backward search, and the "Cited by" link (provided by Google Scholar) was used during forward search. Once again, the aforementioned inclusion and exclusion criteria, and the search filter, were applied. When no new papers were identified, the search stopped. Five papers were added to Group 1 and nine to Group 2 after performing this search. Following this procedure, some papers were repeatedly found, and recent publications were included. This contributes to increase the confidence on the review.

As a result, the final list consists of 52 papers (References R1-R52). Figure 2 shows the gestures used in each study as

[2] Hand positions, such as a hand above the elbow or the head, were not considered as gestures.

[3] The selected papers are included in the reference section with the title "Systematic Review References" [R1-R52].

Operators		Description
T	*Tapping*	Push or move the hand toward the front (i.e. make movements in Z axe).
S	*Swiping*	Move the hand from right to left or vice versa (horizontal swipe), from top to bottom or vice versa (vertical swipe), one time and returning to the starting position.
G	*Gripping*	Grasp, grab, grip or close the hand.
R	*Releasing*	Release or open the hand.
D	*Drawing*	Draw shapes, letters, etc. in the air.

Table 2. Stroke-phase operators.

well as the number of-papers mentioning them. Although *Pointing* is not included in the figure, it is the most studied operation on touchless interaction. It is mainly based on Fitts' Law [10]. Moreover, some authors used diverse shapes for "drawing" gestures, but we did not count each different shape. Besides, we consider unnecessary to mention other gestures with a few occurrences. Finally, due to the diversity of participants' nationalities the reported gestures may be considered culturally independent.

Using these results, the selected operators for the S-phrase are shown in Table 2. Although we have not defined operators for all aforementioned gestures, new operators could be added.

General Operators

*(1) Mentally Prepare (**M**)*: According to Card et al. [7], users spend some time mentally preparing to execute subsequent physical operations. They estimated these mental preparations take 1.35 seconds on the average, but they noted that "the use of a single mental operator is a deliberate simplification" [7]. Moreover, the ***M*** operator perhaps needs revisiting [22]. Despite these cautions, the operator has been successfully used in other works using such value [20, 12]. Moreover, the use of this operator requires following some heuristics provided with KLM [7]. Including mental operators may be tricky and it takes a lot of judgment; Kieras [15] provides some suggestions for how to make these decisions. Thus, we decided to use the existing usage guidelines from [7] and [15] making the necessary interpretations, but we did not adopt the original value for the ***M*** operator.

*(2) Response Time (**R(t)**)*: The last operator represents the time the system needs to respond to user input. This operator is used only when the user must wait before proceeding [7], but s/he can overlap other activities while the system is working [15]. ***R(t)*** is highly variable and application dependent. Therefore, the time is provided as a parameter, *t*, in seconds [7]. Furthermore, we have no evidence for changing the original definition of this operator.

USER STUDY FOR TIME MEASUREMENTS

The duration of each operator must be known in order to be able to use the model and predict required times for tasks. A user study was carried out for estimating these times. For this purpose, the study was divided in six parts with one additional implicit part; the parts are explained in the following subsections. Table 3 summarizes the results of the study showing the THGLM operators with their estimated times.

Method

Participants

36 healthy undergraduate students, 27 male and 9 female (mean age 19 years, σ = 2) took part in the study; 32 participants were right-handed; 29 of them had some basic experience on touchless interaction, such as using a Wii remote or Microsoft Kinect for playing games. The other seven participants had no prior touchless interaction

Operators			Time (s)	SD (s)
H-phrase	***H***, Holding		0.500	0.103[a]
S-phrase	***T***, Tapping		1.108	0.370
	S, Swiping	Mean	0.553	0.211
		Horizontal (***Sh***)	0.613	0.208
		Vertical (***Sv***)	0.493	0.198
	G, Gripping		0.586	0.152
	R, Releasing		0.520	0.172
Movement	***Pr***, Preparation		0.452	0.103
	Re, Retraction		0.746	0.106
	Sp, Swipe preparation	Mean	0.624	0.325
		Horizontal	0.562	0.361
		Vertical	0.685	0.274
	P, Pointing		1.046[b]	NA
General	***MP***, Mentally prepare		0.927	0.116
	R(t), Response Time		*t*	NA

Table 3. Overview of the proposed times for all operators. [a] This value corresponds to the total time of holding (i.e. 1 second according to equation 5). [b] The time was computed from [39].

experience. All participants self-declared their experience on THG and other demographic characteristics in a final questionnaire. Additionally, written informed consent was obtained from all participants.

Apparatus

The hardware setup consisted of a notebook, a Microsoft Kinect sensor and a projected display, mounted in our laboratory. The Microsoft Kinect sensor was connected to a notebook equipped with an Intel Core i7 processor, 8 GB of RAM, to allow tracking users' hand position and recognizing gestures. The Kinect sensor was used with a refresh rate of 30 fps. It was placed at a height of 0.72 cm and below the screen. Participants stood 2.5 meters away from the Kinect while performing the tasks. The notebook was connected to the projected display (with a size of 0.86 × 0.65 meters and a resolution of 1024 × 768 pixels).

A custom software application was developed for directing the experiment. It was developed using Microsoft Visual C# and Kinect for Windows SDK V1.8 on Windows 7. The application logged body tracking data from participants performing gestures and other data (time, users' answers, etc. according to the task performed). Hand movements, joint positions and Dynamic Time Warping algorithm [33] were used for stroke recognition. Also, the application computed the gesture space for each participant based on McNeill's proposal [23] and taking into account the postural comfort zone [18].

The application interface consisted of an augmented video blending user interface controls and the real environment (Figure 3). Augmented video was used trying to avoid participant distractions while performing the tasks. For example, a person may judge his/her movements based on a hand cursor and trying to adjust [35], especially because of sensor noise [19, 31, 39]. We have verified these assumptions in a previous exploratory work. Additionally, visual and auditory feedback was given taking into account the guidelines from [24] and [2].

General Procedure and Design

In general, the participants' task was to answer questions about a subject matter they were studying in the current semester (at the moment the study was carried out). First, they received written instructions on paper. The instructions said they had to answer the questions choosing one from five possible answers, using their dominant hand, and starting (preparation phase) and finishing (retraction phase) with both hands relaxed and below hips. Questions and other experimental conditions were shown in random order. Each question had less than twenty words (13 to 86 characters without spaces). The time for reading the questions was set to 15 seconds taking into account the average speed for reading on computer displays [3] and a pilot study. After that, the question disappeared, and the answers were shown. The answers were represented with green buttons or images labeled "A", "B", "C", "D" and "E". Participants had to perform different hand gestures to choose an answer, according to each part of the study (one gesture per part). If a gesture was wrong, the answer was discarded and the participant had to re-enter it. Also, participants were instructed to perform gestures balancing speed and accuracy. In addition, participants had to answer four practice questions at the beginning of each part of the study. This was enough for learning the gesture. Each participant answered a total of 73 questions plus 24 practice questions.

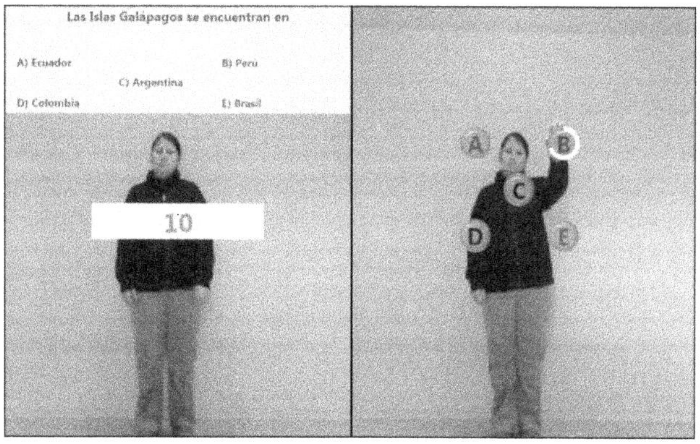

Figure 3. Interface of the experimental software.

A within-subjects design was used where the participants performed six tasks. The task order was counterbalanced using 6 × 6 balanced Latin squares. The whole experiment lasted 1.3 hours per participant on the average.

In addition, observations about interaction mistakes were made. An execution was considered wrong if the participant did not follow the instructions. This allowed discarding wrong executions later (5.6% in the worst case).

Holding (*H*)

This task allowed estimating the time for the *H* operator. For this goal, participants had to hold the hand over an answer button (hovering), and a little timer ring appeared around it indicating the remaining time allowed to select that button. Three button sizes (3.5, 5 and 7 cm. in screen size) and five possible answers were used in this task; it gave a total of 15 questions per participant. The feedback time was set to 500 ms. according to Müller-Tomfelde's findings [25]. If the hand was moved out of the button before completing the feedback time, the subtask was canceled and the participant had to repeat it. Additionally, the button appearance and the color changed when the allowed time was completed. The time for this operator was estimated subtracting the feedback time from the period of time since a participant reached the button until his/her hand moved away from it.

Tapping (*T*)

For estimating this operator time, participants had to put the hand over a button and push it. When the participant reached the button, the color and appearance of the button changed, and changed again when the gesture finished. Although participants were instructed to move the hand toward the front about 15 cm, somebody performed a very long movement (this was annotated as a mistake). Again, three button sizes (3.5, 5 and 7 cm. in screen size) and five possible answers were used in this task (15 questions per participant). The stroke time was computed as the period of time since a participant reached the button until s/he stopped pushing it. This value is approximated to those reported in [30].

Swiping (*S*)

In this section, two parts, horizontal swiping and vertical swiping, are described together because they are similar, although they were performed separately. Participants had to browse the answers moving the hand from right to left or vice versa for horizontal swiping—and up to down or vice versa for vertical swiping— according to an arrow that indicated the direction. They could only browse in one direction at the same time, but they could do it in a cyclical way. For choosing an answer, they had to move the hand down without performing any additional gesture. Ten questions (2 directions × 5 possible answers) were answered in each part. The average time for performing a swipe was computed for every question using only the strokes. In addition, users had to prepare the hand for next swipe, which can be represented using ***Pr*** operators. Alternatively, we decided to include another operator, ***Sp*** (*Swiping preparation*), with other value because the observed time for ***Sp*** was different than the time for ***Pr***. (The ***Sp*** and ***Pr*** operators must not be used together in a same swipe because they are redundant.) As a result, two operators may be used for swipe operations, ***S*** and ***Sp*** (Table 3), although designers can use four operators to distinguish between horizontal and vertical swiping.

Gripping (*G*) and Releasing (*R*)

This task was similar to the tapping task, but participants had to execute other gestures. They had to perform a grip gesture (***G*** operator) followed by a release gesture (***R*** operator). Unlike the other tasks, participants answered 8 questions: 2 button sizes (3.5 and 5 cm. in screen size) × 4 possible answers. The time for the ***G*** operator was estimated computing the time since the participant reached the target until the grip was recognized. Likewise, the time for the ***R*** operator was computed since the grip was detected until the release was recognized.

Drawing (*D*)

In addition, participants performed a "drawing" in the air. They answered 15 questions by drawing a letter inside a red box of three sizes (30, 45 and 60 cm. in motor space) using Graffiti gestures (only for letters A, B, C, D and E). However, we have not used this data yet because a model to predict production time of touchless hand drawing gestures is needed. Thus, we expect to use this data to verify that future model.

Preparation (*Pr*) and Retraction (*Re*)

In each part of the study, participants performed an implicit task for estimating the time of the ***Pr***, ***Re*** and ***M*** (explained below) operators. After answering a question, two circles were shown inside the gesture space. Participants were instructed to "touch" in the air the green circle and then the red one for moving to the next question. The green circle was placed at the center of the gesture space, but the location of the red one was determined using 8 angles (0, 45, 90, 135, 180, 225, 270, 315 degrees). If a participant made a mistake, s/he had to repeat the task. On the one hand, the value of ***Pr*** was estimated as the elapsed time since the participant started to raise the hand until s/he reached the first circle. On the other hand, the ***Re*** time was computed as the elapsed time since the participant moved his/her hand away from the red circle until the return to a rest position below the hip (the hip on the same side of the dominant hand). Although we could get acceptable results, the use of single operators for both preparation and retraction is another deliberate simplification.

Pointing (*P*)

As mentioned above, several research efforts have been performed for analyzing pointing tasks using Fitts' Law and THG [32, 39, 29, 31, 30]. Although we have found no reasons to estimate the time for this operator in a different way that the one in KLM, a value or equation is necessary for using ***P***. However, we have not performed experiments for determining that value or equation. Consequently, we decided to use a value from related works for validating the proposed model. We used the average time observed by Zeng et al. [39] for pointing with the dominant hand and pushing with the other hand. Furthermore, we subtracted our estimated pushing time from their pointing time. Thus, the used value was 1.046 seconds, which is also consistent with the values reported in [30].

Mentally Prepare (*M*)

The mental operator time was estimated using the same task used for the ***Pr*** and ***Re*** operators. It was computed as the time the participant needed to start the task (select the green circle), i.e., the period of time since the answers were shown until the preparation started. Although the estimated value is lower than the proposed by Card et al. [7], it is in the range of 0.6 – 1.35 seconds suggested by Kieras [15].

VALIDATION OF THE MODEL

An empirical validation was performed to test the proposed model. For this goal, we compared predicted times using the model with the observed times collected in three controlled experiments. In all experiments, a within-subjects design and balanced Latin square for determining the order of tasks were used. Similarly, the aforementioned apparatus was employed. The task executions with mistakes were not included (16.7% in the worst case). Details on each experiment are given below.

Experiment 1: NUIPy

In the first experiment, the participants had to use an application developed by us. It was named NUIPy and allowed solving a kind of puzzles using a NUI based on THG. The puzzles were used to represent basic programs written in Python. Each puzzle part corresponded to one statement shown in a rectangle box. The participants had to perform a gesture (tapping or gripping) to select it. If the statement was selected in the right order, it was executed in Python IDLE[4]. If the participant made a mistake, s/he had to repeat the whole puzzle. This allowed ensuring that the participants performed the tasks without errors. The tasks were performed by 18 participants, who took part in the previous user study for time measurements. They received instructions for doing the tasks using their dominant hand (the right hand in most cases). They performed four practice and six experimental tasks (i.e. they solved ten puzzles): five using the tapping gesture and five using the gripping gesture for selecting program statements. (The puzzles used for the model validation had 3, 4 and 5 statements). Swipe gestures were used for browsing between programs (puzzles) and tap gestures for selecting the buttons. Finally, the whole interaction was video recorded and segmented manually to compute duration times.

Experiment 2: OctaNUI

To carry out the second experiment, we developed another application, which was named OctaNUI, based on NUIs and THG to interact with GNU Octave[5]. The application was used by 12 participants, who took part in the previous study for time measurements. Participants received written instructions for performing one practice and four experimental tasks executing two types of gestures with their dominant hand: tap and horizontal swipe. The tasks consisted of select and execute a command with a dataset. If participants made a mistake, they could cancel the task to repeat it. The duration time of each task was automatically logged.

Experiment 3: Other applications

For the third experiment, we used other applications and recruited new participants. The participants were eight graduate students (mean age 32 years, σ = 4; all right-handed; 7 male). They were verbally instructed to use two applications with their dominant hand. The first one, InteractionGallery[6], was used to perform four tasks executing the gestures tapping and scrolling (grip, swipe and release). The second one, Kinect Paint[7], allows painting on a canvas and selecting buttons or options using holding gestures, but this data has not been used yet because a model for drawing gestures is needed. With both applications, the participants performed each task three times. The duration time was computed by videotaping the interactions and segmenting the videos manually.

Results

The predicted times were calculated using equations 1 to 5 and the proposed operator times (Table 3) in order to analyze how well the model works. Figure 4 shows an example of this process. The example task was "solve the puzzle corresponding to program 2 using grip gestures", and two g-units were necessary. The times of the fourteen tasks were computed in a similar way and compared with the observed values (Figure 5). The average prediction error—given as percentage of the estimated time—is 8.2% (min: -19.1%, max: 16.2%), and the root-mean-square error (RMSE) is 10.1%. Figure 6 plots the correlation between estimated and observed execution times (R^2 = 0.936). Then, we performed further analysis to verify whether the model predictions remain acceptable under varying conditions. First, a comparison was made between the predicted values and the observed times in the three repetitions of experiment 3. We obtained RMSEs lower than 16%. (The mean of the three repetitions was used in the comparison shown in Figures 5 and 6.) Second, the following options were used to estimate times and make

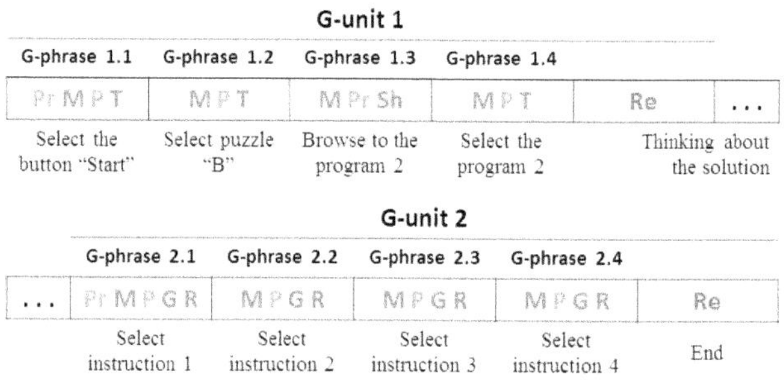

$T_{execute}$ = ({3.533 + 3.081 + 1.992 + 3.081} + 0.746) + ({0.452 + 4 * (3.079)} + 0.746)
$T_{execute}$ = 12.433 + 13.514 = 25.947 seconds

Figure 4. Example of using the THGLM.

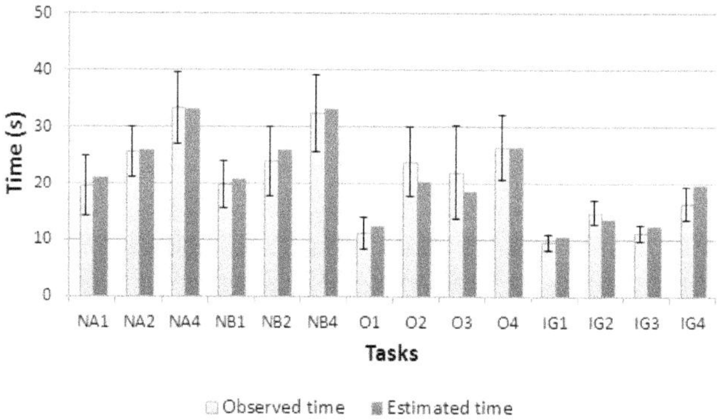

Figure 5. Task execution times: observed vs. predicted. Error bars indicate 1 SD. Task notation: N = NUIPy, using tapping (A) and gripping (B) gestures for selecting puzzle parts; O = OctaNUI; IG = InteractionGallery.

[4] IDLE is the Python IDE (https://www.python.org/)

[5] "GNU Octave is a high-level interpreted language, primarily intended for numerical computations. It is quite similar to Matlab." (http://www.gnu.org/software/octave/)

[6] InteractionGallery is a WPF C# sample distributed with Kinect for Windows SDK (http://msdn.microsoft.com/en-us/library/jj663801.aspx).

[7] Kinect Paint is available at http://paint.codeplex.com/

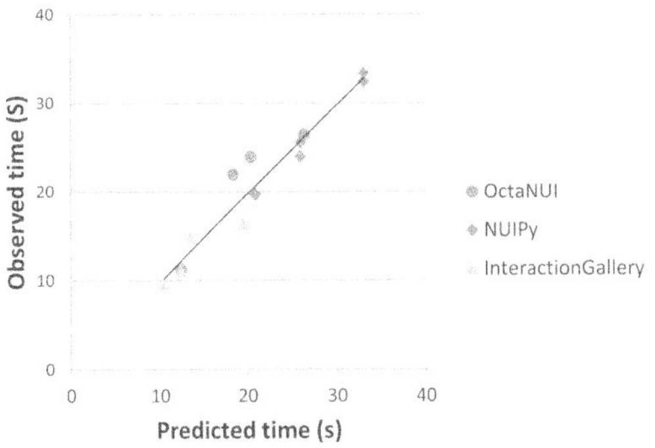

Figure 6. THGLM prediction.

comparisons (one at a time): use Card et al.'s [7] time for the ***M*** operator (1.35 seconds); do not include preparation and retraction phases; use a single operator (***S***) for swiping (i.e. without distinguishing between horizontal and vertical swipe); and use the ***Sp*** operator instead of ***Pr*** for preparing to perform a swipe. The predictions worsened slightly, but they were still acceptable ($R^2 \geq 0.9$, RMSE $\leq$ 19%), and the worst values were obtained when excluding ***Pr*** and ***Re***. These results confirm that the estimated execution times are quite accurate using the THGLM.

DISCUSSION

According to our validation, the proposed model gave promising results. This means that the results are consistent with previous ones. For instance, the RMSE reported by Card et al. [7] for the original KLM is 21%, and the prediction error informed by Luo and John [20] is lower than 8% on handheld interfaces. Nonetheless, we consider necessary to discuss some advantages and limitations.

Similar to KLM, the THGLM is relatively easy to use despite the fact some simplifications were needed. The first one is about the S-phrase operators used. Although actual devices allow detecting and tracking human body and hand fingers, this interaction type has not been considered yet. More importantly, the following question has not been fully answered: Which S-phrase operators should be considered as part of the model? Keeping in mind that the gestures should help the interface appear "natural" to users [38], they should allow reusing existing skills and become transparent [5]. Since there are many studies on NUIs and touchless interaction, the S-phrase operators selection was made by carrying out a bibliographic review. We think this selection may be culture independent because the participants of the selected papers were people from different countries and continents. Therefore, we consider the selected gestures are a starting point towards a "general" gesture set for NUIs based on THG.

Despite the selected gestures may be used to design and implement several application functionalities, there are other gestures that have not been included in the model yet. The gesture "wave" is an example, which may be used for several tasks (e.g. to identify users [11]). Similarly, touchless hand drawing gestures can be used, but there is no comprehensive model to estimate stroke production times. This is not a major limitation because the model is extensible. For this aim, the time it takes to perform the new stroke should be estimated—or find the equations to compute it instead—and included as a new S-phrase operator. This means that stroke time can be computed in different ways, hence the estimate proposed here is only an alternative (equations 3 and 4). Something similar happens with the H-phrase operators (equations 3 and 5), in which case only one operator has been defined.

Other simplifications were made for the movement operators. On the one hand, a constant time, computed from Zeng's et al. work [39], was used for the ***P*** operator for performing the model evaluation. However, keeping in mind that both the use of Fitts' Law on touchless interaction has been verified by other research [29, 39, 32] and Mackenzie's suggestion [22], Fitts' Law should be used for this operator. On the other hand, an average time was estimated for ***Pr*** and ***Re*** operators, although they could be computed in different ways and used in equations 2 and 3. Nevertheless, as preparation and retraction are optional phases, ***Pr*** and ***Re*** may be omitted and still get acceptable results (take care when this choice is made because worse results could be obtained depending on every case).

As it was mentioned above, a deliberate simplification was made for the ***M*** operator similar to Card et al. [7]. Although the estimated value allowed getting acceptable results in our experiments, the mental operator should be revised and maybe "replaced with a set of operators for the diverse interactions requiring user attention and cognition" [22]. Also, the heuristics to place ***M*** operators should be revised and explained in more detail.

Lastly, we consider necessary to mention some details concerning the experiments. First, in general, we could observe a relatively high variation of gesture production times. (The average coefficient of variation among all operators is 30%—and 25% discarding the ***Sp*** operators.) Second, different results may be obtained for users with different characteristics (e.g., users from different cultures, impaired people, etc.) Third, the validation has two limitations that could influence the results: two of three applications were used by the same participants who took part in the study for time measurements, and some tasks were similar. Fourth, the gestures used in the experiments were performed using only the dominant hand (the right hand in most cases), but the used hand could have an effect on time (e.g. [39]), or designers may assume that users can learn with one hand and perform gestures with the other (similar to [1]) without problems. Finally, other subjects' characteristics—such as gender or age—might have a significant impact on the results. Consequently, further research is needed to generalize the model.

CONCLUSIONS AND FUTURE WORK

In this paper, we have described a model that we believe is the first attempt to formulate a comprehensive model to quantitatively evaluate tasks on NUIs based on THG. The model allows estimating performance time a user needs to do a task using his/her dominant hand. It has been built following the proposals to analyze hand gestures looking at their temporal structure [23, 14, 16] and the KLM methodology [7]. The first one confirms that NUIs based on THG can be analyzed by gesture units. The second one means we had to define some operators which correspond to gestures commonly used as part of NUIs. The operator times were estimated by user studies in most cases, and using related works when it was needed. However, these values may change depending on users' characteristics.

The model was empirically validated using three applications and fourteen tasks. According to the metrics used, the obtained results are promising. These metric values should not be considered as definitive because further evaluation is needed. In spite of this, the model will allow software designers to analyze their interfaces at early design stages, without user participation, and in a relatively easy way.

Taking into account the model is easy to extend, we expect to add new operators as future work. In fact, we are currently working on the Drawing operator to estimate stroke times for touchless hand drawing gestures. We also hope to improve other operators such as Mentally Prepare (***M***) considering the aforementioned details. Finally, we hope to use and/or improve the model to predict time of bimanual tasks.

ACKNOWLEDGMENTS

Orlando Erazo appreciates the financial support provided for this research by SENESCYT ("Secretaría de Educación Superior, Ciencia, Tecnología e Innovación", Convocatoria Abierta 2011), Ecuador.

REFERENCES

1. Annett, M., and Bischof, W. Your Left Hand Can Do It Too! Investigating Intermanual, Symmetric Gesture Transfer on Touchscreens. *Proc. CHI 2013*, ACM Press (2013), 1119-1128.
2. Argelaguet, F., and Andujar, C. A survey of 3D object selection techniques for virtual environments. *Comput. Grap. 37*, 3 (2013), 121-136.
3. Ball, R., and Hourcade, J. P. Rethinking Reading for Age From Paper and Computers. *Int. Journal of Human-Computer Interaction 27*, 11 (2011), 1066-1082.
4. Barclay, K., Wei, D., Lutteroth, C., and Sheehan, R. A Quantitative Quality Model for Gesture Based User Interfaces. *Proc. OzCHI 2011*, ACM Press (2011), 31-39.
5. Blake, J. The natural user interface revolution. In *Natural User Interfaces in .Net*, Manning, 2012, 1-43.
6. Cao, X., and Zhai, S. Modeling Human Performance of Pen Stroke Gestures. *Proc. CHI 2007*, ACM Press (2007), 1495-1504.
7. Card, S., Moran, T., and Newell, A. The Keystroke-Level Model for User Performance Time with Interactive Systems. Communications of the ACM 23, 7 (1980), 396-410.
8. Card, S., Moran, T., and Newell, A. *The Psychology of Human-Computer Interaction*. L. Erlbaum Assoc., 1983.
9. Erazo, O., and Pino, J. Estimating the Difficulty of Touchless Hand Gestures. *IEEE Latin America Transactions 12*, 1 (2014), 17-22.
10. Fitts, P. M. The information capacity of the human motor system in controlling the amplitude of movement. *J. of Exp. Psychology 47*, 6 (1980), 381-391.
11. Hayashi, E., Maas, M., and Hong, J. I. Wave to Me: User Identification Using Body Lengths and Natural Gestures. *Proc. CHI 2014*, ACM Press (2014), 3453-3462.
12. Holleis, P., Otto, F., Hussmann, H., and Schmidt, A. Keystroke-Level Model forAdvanced Mobile Phone Interaction. *Proc. CHI 2007*, ACM Press (2007), 1505-1514.
13. Isokoski, P. Model for Unistroke Writing Time. *Proc. CHI 2001*, ACM Press (2001), 357-364. Seattle.
14. Kendon, A. Gesture units, gesture phrases and speech. In *Gesture: Visible action as utterance*. Cambridge University Press, 2004, 108-126.
15. Kieras, D. Using the Keystroke-Level Model to Estimate Execution Times. University of Michigan, 2001. http://www-personal.umich.edu/~itm/688/KierasKLMTutorial2001.pdf.
16. Kita, S., Van Gijn, I., and Van der Hulst, H. Movement Phases in Signs and Co-Speech Gestures, and their Transcription by Human Coders. *Proc. Int. Gesture Workshop on Gesture and Sign Language in Human-Computer Interaction 1998*, Springer (1997), 23-35.
17. Kitchenham, B. Procedures for performing systematic reviews. Dept. Comp. Sc., Keele University, 2004.
18. Kölsch, M., Beall, A. C., and Turk, M. The postural comfort zone for reaching gestures. *Proc. Human Factors and Ergonomics Society 2003*, SAGE Publications (2003), 787-791.
19. Livingston, M. A., Sebastian, J., Ai, Z., and Decker, J. W. Performance Measurements for the Microsoft Kinect Skeleton. *Virtual Reality 2012*, IEEE (2012), 119-120.
20. Luo, L., and John, B. E. Predicting Task Execution Time on Handheld Devices Using the Keystroke-Level Model. *Ext. Abstracts CHI 2005*, ACM Press (2005), 1605-1608.

21. MacKenzie, I. S. Motor Behavior Models for Human-Computer Interaction. In *HCI Models, Theories, and Frameworks*, J. M. Carroll, Ed. Morgan Kaufman, 2003, 27-54.

22. MacKenzie, I. S. Modeling Interaction. In *Human-Computer Interaction: An Empirical Research Perspective*, Morgan Kaufmann, 2013, 233-283.

23. McNeill, D. Guide to Gesture Classification, Transcription, and Distribution. In *Hand and Mind: What Gestures Reveal about Thought*, University of Chicago Press, 1992, 75-104.

24. Microsoft Corporation. Kinect for Windows Human Interface Guidelines v1.8.0. 2013. http://msdn.microsoft.com/en-us/library/jj663791.aspx

25. Müller-Tomfelde, C. Dwell-Based Pointing in Applications of Human Computer Interaction. *Proc. Interact 2007*, Springer (2007), 560-573.

26. Murata, A., and Iwase, H. Extending Fitts' law to a three-dimensional pointing task. *Hum. Movement Sci. 20*, 6 (2001), 791–805.

27. Neff, M., Kipp, M., Albrecht, I., and Seidel, H. P. Gesture Modeling and Animation Based on a Probabilistic. *ACM T. Graphic. 27*, 1 (2008).

28. Norman, D. Natural user interfaces are not natural. *Interactions 17*, 3 (2010), 6-10.

29. Pino, A., Tzemis, E., Ioannou, N., and Kouroupetroglou, G. Using Kinect for 2D and 3D Pointing Tasks: Performance Evaluation. *Proc. HCII 2013*, Springer (2013), 358-367.

30. Polacek, O., Klíma, M., Sporka, A. J., Zak, P., Hradis, M., Zemcik, P., and Procházka, V. A Comparative Study on Distant Free-Hand Pointing. *Proc. EuroiTV 2012*, ACM Press (2012), 139-142.

31. Sambrooks, L., and Wilkinson, B. Comparison of gestural, touch, and mouse interaction with Fitts' law. *Proc. OzCHI 2013*, ACM Press (2013), 119-122.

32. Schwaller, M., and Lalanne, D. Pointing in the Air: Measuring the Effect of Hand Selection Strategies on Performance and Effort. *Proc. SouthCHI 2013*, Springer (2013), 732-747.

33. Senin, P. Dynamic time warping algorithm review. Information and Computer Science Department, University of Hawaii at Manoa, 2008.

34. Song, K., Kim, J., Cho, Y. H., Lee, A., Ryu, H., Choi, J. W., and Lee, Y. J. The Fingerstroke-Level Model Strikes Back: A modified Keystroke-Level Model in developing a gaming UI for 4G networks. *Ext. Abstracts CHI 2013*, ACM Press (2013), 2359-2362.

35. Sutter, C., Müsseler, J., Bardos, L., Ballagas, R., and Borchers, J. (2008). The impact of gain change on perceiving one's own actions. *Mensch & computer 2008*, Oldenbourg Verlag (2008) 147-156.

36. Webb, J., and Ashley, J. NUI. In *Beginning Kinect Programming with the Microsoft Kinect SDK*, Apress, 2012, 170-172.

37. Webster, J., and Watson, R. T. Analyzing the Past to Prepare for the Future: Writing a Literature Review. *MIS Quarterly 26*, 2 (2002), 13-23.

38. Wigdor, D., and Wixon, D. The Natural User Interface. In *Brave NUI World: Designing Natural User Interfaces for Touch and Gesture*, Morgan Kaufmann, 2011, 9-14.

39. Zeng, X., Hedge, A., and Guimbretiere, F. Fitts' Law in 3D Space with Coordinated Hand Movements. *Proc. Human Factors and Ergonomics Society Annual Meeting 2012*, SAGE Publications (2012), 990-994.

SYSTEMATIC REVIEW REFERENCES

R1. Arif, A. S., Stuerzlinger, W., and Gordynski, A. Error Behaviours in an Unreliable In-air Gesture Recognizer. *Ext. Abstracts CHI 2014*, ACM Press (2014), 1603-1608.

R2. Aumi, M. T. I., and Kratz, S. AirAuth: Towards Attack-Resilient Biometric Authentication Using In-Air Gestures. *Ext. Abstracts CHI 2014*, ACM Press (2014), 1585-1590.

R3. Bossavit, B., Marzo, A., Ardaiz, O., and Pina, A. Hierarchical Menu Selection with a Body-Centered Remote Interface. *Interact. Comput.* (2013).

R4. Brown, M. A., and Stuerzlinger, W. The Performance of Un-Instrumented In-Air Pointing. *Proc. GI 2014*, ACM Press (2014), 59-66.

R5. Chattopadhyay, D., and Bolchini, D. Touchless Circular Menus: Toward an Intuitive UI for Touchless Interactions with Large Displays. *Proc. AVI 2014*, ACM Press (2014), 33-40

R6. Cockburn, A., Quinn, P., Gutwin, C., Ramos, G., and Looser, J. Air pointing: Design and evaluation of spatial target acquisition with and without visual feedback. *Int. J. of Human-Computer Studies 69*, 6 (2011), 401-414.

R7. Cohen, L., Haliyo, S., Chetouani, M., and Régnier, S. Intention prediction approach to interact naturally with the microworld. *Proc. AIM 2014*, IEEE (2014).

R8. Dias, T., Variz, M., Jorge, P., and Jesus, R. Gesture Interaction System for Social Web Applications on Smart TVs. *Proc. OAIR 2013*, CID (2013), 225-226.

R9. Drossis, G., Grammenos, D., Birliraki, C., and Stephanidis, C. MAGIC: Developing a Multimedia Gallery Supporting mid-Air Gesture-Based Interaction and Control. *Posters' Ext. Abstracts HCII 2013*, Springer (2013), 303-307.

R10. Garzotto, F., and Valoriani, M. Touchless Gestural Interaction with Small Displays: A Case Study. *Proc. CHItaly 2013*, ACM Press (2013).

R11. Gatto, I., and Pittarello, F. Prototyping a Gestural Interface for Selecting and Buying Goods in a Public Environment. *Proc. AVI 2012*, ACM Press (2012), 784-785.

R12. Giovanni, S., Choi, Y. C., Huang, J., Khoo, E. T., and Yin, K. Virtual Try-On Using Kinect and HD Camera. *Proc. MIG 2012*, Springer (2012), 55-65.

R13. Hartmann, F., and Schlaefer, A. Feasibility of touch-less control of operating room lights. *Int. J. CARS 8*, 2 (2013), 259-268.

R14. Hayashi, E., Maas, M., and Hong, J. I. Wave to Me: User Identification Using Body Lengths and Natural Gestures. *Proc. CHI 2014*, ACM Press (2014), 3453-3462.

R15. Hespanhol, L., Tomitsch, M., Grace, K., Collins, A., and Kay, J. Investigating Intuitiveness and Effectiveness of Gestures for Free Spatial Interaction with Large Displays. *Proc. PerDis 2012*, ACM Press (2012).

R16. Ho, K., and Weng, H. Favoured Attributes of In-Air Gestures in the Home Environment. *Proc. OzCHI 2013*, ACM Press (2013), 171-174.

R17. Hosseini, M., Vallotton, P., Bednarz, T., and Sowmya, A. A study of touchless versus touch-based interactions with bacterial biofilm images. *Proc. VRCAI 2013*, ACM Press (2013), 285-290.

R18. Hötker, A. M., Pitton, M. B., Mildenberger, P., and Düber, C. Speech and motion control for interventional radiology: requirements and feasibility. *Int. J. CARS 8*, 6 (2013), 997-1002.

R19. Jacob, M. G., and Wachs, J. P. Context-based hand gesture recognition for the operating room. *Pattern Recogn. Lett. 36*, (2014), 196-203.

R20. Jalaliniya, S., Smith, J., Sousa, M., Büthe, L., and Pederson, T. Touch-less interaction with medical images using hand & foot gestures. *Proc. UbiComp 2013*, ACM Press (2013), 1265-1274.

R21. Kim, Y., Sim, S., Cho, S., Lee, W. W., Jeong, Y. S., Cho, K., and Um, K. Intuitive NUI for Controlling Virtual Objects Based on Hand Movements. *Future Information Technology*, Springer (2014), 457-461.

R22. Lee, Y. H., Wu, S. K., and Liu, Y. P. Performance of remote target pointing hand movements in a 3D environment. *Hum. Movement Sci. 32*, 3 (2013), 511-526.

R23. Lim, C. J., and Jung, Y. G. A Study on the Usability Testing of Gesture Tracking-Based Natural User Interface. *Posters' Ext. Abstracts HCII 2013*, Springer (2013), 139-143.

R24. Löcken, A., Hesselmann, T., Pielot, M., Henze, N., and Boll, S. User-centred process for the definition of free-hand gestures applied to controlling music playback. *Multimedia systems 18*, 1 (2012), 15-31.

R25. Loehmann, S., Knobel, M., Lamara, M., and Butz, A. Culturally Independent Gestures for In-Car Interactions. *Proc. Interact 2013*, Springer (2013), 538-545.

R26. Markussen, A., Jakobsen, M. R., and Hornbæk, K. Selection-Based Mid-Air Text Entry on Large Displays. *Proc. Interact 2013*, Springer (2013), 401-418.

R27. Mehler, A., vor der Brück, T., and Lücking, A. Comparing Hand Gesture Vocabularies for HCI. *Proc. HCII 2014*, Springer (2014), 81-92.

R28. Meneses, A., and Hernández, E. Kinect©, as Interaction Device with a Tiled Display. *Proc. HCII 2013*, Springer (2013), 301-311.

R29. Nancel, M., Wagner, J., Pietriga, E., Chapuis, O., and Mackay, W. Mid-air Pan-and-Zoom on Wall-sized Displays. *Proc. CHI 2011*, ACM Press (2011), 177-186.

R30. Panger, G. Kinect in the Kitchen: Testing Depth Camera Interactions in Practical Home Environments. *Ext. Abstracts CHI 2012*, ACM Press (2012), 1985-1990.

R31. Pino, A., Tzemis, E., Ioannou, N., and Kouroupetroglou, G. Using Kinect for 2D and 3D Pointing Tasks: Performance Evaluation. *Proc. HCII 2013*, Springer (2013), 358-367.

R32. Polacek, O., Klíma, M., Sporka, A. J., Zak, P., Hradis, M., Zemcik, P., and Procházka, V. A Comparative Study on Distant Free-Hand Pointing. *Proc. EuroiTV 2012*, ACM Press (2012), 139-142.

R33. Re, G. M., and Bordegoni, M. A Natural User Interface for Navigating in Organized 3D Virtual Contents. *Proc. VAMR 2014*, Springer (2014), 93-104.

R34. Ren, G., and O'Neill, E. 3D selection with freehand gesture. *Comput. Grap. 37*, 3 (2013), 101-120.

R35. Ren, G., and O'Neill, E. Freehand Gestural Text Entry for Interactive TV. *Proc. EuroiTV 2013*, ACM Press (2013), 121-130.

R36. Rovelo Ruiz, G. A., Vanacken, D., Luyten, K., Abad, F., and Camahort, E. Multi-Viewer Gesture-Based Interaction for Omni-Directional Video. *Proc. CHI 2014*, ACM Press (2014), 4077-4086.

R37. Rümelin, S., Marouane, C., and Butz, A. Free-hand Pointing for Identification and Interaction with Distant Objects. *Proc. AutomotiveUI 2013*, ACM Press (2013), 40-47.

R38. Salvador, R., Romão, T., and Centieiro, P. A Gesture Interface Game for Energy Consumption Awareness. *Proc. ACE 2012*, Springer (2012), 352-367.

R39. Sambrooks, L., and Wilkinson, B. Comparison of gestural, touch, and mouse interaction with Fitts' law. *Proc. OzCHI 2013*, ACM Press (2013), 119-122.

R40. Sousa, T., Cardoso, I., Parracho, J., Dias, P., and Santos, B. S. DETI-Interact: Interaction with Large Displays in Public Spaces Using the Kinect. *Proc. DAPI 2014*, Springer (2014), 196-206.

R41. Tan, J. H., Chao, C., Zawaideh, M., Roberts, A. C., and Kinney, T. B. Informatics in Radiology: Developing a Touchless User Interface for Intraoperative Image Control during Interventional Radiology Procedures. *Radiographics 33*, 2 (2013), E61-E70.

R42. Tang, J. C., Xiao, R., Hoff, A., Venolia, G., Therien, P., and Roseway, A. HomeProxy: Exploring a Physical Proxy for Video Communication in the

Home. *Proc. CHI 2013*, ACM Press (2013), 1339-1342.

R43. Tian, J., Qu, C., Xu, W., and Wang, S. KinWrite: Handwriting-Based Authentication Using Kinect. *Proc. Annual Network & Distributed System Security Symposium 2013*.

R44. Tuntakurn, A., Thongvigitmanee, S. S., Sa-Ing, V., Hasegawa, S., and Makhanov, S. S. Natural Interactive 3D Medical Image Viewer Based on Finger and Arm Gestures. *Proc. BMEiCON 2013*, IEEE (2013).

R45. Vaidyanathan, V., and Rosenberg, D. "Will Use It, Because I Want to Look Cool" A Comparative Study of Simple Computer Interactions Using Touchscreen and In-Air Hand Gestures. *Proc. HCII 2014*, Springer (2014), 170-181.

R46. Van de Camp, F., Schick, A., and Stiefelhagen, R. How to Click in Mid-Air. *Proc. DAPI/HCII 2013*, Springer (2013), 78-86.

R47. Vatavu, R. D. A comparative study of user-defined handheld vs. freehand gestures for home entertainment environments. *J. of Ambient Intelligence and Smart Env. 5*, 2 (2013), 187–211

R48. Vatavu, R. D. User-Defined Gestures for Free-Hand TV Control. *Proc. EuroiTV 2012*, ACM Press (2012), 45-48.

R49. Vatavu, R. D., and Zaiţi, I. Leap Gestures for TV: Insights from an Elicitation Study. *Proc. TVX 2014*, ACM Press (2014), 131-138.

R50. Wu, H., and Wang, J. User-Defined Body Gestures for TV-based Applications. *Proc. ICDH 2012*, IEEE (2012), 415-420.

R51. Yim, J., Lee, K., and Kim, H. Implementation of a Preliminary Natural User Interface for Video on Demand Systems. *Future Information Technology*, Springer (2014), 475-480.

R52. Zarzuela, M. M., Pernas, F. J. D., Calzón, S. M., Ortega, D. G., and Rodríguez, M. A. Educational Tourism Through a Virtual Reality Platform. *Proc. Computer Science 25*, Elsevier (2013), 382-388.

TouchML: A Machine Learning Toolkit for Modelling Spatial Touch Targeting Behaviour

Daniel Buschek, Florian Alt
Media Informatics Group, University of Munich (LMU)
{daniel.buschek, florian.alt}@ifi.lmu.de

ABSTRACT
Pointing tasks are commonly studied in HCI research, for example to evaluate and compare different interaction techniques or devices. A recent line of work has modelled user-specific touch behaviour with machine learning methods to reveal spatial targeting error patterns across the screen. These models can also be applied to improve accuracy of touchscreens and keyboards, and to recognise users and hand postures. However, no implementation of these techniques has been made publicly available yet, hindering broader use in research and practical deployments. Therefore, this paper presents a toolkit which implements such touch models for data analysis (Python), mobile applications (Java/Android), and the web (JavaScript). We demonstrate several applications, including hand posture recognition, on touch targeting data collected in a study with 24 participants. We consider different target types and hand postures, changing behaviour over time, and the influence of hand sizes.

Author Keywords
Touch; Toolkit; Machine Learning; Gaussian Process

ACM Classification Keywords
H.5.2. Information Interfaces and Presentation (e.g. HCI): Input devices and strategies (e.g. mouse, touchscreen)

INTRODUCTION AND RELATED WORK
Targeting experiments help HCI researchers to assess quantitative aspects of interactions, such as speed-accuracy trade-offs, error rates, and throughput. Participants are asked to point at targets on the screen. The resulting data is commonly analysed with Fitts' Law [5]. Bi et al. [3] refined this approach for targeting with the finger in touch interaction. Other work modelled targeting while typing on touchscreens [1, 7, 14]. A different line of research compensated systematic patterns of touch-to-target errors ("touch offsets") with a polynomial function applied across many mobile device users [6]. More flexible offset models were trained on user-specific recorded touch targeting histories [13]. Touch offsets were also explored to recognise users and hand postures [4], to reveal characteristic screen regions for describing individual touch behaviour [11], and to reduce typing errors [12].

IUI'15, March 29 - April 01 2015, Atlanta, GA, USA
Copyright 2015 ACM 978-1-4503-3306-1/15/03...$15.00
http://dx.doi.org/10.1145/2678025.2701381

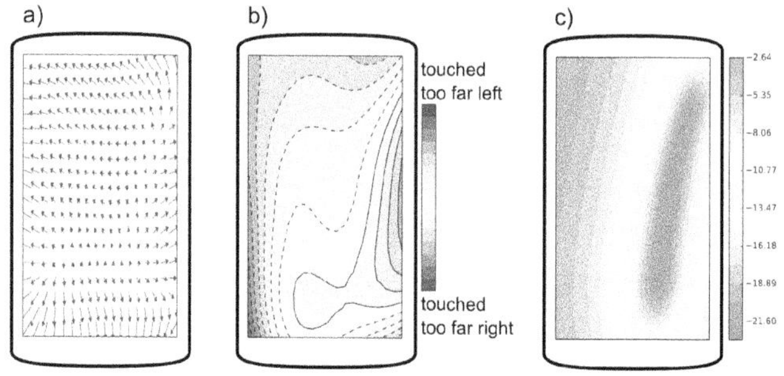

Figure 1. Three visualisations of Gaussian Process touch-to-target offset models: *a)* this arrow plot shows the model's 2D offset predictions across the screen, revealing the user's behavioural pattern for the right thumb when aiming at key-sized targets; *b)* the contour plot shows offset predictions for the same model in just one dimension (here: *x*) in colour; and *c)* shows the log-determinant of the predictive covariance of a model for full width targets, revealing the user's "arc of thumb reach".

These successful applications show the usefulness of modelling users' (individual) behaviour based on touch targeting data. In comparison to Fitts' Law, touch offset models ignore temporal information, but instead capture targeting error patterns across the screen. Hence, they provide an additional *spatial* perspective on user behaviour (Figure 1). However, this perspective is rarely explored, although the required touch and target locations are typically measured in most pointing experiments. In this paper, we present a toolkit which implements touch offset models to facilitate more widespread use in research and practical applications.

In particular, we contribute: 1) an introduction to touch offset models; 2) easy-to-use implementations and visualisations of these models for different use-cases (data analysis, practical deployment); and 3) example applications, including hand posture recognition, analysing more than 150.000 touches from a targeting experiment with 24 participants over two weeks. In contrast to previous studies addressing these models [4, 11, 13], we consider several target shapes and sizes, and also investigate the influence of different hand sizes.

TOUCH OFFSET MODELS
This section reviews touch offset models also employed in related work, introducing and describing linear [4] and non-linear [13] variants.

Touch Input
For the purpose of this paper and toolkit, we describe each touch $\mathbf{t}$ as a point on the plane, in other words as a two-dimensional vector, henceforth denoted as $\mathbf{t} = (x, y)^T \in \mathbb{R}^2$.

Linear Offset Models

A linear touch offset model with quadratic basis functions is described in related work [4]. Basis functions Φ transform the touch location $\mathbf{t}$ into a higher dimensional representation. With this trick, the linear model can account for non-linear relationships between touch and target locations across the screen, although it is still linear in its parameters. By default, the toolkit uses the same transformation Φ as the related work, namely $\Phi(\mathbf{t}) = (1, x, y, x^2, y^2)^T \in \mathbb{R}^5$.

Training

Training data consists of touches and corresponding target locations. Offsets are computed as the distances between touches and targets. The transformed touch locations $\Phi(\mathbf{t})$ of the N training examples are arranged as N rows in a design matrix $\mathbf{X} \in \mathbb{R}^{N\times 5}$. We then solve for the model's parameters $\mathbf{w}_x, \mathbf{w}_y$ with regularised linear regression:

$$\begin{aligned}\mathbf{w}_x &= (\mathbf{X}^T\mathbf{X} + \lambda\mathbf{I})^{-1}\mathbf{X}^T\mathbf{o}_x \\ \mathbf{w}_y &= (\mathbf{X}^T\mathbf{X} + \lambda\mathbf{I})^{-1}\mathbf{X}^T\mathbf{o}_y\end{aligned} \tag{1}$$

The vectors $\mathbf{o}_x$ and $\mathbf{o}_y$ contain the offsets along the x and y dimension of all training examples, respectively. $\lambda \in \mathbb{R}$ is the regularisation parameter. Regularisation helps to avoid overfitting (i.e. fitting noise in the training data).

Prediction

The weights $\mathbf{w}_x, \mathbf{w}_y$, together with the transformation Φ, define the linear touch offset model. For a new touch location $\mathbf{t}'$ the model predicts the offset μ:

$$\begin{aligned}\mu &= (\mu_x, \mu_y)^T \\ \mu_x &= \mathbf{w}_x^T\Phi(\mathbf{t}') \\ \mu_y &= \mathbf{w}_y^T\Phi(\mathbf{t}')\end{aligned} \tag{2}$$

Adding the predicted offset μ to the touch location $\mathbf{t}'$ yields a prediction for the true intended target location. Variances associated with these predictions are given by:

$$\begin{aligned}{\sigma'_x}^2 &= \hat{\sigma}_x^2\Phi(\mathbf{t}')^T(\mathbf{X}^T\mathbf{X} + \lambda\mathbf{I})^{-1}\Phi(\mathbf{t}') \\ \hat{\sigma}_x^2 &= \frac{1}{N}\sum_{i=1}^{N}(o_x^{(i)} - \mathbf{w}^T\Phi(\mathbf{t}_i))^2\end{aligned} \tag{3}$$

Analogously, ${\sigma'_y}^2$ and $\hat{\sigma}_y^2$ can be computed as well. In conclusion, the predicted information can define a bivariate Gaussian distribution $\mathcal{N}(\mathbf{t}' + \mu, \mathbf{\Sigma})$ with:

$$\mathbf{\Sigma} = \begin{bmatrix}{\sigma'_x}^2 & 0 \\ 0 & {\sigma'_y}^2\end{bmatrix} \tag{4}$$

Non-Linear Offset Models

A non-linear modelling approach using Gaussian Process (GP) regression [9] was described by Weir et al. [13]. In contrast to the linear model, GPs offer a more flexible, non-parametric approach. In general, GPs are defined by a mean function μ and a covariance function C. We choose these parameters in line with the related work [13]: μ is set to constant zero. This means that the model predicts zero offsets without data. For C, we combine linear and squared exponential covariance functions, a flexible choice:

$$C(\mathbf{t}_m, \mathbf{t}_n) = a\mathbf{t}_m^T\mathbf{t}_n + (1-a)\exp(-\gamma\|\mathbf{t}_m - \mathbf{t}_n\|_2^2) \tag{5}$$

The mixture of linear and non-linear parts is controlled by a, and γ defines the length-scale of the Gaussian.

Training

We combine the training offsets from both dimensions into one long vector $\mathbf{z}$ and stack up the covariance matrix $\mathbf{C}_{mn} = C(\mathbf{t}_m, \mathbf{t}_n)$ of the training examples accordingly [13]:

$$\begin{aligned}\mathbf{z} &= [o_x^{(1)}, o_x^{(2)}, ..., o_x^{(N)}, o_y^{(1)}, o_y^{(2)}, ..., o_y^{(N)}]^T \\ \hat{\mathbf{C}} &= \begin{bmatrix}\mathbf{C} & \alpha\mathbf{C} \\ \alpha\mathbf{C} & \mathbf{C}\end{bmatrix}\end{aligned} \tag{6}$$

Here, α defines the dependence between x and y. We store $\mathbf{z}$ and the matrix $\mathbf{M} = (\hat{\mathbf{C}} + \sigma^2\mathbf{I})^{-1}$. Assuming noise variance σ^2 helps to map almost identical touches to different offsets.

Prediction

For a new touch location $\mathbf{t}'$, we create the vector $\mathbf{c}$, which contains all covariances of the new touch and the training touches. We then build its stacked up version $\hat{\mathbf{c}}$:

$$\begin{aligned}\mathbf{c} &= [C(\mathbf{t}', \mathbf{t_1}), ..., C(\mathbf{t}', \mathbf{t_N})] \\ \hat{\mathbf{c}} &= \begin{bmatrix}\mathbf{c} & \alpha\mathbf{c} \\ \alpha\mathbf{c} & \mathbf{c}\end{bmatrix}\end{aligned} \tag{7}$$

The model's prediction is a bivariate Gaussian $\mathcal{N}(\mu, \mathbf{\Sigma})$ with:

$$\begin{aligned}\mu &= \hat{\mathbf{c}}\mathbf{M}\mathbf{z} \\ \mathbf{\Sigma} &= \begin{bmatrix}C(\mathbf{t}', \mathbf{t}') & \alpha C(\mathbf{t}', \mathbf{t}') \\ \alpha C(\mathbf{t}', \mathbf{t}') & C(\mathbf{t}', \mathbf{t}')\end{bmatrix} - \hat{\mathbf{c}}\mathbf{M}\hat{\mathbf{c}}^T\end{aligned} \tag{8}$$

Adding the predicted mean offset μ to the sensed touch location $\mathbf{t}'$ can improve touch location. Moreover, $\mathcal{N}(\mathbf{t}' + \mu, \mathbf{\Sigma})$ gives the full predictive distribution.

THE TOOLKIT

A full documentation is provided with the toolkit. Here, we introduce its use in Python. The API style is inspired by the *scikit-learn* machine learning library [8], due to its ease-of-use. For efficiency, we use optimised *numpy* arrays [10].

Data Input

The toolkit uses a simple data format: N touches are given in a $N \times 4$ matrix, with columns *touch x, touch y, target x, target y*. This data could be loaded from a file or database, or collected and stored during runtime in an array. For example, we can load data from a csv-file with these four columns:

```
data = loadData("pointingStudy.csv")
```

As a result, *data* is a $N \times 4$ array containing the provided touch and target locations.

Creating and Applying Models

As a minimal example, creating and training offset models with default or custom hyperparameters could look like this:

```
model = LinearOffsetModel()
model.fit(data)

model2 = GPOffsetModel(gamma=2, noiseVar=0.001,
                       diag=0.9, kernelMix=0.1)
model2.fit(data)
```

After training, offset predictions for given touch locations can be computed as follows:

```
means, covs = model.predict(newTouches)
```

Here, *newTouches* is a $N \times 2$ array containing (new) touch locations. As a result, *means* is a $N \times 2$ array with the predicted offsets for these given touches (see μ in Equations 2 and 8). Complementary, *covs* is a list of N covariance matrices of shape 2×2 (see Σ in Equations 4 and 8).

These predictions can be used, for example, to correct the new touch locations and thus improve touch accuracy. As explained in the previous section, correction is performed by simply adding the predicted offsets to the touch locations:

```
correctedTouches = newTouches + means
```

Visualisation

The Python library also provides several visualisations to explore collected user data and plot the derived models. Figure 1 shows three examples for touch behaviour on a smartphone, visualising offset predictions and variances with arrows and contours. Plots can be created as follows:

```
arrowPlot(model)
contourPlot(model, dim="x")
variancePlot(model)
```

Implementation Aspects

We describe some aspects of our implementation to highlight the benefits of using the toolkit compared to other options:

Optimisation: Computing many predictions is important for data analysis tasks. For instance, consider ten-fold cross-validation to evaluate improving touch accuracy (e.g. Figure 2). On our dataset, such an analysis takes 109s with an implementation of the GP "textbook formulas" - but 18s with the toolkit (measured on i7/2.8Ghz PC, 8GB RAM), achieved by rearranging computations to better utilise matrix routines [10].

Specialisation: Our GP implementation also respects possible dependencies between x and y locations, following related work [13]. Less specialised libraries may not provide these models at all, or they do not implement this special GP variant (e.g. [8]) employed for touch modelling [13]. Moreover, our toolkit's visualisations allow for fast exploration and assessment of the models and the captured behavioural patterns.

Mobile applications: Besides Python, the toolkit provides models in Java/Android and JavaScript, respecting some platform limitations. For example, the models can be used to improve touch accuracy in apps and on websites. Detailed descriptions and examples are provided with the toolkit.

EXPERIMENT AND EXAMPLE APPLICATIONS

As examples for using the toolkit, this section presents three applications to data collected in a targeting experiment.

Dataset

We collected a dataset with over 150.000 touches from 24 participants in a targeting experiment on a Nexus 5 phone. Each participant completed 8 tasks (2 hand postures $\times$ 4 target types). Each task showed 400 targets distributed equally across the screen, displayed one at a time in random order.

The two hand postures were: 1) *thumb*, holding the phone in the right hand, touching with the right thumb; and 2) *index finger*, holding it in the left hand, touching with the right index finger. The phone was always held in portrait orientation. The four target types were (see Figure 2): *crosshair*, *key-sized* (4×7mm), *app-sized* (9×9mm), and *full width* (height 9mm). Task order was varied between participants with a 8×8 latin-square design. Each participant repeated all tasks in a second session one week later.

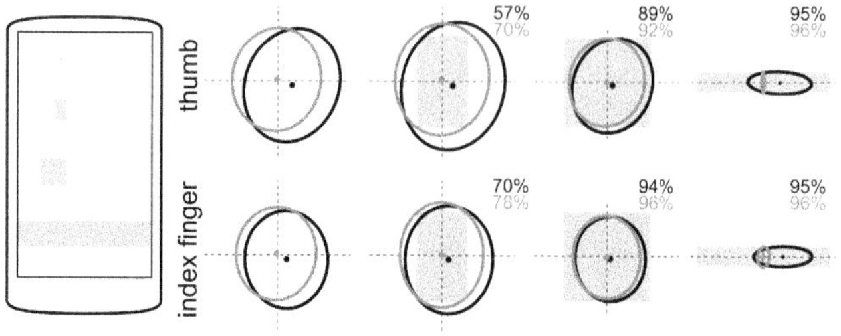

Figure 2. Targets used in the study, shown to scale (left). The plots to the right summarise the distributions of touches from our dataset around these targets for raw touches (black) and touches corrected with offset models (green). The models shifted touches towards the target centres, resulting in a higher overlap of touch distributions and target bounding boxes. Hence, users can hit their intended targets more reliably with offset model corrections (hit rates annotated for targets with an area).

In this note, we focus on three analyses of this dataset to show different uses of offset modelling: 1) improving accuracy, 2) analysing the influence of hand size on targeting behaviour, and 3) predicting hand postures.

Improving Touch Accuracy

In this first application, we address improving touch accuracy by correcting touch locations with the models' predictions. We trained linear offset models on the data from the first session of each user, and then applied these models to correct the touches of each user collected in the second session.

Figure 2 summarises the results, showing distributions of raw and corrected touches around the different targets for both hand postures. Offset models correct touches towards the target centres, improving hit rates.

Analysing the Influence of Hand Size

In our experiment, we also measured participants' hand sizes, using images captured by placing their hands on a scanner. In particular, we measured the distance from the tip of the index finger to the bottom of the palm (Lunate bone). In this way, we obtained hand sizes between 159mm and 194mm.

In this analysis, we are interested in the influence of hand sizes on targeting patterns. In particular, we expect larger y-offsets near the top (left) of the screen with thumb input, since this region is harder to reach on a larger device such as ours (137.8mm $\times$ 69.1mm). Sorting participants by hand size revealed three groups. We focus on the two extremes: small-handed users (N=4, range 159mm to 171mm) and large-handed ones (N=7, range 186mm to 194mm). Using our toolkit, we trained GP models on each groups' thumb touches aiming at *crosshair*, *key-sized*, and *app-sized* targets.

Figure 3 visualises the differences in the lengths of the models' predicted y-offsets: Users with small hands indeed showed longer y-offsets in the upper left corner, but are more

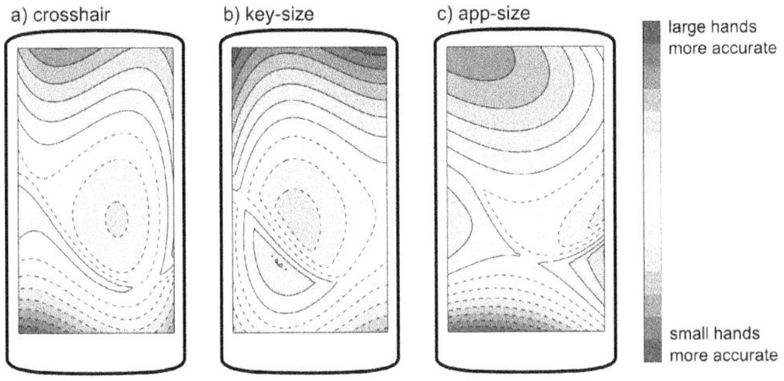

Figure 3. Differences in lengths of the predicted y-offsets of two GP models (for thumb targeting), one representing small-handed users, the other large-handed ones. These plots show that larger hands result in targeting patterns with shorter y-offsets near the top of the screen. In contrast, smaller hands are more accurate near the bottom and centre.

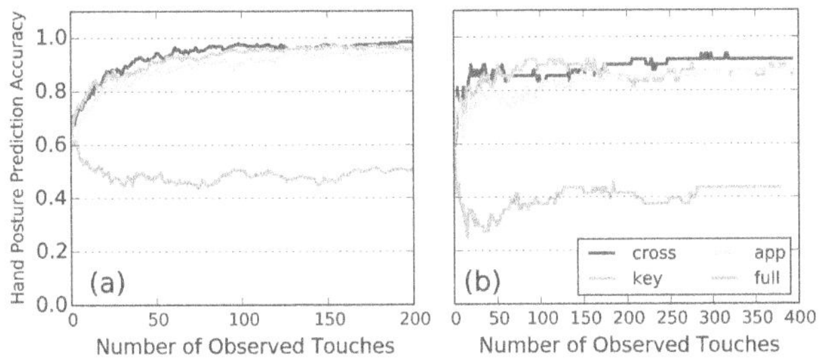

Figure 4. Hand posture prediction accuracy. We deployed offset models to predict hand postures (thumb vs index finger). Our approach achieved 94-98% accuracy within one session *(a)* and 87-92% across sessions *(b)*, for three of four target types. Prediction was not feasible for *full width* targets, indicating little posture-specific information in offset patterns for this target type.

accurate near the bottom of the screen. We also found interesting regions to the bottom left of the centre, where users with large hands were more accurate along the y-dimension. This may indicate an area of comfortable bend for larger thumbs. A future study could investigate this further, for example by filming participants' hands during interaction.

Predicting Hand Postures

We implemented a hand posture recogniser to predict the currently used hand posture after each touch. The general approach follows related work [4], but uses non-linear GP models from our toolkit, joint distributions to accumulate evidence over time, and different target types. Intuitively, we match observed offsets with predictions from one model per posture to decide for the posture whose model provides the best explanation for the observed targeting behaviour.

We evaluated this approach for two cases: *within sessions* - training (testing) models with the first (second) half of the data from one study session; and *across sessions* - training models on data from one session and testing them with touches from the second session collected one week later.

Figure 4 shows that our system predicts the correct hand posture with high accuracy (within: 94-98%, across: 87-92%). It reached >80% after 25-100 touches. These accuracies are comparable to the results from related work on typing posture detection [14]. Predictions were not successful for *full width* targets, which indicates that the corresponding offset patterns were less posture-specific than for the other targets.

DISCUSSION

We discuss the models regarding generalisation and usage scenarios, along with consequences of incorrect predictions:

Generalisation: "In the wild", behaviour will vary more (e.g. different grip, devices, walking), leading to less precise predictions, if the model is not trained on such data. However, related work has shown that offset patterns to some extent transfer across users and devices [4], and that models can improve accuracy even when trained across many users/devices with data collected in a large "in the wild" study [6].

Model robustness: From related work [4, 6], and the investigations of this paper, we find that simpler models seem practically more robust. On the other hand, complex non-linear models can more accurately capture details of behaviour in stable conditions. This can be preferable, for example, when studying behaviour observed in a controlled lab experiment.

Prediction errors: If predictions are not accurate, the touch location might not be shifted directly towards the target. How serious this case is depends on the application. While improving touch accuracy obviously requires accurate predictions, a few imprecise predictions may be acceptable if we can integrate over many touches (e.g. for hand posture detection).

Usage scenarios: Besides the applications shown here, models could help to distinguish users based on touch behaviour for continuous implicit authentication. They could also inform GUI layouts - place important target elements in the user's "comfort zone" of highest touch accuracy. The layout could be dynamically tailored to the individual user and context, as captured by a continuously updated offset model.

CONCLUSIONS AND FUTURE WORK

Targeting experiments help researchers to evaluate and compare different interaction techniques or devices. We have presented a toolkit and example applications for touch offset modelling. These models capture targeting error patterns across the screen, providing a different spatial perspective on user behaviour, which cannot be assessed with more common evaluations, such as Fitts' Law. We have applied the toolkit on a large targeting dataset to improve touch accuracy, to analyse the influence of hand size on targeting patterns, and to predict hand postures. We hope that the presented toolkit facilitates more widespread use of spatial touch modelling.

To the best of our knowledge, we are the first to relate touch offset models to measured hand sizes. Future work could investigate this further, for example to predict the user's hand size from touch offsets, possibly combining it with models for thumb reach from related work [2]. Predicting postures is feasible, as shown in this paper for different target types. We aim to deploy and evaluate the hand posture recogniser in a typical mobile interface, such as a homescreen or keyboard.

Although we have presented the toolkit with touch interactions in mind, it may also be applied to other input methods in which users aim at targets on a two-dimensional surface (e.g. mouse cursor, stylus interaction).

PROJECT RESOURCES

The toolkit, documentation, and study data are available at:
`http://www.medien.ifi.lmu.de/touchml/`

REFERENCES

1. Baldwin, T., and Chai, J. Towards Online Adaptation and Personalization of Key-Target Resizing for Mobile Devices. In *Proceedings of the 17th International Conference on Intelligent User Interfaces* (2012), 11–20.
2. Bergstrom-Lehtovirta, J., and Oulasvirta, A. Modeling the Functional Area of the Thumb on Mobile Touchscreen Surfaces. In *Proceedings of the SIGCHI Conference on Human Factors in Computing Systems* (2014), 1991–2000.
3. Bi, X., Li, Y., and Zhai, S. FFitts Law: Modeling Finger Touch with Fitts' Law. In *Proceedings of the SIGCHI Conference on Human Factors in Computing Systems* (2013), 1363–1372.
4. Buschek, D., Rogers, S., and Murray-Smith, R. User-Specific Touch Models in a Cross-Device Context. In *Proceedings of the 15th International Conference on Human-Computer Interaction with Mobile Devices and Services* (2013), 382–391.
5. Fitts, P. M. The Information Capacity of the Human Motor System in Controlling the Amplitude of Movement. *Journal of Experimental Psychology 47*, 6 (1954), 381–391.
6. Henze, N., Rukzio, E., and Boll, S. 100,000,000 Taps: Analysis and Improvement of Touch Performance in the Large. In *Proceedings of the 13th International Conference on Human Computer Interaction with Mobile Devices and Services* (2011), 133–142.
7. Mock, P., Edelmann, J., Schilling, A., and Rosenstiel, W. User Identification Using Raw Sensor Data From Typing on Interactive Displays. In *Proceedings of the 19th International Conference on Intelligent User Interfaces* (2014), 67–72.
8. Pedregosa, F., Varoquaux, G., Gramfort, A., Michel, V., Thirion, B., Grisel, O., Blondel, M., Prettenhofer, P., Weiss, R., Dubourg, V., Vanderplas, J., Passos, A., Cournapeau, D., Brucher, M., Perrot, M., and Duchesnay, E. Scikit-learn: Machine Learning in Python. *J. Mach. Learn. Res. 12* (Nov. 2011), 2825–2830.
9. Rasmussen, C. E., and Williams, C. K. I. *Gaussian Processes for Machine Learning*. The MIT Press, 2006.
10. van der Walt, S., Colbert, S., and Varoquaux, G. The NumPy Array: A Structure for Efficient Numerical Computation. *Computing in Science Engineering 13*, 2 (March 2011), 22–30.
11. Weir, D., Buschek, D., and Rogers, S. Sparse Selection of Training Data for Touch Correction Systems. In *Proceedings of the 15th International Conference on Human-Computer Interaction with Mobile Devices and Services* (2013), 404–407.
12. Weir, D., Pohl, H., Rogers, S., Vertanen, K., and Kristensson, P. Uncertain Text Entry on Mobile Devices. In *Proceedings of the SIGCHI Conference on Human Factors in Computing Systems* (2014), 2307–2316.
13. Weir, D., Rogers, S., Murray-Smith, R., and Löchtefeld, M. A User-Specific Machine Learning Approach for Improving Touch Accuracy on Mobile Devices. In *Proceedings of the 25th annual Symposium on User Interface Software and Technology* (2012), 465–476.
14. Yin, Y., Ouyang, T. Y., Partridge, K., and Zhai, S. Making Touchscreen Keyboards Adaptive to Keys, Hand Postures, and Individuals - A Hierarchical Spatial Backoff Model Approach. In *Proceedings of the SIGCHI Conference on Human Factors in Computing Systems* (2013), 2775–2784.

From One to Many Users and Contexts: A Classifier for Hand and Arm Gestures

David Costa
Universidade de Lisboa
Lisboa, Portugal
dcosta@lasige.di.fc.ul.pt

Carlos Duarte
Universidade de Lisboa
Lisboa, Portugal
caduarte@fc.ul.pt

ABSTRACT
On-body interaction techniques are gaining traction, and opening up new avenues to control interactive systems. At the same time, they reveal potential to increase the accessibility of systems like touch based smartphones and other mobile devices for visually impaired users. However, for this potential to be realised, it is paramount that these techniques can be used in a multitude of contextual settings, and, ideally, do not impose training and calibration procedures. Our approach intends to optimize signal filtering, feature extraction parameters and classifier configurations for each defined gesture. The results show a 98.35% accuracy for the optimized classifier. We proceeded to conduct a validation study (15 participants) in three contexts: seated, standing and walking. Our findings show that, despite the gesture being trained by someone not participating in the study, the average accuracy was 94.67%. We also concluded that, while walking, false positives can impact its usefulness.

Author Keywords
Gesture recognition; surface electromyography; hand and arm gestures; machine learning; user studies.

ACM Classification Keywords
H5.2. Information interfaces and presentation: Input devices and strategies (e.g., mouse, touchscreen).

INTRODUCTION
Input interaction on mobile devices has been traditionally limited to touch and gestures made directly on the touchscreen or a physical keyboard. While this is not an issue for most people, those that have visual or motor impairments, suffer from limited interaction possibilities with these devices. Recent technological advances and research projects in input sensing have opened up new possibilities for using our body as an interaction platform. These solutions may directly use the skin and body as a means of interaction [10, 16, 23] or understand inputs from arm and forearm gestures: WristFlex [8] makes use of pressure sensors to detect pulse gestures; the Intimate Communication Armband developed by Constanza et al. [6] use surface electromyography (sEMG) signals to capture subtle gestures. However, one aspect that has been neglected so far is how it can improve accessibility.

Our aim is to understand how skin and gesture interaction enabling technologies could improve the accessibility of mobile interfaces for users with different levels of visual impairments. The requirements for such a solution comprise technical and social dimensions. For the latter, the solution must be socially acceptable [28] (e.g. no bulky devices that place the user in awkward situations). For the former, the solution should work equally well in different operating contexts (e.g. sitting, standing or walking) and do not require its user to execute complex training procedures. One possible answer is an sEMG based gesture recognizer. The main benefit of relying on a sEMG solution is that, by being based on muscle activation sensing, it requires a single limb. This means users always have a free limb to do other tasks (this might mean a free hand to hold the cane or a mobile phone). Furthermore, both hands can be free, since muscle activation is not dependent on hand or finger gestures. It is also a vision free activity. Moreover, it does not prevent sensing more fine grained activities, like pinching movements as presented in [26].

sEMG technology, similarly to other solutions, implies several variables that must be taken into account, such as what filters to apply to the raw signal, what sampling window size and overlap, and features to be extracted. The quality of gestural recognition also depends on the classifiers used. All these variables affect the reliability and robustness of gesture recognition. By optimizing their configuration we obtain the best classifier accuracy and therefore improve recognition rates. Through a brute-force approach, over five hundred thousand configurations were tested in training six different classifiers. The result is the configuration with highest accuracy for each classifier, which enables us to have a per-gesture classifier feeding of the sEMG stream. For a wrist bend gesture, we obtained a classifier with an accuracy of 98.35% on a ten-fold cross validation of the data. On a user study, this classifier performed reliably across different users and achieved an accuracy of 94.67%.

In the remainder of the paper we review projects using sEMG technology to recognize arm and forearm gestures. This is followed by a description of our methodology and prototype. To validate the prototype, user trials were held and are

IUI'15, March 29 – April 01 2015, Atlanta, GA, USA

http://dx.doi.org/10.1145/2678025.2701388

described in the Validation Study section. The last section presents the conclusions and the planned future work.

RELATED WORK

Mobile devices' small size and the lack of tactile feedback of touch devices, limits the interaction space which raises accessibility issues especially for visually impaired users. Possibilities to overcome these limitations include: using the surface as a gestural finger input canvas [9]; voice input [17], widely used by visually impaired, but with limited usefulness due to acoustically unpredictable environments, and privacy issues on public spaces; wearable computing [15, 22]. Bio-sensing devices capturing biological signals for input have also been explored, including: heart rate measured by electrocardiographic signals (ECG) [21], galvanic skin response [20], brain activity through electroencephalographic signals (EEG) [18, 1] and eye tracking [12]. More recent approaches are Skinput [10] and PUB [16], which use bio-acoustics and ultrasonic signals respectively, to locate finger taps on body. However, some of these signals are subconsciously driven or involuntary and therefore cannot be controlled with precision and accuracy, while others require high levels of focus and training.

Recognition of gestures using sEMG sensors

Sensing muscle activation [25] also suffers from the aforementioned problems. As Phinyomark et al. state, *Electromyography (EMG) signals have the properties of nonstationary, nonlinear, complexity, and large variation* [24]. However, despite the difficulty in analyzing such signals, sEMG technology has the advantages of being relatively inexpensive and non-intrusive as it makes use of surface electrodes placed on the skin to capture the electrical voltage activity of skeletal muscles. Muscle Computer Interaction (MCI) is already used in a variety of areas from entertainment, industry, to medicine. Examples range from controlling limb prostheses [11], robots [3], diagnosing muscle and nerve diseases [30] to playing games [32]. Our contribution is similar to what Kratzet al. [14] did with accelerometers and gyroscopes, in order to remove the necessity of per-user training of the recognizer, a limitation seen in other works such as [26, 27, 4]. Simultaneously, we achieve better accuracy levels using less hardware. Moreover, we assessed the classifier's performance in three different contexts.

Pattern and Features Extraction

To recognize gestures from sEMG signals there are two important steps: 1) capturing the signal's features; 2) using classifiers to find patterns or using statistical criterion [31]. Phinyomark et al. [24] studied a set of 19 different features. Based on Euclidian distance and standard deviation they concluded that the combined Root Mean Square (RMS), Willinson Amplitude (WAMP) and Waveform length (WL) features are a good set for gestural classification. In their approach, Kim et al. [13] used a different set of features: statistical data such as maximum, minimum and variance values, combined with fundamental frequency ($F0$) and Fourier Variance of the spectrum, and also gestural particular features such as zero-crosses. In their study, Saponas et al. [25] used RMS, Phase Coherence and Frequency Energy features.

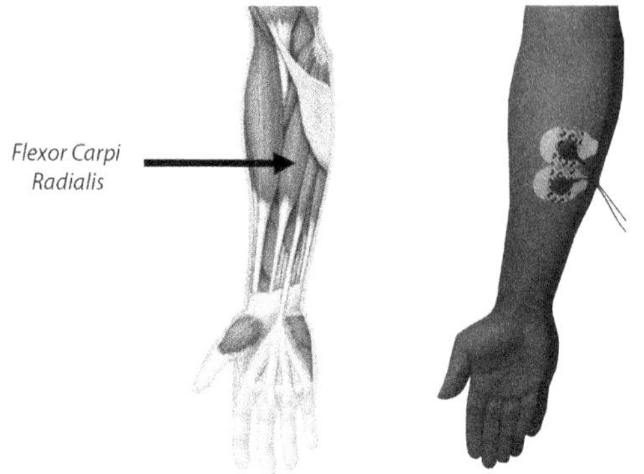

Figure 1. Forearm muscles and sEMG electrodes placement.

Classifiers

Classifiers are an approach used to find patterns and classify, in this particular case, gestures based on the features collected from the signal waveform. The results and performance of these classifiers depend greatly on the characteristics of the data to be classified. There are several types of classifiers: linear (e.g. Naive Bayes), tree based (e.g. Random Tree, Random Forest), rule based (e.g. Decision Table, M5 Rules), function based (e.g. MLP, SVM) amongst others.

Kim et al. [13] uses two simple yet fast classifiers combined in a decision level tree: the K-Nearest Neighbor (K-NN) and the Bayes classifier. Saponas et al. [25] decided for a Support Vector Machine (SVM) algorithm stating that it has a good performance as well. These are examples of supervised classifiers, similar to what we employ in our approach.

BUILDING A sEMG BASED GESTURE RECOGNIZER

Our goal is to build a system that encompasses subtle and non-intrusive technology that allows on-body interaction on mobile contexts. We opted to use sEMG sensors to accomplish these objectives. To enable subtle gestures, sensor's electrodes are placed on the arm's Wrist Flexors Muscle, more specifically on the Flexor Carpi Radialis muscle (Figure 1). This setup gathers signals resulting from forearm and hand gestures with minimal hardware usage as only one sensor is needed. In this section we detail our approach for the development of the sEMG based gesture recognizer.

EMG Hardware

We have used a *Shimmer2r* EMG mounted with a MSP 430 microcontroller (8mHz, 16Bit), with a frequency range of 5Hz to 322Hz and a maximum signal range of 4.4mV. Three electrodes (positive, negative and ground) are used to capture the sEMG data. Communication with the mobile device where the classification takes place is made through Bluetooth-RN42, with maximum range of 10m.

EMG data filtering

The sEMG signal is often contaminated with various noise components which misleads the interpretation of the muscle's activity. To increase the signal's quality, the solution is to eliminate the maximum noise possible without affecting too much the frequency of the muscle's activity signal. This means applying filters in the low and high end frequencies of the signal. An analysis by De Luca et al. [7] established that a Butterworth filter with a corner frequency of 20Hz is recommended for a general use of sEMG signals in order to eliminate the noise artifacts. Although consistent with some works, values differ in several other studies. Merletti [19] suggests a High-pass corner frequency cut of 5Hz while Winter et al. [29] refers 10Hz as the ideal value. As there is not a consensus for these parameters, we opted to test several filters (High-pass, Low-pass, Band-stop) and frequency cut values (1Hz-5Hz and 20Hz for HP, 6Hz for LP and 49-52Hz and 59-62Hz for BS).

Extracting data features

The sEMG features used in our approach were based on the Phinyomark et al. [24] study. Therefore we used the following features: WL (Equation 1), RMS (Equation 2) and WAMP (Equation 3). As the authors state, WAMP registers the number of times the signal's amplitude change surpasses a predefined threshold, which is used to reduce background noise. The suitable value for the threshold is between 10 and 100mV so we decided also to test the suggested range of values for the threshold with increments of 1mV.

$$WL = \sum_{i=1}^{N-1} |x_{i+1} - x_i| \tag{1}$$

$$RMS = \sqrt{(1/N) \sum_{i=1}^{N} x_i^2} \tag{2}$$

$$WAMP = \sum_{i=1}^{N-1} f\left(|x_i - x_{i+1}|\right)$$
$$f(x) = \begin{cases} 1, & if x \geq threshold \\ 0, & otherwise \end{cases} \tag{3}$$

The sample frequency was set to 512Hz. The sampling window size (from 400 to 1200 samples, increments of 100) and overlap (from 25% to 95%, increments of 1%) were also tested in order to obtain the optimized values.

Classifiers' training process

We opted to train several supervised classifiers. Besides Bayes based algorithms and SVM classifiers referenced in other projects, we decided to analyze others, not necessarily faster but possibly more accurate. Therefore we considered a total of six classifiers: 1) Naive Bayes; 2) Bayes Net; 3) SVM; 4) J48; 5) Random Tree; and 6) Random Forest. The classifiers were trained using Weka, a data mining toolkit, API version 3.6 [5]. Accuracy was computed using 10-fold cross-validation.

To train the classifiers, we recruited an healthy male subject of 26 years, with 171cm height and 65Kgs of weight. We asked the subject to perform 60 repetitions of wrist flexion intercalated with 60 pauses while in a sitting position. These two muscle movements (flexion and relaxation) were classified by a human supervisor while observing the subject. The mobile application used to record the gestures automatically saved the sEMG raw data and its classification to a file.

Optimized configuration

Classifiers were trained on a desktop computer, due to the performance requirements of the followed brute force approach. The following steps were applied: 1) The collected data is processed with one of the possible filters and cut-off frequencies. 2) Data is sampled with one possible combination of window size and overlap. 3) Features for each sampled window are computed. 4) Features are converted from numeric to nominal, through a 10 interval unsupervised attribute discretization filter. 5) The accuracy computed over a 10-fold cross-validation, together with the parameter values of the tested configuration are recorded. The process was repeated for every combination of parameter values.

In total 517,563 combinations were used for training. The best configuration achieved the following accuracy: 91.74% for Naive Bayes, 94.21% for Bayes Net and 98.35% for the other four classifiers. This configuration corresponds to a second order Butterworth filter with High-pass corner frequency of 20Hz, with a sampling window size of 1000 samples and 30% overlap, with the WAMP threshold set to 23mV.

VALIDATION STUDY

We conducted a user study to assess if the trained classifier: 1) shows a practical accuracy of the same order of the theoretical one; 2) generalizes to other users; and 3) generalizes to other contexts (standing and walking). Given that our configuration produced four classifiers with the same accuracy, we selected one from that group to use in the study: Random Forest.

Setup and procedure

The hardware used in this study was the Shimmer2r sensor and a Samsung Galaxy SII smartphone. An Android application was installed in the smartphone to receive the data stream from the sensor, apply the elicited configuration and classify the signal.

In order to validate our sEMG recognition prototype, we recruited 15 individuals and interviewed them on age and body characteristics. Each participant was instructed on the gesture to perform (flexion of the wrist) and was able to freely try the recognizer to get acquainted with its operation. Afterwards, participants had to perform 3 tasks, in a randomly assigned order. In each task the participant was asked to execute 15 repetitions of the gesture. The tasks differ by the participant's position: 1) sitting; 2) standing-up still; and 3) walking.

Participants

The participant group was composed of 8 males and 7 females, with ages ranging from 23 to 57 years old (average 30). Height ranged from 152cm to 195cm (average 169.5cm). Average weight was 71.2Kg and ranged from 48Kg to 97Kg. All participants were able to perform the gesture without difficulties. No participant had severe visual impairments. Albeit accessibility is the main concern of this work, in this study we wanted to demonstrate that the trained classifier can be generalized among users and usage contexts, without specific accessibility design concerns.

Data analysis

Across the total of 675 collected gestures, the average accuracy of the recognizer was 94.67% ($Min = 82.22\%, Max = 97.78\%, SD = 5\%$). We also registered 107 false positives, where we considered false positives the occasions when the classifier identified a wrist flexion when the participant was relaxing the wrist, or when after a true positive the classifier did not change classification to a relaxed state.

The classifier's accuracy for each of the 3 tasks was as follows: sitting ($M_1 = 95.11\%, SD = 6.41\%$), standing ($M_2 = 91.56\%, SD = 11.94\%$) and walking ($M_3 = 97.33\%, SD = 4.21\%$). In order to check for any significant differences between them, we began by assessing the normality of the data. The results for all tasks showed that the normality was not verified ($p_1 = 0.002; p_2 = 0.001; p_3 = 0.001$). Following this, we conducted a non-parametric Friedman test between the tasks which revealed that there was not a statistically significant difference in accuracy depending on user's position ($X^2(2) = 2.227, p = 0.328$).

Given that the classifier was trained with data from a male, and Arjunan et al. [2] states there are differences in sEMG signals originating from males or females, we wanted to analyze if the participant's gender had any effect on the accuracy ($M_{male} = 94.29\%, SD = 3.6\%; M_{fem} = 95\%, SD = 6.26\%$). Similarly to the previous results the data was not normal ($p_{male} = 0.019; p_{fem} = 0.011$), thus we conducted a non-parametric Mann-Whitney test. The results show that there is no statistically significant difference between genders ($U = 19.5, p = 0.316$).

Finally, we analyze the occurrence of false positives during each task per person ($M_1 = 0.47, SD = 1.13; M_2 = 1.4, S = 1.92; M_3 = 5.27, SD = 3.93$). Given the non-normality of the data ($p_1 < 0.001; p_2 = 0.001; p_3 = 0.209$), we used the non-parametric Friedman test and found a statistically significant difference between false positives detected in different positions ($X^2(2) = 15.362, p < 0.001$). We proceeded with a Post-Hoc test in order to analyze the different combinations. A Wilcoxon test revealed that the false positives detected on task 3 (walking) in comparison with task 2 (standing) and 1 (sitting) were significantly higher ($Z_{3-2} = -2.906, p_{3-2} = 0.004; Z_{3-1} = -3.066, p_{3-1} = 0.002$). On the other hand, there was no significant difference between tasks 1 and 2 ($Z_{2-1} = -1.691, p_{2-1} = 0.091$).

The same analysis was done comparing gender ($M_{male} = 5.13, SD = 4.32; M_{fem} = 9.43, SD = 4.76$). The data was shown to be normalized ($p_{male} = 0.484; p_{fem} = 0.437$), therefore an unpaired t test was conducted. This study found that the gender does not affect significantly the number of false positives ($t(13) = -1.836, p = 0.089$).

Discussion

Regarding the overall performance of this recognizer, results show that its accuracy on a practical setting is in the same order of the theoretical results, albeit not as good as could be expected. Furthermore, results show that, even though the classifier was trained by someone not participating in the study, it performed accurately when used by the participants in the validation study. This indicates that an sEMG based gesture classifier is capable of generalizing among users, which can be very important for users with impairments.

Moreover, despite the classifier being trained with data collected only in a sitting position, results show that accuracy rates are not affected by the different positions assessed. This is another indication that sEMG based classifiers have the ability to generalize to different contexts of use, which is very relevant for the envisioned mobile usage scenarios.

However, false positives are still a concern. We found that, while walking, the classifier was more prone to recognize a gesture even though the participant was just naturally moving the arm to walk. This happened, on average, more than five times per user during the walking task. We observed that the large majority of these false positives happened right after the participant performed a gesture, with the recognizer not transitioning from the flexion state back to the relaxed state. To trigger this transition we had to ask the participants to briefly stop walking. Only a residual (less than 1%) part of the false positives occurred with the participant's wrist relaxed and the classifier recognizing the execution of a gesture.

CONCLUSION

In this paper we addressed the issue of using minimal technological apparatus, in order to foster social acceptance, for subtle hand and arm gesture recognition. The availability of recognition technology that does not require the use of vision for input, and that is capable to address the requirements for social acceptance (by avoiding the use of speech in public places, the need to perform unsubtle movements, or even having to reach for or hold a device, for example) is bound to increase the accessibility in diverse contexts of use for every person, and in particular for the visually-impaired. In its current state this system is capable of addressing simple scenarios, like being used to subtly and in an easy way turn down a call or accept it.

Furthermore, our approach proves, for a gesture with characteristics similar to what was used, that a classifier can be trained with one person and be used by several other persons without affecting accuracy significantly. Moreover, we could verify that even though training was performed in the seated position, the recognizer worked both in standing and walking contexts.

In the future we plan to address some limitations of this solution and study. We will train classifiers and conduct user studies with more gestures comprising finger, wrist and arm movements. We will focus on measures to avoid false positives to increase the efficacy of the recognizer in all contexts. And even though the sEMG based solution can be fairly easily deployed (e.g. embedding the sensors in an armband), we wish to explore other technical possibilities that are becoming increasingly available, like wearables (e.g. smartwatches or fitness wrist bands). This implies working with different signals (e.g. accelerometer), and looking for other features, in order to evaluate if the proposed approach still holds.

REFERENCES

1. Alba, E. L., Zapirain, B. G., and Zorrilla, A. M. Tennis computer game with brain control using EEG signals. In *16th International Conference on Computer Games, CGAMES 2011, Louisville, KY, USA, 27-30 July, 2011* (2011), 228–234.
2. Arjunan, S., Kumar, D., Kalra, C., Burne, J., and Bastos, T. Effect of age and gender on the surface electromyogram during various levels of isometric contraction. In *Engineering in Medicine and Biology Society,EMBC, 2011 Annual International Conference of the IEEE* (Aug 2011), 3853–3856.
3. Artemiadis, P., and Kyriakopoulos, K. Emg-based control of a robot arm using low-dimensional embeddings. *Robotics, IEEE Transactions on 26*, 2 (April 2010), 393–398.
4. Benko, H., Saponas, T. S., Morris, D., and Tan, D. Enhancing input on and above the interactive surface with muscle sensing. In *Proceedings of the ACM International Conference on Interactive Tabletops and Surfaces*, ITS '09, ACM (New York, NY, USA, 2009), 93–100.
5. Bouckaert, R. R., Frank, E., Hall, M. A., Holmes, G., Pfahringer, B., Reutemann, P., and Witten, I. H. Weka—experiences with a java open-source project. *J. Mach. Learn. Res. 11* (Dec. 2010), 2533–2541.
6. Costanza, E., Inverso, S. A., Allen, R., and Maes, P. Intimate interfaces in action: Assessing the usability and subtlety of emg-based motionless gestures. In *Proceedings of the SIGCHI Conference on Human Factors in Computing Systems*, CHI '07, ACM (New York, NY, USA, 2007), 819–828.
7. De Luca, C. J., Donald Gilmore, L., Kuznetsov, M., and Roy, S. H. Filtering the surface EMG signal: Movement artifact and baseline noise contamination. *Journal of Biomechanics* (Mar. 2010).
8. Dementyev, A., and Paradiso, J. A. Wristflex: Low-power gesture input with wrist-worn pressure sensors. In *Proceedings of the 27th Annual ACM Symposium on User Interface Software and Technology*, UIST '14, ACM (New York, NY, USA, 2014), 161–166.
9. Harrison, C., and Hudson, S. E. Scratch input: Creating large, inexpensive, unpowered and mobile finger input surfaces. In *Proceedings of the 21st Annual ACM Symposium on User Interface Software and Technology*, UIST '08, ACM (New York, NY, USA, 2008), 205–208.
10. Harrison, C., Tan, D., and Morris, D. Skinput: Appropriating the body as an input surface. In *Proceedings of the SIGCHI Conference on Human Factors in Computing Systems*, CHI '10, ACM (New York, NY, USA, 2010), 453–462.
11. He, J., Zhang, D., and Zhu, X. Adaptive pattern recognition of myoelectric signal towards practical multifunctional prosthesis control. In *Intelligent Robotics and Applications*, C.-Y. Su, S. Rakheja, and H. Liu, Eds., vol. 7506 of *Lecture Notes in Computer Science*. Springer Berlin Heidelberg, 2012, 518–525.
12. Kao, C., Yang, C., Fan, K., Hwang, B., and Huang, C. An adaptive eye gaze tracker system in the integrated cloud computing and mobile device. In *International Conference on Machine Learning and Cybernetics, ICMLC 2011, Guilin, China, July 10-13, 2011, Proceedings* (2011), 367–371.
13. Kim, J., Mastnik, S., and André, E. Emg-based hand gesture recognition for realtime biosignal interfacing. In *Proceedings of the 13th International Conference on Intelligent User Interfaces*, IUI '08, ACM (New York, NY, USA, 2008), 30–39.
14. Kratz, L., Morris, D., and Saponas, T. S. Making gestural input from arm-worn inertial sensors more practical. In *Proceedings of the SIGCHI Conference on Human Factors in Computing Systems*, CHI '12, ACM (New York, NY, USA, 2012), 1747–1750.
15. Lawo, M., Herzog, O., and Witt, H. An industrial case study on wearable computing applications. In *Proceedings of the 9th International Conference on Human Computer Interaction with Mobile Devices and Services*, MobileHCI '07, ACM (New York, NY, USA, 2007), 448–451.
16. Lin, S.-Y., Su, C.-H., Cheng, K.-Y., Liang, R.-H., Kuo, T.-H., and Chen, B.-Y. Pub - point upon body: Exploring eyes-free interaction and methods on an arm. In *Proceedings of the 24th Annual ACM Symposium on User Interface Software and Technology*, UIST '11, ACM (New York, NY, USA, 2011), 481–488.
17. Lyons, K., Skeels, C., Starner, T., Snoeck, C. M., Wong, B. A., and Ashbrook, D. Augmenting conversations using dual-purpose speech. In *Proceedings of the 17th Annual ACM Symposium on User Interface Software and Technology*, UIST '04, ACM (New York, NY, USA, 2004), 237–246.
18. McFarland, D. J., and Wolpaw, J. R. Brain-computer interfaces for communication and control. *Commun. ACM 54*, 5 (May 2011), 60–66.
19. Merletti, R. Standards for reporting emg data. *Journal of Electromyography and Kinesiology 9*, III-IV (1999).
20. Moore, M. M., and Dua, U. A galvanic skin response interface for people with severe motor disabilities. In *Proceedings of the 6th International ACM SIGACCESS Conference on Computers and Accessibility*, Assets '04, ACM (New York, NY, USA, 2004), 48–54.
21. Nenonen, V., Lindblad, A., Häkkinen, V., Laitinen, T., Jouhtio, M., and Hämäläinen, P. Using heart rate to control an interactive game. In *Proceedings of the SIGCHI Conference on Human Factors in Computing Systems*, CHI '07, ACM (New York, NY, USA, 2007), 853–856.

22. Ngai, G., Chan, S. C., Ng, V. T., Cheung, J. C., Choy, S. S., Lau, W. W., and Tse, J. T. I*catch: A scalable plug-n-play wearable computing framework for novices and children. In *Proceedings of the SIGCHI Conference on Human Factors in Computing Systems*, CHI '10, ACM (New York, NY, USA, 2010), 443–452.

23. Ogata, M., Sugiura, Y., Makino, Y., Inami, M., and Imai, M. Senskin: Adapting skin as a soft interface. In *Proceedings of the 26th Annual ACM Symposium on User Interface Software and Technology*, UIST '13, ACM (New York, NY, USA, 2013), 539–544.

24. Phinyomark, A., Hirunviriya, S., Limsakul, C., and Phukpattaranont, P. Evaluation of emg feature extraction for hand movement recognition based on euclidean distance and standard deviation. In *ECTI-CON, 2010 International Conference on* (May 2010), 856–860.

25. Saponas, T. S., Tan, D. S., Morris, D., and Balakrishnan, R. Demonstrating the feasibility of using forearm electromyography for muscle-computer interfaces. In *Proceedings of the SIGCHI Conference on Human Factors in Computing Systems*, CHI '08, ACM (New York, NY, USA, 2008), 515–524.

26. Saponas, T. S., Tan, D. S., Morris, D., Balakrishnan, R., Turner, J., and Landay, J. A. Enabling always-available input with muscle-computer interfaces. In *Proceedings of the 22Nd Annual ACM Symposium on User Interface Software and Technology*, UIST '09, ACM (New York, NY, USA, 2009), 167–176.

27. Saponas, T. S., Tan, D. S., Morris, D., Turner, J., and Landay, J. A. Making muscle-computer interfaces more practical. In *Proceedings of the SIGCHI Conference on Human Factors in Computing Systems*, CHI '10, ACM (New York, NY, USA, 2010), 851–854.

28. Shinohara, K., and Wobbrock, J. O. In the shadow of misperception: Assistive technology use and social interactions. In *Proceedings of the SIGCHI Conference on Human Factors in Computing Systems*, CHI '11, ACM (New York, NY, USA, 2011), 705–714.

29. Winter D.A., Rau G., K. R. B. H., and C.J., D. L. *Units, Terms and Standards in the Reporting of EMG Research*. International Society of Electrophysiological Kinesiology, 1980.

30. Yousefi, J., and Hamilton-Wright, A. Characterizing EMG data using machine-learning tools. *Comp. in Bio. and Med. 51* (2014), 1–13.

31. Zardoshti-Kermani, M., Wheeler, B., Badie, K., and Hashemi, R. Emg feature evaluation for movement control of upper extremity prostheses. *Rehabilitation Engineering, IEEE Transactions on 3*, 4 (Dec 1995), 324–333.

32. Zhang, X., Chen, X., Wang, W.-h., Yang, J.-h., Lantz, V., and Wang, K.-q. Hand gesture recognition and virtual game control based on 3d accelerometer and emg sensors. In *Proceedings of the 14th International Conference on Intelligent User Interfaces*, IUI '09, ACM (New York, NY, USA, 2009), 401–406.

Spatio-Temporal Detection of Divided Attention in Reading Applications Using EEG and Eye Tracking

Mathieu Rodrigue,[1] Jungah Son,[2] Barry Giesbrecht,[3] Matthew Turk,[1,2] Tobias Höllerer[1,2]
[1]Computer Science, University of California, Santa Barbara
[2]Media Arts and Technology, University of California, Santa Barbara
[3]Psychological and Brain Sciences, University of California, Santa Barbara
{mathieu, mturk, holl}@cs.ucsb.edu, jungah@umail.ucsb.edu, barry.giesbrecht@psych.ucsb.edu

ABSTRACT
Reading is central to learning and communicating, however, divided attention in the form of distraction may be present in learning environments, resulting in a limited understanding of the reading material. This paper presents a novel system that can spatio-temporally detect divided attention in users during two different reading applications: typical document reading and speed reading. Eye tracking and electroencephalography (EEG) monitor the user during reading and provide a classifier with data to decide the user's attention state. The multimodal data informs the system where the user was distracted spatially in the user interface and when the user was distracted. Classification was evaluated with two exploratory experiments. The first experiment was designed to divide the user's attention with a multitasking scenario. The second experiment was designed to divide the users attention by simulating a real-world scenario where the reader is interrupted by unpredictable audio distractions. Results from both experiments show that divided attention may be detected spatio-temporally well above chance on a single-trial basis.

Author Keywords
Attention classification; EEG; eye tracking; learning tools;

ACM Classification Keywords
H.1.2 Information Systems: User/Machine Systems

INTRODUCTION
It is often easy to become distracted while reading, leaving the reader to not fully understand or acquire knowledge from portions of text. Typically, this happens when distracting sounds are heard or when dividing attention while attempting to multitask. When learning, divided attention creates interference during the encoding process of the brain, thus affecting memory and retrieval of the information [7]. This could have a large, negative impact in fields where sustained attention and understanding is necessary. For example, in an educational or workplace environment, one might be distracted by surrounding peers, causing a decrease in task performance.

IUI'15, March 29–April 1, 2015, Atlanta, GA, USA.

http://dx.doi.org/10.1145/2678025.2701382

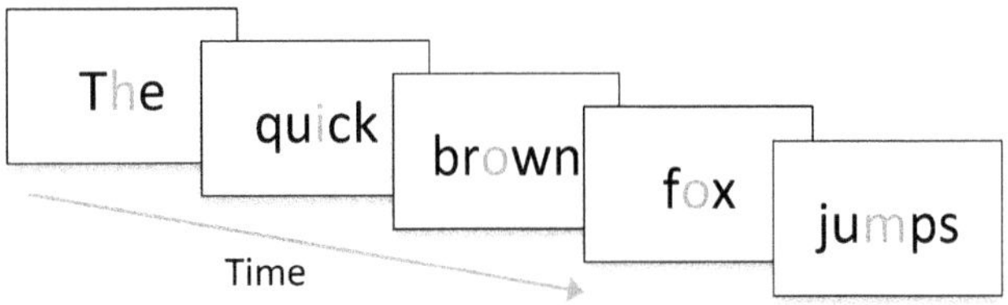

Figure 1. Users focus on the sequential red letters during speed reading.

Interest in reading applications is larger than ever before, given mobile devices with high resolution screens and digital documents such as PDFs and e-books. Digital reading materials are increasingly popular these days due to the fact that they are instantaneously and easily accessible through the internet, and typically cheaper than their physical counterparts. The change from physical to digital reading modalities makes it possible to more easily employ perceptual devices [14] that monitor one's attention state. Here, we discuss two types of reading applications and introduce a novel system to detect divided attention during reading.

Ordinary reading applications are the most common as they are analogous to reading a physical book. In this style of reading application, the user reads from left to right, and top to bottom. Pages are turned by button press or touch gesture. Speed reading has gained recent interest with mobile applications such as Spritz [3]. A speed reading application shows individual, consecutive words to a user (Figure 1), at a rate set by the user. By eliminating saccades and other potentially-distracting words in the periphery, one can read at much higher speeds. Speed reading applications are particularly useful on mobile devices, with screens too small to provide a comfortable reading experience of full-sized documents (e.g. mobile phones, smart watches). By allowing the device to rapidly display consecutive words, the user must be fully attentive at all times. Once a word, sentence, or paragraph is missed, the user may not be able to easily navigate back, or may not be aware of the precise point where attention was lost. This presents a problem to users who are, for example, multitasking or easily distracted by audio within their vicinity.

Novel Attention Monitoring

In this paper, we present a novel system, employing consumer-grade EEG and eye tracking devices, to detect spatially (in the reading application) and temporally if a user is either attending to a reading application or dividing their attention. The contributions of this paper are two-fold: 1) an algorithm for accurately detecting divided attention in reading applications, and 2) the coupling of consumer-grade EEG and eye tracking modalities to improve detection.

To explore the feasibility of classifying between attention and divided attention, two experiments were conducted for each reading task. The first experiment explores to what degree divided attention can be detected in a multitasking scenario. The second experiment explores to what degree divided attention can be detected in the presence of real-world unpredictable distractions.

RELATED WORK

There have been a handful of attempts to accurately measure states of attention using a wide variety of EEG devices. Berka et al. developed one of the first commercial systems, known as B-Alert [6], to detect states of attention (high-engagement, low-engagement, relaxed wakefulness, and sleepy) in real time by a medical grade EEG device, but were not configured to detect divided attention. Hamadicharef et al. were the first to apply the filter bank common spatial pattern (FBCSP) [8] algorithm to an attention task with EEG data. They found that the FBCSP method classified up to 89.4% between states of attention and relaxation using a 15-channel medical grade EEG device. Liu et al. [10] used a consumer-grade EEG device with one electrode (Fp1) to create an attention classifier from pooled subject data. The participants listened to English phrases then answered related questions on a quiz under attentive and distracted conditions. Classification was reported to be on average 76% accurate (55%-60% for the inattention class, 87%-90% for attention, depending on the cost function used). Martínez-Gómez et al. [11] found characteristic features from eye tracking data that describe a subject's level of understanding and English language skill. Putze et al. [13] used the combination of EEG and eye tracking to facilitate video surveillance event selection. They demonstrated accurate event detection in an abstract event selection task, using a set of five electrodes.

The majority of the above attempts were performed unimodally, with devices far too expensive for the average consumer. Similarly, the previously stated work has not attempted classifying divided attention from attention. Hence, we explore the possibility of combining low-cost EEG and eye tracking to detect states of attention from divided attention in popular reading applications.

BRAIN-COMPUTER INTERFACE

The Emotiv Epoc [1], a consumer-grade EEG device, was used for signal acquisition. The device samples at 128hz and is equipped with 14 electrodes (AF3, AF4, F3, F4, F7, F8, FC5, FC6, O1, O2, P7, P8, T7, T8) which are positioned according to the international 10-20 system. The brain-computer interface developed for this system detects changes in power from the frequency bands α (8-13hz), β (14-30hz), and θ (4-7hz) between divided and non-divided attention states.

EEG Preprocessing

EEG data was first low-pass filtered with a cutoff frequency of 50hz and high-pass filtered with a cutoff frequency of 0.16hz, both using a third-order butterworth filter. The data was then segmented into 1.5-second epochs, overlapping each previous epoch by 50%.

Epochs that contained eye blinks were detected using an eye tracker, and filtered according to [15]. An artifact removal algorithm was implemented based on Adaptive SWT-based Denoising (ASWTD). For the detected EEG segments, the wavelet coefficients at level 6 were obtained using the stationary wavelet transform (SWT) and thresholded with the adaptive thresholding mechanism using a hard thresholding function. Denoised signals without artifacts were obtained by computing an inverse SWT on the thresholded wavelet coefficients. Since we were removing ocular artefacts, only the wavelet coefficients from levels 3 to 6 were thresholded. Epochs with other types of artifacts above a predetermined threshold were discarded.

Filter-Bank Common Spatial Pattern

EEG data was spatially filtered according to an adapted FBCSP algorithm [5], which involved IIR filtering the data into frequency bins, then performing the common spatial pattern algorithm on each frequency bin to find the source location of the signal on the scalp. CSP spatially filters the EEG channels by determining a matrix W such that $W\Sigma_1W^\top = D_1$ and $W\Sigma_2W^\top = D_2$ where Σ_1 and Σ_2 are the estimated class covariance matrices, and D_1 and D_2 are diagonal matrices such that $D_1 + D_2 = I$. The first and last n ($n = 6$, in practice) columns of W contain spatial filters that maximally discriminate between the two classes.

Each preprocessed EEG epoch was first band pass filtered, using a third-order butterworth filter, in the α, β, and θ frequency bands. Literature [9] suggests that changes in the chosen frequency bands are correlated with attention. A dedicated portion of the EEG data was deployed to train a corresponding spatial filter W_α, W_β, and W_θ using the common spatial pattern algorithm (CSP). The remaining band-pass filtered epochs were then spatially filtered by their corresponding spatial filter, using the $n = 6$ most discriminative spatial filters as reported by the CSP algorithm.

EEG Classification

Offline EEG data was determined to be representative of attention or divided attention by extracting features from the CSP source signals, and classifying test examples with a trained classifier. Log-variance features were extracted from the spatially filtered data $f_\alpha = \log(\mathrm{var}(W_\alpha X))$, $f_\beta = \log(\mathrm{var}(W_\beta X))$, $f_\theta = \log(\mathrm{var}(W_\theta X))$. 10x10-fold cross validation with a support vector machine (SVM) classifier was employed using the MATLAB implementation with an RBF kernel, to decide if an EEG epoch was in the attention or divided attention state. A grid search was performed to optimize σ for all participants, the remaining parameters were left as default.

EYE TRACKING

The Eye Tribe [4], a consumer-grade eye tracker was used for this work. Raw data was recorded at 60hz and divided into four-second epochs. Each EEG epoch had a corresponding,

Table 1. Average classification accuracy and per-class classification accuracy for EEG, eye tracking and combined modalities.

		EEG			Eye Tracking			EEG + Eye Tracking		
		Average	Att.	Div. Att.	Average	Att	Div. Att.	Average	Att.	Div. Att.
Exp. I_{SR}	Subject 1	95.93%	97.45%	94.40%	63.04%	71.43%	54.05%	96.54%	98.43%	93.74%
	Subject 2	97.68%	97.22%	98.13%	65.99%	54.7%	77.28%	97.79%	96.92%	98.66%
	Subject 3	87.99%	88.21%	87.77%	67.81%	65.88%	69.75%	90.06%	90.97%	89.15%
Exp. I_R	Subject 1	98.16%	99.59%	96.73%	72.26%	69.53%	74.09%	97.8%	99.28%	95.09%
	Subject 2	99.97%	99.95%	100%	74.01%	71.6%	76.42%	99.19%	99.82%	98.56%
	Subject 3	92.41%	93.02%	91.81%	63.14%	51.98%	74.31%	91.25%	93.51%	88.99%
Exp. II_{SR}	Subject 1	84.52%	85.71%	83.33%	66.31%	68.77%	64.02%	83.51%	82.35%	84.60%
	Subject 2	74.82%	73.76%	75.89%	72.34%	75.18%	69.5%	79.43%	75.18%	83.69%
	Subject 3	69.07%	65.56%	73.33%	73.61%	71.48%	75.74%	82.41%	80.0%	84.81%
Exp. II_R	Subject 1	85.71%	88.10%	83.33%	78.57%	73.81%	83.33%	90.48%	95.24%	85.71%
	Subject 2	77.14%	80.0%	74.29%	69.29%	57.14%	81.43%	84.29%	81.43%	87.14%
	Subject 3	75.93%	74.63%	77.22%	71.39%	70.37%	72.41%	80.93%	79.26%	82.59 %

four-second eye tracking epoch, aligned at the last sample. The Eye Tribe eye tracking algorithms are currently in active development. We used version 0.9.41 of the SDK, and a chin rest was used to minimize noise.

Fixation and Saccade Detection

An offline saccade and fixation detection algorithm adapted from [12] was employed. Saccades were found by finding the distance between the mean of two consecutive sliding windows,

$$m_{before}(n) = \left[\frac{1}{r}\sum_{k=1}^{r} s_x(n-k), \frac{1}{r}\sum_{k=1}^{r} s_y(n-k)\right]$$

$$m_{after}(n) = \left[\frac{1}{r}\sum_{k=1}^{r} s_x(n+k), \frac{1}{r}\sum_{k=1}^{r} s_y(n+k)\right]$$

where n is the sample of interest, and r is the window size. The distance d is calculated at every sample in eye tracking data by $d = \sqrt{(m_{after} - m_{before}) \cdot (m_{after} - m_{before})^{\top}}$ which forms a sequence of peaks, where the max of each peak represents a saccade. Once saccades are detected in the epoch, the median of the samples between saccades are marked as fixations. This algorithm may be applied to real-time system where data is processed in epochs.

Eye Tracking Classification

Four of the most discriminative eye tracking features from [11] were used for in our classifier: number of fixations, median saccade length, mean saccade velocity x, and mean saccade velocity y. Among other tested features, the chosen features were found to best characterize between states of attention in this experiment. Median was chosed instead of mean saccade length so that outliers would not affect classification. Additionally, log-variance features for saccade length and mean pupil size were employed after observing discriminative differences in the data. The features were added to their corresponding EEG-epoch feature vector and then classified with the SVM classifier to determine attention states.

EXPERIMENTS

In this section, we'll discuss two experiments to study the effects of distraction from multitasking, and external stimuli on classification. Both experiments required the subject to complete two tasks, both split up into attention and divided attention conditions. The first task involved speed reading a passage of text. Each session lasted approximately two minutes. An open source speed reading application, Spray [2], was used for this task. The second task required the subject to read a normal passage of text, one page at a time. Each session lasted the necessary amount of time for the subject to finish two pages, which was approximately two minutes. Participants were not allowed to go back to a previous page, but were encouraged to read as they normally would. Both tasks were split up into two conditions: attention and divided attention, and required the subjects to wear headphones. After each task, the participant reported a summary of what they had read to ensure the subject was participating in the task. EEG electrodes were checked after each task to ensure proper impedance levels, and eye tracking calibration was checked between experiments, but no recalibration was ever needed.

Experiment I

The first experiment was designed to simulate internal divided attention, such as multitasking. Three participants (one female, two males, ages 25-27) volunteered for the experiment. All had normal or corrected to normal vision. A total of eight sessions were performed, within subjects, for each task. The names of nine different colors were spoken through the headphones in a random order at one-second intervals. The volume of the headphones were set to be as low as possible while still allowing the subject to hear the colors clearly. During the attention condition, the participant was asked to ignore the colors and completely focus on the speed reading task. During the divided attention condition, the participant was told to focus on the reading material but also count the number of times a target color was spoken during the session. The participant reported the number of colors heard after each session, which was compared to ground truth data to ensure the user was dividing attention between both stimuli.

Experiment II

The second experiment was designed to simulate an environment where a reader is distracted by external stimuli. Three participants (three male, ages 22-34) volunteered for the experiment. All had normal or corrected to normal vision. A total of four sessions were performed, within subjects, for each task. The headphones were set to a moderate volume as determined by the participant. During the reading task, the participant heard multiple, unique sound clips that lasted for 30 seconds each and would play randomly, but never overlap.

The sound clips contained distracting noises one might typically hear in their environment while reading, such as energetic music, television shows, movies, dogs barking, or conversations from other people. After each session, the participant reported how distracted they were during audio playback (1-9 Likert scale, 9 being most distracted). Distractions rated below 4 were not used for classification. Three detachable EEG electrodes were found to be damaged and thus excluded from data acquisition: (F3, FC6, P7), (AF3, F3, FC5), and (F7, P7, T7), for subjects one, two and three, respectively.

RESULTS AND DISCUSSION

The objective of this work was to develop algorithms which allow EEG and eye tracking consumer devices to accurately detect divided attention from attention during reading. Additionally, we wanted to provide a proof of concept for mapping human attention into a user interface, so software could intelligently react to and provide useful information about a reader's experience. A user's eye fixations are seen in (Figure 3) which shows a clear discrimination between attention and divided attention conditions.

To avoid any bias in the data, a 10x10-fold cross-validation was used on the feature data for both experiments. Table 1 shows that classification accuracy of EEG and combined modalities in experiment I exceeds those for experiment II for both tasks. Figure 2 shows the higher dimensional EEG features from the highest classification accuracy obtained in experiment I. The feature data was projected onto the two largest principal components in order to visualize the higher dimensional feature space. It is clear from the visualization that the two classes are highly separable, resulting in accurate classification. The first experiment simulated a multitasking scenario, where the reader may be engaging in other activities while they are reading, e.g. listening to a breaking news story on the television while reading. This type of task was designed to keep the subject's attention divided among two sets of stimuli. The EEG classification accuracy is high, most likely due to the fact that the multitasking distraction effect was stronger, resulting in different power in the frequency bands between conditions. This experiment ensured that classification was based on true divided attention and not driven by auditory perception signals in the brain, given that an identical auditory signal (a spoken set of colors in pseudo-random order) was present across both conditions.

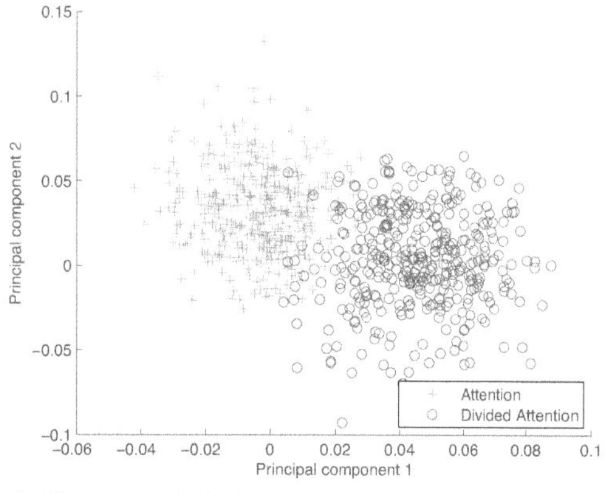

Figure 2. First two principal components of EEG features from subject two during the ordinary reading condition for experiment I.

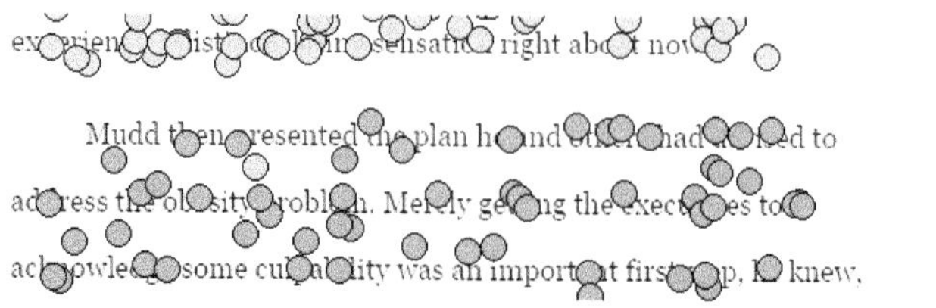

Figure 3. Classified user fixation data visualized from experiment I. Red circles represent divided attention, blue circles represent attention.

Whereas experimenent I was highly controlled to rule out the possibility that auditory brain signals are driving classification results, experiment II was designed to test a more realistic scenario in which a user's attention is divided by unexepected and intrusive auditory distractions. Table 1 shows a lower classification percentage using both modalities for experiment II, but still well above chance. One possibility for lower classification accuracy was the exclusion of three EEG electrodes for each participant. Also, the second experiment did not guarantee that a subject would be distracted during the distraction condition. Given that some people may not have an issue with background noise as they read, e.g. people who commonly read with a running television in the room, this experiment may not have distracted all of the participants equally. This was also observed from the post-session questionnaire, which confirmed that the external stimuli were not fully distracting to all participants. Mean scores for distraction level during the two tasks were (6, 6.25), (7.25,4.75), and (4, 4.5), with their respective standard errors (0.629, 0.722), (0.913, 0.479), (0.408,0.654) for the three participants. Additionally, EEG classification from this experiment may have been partially influenced by the user's perception of hearing different, intermittent audio clips.

CONCLUSION

We proposed a novel approach to detecting attention and divided attention during reading applications, using EEG and eye tracking consumer devices. Results from two experiments show that EEG classification is highly accurate during controlled multitasking scenarios, and still well above chance during unpredictable distraction scenarios. On the other hand, eye tracking data while not as accurate as EEG data, may be effective as a single mode of input for certain types of applications. Additionally, by combining EEG and eye tracking features, classification generally performs better than either modality on its own. Future work will focus on classifying attention from divided attention in real-time. For example, the system could make note of when the user was distracted during speed reading, providing an easy way to navigate to areas the user missed, or warn the user, to regain focus. Similarly, during ordinary reading, the system could make note of spatio-temporal data received from the EEG and eye tracker, and remind the user to go back and review those areas. Other future work involves detection and multiclass classification among other states of attention (e.g. mind wandering), and attention detection in other evironment scenarios.

ACKNOWLEDGEMENTS

This work was partially supported by ONR grants N00014-14-1-0133 and N00014-13-1-0872, as well as NSF grant IIS-0747520.

REFERENCES

1. Emotiv EPOC. `http://www.emotiv.com/`.
2. Spray Open Source Speed Reader. `https://github.com/chaimpeck/spray/`.
3. Spritz. `http://www.spritzinc.com/`.
4. The Eye Tribe Eye Tracker. `http://www.theeyetribe.com/`.
5. Ang, K. K., Chin, Z. Y., Zhang, H., and Guan, C. Filter bank common spatial pattern (FBCSP) in brain-computer interface. In *IEEE International Joint Conference on Neural Networks, 2008. IJCNN 2008. (IEEE World Congress on Computational Intelligence)* (June 2008), 2390–2397.
6. Berka, C., Levendowski, D. J., Cvetinovic, M. M., Petrovic, M. M., Davis, G., Lumicao, M. N., Zivkovic, V. T., Popovic, M. V., and Olmstead, R. Real-time analysis of EEG indexes of alertness, cognition, and memory acquired with a wireless EEG headset. *International Journal of Human-Computer Interaction 17*, 2 (June 2004), 151–170.
7. Fernandes, M. A., and Moscovitch, M. Divided attention and memory: evidence of substantial interference effects at retrieval and encoding. *Journal of Experimental Psychology. General 129*, 2 (June 2000), 155–176.
8. Hamadicharef, B., Zhang, H., Guan, C., Wang, C., Phua, K. S., Tee, K. P., and Ang, K. K. Learning EEG-based spectral-spatial patterns for attention level measurement. In *IEEE International Symposium on Circuits and Systems, 2009. ISCAS 2009* (May 2009), 1465–1468.
9. Klimesch, W. EEG alpha and theta oscillations reflect cognitive and memory performance: a review and analysis. *Brain Research Reviews 29*, 2–3 (Apr. 1999), 169–195.
10. Liu, N.-H., Chiang, C.-Y., and Chu, H.-C. Recognizing the degree of human attention using EEG signals from mobile. *Sensors 13*, 8 (Aug. 2013), 10273–10286.
11. Martínez-Gómez, P., and Aizawa, A. Recognition of understanding level and language skill using measurements of reading behavior. In *Proceedings of the 19th International Conference on Intelligent User Interfaces*, IUI '14, ACM (New York, NY, USA, 2014), 95–104.
12. Olsson, P. Real-time and offline filters for eye tracking. *Master Thesis* (2007).
13. Putze, F., Hild, J., Kärgel, R., Herff, C., Redmann, A., Beyerer, J., and Schultz, T. Locating user attention using eye tracking and EEG for spatio-temporal event selection. In *Proceedings of the 2013 International Conference on Intelligent User Interfaces*, IUI '13, ACM (New York, NY, USA, 2013), 129–136.
14. Turk, M., and Robertson, G. Perceptual user interfaces (introduction). *Commun. ACM 43*, 3 (Mar. 2000), 32–34.
15. Yong, X., Fatourechi, M., Ward, R. K., and Birch, G. E. Automatic artefact removal in a self-paced hybrid brain-computer interface system. *Journal of NeuroEngineering and Rehabilitation 9*, 1 (July 2012), 50.

Principles of Explanatory Debugging to Personalize Interactive Machine Learning

Todd Kulesza[1] **Margaret Burnett**[1] **Weng-Keen Wong**[1] **Simone Stumpf**[2]

[1]Oregon State University
School of EECS
Corvallis, Oregon

[2]City University London
Centre for HCI Design
London, United Kingdom

{kuleszto, burnett, wong}@eecs.oregonstate.edu, Simone.Stumpf.1@city.ac.uk

ABSTRACT
How can end users efficiently influence the predictions that machine learning systems make on their behalf? This paper presents Explanatory Debugging, an approach in which the system explains to users how it made each of its predictions, and the user then explains any necessary corrections back to the learning system. We present the principles underlying this approach and a prototype instantiating it. An empirical evaluation shows that Explanatory Debugging increased participants' understanding of the learning system by 52% and allowed participants to correct its mistakes up to twice as efficiently as participants using a traditional learning system.

Author Keywords
Interactive machine learning; end user programming.

H.5.2. [**Information interfaces and presentation (e.g. HCI)**] User interfaces

INTRODUCTION
In many machine learning applications, the user has a concept in mind—songs he wants to hear, junk mail she doesn't want to see, anomalous transactions he wants to detect—that the machine learning system is trying to identify. An increasing body of research has begun to explore what users can do when their machine learning systems misidentify their concepts [e.g., 1, 2, 18, 26, 38, 45]. Much of this work shares a common challenge: how can end users effectively and efficiently personalize the predictions or recommendations these learning systems make on their behalf?

For example, engineer Alice has email folders for her project group at work, an office sports pool, and individual folders for colleagues she frequently collaborates with; she wants her email program to automatically categorize new email into the appropriate folder. This requires fine-grained control—perhaps she wants email from her colleague Bob to go to the "sports" folder if it mentions something about hockey, the "project" folder if it references something related to their current project, or the "Bob" folder if neither of those conditions are met.

IUI 2015, April 26–May 1, 2015, Atlanta, GA, USA.
Copyright 2015 ACM 978-1-4503-3306-1/15/03...$15.00.
http://dx.doi.org/10.1145/2678025.2701399

However, Alice does not have enough email from Bob to accurately train a learning system to recognize these three concepts, and by the time she acquires it, the hockey season may be over or her group's project may change.

Our proposed solution is *Explanatory Debugging*, which is an explanation-centric approach to help end users effectively and efficiently personalize machine learning systems. We say "debugging" because personalizing a learning system is an end-user debugging problem: as discussed in [14], the user is trying to identify and correct faults in the system's reasoning that are responsible for predictions that failed to meet the user's expectations.

In Explanatory Debugging, the system explains the reasons for its predictions to its end user, who in turn explains corrections back to the system. We hypothesize that this cycle of explanations will help users build useful *mental models*—internal representations that allow people to predict how a system will behave [17]—and thus allow them to personalize their learning system better and faster than traditional black-box systems.

In the earlier example, such an approach could show Alice all the words the system uses to identify email about her group's project, the sports pool, or any other concept. She could then add additional words she knows to be relevant, or remove words that she knows are irrelevant. She would not need to worry that her corrections might confuse the system (e.g., telling it that a message from Bob about hockey belongs in the sports folder and hoping it will identify that the topic is the reason, not the sender), nor would she need to spend weeks or months acquiring new training instances.

In this paper we present the Explanatory Debugging approach and instantiate it in EluciDebug, the first interactive system designed to help end users build useful mental models of a machine learning system while simultaneously allowing them to explain corrections back to the system. We evaluate Explanatory Debugging against a traditional black-box learning system to determine whether Explanatory Debugging helped end users build better mental models, and if so, whether these mental models helped users more efficiently personalize their learning system's behavior.

RELATED WORK
The study of how end users interactively control statistical machine learning systems is gaining increased attention. Fails et al. first popularized the phrase *interactive machine learning*

in a paper describing how an iterative train-feedback-correct cycle allowed users to quickly correct the mistakes made by an image segmentation system [11]. Since then, researchers have explored using this cycle of quick interactions to train instance-based classifiers [5, 13], enable better model selection by end users [2, 12, 40], elicit labels for the most important instances (e.g., active learning) [7, 37], and to improve reinforcement learning for automated agents [21]. These use cases largely treat the machine learning system as a "black box"—users can try to personalize the system by providing it with different inputs (e.g., labeled instances), but are unable to see *why* different inputs may cause the system's outputs to change.

An alternative to the "black box" model is a "white box" model [16], in which the machine learning system is made more transparent to the user. Increased transparency has been associated with many benefits, including increased user acceptance of (or satisfaction with) recommendations and predictions [4, 8, 42], improved training of intelligent agents [41], and increased trust in the system's predictions [10]. In this paper, however, we primarily care about transparency because it has been shown to help users understand how a learning system operates [25, 30].

Recent work has suggested that as end users better understand how a machine learning system operates, they are better able to personalize it [12, 23]. This aligns with work from other domains, which has found that explanation-based debugging approaches can help end users correct a program's faults [22, 36]. Further, research has shown that in the absence of transparency, users experience difficulty building accurate mental models of learning systems [23, 43]. People will still build mental models of the system, but such flawed mental models often lead to misinformed user behavior [19, 32].

Some researchers have sought to expand the types of inputs interactive machine learning systems can process, and this can also increase system transparency. For example, user feedback may take the form of model constraints [18], critiques to the model's search space [45], or adjustments to the model's weights of evidence [26]. In addition to supporting novel user feedback mechanisms, these approaches increase transparency by enabling users to view such facets as the existing model constraints [18], the model's feature set [45], or the weights of evidence responsible for each prediction [26].

All of these works have increased our understanding of how human factors impact machine learning, but none have evaluated the ability of an interactive machine learning system to (1) help users build useful mental models of how it operates such that (2) they can efficiently personalize the system. Kulesza et al. found a link between mental models and personalization ability, but relied on human instructors to help participants build useful mental models [23]. Other work has studied the impact of machine-generated explanations on users' mental models, but did not explore whether this helped participants' personalize their learning systems [8, 25, 30]. In this paper we rely on machine-generated explanations to help users build accurate mental models and then evaluate their resulting ability to personalize a learning system.

EXPLANATORY DEBUGGING

In 2010, Kulesza et al. proposed the idea of Explanatory Debugging—a two-way exchange of explanations between an end user and a machine learning system [24]—but did not provide principles underlying the approach. In this section we build upon that proposal by describing principles to ground and support replication of Explanatory Debugging.

Explainability

Our first principle for Explanatory Debugging is *Explainability*: accurately explain the learning system's reasons for each prediction to the end user. This principle builds upon research showing that end users who received explanations about a learning system's reasoning were able to better personalize classifiers and recommenders [4, 18, 24]. Without explanations, however, users struggle to build accurate mental models of such systems [23, 30, 43]. This suggests *in situ* explanations are a necessary condition to help end users learn how a machine learning system operates. To help users build useful mental models of the learning system, these explanations should observe the following principles:

Principle 1.1: Be Iterative

Research has suggested that users may best personalize a learning system if they build their mental models while interacting with it [23]. Thus, explanations should support an iterative, *in situ* learning process. For example, explanations could take the form of concise, easily consumable "bites" of information—if a user is interested in learning more about the system, he or she can attend to many of these explanations to iteratively build a higher-fidelity mental model.

Principle 1.2: Be Sound

Explanations should not be simplified by explaining the model as if it were less complex than it actually is. In [25] this is referred to as *soundness*: "the extent to which each component of an explanation's content is truthful in describing the underlying system." In [23] the authors found a linear correlation between the quality of a user's mental model and their ability to control the learning system as desired, suggesting that the better someone understands the underlying system, the better they will be able to control it. Further, [25] details the impact of explanation fidelity on mental model development, finding that users did not trust—and thus, were less likely to attend to—the least sound explanations. Because reducing soundness reduces both the potential utility of the explanation and the likelihood that users will invest attention toward it, Explanatory Debugging entails designing explanations that are as sound as practically possible.

One method for evaluating explanation soundness is to compare the explanation with the learning system's mathematical model. How accurately are each of the model's terms explained? If those terms are derived from more complex terms, is the user able to "drill down" to understand those additional terms? The more these explanations reflect the underlying model, the more sound the explanation is.

Principle 1.3: Be Complete

Kulesza et al. describe *completeness* as "the extent to which *all* of the underlying system is described by the explanation" [25], so a complete explanation does not omit important information about the model. In that study, end users built the best mental models when they had access to the most complete explanations, which informed them of all the information the learning system had at its disposal and how it used that information [25]. Also pertinent is work showing that users often struggle to understand how different parts of the system interact with each other [26]. Complete explanations that reveal how different parts of the system are interconnected may help users overcome this barrier.

One method for evaluating completeness is via Lim and Dey's *intelligibility types* [29], with more complete explanations including more of these intelligibility types.

Principle 1.4: But Don't Overwhelm

Balanced against the soundness and completeness principles is the need to remain comprehensible and to engage user attention. Findings from [25] suggest that one way to engage user attention is to frame explanations concretely, such as referencing the predicted item and any evidence the learning system employed in its prediction. In some circumstances, selecting a more comprehensible machine learning model may also be appropriate. For example, a neural network can be explained as if it were a decision tree [9], but this reduces soundness because a different model is explained. Similarly, a model with 10,000 features can be explained as if it only used the 10 most discriminative features for each prediction, but this reduces completeness by omitting information that the model uses. Alternative approaches that embody the Explanatory Debugging principles include selecting a machine learning model that can be explained with little abstraction [e.g., 27, 38, 39] or using feature selection techniques [47] in high-dimensionality domains to prevent users from struggling to identify which features to adjust (as happened in [26]).

Correctability

Our second top-level principle for Explanatory Debugging is *Correctability*: allow users to explain corrections back to the learning system. To enable an iterative cycle of explanations between the system and the user, in Explanatory Debugging the machine-to-user explanation should also serve as the user-to-machine explanation. Research suggests that to elicit corrections from users, this feedback mechanism should embody the following principles:

Principle 2.1: Be Actionable

Both theory [3] and prior empirical findings [6, 23, 25] suggest end users will ignore explanations when the benefit of attending to them is unclear. By making the explanation actionable, we hope to lower the perceived cost of attending to it by obviating the need to transfer knowledge from one part of the user interface (the explanation) to another (the feedback mechanism). Actionable explanations also fulfill three aspects of Minimalist Instruction [44]: (1) people are learning while performing real work; (2) the explanatory material is tightly coupled to the system's current state; and (3) people can leverage their existing knowledge by adjusting the explanation to match their own mental reasoning.

Principle 2.2: Be Reversible

A risk in enabling users to provide feedback to a machine learning system is that they may actually make its predictions worse [e.g., 24, 38]. Being able to easily reverse a harmful action can help mitigate that risk. It may also encourage self-directed tinkering, which can facilitate learning [35]. When combined with Principle 2.4, reversibility also fulfills a fourth aspect of Minimalist Instruction [44]: help people identify and recover from errors.

Principle 2.3: Always Honor User Feedback

As Yang and Newman found when studying users of learning thermostats [46], a system that appears to disregard user feedback deters users from continuing to provide feedback. However, methods for honoring user feedback are not always straightforward. Handling user feedback over time (e.g., what if new instance-based feedback contradicts old instance-based feedback?) and balancing different types of feedback (e.g., instance-based feedback versus feature-based feedback) requires careful consideration of how the user's feedback will be integrated into the learning system.

Principle 2.4: Incremental Changes Matter

In [25], participants claimed they would attend to explanations *only if* doing so would enable them to more successfully control the learning system's predictions. Thus, continued user interaction may depend upon users being able to see incremental changes to the learning system's reasoning after each interaction (i.e., overcoming the *gulf of evaluation* that exists between a user's mental model and a system's actual state [33]). This principle is also related to Principle 1.1 (Be iterative) because our thesis is that users will develop better mental models iteratively, requiring many interactions with the learning system. These interactions may not always result in large, obvious changes, so being able to communicate the small, incremental changes a user's feedback has upon a learning system may be critical to our approach's feasibility.

ELUCIDEBUG: EXPLANATORY DEBUGGING IN ACTION

We instantiated Explanatory Debugging in a text classification prototype we call EluciDebug (Figure 1). We chose text classification because (1) many real-world systems require it (e.g., spam filtering, news recommendation, serving relevant ads, search result ranking, etc.) and (2) it can be evaluated with documents about common topics (e.g., popular sports), allowing a large population of participants for our evaluation. We designed EluciDebug to look like an email program with multiple folders, each representing a particular topic. The prototype's machine learning component attempts to automatically classify new messages into the appropriate folder.

While the principles of Explanatory Debugging primarily deal with the user interface, two principles place constraints on the machine learning model: (1) it must be able to *honor user feedback* in real-time, and (2) it must be explainable with enough soundness and completeness to allow users to build useful mental models of how it operates *without overwhelming*

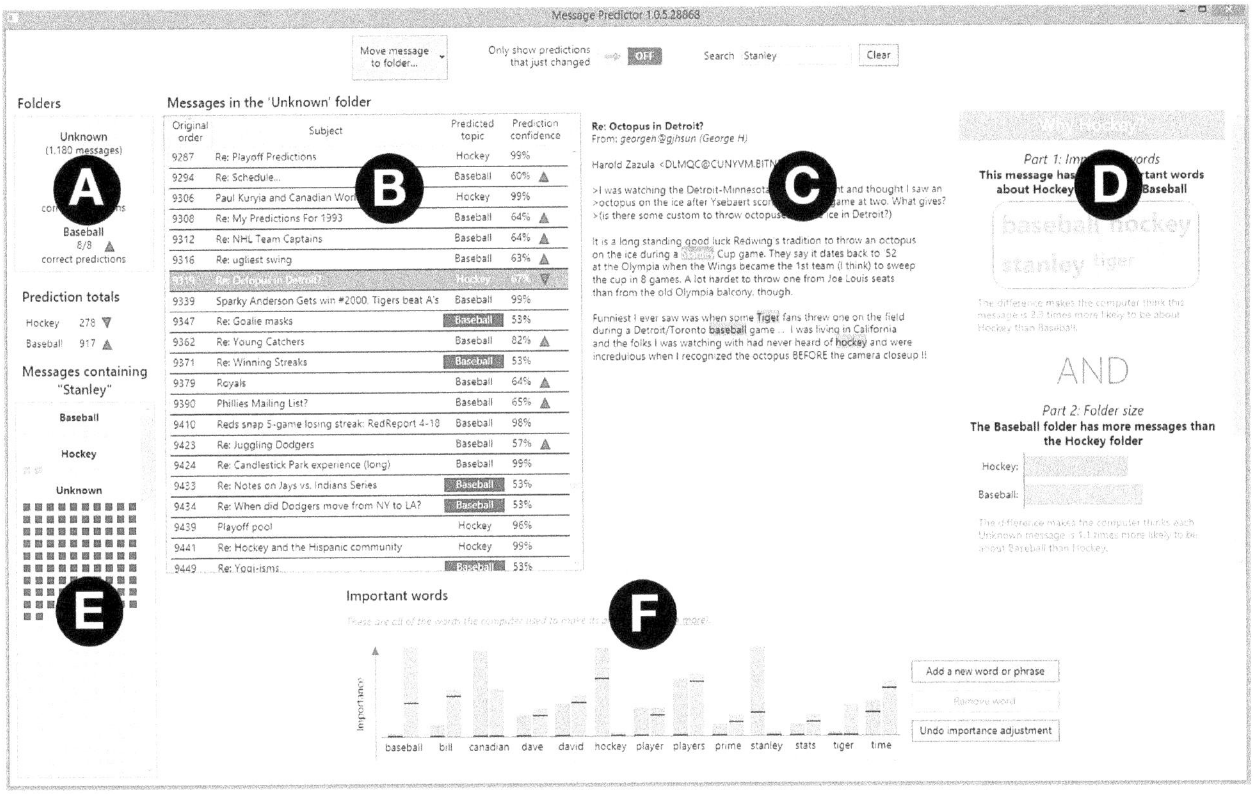

Figure 1. The EluciDebug prototype. (A) List of folders. (B) List of messages in the selected folder. (C) The selected message. (D) Explanation of the selected message's predicted folder. (E) Overview of which messages contain the selected word. (F) Complete list of words the learning system uses to make predictions.

them. Our EluciDebug prototype uses a multinomial naive Bayes model (MNB) [20] with feature selection [47] to meet these constraints. Evaluating the suitability of—or changes necessary to—other models remains an open question.

The Multinomial Naive Bayes Classifier: A Brief Review

Before describing how we integrated MNB with Explanatory Debugging, we first summarize how MNB operates. An MNB classifier computes the probability that a given input (e.g., the document being classified) has of belonging to each output (e.g., the possible labels). The output with the highest probability "wins" and becomes the predicted label for the input. For example, if MNB calculates that a document has a 70% probability of being junk mail and a 30% probability of not being junk mail, the document will be labeled as junk mail. The equations for computing probability, as defined in [20], are shown below. We use c to represent an individual class in the collection of potential output classes C, d_i to represent an individual document to classify, and assume that the only features the classifier uses are individual words in the set of known documents:

$$\Pr(c|d_i) = \frac{\Pr(c)\Pr(d_i|c)}{\Pr(d_i)} \tag{1}$$

The term $\Pr(c)$ represents the probability that any given document belongs to class c and can be estimated by dividing the number of documents in c by the total number of documents in the training set. The term $\Pr(d_i|c)$ represents the probability of document d_i given class c and can be estimated as:

$$\Pr(d_i|c) = \prod_n \Pr(w_n|c)^{f_{ni}} \tag{2}$$

The term f_{ni} is the number of instances of word n in document d_i and the term $\Pr(w_n|c)$ is the probability of word n given class c, estimated with the equation

$$\Pr(w_n|c) = \frac{p_{nc} + F_{nc}}{\sum_{x=1}^{N} p_{xc} + \sum_{x=1}^{N} F_{xc}} \tag{3}$$

where F_{nc} is the number of instances of word n in all of the training documents for class c, N is the number of unique words in the training documents for all classes, and p_{nc} is a smoothing term (usually 1) to prevent the equation from yielding 0 if no documents from class c contain word w_n.

The Explanatory Debugging Principles in EluciDebug

Being Iterative

To help end users iteratively build better mental models, EluciDebug employs two strategies: (1) each explanation focuses on an individual aspect of the learning system, and (2) layered explanations are available if the user wants more information. For example, the *Why* explanation (introduced later) primarily tells users about the system's reasons for a *specific* prediction. Over time, however, the user may learn about the system's general operation by observing commonalities in the reasons for these specific predictions. Further, this *Why* explanation is layered. Part of the explanation shows users which words contributed to the learning system's prediction—if the user wants to know more about why the system associated a particular word with the given topic, hovering over the word yields a tooltip that explains how the system determines which topic a word is associated with.

Being Sound

Soundness means that everything an explanation says is true. Our explanations aim to be sound by accurately disclosing all of the features the classifier used to make its prediction, as well as how each feature contributed to the prediction. EluciDebug's *Why* explanation is responsible for communicating much of this information to users (Figure 2).

Soundly explaining the MNB classifier requires explaining the $\Pr(c)$ and $\Pr(d_i|c)$ terms from Equation 1, as these are the only terms that impact the model's predictions[1]. Because the $\Pr(d_i|c)$ term expands into Equation 2, we also need to explain how word probabilities for each class factor into the prediction. We can further increase soundness by explaining how these probabilities are calculated (i.e., by explaining Equation 3).

In EluciDebug we explain the $\Pr(d_i|c)$ term by using a word cloud to visualize the difference between each feature's probability for the two output classifications (Equation 3) as the following ratio: $\frac{\Pr(w_n|c_1)^{f_{ni}}}{\Pr(w_n|c_2)^{f_{ni}}}$, where c_1 is the class with the larger probability for feature w_n. We use the result to compute the feature's font size, while its font color is based on the class with the larger probability. For example, in Figure 2 the word *stanley* is larger than *tiger* because its ratio of word probability is correspondingly larger, and it is blue because its probability of occurring in the *hockey* class is larger than its probability of occurring in the *baseball* class. Hovering over a word in this cloud shows a tooltip that explains the word's size was determined by a combination of (1) how many times it appeared in each class, and (2) any adjustments the user made to the word's importance (Equation 3).

The second component of a sound explanation of the MNB classifier is the $\Pr(c)$ term from Equation 1. We explain this term via a bar graph visualization of the number of items in each class (Figure 2, middle).

The top-to-bottom design of this entire *Why* explanation, along with the text that describes *Part 1* and *Part 2*, is intended to teach the user that both word presence (the $\Pr(d_i|c)$ term) and folder size (the $\Pr(c)$ term) play a role in each of the classifier's predictions. The result, shown at the bottom of Figure 2, explains how these two parts are combined to determine the classifier's certainty in its prediction.

Being Complete

Completeness means telling the *whole* truth. For the MNB classifier, this means not only explaining each of the terms from Equation 1, but also all of the information the classifier *could* use, where it came from, and how likely it is that each prediction is correct. To help ensure completeness, we turn to

[1]The $\Pr(d_i)$ term in the denominator of Equation 1 is only used to normalize the result to fall within the range 0–1; it does not impact the model's prediction.

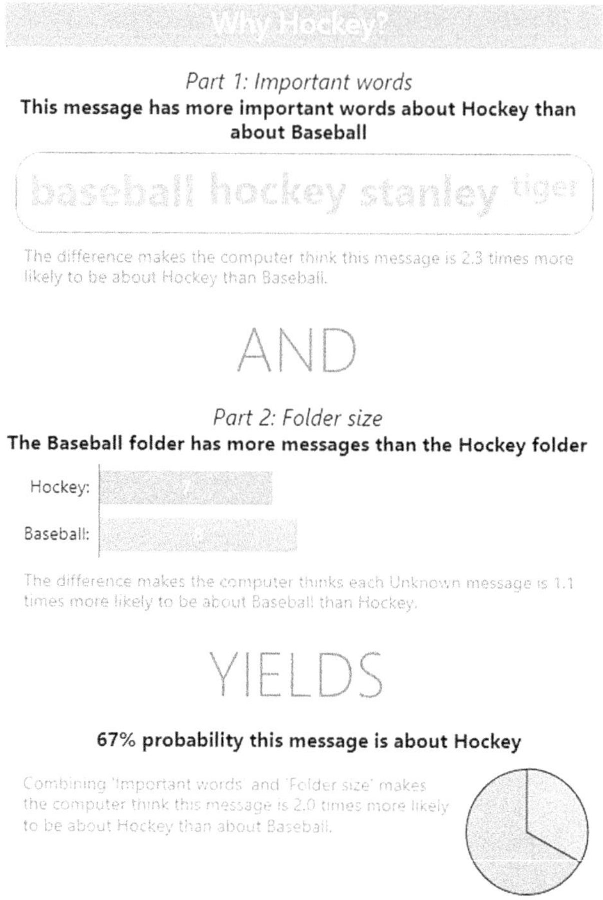

Figure 2. The *Why* explanation tells users how features and folder size were used to predict each message's topic. This figure is a close-up of Figure 1 part D.

Lim and Dey's schema of intelligibility types. The results of [25] suggest that a complete explanation should include Lim and Dey's *why*, *inputs*, *model*, and *certainty* types. Lim's work suggests the usefulness of the *what if* type in scenarios where the user is attempting to change the behavior of a classifier [28], so we included this intelligibility type as well.

We thus designed our EluciDebug explanations to detail all of the information the classifier could potentially use when making predictions. The *Why* explanation shown in Figure 2 tells users that both feature presence and folder size played a role in each prediction (the numerator of Equation 1). The *Important words* explanations (Figure 3) goes even further, telling the user *all* of the features the classifier knows about and may use in its predictions. Because it tells the user about the sources of information available to the classifier, this is also an instantiation of Lim and Dey's *inputs* intelligibility type. To make it clear to users that these features can occur in all parts of the document—message body, subject line, and sender—EluciDebug highlights features in the context of each message (Figure 1, part C).

In [25] the authors found that Lim and Dey's *model* intelligibility type was associated with better mental models, but this intelligibility type was rarely attended to by most participants.

To solve this dilemma, we incorporated the *model* content into our *Why* explanation—it explains all of the evidence the classifiers used, but it also explains where that evidence came from (e.g., words or folder size) and how it was combined to arrive at a final prediction. This approach has the added advantage of making the potentially abstract *model* intelligibility type very concrete; it is now tailored to each specific prediction.

A further aspect of completeness is evident in the *Feature overview* explanation (Figure 1, part E). This explanation shows users how many messages contain a given feature and is intended to help users identify when a feature they think the computer should pay attention to may not be very useful. The explanation updates in real-time as the user types in a potential feature; users do not need to add the feature to view its potential impact on classifications, making this an instance of the *what if* intelligibility type.

We also include the *certainty* intelligibility type, instantiated via the *Prediction confidence* column (Figure 1, part B), which reveals the classifier's confidence in each of its predictions.

Not Overwhelming

To avoid overwhelming users, EluciDebug limits the initial set of features available to the classifier using information gain [47]. Because Principle 1.3 states that explanations should be as complete as possible, users should be able to see all of the classifier's features. Given this constraint, we decided 50 would be the upper limit on feature set size. Offline tests, however, revealed that MNB's F_1 score did not improve while the feature set size increased from 10 to 50, so we decided our classifier would automatically select only the 10 features with the highest information gain (until the user specifies otherwise by adding or removing features).

Being Actionable

The *Important words* explanation (Figure 3) is the primary actionable explanation in EluciDebug. Users can add words to—and remove words from—this explanation, which in turn will add those words to (or remove them from) the machine learning model's feature set. Users are also able to adjust the importance of each word in the explanation by dragging the word's bar higher (to make it more important) or lower (to make it less important), which then alters the corresponding feature's weight in the learning model.

The *Why* explanation (Figure 2) is a likely candidate for actionability, but we have not yet made it actionable in EluciDebug. As this explanation only includes features from the selected message, it cannot replace the *Important words* explanation because doing so would interfere with our explanations' completeness. It could, however, complement the *Important words* explanation by allowing users to directly adjust the importance of features responsible for the given prediction. For example, users could drag out from the center of a word to increase its importance, or drag in toward the center of the word to decrease its importance. Whether such additional actionability would help users, however, remains an open question.

Being Reversible

EluciDebug includes an *undo* button for reversing changes to the *Important words* explanation. There is no limit on how many actions can be un-done because we want users to interact with the system without fear they will harm its predictions; regardless of how much they adjust its reasoning, they can always return to any prior state.

Honoring User Feedback

EluciDebug allows users to provide two types of feedback: traditional *instanced-based feedback*, where the user applies a label[2] to an entire item, and *feature-based feedback*, where the user tells the classifier an item should be labeled in a certain manner because of specific features it contains or feature values it matches. EluciDebug honors instance-based feedback in a straightforward manner: once the user labels an item, the classifier will use it as part of its training set, with no distinction between older versus more recent feedback. Honoring feature-based feedback, however, is more complicated.

The smoothing term p_{nc} from Equation 3 acts as a Bayesian prior, effectively adding some number of virtual occurrences (again, traditionally 1) to the number of actual occurrences of each word in the training data, and we can leverage it to integrate feature-based feedback. By allowing the user to set the value of p_{nc}, we are letting the user increase the number of virtual occurrences of word n in class c. The result is a classifier that considers word n to be stronger evidence in favor of class c than it had before the user's feedback.

Using the smoothing term as a feature-based feedback mechanism, however, has a drawback: F_{nc} may increase as the training set size increases, causing the value of p_{nc} to become a smaller component of Equation 3. Thus, a user's feature-based feedback could account for less and less of the classifier's reasoning as their instance-based feedback increased.

To prevent a user's feature-based feedback from degrading in importance over time, we developed a visual feedback mechanism (Figure 3) that allows users to specify how important their feedback should be relative to the model's internal word probabilities (the F terms in Equation 3). The black lines on the blue and green bars in Figure 3 show the model-computed probabilities for each feature, which serve as a starting point for feature-based feedback. Users can tell the system that the probability of seeing word w_n in class c should be increased by clicking and dragging its bar higher, which will translate to an increased value for p_{nc}. If the user later provides additional instance-based feedback (thus causing F_{nc} to change), p_{nc} will be automatically recalculated such that the ratios of $\sum_{x=1}^{N} p_{xc}$ to $\sum_{x=1}^{N} F_{xc}$ and p_{nc} to F_{nc} remain constant.

Revealing Incremental Changes

There are many components of EluciDebug that may change after each user action, so to avoid confusing users with several

[2] A *label* is a potential output of the learning system, such as *junk mail* or *normal mail*.

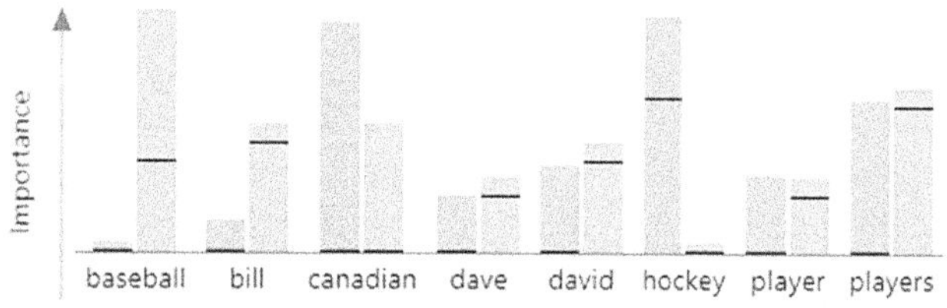

Figure 3. The *Important words* explanation tells users all of the features the classifier is aware of, and also lets users add, remove, and adjust these features. Each topic is color-coded (here, blue for *hockey* and green for *baseball*) with the difference in bar heights reflecting the difference in the word's probability with respect to each topic (e.g., the word *canadian* is roughly twice as likely to appear in a document about *hockey* as one about *baseball*, while the word *player* is about equally likely to appear in either topic). This figure is an excerpt from Figure 1 part F.

different explanation paradigms, we designed a method that consistently reveals changes in terms of *increases* and *decreases*. Increases of any numeric value are identified by green "up" arrows, while decreasing numeric values are identified by red "down" arrows. Examples of each are shown in Figure 1, part B. Hovering over either of these arrow icons yields a tooltip detailing what just changed and how much it changed by, e.g., "Confidence increased by 9%". These indicators reveal changes in the number of messages correctly classified in each folder, the total number of messages the machine learning model currently classified into each folder, and the confidence of each prediction.

In addition to numeric change indicators, we also needed an ordinal change indicator to highlight when a message's prediction flipped from one topic to the other. We used a grey background for these recently-changed predictions (see part B of Figure 1) and included a tooltip explaining that the user's last action resulted in the message's predicted topic changing.

EVALUATION

We evaluated Explanatory Debugging, as instantiated in EluciDebug, to investigate the following research questions:

RQ1: Does Explanatory Debugging help users personalize a classifier *more efficiently* than instance labeling?

RQ2: Does Explanatory Debugging help users personalize a classifier *more accurately* than instance labeling?

RQ3: Does Explanatory Debugging help users build *better mental models* than a traditional black-box approach?

Experiment Design

We used a between-subject, single-factor experimental setup to evaluate Explanatory Debugging. The factor we varied was experiment condition: one condition (*control*) used a variation of EluciDebug with all of its explanation and feature-based feedback capabilities removed (Figure 4), while the second condition (*treatment*) used the EluciDebug prototype described earlier. In both conditions EluciDebug was setup as a binary classifier that attempted to predict whether each message belonged to one of two topics.

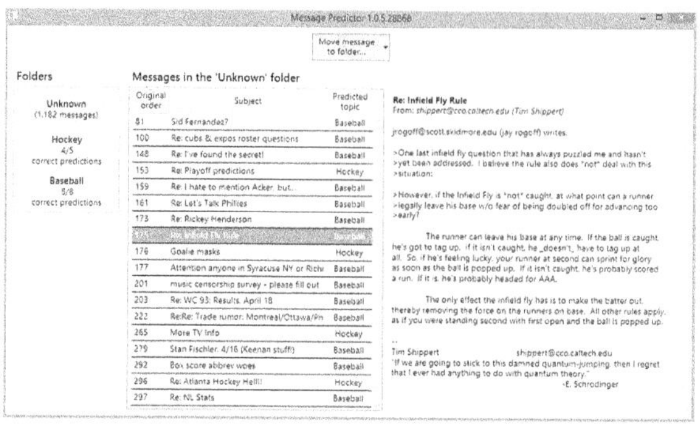

Figure 4. Control participants used this variant of EluciDebug, which lacks explanations and feature-based feedback.

To provide messages for EluciDebug, we selected two concepts from the 20 Newsgroups dataset[3]: *hockey* and *baseball* (the rec.sport.hockey and rec.sport.baseball newgroups, respectively). We used two subgroups of a larger group of related concepts (rec.sport) to ensure overlap in the terminology of each concept (e.g., "player" and "team" may be equally representative of *baseball* or *hockey*). These shared terms help make the classification task more challenging.

To simulate a situation where personalization would be required because sufficient training data does not yet exist, we severely limited the size of the machine learning training set for this experiment. At the start of the experiment this training set consisted of 5 messages in the *Hockey* folder and 5 messages in the *Baseball* folder, with 1,185 unlabeled messages in the *Unknown* folder. The small training set (10 messages) allowed us to evaluate a situation with limited training data, and the large amount of *potential* training data (1,185 messages) allowed us to contrast Explanatory Debugging against black-box instance labeling in a situation where instance labeling could be expected to succeed.

Participants and Procedure

We recruited 77 participants (27 females, 50 males) from the local community and university. To ensure that participants would have little or no prior experience with software debugging or machine learning, we did not accept participants who had more programming experience than an introductory-level course. A total of 37 participants experienced the control condition and 40 participants took part in the treatment condition.

A researcher introduced participants to the prototype via a brief hands-on tutorial that explained how to use it, but did not discuss how it made predictions. Participants then had three minutes to explore the prototype on their own. To avoid learning effects, the tutorial and practice session involved messages about topics (*outer space* and *medicine*) different from the main experiment task.

The main experiment task followed the practice session. Participants were asked to "make the computer's predictions as accurate as possible" and given 30 minutes to work. The software logged all participant interactions and logged evaluations of its internal classifier at 30-second intervals.

[3] http://qwone.com/~jason/20Newsgroups/

After the main task concluded, we assessed participants' mental models via a questionnaire. This test instrument evaluated how well participants understood the two components that contribute to the MNB classifier's predictions: feature presence and class ratios. Because feature presence can be easy to detect given certain words (e.g., the word "hockey" is obviously related to the concept of *hockey*), we evaluated participants' understanding of feature presence using both "obvious" and "subtle" features. We define "subtle" features as words that are not normally associated with a topic, but appear in the classifier's training set and thus will impact classification. Participants were given three short messages about two topics (*swimming* and *tennis*) and told that "these are the only messages the software has learned from". Participants in the treatment condition were also given an *Important words* explanation similar to the one they saw in the prototype. A second sheet displayed 12 messages, each only one or two sentences long, and asked participants which topic the classifier would assign to each message, and why. The messages were constructed such that only one component—either an obvious feature, a subtle feature, or class ratios—was entirely responsible for the classification.

To understand participants' reactions to EluciDebug, the post-task questionnaire also asked participants about various features of the prototype and their perceived task load during the experiment (via the NASA-TLX questionnaire [15]).

Data analysis

We used non-parametric methods for all statistical analyses. As suggested in [31], we used Mann–Whitney U-tests for interval and ordinal data, and Spearman's ρ for correlations.

To analyze participants' mental models, a researcher graded participant responses to the post-task mental model questionnaires. Because some participants may have randomly guessed which topic the classifier would predict for each message, we ignored all predicted topics and only graded the reasons participants' stated for the classifier's prediction. Participants earned two points for correct reasons and one point for partially correct reasons. The researcher graded participant responses without knowing which condition the participant was in (i.e., blindly). Each participants' points were summed to yield a mental model score with a maximum possible value of 24.

We supplemented our evaluation of classifier accuracy with an additional offline experiment using a separate feature selection method. Recall that EluciDebug limits its classifier to the 10 features with the highest information gain. Text classifiers, however, often include most—if not all—of the words in the training set as features. Thus, we analyzed participants' classifiers using both *HighIG* features and *Comprehensive* features. For control participants (who could not provide feature-based feedback), *HighIG* was recomputed after each message was labeled and kept the 10 highest information gain features. For treatment participants, *HighIG* was never recomputed; instead, participants needed to modify it manually by adding, removing, or adjusting features. The *Comprehensive* feature set included all words from the set of labeled messages at the end of the experiment. The classifiers participants interacted with used the *HighIG* features; the *Comprehensive* features were only used for offline analysis.

RESULTS

Explaining Corrections to EluciDebug

EluciDebug includes several methods for users to explain corrections to the classifier, and treatment participants made frequent use of all of them. On average, they added 34.5 new features, removed 8.2 features (including 7.4 of EluciDebug's 10 initial features), and made 18.3 feature adjustments (e.g., increasing or decreasing a feature's importance to a topic). Control participants—who could not provide feature-based feedback—instead relied on instance-based feedback to adjust EluciDebug's predictions, labeling an average of 182 messages vs. the treatment average of 47 ($W = 1395$, $p < .001$). Control participants also examined more messages, averaging 296 message views vs. 151 views ($W = 1306$, $p < .001$). Treatment participants thus provided less feedback overall (and needed to explore less of the dataset while providing it), instead leveraging EluciDebug's abilities to target their feedback at features rather than instances.

This feature-based feedback proved efficient at improving participants' classifiers. We examined the change in F_1 for each participant's classifier during the experiment and divided this by the number of actions the participant made that could influence the classifier's predictions (instances labeled and features added, removed, or adjusted). The results, shown in Figure 5 (left), were that treatment participants performed fewer actions, but each of their actions resulted in larger classifier improvements than those of control participants. Treatment participants' feedback was twice as efficient as control participants' using *HighIG* features (0.16% vs. 0.34% F_1 improvement per action, $W = 207$, $p < .001$), and remained superior when using the *Comprehensive* feature set (0.65% vs. 0.97%, $W = 367$, $p < .001$).

We thus have evidence that when users can only provide a limited amount of feedback to a learning system (such as when labeling instances is expensive, insufficient instances are available for labeling, or the user's time is constrained), Explanatory Debugging can result in better classifiers than a traditional black-box instance labeling approach. Indeed, Figure 5 (right) shows that by the end of the 30-minute experiment, treatment participants had created classifiers that were roughly 10% more accurate than control participants, averaging F_1 scores of 0.85 vs. 0.77 ($W = 237$, $p < .001$).

However, our analysis with the *Comprehensive* feature set suggests that when the user can label many instances, instance labeling with a large feature set may be preferable to Explanatory Debugging—at least to initially train a classifier. The combination of a large training set and many features allowed control participants' classifiers to edge out those of treatment participants by about 8% (Figure 5, right). Even though treatment participants' feedback was up to twice as efficient, control participants provided almost four times as many labeled instances, allowing them to train classifiers with

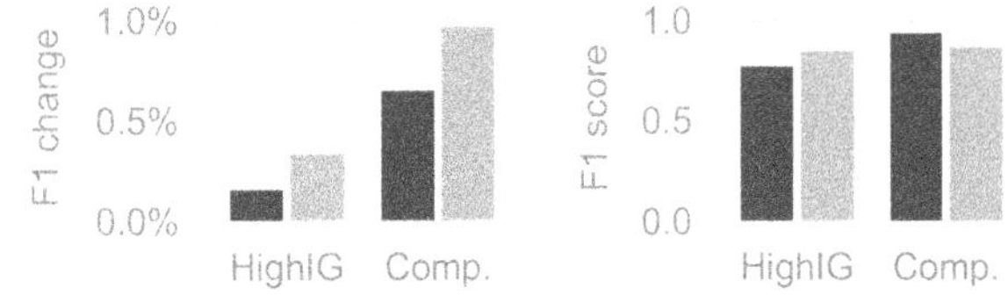

Figure 5. (Left) Average classifier F_1 improvement per user action for control (dark blue) and treatment (light orange); treatment participants controlled their classifiers up to twice as efficiently as control participants. (Right) Average classifier F_1 scores per condition. Control participants needed four times as much data and the *Comprehensive* feature set to create better classifiers than treatment participants.

an average F_1 of 0.94, while treatment participants averaged 0.87 ($W = 1290$, $p < .001$).

To verify it was the amount of instance-based feedback that allowed control participants to outperform treatment participants when *Comprehensive* features were considered, we analyzed the accuracy of their classifiers after the same number of actions had been performed. Figure 6 shows the F_1 scores after *n* feedback actions using the *HighIG* (solid line) and *Comprehensive* (dotted line) feature sets. Given the same number of actions, control participants never outperformed treatment participants. This suggests that when treatment participants did provide instance-based feedback (which was the only type of feedback used for the *Comprehensive* analysis), it was often more useful than control participants' feedback.

We also analyzed participant reactions to the two prototype variations. Treatment participants liked their variant more than control participants, rating its helpfulness as 4.8 vs. 4.3 on a 6-point scale ($W = 474$, $p = .006$). Further, we found no evidence that treatment participants felt Explanatory Debugging involved more work than black-box instance labeling. We used the NASA-TLX survey to measure participants' perceived task load while attempting to improve their classifier, but found no evidence of a difference between conditions.

These classifier measures reveal three findings. First, in situations where large amounts of training data is unavailable or expensive to obtain, Explanatory Debugging (as instantiated in EluciDebug) allows users to successfully train a classifier by telling it about features instead of instances. Second, the mix of feature- and instance-based feedback provided by treatment participants was more efficient than the purely instance-based feedback provided by control participants, suggesting that when an end user has a specific goal in mind (such as our Alice example from earlier), Explanatory Debugging can help the user quickly realize their goal.

Third, control participants' success with using large amounts of instance-based feedback suggests that in domains where labeling instances is quick and practical, some combination of feature- and instance-based feedback may be best. In fact, such systems may need to emphasize the potential usefulness of labeling instances. In our experiment, the mere presence of feature-based feedback tools appears to have biased participants against instance-based feedback: 3 treatment participants did not provide any at all, while the smallest number of labeled

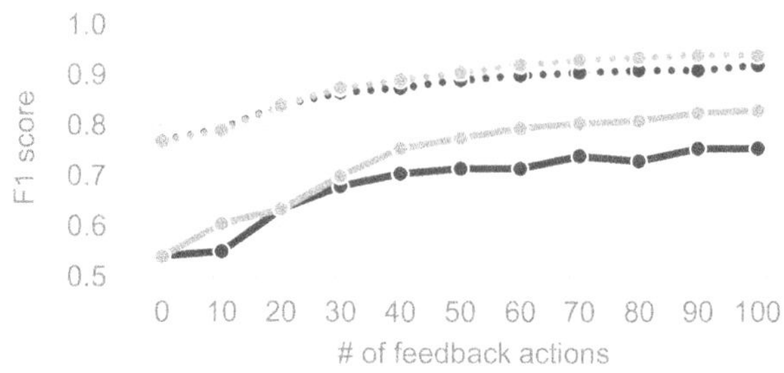

Figure 6. Treatment participants (light orange) created equivalent or better classifiers than control participants (dark blue) using the same amount of feedback. This held for both the *HighIG* (solid) and *Comprehensive* (dotted) feature sets.

instances from a control participant was 56—more than even the treatment *average* of 47 labeled instances.

EluciDebug's Explanations to End Users

Before users can correct a machine learning system's explanation of its reasoning, they must first *understand* the explanation. This understanding is reflected in their mental model.

Treatment participants built significantly better mental models than participants in the control condition. As shown in Table 1, treatment participants scored 52% higher on the mental model assessment than control participants ($W = 259$, $p < .001$). Much of this difference stems from treatment participants identifying *all* of the keywords the classifier used, while control participants often identified only the "obvious" keywords. In fact, treatment participants averaged a score of 14.1 out of 16 (88%) during the keyword assessment, suggesting they firmly understood how the classifier involved keywords—regardless of whether the words had any semantic association with their topics—in its reasoning.

Table 1 also suggests treatment participants better understood that the classifier used class ratios as part of its prediction strategy than participants in the control condition ($W = 619.5$, $p = .099$), but the evidence is weak. Further, a majority of participants in both conditions failed to answer *any* class ratio question correctly, suggesting that this explanation either failed to convey relevant information about how class ratios were used by the classifier, or failed to attract participants' attention.

Many control participants wanted the same information available to the treatment group. As one participant stated:

> *C1: "More information on how emails are sorted would help the user target emails to categorize, which would increase accuracy."*

Another control participant (C15) described the software as *"annoying"*, but that working with it *"would have been easier if we knew how it made predictions"*, while still another (C4) said it was annoying to work with because he *"didn't know what it was basing its predictions off of"*. A fourth participant (C11) even asked for a similar feedback mechanism as was available to treatment participants, saying the software was *"time-consuming"* because there was *"no way to highlight key words/terms"*. A fifth control participant summed it up:

> *C30: "That was a long 30 minutes."*

Model component	Max score	Control mean (SD)	Treatment mean (SD)	*p*-value
Obvious features	8	6.7 (2.7)	7.3 (1.8)	.345
Subtle features	8	2.8 (2.6)	**6.8 (1.9)**	<.001
Class ratios	8	0.6 (1.5)	1.8 (3.0)	.099
Total score	24	10.4 (5.3)	**15.8 (4.6)**	<.001

Table 1. Treatment participants finished the experiment with significantly higher mental model scores than control participants.

Participants in the treatment condition, conversely, appreciated EluciDebug's explanations and feedback mechanisms:

> *T24: "Not difficult to understand/operate, doesn't take a lot of effort."*
>
> *T40: "It was really fast to get a high degree of accuracy."*
>
> *T37: "I felt in control of all the settings."*
>
> *T6: "It was so simple my parents could use it."*

Overall, our principled Explanatory Debugging approach successfully helped participants develop accurate mental models of the classifier they used, and participants benefited from this additional knowledge. Spearman's ρ confirms a link between participants' mental model scores and their classifier's F_1 scores ($\rho[75] = .282$, $p = .013$)

DISCUSSION

RQ1 and RQ2: Efficient and Accurate Personalization

Our results suggest that Explanatory Debugging can be an *efficient* method for users to personalize a machine learning system, but that it may not always result in the most *accurate* classifiers. For example, we found that feature-based feedback was up to twice as effective as instance-based feedback, but instance labeling could still yield more accurate classifiers given enough labels and features (in our experiment, four times as many labels were needed). In situations where labeling instances is considerably easier or faster than providing feature-based feedback, users may be better served by labeling a large number of instances than a small number of features.

However, when users need fine-grained control over a classifier, Explanatory Debugging has two advantages beyond efficiency. First, it does not require much training data to exist, and can thus help bootstrap a learning system. Even a trained system that suddenly needs to support a new output type may benefit from such bootstrapping (this also separates our work from knowledge-based artificial intelligence, which is not retrained post-deployment). Second, the quick improvements—during even the first 10 user actions—treatment participants made to their classifiers suggest that users will remain engaged with Explanatory Debugging. This matters because research has shown that if an end-user debugging technique is not perceived as useful after a small number of interactions, users are unlikely to continue using it [34]. Seeing an immediate improvement after providing feedback suggests that users will continue to view and correct the Explanatory Debugging explanations, while the lack of such an improvement may discourage users of black-box instance labeling systems from continuing to provide feedback.

RQ3: Mental Models

Explanatory Debugging helped participants build useful mental models, and did so without a perceived increase in task load. We found no evidence that treatment participants found the extra information or feedback mechanisms more difficult to understand or use; instead, their responses suggest they appreciated having such information available.

Indeed, the fact that many control participants' requested explanations similar to those the treatment participants saw suggests the need for machine learning systems to be able to explain their reasoning in accordance with Explanatory Debugging's *Explainability* principle. Even if this information is hidden by default, users should be able to view such explanations on demand. Further, because machine learning systems are meant to classify items as their user would, the user must have some method to correct the system's mistakes. Thus, we hypothesize that including Explanatory Debugging-style explanations without also supporting our *Correctibility* principle will frustrate users—they would see what needs correcting, but be powerless to fix it.

CONCLUSION

Overall, Explanatory Debugging's cycle of explanations—from the learning system to the user, and from the user back to the system—resulted in smarter users and smarter learning systems. Participants using Explanatory Debugging understood how the learning system operated about 50% better than control participants, and this improvement correlated with the F_1 scores of participants' classifiers. Each piece of feedback provided by Explanatory Debugging participants was worth roughly two pieces of feedback provided by control participants; even when we expanded our analysis to include a comprehensive feature set, treatment participants still maintained a 50% edge over the control group. Further, participants liked Explanatory Debugging, rating this variant of EluciDebug higher than the control group and responding enthusiastically to the system's explanations.

This work is but one step toward helping users control machine learning systems. How Explanatory Debugging may be applied to more complex problems, such as multiclass classifiers or deep learning algorithms, remains an open question. Future work could also investigate how Explanatory Debugging impacts user interactions over longer time periods and whether end users are able to transfer knowledge of one learning system to more quickly personalize similar systems.

Our results show that when end users want to personalize a machine learning system, Explanatory Debugging is a more controllable and satisfying approach than black-box instance labeling. The approach's focus on users—in which the system explains its reasoning and the user explains back corrections as needed—enables ordinary end users to get the most benefit from learning systems on which they depend.

ACKNOWLEDGMENTS

We thank Irwin Kwan, Charles Hill, Leah Hanen, Renuka Bhatt, and our study participants for their help in conducting this research.

REFERENCES

1. Amershi, S., Cakmak, M., Knox, W. B., and Kulesza, T. Power to the people: The role of humans in interactive machine learning. *AI Magazine* (in press).
2. Amershi, S., Fogarty, J., Kapoor, A., and Tan, D. Examining multiple potential models in end-user interactive concept learning. In *Proceedings of the ACM Conference on Human Factors in Computing Systems* (2010), 1357–1360.
3. Blackwell, A. F. First steps in programming: A rationale for attention investment models. In *Proceedings of the IEEE 2002 Symposia on Human Centric Computing Languages and Environments*, IEEE (2002), 2–10.
4. Bostandjiev, S., O'Donovan, J., and Höllerer, T. TasteWeights: A visual interactive hybrid recommender system. In *Proceedings of the 6th ACM Conference on Recommender Systems* (2012), 35–42.
5. Bryan, N. J., Mysore, G. J., and Wang, G. ISSE: An interactive source separation editor. In *Proceedings of the ACM Conference on Human Factors in Computing Systems* (2014), 257–266.
6. Bunt, A., Lount, M., and Lauzon, C. Are explanations always important? A study of deployed, low-cost intelligent interactive systems. In *Proceedings of the 2012 ACM International Conference on Intelligent User Interfaces* (2012), 169–178.
7. Cakmak, M., Chao, C., and Thomaz, A. L. Designing interactions for robot active learners. *IEEE Transactions on Autonomous Mental Development 2*, 2 (2010), 108–118.
8. Cramer, H., Evers, V., Ramlal, S., van Someren, M., Rutledge, L., Stash, N., Aroyo, L., and Wielinga, B. The effects of transparency on trust in and acceptance of a content-based art recommender. *User Modeling and User-Adapted Interaction 18*, 5 (2008), 455–496.
9. Craven, M. W., and Shavlik, J. W. Using neural networks for data mining. *Future generation computer systems 13* (1997), 211–229.
10. Dzindolet, M. T., Peterson, S. A., Pomranky, R. A., Pierce, L. G., and Beck, H. P. The role of trust in automation reliance. *International Journal of Human-Computer Studies 58*, 6 (2003), 697–718.
11. Fails, J. A., Olsen, D. R., and Jr. Interactive machine learning. In *Proceedings of the 8th International Conference on Intelligent User Interfaces* (2003), 39–45.
12. Fiebrink, R., Cook, P. R., and Trueman, D. Human model evaluation in interactive supervised learning. In *Proceedings of the ACM Conference on Human Factors in Computing Systems* (2011), 147–156.
13. Fogarty, J., Tan, D., Kapoor, A., and Winder, S. CueFlik: Interactive concept learning in image search. In *Proceedings of the ACM Conference on Human Factors in Computing Systems* (2008), 29–38.
14. Groce, A., Kulesza, T., Zhang, C., Shamasunder, S., Burnett, M. M., Wong, W.-K., Stumpf, S., Das, S., Shinsel, A., Bice, F., and McIntosh, K. You are the only possible oracle: Effective test selection for end users of interactive machine learning systems. *IEEE Transactions on Software Engineering 40*, 3 (2014), 307–323.
15. Hart, S. G., and Staveland, L. E. Development of NASA-TLX (Task Load Index): Results of empirical and theoretical research. *Advances in Psychology 52* (1988), 139–183.
16. Herlocker, J. L., Konstan, J. A., and Riedl, J. Explaining collaborative filtering recommendations. In *Proceedings of the 2000 ACM Conference on Computer Supported Cooperative Work* (2000), 241–250.
17. Johnson-Laird, P. N. *Mental models: Towards a cognitive science of language, inference, and consciousness.* Harvard University Press, 1983.
18. Kapoor, A., Lee, B., Tan, D., and Horvitz, E. Interactive optimization for steering machine classification. In *Proceedings of the ACM Conference on Human Factors in Computing Systems* (2010), 1343–1352.
19. Kempton, W. Two theories of home heat control. *Cognitive Science 10* (1986), 75–90.
20. Kibriya, A. M., Frank, E., Pfahringer, B., and Holmes, G. Multinomial naive Bayes for text categorization revisited. In *AI 2004: Advances in Artificial Intelligence.* Springer Berlin Heidelberg, Berlin, Heidelberg, 2004, 488–499.
21. Knox, W. B., and Stone, P. Reinforcement learning from human reward: Discounting in episodic tasks. In *Proceedings of the 21st IEEE International Symposium on Robot and Human Interactive Communication* (2012), 878–885.
22. Ko, A. J., and Myers, B. A. Debugging reinvented. *the 13th international conference* (2008), 301–310.
23. Kulesza, T., Stumpf, S., Burnett, M. M., and Kwan, I. Tell me more? The effects of mental model soundness on personalizing an intelligent agent. In *Proceedings of the ACM Conference on Human Factors in Computing Systems* (2012), 1–10.
24. Kulesza, T., Stumpf, S., Burnett, M. M., Wong, W.-K., Riche, Y., Moore, T., Oberst, I., Shinsel, A., and McIntosh, K. Explanatory debugging: Supporting end-user debugging of machine-learned programs. In *Proceedings of the 2010 IEEE Symposium on Visual Languages and Human-Centric Computing* (2010), 41–48.
25. Kulesza, T., Stumpf, S., Burnett, M. M., and Yang, S. Too much, too little, or just right? Ways explanations impact end users' mental models. *Proceedings of the 2013 IEEE Symposium on Visual Languages and Human-Centric Computing* (2013), 3–10.
26. Kulesza, T., Stumpf, S., Wong, W.-K., Burnett, M. M., Perona, S., Ko, A. J., and Oberst, I. Why-oriented end-user debugging of naive Bayes text classification. *ACM Transactions on Interactive Intelligent Systems 1*, 1 (2011).
27. Lacave, C., and Díez, F. J. A review of explanation methods for Bayesian networks. *The Knowledge Engineering Review 17*, 2 (2002), 107–127.

28. Lim, B. Y. *Improving understanding and trust with intelligibility in context-aware applications*. PhD thesis, Carnegie Mellon University, 2012.
29. Lim, B. Y., and Dey, A. K. Assessing demand for intelligibility in context-aware applications. In *Proceedings of the 11th International Conference on Ubiquitous Computing* (2009), 195–204.
30. Lim, B. Y., Dey, A. K., and Avrahami, D. Why and why not explanations improve the intelligibility of context-aware intelligent systems. In *Proceedings of the ACM Conference on Human Factors in Computing Systems* (2009), 2119–2128.
31. McCrum-Gardner, E. Which is the correct statistical test to use? *British Journal of Oral and Maxillofacial Surgery 46* (2008), 38–41.
32. Norman, D. A. Some observations on mental models. In *Human-Computer Interaction*, R. M. Baecker and W. A. S. Buxton, Eds. San Francisco, CA, USA, 1987, 241–244.
33. Norman, D. A. *The Design of Everyday Things*. Revised and Expanded Edition. Basic Books, 2002.
34. Prabhakararao, S., Cook, C., Ruthruff, J., Creswick, E., Main, M., Durham, M., and Burnett, M. M. Strategies and behaviors of end-user programmers with interactive fault localization. In *Proceedings of the IEEE Symposium on Human Centric Computing Languages and Environments* (2003), 15–22.
35. Rowe, M. B. *Teaching science as continuous inquiry*. McGraw-Hill, 1973.
36. Rugaber, S., Goel, A. K., and Martie, L. GAIA: A CAD environment for model-Based Adaptation of game-playing Software Agents. *Procedia Computer Science 16* (2013), 29–38.
37. Settles, B. Active learning literature survey. Tech. Rep. 1648, University of Wisconsin-Madison, 2010.
38. Stumpf, S., Rajaram, V., Li, L., Wong, W.-K., Burnett, M. M., Dietterich, T., Sullivan, E., and Herlocker, J. Interacting meaningfully with machine learning systems: Three experiments. *International Journal of Human-Computer Studies 67*, 8 (2009), 639–662.
39. Szafron, D., Greiner, R., Lu, P., and Wishart, D. Explaining naïve Bayes classifications. Tech. Rep. TR03-09, University of Alberta, 2003.
40. Talbot, J., Lee, B., Kapoor, A., and Tan, D. S. EnsembleMatrix: Interactive visualization to support machine learning with multiple classifiers. In *Proceedings of the ACM Conference on Human Factors in Computing Systems* (2009), 1283–1292.
41. Thomaz, A. L., and Breazeal, C. Transparency and socially guided machine learning. In *Proceedings of the 5th International Conference on Development and Learning* (2006).
42. Tintarev, N., and Masthoff, J. Evaluating the effectiveness of explanations for recommender systems. *User Modeling and User-Adapted Interaction 22*, 4-5 (2012), 399–439.
43. Tullio, J., Dey, A. K., Chalecki, J., and Fogarty, J. How it works: A field study of non-technical users interacting with an intelligent system. In *Proceedings of the ACM Conference on Human Factors in Computing Systems* (2007), 31–40.
44. van der Meij, H., and Carroll, J. M. Principles and heuristics for designing minimalist instruction. In *Minimalism beyond the Nurnberg funnel*, J. M. Carroll, Ed. MIT Press, Cambridge, MA, 1998, 19–53.
45. Vig, J., Sen, S., and Riedl, J. Navigating the tag genome. In *Proceedings of the 16th International Conference on Intelligent User Interfaces* (2011), 93–102.
46. Yang, R., and Newman, M. W. Learning from a learning thermostat: Lessons for intelligent systems for the home. In *Proceedings of the 2013 ACM International Joint Conference on Pervasive and Ubiquitous Computing* (2013), 93–102.
47. Yang, Y., and Pedersen, J. O. A comparative study on feature selection in text categorization. In *Proceedings of the Twentieth International Conference on Machine Learning* (1997), 412–420.

Binary Space Partitioning Layouts To Help Build Better Information Dashboards

Patrick Hertzog
Nexthink S.A.
Lausanne, Switzerland
patrick.hertzog@nexthink.com

ABSTRACT
Information dashboards are a widely used means to present data at-a-glance and their quality (i.e., their ability to communicate the data in a clear and efficient way) depends not only on the way to represent the data but also on how visual elements are placed on the screen—the dashboard layout. In many cases the dashboards are predefined by the application but we are now in an era where the user wants more freedom. Unfortunately this freedom is today bounded by the applications using layout managers which either do not offer the needed flexibility or are too complex to be used by non-experts.

In this paper, we propose a novel layout manager more suitable for dashboards; it provides layouts based on a binary space partitioning (BSP) and we show how the user can interactively build and modify them. Then we present how we can compute an optimal solution for such layouts, i.e., how to actually compute the position and size of all visual elements in order for them to be as close as possible to their preferred size while respecting the arrangement decided by the user. This is achieved by automatically generating a set of constraints which are then solved to find the optimal solution. Finally we describe the actual implementation of a lightweight constraint solver in JavaScript—named QPSolver—that can be embedded in a web application and we compare its performance with Cassowary [4], a well-known solver for constraint-based GUI layouts notably used by Apple in OS X and iOS.

Author Keywords
Layout manager; information dashboards; constraints generation; constraints solving; quadratic optimization; binary space partitioning; binary tree; QPSolver.

ACM Classification Keywords
H.5.2. User Interfaces: Graphical user interfaces (GUI); Screen design (e.g., text, graphics, color)

ACM 978-1-4503-3306-1/15/03 ...$15.00.
http://dx.doi.org/10.1145/2678025.2701383

INTRODUCTION
In their professional life as well as in their day-to-day life, people encounter more and more information dashboards. In [10], Few gives a formal definition of what a dashboard is:

> "A dashboard is a visual display of the most important information needed to achieve one or more objectives that has been consolidated on a single computer screen so it can be monitored at a glance."

Dashboards are made of several pieces of information, such as metrics and key performance indicators (KPIs) [18], displayed as graphs, tables or even in a purely textual form (in this paper we call them *visual elements*). To design an effective dashboard—i.e., a dashboard that communicates clearly its data—one has to take care of several aspects such as choosing the appropriate display media depending on the kind of information and designing each table and graph properly [9, 31]. A complete guideline to designing effective dashboards can be found in [10].

There are companies selling products dedicated to creating dashboards, such as Tableau Software [30] and Qlik [26]. However dashboards are today used in virtually any application managing data; they include but are not limited to enterprise software (e.g., Salesforce, SAP), analytics tools (e.g., Google Analytics, New Relic) and even personal applications (e.g., Nike+). While most applications provide out-of-the-box hardcoded dashboards, the trend is to let users build their own dashboards. In the latter, the user has not only to choose the data to be displayed—and how to display it—but also to lay it out on the screen. Unfortunately the layout managers used today do not offer the needed flexibility or are too complex for non-experts. To overcome those issues we need to develop a layout manager with the following requirements:

Easy to define We want a layout manager enabling non-experts to easily and interactively build a dashboard, i.e., to place all visual elements at their proper place on the screen.

Flexible A dashboard can be made of visual elements of very different sizes: a full graph requires more space and may have a different aspect ratio than, for example, a number displayed in a textual form.

Predictable On a dashboard, related visual elements are placed close to each other to form groups according to the law of proximity of the Gestalt principles [33]. These groups must be maintained when any modification is made (e.g., the dashboard is resized, a new visual element is added or removed).

Visually coherent Aesthetics, even if often sidelined, play an important part in GUI design as they deal with emotions that are critical for having a successful product [24]. A large part of aesthetics is related to the look and feel of the different visual elements but the visual coherence of the layout plays a role too. To have an aesthetic dashboard, we need to use the whole available space in a well balanced way and all visual elements have to be properly aligned [15]. This also ensures that the layout is more compact and easier to understand.

Related Work

When developing a GUI, one usually uses a layout manager to avoid defining the position of each element in an absolute unit (e.g., in pixels). In this case the developer has to provide a set of simple layout specifications and the layout manager will then automatically compute the position of each element based on different factors (e.g., available space, element sizes, layout specifications). Many different types of layout managers exist and we can classify them into different categories:

1. First of all we have the layout managers that are part of most GUI frameworks such as Java Swing [29], Windows Presentation Foundation [34] or Qt [27]. The *Group* layout enables elements to be placed next to each other, either horizontally of vertically. An evolution of this layout is the *Flow* layout which is basically similar to a horizontal group layout but with elements breaking into multiple rows if not enough space is available. In a *Grid* layout, elements are laid out in a 2-dimensional grid and they can span over several rows/columns. Moreover weights can be assigned to rows and columns to define which amount of space they can use proportionally. More advanced versions of the *Grid* layout, such as Masonry [21], try to automate the positioning of the elements on the grid.

2. Frameworks such as Cocoa [7], CCSS [3], FWL [35] and the Auckland Layout Editor [37] allow the definition of *constraint-based* layouts. In such layouts the user defines a set of constraints in the form of linear equalities or inequalities. An example of constraint can be

   $x_1 = x_2$ where x_i is the horizontal position of element i

   to define that elements 1 and 2 must be left-aligned. Each constraint can be either *hard* (i.e., it must be satisfied) or *soft* (i.e., it can be violated if needed). Soft constraints basically represent preferences. *Group* or *Grid* layouts can be expressed as constraints as well but constraint-based layouts allow even more complex layouts.

3. Finally some more specialized layout managers exist. An example is Packery [25] which automatically lays out elements on a webpage and uses a bin-packing algorithm to minimize the needed amount of space. Other placement strategies are reviewed in [32].

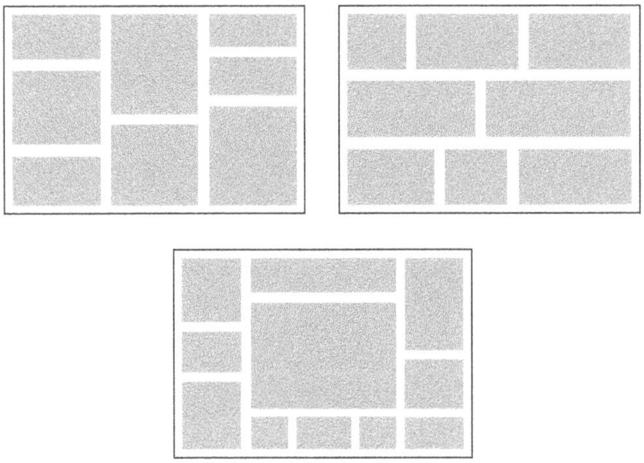

Figure 1. On the top are shown the types of layouts usually available in dashboards: column-based on the left and row-based on the right. On the bottom is the type of layout we would like to achieve.

Unfortunately none of the layout managers mentioned above fulfills the four requirements we want. To remain as easy as possible for the end-user, most dashboards use a layout based on rows or columns—basically a set of *Group* layouts—but they lack the flexibility we need as shown in Figure 1. Such layouts are not predictable neither: for example, in a column-based layout, adding an element to a column will change the position of elements only in that column. Therefore an element that was next to it in another column may not be next to it anymore.

A *Grid* layout would provide the level of flexibility we need but would be more difficult for the user to build: when adding a row or column to the underlying grid, all adjacent elements have to be modified to change their row/column spanning. This is required to ensure a aesthetically pleasing layout by preventing holes (i.e., zones in the layout without any element) and the persistence of the contiguity of the elements for predictability.

Layout managers like Masonry or Packery would be easier for the user as they automate a significant part of the layout process but they have two big drawbacks: firstly these layout algorithms work well only if all elements are of the same size (or a multiple of it), otherwise the resulting layout contains many holes and its aesthetics suffer from it. This means that these layout managers do not provide the level of flexibility we need. Secondly, as the layout is mainly automatic, the result is not predictable so they are not a good fit in our situation: we want to ensure that visual elements placed next to each other stay that way as they may be part of a meaningful group.

Constraint-based layouts offer the flexibility and predictability we need but defining all the different constraints is both a tedious and difficult work especially when constraints have to be defined manually as in OPUS [16], Lapidary [36] or GridStyleSheets (GSS) [14]. Some editors make the process easier [19, 22, 37] but they are made for GUI developers: in such tools constraints are still *visible* to the user to some extent so it is too complex to manage for a non-expert.

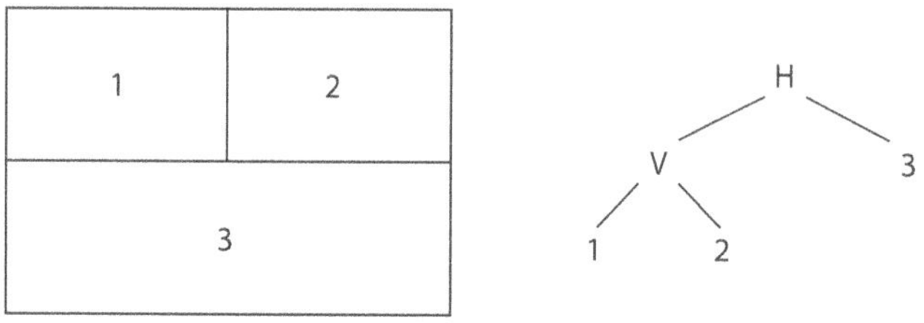

Figure 2. A very simple binary space partitioning (BSP) layout and its tree definition representation. H represents an horizontal edge and V a vertical one.

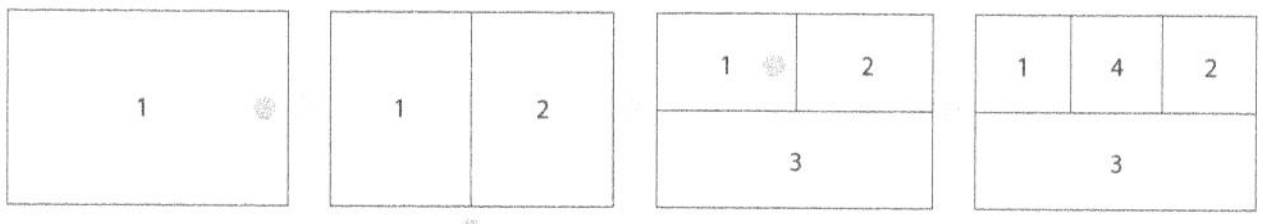

Figure 3. The user builds a layout by adding a tile at the right of tile 1, then one below the whole layout and finally the last one at the right of tile 1.

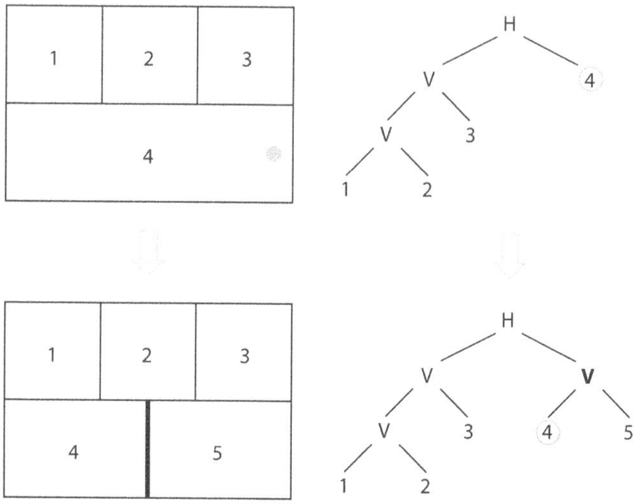

Figure 4. Adding a tile on the right of tile 4 means replacing node 4 by a node V (vertical edge) which has node 4 and the newly created tile as children.

DEFINING A LAYOUT

We want to create a layout manager with the flexibility and predictability of a constraint-based layout but with the ease-of-use of a group-based layout. To achieve it, we propose to use a layout based on binary space partitioning (BSP). In such a layout, the whole available space (i.e., a rectangle) is recursively subdivided by horizontal or vertical lines—called *edges*—into smaller spaces—called *tiles*. Each tile contains one visual element (e.g., a table or a graph) that is automatically resized to fill the available space. A BSP layout can be represented as a binary tree as shown in Figure 2 with each node of the tree being an edge and each leaf a tile. A *sub-layout* is defined as the layout represented by a part of the tree, i.e., one of the children of a node. Two sub-layouts are defined as *siblings* if they share the same parent node. In a similar way, other systems, such as FormsVBT [2], also use a formal (textual) representation of the interface.

In the next subsections we are going to explain how BSP layouts satisfy our requirements stated above: easiness to define, flexibility, predictability and visual coherence.

Easiness to define

A BSP layout can be easily defined in an interactive way by a non-expert user thanks to the recursive nature of the partitioning. To add a new tile, the user has only to choose which tile to subdivide and where to place the new tile relatively to it— on the left, right, top or bottom of it— as shown in Figure 3. The user can also choose to place the new tile on the left, right, top or bottom of the overall layout, i.e., without subdividing an existing tile.

If we consider the tree representation of the layout, adding a new tile is a simple operation as shown on Figure 4. If one takes tile i as a reference:

- Adding a new tile x at its top means replacing node i by a node H—an horizontal edge—with the left child being tile x and the right child tile i.
- Adding a new tile x at its bottom means replacing node i by a node H with the left child being tile i and the right child tile x.
- Adding a new tile x at its left means replacing node i by a node V—an vertical edge—with the left child being tile x and the right child tile i.
- Adding a new tile x at its right means replacing node i by a node V with the left child being tile i and the right child tile x (illustrated in Figure 4).

The same principles apply when adding a new tile not relatively to an existing one but to the overall layout. In that case the root node of the tree is replaced by an edge with its children being the new tile and the former tree.

Removing a tile follows the opposite process: the parent node of the removed tile is replaced by its other child. Sometimes the user may want to move a tile: this case can be simply seen as the succession of the removal of the said tile followed by its addition somewhere else in the layout.

Flexibility

A BSP layout enables us to arrange tiles based on rows and columns as traditional layout managers used for dashboards. As there is no limitation on the size—and the depth—of the tree representing the layout. We can define much more advanced and complex layouts as the one illustrated in Figure 1. However BSP layouts have limitations: not all tile arrangements based on a grid can be modeled by a binary tree. For example, the layout illustrated in Figure 5 can not be represented by a binary tree and is therefore not a BSP layout.

Predictability

To be predictable, a layout has to ensure that tiles displayed close to each other—hence forming a group—remain close to each other no matter which modification is done on the layout. Such modifications include the addition or removal of a tile and the resizing of the whole layout.

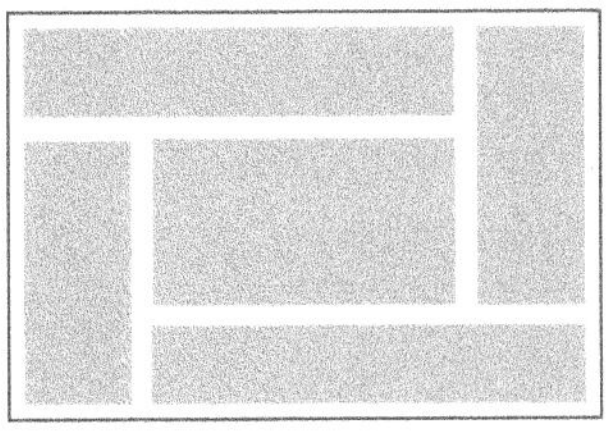

Figure 5. This layout cannot be represented by a binary tree and is therefore not a BSP layout.

In a BSP layout, all tiles belonging to a group are actually tiles located in the same sub-layout, i.e., in the same sub-tree in the tree representation. We have seen above that adding or removing a tile is a simple operation on the tree representation of the layout and has therefore a very limited impact: no sub-layout other than the one in which the modification is done is impacted. This is why all groups are assured to remain together.

When the layout is resized, the visual arrangement of tiles will not be affected: the binary tree representing the layout is independent from the size of the layout. If it changes, the same tree applies, hence the tiles arrangement is guaranteed to be the same. The only change will be the size of each tile.

Visual Coherence

To be aesthetic a dashboard has to fill the whole horizontal available space; a BSP layout uses the whole available space by definition as it is constructed by recursively subdividing this space. It also ensures that all tiles are consistently aligned as each sub-layout is aligned with its sibling. This is also important to ensure that the layout remains as compact as possible and is easy to understand [15].

Another condition to obtain an aesthetic dashboard is to ensure the size of each tile is big enough so that its content has enough space to be displayed and the whole dashboard feels natural and well-balanced. The binary partitioning gives us the arrangement of the tiles but nothing about their sizes—tile sizes are determined by the position of the edges. For this reason we have to set a minimum size for each tile as well as a preferred size which represent the size in which the contained visual element looks the best for the human eye. Finding a solution for the tile sizes will be addressed in the following sections.

GENERATING CONSTRAINTS

Once the layout has been defined (i.e., a tree representation as described in the previous section is defined), we have to actually compute the size and position of each tile. While this task is easy for a human being, doing it programmatically is more difficult. If we look at the simple layout depicted in Figure 2, we can identify two types of constraints: constraints describing the position of the tiles and constraints describing their size.

Tile Position Constraints

Some constraints define the position of the different tiles. For the layout illustrated in Figure 2, tile 1 is the first of the layout so we have the constraints

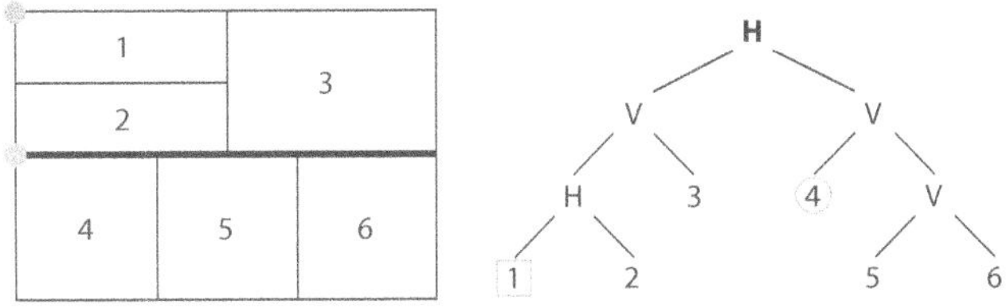

Figure 6. Sub-layouts above and below the edge must be left-aligned, so their first tiles must be left-aligned: it gives us the constraint $x_4 = x_1$.

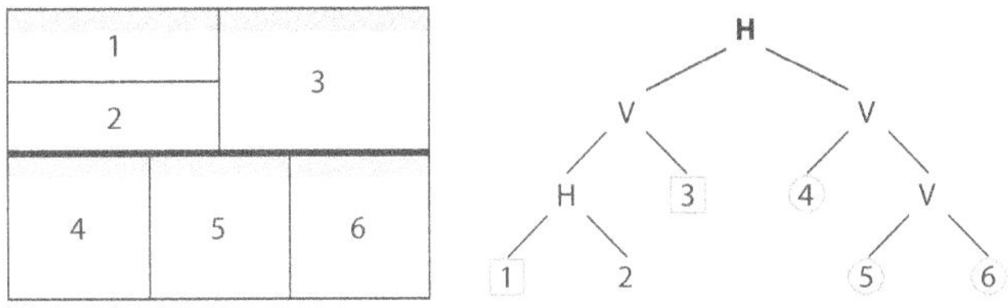

Figure 7. The widths of the sub-layouts above and below the edge must equal: it gives us the constraint $w_4 + w_5 + w_6 = w_1 + w_3$.

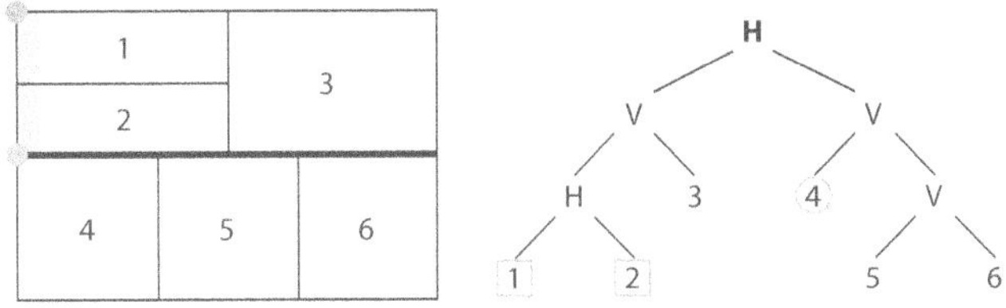

Figure 8. Tile 4 must be positioned below the sub-layout located above the edge: it gives us the constraint $y_4 = y_1 + h_1 + h_2$.

$x_1 = 0$ where x_i is the horizontal position of tile i
$y_1 = 0$ where y_i is the vertical position of tile i

Then we can define the position of the other tiles relative to the first one

$x_2 = x_1 + w_1$ where w_i is the width of tile i
$y_2 = y_1$
$x_3 = x_1$
$y_3 = y_1 + h_1$ where h_i is the height of tile i

Tile Size Constraints

Each tile has a minimum and preferred size, so for the layout depicted in Figure 2, we have the constraints

$$w_i \geq minimum\_width_i$$
$$h_i \geq minimum\_height_i$$
$$w_i \approx preferred\_width_i$$
$$h_i \approx preferred\_height_i$$
$$\forall i \in [1, 2, 3]$$

where $a \approx b$ means that a must have a value as close as possible to the value of b. Additionally the following constraints are derived from the layout

$$h_1 = h_2$$
$$w_3 = w_1 + w_2$$

Finally, as we want the layout to fill all the space horizontally, we add the constraint

$w_1 + w_2 = W$ where W is the available width

Algorithm 1 Retrieving the first tile of a (sub-)layout

```
function FIRSTTILE(node)
    if node is a leaf then
        return node
    else
        return FIRSTTILE(node.leftChild)
```

Automatically Generating Constraints

Based on the tree definition of a layout, it is possible to automatically generate all constraints with a unique deep-first pre-order traversal of the tree. For each visited tree node, a set of constraints has to be generated depending on its type. If it represents a horizontal edge, the constraints are the following:

1. The first tile of the sub-layout above the edge must be left-aligned with the first tile of the sub-layout below the edge (see Figure 6). The sub-layout above an horizontal edge is given by the first child of the tree node representing the said edge; the sub-layout below that edge is given by the second child of the node. The first tile of a sub-layout is determined by Algorithm 1.
2. The sub-layout above the edge must be of an equal width to the one below the edge (see Figure 7). The width of a sub-layout is equal to the sum of the widths of the tiles composing its first row; those tiles can be selected thanks to Algorithm 2.
3. The distance between the first tiles of the both sub-layouts must be equal to the height of the sub-layout above the edge (see Figure 8). The height of a sub-layout is equal to the sum of the heights of the tiles composing its first column; those tiles can be selected thanks to Algorithm 2.

Three similar constraints are generated when the edge is vertical; they are simply defined symmetrically. When a leaf is reached, constraints are added regarding the minimum and preferred width and height of the corresponding tile. If the tile is the first one of the whole layout, two additional constraints are added to set its position to $(0, 0)$. Finally a last constraint is added to ensure that the layout will use all the space available horizontally. The whole algorithm is described in Algorithm 3.

SOLVING THE LAYOUT

In the previous section we have seen how constraints can be automatically generated based on the tree definition of a layout. Now we have to find a way to solve the layout, i.e., finding a value for variables x, y, w and h for each tile of the layout. Those values must of course respect all equality and inequality constraints (hard constraints) but they also have to be optimal, meaning that all tile sizes should be as close as possible to their preferred value (soft constraints). To find an optimal solution, the soft constraints are represented by a scalar objective function that is being minimized while respecting the hard constraints.

The simplest objective function we can use is a linear one such as

Algorithm 2 Retrieving the tiles composing the first row or column of a (sub-)layout

```
function FIRSTROWTILES(node)
    if node is a leaf then
        tiles ← node
    else
        FIRSTROWTILES(node.leftChild)
        if node is a vertical edge then
            FIRSTROWTILES(node.rightChild)
    return tiles
function FIRSTCOLUMNTILES(node)
    if node is a leaf then
        tiles ← node
    else
        FIRSTCOLUMNTILES(node.leftChild)
        if node is an horizontal edge then
            FIRSTCOLUMNTILES(node.rightChild)
    return tiles
```

$$\text{minimize} \sum_{i \in tiles} |w_i - pw_i| + |h_i - ph_i|$$

where pw_i and ph_i are the preferred width and height of tile i. Cassowary [4] is based on such an approach and uses an improved version of the simplex algorithm [8]. Using a linear objective function effectively solves the layout but may provide a layout which is aesthetically not natural for a human (i.e., the human would not come up with that solution if done by hand) as described in [38]. If we consider the simple layout described in Figure 2 and we assume that the preferred width of all tiles is set to x, the solution displayed on the left-hand side of Figure 9 looks the most natural to a human eye: there is no reason why two tiles with the same preferred width (tiles 1 and 2) should be displayed with a different width [33]. However, if we optimize the layout with a linear objective function, we may obtain the solution displayed on the right-hand side as both are equally optimal (i.e., the objective function returns the same value for both solutions).

If we want to obtain an aesthetically natural layout, we have to ensure that each tile individually is as close as possible to its preferred size. This can be done by minimizing a quadratic objective function such as

$$\text{minimize} \sum_{i \in tiles} (w_i - pw_i)^2 + (h_i - ph_i)^2$$

where pw_i and ph_i are the preferred width and height of tile i. Toolkits like QOCA [20] use quadratic objective functions and optimize them thanks to the Active Set method [11].

Our Approach

A toolkit such as QOCA would seem appropriate to find optimal values satisfying the constraints we generate but we want to use layouts as described in this paper inside web applications. To provide a user experience as fluid as in desktop applications, many modern web applications are single-page applications, i.e., everything is run in the client browser, in JavaScript. No implementation of QOCA in JavaScript exist and while porting it in this language is technically feasi-

Algorithm 3 Generating constraints based on a deep-first pre-order tree traversal

function GENERATECONSTRAINTS($node$)
  if $node$ is a leaf **then**
    if $node$ is the tree root **then**
      $constraints \leftarrow x_{node} = 0$
      $constraints \leftarrow y_{node} = 0$
      $tw \leftarrow$ FIRSTROWTILES($node$)
      $constraints \leftarrow \sum_{i \in tw} w_i = width$
    $constraints \leftarrow w_{node} \geq minimum\_width_{node}$
    $constraints \leftarrow h_{node} \geq minimum\_height_{node}$
    $constraints \leftarrow w_{node} \approx preferred\_width_{node}$
    $constraints \leftarrow h_{node} \approx preferred\_height_{node}$
  else
    $leftT \leftarrow$ FIRSTTILE($node.leftChild$)
    $rightT \leftarrow$ FIRSTTILE($node.rightChild$)
    $lw \leftarrow$ FIRSTROWTILES($node.leftChild$)
    $rw \leftarrow$ FIRSTROWTILES($node.rightChild$)
    $lh \leftarrow$ FIRSTCOLUMNTILES($node.leftChild$)
    $rh \leftarrow$ FIRSTCOLUMNTILES($node.rightChild$)
    if $node$ is an horizontal edge **then**
      $constraints \leftarrow x_{rightT} = x_{leftT}$
      $constraints \leftarrow \sum_{i \in rw} w_i = \sum_{j \in lw} w_j$
      $constraints \leftarrow y_{rightT} = y_{leftT} + \sum_{i \in lh} h_i$
    else if $node$ is a vertical edge **then**
      $constraints \leftarrow y_{rightT} = y_{leftT}$
      $constraints \leftarrow \sum_{i \in rh} h_i = \sum_{j \in lh} h_j$
      $constraints \leftarrow x_{rightT} = x_{leftT} + \sum_{i \in lw} w_i$
    GENERATECONSTRAINTS($node.leftChild$)
    GENERATECONSTRAINTS($node.rightChild$)
  return $constraints$

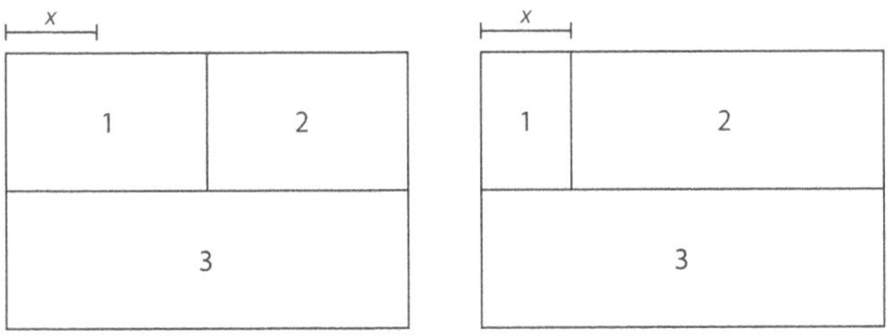

Figure 9. If all tiles have a preferred width of x, both layouts are equally optimal if we use a linear objective function. The one of the left looks however more natural to the human eye because tiles 1 and 2, which have the same preferred width, have the same width.

ble, it would be a daunting task as it is made of approximatively 17,000 lines of code [20]. Moreover the resulting code would be so large (in terms of bytes) that downloading it to the browser would impact the overall performance. A simpler way of solving the constraints has to be found.

As we are automatically generating the constraints, we have a complete control over them: we know exactly the kind of constraints we are going to deal with. The type of layouts we are using, along with their constraints, have the following properties enabling us to propose a simpler and lighter solver:

- There is no cyclic dependencies in constraints. A cyclic dependency would be something similar to $width_i = width_j$, $width_j = width_k$ and $width_k = width_i$
- The widths and heights of the tiles are independent; it means we can optimize them separately (i.e., we find first a solution for the widths and then for the heights).
- Once an optimal solution for the widths and heights is found (i.e., the tile size constraints are solved), finding a solution for the tile position constraints is trivial as it can be reduced to solving a set of linear equations.

Therefore the overall solving strategy can be summarized by the three following steps:

1. Find the optimal solution for all widths
2. Find the optimal solution for all heights
3. Solve the linear equations for the positions

Optimizing Tile Sizes

The first step in solving a layout is to find optimal values for the width and height of all tiles by minimizing the quadratic objective function described above and subject to a set of equality and inequality constraints. Let us consider the layout described in Figure 2 and assume the following values:

$$\forall i \in [1,2,3] : minimum\_width_i = 100$$
$$preferred\_width_1 = 100$$
$$preferred\_width_2 = 200$$
$$preferred\_width_3 = 400$$
$$W = 500$$

To find the optimal solution, we want to find values for w_1, w_2, w_3 that

$$\text{minimize } (w_1 - 100)^2 + (w_2 - 200)^2 + (w_3 - 400)^2$$
subject to
$$w_1 + w_2 = 500$$
$$w_1 + w_2 - w_3 = 0$$
$$w_1 >= 100$$
$$w_2 >= 100$$
$$w_3 >= 100$$

Quadratic programming deals with optimization problems which can be expressed as:

$$\text{minimize } d^T x + \frac{1}{2} x^T D x$$
$$\text{subject to } A^T x \begin{Bmatrix} = \\ \geq \end{Bmatrix} b$$

where x and d are n-vectors, D is an $n \times n$ symmetric positive definite matrix and x^T denotes the transpose of x. A is a $n \times m$ matrix and b is a m-vector and they represent all equality and inequality constraints.

For our sample problem described above, we end up with

$$D = \begin{pmatrix} 1 & 0 & 0 \\ 0 & 1 & 0 \\ 0 & 0 & 1 \end{pmatrix}, x = \begin{pmatrix} w_1 \\ w_2 \\ w_3 \end{pmatrix} \text{ and } d = \begin{pmatrix} 100 \\ 200 \\ 400 \end{pmatrix}$$

to represent the objective function and

$$A = \begin{pmatrix} 1 & 1 & 1 & 0 & 0 \\ 1 & 1 & 0 & 1 & 0 \\ 0 & -1 & 0 & 0 & 1 \end{pmatrix} \text{ and } b = \begin{pmatrix} 500 \\ 0 \\ 100 \\ 100 \\ 100 \end{pmatrix}$$

to represent the equality and inequality constraints—with the first two constraints being equality constraints and the others inequality constraints.

To find the optimal values for vector x, we use the dual method of Goldfarb and Idnani [12, 13], which in our example gives as a result $w_1 = 200$, $w_2 = 300$ and $w_3 = 500$. We use the same approach to find optimal values for variables h_i representing the heights.

Over-Constrained Layouts

Layouts described in this paper can be over-constrained—i.e., no solution respecting all hard constraints can be found. This can happen only because of the overall width constraint which is the one of the form $\sum w_i = W$ where W is the overall desired width. In this situation where the content does not fit inside the available width, we want the layout to take the minimum necessary space even if it implies that the user will have to scroll the viewport. The solution is therefore to relax the constraint by increasing the value of W until a solution can be found. Given the performance of the solving algorithm, it is not an issue to do it incrementally and solve the layout each time. However some heuristics and strategies can be put in place to speed up the search of the minimal required width that satisfies all constraints.

Tiles with Fixed Size

We have seen so far that tiles have minimum and preferred sizes. In some cases we may want them to have a fixed size. The natural way of proceeding would be to add hard constraints of the form $w_i = fixed\_width_i$. The problem is that we would quickly end up with an over-constrained layout; it would even happen when the layout consists of a single tile having a fixed width smaller than the overall available width. We could put in place constraint hierarchies [6] so we can specify which constraints we accept to violate in order to find an adequate result but we wanted to find an simpler solution in order to be able to use our proposed light solver. Our solution is inspired from Weighted Constraint Satisfaction Problems (WCSPs) [5, 28] where constraints have a weight in order to express preferences among solutions. In WCSPs, when one wants to have a constraint satisfied for sure—a hard constraint—its weight is set to ∞; it is the equivalent to say that the cost of having this constraint violated is infinitely high. We apply the same principle and it leads us to add weights to the objective function so at the end we try to

$$\text{minimize} \sum_{i \in tiles} weight_i \times (w_i - preferred\_width_i)^2$$

where $weight_i$ is set to 1 for a *normal* preferred size and to ∞ for a fixed size (in the actual implementation, we approximated ∞ by using a large number). We can represent the problem similarly as described above, simply by adapting the D matrix to

$$D = \begin{pmatrix} weight_1 & 0 & \cdots & 0 \\ 0 & weight_2 & \cdots & 0 \\ \vdots & \vdots & \ddots & \vdots \\ 0 & 0 & \cdots & weight_n \end{pmatrix}$$

and solving it with the same algorithm.

Spring Effect

Because we are optimizing the tile sizes with a quadratic objective function, we may experience a *spring effect* as described in [38] and illustrated in Figure 10. In this example we have four tiles having the same preferred width. Naturally we would expect a result like on the left hand side because as all tiles have the same preferred width, we expected them to have the same actual width (Gestalt law of equality [33]). However we get the result on the right hand side. Preferred size constraints can be seen as springs pulling or pressing tiles to their preferred size. In our exemple we have two columns, the first one with three constraints/springs and the second with only one. The resulting force is therefore three times bigger for the first column.

This effect can be corrected by adjusting the weight of the preferred size in the objective function. When optimizing the widths, the weights would be calculated as

$$weight_i = \frac{1}{\text{number of tiles sharing the same left and right edges than tile } i}$$

and in a same way when optimizing the heights but with taking into account the top and bottom edges.

Determining Tile Positions

The next step is to determine the position of all tiles, i.e., to find a value for their x and y variables respecting the tile position constraints we described above. As we already have optimized the sizes, we can substitute the w and h variables by their corresponding values. In our example based on Figure 2, it gives us

$$\begin{aligned} x_1 &= 0 \\ y_1 &= 0 \\ x_2 &= x_1 + 200 \\ y_2 &= y_1 \\ x_3 &= x_1 \\ y_3 &= y_1 + 100 \end{aligned}$$

if we consider all tiles having a height of 100. These are a set of linear equations that can be represented in the form $Ax = b$

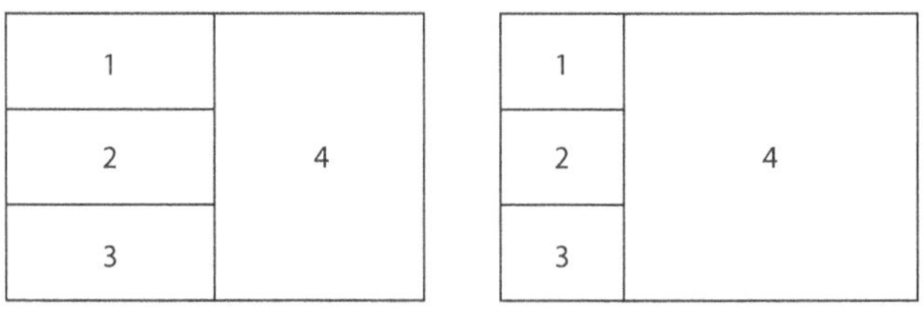

Figure 10. Illustration of the *spring effect*: on the left is what we expect as a result if all tiles have the same preferred width; on the right is the actual result with a quadratic optimization.

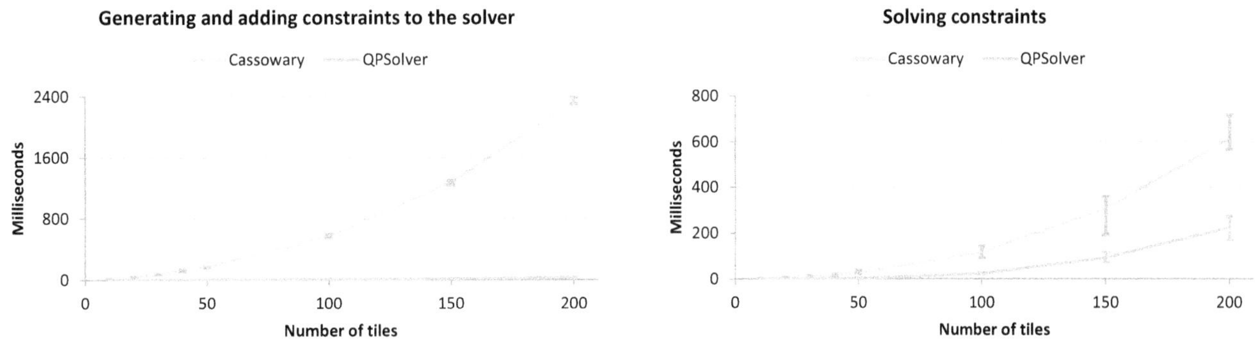

Figure 11. Performance comparison between Cassoway and QPSolver: on the left we compare the time it takes to generate and add the constraints to the solver and on the right the time it takes to solve the constraints. For each layout size we solved 100 random layouts and we plotted the median value as well as the 1st and 3rd quartiles.

where x and b are m-vectors and A is an $m \times n$ matrix with m representing the number of variables and n the number of equations. In our example we have:

$$A = \begin{pmatrix} 1 & 0 & 0 & 0 & 0 & 0 \\ 0 & 0 & 0 & 1 & 0 & 0 \\ -1 & 1 & 0 & 0 & 0 & 0 \\ -1 & 0 & 1 & 0 & 0 & 0 \\ -1 & 0 & 1 & 0 & 0 & 0 \\ 0 & 0 & 0 & 1 & -1 & 0 \\ 0 & 0 & 0 & -1 & 0 & 1 \end{pmatrix}, x = \begin{pmatrix} x_1 \\ x_2 \\ x_3 \\ y_1 \\ y_2 \\ y_3 \end{pmatrix} \text{ and}$$

$$b = \begin{pmatrix} 0 \\ 0 \\ 200 \\ 0 \\ 0 \\ 0 \\ 100 \end{pmatrix}$$

Using the Gaussian elimination algorithm [1] to solve the equations, we get $x_1 = 0$, $y_1 = 0$, $x_2 = 200$, $y_2 = 0$, $x_3 = 0$ and $y_3 = 100$.

Implementation and Performance

We implemented the constraint solver based on the described approach purely in JavaScript as we want our layout manager to be used in web applications; we called it QPSolver. In this section we are comparing it with Cassowary [4]—even if it uses only a linear optimization—because it is the most popular solver for constraint-based GUI layouts (used for example by Apple in OS X and iOS) and an implementation in JavaScript exists. QOCA [20], an evolution of Cassowary, uses a quadratic optimization but implementations only exist in C++ and Java; in [17], Jamil evaluates the performance of different methods for solving constraints but the tests were done in Java and are therefore not comparable to our case.

Our test methodology was the following: we based our tests on layouts with 10, 20, 30, 40, 50, 100, 150 and 200 tiles. For each layout size, we generated 100 random layouts that we solved with Cassowary and QPSolver and we recorded two points of measure: the time it takes to generate and add the constraints to the solver and the time it takes to solve these constraints to find an optimal solution. The tests were performed with Mozilla Firefox version 32.0.3 running on Windows® 7 on an Intel® Core™ i7-2600 (3.4 GHz). The results, displayed in Figure 11, show important differences between Cassoway and QPSolver.

The algorithm to generate the constraints—described in Algorithm 3—is the same used for both solvers so the difference shown in the first chart is only due to the addition of the constraints to the solver. In the case of QPSolver, adding a constraints only means editing some matrices hence the dramatically better performance. On the second chart we can notice that QPSolver is significantly faster than Cassowary for solving the constraints even if it uses a quadratic optimization instead of a linear one. QPSolver can be lighter and faster than Cassowary because it doesn't need to deal with complex issues Cassowary has to (e.g., cyclic dependencies between constraints): QPSolver is tailored to be used for BSP layouts where constraints have been automatically generated.

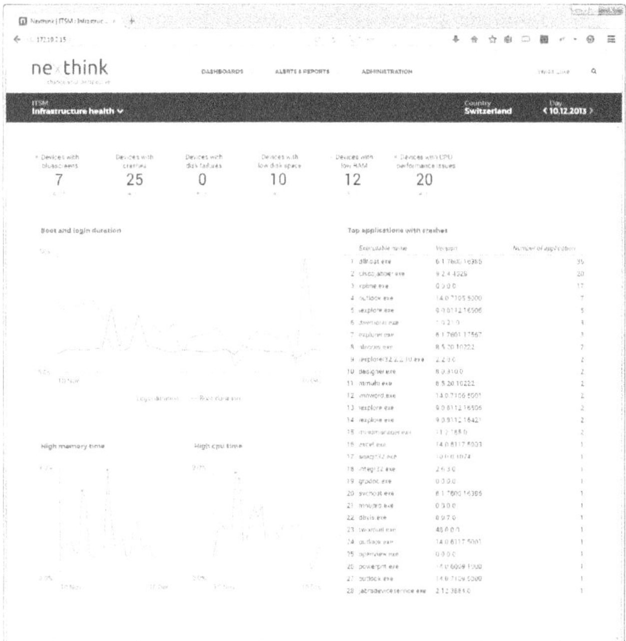

Figure 12. Screenshot of a *beta* version of Nexthink Portal V6 showing a dashboard using the layout manager described in this paper.

It is also worth noting that, besides being fast, QPSolver also has a lightweight implementation in terms of lines of code (around 1,500 versus around 4,600 for Cassowary). This has its importance because web applications will have to download the code that will then be run in the browser: less lines of code means a faster download.

CONCLUSION

In this paper we presented a novel layout manager aimed for information dashboards that satisfies four requirements: *easiness to define*, *flexibility*, *predictability* and *visual coherence*. It is based on BSP layouts that can be represented as binary trees. To be able to actually compute the layout (i.e., to have a computer determine the proper size and position of each tile), we described a way to automatically generate a set of constraints directly from the layout tree representation. Then we proposed a new constraint solver to find the optimal solution for the layout; this solver is light and fast enough to be embedded inside a web application.

The resulting layout manager meets all of our expectations and preliminary tests with users are encouraging. It has been integrated in the upcoming new version of Nexthink Portal [23] that will be released mid-2015 (an example of a real dashboard using it is shown in Figure 12). Our tests indicated that another important aspect to obtain aesthetic dashboards based on our proposed layout manager is to programmatically be able to determine an adequate minimum and preferred size for each tile based on its content. Our layout manager is automatic in the sense that the user only states how to arrange tiles and then an optimal size is computed for each of them. This is the ideal situation and the easiest for the user. However, in some situations, one may want to manually resize tiles—e.g., by dragging edges. This could be achieved by setting additional constraints and a prototype has been developed in that direction. The results are promising but further research has to be conducted to make the process easier and more intuitive.

At a first glance our approach has been devised for information dashboards. Due to the very encouraging results it would be really interesting to apply it in the more generic field of GUI design. In that case, instead of containing for example a table or a graph, each tile would contain a GUI component such as a button or an input field.

ACKNOWLEDGMENTS

The author would like to thank Sébastien Baehni, Kunal Massé, Nicolas Martenet and Samuele Gantner for reviewing the draft of this paper and providing valuable feedbacks. Kudos to the whole Nexthink Portal team for having integrated the layout manager in the product.

REFERENCES

1. Atkinson, K. E. *An Introduction to Numerical Analysis*, 2 ed. John Wiley & Sons, 1989.
2. Avrahami, G., Brooks, K. P., and Brown, M. H. A two-view approach to constructing user interfaces. *SIGGRAPH Comput. Graph. 23*, 3 (July 1989), 137–146.
3. Badros, G. J., Borning, A., Marriott, K., and Stuckey, P. Constraint cascading style sheets for the web. In *Proceedings of the 12th annual ACM symposium on User interface software and technology*, ACM (1999), 73–82.
4. Badros, G. J., Borning, A., and Stuckey, P. J. The Cassowary linear arithmetic constraint solving algorithm. *ACM Transactions on Computer-Human Interaction 8*, 4 (Dec. 2001), 267–306.
5. Bistarelli, S., Montanari, U., and Rossi, F. Semiring-based constraint satisfaction and optimization. *Journal of the ACM (JACM) 44*, 2 (1997), 201–236.
6. Borning, A., Freeman-Benson, B., and Wilson, M. Constraint hierarchies. *LISP and Symbolic Computation 5*, 3 (1992), 223–270.
7. Cocoa. `https://developer.apple.com/technologies/mac/cocoa.html`.
8. Dantzig, G. *Linear Programming and Extensions*. Rand Corporation Research Study. Princeton Univ. Press, Princeton, NJ, 1963.
9. Few, S. *Show Me The Numbers: Designing tables and graphs to enlighten*, vol. 1. Analytics Press Oakland, CA, 2004.
10. Few, S. *Information Dashboard Design: Displaying data for at-a-glance monitoring*. Analytics Press, 2013.
11. Fletcher, R. *Practical Methods of Optimization; (2nd Ed.)*. Wiley-Interscience, New York, NY, USA, 1987.
12. Goldfarb, D., and Idnani, A. Dual and primal-dual methods for solving strictly convex quadratic programs. In *Numerical Analysis*. Springer, 1982, 226–239.
13. Goldfarb, D., and Idnani, A. A numerically stable dual method for solving strictly convex quadratic programs. *Mathematical Programming 27*, 1 (1983), 1–33.
14. GridStyleSheets (GSS). `http://gridstylesheets.org`.
15. Heim, S. G. *The Resonant Interface: HCI foundations for interaction design*. Pearson/Addison Wesley, 2008.
16. Hudson, S. E., and Mohamed, S. P. Interactive specification of flexible user interface displays. *ACM Transactions on Information Systems (TOIS) 8*, 3 (1990), 269–288.
17. Jamil, N. Constraint solvers for user interface layout. *CoRR abs/1401.1031* (2014).
18. Kaplan, R. S., and Norton, D. The balanced scorecard: Measures that drive performance. *Harvard Business Review 70*, 1 (January–February 1992), 71–79.
19. Karsenty, S., Weikart, C., and Landay, J. A. Inferring graphical constraints with Rockit. In *Proceedings of the INTERACT'93 and CHI'93 Conference on Human Factors in Computing Systems*, ACM (1993), 531.
20. Marriott, K., and Chok, S. S. QOCA: A constraint solving toolkit for interactive graphical applications. *Constraints 7*, 3-4 (2002), 229–254.

21. Masonry. `http://masonry.desandro.com`.

22. Myers, B. A., and Buxton, W. Creating highly-interactive and graphical user interfaces by demonstration. In *ACM SIGGRAPH Computer Graphics*, vol. 20, ACM (1986), 249–258.

23. Nexthink. `http://www.nexthink.com`.

24. Norman, D. A. *Emotional Design: Why we love (or hate) everyday things*. Basic books, 2004.

25. Packery. `http://packery.metafizzy.co`.

26. Qlik. `http://www.qlik.com`.

27. Qt. `http://qt-project.org`.

28. Schiex, T., Fargier, H., Verfaillie, G., et al. Valued constraint satisfaction problems: Hard and easy problems. *IJCAI (1) 95* (1995), 631–639.

29. Java Swing. `http://docs.oracle.com/javase/tutorial/uiswing`.

30. Tableau Software. `http://www.tableausoftware.com`.

31. Tufte, E. R. *The Visual Display of Quantitative Information*, 2 ed. Graphics Press, 2001.

32. Vanderdonckt, J., Ouedraogo, M., and Ygueitengar, B. A comparison of placement strategies for effective visual design. In *Proceedings of the Conference on People and Computers IX*, HCI '94, Cambridge University Press (New York, NY, USA, 1994), 125–143.

33. Wertheimer, M. Laws of organization in perceptual forms. *A Source Book of Gestalt Psychology* (1938), 71–88.

34. Windows Presentation Foundation. `http://msdn.microsoft.com/en-us/library/ms754130.aspx`.

35. Yanagida, T., Nonaka, H., and Kurihara, M. Personalizing graphical user interfaces on flexible widget layout. In *Proceedings of the 1st ACM SIGCHI Symposium on Engineering Interactive Computing Systems*, EICS '09, ACM (New York, NY, USA, 2009), 255–264.

36. Zanden, B. V., and Myers, B. A. The lapidary graphical interface design tool. In *Proceedings of the SIGCHI Conference on Human Factors in Computing Systems*, ACM (1991), 465–466.

37. Zeidler, C., Lutteroth, C., Sturzlinger, W., and Weber, G. The Auckland Layout Editor: An improved GUI layout specification process. In *Proceedings of the 26th Annual ACM Symposium on User Interface Software and Technology*, UIST '13, ACM (New York, NY, USA, 2013), 343–352.

38. Zeidler, C., Lutteroth, C., and Weber, G. Constraint solving for beautiful user interfaces: how solving strategies support layout aesthetics. In *Proceedings of the 13th International Conference of the NZ Chapter of the ACM's Special Interest Group on Human-Computer Interaction*, ACM (2012), 72–79.

Counteracting Serial Position Effects in the CHOICLA Group Decision Support Environment

Martin Stettinger
Institute for Software Technology
Inffeldgasse 16b/II
A-8010, Graz, Austria
martin.stettinger@ist.tugraz.at

Alexander Felfernig
Institute for Software Technology
Inffeldgasse 16b/II
A-8010, Graz, Austria
alexander.felfernig@ist.tugraz.at

Gerhard Leitner
Institute for Informatics Systems
Universitätsstraße 65-67
A-9020, Klagenfurt, Austria
gerhard.leitner@aau.at

Stefan Reiterer
Institute for Software Technology
Inffeldgasse 16b/II
A-8010, Graz, Austria
stefan.reiterer@ist.tugraz.at

Michael Jeran
Institute for Software Technology
Inffeldgasse 16b/II
A-8010, Graz, Austria
michael.jeran@ist.tugraz.at

ABSTRACT
Decisions are often suboptimal due to the fact that humans apply simple heuristics which cause different types of decision biases. CHOICLA is an environment that supports decision making for groups of users. It supports the determination of recommendations for groups and also includes mechanisms to counteract decision biases. In this paper we give an overview of the CHOICLA environment and report the results of a user study which analyzed two voting strategies with regard to their potential of counteracting serial position (primacy/recency) effects when evaluating decision alternatives.

Author Keywords
Recommender Systems; Group Decision Making; Group Recommendation; Decision Tasks; Decision Technologies

ACM Classification Keywords
H.5.m. Information Interfaces and Presentation (e.g. HCI): Modelling Environments

INTRODUCTION
Several decisions in everyday life occur in the context of groups, for example, a decision regarding the restaurant to choose for a dinner with business partners or a decision regarding the cinema movie to watch with a group of friends. There exist various decision biases which can negatively influence the quality of group decisions [11]. *Anchoring effects* [9] are responsible for decisions which are biased by a shown reference value. For example, the average rating of other users in the context of rating an item in collaborative filtering scenarios [1] or the evaluation of an item by the first group member shown to other group members can trigger anchoring effects [8, 13]. Anchoring biases in collaborative filtering scenarios can be counteracted with an adaptation of the preference acquisition interface, for example, by an adaptation of the underlying rating scale visualization [2]. In the context of group decision scenarios, anchoring effects can be controlled by not completely disclosing the preferences of other group members in early stages of a decision process [8].

Another example of decision biases are *decoy effects* which denote the fact that irrelevant (inferior) items in an item set significantly influence the selection behavior of users [22]. In the context of recommendation scenarios, decoy effects can occur in the item selection process, i.e., if a set of candidate items is recommended to a user [21]. Decoy effects can be detected and counteracted on the basis of predictive models that estimate dominance relationships between items in a candidate (consideration) set and propose to remove items from the candidate set before showing it to the user [21].

In this paper we focus on *primacy/recency effects* (serial position effects) that represent situations in which items presented at the beginning and the end of the list are evaluated signficantly more often than items in the middle of a list [14]. An explanation of this effect is that users are not interested in evaluating large lists to identify those items that best fit their preferences. Primacy/recency effects are also explained as a cognitive phenomenon since items at the beginning and the end of a list are also recalled more often [6]. In recommendation scenarios these effects have been investigated, for example, by Felfernig et al. [6]. The results of their studies clearly show that item properties shown to a user at the beginning and the end of a recommendation dialog are recalled significantly more often than properties in the middle of a dialog.

IUI 2015, March 29–April 1, 2015, Atlanta, GA, USA.

ACM 978-1-4503-3306-1/15/03 ...$15.00.
http://dx.doi.org/10.1145/2678025.2701391

There exist a couple of online tools that support group decision scenarios. SMARTOCRACY provides support for voting scenarios in social network contexts where information from the social network is applied to rank recommendations [16]. DOODLE[1] focuses primarily on the aspect of coordinating meetings and does not include additional mechanisms to determine recommendations for groups of users. Similarly, VERN [23] is a tool that supports the identification of meeting times based on the idea of unconstrained democracy where individuals are enabled to freely propose alternative dates themselves. DOTMOCRACY[2] deals with larger groups of users and provides a method for collecting and visualizing group preferences. The system is based on the idea of participatory decision making – it's major outcome is a graph type visualization of the group-immanent preferences. Compared to CHOICLA, these tools focus on specific scenarios, i.e., do not allow a flexible definition of decision functionalities depending on the scenario at hand. Furthermore, existing tools do not include recommendation and explanation functionalities which can help to increase trust in recommendations [7] and improve the perceived decision support quality [8].

Typical CHOICLA scenarios range from industrial settings (e.g., selection of conference locations, selection of new employees, and evaluation of project proposals) to decision scenarios in private settings (e.g., selection of a restaurant for a dinner with friends, selection of a hotel for a holiday trip with friends, and the selection of a movie to watch with friends in a cinema). The contributions of this paper are the following. (1) we present CHOICLA which is a novel domain-independent decision support tool for groups of users and (2) we show how to counteract primacy/recency effects occurring in the evaluation of decision alternatives.

The remainder of this paper is organized as follows. In the Section *Choicla Environment* we provide insights to the CHOICLA design process where users (creators of decision apps) can model decision tasks from scratch. In Section *Choicla Decision Apps* we provide an overview of the intelligent management of already created decision apps. In Section *User Study* we report the results of an empirical study which focused on (1) usability aspects and (2) possibilities to counteract serial position (primacy/recency) effects in the evaluation of decision alternatives. Finally, we discuss issues for future work and conclude the paper.

CHOICLA ENVIRONMENT

Configurability of Decision Apps

Since decision scenarios differ in terms of their process design, a variety of parameters (features) is needed to make decision processes configurable (see Figure 1). CHOICLA offers a variety of features that represent user interface elements (and corresponding functionalities) that can be included in a decision process. For example, the creator of a new CHOICLA decision app can select (set) the feature f_{21} which indicates that in the new decision app preferences of other users will be shown in terms of a basic summary (individual user preferences will not be displayed).

[1]doodle.com.

[2]dotmocracy.org.

In order to make decision processes (and corresponding user interface elements) configurable in an intelligent fashion, a configuration model is needed that expresses the set of features and their relationships [4, 20]. This configuration model is an integrative part of CHOICLA. An example of such a relationship is the *requires* constraint between the features f_{14} and f_{15} expressing the fact that the selection of the first one also requires the selection of the latter. An example fragment of the CHOICLA feature model is depicted in Figure 1. We will not discuss this feature model in detail but rather explain major properties on the basis of selected features.[3] An example screenshot of the CHOICLA user interface for defining the parameters of a decision app is depicted in Figure 2.

CHOICLA includes different types of *group recommendation heuristics* that can be selected to be used within the scope of a group decision process. Figure 1 includes the heuristics *Majority* and *Maut* (see [5]). The first one is a basic implementation of majority voting, the second one implements *Multi Attribute Utility Theory* (MAUT) for group-based settings. Both approaches to aggregate group preferences are discussed in Subsection *Recommendation Support*. Solution alternatives can be managed in different ways, for example, if feature f_9 has been selected, only the creator of the corresponding CHOICLA decision app is allowed to add decision alternatives. The scope of a decision app (see also Section *Choicla Decision Apps*) can be *public* or *private*. If it is private, the app cannot be reused by other other users, otherwise it can be reused.

Recommendation Support

CHOICLA includes different group recommendation heuristics (e.g., majority voting and group-based MAUT) that can foster consensus in group decision making (see, e.g., [8, 12]). The degree of perceived decision quality of the participants can be significantly increased by using such aggregation functions – see, for example, [12, 19]. In the following we exemplify group recommendation heuristics (aggregation functions) that can be selected by the creator of a decision app during the corresponding configuration process.

For the explanation of CHOICLA aggregation functions we use a working example which is related to the task of restaurant selection by a group of friends. Table 1 represents the individual restaurant ratings of the participants. For these ratings, group recommendations can be derived on the basis of the CHOICLA group decision heuristics (see Table 2).

restaurant	Martin	Rene	Philip	Stefan
Aphrodite	4	3	4	4
Zeus	5	3	5	4
Hermes	5	3	3	3
Poseidon	3	3	5	3

Table 1. Examples of individual user ratings with regard to the available decision alternatives (restaurants).

Majority Voting (see Formula 1) determines the value (d) that a majority of the users selected as voting for a specific solution s where $eval(u, s)$ denotes the rating for solution s

[3]More details on the CHOICLA feature model can be found in [18].

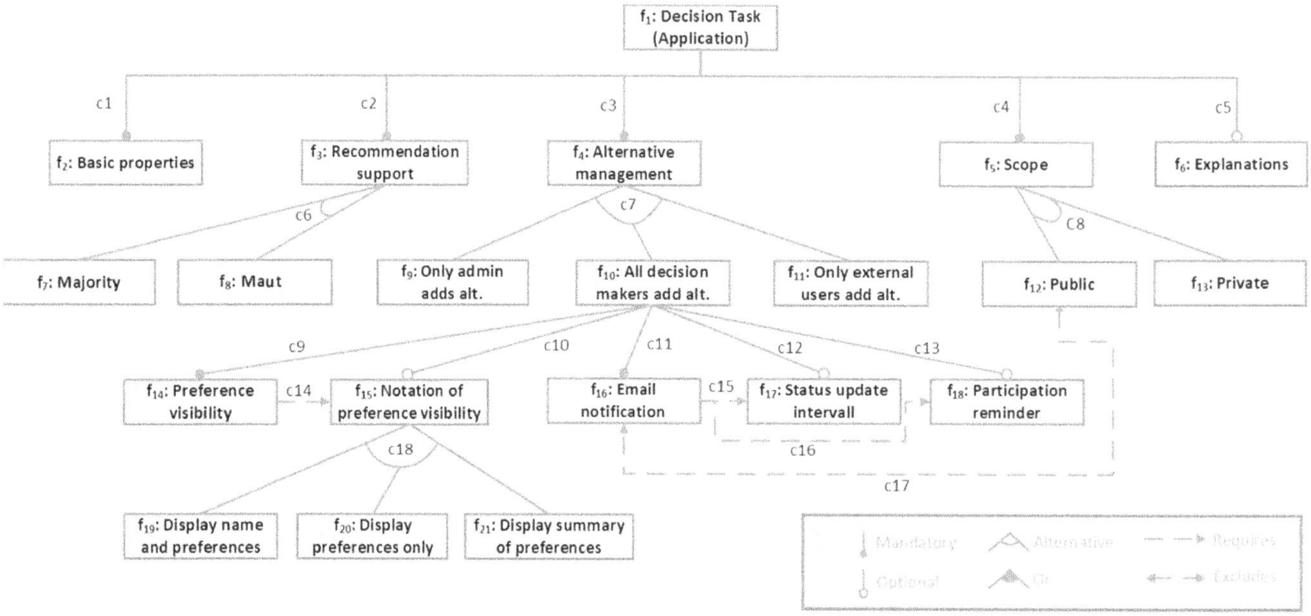

Figure 1. Fragment of the CHOICLA feature model. f_i is used as abbreviation for the individual features, for example, f_3 is the short notation for feature *Recommendation Support*.

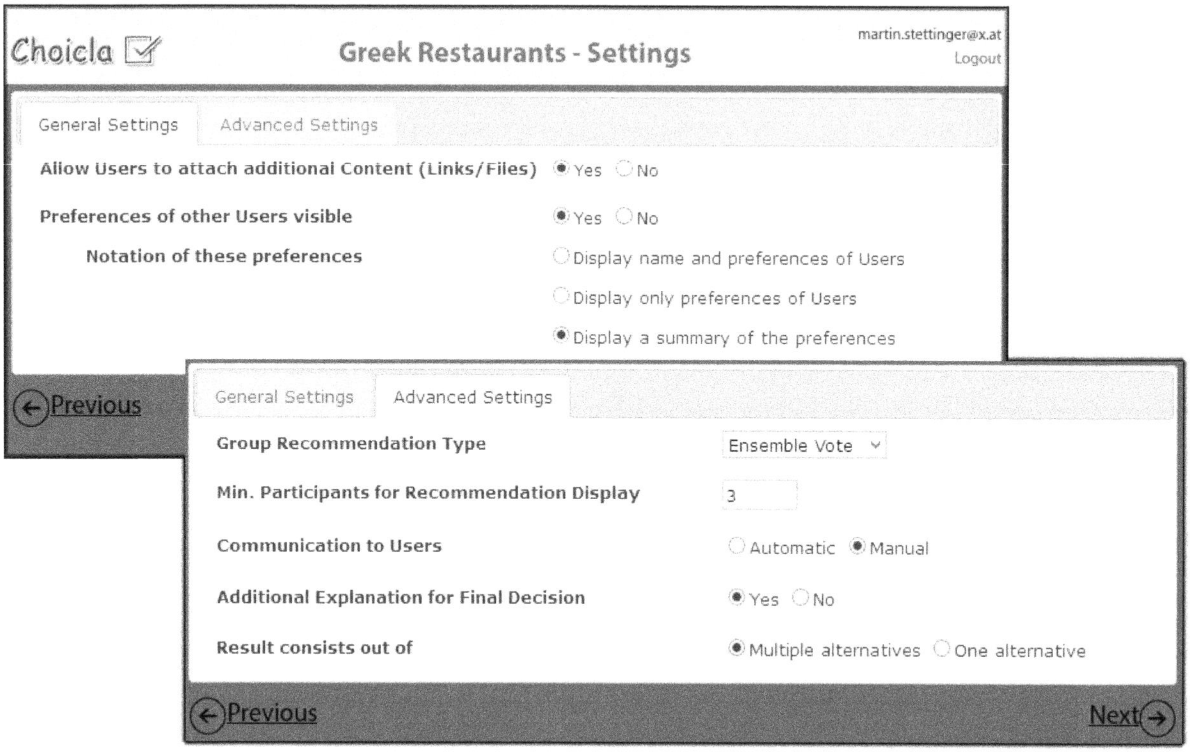

Figure 2. Example set of parameters which can be selected when creating a new CHOICLA decision app.

defined by user u. For example, the majority of votings for *Aphrodite* is 4 (see Table 2).

$$MAJ(s) = maxarg_{(d \in \{1..5\})}(\#(\bigcup_{u \in Users} eval(u,s) = d)) \quad (1)$$

Least Misery (see Formula 2) returns the lowest voting for solution s as group recommendation. For example, the LMIS value for s = *Aphrodite* is 3.

solution	*MAJ*	*LMIS*	*MPLS*	*GDIS*	*ENS*
Aphrodite	4	3	4	4	4
Zeus	5	3	5	5	5
Hermes	3	3	5	3	3
Poseidon	3	3	5	3	3

Table 2. Results of applying the aggregation functions to the individual preferences shown in Table 1. MAJ = Majority Voting; LMIS = Least Misery; MPLS = Most Pleasure; GDIS = Lowest Group Distance; ENS = Ensemble Voting. This example recommendation values are based on the preference information in Table 1.

$$LMIS(s) = min(\bigcup_{u \in Users} eval(u, s)) \quad (2)$$

Most Pleasure (see Formula 3) returns the highest voting for solution s as group recommendation. For example, the MPLS value for the s = *Aphrodite* is 4.

$$MPLS(s) = max(\bigcup_{u \in Users} eval(u, s)) \quad (3)$$

Group Distance (see Formula 4) returns the value d as group recommendation which causes the lowest overall change of the individual user preferences. For example, the GDIS value for s = *Aphrodite* is 4.

$$GDIS(s) = minarg_{(d \in \{1..5\})}(\sum_{u \in Users} |eval(u, s) - d|) \quad (4)$$

Finally, *Ensemble Voting* (see Formula 5) determines the majority of the results of the individual voting strategies H = {MAJ, LMIS, MPLS, GDIS}. For example, the ensemble-based majority voting for *Aphrodite* is 4.

$$ENS(s) = maxarg_{(d \in \{1..5\})}(\#(\bigcup_{h \in H} eval(h, s) = d)) \quad (5)$$

Figure 3 depicts a CHOICLA user interface where a 5-star rating scale can be used to evaluate alternatives. In some cases there is a need for a more detailed evaluation of decision alternatives in terms of *interest dimensions* – this is typically the case in a MAUT-based scenario [5]. Evaluation criteria (MAUT dimensions) differ from decision task to decision task and therefore can be modeled during the creation process of a decision app. A MAUT-based group recommendation for a specific solution s represents the sum of individual MAUT values of participants of the group decision task. A weighted average of all personal ratings of the dimensions of an alternative represents the individual MAUT value of a group member. In our current implementation the attribute values are subjective and the weights of the dimensions are fixed (predefined) which is different in a typical MAUT scenario.

$$MAUT(s) = \sum_{u \in Users} \frac{\sum_{d \in s} eval(u, d) * weight(d)}{|dimensions|} \quad (6)$$

If we look at the individual ratings of the dimensions of the restaurant *Zeus* in Figure 4 we notice the values 9, 7, 8, and 10. For simplification purposes we assume in our example that all dimensions have the same weight ($wd1 = wd2 = wd3 = wd4 = 5$). The current user's individual MAUT value of the restaurant *Zeus* is $(9*5+7*5+8*5+10*5)/4$ which results in 42.5. To display the MAUT-based evaluation of a solution (restaurants in our working example), utility (MAUT) values are transformed to a 5-star scale.

CHOICLA also offers a modified version of the *Group Distance* algorithm (see Formula 8). This modified version of the *Group Distance* algorithm (GD') takes into account past decision outcomes. A user-weighting $w(u)$ is used to ensure that users whose individual ratings often differ from related decisions (represented by $distance(u)$), are privileged. This user-weighting $w(u)$ considers the total sum of all the distances between the individual ratings of a user to the "final decision" in the particular decision situation (see Formula 7). If a history of past decision outcomes is available, the recommendation is influenced by these user-weightings.

$$w(u) = \sum distance(u) + 1 \quad (7)$$

$$GD'(s) = minarg_{(d \in \{1..5\})}(\sum_{u \in Users} w(u) * |eval(u, s) - d|) \quad (8)$$

Decision Alternatives

In CHOICLA, there are different ways in which decision alternatives can be entered into the system. (1) *only the creator* of a decision task can add/modify decision alternatives – this is needed if a person is interested in the opinions of his/her friends about the given alternatives (e.g., alternative candidates for the next digital camera). Another example are so-called "Micro-Polls" where the creator is only interested in knowing the preference distribution of a large group of users. (2) *all decision makers* are allowed to add decision alternatives – a typical example of such a scenario is the group-based decision regarding a restaurant or a hotel [10]. (3) *only external users* are allowed to add alternatives, i.e., users who do not participate in the decision process. For example, job applicants should be able to add a bundle consisting of the application documents as decision alternative to a (personnel) decision task (the application itself is interpreted as a new alternative - see [17]). Another related example is the selection of next year's conference location where proposers submit their material in a similar fashion.

Evaluation of Decision Alternatives

As shown in Figure 4 we used *Ambience*, *Price*, *Quality* and *Location* as dimensions in our working example. The stars

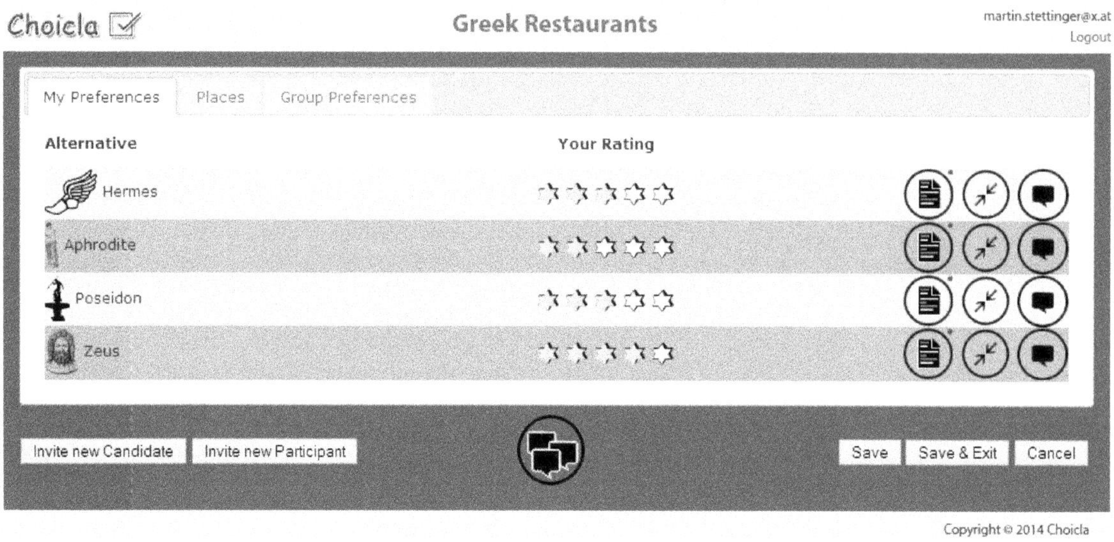

Figure 3. Evaluation of the decision alternatives based on a 5-star scale.

Figure 4. Dimension-based evaluation of the decision alternatives in CHOICLA.

in Figure 4 show the average evaluation based on the values given for the different dimensions of the decision alternatives. To keep the screen in Figure 4 comprehensible, per default only the accumulated ratings of the decision alternatives are shown – the detailed evaluation of the dimensions is hidden and only displayed if users click on the corresponding alternative. The tab *Places* contains, if available, the geographical information of the decision alternatives. The third tab *Group Preferences* only shows up if a (predefined) threshold in terms of the number of participations is reached. It displays the actual group recommendation based on the selected recommendation heuristic (see Section 2) in terms of a bar chart. This threshold prevents the participants from statistical inferences to the individual user preferences, especially if no complete preference visibility is wanted at all. Figure 5 visualizes the current group recommendation.

Explanations

To increase the trust of the participants in the outcome of a decision process, explanations are indispensable [7]. During the design of a CHOICLA decision app explanations can be selected as a feature (see Figure 1).

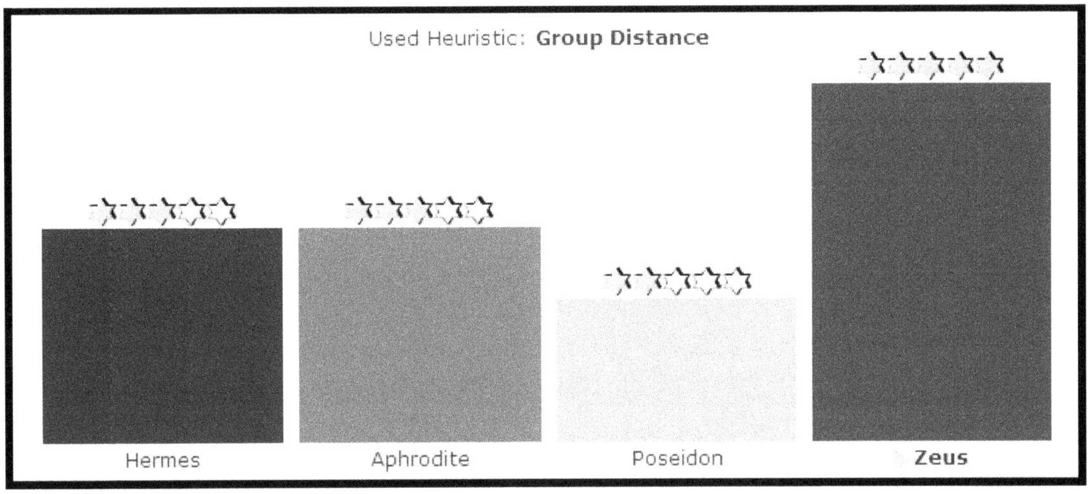

Figure 5. Actual group recommendation based on the *Group Distance* recommendation function (see Formula 4). The group recommendation is highlighted with bold font as well as an green arrow.

CHOICLA supports explanations by allowing the creator of a decision task to attach argumentations as to why an alternative has been selected as group decision. If this feature is selected, the creator has to enter an explanatory text, if not, the entering of such a text remains just an option. If the creator selects the *recommended alternative* as the "final decision", CHOICLA generates an explanation according to the selected recommendation function. For example, if *majority voting* is selected, CHOICLA generates the following explanatory text for the group recommendation *Zeus*: *5-star evaluations were selected more often than other possible evaluations.*

Preference Visibility

The insight to the individual preferences of all participants involved in a decision process can have a significant impact on decision quality (see [10] and [15]). There exist decision tasks where the detailed insight into the preferences of all participants is an advantage and of course others where an opposite effect can occur. If, for example, the decision task deals with finding an appointment for a management meeting it is essential to find a date where all heads of different departments can attend the meeting and therefore it is important to know the individual preferences of the participants.

In some decision scenarios full preference visibility can lead to disadvantages for some participants but some kind of transparency of the preferences is helpful to achieve a reasonable decision. In such cases CHOICLA can support the decision makers by offering the possibility to display solely a summary of all given preferences regarding an alternative. A summary prevents all participants from statistical inferences but still can help participants who are unsure about their preferences. All the mentioned features (see Figure 1) can be configured during the modeling process of a decision app. The interface of a CHOICLA app is automatically generated conform the selected features (see Figure 6).

CHOICLA DECISION APPS

After all features relevant for a new CHOICLA decision app have been selected, the corresponding decision app can be generated automatically. Figure 6 depicts the personal home screen of a CHOICLA user who created four group decision apps (selecting a location, determining an appointment, selecting new hardware, and deciding about new employees). Within each of these apps a user can create new decision tasks (instances) and invite (potential) group members (participants) via email. After a participant has accepted the invitation, the decision app also shows up on the personal home screen of the participant.

The tab *DecisionApp Store* (see Figure 6) contains all publicly available decision apps. Decision apps can be searched and directly installed to the individual home screen. This mechanism can save a lot of effort for very common decision tasks because the creator can reuse/modify an already created decision app instead of creating a new one from scratch. This kind of reuse makes the interaction more intuitive and can also reduce barriers for using CHOICLA. The third tab *Create DecisionApp* offers the possibility to create a completely new decision app from scratch.

USER STUDY

We conducted a user study with the goals (1) to evaluate the usability of the current version of CHOICLA and (2) to investigate whether specific evaluation methods for decision alternatives can counteract serial position (primacy/recency) effects. In this context, the term *item* refers to individual arguments/explanations in descriptions (the difference between descriptions shown to user is the ordering of argumentations, i.e., the same individual argumentations were included in both descriptions). In this study we made CHOICLA accessible to N=44 persons outside our university who were interested in applying a group decision support software but were not aware of the fact that the system has been developed at our university. The participants (34% female, 66% male) had no computer science oriented technical background knowledge.

The participants of the study were organized into groups of 5–6 persons who had the task of evaluating restaurants they would like to visit for a dinner. For this study, the restaurants

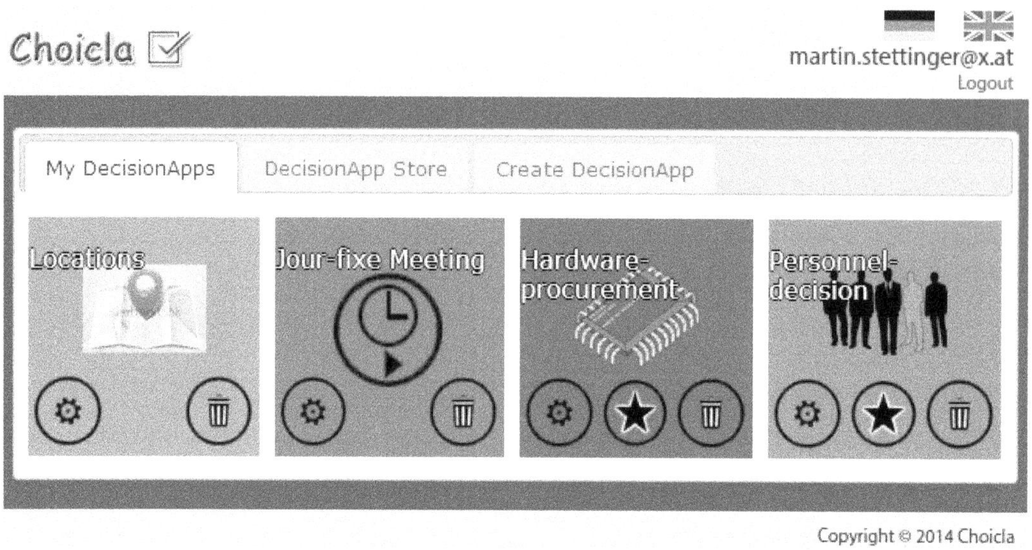

Figure 6. CHOICLA: personal home screen of an registered user. In this setting, the user has installed four different CHOICLA decision apps which are the selection of a location, a meeting time for a jour-fixe meeting, new hardware as well as personnel decisions.

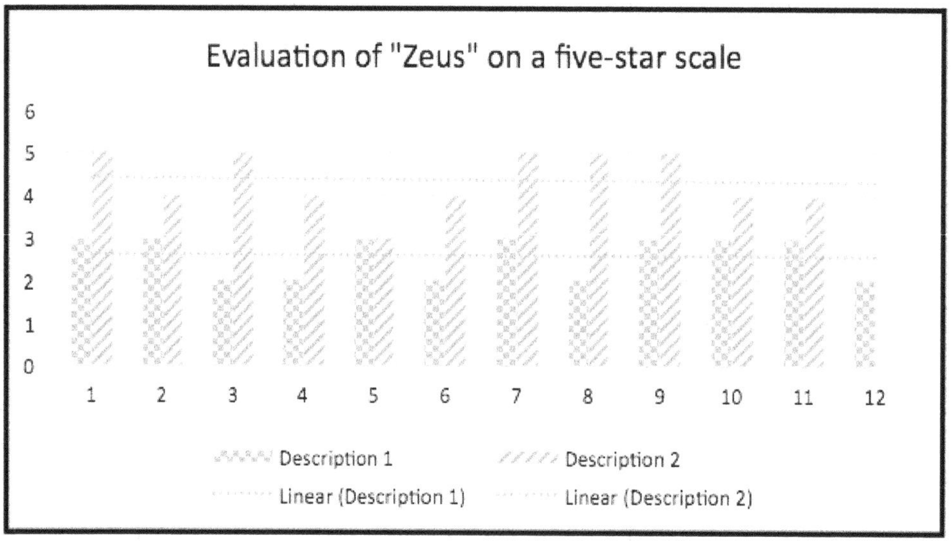

Figure 7. Evaluations of the decision alternative *Zeus* on basis of a 5-star scale. The dotted lines show the average voting value of the alternative. Description 1 states the negative aspects at the very beginning and the end (negative salient) and Description 2 states the positive aspects at the very beginning and the end (positive salient).

were made anonymous, i.e., the names used in our working example (Hermes, Aphrodite, Poseidon, and Zeus) were not disclosed. N=23 participants (groups 1–4: 3 groups with 6 participants and 1 group with 5 participants) had to articulate their preferences on the basis of a 5-star scale, the remaining participants (N=21, groups 5–8: 1 group with 6 and 3 groups with 5 participants) rated the restaurants with regard to the predefined MAUT dimensions (*Ambience*, *Price*, *Quality* and *Location*). We anonymized all restaurants in terms of their name and also made no statement on the type of food (for example "italian", "asian", "steak", ...) to prevent a bias triggered by favorite food tastes. Our major goal was to figure out whether the evaluation based on MAUT [5] can counteract primacy/recency effects (if such effects exist). Before evaluating an alternative (restaurant), each participant had to read the corresponding description which focused on the four mentioned interest dimensions (see Figure 4).

solution	5-star scale	MAUT dimensions
groups 1–2	ns (Description 1)	-
groups 3–4	ps (Description 2)	-
groups 5–6	-	ns (Description 1)
groups 7–8	-	ps (Description 2)

Table 3. Study setting: assignment of groups to different types of preference definition support (5-star scale vs. MAUT dimensions) and descriptions of alternatives (*ns*: negative salient = *Description 1* vs. *ps*: positive salient = *Description 2*).

For each restaurant, two descriptions were available which only differ in terms of the ordering of individual argumen-

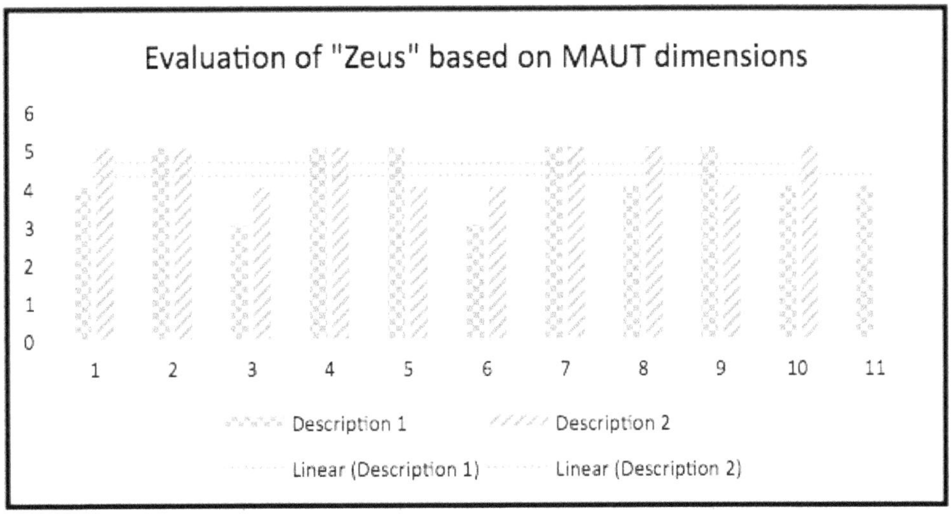

Figure 8. Evaluations (scale: [1..5]) of the decision alternative *Zeus* on basis of MAUT dimensions. The dotted lines show the average voting value of the alternative. Description 1 states the negative aspects at the very beginning and the end (negative salient) and Description 2 states the positive aspects at the very beginning and the end (positive salient).

tations: (1) the *negative salient* description where negative properties of the alternative were positioned at the beginning and the end of the description (*Description 1*) and (2) the *positive salient* description where positive properties of the alternative were positioned at the beginning and the end of the description (*Description 2* – see Table 3).

An example of a positive salient description (restaurant *Zeus*) is depicted in Table 4, Table 5 shows the corresponding negative salient description. With the help of these alternative descriptions we wanted to figure out whether primacy/recency effects exist when evaluating decision alternatives. We hypothesized that the higher effort which comes with an evaluation using MAUT helps to counteract primacy/recency effects. This leads to better decision outcomes because biases such as the primacy/recency effects can be significantly reduced if evaluations are performed more accurately.

As shown in Figure 5, every decision alternative is represented by a bar. To make an easy comparison to the individual preferences possible, the group recommendation displays the alternatives in the same order as the individual preferences (see Figure 3). The bars of the chart in Figure 5 contain also the individual rating information of all participants (displayed by moving the cursor over a corresponding bar). This information is only available if the preference visibility feature has been set correspondingly when creating the decision app.

Results of the User Study

The study shows that the restaurants with negative aspects at the beginning and at the end of the description are rated lower than those with positive aspects at the beginning and the end of the description. This was the case when 5-star ratings were used (on an average 1.5 stars less – see Figure 7). The outcome of a two-sample t-test confirms that the two sample sets have different corresponding mean evaluations ($p < 0.05$). With 5-star rating scales, in 83.2% of the cases restaurants with a *positive salient* description were chosen.

If MAUT dimensions were used to evaluate the alternatives there was no significant difference between the two versions in terms of the average evaluation (see also Figure 8). In this case 53.6% of the participants selected a restaurant with with a *positive salient* description (46.4% selected a restaurant with a *negative salient* description).

Consequently, a MAUT-based evaluation of the decision alternatives can counteract serial position (primacy/recency) effects. Figures 7 and 8 show the results of one decision alternative (*Zeus*) based on a 5-star scale (Figure 7) and on a MAUT dimension evaluation (Figure 8).

After the participants finished their evaluation we asked them whether or not they felt comfortable during the evaluation process on the basis of the systems usability scale (SUS) [3]. This is an important information for us because the MAUT-based evaluation needs more effort and time because all dimensions have to be evaluated separately (see Figure 4).

The usability feedback was very positive and provides a good motivation to continue our work on the extension and improvement of the CHOICLA functionalities. A detailed description of the results and the questionnaire for the evaluation can be found in Figure 9. We did not detect significant differences in the SUS results between the 5-star version and the MAUT-based version. The results indicate that participants spend more time for evaluating alternatives and thus are less susceptible to serial position effects.

CONCLUSIONS AND FUTURE WORK

In this paper we gave an overview of the CHOICLA environment which supports different types of group decision scenarios. Decision apps can be defined on the basis of a feature model that supports the flexible configuration (definition) of decision apps. Within the scope of a user study we detected

Positive salient description (Zeus)
Breathtaking view over the city center. Easily accessible via the highway, plenty of parking opportunities. Terrific ambiente with an open-view kitchen. Side dishes and sauces can be freely customized. Friendly service. Upper price segment. Food quality does not justify the price. Personel leaves the impression of unkemptness. Poor cleanliness. Elegant furniture and a good place for relaxing.

Table 4. Positive salient description (= *Description 2*) of a restaurant.

Negative salient description (Zeus)
Upper price segment. Food quality does not justify the price. Breathtaking view over the city center. Easily accessible via the highway, plenty of parking opportunities. Terrific ambiente with an open-view kitchen. Side dishes and sauces can be freely customized. Friendly service. Elegant furniture and a good place for relaxing. Personel leaves the impression of unkemptness. Poor cleanliness.

Table 5. Negative salient description (= *Description 1*) of a restaurant.

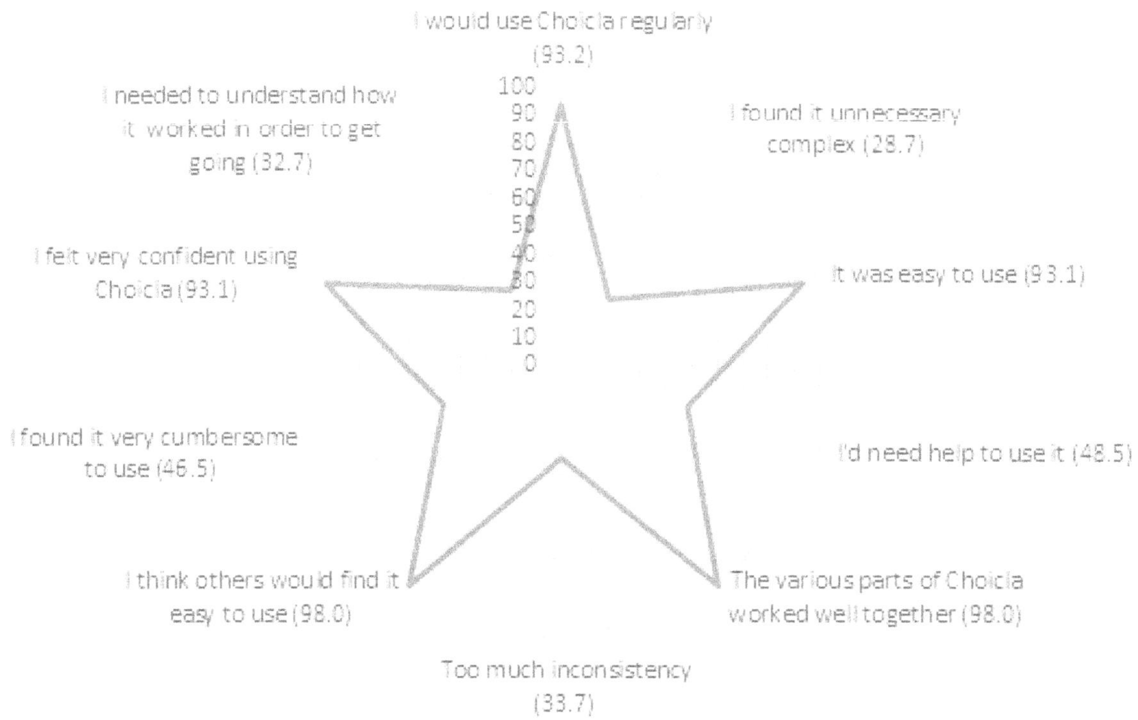

Figure 9. Results of the SUS-based usability study of the second group (MAUT-based evaluation of alternatives) (N=21).

primacy/recency effects in the evaluation of decision alternatives and figured out that a MAUT-based item evaluation approach can help to counteract these effects. Our future work will include the development of group decision technologies for complex products and services, the development of further group decision heuristics which especially focus on fostering consensus among group members, and the investigation of further decision biases that play a role in the context of group decision making.

REFERENCES

1. Adomavicius, G., Bockstedt, J., Curley, S., and Zhang, J. Recommender Systems, Consumer Preferences, and Anchoring Effects. In *RecSys 2011 Workshop on Human Decision Making in Recommender Systems (Decisions@RecSys 2011)* (Chicago, IL, USA, 2011), 35–42.
2. Adomavicius, G., Bockstedt, J., Curley, S., and Zhang, J. De-Biasing User Preference Ratings in Recommender Systems. In *RecSys 2014 Workshop on Interfaces and Human Decision Making for Recommender Systems (IntRS 2014)* (Foster City, CA, USA, 2014), 2–9.
3. Bangor, A., Kortum, P., and Miller, J. An Empirical Evaluation of the System Usability Scale (SUS). *International Journal of Human-Computer Interaction 24*, 6 (2008), 574–594.
4. Benavides, D., Felfernig, A., Galindo, J., and Reinfrank, F. Automated Analysis in Feature Modeling and Product Configuration. In *13th International Conference on Software Reuse*, no. 7925 in LNCS, Springer (Pisa, Italy, 2013), 160–175.
5. Dyer, J. MAUT - Multi Attribute Utility Theory. In *Multiple Criteria Decision Analysis: State of the Art Surveys*, vol. 78 of *International Series in Operations Research & Management Science*. Springer New York, 2005, 265–292.
6. Felfernig, A., Friedrich, G., Gula, B., Hitz, M., Kruggel, T., Leitner, G., Melcher, R., Riepan, D., Strauss, S., Teppan, E., and Vitouch, O. Persuasive Recommendation: Serial Position Effects in Knowledge-Based Recommender Systems. In *Persuasive Technology*, Y. Kort, W. IJsselsteijn, C. Midden, B. Eggen, and B. Fogg, Eds., no. 4744 in LNCS. Springer Berlin Heidelberg, 2007, 283–294.
7. Felfernig, A., Gula, B., and Teppan, E. Knowledge-based Recommender Technologies for Marketing and Sales. *International Journal of Pattern Recognition and Artificial Intelligence (IJPRAI) 21*, 2 (2006), 1–22.
8. Felfernig, A., Zehentner, C., Ninaus, G., Grabner, H., Maaleij, W., Pagano, D., Weninger, L., and Reinfrank, F. Group decision support for requirements negotiation. In *Lecture Notes in Computer Science – Advances in User Modeling*, no. 7138, Springer (2012), 105–116.
9. Jacowitz, K., and Kahneman, D. Measures of Anchoring in Estimation Tasks. *Personality and Social Psychology Bulletin 21*, 1 (1995), 1161–1166.
10. Jameson, A. More than the Sum of its Members: Challenges for Group Recommender Systems. In *Working Conference on Advanced Visual Interfaces*, AVI '04, ACM (New York, NY, USA, 2004), 48–54.
11. Mandl, M., Felfernig, A., Teppan, E., and Schubert, M. Consumer Decision Making in Knowledge-based Recommendation. *Journal of Intelligent Information Systems (JIIS) 37*, 1 (2010), 1–22.
12. Masthoff, J. Group Recommender Systems: Combining Individual Models. *Recommender Systems Handbook* (2011), 677–702.
13. Mojzisch, A., and Schulz-Hardt, S. Knowing Other's Preferences Degrades the Quality of Group Decisions. *Journal of Personality & Social Psychology 98*, 5 (2010), 794–808.
14. Murphy, J., Hofacker, C., and Mizerski, R. Primacy and Recency Effects on Clicking Behavior. *Computer-Mediated Communication 11* (2012), 522–535.
15. Nunamaker, J. F., Dennis, A. R., Valacich, J. S., and Vogel, D. R. Information Technology for Negotiating Groups: Generating Options for Mutual Gain. *Management Science 37*, 10 (1991), 1325–1346.
16. Rodriguez, M., Steinbock, D., Watkins, J., Gershenson, C., Bollen, J., Grey, V., and deGraf, B. Smartocracy: Social Networks for Collective Cecision Making. In *HICSS 2007*, IEEE (Waikoloa, Big Island, HI, USA, 2007), 90.
17. Stettinger, M., and Felfernig, A. Choicla: Intelligent Decision Support for Groups of Users in the Context of Personnel Decisions. *Joint Workshop on Interfaces and Human Decision Making for Recommender Systems co-located with ACM Conference on Recommender Systems (RecSys 2014)* (2014), 28–32.
18. Stettinger, M., Felfernig, A., Ninaus, G., Jeran, M., Reiterer, S., and Leitner, G. Configuring Decision Tasks. *Workshop on Configuration, Novi Sad* (2014), 17–21.
19. Stettinger, M., Ninaus, G., Jeran, M., Reinfrank, F., and Reiterer, S. WE-DECIDE: A Decision Support Environment for Groups of Users. In *Recent Trends in Applied Artificial Intelligence*, M. Ali, T. Bosse, K. Hindriks, M. Hoogendoorn, C. Jonker, and J. Treur, Eds., no. 7906 in LNCS. Springer Berlin Heidelberg, 2013, 382–391.
20. Stumptner, M. An overview of Knowledge-based Configuration. *AI Communications 10*, 2.
21. Teppan, E., and Felfernig, A. Minimization of Decoy Effects in Recommender Result Sets. *Web Intelligence and Agent Systems 10*, 4 (2012), 385–395.
22. Tversky, A., and Simonson, I. Context-dependent Preferences. *Management Science 39*, 10 (1993), 1179–1189.
23. Yardi, S., Hill, B., and Chan, S. VERN: Facilitating Democratic Group Decision Making Online. In *International ACM SIGGROUP Conference on Supporting Group Work (GROUP 2005)*, ACM (Sanibel Island, Florida, USA, 2005), 116–119.

User-directed Non-Disruptive Topic Model Update for Effective Exploration of Dynamic Content

Yi Yang
Northwestern University
yiyang@u.northwestern.edu

Shimei Pan
University of Maryland, Baltimore County
shimei@umbc.edu

Yangqiu Song
University of Illinois at Urbana-Champaign
yqsong@illinois.edu

Jie Lu
IBM T. J. Watson Research Center
jielu@us.ibm.com

Mercan Topkara
JW Player
mercan@jwplayer.com

ABSTRACT

Statistical topic models have become a useful and ubiquitous text analysis tool for large corpora. One common application of statistical topic models is to support topic-centric navigation and exploration of document collections at the user interface by automatically grouping documents into coherent topics. For today's constantly expanding document collections, topic models need to be updated when new documents become available. Existing work on topic model update focuses on how to best fit the model to the data, and ignores an important aspect that is closely related to the end user experience: topic model stability. When the model is updated with new documents, the topics previously assigned to old documents may change, which may result in a disruption of end users' mental maps between documents and topics, thus undermining the usability of the applications. In this paper, we describe a user-directed non-disruptive topic model update system, nTMU, that balances the tradeoff between finding the model that fits the data and maintaining the stability of the model from end users' perspective. It employs a novel constrained LDA algorithm (cLDA) to incorporate pair-wise document constraints, which are converted from user feedback about topics, to achieve topic model stability. Evaluation results demonstrate advantages of our approach over previous methods.

Author Keywords

Statistical Topic Model; Non-disruptive Topic Model Update; User Input; Dynamic Content

ACM Classification Keywords

H.5.m Information Interfaces and Presentation (e.g. HCI): Miscellaneous; I.2.7 Artificial Intelligence: Natural Language Processing-Text analysis

http://dx.doi.org/10.1145/2678025.2701396

INTRODUCTION

In an age of information abundance/explosion, providing interactive interfaces to guide users through the navigation and exploration of the vast information space becomes a necessity for information applications [19, 12]. To achieve this goal, applications commonly employ statistical topic modeling techniques to structuralize content collections by grouping documents into coherent topics, and utilize interactive visualizations at the interfaces to support topic-centric navigation and exploration.

Due to the highly dynamic nature of many content collections where new documents are frequently added, updates to existing topic models are necessary in order to capture the changes to topics (e.g. the emergence of new topics and the evolution of existing topics) over time. When topic model updates introduce substantial changes in the topic assignments of existing documents, the users' mental maps between documents and topics may be disrupted, leading to increased cognitive load of the users and negatively impacting the usability of the applications. Therefore, how to maintain *topic model stability* during updates becomes a critical issue.

Latent Dirichlet Allocation (LDA) is one of the most commonly used approaches to topic modeling due to its capability to uncover hidden thematic patterns in text with little supervision. To handle update, standard (batch) LDA requires the topic model to be regenerated from scratch based on the updated dataset (including old and new content) [25], while online LDA incrementally updates the topic model when new content arrives without requiring a full scan of the entire dataset [9]. Because neither standard LDA nor online LDA explicitly constrains the topic model, the topic assignments of individual documents may vary significantly from one run to the next.

Let us use an example to illustrate why the lack of topic model stability using LDA may pose a serious problem. A user named Jane frequently needs to explore publications in certain fields for her work. She has been using a software tool that trains an LDA topic model on all the papers from a publication database to classify the collection of papers into three topics: Natural Language Processing (NLP), Speech Processing (SP), and Information Management (IM). Realizing that the topic model was created a year ago, Jane requested an update. The tool updated the topic model based on the current publication database, which contains all the previous papers as well as the new papers published since last year. After the update however, Jane cannot locate some of the papers she frequently visited before, because they are re-assigned to a different topic. For instance, some old NLP papers are now under the same topic as other SP papers. In a way, the mental map Jane has built for the paper collection is disrupted, resulting in confusion and frustration. The tool has become less useful to Jane unless she puts in some effort to update her mental map, which significantly increases her cognitive load.

In this paper, we describe a novel user-directed non-disruptive topic model update system (nTMU) to explicitly address topic model stability. It directly incorporates topic stability constraints to minimize the changes to the topic assignments of the same documents before and after model update. As a result, it can effectively maintain the stability of document-to-topic mappings and minimize the disruption to the mental maps of end users. The core module of nTMU runs a novel constrained topic modeling algorithm cLDA. It allows LDA to incorporate pair-wise document constraints such as document must-links and cannot-links. Evaluation on a benchmark dataset as well as a user study have demonstrated the effectiveness of our approach. We believe that both the nTMU system and the cLDA algorithm are significant contributions to the field since as far as we know, there isn't any other system that addresses the topic model stability issue during topic model update, and no existing LDA algorithm can effectively handle document must-link and cannot-link constraints simultaneously.

The rest of the paper is organized as follows. Following a brief review of related work, we use two example scenarios to further illustrate the topic model stability issue and how our system addresses this issue. Then we describe notations used throughout the paper and provides a formal definition of topic model stability. We then present the nTMU system and introduce the cLDA algorithm, which incorporates user feedback into standard LDA as pair-wise document constraints. An algorithmic evaluation and a formal user study are described in the following sections. Lastly, we provide a discussion section and then conclude the paper.

RELATED WORK

Our work is closely related to three areas of research: user interface design, topic model update and topic model with prior knowledge.

User Interface (UI) Design

Usability is critical to the development of a user-friendly interface because it helps users to work in an effective, efficient, and manageable way [6]. Learnability, which is the ease with which a software application or product can be picked up and understood by users, is a key attribute of usability [17]. Because consistency and predictability are considered design factors that contributed to increased learnability [7], they have become two of the most important principles in UI design [18].

Despite being well-established principles in UI design, consistency and predictability have received little attention in the machine learning and data mining communities. New machine learning/data mining algorithms are rarely invented to specifically address these factors. However, for any interactive machine learning/data mining system, without proper backend support, it is impossible to achieve consistency and predictability at the UI level. For example, if the backend algorithm produces inconsistent results at different time intervals due to updates, the UI designed to surface these results will inevitably suffer from low consistency and predictability. More attention is needed during the development of backend algorithms to address these basic usability issues. Our work is the first in this direction.

Topic Model Update

Online LDA has been the main solution to topic model update. It incrementally updates the topic model when new documents arrive. Among existing online LDA algorithms, some use Variational Bayes (VB) [9, 26] to infer latent variables, others employ sampling methods [21, 3, 5]. Although online LDA sometimes can perform as well as batch LDA, it suffers from the same *topic model stability* problem as batch LDA since it mainly focuses on trying to approximate batch LDA's performance without requiring a full scan of the entire dataset. In this paper, we propose a new LDA-based algorithm that employs a novel constrained topic modeling approach to topic model update. With this approach, the algorithm can maintain topic model stability and minimize end user disruption by directly incorporating stability constraints in topic modeling.

Topic Model with Prior Knowledge

Recently, several algorithms have been developed to extend the standard LDA algorithm to incorporate user feedback or domain knowledge. Among them, some support seed constraints (e.g., document topic labels) [4, 20] while others support pair-wise word constraints (e.g., word must-links and cannot-links) [1, 2, 10]. [14] presents a topic modeling framework with network regularization, but it cannot easily handle cannot-links. To ensure topic model stability and at the same time to avoid over-constraining the new topic model, it is desirable to encode the stability constraints as pair-wise document constraints (e.g., document must-link and cannot-link constraints). However, none of these algorithms supports general pair-wise document constraints without further extension.

There have also been works focusing on incorporating specific link relations (e.g., citations between documents) to facilitate social network-based topic analysis [23, 16, 13]. Since all of them employ generative models, they cannot directly formulate cannot-link constraints between documents. Our constrained LDA algorithm is more general and it can handle both types of document constraints (must-links and cannot-links).

EXAMPLE SCENARIOS

In this section, we provide two example scenarios to illustrate the topic model stability problem during dynamic topic-centric exploration of online news articles. For both scenarios, we also show how the nTMU system we have developed aids the user, named Alice, by interactively incorporating her feedback during topic model update to keep the topic model stable.

In the first scenario, news articles related to *Fiscal Cliff* and *Obamacare* are put under two different topics based on the initial topic model created. Alice explores the articles under both topics but focuses more on Obamacare which is more closely related to her personal interests. A few weeks later, as more news articles become available, the topic model needs to be updated. When standard LDA is used to update the model, the *Fiscal Cliff* and *Obamacare* articles are put under a single topic as they are both related to government issues, which means that the articles about two previously separate topics are now mixed together. After this update, Alice is unable to easily relocate the old Obamacare articles and has difficulty identifying the changes happening to Obamacare between several weeks ago and now. In contrast, using the nTMU system which conducts constrained topic model update, Alice can indicate that she wants to keep the *fiscal cliff* and *Obamacare* articles separate since she wants to follow the news on these two events separately. nTMU incorporates this feedback during topic model update, so the articles about *fiscal cliff* and *Obamacare* remain under separate topics after the update to satisfy Alice's preference.

In the second scenario, the initial model includes (among other topics) two topics, one about *Hurricane Sandy* and the other about *Fiscal Cliff*. Alice reads several articles related to Hurricane Sandy. A few weeks later, the topic model is updated to include a new set of news articles. In this new article set, some *Hurricane Sandy* articles discuss government funding situations to aid recovery after the hurricane, which happen to share many common keywords as the articles about *Fiscal Cliff*. As a result, some previous *Hurricane Sandy* articles are put under the same topic as the articles related to *Fiscal Cliff* when standard LDA is used to create the updated model. This totally confuses Alice as she does not understand why those articles about Sandy are not with other Sandy articles but mixed with those about *Fiscal Cliff*. As a result, she questions the accuracy of the system and deems the system not useful. In comparison, the nTMU system will ensure that all *Hurricane Sandy* articles remain together and are not mixed with *Fiscal Cliff* articles after the update.

NOTATIONS AND DEFINITIONS

In this section, we first briefly review topic model representation and topic label assignment based on the standard LDA algorithm (the same notations are also used in later sections). Then we formally define topic model stability.

Topic Model Representation

Statistical topic models derive latent topics from a text collection consisting of a set of documents $d \in D$. Each document is a sequence of words w_n drawn from a vocabulary V of size W. LDA provides a generative topic model where topics are modeled as latent variables $z_n \in \mathcal{K}$ for each word w_n, given a set of topics $\mathcal{K}$. The number of hidden topics in LDA is K.

In LDA, θ_d is the topic distribution for document d which is drawn from a Dirichlet distribution, $\theta_d \sim Dir(\alpha)$; ϕ_k is the topic-specific word distribution which is also drawn from a Dirichlet distribution, $\phi_k \sim Dir(\beta)$. α and β are the hyper-parameters for the two Dirichlet distributions.

We focus on LDA inference using Gibbs sampling. The collapsed Gibbs Sampling algorithm iterates through and updates all the latent variables based on the following formulas:

$$P(z_i = j|\mathbf{z}_{\neg i}, \mathbf{w}) = \frac{(n_{d,j}^{-i} + \alpha)}{n_d^{-i} + K\alpha} \frac{n_{w,j}^{-i} + \beta}{n_j^{-i} + W\beta} \quad (1)$$

where n^{-i} is a count that does not include the current assignment of z_i. The variable $n_{d,j}$ is the count of topic j in document d, and $n_{w,j}$ is the count of word w being assigned to topic j, where $n_d = \sum_j^K n_{d,j}$, and $n_j = \sum_j^W n_{w,j}$.

Finally, we can estimate document d's jth topic probability $\hat{\theta}_{j|d}$ and topic j's word-specific probability of w $\hat{\phi}_{w|j}$ from the topic samples $\mathbf{z}$ by

$$\hat{\theta}_{j|d} = \frac{n_{d,j} + \alpha}{n_d + K\alpha}, \quad \hat{\phi}_{w|j} = \frac{n_{w,j} + \beta}{n_j + W\beta} \quad (2)$$

Topic Label Assignment

Given document d's topic distribution $\hat{\theta_d}$, we can assign d's topic label l_d to be the topic that has the maximum value in $\hat{\theta_d}$. However, it is possible that some topics learned by LDA are only "background" topics which have significant non-trivial probabilities over many documents [22]. Since background topics are often uninteresting ones, a weighted topic distribution could be used to filter them. Therefore, we normalize $\hat{\theta_{dk}}$ by the sum of the kth topic value over all documents. This idea is similar to the inverse document frequency used in tf-idf, which normalizes the weight of a word by its overall occurrences in all documents. A weighted kth component $\hat{\theta}'_{dk}$ for document d is computed as follows:

$$\hat{\theta}'_{dk} = \hat{\theta_{dk}} / \sum_{i=0}^{D} \hat{\theta}_{ik}. \quad (3)$$

Then, instead of assigning the document label to the topic that has the maximum value, we choose the topic that has the maximum normalized value. Therefore, the topic label of document d is $l_d = \arg\max_{k \in K} \hat{\theta}'_{dk}$.

Note that there are other methods of assigning a topic label to a document. For example, we can use the per-document topic distribution as a feature vector in an unsupervised clustering algorithm such as k-means clustering, where the number of clusters equals to the number of topics in LDA. In our work, for simplicity, we utilize the straightforward method described above for topic label assignment, which is commonly used in real-world topic modeling systems.

Topic Model Stability

The topic model stability problem happens when there is new data coming in and the existing topic model needs to be updated. With standard LDA, if an existing model is refreshed with new documents, it is unavoidable that the model's parameters will change. As a result, the top keywords of the same topic and the topic label assignments of old documents may change. Given this, there are two different ways to define topic model stability: (1) keep the top keywords associated with each topic unchanged; (2) keep the topic label assigned to each old document unchanged.

We believe the first definition is too rigid since it does not allow a topic to evolve. For example, early papers on Natural Language Processing (NLP) focused on linguistic methods. As a result, the top keywords of the old NLP topic may include "grammar, syntax, semantics, subject, verb." Nowadays, more and more NLP systems employ data-driven approaches. Statistical and machine learning based NLP methods have become mainstream. Thus, after updating the topic model with new NLP publications, we expect that the top NLP keywords may include "statistics, learning, unigram, frequency, corpus." Since the change of top topic keyword is the result of topic evolution, minimizing the change of top topic keywords does not seem to be a good solution. In this

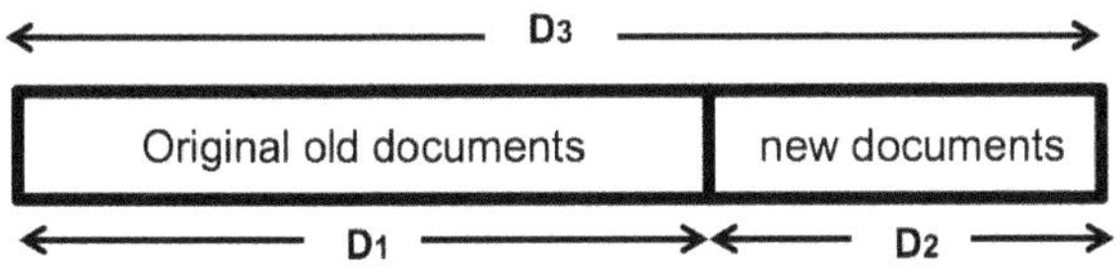

Figure 1. Documents flow in a topic model update system.

work, we adopt the second definition which allows topics to evolve with new content. With this definition, maintaining topic model stability means minimizing the change of topic labels assigned to the same documents before and after an update. Specifically, we use the following formula to define *topic model stability*. Here, we denote D_1 as the dataset used to train the old topic model, D_2 as the new dataset and $D_3 = D_1 \cup D_2$ as the total dataset used to train the new topic model. l_{1i} is the topic label assigned to the ith document based on the old topic model, and l_{2i} is the topic label assigned to the ith document after the model is updated to the new topic model. Figure 1 illustrates the flow of new data.

$$S = (1 - \frac{\sum_{d_i \in D_1} I(l_{1i} \neq l_{2i})}{|D_1|}) * 100\%, \quad (4)$$

where $I(.)$ is the indication function. S equals to 1 when the topic labels for all the documents in D_1 remain the same after the update.

NON-DISRUPTIVE TOPIC MODEL UPDATE (NTMU)

The standard topic model update systems do not have users in the loop. When new data are coming in, based on different topic model update strategies [25], topic models are retrained on either both old data and new data, or only the new data. As we will show in the System Evaluation section, such topic model update systems have poor topic model stability since their main objective is only to fit the data into the model. Figure 2 illustrates our system nTMU (user-directed **n**on-disruptive **T**opic **M**odel **U**pdate). It consists of four main components and includes users as a critical part. Below

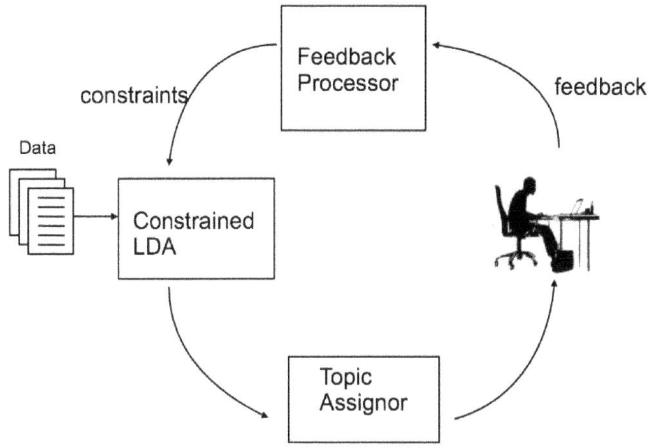

Figure 2. Non-Disruptive Topic Model Update diagram.

we describe these components in counter-clockwise order as shown in the figure.

Data, such as text collections, arrive at the nTMU system in an online fashion. The topic model is created and updated by the *Constrained LDA* component, which employs the cLDA algorithm (described in detail in the next section). Unlike unsupervised standard LDA, cLDA is capable of taking document-level user feedback encoded as document must-links and cannot-links. In the first round when the nTMU system is newly started with an initial set of data and no user feedback, cLDA behaves the same as standard LDA without any constraints. The system does allow users to provide prior domain knowledge/labels, but we assume that there is no prior information available in the current setting.

Given the topic modeling results from the *Constrained LDA* component, the *Topic Assignor* component assigns a topic label to each document using the method discussed in previous section. Since Gibbs sampler randomly initialize topic samples for each document, the topic label of the same topic before and after update can be different, and we need to align the topic label to make the labels consistent. Therefore, Hungarian algorithm[1] is applied to achieve this task by maximizing the label matching. Basically, it will find an optimal matching that maximizes the number of the same document label before and after the update.

Next, the *User Interface* component presents the labeled results to the end users. It displays for each topic the most probable words based on topic-word distributions (Equation 2), along with a treemap-like visualization showing the twenty most representative documents that are assigned to this topic. Users can also click on the "Show More button" to see more representative documents. The title of each document is displayed, and if a user clicks on a document, a summary window will pop out to show the detailed information of this document, including time, author and highlights from the content. Figure 3 provides a screen shot of the user interface.

[1]`http://en.wikipedia.org/wiki/Hungarian_algorithm`

Figure 3. Topic model display interface.

The treemap-like visualization has been demonstrated to be effective to support topic-centric navigation and exploration of document collections [11].

The system allows the user to provide feedback about the topics through the interface. In particular, for each topic, the system asks the user whether the topic is coherent and whether s/he wants to keep it. For example, if the content of the representative documents of the topic is consistent with this topic, the user would respond with *Yes* to the system. However, if the user decides that s/he does not care about the topic or the topic has inconsistent keywords and representative documents, he/she would response *No* to the system.

After the feedback is collected, the *Feedback Processor* component converts the user's *Yes* or *No* feedback to document must-link and cannot-link constraints. A **must-link** constraint between two documents indicates that they should belong to the same topic, and a **cannot-link** constraint indicates that the documents should belong to different topics. For a topic that the user responses with Yes, must-link constraints are added for each pair of the documents that have this topic label, and cannot-link constraints are added between documents with this topic label and documents with a different topic label. In contrast, for a topic that the user responses with No, neither must-links nor cannot-links are added. All the must-links and cannot-links are fed to the *Constrained LDA* component for constrained topic model update, which completes the loop.

CONSTRAINED LDA (CLDA)

In previous section, we introduce nTMU, the Non-Disruptive Topic Model Update system, that is capable of incorporating user feedback into standard LDA, but we treat the Constrained LDA module as a black box. In this section, we will present Constrained LDA algorithm in details.

We focus on two types of document level constraints: must-links and cannot-links. Specifically, we denote $\mathcal{M}_i \in \mathcal{D}$ as the set of documents sharing must-links with document d_i, and $\mathcal{C}_i \in \mathcal{D}$ as the set of documents sharing cannot-links with document d_i. The idea behind cLDA is that, we want to make documents share must-links close to each other, while documents share cannot-links far away from each other, in the K-dimensional space, by controlling documents' topic distribution prior.

The Role of Concentration Parameters

In LDA, the prior of θ is a Dirichlet distribution, which is denoted by $Dir(\vec{\alpha}_g) = Dir(\alpha_{g,1}, ..., \alpha_{g,K})$. $\vec{\alpha}_g$ is the global hyperparameter, and $\alpha_{g,i}$ determines how "concentrated" the probability mass of a sampled θ is likely to be on topic i. If all the $\alpha_{g,i}$ are less than one, the probability mass tends to be concentrated on a few topics. If all the $\alpha_{g,i}$ are greater than one, the probability mass tends to be more uniformly distributed. Meanwhile, smaller $\alpha_{g,i}$ attracts more concentration on topic i. A simple and commonly used Dirichlet distribution is the symmetric Dirichlet distribution, where $\alpha_{g,1} = \alpha_{g,2} = ... = \alpha_{g,K} = \alpha$.

If there is no information about relationships of the documents, the concentration parameters are normally set to be equal. Then the model can update the likelihood by learning the posterior of θ_i. When we have knowledge about a document's topic distribution, e.g., two documents have similar topic distribution, the topic distributions of documents cannot be assumed to be independently sampled. To achieve this, we manipulate the Dirichlet prior over document-topic distribution such that document must-link and cannot-link constraints can be incorporated into the topic model. In such a way, we use an asymmetric Dirichlet prior over document-topic while keep the Dirichlet prior over topic-word symmetric [24]. In the following, we explain how to incorporate the prior knowledge encoded in document must-links and cannot-links into an LDA topic model.

Must-link Constraint

A must-link between two documents d_1 and d_2 suggests that d_1 and d_2 should share the same topics, e.g., both are Sports news. Thus $\hat{\theta}_1$ should be similar to $\hat{\theta}_2$, and both distributions on the K-dimensional space should be close to each other.

Given the documents in $\mathcal{M}_i$, we introduce an auxiliary variable $\vec{\alpha}_i^{\mathcal{M}}$:

$$\vec{\alpha}_i^{\mathcal{M}} = T * \frac{1}{|\mathcal{M}_i|} \sum_{j \in \mathcal{M}_i} \hat{\theta}_j, \quad (5)$$

where T controls the concentration parameters. The larger the value of T is, the closer $\hat{\theta}_i$ is to the average of $\hat{\theta}_j$'s. $\mathcal{M}_i \in \mathcal{D}$ is the set of documents sharing must-links with document d_i

Cannot-link Constraint

A cannot-link between documents d_1 and d_2 suggests that d_1 and d_2 should not have the same topics, for example, one is about Sports and the other is about Politics. Thus, $\hat{\theta}_1$ should *not* be similar to $\hat{\theta}_2$, and both distributions on the K-dimensional space should be really far away from each other.

Given the documents in $\mathcal{C}_i$, we introduce the following auxiliary variable:

$$\vec{\alpha_i}^{\mathcal{C}} = T * \arg_{\hat{\theta}_i} \max \min_{j \in \mathcal{C}_i} KL(\hat{\theta}_i, \hat{\theta}_j), \quad (6)$$

where $KL(\hat{\theta}_i, \hat{\theta}_j)$ is the KL-divergence between two distributions $\hat{\theta}_i$ and $\hat{\theta}_j$. This means we choose a vector that is maximally far away from $\mathcal{C}_i$, in terms of KL divergence to its nearest neighbor in $\mathcal{C}_i$. $\mathcal{C}_i \in \mathcal{D}$ is the set of documents sharing cannot-links with document d_i.

Then in each iteration, we draw a $\hat{\theta}_i$ from the following distribution:

$$\vec{\theta_i} \sim Dir(\eta_g \vec{\alpha}_g + \eta_{\mathcal{M}} \vec{\alpha_i}^{\mathcal{M}} + \eta_{\mathcal{C}} \vec{\alpha_i}^{\mathcal{C}}) = Dir(\vec{\alpha}_i). \quad (7)$$

Here, η_g, $\eta_{\mathcal{M}}$ and $\eta_{\mathcal{C}}$ are the weights to control the trade-off among the three terms. Note that in the first iteration of learning, it is possible that all the $\hat{\theta}_i$'s are initialized by drawing from the global α_g solely. In our experiment, we choose $T = 100$, $\eta_g = \eta_{\mathcal{M}} = \eta_{\mathcal{C}} = 1$.

Inference with Gibbs Sampling

Given a set of document must-links $\mathcal{M}$ and cannot-links $\mathcal{C}$, we infer the values of the hidden variables z using collapsed Gibbs sampling as in LDA [8]. In each iteration, a topic assignment z_i of word w_i in document d is sampled based on all the other variables. We directly present the conditional probability as following distribution:

$$\begin{aligned} P(z_i = j | \mathbf{z}_{\neg i}, \mathbf{w}, \mathcal{M}_d, \mathcal{C}_d) &= \frac{(n_{d,j}^{-i} + \alpha_{d,j})}{n_d^{-i} + \sum_{k=1}^{K} \alpha_{d,k}} \frac{n_{w,j}^{-i} + \beta}{n_j^{-i} + W\beta}, \\ &\propto (n_{d,j}^{-i} + \alpha_{d,j}) \frac{n_{w,j}^{-i} + \beta}{n_j^{-i} + W\beta} \end{aligned} \quad (8)$$

It is worth comparing Equation 8 with Equation 1. In LDA, the hyperparameter $\vec{\alpha}$ is not updated during the training. Moreover, in most of the real world LDA system, for simplicity reason, $\vec{\alpha}$ is a uniformed vector with the same value for each vector component over all documents. However, in cLDA, $\vec{\alpha}$ is not a fixed value but is updated in every iteration based on the constraint sets, and different documents will have different hyperparameter which also reflects the relationship among documents.

The new iterative Gibbs sampling process is shown in Algorithm 2.

Algorithm 1 cLDA Gibbs Sampling for document d with constraint set $\mathcal{M}_d$, $\mathcal{C}_d$

1: $\vec{\alpha}_d = \eta_g \vec{\alpha}_g + \eta_{\mathcal{M}} \vec{\alpha_d}^{\mathcal{M}} + \eta_{\mathcal{C}} \vec{\alpha_d}^{\mathcal{C}}$
2: **for** w_i in d **do**
3:   **for** $j \leftarrow 0$ **to** K **do**
4:     $f(z_i = j | \mathbf{z}_{\neg i}, \mathbf{w}) = (n_{d,j}^{-i} + \alpha_{d,j}) \frac{n_{w,j}^{-i} + \beta}{n_j^{-i} + W\beta}$
5:   **end for**
6:   sample new topic assignment for w_i from $f(z_i)$
7: **end for**

The difference between the cLDA's Gibbs sampling and the standard LDA's Gibbs sampling lies in line 1. In standard LDA, document d's topic distribution prior $\vec{\alpha}_d$ is a vector with fixed values. However, in cLDA, $\vec{\alpha}_d$ is updated in every iteration based on d's constraints set $\mathcal{M}_d$, $\mathcal{C}_d$. If d's constraints set $\mathcal{M}_d$, $\mathcal{C}_d$ are empty sets, then the cLDA Gibbs sampling for d is reduced to LDA Gibbs sampling.

SYSTEM EVALUATION

In this section, we evaluate our nTMU system's performance from two aspects, topic model quality and topic model stability. From a user's standpoint of view, a good topic model update system should not only be able to fit data into model well but can also maintain a stable topic model transition.

For evaluation, we use NIPS dataset[2], a benchmark dataset commonly use in text analysis. It contains 1,740 papers from the NIPS conferences between 1987 and 1999. Documents in the dataset are sorted based on their timestamps. We use the first 844 documents (from 1987 to 1993) as D_1, next 896 documents (from 1994 to 1999) as D_2. Note that the documents in this dataset do not have ground-truth labels. After removing stopwords and stemming, the dataset has 6,448 unique words. For topic modeling parameters, we choose 20 as the number of topics since it is commonly reported in literatures that use NIPS dataset. We also set the global hyperparameter $\alpha_g = 1$, and $\beta = 0.01$. To make sure the Gibbs sampling chain converges, we average over 10 runs for each experiment, and for each run, 500 iterations. The first two experiments are conducted without having user in the loop. Thus, the feedback processor component automatically generates document constraints. Must-links are added for documents with the same topic label, while cannot-links are added between documents with different topic labels. In the experiments, for each document, 10 must-links and 10 cannot-links are randomly sampled.

Experiment 1: Topic Stability

In the first experiment, we test nTMU's capability in maintaining topic stability. We compared nTMU against three baseline systems:

1. Standard LDA: it jointly resamples all topics for the entire collection, including both the old and the new documents, and old documents' topic samples are not reused. Therefore, it retrains the whole topic model one the entire collections from scratch.

2. Fixed Fold-in: it jointly resamples topics for all the new documents, but it keeps old documents' topic samples fixed. Therefore, old documents' topic samples are used to initialize the topic model, but they are not updated. Note that although this method keeps all old documents' topic sample fixed, it does not necessarily mean that the topic labels for the documents will be the same before and after the update. There are two reasons that the topic label would be changed. First, document's topic distribution $\hat{\theta}$ is

[2] `http://psiexp.ss.uci.edu/research/programsdata/toolbox.htm`

a weighted distribution (Equation 3), and its value is normalized over all the documents, including the new documents. Second, since topic labels are aligned by Hungarian algorithm which looks for a "maximum matching" on all documents, it is likely that the old documents' label indexes are swapped, which changes the topic labels for old documents.

3. Rejuvenated Fold-in: in addition to jointly resampling topics for all new documents, it also updates old documents' topic samples. Therefore, after being used to initialize topic model, old documents' topic samples will be updated.

Both (2) and (3) were inspired by the ideas behind sampling-based inference strategies for new documents discussed in [25]. In fact, the difference among three baseline topic model update methods is how to initialize new topic model given old topic model results. In standard LDA, old documents' topic samples have no impact on the new topic model, while in Fixed Fold-in and Rejuvenated Fold-in, old documents' topic samples will have different impacts.

Table 1 shows the topic model stability results on three baseline systems and our nTMU. Among all the topic update methods, nTMU significantly outperforms the other methods in maintaining high topic stability. In particular, it improves the standard LDA's topic model stability by 103%, and it also improves the second best Fixed fold-in method by 46.3%. Note that the results are averaged over 10 runs for each topic model update method.

Model update method	stability
Standard LDA	43.3%
Fixed fold-in	60.2%
Rejuvenated fold-in	57.8%
nTMU	**88.1%**

Table 1. Topic model stability performance of different model update methods.

Experiment 2: Topic Coherence

In addition to topic stability metric, we also evaluate our nTMU using topic coherence metric. Recent research [15] has shown that topic coherence is highly consistent with human judgement than held-out dataset likelihood. Thus, here we use topic coherence to assess a topic model's quality. Following [15], topic t's coherence is defined as $C(t : V^{(t)}) = \sum_{m=2}^{M} \sum_{l=1}^{m-1} \log \frac{F(v_m^{(t)}, v_l^{(t)})+1}{F(v_l^{(t)})}$, where $F(v)$ is the document frequency of word type v, $F(v, v')$ is the co-document frequency of word type v and v', and $V^{(t)} = (v_1^{(t)}, ..., v_M^{(t)})$ is a list of the M most probable words in topic t. In our experiments, we choose the 20 most probable words to compute topic coherence, i.e., $M = 20$. In addition, since LDA usually generates common background topics which appear in many documents and thus un-interesting, we also filtered those topics based on the method proposed in [22] before we compute the coherence scores for all the methods.

As shown in Figure 4, nTMU and Standard LDA achieve similar topic coherence score, and both methods perform better than Fixed Fold-in and Rejuvenated Fold-in methods with statistical significance at $p = 0.05$, using Chi-Square test. Although nTMU is slight worse than standard LDA, but there is no statistical significance. Since this is a simulation experiment, and the constraints are added automatically within each topic label, it is inevitable that 1). mistakes are introduced to the system for inconsistent or uncorrelated topics; 2). the model is over-constrained by the constraints. For example, Fixed Fold-in has the worst topic coherence performance because it does not allow topic samples in old documents to update. Therefore, this system is over-constrained and has a poor topic model quality. However, we can see from the figure that the nTMU system can still achieve topic coherence nearly as good as standard LDA update system, which does not have any constraints applied and have the most freedom to fit new data.

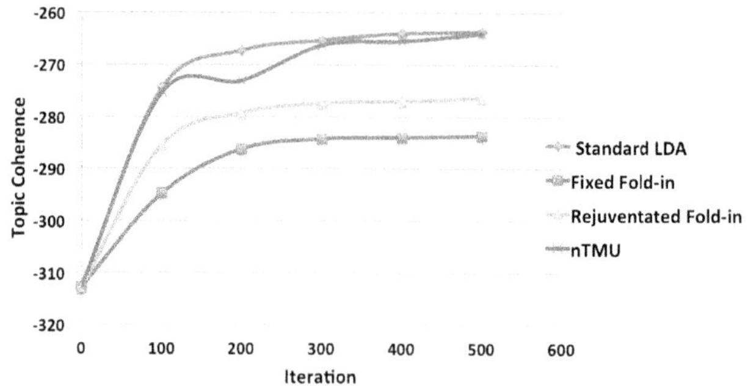

Figure 4. Topic Coherence of different topic model update methods.

To sum up, unlike Fixed Fold-in and Rejuvenated Fold-in who achieve higher topic stability than standard LDA at the cost of lower topic coherence, nTMU achieves the highest topic stability score among all the methods without sacrificing any topic coherence.

Experiment 3: Incorporating User Guidance

In the above two experiments, nTMU system simulates user interaction by adding constraints for each topic automatically. In this experiment, instead of the simulations, we demonstrate the benefit of keeping users in the loop and allowing them to guide topic model update.

Since nTMU employs a constrained topic modeling framework, it needs to satisfy two goals simultaneously: (1) to satisfy as many constraints as possible (2) to derive a topic model that fits the data. In general, if goal (1) matches goal (2), the constraints will help the system to meet goal (2) (e.g., the ground-truth labels). But if goal (1) is competing with goal (2) (e.g., minimizing end user disruption in nTMU), goal (1) may distract the system from meeting goal (2). Here is an example on how goal (1) in nTMU might distract the system from achieving goal (2): With an old topic model, a paper on language modeling was categorized as an SP paper since the method was first adopted in the speech recognition community. Over the years, language modeling became very popular in the NLP community for tasks such as machine translation, POS tagging and parsing. As a result, now, it is more appropriate to categorize this as an NLP paper. But due to the topic stability constraints, our system will insist on categorizing this as an SP paper.

Giving the competing nature of the two goals in nTMU, the more constraints we add to the system, the less freedom it has to fit the topic model to the data. Without user feedback, by default, nTMU will keep all the topics stable. This may over-constrain the system. For example, since not all the topics are equally interesting, there is no need to ensure the stability of topics that a user does not care about. Similarly, not all the topics are equally good. Some of the inferred topics may even be incoherent. Enforcing the stability of incoherent topics can hurt the performance.

To validate the above concerns and to demonstrate the benefit of keeping users in the loop, we designed the following experiment. First, we allowed a user to choose a subset of the topics (e.g., 3) that are important to him. Frequently, user selected topics are coherent topics. In the experiment, this user is one of the authors who is familiar with the topics in this dataset. We also compared this model with two alternatives: (1) a model which kept three incoherent topics stable (b) a model which kept all the topics stable. With this setting, we wanted to verify that (1) keeping incoherent topic stable will hurt the system's capability to adapt to the data (2) keeping all the topics stable will over-constrain the system and prevent it from fitting the data. Here, since we want to measure how well the learned model fits the test dataset, rather than the consistence with human judgement, we use *perplexity*, not topic coherence, as the metric to assess the topic model's quality. As shown in Figure 5, nTMU that uses coherent topic stability constraints performed very well. At the end of the 2000 iterations, there is no difference between the perplexity of this model and the perplexity of a model that has no constraint. In contrast, the performance of the model that enforces the stability of incoherent topics deteriorated noticeably with statistical significance. Finally, the default model that enforces the stability constraints on all the topics had the worst performance. This result has clearly demonstrated the benefit of incorporating user guidance in managing topic model update.

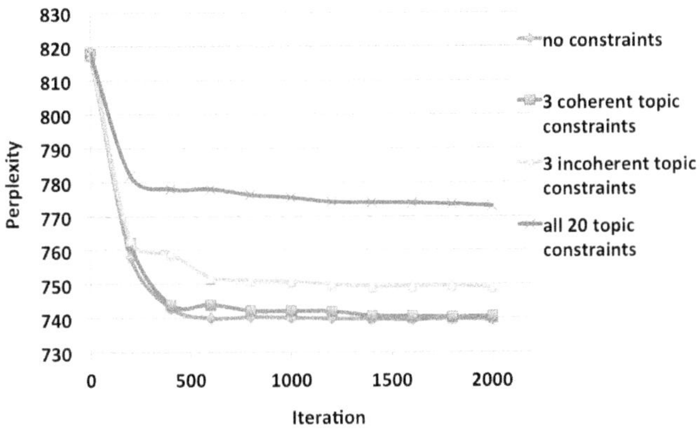

Figure 5. The benefit of human guidance.

Setting Model Parameters

In our current system, we need to set multiple model parameters, such as the number of topics, the value of concentration parameters, and the weights of must-link and cannot-link constraints. Although we can use heuristics to estimate the parameters for a dataset based on its characteristics (e.g., size of the data set), in reality, the parameters will still need to be tuned empirically for each new dataset. Optimizing such parameters for each dataset automatically is an active research topic in Machine Learning and beyond the scope of the paper.

USER STUDY

Experiment Design

We also conducted a user study to evaluate the impact of topic stability in an automated document exploration system. We used Amazon Mechanical Turk (MTurk) as our study platform. In order to design tasks that are not too difficult for the workers (called Turkers), we decided to use a general news dataset instead of a scientific publication dataset. Our news dataset includes CNN news articles from October, 2012 to November, 2013, covering five prominent topics at the time including *"Fiscal Cliff", "Hurricane Sandy", "Violence in Iraq", "Obamacare", and "Syrian Civil War"*. Since it is impossible for a Turker to explore a very large dataset during the time given at the study, we limited the dataset to include 320 articles.

We sorted the articles based on their timestamps and then split the dataset into two halves. The first half was used to train an initial topic model using LDA. Then we added the second half when updating the topic model. We employed a between-subject design, testing two different update algorithms, one used standard LDA, the other used nTMU. Due to the similarities of some of the topics in the dataset (e.g., both "Obamacare" and "Fiscal Cliff" are about US politics), the topic model was not very stable during update. For example, before update, "Fiscal Cliff" and "Obamacare" were two different topics. After the update using LDA, they merged into one general topic of "US Government Affairs". With nTMU, the system still maintained two separate topics in the updated topic model.

We designed two Human Intelligence tasks (HITs), one for each test condition. Each HIT was divided into two parts: before-update tasks and after-update tasks. Before-update tasks were designed to help a Turker to build a mental model of the system. The before-update tasks were exactly the same in two test conditions. For example, before an update, a Turker was asked to choose the best label for a given topic by inspecting the top topic keywords and the top articles on that topic, both inferred by the system. S/he was also asked to select a few articles s/he would like to read and write down a few details from each article such as its title. The after-update tasks were designed to test how topic stability affects (a) a Turker's comprehension of the topics in the updated model (2) a Turker's ability to recall and relocate the articles s/he has chosen before the update.

We used both subjective and objective metrics to evaluate the effectiveness of these methods. Our objective evaluation metrics included

1. *KTLA_BU* (Keyword-based topic label accuracy before update). This measures whether a Turker is able to pick a correct topic label based on the top topic keywords before model update.
2. *ATLA_BU*(Article-based topic label accuracy before update). This measures whether a Turker is able to pick a correct topic label based on the top articles in a topic before model update. The top articles were automatically inferred by the system.
3. *BTLA_BU* (Topic label accuracy based on both topic keywords and top articles before model update). This measures whether a Turker is able to pick a correct topic label based on both the topic keywords and the top articles in a topic before model update.
4. *KTLA_AU*(Keyword-based topic label accuracy after model update). This measures whether a Turker is able to pick a correct topic label based on the top topic keywords after model update.
5. *ATLA_AU*(Article-based topic label accuracy after model update). This measures whether a Turker is able to pick a correct topic label based on the top articles in a topic after model update.
6. *BTLA_AU*(Topic label accuracy based on both topic keywords and top articles after model update). This measures whether a Turker is able to pick a correct topic label based on both the topic keywords and the top articles in a topic after the model update.
7. *ARSR_AU*(Article relocating success rate after update) This measures whether a Turker is able to relocate the articles s/he found before an update.

In addition, we included four subjective evaluation metrics :

1. *TD* (Topic difficulty) This measures how difficult it is to understand the system-derived topics.
2. *ARD*(Article relocating difficulty) This measures how difficult it is to relocate the articles a user found before.
3. *UA*(Use Again) This measures the likelihood of a user to use the system if it is available.
4. *RF*(Recommend Friends) This measures the likelihood of a user to recommend the system to others.

All the survey questions are rated on a 5-point Likert scale with 1 being the least desirable and 5 the most desirable.

Experiment Results

Overall, we have collected data from 80 Turkers, 40 for each test condition. Figure 6 shows the before-update objective metrics. Since the before-update tasks are exactly the same in the two test conditions, we did not expect much differences. Moreover, any significant difference in these scores may indicate an irregularity of the test conditions and thus require further investigation.

As shown in Figure 6, since there isn't any statistically significant differences between the test conditions, we are assured of the validity of the data . In contrast, since the after-update metrics are design to capture the impact of topic stability on a user's ability to comprehend topics and recall articles, if maintaining topic stability is important and our system is effective, we expect that our method will result in better scores than those using the LDA method. Our study results have also confirmed this. With our method, the topic keywords are more coherent, which makes it easier for a user to understand a topic and select a correct topic label for it (0.688 with nTMU v.s. 0.338 with LDA). Since the top articles selected by the system are also more topic-relevant, which makes it easier for a user to pick the correct topic label based on top articles (0.875 with nTMU versus 0.388 with LDA). Finally, keeping the topic model stable can also significantly improve a user's chance to relocate an article (0.775 with nTMU v.s. 0.525 with LDA). As shown in Figure 7, our system outperformed the baseline in all the after-update evaluation dimensions. The differences are all statistically significant with $p < 0.001$ based on independent sample t-test. Therefore, it again demonstrated that our nTMU system can provide users a non-disruptive topic model update process, compared to the real world system that based on standard LDA.

In addition,as shown in Figure 8, our system also outperformed the baseline in three out of the four subjective evaluation dimensions. For example, with our system, the users think that they can understand the topics better. It is also easier for them to relocate an article they found before. They are also more likely to recommend the system to their friends.

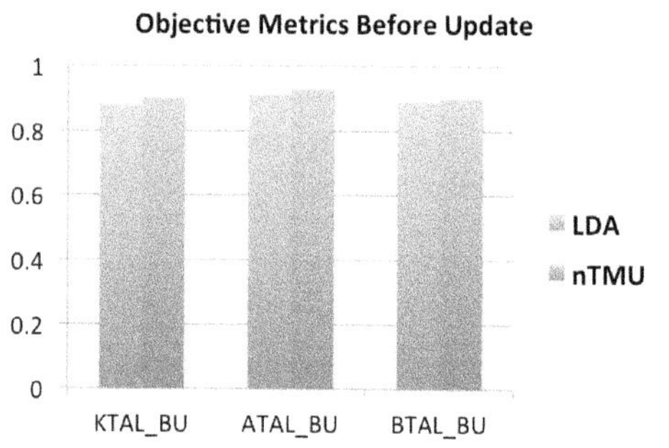

Figure 6. Before-update Objective Evaluation Metrics.

DISCUSSION

Scalability

For today's constantly expanding document collections, a topic modeling system that supports topic-centric navigations and explorations of the collections needs to be quickly updated when new documents arrive in an online fashion. Therefore, scalability is a critical issue for any topic modeling update system. For example, online LDA [9] incrementally updates the topic model without requiring a full scan of the entire dataset. However, as we mentioned before, online

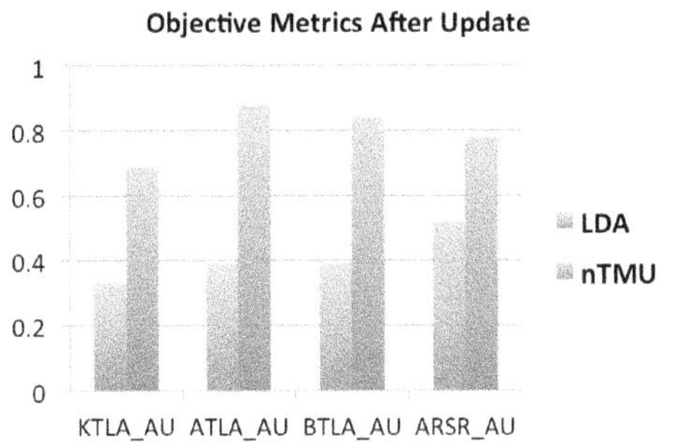

Figure 7. After-update Objective Evaluation Metrics.

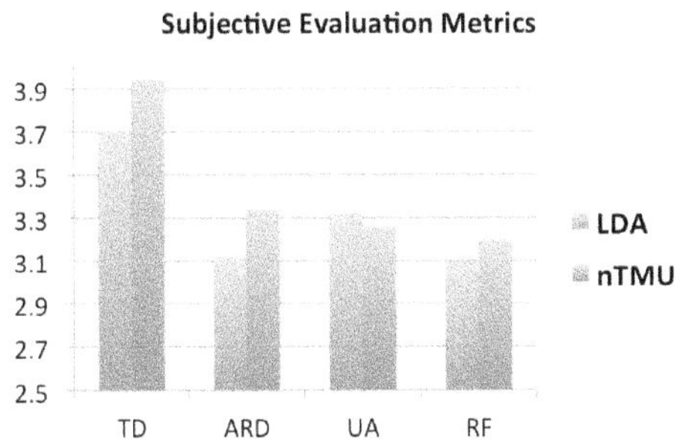

Figure 8. Subjective Evaluation Metrics.

LDA suffers from topic stability problem that undermines the system's usability. Unlike online LDA, our nTMU system can not only update the topic model without a full scan of the entire dataset when new content arrives, but also maintain a good topic model stability based on user feedback. A user has both the freedom to choose a topic that he/she wants to keep stable and specify a set of documents that are supposed to have the same label after the model is updated. Thus, the user can control the size of old documents that are trained with the new data. The *Feedback Processor* in nTMU system can consume users' feedback and generate document-level constraints accordingly. Therefore, at the expense of adding a subset of old documents and their constraints, the nTMU system can achieve the same scalability as online LDA, but with a better stability performance. The only issue is that online LDA uses variational inference method while nTMU's cLDA component utilizes Gibbs sampling for inference. It is not very straightforward to develop a variational inference version of cLDA to incorporate document-level constraints. Therefore, it needs further investigation for cLDA to achieve same converge speed as online LDA.

Personalization

In addition to a non-disruptive topic model update, the proposed constrained topic modeling, cLDA, can also be used for personalized topic modeling. In practice, different users may have different expertise or interests. For example, let us assume two users want to explore a newsgroup dataset, such as New York Times news article dataset. The first user who is a sports fan may be looking for a fine-grained topic exploring all sports articles. As a result, this user will likely add a cannot-link between Baseball documents and Hockey documents. However, the second user who has little interest in sports may just want a coarse-grained topic for sports articles. Therefore, this user will likely add a must-link between Baseball and Hockey documents. Although these two users are training the same dataset with cLDA, they will get different topic summarizations based on their different feedback. The personalized topic model would be very useful in practice by providing individual users the freedom to explore the dataset to match their own tastes and preferences. We also believe personalization along with user interaction is an important future research direction.

CONCLUSION

Existing topic model update methods (e.g., online LDA) have long neglected an important issue which has a significant impact on the usability of a topic modeling system: How to maintain topic model stability to minimize end user disruption? In this paper, we presented an approach to topic model update which directly addresses topic model stability. Included in this approach are 1) a novel constrained LDA algorithm cLDA which enables LDA to incorporate general pairwise document constraints that none of the existing methods are capable of handling effectively, and 2) a new user-directed non-disruptive topic model update system nTMU which collects user feedback, converts them to pair-wise document constraints and employs cLDA to achieve a smooth topic model transition. Evaluation results on both simulation experiments and user studies indicated that our approach significantly outperforms baseline systems in achieving high topic model stability while still maintaining high topic model quality.

ACKNOWLEDGMENTS

This work was supported by DARPA contract D11AP00268.

REFERENCES

1. Andrzejewski, D., Zhu, X., and Craven, M. Incorporating domain knowledge into topic modeling via dirichlet forest priors. In *ICML* (2009), 25–32.
2. Andrzejewski, D., Zhu, X., Craven, M., and Recht, B. A framework for incorporating general domain knowledge into latent dirichlet allocation using first-order logic. In *IJCAI* (2011), 1171–1177.
3. Banerjee, A., and Basu, S. Topic models over text streams: A study of batch and online unsupervised learning. In *SDM* (2007).
4. Blei, D., and McAuliffe, J. Supervised topic models. In *NIPS* (2008), 121–128.
5. Canini, K. R., Shi, L., and Griffiths, T. L. Online inference of topics with latent dirichlet allocation. In *AISTAT* (2009).
6. Crowther, M. S., Keller, C. C., and Waddoups, G. L. Improving the quality and effectiveness of computer-mediated instruction through usability evaluations. In *British Journal of Educational Technology, 35(3)* (2004), 289–303.

7. Dix, A., Finlay, J., Abowd, G., and R, B. Human-computer interaction. In *Prentice Hall, Upper Saddle River, NJ, USA.* (1998).
8. Griffiths, T. L., and Steyvers, M. Finding scientific topics. *Proceedings of the National Academy of Sciences 101*, Suppl. 1 (2004), 5228–5235.
9. Hoffman, M. D., Blei, D. M., and Bach, F. Online learning for latent dirichlet allocation. In *NIPS* (2010).
10. Hu, Y., Boyd-Graber, J., and Satinoff, B. Interactive topic modeling. In *ACL* (2011), 248–257.
11. Lai, J., Lu, J., Pan, S., Soroker, D., Topkara, M., Weisz, J., Boston, J., and Crawford, J. Expediting expertise: Supporting informal social learning in the enterprise. In *IUI* (2014), 133–142.
12. Liu, S., Zhou, M. X., Pan, S., Song, Y., Qian, W., Cai, W., and Lian, X. Tiara: Interactive, topic-based visual text summarization and analysis. *ACM Trans. Intell. Syst. Technol. 3*, 2 (2012), 25:1–25:28.
13. Liu, Y., Niculescu-Mizil, A., and Gryc, W. Topic-link lda: Joint models of topic and author community. In *ICML* (2009), 665–672.
14. Mei, Q., Cai, D., Zhang, D., and Zhai, C. Topic modeling with network regularization. In *WWW* (2008), 101–110.
15. Mimno, D., Wallach, H. M., Talley, E., Leenders, M., and McCallum, A. Optimizing semantic coherence in topic models. In *EMNLP* (2011), 262–272.
16. Nallapati, R. M., Ahmed, A., Xing, E. P., and Cohen, W. W. Joint latent topic models for text and citations. In *KDD* (2008), 542–550.
17. Nielsen, J. Usability engineering. In *Academic Press, Boston, MA, USA.* (1993).
18. Norman, D. A., and Nielsen, J. 10 heuristics for user interface design. `http://www.nngroup.com/articles/ten-usability-heuristics/`, 2013. [Online; Retrieved 31-August-2013].
19. Pan, S., Zhou, M. X., Song, Y., Qian, W., Wang, F., and Liu, S. Optimizing temporal topic segmentation for intelligent text visualization. In *IUI* (2013), 339–350.
20. Ramage, D., Hall, D., Nallapati, R., and Manning, C. D. Labeled lda: A supervised topic model for credit attribution in multi-labeled corpora. In *EMNLP* (2009), 248–256.
21. Song, X., Lin, C.-Y., Tseng, B. L., and Sun, M.-T. Modeling and predicting personal information dissemination behavior. In *KDD* (2005), 479–488.
22. Song, Y., Pan, S., Liu, S., Zhou, M. X., and Qian, W. Topic and keyword re-ranking for lda-based topic modeling. In *CIKM* (2009), 1757–1760.
23. Stephen, E. E., Fienberg, S., and Lafferty, J. Mixed membership models of scientific publications. In *Proceedings of the National Academy of Sciences* (2004), 2004.
24. Wallach, H. M., Mimno, D. M., and McCallum, A. Rethinking lda: Why priors matter. In *NIPS* (2009), 1973–1981.
25. Yao, L., Mimno, D., and McCallum, A. Efficient methods for topic model inference on streaming document collections. In *KDD* (2009), 937–946.
26. Zhai, K., and Boyd-Graber, J. L. Online latent dirichlet allocation with infinite vocabulary. In *ICML* (2013), 561–569.

ConVisIT: Interactive Topic Modeling for Exploring Asynchronous Online Conversations

Enamul Hoque and Giuseppe Carenini
Department of Computer Science
University of British Columbia, Canada
{enamul, carenini}@cs.ubc.ca

ABSTRACT
In the last decade, there has been an exponential growth of asynchronous online conversations thanks to the rise of social media. Analyzing and gaining insights from such conversations can be quite challenging for a user, especially when the discussion becomes very long. A promising solution to this problem is topic modeling, since it may help the user to quickly understand what was discussed in the long conversation and explore the comments of interest. However, the results of topic modeling can be noisy and may not match the users current information needs. To address this problem, we propose a novel topic modeling system for asynchronous conversations that revises the model on the fly based on user's feedback. We then integrate this system with interactive visualization techniques to support the user in exploring long conversations, as well as revising the topic model when the current results are not adequate to fulfill her information needs. An evaluation with real users illustrates the potential benefits of our approach for exploring conversations, when compared to both a traditional interface as well as an interactive visual interface that does not support human-in-the-loop topic model.

Author Keywords
Interactive topic modeling; asynchronous conversation; text visualization; computer mediated communication;

ACM Classification Keywords
H.5.2 Information Interfaces and Presentation: User Interfaces
I.2.7 Natural Language Processing: Text analysis

INTRODUCTION
With the proliferation of Web-based social media, asynchronous conversations have become very common for supporting online communication and collaboration. An asynchronous conversation such as a blog may start with a news article or an editorial opinion, and later generate a long and complex thread as comments are added by the participants [2]. Consider a reader who opens a blog conversation about Obama's healthcare policy. She wants to know why people are supporting or opposing 'ObamaCare'. However, since the conversation is quite long (e.g., 100 comments) and some other related discussion topics like 'student loan' and 'job recession' were introduced, she finds it hard to keep track of the comments about 'ObamaCare', which end up being buried in the long thread. This and similar scenarios often lead to information overload, where the reader gets overwhelmed, starts to skip comments, and eventually leaves the conversation without satisfying her information needs [17].

Integrating Natural Language Processing (NLP) and Information Visualization (InfoVis) techniques has been proposed as a promising solution to this and similar problems [34, 36]. It has been found that when the results of topic modeling and sentiment analysis are presented in a visual interface, they can support most of the reading tasks identified in the domain of asynchronous conversations [15]. For instance, topic modeling can group sentences into different semantically coherent clusters and then assign descriptive keyphrases to each of them [18], such as 'ObamaCare' and 'student loan'. When these topics are presented within an interface, the user can select the one(s) she is interested in (e.g., 'ObamaCare') and then quickly navigate through its related comments. In addition, if information about sentiment (e.g., positive vs negative opinions) is visually encoded along with the topics, the user can assess what comments were in favor or against a particular issue.

While topic models can provide attractive solution in understanding large conversations, they may not be always useful to the end users [2, 15, 16]. This could be due to three different reasons. First, sometimes the current information seeking tasks may require a topic model at a different level of granularity, e.g., if the user needs more specific information about 'ObamaCare' she might be interested in exploring its potential sub-topics such as 'health insurance', 'healthcare cost' and 'drugs'. Second, the interpretation of topics may vary among users according to their expertise and mental model. In fact, in a topic annotation study humans sometimes disagreed on the number of topics and on the assignment of sentences to topic clusters [18]. For instance, for one of the conversations from their corpora, one annotator produced 22 topics, while another annotator reported only 8 topics. Finally, in some cases the results of topic modeling can be simply incorrect, in the sense that the generated topics would not make sense to any user [5, 18]. For example, two semantically different topics 'Obama health policy' and 'job reces-

IUI'15, March 29 - April 01, 2015, Atlanta, GA, USA.

http://dx.doi.org/10.1145/2678025.2701370

sion' might be wrongly grouped together with the misleading topic 'Obama recession'.

In this paper, we present an interface in which the user can explore a conversation by relying on topics that make sense to her, that are semantically coherent and match her expertise, mental model and current task. Our solution is to support the user in revising the topic model, while she is exploring the conversation. To achieve this, user feedback is incorporated within the topic modeling loop in real-time through a visual interface, named ConVisIT. The interface is designed by extending ConVis [15], which was developed to satisfy a comprehensive set of the user requirements in the domain of asynchronous conversation. ConVis presented topics, sentiment and a set of metadata to support the user in exploring and navigating through the conversation. However, a preliminary evaluation of ConVis suggested that the user could benefit from a greater control over the topic modeling process [15]. This was particularly evident from the interviews and observational data, where users expressed a pressing need for enhancing their ability to revise the topic model according to their own information needs. Motivated by this experience, we aim to support users in taking an even more active role in exploring conversations through an interactive topic modeling approach.

Figure 1 illustrates our proposed topic modeling framework. Given an asynchronous conversation (e.g., blog), the system generates the initial set of topics, which are presented in the visual interface along with other conversational data. The interface then supports the user in exploring the conversation. However, whenever the user realizes that the current topic model is not helping her, she can provide topic revision feedback to the system through interactions. Subsequently, the system updates the topic model and the new results are presented in the interface.

The primary contributions of our work are three-fold:

1) A novel interactive topic modeling system specifically designed for asynchronous conversation. Existing systems (e.g., [4, 16, 22]) are mainly devised for generic documents without considering the unique features of conversations. On the contrary, we analyze the information seeking tasks in our target domain to select a minimum set of topic revision operations that are critical to the user. Then, we devise computational methods for each of these operations to be performed by the system.

2) ConVisIT, a visual interface which provides a set of interactive features that allow the user to revise the current topic model. In response, the interface updates and re-organizes the modified topics by means of intuitive animations, so that the user can better fulfill her information needs.

3) A user study to understand how the visual interfaces for exploring conversations (ConVis and ConVisIT) may influence user performance and subjective opinions when compared to more traditional interfaces. This evaluation also provides insights into the potential advantages and relative trade-offs of interactive topic visualization approaches (i.e., ConVis vs. ConVisIT).

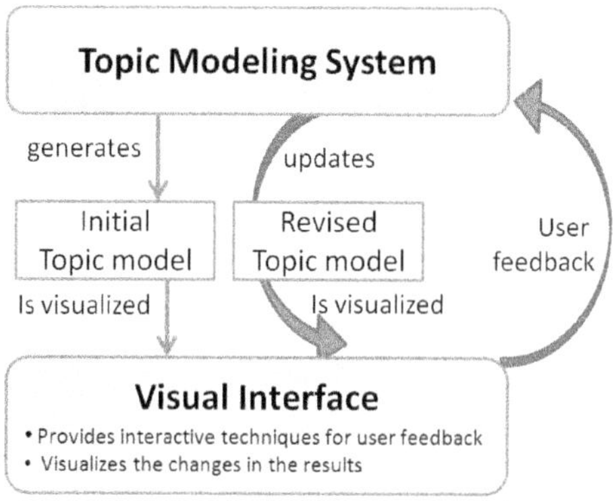

Figure 1. Interactive topic modeling framework for exploring asynchronous conversation.

RELATED WORKS

Visualizing asynchronous conversations

Earlier works on visualizing asynchronous conversations primarily investigated how to reveal the thread structure of a conversation using tree visualization techniques, such as using a mixed-model visualization to show both chronological sequence and reply relationships [33], thumbnail metaphor using a sequence of rectangles [35, 20], and radial tree layout [26]. However, such visualizations did not focus on analyzing the actual content (i.e., the text) of the conversations, therefore they are arguably inadequate to support users in most of the information seeking tasks identified in [15].

Recently, there has been more focus on performing content analysis of the conversations, such as identifying primary themes (or topics) within conversations [28, 9], and visualizing the content evolution over time [34, 36, 10]. Commonly, these approaches use probabilistic topic models such as Latent Dirichlet Allocation (LDA), where topics are defined as distributions of words and documents are represented as mixture of topics. For instance, the TIARA system applies the Themeriver metaphor [13], where each layer in the graph represents a topic and the keywords of each topic are distributed along time. From the height of each topic and its content distributed over time, the user can see the topic evolution. The underlying temporal topic segmentation of TIARA was further improved by applying a set of semantic, temporal, and visualization constraints simultaneously [25]. More recently, a hierarchical version of the Themeriver metaphor was also designed to explore the temporal changes of topics [10], by generating a topic tree based on computing the distance between the probability distributions of topics.

Although the aforementioned approaches do combine text analysis with InfoVis methods to support the user in making sense of conversational data, they suffer from two major limitations. First, often the visual encodings and interactive techniques are not derived from task and data abstractions based on a detailed analysis of specific user needs and requirements in the target domains, which has been identified as crucial according to the InfoVis design study methodology literature [23, 29]. Second, the text analysis methods employed by these approaches are not designed to exploit the specific characteristics of asynchronous conversations (e.g., use of quotation), while it has been shown that topic models are more accurate when these specific characteristics are taken into account [18]. In order to address these two limitations, ConVisIT was designed based on data and tasks analysis specific to the domain of asynchronous conversation [15], and by applying a topic modeling approach that takes advantage of the conversational feature [18].

Human-in-the-loop topic model

Since system-generated topic models can be noisy, some recent work investigate how user supervision can be introduced to improve the results. These works mainly focused on answering two research questions: 1) How to incorporate user feedback in the topic model? 2) How an interface can support the user in expressing such feedback? To answer the first question- in the dominant LDA topic modeling framework, the original unsupervised LDA method was modified to allow the introduction of human supervision [1, 16, 27]. For instance, Andrzejewski et al. incorporates user's domain knowledge in LDA by adding constraints in the form of must-link (enforces that sets of words must appear together in the same topic) and cannot-link (enforces that sets of words must be in different topics) using Dirichlet forest prior [1]. However, this method requires to rerun Gibbs sampling from scratch after a set of constraints is added, leading to high latency. Since, such latency is undesirable for real-time interactions, [16] proposes an efficient inference mechanism that aims to minimize user's waiting time. Unfortunately, all these approaches were designed for generic documents. In contrast, we devise a new interactive topic modeling framework that is designed to take advantage of conversational features.

The question of how a visual interface can support the user in expressing her feedback has been addressed in [6, 4, 22]. Chuang et al. extend Termite [7], which visualizes the term-topic distributions produced by LDA topic models, and allows the user to revise the model by clicking on words to promote or demote a words usage in a topic [6]. Similarly, [22] visualizes topic modeling results from LDA, and allows the user to interactively manipulate the topical keyword weights and to merge/split topic clusters. More recently, user feedback was incorporated through a scatter plot visualization, that steers a semi-supervised non-negative matrix factorization (NMF) method for topic modeling [4]. The authors show that the NMF-based approach has faster empirical convergence and offers more consistency in the results over traditional LDA-based approach. They visually present each topic cluster and then allows the user to directly manipulate the documents and keywords within each cluster to specify topic revisions. A fundamental limitation of most of these works is that the visual interfaces for interactive topic model were not evaluated with real users. Therefore, a set of critical research questions remained unanswered. For instance, would users be really interested in performing all the operations provided with such a complex interactive visualizations? What operations are actually useful to the users for performing exploratory tasks in a specific domain? To answer these questions, we applied a systematic approach, where we first devised a set of topic revision operations which are most useful according to our tasks analysis, and then performed a user study to measure the utility of these operations.

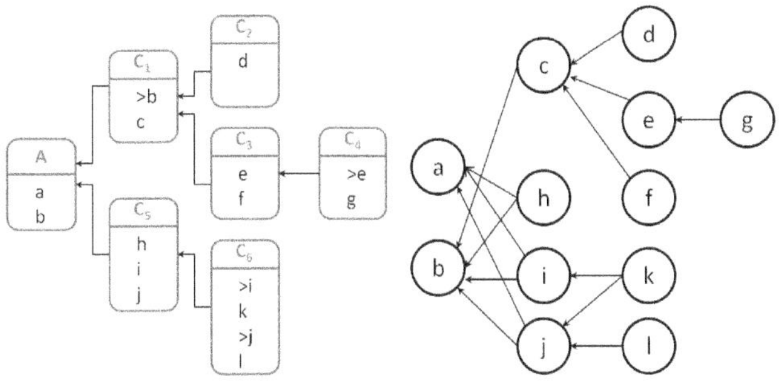

(a) (b)

Figure 2. a) Reply-to relationships between the initial post A and the comments $C_1, C_2, ..., C_6$ (left). Here, '>' represents the quotation mark and each lowecase letter corresponds to a text fragment that may comprise one or more sentences. b) the corresponding FQG (right) where each node represents a text fragment and the edges represents replying relationships between fragments.

INTERACTIVE TOPIC MODELING SYSTEM

As illustrated in Figure 1, interactive topic modeling system performs two primary functions: 1) generating the initial topic model, 2) revising the topic model based on user feedback. Here, we discuss these two functions in details:

The initial topic model

Initially, we group the sentences of a conversation into a number of topical clusters (*segmentation*) and label each cluster by generating semantically meaningful descriptor (*labeling*). We adopt a novel topic modeling approach for asynchronous conversations that captures finer level conversation structure in the form of a graph called Fragment Quotation Graph (FQG) [18]. We extract all the distinct fragments (both new and quoted) within a conversation as the nodes of the FQG (see Figure 2). Then the edges are created to represent the replying relationship between fragments. If a comment does not contain any quotation, then its fragments are linked to the fragments of the comment to which it replies, capturing the original reply-to relation. Here we briefly describe how topic segmentation and labeling can take advantage of the FQG, interested readers are directed to [18] for a more detailed description.

Topic Segmentation

First, a Lexical Cohesion-based Segmenter (LCSeg) [12] is applied to find the segmentation boundary within each path (from roots to the leaves) of a FQG (see Figure 2). Then an undirected weighted graph $G(V, E)$ is constructed, where each node in V represents a sentence within the conversation, and each edge $w(x, y)$ in E represents the number of segments on different paths in which the two sentences appear together. If x and y do not appear together in any segment, their cosine similarity (always between 0 and 1) is used as edge weights. By construction, any subgraph of G whose nodes are strongly connected represent a set of sentences that should belong to the same topical segment.

To identify subgraphs whose nodes are strongly connected, a k-way min-cut graph partitioning algorithm is applied on the graph $G(V, E)$ with the normalized cut (Ncut) criteria.

No	Operation	Why?	Criteria			Reference
			Task relevancy	Topic Model relevancy	Redundancy	
1	Split a topic	This topic is too generic	high	yes	no	[4, 22]
2	Merge by joining	These topics are talking about similar things	high	yes	no	[4, 22]
3	Merge by absorption	A group of sentences are wrongly clustered into a different topic	high	yes	no	[4]
4	Split by keyword	This keyword should be separated into a new topic	medium	yes	yes	[4]
5	Change the overall granularity level of topics	Too few topics/ too many specific topics are generated	medium	yes	yes	-
6	Remove the topic from the display	This topic does not make any sense (i.e., off-topic)	low	yes	yes	[22]
7	Assign a label for this topic	The current label of this topic does not represent the actual topic	low	yes	yes	[11]
8	Increase the weight of this keyphrase	This keyphrase should be included in the topic label list	low	yes	yes	[11]
9	Apply must-link constraint	Those words **must be** in the same topic	low	no	no	[1, 16]
10	Apply cannot-link constraint	Those words **must not be** in the same topic	low	no	no	[1, 16]
11	Change keyword weights	This keyword is more related to the topic	low	no	yes	[4, 22]

Table 1. Different possible topic revision operations.

Since Ncut is a NP-complete problem, an approximate solution is found following an efficient method proposed by Shi and Malik [30]. At the end of this process, each sentence of the conversation is assigned to one of the topical segments.

Topic Labeling

Topic labeling takes the segmented conversation as input, and generates keyphrases to describe each topic in the conversation. The conversation is first tokenized and a syntactic filter is applied to select only nouns and adjectives from the text. Then a novel graph based ranking model is applied that exploits two conversational features: information from the leading sentences and the FQG. For this purpose, a heterogeneous network is constructed that consists of three subgraphs: the FQG; the word co-occurrence graph (Wc) generated from computing the co-occurrence of each word with respect to the leading sentence and the topical segment; and a bipartite graph that ties these two graphs together. A co-ranking method [37] is then applied to this heterogeneous network to generate the ranked list of words for each topic. The top-M selected keywords from the ranked list are then marked in the text, and the sequences of adjacent keywords are collapsed into keyphrases. Finally, to achieve broad coverage of the topic, the Maximum Marginal Relevance (MMR) criterion is used to select the labels that are most relevant, but not redundant.

Corpora and preprocessing

For our analysis and experiments, we used twenty blog conversations from the Slashdot [1] corpora [18]. For each conversation, we generated a topic model comprising of x topics, where x represents the average number of topics produced by the annotators for that conversation. To determine the sentiment polarity of each sentence of the conversation we used SoCAL [32], which has been shown to work well on user-generated content. We defined five different polarity intervals (-2 to +2), and for each comment we counted how many sentences fall in any of these polarity intervals to compute the polarity distribution for that comment.

[1] http://slashdot.org

Interactive topic revisions

Although the initial topic model is more accurate than models generated by traditional methods for non-conversational text [18], still the extracted topics may not always match the user's information needs. Depending on user's mental model and current tasks, the topic modeling results may not be adequate. For instance, more specific topics may be more useful in some cases, while more generic ones in other cases. Therefore, we incorporate a set of topic revision operations by which users can iteratively modify the initial topic model to better fulfill their information needs.

Since it may take some effort from the users to express different topic revision operations, it is important to devise the minimal set of operations that would be both intuitive and sufficient to support user's tasks [6]. For this purpose, we first identified eleven different possible topic revision operations (see Table 1) based on reviewing existing work on interactive topic model [1, 4, 16, 22]. Next, we prioritized the operations based on the following criteria ordered by their importance: 1) *Task relevancy:* To what extent this operation is relevant to the tasks involved in exploring conversation as identified in [15]? 2) *Topic model relevancy:* Is this operation applicable to our topic model approach? 3) *Redundancy:* Is this operation already covered by other operations, which are stronger on the previous two criteria?

The three operations at the bottom of Table 1 (9-11) are eliminated based on both task and topic model relevancy criteria. Not only these operations are designed to fix the term-topic distribution which is not applicable to our topic modeling approach; but more importantly they are arguably not very useful to support the high level exploratory reading tasks as identified in [15] and therefore the users may not be motivated to perform such operations. On the contrary, we selected the top three operations in Table 1 (i.e., 'split a topic', 'merge topics by join', and 'merge topics by absorption'), because we identified them as the most relevant to our exploratory reading tasks that require the user to dynamically change the granularity level of different topics. Also, by selecting them some

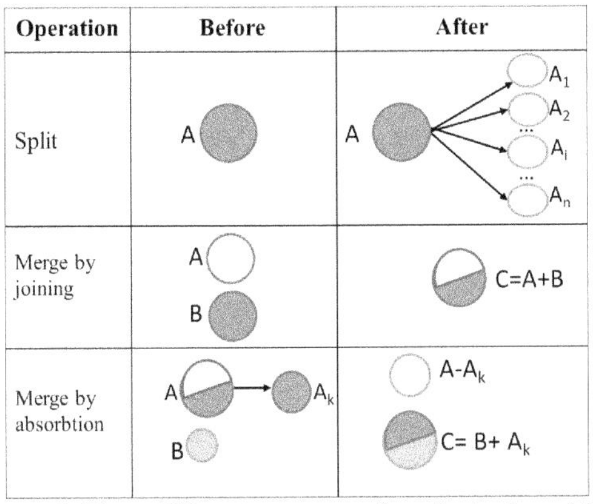

Figure 3. Three different user operations for topic revision

other candidate operations with lower task relevancy become redundant and therefore they are eliminated, such as 'change the overall granularity level of topics' (covered by topic splitting and merging) and 'split by keyword' (covered by topic splitting). In the reminder of the section, we describe how each of these operations support user's tasks, and how the underlying topic model is revised according to these operations.

Split a topic

Topic splitting allows the user to explore more specific subtopics of a given topic, thus changing the topic granularity to a finer level. Consider an example, where initially the system creates a topic named 'military security'. As the user starts exploring this topic, she finds it to be too generic with respect to her information needs and therefore she wants to split it into more specific sub-topics.

Method: Assume that the user wants to split a topic A into multiple sub-topics (see Figure 3). Upon user's request, the underlying topic model creates a sub-graph $G_A(V_A, E_A) \subset G(V, E)$ from the original graph $G(V, E)$ generated in the initial topic segmentation, where V_A represents the vertices (sentences) of topic A, and and each edge $w(x, y)$ in E_A represents the edge weights of topic A.

Next, the system splits the chosen topical cluster A into further n sub-clusters $A_1, A_2, ..., A_n$, by applying the same graph partitioning algorithm used in the initial topic segmentation phase, i.e., approximate solution to n-Cut [30] on $G_A(V_A, E_A)$. Here, n is the optimal number of sub-topics, which is automatically determined by finding the value of n for which an objective function Q is maximized according to the formula proposed by Newman and Girvan [24],

$$Q_n = \sum_{c=1}^{n} \frac{\sum_{x \in V_c, y \in V_c} w(x,y)}{\sum_{x \in V_A, y \in V_A} w(x,y)} - \left(\frac{\sum_{x \in V_c, y \in V_A} w(x,y)}{\sum_{x \in V_A, y \in V_A} w(x,y)} \right)^2 \quad (1)$$

Here, Q_n measures the quality of a clustering of nodes in the graph $G_A(V_A, E_A)$ into n groups, where $\sum_{x \in V_c, y \in V_c} w(x, y)$ measures the within-cluster sum of weights, $\sum_{x \in V_A, y \in V_A} w(x, y)$ measures the sum of all edge weights in the graph, and $\sum_{x \in V_c, y \in V_A} w(x, y)$ measures the sum of weights over all edges attached to nodes in cluster c. In essence, according to (1), the nodes in high quality clusters should have much stronger connections among themselves than with other nodes in the graph.

We apply equation (1) for the value of $n = 2, 3, 4, 5$ and select the value of n, for which Q_n is maximum. The highest possible value is capped to 5 because of time constraint imposed by the interactive nature of the operation. Notice however, that this limitation is not too penalizing. Our analysis of the Slashdot corpus shows that in 86% cases of splitting a topic, the best value of Q_n is with $n \leq 5$.

Once the parent topic is segmented into n different subclusters, representative keyphrases are generated for each sub-topic. This is done by running our topic labeling method only on the sub-conversation covered by A.

Merge by joining

This operation allows the user to aggregate multiple similar topics into a single one. As opposed to topic splitting, the result is a topic with coarser granularity level. Consider an example, where the initial topic model produces two different topics namely 'secure code' and 'simple sql server injection'. The user may find that both topics are too specific, therefore joining them into a more generic topic may help her to better perform the subsequent tasks.

Method: Assume that the user decides to merge by joining two topics A and B (see Figure 3). To perform this operation, the topic modeling system creates another topic C and assigns its vertices as $V_C = V_A \bigcup V_B$ and edges as $E_C = E_A \bigcup E_B$. After that, a label for C is generated. This is done by running our topic labeling method only on the sub conversation covered by C.

Merge by absorption

If a sub-topic is more related to a different topic than its current parent topic, merge by absorption allows the user to separate this sub-topic from its current parent and merge it with the one to which it is more related. Unlike the previous merge operation (which joins two independent topics), this operation allows a sub-topic that is already placed under a topic to be absorbed by a different parent topic. Consider an example, where the sentences related to two different topics, namely 'Obama health policy' and 'job recession' are wrongly grouped together under the topic 'Obama recession'. The user may realize that the sub-topic 'job recession' should be separated from its parent topic and merged with the 'unemployment' topic to which it is more related.

Method: Upon receiving a merge by absorption feedback from the user on A_k and B, the topic modeling system removes the sub-topic A_k from its current parent A and merge it with the topic B (see Figure 3). The system then creates a new parent topic C and then assigns vertices such that,

$$V_C = V_{A_k} \cup V_B, V_A = V_A \setminus V_{A_k} \quad (2)$$

and edges such that,

$$E_C = E_{A_k} \cup E_B, E_A = E_A \setminus E_{A_k} \quad (3)$$

After that, the topic labeling method takes the portion of the conversation that consists of the sentences in V_C, thus generating a label for C that potentially represents descriptive keyphrases from both topics A_k and B.

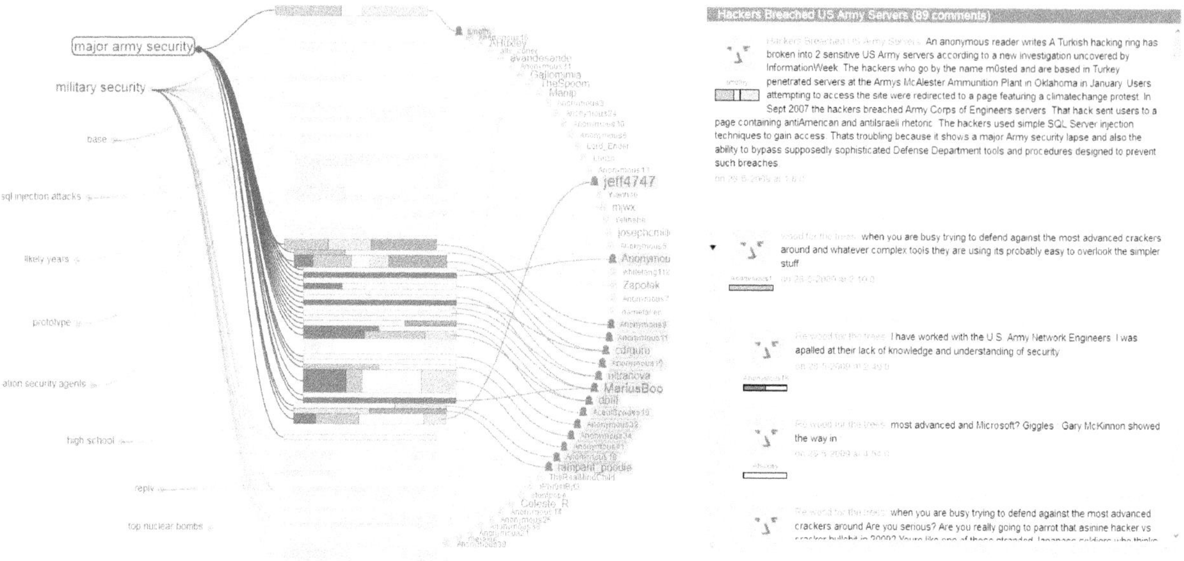

Figure 4. A snapshot of ConVisIT showing a blog conversation from Slashdot: the Thread Overview visualizes the whole thread and how the sentiment is expressed for each comment (middle-left); the Facet Overview presents topics and authors circularly around the Thread Overview; and the Conversation View presents the actual conversation (right). Here, the user hovers the mouse over the topic element ('major army security'). This action highlights the connecting visual links, brushing the related *authors*, and providing visual prominence to the related comments in the Thread Overview.

CONVISIT: EXPLORING CONVERSATIONS USING INTERACTIVE TOPIC MODEL

In order to effectively support the user in exploring conversations, we enable the three interactive topic revisions by redesigning the ConVis interface [15], which was originally designed to present static topic model results as a linear list. In this section, we first provide an overview of the visual interface features common in both ConVis and ConVisIT, along with their justification in term of visual encoding and interactions. Next, we describe the interaction redesign made in ConVisIT to incorporate topic revision operations.

Features common to both Interfaces

The interface starts with visualizing the initial topic model, the sentiments being expressed and a set of metadata of the given conversation (See Figure 4). It is primarily an overview + details interface, since this design has been found to be more effective for text comprehension tasks than other approaches such as zooming and focus+context [8]. The overview consists of the whole thread as well as the topics and authors of the conversation. The Thread Overview visually represents each comment of the discussion as a stacked bar, where each stacked bar encodes three different metadata (comment length, position of the comment in the thread, and depth of the comment within the thread). A set of five diverging colors was used to visualize the distribution of sentiment orientation of a comment in a perceptually meaningful order, ranging from purple (highly negative) to orange (highly positive). Thus, the distribution of colors in the Thread Overview can help the user to perceive the kind of conversation they are going to deal with. For example, if the Thread Overview is mostly in strong purple color, then the conversation has many negative comments.

The primary facets of the conversations, namely topics and authors are presented in a circular layout around the Thread Overview (Figure 4). Both topics and authors are positioned according to their chronological order in the conversation starting from the top, allowing the user to understand how the conversation evolves as the discussion progresses. The font size of facet items helps the user to quickly identify what are the mostly discussed themes and who are the most dominant participants within a conversation. To indicate topic-comment-author relationship, the facet elements are connected to their corresponding comments in the Thread Overview via subtle curved links. These visual links allow the user to perceive the related entities more quickly and with greater subjective satisfaction than plain highlighting [31]. Finally, the Conversation View displays the actual text of the comments in the discussion as a scrollable list.

The user can start exploring the conversation by hovering the mouse on topics, which highlights the connecting curved links and related comments in the Thread Overview. As such, one can quickly understand how topics may be related to different comments and authors. Then, if the reader becomes further interested in specific topic/author, she can click on it. As a result, a thick vertical outline is drawn next to the corresponding comments in the Thread Overview. Such outlines are also mirrored in the Conversation View. Besides exploring by the topics/authors, the reader can browse individual comments by hovering and clicking on them in the Thread Overview. In particular, when the user hovers over a comment its topic is highlighted, while when the user clicks on a comment, the actual text for that comment is shown in the Conversation View (by scrolling). In this way, the user can easily locate the comments that belong to a particular topic.

Interactive visualization for topic revisions

As the user explores the conversation, she may realize that the initial topic model is not helping her anymore, and may want to revise it. To support such situation, ConVisIT provides a set of interactive topic revision operations within the interface

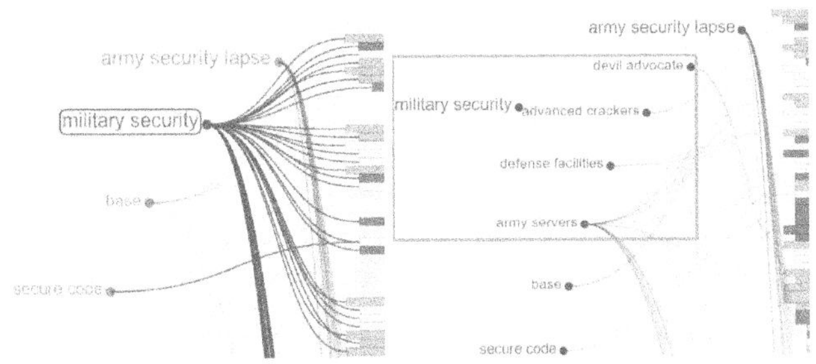

(a) Before splitting (b) After splitting

Figure 5. An example showing: (a) The user hovers over the topic 'military security' and decides to perform the split operation. (b) As a result, the topic moves to its left while the rest of the topics are pushed along the perimeter of the circular layout to create space for the new children.

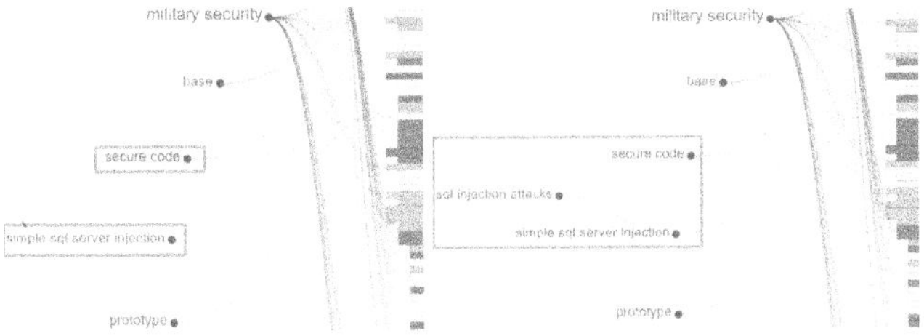

(a) Before merge by joining (b) After merge by joining

Figure 6. An example showing: (a) The user decides to merge two topics by joining (indicated by orange color). (b) As a result, ConVisIT updates the topic organization where these two topic nodes are merged under the parent topic 'subject sql injection attack'.

through some intuitive direct manipulation methods. As the user performs these operations, the system updates the topic model and changes the visual encoding of the topic list from the initial flat list of topics into a multi-rooted tree organization. Such updates to the topic organization becomes visible to the user through perceptually meaningful animations, following the design guidelines of effective animation presented in [14]. In particular, we have designed staged animation for each operation, i.e., we break up the corresponding transition into a set of simple sub-transitions, allowing multiple changes to be easily observed.

For instance, when the user splits a topic by double clicking on it, the following sub-transitions occur. First, the clicked topic A moves to the left along with its parent node(s) (if any), while existing nodes at the deepest level are pushed towards their new positions (up/down) around the circular layout to create angular spaces for the new sub-topics. Second, the new sub-topics $A_1, A_2, ...A_n$ appear and move from their parent's position (A) to their new positions. Third, labels appear for these sub-topics (see Figure 5(b)). Double clicking on A again causes it to collapse by following the exact reverse order of animation, i.e., the labels of the children move from their current positions to their parent and fade away, and then the parent moves to its previous position while other nodes move closer to the parent node to fill the gaps left by the removed children nodes.

Merging of two topics can be performed by dragging a topic A over another topic B, which causes the system to update the topic model. As a result, a new parent topic C appears to the left and curved links are drawn from C to A and B to in-

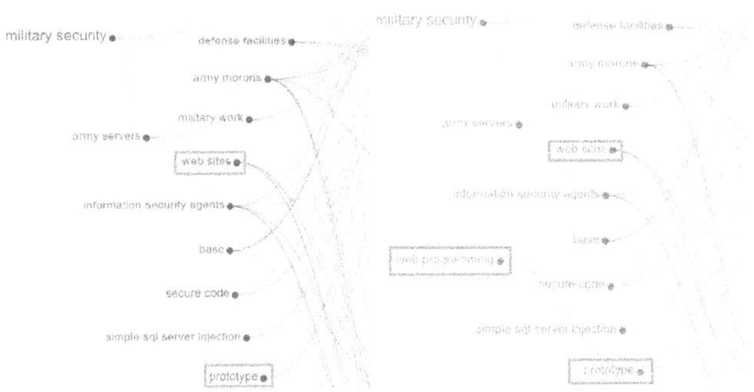

(a) Before merge by absorption (b) After merge by absorption

Figure 7. An example showing: (a) The user decides to perform merge by absorption on two topics 'web sites' and 'prototype'. (b) ConVisIT updates the topic organization where the previous link from 'web sites' to 'army server' is removed, and then 'web sites' is absorbed into a more generic parent topic 'web programming' along with 'prototype'.

dicate parent-child relationship (see Figure 6). The user can subsequently double click on C to collapse it, which hides its sub-topics. Finally, if a child topic A_k is discovered to be wrongly placed under a topic A instead of under a more appropriate topic B, the user can drag A_k over B. As a result, the link of A_k with its parent A is removed and then a new parent node C appears that connects both A_k and B (see Figure 7).

As the user continues to perform interactive topic revisions, the topic organization can potentially grow quickly to multiple levels of hierarchy due to iterative splitting and merging. The current implementation can reasonably show a topic organization having a tree depth up to four levels, when the visualization is used on a 1920 x 1080 screen. This seems adequate for conversations with no more than a few hundreds comments, because the number of sub-topics grows exponentially with the depth of the topic hierarchy, and topics at the bottom of a hierarchy of depth four becomes so specific (i.e., cover so few sentences) that further splitting would be inappropriate. For instance, if we assume that the avg. branching factor in a single-rooted topic hierarchy is 3 and the conversation contains 300 sentences, each leaf of the topic hierarchy of depth 4 will contain on avg. $(300/3^4) = 3.7$ sentences.

IMPLEMENTATION

A server side component (in php) communicates with the topic modeling system (in python) to produce the updated results. The visualization component, on the other hand, is implemented in Javascript (using D3 and JQuery library), which is sufficiently fast to respond in real time to the user actions. The system runs on a laptop computer with a 2.4 GHZ processor and 16 GB RAM. The average processing time for topic splitting operation is 6.92 sec. and for topic merging operation is 2.74 sec. (over the initial set of topics in our corpora). In order to increase the response time, topic split results were cached by the system for all the topics in the initial topic model, as well as for the sub-topics as soon as they were created upon topic revision operations.

USER STUDY

The goal of the study is to understand how the introduction of visual interfaces for exploring conversations may influence the user performance and subjective opinions compared to more traditional interfaces. In this paper, we have introduced ConVisIT, which is highly interactive, providing the capability to revise topic models. Its precursor, ConVis [15] is also an interactive visualization for exploring conversations, however it does not support the topic revision operations. Finally, as a traditional interface for exploring conversation, we have re-implemented the interface to the popular Slashdot blog. The user study aims to answer the following two questions:

(1) When we compare ConVisIT, ConVis and the Slashdot interface, is there any difference in user performance and subjective reactions?

- Does one interface help to find more insightful comments in a conversation?
- Is one interface perceived as more useful and easy to use?
- Is reading behavior influenced by the interfaces? If the answer is 'Yes' then how?

(2) What specific visualization features/components of the three different interfaces are perceived as more/less beneficial by the potential users (e.g., interactive topic revision, Thread Overview, and relations between facets)?

Methodology

Since the above research questions require comparisons among different user interfaces, we perform a summative evaluation through controlled experiments [21]. The study was designed with three interfaces as conditions: a) *Slashdot*, b) *ConVis*, and c) *ConVisIT*. The Slashdot interface follows a typical blog reading interface design and it serves as a suitable baseline for our experiments. It provides an indented list based representation of the whole conversation as well as common functionalities of blog interfaces such as scrolling up and down, collapsing a sub-thread, and searching for terms. The primary reason for comparing between ConVis and ConVisIT was to verify whether any potential influence in performance and user behaviour are due to the visualization features common between them, or due to the interactive topic revision feature (which is only present in ConVisIT). For fair comparison, different interface parameters such as screen size and font size were kept the same across all the interfaces. Moreover, a within-subject design was used for this experiment with interface as the within-subject factor, allowing us to directly compare the performance and subjective measures of each participant with respect to all three interfaces. Finally, all study aspects, including instructions and setup, went through several iterations of evaluation and pilot testing with two users, who did not participate in the actual study.

Participants

20 subjects (aged 19-43, 8 females) with considerable prior experience of reading blogs participated in the study. They held a variety of occupations including engineer, software developer, and students at undergraduate, masters, and PhD levels, mostly with strong Science background. They were recruited through emails and Reddit posts.

Task and procedure

At the beginning, a pre-study questionnaire was administered to capture demographic information and prior experience with blog reading. Then, the user went through the following steps for each of the three interfaces: 1) In a warm-up session, the interface was introduced to the participant using a sample conversation; 2) The participant was then asked to perform a task on a given conversation (a different conversation was provided for each interface). Rather than asking some specific questions, we provided an open-ended task to reflect the exploratory nature of blog reading. We asked the participant to explore the conversation according to her own interests using the given interface and write down a summary of the keypoints found while exploring the conversation. The study lasted approximately 90 minutes and each participant was paid $20 to participate.

We carefully selected three different conversations from the Slashdot blog corpora having similar number of comments (89, 101, and 89) to avoid potential variations due to the conversation length or complexity of the thread. Also, to counterbalance any potential learning effects due to the order of exposure to specific interfaces and conversations, the order was varied using a 3 x 3 Latin square.

During the study, we collected both quantitative data such as task completion time and qualitative data such as observations and questionnaires. After completing the task with each interface, participants rated the following measures on a 5 point Likert scale: 1) *usefulness*: 'I found this interface to be useful for browsing conversations'; 2) *easeofUse*: 'I found this interface to be easy to use'; 3) *enjoyable*: 'I found this interface enjoyable to use'; and 4) *findInsightfulComments*: 'This interface enabled me to find more insightful comments'. At the end of the study, post-study questionnaires followed by and semi-structured interviews were administered regarding the individual features and overall interfaces. The recorded interviews were transcribed and coded to facilitate analysis. Finally, we logged interface actions to better compare the usage patterns of the three different interfaces.

Results analysis

Quantitative analysis

The results of the in-study questionnaires are presented in Figure 8, showing the average rating expressed by the participants on four different measures. Since the data was collected using a standard 5 point Likert scale, standard parametric analysis is not suitable due to the lack of normality [19]. Instead we perform nonparametric analysis i.e., Mann-Whitney's U tests on the responses for each of these measures. Finally, all reported pairwise comparisons are corrected with the Bonferroni adjustment.

The analysis reveals that the interfaces significantly affected *findInsightfulComments*, with pairwise comparisons showing that ConVisIT was perceived to help them in finding more insightful comments than the ConVis and the Slashdot interfaces. This is an important result because it supports our intuition that by allowing the user to dynamically modify the topic organization (in ConVisIT), we enable her to find more insightful comments. There were also significant effects of interface on *usefulness* (see Table 2), with pair-wise tests showing that ConVisIT and ConVis were perceived to be significantly more useful than the Slashdot interface (see Table 2). Also, ConVisIT was rated slightly more useful than ConVis, although the difference was not significant. Similar

Measures	Slashdot vs ConVis	Slashdot vs ConVisIT	ConVis vs ConVisIT
usefulness	$Z = -3.423; p < 0.001$	$Z = -3.725; p < 0.001$	$Z = -0.560; p = 0.575$
easeofUse	$Z = -0.646; p = 0.518$	$Z = -0.657; p = 0.511$	$Z = -0.144; p = 0.885$
findInsightfulComments	$Z = -3.855; p < 0.001$	$Z = -4.792; p < 0.001$	$Z = -2.003; p < 0.05$
enjoyable	$Z = -3.770; p < 0.001$	$Z = -3.888; p < 0.05$	$Z = -.652; p = 0.24$

Table 2. Statistical analysis (Mann-Whitney's U test) on *usefulness*, *easeofUse*, *enjoyable* and *findInsightfulComments* measures.

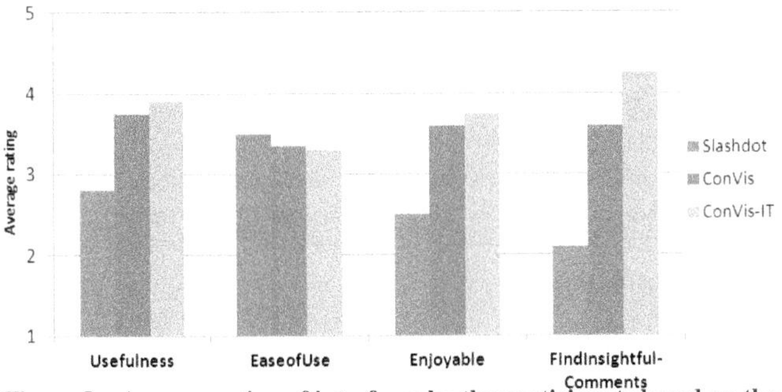

Figure 8. Average rating of interfaces by the participants based on the following measures: *usefulness*, *easeofUse*, *enjoyable* and *findInsightful-Comments*. Longer bars indicate better rating.

results were obtained on *enjoyable* measure, where ConVis and ConVisIT were rated significantly higher than Slashdot (see Figure 8). Finally, the *easeofUse* measure is not significantly affected by the interfaces, indicating that none of the interfaces was superior on this measure. However, this is a favorable outcome for ConVisIT in that even though its interactive features are more complex than in ConVis, the participants did not report ConVisIT as being significantly more difficult to use. Similarly, it is also a favorable outcome for both ConVisIT and ConVis, since, in spite of their complexity, they were found to be as easy to use as the simpler traditional blog interface.

Interface Features

The in-study questionnaire also included a number of questions regarding the usefulness of specific features of the three interfaces. To complement this data, we also analyzed the interaction log data of ConVis, ConVisIT, and Slashdot. The quantitative results of the subjective responses are provided in Figure 9. We can readily see that the majority of the responses regarding features of the Slashdot interface range from strongly disagree to neutral. In contrast, responses regarding ConVis and ConVisIT features are dominated by strongly positive to neutral ratings.

Regarding topic revision operations, *Split* was found to be more useful (35 % strongly agree and 40 % agree) than *Merge* (20 % strongly agree and 25 % agree). This is also evident from the usage of these operations, as the split operation was used more frequently (5.3 times on average) than merge (1.6 times on average). Moreover, 16 out of 20 users performed split operation prior to performing any merge operation. A possible explanation is that participants generally found the initial topic model results to be coarse grained with respect to their information needs, expertise and metal model, and therefore they tended to apply split operation both earlier on and more frequently than the merge operation so that they could read at finer topic granularity.

An interesting observation from the log data is that even though some features were common in both ConVis and Con-

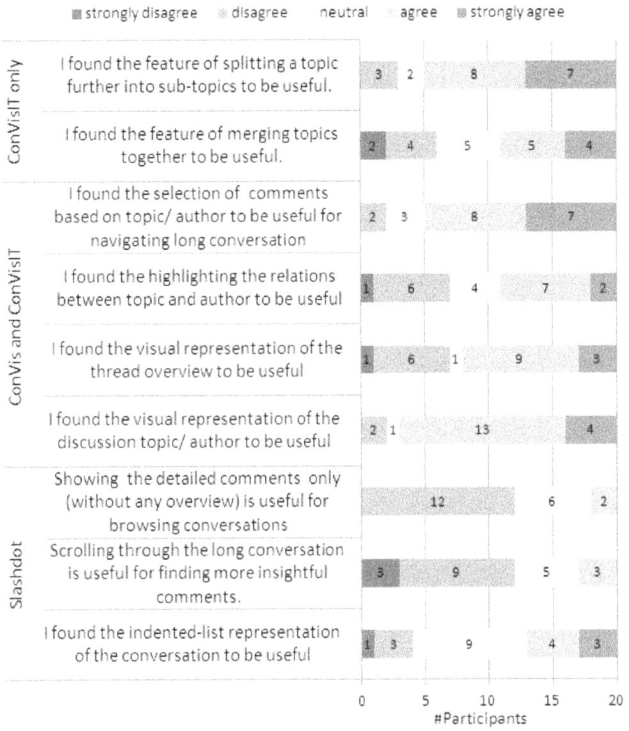

Figure 9. Responses to statements regarding specific features of the three interfaces under investigation.

VisIT, they were used more frequently with ConVisIT. For example, participants hovered and clicked on topics significantly more times on average using ConVisIT (60.4 and 82.0 respectively) than using ConVis (11.6 and 19.1 respectively). A possible explanation is that due to the presence of interactive topic revision features, the participants could create topics that were more useful to them and therefore they relied on topics more frequently in their exploration.

Time

Interestingly, the average time required to complete the tasks was not significantly affected by the interfaces, with Slashdot, ConVis, and ConVisIT requiring 1056, 1240 and 1159 secs respectively. This result is rather promising, because it indicates that participants were not slowed down by the fact that they were unfamiliar with the topic revision operations and by the overhead involved in performing those operations. On the contrary, they perceived to find more insightful comments as reported before.

Qualitative Analysis

Overall Preference

At the end of the study, participants were asked to indicate their overall preference for a blog reading interface and then justify their choice. 60 % of the participants indicated a preference for ConVisIT, 25 % for ConVis, and 15 % for Slashdot. Most of the participants who chose ConVisIT felt that the topic revision operations were very helpful in finding relevant comments: *"ConVisIT is the most convenient interface because of its splitting and merging features. Using this interface to understand the conversation, I really did not have to go through all the comments" (P19).* It was also evident that when the granularity level of the topics did not match the user's information needs, ConVisIT was especially helpful for navigation: *"Sometimes the first-level keywords are way too generic, so it's better to navigate via second-level categories (P11)".* However, participants did become frustrated in a few cases, when ConVisIT could not accurately split the topics into meaningful list of sub-topics as mentioned by P13: *"...I enjoyed the ability to split apart topics, though I think it would benefit from better categorization of topics as I felt like some were misclassified".*

Those participants who chose the ConVis interface over its counterparts emphasized the utility of its visual components, i.e., the visual representation of the thread and highlighting the relations between topics and comments, which *"...makes it easier to find out which comments are more interesting"* , and *"...allowed me to see more of what was going on, how comments were inter-related, as well as kept me interested and focused on the thread as a whole." (P4).* The primary reason for preferring ConVis over ConVisIT was that sometimes the revised topic organization became too cluttered or made the navigation too complex: *"... drilling down to a subtopic made the graph look too cluttered up. Sometimes, it was harder to figure out if two topics were at the same level or not based on the layout." (P7),* and *"It felt like a good mix, others were too complex (ConVisIT) or too simple (Slashdot)." (P2).*

Three participants who preferred the Slashdot interface felt that it was easier to use, although *"...it is not giving me the structural information that I am interested about " (P16).* Another reason was that they were so much familiar with this interface: *"Scrolling through the conversation was good enough for me to find important topics in it, maybe because I am used to reading things this way." (P15).*

DISCUSSION

Summary of findings

Based on our analysis of the study results, we now revisit our research questions. Our first research question was whether there is any difference in user performance and subjective reactions due to the interface condition. We found that overall ConVisIT was the most preferred interface, and was rated higher over its counterparts on the *findInsightfulComments* measure. On the contrary, Slashdot was the least preferred interface, and it received significantly lower rating on three different measures. As for ConVis, it seems to provide a middle ground between the other two interfaces and its topic organization, although static, was found to be visually less cluttered than the one of ConVisIT. In general, this shows that while interactive topic model can be beneficial to the user, such feature may introduce visual clutter and interaction costs at least for some users. Finally, there were no significant differences among the interfaces in terms of *easeOfuse*, in spite of the higher complexity of ConVis and ConVisIT.

The second key research question was what specific visualization features/ components of the interfaces are perceived as more/less beneficial by the potential users (e.g., interactive topic revision, Thread Overview, and relations between facets)? We found that in general, the visualization features of ConVis and ConVisIT received higher rating than the ones of Slashdot. Interestingly, we found that subjective reactions about different features of the interfaces such as split, merge, and clicking on topic directly correlates with their frequency of use. More importantly, we found that not all interactive topic revision operations were equally received. For example, the split operation was used more frequently than its counterparts. This issue needs to be further investigated.

Study limitations

Even though a controlled study is suitable for comparing different interfaces, it may not accurately capture real world uses scenario [21]. Although we carefully recruited participants who were frequent blog readers, still different settings were controlled to make a fair comparison among interfaces (e.g., they were not allowed to choose a conversation according to their own interest). In this context, a more ecologically valid evaluation [3] would be to allow the users to explore their own conversations of interest over an extended period of time. Such longitudinal study would provide valuable insights regarding the utility of the interface. For instance, one possible way of enhancing the ecological validity could be to make the system publicly available and invite potential participants to carry out their usual reading activity with ConVisIT interface.

CONCLUSIONS AND FUTURE WORK

This paper presents a novel human-in-the-loop topic modeling approach combined with a visual interface to support the exploration of large conversations. With ConVisIT, users can explore and revise the topic model to better fulfill their information needs. Our evaluation suggests that ConVisIT can enhance the user's ability to find more insightful comments, even if they are buried in a long conversation. Remarkably, ConVisIT was preferred by the majority of the participants over the other two interfaces (i.e., ConVis and Slashdot) that do not support interactive topic revision, indicating that users benefit from getting more control over the topic modeling process while exploring conversations.

There are several important avenues for extending ConVisIT. While our approach has been found to be useful for Slashdot conversations about technology, we plan to investigate its potential utility in other domains, ranging from political to health related blogs, to education forums for Massive Open Online Courses (MOOC). In this regard, we plan to conduct longitudinal case studies with real users for each of these domains. Finally, exploring a large set of conversations is arguably even more challenging task than when with only one conversation, because the volume and complexity of the textual data may drastically increase and the information overload problem could be even more prevalent among users [17]. Therefore, we aim to extend our interactive topic modeling approach to handle a large collection of asynchronous conversations, where the user will be able to explore topics that are discussed over many different threads.

REFERENCES

1. Andrzejewski, D., Zhu, X., and Craven, M. Incorporating domain knowledge into topic modeling via dirichlet forest priors. In *Proc. International Conf. on Machine Learning* (2009), 25–32.
2. Carenini, G., Murray, G., and Ng, R. *Methods for Mining and Summarizing Text Conversations*. Morgan Claypool, 2011.
3. Carpendale, S. Evaluating information visualizations. In *Information Visualization*. Springer, 2008, 19–45.
4. Choo, J., Lee, C., Reddy, C. K., and Park, H. Utopian: User-driven topic modeling based on interactive nonnegative matrix factorization. *IEEE Trans. Visualization & Comp. Graphics 19*, 12 (2013), 1992–2001.
5. Chuang, J., Gupta, S., Manning, C., and Heer, J. Topic model diagnostics: Assessing domain relevance via topical alignment. In *Proc. Conf. on Machine Learning* (2013), 612–620.
6. Chuang, J., Hu, Y., Jin, A., Wilkerson, J. D., McFarland, D. A., Manning, C. D., and Heer, J. Document exploration with topic modeling: Designing interactive visualizations to support effective analysis workflows. In *NIPS Workshop on Topic Models: Computation, Application and Evaluation* (2013).
7. Chuang, J., Manning, C. D., and Heer, J. Termite: Visualization techniques for assessing textual topic models. In *Proc. International Working Conf. on Advanced Visual Interfaces* (2012), 74–77.
8. Cockburn, A., Karlson, A., and Bederson, B. B. A review of overview+ detail, zooming, and focus+ context interfaces. *ACM Computing Surveys (CSUR) 41*, 1 (2008), 2.
9. Dave, K., Wattenberg, M., and Muller, M. Flash forums and forumreader: navigating a new kind of large-scale online discussion. In *Proc. ACM Conf. on CSCW* (2004), 232–241.
10. Dou, W., Yu, L., Wang, X., Ma, Z., and Ribarsky, W. Hierarchicaltopics: Visually exploring large text collections using topic hierarchies. *IEEE Trans. Visualization & Comp. Graphics 19*, 12 (2013), 2002–2011.
11. Endert, A., Fiaux, P., and North, C. Semantic interaction for visual text analytics. In *Proc. Conf. CHI* (2012), 473–482.
12. Galley, M., McKeown, K., Fosler-Lussier, E., and Jing, H. Discourse segmentation of multi-party conversation. In *Proc. Annual Meeting on Association for Computational Linguistics* (2003), 562–569.
13. Havre, S., Hetzler, E., Whitney, P., and Nowell, L. Themeriver: visualizing thematic changes in large document collections. *IEEE Trans. Visualization & Comp. Graphics 8*, 1 (2002), 9–20.
14. Heer, J., and Robertson, G. G. Animated transitions in statistical data graphics. *IEEE Trans. Visualization & Comp. Graphics 13*, 6 (2007), 1240–1247.
15. Hoque, E., and Carenini, G. Convis: A visual text analytic system for exploring blog conversations. *Computer Graphics Forum 33*, 3 (2014), 221–230.
16. Hu, Y., Boyd-Graber, J., Satinoff, B., and Smith, A. Interactive topic modeling. *Machine Learning 95*, 3 (2014), 423–469.
17. Jones, Q., Ravid, G., and Rafaeli, S. Information overload and the message dynamics of online interaction spaces: A theoretical model and empirical exploration. *Information Systems Research 15*, 2 (2004), 194–210.
18. Joty, S., Carenini, G., and Ng, R. T. Topic segmentation and labeling in asynchronous conversations. *Journal of Artificial Intelligence Research 47* (2013), 521–573.
19. Kaptein, M. C., Nass, C., and Markopoulos, P. Powerful and consistent analysis of likert-type ratingscales. In *Proc. Conf. CHI* (2010), 2391–2394.
20. Kerr, B. Thread arcs: An email thread visualization. In *IEEE Symposium on Information Visualization* (2003), 211–218.
21. Lam, H., Bertini, E., Isenberg, P., Plaisant, C., and Carpendale, S. Empirical studies in information visualization: Seven scenarios. *IEEE Trans. Visualization & Comp. Graphics 18*, 9 (2012), 1520–1536.
22. Lee, H., Kihm, J., Choo, J., Stasko, J., and Park, H. ivisclustering: An interactive visual document clustering via topic modeling. In *Computer Graphics Forum*, vol. 31, Wiley Online Library (2012), 1155–1164.
23. Munzner, T. A nested model for visualization design and validation. *IEEE Trans. Visualization & Comp. Graphics 15*, 6 (2009), 921–928.
24. Newman, M. E., and Girvan, M. Finding and evaluating community structure in networks. *Physical review E 69*, 2 (2004), 026113.
25. Pan, S., Zhou, M. X., Song, Y., Qian, W., Wang, F., and Liu, S. Optimizing temporal topic segmentation for intelligent text visualization. In *Proc. International conf. on Intelligent User Interfaces)* (2013), 339–350.
26. Pascual-Cid, V., and Kaltenbrunner, A. Exploring asynchronous online discussions through hierarchical visualisation. In *IEEE Conf. on Information Visualization* (2009), 191–196.
27. Ramage, D., Hall, D., Nallapati, R., and Manning, C. D. Labeled LDA: A supervised topic model for credit attribution in multi-labeled corpora. In *Proc. Conf. on EMNLP* (2009), 248–256.
28. Sack, W. Conversation map: an interface for very-large-scale conversations. *Journal of Management Information Systems 17*, 3 (2000), 73–92.

29. Sedlmair, M., Meyer, M., and Munzner, T. Design study methodology: reflections from the trenches and the stacks. *IEEE Trans. Visualization & Comp. Graphics 18*, 12 (2012), 2431–2440.

30. Shi, J., and Malik, J. Normalized cuts and image segmentation. *IEEE Trans. on Pattern Analysis and Machine Intelligence 22*, 8 (2000), 888–905.

31. Steinberger, M., Waldner, M., Streit, M., Lex, A., and Schmalstieg, D. Context-preserving visual links. *IEEE Trans. Visualization & Comp. Graphics 17*, 12 (2011), 2249–2258.

32. Taboada, M., Brooke, J., Tofiloski, M., Voll, K., and Stede, M. Lexicon-based methods for sentiment analysis. *Computational linguistics 37*, 2 (2011), 267–307.

33. Venolia, G. D., and Neustaedter, C. Understanding sequence and reply relationships within email conversations: a mixed-model visualization. In *Proc. Conf. CHI* (2003), 361–368.

34. Viégas, F. B., Golder, S., and Donath, J. Visualizing email content: portraying relationships from conversational histories. In *Proc. Conf. CHI* (2006), 979–988.

35. Wattenberg, M., and Millen, D. Conversation thumbnails for large-scale discussions. In *extended abstracts on CHI* (2003), 742–743.

36. Wei, F., Liu, S., Song, Y., Pan, S., Zhou, M. X., Qian, W., Shi, L., Tan, L., and Zhang, Q. Tiara: a visual exploratory text analytic system. In *Proc. ACM Conf. on Knowledge Discovery and Data Mining* (2010), 153–162.

37. Zhou, D., Orshanskiy, S. A., Zha, H., and Giles, C. L. Co-ranking authors and documents in a heterogeneous network. In *Seventh IEEE International Conf. on Data Mining* (2007), 739–744.

Applying the CASSM Framework to Improving End User Debugging of Interactive Machine Learning

Marco Gillies
Embodied Audio-Visual Interaction, Department of Computing, Goldsmiths' University of London
London SE14 6NW
m.gillies@gold.ac.uk

Andrea Kleinsmith
Department of Computer and Information Science and Engineering
University of Florida,
Gainsville, Florida, USA
alk@cise.ufl.edu

Harry Brenton
Embodied Audio-Visual Interaction, Department of Computing, Goldsmiths' University of London
London SE14 6NW
h.brenton@gold.ac.uk

ABSTRACT
This paper presents an application of the CASSM (Concept-based Analysis of Surface and Structural Misfits) framework to interactive machine learning for a bodily interaction domain. We developed software to enable end users to design full body interaction games involving interaction with a virtual character. The software used a machine learning algorithm to classify postures as based on examples provided by users. A longitudinal study showed that training the algorithm was straightforward, but that debugging errors was very challenging. A CASSM analysis showed that there were fundamental mismatches between the users concepts and the working of the learning system. This resulted in a new design in which aimed to better align both the learning algorithm and user interface with users' concepts. This work provides and example of how HCI methods can be applied to machine learning in order to improve its usability and provide new insights into its use.

Author Keywords
Interactive Machine Learning; Movement Interfaces; Gesture Design; Conceptual Models;

ACM Classification Keywords
H.5.2. Information interfaces and presentation (e.g., HCI): User Interfaces: Evaluation/methodology

General Terms
Human Factors; Design; Experimentation.

INTRODUCTION AND RELATED WORK
Full body and gestural interfaces can be a compelling and engaging way of interacting with games and other software[1]. One important application of full body interfaces is the ability to interact with an animated virtual character using natural body language, examples range from Thórisson's early work [7] to Huang et al's [5] sophisticated responsive listening agent. Recent research has focused on how to support end users in designing their own bodily and gestural interfaces[4, 8]. These methods use Interactive Machine Learning (IML) [3] in which users provide examples of interactions that are used to train a machine learning classifier. This has the benefit that users can create interaction systems by performing movement without having to analyze it into low level components of features [4]. However, this does not mean that this approach is automatically easy to use. Machine learning algorithms can be very complex and it can be difficult for end users to build adequate conceptual models of how they work.

In this paper we present a system that users were able to use effectively to train a system, however, debugging the system when it did not work effectively was challenging. This is interesting as debugging relies greatly on effective conceptual models (an issue also highlighted by Kuleaza et al.[6]). We applied CASSM (Concept-based Analysis of Surface and Structural Misfits) framework by Blandford et al [2] to understanding our users' difficulties and redesigning the system to better support them. CASSM is a method of evaluating the concepts inherent in a piece of software and how they may mismatch with users' concepts, and so better support users in creating effective conceptual models. The method involves identifying concepts that are important to users and present in a system and identifying how these concepts match between users' understanding, the software interface and the system itself. In each of these three elements a concept may be "present", "absent" or "difficult", meaning that the concept is not straightforward to understand or mismatched relative to another element.

USER CENTRED DESIGN
We performed a longitudinal user centred design process to inform the design of our system. The process was driven by one expert user: an actor and physical performer. The aim of this process was to understand how a body movement expert, with no computer science training, might learn to use Interactive Machine Learning software. We designed and tested a software platform to allow him to design a game in which a player interacts with a virtual character via body movements. The performers task was to design a character from scratch. This character would interact with with a game player via body movement. During the user centred design process the actor worked with 8 non-expert participants (all students in

ACM 978-1-4503-3306-1/15/03 ...$15.00.
http://dx.doi.org/10.1145/2678025.2701373

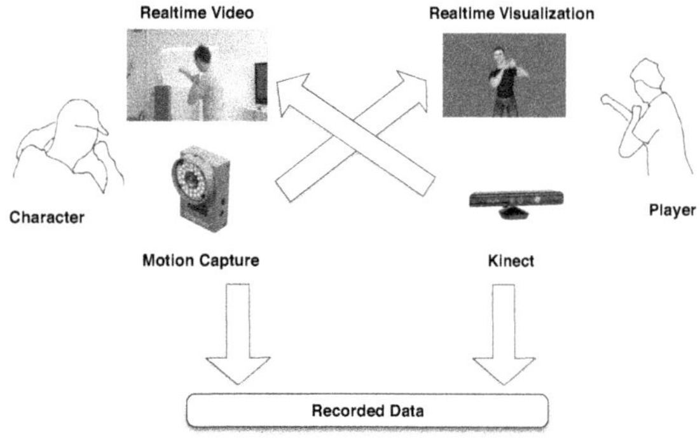

Figure 1. The capture process.

the Department of Computing at Goldsmiths, University of London, 6 male and 2 female) who played the part of the player, either interacting directly with the performer or with our software.

In the initial phase of the study we observed the performer interacting with two of the participants (both male) to design the character's behavior. The core of the performer's method was identifying actions by the player and responses by the character, for example, the player looks threatening and the character cowers in fear. Action-response pair is a central concept in how he organized his work. In preparation for a session he would write down a sequence of pairs (e.g. "applaud-bow", "punch-fall") and the study included a lot of discussion of the suitability and effectiveness of individual pairs. This approach seemed to map naturally onto a machine learning methodology, in which a classifier could be used to classify actions from the player and the results used to generate responses in the character. The examples of actions and responses performed by the participants during improvisation could serve as training data for the classifier.

These results were used to design software to support the design of the character. It used the concept of action and response as the basis of a classifier based machine learning system described above. In the rest of the paper we will use the term **action** to describe a meaningful movement performed by the player and **response** for the movement to be performed by the virtual character in response to the action. Responses are represented as short clips of animation data extracted from the motion capture. Actions are detected using a machine learning classifier. The purpose of the classifier is to analyse novel movement data from the player and determine which of a number of discrete classes it belongs to. Each class is designed to correspond to a type of action. However, the two will not be in perfect correspondance the classifier will sometimes classify movements in ways that do not correspond with the performer's understanding of a particular type of action. This distinction is critical as we shall see later in the paper. In the rest of the paper we will use the term **class** to mean what it learned by the machine learning classifier and **type of action** to mean the user's concept.

Figure 1 shows outlines the process for designing a virtual character. Two people, one acting the part of the character (the performer), the other acting the part of the player, interact with each other video a live link. The performer saw a live video of the player while the player saw the performer represented as a 3D virtual character. Their movement is recorded, the character via optical motion capture, the player via a Microsoft Kinect^{TM}. The resulting data is then accessible via a labeling interface (figure 2, left). Users can select sequences of the character's movements together with the corresponding action by the player. These are used to train a Decision Tree classifier which learns a mapping between player's actions and the character's responses. The performer used this interface over 3 sessions each lasting about 3 hours. He designed a character and tested it with 6 of the participants (2 female, 4 male) acting the part of the player.

RESULTS

There were a number of positive outcomes of these studies. Firstly, the performer and other participants were able to follow the process and found the interface quick to learn, as the performer commented: *"technically it is quite easy to learn, you learn it fast. All the people that came in after a few seconds everybody was able to add clips, add classes"*. In all sessions, the performer created an interactive character and was able to test it. Some responses were very successful. For example, one participant commented *"It was very good at ... when I laughed at it, it would walk away disappointed"*.

However, overall, the performance of the interactive character was disappointing. While some actions were recognized reliably others were not. As one participant describes *"about 60% of the time it did what I wanted it to do. The other 40% of the time it was insulted"*. What is more the performer and the other participants were not able to clearly identify specific causes of problems (*"about the clips I'm still not clear what ... the problem [is]"*) and therefore any proposed solutions were vague and often inappropriate. The performer proposed solutions mostly related to the physical performance rather than the labeling process. Examples of his ideas include being aware of the body shapes of participants (he suggested that one session worked better because *"the two people we worked with today had a more similar physicality"*) or taking more control himself by playing both parts (*"I would like to be the block man too"*). This shows that while he was well aware that the performance was poor but was not able to improve it. This shows that the most difficult task was debugging the model when it did not work correctly, a key issue for IML as noted by Kulesza et. al.[6]. Debugging requires users to have a correct conceptual model of the system, and how it might fail, in order to formulate an appropriate solution. Making a system easier to debug therefore means supporting users in creating better conceptual models of software.

We applied the CASSM methodology to analyzing the conceptual model implicit in the software. Table 1 shows a simplified CASSM analysis of the first prototype. It only covers concepts and not the action elements of the CASSM framework nor does it distinguish the types of concept (entity, attribute) proposed in CASSM. While the generic CASSM framework includes three loci at which concepts can be represented (user, interface and system) we focus on analyzing

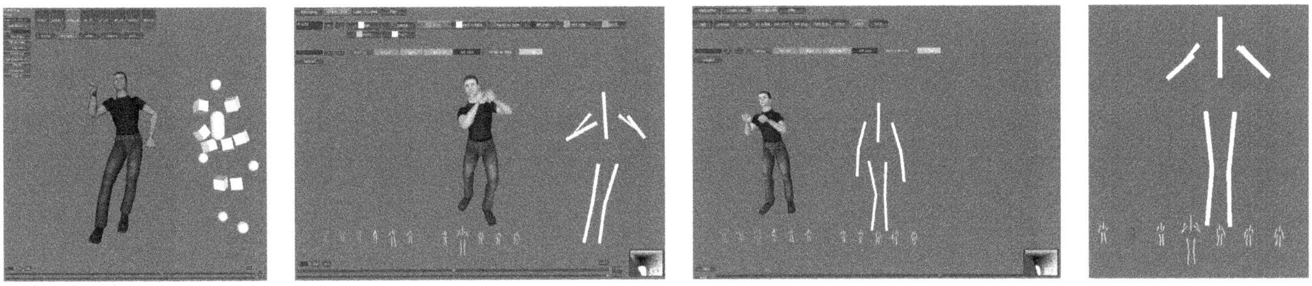

Figure 2. The evolution of the user interfaces. From left to right: the labeling interface of the first prototype the layout of the second prototype of our software which more clearly separates out different aspects of the process. Left, the screen for selecting clips; the screen for labeling feature data; the dynamic visualization of the nearest neighbor algorithm. Each data item is displayed as a stick figure. The figures are scaled in proportion to the amount of probability each contributes to the classification of the current posture.

concept	user	interface	classifier
action	present	*difficult*	*absent*
response	present	present	present
a-r pair	*difficult*	present	*absent*
class	present	present	present
feature	*difficult*	*absent*	present

Table 1. A CASSM analysis of the first prototype

the classifier rather than the system as a whole as this is the element of the system where the difficulty seems to lie and analyzing it separately allows us to identify conceptions such as "action" that are present in the system as a whole but (problematically) absent in the classifier.

The key finding of the first phase of this study was that the performer's key working concepts were actions and responses. Responses are clearly represented in the interface as animation clips that are selected by users and also in the classifier as sets of clips that can be played in response to a particular classification. However, there are a number of conflicts between participants concepts of actions and how they are represented in the system.

While actions and types of action are central to users' understanding of the process and the interface, they are not well represented in the classifier itself. The classifier used was a decision tree which uses the data from individual actions to train a generic model, and once no longer uses them once it has done so. The classifier does not even use the concept of a holistic pose in its classification, but makes a sequence of decisions based on individual features (e.g. left shoulder rotation about the x-axis). The central concept of the classifier is therefore the feature, not the whole action. This conflicts with the interface, which deals in action and also with the performer's working practices. While users were able to think about individual features to a degree (or at least individual body parts), most of the discussions between the performer and other participants were at the level of holistic actions; discussions of individual body parts were rare.

A second mismatch relates to pairing actions and responses. As noted above, action-response pairs were central to the performer's way of work in the project, for this reason the action-response pair concept was built in to the interface. Users provide training data by selecting an action-response pair from the recorded data. A section of data represents both an action (the Kinect data at the start of the section) and a response (a clip formed of the entire selected motion capture data). However, in the classifier action data and response data are treated entirely separately. Presenting action-response pairs therefore conflates two concepts which are distinct within the system and discourages users from considering them independently. What happened initially was that the performer and other participants concentrated primarily on responses rather than actions. The performer said that *"I didn't know about the block man, I understood the block man towards the real end"*. Pairing actions and responses can make it more challenging to train an effective model as it may not be possible to find clips that are good both as training data and as animation clips. Action response pairs are not the only concepts that link actions and responses. The performer did not think solely in terms of individual instance of actions and responses but in types of action and response (such as "applaud" and "punch"). A generic type of response was linked to a generic type of action, but the individual response movement were not specific to an individual action movement. Action type - response type pairs are therefore the key concept, not action-response pairs. Types of action are well represented in both the interfaces and classifier in the form of classes. The pairing of types of action with classes in the classifier therefore forms the major bridge between the perfumer's working practice and the machine learning algorithm.

REDESIGNING THE PROTOTYPE

The CASSM analysis was used to inform a redesign of the system, with a new interface shown in figure 2 (center). As noted, the classification algorithm used is key in supporting or not supporting user concepts. Changing the algorithm can have an important effect on how understandable the system is. Classification algorithms embody concepts of the domain that can either match or mismatch with user concepts. Mismatched concepts can lead to situations in which the algorithm does not effectively support users or in which users are not able to use the algorithm effectively. Concepts that match closely are more likely to support users' work, but even systems that are close to user concepts will not immediately be understood unless they are communicated effectively in the interface. Therefor all of the concepts we have discussed need to be well represented both in the classifier and the interface.

The new classifier uses a weighted nearest neighbor method. Nearest neighbour methods directly use the examples in the original dataset, new items are classified based on the most similar training examples. A standard nearest neighbor algorithm selects a fixed number of neighbors (e.g. 3) and treats them equally. The classification will be the majority vote of the neighbors. On the other hand a weighted approach applies a weight to the influence of a data example based on it's distance form the item to be classified. Our classifier uses all the examples but weights them by distance. A weighted approach is likely to work better when there are a small number of data items. If the data is very sparse, a standard nearest neighbor approach is likely to select neighbors that are very different from the item to be classified. If these are all treated equally, they are likely to result in poor performance. If they are weighted by distance, they are less likely to affect the performances. The use of a weighted algorithm was also motivated by the intuition that users are more likely to think in terms of examples being more or less similar rather than in terms of an arbitrary cut off where some examples are similar and some are not.

The classifier was implemented as a Gaussian Mixture Model, a probabilistic model that gives an estimated probability of a data item being in each class. The probability is the sum of a number of multi-variate Gaussian distributions:

$$P = \sum_i \mathcal{N}(\mu_i, \sigma_i)$$

μ_i is the mean of the ith distribution and σ_i is it's variance. Each class has it's own Gaussian Mixture Model which gives the probability of an item being in that class. There is a Gaussian for each training example that belongs to that class. The mean of that distribution is the feature vector for that example. The Gaussian therefore gives an exponentially weighted measure of the distance from each example and therefore particularly privileges similar examples, and virtually ignores distant ones. σ_i is the same for all examples and is spherical (i.e. it is the same for all dimensions of the feature vector). It could be used as a tunable parameter, or varied between examples, to give greater weight to certain example, but we did not explore these possibilities in this prototype.

This new algorithm aims to align the working of the algorithm with users' conceptual models, because actions are represented directly. It is likely to perform better with a small number of data items, as long as they are well chosen. More importantly, it makes it possible to provide better visual feedback to users about the functioning of the algorithm. As the classifier is defined by all of the training examples, it can be visualized simply by presenting all of the actions used to train the system. This visualization should map very directly onto user concepts as it directly displays the actions they have selected. Figure 2, far right, shows the new visualization. Each training example is represented using the same stick figure representation as is used for the live and recorded Kinect data. The examples are color coded to represent classes (the same colors are used in the class buttons shown in Figure 2, center). In order to give real time feedback about the system, the visualization needs to represent the reasons why the classifier is classifing particular instances the way it does. To do this visualization shown in Figure 2, far left, scales each example in proportion to the weight assigned to that example by the classifier (plus a constant to ensure that even components that contribute zero weight are still visible). This scaling is done during live testing, but also on the labeling screen, so users can see how the classification changes as they scrub through their data.

Other mismatches can be solved by changing the interface rather than the classifier. The first interface was built around the concept of action-response pair that is not present in the classifier. The second prototype separates the two concepts with different interfaces for selection response clips and labeling feature data containing actions. (figure 2 center left and center right). This separation aimed to make the distinction conceptually clearer. It also allowed users to select the most suitable clips and Kinect poses independently, and therefore be able to select the best of each.

CONCLUSIONS

This paper has presented an example of how a CASSM analysis can support researchers in understanding difficulties in an Interactive Machine Learning interface and redesigning that interface. It was particularly useful in understanding how machine learning can fit into users conceptual understanding. CASSM is valuable here because it forces designers to think about conceptual models not simply in terms of the interface but also at the level of machine learning system, which is all too often treated as a black box. While a black box approach can seemingly simplify the user experience, it can lead to confused conceptual models and hinder users when they must debug the learning system. CASSM's focus on how conceptual models map into the computational system may be able to help overcome this problem by encouraging designers to align the learning algorithm used with users' conceptual models. However, it is important to note that analysis like CASSM, while it can result in a plausible design, is not sufficient to demonstrate that this design is actually usable in pracitce. Considerable further work is needed. The next step is to perform a large scale controlled trial to test whether the system is usable. This work will no doubt result in many changes and iterations before a fully usable interactive machine learning system is achieved.

More generally, this work is an example of how established HCI methodologies can be applied to Machine Learning, to improve its usability but also to provide new ways of understanding learning algorithms: not simply in terms of efficiency or accuracy but also how they are understood by users. This is an important step in making Machine Learning accessible to a wide public, beyond the academic and industry research labs to which it is currently largely confined.

ACKNOWLEDGMENTS

This work is supported by the UK Engineering and Physical Sciences Research Council, under grant EP/H02977X/1, Performance based expressive virtual characters.

REFERENCES

1. Bianchi-Berthouze, N., Kim, W. W., and Patel, D. Does body movement engage you more in digital game play? and why? In *Proceedings of Affective Computing and Intelligent Interaction, ACII 2007*, A. Paiva, R. Prada, and R. W. Picard, Eds., vol. 4738 of *Lecture Notes in Computer Science*, Springer (2007), 102–113.

2. Blandford, A., Green, T. R. G., Furniss, D., and Makri, S. Evaluating system utility and conceptual fit using cassm. *Int. J. Hum.-Comput. Stud. 66*, 6 (June 2008), 393–409.

3. Fails, J. A., and Olsen, Jr., D. R. Interactive machine learning. In *Proceedings of the 8th international conference on Intelligent user interfaces*, IUI '03, ACM (New York, NY, USA, 2003), 39–45.

4. Fiebrink, R., Cook, P. R., and Trueman, D. Human model evaluation in interactive supervised learning. In *Proceedings of the 2011 annual conference on Human factors in computing systems*, CHI '11, ACM (New York, NY, USA, 2011), 147–156.

5. Huang, L., Morency, L.-P., and Gratch, J. Learning backchannel prediction model from parasocial consensus sampling: a subjective evaluation. In *Proceedings of the 10th international conference on Intelligent virtual agents*, IVA'10, Springer-Verlag (Berlin, Heidelberg, 2010), 159–172.

6. Kulesza, T., Stumpf, S., Wong, W.-K., Burnett, M. M., Perona, S., Ko, A., and Oberst, I. Why-oriented end-user debugging of naive bayes text classification. *ACM Trans. Interact. Intell. Syst. 1*, 1 (Oct. 2011), 2:1–2:31.

7. Thórisson, K. Real-time decision making in multimodal face-to-face communication. In *second ACM international conference on autonomous agents* (1998), 16–23.

8. Zamborlin, B., Bevilacqua, F., Gillies, M., and D'inverno, M. Fluid gesture interaction design: Applications of continuous recognition for the design of modern gestural interfaces. *ACM Trans. Interact. Intell. Syst. 3*, 4 (Jan. 2014), 22:1–22:30.

Path Bending: Interactive Human-Robot Interfaces With Collision-Free Correction of User-Drawn Paths

Jared Alan Frank and Vikram Kapila
NYU Polytechnic School of Engineering, Brooklyn, NY 11201
jared.alan@nyu.edu, vkapila@nyu.edu

ABSTRACT

Enabling natural and intuitive communication with robots calls for the design of intelligent user interfaces. As robots are introduced into applications with novice users, the information obtained from such users may not always be reliable. This paper describes a user interface approach to process and correct intended paths for robot navigation as sketched by users on a touchscreen. Our approach demonstrates that by processing video frames from an overhead camera and by using composite Bézier curves to interpolate smooth paths from a small set of significant points, low-resolution occupancy grid maps (OGMs) with numeric potential fields can be continuously updated to correct unsafe user-drawn paths at interactive speeds. The approach generates sufficiently complex paths that appear to bend around static and dynamic obstacles. The results of an evaluation study show that our approach captures the user intent while relieving the user from being concerned about her path-drawing abilities.

Author Keywords

Interactive; path; replanning; robot; user interface; vision

ACM Classification Keywords

I.2.9. Artificial Intelligence: Robotics—*Operator interfaces*

INTRODUCTION

Natural and intuitive communication between a user and a robot requires the design of an intelligent user interface. Through intuitive, multi-modal input mechanisms and interactive displays, user interfaces have made the command, control, and monitoring of mobile robots accessible to inexperienced and even disabled users [18, 20, 29]. This is important since robotic platforms are increasingly appearing in public domains, such as domestic applications, where they operate outside of the controlled laboratory environment [6]. However, novice users with limited training and experience with the robot may not always provide reliable commands for the robot operation. Untrained users may exhibit varying degrees of fine motor skills. Specifically, with a sketch interface, a user trying to convey spatial information to guide a mobile robot may suffer from limited dexterity, dygraphia (poor handwriting), or a developed coordination disorder such as muscular dystrophy or Parkinson's disease. Moreover, a user may suffer from situational impairment by being distracted while using the interface. The problem of allowing interactions between novice or disabled users and robots has led to novel interfaces (e.g. brain-computer interface [4]), technologies, and algorithms for safe and reliable operation of robots with higher levels of autonomy. However, such new approaches are not commonly available and increases in robot autonomy are often accompanied by increases in platform size, weight, cost, and computational complexity.

Recent years have seen the development of sketch interfaces on several platforms for commanding robots, and have demonstrated that such a graphical approach may be used to directly and intuitively communicate spatial information to robots. Interfaces that provide environmental maps and represent robots with graphical icons, that users may interact with using a touch pen [22] or finger-based gestures [2], have been developed, but require an *a priori* map of the environment to be hard-coded into the interface. Other interfaces require users to sketch an approximate representation of the robot's environment on a blank canvas [24, 25], which involves identifying and providing the approximate size, shape, and relative locations of robots and landmarks. Thus, interfaces that require the map to be known or sketched by the user from scratch are unsuitable for novice users and ill-equipped to deal with complex or dynamic environments. Therefore, sketch applications have been developed to command home robots by drawing paths on a live view of the robot in its environment as it is streamed by an overhead camera [21]. However, prior research has not considered the issue of poorly drawn paths that cause the robot to collide with obstacles. Use of a reactive motor schema method for on-line modification of a robot trajectory generated from a user-drawn path, approximated by piecewise Bézier curves, has been considered in [10]. However, the work of [10] was evaluated only in simulation. For static and known environments, several path planning approaches have been considered, e.g., graph search [19], potential fields [11], visibility graphs [15], and Voronoi diagrams [15]. Recently, techniques have been considered for dynamic or unknown environments, e.g., artificial neural networks [31], genetic algorithms [28], incremental replanning [12, 16, 26, 27], and on-line deformation of previously planned paths [5, 13, 14]. However, these approaches have

IUI 2015, March 29–April 1, 2015, Atlanta, GA, USA.

http://dx.doi.org/10.1145/2678025.2701402

been devised to handle path generation on the robot rather than correct user-drawn paths at the interface level.

In this paper, we suggest an interface approach that processes user input and takes preventive action to shift the burden of collision avoidance from the robot to the user interface. A semi-autonomous robot has been programmed to travel along a path provided by the user. An overhead camera captures a live view of the robot navigating in its environment and streams it to the touchscreen of the user interface on a tablet computer. Augmented reality (AR) is used to overlay onto the live view a virtual representation of the robot, whose location and orientation correspond to the location and orientation of the actual robot as determined by image processing. The AR also includes additional graphical content relevant to the robot's mission goals. To command the robot, a user sketches an intended path on the touchscreen interface. Using a vision-based OGM and a numeric potential function, the interface implements graph search to replan path segments that require collision avoidance. The resulting path contains information from both the original user-drawn path, which has spatial information regarding user intent but may be sloppily drawn or cause collisions with obstacles, and the planned sections, which are sufficiently short and at safe distances from obstacles. Regenerating the OGM and potential function from the overhead video frames and replanning results in paths that appear to bend around dynamic obstacles in real-time. This vision-based robot control approach, as outlined in this study, is applicable to indoor environments. Moreover, a Roomba-like robot and maze-like environment are used in this study to demonstrate the utility of the interface with the types of robots and narrow passageways that can be encountered in homes and offices.

The main contributions of this paper are as follows. Our interface enhances the interaction between untrained users and robots via the user's own personal mobile device. The interface feels natural to users regardless of their path-drawing abilities and can correct user-drawn paths such that the robot is always sent reliable, collision-free paths that respect the user's original intent for the robot. The approach shows that smart mobile devices, such as tablet computers, are now powerful enough to run user interfaces that can offload some of a robot's computataional load and intelligence.

SYSTEM OVERVIEW

Since indoor environments are common application areas for robots, overhead vision-based methods are convenient solutions that can provide a user interface with an exocentric view of the robot. Such an approach can relax the requirements on robot design by simplifying the localization and mapping approaches. To provide users with an AR interface to interact with a robot by directly sketching paths on the touchscreen of a tablet device, and to generate vision-based maps to be used to correct the user-drawn paths, a Logitech Quickcam Pro 9000, with 1,600$\times$1,200 resolution, is fixed on the ceiling 2.6 m above the robot obstacle course (see Figure 1). The camera is connected to a host PC that runs the software for vision-based map generation, user-drawn path correction, and wheel velocity computation [7] to control the mobile robot to follow the corrected paths. A wireless router is attached so that the user interface on a tablet computer and the robot driven through the obstacle course by wheel velocity commands can be wirelessly connected to the host PC. The host PC also acquires images from the overhead camera and streams them over the network to the tablet interface for display. This study uses a Quanser Qbot [9] (see Figure 2(a)), which is based on an iRobot Create platform with a Quanser Controller Module (QCM). The QCM includes a data acquisition card (DAC) and a Gumstix Verdex computer to run a real-time control software. The host PC is interfaced to the QCM through a MATLAB-Simulink interface. The host PC is a desktop computer running a Linux Ubuntu operating system. It is physically connected to the overhead camera and to a wireless router, and runs image processing and control algorithms that: (1) acquire video frames from the overhead camera; (2) save video frames for post-processing; (3) stream video frames to be displayed on the user interface; (4) process video frames to determine the location and orientation of the mobile robot and to generate an OGM of the robot's environment in real-time, which is displayed using the SDL graphics library; (5) wirelessly receive user-drawn paths from the user interface and send back corrected paths; (6) perform the path correction algorithm proposed in this paper; (7) implement a virtual line following control algorithm to compute the wheel velocity commands for the mobile robot to track the path; and (8) wirelessly issue the wheel velocity commands to robot. By implementing port forwarding on the wireless router, the user can interact with the robot from both inside or outside of the laboratory. The obstacle course used in this study is shown in Figure 2(b). It is a square, 2.1 m $\times$ 2.1 m environment with three interior walls creating narrow passageways that the robot can navigate through to complete a task. While most of the components involved in the setting (smart mobile device, Wi-Fi network, camera, PC to run host software) can usually be found in the average home, office, or factory seeking to incorporate a service robot, sometimes they aren't and need to be purchased.

APPROACH

Overhead Vision-Based Localization and Mapping

Two colored circular markers are placed on the robot to determine its location and orientation. The OpenCV library is used to perform binary thresholding and morphological filtering operations on the video frames of the overhead camera to retrieve a position and orientation estimate of the robot. The environment is painted to make reachable space white and obstacles, such as walls, black, so that video frames can be converted to grayscale and a thresholding operation can yield a binary image of the environment. The image is resized to a small resolution so that each pixel in this image corresponds to a square cell of pixels in the original image. OpenCV's distance transform function is used to calculate the distance to the closest black pixel (obstacle pixel) for each pixel in the image. This allows a numeric potential field to be generated, applied as shades of gray in the image, and used to consider the closeness to obstacles in the planning process [32]. The intensity values of each pixel in the image are used to create and update the OGM of the robot's environment.

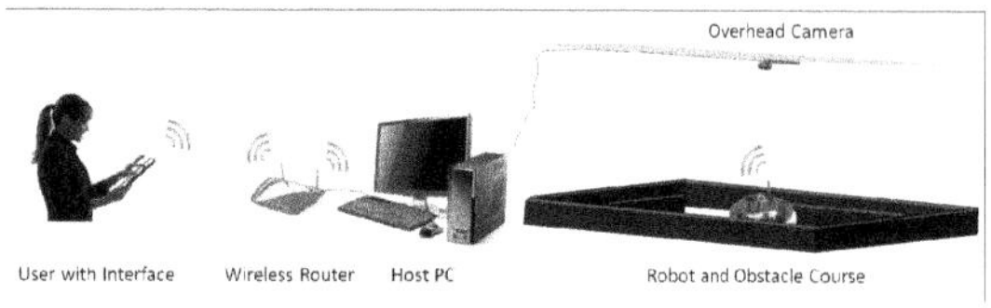

Figure 1: Schematic of the components used.

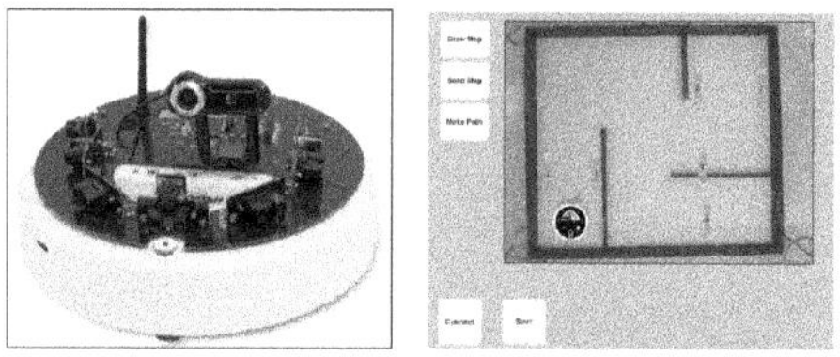

(a) (b)

Figure 2: (a) Mobile robot and (b) the tablet application.

Interface Design

The user interface (Figure 2(b)) is developed on an Apple iPad. It features a 640×480 pixel overhead view of the robot navigating the obstacle course with an animated representation of the robot projected onto the video. A button for connecting to the host PC is provided. To conduct an evaluation of the interface, a start button is provided to begin collecting performance metric data. AR is used to project additional task-relevant graphics onto the live view. These include red goal posts which aid the user to perform navigational tasks. To command the motion of the robot, the user can tap on the virtual robot and drag it to draw a path for the robot to follow. All paths begin from the current location of the robot. The user is free to draw any length or shape path she wishes. Touch gesture recognition classes are used to detect the coordinates of the pixels that the finger contacts during the drawing. These coordinates are stored into an array and the pixels are colored neon green as the path is drawn to be discernible by the user. As the user traces the path on the screen, the interface displays a semi-transparent duplicate of the virtual robot, called the "ghost robot," at the coordinates underneath the user's finger. The ghost robot is meant as a guidance tool to make the user aware of robot clearance at a given location to help protect against the drawing of paths that cause collisions. At any moment, the user may redraw the path, which causes the previously drawn path to disappear as it is replaced by the new one. Currently, users cannot make small local changes to an already drawn path. This feature will be considered in the next prototype of the interface.

Bézier Curves

By reducing the number of points in the user-drawn paths and storing and operating on just a subset of significant points, path information can be efficiently represented, communicated, and operated on from both the user interface and the host PC. Various geometric curves have been considered in generating smooth continuous paths for mobile robots between such sets of points. The most popular of these curves, the cubic Bézier curve, is described by the locations of its four control points according to the following parametric equation

$$\mathbf{P}(t) = (1-t)^3\mathbf{P}_0 + 3(1-t)^2 t\mathbf{P}_1 + 3(1-t)t^2\mathbf{P}_2 + t^3\mathbf{P}_3. \tag{1}$$

Bézier curves are contained within the convex hull of its control points, a desirable property for obstacle-avoidance. As seen through [3, 17, 23, 30], Bézier curves play an important part in the planning and smoothing of robot paths. In the proposed approach, an algorithm is used to generate composite Bézier curves, a piecewise series of cubic Bézier curves stitched end-to-end, from sets of discrete points.

Path Correction Algorithm

Use of human-robot interfaces by novice users can result in unreliable commands. Sketching user interfaces to command the motion of mobile robots can be made available to users with a wider range of dexterous abilities if sketched paths are checked and the segments which would cause collisions are automatically corrected. Below, we describe the algorithm performed on the user-drawn path that computes a final collision-free path composed of both automatically-corrected and originally-drawn segments stitched together. Screenshots of the map on the host PC show each step of the algorithm being performed on a user-drawn path in Figure 3.

Transform Path and Remove Colliding Points: After the user-drawn path is received, the coordinates of each point are transformed from the frame of the drawing window on the tablet to the frame of the reduced resolution OGM (Figure 3(a)). Then, each point in the path that would cause a collision between the robot and an obstacle is removed from the path (Figure 3(b)). This is done by checking the cost of each cell in the map that is occupied by a point in the path and comparing it to an empirically determined threshold, $c_{\max}$.

Significant Point Extraction of User-Drawn Path: To correct a sloppily-drawn path and to allow the algorithm to run more efficiently, we reduce the number of points in the drawn path to a subset. Such an approach is referred to as significant point extraction in the literature [10]. This is done by iterating through the set of points and removing successive points that are within a minimum distance tolerance, $d_{\min}$ (Figure 3(c)).

Locating and Planning Around Collision Areas: To locate which portions of the path are being disrupted by an obstacle, the points that make up a straight line segment between each pair of successive significant points are located using Bresenham's line algorithm [1] and checked against the OGM. If any straight line segment drawn between a pair of successive significant points contains a point that causes a collision, the A* algorithm [8] is implemented to plan a path between those two significant points. The result is a path where problem areas have been avoided (Figure 3(d)).

Significant Point Extraction of Planned Sections: Using the same significant point extraction method discussed above, the planned portions of the path are reduced such that the path is simplified without distorting its overall shape. The result is a reduced set of points that will still be pleasing to the eye and be easy for the robot to follow (Figure 3(e)).

Send to Interface: The coordinates of the final set of significant points, consisting of appropriately drawn points from the original path and planned segments of the path, are sent to the interface to be displayed to the user.

Bézier Interpolation: To generate a smooth corrected path, both the interface and host PC use an interpolation algorithm to generate a set of control points so that the set of points from the last step act as waypoints for a composite Bézier curve. Next, the interface and host PC use Eq. (1) at incremental values of t to compute intermediate points in each segment of the curve (Figure 3(f)). Paths are drawn on the interface with small line segments connecting each intermediate point.

The above algorithm entails a trade-off between collision avoidance and user intention. The parameters $c_{\max}$ and $d_{\min}$ may be tuned so that the final path is dictated entirely by the user or by the planner. Intermediate values of the parameters can be chosen that respect the user-drawn path to varying degrees. Empirically determined values of the parameters were found that results in a path that respects the user intention while keeping final paths collision-free.

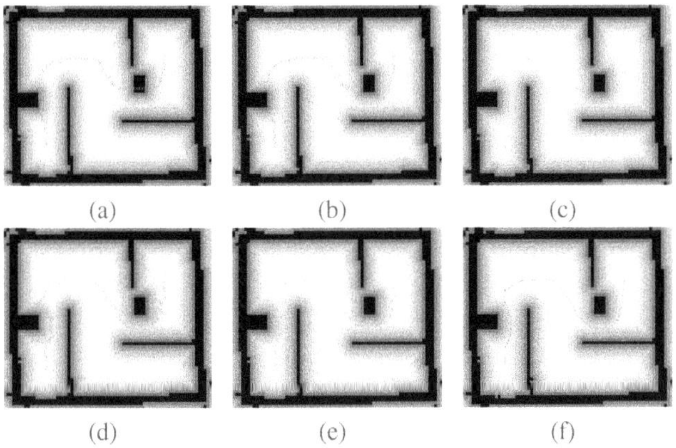

Figure 3: Screenshots of the map on the host PC showing (a) a user-drawn path and the path after (b) removing colliding points, (c) significant point extraction, (d) joining significant points, (e) second significant point extraction, and (f) Bézier curve computation.

EVALUATION

To evaluate the need for the proposed path correction approach, 30 participants, ranging in age from 11 to 54 years with 22 males and 8 females, were asked to complete a navigation task using the interface before the path correction algorithm had been developed. The task involved driving the robot through the three pairs of red goal posts (shown in Figure 2(b)) until all three had been crossed by the robot. As the robot passed through each goal post, it turned green on the user interface to indicate that this part of the task had been accomplished. The robot was observed colliding into a wall while being controlled by 10 of the 30 participants. After the development of the path correction algorithm, 5 participants were given the interface and asked to perform the same navigation task, this time with different numbers of rectangular obstacles randomly placed in the course. Figures 4 and 5 show screenshots during two trials. In Figure 4(a), the user has drawn a sloppy path through areas where the robot will not fit and will collide with obstacles. Figure 4(b) shows that the path correction algorithm smoothens the path, avoids areas where the robot will collide with obstacles, and still retains the shape of the user drawn path. In another trial, a user draws a path shown in the OGM in Figure 3(a). The path correction algorithm provides an appropriate course of action (Figure 5(a) and 3(f)). However, before the robot begins following the corrected path, the evaluator introduces a third obstacle (Figure 5(b)), moves one of the original obstacles (Figure 5(c)), and moves an obstacle in the way of the second goal (Figure 5(d)) to demonstrate the path correction algorithm's ability to compensate for these changes. Figure 5(d) shows the algorithm ends the path short of the robot's destination until the obstacle is moved away from the goal.

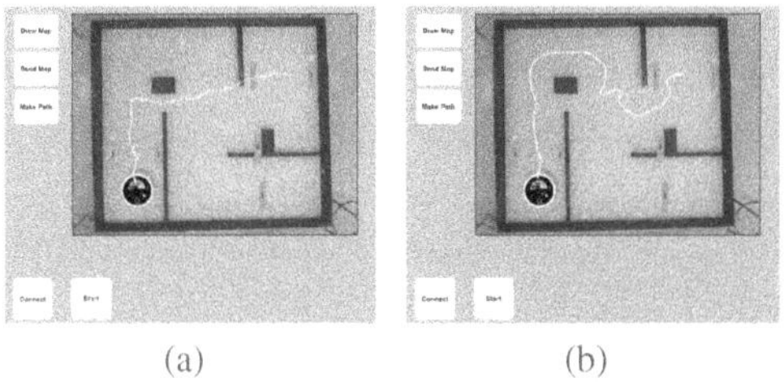

Figure 4: Screenshots of the tablet application after (a) a sloppy, collision causing path is drawn by a user and (b) the corrected path is generated on the screen.

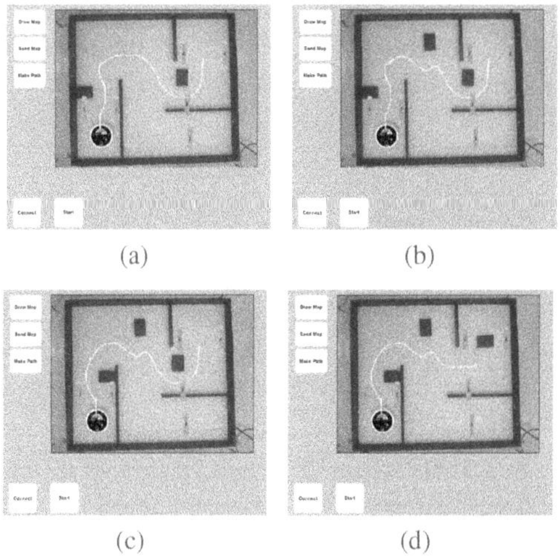

Figure 5: Screenshots of the tablet application after (a) an original drawn path is corrected, (b) a third obstacle is introduced, (c) one of the original obstacles is moved, and (d) an obstacle is moved in the way of the second goal.

CONCLUSION

In this paper, we described an approach to develop a user interface that can produce collision-free paths for robots to follow from potentially unreliable user-drawn paths. The highly interactive, computationally efficient path correction algorithm allows for more reliable communication between nontechnical users and robots by combining interpreted user intention with intelligent planning. A pilot test with users showed that such an approach allows users with no training or experience to control mobile robots with ease.

ACKNOWLEDGMENTS

This work is supported in part by the National Science Foundation awards RET Sites EEC-0807286 and EEC-1132482, GK-12 Fellows DGE: 0741714, and DRK-12 DRL: 1417769, and NY Space Grant Consortium grant 48240-7887.

REFERENCES

1. Bresenham, J. E. Algorithm for computer control of a digital plotter. *IBM Sys. J.*, 4(1):25–30, 1965.
2. Burke, D. *et al.* Multimodal interaction for human-robot teams. In *Proc. SPIE Defense, Security, and Sensing*, pp. 87410E–87410E, 2013.
3. Choi, J.-W., Curry, R., and Elkaim, G. Path planning based on Bezier curve for autonomous ground vehicles. In *Proc. World Cong. on Eng. and Computer Science*, pp. 158–166, 2008.
4. Cincotti, F. *et al.* Non-invasive brain–computer interface system: Towards its application as assistive technology. *Brain Research Bulletin*, 75(6):796–803, 2008.
5. Delsart, V. and Fraichard, T. Navigating dynamic environments with trajectory deformation. *J. of Computing and Information Tech.*, 17(1):27–36, 2009.
6. Forlizzi, J. and DiSalvo, C. Service robots in the domestic environment: A study of the roomba vacuum in the home. In *Proc. ACM SIGCHI/SIGART Conf. Human-Robot Interaction*, pp. 258–265, 2006.
7. Frank, J., Sahasrabudhe, Y., and Kapila, V. An augmented reality approach for reliable autonomous path navigation of mobile robots. In *Proc. Indian Control Conf.*, 2015.
8. Hart, P. E., Nilsson, N. J., and Raphael, B. A formal basis for the heuristic determination of minimum cost paths. *IEEE Trans. Sys. Science and Cybernetics*, 4(2):100–107, 1968.
9. Huq, R. *et al.* Qbot: An educational mobile robot controlled in Matlab Simulink environment. In *Proc. Canadian Conf. Electrical and Computer Eng.*, pp. 350–353, 2009.
10. Hwang, J.-H., Arkin, R. C., and Kwon, D.-S. Mobile robots at your fingertip: Bezier curve on-line trajectory generation for supervisory control. In *Proc. IEEE/RSJ Int. Conf. Intelligent Robots and Sys.*, pp. 1444–1449, 2003.
11. Khatib, O. Real-time obstacle avoidance for manipulators and mobile robots. *The Int. J. of Robotics Research*, 5(1):90–98, 1986.
12. Koenig, S. and Likhachev, M. Fast replanning for navigation in unknown terrain. *IEEE Trans. Robotics*, 21(3):354–363, 2005.
13. Kurniawati, H. and Fraichard, T. From path to trajectory deformation. In *Proc. IEEE/RSJ Int. Conf. Intelligent Robots and Sys.*, pp. 159–164, 2007.
14. Lamiraux, F., Bonnafous, D., and Lefebvre, O. Reactive path deformation for nonholonomic mobile robots. *IEEE Trans. Robotics*, 20(6):967–977, 2004.
15. Latombe, J. *Robot Motion Planning*. Kluwer Academic Publishers, New York, NY, 1991.
16. Likhachev, M. *et al.* Anytime dynamic A*: An anytime, replanning algorithm. In *Int. Conf. Automated Planning and Scheduling*, pp. 262–271, 2005.
17. Linquan, Y. *et al.* Path planning algorithm for mobile robot obstacle avoidance adopting Bezier curve based on genetic algorithm. In *Proc. Chinese Control and Decision Conf.*, pp. 3286–3289, 2008.
18. Micire, M. *et al.* Multi-touch interaction for robot control. In *Proc. Int. Conf. Intelligent User Interfaces*, pp. 425–428, 2009.
19. Nilsson, N. J. *Principles of Artificial Intelligence.* Springer, 1982.
20. Perzanowski, D. *et al.* Building a multimodal human-robot interface. *IEEE Intelligent Sys.*, 16(1):16–21, 2001.
21. Sakamoto, D. *et al.* Sketch and run: A stroke-based interface for home robots. In *Proc. SIGCHI Conf. Human Factors in Computing Sys.*, pp. 197–200, 2009.
22. Sato, N., Kon, K., and Matsuno, F. Navigation interface for multiple autonomous mobile robots with grouping function. In *Proc. IEEE Int. Symp. Safety, Security, and Rescue Robotics*, pp. 32–37, 2011.
23. Škrjanc, I. and Klančar, G. Optimal cooperative collision avoidance between multiple robots based on bernstein–bézier curves. *Robotics and Autonomous Sys.*, 58(1):1–9, 2010.
24. Skubic, M., Bailey, C., and Chronis, G. A sketch interface for mobile robots. In *Proc. IEEE Int. Conf. Sys., Man and Cybernetics*, pp. 919–924, 2003.
25. Skubic, M. *et al.* Using a hand-drawn sketch to control a team of robots. *Autonomous Robots*, 22(4):399–410, 2007.
26. Stentz, A. Optimal and efficient path planning for partially-known environments. In *Proc. IEEE Int. Conf. Robotics and Automation*, pp. 3310–3317, 1994.
27. Stentz, A. The focussed D* algorithm for real-time replanning. In *Proc. Int. Joint Conf. Artificial Intelligence*, pp. 1652–1659, 1995.
28. Sugihara, K. and Smith, J. Genetic algorithms for adaptive motion planning of an autonomous mobile robot. In *Proc. IEEE Int. Symp. Computational Intelligence in Robotics and Automation*, pp. 138–143, 1997.
29. Yanco, H. A. Wheelesley: A robotic wheelchair system: Indoor navigation and user interface. In *Proc. Assistive Tech. and Artificial Intelligence*, pp. 256–268. 1998.
30. Yang, K. and Sukkarieh, S. 3D smooth path planning for a UAV in cluttered natural environments. In *Proc. IEEE/RSJ Int. Conf. Intelligent Robots and Sys.*, pp. 794–800, 2008.
31. Yang, S. X. and Meng, M. An efficient neural network method for real-time motion planning with safety consideration. *Robotics and Autonomous Sys.*, 32(2):115–128, 2000.
32. Zelinsky, A. and Yuta, S. Reactive path planning for a mobile robot using numeric potential fields. In *Proc. Int. Conf. Intelligent Autonomous Sys.*, pp. 84–93, 1993.

Unsupervised Modeling of Users' Interests from their Facebook Profiles and Activities

Preeti Bhargava
University of Maryland
College Park, MD, USA
prbharga@cs.umd.edu

Oliver Brdiczka
Vectra Networks, Inc.
San Jose, CA, USA
brdiczka@acm.org

Michael Roberts
Palo Alto Research Center
Palo Alto, CA, USA
michael.roberts@parc.com

ABSTRACT
User interest profiles have become essential for personalizing information streams and services, and user interfaces and experiences. In today's world, social networks such as Facebook or Twitter provide users with a powerful platform for interest expression and can, thus, act as a rich content source for automated user interest modeling. This, however, poses significant challenges because the user generated content on them consists of free unstructured text. In addition, users may not explicitly post or tweet about everything that interests them. Moreover, their interests evolve over time. In this paper, we propose a novel unsupervised algorithm and system that addresses these challenges. It models a broad range of an individual user's explicit and implicit interests from her social network profile and activities without any user input. We perform extensive evaluation of our system, and algorithm, with a dataset consisting of 488 active Facebook users' profiles and demonstrate that it can accurately estimate a user's interests in practice.

ACM Classification Keywords
C.3.2 [Special-Purpose and Application-based Systems]: Real-time and embedded systems

General Terms
Algorithms; Design; Experimentation; Performance

Author Keywords
User Interest Modeling; User Profiling; Personalization; Social network profiles and activities;

INTRODUCTION
As the amount of information available to us increases, a common phenomenon that occurs among users is information overloading. This can be addressed by personalizing information streams and services, and user interfaces and experiences for individual users. User interest profiles are essential for such personalization as they enable recommender systems to provide users with highly personalized content in several domains (such as sports, music etc.). Automated user interest modeling that involves extracting and inferring user interests without any user input presents a burden free method for generating such profiles.

IUI 2015, March 29–April 1, 2015, Atlanta, GA, USA.

http://dx.doi.org/10.1145/2678025.2701365

As a simplest formulation, user interest profiles can be modeled as a *Utility Matrix* where rows represent users, columns represent items and the values represent the users' levels of interest in those items on a scale, say, 1 - 5 [28]. For instance, it is possible to generate a utility matrix for users from their interaction with a movies website and the movie ratings provided by them. Furthermore, these ratings can be leveraged to predict users' preferences for new unseen movies using a technique such as *Collaborative Filtering* [8, 23] that exploits user -user and movie -movie similarity information. Ultimately, this enables a movie recommender system to make personalized movie recommendations based on the users' derived and predicted movie preferences.

User interest profiles can also be developed by utilizing domain knowledge about the users or about the items they have expressed interest in. These approaches are referred to as *Content-based approaches* [23] which model user preferences by representing the item, that the user has expressed interest in, in terms of its attributes and building the user's interest profile based on that (for instance, movies can be represented by genre, cast etc.) They are particularly useful when data from similar users may not be readily available due to privacy reasons. Moreover, they are capable of recommending information that has not been rated before by any user and can also accommodate differences between individual users.

A popular content source for such approaches is users' interaction (such as time spent on web pages or click history) with various websites, for instance, news websites [21]. The websites' content can then be mined to derive their interests and preferences. However, most websites offer very specific content (movie reviews, news articles etc.) and hence, only a limited set of user interests can be modeled from them. To address this, modeling users' interests based on their entire web search and browsing history has been researched extensively [9, 27, 31].

In today's world, social networks and media such as Facebook or Twitter provide users with a powerful platform for interest expression across several domains. They have become a popular medium for users to connect, explore, share content and express themselves. For instance, Facebook users can 'like' (described as a way to *"give positive feedback and connect with things a user cares about"*) items such as Facebook pages. They can share URLs and videos, or post status updates and comments about topics that interest them. Thus, user profiles and activities on these social networks can act as a rich content source for automated user interest modeling.

However, a significant challenge in modeling user interests from their social network profiles and activities is that the user generated content on them (such as posts, tweets etc.) often consists of free unstructured text which is far from any form of items and user interest levels. Moreover, in practice, users may not explicitly tweet or post on these networks about everything that interests them. In addition, their profiles and activities evolve over time based on their dynamic interests. As a result, new algorithms and techniques need to be developed in order to build accurate and exhaustive user interest profiles from their activities on social networks.

In this paper, we address these challenges and present an approach for building comprehensive hierarchical user interest profiles from their social network profiles and activities. These interest profiles represent the users' levels of interest in over 200 coarse to fine-grained categories covering a wide spectrum of popular interests. To this end, we extract users' *explicit* interests (that have been directly expressed through tweets or posts) from user generated content on a social network platform such as Facebook. We further infer their *implicit* interests in order to augment their interest profiles. Thus, our contributions in this paper are:

1. We propose a novel unsupervised algorithm and system, that utilizes several Natural Language Processing (NLP) techniques, to model an individual user's explicit and implicit interests from her social network profile and activities without any user input. The NLP techniques that we have employed include named entity recognition, document categorization, sentiment analysis, semantic relatedness and social tagging.
2. We perform extensive evaluation of our system, and its underlying algorithm, with a dataset consisting of 488 active Facebook users' profiles and demonstrate that it can accurately estimate a user's interests.
3. We compare our algorithm with several baselines and show that it outperforms all of them.
4. We establish the value of using techniques such as Semantic Relatedness for inferring implicit user interests, and using features such as social tags and document categories for modeling her fine-grained interests. We demonstrate that this enhances interest prediction.
5. We also consider temporal dynamism of users' interests and demonstrate that it improves prediction of their interest levels.

We note that while we have used Facebook profiles as a primary and motivating dataset, our approach can be easily extended to other social network profiles.

RELATED WORK

In this section, we first briefly discuss related work in user interest modeling from search and browsing history. Since existing literature in user interest modeling from social media and networks is more pertinent to our work, we discuss it in detail after that. We highlight their shortcomings as well as differences with our approach.

User interest modeling from search and browsing history

Modeling users' interests from their browsing history has received significant attention recently. Eichstaedt et al. [9] present a method for generating user interest profiles from structured documents such as browsed web pages. The profiles include a hierarchy of interest categories with a score for each category (representing the user's interest level) assigned based on the text content and classification of the viewed documents. The hierarchy is periodically refined to reflect dynamically changing interests. Kim and Chan [19] model hierarchical user interests by clustering user's bookmarked web pages.

Qiu and Cho [27] personalize search results and improve ranking mechanisms, by automatically learning a user's preferences based on past click history. Liu et al. [21] present a hybrid approach, that combines a content based approach with collaborative filtering, for personalized news recommendations based on users' click behavior. White et al.[31] map a user's browsing history URLs into Open Directory Project Ontology Concepts[1]. They further utilize the browsing behavior of several users, over a window of time, in order to predict the user's interests. Ramanathan et al. [29] create a hierarchical user profile from Wikipedia pages visited by a user. Min and Jones [24] employ unsupervised clustering of Wikipedia pages to infer a user's coarse-grained interests.

User interest modeling from social media and networks

Social network profiles, such as Facebook profiles, offer a wealth of information for modeling users. Golbeck et al. [12] and Bachrach et al. [7] derive the personalities of users (in terms of the Big Five personality model) based on characteristics of their Facebook profiles such as the size and density of their friendship network, number of uploaded photos, number of events attended, etc. Viswanath et al. [30] examine the evolution of activity and interactions between 60,000 Facebook users over a period of 2 years. Kosinski et al. [20] predict personal attributes of users such as ethnicity, religious and political views, based on the pages that they liked on Facebook. However, these approaches do not attempt to model individual user interests and preferences.

Mislove et al. [25] propose an approach, based on community detection in social networks, to infer user attributes from their friends' attributes. Ho et al. [17] explore how friendships and conversations on Facebook are influenced by users' shared interests. They estimate shared interests based on whether users liked the Facebook pages for four popular interests such as 'Camping' etc. On the other hand, in our work, we employ a content-based approach and utilize an individual user's Facebook profile, instead of profiles of other users in her network, to model a wide spectrum of her interests.

Abel et al. [6] employ a bag of words approach to explore whether a user's professional scientific interests overlap with her social web interactions and if this overlap can be used to recommend relevant publications. Abel et al. [5] utilize a user's Tweets in order to construct different user profiles based on extracted hashtags, entities and topics. They also examine how these profiles perform with respect to personalized news recommendations. They further analyze temporal patterns (such

[1] http://www.dmoz.org/

Questions on a Likert Scale of 1 (Highest) to 5 (Lowest)
How often do you listen to music? For the following genres, rate your interest: Asian, Rock, Easy Listening, Rhythm and Blues, Jazz, Hip Hop, Electronic, Pop, Country or Folk, Avant-Garde
How often do you read books? For the following genres, rate your interest: Romance, Travel, Horror, Children's, Nonfiction, Fantasy, Historical/ Realistic/ Science Fiction, Short story, Mystery, Humor, Biography, Poetry etc.

Table 1. Sample questions from the survey administered to Facebook users

as weekday/weekend differences) in users' tweeting behavior and their effect on personalization. Esparza et al. [10] explore the idea of using user generated content on real time web, such as Twitter, as a source of knowledge for building recommender systems. Esparza et al. [11] present a user profiling approach based on topical categorization of URLs present in Tweets. They achieve a mean profile prediction accuracy of 0.73 for 32 users over 18 coarse-grained interest categories (such as music, food etc.). Pennacchiotti and Popescu [26] proposed a supervised learning approach to classify Twitter users into 3 attribute based categories representing political affiliation, ethnicity and business fans. They employed features such as user's Twitter profile, tweeting behavior and content, and social graph. Even though our system shares some similarities with the content source being used in these works (Facebook profile and activities etc. vs Twitter profile and Tweets), we propose an unsupervised approach. Moreover, we models users' interests in over 200 hierarchical, coarse to fine-grained categories covering different domains such as food, entertainment etc. This is a significantly challenging task. In addition, we consider dynamic changes in users' interests with time. Also, our approach employs several NLP techniques in addition to topical categorization and entity recognition. As we demonstrate in our evaluation, these techniques improve interest prediction accuracy.

Ma et al. [22] model users' interests based on terminology specific keywords extracted from their personal webpage and profiles on social networks such as Facebook, LinkedIn, etc. They further infer higher level interests from those keywords using a pre-defined ontology. This supervised approach has limits as keyword extraction is domain-specific. Moreover, it requires ontology generation for each domain. These limitations motivate a deeper exploration of how a broad range of interests can be modeled in an unsupervised manner from a user's social network profiles and activities.

FACEBOOK USER PROFILES

Facebook is one of the most ubiquitous and popular social networks. Recent Facebook statistics [2, 3] show that it has around 1.11 billion active users. It processes 2.5 billion pieces of content and 500+ terabytes of data each day. It has 2.7 billion Likes. A Facebook user creates 90 pieces of content every month on an average.

Though the Facebook social network has a number of features [1], we focus predominantly on the text content of an individual user profile. Each user profile consists of several sections such as basic profile information (personal and professional), *check-ins* which represent all the places/locations that the user has visited, *notes* which are user generated write ups, photos that the user has taken etc. The two most significant sections that we analyze are liked *Pages* and *Timeline*. A page can represent any entity and contains detailed information about it. In addition, each page also has a category such as 'Book', 'Movie' etc. assigned to it from among the Facebook Page categories[2]. The Timeline reflects the user's Facebook activity such as her status updates and posts along with comments and likes, posts from another Facebook user etc. Most of the profile sections remain static or expand as the user adds more content or likes more pages[3]. However, the timeline is dynamic and varies temporally depending on how active a user is.

A technique to infer explicit coarse-grained interests for a user would be to utilize the names and categories of liked pages in her profile. However, as we show later in our evaluation, this approach performs fairly in comparison to our approach which infers implicit user interests in addition to such explicit interests. Moreover, we also address modeling fine-grained interests such as specific genres of books and movies etc.

DATA COLLECTION

Since Facebook has no public API, we recruited 728 Facebook users through tasks posted on Amazon Mechanical Turk. The recruitment criteria were: (i) they should be based in the US (so that their profiles would be predominantly in English), and (ii) they should be currently active Facebook users with at least 500 or more Facebook activities such as liked pages and posts (as modeling users with sparse profiles can be error prone). Each task lasted an hour on an average and each user was paid $1 each for successfully completing it. Through the task, the users had to authorize a Facebook application to allow access to their profile. Once authorized, it directed them to a secure server where a deployed web application retrieved their Facebook profile data. They also completed a web-based survey that gathered their demographic, Facebook activity frequency, and interests and preferences information. The survey consisted of 44 quantitative questions which were either open ended, choice based, or Likert scale based. Table 1 lists a few survey questions.

Out of the 728 users, 472 (64.9%) were women and 255 (35.1%) were men. The largest group consisting of 266 (36.6%) users was working full time while 174 (23.9%) users had completed university. 704 (96.7%) users listed English as their native language. 417 (57.3%) users admitted visiting Facebook 2-10 times a day, while 375 (49.1%) participants said they spent 10 - 60 minutes per day on Facebook. 295 (40.5%) participants stated that they posted status updates several times a month.

From the collected dataset, we invalidated the data of 240 users. For these users, either the profile data was

[2] `https://www.facebook.com/pages/create/` [3] We assume that once a user has liked a page, he will rarely 'unlike' it.

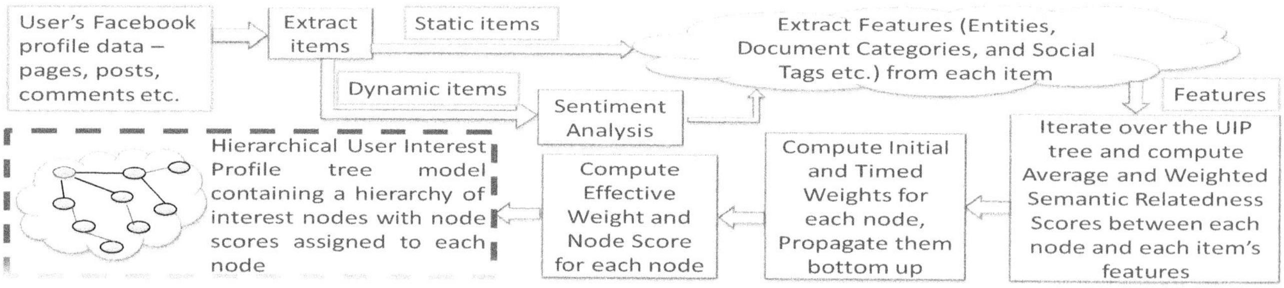

Figure 1. User Interest Profile Generation Pipeline

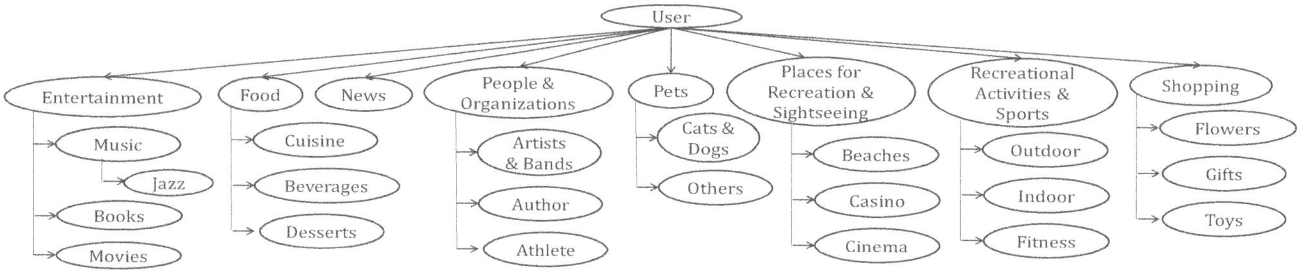

Figure 2. Partial view of the User Interest Hierarchy showing all depth 1 nodes and a few depth 2 and depth 3 nodes

too sparse (for instance, very few posts and liked pages), incomplete (e.g. all posts missing) or we found missing or contradictory responses in their surveys indicating that they did not fill it out properly (incomplete surveys). Our final dataset consists of 488 users, each of whom had an average of over 2000 pages and posts etc.

USER INTEREST MODELING

Figure 1 shows an overview of the User Interest Profile Generation system pipeline. It generates a hierarchical **User Interest Profile (UIP)** tree model, for each user, from the user's Facebook profile data. Each user's UIP tree is structured as our User Interest Hierarchy (Figure 2) with a score assigned to each node, which represents the user's level of interest in the node category.

User Interest Hierarchy

Figure 2 shows a partial view of our User Interest Hierarchy. It has been derived from the Yelp category list[4] and the Facebook Page categories, which cover a wide range of popular lifestyle and interest categories. The Yelp category list is hierarchical while Facebook Page categories are generic, coarse-grained and flat. As a result, we have attempted to build a hierarchy that would cover a significant range of popular user interests (without being too specific) by merging the two lists and filtering out very fine grained categories.

Our hierarchy has a tree structure with depth 3 and contains 204 nodes including the root node 'User'. There are 8 high-level (depth 1) categories which branch out into 58 coarse-grained categories (depth 2). A few coarse-grained categories at depth 2 are further categorized into 137 fine-grained categories (depth 3). The high-level categories, and some of the coarse-grained and fine-grained categories that they include, are shown in Figure 2. For instance, 'Entertainment' (depth 1) subsumes 'Music' (depth 2) which further subsumes 'Jazz' (depth 3).

[4] `http://www.yelp.com/developers/documentation/category_list`

It is possible that a user may be interested in a category not included in our hierarchy. As explained later, it will be added as a newly discovered interest category in that user's profile.

User Interest Profile Generation

The pipeline for user interest profile generation employs the proposed User Interest Profile Generation Algorithm (Algorithm 1) and consists of the following phases (for some phases, the design choices are explained in 'Selection and Tuning of design schemes and parameters'):

Item Extraction

As mentioned earlier, most of the profile sections remain static or expand while the timeline varies dynamically with time. We extract all such user generated *static items* (profile content such as notes, liked pages, etc.) and *dynamic items* (contents of the timeline such as status updates, posts and comments etc.) from a user's Facebook profile. Each dynamic item also has a timestamp indicating when it was generated or last updated.

Sentiment Analysis

Each dynamic item is subjected to sentiment analysis (a technique to determine the attitude or emotional state of a speaker or writer with respect to some topic). We determine the item's sentiment polarity, which can be negative (< 0.0), neutral (0.0) or positive (> 0.0), using a well-known tool called Alchemy[5].

In our current implementation, we utilize only those dynamic items for a user that have neutral or positive sentiment as we are estimating her likes rather than her dislikes. This is not required for static items such as liked pages as liking implies positive interest.

[5] `http://www.alchemyapi.com/`

Algorithm 1: User Interest Profile Generation Algorithm

Input: Facebook profile text data, User Interest Hierarchy (UIH)
Output: User Interest Profile (UIP)
Initialize UIP tree using UIH with Initial Weights = 0.0 and Node Scores = 0.0 for all nodes;
Extract user generated static and dynamic items from a user's Facebook profile such as liked pages, posts etc.;
foreach *item* i **do**
  Extract *features* from i such as Named entities and their types, Document categories etc.;
  Calculate Item Weight of i: w_i;
  `// Traverse the UIP tree`
  foreach *Node n in the UIP tree* **do**
    Compute ASR_n = Average Semantic Relatedness score between n and features of i;
    if $ASR_n < SR_{threshold}$ *(threshold SR score)* **then**
      replace ASR_n with 0.0;
    Compute Weighted Average Semantic Relatedness score: $WSR_n = w_i \times ASR_n$;
    if i *is a static item* **then**
      Compute Initial Weight (IW) of n: $IW_n = \arg\max$ (Current IW_n, WSR_n);
      `// Propagate Initial weights up to parent node of n (denoted by n_parent)`
      if *n is a leaf node* **then**
        Compute IW of n's parent: $IW_{n\_parent} = \arg\max$(Current IW_{n_parent}, $\arg\max$(IW of n and siblings));
      else
        $IW_{n\_parent} = \arg\max$ (Current IW_{n_parent}, Average IW of n and siblings);
    else if i *is a dynamic item with positive or neutral sentiment* **then**
      Compute kth Timed Weight (TW) of n: $TW_{n,k} \leftarrow <T_{i\_LastUpdate}$ (LastUpdate Timestamp of i), $WSR_n>$;
      `// Propagate Timed weights up to parent node of n (denoted by n_parent)`
      if *n is a leaf node* **then**
        Compute k'th TW of n's parent: $TW_{n\_parent,k'} = <T_{i\_LastUpdate}, \arg\max(TW_{n,k}$ of n and siblings$)>$;
      else
        $TW_{n\_parent,k'} = < T_{i\_LastUpdate}$, Average $TW_{n,k}$ of n and siblings$>$;
  end
  `// Discovering new category of interest`
  if $\arg\max(ASR_n) < SR_{threshold}$ **then**
    Create a new node for i in the UIP tree;
end
foreach *Node n in the UIP tree* **do**
  Compute Effective Weight: $EW_n = IW_n \times \prod_{j=1}^{k} (1 - TW_j \times e^{-\lambda(T_{Current} - T_{j\_LastUpdate})})$;
  Node Score of node $n \leftarrow EW_n$ mapped to a linear scale of 1-5;
end
return *User Interest Profile tree;*

Feature Extraction

From each item, we extract *features* such as page category (available only for liked pages), and other rich semantic information that includes named entities, document categories and social tags. This semantic information is obtained using three NLP techniques:

- Named Entity Recognition - a subtask of information extraction that identifies names of persons, organizations etc. in a given text or sentence
- Document Categorization - a task that classifies the subject or topic of the text, and
- Social Tagging - the practice of generating tags or keywords by users rather than experts to classify and describe online content.

We employ a tool called OpenCalais[6] which can recognize up to 39 entities from the text. It also categorizes the text into one or more 18 document categories such as Finance, Entertainment etc. In addition, it associates one or more social or common sense tags with the text. The use of these techniques ensures that a large amount of world knowledge is exploited for feature extraction. For instance, consider the Facebook page for 'Pride and Prejudice'[7]. Some of the features generated from it:

- Entities (Type): Pride and Prejudice (Book), Elizabeth Bennet (Person), United Kingdom (Country)
- Document Category: Education
- Page Category: Book
- Social Tags: Film, Literature etc.

These features provide a valuable insight into a user's interests. Thus, if a user has liked this particular page, we can infer from the extracted features that the user is interested in books and literature. An important observation to note here is that if we use only the Facebook page category i.e. 'Book', it can help infer the user's coarse-grained interest (in books). However, additional

[6] http://www.opencalais.com/

[7] http://on.fb.me/1BVX8Yo

features such as tags further enable inferring his fine-grained interests in 'Literature' (a specific book genre).

Computing Normalized Item Weights
Each item is assigned a normalized Item Weight w_i (explained in the 'Selection and Tuning of design schemes and parameters' section) which represents its contribution, with respect to other items, to the user's interest profile. This normalization also ensures that the scores remain comparable across users.

Computing Semantic Relatedness Scores
For each item, we iterate over the UIP tree model (initialized from the User Interest Hierarchy with all node scores set to 0.0) and compute the Semantic Relatedness (SR) scores between each of the the item's features and the node category. Semantic Relatedness[8] [4] is a metric for determining similarity of two documents or phrases based on their semantic meaning. It is often normalized to a value between 0 (no relatedness) and 1 (extremely high relatedness). Harispe et al. [14] present a detailed discussion of various Semantic Relatedness metrics and techniques such as Latent Semantic Analysis (LSA). We employ the Semantic Textual Similarity (STS) system [13] for computing the SR scores. STS is based on LSA along with WordNet knowledge and is trained on LDC Gigawords and Stanford Webbase corpora.

The SR metric enables inferring implicit interests of users which they have not expressed explicitly (through liking or posting etc.) on Facebook. For instance, the semantic relatedness between 'Movies' and 'Cinema' is 0.9. Thus, if a user has expressed significant interest in the category 'Movies' by liking items pertaining to movies or by posting about movies, it is highly likely that her level of interest in going to 'Cinema' (categorized under 'Places for Recreation and Sightseeing') would be high.

For each node, we average the SR scores calculated between the item's features and the node category to compute the Average Semantic Relatedness (ASR) score for that node. As explained earlier, the ASR score is used to predict the likelihood of the user being interested in the node's category, given her level of interest in that item. If the ASR score for a node calculated from an item is below a certain threshold score, $SR_{threshold}$, we set it to 0.0. This helps in reducing noise and false positives. Since SR is a cosine similarity measure, a threshold of 0.293 (1 - cos 45°) is generally considered an appropriate threshold and we use that in our current implementation.

Computing Initial and Timed Weights for each node
Each node in a user's UIP tree has one 'Initial' weight (initialized as 0.0) and zero or more 'Timed' weights assigned to it. The Initial Weight represents the weight obtained from static items in the user's Facebook profile. The Timed Weights represent the weights obtained from dynamic items and also consist of the time at which the weights were generated i.e. the time at which the items were posted or updated in the user's Facebook profile. These Timed Weights signify decaying interests in the dynamic items with the decay being a function of time (decay scheme explained in the next section) that has passed since the item was generated or updated. Intuitively, if a user has posted recently about a category, for instance 'Cricket', as opposed to a year back, her current level of interest in 'Cricket' would be high.

[8] Semantic Relatedness and Semantic Similarity have often been used interchangeably in literature. We use Semantic Relatedness in this paper to refer to the metric.

The ASR score between an item and a node is multiplied with the item's normalized weight to generate a Weighted Average Semantic Relatedness (WSR) score for that node. The WSR score calculated from each static item is compared with the current Initial weight of each node and the maximum of the two values is assigned as the node's current Initial weight. The WSR score calculated from each dynamic item is used to generate a <key,value> pair of Timed weight for each node where the timestamp of the item is the unique key. The generated Timed Weight is added to the existing set of Timed Weights for each node.

Propagating weights bottom up in the tree
The Initial and Timed weights assigned to children nodes are propagated bottom up in the UIP tree to their parent node (propagation scheme explained in the next section). The upward propagation of weights ensures that implicit high-level interests are inferred from explicit low-level interests that they subsume. For instance, if a user has explicitly expressed interest in a fine-grained node category such as 'Jazz Music', she has implicitly expressed interest in its parent node category 'Music'.

The Initial weight, propagated from the children nodes, is compared with the existing Initial weight of the parent node and the maximum of the two values is assigned as the parent node's current Initial weight. The propagated Timed weights are added to the existing set of Timed weights of the parent node.

Discovering new category of interest
If the maximum ASR score between an item and any of the nodes in a user's UIP tree is $< SR_{threshold}$, it implies that the item is not related to any of the categories in the profile. Hence, we add that item as a new node in the user's UIP tree, thus, representing a newly discovered category of interest for that user.

Computing Effective Weight from Initial and Timed Weights
To compute an aggregated weight from the Initial and decayed Timed weights assigned to a node, we compute an 'Effective Weight' for it.

Computing Node Score from Effective Weight
Since the SR score is a non-linear score, the weights computed from it are non linear. In order to compare them with Likert scale scores, we map the effective weight for each node to a linear scale of 1-5 using the inverse cosine function, round it and assign it as the Node Score.

Selection and Tuning of design schemes and parameters
We experimented with various design parameters and schemes for Algorithm 1 on a validation dataset consisting of about 10% of the users from the entire dataset i.e. 50 randomly chosen users. We then tuned the parameters and schemes based on empirical performance.

	No Decay	Decay with $\lambda =$				
		0.002	0.008	0.03	0.14	0.8
MAE	1.4	1.28	1.21	1.32	1.27	1.25

Table 2. MAE Comparison of Temporal Decay schemes

The performance measure used was the Mean Absolute Error (MAE), which is one of the most commonly used metrics in the literature [16, 23]. We computed MAE over all nodes for all users in the validation dataset.

The Absolute Error for a node j in a UIP tree for a user i is computed as: $err_{i,j} = |s_{i,j}^{actual} - s_{i,j}^{estimated}|$ where $s_{i,j}^{actual}$ is the actual Likert scale score assigned by user i to node j and $s_{i,j}^{estimated}$ is the node score estimated by our algorithm for node j for user i. The MAE for the entire population of users is defined as: $\sum_{i=1}^{N} \frac{\frac{\sum_{j=1}^{n} err_{i,j}}{n}}{N}$ where n is the number of nodes (203) and N is the number of users in the population.

Item Weight Normalization Scheme

We experimented with two schemes for item weight normalization for each item i:

1. Constant item weight scheme: The item weight is constant and same for each item i.e. $w_i = 1$.
2. Normalized item weight scheme: The item weight is normalized as,

$$w_i = \frac{\text{\# of similar items in a section of a user profile}}{\text{Total \# of items in that section of the user profile}}$$

For instance, w_i for an item such as a liked movie page would be the ratio of the number of liked movie pages to the total number of liked pages. This is intuitive because if a user has liked 100 pages on Facebook and 50 of them are movie pages, her interest in movies is significantly high.

Scheme 1 has a MAE of 1.71 while Scheme 2 has a MAE of 1.28. Hence, we implemented scheme 2 in our system.

Upward Weight Propagation Scheme

We experimented with three schemes for propagating weights upwards:

1. No weight propagation - In this scheme, there is no bottom up weight propagation.
2. Average weight propagation - In this scheme, the averaged Initial and Timed weights of children nodes are propagated up to the parent node at all depths.
3. Average and maximum weight propagation - In this scheme, if the children nodes are leaves, then the maximum Initial and Timed weights of the children nodes are propagated up to the parent node. At all other depths, the averaged Initial and Timed weights of the children nodes are propagated upwards.

As stated earlier, the upward weight propagation ensures that implicit high-level interests are inferred from subsumed low-level interests. We observed that if a user expresses a significant interest in any of the fine-grained categories, say 'Jazz Music', she often expresses a significant interest in its parent coarse-grained category, 'Music'. Hence, we experimented with propagation of both average and maximum weights. Scheme 1 has a MAE of 1.68, Scheme 2 has a MAE of 1.41 and Scheme 3 has a MAE of 1.21. We have implemented Scheme 3.

Temporal Decay scheme and parameters

We experimented with two temporal decay schemes:

1. A no decay scheme - In this scheme, the Timed weights do not decay. The Effective Weight for each node is the maximum of its Initial and Timed weights.
2. An Exponential decay scheme - In this scheme, a decayed Timed weight obtained from item i is

$$TWDec_i = TW_i \times e^{-\lambda(T_{Current} - T_{LastUpdate})}$$

where TW_i is the Timed weight generated from item i, λ is the exponential decay constant, $T_{Current}$ is the time at which the interest score is being calculated and $T_{LastUpdate}$ is the time at which i was updated. The time difference is measured in days. The Effective weight for node n is calculated as

$$EW_n = IW_n \times \prod_{i=1}^{k}(1 - TWDec_i)$$

where IW_n is the Initial weight and k is the number of Timed weights assigned to node n.

Table 2 shows the MAE for the two schemes. For the Decay scheme, we varied the values [9] of λ. As shown, the no decay scheme performs worse than the exponential decay schemes, thus, validating our intuition that the timeline represent dynamic interests of users that evolve with time. For the exponential decay scheme, $\lambda = 0.008$ has the lowest MAE of 1.21. Hence, we use that in our current implementation. Henceforth, all experimental results will be based on the aforementioned design choices.

Discussion

In order to apply this approach to other social media profiles, such as Twitter, the user's Twitter profile and content of tweets (including URLs etc.) will be utilized as items. These items will be presented as input to the UIP Generation Pipeline which will extract features (such as hashtags, entities, social tags and categories) and employ Algorithm 1 to build the user interest profile.

CHALLENGES IN PROCESSING AND ANALYSIS OF FACEBOOK TEXT DATA

Before we evaluate our algorithm, we first identify some of the challenges that we faced while processing and analyzing text data retrieved from a user's Facebook profile:

- As mentioned earlier, Facebook profile text is unstructured user generated content. Hence, it is noisy and unnormalized. Moreover, it can be grammatically incorrect, and can contain misspellings and slangs. Unlike Twitter, where research has been conducted in syntactic and lexical text normalization [18], Facebook text has not been studied extensively.
- A Facebook user's profile may have content in several languages in addition to English. Hence, most NLP techniques, that have been developed using English as a base language, cannot be directly applied to such multi-lingual content.

[9] We experimented with several values of λ but have shown only a few.

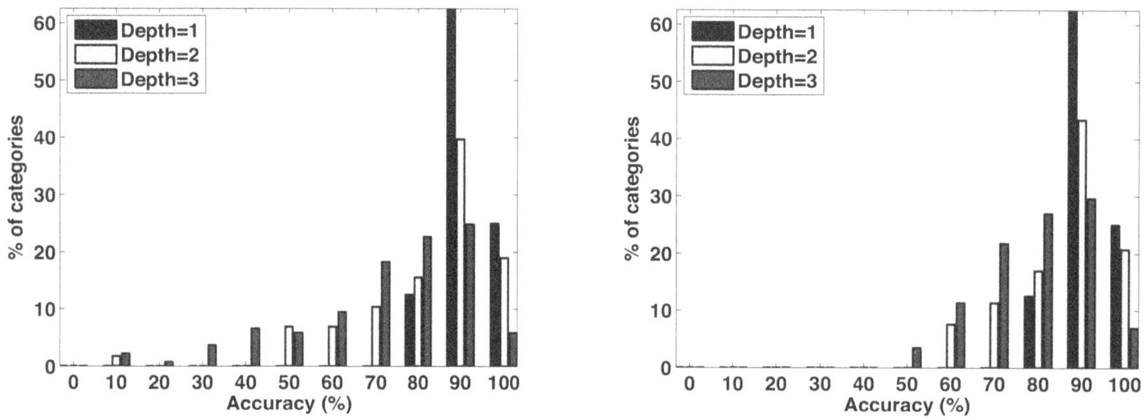

(a) Interest prediction accuracy for all categories (b) Interest prediction accuracy for relevant categories

Figure 3. Histogram of interest prediction accuracy for all and relevant categories for all users

- As stated earlier, Facebook page categories are coarse-grained and flat. Moreover, they are not clearly documented and are often inconsistent. Multiple pages representing the same entity are categorized differently. For instance, a sportsperson can have a page with category 'Public figure' and another with category 'Athlete'. A page may have the generic category 'Interest' which doesn't indicate anything useful. Hence, relying solely on the page category feature does not lead to high interest prediction accuracy. The use of additional features such as social tags and document categories, as we have done, improves performance. This is demonstrated later in the Evaluation section.
- Facebook data is retrieved as a JSON object with no defined format. Hence, individual parsers have to be implemented to parse the text data from each section.

EXPERIMENTAL EVALUATION

Methodology and Goals

The goal of this evaluation is to determine how accurately our system, and its underlying algorithm, can estimate a user's interest in a category. As mentioned earlier, we asked the Facebook users participating in our study to fill out a survey and enumerate their levels of interest in the 203 interest categories, in our User Interest Hierarchy, on a scale of 1-5 (1 = To a great extent, 2=Very much, 3=Somewhat, 4=Very little, 5 =Not at all). These values were used as *Ground Truth* for the users and were then compared with the User Interest Profiles generated by our system from their Facebook profiles. Figure 4 shows partial views of the ground truth and generated UIP trees for a randomly chosen user.

Ground Truth Characteristics

The ground truth exhibits some interesting characteristics: The global average score assigned by all 488 users over all category nodes is 3.2. The average score for nodes at different depths increases as depth increases (2.6 at depth 1, 2.98 at depth 2, and 3.3 at depth 3). The most popular categories (average user score < 2.0) were:

- Depth 1 - 2 categories ('Entertainment' and 'Pets')

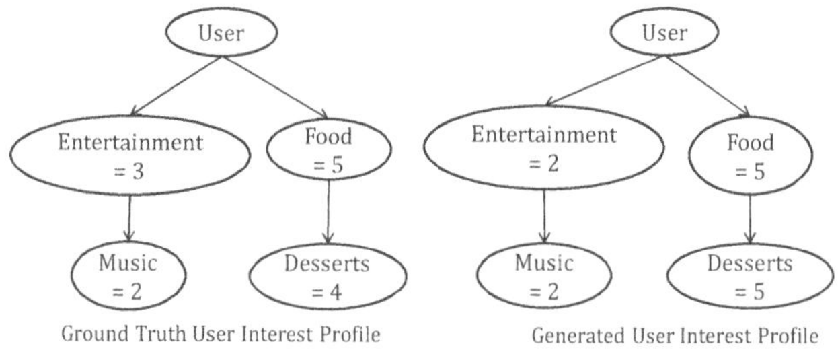

Figure 4. Partial view of Ground Truth and Generated UIPs for a randomly chosen user

- Depth 2 - 10 categories including 'Music', 'Television shows', 'Movies', 'Desserts', 'Fruits', 'Cats and Dogs'
- Depth 3 - 15 categories including 'Comedy Television shows' and 'Comedy movies'

Least popular categories (average user score > 4.0) were:

- Depth 2 - 5 categories including 'Landmarks and Historical Buildings' and 'Financial services'
- Depth 3 - 22 categories including 'Asian Music', 'Avant-Garde Music', 'Religious Television Shows', 'Religious Movies' and 'Chess'

Results

We evaluate the performance of our system, and proposed algorithm, on the entire dataset of 488 users using 3 standard performance measures that have been widely employed in existing literature [16, 23]:

Interest Prediction Accuracy

This measure evaluates how accurately the proposed algorithm can estimate whether a user is interested in a category or not. As suggested by Herlocker et al. [15], we use the ground truth scores provided by the users to identify whether they are interested in a category or not. We divided the ground truth and estimated node scores into two classes 'Interested' and 'Not Interested' using a classification threshold. Since we use a 5 point Likert scale (which has also been employed in [15]), we set the threshold as t=3.0 as a score <= 3.0 represents some interest level. Thus, a node score <= 3.0 represents the

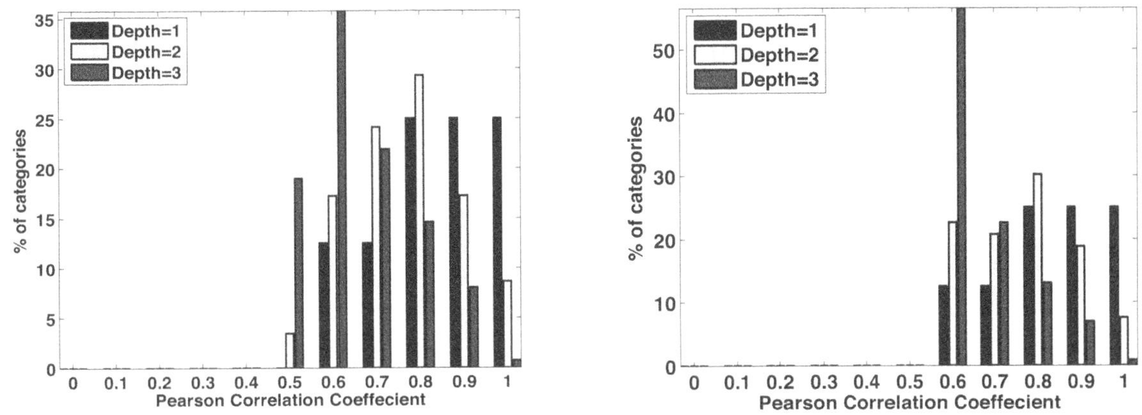

(a) Pearson Correlation coefficient between actual and predicted values for all categories (b) Pearson Correlation coefficient between actual and predicted values for relevant categories

Figure 5. Interest Prediction accuracy expressed by the Pearson correlation coefficient between estimated and actual values, for all and relevant categories

positive class 'Interested' and a node score > 3.0 represents the negative class 'Not Interested'. Accuracy a is defined as $\frac{t_p+t_n}{t_p+t_n+f_p+f_n}$ where t_p is number of true positives, t_n is number of true negatives, f_p is number of false positives and f_n is number of false negatives.

Since our interest categories have a hierarchical structure, we analyze the accuracy at individual depths as well as all depths taken together. Table 3 summarizes the accuracy (higher the better) of our algorithm for all categories at different depths and at all depths. Figure 3(a) shows the histogram of accuracy for Algorithm 1 for categories at different depths[10]. As evident, the algorithm performed very well when predicting a user's interests in high-level and coarse-grained categories (Depths 1 and 2) and reasonably well for fine-grained categories (Depth 3). Though a direct comparison with CatStream[11] is not possible because of the differences in our approach, dataset, and structure and number of categories, our algorithm's overall accuracy is higher.

For most real world recommender systems, the primary concern is to accurately predict user interests in the *relevant* or *good* categories [23]. For our evaluation, we consider irrelevant categories as those which have a high average user assigned ground truth score (> 4.0) as this indicates a low average user population interest (See the Ground Truth Characteristics section for a discussion of popular and unpopular categories.). As mentioned earlier, there were no irrelevant categories at depth 1, 5 (out of 58) irrelevant categories at depth 2, and 22 (out of 137) irrelevant categories at depth 3. Hence, we remove the irrelevant categories and compute accuracy over the relevant categories only. Figure 3(b) shows the histogram for accuracy at different depths for only the relevant categories. Table 3 summarizes the accuracy for relevant categories at individual depths and at all depths. As evident, the accuracy of our algorithm is high for relevant categories. Thus, in practice, our system and algorithm can predict a user's interests accurately.

[10] Due to large number of categories in our hierarchy (203), it is not possible to show accuracy for each individual category

Categories	Accuracy (%) for	
	all categories	relevant categories
Depth 1	90.19	90.19
Depth 2	81.67	85.53
Depth 3	71.72	78.85
All depths	75.29	81.2

Table 3. Accuracy for all and relevant category nodes at individual depths and all depths taken together

Categories	MAE for	
	all categories	relevant categories
Depth 1	0.88	0.88
Depth 2	0.91	0.89
Depth 3	1.0	0.93
All depths	0.97	0.91

Table 4. MAE for all and relevant category nodes at individual depths and all depths taken together

Categories	Algorithm 1	Baseline			
		1	2	3	4
Depth 1	**0.88**	1.12	1.17	1.2	1.5
Depth 2	**0.91**	1.21	1.27	1.33	1.66
Depth 3	**1.0**	1.26	1.32	1.59	1.77
All depths	**0.97**	1.24	1.35	1.49	1.74

Table 5. MAE Comparison of Algorithm 1 with baselines for all category nodes at individual depths and all depths taken together

Pearson's Correlation Coefficient

Figure 5(a) presents the accuracy of predicting interest as expressed by the Pearson product-moment correlation coefficient (ρ) between the actual and estimated interest levels for all categories. As shown, more than 75% of depth 1 categories have $\rho > 0.75$ which indicates that the actual and estimated interest levels are highly correlated. At depth 2, 67% of the categories have $\rho > 0.7$ and at depth 3, 63.5% of the categories have $\rho > 0.6$. This too indicates that the algorithm has high accuracy when predicting interests in high-level and coarse-grained categories and reasonable accuracy for fine-grained categories, corroborating the results presented previously.

Similar to interest prediction accuracy measure, we computed the Pearson correlation coefficient for relevant categories. Figure 5(b) presents the accuracy at different depths for relevant categories only. As shown, more than 75% of depth 1 categories have $\rho > 0.75$ which indicates that the actual and estimated interest levels are highly correlated. At depth 2, 70% of the categories have $\rho > 0.7$ and at depth 3, 70% of the categories have $\rho > 0.6$.

Mean Absolute Error (MAE)

The Absolute Error evaluates how accurately the proposed algorithm can estimate the level of interest of a user in a category. For instance, for the node with category 'Entertainment' in the ground truth and estimated profiles of a randomly chosen user shown in Figure 4, the absolute error will be | 3 - 2 | = 1.0.

We use the definition of MAE mentioned earlier and compute it for all categories for all 488 users in our dataset. Table 4 shows the MAE (the lower the better) for categories at individual depths and all depths for all users. When considering only relevant categories, the MAE decreases even further. This too demonstrates that, for practical purposes, our system and algorithm can accurately predict a user's level of interests.

Discussion

The MAE is higher and the accuracy is lower as the categories become more specific at each depth. A possible reason for this could be that even though our algorithm employs various techniques to infer fine-grained interests, we do not have enough information to estimate a user's levels of interest in all the fine-grained categories in our hierarchy. For instance, a user can be interested in various genres of books but may post only about a few. A hybrid approach that also employs collaborative filtering techniques (which exploit user or item similarity) can be used to overcome this limitation. Moreover, the challenges mentioned earlier (such as unnormalized text and multi-lingual content) highlight some of the difficulties involved in user interest profiling from Facebook data. We will address these limitations in future work.

Comparison with baselines

To put the accuracy of our proposed Algorithm 1 in perspective, we compare its performance with 4 baselines. These have been constructed using different sets of features or techniques to evaluate and demonstrate their impact on accuracy. These baselines are:

1. Baseline 1 - An algorithm similar to Algorithm 1 which utilizes Facebook page category and page name as the only features to generate the user's interest profile. Since only the liked pages in a user's Facebook profile have a page category, they are the only items used.
2. Baseline 2 - An algorithm similar to Algorithm 1 which performs lexical comparison (instead of using Semantic Relatedness) of each feature with the interest categories to generate the user's interest profile. Here, the SR score = 1 if a match is found and 0 otherwise.
3. Baseline 3 - An algorithm that assigns the global average user score for all categories i.e. 3.2 to each node in the UIP tree for a user.
4. Baseline 4 - An algorithm that selects a random value between 1 and 5 and assigns that as the score to each node in the UIP tree for a user.

Table 5 compares the MAE for Algorithm 1 and the baselines (lower MAE indicates superior performance) for all categories for all users in our dataset. As shown, Algorithm 1 outperforms all the baselines at all depths. It is evident from the higher overall MAE for Baseline 1 that even though Facebook page categories are valuable for inferring coarse-grained interests, they are not sufficient for inferring fine-grained interests. Additional features such as social tags and document categories utilized by our Algorithm proved to be useful in this case and improved performance by almost 6.75% (on a scale of 1-5). Moreover, this also demonstrates that exploiting the temporally dynamic nature of the user's Facebook timeline is beneficial for augmenting her user interest profile and improving interest prediction accuracy. Similarly, we can see from the performance of Baseline 2 that even though lexical equality serves to identify explicit interests, Semantic Relatedness helps infer implicit interests as well which further enhances interest prediction for all categories at all depths by a margin of 9.5%.

CONCLUSION AND FUTURE WORK

In this paper, we presented an approach for building comprehensive hierarchical user interest profiles, that cover a wide spectrum of popular interests, from users' social network profiles and activities. We proposed a novel unsupervised algorithm and system to model an individual user's explicit and implicit interests from her social network profile and activities without any user input. We performed extensive evaluation of our system, and its underlying algorithm, with a dataset consisting of 488 active Facebook users' profiles and demonstrated that it can accurately estimate a user's interests in practice. We also compared our algorithm with several baselines and showed that it outperforms all of them. We established the value of using techniques such as Semantic Relatedness for inferring implicit user interests and using features such as social tags and document categories for modeling fine-grained interests. We showed that employing these techniques and features enhances interest prediction performance. We further demonstrated that considering temporal dynamism of users' interests improves prediction of their interest levels.

We now plan to deploy this system in a live environment and update the user interest profiles based on the users' real-time Facebook profile activity and feedback. We are also working on several enhancements to this system. For instance, topic modeling could be used to generate topic words from the items to augment the list of features. Different mechanisms can be used to analyze the temporal decay of a user's interests. Finally, a hybrid method which combines this content based approach with collaborative filtering could be used to improve performance. This approach would also address cold start for such a system.

REFERENCES

1. Facebook features. http://en.wikipedia.org/wiki/Facebook_features.
2. Facebook's growth since ipo in 12 big numbers. http://techcrunch.com/2013/05/17/facebook-growth/.
3. How big is facebook's data? http://techcrunch.com/2012/08/22/how-big-is-facebooks-data-2-5-billion-pieces-of-content-and-500/-terabytes-ingested-every-day/.
4. Semantic similarity. http://en.wikipedia.org/wiki/Semantic_similarity.
5. Abel, F., Gao, Q., Houben, G.-J., and Tao, K. Analyzing user modeling on twitter for personalized news recommendations. In *User Modeling, Adaption and Personalization*. Springer, 2011, 1–12.
6. Abel, F., Herder, E., and Krause, D. Extraction of professional interests from social web profiles. *Proc. UMAP* (2011).
7. Bachrach, Y., Kosinski, M., Graepel, T., Kohli, P., and Stillwell, D. Personality and patterns of facebook usage. In *Proceedings of the 3rd Annual ACM Web Science Conference* (2012).
8. Bennett, J., and Lanning, S. The netflix prize. In *Proceedings of KDD cup and workshop* (2007).
9. Eichstaedt, M., Lu, Q., and Teng, S.-H. Automatic user interest profile generation from structured document access information, May 7 2002. US Patent 6,385,619.
10. Garcia Esparza, S., O'Mahony, M. P., and Smyth, B. On the real-time web as a source of recommendation knowledge. In *Proceedings of the fourth ACM conference on Recommender systems*, ACM (2010), 305–308.
11. Garcia Esparza, S., O'Mahony, M. P., and Smyth, B. Catstream: categorising tweets for user profiling and stream filtering. In *Proceedings of the ACM International conference on Intelligent user interfaces* (2013).
12. Golbeck, J., Robles, C., and Turner, K. Predicting personality with social media. In *CHI'11 Extended Abstracts on Human Factors in Computing Systems* (2011).
13. Han, L., Kashyap, A., Finin, T., Mayfield, J., and Weese, J. Umbc ebiquity-core: Semantic textual similarity systems. In *Proceedings of the Second Joint Conference on Lexical and Computational Semantics* (2012).
14. Harispe, S., Ranwez, S., Janaqi, S., and Montmain, J. Semantic measures for the comparison of units of language, concepts or instances from text and knowledge representation analysis. *arXiv preprint arXiv:1310.1285* (2013).
15. Herlocker, J. L., Konstan, J. A., Borchers, A., and Riedl, J. An algorithmic framework for performing collaborative filtering. In *Proceedings of the 22nd annual international ACM SIGIR conference on Research and development in information retrieval*, ACM (1999), 230–237.
16. Herlocker, J. L., Konstan, J. A., Terveen, L. G., and Riedl, J. T. Evaluating collaborative filtering recommender systems. *ACM Transactions on Information Systems (TOIS) 22*, 1 (2004), 5–53.
17. Ho, Q., Yan, R., Raina, R., and Xing, E. P. Understanding the interaction between interests, conversations and friendships in facebook. *arXiv preprint arXiv:1211.0028* (2012).
18. Kaufmann, M., and Kalita, J. Syntactic normalization of twitter messages. In *International conference on natural language processing, Kharagpur, India* (2010).
19. Kim, H. R., and Chan, P. K. Learning implicit user interest hierarchy for context in personalization. In *Proceedings of the 8th international conference on Intelligent user interfaces*, ACM (2003), 101–108.
20. Kosinski, M., Stillwell, D., and Graepel, T. Private traits and attributes are predictable from digital records of human behavior. *Proceedings of the National Academy of Sciences 110*, 15 (2013), 5802–5805.
21. Liu, J., Dolan, P., and Pedersen, E. R. Personalized news recommendation based on click behavior. In *Proceedings of the 15th international conference on Intelligent user interfaces*, ACM (2010), 31–40.
22. Ma, Y., Zeng, Y., Ren, X., and Zhong, N. User interests modeling based on multi-source personal information fusion and semantic reasoning. In *Active Media Technology*. Springer, 2011, 195–205.
23. Melville, P., and Sindhwani, V. Recommender systems. In *Encyclopedia of machine learning*. Springer, 2010, 829–838.
24. Min, J., and Jones, G. J. Building user interest profiles from wikipedia clusters. *SIGIR 2011 Workshop on Enriching Information Retrieval (ENIR 2011)* (2011).
25. Mislove, A., Viswanath, B., Gummadi, K. P., and Druschel, P. You are who you know: inferring user profiles in online social networks. In *Proceedings of the third ACM international conference on Web search and data mining*, ACM (2010), 251–260.
26. Pennacchiotti, M., and Popescu, A.-M. Democrats, republicans and starbucks afficionados: user classification in twitter. In *Proceedings of the 17th ACM SIGKDD international conference on Knowledge discovery and data mining* (2011).
27. Qiu, F., and Cho, J. Automatic identification of user interest for personalized search. In *Proceedings of the 15th international conference on World Wide Web* (2006).
28. Rajaraman, A., and Ullman, J. D. *Mining of massive datasets*. Cambridge University Press, 2011.
29. Ramanathan, K., Giraudi, J., and Gupta, A. Creating hierarchical user profiles using wikipedia. *HP Labs* (2008).
30. Viswanath, B., Mislove, A., Cha, M., and Gummadi, K. P. On the evolution of user interaction in facebook. In *Proceedings of the 2nd ACM workshop on Online social networks* (2009).
31. White, R. W., Bailey, P., and Chen, L. Predicting user interests from contextual information. In *Proceedings of the ACM SIGIR conference on Research and development in information retrieval* (2009).

Personalized Search: Reconsidering the Value of Open User Models

Jae-wook Ahn
IBM T.J. Watson Research Center
1101 Kitchawan Rd
Yorktown Heights, NY 10538
jaewook.ahn@us.ibm.com

Peter Brusilovsky
University of Pittsburgh
135 North Bellefield Avenue
Pittsburgh, PA 15260
peterb@pitt.edu

Shuguang Han
University of Pittsburgh
135 North Bellefield Avenue
Pittsburgh, PA 15260
shh69@pitt.edu

ABSTRACT
Open user modeling has been perceived as an important mechanism to enhance the effectiveness of personalization. However, several studies have reported that open and editable user models can harm the performance of personalized search systems. This paper re-examines the value of open and editable user models in the context of personalized search. We implemented a personalized search system with 2D user manipulatable visualization and concept-based user model components. A user study result suggests that the proposed visualization-based open user modeling approach can be beneficial for adaptive search.

Author Keywords
Adaptive Visualization; Concept-based User Modeling; Named-Entity; Information Retrieval; VIBE

ACM Classification Keywords
H.3.1 [Content Analysis and Indexing]: *Indexing method*; H.3.3 [Information Search and Retrieval]: *Information filtering*; Relevance feedback]; H.3.5 [Online Information Services]: *Web-based services.*

INTRODUCTION
Open user models are recognized as an important direction of research in the area of user modeling and personalization. User models are an internal representation of user knowledge, interests, goals, or other essential features that user-adaptive systems apply to produce the personalization effect, i.e., make the systems look or behave differently for different users [25]. In the majority of user-adaptive systems, user models are hidden from the users and and have no other function beyond providing data to the personalization mechanism. Adaptive systems with open user models provide an interface for the user to view the content of their models and sometimes also edit it (in the latter case these models are also called editable). Multiple arguments have been provided in favor of open and editable user models. It has been claimed that these models make personalization more transparent, support self-reflection, allow the user to stay in control, and improve the quality of user representation and personalization. In the area of personalized e-learning systems where these models have been explored for almost 20 years [12, 28, 14, 27], all of these claims were gradually confirmed and open user models (also known in this area as open student models) became almost a standard feature.

In contrast, in the area of adaptive search and filtering systems, open user models originally failed to deliver the expected value. On the contrary, a pioneer study [24] demonstrated that making user models open and editable might harm the performance of an adaptive search system. A follow-up experiment in a different context confirmed this unexpected result [6]. After these two studies one might have concluded that open user models are not applicable to adaptive search. In other words, open models could be beneficial when modeling user *knowledge* (as educational systems do) and harmful when modeling user *interests* (as search/filtering systems do).

A comparison of successful open student models [11] and failed open user models in information access studies [24, 6] hinted that the cause of the problems might not be the kind of modeled user characteristics, but the kind of open models applied. Successful open student models have at least two other noticeable differences with respect to open user models applied in information retrieval [24, 6]. First, most open student models use highly visual 2-dimensional representation of user knowledge, while open models in [24, 6] used simple one-dimensional text-based visual representation. Second, open student models modeled user knowledge in terms of semantic categories (concepts and topics of the course) while open models in [24, 6] modeled user interests in terms of preferred keywords. This comparison indicated that a switch to visual and semantic-level open models for adaptive information access could lead to more successful models.

The first evidence in favor of visual and semantic level models was provided just a few years later in [9, 2]. Both papers introduced an important innovation. Instead of simple text-based models, the papers suggested two different approaches to present models of user interest in a visual 2-dimensional form with natural and responsive drag-and-drop manipulation. In addition, Bakalov et al. [9] switched to a semantic-level user model representing user interests over a set of ontology concepts while [2] retained more traditional keyword-level models. Both studies provided early evidence that open

IUI 2015, March 29April 1, 2015, Atlanta, GA, USA.

http://dx.doi.org/10.1145/2678025.2701410

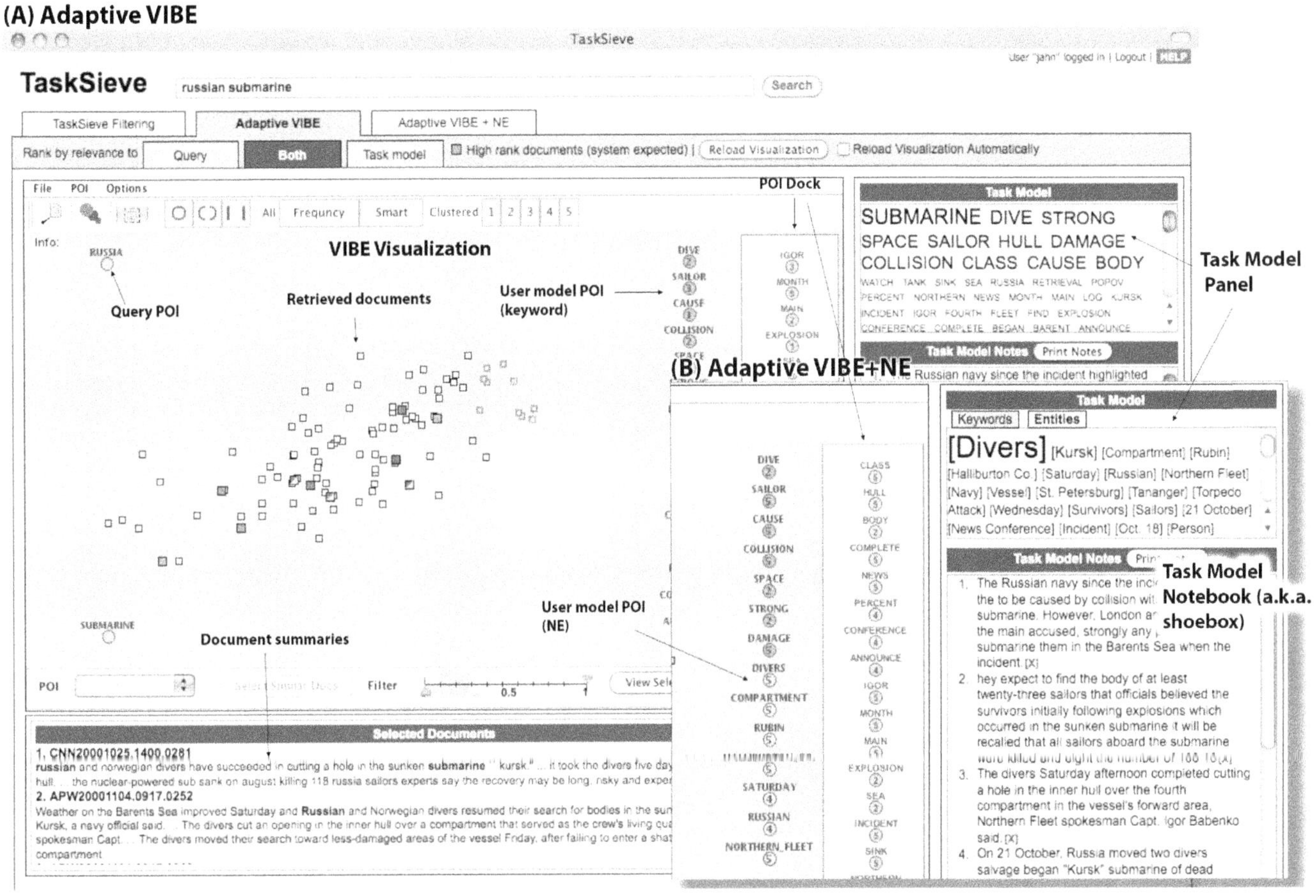

Figure 1: (A) Adaptive VIBE versus (B) Adaptive VIBE with Named-Entity POIs (Adaptive VIBE+NE). (A) has only keyword POIs but (B) has both keyword and NE POIs. Keyword POIs are painted in blue (e.g., "DIVE") and NE POIs are painted in green (e.g., "HALLIBURTON CO."). Users select and save text passages from document summaries or fulltexts (not shown here) into Task Model Notebook. From the notebook keywords and NEs are automatically extracted on the fly and displayed in Task Model Panels and in the VIBE visualization. (B)'s Task Model Panel includes both keywords and NE tabs.

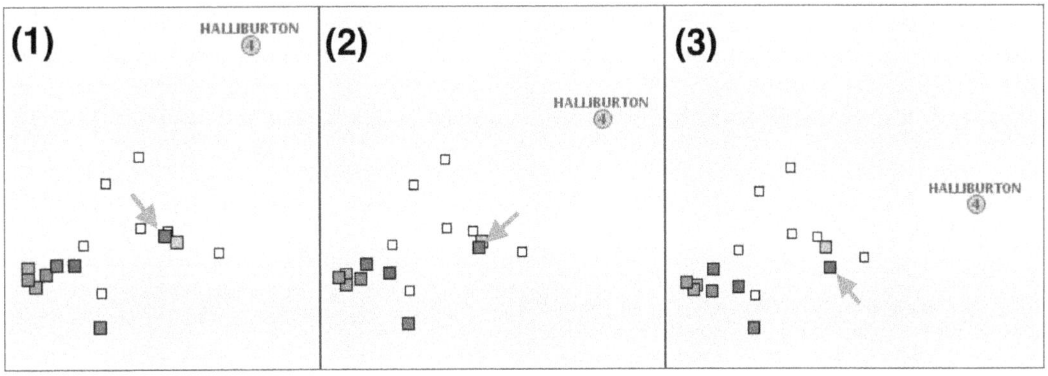

Figure 2: Dragging a POI dynamically updates visualization. A user drags POI "HALLIBURTON" and the similar documents to the POI instantly follow its movement (e.g., arrow-marked square), whereas other non-similar documents remain static.

models are able to provide an advantage in this context of information helping to locate relevant documents. Over the next few years this work was expanded by the original teams and other researchers [10, 15, 4] who offered more extensive studies of open visual user models and provided additional evidence in favor of this approach.

While this work provided important evidence that more advanced open user models can be efficiently applied in the search context, it had several shortcomings. First, a separate value of two major components of this approach (visual 2D open modeling and conceptual-level user models) has not been explored. Two of the papers [2, 4] demonstrated benefits of one form of visual keyword-level models in a news search context and three others [9, 10, 15] stressed benefits of another form of visual semantic-level model in a publication search context. It has not been demonstrated whether the use of semantic model offers any additional advantage over keyword-level models in any of the explored contexts. Second, it remains unclear whether the user manipulation with open models can improve (or at least not degrade) information retrieval performance. The majority of cited papers did not even explore the performance aspect focusing instead on user perception parameters and other forms of indirect evidence. Given that the originally discovered problems of open user modeling in search context were related with performance degradation, especially in case of extensive manipulation with open models, the proof of new approaches cannot compete without performance evaluation and analysis of model manipulation impact.

This paper reports our attempt to bridge this gap in research on open user modeling in search context. We explored whether a combination of a concept-level user model and a 2D visual open user modeling interface with drag-and-drop manipulation could have positive impact on personalized search context. To close the gap left by the earlier studies, we focused on performance evaluation and designed an experiment in a way that could separately assess the impact of "visual" and "semantic" innovations. In addition, we performed our study in a news search domain, which is exactly where the original negative results were obtained. This allows a more direct comparison of our new study with the earlier work making our re-assessment more reliable. The next section reviews related studies on open user modeling and named-entity based user modeling. Then we introduce the 2D visualization based personalized search system Adaptive VIBE and Adaptive VIBE+NE that supports named-entity based user modeling. The remaining sections outline the user study design, present analysis results, and conclude this paper by discussing the study implications.

RELATED STUDIES

Open User models aim to transparently reveal the personalization process so that users can easily understand the internal mechanism and anticipate the behavior of the system. By overcoming the limitations of traditional blackbox-based personalization systems, users can build mental models and increase their trust in the systems. Open user modeling has been widely adopted by the personalized e-learning community [11] and has been explored in several other domains such as news recommendation [6], Wikipedia page recommendation [17], and restaurant menu recommendation for mobile devices [26]. Several personalized systems went beyond simple text-based open user models and explored benefits of 2D visualization for open user modeling. For example, IntrospectiveView [9] visualized user interests in domain concepts using 2D "radar" representation.

While the results of existing studies support the assumption that open user models are beneficial for adaptive systems, there is less consistency in respect to editable user models, a subclass of open models that go beyond passive visualization and let users edit or manipulate the user model contents. Following some positive experience with editable models in adaptive educational systems, YourNews [6] explored an on-line news filtering system that was equipped with a user model viewer/editor. Unlike the expectations, the result showed that the user model manipulation from the user side could lead to degraded system performance. Waern [24] reported similar results based on an offline experiment as well. On the other hand, more recent studies reported different results. IntropectiveView [10] reported positive results with its interactive 2D "radar" user model and Glowacka et al. [15] proposed a similar user manipulable model to direct the search process and reported improved performance.

Named-entities (NEs) are information units important to recognize names and numeric expressions from unstructured text [22]. Even though they are called *named*-entities, they can represent semantic categories and pointers to real world entities [20] that are richer in semantic content than simple keywords. For example, the NE "ski lovers" delivers the exact meaning of real objects in a news story whereas the individual keywords "ski" or "lovers" lose the real meaning. The NE extractor we used in this study can recognize 32 types of entities and their categories (e.g., `PERSON`, `LOCATION`, or `TIME`) and 13 types of events. Moreover it understands *cross-references* between entities, so that it can link identical entities with different representations (e.g., "He," "him," and "President Kennedy"). Such features greatly improve the ability of search systems to understand the semantic meanings of objects found in news stories. To our knowledge, there are just a few attempts to directly incorporate NEs for user model construction. Abel et al. [1] incorporated semantic entity and topic-based user modeling for Twitter personalization, which reported enhanced variety of constructed profiles and improved news article recommendation accuracy. Aktolga et al. [8] reported that employing related terms and NEs for user search query profiling provided the best performance. A previous attempt [5] constructed an NE based news search system and [18] used NEs extracted from textual metadata for photo exploration and retrieval. They could observe boosted performances compared to baseline keyword-based search systems. Therefore, we expect NEs to perform as high quality semantic representations for open user modeling.

ADAPTIVE VIBE+NE: PERSONALIZED VISUAL SEARCH WITH CONCEPT-BASED OPEN USER MODELING

Adaptive VIBE+NE extends keyword-based Adaptive VIBE [4] by incorporating NEs as semantic entities. Adaptive VIBE is a personalized search system with a 2D adaptive visualization (Figure 1) that replaces traditional one-dimensional ranked lists [4]. It displays (1) retrieved documents (squares in Figure 1), (2) user query terms (*yellow* disks), and (3) user model terms (*blue* or *green* disks) to implement an adaptive visualization based personalized search system. The system operates in the following sequence.

1. Retrieve documents using Indri search engine [23] with user queries.
2. If a user model exists, calculate similarities between user model terms (keywords or NEs) and the retrieved documents.
3. Visualize the documents, query terms, user model terms using VIBE visualization algorithm [19] and the similarity scores calculated in step 2.
4. Users collect important text fragments and save them into a "Task Model Notebook."
5. The system extracts important keywords and NEs from the notebook and user models (or task models) are created or updated on the fly. The visualization is updated following the user mode update.

The terms (disks in the Figure) are called POIs (Points of Interest), which establish the core of the VIBE (Visual Information Browsing Environment) visualization algorithm [19]. VIBE allocates visual objects (documents) on a 2D space according to their similarity ratios to multiple POIs. For example, if a document is two times more similar to a POI, it is placed two times closer to the POI. Therefore, users can directly understand the relatedness of a document to POIs by visually comparing the distances from them. If a document is closer to a POI (or concept A) than another POI (or concept B), then she can immediately guess that the document is more about concept A than concept B. If another concept C is at an opposite position on the screen, she can simply ignore the concept as the relatedness would be very low.

In Adaptive VIBE, user queries and user model terms are defined as POIs and placed in separate groups. In Figure 1 the query terms ("RUSSIA" and "SUBMARINE") are placed on the left side of the screen and the user model terms that estimate the user's current task ("DIVE", "SAILOR", etc.) are placed on the right side. By spatially separating the two POI groups, documents are separated according to their similarities to the group of POIs as well. The system can visually suggest that the documents closer to the user model terms (right) are more related to the system's estimation about their tasks rather than their own query terms (left). The document positions not only indicate the relatedness either to user query or user model terms but also indicate the relatedness to each individual POI. In the figure, many documents in the query side (left) are skewed to "SUBMARINE" rather than "RUSSIA," which means the latter query term has more effect on the documents. Also, Adaptive VIBE is dynamically manipulable. Users can drag POIs and documents smoothly follow the movements of similar POIs on the fly (Figure 2). Visually tracking the document movements, users can easily estimate their similarities to POIs.

The property of VIBE visualization, makes the user model (UM) terms presented as a set of POIs fully open, i.e., inspectable and editable. Manipulating the UM POIs, users can change the effect of the user model on the presentation of the documents helping in separation of relevant and non-relevant documents. While it is a direct analogy to the traditional editing of user models in adaptive search system [24, 6] where increase or decrease of UM term weight affects the ranking of retrieved documents to help separate relevant documents, visual manipulation of UM terms in systems like Adaptive VIBE, IntrospectiveViews [10], and SciNet [15] is more powerful since it affects document presentation not in one, but in two dimensions.

User models can be constructed either implicitly by observing user activities or explicitly by asking for user feedback. We adopted an explicit method for Adaptive VIBE. Users were asked to save important passages from document summaries or fulltexts into a "Task Model Notebook" (lower-right corner in Figure 1), by selecting text fragments and clicking on a "Save" button. The system observes the notebook and instantly calculates the scores of the keywords contained in the notebook contents (words, phrases, or sentences). The score is defined as the sum of frequencies of a given term in the notebook. It selects high-score keywords to construct *task models*, specialized user models for solving specific tasks rather than representing general user interests. *Task models* are updated immediately whenever the notebook contents are changed and the updated contents are shown to users in the "Task Model Panel" (upper-right corner in Figure 1). In the "Task Model Panel" more frequent user model terms are rendered in bigger/bolder fonts in a term-cloud format. Unlike the "Task Model Panel" users can select whether to update the VIBE visualization manually or automatically.

Adaptive VIBE+NE adds semantic NE POIs in addition to keyword POIs. They are painted as *green disks* and presented in the second tab of the "Task Model Panel" (Figure 1 smaller window). As Figure 1 shows, the NE-based task model can contain concept-richer information than simple keywords. It includes person or location names, date and time, and objects in the form of phrases as well as one-word keywords. We preprocessed the entire news story texts in the corpus, extracted NEs, and stored them into a database with location information so that the system could instantly retrieve NEs from any text segments saved into the notebook. We used an NE extractor developed by our project partner at IBM [5], which uses a statistical maximum-entropy model to recognize 32 types of named, nominal and pronominal entities (`PERSON`, `ORGANIZATION`, `FACILITY`, `LOCATION`, etc), and 13 types of events. Interested readers can refer to [5, 4] for more details and examples.

STUDY DESIGN

A user study was conducted to test the advantages of Adaptive VIBE+NE's concept-based visual open user modeling. The study was designed to simulate the work situation of an information analyst engaged in a sufficiently complex exploratory search with information foraging and sense-making stages [21]. The tasks and the documents were provided by an expanded TDT4 (Topic Detection and Tracking) document collection that contains 28,390 English documents published from October 2000 to January 2001. The original TDT4 topics were enriched to resemble the tasks performed by intelligence analysts [16] with 18 topics and ground-truth information. In order to select as equally difficult topics as possible and to make them comparable with each other, we devised a measure considering the ground-truth information distribution in the corpus. In some topics, answers are concentrated in a small number of documents (easier because it reduces user efforts to explore more documents) whereas other topics disperse answers across many documents (more difficult). Therefore, we defined the standard deviation of relevant passage count per document as a pseudo topic complexity measure (Equation 1). Three TDT4 topics with equivalent topic complexity were selected as the study topics (Table 1).

$$Complexity_{topic} = \sqrt{\frac{1}{|Doc_{rel}|} \sum_{i=1}^{|Doc_{rel}|} (|Passage_{rel}| - \mu))^2} \quad (1)$$

The participants were recruited from the University of Pittsburgh and Carnegie Mellon University. They were expected to play the role of information analysts who could proficiently operate the search systems for the task completion and were required to meet the following criteria: (1) native English speakers or equivalent language abilities; (2) sufficient information retrieval skills; (3) sufficient intellectual ability as analysts from their educational backgrounds [4]. Thirty three participants (23 males and 10 females) were recruited and were asked to complete search tasks across two sessions. The average age of the participants was 26.1 with standard deviation = 6.5.

They were asked to solve two tasks under two conditions: (1) Adaptive VIBE and (2) Adaptive VIBE+NE.[1] The order of the systems was randomized by Latin square design to avoid learning or fatigue effects. They read an one-page introductory statement and completed a demographic questionnaire focusing on their search experience and consumption of news. 50 minute training sessions were given to them where the experiment coordinator explained the system features and allowed them to solve a realistic training task. The training session is important because the Adaptive VIBE visualization systems were new to the participants and they needed practice. The main search sessions were 20 minutes each (40 minutes in total) and no attempt to complete the tasks after the given time was allowed. After the sessions they were asked to fill out post-task questionnaires and took 10-minute exit interviews.

[1]For simplicity, they are referred to as "VIBE" and "VIBE+NE" henceforth.

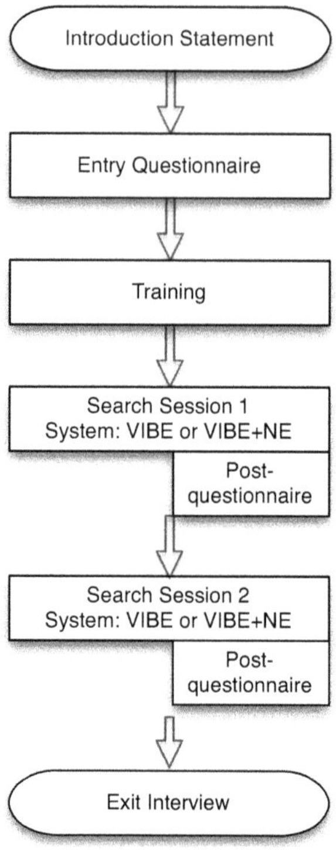

Figure 3: Study procedure

Table 1: Topic difficulty: distribution of relevant information

Topic ID	40009	40021	40048
$Complexity_{topic}$	71.46	73.98 (most difficult)	64.12 (least difficult)

RESULT ANALYSIS

System Performance Analysis

Traditional information retrieval systems presenting search results with one-dimensional ranked lists try to assure that relevant documents are placed higher in the lists, where users have more chances to access them. However, Adaptive VIBE attempts to visualize the retrieved documents on a 2D plane and to spatially separate relevant documents from non-relevant ones to eventually draw user attention to the relevant document group. In this section we explore two parameters – clustering and positioning – that measure how successfully the system visualizes relevant documents. It assesses two questions: (1) to what extent the performance improvement can be attributed to the user model, i.e., if the performance increases with the gradual improvement of the user model over time and (2) whether the NE POI can lead to better system performance.

Visual separation of relevant documents. An important attribute of Adaptive VIBE is the ability to spatially separate

Table 2: Comparison of x-coordinates of relevant and non-relevant document cluster centroids

Mean x-coord	Rel	Non-rel	diff
Overall	458.03	379.55	78.48
VIBE	414.43	372.36	42.07
VIBE+NE	492.58	397.66	94.92

relevant and non-relevant documents and place relevant document clusters closer to the user model (to the right in Figure 1). It is similar to the behavior of search systems that promote the relevant documents to the top of the lists. However, Adaptive VIBE displays the documents in a 2D space so the POIs play the equivalent role with the *top* position of the ranked lists. This feature is achieved by the layouts that spatially separate the query and the user model POIs in the visualized document space. Previous studies [2, 4] have already observed this property for keyword-only VIBE user models. In particular the separation was amplified by adding NEs to the VIBE user models in [3]. Yet the result was observed in a simulation using log data from a text-based personalized search study [7]. Therefore, we examined if the simulation results could be replicated in a user study.

For VIBE and VIBE+NE, we recorded all visualization snapshots shown to the participants during the user study and examined if the same results were observed in actual search tasks. Table 2 compares the centroid locations of relevant and non-relevant document clusters. Of course, the relevance of the documents was invisible to the user study participants and was marked for the post-study analysis. The locations represent the x-coordinates of the documents. Because the user model POIs are located to the right of the visualization and the coordinate follows the usual Java 2D coordinate system where a top-leftmost point has ($x = 0$, $y = 0$), bigger values in this table mean the centroids are located closer to the user models. It is clearly observed that the relevant document cluster centroids were formed closer to the user models (458.03 versus 379.55) than the non-relevant document clusters (Wilcoxon rank sum test, $p < 0.001$). Moreover, NE-based user models (VIBE+NE) show bigger separation (around 100 pixels) than keyword-based user models (VIBE, around 69 pixels) and the relevant document cluster in VIBE+NE is even closer to the user models than VIBE (492.58 versus 414.43). The difference is statistically significant (Kruskal-Wallis rank sum test, $p < 0.001$). This result confirms the aforementioned simulation result [3] and suggests that VIBE+NE has stronger relevant document discrimination power than baseline VIBE. Table 3 provides another metric regarding the document cluster quality. The Davies-Bouldin Validity Index (DB-index) [13] measures the clustering quality by comparing the within document-centroid distances versus between-cluster centroid distances. A smaller

Table 3: Comparison of DB-index between systems

System	VIBE	VIBE+NE	p
Overall	1.70	1.69	< 0.001

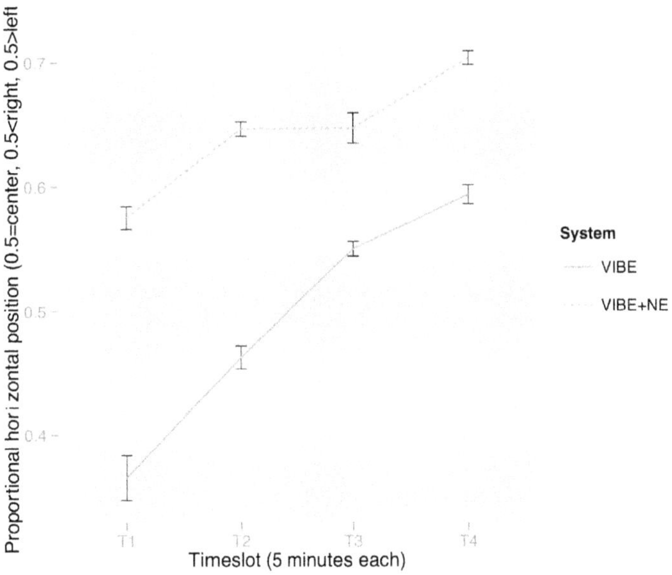

Figure 4: Movement of top-10 documents through search progress: compared by system (VIBE vs. VIBE+NE)

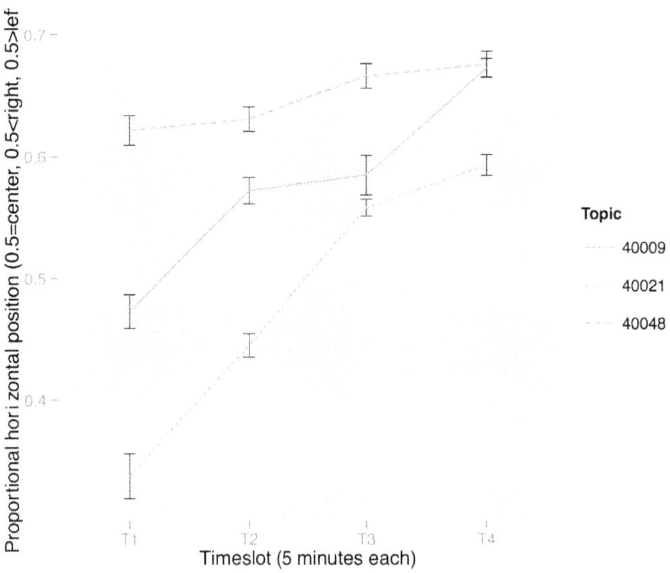

Figure 5: Movement of top-10 documents through search progress: compared by topic

DB-index value means a better clustering result. Overall, VIBE+NE shows significantly better DB-index even though the difference is small (Kruskal-Wallis rank sum test, $p < 0.001$).

Position of system recommended documents. In addition to the ability that can guide users to relevant documents closer to visual user models, Adaptive VIBE estimates document relevance by combining query-document and user model-document similarity scores. The top-most highly scored documents are painted in blue (see Figure 1), so that users can easily identify system-recommended documents. It is important to examine how these documents are represented because they are equivalent to top-10 high-scored documents in textual ranked-list based systems. Figure 4 compares how top-10 document locations change over time in VIBE and VIBE+NE. The y-axis is the relative horizontal position in the visualizations. 0.5 is the exact center of the visualization, above 0.5 is the right-half, and below 0.5 is the left-half. The 20-minute sessions are broken down into four 5 minute time-frames in order to observe temporal changes of the document locations. It is interesting to note that both VIBE and VIBE+NE show top-10 documents moving to the right-half area of the visualization (> 0.5). It means that the user model POIs placed to the right in the visualization attract the top-10 documents as the user model learns more about the user tasks. The difference between VIBE and VIBE+NE is noticeable as well. VIBE+NE could attract the top-10 documents from the very beginning of the sessions (> 0.5) and their relative positions are always closer to the user model side compared to VIBE (higher relative horizontal position). Another interesting aspect is the comparison across the three search task topics (Figure 5), which shows the consistency between the user perceived topic difficulty (See Table 8) and the location of the top-10 documents. Topic 40021 was perceived as the most difficult by the participants and it shows the least closeness to the user model side (below 0.3 in T1 and below 0.6 in T4). These results re-confirm the relationships between the visual separation of the relevant and non-relevant document clusters and their orientations to the user models.

User Performance Analysis

This section examines user performance, which represents to what extent the improved system performance (ability to guide users to relevant documents) contributed to the user performance improvement (user ability to recognize relevant documents and retrieve relevant information from them).

Open document precision. The first metric to measure the user performance is *open document* precision, which is defined as Equation 2.

$$P_{open} = \frac{|Doc_{rel}|}{|Doc_{open}|} \qquad (2)$$

It measures the fraction of relevant documents among the ones users explicitly opened and read. Table 4 shows that the users marked the same precision scores with VIBE and VIBE+NE. This means they opened relevant documents for the search tasks in the same chances across the two systems. However, if we count the number of relevant documents, the experiment system (VIBE+NE) shows higher productivity (Table 5; 315 versus 369). It is 1.64 more documents per each search session on average. This difference is not ignorable because the document open activities usually take place after a long sequence of various search activities in Adaptive VIBE such as `move_POI` and `mouseover_on_document`. A deeper investigation reveals an interesting observation. The standard deviation of VIBE+NE is greater than VIBE (7.72 versus 5.53), which suggests there may exist individual differences in terms of the number of relevant document opening actions. Figure 6 compares the CDF (cumulative distribution function) of the relevant document opening counts between VIBE and VIBE+NE. They opened almost the same number of relevant documents until document count=20. However VIBE+NE shows higher probability beyond count=20 and only VIBE+NE scores the very high level of relevant document opening count (> 22). This suggests that even though the mean open document precision does not show significant statistical difference, VIBE+NE could support high-level productive document opening actions while maintaining low- or mid- level productivity compared to VIBE.

Table 4: Open document precision

System	VIBE	VIBE+NE
Overall	0.875	0.875
40009	0.790	0.843
40021	0.897	0.935
40048	0.884	0.889

Table 5: Opened relevant documents

System	VIBE	VIBE+NE
Count	315	369
Mean	9.55	11.18
SD	5.53	7.72

Table 6: Note precision

System	VIBE	VIBE+NE	p
Overall	0.817	0.866	0.110
40009	0.769	0.784	0.66
40021	0.789	0.888	<0.001
40048	0.865	0.931	1

User generated note precision. Note precision measures the precision of user notes in the "Task Model Notebook" at the passage level whereas the previous analysis investigated the document level precision. The passage level precision was calculated as in [7, 16, 4]. Table 6 compares the note precision between VIBE and VIBE+NE. The overall mean scores does not show significant difference (Kruskal-Wallis rank sum test). However, if we break down the note precision by topic, VIBE+NE shows significantly better performance with Topic 40021 ($p < 0.001$). Topic 40021 was the most difficult topic either subjectively perceived by the participants (See Table 8) or estimated objectively by tracking the locations of the top-10 documents (See the System Performance Analysis section).

User Model Manipulation versus Search Performance

Previous studies on open user modeling have shown that user model content manipulation could harm the search performance [24, 6]. However the result was derived from an one-dimensional text-based user model and we attempt to re-examine 2-dimensional visual user model manipulation effects with Adaptive VIBE. In Adaptive VIBE, the most evident user model manipulation action is *moving POIs*. As explained in the previous sections, the documents are placed

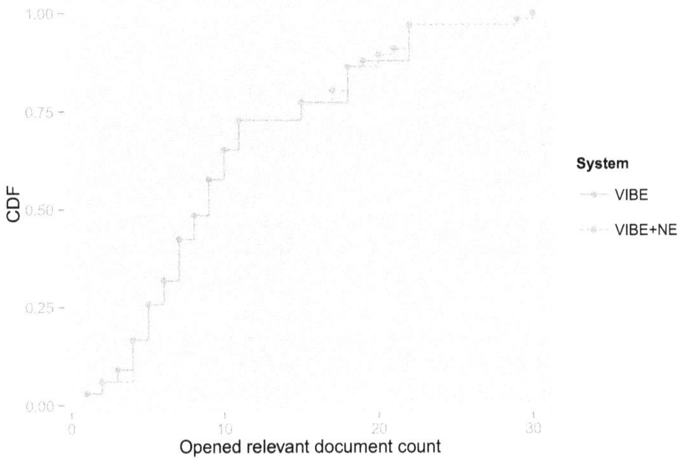

Figure 6: Comparison of relevant document open count

closer to more similar POIs in Adaptive VIBE and their positions are updated dynamically while users drag related POIs. This dynamic visualization feature can let users manipulate the layout of the user model POIs and instantly learn the effect of the manipulation on the retrieved documents. Therefore, we compared the participants' POI movement (or POI dragging) event counts with system and user precision. System precision was calculated as the precision of top-10 documents and user precision was calculated as the precision of user opened documents. Figure 7 shows the correlation between POI manipulation counts and system/user precision. The regression lines suggest no statistical evidence that POI manipulation degraded system or user performance. Figure 8 and 9 break down the overall correlations into keyword POI and NE POI correlations respectively. Among them only keyword-user precision shows significantly negative result (Figure 8 (below), $p = 0.0179$). However the system precision (Figure 8 (above)) still does not show any significant degradation. It suggests the system could maintain high performance regardless of user POI manipulation but the users eventually made wrong decisions. In fact the R-square score is relatively low ($R^2 = 0.179$) and the graph shows that a few outliers resulted in negative results. Moreover NE POI manipulations show no performance degradation (Figure 9), which hints at the advantages of semantic named-entities during the user manipulation of visual user model elements. These analyses suggest that the visualization-based open user model manipulation could overcome the disadvantage of the text-based open and editable user modeling, which was observed in the previous studies.

Table 7: Subjective feedback: positive reactions

System	VIBE	VIBE+NE
Average Score	3.18	3.39
SD	0.98	0.93
Positive count	4	9

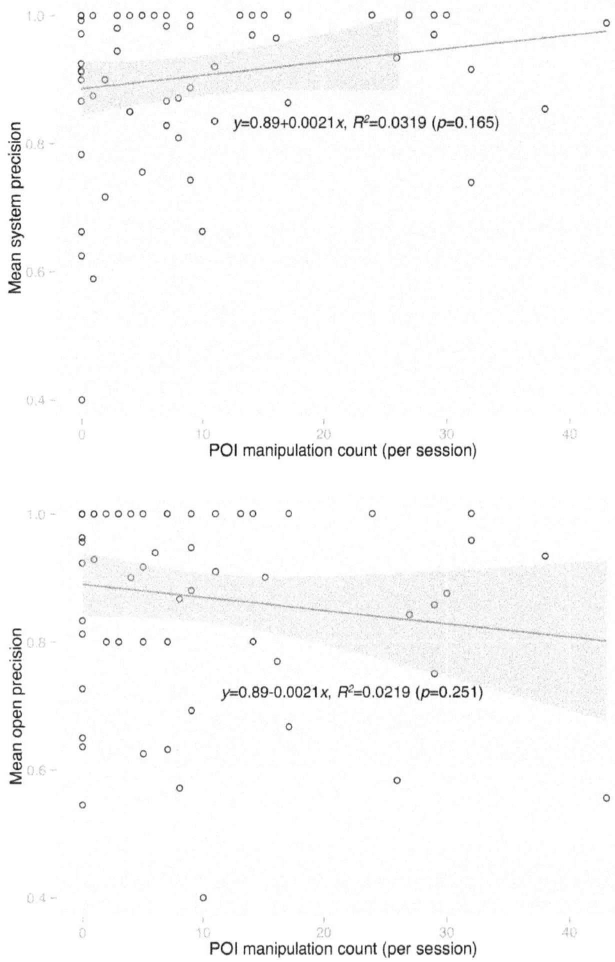

Figure 7: POI movement versus performance (all POIs)

Table 8: Subjective feedback: topic difficulty

Topic	40009	40021	40048
Mean Topic Difficulty	2.77	3.27	2.68

Subjective Feedback

We asked the participants to rate VIBE and VIBE+NE in the 5-point Likert scale (1=dislike, 5=like). The average difference was close to significant between the two systems (Table 7, Kruskal-Wallis rank sum test, $p = 0.053$). Table 7 also compares relative positive reactions, showing how many subjects preferred VIBE or VIBE+NE. More participants (9) preferred VIBE+NE to VIBE (4) when they were not tied (20). Table 8 compares topic difficulty scores returned by the participants (1=easy, 5=difficult). Despite our attempt to make the three topic difficulties equivalent, the participants perceived differences. The most difficult topic was 40021 and the easiest one was 40048. This result was statistically significant (Kruskal Wallis rank sum test, $p = 0.032$).

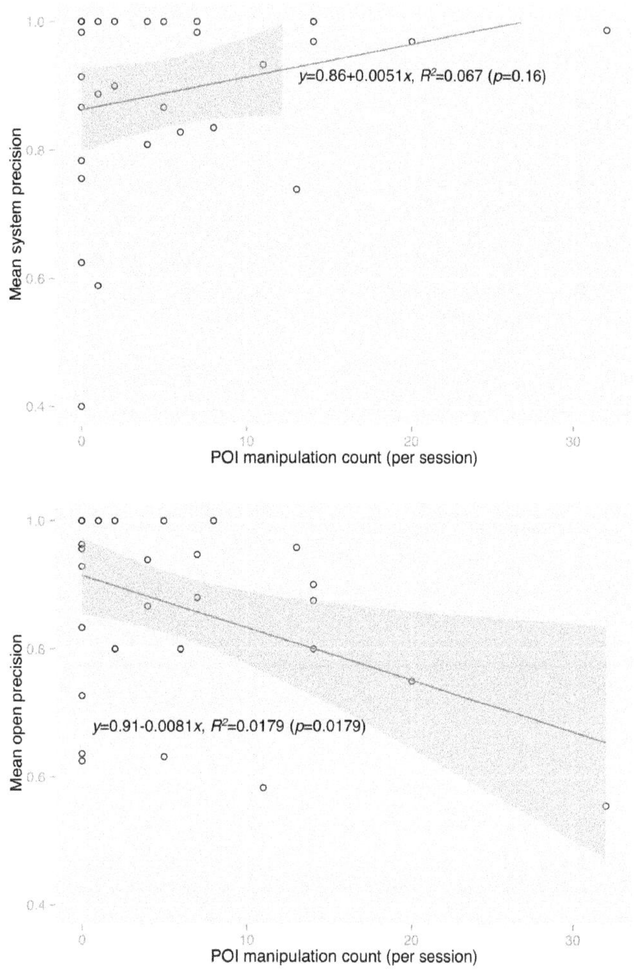

Figure 8: POI movement versus performance (Keyword POIs)

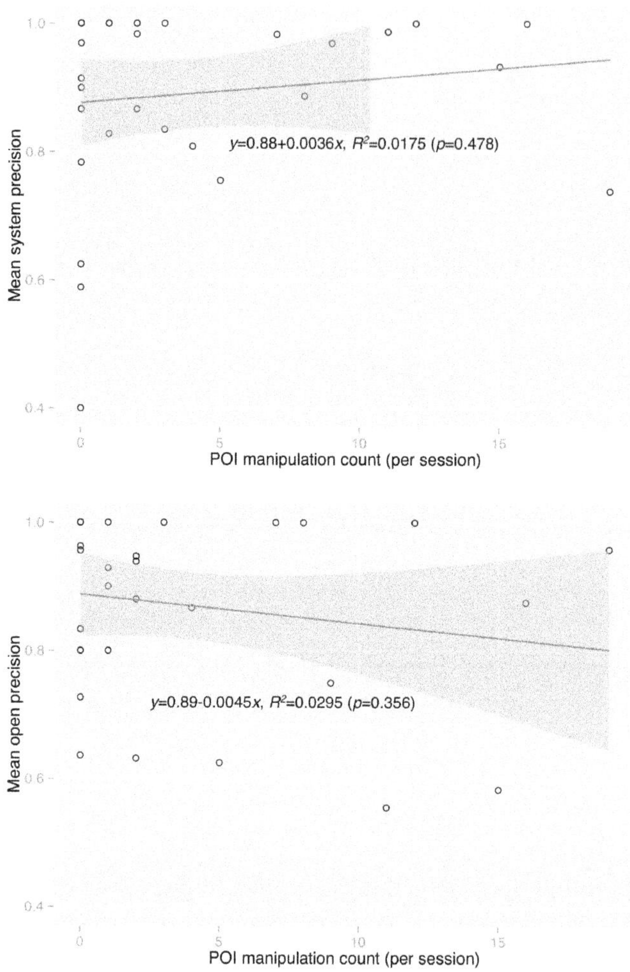

Figure 9: POI movement versus performance (NE POIs)

CONCLUSIONS

This study re-examined the value of open and editable user models in the context of adaptive search. While early studies indicated that any manipulations with an open user model cam harm the performance of an adaptive search system, more recent research [10, 15] indicated that a combination of semantic-level open user models with a visual 2D drag-and-drop interface to manipulate these models might lead to positive results. In our study we attempted to separately assess the value of semantic-level modeling and a visual interface in a news access domain where the original negative results were obtained. Unlike the cited earlier studies that focused on user subjective parameters, our study examined a range of different aspects with the main focus on system and user performance issues.

The results of the study provide several arguments in favor of concept-level open user models with advanced 2D visualization. The analysis of the system performance indicated that the visual open user models ensured a considerable level of visual separation between relevant and non-relevant documents with the semantic-level open model delivering a significantly better performance. A time-based analysis demonstrated that the separation of the relevant documents could be attributed to the presence of the user model: the system ability to move relevant documents to the user focus was gradually improved over the session duration as the quality of user model improved by accumulating more information about user interests. Again, the semantic-level open user model delivered a considerably better performance than the pure keyword-level model. We also showed that the user model manipulation in our 2D visualization did not harm the system performance at all, by comparing users' actual POI manipulation counts and the performance measures.

In brief, the study provided additional evidence that, in contrast to the traditional text-based open user models, visual 2D open user models with direct manipulation could be beneficial in the adaptive search context. Our data confirms several benefits while failing to connect user model manipulation with decreased performance. In combination with the earlier work in two different domains [10, 15] our result hints that rich 2D representation together with drag-and-drop manipulation might break the usefulness barrier of open user models in search context. In addition, the study demonstrated the added value of semantic-level models. We believe that along with the cited recent work, this study opens a new page in the exploration of open user models in adaptive search.

At the same time, by the very nature of this study, it has some limitations. Since the study simulated the work of professional information analysts, we recruited subjects with higher level of information retrieval proficiency. Even though no performance difference was found between participants with different educational backgrounds and computing skills, it is not clear whether the more general public will be as comfortable with sophisticated and novel visualizations as our subjects. More studies with less technology-proficient audience are required to understand the broader applicability of or our approach. It is also likely that more work will be required to reduce the complexity of the visual interaction mechanism. We leave this for the future work. In addition, just two kinds of visual models were explored along with three kinds of semantic entities for modeling. We believe that more approaches should be explored to discover the true value of different open user models and to determine what kind of open models could be the best in each specific search context.

REFERENCES

1. Abel, F., Gao, Q., Houben, G.-J., and Tao, K. Analyzing user modeling on twitter for personalized news recommendations. In *User Modeling, Adaption and Personalization*, J. Konstan, R. Conejo, J. Marzo, and N. Oliver, Eds., vol. 6787 of *Lecture Notes in Computer Science*. Springer Berlin Heidelberg, 2011, 1–12.
2. Ahn, J., and Brusilovsky, P. Adaptive visualization of search results: Bringing user models to visual analytics. *Information Visualization 8*, 3 (2009), 167–179.
3. Ahn, J., and Brusilovsky, P. Can concept-based user modeling improve adaptive visualization? In *18th International Conference on User Modeling, Adaptation, and Personalization (UMAP 2010)* (2010), 4–15.
4. Ahn, J., and Brusilovsky, P. Adaptive visualization for exploratory information retrieval. *Information Processing & Management 49*, 5 (2013), 1139 – 1164.
5. Ahn, J., Brusilovsky, P., Grady, J., He, D., and Florian, R. Semantic annotation based exploratory search for information analysts. *Information Processing and Management 46*, 4 (July 2010), 383–402.
6. Ahn, J., Brusilovsky, P., Grady, J., He, D., and Syn, S. Y. Open user profiles for adaptive news systems: help or harm? In *WWW '07: Proceedings of the 16th international conference on World Wide Web*, ACM Press (New York, NY, USA, 2007), 11–20.
7. Ahn, J., Brusilovsky, P., He, D., Grady, J., and Li, Q. Personalized web exploration with task models. In *WWW '08: Proceedings of the 17th international conference on World Wide Web*, ACM (New York, NY, USA, 2008), 1–10.
8. Aktolga, E., Jain, A., and Velipasaoglu, E. Building rich user search queries profiles. In *User Modeling, Adaptation, and Personalization*, S. Carberry, S. Weibelzahl, A. Micarelli, and G. Semeraro, Eds., vol. 7899 of *Lecture Notes in Computer Science*. Springer Berlin Heidelberg, 2013, 254–266.
9. Bakalov, F., König-Ries, B., Nauerz, A., and Welsch, M. IntrospectiveViews: An Interface for Scrutinizing Semantic User Models. *18th International Conference on User Modeling, Adaptation, and Personalization (UMAP 2010)* (2010), 219–230.
10. Bakalov, F., Meurs, M.-J., König-Ries, B., Sateli, B., Witte, R., Butler, G., and Tsang, A. An approach to controlling user models and personalization effects in recommender systems. In *Proceedings of the 2013 international conference on Intelligent user interfaces*, IUI '13, ACM (New York, NY, USA, 2013), 49–56.
11. Bull, S. Supporting learning with open learner models. In *4th Hellenic Conference on Information and Communication Technologies in Education,* (September 29 - October 3 2004), 47–61.
12. Bull, S., Brna, P., and Pain, H. Extending the scope of the student model. *User Modeling and User-Adapted Interaction 5*, 1 (1995), 45–65.
13. Davies, D. L., and Bouldin, D. W. A cluster separation measure. *IEEE Transactions on Pattern Analysis and Machine Intelligence PAMI*, 2 (January 2009), 224–227.
14. Dimitrova, V., Self, J., and Brna, P. Applying interactive open learner models to learning technical terminology. In *User Modeling 2001*, M. Bauer, P. Gmytrasiewicz, and J. Vassileva, Eds., vol. 2109 of *Lecture Notes in Computer Science*. Springer Berlin Heidelberg, 2001, 148–157.
15. Glowacka, D., Ruotsalo, T., Konuyshkova, K., Athukorala, k., Kaski, S., and Jacucci, G. Directing exploratory search: reinforcement learning from user interactions with keywords. In *Proceedings of the 2013 international conference on Intelligent user interfaces*, IUI '13, ACM (New York, NY, USA, 2013), 117–128.
16. He, D., Brusilovsky, P., Ahn, J., Grady, J., Farzan, R., Peng, Y., Yang, Y., and Rogati, M. An evaluation of adaptive filtering in the context of realistic task-based information exploration. *Information Processing & Management 44*, 2 (March 2008), 511–533.
17. Lehmann, S., Schwanecke, U., and Dörner, R. Interactive visualization for opportunistic exploration of large document collections. *Information Systems 35*, 2 (2010), 260–269.
18. Lin, Y., Ahn, J.-W., Brusilovsky, P., He, D., and Real, W. Imagesieve: Exploratory search of museum archives with named entity-based faceted browsing. *Proceedings of the American Society for Information Science and Technology 47*, 1 (2010), 1–10.

19. Olsen, K. A., Korfhage, R. R., Sochats, K. M., Spring, M. B., and Williams, J. G. Visualization of a document collection: the vibe system. *Information Processing & Management 29*, 1 (1993), 69–81.

20. Petkova, D., and Croft, B. W. Proximity-based document representation for named entity retrieval. In *CIKM '07: Proceedings of the sixteenth ACM conference on Conference on information and knowledge management*, ACM (New York, NY, USA, 2007), 731–740.

21. Pirolli, P., and Card, S. The sensemaking process and leverage points for analyst technology as identified through cognitive task analysis. In *Proceedings of International Conference on Intelligence Analysis* (2005), 2–4.

22. Sekine, S. Named entity: History and future. *New York University* (2004).

23. Strohman, T., Metzler, D., Turtle, H., and Croft, W. B. Indri: A language model-based search engine for complex queries. In *Proceedings of the International Conference on Intelligent Analysis*, vol. 2, Citeseer (2005), 2–6.

24. Wærn, A. User involvement in automatic filtering: An experimental study. *User Modeling and User-Adapted Interaction V14*, 2 (June 2004), 201–237.

25. Wahlster, W., and Kobsa, A. *User models in dialog systems*. Springer, 1989.

26. Wasinger, R., Wallbank, J., Pizzato, L., Kay, J., Kummerfeld, B., Böhmer, M., and Krüger, A. Scrutable user models and personalised item recommendation in mobile lifestyle applications. In *User Modeling, Adaptation, and Personalization*, S. Carberry, S. Weibelzahl, A. Micarelli, and G. Semeraro, Eds., vol. 7899 of *Lecture Notes in Computer Science*. Springer Berlin Heidelberg, 2013, 77–88.

27. Weber, G., Brusilovsky, P., et al. Elm-art: An adaptive versatile system for web-based instruction. *International Journal of Artificial Intelligence in Education (IJAIED) 12* (2001), 351–384.

28. Zapata-Rivera, J.-D. Supporting negotiated assessment using open student models. In *User Modeling 2001*, M. Bauer, P. Gmytrasiewicz, and J. Vassileva, Eds., vol. 2109 of *Lecture Notes in Computer Science*. Springer Berlin Heidelberg, 2001, 295–297.

Learning Higher-Order Interactions for User and Item Profiling Based on Tensor Factorization

Xiaoyu Tang, Yue Xu, Shlomo Geva
Queensland University of Technology,
Brisbane, Australia
xiaoyu.tang@connect.qut.edu.au, {yue.xu, s.geva}@qut.edu.au

ABSTRACT

User profiling techniques play a central role in many Recommender Systems (RS). In recent years, multidimensional data are getting increasing attention for making recommendations. Additional metadata help algorithms better understanding users' behaviors and decisions. Existing user/item profiling techniques for Collaborative Filtering (CF) RS in multidimensional environment mostly analyze data through splitting the multidimensional relations. However, this leads to the loss of multidimensionality in user-item interactions; whereas the interactions are naturally multidimensional since users' choices are often affected by contextual information. In this paper, we propose a unified profiling approach which models users/items with latent higher-order interaction factors. We demonstrate that the proposed profiling approach is intimately related to two-dimensional profiling based on Matrix Factorization techniques. We further propose to integrate the profiling approach into three neighborhood-based CF recommenders for item recommendation. Finally, we empirically show on real-world social tagging datasets that the proposed recommenders outperform state-of-the-art CF recommendation approaches in accuracy.

Author Keywords

User profiling; higher-order interactions; tensor factorization; recommender systems; collaborative filtering.

ACM Classification Keywords

H.3.3. Information Search and Retrieval: Information filtering

General Terms

Algorithms; Performance; Experimentation.

IUI'15, March 29 - April 01, 2015, Atlanta, GA, USA.

ACM 978-1-4503-3306-1/15/03…$15.00
http://dx.doi.org/10.1145/2678025.2701369

INTRODUCTION

Multidimensional data is becoming a goldmine for web personalization and Recommender Systems (RS) in recent years. For example, in Social Tagging Systems (STS), users employ self-defined keywords to organize content voluntarily. Also, mobile techniques and the recent wearable techniques are vigorously promoting the use of context-aware applications [26]. In these typical settings users' decisions are often related to multiple contextual variables. Against this background, user profiling and recommendation techniques need to consider the multifaceted nature of users' choices and decisions in order to provide desirable services.

Collaborative Filtering (CF) RS for multidimensional data can be mostly categorized into two families: neighborhood-based methods and Tensor Factorization (TF) models. TF models [13, 24, 29] discover holistic latent relations between all dimensions to predict new user-item correlations. However TF models usually do not create or use user profiles explicitly. Also, they are limited when considering strong localized relations which instead are the natural specialty of neighborhood-based approaches. For neighborhood-based CF which focuses on neighborhood relations, various ways to utilize multidimensional data in user/item profiling have been proposed, which are mostly based on explicit mapping from multidimensional to two-dimensional spaces [20, 23, 31]. However, the dimension mapping solutions result in the loss of holistic interactions between all dimensions. This leads to less accurate user profiles and recommendations. Despite the various recommendation models proposed for multidimensional context, they essentially only emphasize on partial structures of data.

Traditionally content-based profiling approaches modeling users/items as weighted keywords, semantic networks or ontologies are widely used in content-based filtering recommender systems [21] and web personalization [9]. However, in this paper we focus on collaborative filtering. For neighborhood-based CF, traditionally user/item profiles are constructed from user-item matrix built on implicit or explicit user feedback. With multidimensional data, most user/item profiling techniques explicitly split and convert the multidimensional relations into vector spaces so as to employ conventional CF approaches. This however discards the holistic interrelations between the dimensions and thus cannot preserve the multidimensionality nature of users' decisions and choices. Also, since most of these user/item profiles are created one-by-one, the profiling and updating procedure can be very time- and resource-consuming.

To the best of our knowledge, there has not been any profiling research in neighborhood-based CF which preserves higher-order interactions, while this can represent users more holistically than the projection-based vector representations. Also, the existing multidimensional TF based recommendation approaches do not incorporate localized neighborhood and latent holistic interactions simultaneously. These two are the motivations of our work. In this paper, we propose a unified user/item profiling approach based on TF and further propose modified CF recommendation algorithms based on that. Our contributions are as follows:

- We propose a unified profiling approach for multidimensional data which accurately models users/items with latent higher-order interaction factors. The proposed profiling approach is straightforwardly extendable to N-dimensional data and generalizable to entities other than users and items.
- We prove that the proposed profiling approach is a compatible higher-order extension of the conventional user/item profiling approaches based on Singular Value Decomposition (SVD) and based on Eigenvalue Decomposition (EVD).
- We present three neighborhood-based CF approaches based on the proposed profiling approach. They incorporate holistic latent relations and different local neighborhood relations for making more accurate recommendations.

Extensive experiments showed that the proposed profiling method helps achieve substantially improved performance in top-N item recommendation task. In the rest of this paper, we first provide a brief discussion of the related work. We then introduce our unified profiling approach and three enhanced CF algorithms. Finally we present our experiments and the results.

RELATED WORK

Various efforts have been made to incorporate more dimensions of information in user-item interactions for user profiling and item recommendations. Neighborhood-based CF and TF models are two most important categories in the CF field in recent years.

Marinho et al. [23] discussed how traditional neighborhood-based CF can be applied for making recommendations with multidimensional data through dimension projection. They referred to this type of approaches as projection-based CF. The approaches that fall into this category usually explicitly project data to two-dimensional spaces for user profiling and neighborhood formation. Tso-Sutter et al. [31] proposed to extend user-item matrix with tags through projection for better profiling users/items. A fusion algorithm is applied to unify two neighborhood-based CF. Liang et al. [20] proposed to construct tag-based user profiles in CF through splitting the ternary relations between users, items and tags in STS to find personalized semantic meaning of each tag. Tagommenders [27] predicts users' item preferences based on their inferred preferences for tags. They combine tag preference inference algorithms with tag-aware recommenders and showed that their approach outperforms classic CF algorithms. Although focused on three-dimensional user-item-tag data, these approaches discard the nature of multimodal user-item interactions and cannot directly utilize more dimensions of information. Besides, most of these approaches do not incorporate latent multidimensional relations in the data. These disadvantages limit their recommendation capacity. Differently, our profiling approach tackles this problem by decomposing the multidimensional relations and retaining the refined higher-order interaction factors in profiles. Our recommendation approaches differ with them in that our approaches incorporate latent higher-order relations and localized neighborhood relations at the same time.

Different to neighborhood-based CF, TF models exploit holistic latent relations for making recommendations. Multiverse Recommendation [13] utilizes Tucker model for context-aware item recommendations. Time is used as the context in their model. Factorization Machines (FM) [25] also targets on context-aware rating prediction and it can be computed in linear time with the number of context variables and the factorization size. However, these models target on rating prediction and do not model users explicitly, which is different with our work. Rendle et al. [24] proposed a post-based ranking interpretation scheme for better interpreting social tagging data and a Ranking with Tensor Factorization (RTF) model for optimizing tag recommendation. Symeonidis et al. [29] introduced a unified framework for making recommendations in STS based on Higher-Order Singular Value Decomposition (HOSVD). Although these approaches effectively employ the higher-order relations of data, they neglect the localized relations which mostly represent the specialty of the approaches based on nearest neighborhoods. Strong local neighborhood relations can make up a sound complement to holistic latent relations for item recommendation, which has been studied with MF models for rating prediction task [4, 16]. In addition, neighborhood specially facilitates user-to-user recommendation based on shared interests [5], such as the "Neighbours" function in Last.fm. Our profiling approach has a strong relation with the TF models in that our profiling approach analyses the multidimensionality of user tagging behavior based on a Tucker model. However, different to the TF recommendation models, our recommendation approaches also employ neighborhood relations for better recommendation quality.

BACKGROUND OVERVIEW

Tensors and Tucker Models

In this subsection, we introduce some concepts of tensors and the Tucker model.

Tensors. A tensor is a multidimensional matrix. The order of a tensor is the number of dimensions or modes. An *N*th-order tensor $\mathcal{X}$ is denoted as $\mathcal{X} \in \mathbb{R}^{I_1 \times \cdots \times I_N}$.

Tensor unfoldings. An *N*th-order tensor $\mathcal{X}$ can be unfolded as a matrix by the nth mode [7], denoted as $\mathcal{X}_{(n)}$. This operation is also called matricization, which is the process of reordering the elements of an *N*th-order tensor into a matrix [1, 15]. Formally, in the mode-n matricization $\mathcal{X}_{(n)}$ of an *N*th-order tensor $\mathcal{X} \in \mathbb{R}^{I_1 \times \cdots \times I_N}$, the tensor element $(i_1, \cdots, i_n, \cdots, i_N)$ maps to the matrix element (i_n, j) [15], where

$$j = 1 + \sum_{\substack{k=1 \\ k \neq n}}^{N} (i_k - 1) J_k \tag{1}$$

in which $J_k = \prod_{\substack{m=1 \\ m \neq n}}^{k-1} I_m$, $1 \leq n \leq N$.

***n*-mode product of a tensor by a matrix**. The n-mode product of an Nth-order tensor $\mathcal{X} \in \mathbb{R}^{I_1 \times I_2 \times \cdots \times I_N}$ with a matrix $\mathcal{Q} \in \mathbb{R}^{J \times I_n}$ [7] is an Nth-order tensor, denoted by $\mathcal{X} \times_n \mathcal{Q}$. The element of the product is calculated as:

$$(\mathcal{X} \times_n \mathcal{Q})_{i_1, \cdots, i_{n-1}, j, i_{n+1}, \cdots, i_N} = \sum_{i_n=1}^{I_n} (\mathcal{X})_{i_1, \cdots, i_n, \cdots, i_N} (\mathcal{Q})_{j, i_n} \tag{2}$$

where $(\mathcal{X})_{i_1, \cdots, i_n, \cdots, i_N}$ and $(\mathcal{Q})_{j, i_n}$ are the elements of $\mathcal{X}$ and $\mathcal{Q}$ respectively. The n-mode product $\mathcal{Y} = \mathcal{X} \times_n \mathcal{Q}$ has the following unfolding form [15]:

$$\mathcal{Y} = \mathcal{X} \times_n \mathcal{Q} \Leftrightarrow \mathcal{Y}_{(n)} = \mathcal{Q} \cdot \mathcal{X}_{(n)} \tag{3}$$

Tucker model. Tucker model [17, 22] is a higher-order generalization of SVD for tensors. Tucker model was first introduced by Tucker in 1960s [32, 33]. The Tucker decomposition is a form of higher-order PCA [15]. It decomposes an *N*th-order tensor $\mathcal{X}$ into a core tensor $\mathcal{S}$ multiplied by a component matrix along each mode:

$$\mathcal{X} = \mathcal{S} \times_1 \mathcal{U}^{(1)} \times_2 \mathcal{U}^{(2)} \times_3 \cdots \times_N \mathcal{U}^{(N)} \tag{4}$$

where the mode-n component matrix $\mathcal{U}^{(n)}$ is a matrix often assumed to have orthonormal column vectors.

Higher-Order Singular Value Decomposition (HOSVD) [7] is an algorithm of Tucker model, in which the mode-n component matrix $\mathcal{U}^{(n)}$ is computed as the left singular vectors of the SVD of $\mathcal{X}_{(n)}$, and the core tensor is:

$$\mathcal{S} = \mathcal{X} \times_1 \left(\mathcal{U}^{(1)}\right)^T \times_2 \left(\mathcal{U}^{(2)}\right)^T \times_3 \cdots \times_N \left(\mathcal{U}^{(N)}\right)^T \tag{5}$$

For third-order tensors, the terms Tucker3, Tucker2, and Tucker1 have been coined [18]. Equation (4) with $N = 3$ is the Tucker3 model. Tucker2 is a variation of Tucker3 where one of the component matrices is an identity matrix. For instance, a Tucker2 model is

$$\mathcal{X} = \mathcal{S} \times_1 \mathcal{U}^{(1)} \times_2 \mathcal{U}^{(2)} \times_3 I^{(3)} = \mathcal{S} \times_1 \mathcal{U}^{(1)} \times_2 \mathcal{U}^{(2)} \tag{6}$$

Similarly, the Tucker1 model sets two of the component matrices to be identity matrices. For example, if the second and third component matrices are the identity matrices, then we have

$$\mathcal{X} = \mathcal{S} \times_1 \mathcal{U}^{(1)} \times_2 I^{(2)} \times_3 I^{(3)} = \mathcal{S} \times_1 \mathcal{U}^{(1)} \tag{7}$$

These concepts extend easily to the N-way case, i.e., we can set any subset of the component matrices to the identity matrix [15].

User/Item Profiling Approaches Based on Matrix Factorization on User-Item Matrix

Traditionally some two-dimensional CF approaches apply SVD on user-item matrix to compute user/item profiles and identify similar users/items [30, 36]. In these approaches, user-item matrix $\mathcal{M} \in \mathbb{R}^{|U| \times |I|}$ is decomposed and approximated by the truncated SVD:

$$\mathcal{M}_{|U| \times |I|} \approx \widehat{\mathcal{M}}_{|U| \times |I|} = \mathcal{U}_{|U| \times k} \cdot \mathcal{S}_{k \times k} \cdot \left(\mathcal{V}_{|I| \times k}\right)^T \tag{8}$$

Taking user-based CF for example, $\mathcal{U}_{|U| \times k} \cdot \mathcal{S}_{k \times k}$ is used to project each user's data from an $|I|$-dimensional space to a k-dimensional space, where k principal components of the data are preserved. Thus the user profile matrix in the SVD-based user profiling is computed as:

$$\mathcal{SUP}_{|U| \times k} = \mathcal{U}_{|U| \times k} \cdot \mathcal{S}_{k \times k} \tag{9}$$

Each row in the user profile matrix $\mathcal{SUP}_{|U| \times k}$ is a user's profile in the k-dimensional space. That is, the vth user u_v's profile $UP^{\mathcal{SUP}}(u_v)$ is defined as:

$$UP^{\mathcal{SUP}}(u_v) = \left(\mathcal{SUP}_{|U| \times k}\right)_{v,:} \tag{10}$$

A colon is used to indicate all elements of a dimension. Then, user similarities can be computed in the reduced k-dimensional vector space.

A different MF approach for user/item profiling is based on Eigenvalue Decomposition (EVD), e.g., Eigentaste algorithm [10], which uses the EVD of covariance matrix $\mathcal{M}^T \cdot \mathcal{M}$:

$$\left(\mathcal{M}_{|U| \times |I|}\right)^T \cdot \mathcal{M}_{|U| \times |I|} = \mathcal{V}_{|I| \times |I|} \cdot \left(\mathcal{S}_{|I| \times |I|}\right)^2 \cdot \left(\mathcal{V}_{|I| \times |I|}\right)^{-1} \tag{11}$$

Then the user profile matrix $\mathcal{EUP}_{|U| \times k}$ is computed by:

$$\mathcal{EUP}_{|U| \times k} = \mathcal{M}_{|U| \times |I|} \cdot \mathcal{V}_{|I| \times k} \tag{12}$$

where k is the dimension reduction parameter.

THE PROPOSED PROFILING APPROACH

In this section, we propose a unified profiling approach for modelling entities (e.g., users, items) in multidimensional data with reduced higher-order interaction factors. In the following, we first define some key concepts related to the social tagging data scenario and recommendation which will be used in the rest of this paper. Then, the procedure of the proposed profiling approach is introduced in four steps. Finally, we reveal the inherent relevance of our profiling approach with the MF-based profiling approaches for user-item matrix.

Definitions

For the sake of simplicity, we frame the proposed approaches for multidimensional data in the context of STS, in which three dimensions are usually given: user, item and tag. We define U, I and T as disjoint non-empty finite sets, in which the elements are users, items and tags respectively. We define the following concepts for the rest of the paper:

- **Tag assignments**. The basic tagging behavior, namely tag assignment, is defined as a 3-tuple $e: U \times I \times T \in \{0,1\}$. If user u_v collected item i_j with tag t_p, then $e_{u_v,i_j,t_p} = 1$, otherwise $e_{u_v,i_j,t_p} = 0$.
- **Item preferences**. An item preference with respect to a user, denoted by $p(u_w, i_j)$, represents the measure of user u_w's interest in a used item i_j. We define the item preference for social tagging data: $p(u_w, i_j) = 1$ if user u_w collected item i_j with at least one tag, otherwise $p(u_w, i_j) = 0$ indicating that the interest of user u_w to item i_j is unknown.
- **Predicted item preferences**. For user u_w, a predicted item preference $\hat{p}(u_w, i_k)$ is computed for an unused item i_k. This value is used for ranking the top-N item recommendations for user u_w.

A Unified Profiling Approach Based on Tucker Model in Third-Order Tensor

Our profiling approach first models the social tagging data as a third-order tensor, then extracts principal components for each mode of the tensor. Based on this, we proceed to compress the initial tensor to a reduced multilinear subspace, from which we create the profiles of users/items with reduced higher-order interaction factors.

Initial Tensor Construction for Social Tagging Data

We model the social tagging data as a third-order tensor $\mathcal{A} \in \mathbb{R}^{|U|\times|I|\times|T|}$. In this paper, we specify the user, item and tag dimensions as the first, second and third mode of $\mathcal{A}$ respectively. In $\mathcal{A}$, a tensor element with indices (v, j, p) is associated with a value $(\mathcal{A})_{v,j,p}$, which is defined as:

$$(\mathcal{A})_{v,j,p} = \begin{cases} 1, & if\ e_{u_v,i_j,t_p} = 1 \\ 0, & otherwise \end{cases}$$

In the next, we unfold the tensor $\mathcal{A}$ to reveal the initial ternary interactions against each of the tensor modes.

Tensor Unfoldings

As discussed, a tensor can be matricized using Equation (1). Figure 1 shows the mode-1 unfolding of $\mathcal{A}$, denoted as $\mathcal{A}_{(1)} \in \mathbb{R}^{|U|\times|I||T|}$, which is the unfolding of the tensor against the first mode. Each row in $\mathcal{A}_{(1)}$ corresponds to all tag assignments of a user. Note the order of the columns in $\mathcal{A}_{(n)}$ is trivial as long as it is consistent across all users.

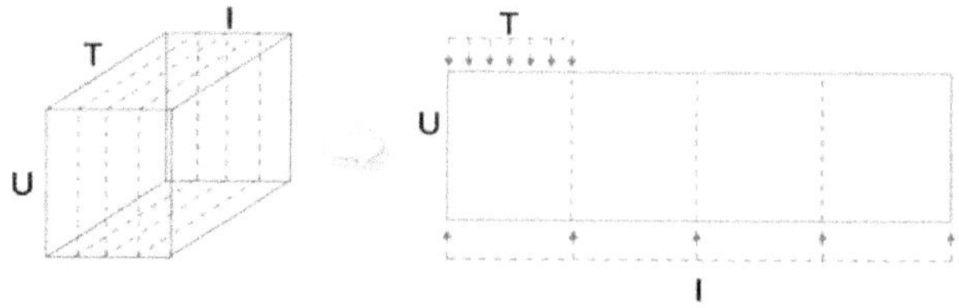

Figure 1. Mode-1 matricization of the tensor $\mathcal{A}$.

Analogously, we can unfold the tensor $\mathcal{A}$ by the item and tag mode, from which we obtain the other two unfolding matrices: $\mathcal{A}_{(2)}$ and $\mathcal{A}_{(3)}$, where each row corresponds to an item and a tag respectively.

Application of SVD on Each Mode

The three tensor unfoldings $\mathcal{A}_{(1)}$, $\mathcal{A}_{(2)}$ and $\mathcal{A}_{(3)}$ represent the mode-wise matrix forms of the original data. For example, each row in $\mathcal{A}_{(1)}$ corresponds to one user and consists of all tag assignments of this user. However, the three matrices are too sparse and noisy for directly revealing relations between the three dimensions. We apply SVD on each of the three unfoldings to obtain the component matrices of each mode. In the following, we take $\mathcal{A}_{(1)}$ as an example of the three.

The following equation is the full SVD of $\mathcal{A}_{(1)}$:

$$\mathcal{A}_{(1)} = \mathcal{U}^{(1)}_{|U|\times|U|} \cdot \mathcal{S}^{(1)}_{|U|\times|I||T|} \cdot \left(\mathcal{V}^{(1)}_{|I||T|\times|I||T|}\right)^T \quad (13)$$

In the decomposition, the columns of $\mathcal{U}^{(1)}_{|U|\times|U|}$ are the left singular vectors, which are the orthonormal bases of the users in the matrix $\mathcal{A}_{(1)}$. We call the orthonormal matrix $\mathcal{U}^{(1)}_{|U|\times|U|}$ the user component matrix.

In matrix dimensionality reduction, low-rank approximation is used to filter out the small singular values that introduce noises or less relevant information, where the SVD of a matrix is truncated to a number of top largest singular values and the corresponding singular vectors. The rank-k_u approximation of $\mathcal{A}_{(1)}$, i.e., the truncated SVD is:

$$\hat{\mathcal{A}}_{(1)} = \mathcal{U}^{(1)}_{|U|\times k_u} \cdot \mathcal{S}^{(1)}_{k_u\times k_u} \cdot \left(\mathcal{V}^{(1)}_{|I||T|\times k_u}\right)^T \quad (14)$$

Similarly, for $\mathcal{A}_{(2)}$ and $\mathcal{A}_{(3)}$, we can compute the rank-k_i item component matrix $\mathcal{U}^{(2)}_{|I|\times k_i}$, and rank-$k_t$ tag component matrix $\mathcal{U}^{(3)}_{|T|\times k_t}$. In the next step we will employ the user component matrix, the item component matrix and the tag component matrix, in the proposed profiling approach for dimension reduction.

User/Item Profiling as Third-Order Interaction Models

In this subsection, we propose a method for modelling users/items in the third-order tensor of social tagging data based on the Tucker Model (TM).

The information of each user in the initial tensor $\mathcal{A}$ is about what tags were used by the user to collect which items, that is, a matrix representing the explicit item-tag relations with

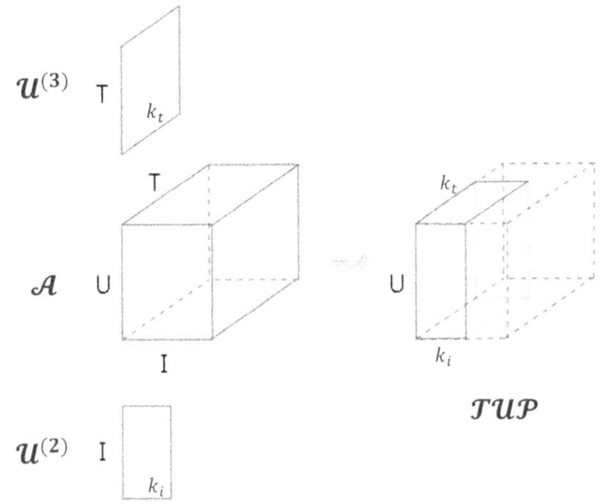

Figure 2. TM-based user profiling.

respect to that user. The fact that this matrix is large and sparse makes it very inaccurate, insufficient and inefficient to be used for user profiling directly. Factorization models often assume the interactions between different dimensions can be reduced into a smaller number of factors.

For the third-order tensor $\mathcal{A} \in \mathbb{R}^{|U|\times|I|\times|T|}$ where user, item and tag are the three modes, we propose to multiply the tensor $\mathcal{A}$ with the item and tag component matrices for modeling users in a reduced second-order subspace. We refer to this profiling method as TM-based user profiling, which is given as follows:

$$\mathcal{TUP}_{|U|\times k_i\times k_t} = \mathcal{A}_{|U|\times|I|\times|T|} \times_2 \left(\mathcal{U}^{(2)}_{|I|\times k_i}\right)^T \times_3 \left(\mathcal{U}^{(3)}_{|T|\times k_t}\right)^T \quad (15)$$

where $1 \le k_i \le |I|$, $1 \le k_t \le |T|$.

In fact, $\mathcal{TUP}$ is equivalent to the core tensor in the following Tucker2 decomposition [15] of $\mathcal{A}$:

$$\hat{\mathcal{A}}_{|U|\times|I|\times|T|} = \mathcal{TUP}_{|U|\times k_i\times k_t} \times_2 \mathcal{U}^{(2)}_{|I|\times k_i} \times_3 \mathcal{U}^{(3)}_{|T|\times k_t}$$

The tensor $\mathcal{TUP} \in \mathbb{R}^{|U|\times k_i\times k_t}$ can be seen as a compression of the initial tensor $\mathcal{A} \in \mathbb{R}^{|U|\times|I|\times|T|}$. Figure 2 illustrates the computation of Equation (15). As we can see, the profiling procedure is a tensor-to-tensor projection (TTP) [22] of the same order.

Definition 1 (TM-based user profile). We define the vth user u_v's profile to be represented by $UP^{\mathcal{TUP}}(u_v)$, which is a second-order tensor (i.e., matrix). Formally, $UP^{\mathcal{TUP}}(u_v)$ is defined as:

$$UP^{\mathcal{TUP}}(u_v) = \left(\mathcal{TUP}_{|U|\times k_i\times k_t}\right)_{v,:,:} \quad (17)$$

Element-wise, $\left(UP^{\mathcal{TUP}}(u_v)\right)_{p,q} = \left(\mathcal{TUP}_{|U|\times k_i\times k_t}\right)_{v,p,q}$, where p and q are the indices in first and second mode of $UP^{\mathcal{TUP}}(u_v)$ respectively, $1 \le p \le k_i$, $1 \le q \le k_t$. Each element in $UP^{\mathcal{TUP}}(u_v)$ represents a latent interaction relation between the item and the tag modes regarding u_v.

In Equation (15), we assume for each user, the item-tag relations are essentially determined by a much smaller number of ternary interaction factors, which are the essence of the tag assignments of this user. These ternary interaction factors reveal this user's personalized attention or interests for the relevance between items and tags on a level deeper than explicit tagging connections. And through this deeper level of relevance, we can predict relations between users and between users and items more effectively. Consider an example in the MovieLens website. A user collected the movie *Titanic* with the tag "disaster", and a different user collected the movie *Poseidon* with the tag "natural While "love story" and "romance" are popular tags for *Titanic* used by other users in the website, they are not on the top tag list of *Poseidon*. Therefore, the two users may well be intrinsically motivated by similar interests behind the tag assignments they created, since the two movies are both of sea disaster topic, and the two tags are also semantically related. While in the "raw" explicit relations in the initial tensor $\mathcal{A}$, those inherent interaction factors are dispersed in a much larger data space, which makes comparing user profiles difficult. The proposed TM-based user profiling method analyzes the linear relations in the input space of items and of tags through mode-wise SVD, so as to discover the essential interaction factors and thus represent the item-tag interactions in a much lower subspace. In this way, the most important ternary interaction factors are revealed and preserved in the representation of each user profile.

In more complex settings where multiple contextual variables like time, locations, etc. are available, we can model the data as an *N*th-order tensor. The extension of the TM-based user profiling approach using Equation (15) to *N*th-order tensor is straightforward through Equation (2). For an *N*th-order tensor where user is the first mode, user profiling is done with $(N-1)$ steps of tensor-matrix multiplication, of which in the nth step each $(\mathrm{n}+1)$-mode vector is projected to a lower dimension by the $(\mathrm{n}+1)$-mode component matrix. A user profile is a $(N-1)$th-order tensor, where each element is an interaction factor of other modes with respect to an individual user. The formalization of user profiling in *N*-dimensional data space is omitted here due to space limitation.

Similarly, we propose the following equation for TM-based item profiling in the third-order tensor $\mathcal{A}$:

$$\mathcal{TIP}_{k_u\times|I|\times k_t} = \mathcal{A}_{|U|\times|I|\times|T|} \times_1 \left(\mathcal{U}^{(1)}_{|U|\times k_u}\right)^T \times_3 \left(\mathcal{U}^{(3)}_{|T|\times k_t}\right)^T \quad (18)$$

Accordingly, we define jth item i_j's TM-based item profile to be represented by $IP^{\mathcal{TIP}}(i_j) \in \mathbb{R}^{k_u\times k_t}$. Formally,

$$IP^{\mathcal{TIP}}(i_j) = \left(\mathcal{TIP}_{k_u\times|I|\times k_t}\right)_{:,j,:} \quad (19)$$

Element-wise, $\left(IP^{\mathcal{TIP}}(i_j)\right)_{p,q} = \left(\mathcal{TIP}_{k_u\times|I|\times k_t}\right)_{p,j,q}$, $1 \le p \le k_u$, $1 \le q \le k_t$.

The proposed TM-based user/item profiling approach preserves the essential part of multidimensional interactions between all dimensions. Consequently, the holistic latent interaction factors constitute tensors or matrices which formulate the user/item profiles. This helps retain rich dimensional information for user/item representation due to the multimodal nature of user-item interactions.

The Connections between TM-Based Profiling Approach and Two-Dimensional MF-Based Profiling Approaches

Now let's go back to the MF-based user/item profiling approaches in the two-dimensional case. First, we propose the following Theorem 1 for Equation (9) and (12), and then we prove that the proposed TM-based profiling approach is a higher-order generalization of the SVD-based and EVD-based profiling approaches.

Theorem 1. The SVD-based profiling approach in Equation (9) and the EVD-based user profiling in Equation (12) are equivalent, i.e.,

$$\mathcal{U}_{|U|\times k}\cdot \mathcal{S}_{k\times k} = \mathcal{M}_{|U|\times|I|}\cdot \mathcal{V}_{|I|\times k} \quad (20)$$

Proof of Theorem 1. In the following, we use block matrix multiplication to prove the equation from the right side.

$$\mathcal{M}_{|U|\times|I|}\cdot \mathcal{V}_{|I|\times k} = \mathcal{U}_{|U|\times|U|}\cdot \mathcal{S}_{|U|\times|I|}\cdot\left(\left(\mathcal{V}_{|I|\times|I|}\right)^T\cdot \mathcal{V}_{|I|\times k}\right) =$$

$$\mathcal{U}_{|U|\times|U|}\cdot\left(\left[\mathcal{S}_{|U|\times k}\quad \mathcal{S}_{|U|\times(|I|-k)}\right]\cdot\begin{bmatrix} I_{k\times k}\\ 0_{(|I|-k)\times k}\end{bmatrix}\right) =$$

$$\left[\mathcal{U}_{|U|\times k}\quad \mathcal{U}_{|U|\times(|U|-k)}\right]\cdot\begin{bmatrix}\mathcal{S}_{k\times k}\\ 0_{(|U|-k)\times k}\end{bmatrix} = \mathcal{U}_{|U|\times k}\cdot \mathcal{S}_{k\times k}$$

■

In the following, we propose the tensor form of the two MF-based profiling approaches in Equation (9) and (12).

Theorem 2 (Tensor form of MF-based user profiling). By taking the matrix $\mathcal{M} \in \mathbb{R}^{|U|\times|I|}$ as a second-order tensor, the MF-based user profiling approach in Equation (12) can be reformulated in the following tensor form:

$$\mathcal{SUP}_{|U|\times k} = \mathcal{EUP}_{|U|\times k} = \mathcal{M}_{|U|\times|I|}\times_2\left(\mathcal{V}_{|I|\times k}\right)^T \quad (21)$$

Proof of Theorem 2. We derive Equation (12) as follows.

$$\mathcal{EUP}_{|U|\times k} = \mathcal{M}_{|U|\times|I|}\cdot \mathcal{V}_{|I|\times k}$$

$$\Rightarrow \left(\mathcal{EUP}_{|U|\times k}\right)^T = \left(\mathcal{V}_{|I|\times k}\right)^T\cdot\left(\mathcal{M}_{|U|\times|I|}\right)^T$$

In fact, the matrix transpose can be considered as the mode-2 unfolding, then,

$$\Rightarrow \left(\mathcal{EUP}_{|U|\times k}\right)_{(2)} = \left(\mathcal{V}_{|I|\times k}\right)^T\cdot\left(\mathcal{M}_{|U|\times|I|}\right)_{(2)}$$

According to Equation (3), we thus have

$$\Rightarrow \mathcal{EUP}_{|U|\times k} = \mathcal{M}_{|U|\times|I|}\times_2\left(\mathcal{V}_{|I|\times k}\right)^T$$

■

In Equation (7) we have introduced the concept of a Tucker1 model. Similarly, a truncated Tucker1 model of $\mathcal{M}_{|U|\times|I|}$ where the mode-1 component matrix $\mathcal{U}^{(1)}$ is an identity matrix, and k is the dimension reduction parameter, can be computed as:

$$\widehat{\mathcal{M}}_{|U|\times|I|} = \mathcal{G}_{|U|\times k}\times_2 \mathcal{U}^{(2)}_{|I|\times k} \quad (22)$$

where

$$\mathcal{G}_{|U|\times k} = \mathcal{M}_{|U|\times|I|}\times_2\left(\mathcal{U}^{(2)}_{|I|\times k}\right)^T \quad (23)$$

Note here the matrix $\mathcal{M}_{|U|\times|I|}$ is taken as a second-order tensor again. Thus, Equation (21) is in fact the core tensor $\mathcal{G}_{|U|\times k}$ of the truncated Tucker1 model in Equation (22), where $\mathcal{U}^{(2)}_{|I|\times k} = \mathcal{V}_{|I|\times k}$. Since Tucker1 model can be seen as a special case of Tucker2 model as we presented in the beginning, the proposed TM-based profiling approach is in fact a higher-order (third-order) generalization of the two MF-based profiling methods in Equation (9) and (12).

In summary, we proved that the SVD-based and EVD-based profiling approaches are equivalent, and they are all equivalently based on a truncated Tucker1 model of a matrix. Meanwhile the proposed TM-based profiling approach is based on the Tucker2 model. Thus the proposed TM-based profiling approach is a higher-order generalization of the SVD-based and EVD-based profiling approaches.

NEIGHBORHOOD-BASED CF ITEM RECOMMENDATION BASED ON TM-BASED PROFILES

In this section, we propose to integrate neighborhood-based CF approaches with the TM-based user/item profiles. We present a user-based CF approach integrated with the TM-based user profiles, denoted as $uCF - TM$, an item-based CF approach integrated with the TM-based item profiles, denoted as $iCF - TM$, and a CF fusion algorithm denoted as $CFF - TM$, for social tagging data.

User-Based and Item-Based CF with TM-Based Profiles

In the following, we present a user-based CF recommendation approach integrated with the TM-based user profiles for STS. An item-based CF approach can be similarly integrated with the TM-based item profiles. Based on the standard user-based CF algorithm [28], our user-based CF algorithm works with the following procedure:

Firstly, compute TM-based user profiles for all users together as we presented in the previous section.

Secondly, for each active user, generate k most similar users as his/her neighborhood according to a predefined similarity measure method. Since the TM-based user profiles computed from social tagging data are matrices or second-order tensors, user similarities can be defined as a measure of the distance or difference between two matrices. Tensor/matrix distance can be directly measured by the Frobenius norm of tensor/matrix subtraction [22]. In our approaches, to facilitate the recommendation process, we use following cosine similarity to measure user similarities:

$$sim(u_v, u_w) = \frac{vec\left(UP^{\mathcal{TUP}}(u_v)\right) \cdot vec\left(UP^{\mathcal{TUP}}(u_w)\right)}{\left\|vec\left(UP^{\mathcal{TUP}}(u_v)\right)\right\| \cdot \left\|vec\left(UP^{\mathcal{TUP}}(u_w)\right)\right\|} \quad (24)$$

where $vec\left(UP^{\mathcal{TUP}}(u_v)\right)$ is the vectorization [6, 22] of $UP^{\mathcal{TUP}}(u_v)$:

$$vec\left(UP^{\mathcal{TUP}}(u_v)\right) =< \left(UP^{\mathcal{TUP}}(u_v)\right)_{1,1}, \left(UP^{\mathcal{TUP}}(u_v)\right)_{1,2}, \cdots, \left(UP^{\mathcal{TUP}}(u_v)\right)_{k_i,k_t} > \quad (25)$$

Note the specific permutation of elements is not important so long as it is consistent across all users in the vectorization.

Finally, for each active user, based on the item preferences of his/her neighbor users, compute a predicted item preference for each item unknown to him/her. Then produce a ranked list of top-N items as the recommendations. The predicted item preference $\hat{p}^{uCF-TM}(u_v, i_j)$ for user u_v to item i_j is:

$$\hat{p}^{uCF-TM}(u_v, i_j) = \sum_{u_w \in N(u_v,k), i_j \in I_{u_w}} \left(p(u_w, i_j) \cdot sim(u_w, u_v)\right) \quad (26)$$

where $N(u_v, k)$ is the set of top k neighbor users of u_v. I_{u_w} is the set of items used by a neighbor u_w and unknown to u_v. $p(u_w, i_j)$ is neighbor u_w's item preference for item i_j.

Likewise, the predicted item preference computed from the item-based CF based on TM-based item profiles can be formulated as:

$$\hat{p}^{iCF-TM}(u_w, i_l) = \sum_{i_j \in I_{u_w}, i_l \in N(i_j,k)} \left(p(u_w, i_j) \cdot sim(i_j, i_l)\right) \quad (27)$$

where $N(i_j, k)$ are the top k neighbor items of a used item i_j of the active user u_w. I_{u_w} is the set of items collected by user u_w, and $sim(i_j, i_l)$ is the similarity between i_j and i_l.

Thereby, two neighborhood-based CF approaches integrated with TM-based profiles are proposed. They are able to make recommendations by collaborating the user/item profiles based on multidimensional interaction factors with nearest neighborhood relations. This is a distinctive advantage compared to conventional neighborhood-based CF approaches. We will empirically demonstrate that the proposed TM-based profiles enhance the two neighborhood-based CF approaches to perform apparently better compared to their two-dimensional counterparts. Besides, we will also show that the more ternary transactions there exist in the data, the more the recommendation quality will be improved.

CF Fusion Model with TM-based Profiles

Tags can be seen as explicit attributes specific to user-item interactions, that is, they are local to each transaction. In this way, the relations in the social tagging data observed from the aspect of users can be different to that from items. For instance, two users may have rather different personal standpoints for two items they both collected, while the two items are however closely related. This indicates a recommendation model which can properly capture both users' and items' standpoints may lead to the improvement of recommendation quality. This lays the foundation of some previous works [3, 19, 31].

As aforementioned, the exploitation of various relations or effects is the key of most CF approaches to quality recommendation. In the previous subsection, two neighborhood-based CF approaches with TM-based profiles have been proposed. A CF fusion approach can be used to unify them, so as to benefit from the holistic latent relations in the TM-based profiles and the local user-user and item-item neighborhoods simultaneously.

The CF fusion for the top-N item recommendation task can be done by combining the predicted item preferences of user-based and item-based CF approaches. Since the predicted item preferences computed by user-based and item-based CF come from different computation methods, they have different scales of values. A normalization process is needed to unify the recommendations from the two, which produces the final item preference prediction:

$$\hat{p}^{CFF-TM}(u_v, i_j) = \lambda \cdot \frac{\hat{p}^{uCF-TM}(u_v, i_j)}{\sum_{i_l} \hat{p}^{uCF-TM}(u_v, i_l)} + (1-\lambda) \cdot \frac{\hat{p}^{iCF-TM}(u_v, i_j)}{\sum_{i_l} \hat{p}^{iCF-TM}(u_v, i_l)} \quad (28)$$

where $0 \leq \lambda \leq 1$. Note the neighborhood sizes of users and items are specified by the same parameter k [31].

The CF fusion approach integrated with the TM-based profiles can reasonably enhance recommendation quality, since it not only efficiently utilizes latent ternary relations in the profiles, but also brings out the recommendation power of both localized user-user and item-item neighborhood relations. The profiling procedure effectively removes redundant information and reveals principal implicit relations. In fact, empirical analysis has shown that our CF fusion approach provides superior performance than state-of-the-art recommendation approaches for multidimensional data.

EXPERIMENTAL EVALUATION

In this section, we present empirical analysis using real-world datasets collected from Bibsonomy and Delicious. We compare the user-based/item-based CF and CF fusion approaches integrated with the TM-based profiles against a series of benchmarking CF recommendation approaches.

Datasets

We used popular social tagging datasets from Bibsonomy [14] and Delicious [34]. The basic data record in the two datasets is a user-item-tag 3-tuple, corresponding to a tag assignment as we previously defined. The two datasets are publicly available and originally collected on April 30, 2007 and in January, 2004 respectively by their researchers [14, 34]. The Bibsonomy dataset contains 1037 users, 86563 items and 28648 tags; the Delicious dataset contains 2419 users, 30838 items and 10926 tags. Following a common practice in the works of this area [12, 24, 29], the notion of p-core [12] was applied to the datasets. The p-core of level k indicates that each user, tag and item has to occur in at least k posts. A post is a user-item pair (u, i) representing that the user u has tagged the item i using any number of tags. Following the experiments for the HOSVD model of Symeonidis et al. [29], we used $k = 5$ for both of the two datasets. After this, the Delicious dataset contains 216 users, 337 items, and 247 tags; the Bibsonomy dataset contains 116 users, 361 items and 412 tags. The sizes of the datasets after pruning are the same or close to the ones used in existing works [12, 13, 24, 29, 35]. We define the density of a dataset as the percentage of the number of non-zero (NNZ) elements in the data tensors [35], i.e., $Density = \frac{\#NNZ}{|U|\times|I|\times|T|}$. Then the densities of the Bibsonomy and Delicious datasets after pruning are 0.0588% and 0.0278% respectively. Yet these are still lower than traditional recommender systems in commercial area where the density of data is approximately 1% [35].

Evaluation Settings

Evaluation Metrics

We adopted F1 score [11] as the metric for evaluating top-N item recommendations: $F_1 = \frac{2\cdot precision\cdot recall}{precision+recall}$. We conducted 5-fold cross validation. For each run, we randomly choose 75% observed data of each user as training set, and the remaining 25% are used as testing data for evaluation.

Recommendation Models

Following are the proposed approaches integrated with the TM-based profiles to be evaluated:

- **iCF-TM**. This is the item-based CF approach integrated with the TM-based item profiles.
- **uCF-TM**. This is the user-based CF approach integrated with the TM-based user profiles.
- **CFF-TM**. This is the CF fusion approach integrated with the TM-based user/item profiles.
- **CFF-TM2**. This is a modified version of CFF-TM. In order to validate the effectiveness of the TM-based profiles and compare with the tag-aware CF fusion model [31] fairly, we follow the method in [31] to specially compute item preference predictions of the user-based CF part in the fusion approach as in the following equation. We keep the rest of the approach the same to CFF-TM.

$$\hat{p}^{uCF-TM2}(u_v, i_j) = \frac{|\{u_w|u_w \in N(u_v,k), i \in I_{u_w}\}|}{|N_{u_v}|} \quad (29)$$

We adopted the following models as the baselines in our experiments:

- **iCF**. This is the two-dimensional item-based CF approach [8] with the implicit item preferences as input.
- **uCF**. This is the two-dimensional user-based CF approach [2] with the implicit item preferences as input.
- **tCFF**. This is the tag-aware CF Fusion model [31]. It extends its profiling ability by projecting tags onto user dimensions as pseudo users in item-based CF and onto item dimensions as pseudo items in user-based CF. A CF fusion method is applied to unify the two parts.
- **TF**. Symeonidis et al. [29] proposed a HOSVD-based TF recommendation model in STS. They adopted kernel-SVD smoothing technique in the model to further enhance the recommendation accuracy.

Parameter Settings

Following are the specific settings for the proposed approaches and the baseline models. For each model which involves neighborhood, we tried the neighborhood size parameter k from 5 to 300 by an interval of 5. For each model with the λ parameter, we varied λ from 0 to 1 by an interval of 0.1.

- **iCF-TM**. For the Bibsonomy dataset, we found the best results came with factor number parameter k_u as 99, k_t as 246 and item neighborhood size as 20. For the Delicious dataset, we found the best results came with factor number parameter k_u as 105, k_t as 48 and item neighborhood size as 20.
- **uCF-TM**. For the Bibsonomy dataset, we found the best results came with factor number parameter k_i as 288, k_t as 410 and user neighborhood size as 60. For the Delicious dataset, we found the best results came with factor number parameter k_i as 176, k_t as 80 and user neighborhood size as 25.
- **CFF-TM**. For the Bibsonomy dataset, we found the best λ was 0.2 and k was 20. For the Delicious dataset, we found the best λ to be 0.9 and k to be 50. With regard to the profiles of users and items, we used the best factor number settings of iCF-TM and uCF-TM.
- **CFF-TM2**. For the Bibsonomy dataset, we found the best λ was 0.6 and k was 20. For the Delicious dataset, we found the best λ to be 0.8 and k to be 25.
- **iCF**. For the Bibsonomy dataset, the best result was achieved with the item neighborhood size being 100. For the Delicious dataset, the best result was achieved with the neighborhood size being 40.
- **uCF**. For the Bibsonomy dataset, the best result was achieved with the neighborhood size being 30. For the Delicious dataset, the best result was achieved with the neighborhood size being 30.
- **TF**. We followed their approach to determine the factor number parameters of core tensor in the model. For the Bibsonomy dataset, we found when the three parameters were set as 96, 60 and 274 this model achieved its best

result. For the Delicious dataset, we found when the three parameters were set as 61, 96 and 211 this model achieved its best result.

Top-N	TF	tCFF	CFF-TM	Imp. (%)	CFF-TM2	Imp. (%)
1	0.048	0.042	**0.086**	78%	0.082	69%
2	0.080	0.075	**0.129**	60%	0.113	40%
3	0.096	0.100	**0.153**	52%	0.152	51%
4	0.097	0.116	**0.165**	42%	0.163	40%
5	0.108	0.123	0.166	34%	**0.167**	35%
6	0.108	0.123	0.170	38%	**0.170**	38%
7	0.113	0.126	0.164	30%	**0.171**	35%
8	0.113	0.120	0.163	35%	**0.167**	38%
9	0.110	0.119	**0.159**	33%	0.158	33%
10	0.108	0.113	**0.153**	35%	0.152	34%

Table 1. F1 scores of the four recommendation models for the Bibsonomy dataset.

Top-N	TF	tCFF	CFF-TM	Imp. (%)	CFF-TM2	Imp. (%)
1	0.029	0.041	**0.043**	5%	0.039	-6%
2	0.042	0.047	**0.062**	32%	0.055	16%
3	0.046	0.053	**0.064**	19%	0.064	18%
4	0.050	0.059	**0.072**	21%	0.067	13%
5	0.053	0.064	**0.070**	8%	0.066	2%
6	0.055	0.062	**0.069**	11%	0.069	11%
7	0.055	0.060	0.066	11%	**0.067**	13%
8	0.055	0.059	0.065	10%	**0.066**	12%
9	0.056	0.059	0.062	5%	**0.062**	5%
10	0.053	0.059	0.060	1%	**0.061**	4%

Table 2. F1 scores of the four recommendation models for the Delicious dataset.

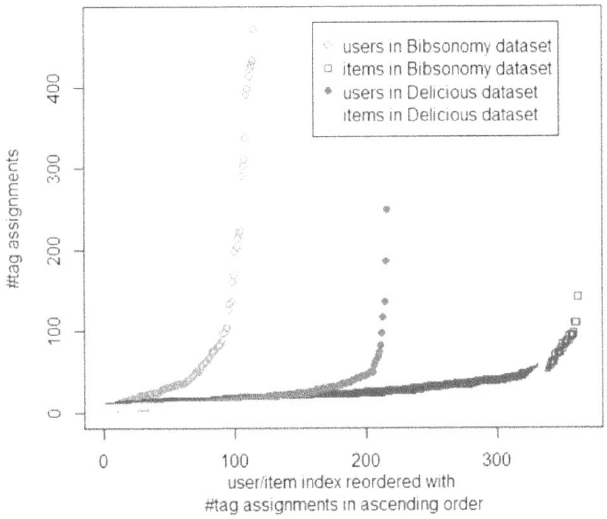

Figure 3. Distribution of tag assignments per user/item.

- **tCFF**. For the Bibsonomy dataset, we found the best λ to be 0.8 and k to be 20. For the Delicious dataset, we found the best λ to be 0.7 and k to be 70.

Experiment Results and Discussion

In this section, we present detailed experiment results and discuss the performance of the recommendation models.

Multidimensional Recommendation Models

In this subsection, we compare the proposed CF fusion models CFF-TM and CFF-TM2 against two multidimensional CF models: TF and tCFF. Table 1 and Table 2 present the F1 scores of the four models for the Bibsonomy and the Delicious dataset, respectively. For each top-N value in the two tables, the largest value in each row is highlighted in bold. The percentages of improvements by CFF-TM and CFF-TM2 against the larger one between TF and tCFF are also given for each row.

As shown in the two tables, although all of the four recommendation models utilize three-dimensional user-item-tag relations, they achieved different accuracies. Basically for all top-N values, CFF-TM and CFF-TM2 have shown significantly better results compared to TF and tCFF for Bibsonomy dataset. For Delicious dataset, except the result of CFF-TM2 in Top-1, CFF-TM and CFF-TM2 outperform both TF and tCFF with notable improvements. The reason for CFF-TM and CFF-TM2 being superior is mostly because they utilize more relations in data. They use TM-based profiles, where the ternary interactions are modelled as latent factors. This makes the profiles in CFF-TM and CFF-TM2 more accurate than those in tCFF. They also take into consideration both localized user and item neighborhoods, which however is a shortage of TF.

The results of CFF-TM and CFF-TM2 for each dataset are a quite close due to the similarity of the two approaches. Meanwhile CFF-TM seems showing better performance than CFF-TM2 in top recommendations. This may be attributable to that CFF-TM2 discards the user similarity values in the recommendation algorithm of its user-based CF part. It is also obvious to observe that, CFF-TM and CFF-TM2 evaluated on Bibsonomy dataset have shown more improvements than on Delicious dataset. This is because in Bibsonomy dataset, there're more tag assignments averagely per user/item. In Figure 3, we plot the distribution of the number of tag assignments of each user and of each item in the two datasets. We have reordered the indices of users and items by the corresponding numbers of tag assignments in ascending order to make the curves smooth. This indicates that CFF-TM and CFF-TM2 are more effective when there're more existing user-item-tag relations in the data to supply to TM-based profiles.

Single Neighborhood-Based CF Models

In this subsection, in order to evaluate the effectiveness of the proposed TM-based profiling approach, we compare the proposed uCF-TM and iCF-TM with popular two-dimensional neighborhood-based CF approaches, uCF and iCF. Specifically, in Figure 4 and Figure 5, we plot the F1 scores of the approaches for the Bibsonomy dataset and the Delicious dataset respectively.

As we can see, uCF-TM and iCF-TM show consistently superior performance than uCF and iCF respectively. This is because the user/item profiling approach in uCF-TM and iCF-TM is able to take into consideration the additional tag information and to incorporate the three-dimensional latent relations effectively, which leads to highly refined user/item profiles. In this way, neighborhood formation is more accurate and thus the recommendation results show obvious improved accuracy. This indicates the TM-based user/item profiles are effective for improving recommendation quality.

Overall Comparison of All Models

Figure 6 and Figure 7 show the experimental results of all recommendation models for the two datasets. In both figures, the top recommendation models are all based on the proposed TM-based profiles. As we can see, CFF-TM shows better performance than uCF-TM and iCF-TM although the extent of the improvements are different. This indicates CFF-TM successfully unifies user-user and item-item neighborhood relations to complement each other. Also, generally CFF-TM outperforms all other tag-aware baseline models especially in top-ranked recommendations. This indicates, the proposed TM-based profiling approach has created users and items profiles of higher quality, which leads to more accurate user/item similarities and neighborhood formation in CFF-TM. These are the advantages of CFF-TM and the TM-based profiles.

CONCLUSION AND FUTURE WORK

The increasing availability of multidimensional data has provided user profiling techniques and recommender systems with new opportunities and challenges. In this paper, we proposed a novel unified profiling approach for entities in multidimensional data based on a Tucker model. We proved that the proposed TM-based profiling approach is a higher-order generalization of the traditional SVD-based and EVD-based profiling approaches. We further presented three new CF approaches based on user-based, item-based and CF fusion approaches with the integration of the proposed TM-based profiles. Our profiling approach distinguishes itself from existing profiling approaches by representing users/items as third-order interaction models, where the multidimensionality of user-item interactions is retained and refined. The proposed profiling approach is generic. Other types of entities also can be modelled with the same approach. Also, other types of entities can be added into the approach as new modes. Experimental studies on the Bibsonomy and Delicious datasets showed significant improvements in recommendation making using the proposed profiling approaches. This confirms the TM-based profiles are very effective.

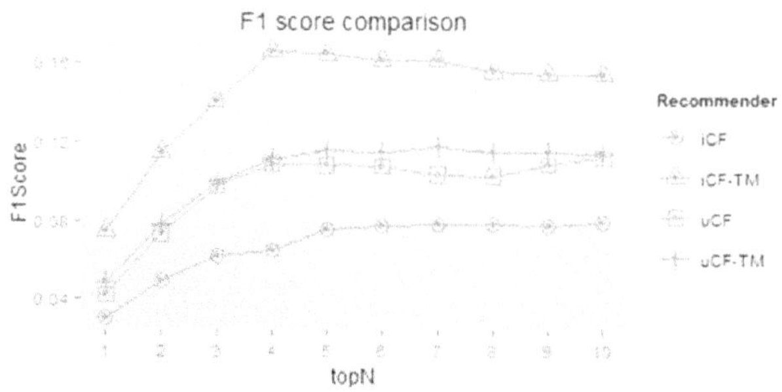

Figure 4. F1 score comparison for the single neighborhood-based CF models for the Bibsonomy dataset.

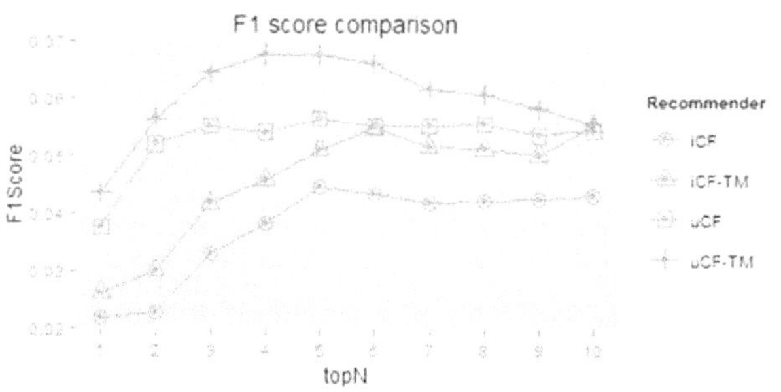

Figure 5. F1 score comparison for the single neighborhood-based CF models for the Delicious dataset.

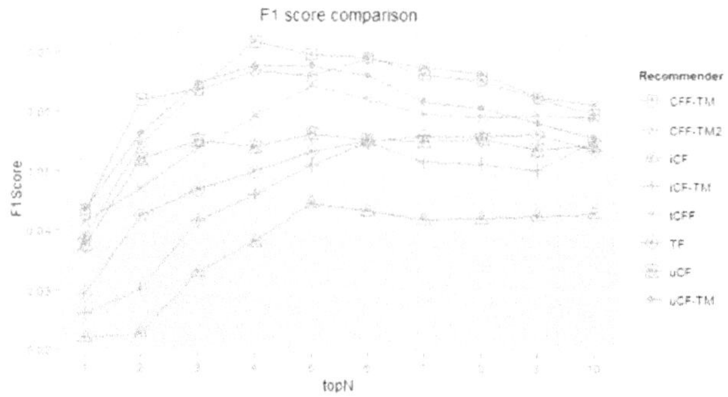

Figure 6. F1 scores of all recommenders for the Bibsonomy dataset.

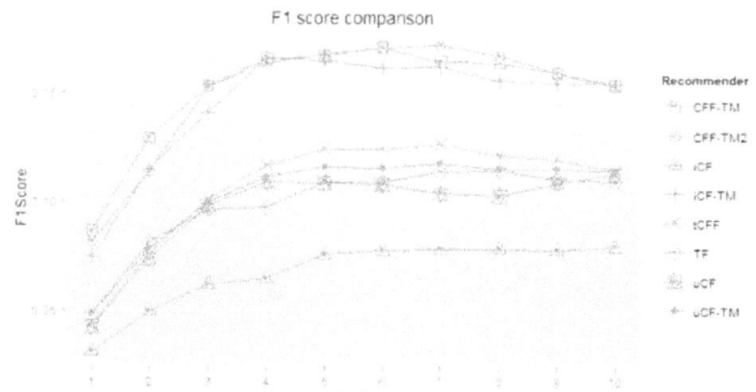

Figure 7. F1 scores of all recommenders for the Delicious dataset.

For the future work, we intend to explore the integration of various types of contextual variables in the TM-based profiling approach. Also, we plan to further apply the profiling method in user recommendation task.

REFERENCES

1. Acar, E. and Yener, B., Unsupervised multiway data analysis: A literature survey. *Knowledge and Data Engineering, IEEE Transactions on* 21, 1 (2009), 6-20.
2. Adomavicius, G. and Tuzhilin, A., Toward the next generation of recommender systems: A survey of the state-of-the-art and possible extensions. *Knowledge and Data Engineering, IEEE Transactions on* 17, 6 (2005), 734-749.
3. Bar, A., Rokach, L., Shani, G., Shapira, B., and Schclar, A., Improving simple collaborative filtering models using ensemble methods, in *Multiple Classifier Systems*. 2013, Springer. p. 1-12.
4. Bell, R.M. and Koren, Y., Lessons from the Netflix prize challenge. *ACM SIGKDD Explorations Newsletter* 9, 2 (2007), 75-79.
5. Chen, J., Geyer, W., Dugan, C., Muller, M., and Guy, I. Make new friends, but keep the old: recommending people on social networking sites. In *Proc. Proceedings of the SIGCHI Conference on Human Factors in Computing Systems*. ACM (2009). 201-210.
6. Cichocki, A., Zdunek, R., Phan, A.H., and Amari, S.-i., *Nonnegative matrix and tensor factorizations: applications to exploratory multi-way data analysis and blind source separation*. 2009: John Wiley & Sons.
7. De Lathauwer, L., De Moor, B., and Vandewalle, J., A multilinear singular value decomposition. *SIAM journal on Matrix Analysis and Applications* 21, 4 (2000), 1253-1278.
8. Deshpande, M. and Karypis, G., Item-based top-n recommendation algorithms. *ACM Transactions on Information Systems (TOIS)* 22, 1 (2004), 143-177.
9. Gauch, S., Speretta, M., Chandramouli, A., and Micarelli, A., User profiles for personalized information access, in *The adaptive web*. 2007, Springer. p. 54-89.
10. Goldberg, K., Roeder, T., Gupta, D., and Perkins, C., Eigentaste: A constant time collaborative filtering algorithm. *Information Retrieval* 4, 2 (2001), 133-151.
11. Herlocker, J., Konstan, J., Terveen, L., and Riedl, J., Evaluating Collaborative Filtering Recommender Systems. *ACM Transactions on Information Systems* 22, 1 (2004), 5-53.
12. Jäschke, R., Marinho, L., Hotho, A., Schmidt-Thieme, L., and Stumme, G., Tag recommendations in folksonomies, in *Knowledge Discovery in Databases: PKDD 2007*. 2007, Springer. p. 506-514.
13. Karatzoglou, A., Amatriain, X., Baltrunas, L., and Oliver, N. Multiverse recommendation: n-dimensional tensor factorization for context-aware collaborative filtering. In *Proc. Proceedings of the fourth ACM conference on Recommender systems*. ACM (2010). 79-86.
14. Knowledge and Data Engineering Group, University of Kassel. *Benchmark Folksonomy Data from BibSonomy*. 2007 [cited 2007 30 June]; Available from: http://www.kde.cs.uni-kassel.de/bibsonomy/dumps/.
15. Kolda, T.G. and Bader, B.W., Tensor decompositions and applications. *SIAM review* 51, 3 (2009), 455-500.
16. Koren, Y. Factorization meets the neighborhood: a multifaceted collaborative filtering model. In *Proc. Proceedings of the 14th ACM SIGKDD international conference on Knowledge discovery and data mining*. ACM (2008). 426-434.
17. Kroonenberg, P.M., *Applied multiway data analysis*. Vol. 702. 2008: John Wiley & Sons.
18. Kroonenberg, P.M. and De Leeuw, J., Principal component analysis of three-mode data by means of alternating least squares algorithms. *Psychometrika* 45, 1 (1980), 69-97.
19. Lee, J.-S. and Olafsson, S., Two-way cooperative prediction for collaborative filtering recommendations. *Expert Systems with Applications* 36, 3 (2009), 5353-5361.
20. Liang, H., Xu, Y., Li, Y., Nayak, R., and Tao, X., Connecting users and items with weighted tags for personalized item recommendations, in *Proceedings of the 21st ACM conference on Hypertext and hypermedia*. 2010, ACM: Toronto, Ontario, Canada. p. 51-60.
21. Lops, P., De Gemmis, M., and Semeraro, G., Content-based recommender systems: State of the art and trends, in *Recommender systems handbook*. 2011, Springer. p. 73-105.
22. Lu, H., Plataniotis, K.N., and Venetsanopoulos, A., *Multilinear Subspace Learning: Dimensionality Reduction of Multidimensional Data*. 2013: CRC Press.
23. Marinho, L.B., Hotho, A., Jäschke, R., Nanopoulos, A., Rendle, S., Schmidt-Thieme, L., Stumme, G., and Symeonidis, P., *Recommender systems for social tagging systems*. 2012: Springer.
24. Rendle, S., Balby Marinho, L., Nanopoulos, A., and Schmidt-Thieme, L. Learning optimal ranking with tensor factorization for tag recommendation. In *Proc. Proceedings of the 15th ACM SIGKDD international conference on knowledge discovery and data mining*. ACM (2009). 727-736.
25. Rendle, S., Gantner, Z., Freudenthaler, C., and Schmidt-Thieme, L. Fast context-aware recommendations with factorization machines. In *Proc. Proceedings of the 34th international ACM SIGIR conference on Research and development in Information Retrieval*. ACM (2011). 635-644.
26. Schmidt, A., Context-aware computing: context-awareness, context-aware user interfaces, and implicit interaction. *The Encyclopedia of Human-Computer Interaction, 2nd Ed.* (2013).

27. Sen, S., Vig, J., and Riedl, J. Tagommenders: connecting users to items through tags. In *Proc. Proceedings of the 18th international conference on World wide web*. ACM (2009). 671-680.

28. Su, X. and Khoshgoftaar, T.M., A survey of collaborative filtering techniques. *Advances in artificial intelligence* 2009, (2009).

29. Symeonidis, P., Nanopoulos, A., and Manolopoulos, Y., A unified framework for providing recommendations in social tagging systems based on ternary semantic analysis. *IEEE Transactions on Knowledge and Data Engineering* 22, 2 (2010), 179-192.

30. Symeonidis, P., Nanopoulos, A., Papadopoulos, A., and Manolopoulos, Y. Scalable collaborative filtering based on latent semantic indexing. In *Proc. Proc. 21st Assoc. for Advancement of Artificial Intelligence (AAAI) Workshop Intelligent Techniques for Web Personalization (ITWP'06)*. AAAI (2006). 1-9.

31. Tso-Sutter, K.H.L., Marinho, L.B., and Schmidt-Thieme, L. Tag-aware recommender systems by fusion of collaborative filtering algorithms. In *Proc. Proceedings of the 2008 ACM symposium on Applied computing*. ACM (2008). 1995-1999.

32. Tucker, L.R., Implications of factor analysis of three-way matrices for measurement of change. *Problems in measuring change* (1963), 122-137.

33. Tucker, L.R., Some mathematical notes on three-mode factor analysis. *Psychometrika* 31, 3 (1966), 279-311.

34. Wetzker, R., Zimmermann, C., and Bauckhage, C. Analyzing social bookmarking systems: A del. icio. us cookbook. In *Proc. Proceedings of the ECAI 2008 Mining Social Data Workshop*. IOS Press (2008). 26-30.

35. Zhang, M., Ding, C., and Liao, Z. Tensor Fold-in Algorithms for Social Tagging Prediction. In *Proc. Data Mining (ICDM), 2011 IEEE 11th International Conference on*. IEEE (2011). 1254-1259.

36. Zhang, M. and Hurley, N. Novel item recommendation by user profile partitioning. In *Proc. Proceedings of the 2009 IEEE/WIC/ACM International Joint Conference on Web Intelligence and Intelligent Agent Technology-Volume 01*. IEEE Computer Society (2009). 508-515.

Exploring Personalized Command Recommendations based on Information Found in Web Documentation

Md Adnan Alam Khan, Volodymyr Dziubak, Andrea Bunt
Department of Computer Science
University of Manitoba
Winnipeg, MB
{akhan, vdziubak, bunt}@cs.umanitoba.ca

ABSTRACT

Prior work on command recommendations for feature-rich software has relied on data supplied by a large community of users to generate personalized recommendations. In this work, we explore the feasibility of using an alternative data source: web documentation. Specifically, our approach uses QF-Graphs, a previously proposed technique that maps higher-level tasks (i.e., search queries) to commands referenced in online documentation. Our approach uses these command-to-task mappings as an automatically generated plan library, enabling our prototype system to make personalized recommendations for task-relevant commands. Through both offline and online evaluations, we explore potential benefits and drawbacks of this approach.

Author Keywords

Feature-rich software; Software learnability; Recommender systems; Web-based documentation

ACM Classification Keywords

H.5.m. Information interfaces and presentation (e.g., HCI): Miscellaneous.

INTRODUCTION

Feature-rich software applications (e.g., image-manipulation programs, spreadsheet software and statistical analysis packages) are highly versatile, in part owing to the hundreds (or even thousands) of commands or features that they make available. At the same time, this high volume of commands can make feature-rich software difficult for users to master [17]. For example, studies of long-term application use have shown that most users have fairly limited *command vocabularies* [14], typically using much less than one quarter of the available command set (e.g., [26, 30]).

IUI 2015, March 29–April 1, 2015, Atlanta, GA, USA.

ACM 978-1-4503-3306-1/15/03…$15.00.
http://dx.doi.org/10.1145/2678025.2701387

One promising approach to increasing a user's awareness of the available command set is to present them with intelligently generated, personalized command recommendations (e.g., [30, 31, 35]). Central to this approach is an understanding of the potential relationships between commands – knowledge that enables an intelligent system to recommend commands that could complement those currently being used. Most prior work has extracted this relevancy information from community usage logs, for example, by applying collaborative filtering algorithms to a large corpus on logged data (e.g., [30, 31, 35]). While these usage-data centric approaches have shown a great deal of promise, their practical success hinges on the existence of a large community of users willing to upload their usage data to a central repository.

In this work, we propose an alternative approach to personalized command recommendations that uses command-to-task mappings mined from online documentation. Specifically, our approach uses Query-Feature Graphs (QF-Graphs) [13], a technique that maps common web search queries to collections of interface elements referenced in the resulting online documentation. Within the context of the GNU Image Manipulation Program (GIMP), we illustrate how our prototype recommender system uses a QF-Graph as an automatically generated plan library.

Through offline experimentation with previously collected usage data, we explore this documentation-centric approach's potential to both increase a user's command awareness through task-relevant recommendations, and to enable a system to provide efficient access to needed commands. In a controlled laboratory experiment, we also explore the impact of two alternative recommendation presentation techniques on immediate task performance as well as on incidental awareness of relevant commands not selected during the primary task [10].

Our results suggest that web documentation can be leveraged to generate recommendations for commands that are relevant to the task at hand. In terms of its ability to streamline access to needed commands, our findings indicate that the approach works best for users with diverse feature usage. Frequency-based approaches, on the other hand, achieve higher predictive accuracy for users with stable and homogenous usage patterns. The results of our laboratory evaluation reveal that presenting recommendations in-place, as opposed to in a separate palette, increases users' incidental command awareness without negatively impacting their immediate task performance.

The contributions of this work are as follows. We present a novel approach to intelligent command recommendation that uses web documentation as a knowledge source. We demonstrate potential strengths and weaknesses of this approach given a variety of command usage patterns. Finally, we present an initial empirical exploration of how such a system could display its recommendations within the interface.

RELATED WORK

Prior work on supporting feature-rich software use has focused on three main areas: supporting application learning through improved tutorials, providing in-application assistance, and techniques for streamlining access to needed commands. We describe each of these bodies of work below. We conclude the section with a brief description of techniques for mining web documentation for command-to-task mappings, one of which we apply in our work.

Improved Tutorial Interfaces

Prior work has shown that tutorials play a large role in application learning (e.g., [7, 25]), but that authoring effective tutorials can be difficult [32]. Consequently, prior research has focused on automated or semi-automated tutorial authoring (e.g., [5, 16]), and creating novel and engaging tutorial formats (e.g., [6, 8, 18, 29]). Work has also begun to explore ways to harness crowds or community contributions to improve the utility of web-based tutorials, for example, through integrated community refinements [3], by augmenting tutorials with community demonstrations [27], and by using crowds to help segment video tutorials into steps to permit easier tutorial navigation [23]. Finally, prior work has sought to make it easier for users to select appropriate tutorials, by highlighting the commands used [7, 24].

In-Application Assistance

As is the case with our work, prior research has also sought to improve software learning from within the application itself. One approach has focused on helping users understand how to use commands through, for example, intelligent task assistants [20], Q&A forums embedded within the interface [34] and video-based tool-tips [19].

Most relevant to our work are systems that provide unobtrusive personalized command recommendations by mining large corpuses of community usage data. For example, the OWL system used long-term usage histories from individuals within an organization to recommend commands that were underused in comparison to their peers. Similarly, CommunityCommands [30, 35] used collaborative filtering algorithms on a large corpus of usage data to generate personalized command recommendations. Patina, on the other hand, provided subtle command recommendations by overlaying heat maps on the interface to highlight commands commonly used by the community [33]. We extend this prior work by exploring a new data source for task-relevant command recommendations – web-based documentation. We also further explore the question of how to present these types of command recommendations within the interface.

Providing Efficient Access to Needed Commands

Given that users of feature-rich software tend to use only a small subset of the available command set (e.g., [26, 30]), prior work has examined ways to provide more efficient access to needed commands by reducing the search space. These approaches have ranged from user-customizable subset interfaces (e.g., [2, 36]), to community-authored task-specific interfaces accessible through in-application keyword search [28], to interfaces that adaptively promote commands according to recency and frequency information (e.g., [10, 15]). Our recommendation presentation techniques are informed by this body of work. We also extend this prior research by exploring a new way to compute relevant command subsets.

Extracting Command-to-Task Mappings from Online Documentation

Given the prevalence of online documentation for feature-rich software, prior work has explored the feasibility of using these resources to generate task-specific command groupings. For example, Fourney *et al.* [13] proposed Query-Feature Graphs (QF-Graphs) as a way to relate users' search queries for feature-rich applications to individual interface elements referenced in the resulting webpages. The very recent CommandSpace work also uses web documentation to model the relationships between tasks and commands, but does so using a vector-space representation as opposed to a graph [1]. We extend this work by systematically exploring the potential of these mappings to support personalized command recommendations.

PROTOTYPE DESCRIPTION

The core component of our system, which we refer to as QFRecs (see Figure 1), is the Query-Feature Graph that was originally introduced by Fourney *et al.* [13]. As illustrated in the simplified example in Figure 2, a Query-Feature Graph (QF-Graph) is a weighted bipartite graph, which associates user search queries (i.e, natural language descriptions of high-level tasks [26], Figure 2 a, left), with the features of a target application (Figure 2 a, right). The weight of the edge between a query node and a feature node represents their strength of association (see Table 1 for example weights).

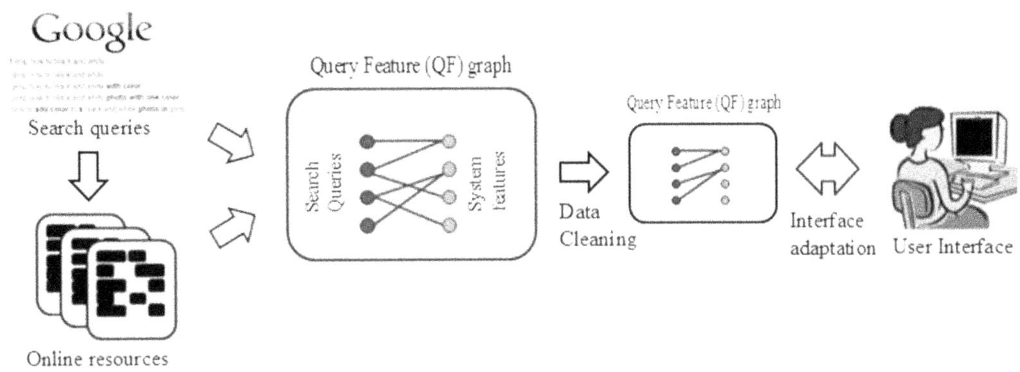

Figure 1. The general architecture for our prototype command recommender system QFRecs.

The process of building a QF-Graph starts with collecting common user search queries issued for a target application using an application of the CUTS method [12], which leverages the Google Suggest API. These queries are then executed and the resulting webpages are examined for occurences of application-specific features (using a list of features that can be generated semi-automatically using the application's localization data).

	Blur/sharpen	Blend	…	Color balance
how to blur image background in GIMP	9.33	6.82	…	0
…	…	…	…	…
Gimp make image black and white	0	0	…	8.77

Table 1. Example connection weights between tasks and features.

QFRecs's general architecture is depicted in Figure 1. As a starting point, we use the "raw" QF-graph generated by Fourney *et al.* [13] for the GNU Graphics Manipulation Program (GIMP). We focus on GIMP for two reason: it allows for greater modification possibilities than propietary software, and we are able to perform offline evalutations of our approach using data previously collected through the Ingimp project [26, 37]. In the next section we describe some of the steps that we took to clean this raw QF-Graph. We follow this by describing how our approach uses the cleaned QF-Graph to generate personalized command recommendations.

Data Preparation

In moving from the original QF-Graph concept to a concrete application, we discovered two sources of noise that impacted the quality of our prototype's recommendations requiring that we "clean" this original QF-Graph for it to be suitable for our purposes. As an overview, our cleaning process took part in two steps. First, we pruned tasks from the left-hand side of the QF-Graph that were not representative of high-level tasks. Second, since the goal was to recommend specific GIMP commands, we made sure that all system features on the right-hand side of the graph corresponded to actual elements in the GIMP interface. We describe these sources of noise and our methods for cleaning the data in further detail here to illustrate some of the challenges of using the document-based approach to command recommendation in practice.

In terms of the high-level tasks (see Figure 2 a, left for examples), manual exploration of 12,311 search queries used to build the original QF-Graph revealed that many queries were not actually representative of high-level tasks. Therefore, we removed queries from this original graph if they met any of the following criteria: they contained digits (e.g. "gimp review 2010", "gimp 2.6 fonts", etc.), operating system names (e.g. "gimp for mac

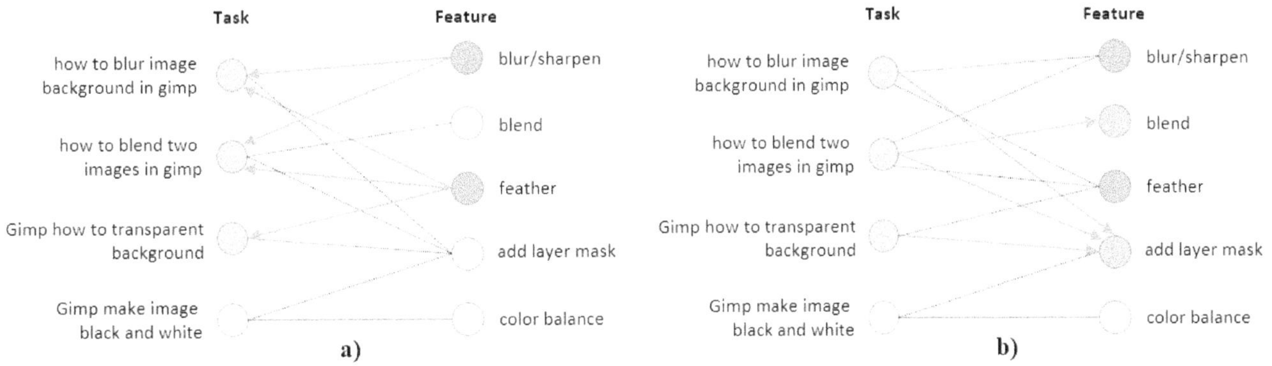

Figure 2. A simple illustration of the QF-Graph based approach.

OS x"), or the "vs" string (e.g. "gimp vs adobe", "adobe illustrator vs gimp"). This left us with 9889 queries. An altnerative would have been to restrict the search queries to those containing the string "GIMP how to", however, this strategy appeared to result in unnecessary information loss (e.g., it removed over 90% of the queries).

The second source of noise concerned the features themselves (see Figure 2 a, right for example features in a QF-Graph). We found that not all the features extracted from the Web documentation mapped to commands in the actual GIMP interface. The primary cause was minor textual differences in labelling (e.g., "by color select" vs. "select by colour"). Most differences were resolved automatically by string matching using regular expressions. The matching rules for the regular expressions were crafted manually based on actual command names from the GIMP menus. After this process, there remained 40-50 unmapped features (of the original 617 distinct features in the raw QF-Graph). For these remaining features, the mapping was done manually based on our knowledge of the target application. Manual inspection also revealed that a feature's parent entity (e.g., menu name) was sometimes present in the raw data in addition to the command itself. This is because Web documentation will often specify a command's full path. For example, the line "Tools > Paint Tools > Paintbrush" would lead both "Tools" and "Paint Tools" to appear in the graph. We removed such menu names from the graph.

Generating Recommendations

To generate personalized, contextually relevant command recommendations, QFRecs uses the cleaned QF-graph as an automatically generated plan library. Based on a user's last x command selections (i.e., the history size), QFRecs "activates" the corresponding nodes in the graph (i.e., the recently used features/commands). Our system currently uses the last 5 distinct observed commands for this initial activiation phase, however, this history size is a configurable parameter. Larger history sizes will mean recommendations tailored more to the user's overall usage than their current context. After the the user's last x commands are activiated, QFRecs "activites" possible task (query) nodes based on their connection weights. This step amounts to estimating which of the tasks in the graph are most likely to be the user's current task. Using these estimations, QFRecs then "activates" other relevant commands for those candidate tasks.

This process is illustrated in Figure 2. In this example, the history is size 2 and the last two observed commands are "Blur/Sharpen" and "feather". QFRecs first finds the set of tasks that are strongly associated those two features (see the left-hand nodes in Figure 2 a) using the edge weights in Table 1. In the next step, QFRecs uses those strongly associated tasks to isolate other features (see the right-hand nodes in Figure 2 b) associated with those tasks. These features are then ranked according to the summed weights of all of their associated tasks activated in the previous step, enabling the system to recommend the top k features. In this small example ($k = 2$) QFRecs recommends "blend" and "add layer mask" to the user.

Recommendation Types

Using the process described above, the recommended commands will be one of the following two types:

1. *"Familiar" Recommendations:* These are commands in the user's existing command vocabulary that are predicted to be most relevant to the current usage context.
2. *"Unfamiliar" Recommendations:* These are contextually-relevant recommendations for commands that are not yet in the user's command vocabulary.

These recommendations serve different purposes. "Familiar" recommendations will not introduce users to new commands, but if promoted effectively, have the potential to improve task effeciency. "Unfamiliar" recommendations, on the other hand, have the potential to enhance feature awareness. That this method is capable of generating both types of recommendations raises a number of interesting interface presentation questions, which we begin to explore in our laboratory evaluation. However, we first explore the accuracy and potential utility of these document-based recommendations using offline analysis.

OFFLINE EVALUATION

We evaluated our QF-Graph approach on a corpus of GIMP usage data that was collected as part of the Ingimp project [26, 36]. This corpus contains feature usage histories (or logs) from 207 users, collected over a period of approximately two years. We used this data to evaluate our prototype along two dimensions. The first was its ability to generate relevant recommendations, to gain an initial understanding of the approach's potential to improve users' feature awareness. We also evaluated the approach's accuracy in predicting a user's next command selection, comparing our approach to frequency- and recency-based prediction algorithms (e.g., [9. 15]).

Potential to Promote Awareness of Relevant Commands

In assessing the approach's potential to make users aware of new commands, we first examined (according to the definitions above), how many of the generated recommendations could be classified as "unfamiliar". Figure 3 illustrates the mean breakdown of the recommendations into the two types when QFRecs generates 5, 10, 15 and 20 recommendations (Recommendation Size in Figure 3). These results indicate that the QF-based approach tends to favor "unfamiliar" recommendations, particularly as the number of recommendations increases.

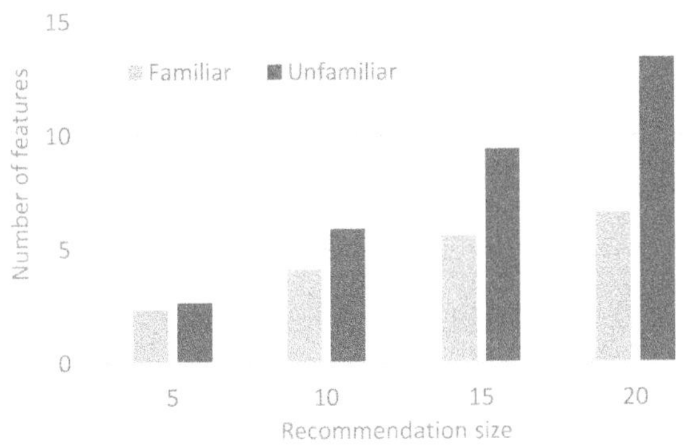

Figure 4. The mean number of familiar features and novel unfamiliar features for different recommendation sizes.

As a measure of recommendation relevance, we used a modified version of the K-tail evaluation method, introduced by Li *et al.* to evaluate their CommunityCommands recommender system [30, 35]. A K-tail evaluation divides a series of used features F into two sets: a training set (F_{train}) and a test set (F_{test}), such that the test set F_{test} contains *k* distinct features which are not in F_{train}. The training set is then used as the user's history and the prediction algorithm's performance is measured according to how well it predicts those k-distinct features in F_{test}. As an initial measure of the relevance of the "unfamiliar" recommendations to the user's current usage context, we adapted this evaluation method as follows: We measured whether or not our system's recommendations predict at least one new feature in the next *k* feature invocations (i.e., whether or not at least one "unfamiliar" recommendation appears in the next k feature invocations).

Figure 4 depicts our results for a range of recommendation and tail sizes. With a recommendation size of 20, QFRecs achieves a k-tail "accuracy" that is up to 80%. We also analyzed the k-tail accuracy of QFRecs's "familiar" recommendations, with Figure 5 illustrating similar trends.

To provide further insight into the relevance of the novel command recommendations, we also examined how

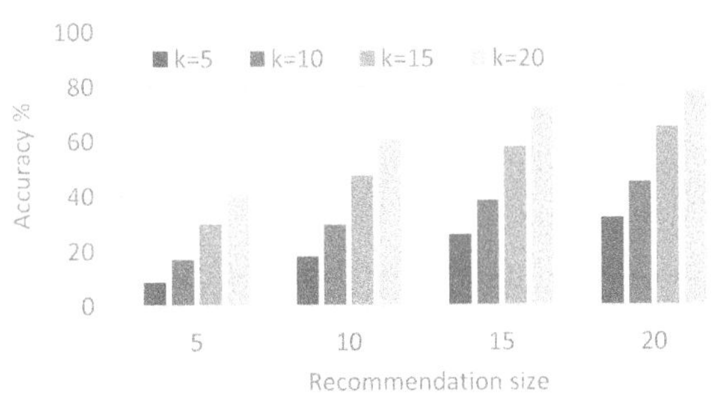

Figure 3. Performance of our QF-based approach recommending an "unfamiliar" feature that is then used in the next k feature invocations.

many of the "unfamiliar" recommendations are "accurate" according to the above definition. Table 2 illustrates that, on average, 3 - 9% of "unfamiliar" recommendations in a given set appear in the user's next k commands. The table also illustrates a large variability in accuracy, with up to 80% of the recommendations appearing in the user's next k selections. In some respects, the results in Figure 4 and Table 2 represent a lower bound on the relevance of the system's recommendations; users may be failing to use certain features not because of lack of relevance, but because of lack of awareness.

Combined, these results suggest that the QF-based approach (as currently instantiated in our QFRecs system) is able to recommend at least some relevant commands. The results also suggest that if promoted effectively within the interface, the recommendations could potentially aid users in completing their current task. We explore this question of presentation in our laboratory study and describe potential ways to improve the recommendations in the Discussion.

Predicting the Next Command

The above results provide an initial indication that the QF-based approach does generate some user-relevant recommendations in that they appear later in the user's command stream. In this section, we explore the approach's potential to immediately streamline access to needed commands, by analyzing the degree to which the recommended set accurately predicts the next command in the stream. We also compared our QF-based approach with two algorithms commonly used in prior work on adaptive interfaces (e.g. [9, 15]): frequency-based predictions, and recency-based predictions. In this case, we defined an "accurate" prediction as one where the user's next action is within the recommended set of commands.

When considering all users' data, we found that the frequency-based algorithm dramatically outperformed the others when it came to predicting the user's next command (see Figure 6). When examining the reasons why, we found that the users in this particular dataset tended to have very homogenous and stable command

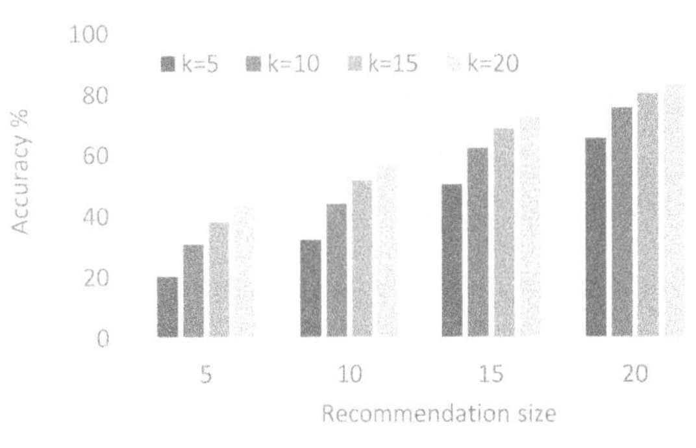

Figure 5. Performance of our QF-based approach in recommending a "familiar" feature that is then used again in the next k feature invocations.

	K = 5			K = 10			K = 15			K = 20		
	Accuracy %	Max %	Standard deviation	Accuracy %	Max %	Standard deviation	Accuracy %	Max %	Standard deviation	Accuracy %	Max %	Standard deviation
R = 5	3.3	60	10.79	5.79	80	11.95	6.68	80	12.75	7.25	80	13.76
R=10	3.85	40	6.11	5.81	50	7.54	7.3	50	8.46	8.53	50	9.13
R=15	4.39	33.33	5.05	6.39	40	6.29	7.68	40	7.07	8.7	40	7.64
R=20	4.52	25	4.07	6.38	30	5.1	7.84	35	5.76	9	35	6.24

Table 2. Average and maximum percentage of correct recommendations for each tail (k) and recommendation set size (R).

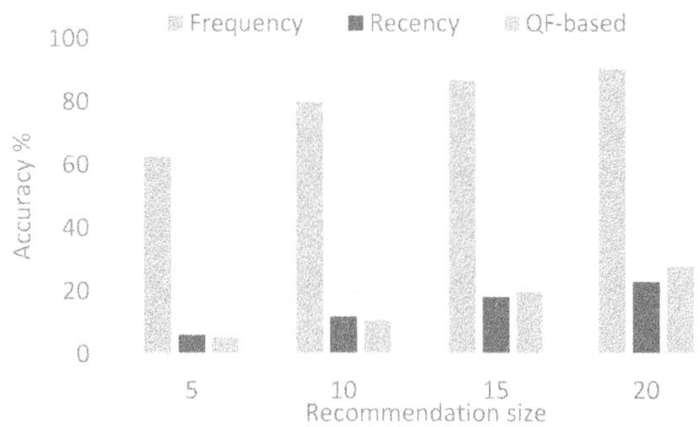

Figure 6. The overall accuracy in predicting the next command of the Frequency-based, Recency-based and QF-based approaches for different recommendation sizes.

usage, which naturally favors the frequency-based approach. As an example, consider a feature invocation sequence of length 149, but that consists of only 10 distinct features. With a recommendation size of 10, once these 10 features are observed, the algorithm will never fail.

To better characterize and explore the dataset, we defined a user's feature usage diversity, R_d, as follows

$$R_d = \frac{Number\ of\ Distinct\ Features\ Used}{Sequence\ Length}$$

In this dataset, the mean R_d for all 178 users with usage sequences longer than 20 is 0.1668 with a standard deviation of 0.1329. The max(R_d) was 0.6666 (sequence length = 42 and number of distinct commands = 28) and min(R_d) was 0.0043 (sequence length = 23459 and number of distinct commands = 101). Whereas the frequency-based approach substantially outperformed the QF-Graph approach for users with low feature diversity, the results are much more promising for users with high feature diversity. As an example, Figure 7 compares the accuracy of the different algorithms for a user with near mean feature diversity (0.1667). In this case, the QF-based approach actually outperforms the alternatives when the recommendation size is 5.

A second potential downside of the frequency-based approach is that it requires usage patterns to stabilize before it can be effective. For example, Figure 8 compares the frequency-based approach's accuracy over its first 30 feature invocations to its overall performance. Our QF-based approach, on the other hand, requires less start-up time; it is currently set to generate recommendations based on the last five commands.

Thus, to summarize, we found that a frequency-based or any history-based approach is sensitive to the usage diversity and session length. While the QF-based approach may not be an effective predictor when faced with long, homogenous sessions, it has advantages for short, diverse user sessions. Further, a frequency- or recency-based approach is (by definition) unable to recommend "unfamiliar" commands.

Given the potential for the QF-based approach to produce recommendations that are both needed and novel, in the

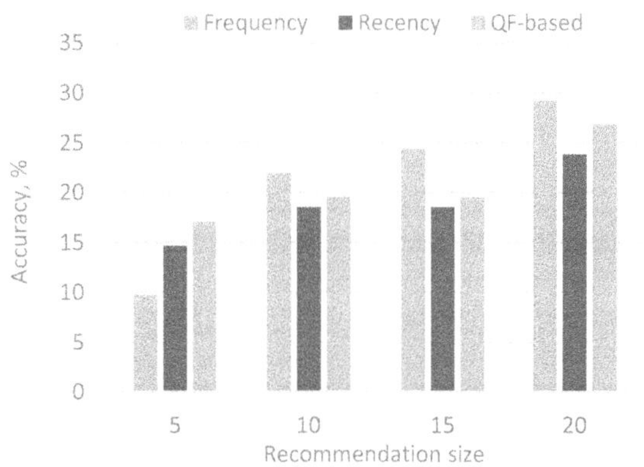

Figure 7. Accuracy of the Frequency-based, the Recency-based and QF-based approach for an average diverse session.

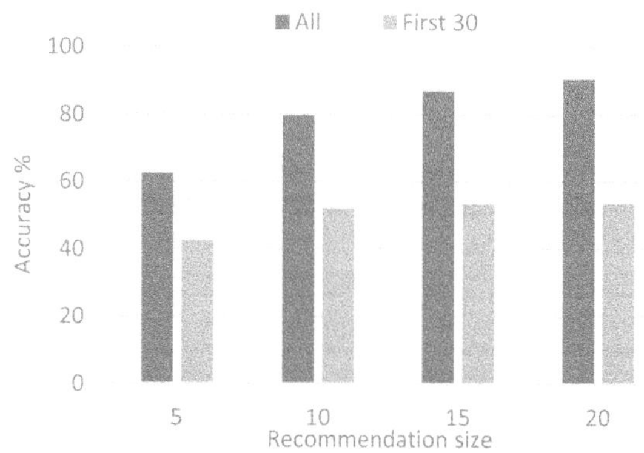

Figure 8. The accuracy of frequency-based approach over users' first 30 command invocations and over all command invocations.

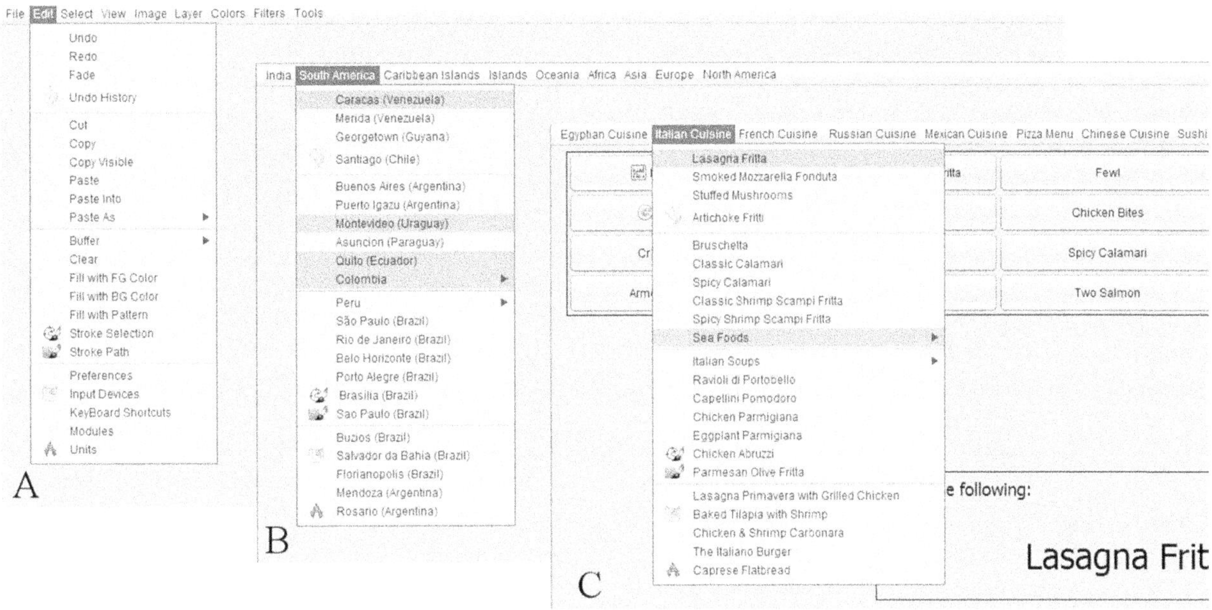

Figure 9. Sample snapshot of the interface variants used in study: Basic interface (A), Combined interface (B), and Separated interface (C). The recommendations highlighted in pink are the "familiar" features and the features highlighted in blue are "unfamiliar" features.

next section, we explore how the system might present these recommendations to the user.

LABORATORY EVALUATION

The goal of our laboratory evaluation was to explore two different ways to present the system's recommendations. As described in the section "Recommendation Types", QFRecs's recommendations can be divided into two types: commands that are "familiar" to the user (i.e., they are part of the user's usage history) and those that are "unfamiliar" (i.e., they are not part of the usage history). We experimented with two different ways to present these recommendations and compared both presentation techniques to a control condition with no recommendations. We explore the impact of the presentation techniques on both primary task performance and on incidental awareness of recommended features not part of the primary task.

Participants

Eighteen participants (2 females) were recruited from a university campus. Participants were between the ages of 18-25 and were rewarded with a 15$ gift card.

Conditions

Our three interface variants were as follows:

1. **Basic Interface:** A control condition with traditional static menus (Figure 9 A).
2. **Combined Interface:** Recommendations for both "familiar" and "unfamiliar" features were highlighted in place (i.e., within the menus) using one of the best known visual highlighting techniques: ephemeral adaptation [11]. With ephemeral adaptation, recommended items appear immediately when a menu is opened, with the remaining items gradually appearing after an initial delay (500 ms as in [11]). The two types of recommendations ("familiar" vs. "unfamiliar") were distinguished only by colour: the "familiar" features were highlighted with a pink overlay and the "unfamiliar" features were highlighted with a blue overlay (Figure 9 B).
3. **Separated Interface:** "Familiar" recommendations were ephemerally highlighted within the menus (using also a blue overlay) but "unfamiliar" recommendations were presented in a separate palette (as well as appearing as non-recommended features in the menus) (Figure 9 C). In the separate palette, the full command path each feature was also available on mouse over. In comparison to the Combined Interface, with the Separated Interface, users could choose to ignore these "unfamiliar" recommendations completely in favor of focusing on their primary task. This palette-based approach has been commonly explored in prior work on novel command recommendations (e.g. [30, 31]).

To enable our system to make recommendations using real GIMP usage data (see the "Tasks" section), and our QF-graph to be built from actual web queries and documentation, the menu hierarchy in all interfaces was modeled after The GNU Image Manipulation Program (GIMP) version 2.8.6. To simplify the interface slightly for our participants, we excluded the "Windows" and "Help" menus, resulting in 9 top-level menus containing a total of 368 features.

Design, Tasks, and Procedure

The experimental task was a sequence of menu selections using each of the three interfaces described above. In other words, our study used a within-subjects design, where all participants experienced all three interface variants. The menu selections were based on a real user's data from the Ingimp dataset described in the "Offline Evaluation" section. We selected data from a user with a sufficiently long sequence that was also close to the data set's mean diversity. The selected usage sequence was 74 selections long and had a diversity of .2065 (defined in the "Offline Evaluation" section). From this sequence, we used the first 20 selections as "training", and the next 50 features as the main task (discarding last 4 selections in the interest of participant time).

For each feature selection, our experimental interface provided participants with the name of the feature, but not the menu name. As a result, participants had to explore the interface (using the top-level menu names as a guide) to find their needed commands. Once the participant correctly selected the displayed feature, the next feature to be selected was displayed. We used the same selection sequence in all interface variants, but used different interface "masks" (the GIMP menus, Geography-related menus, and Cuisine-related menus) to mitigate learning effects between conditions. The structure of all three masks was identical. To further account for potential order effects, the order of interface and the assignment of masks to interface were counterbalanced using a Latin Square.

After each main task, we measured incidental command awareness [11], by having participants perform a recall test. During this recall test participants selected 24 distinct commands that were recommended by the QF-based system but that was not part of the main task.

The procedure for the 1.5 hour experiment was as follows: Participants first completed a background and demographics questionnaire. Then, for each interface variant, participants completed a training task consisting of 20 selections, followed by the main task consisting of 50 selections. After the main task, participants completed

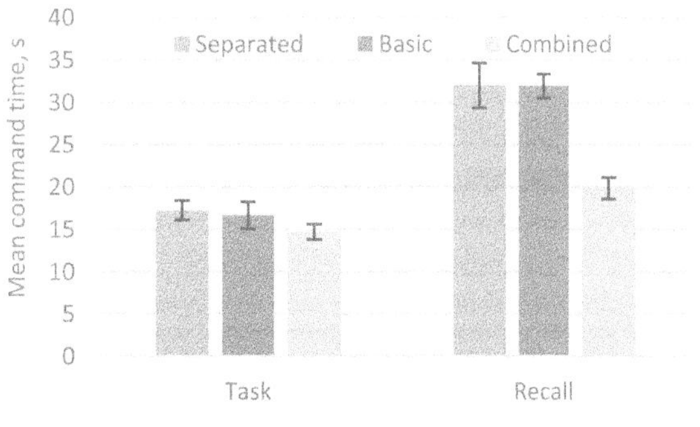

Figure 10. Mean selection time between commands (with standard errors) for the main task (left) and the recall task (right)

the NASA-TLX [22], which measures perceived workload. Participants then completed the recall test described above prior to repeating the above steps with the next interface variant. The session concluded with a comparative questionnaire.

In the Combined and Separated interfaces, our prototype system presented its top 20 recommendations based on the user's last 5 command selections. With this particular usage stream, this recommended set accurately predicted the next command in the stream 18% of the time.

Apparatus

An Intel Core i7 desktop with 8 GB of RAM and Microsoft Windows 7 was used for the experiment. The system was connected to a 22'' LCD monitor with a 1920x1080 resolution. The experiment software recorded all timing and selection data.

Hypotheses

Given the low predictive accuracy of QFRecs's recommended set in comparison to those studied in prior work (e.g., [11]), we did not have any apriori hypotheses on the effect of interface on selection speed during the primary task. We did, however, have the following hypotheses with respect to recall selection speed, perceived workload and user preference:

H1 (Recall Speed): The Combined interface will have faster recall times than both the Basic interface and the Separated interface. We expect no difference between the Basic interface and the Separated interface.

H2 (Perceived Workload): Perceived workload will be lower with the Combined interface than with the Separated interface.

H3 (User Preference): Users will prefer the Combined interface over the Separated interface.

Results

We performed our analysis with a one-way RM-ANOVA with *Interface* (Basic, Combined, Separated) as the within-subjects factor. We used $p > 0.05$ as our threshold for significance, and Bonferroni corrections were applied to all post-hoc comparisons. Error bars in the figures represent Standard Error.

Primary Task Selection Time

As expected, we did not find a significant main effect of Interface on primary task selection time ($F_{2,34} = 1.064$, $p = .356$, $\eta^2 = .059$, Figure 10 left). The fact that the recommendations did not significantly improve immediate task performance is consistent with prior results on low accuracy predictors (e.g., [11]). Despite having only limited immediate accuracy, the recommendations did not hurt task performance, and perhaps even helped it slightly (as indicated by the means and effect size), when presented in-place.

Recall Speed (H1)

In the case of the incidental awareness task (i.e., the Recall test), we found the main effect of Interface was statistically significant ($F_{2,34}$ = 12.731, p < .001, η^2 = .428, Figure 10 right). Moreover, the post-hoc comparisons revealed significantly faster selections using the Combined interface (19.8s, se 1.3s) when compared to either the Basic (32.0s, se. 1.4s, p < 0.001) or Separated (32.0s, se. 2.7s, p = 0.005) conditions. The difference between the Basic and Separated conditions was not statistically significant (p = 1.00). Therefore, we find support for *H1*.

Perceived workload (H2)

As a measure of a perceived workload, we used the data from NASA-TLX questionnaires. Table 3 shows significant main effects of Interface on two of the NASA-TLK categories: "hard work" and "frustration". For these categories, participants reported experiencing lower workload with the Combined interface, however, the only significant pairwise difference revealed by the post-hoc comparisons was that of frustration for the Combined and Basic interface variants (p = 0.038). Therefore, we could not fully support *H2*.

User Preference (H3)

Regarding subjective preferences, in the post study questionnaire we asked our participants to rank the different interface types based on their overall performance. The analysis of results showed high inclination towards the Combined option, with 13 participants ranking it as their most preferred interface variation. For comparison, 3 users rated the Separated interface as their primary choice and only two preferred the Basic one (this difference was significant with χ^2 = 16.0, p = 0.002). Therefore we find support for *H3*.

DISCUSSION

Combined, the results of our offline and laboratory evaluations suggest that recommendations generated based on information mined from web documentation is a promising approach to improving command awareness in feature-rich software. They also highlight a number of important considerations moving forward.

Assessing the Utility of Novel Recommendations

Our offline evaluation indicates that for our target application (GIMP), the QF-based approach was able to generate at least some contextually relevant recommendations. For example, when providing the user with 20 recommendations (which would be distributed throughout the entire menu hierarchy), previously collected GIMP usage data indicated that at least one recommended command would subsequently be used within a user's next 15 selections. Further work is required, however, to assess the relevance and utility of recommended commands that do not later appear in the user's command stream, since their omission does not imply a lack of utility. A potential first step in this direction would be to collect relevance ratings from application experts; however, a longer-term experiment is necessary to fully assess the value of these recommendations from the user's perspective. A longer-term experiment would also enable us to compare the QF-based approach to the collaborative filtering approaches explored in prior work [30, 35].

	Basic	Separated	Combined	F	Sig
Mental demand	13.1 (.78)	12.8 (.96)	11.3 (.94)	1.756	0.188
Physical demand	4.5 (1.0)	4.9 (.94)	4.0 (.81)	1.125	0.336
Temporal demand	10.8 (1.3)	10.8 (1.1)	9.7 (1.1)	0.98	0.386
Success	6.2 (1.1)	4.6 (.95)	4.8 (1.0)	1.717	0.195
Hard work	**14.3 (1.0)**	**12.9 (1.0)**	**10.4 (1.2)**	**3.754**	**0.034**
Frustration	**10.9 (.86)**	**9.4 (1.1)**	**7.1 (1.0)**	**5.251**	**0.01**

Table 3. Mean (st. err.) NASA-TLX values (1=low, 20=high). Rows in bold indicate significant differences.

Prototype Extensions and Improvements

Motivated by our initial feasibility study, there are a number of system-related improvements worth exploring. Aside from culling queries from the original QF-Graph that were clearly not representative of high-level tasks, we did little to optimize the graph's suitability to act as a recommender. More sophisticated lexical analysis or machine learning could enable the system to focus its recommendations on a more informative set of high-level tasks. It also possible that restricting the documentation set to specific tutorial repositories would improve the precision of the command-to-task mappings. Finally, there are numerous avenues that could be explored to improve the approach's predictive capabilities, such as incorporating command usage frequency.

In addition improving the algorithmic component, there is also the potential to make the interaction between the system and the user more of a mixed-initiative one [21]. In particular, the system could leverage the human-readable format of the high-level tasks to display its task assessments to the user. The user could then refine these assessments to obtain more tailored recommendations.

Presentation Techniques

Our laboratory evaluation is one of few systematic explorations of how to present command recommendations designed to promote command awareness (as opposed to short-term efficiency). Our results indicate that presenting these types of recommendations in-place can significantly improve incidental command awareness over a palette-based approach. This is perhaps not surprising given that this presentation technique is more obtrusive. What is perhaps more surprising is that the extra visual complexity introduced into the main interface did not appear to negatively impact short-term task efficiency. Users also preferred this in-place presentation strategy and reported lower levels of frustration. Further exploration is needed to determine the sensitivity of these results to factors such as the number of recommendations, their distribution across the menus, etc.

While our results show initial promise for an in-place presentation technique, there are a number of open questions concerning how to present recommendations in a way that will eventually lead to their adoption. For example, with the palette approach, it would be easier to provide rich supplemental information on why the command is recommended and how it might be used in practice. In a palette, the system could display its confidence in each recommended command, the list of tasks to which the command relates, and links to documentation that illustrate how to use the command. Such information could also potentially be integrated within the main interface (available, for example, on mouse over), but at the risk of impacting immediate task performance. A palette-based approach could also potentially do more to promote command location awareness than simply displaying the command path on mouse over. For example, users could be provided with an animated location cue when they select a command in the palette.

Understanding the above types of presentation-level tradeoffs will be important to the ultimate success of all approaches to command recommendation, not just ones based on Web documentation. It is also possible that a more static presentation technique is desirable. For example, the system could recommend entire task-centric interface that corresponds to the user's most probable high-level tasks [28].

Generalizability

Finally, it would be interesting to explore the generalizability of the QF-based approach to command recommendations to feature-rich applications other than GIMP. Fourney *et al.*'s original QF-Graph graph results suggest that the technique will extend to other applications with a large Web presence [13]. Exploring generalizability to other applications, however, could provide insight on how properties of the graphs themselves affect their abilities to generate useful recommendations, such as the range of high-level tasks present, and the connectedness of the graphs.

In addition to exploring the generalizability of our approach to other feature-rich applications, it will also be important moving forward to explore the generalizability of our study results to a more diverse user population.

SUMMARY

In this paper we have created a prototype recommender system that leverages a new form of information on command relevance: command-to-task mappings mined from Web documentation. Our offline evaluation suggests that this technique has the potential to expose users to a number of new and relevant commands, while our online evaluation suggests value in integrating the recommendations within the main interface. Our work also suggests a number of promising avenues for future research, included developing a more detailed understanding of the design space for recommendation presentation and exploring ways to tailor the system's recommendations according to user feedback. Long-term evaluations of deployed technologies are also needed to assess the impact of these document-based recommendations on command use.

ACKNOWLEDGEMENTS

This work was supported by the GRAND Network Centre of Excellence and the Natural Sciences and Engineering Research Council (NSERC). We also thank Adam Fourney for his invaluable help in providing data for building the QF graph.

REFERENCES

1. Adar, E., Dontcheva, M., and Laput, G. CommandSpace : Modeling the Relationships Between Tasks , Descriptions and Features.In *Proc. UIST 2014*, 167-176.
2. Bunt, A., Conati, C. and McGrenere, J. Supporting Interface Customization Using a Mixed-Initiative Approach. In *Proc. IUI 2007*, 92-10.
3. Bunt, A., Dubois, P., Lafreniere, B., Terry, M. and Cormack, D. TaggedComments: Promoting and Integrating User Comments in Online Application Tutorials. In *Proc. CHI 2014*, 4037-4046.
4. Charles L. A. Clarke, Gordon V. Cormack, and Thomas R. Lynam. Exploiting redundancy in question answering. In Proc. *SIGIR* Research and Development in Information Retrieval 2001, 358-365.
5. Chi, P.P., Ahn, S., Ren, A., Dontcheva, M., Li, W., and Hartmann, B. MixT: Automatic Generation of Step-by-Step Mixed Media Tutorials.In *Proc. UIST 2012*, 93–102
6. Dong, T., Dontcheva, M., Joseph, D., Karahalios, K., Newman, M.W., and Ackerman, M.S. Discovery-Based Games for Learning Software. In *Proc. CHI 2012,* 2083–2086.
7. Ekstrand, M., Li, W., Grossman, T., Matejka, J., and Fitzmaurice, G. Searching for Software Learning Resources Using Application Context. In *Proc. UIST 2011*, 195–204.
8. Fernquist, J., Grossman, T., and Fitzmaurice, G. Sketch-Sketch Revolution: An Engaging Tutorial System for Guided Sketching and Application Learning.In *Proc. UIST 2011*, 373–382.
9. Findlater, L. and McGrenere, J. A Comparison of Static, Adaptive, and Adaptable Menus. In Proc. *CHI 2004*, 89-96.

10. Findlater, L., Mcgrenere, J., Evaluating Reduced-Functionality Interfaces According to Feature Findability and Awareness. In *Proc. Interact 2007*, 592-605.
11. Findlater, L., Moffatt, K., Mcgrenere, J., and Dawson, J. Ephemeral Adaptation: The Use of Gradual Onset to Improve Menu Selection Performance. In *Proc. CHI 2009*, 1655–1664.
12. Fourney, A., Mann, R., and Terry, M. Characterizing the Usability of Interactive Applications through Query Log Analysis.In *Proc. CHI 2011*, 1817–1826.
13. Fourney, A., Mann, R., and Terry, M. Query-feature graphs: bridging user vocabulary and system functionality. In *Proc. UIST 2011*, 207-216.
14. Greenberg, S. The Computer User As Toolsmith: The Use, Reuse, and Organization of Computer-based Tools. Cambridge University Press, 1993.
15. Gajos, K., Czerwinski, M., Tan, D. and Weld, D. Exploring the design space for adaptive graphical user interfaces. In *Proc. AVI 2006*, 201-208.
16. Grabler, F., Agrawala, M., and Erato, J.S.T. Generating Photo Manipulation Tutorials by Demonstration. In *Proc. SIGGRAPH* 2009, 1–9.
17. Grossman, T.; Fitzmaurice, G. and Attar, R. A survey of software learnability: metrics, methodologies and guidelines. In *Proc. CHI* 2009, 649-658.
18. Grossman, T., Matejka, J., and Fitzmaurice, G. Chronicle: Capture, Exploration, and Playback of Document Workflow Histories.In *Proc. CHI* 2010, 143–152.
19. Grossman, T. and Fitzmaurice, G. ToolClips: An investigation of contextual video assistance for functionality understanding. In *Proc. CHI* 2010, 1515-1524.
20. Horvitz, E., Breese, J., Heckerman, D., Hovel, D., and Rommelse, K. The Lumiere Project: Bayesian User Modeling for Inferring the Goals and Needs of Software Users. In *Proc. UAI* 1998, 256–265.
21. Horvitz, E. Principles of mixed-initiative user interfaces. In *Proc CHI 99*. 159-166.
22. Hart, S.G., Staveland, L.E.: Development of NASA-TLX (Task Load Index): Results of Empirical and Theoretical Research. Human Mental Workload 1, 139–183 (1988)
23. Kim, J., Nguyen, P.T., Weir, S., Guo, P.J., Miller, R.C., and Gajos, K.Z. Crowdsourcing Step-by-Step Information Extraction to Enhance Existing How-to Videos.In *Proc. CHI 2014*, 4017–4026.
24. Kong, N., Grossman, T., Hartmann, B., Fitzmaurice, G., and Agrawala, M. Delta: A Tool For Representing and Comparing Workflows.In *Proc. CHI 2012*, 1027–1036.
25. Lafreniere, B., Bunt, A., Lount, M. and Terry, M. Understanding the Roles and Uses of Web Tutorials. In *Proc ICWSM 2013*, 303-310.
26. Lafreniere, B., Bunt, A., Whissell, J., Clarke, C., and Terry, M. Characterizing Large-Scale Use of a Direct Manipulation Application in the Wild. In *Proc GI 2010*, 11-17.
27. Lafreniere, B., Grossman, T., and Fitzmaurice, G. Community Enhanced Tutorials: Improving Tutorials with Multiple Demonstrations. *In Proc. CHI 2013*, 1779–1788.
28. Lafreniere, B., Krynicki, F., Terry, M., Bunt, A. and Lount, M. AdaptableGIMP: Designing a Socially-Adaptable Interface, In *Proc. UIST 2011*, 89-90.
29. Li, W., Grossman, T., and Fitzmaurice, G. GamiCAD: A Gamified Tutorial System For First Time AutoCAD Users.In *Proc. UIST 2012*, 103–112.
30. Li, W., Matejka, J., Grossman, T., Konstan, J. A. and Fitzmaurice, G. Design and Evaluation of a Command Recommendation System for Software Applications. In ACM Trans. Comput.-Hum. Interact., ACM, 2011, 18, 6:1-6:35.
31. Linton, F. and Schaefer, H.-P. Recommender Systems for Learning: Building User and Expert Models Through Long-Term Observation of Application Use. User Modeling and User-Adapted Interaction, Kluwer Academic Publishers (2000), 181-208.
32. Lount, M., and Bunt. A., Characterizing web-based tutorials: Exploring quality, community, and showcasing strategies. In *Proc. SIGDOC 2014*.
33. Matejka, J., Grossman, T., and Fitzmaurice, G. Patina: Smart Heatmaps for Visualizing Application Usage.In *Proc. CHI 2013*, 3227-3236.
34. Matejka, J., Grossman, T., and Fitzmaurice, G. IP-QAT: In-Product Questions, Answers & Tips. In *Proc. UIST 2011*, 175–184.
35. Matejka, J., Li, W., Grossman, T., and Fitzmaurice, G. CommunityCommands: Command Recommendations for Software Applications. In *Proc. UIST 2009*, 193–202.
36. McGrenere, J., Baecker, R.M., and Booth, K.S. An Evaluation of a Multiple Interface Design Solution for Bloated Software. In *Proc. CHI 2002*, ACM Press (2002), 163–170
37. Terry, M., Kay, M., Van Vugt, B., Slack, B., and Park, T. 2008. Ingimp: introducing instrumentation to an end-user open source application. In Proc. *CHI 2008*. 607-616.

Minimal Interaction Search in Recommender Systems

Branislav Kveton
Adobe Research
321 Park Ave, San Jose, CA, United States
kveton@adobe.com

Shlomo Berkovsky
CSIRO
Vimiera Rd, Marsfield, NSW, Australia
shlomo.berkovsky@csiro.au

ABSTRACT

While numerous works study algorithms for predicting item ratings in recommender systems, the area of the user-recommender interaction remains largely under-explored. In this work, we look into user interaction with the recommendation list, aiming to devise a method that allows users to discover items of interest in a minimal number of interactions. We propose *generalized linear search* (GLS), a combination of linear and generalized searches that brings together the benefits of both approaches. We prove that GLS performs at least as well as generalized search and compare our method to several baselines and heuristics. Our evaluation shows that GLS is liked by the users and achieves the shortest interactions.

Author Keywords

Human-computer interaction; interactive search; generalized binary search; recommender systems; active learning

ACM Classification Keywords

H.5.m. Information Interfaces and Presentation (e.g. HCI): Miscellaneous

INTRODUCTION

Recommender systems are widely used in eCommerce sites and online social networks as a means to help users cope with the information overloading. The recommenders select, in a personalized manner, a set of items from a substantially larger set of candidate items and present the recommended items to users. The selection is based on the predicted ratings, reflecting the match of the items to the preferences and needs of the users. Normally, N top-scoring items are included in the recommendation list.

Although numerous works focused on the algorithms for improving the accuracy of item selection [20], little research looked into the intricacies of the presentation of recommendations [11]. The canonic way of presenting the recommendations is through a list, the items of which are ordered according to their predicted rating. The choice of the item to consume – a movie to watch, a product to buy, or a song to listen to – is done by the user upon examining the recommendation list. To ease navigation, the list is normally is split into small-size batches, such as 10 items per screen for a desktop interface or 3-4 items for a mobile app.

For a large N, the examination of the recommendation list can be tedious. Consider also the challenge of choosing the desired item out of a set of attractive recommendations, and the importance of the recommendation list presentation that allows easy discovery of items of interest becomes clear.

In this work, we focus on minimizing the length of user interaction with the recommender. We assume that the predicted item ratings are computed by the recommender and leave the details of rating computation beyond the scope of our work. Given the predicted ratings, we focus on N top-scoring items, assuming that an item of interest is included there. Note that the user may not know the exact item they are looking for and therefore cannot use the search functionality. However, the user may be able to describe the features of the item of interest (e.g., "something like that Irish black comedy I watched last week") and answer questions about the target item. We aim at developing a method for the recommendation list presentation that facilitates the discovery of the target item in least interactions (clicks, scrolls, etc.) between the user and the recommender.

The simplest approach to searching recommended items is what we refer to as *linear search* (LS): the items are ranked according to their predicted ratings and the users scroll through batches of items until they find the target item. A natural generalization of LS is *linear search with item categories* ($\mathtt{LS}_{\mathtt{cat}}$), which capitalizes on the knowledge of item categories. Here, the users are first shown the list of item categories, out of which they choose the category that best matches the target item. Then the users search for the target item in a smaller list of items in the selected category. This approach is adopted by several recommenders, e.g., the 'bands' interface deployed by Netflix. However, our simulations show that the discovery of the target item with LS and $\mathtt{LS}_{\mathtt{cat}}$ requires many user-recommender interactions.

But why does the item category selection occur only once? Can this be repeated in order to carry out a hierarchical search over dynamically computed item categories? This kind of search can be considered as a question-answering game [26]. At each round of the game, the recommended items are dynamically split into K item categories, which are presented to the user who selects the category of the target item. The game stops when only a single item – the target item – is left. This game is a form of *active learning* and is known as *generalized*

IUI 2015, March 29–April 1, 2015, Atlanta, GA, USA.

http://dx.doi.org/10.1145/2678025.2701367

Interaction 1 of GLS User is shown 8 categories (GS)	Interaction 2 of GLS User is shown 8 categories (GS)	Interaction 3 of GLS User is shown 8 categories (GS)	Interaction 4 of GLS User is shown 8 movies (LS)
Action Thrillers	Romance Classics	Contemporary Literature	Misery (1990)
Foreign Regions	Mobster	Crime Thrillers	**Primal Fear (1996)**
Ages 11-12	**Thrillers**	Mystery	General's Daughter (1999)
20th Century Period	Based on Bestsellers	Courtroom Dramas	Silence of the Lambs (1991)
Based on the Book	Crime Dramas	Sci-Fi Horror	Dolores Claiborne (1994)
Classics	Drama	Crime Dramas	Pelican Brief (1993)
Drama	Classic Dramas	**Based on Bestsellers**	Boys from Brazil (1978)
Something Else	Something Else	Something Else	Instinct (1999)

Figure 1. Searching for a movie like *Silence of the Lambs (1991)* with GLS. The choices of the user are highlighted in bold.

search (GS) [10, 12, 18, 5, 25]. In large-scale problems, GS is expected to find the target item in less user interactions than LS and LS_{cat}. The main limitation of GS is that the number of interactions can be high when the space of recommended items cannot be partitioned well into item categories.

In this work, we propose a combination of GS and LS, which brings together the benefits of both approaches. GS is a hierarchical approach and therefore it converges in $O(\log(N))$ interactions when the categories of recommended items are sufficiently diverse. However, in the worst-case, all N items may belong to the same category and GS may need $\Omega(N)$ interactions to find the target item. On the other hand, LS does not depend on the item categories and is efficient when some recommended items are more likely to be chosen than others. We combine the two approaches and suggest switching from GS to LS when the former is suboptimal. The pivotal question here refers to the *switching criterion*, i.e., when to switch from GS to LS. We argue that GS should be applied as long as the *expected length* of user interaction in GS is shorter than that in LS. We denote the proposed combined approach as *generalized linear search* (GLS).

We illustrate GLS with an example of searching for a movie like "Silence of the Lambs" (Figure 1). At the first interaction, GS suggests 8 movie categories and the user selects the best matching category, "Based on the Book". The search space gets reduced accordingly. At the second interaction, the expected cost of GS is smaller than that of LS. Therefore, GS suggest another 8 categories, the user selects the best matching category, "Thrillers", and the search space gets reduced again. The third interaction is still GS and the user selects again a movie category. At the fourth interaction, the expected cost of GS is larger than that of LS. Therefore, GLS switches to LS and the user is shown 8 movies that are consistent with the user's previous answers. Then the user selects "Primal Fear" as the desired movie. Overall, the length of this user interaction is 4.

In this work, we prove that GLS performs at least as well as GS, and compare it experimentally with GS and several heuristic search methods. We evaluate the expected length of user interaction with the recommender using two datasets and show that GLS achieves shorter interactions than GS. We also show that the expected length of GLS interaction is never longer than that of the heuristic methods. However, the performance of the heuristic methods requires an a-priori parameter tuning, whereas GLS is parameter-free. We also conduct an intra-group user study that compares the binary variants of GLS and GS. The study shows that GLS achieves shorter interactions and is easier to use. The subjects also express their direct preference towards GLS.

Overall, the proposed GLS approach combines the state-of-the-art in active learning with a widely used practical technique, and shows a significant improvement in using both. It should be highlighted that GLS combines two existing search methods, GS and LS, in an optimal way. The presented combination has several notable properties and contributions. First, GLS is guaranteed to perform no worse than each of its parts, GS and LS, and we prove this formally. Second, GLS requires no tunable parameters and can be easily applied in practice. Third, GLS improves significantly over both GS and LS, and we show this by both offline experiments and a live user study. In the experiments, we report improvements as large as 50%.

PRELIMINARIES

In this section, we discuss two policies for searching a list of recommended items, LS and LS_{cat}. We evaluate the policies on one problem and use this to motivate our work.

We formalize the problem of minimal interaction search as follows. The user has a *target item* e^* in mind, which belongs to a set of N *recommended items* $E = \{1, \ldots, N\}$. The user cannot express what the item is, otherwise the user could find the item using conventional search techniques, like text search. The target item e^* is drawn i.i.d. from the distribution π over items E. The distribution π is generated by a recommender and is known, but the target item e^* is unknown. The goal is to present items E to the user such that e^* can be discovered in *least interactions*. More formally, let A be an interface for searching items E and $N_A(e^*)$ be the number of user interactions with A until e^* is discovered. Then our goal is to design an interface that minimizes $\mathbb{E}_{e\sim\pi}[N_A(e)]$.

Our abstraction of interactive search can model various problems. For instance, the search interface A can be a list of items, which are ordered according to their popularity, or an assistant on a mobile device that asks natural language questions. The interaction can be clicking on the screen of a device, scrolling down the list of items, or answering a natural-language question.

Linear Search

Linear search (LS) is a form of search, where items E are sorted in descending order according to their score. The sorted items are then scanned by the user until the target item e^* is discovered. This search interface is prevalent in existing recommender systems.

Algorithm 1 LS: Linear search.

Input:
Items $V \subseteq E$
Number of shown items L

Let $e_1, \ldots, e_{|V|}$ be an ordering of items V such that:
$\pi(e_1) \geq \ldots \geq \pi(e_{|V|})$
$\ell \leftarrow 0$
repeat
$A \leftarrow \{e_i \in V : \ell L < i \leq (\ell + 1)L\}$
Show items A to the user
$\ell \leftarrow \ell + 1$
until $(e^* \in A)$

Output: Target item $e^* \in A$

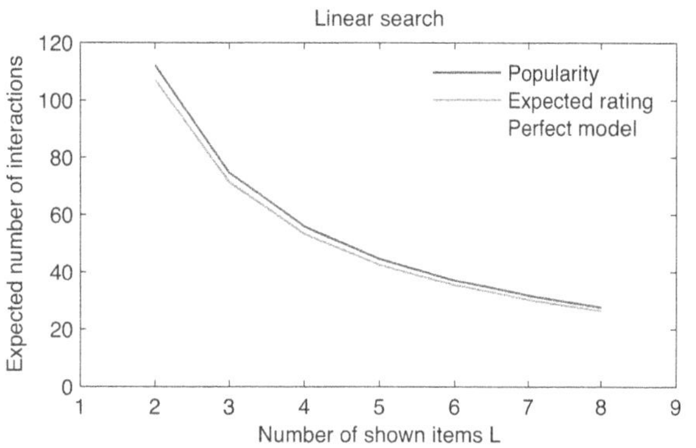

Figure 2. The length of interaction for three LS policies.

In this work, we assume that the items are divided into batches of size L. For the sake of concreteness, and without loss of generality, we assume that L is the number of items displayed on the screen of a device. Therefore, the length of interaction to find item e^* is the number of screens that the user has to scan until the target item e^* appears on the screen. The pseudocode of LS is in Algorithm 1. The score of item e is the probability of choosing the item, $\pi(e)$.

We present a motivational simulation, which compares three LS policies that differ in the computation of the item scores. The first policy scores items by their popularity, i.e., the number of times that the item was consumed. We refer to this policy as *popularity*. The second policy scores items by their expected rating, which is computed by averaging all the available ratings for the item. We refer to this policy as *expected rating*. In the last policy, the score of the item is the actual rating assigned by the user. The score of unrated items is 0. This policy is obviously unrealistic and cannot be implemented in practice, because the ratings of recommended items are typically unknown. However, the policy can be viewed as a lower bound on the length of interaction of any LS policy, under the assumption that the true preferences of the user are known. Therefore, we refer to this policy as *perfect model*.

We evaluate the expected length of user interaction with all three policies using the *MovieLens* dataset, which is described in detail in the evaluation section. The expected interaction length is computed as follows. Initially, we randomly choose a target user. Then, we randomly choose a target item e^* from the movies that the user liked, i.e., rated with 4 or 5 stars. All movies are scored according to the chosen policy: *popularity*, *expected rating*, or *perfect model*. Finally, we rank the movies according to their scores and simulate LS until the target item e^* is found. The length of interaction is averaged over all users and target items, and we vary the number of shown items L from 2 to 8. The results of the simulation are reported in Figure 2.

We observe two trends. First, the expected length of interaction in all three policies decreases with the number of displayed items L. This is expected; as L increases, the length of interaction required to find a target item cannot increase. Second, we observe that the predicted item score affects the expected length of interaction. In particular, the *popularity* policy consistently performs worse than the *expected rating* policy, which performs worse than the *perfect model* policy. Interestingly, *popularity* performs only slightly worse than *expected rating*, while *perfect model* significantly outperforms the other two policies. On average, it finds the target item in about 20% of interactions of the *popularity* policy.

Linear Search with Item Categories

Linear search with item categories (LS_{cat}) is a variant of LS, where the users are first asked to choose the category of the target item e^*, out of K item categories. After the category is chosen, all items in that category are searched using LS. Note that LS_{cat} involves two types of user interaction. The first interaction is choosing one item category out of K. The remaining interactions are identical to LS – scanning the items until the target item e^* is discovered. This type of an interface is not unusual; e.g., Netflix 'bands' allow users to choose a movie genre and then scan through the movies in that genre.

LS_{cat} is parameterized by the number of item categories K that are shown to the user. We represent each category as a set $q \subseteq E$ such that $e \in q$ if and only if item e belongs to category q. The problem of choosing K item categories is an optimization problem. Loosely speaking, the best K categories partition the set of items E into K disjoint sets of cardinality N/K each. In this case, the set E is reduced to N/K items regardless of the item category chosen by the user. In practice, such a partitioning is typically impossible because the categories are not sufficiently diverse.

How to partition E into K item categories? We implement a greedy strategy for choosing the categories that was proposed by Bhamidipati *et al.* [5]. For a given K, we greedily select $K - 1$ item categories $q_1, \ldots, q_{K-1}$ whose cardinality is closest to N/K. In addition, we define a special category, $q_K \leftarrow \overline{(q_1 \cup \ldots \cup q_{K-1})}$, which includes all items that do not belong to any of the first $K - 1$ categories. The key advantage of this strategy is that any item in E is guaranteed to belong to at least one category q_k. Therefore, the user can always choose a category that matches the target item e^*. After the category q_k is chosen, the set of candidate items is reduced to $q_k \cap E$ and we apply LS. The pseudocode of LS_{cat} is shown in Algorithm 2.

Algorithm 2 $\texttt{LS}_{\texttt{cat}}$: Linear search with item categories.

Input:
Number of item categories K in a question
Number of shown items L

Choose $K-1$ categories $q_1, \dots, q_{K-1}$ given E and π
$q_K \leftarrow \overline{(q_1 \cup \dots \cup q_{K-1})}$
Ask the user to choose one category
The user chooses category q_k
$e^* \leftarrow \texttt{LS}(q_k \cap E, L)$

Output: Target item e^*

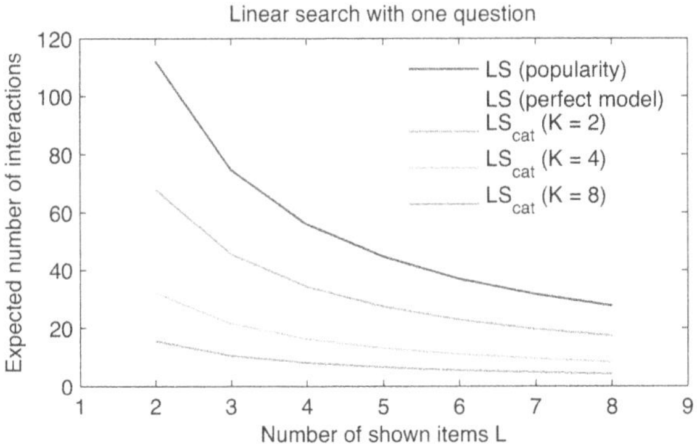

Figure 3. The expected length of $\texttt{LS}_{\texttt{cat}}$ interaction.

We evaluate $\texttt{LS}_{\texttt{cat}}$ using the same methodology as in the earlier evaluation of the LS policies. We simulate $K = 2$, $K = 4$, and $K = 8$ item categories being shown to the user, and compare $\texttt{LS}_{\texttt{cat}}$ with these values of K to the *popularity* and *perfect model* policies of LS. The results of the simulation are reported in Figure 3.

We observe that splitting items into K categories and then performing LS substantially decreases the length of user interaction. A split into $K = 2$ categories decreases the length of interaction by about 30%, consistently for any number of shown items L. Notably, for $K = 8$, the expected length of interaction by $\texttt{LS}_{\texttt{cat}}$ is on par with the *perfect model* LS policy. In other words, we show that a single piece of additional information provided by the user (choosing one item category out of K) reduces the expected length of interaction as much as knowing the exact ratings for the set of items that are recommended to the user.

MINIMAL INTERACTION SEARCH

In this section, we present the generalized search and our main contribution, *generalized linear search* (GLS).

Generalized Search

Generalized binary search (GBS) [10, 12, 18] is a greedy algorithm for active learning, where the goal is to identify an item of interest e^* by asking a sequence of binary questions. A question-answering policy that minimizes the expected number of asked questions is NP-hard to compute, and GBS is its computationally efficient approximation. In particular, GBS always asks a question that partitions the *version space* V, the set of the items that are consistent with the past questions and answers, most evenly in expectation. A remarkable property of GBS is its theoretical guarantee to ask, in expectation, at most $\log(1/\pi_{\min})$ times more questions than the optimal policy, where $\pi_{\min} = \min_{e \in E} \pi(e)$ is the probability of choosing the least likely item.

Algorithm 3 GS: Generalized search.

Input:
Number of item categories K in a question

$V \leftarrow E$
repeat
Choose $K-1$ categories $q_1, \dots, q_{K-1}$ given V and π
$q_K \leftarrow \overline{(q_1 \cup \dots \cup q_{K-1})}$
Ask the user to choose one category
The user chooses category q_k
$V \leftarrow q_k \cap V$
until $(|V| = 1)$

Output: Target item $e^* \in V$

In this work, we consider a generalization of GBS to multiway questions [5], which we refer to as *generalized search* (GS). The search for the target item e^* proceeds as follows. The user is presented K item categories $q_1, \dots, q_K$ and asked to choose one. After the user chooses a category q_k, the search space V is reduced to the items that belong to that category, $q_k \cap V$. Then the user is presented another K item categories. These categories may, and typically do, depend on the previously chosen categories. The user chooses again one category and this question-answering game continues until the cardinality of the version space V is one, and the target item e^* is found. Each round of this game is considered as an interaction. The pseudocode of GS is shown in Algorithm 3.

GS can search high-dimensional spaces efficiently when the item categories permit good partitioning of the version space. This is not always possible in practice. For instance, consider $N = 100$ items, where the probability of choosing the most likely item is $\pi(1) = 0.99$ and the item cannot be separated from the rest of the items by a single question. In this case, LS can identify the target item in a single interaction with at least 0.99 probability, because in 99% of cases the highest ranked item by $\pi(e)$ is the target item. On the other hand, GS needs to ask multiple questions to eliminate other items with at least 0.99 probability.

In previous section, we showed that a single split into K item categories in $\texttt{LS}_{\texttt{cat}}$ gains as much information about the target item e^* as knowing the exact item ratings. A natural question to ask is "what happens if the user is asked to choose a category of interest more than once". Will the expected length of interaction further decrease? To answer this question, we simulate a modified variant of GS with $K = 2$ item categories. Specifically, we fix the number of GS questions and switch to LS either after this number of questions or when the cardinality of the version space is one. The methodology for choosing users and items is identical to that in our earlier simulations.

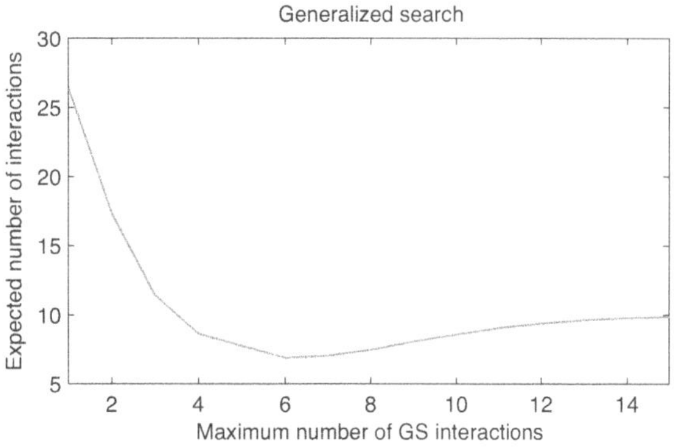

Figure 4. The expected length of interaction as a function of the number of GS steps.

The overall length of interaction is the sum of the number of interactions in GS and LS. The results of the simulation are reported in Figure 4.

Interestingly, the expected length of interaction does not always decrease with the number of asked GS questions. In fact, it starts increasing when GS asks more than 6 questions. For instance, the expected length of interaction at 9 questions is larger by one than at 6 questions. The reason for this behavior is that asking questions is beneficial only if the version space can be partitioned sufficiently well into K item categories. Loosely speaking, if this cannot be done, it is preferable to order items according to their popularity, from the most popular to the least popular, and ask the user to discover the target item by scanning the items.

Generalized Linear Search

This observation motivates our work on the hybridization of GS and LS that leverages the strengths of both approaches to minimize the length of user interaction. Specifically, we propose to perform GS up to the point where it is not effective, because the version space V cannot be partitioned well, and then switch to LS, which does not rely on the features of items. A pivotal question in this hybridization is "how to choose the sweet spot where GS should switch to LS". For instance, one suitable switching criterion may be when the number of items in the version space V is small. Another suitable criterion may be when the probability mass in V is small. In other words, there are many ways to combine the two methods and it is not obvious which one to apply.

In this work, we propose a new hybrid method that we call *generalized linear search* (GLS). GLS switches from GS to LS when the *expected length of interaction* to discover the target item using GS is greater than that of LS. We choose this switching oracle for several reasons. First, this criterion naturally captures the fact that GS outperforms LS in minimizing the expected length of interaction. Second, the oracle can be implemented computationally efficiently. Third, we can incorporate the oracle in the analysis of GLS and show that the expected length of interaction decreases. Finally, as we demonstrate in the experimental evaluation, this approach performs well in practice.

Algorithm 4 GLS: Generalized linear search.

Input:
Number of item categories K in a question
Number of shown items L

$V \leftarrow E$
repeat
Choose $K-1$ categories $q_1, \dots, q_{K-1}$ given V and π
$q_K \leftarrow \overline{(q_1 \cup \dots \cup q_{K-1})}$
Ask the user to choose one category
The user chooses category k
$V \leftarrow q_k \cap V$
until $(\texttt{costGS}(V, K) \geq \texttt{costLS}(V, L))$
$e^* \leftarrow \texttt{LS}(V, L)$

Output: Target item e^*

Algorithm 5 costLS: Expected cost of linear search.

Input:
Items $V \subseteq E$
Number of shown items L

Let $e_1, \dots, e_{|V|}$ be an ordering of items V such that:
$\pi(e_1) \geq \dots \geq \pi(e_{|V|})$
$c \leftarrow 0$
for all $i = 1, \dots, |V|$ **do**
$c \leftarrow c + \lceil i/L \rceil \pi(e_i)$
end for

Output: Expected cost c

The pseudocode of GLS is in Algorithm 4. Note that GLS differs from GS in two aspects. First, GS stops when the expected cost of GS is higher than that of LS. Second, when GS stops, we switch to LS. The pseudocodes for computing the expected costs of LS and GS are in Algorithms 5 and 6, respectively.

GLS can be implemented efficiently. In particular, note that GS can be represented as a decision tree [12], where each node is a version space associated with K item categories. Similarly, GLS can be viewed a pruned version of this tree, where each leaf node is an instance of LS. The pruned tree is built as follows. First, we build the tree for GS and recursively compute the expected cost of GS in each node. Second, we compute the expected cost of LS in each node and prune the tree at the nodes where $\texttt{costGS}(V, K) \geq \texttt{costLS}(V, L)$. The expected cost of LS in each node can be computed in $O(N \log N)$ time, because it requires sorting at most N items.

Analysis

Let π be the distribution over items E and $\pi(e)$ be the probability that item e is chosen. Let $V \subseteq E$ be a version space and $\mathcal{V}$ be the set of all version spaces where GLS switches from GS to LS, $\texttt{costGS}(V, K) \geq \texttt{costLS}(V, L)$. Then $\mathcal{V}$ is a partitioning of E:

$$E = \bigcup_{V \in \mathcal{V}} V \qquad \forall V \in \mathcal{V}, U \in \mathcal{V} \setminus V : V \cap U = \emptyset$$

Algorithm 6 costGS: Expected cost of generalized search.

Input:
Items $V \subseteq E$
Number of item categories K in a question

$c \leftarrow 1$
if $(|V| > 1)$ **then**
Choose $K - 1$ categories $q_1, \dots, q_{K-1}$ given V and π
$q_K \leftarrow \overline{(q_1 \cup \dots \cup q_{K-1})}$
for all $k = 1, \dots, K$ **do**
$c \leftarrow c + \pi(q_k \cap V) \times \texttt{costGS}(q_k \cap V, K)$
end for
end if

Output: Expected cost c

because GLS is guaranteed to switch to LS, at the latest when the cardinality of the version space is one. Let $N(e)$ be the length of interaction to find item e by GLS and $N(V)$ be the length of interaction until GLS reaches V. Let $\pi(V) = \sum_{e \in V} \pi(e)$ be the probability mass of all items in V.

THEOREM 1. *The expected cost of* GLS *is smaller or equal to the expected cost of* GS.

PROOF. Note that the expected cost of GS is defined as

$$\mathbb{E}_{e \sim \pi}[N(e)] = \sum_{e \in E} \pi(e) N(e). \qquad (1)$$

For any target item e^*, Algorithm 4 switches from GS to LS at one particular point, where $e^* \in V$ for some $V \in \mathcal{V}$. Based on this, the expected cost can be written as:

$$\sum_{V \in \mathcal{V}} \left[\pi(V) N(V) + \sum_{e \in V} \pi(e)(N(e) - N(V)) \right]. \qquad (2)$$

The first term is the expected cost of GS before $V \in \mathcal{V}$ is reached. The second term is the expected cost of GS after V is reached. Equation 2 can be further rewritten as:

$$\sum_{V \in \mathcal{V}} \pi(V) \left[N(V) + \sum_{e \in V} \frac{\pi(e)}{\pi(V)} (N(e) - N(V)) \right], \qquad (3)$$

where $\sum_{e \in V} \frac{\pi(e)}{\pi(V)} (N(e) - N(V))$ is the expected cost of GS applied in V. Let $N_{\mathrm{LS}}(V)$ be the expected cost of LS from V. By our assumption:

$$N_{\mathrm{LS}}(V) \leq \sum_{e \in V} \frac{\pi(e)}{\pi(V)} (N(e) - N(V)) \qquad (4)$$

because $\texttt{costGS}(V, K) \geq \texttt{costLS}(V, L)$ for all $V \in \mathcal{V}$. Finally, we chain all inequalities and get:

$$\mathbb{E}_{e \sim \pi}[N(e)] \geq \sum_{V \in \mathcal{V}} \pi(V) \left[N(V) + N_{\mathrm{LS}}(V) \right], \qquad (5)$$

where the right-hand side is the expected cost of GLS. This concludes the proof. ■

Non-Unit Costs of Interaction

So far we assumed that each type of interaction bears the same cost. Our work can be easily generalized to the setting where the costs of GS and LS interactions differ. Without loss of generality, let the cost of GS interactions be one and the cost of LS interaction be α. Note that when $\alpha > 1$, LS interactions are more costly than GS interactions, and vice versa. Then GLS can be straightforwardly adapted to minimize the weighted length of interactions, by replacing c with αc in costLS (Algorithm 5). Similarly, it is straightforward to adapt the proof of Theorem 1, by replacing $N_{\mathrm{LS}}(V)$ with $\alpha N_{\mathrm{LS}}(V)$.

OFFLINE EVALUATION

We conduct offline evaluation of the proposed GLS method using two public recommender systems datasets and compare it to several baselines and heuristics.

Experimental Setting

We compare GLS to five baselines. The first two baselines are standalone LS and GS, which were presented in previous sections. The other three baselines are heuristic combinations of GS and LS, which we call GS-step, GS-num, and GS-ent. These baselines differ in how they switch from GS to LS. GS-step switches to LS after Δ iterations of GS. GS-num switches to LS when the version space contains less than Δ items. GS-ent switches to LS when the entropy of the probability mass of the items in the version space is smaller than Δ. Intuitively, the heuristics address the pivotal question of when to switch to LS: when the version space has been refined enough times in GS-step, when the version space is sufficiently small in GS-num, and when the probability mass is concentrated in just a few items in GS-ent. In all three cases, Δ is the external parameter for the heuristic method.

The performance of all methods is measured by the expected length of interaction. This quantity is computed as follows. First, we randomly choose a user, proportionally to the number of items that the user consumed in the dataset. Second, for a given user, we randomly choose a target item e^*, proportionally to the number of times that this item is consumed by the user. Finally, we compute the length of interaction to find e^*. The length of interaction is averaged over 10^6 randomly chosen pairs of user and item. Therefore, all error bars in the experiments are on the order of $1/\sqrt{10^6} = 10^{-3}$, and most differences in the expected lengths of interaction are statistically significant. We experiment with three different numbers of item categories that are shown: $K = 2$, $K = 4$, and $K = 8$. In the all experiments, the number of shown items in LS is $L = 8$. We observed similar trends for other values of L and do not report these due to space constraints.

The proposed methods are evaluated on two datasets: *MovieLens*[1] and *Lastfm*[2]. The *MovieLens* dataset contains the ratings of 6K users for 3.9K movies. We preprocess this dataset as follows. The items E are movies and $\pi(e)$ is the probability that movie e is watched. This probability is estimated as the number of times that e is rated with 4 or 5 stars divided by

[1]MovieLens dataset: http://www.grouplens.org/node/73
[2]Last.fm dataset: http://www.lastfm.com

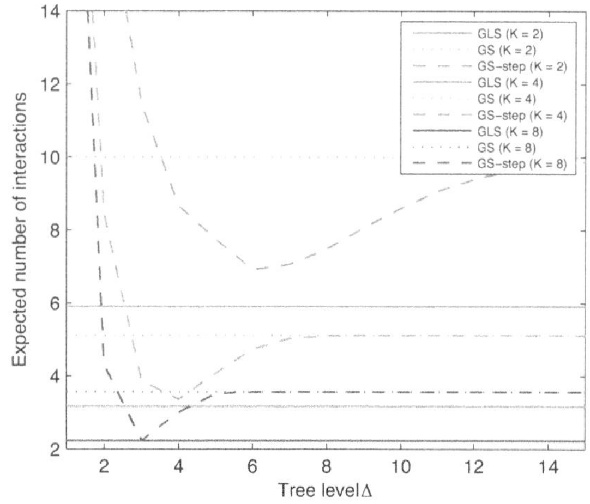

Figure 5. Comparison of GLS to GS and GS-step for *MovieLens*.

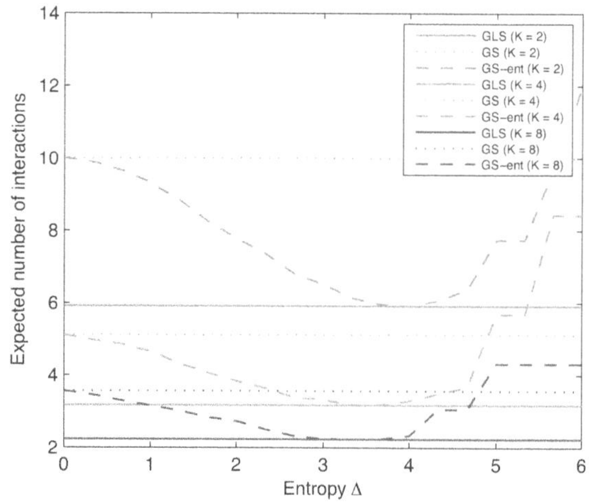

Figure 7. Comparison of GLS to GS and GS-ent for *MovieLens*.

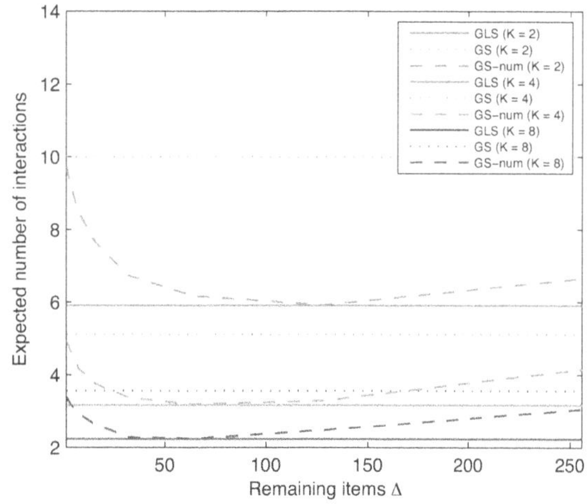

Figure 6. Comparison of GLS to GS and GS-num for *MovieLens*.

the total number of 4 and 5 star ratings. The item categories q are the genres of movies. *MovieLens* contains 18 movie genres, which is insufficient for our purpose. Therefore, we replaced the genres of each movie by its Netflix genres. There are 335 distinct Netflix genres in our dataset. We eliminate the movies that are described by less than 5 genres. These are unsuitable for GS-style methods because they are not described by a sufficient number of features. We end up with a dataset of 1.4K movies.

Lastfm is a music dataset of 2K users who listen to 18K artists. We preprocess this dataset as follows. The items E are artists and $\pi(e)$ is the probability that artist e is listened to. This probability is estimated as the number of times that artist e is listened to divided by the total number of the artist listening events. The item categories q are the tags assigned to the artists. We eliminate the artists that are described by less than 5 tags. Again, these are unsuitable for GS because they are not described by a sufficient number of features. We end up with a dataset of 6K artists.

Experimental Results

In Figure 5, we compare GLS to GS and heuristic GS-step on the *MovieLens* dataset, for three values of K. We observe two major trends. First, the length of interaction decreases with K, as larger values of K allow for a fine-grained partitioning of the version space. Second, for all values of K, GLS significantly outperforms GS. For example, for $K = 2$, the expected length of GLS interaction is 5.93, 40% shorter than that of GS, 9.85. For $K = 4$ and $K = 8$, the expected length of GLS interaction is, respectively, 36% and 34% shorter than that of GS. Third, GLS always performs better than or on par with GS-step. Fourth, we observe that the performance of GS-step depends on the parameter Δ. For instance, for $K = 2$, GS-step(6) performs the best, while GS-step(3) is already worse than GS. We observe the same trend for other values of K. For instance, GS-step(3) performs comparably to GLS for $K = 8$, but worse than GS for $K = 2$.

In Figure 6, we compare GLS to GS and GS-num on the *MovieLens* dataset. We observe the same trends as in Figure 5. First, the length of interaction is inversely correlated with K. Second, GLS always outperforms GS. Third, GLS always outperforms or is on par with GS-step. Fourth, the performance of GS-num depends on the value of Δ: for $K = 2$, the shortest GS-num interaction is obtained for $\Delta = 130$; while for $K = 4$ and $K = 8$, it is obtained for $\Delta = 70$ and $\Delta = 50$, respectively. Also note that for all values of K, at the optimal operating point GS-num performs on par with GLS, whereas for GS-step this was observed only for $K = 8$. This is attributed to the fact that the number of items in the version space is a finer indicator of the suboptimal performance of GS than the number of GS steps.

In Figure 7, GLS is compared to GS and heuristic GS-ent on the *MovieLens* dataset, for the same three values of K. We observe the same trends that were observed in Figures 5 and 6, although in this case the performance of GS-ent does not vary with K as widely as previously.

We conduct the same experiments on the *Lastfm* dataset, and our results are reported in Figures 8, 9, and 10. Our findings

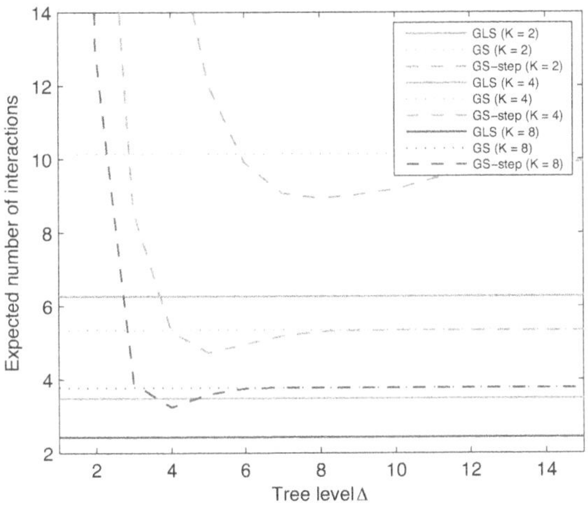

Figure 8. Comparison of GLS to GS and GS-step for *Lastfm*.

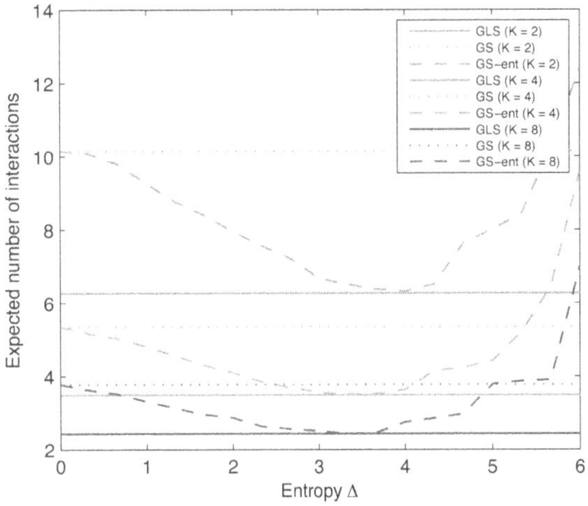

Figure 10. Comparison of GLS to GS and GS-ent for *Lastfm*.

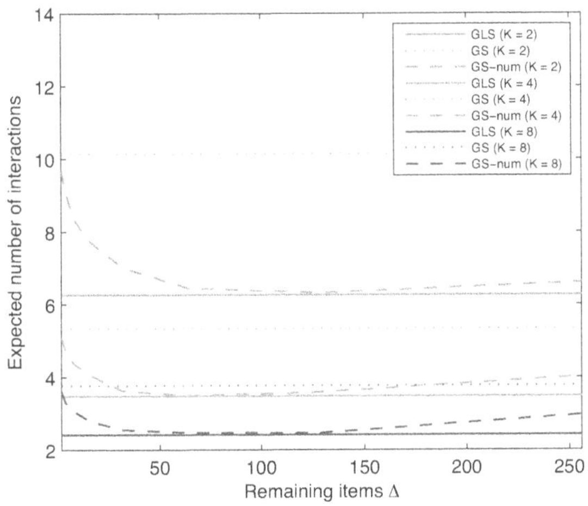

Figure 9. Comparison of GLS to GS and GS-num for *Lastfm*.

resemble those in the *MovieLens* dataset. The expected length of GLS interaction is always shorter than that of GS, and GLS is either superior or comparable to the three heuristic methods, whose performance depends on their parameter Δ. Also note that the optimal operating points of the heuristics are obtained for different values of Δ. For example, on the *MovieLens* dataset, GS-step performs the best for $\Delta = 3$, $\Delta = 4$, and $\Delta = 6$; when $K = 2$, $K = 4$, and $K = 8$, respectively. On the other hand, on the *Lastfm* dataset, GS-step performs the best for $\Delta = 4$, $\Delta = 5$, and $\Delta = 8$ for the same values of K. Similar differences across the datasets are observed also for the GS-num and GS-ent heuristics.

We conclude that GLS performs better than its individual components, GS and LS. This superiority is statistically significant and holds for the *MovieLens* and *Lastfm* datasets under evaluation, and for various values of K. A more intricate question deals with the comparison of GLS to the heuristic methods. We conclude that GLS steadily outperforms GS-step, and performs comparably with GS-num and GS-ent, but only when these two are parameterized optimally. However, the optimal operating points Δ of the heuristics depend on the applied heuristics, the dataset in hand, and the number of categories K. In practice, a suitable value of Δ has to be chosen a priori and this is not trivial. On the other hand, GLS is parameter free and never performs worse than GS-step, GS-num, and GS-ent. Hence, GLS should be preferred not only to GS and LS, but also to the three evaluated heuristic methods.

LIVE USER STUDY

We conduct a user study of GLS on Amazon's Mechanical Turk[3], a public crowd-sourcing service. For the sake of simplicity, we only compare the binary variants of GLS and GS, with $K = 2$ and $L = 10$. The study is intra-group: each subject experiences both searches and is asked to compare them.

Experimental Setting

We experiment with 253 subjects. Each subject interacts with GLS and GS in a random order, and is asked to compare the searches. The recommended items E are 200 most rated movies from the *MovieLens* dataset.

The experiment is organized as follows. At the beginning of the experiment, we randomly select 10 movies from E, present them to the subject, and ask the subject to choose a target movie that the subject is familiar with (top of Figure 11). Upon selecting the target movie, the subject interacts with the first search. This search is chosen at random to eliminate position bias. In the GLS search, the subject is asked to answer binary GS questions (middle of Figure 11) until GLS switches to LS. When this happens, the subject is shown a list of recommended movies, requested to examine it, and asked if the target item is in the list (bottom of Figure 11). Likewise, in the GS search, the subject answers binary GS questions until the search space is sufficiently small, and then is shown a list of movies and asked whether the target movie is in the list. Upon completing both searches, the subject is asked to answer four questions that compare the searches (Table 1).

[3]`http://mturk.com`

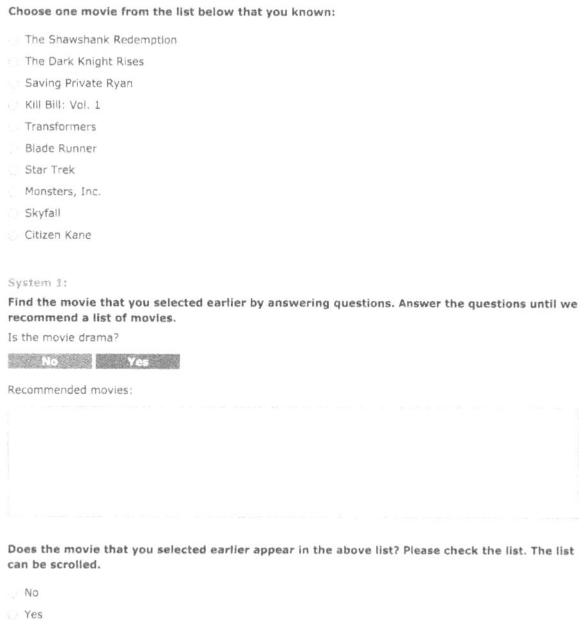

Figure 11. A portion of the user study.

For each search, we compute four metrics. The first is the *hit rate*, i.e., the fraction of searches in which the target movie appears in the final list, which communicates how good the search is in finding the target movie. The second metric is the *number of questions* that the subject was asked during the search. The third metric is the *duration of interaction*, i.e., the time (in seconds) between answering the first question and examining the final list. The fourth metric is the *length of the final list* of recommended movies.

Experimental Results

In Table 2, we report the values of the four metrics for each search as well as the distribution of the answers to the comparison questions from Table 1. We observe several trends. First and foremost, GLS is preferred over GS by more subjects, 61.3% vs 38.7%. What are the reasons for this preference?

Table 2 clearly shows that GLS requires significantly less interaction than GS, as reflected by both the number of asked questions and the duration of the search. This is noted by the subjects. Specifically, 46.7% of the subjects prefer GLS because it asks less questions (C1). Most of these subjects also find GLS easier to use (C3) and prefer it overall (C4).

Also, Table 2 shows that GLS produces much longer lists of movies than GS. Although the examination of these lists does not overload the subjects, as indicated by the duration of the search, 38.3% of the subjects prefer shorter lists that are produced by GS (C2), and most of these subjects also prefer GS overall. Nevertheless, the benefits of C1 and C3 outweigh the shortcomings of C2, as more subjects prefer GLS over GS.

We also observe that a large portion of the subjects has no clear preference towards the three criteria: 39.5% (C1), 43.9% (C2), and 55.7% (C3). This is not surprising, since both searches are similar and differ only in the last few steps, when GLS terminates before GS and produces a longer list of movies. Finally, note that GLS achieves a substantially higher hit rate than GS. This is due to the fact that GLS asks less questions than GS and is less likely to eliminate the target movie due the incorrect answer of a subject to a question.

Which system do you prefer with respect to the following:

(C1) Number of asked questions
- No preference
- I prefer System 1 because it asks less questions
- I prefer System 2 because it asks less questions

(C2) Length of the final list
- No preference
- I prefer System 1 because it produces a shorter list
- I prefer System 2 because it produces a shorter list

(C3) Ease of use
- No preference
- I prefer System 1 because it is easier to use
- I prefer System 2 because it is easier to use

(C4) Overall
- I prefer System 1 to System 2
- I prefer System 2 to System 1

Table 1. Search comparison questions.

	GS	GLS	Neither
Hit rate	0.32	0.53	
Number of questions	6.12	2.30	
Search duration	9.69	3.52	
Length of the final list	3.74	29.41	
(C1) Number of questions	13.8%	46.7%	39.5%
(C2) Length of the final list	38.3%	17.8%	43.9%
(C3) Ease of use	13.8%	30.5%	55.7%
(C4) Overall preference	38.7%	61.3%	

Table 2. Summary of the user study results.

RELATED WORK

Recommendations produced by a recommender system are typically shown as a ranked list of items. The ranking of items in the list communicates their fit to the target user, such as the top-ranked items are supposedly the best recommendations [17]. Limiting the size of the list reduces the choice difficulty and helps the user to cope with information overloading [6].

Several issues around recommendation interfaces have been investigated in early recommendation works. Cosley *et al.* [9] studied how the display and the scale of item predictions affect the ratings provided by users. It was found that users were influenced by the displayed predictions, while the scale had no apparent effect. Ziegler *et al.* [28] argued that the recommendation list should incorporate a degree of diversity, to reflect the breadth of user interests [1, 2]. It was shown that, despite decreasing the accuracy of the recommendations, diversification increased the overall user satisfaction.

Often, the recommendation list can be grouped or categorized, to simplify user navigation and item exploration. Hu and Pu [15] evaluated the "organizational" recommendation interface that allowed users to group and filter items according to a set of domain features. A comparison between the organizational and list interfaces indicated that the former improved the perceived usefulness and diversity of the recommendations, increased user confidence, and was found to be more intuitive than the latter.

In addition to the LS and GS approaches that were elaborately discussed earlier, another related search is *faceted search* [14]. This is a search, where the user first chooses a facet, a group of semantically related attributes, and then a desired attribute in that facet. In our work, we have only one group of semantic attributes, either movie or music genres. That is, our approach can be viewed as a degenerate case of faceted search with only one group, and we do not perform experimental comparison work to faceted search.

The importance of an easy-to-use interface is paramount in critique-based recommendations [8]. Chen and Pu developed an interface that grouped items, compared the groups to the recommended items, and suggested critiques reflecting these comparisons [7]. The accuracy of the critiques and the usability of the interface were evaluated in a user study. The results showed that users preferred the suggested critiques and provided them more frequently, which reduced the duration of interactions and increased the perceived user confidence.

Another functionality availed by the recommender's interface is explanation and persuasion [4]. These are used to justify the recommendations, cultivate user trust, and convince users to follow the recommendations. Tintarev and Masthoff [22] developed several interfaces complementing the recommended items with explanations. Their evaluation confirmed that explanations boost user satisfaction, whereas the highest satisfaction was achieved when the explanations referred to item features that were important for users.

Although much research has been devoted to exploration interfaces in the general HCI context [3], this has received relatively little attention in recommender systems [21, 23]. In a recent work, Verbert *et al.* [24] developed TalkExplorer, an interactive academic conference visualization tool, building upon graph-based information exploration libraries, like PeerChoser [19] and SmallWorlds [13]. TalkExplorer allowed users to explore various relevance perspectives, e.g., tags assigned to recommended papers, users who bookmarked these papers, and other papers tagged by these users. The evaluation indicated that TalkExplorer was perceived more insightful that the standard list of recommended items.

The above interface components and visualization tools supply various information complementing the recommendations. However, none of them looks into optimizing user experience in recommender systems [16]. This issue is addressed by general user interaction design guidelines, and we observe successful practical solutions in industrial products, such as movie recommendation interface by Netflix[4] or contact recommendations by LinkedIn[5]. However, to the best of our knowledge, no evidence-based research that articulates the development of these interfaces, in particular, considering the recommendation scenarios, has been published.

CONCLUSIONS

The claim that a usable interface may improve user's subjective perception of a recommender is well established [20]. In spite of this, recommender systems research has mainly focused on algorithmic techniques for rating predictions, rather than on interface and user interaction matters.

In this work, we devised the GLS method that minimizes the length of user interaction with the recommender, to find a target item in a recommendation list. GLS combines two established search methods, GS and LS, and successfully leverages their advantages. We investigated the switching criterion from GS to LS and concluded that GS should be applied as long as its expected cost is lower than that of LS, and should be abandoned afterwards. We prove that GLS performs at least as well as GS.

We demonstrate in an offline and live evaluation that the proposed GLS method is superior not only to its individual components, GS and LS, but also to several heuristic methods. Having said that, GLS does not require any parameter tuning and can be deployed in a practical recommender system. We also conduct a user study that demonstrates steady user preference towards GLS over the baseline GS method.

Future questions for investigation refer to a thorough user evaluation of GLS. While it was found to lead to the shortest interactions and was preferred by users, it combines item categories with individual items in the same search process. Hence, it is critical to ascertain whether users find the GLS interactions intuitive and enjoyable [16]. Also, it is not obvious how GLS, and specifically the item categories in the GS stages, should be visualized [27]. On one hand, textual titles may not be as appealing as pictorial thumbnails. On the other hand, showing the thumbnails may not properly communicate the very notion of categories.

Apart from this, it is important to address the cost of answering questions. In our user study, we show that GLS recommends a much longer list of items than GS. This may put a significant burden on users [6], which may be comparable with answering a few GS questions, and practically factor out the advantages of GLS. Therefore, it is important to thoroughly study the cost, both in terms of time and cognitive effort, of answering different types of questions.

Finally, another aspect that asks for further research is the integration of GLS with a variety of interface and user-related topics, such as decision support, provision of critiques, content discovery, and explanation of recommendations [11]. It is, therefore, necessary to conduct user studies and evaluate the compound effect of GLS in these use cases.

[4]Netflix recommendations: Beyond the 5 stars, http://techblog. netflix. com/2012/04/netflixrecommendations-beyond-5-stars.html

[5]Navigating LinkedIn's New User Interface, http://randomactsofleadership.com/navigating-linkedins-new-user-interface/

REFERENCES

1. Ashkan, A., Kveton, B., Berkovsky, S., and Wen, Z. Diversified utility maximization for recommendations. In *RecSys Posters* (2014).
2. Ashkan, A., Kveton, B., Berkovsky, S., and Wen, Z. DUM: Diversity-weighted utility maximization for recommendations. *CoRR abs/1411.3650* (2014).
3. Baldonado, M. Q. W., and Winograd, T. Sensemaker: An information-exploration interface supporting the contextual evolution of a user's interests. In *CHI* (1997), 11–18.
4. Berkovsky, S., Freyne, J., and Oinas-Kukkonen, H. Influencing individually: Fusing personalization and persuasion. *ACM Trans. Interact. Intell. Syst. 2*, 2 (2012), 9.
5. Bhamidipati, S., Kveton, B., and Muthukrishnan, S. Minimal interaction search: Multi-way search with item categories. In *ITWP* (2013), 9–15.
6. Bollen, D. G. F. M., Knijnenburg, B. P., Willemsen, M. C., and Graus, M. P. Understanding choice overload in recommender systems. In *RecSys* (2010), 63–70.
7. Chen, L., and Pu, P. Experiments on the preference-based organization interface in recommender systems. *ACM Trans. Comput.-Hum. Interact. 17*, 1 (2010), 5.
8. Chen, L., and Pu, P. Critiquing-based recommenders: survey and emerging trends. *User Model. User-Adapt. Interact. 22*, 1-2 (2012), 125–150.
9. Cosley, D., Lam, S. K., Albert, I., Konstan, J. A., and Riedl, J. Is seeing believing?: how recommender system interfaces affect users' opinions. In *CHI* (2003), 585–592.
10. Dasgupta, S. Analysis of a greedy active learning strategy. In *Advances in Neural Information Processing Systems 17* (2005), 337–344.
11. Felfernig, A., Burke, R. D., and Pu, P. Preface to the special issue on user interfaces for recommender systems. *User Model. User-Adapt. Interact. 22*, 4-5 (2012), 313–316.
12. Golovin, D., and Krause, A. Adaptive submodularity: Theory and applications in active learning and stochastic optimization. *Journal of Artif. Intell. Research 42* (2011), 427–486.
13. Gretarsson, B., O'Donovan, J., Bostandjiev, S., Hall, C., and Höllerer, T. Smallworlds: Visualizing social recommendations. *Comput. Graph. Forum 29*, 3 (2010), 833–842.
14. Hearst, M. Design recommendations for hierarchical faceted search interfaces. In *SIGIR Workshop on Faceted Search* (2006).
15. Hu, R., and Pu, P. Enhancing recommendation diversity with organization interfaces. In *IUI* (2011), 347–350.
16. Knijnenburg, B. P., Willemsen, M. C., Gantner, Z., Soncu, H., and Newell, C. Explaining the user experience of recommender systems. *User Model. User-Adapt. Interact. 22*, 4 (2012), 441–504.
17. McNee, S. M., Riedl, J., and Konstan, J. A. Being accurate is not enough: how accuracy metrics have hurt recommender systems. In *CHI* (2006), 1097–1101.
18. Nowak, R. The geometry of generalized binary search. *IEEE Transactions on Information Theory 57*, 12 (2011), 7893–7906.
19. O'Donovan, J., Smyth, B., Gretarsson, B., Bostandjiev, S., and Höllerer, T. Peerchooser: visual interactive recommendation. In *CHI* (2008), 1085–1088.
20. Ricci, F., Rokach, L., and Shapira, B. Introduction to recommender systems handbook. In *Recommender Systems Handbook*. Springer, 2011, 1–35.
21. Tintarev, N., Hu, R., and Pu, P. Recsys'12 workshop on interfaces for recommender systems. In *RecSys* (2012), 355–356.
22. Tintarev, N., and Masthoff, J. Evaluating the effectiveness of explanations for recommender systems - methodological issues and empirical studies on the impact of personalization. *User Model. User-Adapt. Interact. 22*, 4-5 (2012), 399–439.
23. Tintarev, N., O'Donovan, J., Brusilovsky, P., Felfernig, A., Semeraro, G., and Lops, P. Recsys'14 workshop on interfaces and human decision making for recommender systems. In *RecSys* (2014), 383–384.
24. Verbert, K., Parra, D., Brusilovsky, P., and Duval, E. Visualizing recommendations to support exploration, transparency and controllability. In *IUI* (2013), 351–362.
25. Wen, Z., Kveton, B., Eriksson, B., and Bhamidipati, S. Sequential Bayesian search. In *ICML* (2013), 226–234.
26. Winterboer, A., Tietze, M., Wolters, M., and Moore, J. The user model-based summarize and refine approach improves information presentation in spoken dialog systems. *Comput. Speech and Lang. 25*, 2 (2011), 175–191.
27. Zhang, J., Jones, N., and Pu, P. A visual interface for critiquing-based recommender systems. In *EC* (2008), 230–239.
28. Ziegler, C.-N., McNee, S. M., Konstan, J. A., and Lausen, G. Improving recommendation lists through topic diversification. In *WWW* (2005), 22–32.

Improving Controllability and Predictability of Interactive Recommendation Interfaces for Exploratory Search

Antti Kangasrääsiö
Helsinki Institute for
Information Technology HIIT
Dept. of Computer Science
Aalto University
antti.kangasraasio@hiit.fi

Dorota Głowacka
Helsinki Institute for
Information Technology HIIT
Dept. of Computer Science
University of Helsinki
dorota.glowacka@hiit.fi

Samuel Kaski
Helsinki Institute for
Information Technology HIIT
Dept. of Computer Science
Aalto University;
Dept. of Computer Science
University of Helsinki
samuel.kaski@hiit.fi

ABSTRACT
In exploratory search, when a user directs a search engine using uncertain relevance feedback, usability problems regarding controllability and predictability may arise. One problem is that the user is often modelled as a passive source of relevance information, instead of an active entity trying to steer the system based on evolving information needs. This may cause the user to feel that the response of the system is inconsistent with her steering. Another problem arises due to the sheer size and complexity of the information space, and hence of the system, as it may be difficult for the user to anticipate the consequences of her actions in this complex environment. These problems can be mitigated by interpreting the user's actions as setting a goal for an optimization problem regarding the system state, instead of passive relevance feedback, and by allowing the user to see the predicted effects of an action before committing to it. In this paper, we present an implementation of these improvements in a visual user-controllable search interface. A user study involving exploratory search for scientific literature gives some indication on improvements in task performance, usability, perceived usefulness and user acceptance.

Author Keywords
Controllability; exploratory search; information retrieval; interactive user modelling; predictability; probabilistic user models; user interfaces

ACM Classification Keywords
H.3.3 Information Search and Retrieval: Relevance feedback; H.5.2 Information Interfaces and Presentation: User Interfaces

IUI 2015, March 29–April 1, 2015, Atlanta, GA, USA.

http://dx.doi.org/10.1145/2678025.2701371

INTRODUCTION
Traditionally, research in information retrieval systems focuses on improving the predictive accuracy of recommendations mostly by developing new algorithms. Recent studies [9, 13] have shown that visual features and enhanced interaction can greatly improve the user engagement in the search process, and consequently also the performance of the retrieval system. Some of the interface characteristics studied are transparency, explainability, predictability and controllability, of which user controllability is the least explored aspect of information retrieval systems.

In this paper, we concentrate on user controllability and system predictability in the context of exploratory search. In exploratory search, the user searches for information in a domain that she is not initially familiar with. Because of this, search interfaces assisting the user in exploratory search are faced with a difficult problem: how to help the user direct the exploratory search with uncertain feedback. If the user were an expert and the feedback certain, it could be interpreted in a purely exploitative manner. However, since this is not the case in exploratory search, there needs to be a suitable amount of exploration mixed in to help the user with the search task.

Probabilistic user models can be used to handle the exploration/exploitation trade-off, but there can be usability problems if the user feedback is interpreted simply as datapoints to fit a model. As the user is not a passive function that is sampled by the system, but an active entity that is trying to steer the system through iteratively improving the model, there needs to be a layer of interpretation between the user and the system. In this work we propose a layer which translates the user input into requirements for the state of the system, and makes the system better predictable by showing the user on-line estimates of the effects her actions will have on the system.

A user study gives some indication that by implementing this layer of interpretation, users are able to perform better in focused exploratory information retrieval tasks, they are able to better predict the consequences of their actions, and to understand the connections between different feedback items in the search interface. There is also some evidence of improvement in the usability and perceived usefulness of the search system.

RELATED WORK

In recent years, exploratory search has attracted attention from, among others, information retrieval (IR), Human Computer Interaction (HCI), and Machine Learning (ML) communities, which have proposed several techniques and systems to facilitate exploratory search.

Some of the initial solutions include result clustering [4], relevance feedback [7], query suggestion [1], and faceted search [15]. However, the proposed techniques are rarely used in practice due to the high cognitive load of going through a large list of suggestions or providing feedback for a large number of items [7].

There have also been numerous attempts to engage the user into the feedback loop through interactive visualizations combined with learning algorithms to support users to comprehend the search results [3], and visualization and summaries of results [8]. These solutions give users more control; however, they do not adapt to the evolving information needs of the user [12]. Recently, reinforcement learning (RL) techniques have been applied to facilitate exploratory search [5, 6, 11]. The RL-based systems prevent the user from getting trapped in a local context and expose the user to a larger area of the information space. However, they do not allow the user to anticipate the effects of their actions.

One approach to improve the controllability of recommendation interfaces is by allowing the user to interactively combine different recommendation algorithms using weights [9]. We deal with the same problem through improving the user's control over a single algorithm.

PROPOSED APPROACHES

User Feedback as a Goal for an Optimization Problem

The user feedback will have the effects intended by the user, if the feedback values are interpreted as the goal for an optimization problem regarding the next state of the system, instead of just additional datapoints to fit a model. This way the user in effect has an automatic assistant that steers the system towards the desired target indicated by the user. In this modelling approach the user is assumed to be an active entity trying to steer the system, instead of a passive entity that is sampled by the system, as is usual in reinforcement learning approaches. In general, we formalize the problem of interfacing users with reinforcement learning based systems as follows: "What feedback values should be given to the model update algorithm so that the resulting model fulfills certain optimality criterion, which is parametrized by the feedback values given by the user?"

Solving this problem requires making three design choices: what optimality criterion to use, from what space the optimal feedbacks are sought and what algorithm to use for solving the optimization problem.

Predicting Effects of Feedback Actions

When the user is giving feedback, it is not obvious that she will be able to predict the effects these actions will have on the system, given that the behavior of the system relies on a potentially complex underlying user model. If making the user model simpler is not possible without sacrificing performance, one way to solve this problem is to enable the user to see a prediction of the effects of any action available to her before she commits to it. This way the user will be less surprised by the effects of the action and is able to choose the action based on the expected consequences.

However, there are some practical problems with accurately predicting the effects of different actions. For example, the system may be so complex that accurately simulating and visualizing the effects for any possible action is infeasible in real time. Further problems may arise if the system has randomized elements in it, for example in order to support exploration, because in this situation the number of possible future states may be practically infinite.

It is thus more practical to use approximate prediction. The interface should visualize the probable effects of the action, while still being computationally feasible in real time. Our solution for the approximate prediction is to sample the possible future states of the system, fit a simpler function approximation to these samples and use it for visualizing the effects.

Constructing this approximation requires making two main choices: which points to sample and what function family to use for constructing the approximation based on these samples.

SYSTEM ARCHITECTURE

Introduction to the system

We use an existing search engine, the SciNet [5], as a case study and implement these new approaches in it. SciNet allows the user to direct the search by interacting with a visualization of the search intent model of the user, composed of keywords and their estimated relevances. The model is visualized to the user using an Intent Radar, where the top 10 relevant keywords are shown on a circular layout so that the closer to the center a keyword is, the more relevant it is. Additional keyword suggestions are also visualized on the edge of the radar view. An example of the visualized user model is shown in Figure 1, along with a scenario illustrating one of the problems with the baseline system, resulting from the user feedback being interpreted only as additional datapoints.

The user gives feedback on the user model by moving one keyword at a time to a new location on the radar. When the user lets go of the keyword, feedback for this keyword is calculated based on the distance from the center. The user model is then updated, new articles are retrieved, and the new state is visualized to the user.

Implementation of the Proposed Approaches

We implemented the optimization of the user model as a linear greedy incremental search, illustrated in Algorithm 1. This algorithm was motivated by the underlying user model being approximately linear. At each step, first the maximal and minimal relevance feedback values (r_{max}, r_{min}) for the keyword (k) the user moved are used to tentatively update the current model ($\mathbf{M}_{t+1}$), to get the estimates of the corresponding error values (e_{max}, e_{min}). Then, the next approximation for optimal relevance feedback (r') is chosen by linear

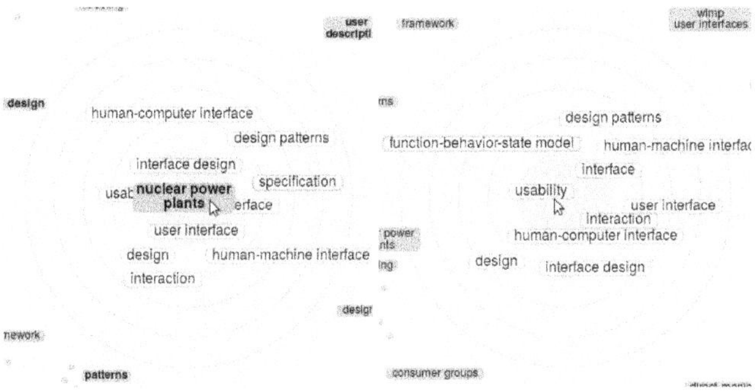

Figure 1. In the baseline system, sometimes even giving maximal relevance feedback to a keyword by dragging it to the center of the Intent Radar (left) may result in a new model that does not contain this keyword within the top 10 keywords (right). The central keywords represent the top 10 keywords.

interpolation, or at the maximum values. This value is then used to update the current model, and the relevance value is appended to a list containing the relevance values used to update the model (**r'**). The algorithm terminates either when the model is close enough (ϵ) to the optimum ($|\tilde{o}(\cdot)|$), or when a maximum number of iterations (N_{max}) has been reached.

We implemented the approximate prediction as a per-keyword linear interpolation. The idea of the algorithm is to calculate two possible user models using the extreme feedback values (r_{min}, r_{max}) for the keyword the user is dragging, and to use a linear interpolation as the predicted user model for any relevance value between the extremes. As the user is dragging any single keyword over the radar, the (other) central keywords will be moved on the radar, in the radial direction, to the place corresponding to the predicted new relevance value, as illustrated in Figure 2.

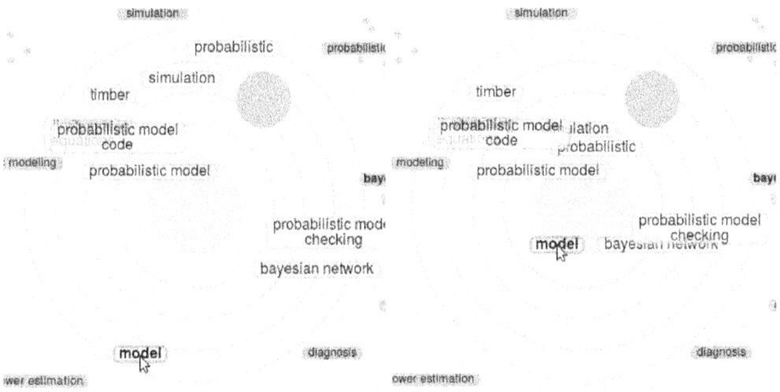

Figure 2. In the improved system, while the user is dragging a keyword over the Intent Radar, the locations of (other) central keywords move simultaneously according to the prediction model. The purple dot indicates the original location of the keyword, and the user can move the keyword back there to cancel the prediction for the current keyword if she wants to try out another one.

EVALUATION

We conducted a preliminary user study on 12 naïve university students and staff members. Each user performed two search tasks, one using the search engine without the proposed improvements (baseline system) and another where the improvements were implemented (improved system). One task was a focused exploratory task and the other a broad exploratory task. Both tasks were about fact retrieval regarding topics the users were not very familiar with. Familiarity in the topic was rated in 1 to 5 Likert scale and all the users reported familiarity less than 5, with average rating of 2.0. In the broad task the questions had multiple correct answers, whereas in the focused task the question scopes were more narrow. The study was balanced with respect to the combination of the type of interface, task and order. The users answered a standard SUS [2] and a modified 15-question ResQue [10] questionnaire after each task. After both tasks a short semi-structured interview was conducted.

Input: user model $\mathbf{M}_t$, keyword k, relevance feedback r, model update rule $u(\cdot)$, accuracy ϵ, maximum number of iterations N_{max}, limits for relevance values (r_{max}, r_{min})
Output: new user model $\mathbf{M}_{t+1}$, relevance feedback values **r'**

$\tilde{o}(\mathbf{M}) = $ (relevance value of keyword k in $\mathbf{M}$) $- r$
$\mathbf{M}_{t+1} \leftarrow \mathbf{M}_t$
r' $\leftarrow$ empty list
while $|\tilde{o}(\boldsymbol{M}_{t+1})| > \epsilon$ **do**
  $e_{max} \leftarrow \tilde{o}(u[\mathbf{M}_{t+1}, k, (\mathbf{r'}, r_{max})])$
  $e_{min} \leftarrow \tilde{o}(u[\mathbf{M}_{t+1}, k, (\mathbf{r'}, r_{min})])$
  if $e_{max} e_{min} < 0$ **then**
    $r' \leftarrow \dfrac{r_{min} e_{max} - r_{max} e_{min}}{e_{max} - e_{min}}$
  else
    if $|e_{max}| < |e_{min}|$ **then**
      $r' \leftarrow r_{max}$
    else
      $r' \leftarrow r_{min}$
    end
  end
  $\mathbf{M}_{t+1} \leftarrow u(\mathbf{M}_{t+1}, k, r')$
  $\mathbf{r'} \leftarrow (\mathbf{r'}, r')$
  if number of iterations $\geq N_{max}$ **then**
    break
  end
end

Algorithm 1: Our implementation of user model state optimization. The M_t is (the data structure representing) the user model at time t. The pair (k, r) is the feedback, indicating that keyword k has relevance r for the user's search intent. The model update rule $u(\cdot)$ takes a model, a keyword and one or more relevance feedback values for that keyword, and returns an updated model. The r' is a list containing the optimal relevance values (length less than or equal to N_{max}). The accuracy ϵ defines the limit for acceptable error in the optimality criterion $o(\cdot) = |\tilde{o}(\cdot)|$. The r_{max} and r_{min} are the maximum and minimum relevance values the user can give, e.g. 1 and 0. The result of appending value b to list a is denoted by (a, b).

The answers to the task questions were rated in a double-blind manner by an expert in both fields. The grading was done in a 1 to 5 Likert scale per question where 5 corresponded to an excellent answer and 1 to a completely wrong answer. One third of the answers were rated separately by another expert. The average inter-rater reliability based on Spearman rho was 0.75, which can be considered adequate. Also the keywords and articles viewed by the users were rated for relevancy by an expert. P-values for the results were calculated using the two-sided Wilcoxon rank-sum algorithm. The interviews were analyzed using content analysis [14].

RESULTS

Based on the results we deemed two users as outliers because on one task they received the lowest possible points on task performance and over 80 % of the articles they viewed were rated irrelevant. It was likely that these tasks were too difficult for these users. These two users were excluded from the analysis.

The improved system resulted in better performance in the focused exploratory task (3.1 for improved, 2.2 for baseline) and worse performance in the broad exploratory task (3.0 for improved, 3.8 for baseline), but these differences were not statistically significant ($p = 0.2$ and $p = 0.1$ respectively). However, the difference of task performances for the baseline between the two tasks was significant ($p = 0.01$). This indicates that the baseline is more efficient in broad than focused exploratory tasks. For the improved system this difference did not exist ($p = 0.6$).

The improved system had slightly better SUS score (64.5 for improved, 62.8 for baseline) and ResQue score (36.0 for improved, 32.7 for baseline). However, the differences were not statistically significant ($p = 0.8$ and $p = 0.7$ respectively). The per-question scores for SUS are shown in Table 1 and for ResQue in Table 2.

I	B	Question
3	3	I think that I would like to use this system frequently
2.2	**1.9**	I found the system unnecessarily complex
3.9	3.3	I thought the system was easy to use
1.6	1.6	I think that I would need the support of a technical person to be able to use this system
3.3	3	I found the various functions in this system were well integrated
2.8	**2.7**	I thought there was too much inconsistency in this system
3.8	3.7	I would imagine that most people would learn to use this system very quickly
2.7	2.7	I found the system very cumbersome to use
3.2	3.1	I felt very confident using the system
2.1	2.1	I needed to learn a lot of things before I could get going with this system

Table 1. SUS score question averages for improved (I) and baseline (B) system. Questions were answered in 5-point Likert scale from 1 (disagree) to 5 (agree). The better value on each row has been boldfaced; higher is better for odd numbered questions and lower is better for even numbered questions.

In the interviews 7 out of 10 users reported that they felt that the visualized prediction helped them in the task. The main stated reason for this was that it helped them predict the effects of their actions, but it was also felt useful for illustrating which keywords were related to each other, as dragging a keyword over the Intent Radar would cause related keywords to move in a similar fashion.

Based on the interviews, the majority of the users stated that they prefer the improved interface over the baseline. Five users preferred the improved system overall, 2 had mixed preferences depending on the situation, 1 preferred the baseline system overall and 2 indicated no explicit preference.

I	B	Question
3.1	3	The items recommended to me matched what I was searching for
3.7	3.4	The recommender system helped me discover new items
4.2	**4.3**	The items recommended to me are diverse
3.4	3.2	The layout of the recommender interface is adequate
2.7	2.3	The recommender explains why the items are recommended to me
3.4	2.6	The information provided for the recommended items is sufficient
3.1	2.8	I found it easy to tell the system what I want / don't want to find
4.1	4	I became familiar with the recommender system very quickly
3.4	3.1	I found it easy to modify my search query in the recommender
3.1	2.9	I understood why the items were recommended to me
3.3	3	Using the recommender to find what I like is easy
3.4	3.4	The recommender gave me good suggestions
3.1	2.9	Overall, I am satisfied with the recommender
3.3	3.3	The recommender can be trusted
3.7	3.5	I would use this recommender again, given the opportunity

Table 2. ResQue score question averages for improved (I) and baseline (B) system. Questions were answered in 5-point Likert scale from 1 (disagree) to 5 (agree). The better value on each row has been boldfaced; higher is better.

DISCUSSION AND FUTURE WORK

In this paper we identified two problems with the usability of interactive search engines where the user is assumed to be a passive provider of feedback, and has no practical means to anticipate the effects of her feedback actions on the system. We proposed a solution for improving the usability of these kinds of systems, demonstrated how it can be implemented in practice, and presented results indicating improvements in task performance, usability, perceived usefulness and user acceptance. We intend to carry out a larger user study with the next generation of the system to confirm these results.

ACKNOWLEDGEMENTS

This work has been partly supported by the Academy of Finland (Finnish Centre of Excellence in Computational Inference Research COIN, 251170) and TEKES (Re:Know). The research leading to this results has received funding from the European Union Seventh Framework Programme (FP7/2007-2013) under grant agreement no 611570. Certain data included herein are derived from the Web of Science prepared by THOMSON REUTERS, Inc., Philadelphia, Pennsylvania, USA: Copyright THOMSON REUTERS, 2011. All rights reserved. Data is also included from the Digital Libraries of the ACM, IEEE, and Springer.

REFERENCES

1. Anick, P. Using terminological feedback for web search refinement: A log-based study. In *Proc. of SIGIR*, ACM (2003), 88–95.

2. Brooke, J. SUS–A quick and dirty usability scale. *Usability Evaluation in Industry 189* (1996), 194.
3. Chau, D. H., Kittur, A., Hong, J. I., and Faloutsos, C. Apolo: making sense of large network data by combining rich user interaction and machine learning. In *Proc. of CHI*, ACM (2011), 167–176.
4. Cutting, D. R., Karger, D. R., Pedersen, J. O., and Tukey, J. W. Scatter/gather: A cluster-based approach to browsing large document collections. In *Proc. of SIGIR*, ACM (1992), 318–329.
5. Głowacka, D., Ruotsalo, T., Konyushkova, K., Athukorala, K., Kaski, S., and Jacucci, G. Directing exploratory search: Reinforcement learning from user interactions with keywords. In *Proc. of IUI*, ACM (2013), 117–128.
6. Karimzadehgan, M., and Zhai, C. Exploration exploitation tradeoff in interactive relevance feedback. In *Proc. of CIKM*, ACM (2010), 1397–1400.
7. Kelly, D., and Fu, X. Elicitation of term relevance feedback: An investigation of term source and context. In *Proc. of SIGIR*, ACM (2006), 453–460.
8. Kules, B., Wilson, M., Schraefel, M. C., and Shneiderman, B. From keyword search to exploration: How result visualization aids discovery on the web. Tech. rep., 2008.
9. Parra, D., Brusilovsky, P., and Trattner, C. See what you want to see: Visual user-driven approach for hybrid recommendation. In *Proc. of IUI*, ACM (2014), 235–240.
10. Pu, P., Chen, L., and Hu, R. A user-centric evaluation framework for recommender systems. In *Proc. of RecSys*, ACM (2011), 157–164.
11. Radlinski, F., Kleinberg, R., and Joachims, T. Learning diverse rankings with multi-armed bandits. In *Proc. of ICML*, ACM (2008), 784–791.
12. Teevan, J., Alvarado, C., Ackerman, M. S., and Karger, D. R. The perfect search engine is not enough: a study of orienteering behavior in directed search. In *Proc. of CHI*, ACM (2004), 415–422.
13. Verbert, K., Parra, D., Brusilovsky, P., and Duval, E. Visualizing recommendations to support exploration, transparency and controllability. In *Proc. of IUI*, ACM (2013), 351–362.
14. Weber, R. *Basic content analysis*. Sage, 1990.
15. Yee, K.-P., Swearingen, K., Li, K., and Hearst, M. Faceted metadata for image search and browsing. In *Proc. of CHI*, ACM (2003), 401–408.

Adaptive Recommendation-based Modeling Support for Data Analysis Workflows

Dietmar Jannach
TU Dortmund
44227 Dortmund, Germany
dietmar.jannach@udo.edu

Michael Jugovac
TU Dortmund
44227 Dortmund, Germany
michael.jugovac@udo.edu

Lukas Lerche
TU Dortmund
44227 Dortmund, Germany
lukas.lerche@udo.edu

ABSTRACT
RapidMiner is a software framework for the development and execution of data analysis workflows. Like many modern software development environments, the tool comprises a visual editor which allows the user to design processes on a conceptual level, thereby abstracts technical details, and thus helps the user focus on the core modeling task. The large set of pre-implemented data analysis operations available in the framework, as well as their logical dependencies, can, however, be overwhelming in particular for novice users.

In this work we present an intelligent add-on to the RapidMiner framework that supports the user during the modeling phase by recommending additional operations to insert into the currently developed data analysis workflow. In the paper, we first propose different recommendation techniques and evaluate them in an offline setting using a pool of several thousand existing workflows. Second, we present the results of a laboratory study, which show that our tool helps users to significantly increase the efficiency of the modeling process.

Author Keywords
Visual Process Modeling; Recommendation; User Interfaces

ACM Classification Keywords
H5.3 Information Interfaces and Presentation: Interaction Styles

INTRODUCTION
RapidMiner[1] is a wide-spread open-source software framework for the design and execution of data analysis workflows. The framework comprises a number of pre-implemented software components that provide often-required functionalities for data mining and data analysis including, for example, methods for data retrieval and data pre-processing, feature selection techniques, various machine learning algorithms, as well as methods for performance evaluation.

[1] `http://www.rapidminer.com`

IUI 2015, March 29–April 1, 2015, Atlanta, GA, USA.

ACM 978-1-4503-3306-1/15/03 ...$15.00.
http://dx.doi.org/10.1145/2678025.2701380

In contrast to many other data processing frameworks or machine learning libraries, RapidMiner includes a visual modeling environment (Figure 1) that supports the definition of complete data analysis workflows (processes). The elements of the processes are (1) a set of process steps called "operators" and (2) a set of edges connecting the operators. The operators are used to model data processing tasks and the control flow; the edges specify the required data flows.

The right-hand side of Figure 1 shows a small example of a process in RapidMiner consisting of three operators and their pre-defined input and output ports. The "preprocessing" operator in this case is by the way not an atomic step, but rather a subprocess that encapsulates other operators. The left-hand side of the screenshot shows the set of available operators.

While tools like RapidMiner make it easier for users to incrementally develop and immediately test the data analysis workflows, the variety of available process steps can be challenging, in particular for novice users: a standard installation of RapidMiner without extensions already comprises several hundred operators. Furthermore, some operators are semantically or logically connected and often only make sense in a process when used in combination. In the example, a "rule generation step" would typically follow after the association rule mining operator "FP-Growth". Rule mining, on the other hand, might require some preceding data transformation step.

To better support the users, we propose a user interface (UI) extension for RapidMiner which makes adaptive recommendations to the user regarding suitable operators to extend the currently developed data analysis process. The new UI component bases its suggestions on a prediction model that is learned in a pre-processing phase using a pool of several thousand real-world data analysis workflows. The "operator recommender" is fully integrated into the RapidMiner modeling framework as a plug-in component, supports standard drag & drop operations, and constantly updates the recommendations depending on the user's recent actions.

The paper is organized as follows. In the next section, we propose new algorithms for operator recommendation that take the user's current modeling *context* into account and benchmark these methods with the algorithms presented in [12]. After outlining the technical architecture of the overall recommendation framework, we report the results of a laboratory study that aimed to assess the utility of the system during the modeling process. The paper ends with a discussion of previous works and an outlook on future developments.

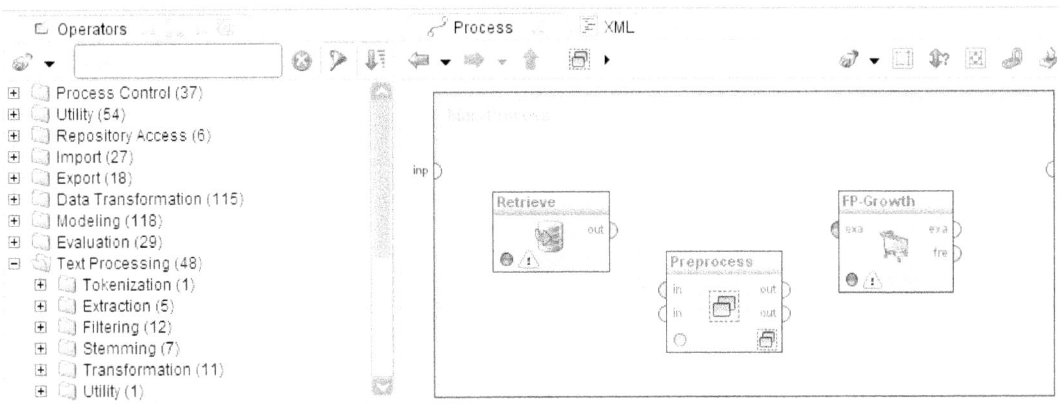

Figure 1. A process fragment developed in RapidMiner

CONTEXTUALIZED OPERATOR RECOMMENDATION

Results from a previous study

In [12], the results of an experimental evaluation of different operator recommendation schemes were presented. The evaluation was based on an offline experimental design in which the goal was to predict additional operators given a partial data mining workflow. We will use the same experimental procedure in this paper; details will be given in a later section.

The prediction approaches in [12] were mostly based on operator co-occurrence patterns within a larger pool of historical data analysis workflows. Among others, different association rule mining techniques like FP-Growth [1], sequential patterns [9], or CFP-Growth [11] were evaluated.

A k-nearest neighbors method

The most successful approach in most settings tested in [12] was a weighted *k-nearest-neighbor* (kNN) based technique, which was designed as follows.

1. Neighborhood formation: Each historical process p was represented as a vector containing boolean values. Each vector element corresponds to one of the operators and is set to "1" if the operator is contained at least once in p. The similarity of two processes was then determined by calculating the cosine of the angle between the vectors.

2. Scoring function: To determine the prediction *score* for an operator op for a given partial process $\hat{p}$, the k most similar processes to $\hat{p}$ were considered and the similarity values for those "neighbors" that contained the operator op were summed up. More formally, given a target process $\hat{p}$, its k nearest neighbors $N_k(\hat{p})$, and an operator op,

$$score(op, \hat{p}) = \frac{\Sigma_{p_i \in N_k(\hat{p})} sim(\hat{p}, p_i)}{|N_k(\hat{p})|} \quad (1)$$

   where $sim(\hat{p}, p_i)$ is zero if p_i does not contain op, and the cosine similarity of $\hat{p}$ and p_i otherwise.

3. The operators are finally ranked and recommended based on their score as computed in Equation 1 in decreasing order.

The main idea of the *kNN* method is therefore that operators that appeared in processes that are similar to the currently developed one, are likely to appear in the current process as well.

Using pairwise co-occurrences

In [12], additional experiments with a quite simple method called COOCCUR were made. The method relies on co-occurrence probabilities for any pair of operators, which can be efficiently determined offline by scanning all historical processes once. To create an operator recommendation list for a given process $\hat{p}$, we can iterate over all operators of $\hat{p}$ and return a ranked list of other operators that co-occurred with the elements of $\hat{p}$ most often. The experiments in [12] showed that COOCCUR performed surprisingly well and was often better than the computationally more expensive rule mining techniques.

Context-Aware Algorithms

The different techniques presented in [12] significantly outperformed the "popularity"-based baseline with respect to their ability of predicting which operator was hidden from an existing process during the evaluation procedure. The predictions made by the proposed algorithms were mostly based on co-occurrence patterns.

In this work, we build on these co-occurrence based approaches but in addition try to take the current stage of the modeling process – the "context" – into account. The development of a complex data analysis workflow is an incremental and possibly iterative process. A recommendation tool should therefore take into account which part of the process the designer is currently working on.

Consider, for example, a situation in which the user is working on the details of a multi-element *subprocess* of a larger process. The recommendations made in this context should therefore be based on the operators used in the subprocess; other operators appearing in the overall workflow might be less relevant. Another example is shown in Figure 2, where we have a process with multiple execution threads. If we assume that the last user action was the insertion of the "FP-Growth" operator, then it is reasonable to give more weight to operators in the recommendation process that co-occurred

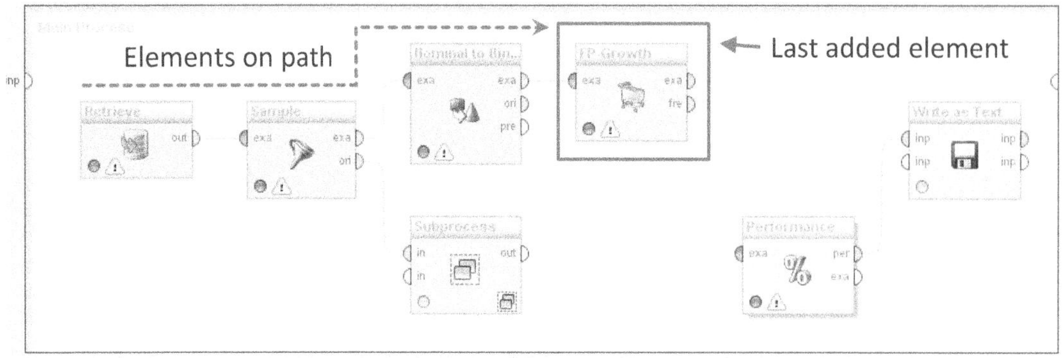

Figure 2. Looking at the most recently added elements

with this operator in the past. One assumption here is that the user is about to proceed with the construction of the process where the last operator insertion took place. Another reason to give more weight to these more "recent" operators is that maybe the user has already finished modeling the data preparation phase at the beginning of the process.

Adding context information

In the following, we propose new context-aware versions of the discussed methods, which receive the current modeling context as an additional parameter. In our experimental setup, we consider the set of operators that precede the last inserted one as the context. The list of preceding operators is determined by following the incoming edges backwards until an operator is reached which has no inputs. In the example in Figure 2, we would pass the last added operator and the three other elements on the path to the recommender. In case there are multiple input paths for an operator, we return the elements on the longest path. If the last added operator is not yet connected with the rest, the additional context information would be empty[2].

Note that while the context information passed to the recommendation algorithms contains all the elements of the path, not all of them might actually be useful to adapt the recommendations. Operators appearing at the very beginning of the process could even be misleading the algorithms as this part of the process model might already be completed. An algorithm could therefore try to focus on the operators that immediately precede the last operator.

A context-aware kNN method

The general idea of the proposed KNN-CTX method is to increase the weight (importance) of neighbors that contain an operator that is also part of the context of the currently constructed process, i.e., we assume that these neighbors are better predictors for the current situation than others that are similar as well but have no overlap with the recent context. The score function shown in Equation 2 correspondingly has an additional parameter – the context – and uses an updated similarity function sim_{ctx}.

$$score(op, \hat{p}, ctx) = \frac{\Sigma_{p_i \in N_k(\hat{p})} sim_{ctx}(\hat{p}, p_i, ctx)}{|N_k(\hat{p})|} \quad (2)$$

[2]Alternative ways of determining the context are of course possible.

Various ways of adding more weight to certain neighbors are possible. In our experiments we used a scheme which increases the weight by a factor α for favorable neighbors (which contain elements of the current context) and decreases the weight of other neighbors using a factor β. The context-based weighting scheme is shown in Equation 3:

$$sim_{ctx}(\hat{p}, p_i, ctx) = \begin{cases} sim(\hat{p}, p_i) \cdot \alpha \cdot (1 + sim(p_i, ctx)), & \text{if } p_i \text{ overlaps with } ctx \\ sim(\hat{p}, p_i) \cdot \beta, & \text{otherwise} \end{cases} \quad (3)$$

where $\alpha > 0$; $0 < \beta < 1$; and *sim* is again calculated as the cosine similarity, in this case between the context and the neighbor process p_i, which allows us to take the degree of overlap into account in the weighting scheme.

A context-aware co-occurrence method

Since the computationally simple but comparably effective method of looking at pairwise operator co-occurrences (COOCCUR) led to good results in [12], we created a context-aware version of it (COOCCUR-CTX). The difference to the original method is that we only consider co-occurrence scores for operators that are part of the current context *ctx*, i.e., for the elements on the path in Figure 2. Because this context-based approach is independent of operators outside of the context, it requires even less computation time than its non-contextualized counterpart.

LINK-CTX: *Considering linked operators*

So far, we only looked at operator co-occurrences but did not take the structure of the processes into account. The proposed method LINK-CTX is a first step to look at such structural process characteristics for recommendations.

Specifically, the idea again is to look at the current modeling context and count in the training set which other operators were *frequently linked* with the context elements. Following this approach, we try to rank those operators higher which are "closer" to the current modeling area. At the same time, we hope to rule out frequently used elements (e.g., for input data retrieval) which have high co-occurrence statistics but are no longer relevant at the current stage of modeling.

The algorithm LINK-CTX uses the following score function, in which P is the set of all training processes, *op* is the operator to be scored, and ctx is the given context (of the currently constructed process $\hat{p}$):

$$score(op, \hat{p}, ctx) = \Sigma_{p_i \in P} \Sigma_{op_j \in p_i} linkScore(op, op_j, ctx) \quad (4)$$

The function *linkScore* can implement different strategies to assign scores to the linked operators depending, e.g., on the position of the compared element in the context. One possible strategy is to simply look at the last element of the context (*ctx.last*()) and return 1 if the operator op was a direct successor of this element in a training process or 0 otherwise (Equation 5).

$$linkScore(op, op_j, ctx) = \begin{cases} 1, & \text{if } (op_j = ctx.last() \wedge \\ & \quad linked(op_j, op)) \\ 0, & \text{otherwise} \end{cases} \quad (5)$$

The score for a given operator *op* is therefore determined by the number of times it is a successor in all training processes to the operators in the context. In case no or only a few connected operators can be found (e.g., because the last operator is a rarely used or it is a custom operator), we append elements from the standard COOCCUR method to the recommendation list.

A hybrid strategy

The last recommendation strategy evaluated in this paper, HYBRID-CTX, combines the two contextualized strategies KNN-CTX and LINK-CTX because the two methods focus on different patterns in the training data. We use a weighting strategy, where the weight factor w is dependent on the number of operators in the process. The more operators exist, the more weight is given to the KNN-CTX method. For shorter processes, our experiments show that the link-based method is preferable; for longer processes the kNN method performs better. Thus, we devised the following scheme to distribute the algorithm's weights:

$$w(\hat{p}) = \begin{cases} log_{10}(|\hat{p}|) \cdot \gamma, & \text{if } |\hat{p}| \leq 5 \\ \gamma, & \text{otherwise} \end{cases} \quad (6)$$

in which $|\hat{p}|$ corresponds to the number of operators in $\hat{p}$ and γ is an empirically determined maximum weight. The score for a target operator *op* is given in Equation 7.

$$\begin{aligned} score(op, \hat{p}, ctx) = \quad & w(\hat{p}) \cdot score_{kNN-Ctx}(op, \hat{p}, ctx) + \\ & (1 - w(\hat{p})) \cdot score_{Link-Ctx}(op, \hat{p}, ctx) \end{aligned} \quad (7)$$

EXPERIMENTAL EVALUATION

Evaluation protocol

We adopt the evaluation approach from [12]. The evaluation is based on a pool of several thousand existing data mining workflows, which are split into training and test datasets. The task of the algorithm is to predict operators that were hidden in the processes from the test dataset. Ten-fold cross validation was applied in all experiments.

The following protocol variants were examined.

- *Leave-one-out*: In this setting, we remove one operator from each process in the test set and use the following strategies to determine the element to be removed: RANDOM, FIRST, MIDDLE, SECOND-TO-LAST, LAST. Removing and predicting the first and the last element is, however, not very informative because these operations are typically related to raw data retrieval (e.g., from a file) and result output. In this paper we will report the results of the SECOND-TO-LAST variant; the results are similar for the RANDOM and MIDDLE strategy.

- *Given-n*: The idea of this evaluation variant is to remove all but the first n elements from the process. By increasing the value of n step by step, we can simulate the incremental development of the data mining workflow by the user. This evaluation procedure can thus also help to determine how good the individual algorithms are in the "cold-start" setting, in which limited information is available for the recommendation process.

Beside the incomplete partial test processes, the recommendation algorithms were also provided with the information about the current context as described above, i.e., they received the list of operators that preceded the hidden one.

As evaluation measures, we use *Recall* and the *Mean Reciprocal Rank* (MRR). Since we only hide one element in each test process, Recall has the value of "1", in case the recommendation algorithm puts the hidden operator in the top n list. Otherwise, no hit was made and the Recall is zero. The MRR measure in addition takes the position of the "hit" in the list into account. The MRR value for a given recommendation is 0, if the hidden element is not in the list, and $1/pos$ otherwise, where pos denotes the position of the hit in the recommendation list. Both for Recall and the MRR we report the mean value over all examined data mining processes.

Dataset

The data that was used for the evaluation consisted of a collection of several thousand real-world data analysis workflows created with RapidMiner. The process definitions contained both processes that were publicly shared by users on the "myexperiment" web site[3], the example process sets from the RapidMiner framework, and data from other sources.

Since there were a number of duplicate processes stemming from, e.g., duplicate posts on the forums, we applied a comparably strict de-duplication strategy. Specifically, we considered process definitions to be duplicates when they contained the same operator sequences. Furthermore, we ignored all processes that consisted only of one operator. Table 1 shows some statistics of the final dataset.

Note that the average number of unique operators per process is lower than the average number of operators per process. This means that the same operator is used multiple times in several processes. The recommendation of an operator that is already used in the process might therefore be reasonable.

[3]http://www.myexperiment.org/

Number of processes	6,385		
Number of unique operators	833		
	Mean	*Median*	*St. dev.*
Operators per process	20.7	14	20.2
Unique operators per process	11.8	10	7.3
Longest connected path	6.5	5	4.4

Table 1. Dataset Characteristics

The average number of operators per process is also much lower than the average length of the longest path of connected operators. This indicates that processes are often not entirely linear but contain branches and subprocesses. Finally, the majority of the processes is fairly short and about 50% of the processes have a length between 6 and 15 operators. Some processes, however, comprise a comparably large number of operators. These processes are typically organized in subprocesses.

Another important aspect to note is that the distribution of how often certain operators are used is highly skewed. Many of the several hundred operators are only used in a small number of processes. Others, e.g., those for data import, sampling, or the computation of derived attributes, are part of a major fraction of the processes. As a result, using a popularity-based recommendation strategy and recommending the most frequently used operators can be a comparably hard baseline.

The distribution of operator usage frequencies is shown in Figure 3.

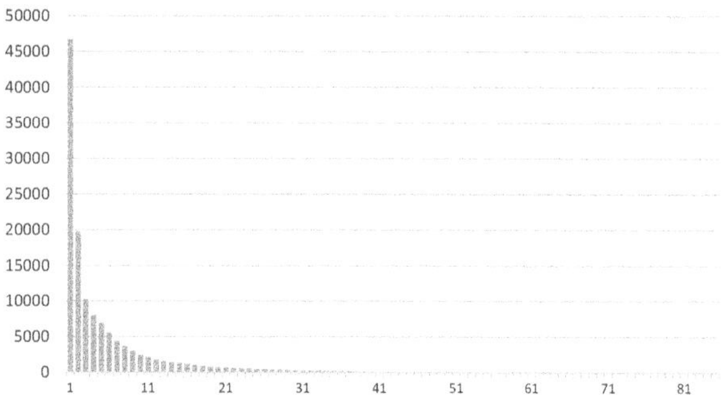

Figure 3. Distribution of the usage frequencies of the operators (each step on the x-axis represents a bin of 10 operators)

To visualize the unevenness of the distribution, we sorted the operators based on their absolute usage frequency in the process pool in descending order and grouped them in bins of size 10. The first bin (left-most bar in the chart) therefore contains the most frequently used operators. Overall, about 40% of all operator usages in the processes correspond to these first ten very general operator types. On the other hand, the long-tail distribution shown in Figure 3 indicates that many of the operators are used less than 10 times in the several thousand process definitions.

Evaluation Results and Discussion

We compared the best performing algorithms from [12] with the context-aware ones proposed in the previous section using the above described protocols and evaluation measures.

Results for the Leave-One-Out setting

Table 2 shows the obtained Recall and MRR results using the best parameter settings for each algorithm, which we obtained through a manual fine-tuning process. We chose a list length of 10, assuming that this corresponds to a number users would probably inspect and will not require scrolling in the UI. Experiments with different list lengths did not lead to different results in terms of the ranking of the algorithms.

The numbers provided in Table 2 correspond to a setting in which we hid the second-to-last element in the process. Different hiding strategies – e.g., hiding a random element – led to different absolute values for the measures but not to a different algorithm ranking.

Beside the accuracy measures the average time required to compute one recommendation list[4] is shown. We implemented the context-aware algorithms in such a way that a context-agnostic algorithm of the same family is used as fallback in case the contextualized variant did not produce enough results.

Algorithm	Recall	MRR	RecTime
MOSTFREQ	0.414	0.143	0.01 ms
COOCCUR	0.542	0.234	0.43 ms
KNN	0.669	0.228	3.77 ms
COOCCUR-CTX	0.540	0.262	0.27 ms
KNN-CTX	0.843	0.567	3.94 ms
LINK-CTX	0.673	0.394	0.14 ms
HYBRID-CTX	**0.852**	**0.573**	4.07 ms

Table 2. Recall, MRR (top-10) and recommenation time

Accuracy results: The results clearly show that all context-aware methods (except COOCCUR-CTX) by far outperform the non-contextualized versions from [12] and that the hybrid method leads to the overall best results. A t-test ($p < 0.05$ with Bonferroni correction for multiple testing) revealed that all pairwise differences between the algorithms are statistically significant except between (a) LINK-CTX and KNN (Recall), (b) COOCCUR and COOCCUR-CTX (Recall), (c) COOCCUR and KNN (MRR), and (d) HYBRID-CTX and KNN-CTX (Recall and MRR).

Computation times: Due to our internal bitset encoding of the processes, the computation times required to compute one recommendation list are very low even for the *kNN* approaches.

Parameter settings: We determined optimal neighborhood sizes of 5 for the KNN method and 9 neighbors for KNN-CTX, for which we used $\alpha = 0.5$ and $\beta = 0.001$. The optimal context-lengths were 2 (COOCCUR-CTX) and 1 (LINK-CTX). The value of 0.9 for γ led to the best results for the hybrid.

Results for the Given-n setting

Table 3 shows the results when using the GIVEN-N procedure to simulate the incremental development process.

Precision and Recall: The results reveal that the proposed hybrid method HYBRID-CTX performs best even in cold-start

[4]The computer used in our experiments was equipped with 16GB RAM and an Intel i5 CPU.

Algorithm	Given-1	Given-3	Given-5
MostFreq	0.378/0.158	0.412/0.177	0.390/0.148
CoOccur	0.504/0.221	0.557/0.247	0.504/0.217
kNN	0.228/0.088	0.542/0.170	0.586/0.175
CoOccur-Ctx	0.504/0.221	0.555/0.245	0.509/0.209
kNN-Ctx	0.293/0.167	0.639/0.386	0.684/0.439
Link-Ctx	**0.640/0.296**	0.713/0.385	0.718/0.383
Hybrid-Ctx	**0.640/0.296**	**0.765/0.444**	**0.803/ 0.468**

Table 3. Recall/MRR for different given-n configurations

situations, in which only the first few elements are known. The kNN methods alone perform better than the frequency-based technique as soon as three elements of the process are known. In the extreme *Given-1* case, the structure-based Link-Ctx method yields very good results. Most observed differences are again statistically significant using pairwise t-tests with Bonferroni correction, $p < 0.05$; in particular the difference between the hybrid method and Link-Ctx and all other techniques for the *Given-3* and *Given-5* situations are significant both in terms of Recall and MRR.

Overall, the results of the offline evaluation indicate that combining different aspects like process structure and neighborhood-based co-occurrence patterns – as done in Hybrid-Ctx – is the most promising approach to obtain high recommendation accuracy.

IMPLEMENTATION ARCHITECTURE

In addition to the offline analysis, we carried out a laboratory study in order to assess to which extent the automated system-side recommendation of operators can actually help to make the design process for data mining workflows more efficient. To be able to conduct such a test, we developed a fully-functional plug-in to RapidMiner with which (parts of) the participants of the study interacted. The developed software is not yet in productive use. An evaluation with real users is, however, planned in the near future.

Before we describe the details of the laboratory study, we will first outline the overall architecture of the recommendation service of RapidMiner (Figure 4).

The end user's view

The recommendation service is visible to the end user (process designer) as one additional "view" (UI plug-in), which is integrated into the Graphical User Interface of RapidMiner, see Figure 4. Once activated, the plug-in monitors the user actions related to the process definition, in particular the insertion or removal of operators. After such a relevant user action is observed, the UI component collects the information about the currently modeled process and forwards it to a remote recommendation service to receive a new set of recommendations.

The server responds with a ranked list of operators which – together with a confidence value[5] – is then presented in the designated area of RapidMiner. Figure 4 shows our default position of the recommendation lists, which is close to the existing tree- or search-based operator selection window. In case the user finds a relevant operator in the recommendation list, they can drag & drop the operator into the modeling window, which in turn leads to a request to the server for a new recommendation list. The purpose of the plug-in component is therefore to help the user find suitable operators more quickly than by scanning the entire hierarchical list of operators and their descriptions. In addition, the recommender will eventually make recommendations for operators that the user might have forgotten to include in the process otherwise.

An adaptive recommendation service

The recommendation algorithms run on a dedicated server, which receives requests for recommendations from the clients over a REST and JSON-based Application Programming Interface. The requests contain the current partial process model developed by the user[6]. The server then creates the recommendations and also updates the new partial process received by the client in the pool of known processes. This helps us to constantly grow our "knowledge base" of training process models.[7] It furthermore allows us to make recommendations for new operators that are added to the RapidMiner system over time.

As stated earlier, each recommendation list can be computed in a fraction of a second. This nearly unnoticeable delay is more than sufficient to stay within the narrow time frame required in this interactive application setting. Scalability for situations of heavy parallel access to the recommendation server can be easily achieved by running the algorithms on a cluster of servers.

LABORATORY STUDY

In the following, we will describe the details of the laboratory study which we conducted to better understand the value of the proposed recommendation service within RapidMiner and get additional feedback from the users regarding, e.g., the general usability. The experiment consisted of a workflow modeling exercise, in which half of the participants had to accomplish the task with the plug-in and the other half was not supported by the plug-in (i.e., the plug-in was not visible in the UI at all for them).

Inspired by the work presented in [14], who made a comparable user study in the domain of business process modelling, we specifically aimed to verify the following expectations with our experiment.

Expected differences between the groups (with and without recommendation support):

- (E1) Participants that use the plug-in are more efficient than the other group in terms of required system interactions and the overall task completion time.
- (E2) Plug-in users are more confident in their solution as their solution was based on system-side recommendations.

[5]The confidence values presented to the user depend on the chosen algorithm.

[6]All specific pieces of information like parameters, data source names etc. are removed for privacy reasons before the transmission to the server.

[7]This feature was switched off for the user study.

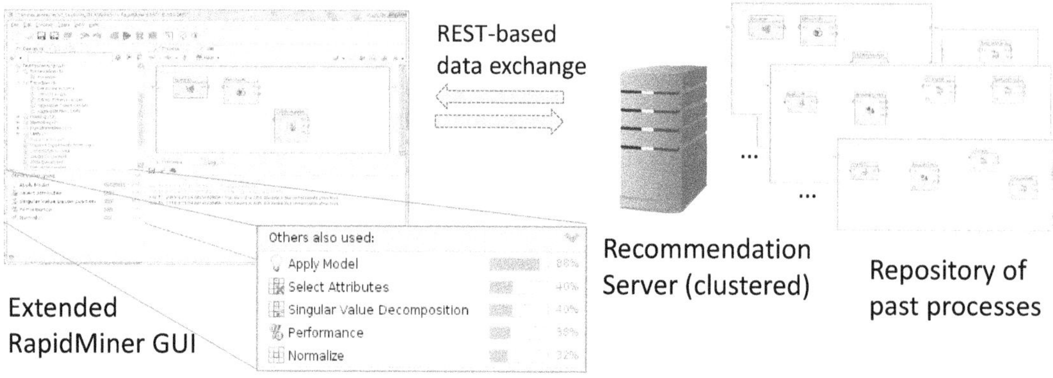

Figure 4. Architecture of the recommendation service for RapidMiner

- (E3) Participants that use our tool perceive the modeling exercise to be easier and the overall task to be more understandable than the other group.

Expected differences within subgroups of plug-in users:

- (E4) Non-experienced users find the recommendations to be more helpful than experienced ones and have a higher tendency to recommend the tool to others.
- (E5) The plug-in leads to efficiency improvements both for experienced and inexperienced users.

Experimental procedure

The experiment had three phases. In the first phase, the users were instructed in the use of RapidMiner. In the second phase, the participants had to complete a partial workflow model according to a written specification. At the end of the experiment, the participants had to fill out a questionnaire.

All subjects completed the task individually in the same office room at our department and used the identical computer equipment. We screen-recorded the interactions of the subjects with RapidMiner. We furthermore encouraged the users to comment on what they are thinking during the exercise in the sense of a "think-aloud" protocol and recorded the user utterances.

Tutorial phase

The goal of this phase was to make the participants acquainted with the RapidMiner system. We used detailed scripts that were used by the experimenter and the participant to make the process independent of the experimenter. In the tutorial, the participants completed a partial process with the tool. In case the participant was part of the group using the plug-in, the tutorial included a step that showed how to use the recommendations.

Modeling exercise

All participants received the same detailed and written task description which did not mention the recommendation tool. The experimenter was not allowed to help the subject in any form. The experimenter was instructed to stop the experiment after a time limit of 15 minutes was reached.

The problem to solve in the exercise itself consisted of a partial four-element data mining workflow to which three more operators had to be added to achieve the described process goals that were specified in the task description. The exact names of the operators to be inserted into the process were not provided in the task description. Beside the retrieval of the correct operators, the participants were asked to connect the operators via their input and output ports. Overall, the process to model therefore contained 7 operators which is a realistic and common size as mentioned above. Figure 5 shows a screenshot of a correctly completed process.

At the server side, we used the *kNN* method from [12] to compute the operator recommendations since this was the best performing method we had available at the time of the study.

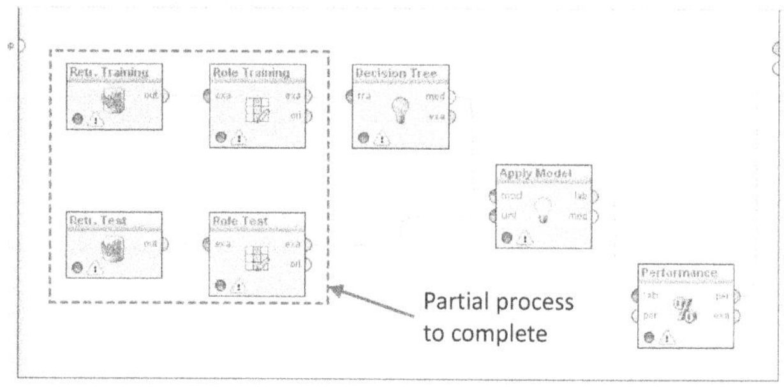

Figure 5. A correct solution to the modeling exercise

Questionnaire

In the post-experiment questionnaire, we asked several questions to validate our hypotheses. We asked questions around the following topics: (a) experience in data mining in general and with RapidMiner, (b) the perceived complexity of the modeling task, (c) the user's self-assessment of the quality of the final process and the level of encountered difficulties, and (d) their satisfaction with the tutorial material. The users that could use the recommendation plug-in were additionally asked (i) whether they found the tool helpful, (ii) if they felt well-supported by the tool, and (iii) if they would recommend the use of the plug-in to others. For all questions we used five-point or ten-point Likert scales.

Participants

In total, 28 subjects participated in the study. All of them had at least basic knowledge in the field of computer science (CS).

Some of them had some experience in data mining, workflow processes or RapidMiner. The participants were split randomly into two groups of 14 subjects. One group could complete the modeling task with the help of the recommendation plug-in but they could also use the standard operator browsing and search feature of the tool. The other group did not have the plug-in at their disposal at all. We recruited the students via an announcement to a mailing list for CS students. We conducted a raffle and one participant received a price worth 100 € after the study was completed.

Study results

Efficiency of modeling (E1)

As a measurement method for testing our expectation E1, i.e., for determining how quickly users can complete the task, we measured (a) the elapsed time until all required operators were correctly inserted by the participant and (b) the number of required clicks to insert the operators (either through the recommender or through the standard tree-based representation of RapidMiner). Table 4 summarizes these observations.

Note that all subjects could successfully identify and insert the three missing operators within the 15 minute time limit. Not all subjects however managed to correctly wire the operators in time. Since the purpose of the plug-in is to point users to relevant operators and is not related to the wiring of the operators, our measurement covers the time from the beginning of the task until the moment when the operators were successfully inserted[8].

Group	Time (sec)	Std. dev.	Clicks	Std. dev.
no plug-in	290.85	105.55	35.77	6.34
with plug-in	119.94	104.70	9.86	16.76

Table 4. Efficiency results

The observations show that the users that were supported by the plug-in needed significantly ($p < 0.05$) less time and number of clicks to find and insert the correct operators. The average task completion time without the plug-in was close to 5 minutes. The provision of recommendations helped to reduce the average time to about 2 minutes. The comparably large variance observed for the plug-in users is explained by the fact that two of the subjects found and inserted the three operators into the model in less than 30 seconds.

Confidence in results (E2)

For this measurement, we compared the self-reported confidence of the users after the experiment in the quality of their solution (Table 5). The mean value reported by plug-in users was at 3.93 on the 5-point Likert scale which means that most of them were highly confident that their solution was correct. The mean value for users without recommendation support was slightly lower (3.36). A t-test reveals that the differences are marginally significant ($p < 0.1$). Nonetheless, we see this as some indication that the participants assumed that the recommendations made by the system were correct.

[8]Given that all participants at the end had correctly inserted the three required operators, no differences in the final solution quality were observed. Testing whether our tool leads to higher quality solutions, was not in the focus of the study.

Group	Confidence in result	Std. dev.
no plug-in	3.36	1.23
with plug-in	3.93	0.64

Table 5. Confidence in results

Perceived task complexity (E3)

Our expectation before the experiment was that through the recommendation support, users (a) perceived the construction of the specific workflow to be less complex when guided by the tool and (b) that they found it overall clearer from the beginning what they were supposed to do in general, i.e., find and connect the right operators and complete the workflow. The mean values of the provided answers in the questionnaire are shown in Table 6.

Group	Ease of task	Comprehens. of task
no plug-in	3.42	3.29
with plug-in	3.72	4.29

Table 6. Perceived ease/comprehension of modeling task

As for the modeling complexity, plug-in users found the exercise on average (3.72) to be easier than the other group (3.42); note that higher values for this questionnaire item correspond to lower complexity. The differences were however not statistically significant at $p < 0.05$ and our expectation was therefore not fulfilled. However, plug-in users found the overall task significantly clearer (4.29 vs. 3.29, $p < 0.05$) than users who were not supported by the tool. We see this as an indicator that the tool can be particularly useful for novice users as the system guides the user through the model development process.

Utility of plug-in for different user groups (E4)

We differentiate between experienced and non-experienced users based on their self-reported assessment at the beginning of the experiment. We expect that non-experienced users find the tool more helpful than experienced ones and would also have a higher tendency to recommend the tool to others.

The general acceptance of the tool was very high. The mean answer for the questions regarding the helpfulness of the recommendations in general and whether the users felt well supported by the recommendations was at about 4.8, which is close to the optimum on the given 5-point scale. The average value for the answer regarding the recommendation of the plug-in to friends was at 8.75 on a ten-point scale.

A correlation analysis using the Bravais-Pearson coefficient showed that the questionnaire answer regarding the helpfulness of the recommendations correlated with the self-reported expertise values. Lower expertise in RapidMiner for example led to higher values for perceived helpfulness (r=*–0.85*) and a higher tendency to recommend the tool to friends (r=*–0.56*). Lower general experience in Data Mining correlated with a slightly higher friend-recommendation tendency (r=*–0.23*).

In general, the mean self-reported value regarding experience in Data Mining was modest (2.46 on a 5-point scale). Further experiments involving a larger group of more advanced and experienced users are therefore required to better assess the helpfulness of the tool for this user group.

Efficiency gains for different user groups (E5)

To analyze whether both experienced and novice users profit from the tool, we made the following comparison. First, we split all participants into experienced users and non-experienced ones. We used the mean self-reported value as a split point. Then, we looked at the average time needed for these two groups when the plug-in was *not used*. Experienced users required about 217 seconds and inexperienced about 301 seconds. *With* the plug-in, the average time needed by experienced users went down to about 52 seconds. Inexperienced users needed about 111 seconds. As a result, the relative efficiency gain was about three fourths for experienced users and more than two thirds for inexperienced users. Table 7 summarizes these effect.

Overall, the results suggest that efficiency gains are even stronger for experienced users, at least when they are given a task which might be relatively easy for them.

Group	Experienced	Inexperienced
no plug-in	214.6	301.2
with plug-in	52.5	111.25
rel. improvement	75.5%	63.0%

Table 7. Rel. efficiency improvement (experienced vs. inexperienced)

General observations regarding the user interfaces

According to the user utterances during the experiments, the UI of RapidMiner was generally considered to be quite complex in particular by the inexperienced participants. The default UI layout of RapidMiner contains six subwindows, of which four have more than one tab. The recommendation functionality was implemented as an additional "view", which can be activated and positioned floating on the whole screen or in *docked* mode within the UI.

The recommendations therefore further add to the complexity of the UI and "compete" with the other subwindows for the attention of the user. We conducted initial experiments regarding the best positioning of the recommendations because we observed in a pilot study that they were often overlooked by users. For example, users paid less attention to the recommendations when they were displayed on the right hand side of the screen, even though this is a typical position for recommendations on e-commerce sites. Even when positioned between the operator selection tree and the main drawing window – which was our choice for the experiments – some users only noticed the recommendations after the list was automatically updated when the first operator was added by the user[9]. Further experiments are therefore required to determine the optimal default position and a layout of the recommendations that does not overwhelm the users.

[9]On average, the participants selected about 2.4 (out of 3) of the inserted operators from the recommendation plug-in.

Research limitations

The size of the user study is clearly a limitation of our research. As for the selection of the participants, we have recruited mostly computer science students. Some of them had some background in Data Mining, a small number already knew the RapidMiner tool, one of them worked with it professionally. The group is therefore probably not representative of the average professional RapidMiner user. Still, graduates in computer science might be well representative of inexperienced (new starters) or infrequent users of RapidMiner.

In this study, we have mainly focused on the efficiency improvements that can be achieved through the recommendations for a specific modeling problem. A detailed study on how the recommendations possibly affect the quality of the resulting models has not been done so far. Furthermore, experiments with professional users – as planned in our future work – are needed to better assess the utility of the plug-in for experienced process modelers.

RELATED WORK

The use of recommendation techniques to support the user in the specific area of modeling data mining workflows has – to the best of our knowledge – not been explored so far. There are, however, a number of research works that have focused on techniques for assisting the user in the development of more general process models, in particular for business processes. According to the overview of such approaches in this area from [13], our work would fall into the category of *single-element, structural recommendations*. Our Given-n simulation corresponds to a "forward-completion" approach.

In [14], Koschmieder et al. present a visual and recommendation-based modeling system for business processes. The environment supports both a search interface for process model fragments based on semantic annotations (tags) as well as a recommendation-based ranking component which is based on a combination of factors such as a query-based score, process fragment usage frequencies, and indicators of the structural match or the quality of the recommended fragments. The work is similar to ours in that the recommendations are based on a repository of past models (fragments) and that the current modeling state is essential to determine suitable suggestions for process extensions. Similar to our work, the authors conducted a laboratory study involving 24 pairs of students who had to accomplish a modeling exercise with and without tool support to assess the value of the recommendation support.

The evaluation in [14] was based only on one recommendation technique and a comparably small repository of process fragments that were developed for the particular modeling exercise. In our work, in contrast, we could rely on a pool of thousands of real-world workflows and additionally compare a number of different strategies in an offline experimental design.

Generally, however, there are several approaches in the area of business process modeling support that we plan to explore in the future in our specific application domain. This includes, for example, the use of semantic information to identify the user's modeling *intention*, see [10] or [14]. In our application domain, semantic information is, for example, available in terms of operator descriptions, user-specified operator names, or the given operator hierarchy.

Furthermore, we plan to go beyond our first link-based analysis and explore more complex *structural* patterns in the currently developed process and the process fragments in the repository. Such analyses were done, e.g., in [16] through an efficient encoding of the graph matching problem or can rely on other process similarity measures as proposed in [7].

Several approaches in the literature like the ones mentioned above or the Bayesian Networks one proposed in [2] aim at the *recommendation of process fragments* or more complex structures instead of single elements (operators) as done in our approach. In our application domain, we plan to specifically look at patterns in subprocesses that are used for common tasks like cross-validation. The possibly required adaptation according to the specific process could then be supported, e.g., by a case-based reasoning approach as proposed in [19].

Finally, some other modeling support approaches in the literature in the domain of business processes aim to the suggestion of appropriate textual names [15] or present recommendations based on the syntactical rules of the used modeling language [18]. These approaches seem to have limited applicability in our domain in which (a) the modeling language has only a few syntactic rules and operators have quite a limited set of connection types, and (b) the activities already have defined semantics and names.

An alternative path potentially worth exploring in the context of our work is to apply ideas from "information foraging", where the goal is to aid the user in their "hunt for information" (see [20]). For our scenario, this means that instead of supporting the search process by immediately providing potential results, our tool would rather support the user in their natural search process, e.g., by highlighting search paths that contain the most promising operators. Such an approach may therefore help to combine the advantages of the user's own search abilities with the information reduction capabilities of the recommender algorithms.

During the last decade, inter-organizational business processes, service oriented architectures, and the integration of applications through web services gained in importance. Recommendation-based modeling support approaches have been applied in that context, e.g., for process completion, the recommendation of alternatives for broken services, or web service discovery [3, 5, 21]. The discovery approach presented in [3], for example, tries to identify fragments (composite services) in past processes that are *structurally* similar to the currently modeled one. In contrast to our work, the evaluation in [3] was made on a small set of purposely created fragments, while in our work we can rely on a larger set of real-world process definitions.

A different strategy for web service discovery was proposed in [5]. Instead of relying on text-based (content-based) matching as done, e.g., in [8], they try to apply historical usage data and classical collaborative and content-based filtering techniques to determine suitable recommendations, e.g., by comparing user profiles. Our kNN method has some similarity with the process-similarity based approach in [5]. We have however not looked at the behavior of individual users over time in our approach, as no author information is available in our workflow repository and collecting such information raises privacy issues.

A different approach to generate recommendations using historical data was made in [4], where process *execution logs* were used instead of the models as a basis for mining co-occurrence patterns. Thereby, actual usage frequencies are taken into account, which is also the case in our recommendation techniques. Similar to our work, the authors of [4] propose to take the current modeling context into account and to generate recommendations depending on the selected activity in the workflow. The evaluation in [4] was based on artificially created execution logs as real-world execution logs were not available. Generally, estimating the "relevance" of individual workflow models based on their usage (execution frequencies) could also be an interesting approach in our domain if such information were available.

Finally, adaptive action recommendation mechanisms that are based on historical interaction data can also be found in other types of software applications not related to process modeling. One example is the *CommunityCommands* system proposed in [17], which recommends new software functionality in terms of helpful commands to users of the AutoCAD design software. As a recommendation technique, user- and item-based collaborative filtering techniques were evaluated based on automatically collected command usage data. Similar to our work, *CommunityCommands* in some form recommends user actions[10]. The main goal of the AutoCAD extension, however, is to point users to newly introduced functionality in the system in a personalized way. Even though our approach can also help users discover new operators, our work aims to point the user to operators that are supposed to be helpful in the current modeling context rather than recommendations based on the user's past actions.

CONCLUSIONS

We have presented an extension to the wide-spread RapidMiner software environment for modeling data mining workflows, which recommends additional operators to the user during the modeling process. An offline evaluation revealed that taking the current modeling context into account is advisable to increase the prediction accuracy. A first user study showed that the tool actually helps both experienced and inexperienced users to develop the processes in a more efficient way. In our future work, we will further explore semantic and more complex structure-based approaches to identify patterns in the data and investigate the recommendation of process fragments (skeletons) in addition to the current single-element recommendations.

[10] See also [6] for an earlier work on predicting user actions.

REFERENCES

1. Agrawal, R., and Srikant, R. Fast algorithms for mining association rules in large databases. In *Proceedings of VLDB '94* (1994), 487–499.
2. Bobek, S., Baran, M., Kluza, K., and Nalepa, G. J. Application of bayesian networks to recommendations in business process modeling. In *Proceedings of AIBP '13* (2013), 41–50.
3. Chan, N., Gaaloul, W., and Tata, S. Composition context matching for web service recommendation. In *Proceedings of SCC '11* (2011), 624–631.
4. Chan, N., Yongsiriwit, K., Gaaloul, W., and Mendling, J. Mining event logs to assist the development of executable process variants. In *Proceedings of CAiSE '14*. 2014, 548–563.
5. Chan, N. N., Gaaloul, W., and Tata, S. A recommender system based on historical usage data for web service discovery. *Service Oriented Computing and Applications 6*, 1 (2012), 51–63.
6. Davison, B. D., and Hirsh, H. Predicting sequences of user actions. In *Proceedings of AAAI '98 Workshop on Predicting the Future: AI Approaches to Time Series Analysis* (1998), 5–12.
7. Dijkman, R., Dumas, M., van Dongen, B., Käärik, R., and Mendling, J. Similarity of business process models: Metrics and evaluation. *Information Systems 36*, 2 (2011), 498–516.
8. Dong, X., Halevy, A., Madhavan, J., Nemes, E., and Zhang, J. Similarity search for web services. In *Proceedings of VLDB '04* (2004), 372–383.
9. Fournier-Viger, P., Faghihi, U., Nkambou, R., and Nguifo, E. M. CMRules: Mining sequential rules common to several sequences. *Knowledge-Based Systems 25*, 1 (2012), 63–76.
10. Hornung, T., Koschmider, A., and Lausen, G. Recommendation based process modeling support: Method and user experience. In *Proceedings of ER '08* (2008), 265–278.
11. Hu, Y.-H., and Chen, Y.-L. Mining association rules with multiple minimum supports: a new mining algorithm and a support tuning mechanism. *Decision Support Systems 42*, 1 (2006), 1–24.
12. Jannach, D., and Fischer, S. Recommendation-based modeling support for data mining processes. In *Proceedings of RecSys '14* (2014), 334–340.
13. Kluza, K., Baran, M., Bobek, S., and Nalepa, G. J. Overview of recommendation techniques in business process modeling. In *Proceedings of KESE9* (2013), 46–57.
14. Koschmider, A., Hornung, T., and Oberweis, A. Recommendation-based editor for business process modeling. *Data and Knowledge Engineering 70*, 6 (2011), 483–503.
15. Leopold, H., Mendling, J., and Reijers, H. A. On the automatic labeling of process models. In *Advanced Information Systems Engineering*, vol. 6741 of *Lecture Notes in Computer Science*. 2011, 512–520.
16. Li, Y., Cao, B., Xu, L., Yin, J., Deng, S., Yin, Y., and Wu, Z. An efficient recommendation method for improving business process modeling. *IEEE Transactions on Industrial Informatics 10*, 1 (2014), 502–513.
17. Matejka, J., Li, W., Grossman, T., and Fitzmaurice, G. W. CommunityCommands: Command recommendations for software applications. In *Proceedings of UIST '09* (2009), 193–202.
18. Mazanek, S., and Minas, M. Business process models as a showcase for syntax-based assistance in diagram editors. In *Model Driven Engineering Languages and Systems*, vol. 5795 of *Lecture Notes in Computer Science*. 2009, 322–336.
19. Minor, M., Bergmann, R., Görg, S., and Walter, K. Towards case-based adaptation of workflows. In *Case-Based Reasoning. Research and Development*, vol. 6176 of *Lecture Notes in Computer Science*. 2010, 421–435.
20. Piorkowski, D., Fleming, S., Scaffidi, C., Bogart, C., Burnett, M., John, B., Bellamy, R., and Swart, C. Reactive information foraging: An empirical investigation of theory-based recommender systems for programmers. In *Proceedings of CHI '12*, ACM (New York, NY, USA, 2012), 1471–1480.
21. Sellami, M., Tata, S., Maamar, Z., and Defude, B. A recommender system for web services discovery in a distributed registry environment. In *Proceedings of ICIW '09* (2009), 418–423.

Intelligent Computing in Personal Informatics: Key Design Considerations

Fredrik Ohlin and Carl Magnus Olsson

Department of Computer Science
Malmö University
Malmö, Sweden

Internet of Things and People Research Center
Malmö University
Malmö, Sweden

{fredrik.ohlin, carl.magnus.olsson}@mah.se

ABSTRACT
An expanding range of apps supported by wearable and mobile devices are being used by people engaged in personal informatics in order to track and explore data about themselves and their everyday activities. While the aspect of data collection is easier than ever before through these technologies, more advanced forms of support from personal informatics systems are not presently available. This lack of next generation personal informatics systems presents research with an important role to fill, and this paper presents a two-step contribution to this effect. The first step is to present a new model of human cooperation with intelligent computing, which collates key issues from the literature. The second step is to apply this model to personal informatics, identifying twelve key considerations for integrating intelligent computing in the design of future personal informatics systems. These design considerations are also applied to an example system, which illustrates their use in eliciting new design directions.

Author Keywords
Personal informatics; quantified self; cooperative computing; augmented computing; ambient computing; cooperative action orchestration

ACM Classification Keywords
H.5.m Information Interfaces and Presentation (e.g. HCI): Miscellaneous; I.2.m Artificial Intelligence: Miscellaneous

INTRODUCTION
Activity trackers, smart watches, and large selections of sensor-powered smartphone applications all exemplify current technology supporting personal informatics. Using such technology, people can explore, strive to understand, and improve their behavior in ways not previously feasible due to the cumbersome data collection otherwise. Further contributing to the wave of interest in this technology is the *quantified self* movement, wherein enthusiast champion a 'data-driven life' [41], and publicly reflect upon appropriate practices and tools through meetups and on the web. Aside from private consumer use, the medical area has started showing significant interest in the possibilities of patient-driven longitudinal data collection [42] using this technology. Computing system support is therefore widely considered as an enabling factor for personal informatics [25, 26], and as a driver for adoption [38].

Nevertheless, current personal informatics systems often holds a simple focus on recording data and displaying it in statistical form to the user for post-activity viewing. In such cases, system support mostly takes the form of automation of previously manual tasks with automatic data collection being the most prominent example. More advanced forms of system support, informed by techniques from intelligent computing, are currently underexplored. This becomes a notable omission when considering that personal informatics is an area where engaged users willingly contribute increasingly rich data (cf. [8]) and thus offers a strong case for intelligent computing to be applied.

The purpose of this paper is to illustrates how intelligent computing could be included as a core part of personal informatics and thereby act as a catalyst for new forms of system support that may provide a richer understanding of the tracked activities to users than present systems allow. We begin our work towards this goal in the next section, by identifying related challenges and opportunities from current personal informatics research. The following section then contains a survey of established techniques and approaches from several areas of intelligent computing. The findings of this review is then used to inform a new model of cooperative action orchestration for human-centered intelligent computing, which is developed in the subsequent section. The model collates issues regarding how human and computing system both may drive cooperation, and mutually revise their behavior as part of a cooperative process. Finally, we present our main contribution of this paper, which is to apply the cooperative action orchestration model to personal informatics in order to identify key design considerations for incorporating intelligent computing into this area. As the design considerations are general to personal informatics, we also illustrate their use in eliciting new design directions for the specific example system *Ski Tracks* (shown in Figure 1).

IUI 2015, March 29–April 1, 2015, Atlanta, GA, USA.

ACM 978-1-4503-3306-1/15/03 ...$15.00.
http://dx.doi.org/10.1145/2678025.2701378

Figure 1. Ski Tracks is an example of a traditional personal informatics system. It provides convenient data collection via GPS, and simply presents the resulting data for post hoc analysis.

PERSONAL INFORMATICS

A substantial part of the current personal informatics research is focused on examining the real-world practices of users, and framing the resulting insights in terms of possibilities for system design. As a prominent example, Li et al. [25] describe five stages of personal informatics processes. Before collecting any data, users are in what Li et al. describe as the preparation stage, which deals with motivations for data collection, and defining what and how to collect data. The subsequent collection stage is when data is recorded during everyday use, and is followed by the integration stage where data is prepared for analysis. When data is deemed to be in a suitable form for analysis, users may then transition to the reflection stage. This reflection stage is were analyzed data is considered both in terms of reliability and to decide upon potential action-taking. This action stage is the final stage where users make informed choices of what to do given the insight obtained through the personal informatics process. The stages Li et al. describe are intended as iterative stages, and each stage has many potential barriers to users. These barriers cascade through the sequence of stages, meaning that problems in an earlier stage is likely to negatively impact the latter ones. Users may address barriers as part of their ongoing practices, or – if they fail to overcome them – simply give up. Identifying and overcoming barriers subsequently becomes one of the most important aspects of successful personal informatics practices.

Notably to the context of this paper, the stage-based model [25] of personal informatics includes the notion that each stage can be user-driven, system-driven, or driven in a hybrid fashion. This means that system autonomy and proactive behavior already are implied as key aspects of personal informatics systems. However, the stage-based model shares a limitation with other research, as we shall see in a moment, as it does not elaborate on the system autonomy implications. We do know that including system autonomy in personal informatics is not simple, as shown by Choe et al. [8]. From their analysis of 52 expert presentations from quantified self meetup groups, they find a tension between the convenience of automation and user engagement. They find this even for automated data collection, and "envision striking a balance between fully automated sensing and manual self-report that can increase awareness, achieve better accuracy, and decrease mental workload" [8].

Parts of personal informatics is criticized by Rooksby et al. [35] for being overly technology-centric, and for assuming rational and systematic behavior that does not match the messy and intertwined activities and contexts of everyday life. As they put it, "do not expect people to act as rational data scientists" [35]. This is in line with Choe et al. [8], who argue that users need system support designing their self-tracking experiments. Consequently, Rooksby et al. [35] recommend evaluating personal informatics systems not only by the resulting behavior change, but also from a broader experiential perspective. Calvo and Peters [7] also point to complexities in how people use personal informatics data, by using frameworks and evidence from psychology. Specifically, they show that goals may become obstacles to behavior change – contrary to the intention of them – and that we continually reinterpret data, leading to reduced predictability in how we behave.

An important discussion related to personal informatics is about the extent to which system design should be normative. The question posed is essentially: Should the system provide an objective starting point for personal reflection, or should it promote behavior found to be positive by its designers? The latter approach corresponds to what is argued for and described as persuasive technology. Such technology overlaps with what is used in personal informatics and is particularly common in health-related applications (cf. [17]). The former approach is more consistent with research examining self-reflection in personal informatics or interactive systems in general [34, 2, 22]. In their review, Baumer et al. [2] find such self-reflection to be positive for increased self-knowledge, which is the traditional goal of personal informatics [25].

Difficulties in performing sound data analyses is a barrier in many personal informatics systems. While different appropriate data visualizations techniques play a key role (cf. [14]), Bentley et al. [4] note that the general population has low chart literacy. This poses a considerable problem to personal informatics as such techniques dominate data visualization presently. Furthermore, and as individuals may be uncomfortable analyzing their own data [27], Bentley et al. [4] instead propose a system that provides textual descriptions of correlations found in the data. More conventional graphs are thus combined with statements such as 'on weeks when you are happier you walk more (quite likely)'. They argue that this is a promising direction in cases where the personal informatics system acts as a cooperative agent.

Summarizing the review of personal informatics research, we find several challenges and opportunities related future directions informed by intelligent computing.

- Various forms of computing system support is key in personal informatics. There are opportunities for autonomous and proactive system behavior, both for collection and analysis of data. The full range of appropriate forms of system behavior is not known.
- Personal informatics relies on active user engagement and ongoing reflection. System design needs to strike a balance workload-reducing automation and promoting user engagement. Autonomous system functionality specifically to promote engagement and reflection is underexplored.
- System design needs to be mindful of the types of behavior change it promotes – and consider how this can to evolve in cooperation with the user.
- The need for flexibility is apparent from several perspectives – individualization between users, and over time.

HUMAN-CENTERED INTELLIGENT COMPUTING

Intelligent computing is being integrated in everyday life through appliances, entertainment systems, wearable and mobile devices, and similar everyday use technology. As a consequence, there is a shift in focus from 'performing tasks efficiently and safely' to 'enhancing the lived experiences of individuals'. This experiential shift can be seen in much contemporary research, including ambient intelligence [10, 18]; cyber-physical systems [9, 37]; human-automation interaction [20]; and intelligent user interfaces. What can be learnt, so far, from this growing body of research? To answer this, we performed a review of related literature that identifies key design issues for intelligent computing and its integration in everyday life. In later sections we will use these show their usefulness in informing intelligent personal informatics systems.

In the survey of related research, three basic relationships between human and computing were found. In the first relationship, *cooperation*, intelligent computing is viewed as an agent of its own and with which humans interact (cf. [29, 16, 5]). In the second relationship, *augmentation*, human experience is partly shaped through the computing system (cf. [43, 13, 12]). The third form of relationship centers on system autonomy, where intelligent computing exists *ambient* to humans by being embedded in the environment and acting in the background of human actions (cf. [10, 18, 9]). The human-computing relationship is one major factor in the design of intelligent computing, and the following review of the literature consequently includes all three relationship types. The relationship types are perspectives on design in and of themselves, and their related research serves to highlight partly different concrete issues.

Cooperative relationship

Humans and computing systems have fundamental, and complementary, asymmetries [21, 6]. In essence, the argument this relies upon is that many tasks are best achieved by human and computer working collaborating based on the inherent strengths of each agent. Determining how such a collaboration can be designed is part of an ongoing discourse of autonomous computing, with early research dating back to the 50s and 60s [20].

One common concept is describing and analyzing the *level of automation*, commonly classified according to a ten level scale such the one given by Miller et al. [29]. This allows discussion and analysis of the degree of manual supervision required for a given system, ranging from "1. Human does it all", via "5. Computer executes alternative if human approves", to "10. Computer acts entirely autonomously" [29]. Automation classification schemes are often (e.g. [15]) informed by the early work of Sheridan and Verplank [36]. This early work did not intend for a specific level of automation to be assigned to systems as a whole. Instead, their original ten level scale was rather intended to be applied for a delimited step in the cooperative process.

From the discourse on scale as an elemental step follows the second key concept – the *concern of automation*. Parasuraman et al. [32] identified four concerns (acting as stages) of automation, from 'information acquisition', and 'information analysis', to 'decision and action selection', and 'action implementation'. These represent a step towards acknowledging how humans and automation can cooperate in more nuanced ways, and are often cited to show how the level of autonomy can vary within one system.

A third key concepts is *adaptive autonomy* [19], which dictates that the appropriate level of autonomy should be decided based on the specific situation. This can reduce the need for human involvement, e.g. by only requiring supervision on tasks that are determined highly critical, or increase the level of automation when human performance is degrading. Miller et al. [29] show how adaptive autonomy is related to trade-offs with regards to the human operator, namely to unpredictability and mental workload. The workload "can be reduced by allocating some functions to automation, but only at the expense of increased unpredictability" [29]. A corollary is that increased human management, described as adaptable autonomy, may sometimes be preferable. For instance, Ball and Callaghan [1] show adaptable autonomy to be necessary based on large variations of user preferences.

At this point, a final set of concepts relevant to a cooperative relationship between human and computer is starting to emerge from the discourse on autonomous computing. Similar to adaptive and adaptable autonomy is the notion of *mixed-initiative systems*, which focuses on effective and natural man-machine cooperation [16, 5]. In mixed-initiative systems, we can consider actions as possible, available or obligated – either independently by each actor or through joint effort [5]. Ferguson and Allen [16] describe how mixed-initiative systems rely on the human and the computing system agreeing on allocation of responsibility, and jointly committing to achieving tasks. The system can then exhibit proactive behavior in service of goals committed to, including communicating with the user to gather new knowledge deemed

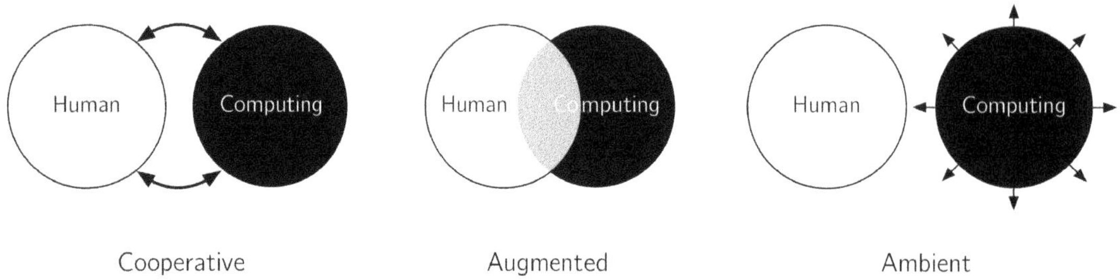

Figure 2. Three relationships between human and intelligent computing.

required. Shared awareness of the process, and alignment of the parties' intentions are identified as key issues. This is not unlike the shared task model [30] (extended further in [29]) which focuses on achieving a shared vocabulary of goals and plans - or 'task hierarchies' as the authors refer to these. More recently, Pacaux-Lemoin and Vanderhaegen [31] present a general model of human-machine cooperation, which features a core focus on mutual awareness between human and computing agent.

Augmented relationship

Augmentation is a second type of relationship between humans and intelligent computing. From this perspective, intelligent computing is not a separate agent, but something integrating with and enhancing human capabilities. The augmentation literature often uses Engelbart's [13] early work on 'augmenting human intellect' as a starting point, and his notion of 'coupled processes' still serves to highlight the quest for tight integration of human and artifact.

In light of the emergence of wearable computing, with intelligent computing facilitating personalized functionality, Xia and Maes [43] show that a personal enhancement view of augmentation is appropriate. They point to key questions that emerge from such a view, notably "How would I like to change myself?" and "What program can I employ to change myself?" – making clear connections to personal informatics. In their elaboration if augmentation research in that direction, Xia and Maes show how three cognitive domains are especially relevant: memory, motivation, and decision making. Each of these domains contains processes suitable for augmentation:

- Memory: event recording (information should not be lost or distorted); handle attachment (relevant handles should be attached to facilitate retrieval of stored information); handle usage (handles relevant to the current situation should be identified); and event playback (store information should be read correctly).
- Motivation: self-evaluation of performance (relate personal performance to goals); reminder of goal (remember and stick to goals); task identification (convert long-term goals into actionable tasks); and task evaluation (determine whether a task is worthwhile).
- Decision making: knowledge acquisition (consider knowledge relevant to the decision); value system formation; decision recognition (determine decision appropriate to context); decision framing (relate decision to time and choices available); and value system reconciliation.

Augmentation is also one emerging direction within personal informatics. Swan [40] uses the notion of 'the extended exoself' to refer human senses heightened by the real-time integration of personal informatics. This could mean more than simply showing current sensor values – the current status can also be related to goals, projections, and previous experiences. Swan joins Xia and Maes [43] in pointing to the importance of interaction technologies that support augmentation, discussing smart glasses and haptics as notable current examples.

Personal informatics augmentation can in this light be seen as a specialized version of situation awareness [39] – a version that is focused on the *self*. Traditional situation awareness is focused on enhancing comprehension of the current situation, with strong ties to fields like aerospace, military, and safety-critical systems (cf. [12, 28]), and does not highlight the self as focal point in the same manner as personal informatics. Situation awareness is commonly characterized according to three levels, each of which can be enhanced through computing system support: perception, comprehension, and projection [12]. Perception is the sensing and gathering of potentially important information, comprehension is the subsequent interpretation and understanding of this information, and projection is the forecasting of future events.

Ambient relationship

In the third relationship, intelligent computing exists in the background, ambiently acting autonomously as a mindful monitoring agent of human activity. Often, this is framed as placing the intelligence in the environment, as is done within ambient intelligence systems–defined by Cook et al. [10] as "a digital environment that proactively, but sensibly, supports people in their daily lives". Several types of environments make up the focus of ambient intelligence, including the home, workplace, healthcare, and transportation [10]. In all cases, this includes sensing, reasoning and acting based on the behavior of people present.

Enabling automatic sensing is a strength in personal informatics, but there is much to learn from the approaches to computational reasoning found within ambient intelligence. Key issues in this regard include the design of domain and activity models, as well as activity recognition and predictions [10].

Related to this is the importance of system designers understanding the situation of use [18].

Intelligent computing coexists with people not only as embedded in the physical environment, but also as part of the *digital environment*. The ongoing realization of ubiquitous computing and the Internet of Things results in a convergence of the digital and physical [9, 11]. This means that the digital part of everyday life increases as the worlds become less separated and subsequently not easily opted out of or ignored. Intelligent computing can be used to guard the interest of individuals through processes, preferences, and filtering mechanisms running in the background. A key issue is enabling people to understand and control such processes, and creating a scrutable system can be an explicit design goal. Making system models scrutable can serve to increase engagement and trust, as well as to facilitate user-driven identification of inappropriate system behavior [24].

A key issue for most forms of ambient intelligent computing is striking a balance between the system actively interacting with the user ('intervening') and autonomous action [10, 18]. This also relates to the broader discussion within ambient intelligence and ubiquitous computing of 'calm' or 'invisible' services. For instance, Jonsson [23] shows that users may strive to make such services more visible, in spite of designer intentions of keeping the computing in the background. Bellotti and Edwards [3] further establish intelligibility as a key design considerations for all forms of context-aware systems – meaning to design for the ability of computing systems to "represent to their users what they know, how they know it, and what they are doing about it".

COOPERATIVE ACTION ORCHESTRATION

The relationships presented earlier are all concerned with people working (or living) together with intelligent computing. The behaviors of the human actor and the computing system are, to varying extents and forms, dependent on each other in the three relationships. The computing system may make certain actions more likely, for instance by interjecting with a now-relevant piece information or recommendation. This in turn may cause the human to interact with the computing system to instruct or otherwise affect future system behavior, and so forth. This ongoing process can be characterized as a form of *cooperative action orchestration*.

In this section, we introduce a model of action orchestration which draws upon the human-computing relationships described earlier. We use the term *orchestration* as it emphasizes a mindful stance (from user as well as system) towards future progression of the cooperative process, rather than for instance a master-slave stance where one agent (human or system) would blindly follow the other's instructions. The model seeks to inform design of intelligent computing which enables such a stance from both individual and computing system. At the core of the model, there are four basic types of action (Table 1). These types are identified based on the work by Parasuraman et al. [33] and Bradshaw et al. [5], and separates the initiating party of an action from the executing party to identify the action types this results in.

		Initiating party	
		H	C
Acting party	H	$I_H A_H$ Human autonomy	$I_C A_H$ Computing-directed human action
	C	$I_H A_C$ Human-directed computing system action	$I_C A_C$ Computing system autonomy

Table 1. Four basic types of cooperative actions (H = Human, C = Computing system).

As a result of separating initiating from executing party, autonomous action may be performed by both the human ($I_H A_H$) and the computing system ($I_C A_C$). Such autonomous actions are by nature self-initiated and self-regulated, but they also occur in an environment of other agents. In the human case, action is situated, meaning that conscious and unconscious thought is given to the current context as the action is taken. Computing system autonomy similarly relies on system perception, as dictated by sensors and computing models for the state of the world as viewed by the system.

The computing system can also be instructed, or otherwise explicitly be engaged with, in order for the human to initiate an action ($I_H A_C$). Doing so not only depends on what the computing system's capabilities are, but also the interfaces through which the capabilities are exposed. The human user must have a way to express intent or instructions in mutually understandable form. The computing system can also ask the human to take action ($I_C A_H$), or more subtly provide information which indirectly affects human behavior. Computing-directed human action is limited and enabled by the interaction channels available to the computing agent. It also highlights issues of when it is appropriate for the computing agent to interject.

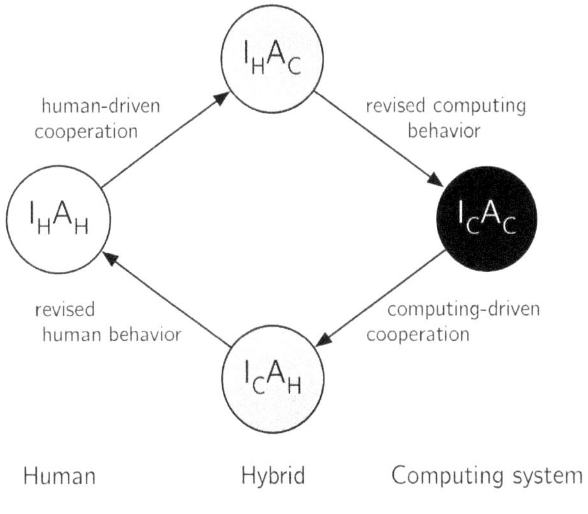

Figure 3. Transitions facilitating cooperative action orchestration.

While the types of cooperative action (Table 1) are important to note for orchestration, the possible transitions between the action types should also be considered as an ongoing process (Figure 3). By examining these transitions we can reveal aspects that constrain or enable the cooperative process to progress. For example, the human actor must be able to move from autonomous action to directing the computing system, which in turn must be able to revise its behavior. This revised behavior may then directly or indirectly affect future human interaction with the system, which illustrates why this is an ongoing process. The same example may be considered in the other direction as well, where the computing system must be able to engage with the user to affect its future behavior, and so forth.

In an intelligent computing informed personal informatics system, the four transitions are played out during the entire life-time of the human-system and not only during active use. Below, key considerations in terms of constraints and enablers are presented for each transition. These are not meant as an exhaustive lists of all possible considerations but rather to cover a core set of aspects from the literature. Prior to each set of aspects and related considerations, we provide a summary of the general issues.

Human-driven cooperation: $I_H A_H \rightarrow I_H A_C$

For transitions that show human-driven cooperation, an individual may contribute and drive the cooperative process based on the understanding this individual has of how the computing system analyses (i.e. makes sense) of human actions, as well as the individual's understanding of the orchestration process as a whole. An important issue therefore concerns how to facilitate human knowledge of the capabilities that the computing system holds, and understanding of the computing system's current state. Considerations related to this include making the system models visible and understandable [24]; explicitly highlighting current choices available [12, 43]; and the human learning based on observable behavior [31].

At a more basic level lies the issue of the conceptual design of cooperation and the subsequent framing of this that is presented to the human. One direction would be an outcome-focused presentation, meaning that goals are established and worked towards. Goals can concern either – or both – the human and the computing system (cf. [16, 29]). Cooperation can also hold a process-focused presentation, emphasizing how the human and the computing system influence each other's behaviors. Further, an assistance-focused presentation of cooperation represents a background relationship between human and computing system which is enabled by computational reasoning techniques [10]. Regardless which presentation form is used, it is not the specific design and inherent quality of this design of computational intelligence that is in focus but rather the *effects* of such choices upon the user.

For the human to actively engage with the computing system, there must be enabling interaction technologies, e.g. a smartphone application or physical controls (cf. [40, 10]). The user interfaces provided through these technologies further enable and constrain what is possible for the human to express.

Aspect	General issues	Considerations
Human understanding and motivation	Knowledge of computing system capabilities Knowledge of computing system state Trust in computing system Understanding current options for interacting with the computing system	Scrutable models [24] Intelligibility [3] 'Know-how', 'Know-how-to-cooperate' [31] Situation awareness: perception and comprehension [12] Decision framing augmentation [43]
Outcome-focused cooperation	Goals of H documented to C Goals of C programmed by H Shared goals	Mixed initiative: allocation of responsibility [16] Adaptive autonomy [29] Task identification augmentation [43]
Process-focused cooperation	Behavior of C programmed by H Behavior of H regulated by C	Concern of automation [32] User-adaptable autonomy [29] Task recognition [10]
Assistance-focused cooperation	Proactive stance from computing system	Concern of automation [32] User-adaptable autonomy [29] Task recognition [10]

Table 2. Key issues and related considerations for enabling human-driven cooperation.

Revised computing system behavior: $I_H A_C \rightarrow I_C A_C$

While the previous transition deals with enabling human-driven input into the cooperative process, the transition that follows such input is concerned with how the computing system revises its behavior as a result. This means that the transition covers the issues of mapping interpretations of human intentions – as communicated via what the interaction interface permits – to the internal functions and models of the computing system.

System designers must here tackle the possible scope of revised behavior (as in: what is the action space?), and what the sources of revised behavior are. This means considering possible and appropriate levels of automation, how and in which situations the level of autonomy changes, and the levels of explicit user control (cf. [19, 29, 5]).

Enabling more intelligent autonomous action requires understanding of both application domain and user behavior (cf. [10, 37]). Related considerations concern the design of models used by the system, which may have a very limited scope and dealing with only a limited set of highly specific concepts. This can come at the expense of being too constraining for the user, and models could therefore instead opt to include rich descriptions of the domain and individual user, at the possible risk of becoming overly complex and thus hard to understand and use. Related design considerations also concern the intended levels of flexibility between different users and over time (cf. [24, 29]).

Aspect	General issues	Considerations
Source of revised behavior	Explicit instruction Independent learning Mapping of user interface vocabulary to computational models	Levels of automation [19, 29] Adaptive and adaptable autonomy [29]
Scope of revised behavior	What can the computing system achieve?	Independently possible, available and obligated actions [5] Predictability [29]
Enabling autonomous action	Understanding of domain and user behavior Understanding of role in cooperation	Domain and activity models [10, 37]
Flexibility	Variations between users Variations over time	Scrutability [24] User-adaptable autonomy [29]

Table 3. Key issues and related considerations for enabling revised computing system behavior.

Computing-driven cooperation: $I_C A_C \rightarrow I_C A_H$

This transition covers considerations related to how the computing system move from existing ambiently in the background to actively engaging with the human. For such interjections to be possible, there needs to be supporting interaction technologies such as the push notifications on smartphones or haptic feedback from a wearable bracelet (cf. [10]). Different forms of interaction are associated with different user expectations that need to be taken into account. Experience and understanding of the particular computing system further affect such expectations [31].

Aspect	General issues	Considerations
Human openness to interaction	Knowledge and expectations on how the computing system behaves Possibilities to interact	'Know-how-to-cooperate' [31] Variation of interaction technologies [10]
Promoting human engagement	Knowledge about actions available Ease of affecting computing system behavior Actionable interjections Frequency of interjections	Decision making augmentation [43] Intelligibility [3] Adaptive autonomy [29]
Cost of interjection	Immediate cost: is interjection contextually appropriate Long term cost: is the ongoing amount and type of interjections appropriate	Automation: unpredictability and mental workload [32, 5] Type of interaction technology [10] User-adaptable autonomy [29]

Table 4. Key issues and related considerations for enabling computing-driven cooperation.

An underexplored but important aspect of this transition concerns the design of computing system interjections for promoting future human engagement (cf. [43, 29]). This includes facilitating more immediate engagement through actionable interjections, and promoting long-term engagement through techniques such as adaptive autonomy [29].

Too frequent or irrelevant interjections may incur an higher than acceptable cost to the user experience. The cost of interjections on human engagement may either be immediate, such as when they come at an inappropriate time (and thus go ignored or cause frustration). The cost/value ratio of interjections is also experienced over longer periods of time, meaning that a slight value of each interjection may not be enough to justify the process as a whole. Overall, there is a need for human-centered interjection protocols as the user should experience interactions as valuable, either through some instrumental value, or through understanding of the interjections' larger role in promoting end-user value (cf. [32, 5, 10, 29]).

Revised human behavior: $I_C A_H \rightarrow I_H A_H$

The final transition in the cooperative action orchestration process concerns how human practice changes as a result of the interactions with the computing system. The intent of computing system interactions needs to be understandable during use–e.g. is it a call to action to perform an immediate task, or is it simply a piece of information to consider, or is it only used to show that the computing system is active (cf. [12, 31])?

Revised behavior can also stem from a increased insight into how current behavior relates to possible outcomes. It can, however, be challenging to ongoingly understand one's behavior in terms of beneficial goals, which points to several considerations related to augmentation technology (cf. [12, 3, 43]).

Aspect	General issues	Considerations
Cooperative stance	Understanding of and engagement in cooperation Shared goals	Mixed initiative: agree on responsibilities [16] Shared task modelling [30, 29] Independently possible, available and obligated actions [5]
Immediate action	Communication of computing system intent Actionable interjections	Situation awareness: direction of attention [12] 'Know-how-to-cooperate' [31]
Informed change	Understand relationship between behavior and set goals Frame behavior in terms of possible goals	Situation awareness: perception and comprehension [12] Feedforward [3] Motivation augmentation [43]

Table 5. Key issues and related considerations for enabling revised behavior.

Additionally, human actors can of course revise their behavior independently of explicit interactions from the system. Revised human behavior may or may not affect the computing system and the cooperative process, depending on the system's ability to note this behavior change and adapt accordingly, rather than continue along the progression and data analysis path that the system had predicted previously as relevant. System designers therefore have considerations related to increasing the coupling between behavior change and cooperation with the system. In essence this implies striving to enable human behavior change that promotes further system cooperation (cf. [16, 30, 29, 5]).

INTELLIGENT COMPUTING IN PERSONAL INFORMATICS

Having identified key considerations for intelligent computing it is time to position these towards personal informatics. To do this, we again use the basis of the cooperative action orchestration model and the aspects of human-centered intelligent computing it highlights. The broad goal of this step is to move personal informatics beyond convenient data collection and visualization, to include proactive and cooperative behavior from the computing system. While our introduction of the cooperative action orchestration model earlier is an important step of this paper, it is how we use the model (to identify key considerations from intelligent computing) and its application to personal informatics (i.e. this section) that is the core contribution of this paper.

The resulting design considerations are described with a practical design orientation, as our intention is for them to be useful guides for actual design and development of future intelligent computing informed personal informatics systems, and not strictly as academic reflection guidelines. As the area of personal informatics is quite heterogenous – spanning from casual logging of everyday activities, via professional sports tracking, to health-critical applications – it may be inappropriate to strive for too overarching and generally applicable guidelines. As a consequence, we have kept to design considerations that need elaboration in the specific case. In their elaboration, these considerations will serve to highlight questions not commonly reflected in personal informatics.

From our review of personal informatics research, we know that people may benefit from system support in all stages of their personal informatics practices (cf. [25]). Research on e.g. automation design [5] and mixed-initiative systems [16] indicates that intelligent and proactive system behavior should not be approached as 'adding a feature' but rather a core conceptual design which should define *what the system is*. This points to possibilities for a broader reframing of what constitutes a personal informatics system, and we return to discuss this direction as a concluding element of this section. Such a reframing can also be seen as a theme behind the presentation of design considerations which follows. We will start, however, by identifying what the four transition stages of the cooperative action orchestration process mean in terms of personal informatics systems.

The key design considerations we present below for each transition are based on a synthesis of the existing research presented earlier in this paper. While the considerations are clearly situated within the context of personal informatics, Tables 2-5 contain the corresponding issues and references from intelligent computing.

The first transition from the cooperative action orchestration model concerns how to enable human-driven cooperation. In terms of personal informatics, this means enabling users to think not only of themselves and their behavior, but to couple these things with potential system support. Based on the intelligent computing issues reported for this transition (Table 2), the following considerations may be viewed key for personal informatics systems:

1. *Explore framings of personal informatics as cooperation between human and computing system.* Goals in personal informatics are traditionally framed as a concern for the human, and the computing system's role is to 'keep track' of them. In the alternative framings of cooperation, presented as part of this first transition, goals are an equal concern of both parties, and serve to establish agreements on who should do what.

2. *Consider conceptual designs which shift the focus of behavior change to a joint human-system effort.* Insight gained from data analysis would then equally be used to update future behavior of the personal informatics system. This may require user interfaces for data analysis to better highlight possible contributions from the system.

3. *Consider the effect of increased focus on cooperation in terms of human engagement and motivation.* Expose what the autonomous capabilities of the personal informatics system are, as well as its earlier contributions.

4. *Evaluate when and how the computing system should to be available to the human, and focus on interaction technologies accordingly.* What will the relationship between human and personal informatics system be (cooperation, augmentation, coexistence) and how will this vary over the course of use?

The second transition from the cooperative action orchestration model concerns enabling revised behavior from the computing system. For personal informatics systems, this can mean an increased focus on richer models of both application domain and user activity as these enable independent reasoning. Key design considerations thus include (see Table 3 for the underlying issues from intelligent computing):

5. *Focus not only on models of the domain (e.g. specific type of exercise or biometric factor), but also on models of how people use the personal informatics system itself.* This would enable reasoning about the cooperative process and more sophisticated system behavior like adaptive autonomy.

6. *Include explorations autonomous behavior in the design process of personal informatics systems.* Further consider collecting ongoing use data or feedback to identify pain points, e.g. in terms of too much manual work.

In the third transition of cooperative action orchestration, focus is on enabling the computing system to initiate interactions. As with the human-driven perspective, this requires supporting interaction technologies which make the human available. Unless the personal informatics system has its own hardware component, it must rely on the equipment commonly used – which will likely mean the smartphone remains a primary enabler for the foreseeable future. Regardless of the enabling interaction technologies, several design considerations relate to the design of the system interjections themselves, as they make up a primary channel through which the system can keep the user in the loop. Key design considerations for computing-driven cooperation in personal informatics systems (based on the core issues in Table 4) are:

7. *Explore forms of real-time system-provided feedback to decrease the need for sophisticated post hoc data analysis by the user.* This implies a shift of personal informatics system from context-recording to context-aware.

8. *Explore ways of grounding real-time feedback in past performance, projections, and/or goals.* Simply showing current sensor data readings does not sufficiently promote increased insight into potential behavior change – designs should strive for heightened understanding of the current situation.

9. *Explore ways including users in processes of automatic data collection.* Insight into the autonomous behavior of the system may promote user engagement, although the frequency and type of interjections will likely have to vary (related to next point).

10. *Consider ways of letting users give feedback on interjections from the personal informatics system.* System interjections provide a natural opportunity to allow the user to tweak system behavior, potentially making for low cost user-adaptable autonomy.

The final transition of cooperative action orchestration, revised human behavior, establishes a new perspective on behavior change in personal informatics by making it inclusive of user-system cooperation. We have already discussed the possibility of adopting conceptual designs in this direction, which would promote the aspect of cooperative stance found in this transition as well. Considerations specific to this transition are as follows (see Table 5 for the underlying issues from intelligent computing):

11. *Include possibilities for immediate action with interjections from the personal informatics system.* This can facilitate the user opportunistically engaging in the cooperative process.

12. *Explore more sophisticated relationships between personal informatics data and goals.* One direction is towards answering the user question: based on my current status, what goals can be appropriate to work towards? (Or, as has been discussed, which goals should *we*, the user and the personal informatics system, adopt together?)

Taking a step back from the four transition stages, we can now return to the matter of incorporating intelligent computing as more than adding a feature. Overall, our analysis points to a reframing of what constitutes a personal informatics system. New systems powered by intelligent computing are not simply advanced versions pen and paper, but represent active participants in the ongoing personal informatics practice. In this reframing, hybrid actions between user and computing system – which make up the core of the cooperative action orchestration model – subsume the earlier human-only, or tool-only, focus. As a result, the established notions of 'activity tracking' and 'self-quantification' may be inadequate for future personal informatics systems informed by intelligent computing.

Example: Applying the Considerations in Practice

The presented design considerations are intended to be applied in the context of a specific personal informatics system. To illustrate such a process and potential outcome, we will use the Ski Tracks smartphone application shown in the introduction of this paper (Figure 1). The application may be described as continuously tracking the user's movements via GPS, once the user has activated it. When the skiing session is over, the user stops the tracking and may then access key statistics and simple visualizations that are relevant to downhill skiing. The application thus enables convenient logging and analysis that would be cumbersome or impossible to do manually. The application is made with particular care to the needs of skiers and snowboarders, and can be considered a strong implementation and functional application when compared to other similar applications. Thus, what would it mean to include lessons from intelligent computing in the particular case of Ski Tracks? To answer this, we will elaborate on each of the presented design considerations (C1-C12).

C1 and C2 both suggest that we consider what the application is, in terms of how it is experienced by the user. As is the case for many personal informatics systems, Ski Tracks is conceptually designed as tool for data tracking, and in light of this, personal informatics becomes human-driven. C1 asks us instead to explore how Ski Tracks can be framed as a cooperative agent with more active participation. One primary direction to consider, as included in C1, is designing goals such that they are of concern for both human and computing system. Goals could be included in Ski Tracks as part the current logging and analysis. For instance, the user might configure a goal of 10000 meters descent per day, with an evaluation of this goal being added to the analysis screen ("Achieved 81 % of 10 k descent goal"). This would not, however, promote increased participation of the computing system, as C1 asks. Instead, we can expand on the goal example to include the application helping in goal achievement. This may entail configuring Ski Tracks to notify of progress ("Skiing for 3.5 hours and currently at 51 % of descent goal with 3 hours before the lifts close") or advise on behavior ("Do 3 more runs to achieve descent goal" or "Stop current break soon to if you want to achieve descent goal at your average pace for today").

Further, C2 then asks for ways to include contributions from the computing system as a perspective during data analysis, complementing data describing only the user. This implies a future design that complements visualization of ski data by also showing when system notifications occurred. Such a change would allow the user to evaluate if revised system behavior is appropriate, and may also lead the user to notice where the system could have helped but did not.

Ski Tracks taking a more active role may have both positive and negative effects on user engagement and motivation, which C3 asks us to consider. Specifically, C3 suggest managing user expectation by clearly exposing what system-initiated behavior is possible. To address this, the application could for instance include a textual description when creating the type of goal illustrated above ("Ski Tracks will let you know if you have to increase the pace to reach the day's goal").

Skiing is an activity which inherently exemplifies an activity that may prohibit typical phone usage, which means that system-driven interactions are particularly important that they come at a contextually appropriate time, such as when stopping to get on a lift rather than during the actual descent. C4 asks us to examine what those situations may be, and what supporting interaction technologies to use as a consequence. In this situation, the phone notification model may be considered inadequate for ongoing interaction, which instead suggest that future designs explore more substantial changes such as integration with smart watches or goggles with heads-up display, thereby facilitating an augmentation relationship (cf. Figure 2).

The Ski Tracks application includes models of the activity of skiing allowing it to e.g. determine when the user is riding a lift. C5 asks us to go beyond this and also explore models of how the application itself is used. For instance, this can include adapting what data is highlighted based on previous user behavior during data analysis. C6 further focuses on identifying user pain points that can be alleviated through autonomous system behavior. In its current design, users must activate Ski Tracks manually, or re-activate after pausing, and this seemingly simple step may result in significant data loss if not performed. A simple form of proactive system behavior could target this specific pain point, e.g. by considering time of day or specific user instructions.

C7 and C8 both concern real-time feedback, as opposed to Ski Tracks' current focus on post hoc analysis. In exploring contextually-relevant feedback in real-time, starting with determining contexts which the application already has data to identify – such as "having stopped after the fastest run of the season", or "going on the same slope for the third time in a row" – would pragmatically be useful. However, providing contextual feedback is further enabled by the available interaction technologies (as discussed with C4) and may thus not be feasible only through the smartphone. Similarly, when considering C9, which asks for increased user engagement in automatic data collection, we may find it unnecessary for this particular application. This is because Ski Tracks, in contrast with general always-on fitness trackers, has a very clear connection to a particular type of activity. In other words, users are likely to be highly engaged in the activity of skiing, with which the application is closely tied. If system-initiated interactions are added to Ski Tracks, C10 suggests including the option of immediate user feedback – e.g. "do not show notifications like this" or "keep me posted on this goal".

The two final concerns relate to revised human behavior. C11 emphasizes that notifications from the application should not only be understandable, but also actionable when appropriate. In listing what types of actions that may be appropriate for Ski Tracks to suggest, we can note that some actions are human-only (e.g. skiing a particular slope), while others are cooperation with the system (e.g. "compare future runs to this previous one"). Finally, in considering C12, choosing and setting goals in Ski Tracks should not be the sole responsibility of the user. Given some initial use, the application may suggest goals that are likely to be attractive (based on the domain of skiing), and fitting (based on user data).

As presented here, the design considerations for personal informatics systems have been applied to the Ski Tracks application, in order to illustrate how the consideration may be used to elicit future design directions that build upon state-of-the-art opportunities that are recognized within intelligent computing. This implies that the presented design directions do not represent a complete list, as they are based on the domain for inquiry identified as relevant to this paper. Additional domains for inquiry would add further design considerations, and represents an obvious way to expand upon this paper.

CONCLUSIONS

This paper set out to explore how intelligent computing could be included as a core part in personal informatics and thereby act as a catalyst for new forms of system support that may provide a richer understanding of the tracked activities than present systems allow. To form a basis for this exploration, we have surveyed current research on personal informatics to more concretely reveal the related challenges and opportunities. We have also presented established techniques and approaches from several areas of intelligent computing, resulting in the new cooperative action orchestration model.

The model of cooperative action orchestration is combined with the insights from personal informatics to form the domain-specific key design considerations. These can be used to elicit new design directions for individual personal informatics systems, as illustrated with the Ski Tracks example. Neither the list of design considerations, nor the core action orchestration model, can ever be said to be fully exhaustive. This does not diminish the value of what has been presented, however, and we see a promising research direction in iteratively revising both model and considerations as part of future design and development. In light of these results, we also see the need for a consistent vocabulary facilitating clear comparison between different personal informatics systems. Another intriguing possibility is using the action orchestration model to form consideration for domains other than personal informatics, thus contributing broader insight into how humans and computing systems can complement each other in practice.

REFERENCES

1. Ball, M., and Callaghan, V. Explorations of Autonomy: An Investigation of Adjustable Autonomy in Intelligent Environments. In *Proc. IE 2012*.

2. Baumer, E. P. S., Khovanskaya, V., Matthews, M., Reynolds, L., Sosik, V. S., and Gay, G. Reviewing reflection: on the use of reflection in interactive system design. In *Proc. DIS 2014*.

3. Bellotti, V., and Edwards, K. Intelligibility and Accountability: Human Considerations in

Context-Aware Systems. *Human-Computer Interaction 16*, 2 (2001), 193–212.

4. Bentley, F., Tollmar, K., Stephenson, P., Levy, L., Jones, B., Robertson, S., Price, E., Catrambone, R., and Wilson, J. Health Mashups: Presenting Statistical Patterns between Wellbeing Data and Context in Natural Language to Promote Behavior Change. *Transactions on Computer-Human Interaction (TOCHI) 20*, 5 (2013).

5. Bradshaw, J. M., Feltovich, P. J., Jung, H., Kulkarni, S., Taysom, W., and Uszok, A. Dimensions of Adjustable Autonomy and Mixed-Initiative Interaction. In *Agents and Computational Autonomy*, M. Nickles, M. Rovatsos, and G. Weiss, Eds. Springer Berlin Heidelberg, 2004, 17–39.

6. Bradshaw, J. M., Sierhuis, M., Acquisti, A., Feltovich, P., Hoffman, R., Jeffers, R., Presott, D., Suri, N., Uszok, A., and van Hoof, R. Adjustable Autonomy and Human-Agent Teamwork in Practice: An Interim Report on Space Applications. In *Agent Autonomy*. Springer US, 2003, 243–280.

7. Calvo, R. A., and Peters, D. The irony and re-interpretation of our quantified self. In *Proc. OzCHI 2013*.

8. Choe, E. K., Lee, N. B., Lee, B., Pratt, W., and Kientz, J. A. Understanding quantified-selfers' practices in collecting and exploring personal data. In *Proc. CHI 2014*.

9. Conti, M., Das, S. K., Bisdikian, C., Kumar, M., Ni, L. M., Passarella, A., Roussos, G., Tröster, G., Tsudik, G., and Zambonelli, F. Looking ahead in pervasive computing: Challenges and opportunities in the era of cyber-physical convergence. *Pervasive and Mobile Computing 8*, 1 (2012), 2–21.

10. Cook, D. J., Augusto, J. C., and Jakkula, V. R. Ambient intelligence: Technologies, applications, and opportunities. *Pervasive and Mobile Computing 5*, 4 (2009), 277–298.

11. Crabtree, A., and Rodden, T. Hybrid ecologies: understanding cooperative interaction in emerging physical-digital environments. *Personal and Ubiquitous Computing 12*, 7 (2008).

12. Endsley, M. R. Theoretical Underpinnings of Situation Awareness: A Critical Review. In *Situation Awareness Analysis and Measurement*, M. R. Endsley and D. J. Garland, Eds. Lawrence Erlbaum Associates, 2000, 1–24.

13. Engelbart, D. C. Augmenting Human Intellect: A Conceptual Framework. Tech. Rep. AFOSR-3223, Oct. 1962.

14. Epstein, D., Cordeiro, F., Bales, E., Fogarty, J., and Munson, S. Taming data complexity in lifelogs: exploring visual cuts of personal informatics data. In *Proc. DIS 2014*.

15. Fereidunian, A., Lehtonen, M., Lesani, H., Lucas, C., and Nordman, M. Adaptive autonomy: Smart cooperative cybernetic systems for more humane automation solutions. In *Proc. SMC 2007*.

16. Ferguson, G., and Allen, J. Mixed-initiative systems for collaborative problem solving. *AI Magazine 28*, 2 (2007), 23–32.

17. Fritz, T., Huang, E. M., Murphy, G. C., and Zimmermann, T. Persuasive technology in the real world: a study of long-term use of activity sensing devices for fitness. In *Proc. CHI 2014*.

18. Gross, T. Towards a new human-centred computing methodology for cooperative ambient intelligence. *J Ambient Intell Human Comput 1*, 1 (2009), 31–42.

19. Hancock, P. A., Chignell, M. H., and Lowenthal, A. An adaptive human-machine system. In *Proc. SMC 1985*.

20. Hancock, P. A., Jagacinski, R. J., Parasuraman, R., Wickens, C. D., Wilson, G. F., and Kaber, D. B. Human-Automation Interaction Research: Past, Present, and Future. *Ergonomics in Design: The Quarterly of Human Factors Applications 21*, 2 (2013), 9–14.

21. Hoffman, R. R., Feltovich, P. J., Ford, K. M., and Woods, D. D. A rose by any other name...would probably be given an acronym. *Intelligent Systems, IEEE 17*, 4 (2002), 72–80.

22. Huldtgren, A., Wiggers, P., and Jonker, C. M. Designing for Self-Reflection on Values for Improved Life Decision. *Interacting with Computers 26*, 1 (2014)

23. Jonsson, K. Making IT Visible: The Paradox of Ubiquitous Services in Practice. In *Industrial Informatics Design, Use and Innovation Perspectives and Services*. IGI Global, 2010, 30–43.

24. Kay, J., and Kummerfeld, B. Creating personalized systems that people can scrutinize and control: Drivers, principles and experience. *Transactions on Interactive Intelligent Systems (TiiS) 2*, 4 (2012).

25. Li, I., Dey, A., and Forlizzi, J. A stage-based model of personal informatics systems. In *Proc. CHI 2010*.

26. Li, I., Dey, A. K., and Forlizzi, J. Understanding my data, myself: supporting self-reflection with ubicomp technologies. In *Proc. UbiComp 2011*.

27. Mamykina, L., Mynatt, E., Davidson, P., and Greenblatt, D. MAHI: investigation of social scaffolding for reflective thinking in diabetes management. In *Proc. CHI 2008*.

28. Matheus, C. J., Kokar, M. M., and Baclawski, K. A core ontology for situation awareness. In *Proc. Fusion 2003*.

29. Miller, C. A., and Parasuraman, R. Designing for Flexible Interaction Between Humans and Automation: Delegation Interfaces for Supervisory Control. *Human Factors: The Journal of the Human Factors and Ergonomics Society 49*, 1 (2007), 57–75.

30. Miller, C. A., Pelican, M., and Goldman, R. "Tasking" interfaces to keep the operator in control . In *Proc. Human Interaction with Complex Systems 2000*.

31. Pacaux-Lemoine, M.-P., and Vanderhaegen, F. Towards Levels of Cooperation. In *Proc. SMC 2013*.

32. Parasuraman, R. Designing automation for human use: empirical studies and quantitative models. *Ergonomics 43*, 7 (2000), 931–951.

33. Parasuraman, R., Sheridan, T. B., and Wickens, C. D. A model for types and levels of human interaction with automation. *IEEE Transactions on Systems, Man and Cybernetics, Part A: Systems and Humans, 30*, 3 (2000), 286–297.

34. Pirzadeh, A., He, L., and Stolterman, E. Personal informatics and reflection: a critical examination of the nature of reflection. *Proc. CHI EA 2013*.

35. Rooksby, J., Rost, M., Morrison, A., and Chalmers, M. C. Personal tracking as lived informatics. In *Proc. CHI 2014*.

36. Sheridan, T. B., and Verplank, W. L. Human and Computer Control of Undersea Teleoperators. Tech. rep., 1978.

37. Sheth, A., and Anantharam, P. Physical cyber social computing for human experience. In *Proc. WIMS 2013*.

38. Shilton, K. Participatory personal data: An emerging research challenge for the information sciences. *Journal of the American Society for Information Science and Technology 63*, 10 (2012), 1905–1915.

39. Smith, K., and Hancock, P. A. Situation Awareness is Adaptive, Externally-Directed Consciousness. In *Situational Awareness in Complex Systems*, R. D. Gilson, D. J. Garland, and J. M. Koonce, Eds. Aeronautical University Press, 1994, 59–68.

40. Swan, M. The Quantified Self: Fundamental Disruption in Big Data Science and Biological Discovery. *Big Data 1*, 2 (2013), 85–99.

41. Wolf, G. The Data-Driven Life *New York Times Magazine*, Apr. 2010.

42. Wright, A. Patient, heal thyself. *Commun. ACM 56*, 8 (Aug. 2013).

43. Xia, C., and Maes, P. The design of artifacts for augmenting intellect. In *Proc. AH 2013*.

Aurigo: An Interactive Tour Planner for Personalized Itineraries

Alexandre Yahi,* Antoine Chassang,* Louis Raynaud,* Hugo Duthil,* Duen Horng (Polo) Chau
Georgia Institute of Technology
{alexandre.yahi, antoine.chassang, l.raynaud, hduthil, polo}@gatech.edu

ABSTRACT

Planning personalized tour itineraries is a complex and challenging task for both humans and computers. Doing it manually is time-consuming; approaching it as an optimization problem is computationally NP hard. We present Aurigo, a tour planning system combining a recommendation algorithm with interactive visualization to create personalized itineraries. This hybrid approach enables Aurigo to take into account both quantitative and qualitative preferences of the user. We conducted a within-subject study with 10 participants, which demonstrated that Aurigo helped them find points of interest quickly. Most participants chose Aurigo over Google Maps as their preferred tools to create personalized itineraries. Aurigo may be integrated into review websites or social networks, to leverage their databases of reviews and ratings and provide better itinerary recommendations.

Author Keywords

User Interfaces; Visualization; Recommendation; Tour itinerary planning

ACM Classification Keywords

H.3.3 Information storage and retrieval: Information Search and Retrieval; H.5.2 Information interfaces and presentation (e.g. HCI): User interfaces

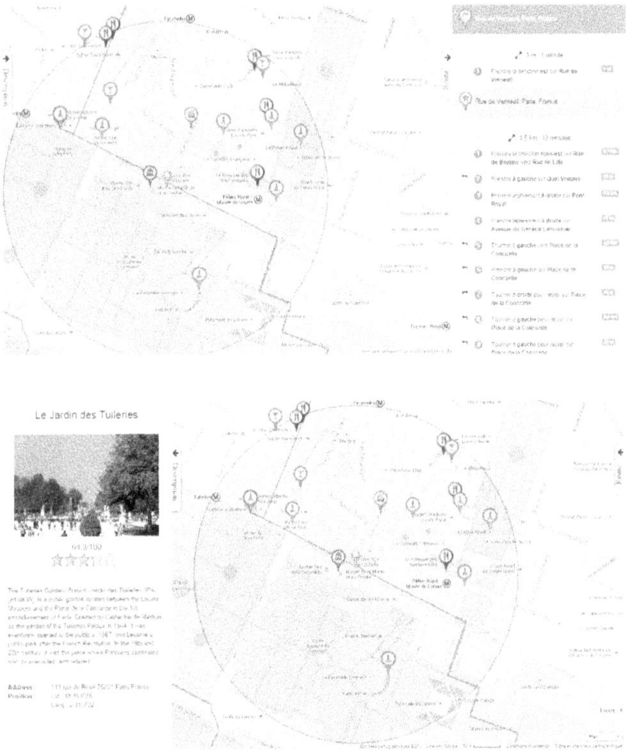

Figure 1. Screenshots of Aurigo showing the path of an itinerary generated by its recommendation algorithm. Points of Interest (POIs) are displayed within the blue area of the *Pop Radius*, a novel feature provided by Aurigo for interactively selecting POIs to fine-tune a path. The collapsible right panel (top image) shows the directions of the itinerary. The left panel (bottom image) describes a POI ("le jardin des Tuileries") with a picture, rating and text description.

INTRODUCTION

The Internet has become the leading source of information for trip planning [18], dramatically transforming how travel planning would be performed, prompting users to shift from using printed materials like travel guides and brochures, to leveraging more online resources, like travellers' comments and suggestions on online forums, review websites, and blogs.

Trip planning is a challenging problem that has been widely studied. From a mathematical point of view, trip planning can be viewed as an optimization problem under constraints (e.g., in time, costs, popularity of places), its simplest version being the famous travelling salesman problem (TSP). However, this optimization problem is NP hard [3], which led to two predominant streams of research: 1) developing algorithmic solutions that try to find the best possible itineraries, often through approximation and heuristics; and 2) learning from human behaviors. The latter appears as a reasonable solution to mitigate this parameter-intensive optimization problem.

In the tourism industry, it has been widely acknowledged that tour planning tools should be designed to allow users to develop *memorable experiences* (ME) while building their itineraries [16], which means that besides considering quantitative data and objective requirements like price, duration, or distance, a desirable itinerary building process should also take into account the user's cognitive, behavioral and affective experiences. The Internet and online social media have

*The four first authors contributed equally to this work

IUI 2015, March 29–April 1, 2015, Atlanta, GA, USA.

http://dx.doi.org/10.1145/2678025.2701366

made the sharing of such information possible and often enjoyable, where users' participation is often driven by altruism or community-related motivations [12, 17]. Nowadays, people often share their personal experiences through microblogs (e.g., Twitter), blogs (e.g., Tumblr), social network sites (e.g., Facebook, Google+), media-sharing sites (e.g., Instagram), and review sites (e.g., Yelp, TripAdvisor) [12].

Not surprisingly, some research aimed to leverage this wealth of social media data to tackle the trip planning problem, from mining geotagged photos and check-ins on social networks [8, 4, 9, 6] to crowdsourcing recommendations by using the Amazon Mechanical Turk and other related systems [20, 14], combining human contributions to collectively build better itineraries.

In this paper, we present Aurigo (Figure 1), a novel system for tour planning that aims to strike a balance between automated approaches and purely manual approaches. Aurigo combines data-driven recommendations, interactive visualization, and personalization features that are highly configurable to help the user quickly build desirable itineraries.

Aurigo's recommendation engine suggests itineraries based on the user's personal preference (e.g., prefer museums) and data such as reviews and ratings extracted from review websites. Using Aurigo, the user can fine-tune a recommended itinerary's route using an interactive user interface (UI). The user may also build his or her own itinerary incrementally and interactively through the same UI. We designed Aurigo to tackle two common types of tour planning:

- **The efficient itinerary problem**: *How to efficiently go from point A to point B, visiting points of interest (POIs) along the way, while having the option to fine-tune and select which POIs to visit?*

- **The assisted exploration problem**: *How to rapidly create my own itinerary, assisted by an interface that relevantly displays POIs and information about my trip?*

Aurigo's major contributions include:

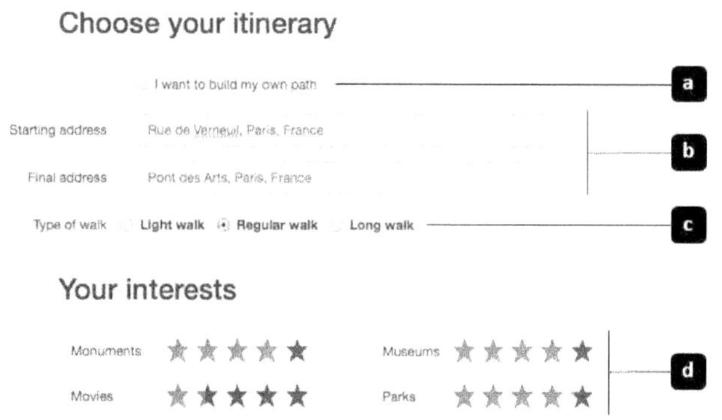

Figure 2. Aurigo's homepage with (a) the "I want to build my own path" option linking to the S2S (step-by-step) mode when checked, (b) the starting and ending address for the E2E (end-to-end) mode, (c) the style of walk indicating the qualitative length of the tour, and (d) the user's preferences towards the four types of attractions offered.

- Addressing two fundamental issues of trip planning with: an *end-to-end* mode (E2E) where Aurigo constructs a recommended itinerary based on a start and end points provided by the user; and an *step-by-step* mode (S2S) that allows the user to build a personalized itinerary interactively and incrementally, step by step.

- An original itinerary recommendation algorithm (used in E2E mode) that incorporates the user's *quantitative* preferences (e.g., desired tour length, preferred types of POIs, start and end points).

- An interactive user interface for building and fine-tuning the itinerary path based on the user's personal *qualitative* tastes and desires, with novel features such as the *Pop Radius* overlay (see Figure 1) which is a lightweight interaction technique for the user to interactively explore and select POIs within a short walking distance from a point on the map.

Currently, Aurigo uses the Yelp API to obtain data about POIs, the Google Maps API to localize them, and the Wikipedia API to obtain photos and descriptions about POIs. However, our general approach is database-agnostic and could be generalized to work with other databases POIs, reviews and ratings.

INTRODUCING AURIGO

Aurigo's main interface

Aurigo's user interface is composed of two main pages: a *homepage* (Figure 2), and an *exploration page* (Figure 3). The *homepage* allows the user to choose between two modes:

- *End-to-end* (E2E), where the user provides the start and end points and Aurigo's recommendation algorithm generates an itinerary based on the user's preferences.

- *Step-by-step* mode (S2S), where the user interactively build an itinerary by adding POIs incrementally, beginning from a start point.

In the E2E mode, two fields are available by default under "Choose your itinerary" to specify the starting address and the destination address (Figure 2, at b) and to indicate personal preferences through the style of walk: light, regular or long (at c). Under "Your interests", the user can specify his or her preferences for the four types of POIs that Aurigo supports (Monuments, Museums, Movie filming locations, and Parks) through a 5-star rating scale (at d). Alternatively, the user can enter the step-by-step mode by checking the box "I want to build my own path" (at a), where the user would only need to enter the starting address before moving on to the next page (i.e., the exploration page).

The *exploration page* (Figure 3) shows a map of the city, centered at the address the user has provided. The user can zoom in and out of the map. The current total distance of the itinerary is displayed at the top of the page ("). The map is the main interactive area through which the user would construct his or her itinerary (at e). It contains two collapsible panels: the *description panel* on the left (at d), and the *route panel* on the right (at f).

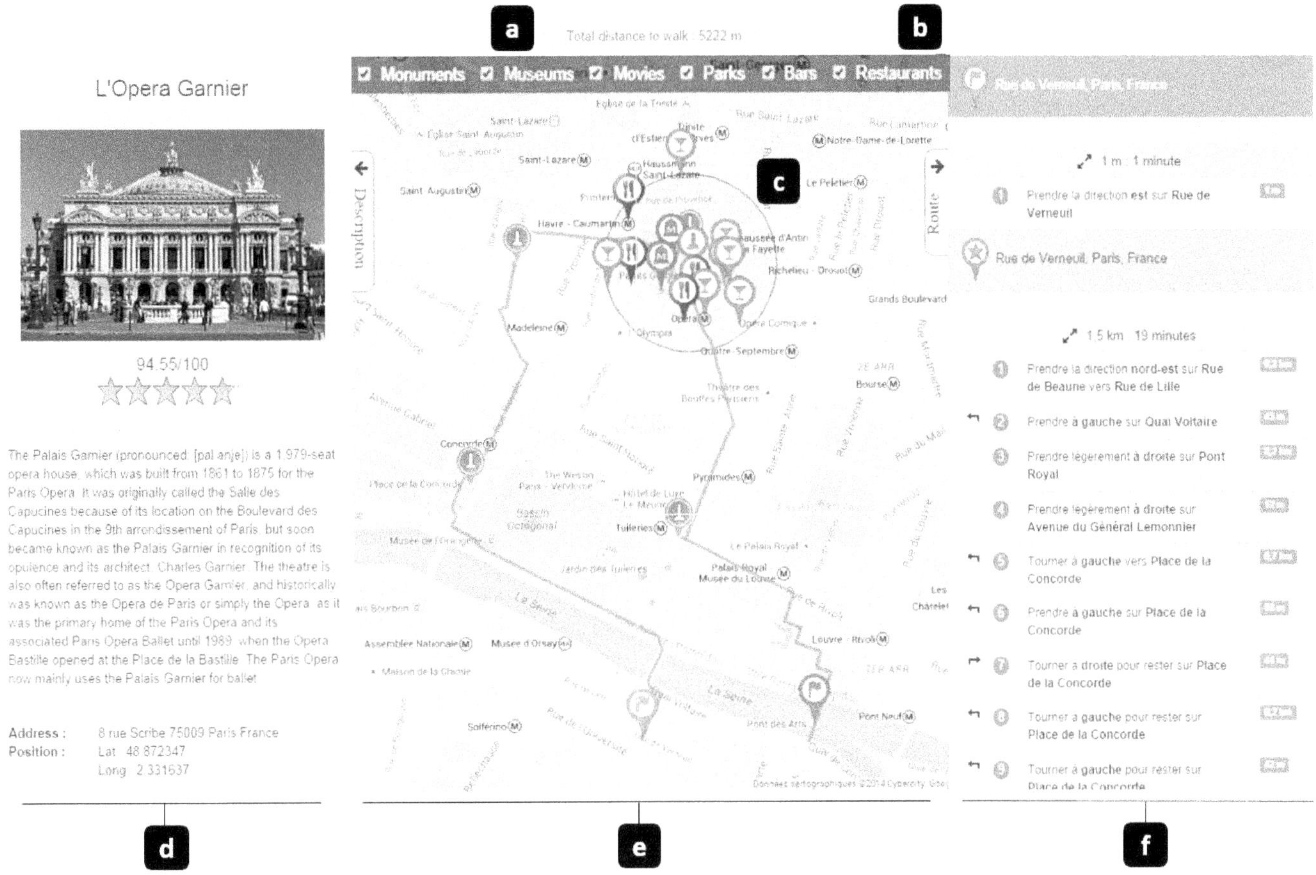

Figure 3. Aurigo's exploration page, with a tour constructed with the end-to-end mode (E2E, where the user provides the start and end points), composed of (a) the total distance, (b) the filter bar, (c) the Pop Radius, (d) the Description panel, (e) the map and (f) the Route panel.

A top filter bar (at b), right below the total distance, allows the user to select the types of POIs to display on the map. We included *bars* and *restaurants*, in addition to the four POI types listed on the homepage, since the user may want to find them on an ad hoc or on-demand basis.

POIs are displayed on the map as colored icons (see Table 1, and Figure 3, at c). The route panel (at f) shows the directions of the itinerary and is collapsible. The description panel (at d) provides a small paragraph about the selected POI with its photo (extracted from Wikipedia), its popularity score on a 0-to-100 scale, its address and its geographical location with latitude and longitude. We describe how all this information is extracted or derived from online websites and databases in a later section.

The map area (Figure 3, at e) offers multiple interactive features for the user to explore the surroundings of the itinerary and to personalize it by adding and removing POIs. Mousing over a POI will show its name in a pop up label (Figure 4, at c). Clicking a POI will cause a *Pop Radius* to show up as a transparent blue disk, centered at the clicked POI (at a). Within the Pop Radius, Aurigo displays all POIs of types that are selected in the filter bar. The user can then add or remove POIs in the Pop Radius and the itinerary will automatically adapt to the modifications and update the Route in the right panel.

Bar	Monument	Filming Location
Museum	Park	Restaurant

Table 1. Icons for each POI on the map

The Pop Radius represents the core feature of the step-by-step mode: beginning at a starting location, through consecutive invocations of the Pop Radius, the user can incrementally build an itinerary by adding or removing POIs, while exploring attractions in the city. The route shown on the right automatically updates after each user interaction with the Pop Radius.

ILLUSTRATIVE SCENARIOS: AURIGO IN ACTION

Below, we describe two scenarios to illustrate each of the two modes that Aurigo supports in tour planning.

Scenario 1: Gina does not know anything about Paris

Gina is visiting Paris for the first time. She prefers to walk around to better immerse herself in the city rather than joining a bus tour. She only knows that she will start her walk near her hotel and finish it near a cafe where she will meet her friend Kat who lives in Paris. She will use the end-to-end mode (E2E). While Gina enjoys walking, we does not

Figure 4. Illustration of the S2S mode (step-by-step) and the use of the Pop Radius: (1) the user has selected a starting point, shown by a green flag, and added two POIs. The last POI added is a temporary end point, shown as a red flag. (2) The user clicks on the POI indicated by a blue star to display a Pop Radius shown as a transparent blue circle (at a) that reveals all POIs within its radius; the route panel on the right (at b) shows directions for the current itinerary; mousing over a POI shows its names (at c). (3) The user has selected a new POI which becomes the new end point and the route is update automatically.

want to overdo it, so she chooses a *regular* walk on Aurigo's homepage (Figure 2).

Gina prefers to spend her day outdoors to visit historic sites and sees monuments rather than staying inside museums and buildings. The problem is that there are just too many monuments in the city. To indicate what she prefers, Gina rates each POI type (i.e., museums, parks, monuments, movie filming locations) using a 5-star scale on the homepage. Then she presses "Go" and Aurigo brings her to the exploration page.

Now she sees the map of the city on which Aurigo has displayed the recommended itinerary in blue, with all the selected POIs. The start and end points are indicated with a green and a red flag respectively. The path has been drawn using Google Maps API and each POI has a type-specific icon. Now Gina can use Aurigo's interactive visualization features to personalize this itinerary further.

On the recommended itinerary, Gina sees the Louvre museum as a suggested POI (Figure 5). She does not want to visit it yet since she promised to go there with Kat, so she clicks on the POI to remove it from the path. (If she wants to undo that, she can double click on it to add it back.) Instantly, the path is updated by the Google Maps API, which now excludes the Louvre museum from her itinerary.

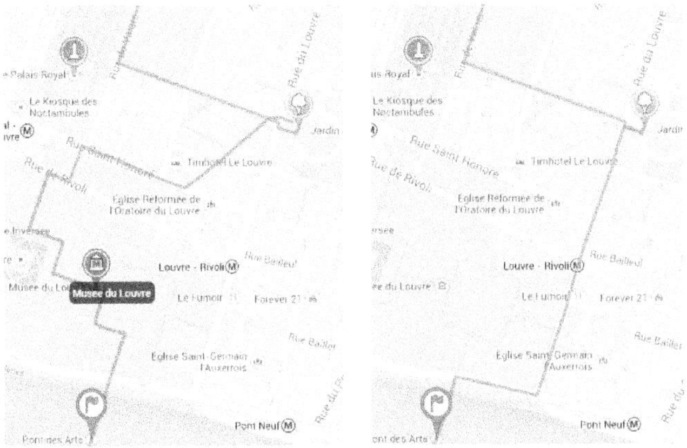

Figure 5. Gina does not want to go to the Louvre museum, but it is part of her recommended itinerary. She double clicks on it to delete it.

Gina can iterate this process until she is satisfied with her itinerary. Starting with an itinerary close to her expectations, it takes very little work for her revise the itinerary. She can easily revise it by integrating her subjective preferences. With Aurigo, Gina can craft her itinerary on a single-page user interface, instead of browsing many different sources of information, which can be difficult to navigate and summarize.

Scenario 2: Patrick knows a little bit about Paris and wants to create his own tour

Patrick has been reading a lot about Paris, and he knows the in which areas that he wants to spend his weekend with his wife. However, he is not sure how to organize his tour and is also not sure if he has enough places to visit for his two-day visit. Since he wants to begin their trip near their hotel, he enters the hotel's starting address on Aurigo's homepage, and starts building his path. Patrick selects "I want to build my own path" and enters "L'hotel Paris" as the starting point.

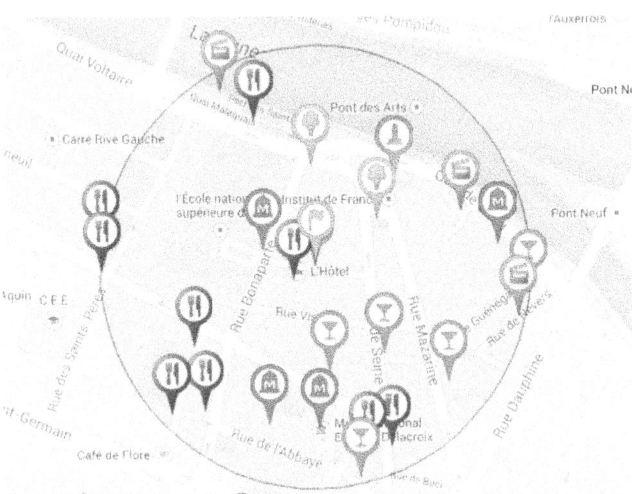

Figure 6. The Pop Radius is centered on the POI that has been clicked on. All the POIs inside this area are shown with an icon according to their category (or type of attraction). The starting point has a green flag. By double clicking on a POI, it adds it to the POI list and makes it the temporary ending point.

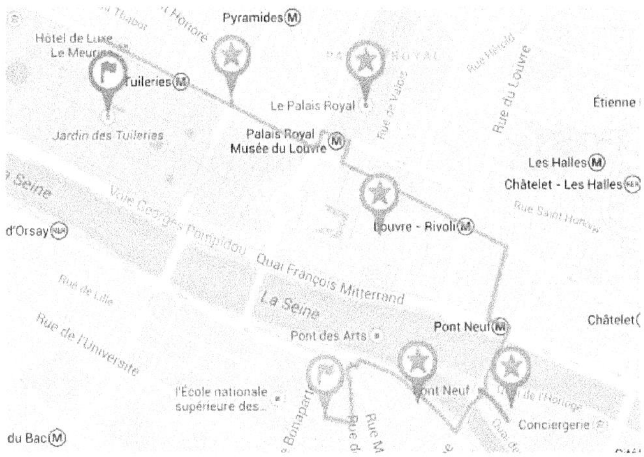

Figure 7. Candidate itinerary for Patrick's tour. The green flag is the starting point, the red flag is the ending point, and the blue stars are the intermediate POIs that Patrick has selected.

Once he clicks the "Go" button, a map is displayed on the exploration page. Thanks to the Pop Radius that has appeared at his starting location (Figure 6), he can choose his first place to visit. Since Patrick spent his previous day visiting monuments, he is eager to try something new. We wants to visit some movie filming locations. Within the Pop Radius, he looks for the POIs with the movie icons, and makes his choice. Patrick chose "Le Pont Neuf" because it would please his wife (he forgot their last wedding anniversary).

As he selected "Le Pont Neuf", it becomes the center of a new Pop Radius, which allows Patrick to select a new checkpoint. He wants to mix things up a little; he wants to visit the Louvre museum. Right after adding the museum to his itinerary, the new Pop Radius centered at the museum shows a restaurant which he recalls is a very nice one, with a great romantic setting, which his wife would surely enjoy dining in.

After a few minutes and some descriptions reading, Patrick has built a perfect itinerary step by step. Patrick takes note of the route, and gets ready for a great trip in Paris. He is fully prepared this time!

AURIGO'S KEY FEATURES

Popularity Function

Our popularity function combines the ratings and the number of reviews for each POIs. We used two different sources: (1) Yelp for museums, monuments and parks; (2) a movie database website for the filming locations (see *Data sources and implementation*). Movies are rated out of five points so we scaled them to a 0-to-100 scale. Concerning the Yelp POIs', we used a weighted scoring approach to balance the two quantitative parameters we extracted (i.e., ratings and number of reviews):

- 80 points derived from the star rating (1 to 5);
- 20 points derived from the review count (normalized).

The popularity formula for a POI p is the following:

$$popularity(p) = (stars(p) - 1) \times 20 + \ldots$$
$$\ldots + [\frac{nb_{reviews}(p)}{max_{reviews}(cat(p))}] \times 20$$

Where:

- $stars(p)$ is the number of stars (1 to 5) for the POI p (i.e., ratings);
- $nb_{reviews}(p)$ is the number of reviews for this POI;
- $max_{reviews}(cat(p))$ is the maximum number of reviews for this number of stars over all the POIs sharing the same category as p (for normalization).

In addition, a POI p with $stars(p) = 0$ (i.e., no ratings or null ratings) will return a zero popularity score. The formula above ensures that there is no score overlap between places with different ratings due to the number of reviews: 1 star will return a score in the interval $(0, 20]$, 2 stars $(20, 40]$, 3 stars $(40, 60]$, 4 stars $(60, 80]$ and 5 stars $(80, 100]$.

The Recommendation Algorithm

For the end-to-end mode (E2E), we designed a recommendation algorithm that constructs an itinerary path that goes through a sequence of POIs that are selected based on the users preferences. The algorithm first identifies and orders the candidate set of POIs, and then uses the Google Maps API to find a route to connect these POIs.

Our algorithm is fast and scalable. Its runtime is linear in the number of POIs specified. Empirically, it takes less than 0.5 second to run on more than 2,000 POIs. In the algorithm, the most computationally expensive step is the creation of the path itself (database accesses are instantaneous). The algorithm takes into account the following parameters from the user:

- Start and end points (both are addresses)
- Style of walk: *light walk*, *regular walk*, or *long walk*
- POI Preferences: expressed as 5-star ratings for *Monuments*, *Museums*, *Movies* (filming locations), and *Parks*
- POIs' popularity, computed with our popularity function

Other parameters concerning POI data include: POIs' geographical locations and popularity. We designed a scoring function to compute the popularity for each POI, which takes into account the reviews and ratings that the POI is associated with.

$$Score(p, path, taste, walkFactor) = distToPath(p, path)$$
$$-\lambda \times popularity(p) \times taste(cat(p)) \times walkFactor$$

Where:

- $distToPath(p, path)$ is the shortest distance of a point to the path (i.e., minimum of the distances from the orthogonal projections to each segment of the path using euclidian norm in the latitude-longitude plan);
- λ is empirical coefficient to balance popularity versus distance in the score function. We selected $\lambda = 0.0002$ after iterative testings;
- $popularity(p)$ is the score of the place given out of 100 as explained above; $taste(cat(p))$ is the the number of stars given to the corresponding category (higher means more preferred by the user);
- $walkFactor$ is a distance criterion, it allows us to tune the importance of the popularity of the place with respect of the distance. Long walks have higher values than short walks. By doing so, a path can include new points that are further away. The associated coefficients are 1 for a short walk, 2 for a medium walk and 3 for a long walk.

Since we do not expect reviews and ratings to change frequently, Aurigo pre-computes the popularity scores of all POIs. These popularity scores are then normalized using a scale of 0 to 100, with 100 before the score for the most popular place in the POI database.

Our algorithm is designed to find an itinerary in the form of a **natural** path connecting a list of POIs. For example, we would not want the user to walk through the same place twice, and we also would not want to an itinerary to consist of lengthy detours from the shortest path between the start and end points.

Given these design rationale, the trajectory obtained by linking the selected POIs from a birds-eye view should ideally be smooth. The first step of the algorithm (see Algorithm 1) is to draw a line between the start and end points. As we add POIs, we break the path down into Piecewise Linear (PwL) segments. From the initial straight line, the algorithm iteratively computes the Euclidean distance of all the POIs relative to this trajectory, selects the POI that minimizes the distance and maximizes a custom weighted objective function (with the parameters described above). The algorithm loops through the above steps (Algorithm 1, line 4-8), computing distances and picking a new POI in each iteration, until the path has 8 POIs, a limit imposed by the Google Maps API that the algorithm uses to get the turn-by-turn directions between consecutive POIs. We plan to investigate methods to overcome this limitation in our future work (e.g., break the itinerary into sub-itineraries).

The Pop Radius

The **Pop Radius** is one of Aurigo's key interaction techniques for locally exploring POIs. It allows the user to select any point along a path to display all POIs within a context-dependant radius, visually shown as a circular translucent blue overlay. It also allows the user to add and remove POIs from the tour itinerary, based on subjective preferences.

The area of the Pop Radius is computed based on the style of walk selected, using the following formula.

$$r = d(2i + 1)$$

Where r is the radius in meters, d a scaling factor (constant) set to 60m, and i depends on the walk: $i = 1$ for light, 2 for standard, and 3 for a long walk. If there are fewer than 5 POIs within the circle of radius r, it will be expanded with a new radius r' as follows:

$$r' = r + 2d$$

Clicking a POI within the Pop Radius selects it and displays its description on the Description panel. If the user clicks on it once more, it will be added to the path. Similarly, the user can remove a POI that is already on the path by clicking on it. The tour itinerary will be instantly updated.

DATA SOURCES AND IMPLEMENTATION

The current Aurigo prototype focuses on the city of Paris. We extracted a total 2204 POIs from various online websites and databases: from Yelp, we extracted 626 bars, 236 monuments, 187 museums, 150 parks, 714 restaurants; and from an open-source website[1], we extracted 282 filming locations. For each POI, Aurigo extracted its name, address, number of reviews, and its ratings using the Yelp API. For movie filming locations, we derived their popularity scores from ratings of the movies filmed at those sites by extracting data from *the movie database* website[2]. We used the Google Maps API to find the geolocation of each POI, and Wikipedia for the POI's description and photos.

EVALUATION

Hypothesis

Aurigo aims to assist users during the creation of tour itineraries in cities where there is a high density of POIs. We conducted a user study to assess how users would take advantage of the various features provided by Aurigo to build their own itineraries, and to test the usability of Aurigo's features and the system overall. Our study was designed to compare Aurigo with currently available solutions and evaluate the impact of Aurigo's unique features on its performances. We hypothesized that Aurigo is easier to use and provides more personalized itineraries in similar time constrains. We selected Paris for this user study, since it is one of the most visited city in the world, and it has a wide variety of monuments, museums, parks and other featured POIs types to visit.

[1]http://opendata.paris.fr/
[2]https://www.themoviedb.org/

Algorithm 1: Building an itinerary (a path of POIs), with a *Score* function that determines how much a user may like it

Data: path, POIs, Score, Insert
Result: path

$p_{min} \longleftarrow POIs[0]$;
while $POIs.length < 8$ **do**
  $score_{min} \longleftarrow +\infty$;
  for $p \in POIs$ **do**
    $score = Score(p, path)$;
    if $score < score_{min}$ **then**
      $score_{min} \longleftarrow score$;
      $p_{min} \longleftarrow p$;
  $path = Insert(p_{min}, path)$;

Design

We used a within-subjects design with two conditions: (1) *Aurigo* and (2) *Google Maps* where participants used Google Maps to find interesting places and build their itineraries. This design allowed the participants to compare their experiences with both tools. We decided to only evaluate Aurigo's end-to-end mode (with recommendation algorithm) against Google Maps for two reasons: (1) Aurigo's step-by-step mode (S2S) does not have a counterpart in Google Maps; (2) Aurigo's E2E mode includes most interaction and algorithmic functionality used in the S2S mode.

Participants

We recruited 10 volunteers for this user study by word-of-mouth from our professional and academic networks. The first inclusion criterion for a user to participate is that he or she should have travelled at least once in his or her life. There were 4 males and 6 females, ranging from 18 to 27 years old, averaging at 23 years old. Most of them were graduate students, a few were consultants, and one was an undergraduate student. Every participant had used Google Maps before, from once a week and more than once a day. However, most participants had not used Google Maps for planning tours.

Every participant had at least travelled once in the past 3 years, domestically or internationally. Only one participant was not used to preparing his or her own trip. The other participants used tour guides or web searches to help them prepare (80%) (Figure 8). The participants commented that they usually needed about an hour to design a satisfying itinerary. Each session lasted for about 75 minutes, and each participant was paid $10 in compensation for his or her time.

Apparatus and Materials

All participants used laptops that we provided. Every session was conducted in a "Incognito" window of the Google Chrome web browser (i.e., private browsing mode) so as not to keep any history or preferences from a previous participant. When using Google Maps and Aurigo, all Google accounts were disconnected, so that all participants will be using the tools in their default settings. The database Aurigo used from Yelp and open source websites contained 2,204 POIs. Aurigo was run on a localhost (e.g., the laptop the participant was using).

Procedure

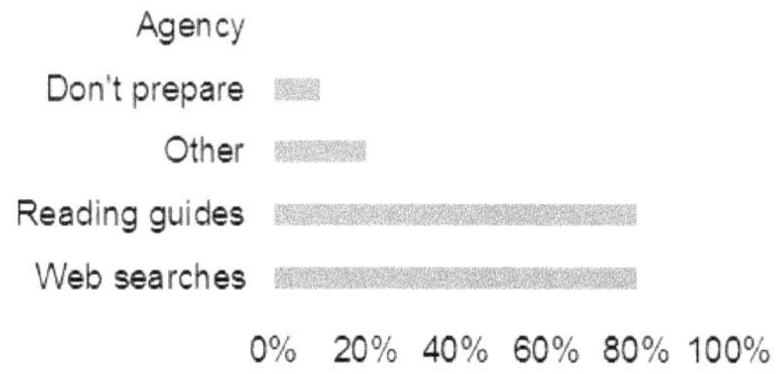

Figure 8. Types of tools used by our participants for tour planning. Tour guides and web searches are most frequently used. None of the participants consulted travel agency for tour preparation.

We first asked all the participants to fill out a background questionnaire to evaluate how much they were used to travelling and itinerary building. Then, we explained the main purpose of this study to the participants. Next, we asked the participants to imagine that they were tourists about to arrive in Paris, or that they were already in the city, but they do not know much about the city. With this scenario, they wanted to visit the city by walking and they would use the Internet to find interesting information about the attractions available. They would focus on where they wanted to start, and their preferences considering their walking style (e.g., short walk, moderate walk, long walk) but also the type of places they wanted to visit (e.g., museums, parks, monuments, famous movies shooting locations).

All participants were free to choose their own start and end points. In fact, if we were to tell all participants to do exactly the same things, user preferences would become irrelevant, and it would be unlikely for them could build satisfying itineraries. Before starting with each condition, we briefly explain how to use the tool by showing a demo. Finally, we randomly assign half of the participants to start with the Aurigo condition, to counter balance for condition order.

For each condition, participants were given about 15 minutes to find interesting places and design their itineraries. Then they were asked to fill out another questionnaire that asked for their subjective opinions about Aurigo, how it compared to Google Maps, and any feedback and suggestions that they might have about Aurigo.

Results

Quantitative results

For each condition, the participants used the tool for a maximum of 15 minutes. If the participant was satisfied with her itinerary, she could let us know and we would stop the timer. The number of places chosen for the itineraries was interesting to us because it showed us how complex the itineraries might be. This number has an upper bound however: Google Maps only allows up to 10 places for an itinerary, while Aurigo supports up to 8 (due to limitations of the Google Maps API which Aurigo uses). We recorded these numbers for each participant; if a participant gave up for a condition, the time was noted and the number of places set to 0 (Figure 9).

In our evaluation, we saw that participants had similar behaviors using Google Maps and Aurigo. We believed Google-Maps based Aurigo's interface might not be the only factor that contributes to this, but that we also believed it was due to participants quickly becoming familiar with Aurigo's usage. Before the study, we had the hypothesis that Aurigo participants would need to spend more time than Google Maps participants. However, using a one-tailed test, we found that this hypothesis was not supported ($p > .1$). Despite the similarity in timing results, we observed an important difference between the Aurigo and the Google Maps conditions: whereas the Aurigo participants spent most of their time on designing itineraries by adding or removing points to adjust locally the itinerary, Google Maps participants spent most of their time on finding places, often leaving little time in the end on building their itineraries. This observation implies that the itineraries built by the Google Maps participants might not be satisfactory.

We also observed that the number of places chosen for Aurigo were really close to the maximum allowed. Indeed, every participant chose at least 7 places, and over half of them stopped at 8 places, whereas we only suggested 6 places at the beginning of each itinerary designed with Aurigo's algorithm. Before the study, we hypothesized that Aurigo participants would be able to find more places than Google Maps participants since Aurigo suggested multiple places to start 9. Using a one-tailed test, we find that this effect to be statistically significant ($p < .002$), proving our hypothesis. Nevertheless, we could not find any correlation between the time spent and the number of places chosen. Indeed, every participant has his or her own rhythm when it comes to exploring the map, reading descriptions and choosing his or her POIs. Moreover, a satisfactory itinerary does not necessarily require a lot of POIs.

Subjective results

We asked our participants to compare Aurigo with Google Maps (Figure 10), and to rate Aurigo on several criteria (Figure 11). Aurigo was rated favorably. All participants, except one, would choose Aurigo over Google Maps when asked which tool they would prefer to use in the future for tour planning. Most Aurigo participants seemed to enjoy using it.

POIs and paths seem to be more easily found using Aurigo (80% of participants agree), and Aurigo's user interface seems more enjoyable to use as well. Knowing that Aurigo's design is not only based on building an itinerary but

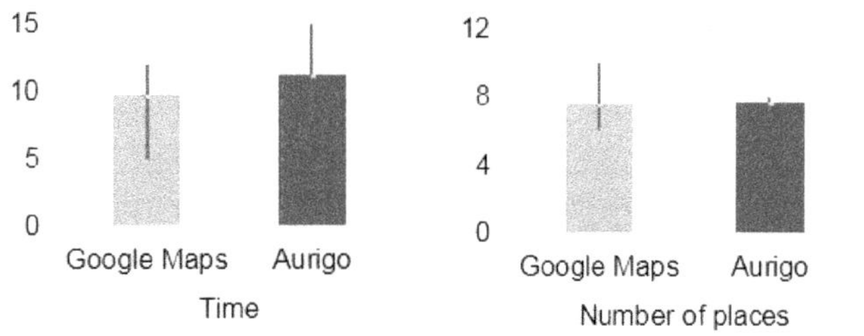

Figure 9. Time taken and number of places found on average for each condition with 95% error bar. Results were similar for Aurigo and Google Maps in term of the average number of places.

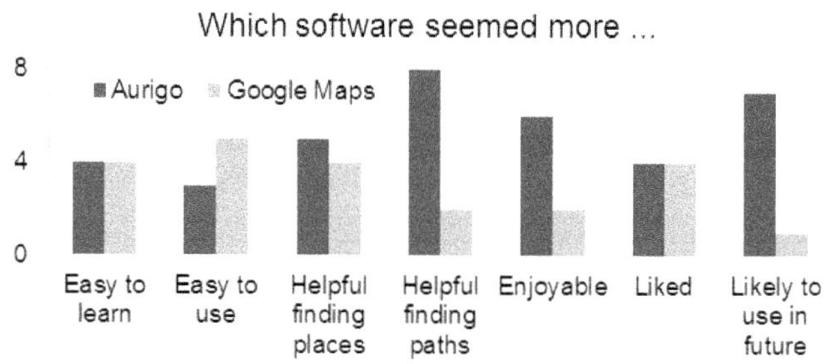

Figure 10. Impressions about the different conditions after testing them. Aurigo was rated favorably comparing to Google. Only one user chose Google Maps over Aurigo, when asked which tool they prefer to use in the future.

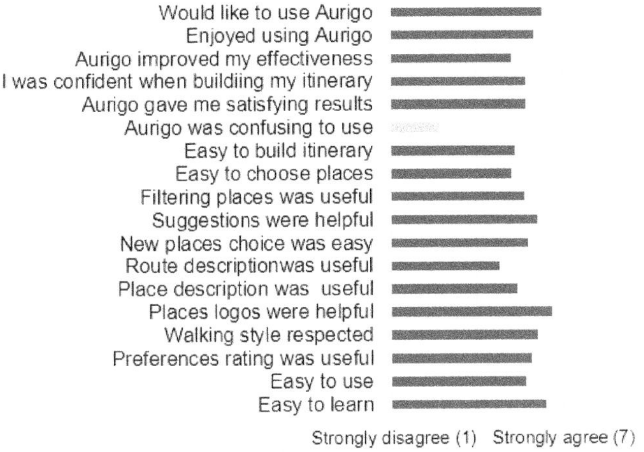

Figure 11. Subjective ratings of Aurigo. Participants rated Aurigo favorably. It didn't seem confusing, the best features for the participants being the places logos, the walking style and the suggestions.

also on finding interesting places to put in it, participants seem to have preferred it over Google Maps. One participant said "choosing my preferences and being able to modify my itinerary by picking some new places were the features I liked the most about Aurigo".

An exciting piece of feedback from the participant was that Aurigo did not seem to be confusing to use. Participants were able to learn to use its features in a very short amount of time. The top three features that interested participants were the icon design for the POIs, the choice of their walking style and the suggestions given by the "Pop Radius". These features have been developed to help users find POIs that best match their preferences, and they seem to play their part very well.

The overall impression about Aurigo seems to be very positive. However, some technical details like a wider "Pop Radius" has been identified as wishes by some of them and we plan to improve on them. The description content was also discussed. Some participants suggested that the POI descriptions should also include opening hours, and ticket prices.

RELATED WORK

Tour planning, a practical everyday activity and challenge, has received a lot of attention in research. Initially considered as an optimization problem under multiple constraints, a wide variety of studies have tried to take advantage of data and metadata available on social networks such as Flickr, Panoramio, Facebook or FourSquare.

While most approaches focus on displaying only points of interest (POIs) close to the user's location, INTRINGUE represents an early foray of intelligent information systems in tourism [2] by offering trip recommendations personalized for single individuals or groups with a user interface on Web browers and WAP minibrowers. Stimulated by those early prototypes, the tour planning problem has aroused a significant interest within the intelligent user interface community. Trip-Mine has introduced the travel time constraints and scalability of travel region to offer a broader tour planning experience [10]. The trip map, the set of potential POIs considered, was modeled by a weighted graph and Lu et al. proposed three optimization mechanisms for their cost function. Taking time constraints into account has been further developed with a study dealing with transfer connections in public transportation [7], taking into account the network togy, the schedules and the passengers' distribution over time to develop a trip planning system based on this algorithm for passengers. Tour planning problem has evolved to a Multi Constrained Team Orienteering Problem with Time Windows (MCTOPTW) by combining time with all other quantitative parameters [15]. Sylejmani et al. adopted the local search meta-heuristics of "tabu" planning, which keeps track of moves that cannot be performed to ensure high constraints on the neighborhood candidates to the trip schedule and facilitate the diversification of search process into unexplored part of the map. Aurigo's planning approach seems to be the next step of these evolutions, taking quantitative parameters (users' preferences, POIs' score) but also time restriction (type of walk desired by the users) into account to propose the best itinerary within a known map.

But those planning algorithms are NP hard [3], hence justifying the need for mining human behaviors to recommend natural trips more than mathematically optimal ones. Geotagged photos have represented a valuable and reliable source of metadata to track millions of tourists on their itineraries. However, these metadata appeared to be noisy and needed efficient filtering methods [13]. Efficiently collecting those metadata allows to leverage temporal information regarding tourist attractions. By mining trips on these large scale geotagged photos databases, it was possible to segment photo collections into trip patterns [1], and label them using tags under themes such as landmarks, events, nature or food tasting. However, to fully take advantage of those metadata (e.g., location, time, tags), Chareyron et al. developed methodologies to rebuild a photographer's path from Flickr (a hosting website allowing people to tags and share their photos and videos) [5], hence recreating the photographer's spatial and temporal trace. Aurigo also uses raw data in order to build itineraries and propose the best one with the close difference that the building part of the itineraries is achieved by the algorithm. The itineraries stay as natural as possible with the consideration of the user's preferences but also the "Pop Radius" functionality allowing the user to tune his or her itinerary. Using Panoramio, a geolocation-oriented photo sharing website, another initiative called Photo2Trip [11, 19], indexed paths generated from photos' metadata and computed a distance to evaluate the similarity between two paths. Then, using path enrichment technique, it suggested to the user itineraries resulting from the merge of several paths to ensure a longer and denser tour. Therefore, this approach offers tours that are more representative of people behavior.

Studies have been combining these behavioral trip mining with recommendation algorithms to provide knowledge-based tour planning tools. Among them, Antourage [8], proposed a distance-constrained recommendation algorithm relying on the mining of large volumes geotagged photos databases like Flickr and Panoramio. Given a starting point, which is usually the user's hotel, the algorithm applied max-min ant system (MMAS) derived from classic "ant colony optimization" (ACO) meta-heuristic to suggest tours looping back to the starting point. Aurigo presents another approach where our recommendation algorithm selects an ordered list of POIs and Google API trace the route between them. Another framework, TripBuilder [4], mined itineraries from Flickr and matched the POIs available on Wikipedia. Then it applied classic generalized maximum coverage developing its own cost function for path recommendation.

Other studies have exploited users' "check-in" activities on Location-Based Social Networks (LBSN) such as Gowalla, FourSquare or Facebook. For example, Lu et al. [9] used data from these 3 social networks non-distinctively to attribute popularity and temporal-based properties to points of interest (POIs). Then they combined a recommendation algorithm based on parallel computing with these data to extract social relationships and temporal properties. In addition to using these "social breadcrumbs" [6], De Choudhury et al. proposed to validate the itineraries with Amazon Mechanical Turk (AMT) for better recommendations.

The use of AMT was fully exploited in Mobi [20], a crowd-powered trip planning application using natural language input and quantitative constraints to ask the crowd for asynchronous contributions. With Crowdcierge [14], Rafidi et al. suggested the application of the retainer model to keep a pool of workers and therefore offer synchronous AMT where workers tag ideas to plan the itinerary and re-plan in response to problems that can arise during the trip. Aurigo uses large pools of workers with the scores being extracted from popular touristic social networks, that let the data respect to the extent possible the tourists' opinion of every places.

DISCUSSION, LIMITATIONS AND FUTURE WORK

We believe that interactive visualization is complementary to planning algorithms for providing efficient and personalized tour itineraries. The interface we built provides features to empower the user: (i) information and visualization to guide his or her choices and (ii) means of action to locally modify his or her itinerary. Thanks to those elements, only a small amount of quantitative preferences is required from the user in the departure-arrival mode. Our approach merges smoothly the crowd-sourcing by taking into account popularity in POIs' scores without depriving completely the user from making his or her own choices.

Due to the limited amount of participants in the user study, it has been difficult to establish significant results. However, Aurigo appears to take significantly more advantage of the maximum number of places possible to visit. Users also spent significantly more time on the Aurigo condition, mainly due to the interactive path they liked to tuned as much as much. This feature and Aurigo's interactive interface including the Pop Radius function were overall appreciated by the majority of participants. A User study at a larger scale would help us evaluate further the quantitative performances.

Aurigo currently relies on POIs' ratings, reviews and location, and displays pictures, descriptions and ratings. In the future we would like to enable our system to use more data and allow users to visualize more information on the interface. Aurigo does not take yet into account the time of departure nor provides a time estimation in addition to the total distance outside of the Route in the right panel. We could integrate the opening timetables of museums, restaurants and other time dependant types of POIs to recommend our path. With appropriate data, we could also integrate prices as a user's parameter and estimate the expends of the tour. Aurigo does not integrate either a public transportation module that would allow a user to assemble interactively several tour itineraries by taking recommended route by train or bus within the same city.

In terms of interface, we consider to improve the Pop Radius in the future by letting the user customize in some extends the size of the disk, along with allowing the creation of a Pop Radius anywhere on the map. We have also been working on creating a heat map that would be superimposed on the plan indicating the density of parameters such as popularity by type. This heat map could also be the first brick of a system that not only suggests POIs for a tour itinerary but also adapts the path to walk in streets that are more likely to interest the user between each POI (e.g., famous avenue instead of small street even if it increases the distance walked).

However those new features strongly depends on the provided data sources. We do not aim to create our own user platform but we want to demonstrate the potential of Aurigo in this proof of efficacy. Aurigo is an interactive system fed by data that can be integrated by a review website or a social network that references POIs, and uses reviews and ratings.

CONCLUSIONS

This paper introduces Aurigo, a novel system for tour planning. Aurigo helps the user create personalized itineraries through a mixed-initiative approach, by combining data-driven recommendations, interactive visualization, and customizable features. We illustrated the utility of Aurigo through two scenarios: the *end-to-end* mode (E2E) where Aurigo constructs an itinerary based on a start and end points provided by the user; and the *step-by-step* mode (S2S) that allows the user to build an itinerary interactively and incrementally.

We performed a user study with 10 participants, where most users found Aurigo and its features, such as the algorithmically-suggested POIs, and the Pop Radius, highly enjoyable and easy to use. In the current prototype, Aurigo uses data from Yelp and Wikipedia, and the Google Maps APIs. We look forward to integrating Aurigo with other crowd-sourced POI databases and deploying Aurigo for more people to try it out.

REFERENCES

1. Arase, Y., Xie, X., Hara, T., and Nishio, S. *Mining people's trips from large scale geo-tagged photos*. ACM, New York, New York, USA, Oct. 2010.
2. Ardissono, L., Goy, A., Petrone, G., Segnan, M., and Torasso, P. Intrigue: Personalized recommendation of tourist attractions for desktop and hand held devices. *dx.doi.org 17*, 8-9 (Nov. 2010), 687–714.

3. Bao, J., Yang, X., Wang, B., and Wang, J. An Efficient Trip Planning Algorithm under Constraints. In *Web Information System and Application Conference (WISA), 2013 10th*, IEEE (2013), 429–434.
4. Brilhante, I., Macedo, J. A., Nardini, F. M., Perego, R., and Renso, C. Where shall we go today?: planning touristic tours with tripbuilder. In *CIKM '13: Proceedings of the 22nd ACM international conference on Conference on information & knowledge management*, ACM Request Permissions (New York, New York, USA, Oct. 2013), 757–762.
5. Chareyron, G., Da-Rugna, J., and Branchet, B. Mining tourist routes using Flickr traces. In *ASONAM '13: Proceedings of the 2013 IEEE/ACM International Conference on Advances in Social Networks Analysis and Mining*, ACM (New York, New York, USA, Aug. 2013), 1488–1489.
6. De Choudhury, M., Feldman, M., Amer-Yahia, S., Golbandi, N., Lempel, R., and Yu, C. *Automatic construction of travel itineraries using social breadcrumbs*. ACM, New York, New York, USA, June 2010.
7. Guo, J., Jia, L., Xu, J., and Qin, Y. An Algorithm for Trip Planning with Constraint of Transfer Connection in Urban Mass Transit Network. *Distributed Computing and Applications to Business, Engineering & Science (DCABES), 2012 11th International Symposium on* (2012), 341–344.
8. Jain, S., Seufert, S., and Bedathur, S. *Antourage: mining distance-constrained trips from flickr*. mining distance-constrained trips from flickr. ACM, New York, New York, USA, Apr. 2010.
9. Lu, E. H.-C., Chen, C.-Y., and Tseng, V. S. *Personalized trip recommendation with multiple constraints by mining user check-in behaviors*. ACM, New York, New York, USA, Nov. 2012.
10. Lu, E. H. C., Lin, C.-Y., and Tseng, V. S. Trip-Mine: An Efficient Trip Planning Approach with Travel Time Constraints. In *Mobile Data Management (MDM), 2011 12th IEEE International Conference on*, IEEE (2011), 152–161.
11. Lu, X., Wang, C., Yang, J.-M., Pang, Y., and Zhang, L. *Photo2Trip: generating travel routes from geo-tagged photos for trip planning*. generating travel routes from geo-tagged photos for trip planning. ACM, New York, New York, USA, Oct. 2010.
12. Munar, A. M., and Jacobsen, J. K. S. Motivations for sharing tourism experiences through social media. *Tourism management 43* (Aug. 2014), 46–54.
13. Popescu, A., and Grefenstette, G. Deducing trip related information from flickr. *Proceedings of the 18th international conference on World wide web* (2009).
14. Rafidi, J. *Real-time trip planning with the crowd*. ACM, New York, New York, USA, Apr. 2013.
15. Sylejmani, K., Dorn, J., and Musliu, N. A Tabu Search approach for Multi Constrained Team Orienteering Problem and its application in touristic trip planning. In *Hybrid Intelligent Systems (HIS), 2012 12th International Conference on*, IEEE (2012), 300–305.
16. Tung, V. W. S., and Ritchie, J. R. B. Exploring the essence of memorable tourism experiences. *Annals of Tourism Research 38*, 4 (Oct. 2011), 1367–1386.
17. Xiang, Z., and Gretzel, U. Role of social media in online travel information search. *Tourism management 31*, 2 (Apr. 2010), 179–188.
18. Xiang, Z., Wang, D., O'Leary, J. T., and Fesenmaier, D. R. Adapting to the Internet: Trends in Travelers' Use of the Web for Trip Planning. *Journal of Travel Research* (Feb. 2014), 0047287514522883.
19. Yin, H., Wang, C., Yu, N., and Zhang, L. Trip Mining and Recommendation from Geo-tagged Photos. In *Multimedia and Expo Workshops (ICMEW), 2012 IEEE International Conference on*, IEEE (2012), 540–545.
20. Zhang, H., Law, E., Miller, R., Gajos, K., Parkes, D., and Horvitz, E. *Human computation tasks with global constraints*. ACM, New York, New York, USA, May 2012.

Rhema: A Real-Time In-Situ Intelligent Interface to Help People with Public Speaking

M. Iftekhar Tanveer
ROC HCI, Electrical and Computer Eng.
University of Rochester
itanveer@cs.rochester.edu

Emy Lin
ROC HCI, Computer Science
University of Rochester
elin9@u.rochester.edu

Mohammed (Ehsan) Hoque
ROC HCI, Computer Science
University of Rochester
mehoque@cs.rochester.edu

ABSTRACT
A large number of people rate public speaking as their top fear. What if these individuals were given an intelligent interface that provides live feedback on their speaking skills? In this paper, we present Rhema, an intelligent user interface for Google Glass to help people with public speaking. The interface automatically detects the speaker's volume and speaking rate in real time and provides feedback during the actual delivery of speech. While designing the interface, we experimented with two different strategies of information delivery: 1) Continuous streams of information, and 2) Sparse delivery of recommendation. We evaluated our interface with 30 native English speakers. Each participant presented three speeches (avg. duration 3 minutes) with 2 different feedback strategies (continuous, sparse) and a baseline (no feeback) in a random order. The participants were significantly more pleased ($p < 0.05$) with their speech while using the sparse feedback strategy over the continuous one and no feedback.

Author Keywords
Public Speaking; Google Glass; Live Feedback; Design Techniques; Human Factor; User Study.

ACM Classification Keywords
H.5.m. Information interfaces and presentation (e.g., HCI): Miscellaneous.

INTRODUCTION
Humans intuitively understand the elements of a well-presented speech. In addition to presenting meaningful content, the speaker needs to modulate his or her volume and vary speaking rate to retain the audience's attention [11]. Yet many presenters forget to do this in the delivery. During the act of publicly speaking, the speaker becomes the center of attention. In these kinds of scenarios, many people feel afraid and conscious of judgment, which often results in an overwhelming, uncomfortable, and stressful speaking experience. As a result, people rate public speaking as their number one fear (higher than the fear of death) [24]. With the advent of new and comfortable wearable technologies (e.g. Google Glass) and smart interfaces, a whole new realm of opportunities have arose to enable users to increase awareness of their nonverbal behavior during public speaking.

IUI 2015, March 29 - April 01, 2015, Atlanta, GA, USA.
Copyright 2015 ACM 978-1-4503-3306-1/15/03…$15.00.
http://dx.doi.org/10.1145/2678025.2701386

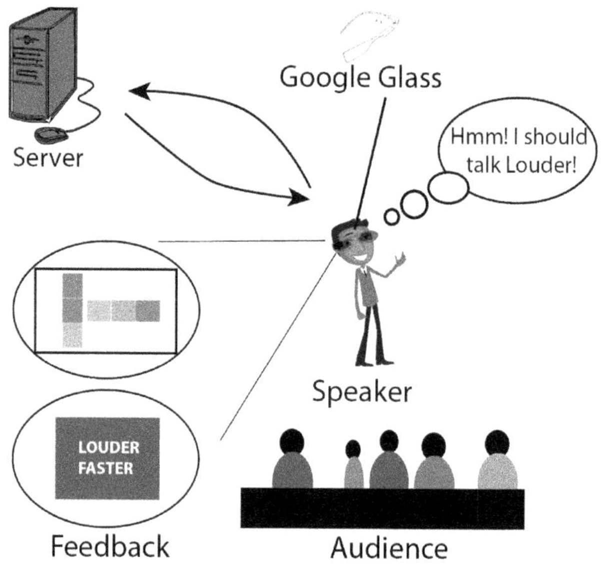

Figure 1: Usage scenario for Google Glass based real-time feedback system

In this paper, we present the design, development and evaluation of a smart user interface, Rhema[1], which presents live feedback on users' speaking styles through a wearable Google Glass. We have implemented a framework to record the live speech of the speaker using the Glass, transmit the audio to a server for automated processing of volume and speaking rate, and then present the data to the user. The analysis occurs in real time, allowing the interface to function during an actual speech delivery. The data is presented to the user in a format that is intuitive and informative about his or her voice modulation, without distracting them from delivering the speech and engaging with the audience.

[1] www.cs.rochester.edu/hci/currentprojects.php?proj=rh

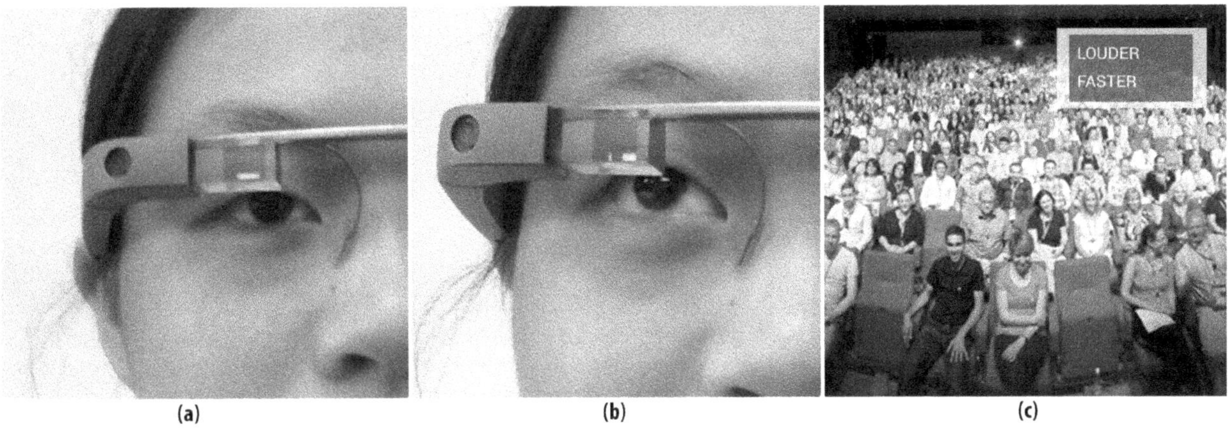

Figure 2: Demonstration of Google Glass as a secondary display (a) Eye position while looking forward (b) Eye position while looking at the glass display (c) User's view

Providing feedback during a live speech has a number of design challenges. One challenge is to keep the speakers informed about their speaking performance without distracting them from their speech. A significant enough distraction can introduce unnatural behaviors, such as stuttering or awkward pausing. Because the human brain is not particularly adept at multitasking [19,22], this is a significant issue to address in our feedback design. Secondly, the head mounted display is positioned near to the eye, which might cause inadvertent attention shifts [2]. Human attention is a limited resource [20], and the user might completely ignore the interface if the interaction requires too much attention. Additionally, if the user continuously stares at the feedback screen, the speaker will lose eye contact with the audience, causing the quality of the presentation to disintegrate.

We address these concerns by designing the interface in the form of "*Secondary Display*" [16], which avoids cognitive overload from multitasking and significantly improves the quality of the presentation. Information presented in secondary display is perceived and interpreted through a quick glance or a series of short glances. Unlike usual computer displays, it does not require a lengthy period of the users' attention. As a result, information presented in this form is less intrusive and minimizes the level of distraction. Physically, Google Glass works well as a secondary type because it is positioned in the periphery of the user's field of vision (Figure 2). The user must look upwards to actually see the display. In effect, it enables the users to usefully "*tradeoff attention for utility*" [16]. They make a glance towards the display if needed but do not lose attention inadvertently. A low requirement in attention makes the task cognitively less demanding, which results in more effective delivery of information. This is reflected in the results of our quantitative user study, in which the participants rated themselves significantly more satisfied ($p < 0.05$) with their speech while using the sparse feedback strategy than with the continuous one. They also strongly appreciated the minimization of distraction in comparison to what they had expected.

We came to an effective design decision by involving the potential users early and often in the design process. Starting with the brainstorming session, we reached out to a potential user group via social media and online forums. This enabled us to evaluate wide varieties of possibilities for the feedback design. We identified two main approaches for information delivery. The first approach consisted of continuous and slowly changing feedback schemes. This type of interface was designed to constantly deliver information through various plots, graphs or icons. To minimize distractions arising from movements in peripheral vision, this approach required the interface to change slowly [8]. The second approach was designed to deliver information sparsely over time. We designed a feedback scheme named "Words" which falls under this category. This feedback scheme shows nothing for 20 seconds. After 20 seconds, words such as "Louder", "Faster", "Good" (depending on the speaker's volume and/or speaking rate) are displayed. The words are shown for three seconds and then the display is blank again for the next 20 seconds.

We conducted a within-subject study with these two different types of feedback schemes along with a baseline case where Google Glass was turned off. 30 native speakers of English participated in this experiment. We collected qualitative and quantitative data from the participants. In addition, we collected quantitative ratings from 10 different Mechanical Turk workers for each speech to gain a sense of audience perception. The experiment demonstrated that the subjects found the system effective for adjusting their speaking rate. They also rated the sparse version of the feedback scheme significantly higher than the continuous version.

In summary, we contribute the following in this paper:

- We present a Google Glass interface to help people with public speaking by providing live feedback during the delivery of the speech. This information enables the speakers to modulate their volume and speaking rate.

- We demonstrate that providing quick recommendations in regular intervals during the live speech delivery is more useful than continuously presenting the data to the users.
- Our experiment with 30 participants shows that the Google Glass interface adds value during the actual speech delivery in regards to voice modulation and speaking rate.

RELATED LITERATURE

Designing an interactive system that can capture and analyze a live speech and provide feedback using a wearable device draws on areas from Wearable Computing, Human Factors, Human-Computer Interaction, and Virtual Reality. Teeters et al. from MIT Media Lab demonstrated the use of self-cam [23], a custom built prototype where a camera hangs out from a person's neck and analyzes the facial expressions of the wearer. The prototype was developed with the need of individuals with autism to interpret their own emotions. This project allowed users to become self-aware by providing real time feedback on social behavior. While the prototype successfully demonstrated the feasibility of such technology, no user studies have been reported to measure its efficacy.

There is a growing body of literature in the area of Human Factors that focuses on developing ways to present live information to people while they are engaged in a cognitively overloading task. For example, Ofek et al. [18] studied the mode and the amount of information that can be consumed during a conversation. Their study suggested that it is possible to process information while a person is engaged in a conversation. However, people consume more information when the data is presented in small batches of visual elements. McAtamney and Parker reported that wearable technologies with active display (e.g. the display of handheld smart phones) significantly disrupt social interactions because users lose the element of eye-to-eye contact [15]. We kept these findings in mind while designing our interface, and they also guided our decision to use Google Glass as a secondary display instead of an active head-mounted display.

Researchers continue to study both verbal and nonverbal behaviors during public speaking in an effort to find ways to improve speaking skills. Eva et al. described a study in which they analyzed the effect of acoustic features of individuals perceived as excellent speakers [21]. They conducted a perceptual evaluation by manipulating the F0 dynamics, fluency, and speech rate in a synthesized animation of a speaker. They noted that the amount of manipulation is highly correlated with the ratings of the speaker. Koppensteiner et al. [13] reported the effect of "dominant activation of body parts" with different personality traits. However, scopes of all these previous efforts are limited to manually inspecting and understanding positive and negative behaviors of public speaking. There is room for further research by automating the analysis and providing feedback.

A considerable amount of effort has taken place related to public speaking in the virtual reality domain as well. In 1998, North et al. described a study in which virtual reality was used as a therapy to treat phobia associated with public speaking [17]. In the study, a group of people was exposed to a virtual public speaking scene. The group showed significant improvements after five weeks of treatment. This experiment provided evidence in support of virtual reality therapy for improving public speaking skills.

Researchers have also worked on virtual environments to enable people to practice public speaking. Chollet et al. from University of Southern California developed an interactive virtual audience program for public speaking training [5]. The program collects a dataset of public speaking performances under different training conditions. The same team of researchers is currently working to build a fully multimodal platform named "Cicero" [1] to automatically analyze and train a user's behavior during public speaking. Cicero can identify some nonverbal descriptors that are considered characteristics of speakers' performances. However, providing any user level feedback to improve speaking performances remains part of their future work. Hoque et al. developed an intelligent avatar coach named MACH, "My Automated Conversation coacH" [12], to help people practice job interviews. Their results suggested that a virtual coach might be more effective than traditional behavioral interventions. However, all the aforementioned applications only allow participants to practice social interactions offline. In this paper, we take on the challenge of providing live feedback during the actual interaction.

TECHNICAL DETAILS

In order to validate whether real time feedback would actually elicit measurable improvements, we implemented working prototypes on Google Glass using the Android platform. We chose Google Glass as it is lightweight and comfortable to wear and comparatively cheaper than other head mounted displays. We hoped that people using this form factor would not become overwhelmed from the discomfort of a traditional head-mounted display. In addition, as shown in Figure 2, the position of Google Glass display worked effectively for communicating information in real time without inadvertently distracting the user. Unfortunately, Google Glass is not designed to run computationally intensive programs [10]. It does not have any suitable heat dissipation mechanism. As a result, running intensive algorithms to process the speakers' speeches made the glass hot and uncomfortable for long continuous use.

To overcome this problem, we used a local server for leveraging the computational capabilities. The server

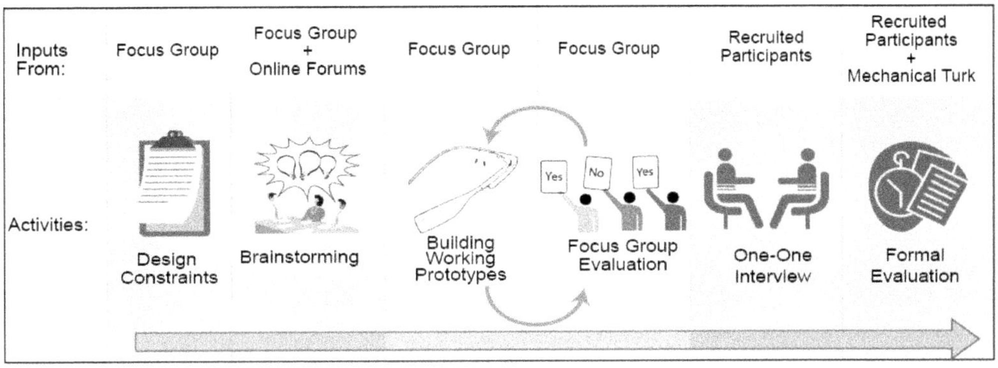

Figure 3: Chronological list of actions taken for finding a suitable design of a live feedback scheme

analyzed the audio data for loudness (in decibels) and speech rate (in words per second) and sent the results back to the glass. We experimented with Transfer Control Protocol (TCP), Real-time Transport Protocol (RTP) and User Datagram Protocol (UDP) to transmit each second of audio clips to the local server. The use of streaming protocols like RTP caused the Glass to overheat. On the other hand, UDP datagrams were too unreliable for accurate calculation of loudness and speaking rate as there is no guarantee for packet delivery, ordering and duplicate protection. Therefore, TCP was suitable for our application as the audio clips were only used in calculation of loudness and speaking speed and not for playing them in real-time. Offloading the computationally expensive tasks to a local server enabled us to use the Google Glass for about an hour without overheating it. However, with further upgrade to the hardware, it may be possible to extend the battery life in the future.

On the server-side, we calculated the perceived loudness from the audio signal energy. Because we recorded the audio signal from the microphone embedded in Google Glass, the recorder settings remained consistent for each participant. As a result, calibrating the intensity levels once for a single user gives us highly accurate loudness estimates for all of the participants. We used an open source audio processing library named PRAAT [4] to calculate the loudness levels for the participants. In order to run experiments to validate the interface, we calibrated the app based on the audio settings in our lab, where the ambient loudness was 30dB. As a result, we empirically determined that a range of 54dB to 58dB to be a medium range for giving a speech. Less than 54dB was regarded as "quiet" and greater than 58dB as "loud". We empirically adjusted these ranges and remained constant throughout the formal evaluation period. However, the application has the functionality to automatically calibrate these thresholds levels for each individual's natural level of loudness, allowing it to be deployed outside of the lab.

We employed an estimation of fundamental frequency to detect the voiced and unvoiced regions in the audio signal. From these regions we calculated the speaking rate of the participants. We used the pitch detection algorithm available in PRAAT proposed by Paul Boersma [3]. We created a routine to count the number of discontinuities within the pitch contour. This count gave a rough estimate of the number of words per second. This was a simple metric and fast enough for our application. The server stored the loudness and speaking rate values of the last five seconds to calculate a weighted average of the samples. We used appropriate weights to resemble the effect of a "leaky integrator" so that it removed the effect of high frequency noise from the calculated values of speaking rate.

METHODS

One of the fundamental challenges of this research was to design a feedback interface that can convey loudness and speaking rate measurements to a speaker with minimal distraction. To achieve this goal, we performed a principled design strategy as illustrated in Figure 3. We involved our users early on in the design process. In this regard, we formed a focus group for quick evaluation and redesign of the prototypes. The participants of the focus group were students and faculty members who regularly met during weekly Human-Computer Interaction (HCI) meetings at the department of Computer Science over the summer of 2014. Members of this focus group included two professors in Computer Science, two PhD students, one research programmer, and five undergraduate students. We describe each activity in the following sections.

Design Constraints

Based on our theoretical understanding, we decided that the intended feedback interface should use a secondary form of information delivery to avoid cognitive overload. Additionally, the feedback scheme should contain as few movements as possible in order to avoid unintentional attention drift. Lastly, the interface should contain temporal history of the user's performance. As we wanted to encourage the users to modulate their voice, showing only an instantaneous value of loudness and speaking rate was not enough to understand how they were modulating their voice.

Brainstorming Session

Before brainstorming the possible ideas and design choices for the interface, we solicited ideas from Reddit.com in the

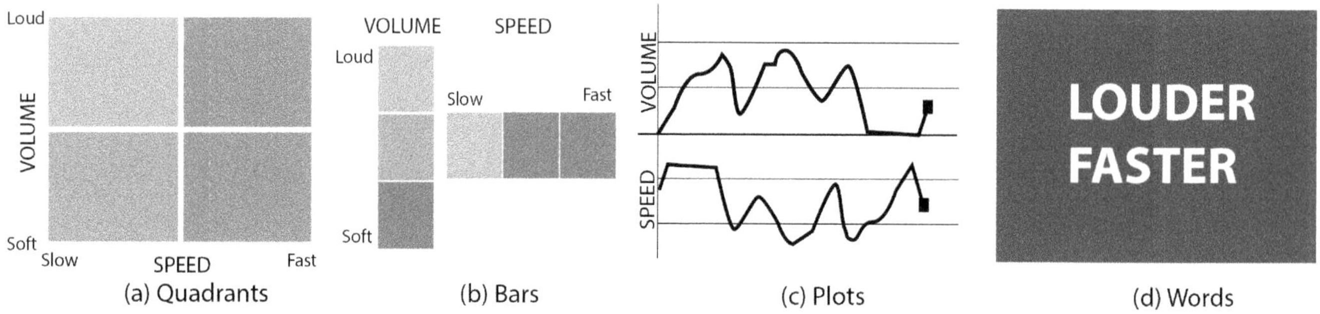

Figure 4: A few Feedback schemes that we explored for our interface

form of a survey. We particularly chose the forums "Futurama" and "HackerNews" since these communities are open to new and innovative ideas. We obtained a mixed response in this survey. 4 people out of 28 total respondents mentioned that it would be a bad idea to provide any information while a person is speaking because it would severely distract the speaker. However, many others proposed several feedback schemes. Seven respondents proposed displaying only raw numbers in decibels and words per second as a feedback scheme. Five participants proposed various forms of bar graphs (horizontal for speed, vertical for loudness, bars changing colors, decibel meters, etc.). Others proposed various icons, line graphs or traffic colors to represent volume and speaking rate.

In the brainstorming session with the focus group, we reviewed the proposed feedback schemes. Everyone in the focus group agreed that raw values or simple bar graphs would not be sufficient according to the design constraints because they do not contain enough temporal history. We converged on a few potentially viable designs from the brainstorming session as shown in Figure 4. The "*Quadrant*" feedback scheme (Figure 4a) resembles a 2D graph. The volume is on the y-axis and speed is on the x-axis. This graph is divided into four quadrants, each representing a range in volume and speed. When the user's voice is within a certain range, the corresponding box fades to green. If the user's voice hits a different range, that range will begin to fade to green and the previous range will start to fade back to red. The fading is slow enough so that more than one box can be green at once. Ideally, all the boxes turn green during a speech, indicating an appropriate amount of voice modulation. Presence of red boxes indicates that the user is not hitting that range for a considerable amount of time. The "*Bars*" feedback scheme (Figure 4b) involves two bars, each segmented into three regions. The vertical bar represents volume and the horizontal one is speed. The fading between red and green works the same way as in the Quadrant feedback scheme. Orientations of the bars were decided from people's natural tendency to associate high/low volume with up/down and fast/slow speed with left/right. This design allowed the users to immediately identify in a quick glance which bar is for volume and which one is for speaking rate. These two bars change independently of one another. The "*Plot*" feedback scheme (Figure 4c) plots raw data on two separate line graphs, one of volume on the top half of the display and one of speed on the bottom half. The Plot Feedback Scheme was selected for its ability to present temporal information and its intuitive representation of data, thus eliminating the learning curve. The "*Words*" feedback scheme (Figure 4d) displays nothing for 20 seconds; during this period, the system measures the speaker's voice modulation. For example, if the speaker spoke too quietly for a significant portion of the 20 seconds, then the word "LOUDER" will be displayed on the screen. Similarly, if the speaker spoke too loudly during the 20 seconds, the word "SOFTER" will appear on the screen. The same goes for speed ("FASTER" or "SLOWER"). If the speaker has adequately modulated their voice, either in volume or speaking rate or both, "good!" is displayed. These words are displayed for three seconds and then the Glass display becomes blank again for another 20 seconds. The 20 seconds of time interval was decided in our iterative informal evaluations. We found that any additional increase in this duration causes the user to question whether the app is working.

Iterative Implementation and Evaluation of Prototypes

In the next step, we started an iterative implementation and evaluation cycle. We implemented different versions of the Quads, Bars, Plots, and Words feedback scheme and evaluated empirically in the focus group discussions. We also built a number of other innovative feedback schemes. For example, we implemented "Audio Feedback" which functions like a metronome. It produces a ticking noise at a rate determined by the user's speaking rate. When the user talks too quickly for too long, the system starts ticking at a slower pace to encourage the user to slow down, and vice versa. Another feedback method we implemented is "Black and White". The display fades between black and white depending on the loudness of the user's voice. However, the last two prototypes could deliver only one variable (either volume or loudness) at a time. Using both schemes together was found to be too distracting and overwhelming.

One-to-One Interview Session

As we wanted to select only two feedback schemes for the formal evaluation, we needed to rank among the prototypes in terms of their efficacy. We arranged one-to-one

Figure 5: The setup for formal evaluation

interview sessions with 13 students to rank these prototypes. Before the interview session, all the participants were unfamiliar with the project. In total, 9 female and 4 male students participated. The participants ranged from 19 to 25 years old. We presented them with the Google Glass prototypes, explained the goal of the project, and allowed each participant to try each of the feedback schemes while reciting a poem or talking about him or herself. Once they were accustomed with all the prototypes, we asked them to choose their top two preferred versions of the interface and explain their choice. From their feedback, we found the following ranking: Words (11), Bars (8), Quadrant (6), and Plots (1). The quantitative data highlights the users' preference for sparse feedback over continuous feedback. This was further echoed in the participants' qualitative responses.

Statements related to speech	Overall, I am happy with the quality of my speech; I varied my volume appropriately; My speech was well paced; I showed appropriate body language; I maintained eye contact with audience
Statements related to Feedback Scheme	**Efficacy:** I found this feedback to be very helpful; The quality of my speech improved due to the feedback; The feedback was useful in helping me modulate my volume; The feedback was useful in helping me vary my speed; I felt distracted by the feedback; The usefulness of the feedback outweighed any distractions; **Learnability:** The feedback scheme was easy to learn; It was easy to follow while delivering my speech; The learning curve for using the feedback system is huge; **Future Use:** If available, I would love to use this feedback system in an actual speech

Table 1: List of statements as in the post-speech survey. The live form is available at http://tinyurl.com/rhemaSurvey

Figure 6: Sample snapshot from a recorded video of public speaking

EVALUATION

We evaluated Rhema in order to seek answers to the following questions:

- What value, if any, is added to the participants' performance while using the interface?
- Do the participants find the interface effective and easy to learn?
- Are there any noticeable side effects or distractions from the usage of Rhema?

Procedure

In order to answer these questions, we designed a formal user study where we asked the participants to deliver three speeches, three minutes in duration, while wearing Google Glass. Two speeches were delivered with the Google Glass display on, one with the "Words" feedback scheme and the other with the "Bars" feedback scheme. Another speech was delivered with the Google Glass display turned off, which served as a baseline. The participants wore Google Glass for the baseline to ensure that the results would not be influenced due to the mere existence of the Glass. Before the participants delivered the speeches with the Bars and Words feedback schemes, we explained the use of the interface to the users and set aside at least five minutes so that they may practice and familiarize themselves with it. We began the actual speech only when the participants said they were comfortable with the feedback scheme. The speakers chose three topics from a list of sample topics (e.g. favorite pastime, favorite book/movie/superhero, etc.) that we supplied for convenience. The topics were decided at least two days ahead of the presentation time to allow the participants to prepare. The order of both the topics and the Google Glass feedback schemes were counterbalanced to remove any ordering effects.

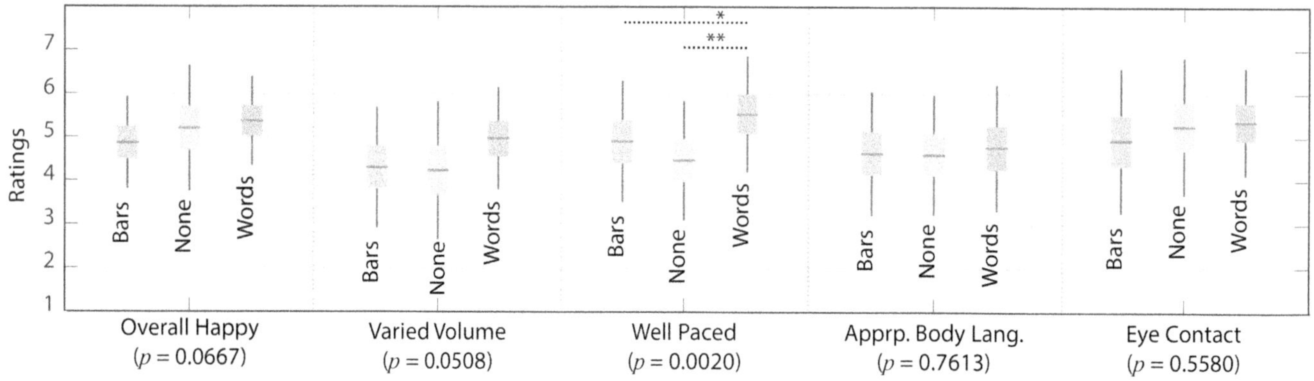

Figure 7: Boxplot of responses for each measure enlisted in the first row of Table 1

The study was conducted in a lab environment where each speech was recorded using a high definition video camera, as shown in Figure 5. Figure 6 shows a sample snapshot of the videos that we recorded. The camera was placed to capture the participant and a part of the audience's head. This allowed the viewers of the videos to judge if the speaker was maintaining eye contact with the audience. A brief interview session regarding the participants' experiences with the feedback schemes took place at the end of each study session.

Participants

We recruited 30 students from University of Rochester, of which 17 were male and 13 female. Their ages ranged from 18 to 32 and average age was 20. There were 10 freshmen, 4 sophomores, 4 juniors, 5 seniors, 4 graduate students, and 3 others. We posted flyers at different places throughout the campus, and we also posted recruitment messages in different Facebook groups associated with student activities. The study was limited to native speakers of English of at least 18 years of age.

Measures

To assess the extent of value that Rhema added to the participants' experiences, we asked our participants to fill out a survey related to their speaking performance. Participants filled it out immediately after delivering each speech. These measures are listed in the first row of Table 1 and are related to the participant's overall speech.

We asked the participants to fill out a different set of measures to assess the efficacy, learnability, and future use of the interface (Listed in the second row of Table 1). All the measures were answered in a 7-point Likert scale where 7 represents 'strongly agree.' Since these measures are only related to a particular feedback scheme (e.g. easy to follow, the associated learning curve, etc.), these are not applicable when no feedback exists. Thus, we have responses in these measures for Bars and Words feedback only.

Finally, to assess any noticeable effects of distractions arising from Rhema, we posted each video to Amazon Mechanical Turk. Ten different workers evaluated the videos. Table 2 presents the measures of ratings. The measures were selected to identify any possible effect of distraction. In order to ensure the quality of Mechanical Turk ratings, we opened the assignments only to workers with a good working history (i.e. master workers with >95% HIT acceptance rate and a total of >5000 accepted HITs). We considered the ratings from Mechanical Turk workers as anonymous opinions from a general audience.

RESULTS

Figure 7 illustrates a boxplot representing the participants' responses to the questions related to their speech. The responses are shown under three different groups representing three different feedback schemes. In the boxplot, the red horizontal line represents sample mean, the blue vertical line represents 1 standard deviation range and the box represents 95% confidence interval in t-test (for illustration purpose only). As the users rated on an ordinal scale (7-point Likert), we used non-parametric methods of calculating statistical significance. We used Friedman's test [9] to detect the differences among the groups. The p-value for this test is given within parentheses along the horizontal axis. Upon finding any significant differences among the groups, we used Wilcoxon's Signed Rank [25] test for pairwise comparison. We applied Bonferroni correction [7] to counteract the problems of multiple comparisons. In the box plot, we used one or two asterisks to represent differences with significance level 0.05 and 0.01

Statements	$K\alpha$
This person did not pause too often during the speech	0.28
This person maintained eye contact with whomever he or she was talking to	0.35
This person did not use a lot of filler words (Um, uh, basically etc.) during the speech	0.39
This person does not appear distracted	0.22
This person did not appear stiff during the speech (i.e. looks spontaneous)	0.30

Table 2: List of statements in the Mechanical Turk worker's questionnaire. $K\alpha$ represents the inter-rater agreement using Krippendorff's Alpha [14].

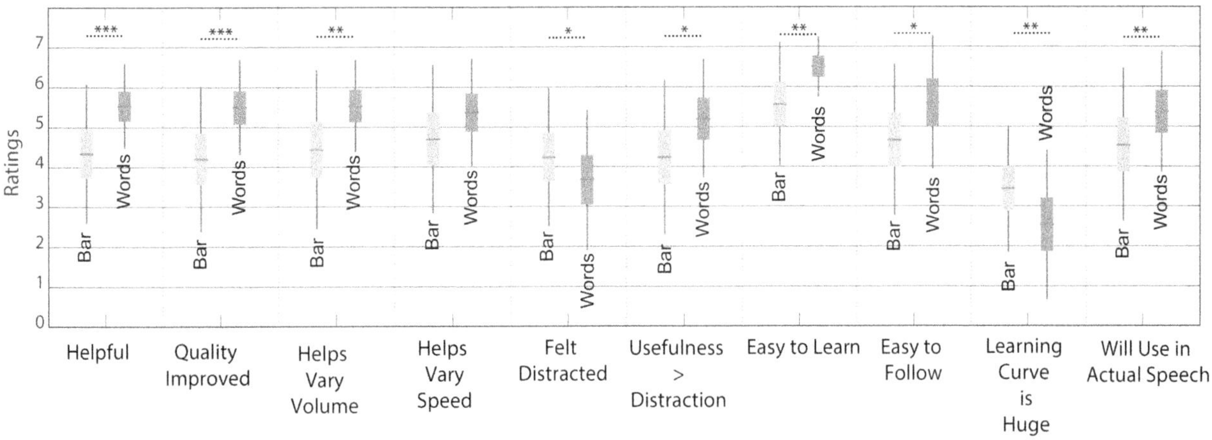

Figure 8: Boxplot of responses for each statement listed in the second row of Table 1

respectively. The plot illustrates that the participants rated their speech to be significantly well paced while using the Words feedback scheme. The Friedman's test rejects the null hypothesis with a p-value of 0.002 for this case. The p-value for the measure on whether the participants varied their volume was slightly higher than the significance level and thus failed to reject the null hypothesis.

Figure 8 represents the boxplots of responses to the measures related to the interface. As there are only two groups to be compared in this plot, we used Wilcoxon's Signed Rank test [25] to calculate the statistical significance. In the figure, we used one, two, or three asterisks to represent 0.05, 0.01, and 0.001 significance level. The plot shows that the Words feedback scheme is rated significantly better in most of the survey measures.

Measures from Mechanical Turkers

We considered the ratings provided by the Mechanical Turk workers in order to assess viewer's opinion (10 viewers per participant). While it is easy to get Mechanical Turk ratings, the workers are less likely to be experts in public speaking. Therefore, it was important to assess the reliability of the ratings. To determine the quality of the ratings, we calculated inter-rater agreement using Krippendorff's Alpha [14] as shown in Table 2. Kippendorff's alpha is a better metric than other methods of calculating inter-rater agreement (e.g. Cohen's Kappa [6]) because it allows any number of raters, missing data, and any type of measurement values (e.g. binary, nominal, ordinal, interval, etc.).

In our results, the agreement varied from 0.229 to 0.395 for different survey measures. We noticed that the agreement was highest for objective questions that asked the Turkers to rate the quality of eye contact and the use of filler words. On the other hand, it was lowest for the question on the speakers' level of distraction. We suspect different people might consider different criteria for assessing distraction (e.g. it might mean not making eye contact, not moving, or repeating the same words), which may have led to this poor agreement between the raters in this measure. Figure 9 shows the box plot of the responses.

To calculate the statistically significant differences in the ratings under different feedback schemes, we conducted Friedman's test. The p-values are reported within parentheses in Figure 9. Unfortunately, the test failed to reject the null hypothesis for any of the measures. This may result from the fact that the Turkers are not as trained as public speaking experts to identify nuance differences in a public speaker's performance. The suboptimal agreement in Turker's ratings also indicate that possibility.

Post Study Interview Results

As evidenced in the brief post-study interview sessions with the formal evaluation of participants, some form of real-time feedback during a live speech certainly has a beneficial effect. We asked each participant, "*Was x feedback useful or effective in reminding you to modulate your voice?*" All replied yes to either one or both of the feedback schemes they tried. Several reflected on their three speeches and concluded that the feedback "*definitely*

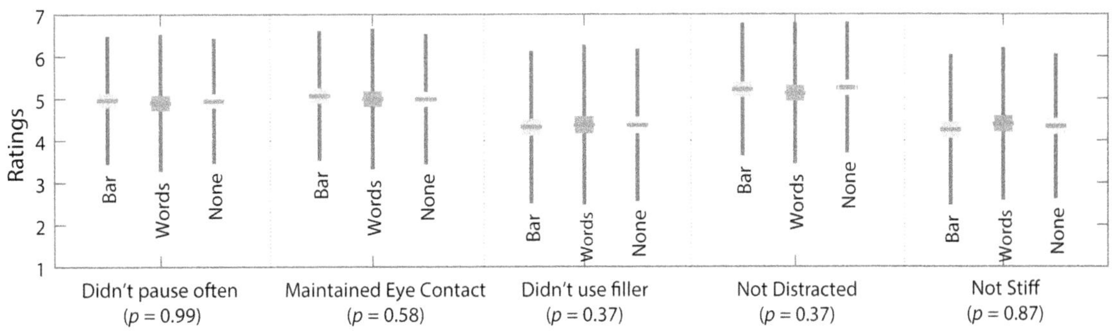

Figure 9: Boxplot of responses from Mechanical Turk Workers

helped" and "*made [them] more aware*" of their voice modulation, especially when they compared their speech with feedback to that with no feedback. Regardless of the type of feedback scheme, all participants said that the customized feedback "*actively changed how I spoke more*" or that "*it reminded me that I was supposed to change something*".

We also asked the participants about their preferred feedback scheme. 22 of the 30 participants preferred the Words feedback scheme, rather than the Bars, because the Words feedback was straightforward and simpler. Those who did not like Words complained that the feedback required additional effort from the language part of the brain since they were already using it for the content of their speech. However, other participants disagreed. One stated that the Words feedback scheme was "*less cognitively demanding while giving a speech*" as it was "*more straightforward.*" Several found it useful that the Words feedback scheme displayed "*information that could be parsed a little more quickly*" as it only showed two pieces of data for a few seconds at a time.

> *"It was just enough information that I could take in while also talking, but not too much information that it was overwhelming."*

Eight of the 30 participants preferred the Bars feedback scheme rather than the Words. Some preferred it because it contained more information that was always readily available on the screen, and this constant feedback felt reassuring to them. They also liked the visual aspect of it and that the "*visual nature of it didn't interfere with the words [they] were thinking of.*" However, many did not find the Bars useful or effective. Several participants did not know how to interpret or apply the information to their voice. The Bars feedback scheme was also clearly confusing; two participants explicitly told us during the post-speech interview that they wondered, "*What am I supposed to do with this?*" and "*What does it mean?*" while using the Bars feedback. Some found it too overwhelming and complex and ended up completely ignoring it. One participant explained that

> *"It was so complicated that I couldn't use it. The pause I would have to take to process the information was so great that I couldn't maintain my speech."*

Aside from these general overall trends in opinions on the feedback schemes, personal preferences drove many of the participants' responses. For example, some are more receptive to visuals – those who preferred the Bars feedback scheme thought it worked well because they consider themselves "*visual thinker[s]*". They also varied in the amount of information they wanted to see: one participant suggested using less boxes in the Bars feedback system, and another suggested using many more boxes; some wanted to see the words appear more frequently, whereas others thought the implemented frequency was good. Some participants thought the Bars feedback was easier to ignore, while others were more likely to disregard the Words feedback. From this, we concluded that the efficacy, usefulness, and level of distraction of the different feedback schemes vary largely as a result of the users' personal preferences and tendencies.

DISCUSSIONS AND CONCLUSION

In this work, we implemented a fully functional, real time Google Glass interface to help people with public speaking. The interface provides live feedback regarding the user's volume and speaking rate. The primary objective was to maximize the usefulness of our system by minimizing the level of distraction.

From the quantitative and qualitative evaluations of our system, we can safely conclude that the participants found the interface valuable to their speaking performance. The qualitative study reflects that the participants rated the Words feedback to be effective in varying their speaking rate and significantly easier to learn than the Bars feedback scheme. We hypothesize that this is the effect of our Sparse information delivery strategy and recommendation-based feedback scheme. Unfortunately, we could not conclusively measure the level of distraction from the audience's perception. As the Mechanical Turk raters were not experts in public speaking, their ratings did not agree and also failed to pass any hypothesis tests. It is possible to address this in the future by involving expert opinions from the Toastmasters International Organization.

We collected Kinect [26] depth information while the participants delivered their speech, and we will leverage this dataset to train machine learning algorithms that can analyze and predict speaking performance from a combination of the speaker's voice patterns, facial expressions, and body language. We will show these predicted performances to the users and offer live recommendations to help them further improve their public speaking skills and speech delivery.

This research also has a number of implications for future endeavors. Presenting information sporadically through secondary display might be a generic strategy in situations with cognitive or attentional overload. The preliminary observation described in this paper calls for further investigation in this area. In addition, we see room to explore the potential for haptic feedback schemes in similar situations.

Our current prototype was originally designed to give novice speakers real-time feedback on voice modulation. However, as the system already sends the audio data to a server, this data could be used to provide post-speech feedback to the user. Such a system could be useful for even expert users because it would allow them to review the speech and check for mistakes in retrospect. Without the need for instantaneous feedback, such a system could be adapted to a range of wearable technologies including smart

phones. Rhema is available for download in the following webpage:
www.cs.rochester.edu/hci/currentprojects.php?proj=rh

ACKNOWLEDGEMENT

This research was developed through a generous gift from the Google Faculty Research Award. We would like to thank all the participants in the research study. We thank our anonymous reviewers for many helpful comments.

REFERENCES

1. Batrinca, L., Stratou, G., Shapiro, A., Morency, L.-P., and Scherer, S. Cicero-towards a multimodal virtual audience platform for public speaking training. *Intelligent Virtual Agents*, Springer (2013), 116–128.
2. Biocca, F., Owen, C., Tang, A., and Bohil, C. Attention Issues in Spatial Information Systems: Directing Mobile Users' Visual Attention Using Augmented Reality. *Journal of Management Information Systems 23*, 2007, 163–184.
3. Boersma, P. Accurate short-term analysis of the fundamental frequency and the harmonics-to-noise ratio of a sampled sound. *IFA Proceedings 17*, (1993), 97–110.
4. Boersma, Paul ;Weenink, D. Praat: Doing Phonetics by Computer. *Ear and Hearing 32*, 2011, 266.
5. Chollet, M. et al. An interactive virtual audience platform for public speaking training. *Autonomous agents and multi-agent systems*, (2014), 1657–1658.
6. Cohen, J. A coefficient of agreement of nominal scales. *Educational and Psychological Measurement 20*, (1960), 37–46.
7. Dunn, O.J. Multiple Comparisons Among Means. *Journal of the American Statistical Association 56*, (1961), 52–64.
8. Finlay, D. Motion perception in the peripheral visual field. *Perception 11*, 1982, 457–462.
9. Friedman, M. A comparison of alternative tests of significance for the problem of m rankings. *The Annals of Mathematical Statistics 11*, 1 (1940), 86–92.
10. Ha, K., Chen, Z., Hu, W., Richter, W., Pillai, P., and Satyanarayanan, M. Towards wearable cognitive assistance. *MobiSys '14*, (2014), 68–81.
11. Hoogterp, B. *Your Perfect Presentation: Speak in Front of Any Audience Anytime Anywhere and Never Be Nervous Again*. McGraw Hill Professional, 2014.
12. Hoque, M., Courgeon, M., and Martin, J. Mach: My automated conversation coach. *Proceedings of the 2013 ACM international joint conference on Pervasive and ubiquitous computing*, (2013), 697–706.
13. Koppensteiner, M. and Grammer, K. Motion patterns in political speech and their influence on personality ratings. *Journal of Research in Personality 44*, (2010), 374–379.
14. Krippendorff, K. *Content Analysis: An Introduction to Its Methodology*. 2004.
15. McAtamney, G. and Parker, C. An examination of the effects of a wearable display on informal face-to-face communication. *Proceedings of ACM CHI 2006 Conference on Human Factors in Computing Systems*, (2006), 45–54.
16. McCrickard, D.S., Catrambone, R., Chewar, C.M., and Stasko, J.T. Establishing tradeoffs that leverage attention for utility: Empirically evaluating information display in notification systems. *International Journal of Human Computer Studies 58*, (2003), 547–582.
17. North, M.M., North, S.M., Coble, J.R., et al. Virtual reality therapy: an effective treatment for the fear of public speaking. *The International Journal of Virtual Reality 3 (1998), 1 3*, (1998).
18. Ofek, E., Iqbal, S.T., and Strauss, K. Reducing disruption from subtle information delivery during a conversation: mode and bandwidth investigation. *Proceedings of CHI 2013*, (2013), 3111–3120.
19. Pashler, H. Dual-task interference in simple tasks: data and theory. *Psychological bulletin 116*, (1994).
20. Shiffrin, R.M. and Gardner, G.T. Visual processing capacity and attentional control. *Journal of experimental psychology 93*, (1972), 72–82.
21. Strangert, E. and Gustafson, J. What makes a good speaker? subject ratings, acoustic measurements and perceptual evaluations. *INTERSPEECH*, (2008), 1688–1691.
22. Strayer, D.L., Drews, F.A., and Crouch, D.J. Fatal distraction? A comparison of the cell-phone driver and the drunk driver. *Human Factors: The Journal of the Human Factors and Ergonomics Society 48*, (2006), 381–391.
23. Teeters, A., Kaliouby, R. El, and Picard, R. Self-Cam: feedback from what would be your social partner. *ACM SIGGRAPH 2006 Research posters*, (2006).
24. Wallechinsky, D. *The book of lists*. Canongate Books, 2009.
25. Wilcoxon, F. Individual comparisons of grouped data by ranking methods. *Journal of economic entomology 39*, (1946), 269.
26. Zhang, Z. Microsoft kinect sensor and its effect. *MultiMedia, IEEE 19*, 2 (2012), 4–10.

Managing Smartphone Interruptions through Adaptive Modes and Modulation of Notifications

Hugo Lopez-Tovar
UCL Interaction Centre
University College London
h.tovar.11@ucl.ac.uk

Andreas Charalambous
Dept. of Computer Science
University College London
andreas.charalambous.10@ucl.ac.uk

John Dowell
UCL Interaction Centre
University College London
j.dowell@cs.ucl.ac.uk

ABSTRACT
Smartphones are capable of alerting their users to different kinds of digital interruption using different modalities and with varying modulation. Smart notification is the capability of a smartphone for selecting the user's preferred kind of alert in particular situations using the full vocabulary of notification modalities and modulations. It therefore goes well beyond attempts to predict if or when to silence a ringing phone call. We demonstrate smart notification for messages received from a document retrieval system while the user is attending a meeting. The notification manager learns about their notification preferences from users' judgements about videos of meetings. It takes account of the relevance of the interruption to the meeting, whether the user is busy and the sensed location of the smartphone. Through repeated training, the notification manager learns to reliably predict the preferred notification modes for users and this learning continues to improve with use.

Author Keywords
Adaptation; Smartphone notification; Interruption; Alert modality; Machine learning.

ACM Classification Keywords
H.5.m. Information Interfaces and Presentation (e.g. HCI): Miscellaneous

INTRODUCTION
Managing their digital interruptions is a pressing issue for smartphone users. All leading operating systems allow users to customize notification protocols and some third party apps considerably extend customization capabilities. But customized notifications are only a partial solution to the interruption issue. Apart from the overhead for users of learning to configure notification settings and continuing to maintain them [6], customized notifications do not discriminate between interruptions of varying importance and urgency in different contexts where users' receptivity varies [2]. Smart notification is the idea of an automatic personalisation of notifications, notifications adapted and optimised to the individual user. It would manage the user's digital interruptions either by selectively delaying notifications to a more suitable moment, or by selecting an appropriate modality or modulation for the notification, for example, by turning off alert sounds.

IUI'15, March 29 - April 01, 2015, Atlanta, GA, USA
Copyright 2015 ACM 978-1-4503-3306-1/15/03:...$15.00.
http://dx.doi.org/10.1145/2678025.2701390

Smart notification has demonstrated that it is able to predict users' preferences for delaying phone call notifications in different contexts. The InterruptMe system [7] used explicit experience sampling to model a user's interruptibility in relation to context and then used this model to predict which notifications should be delayed. Approaches have also been demonstrated that mitigate the interruption caused by phone calls by silencing the notification but leaving the visual alert. The Ringlearn system [9] learned preferences for when to silence phone call notifications in different settings whilst the In-Context system [3] learnt when to silence phone call notifications taking account of different levels of user interruptibility.

The study of managing interruptions by smartphones follows the path of investigation in other contexts, for example performing office tasks with desktop computers [4, 8]. These studies have most often focused on managing phone calls, for example the Bayesphone system [5] demonstrated the use of the mobile device as a way to calculate interruption cost of incoming calls in the office context. However, phone calls are only one source of interruption for smart phone users who now must contend with notifications from a wide variety of digital services. These new kinds of interruption extend the vocabulary of notification with multiple modalities, formats and levels. For example, an interruption from a social network will often require a more nuanced notification than a phone call. Rather than simply a binary choice of alert now or later, or of let ring or silence [9], notifications require more carefully calibrated alert cues in visual, auditory and tactile modalities.

We demonstrate smart notification where the appropriate intervention is to adapt the notification modality and to modulate the alert cue. The notifications are messages from a simulated document retrieval agent system within a smart meeting room offering the user documents relevant to the meeting they are attending at particular junctures in the meeting. The system uses a Bayes Network to calculate the preferred notification method based on context where the data is obtained from participant analysis of videos of meetings. Evaluation showed the system to be capable of anticipating a majority of users' notification preferences and will continue adapting to changes in the user's preferences.

STUDY AND DATA COLLECTION

To train the notification manager to predict a person's preferences for alerts while they are attending a meeting, we used recordings of meetings and asked participants to judge those meetings as though they themselves were present. We selected short videos of meetings [Fig. 1] from the AMI corpus [1] covering 22 different kinds of scenario. 70 participants were asked to watch the videos and for each they were asked to choose their preferred notification method given the context: imagining they were present in the meeting and either speaking or listening; supposing their mobile device was in a particular position (in their pocket; face down on the table; on a stand on the table; holding it) and expecting a given level of notification relevance (i.e. high/low). In this study, we have considered loud and discrete modulations for the sound modality. The rest of the modalities (i.e. text notification, flashing LED, vibration) don't allow different modulation levels.

The results showed that in only 45% of the scenarios would a binary classification of notification method (e.g. vibration and audible notification) be appropriate, while for the remainder, participants preferences were more or less equally distributed among the many available notification methods. Figure 2 shows examples for both situations and graphically confirms the argument for adapting mode and modulation of notifications to better calibrate the disturbance, rather than relying on a binary choice. Table 1 lists the summary of preferred notification methods by specific scenarios.

The full participants' responses have been aggregated to produce the default profile of preferences for our evaluation system, assuming it represents the notification preferences for the average user. This default profile of preferences consists of the probability distributions for each notification method given the context.

Figure 1. Example of meeting video presented to study participants. ©*Image from the AMI meeting corpus.*

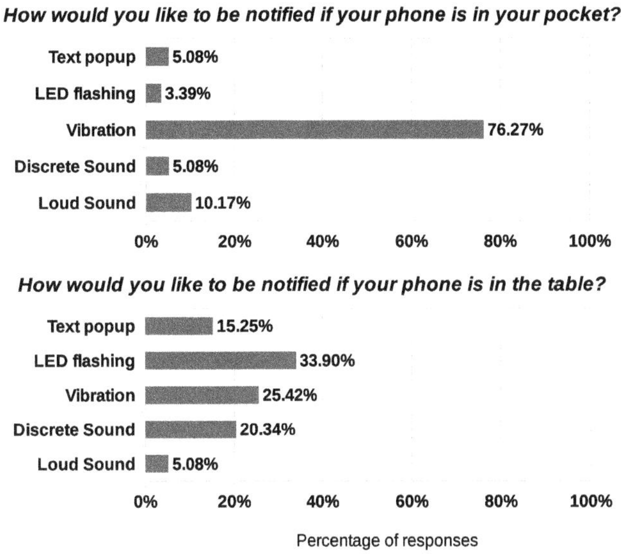

Figure 2. Above, a case where most of participants agree in a single notification method. Below, a case where participants' preferred method varies along the different notification methods.

ADAPTATION PROCEDURE

To infer the preferred notification mode given the context, a Bayesian Network is used as our statistical model, allowing us to represent the context as variables and their relationships as dependencies. The set of variables includes the relevance (low/high) of the interruption (i.e., whether the message from the document agent is currently relevant to the meeting), whether or not the person is speaking, and the mobile device position (pocket, stand, holding and table). Separate tests have shown that it is possible to reliably discriminate these different positions from a combination of accelerometer, gyroscope and ambient light sensor states.

The probability distributions of our model are initialised using the default profile generated from the collected data during our study and are updated with every feedback obtained from the user, i.e. whether they confirm that the proposed notification is acceptable. We have included a general probability distribution over the success of the notification methods considering only the device position (i.e. independent of notification relevance and speaking status) to overcome the problem of not having feedback on unseen scenarios, which is also updated with the participant responses.

Phone Loc.	High Relevance		Low Relevance	
In pocket	Vibr 71%	Vibr 76%	*Vibr 42%	*Vibr 47%
On the table	*LED 40%	*LED 34%	*LED 44%	LED 52%
On a stand	*LED 40%	*LED 49%	*LED 44%	*LED 45%
Holding it	Vibr 65%	Vibr 69%	*Vib 42%	*Vib/text 39%

Table 1. Summary of preferred notification methods from the initial collection of users' preferences, including the percentage of participants that selected the given notification method based on the notification relevance. Entries marked with * denote scenarios where other methods have also been selected by a significant number of participants.

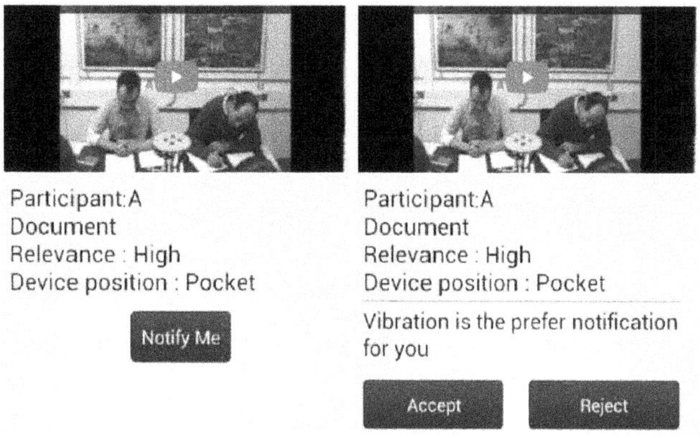

Figure 3. Left (3a), presented context scenario, allowing users to think about their preferred notification method. Right (3b), inferred notification method which can be accepted or rejected. ©*Images from the AMI meeting corpus.*

In the case of an accepted notification, the probability distributions are updated to give advantage to this particular notification method given the variable values. When the participant rejects the notification mode, their response doesn't include information about their actual preferred mode, so in this case the probability distributions are adjusted to reduce the likelihood of this particular notification method, favouring the others. To allow the agent to adapt to the participant's current preferences, we have implemented an ageing process to give more weight to recent user feedback. We calculate the weight w by a decreasing function of the form $w = k(x^2)$ where x is the number of days a decision-response pair was given as feedback by the user, and k is a constant inversely proportional to the maximum number of days being considered.

EVALUATION

Setup

To evaluate our prototype smart notification manager, ten participants were asked to confirm its predictions about their preferred notifications, again using a set of meeting videos. At this stage of course the Bayesian Network model was using the default profile generated from the study data and so its predictions were for a nominal average user. Its ability to adapt to the personal preferences of individual participants would be a key criterion for the system's success.

For the system's training phase, participants were presented with a set of short meeting videos representing different scenarios. For each video, the participants would first be presented with the context information, allowing them to picture themselves in the given situation [Fig. 3a]. They were told which person they should consider themselves to be in the video (e.g. person A), how relevant to the meeting is the document being offered, and the current position of their smartphone. The notification manager then proposes to them the method of notification it predicted they would prefer in this precise situation (e.g., "Vibration is the preferred notification for you"). The participant would then confirm whether this prediction was correct [Fig. 3b]. The feedback obtained from each scenario was used to update the probability distributions

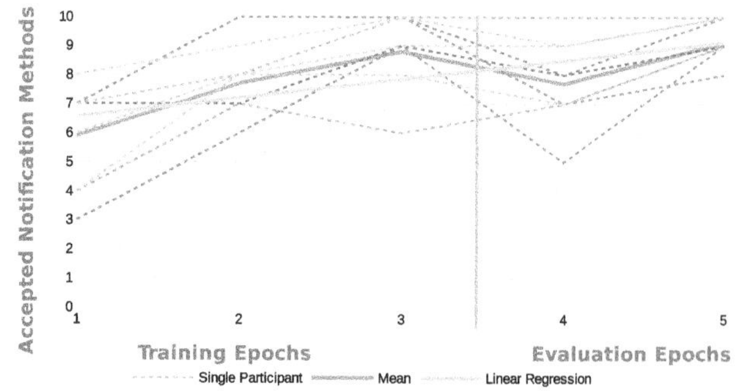

Figure 4. Number of accepted inferred notification methods by epoch. Each dotted line represents a single evaluation participant, solid lines represent the average acceptance and the linear regression.

for the next videos. To evaluate the progress of adaptation, we grouped the presented videos in sets of 10, each group constituting an 'epoch'. For the training phase, we presented the same 10 videos during three epochs to evaluate the adaptation on previously seen videos. We then presented two more epochs of 10 unseen videos each to evaluate adaptation on unseen scenarios. This made a total of 30 videos (i.e. 10 for training, 20 for evaluation).

Results

Figure 4 shows a plot with the evaluation results by epoch, indicating that:

- By the end of the training phase, every participant accepted from 2 to 6 more proposed notifications methods.
- By the end of the evaluation phase, most participants accepted from 2 to 6 more proposed notifications methods than before adaptation, except one which began and ended in 80% acceptance (reaching 100% at the end of training phase).

By analysing the mean of the participants' responses, we can see that:

- By using the default profile (i.e. no adaptation), the initial notification method was accepted in 5.92 out of 10 scenarios with a dispersion in the range of 3 to 8.
- By the end of the training phase, the number of accepted notification methods had increased to an average of 8.8 in 10 scenarios (a 60% improvement).
- By the end of the evaluation phase, the number of correctly predicted notification methods had increased to 9.1 (a 70% improvement compared to no adaptation).

Using linear regression analysis, we calculate a Correlation Coefficient r of 0.8056, confirming strong positive correlation between the epoch and the amount of accepted notification methods. In other words, as the number of epochs increase, more notification methods are accepted. Analysis of variance over all the epochs shows that the number of accepted notifications increases significantly ($F = 7.587$, $P < 0.0001$).

These results show that the default profile is an appropriate starting point and that the system continues to adapt to the user's preferences in an agile way. They also demonstrate that it is possible to adapt by exploiting feedback limited to acceptance or rejection, without requiring the user to provide their actual preferred notification method.

CONCLUSIONS

Smartphones are capable of providing notifications in many different ways for different kinds of situation. That capability is under-exploited and typically only a manual switching between ringing and vibrating notifications for phone calls is used. The idea of smart notification is of a smartphone able to learn a user's preferences for notifications of different kinds in different situations. Notification would adapt to the type of interruption, the user's receptivity to interruptions and the particular context including where the device itself is currently positioned.

Research on smart notification has to date focused narrowly on managing phone call notifications. We have investigated document delivery notifications by smartphones in the setting of a smart meeting room. We have confirmed the need for adapting notifications to multiple modalities and modulations through a study where participants were asked to watch short videos of meetings and to identify their preferred notification method given the context as though they themselves were present in the meeting. Results show that in slightly more than half of the scenarios, users' preferred notification methods cannot be categorised only in two modalities.

For our adaptation model we chose a Bayesian Network that allows us to define the context as variables and their relationships as dependencies. The Bayesian Network is initialised with the probability distributions of the consensus data collected from the study. This proved to be a suitable starting point for our model which reached an average of 59% of accepted notifications before adaptation took place, in a range of 30% to 80%, which shows the dispersion of users' preferences.

For the evaluation of our model the results show that the system continuously adapts to the user's preferences in an agile way for both already experienced and unseen scenarios. Results also show that acceptance/rejection feedback is enough for our system to adapt, easing the work to the users.

The presented work contributes to research on smart notification by:

- expanding the scope of work to exploit the tasks and events that smartphones now make available, beyond simply incoming calls.
- demonstrating that broadening the vocabulary of notification modalities and modulations improves adaptation to manage users' interruptions by their smartphones.

Although conducting the validation in the laboratory using meeting videos rather than in a trial involving real meetings does not fully validate the efficacy of the system, it provides nevertheless quite compelling evidence. Whilst a field trial would offer much greater ecological validity, the lack of controls would mean that the effects of the adaptation process we have developed would be observed together with effects from other contextual factors, hence the importance of clear results in the laboratory. Having established these results in the laboratory, a field trial of the system should now be conducted.

In our model, our interpretation of users' interruptibility is limited to whether or not they are talking. Broadening this concept, as well as the representation of the context, could help to improve the adaptation to more specific situations. It also remains to investigate to what degree users are tolerant of adaptation inaccuracy.

REFERENCES

1. Carletta, J., Ashby, S., Bourban, S., Flynn, M., Guillemot, M., Hain, T., Kadlec, J., Karaiskos, V., Kraaij, W., Kronenthal, M., et al. The ami meeting corpus: A pre-announcement. In *Machine learning for multimodal interaction*. Springer, 2006, 28–39.
2. Fischer, J. E., Yee, N., Bellotti, V., Good, N., Benford, S., and Greenhalgh, C. Effects of content and time of delivery on receptivity to mobile interruptions. In *Proceedings of the 12th international conference on Human computer interaction with mobile devices and services*, ACM (2010), 103–112.
3. Fisher, R., and Simmons, R. Smartphone interruptibility using density-weighted uncertainty sampling with reinforcement learning. In *Machine Learning and Applications and Workshops (ICMLA), 2011 10th International Conference on*, vol. 1, IEEE (2011), 436–441.
4. Horvitz, E., and Apacible, J. Learning and reasoning about interruption. In *Proceedings of the 5th international conference on Multimodal interfaces*, ACM (2003), 20–27.
5. Horvitz, E., Koch, P., Sarin, R., Apacible, J., and Subramani, M. Bayesphone: Precomputation of context-sensitive policies for inquiry and action in mobile devices. In *User Modeling 2005*. Springer, 2005, 251–260.
6. Khalil, A., and Connelly, K. Context-aware configuration: A study on improving cell phone awareness. In *Modeling and Using Context*. Springer, 2005, 197–209.
7. Pejovic, V., and Musolesi, M. Interruptme: designing intelligent prompting mechanisms for pervasive applications. In *Proceedings of the 2014 ACM International Joint Conference on Pervasive and Ubiquitous Computing*, ACM (2014), 897–908.
8. Shrot, T., Rosenfeld, A., Golbeck, J., and Kraus, S. Crisp: an interruption management algorithm based on collaborative filtering. In *Proceedings of the 32nd annual ACM conference on Human factors in computing systems*, ACM (2014), 3035–3044.
9. Smith, J., and Dulay, N. Ringlearn: Long-term mitigation of disruptive smartphone interruptions. In *Pervasive Computing and Communications Workshops (PERCOM Workshops), 2014 IEEE International Conference on*, IEEE (2014), 27–35.

IntentStreams: Smart Parallel Search Streams for Branching Exploratory Search

Salvatore Andolina[1], Khalil Klouche[1,4], Jaakko Peltonen[2,3], Mohammad Hoque[1], Tuukka Ruotsalo[2], Diogo Cabral[1], Arto Klami[1], Dorota Głowacka[1], Patrik Floréen[1,2], and Giulio Jacucci[1,2]
Helsinki Institute for Information Technology HIIT
[1]University of Helsinki, Department of Computer Science, Finland
[2]Aalto University, Finland [3]University of Tampere, School of Information Sciences, Finland
[4]Aalto University, Media Lab, Finland

ABSTRACT
The user's understanding of information needs and the information available in the data collection can evolve during an exploratory search session. Search systems tailored for well-defined narrow search tasks may be suboptimal for exploratory search where the user can sequentially refine the expressions of her information needs and explore alternative search directions. A major challenge for exploratory search systems design is how to support such behavior and expose the user to relevant yet novel information that can be difficult to discover by using conventional query formulation techniques. We introduce IntentStreams, a system for exploratory search that provides interactive query refinement mechanisms and parallel visualization of search streams. The system models each search stream via an intent model allowing rapid user feedback. The user interface allows swift initiation of alternative and parallel search streams by direct manipulation that does not require typing. A study with 13 participants shows that IntentStreams provides better support for branching behavior compared to a conventional search system.

Author Keywords
User interface design; information exploration; parallel browsing.

ACM Classification Keywords
H.5.m. Information Interfaces and Presentation (e.g. HCI): Miscellaneous

INTRODUCTION
Exploratory search activities confront users with problems in formulating queries and identifying directions for information exploration. Studies show that searchers tend to perform more than one task simultaneously: approximately 75% of submitted queries involve a multitasking activity [22, 21]. Users engage in multitask search with and without parallel browsing, but parallel browsing is a common activity and more prevalent than linear browsing. In parallel browsing, also called branching [13], users visit web pages in multiple concurrent threads, for example, by opening multiple tabs or windows in web browsers [14]. Branching in browsing has been studied extensively [6], but little has been done to support nonlinear and parallel browsing. Recent visual search user interfaces have shown the effectiveness of interacting visually with query elements, however, there are no solutions to support fluid branching and parallel search.

We introduce IntentStreams, a system supporting parallel browsing and branching during search without the need to open new tabs. It presents parallel streams of searches, where each stream shows a list of resulting documents and keywords, and a display of the underlying queries as keywords representing the search intent of the stream. New streams are initiated by the user, where the search intent of a new stream is initialized by typing a traditional query or by dragging keywords available in any of the streams. In each stream, in addition to the user-chosen keywords, the system proposes other relevant keywords and orders them vertically by their predicted relevance. The users can change the relative relevance of keywords in the query intent of each stream and branch new streams by simply dragging keywords. IntentStreams was tested using 25 million news articles crawled from public news sources in a comparative study with 13 subjects.

The experimental results show that IntentStreams better supports parallel search and branching behavior when compared to a conventional search system.

Exploratory search is commonly distinguished from lookup search and has been described as combining exploratory browsing and focused searching [23, 5]. These and other information seeking frameworks [23, 27] partially overlap, emphasizing different aspects but similarly trying to characterise iterative sense making and refinement of search intents. As a response, personalization techniques have been developed to support query formulation and relevance feedback. Several techniques exist for supporting query formulation or for processing results to help re-rank, filter [31] or expand the query [8, 26]. For example, relevance feedback [16] and query or term suggestions [17] can be effective in short-term navigational search, but give limited support for exploratory

IUI 2015, March 29–April 1, 2015, Atlanta, GA, USA.

http://dx.doi.org/10.1145/2678025.2701401

search. However, increasing evidence in information retrieval research suggests relevance feedback in exploratory search often leads to a context trap where after a few iterations of feedback users have specified their context so strictly the system is unable to propose anything new [12, 23].

Visual search interfaces. Recently, search systems use visualization of the resulting information for faster relevance judgment and effective feedback [11, 15, 20, 24, 32]. Several approaches to visualize results have been explored, including multiple linked lists, scatter plots, graphs and their combinations [30, 20]. Such visual search systems are distinguished from traditional query composition ones through their emphasis on rapid filtering to reduce result sets, progressive refinement of search parameters, continuous reformulation of goals, and visual scanning to identify results [1]. Visual approaches provide better support for exploration in a variety of ways: supporting sense making by incrementally and interactively exploring the network of data [7], showing how visualization supports user involvement in the recommendation providing rationale behind suggested items [34], visualizing relations of different queries and result sets [2], supporting entity search on touch devices [18]. Recent work shows how users can view and manipulate their search intent models provided by the system [2, 3, 29, 9, 28]. However, there is still a lack of solutions that specifically address branching behavior while supporting query formulation.

INTENTSTREAMS

A user performing exploratory search typically needs to steer the exploration by query refining or reformulating as she makes better sense of the information space. We identified two challenges impairing a proper steering support:

1. Supporting information comparison from several queries: Traditional search systems show one set of results at a time. To compare information from distinct queries, one must rely on memory or complicated browser windows arrangements.

2. Formulating queries in unknown areas: Exploratory search tasks usually require the user to iteratively formulate queries in a field she is unfamiliar with. To progress with the search, the used needs to go through long lists of results with low information gain to acquire new terms and notions to reformulate the query.

We tackle these challenges through a combination of a user interface supporting parallel search streams, and user intent modeling.

The User Interface

IntentStreams provides a unique horizontally scrollable workspace divided in two areas: the keywords area at the bottom and the results area on top (Figure 1). By clicking the workspace, the user is prompted to type a first query. The system returns a list of relevant documents in the results area and a set of related keywords in the keywords area. Keywords are positioned vertically by weight and horizontally by topic proximity. The vertical arrangement is called a stream and can be easily manipulated, modified and refreshed. The content of a document can be seen by clicking the title. A click and hold on a document highlights keywords directly related to it. A click and hold on a keyword highlights related documents. By moving keywords vertically, the user can change their weight; by hitting the refresh button, the stream then updates and presents a new set of documents and keywords. New parallel streams can be created by clicking next to an existing stream and typing a new query, or simply by dragging a keyword outside of its stream. Since the workspace is horizontally scrollable, the amount of parallel streams a user can create is limited only by computer memory. The amount of parallel streams that can be shown simultaneously is determined by the display resolution. Streams can be dragged and rearranged. A button lets the user delete streams.

Interactive Intent Model

For each search stream, the interactive intent model is similar to the model in a previous non-parallel system [29] and has two parts: a model for retrieval of documents, and a model for estimating the user's search intent (relevance of keywords to the user's information need). We describe both below.

Document retrieval model. For each stream, we estimate a relevance ranking where documents are ranked by their probability given the intent model for the stream. We use a unigram language model. The intent model yields a vector $\hat{\mathbf{v}}$ with a weight $\hat{v}_i$ for each keyword k_i. The $\hat{\mathbf{v}}$ is treated as a sample of a desired document. Documents d_j are ranked by probability to observe $\hat{\mathbf{v}}$ as a sample from the language model M_{d_j} of d_j. Maximum likelihood estimation yields $\hat{P}(\hat{\mathbf{v}}|M_{d_j}) = \prod_{i=1}^{|\hat{\mathbf{v}}|}(\hat{P}_{mle}(k_i|M_{d_j}))^{\hat{v}_i}$. We regularize probabilities $\hat{P}_{mle}(k_i|M_{d_j})$ in d_j towards overall keyword proportions in the corpus by Bayesian Dirichlet smoothing. In each stream the d_j are ranked by $\alpha_j = \hat{P}(\hat{\mathbf{v}}|M_{d_j})$. To expose the user to more novel documents we sample a document set from the ranking and show them in rank order. As in [9, 29] we use Dirichlet Sampling based on the α_j, and favor documents whose keywords got positive feedback by increasing their α_j [10].

User intent model. For each stream, the intent model estimates relevance of keywords from feedback to keywords. For a stream launched by a typed query, we use the query with weight 1 as the initial intent model; for a stream launched by dragging a keyword we use the keyword with weight 1. The user gives feedback as relevance scores $r_i \in [0, 1]$ for a subset of J keywords $k_i, i = 1, \ldots, J$ in the stream; $r_i = 1$ means k_i is highly relevant and the user wishes to direct the stream in that direction, and $r_i = 0$ means k_i is of no interest.

Let $\mathbf{k}_i$ be binary $n \times 1$ vectors telling which of the n documents k_i appeared in; to boost documents with rare keywords we convert the $\mathbf{k}_i$ to *tf-idf* representation. We estimate the expected relevance r_i of a keyword k_i as $\mathbb{E}[r_i] = \mathbf{k}_i^\top \mathbf{w}$. The vector $\mathbf{w}$ is estimated from user feedback by the LinRel algorithm [4]. In each search iteration, let $k_1, \ldots, k_p$ be the keywords for which the user gave feedback so far, let $\mathbf{K} = [\mathbf{k}_1, \ldots, \mathbf{k}_p]^\top$ be the matrix of their feature vectors, and let $\mathbf{r}^{feedback} = [r_1, r_2, \ldots, r_p]^\top$ be their relevance scores from the user. LinRel estimates $\hat{\mathbf{w}}$ by solving $\mathbf{r}^{feedback} = \mathbf{K}\mathbf{w}$, and estimates relevance score for each k_i as $\hat{r}_i = \mathbf{k}_i^\top \hat{\mathbf{w}}$.

Figure 1. a. The first query (in this case mobile phone") returns a search stream composed of news articles most relevant to the query, as well as a set of most relevant keywords extracted from a larger set of related articles. b. The user can modify the weight of the keywords by sliding them vertically, after which the stream will refresh, updating articles and keywords accordingly. If dropped outside their initial stream, keywords can either trigger a new search stream or be passed to an already existing parallel stream.

To expose the user to novel keywords, in each stream we show keywords k_i not with highest $\hat{r}_i$, but with highest upper confidence bound for relevance, which is $\hat{r}_i + \alpha\sigma_i$, where σ_i is an upper bound on standard deviation of $\hat{r}_i$, and $\alpha > 0$ is a constant for adjusting the confidence level. In each iteration, we compute $\mathbf{s}_i = \mathbf{K}(\mathbf{K}^\top\mathbf{K}+\lambda\mathbf{I})^{-1}\mathbf{k}_i$ where λ is a regularization parameter, and show the k_i maximizing $\mathbf{s}_i^\top\mathbf{r}^{feedback} + \frac{\alpha}{2}\|\mathbf{s}_i\|$ representing estimated search intent. We optimize horizontal positions of the shown k_i by dimensionality reduction [33]; k_i get similar positions if their relevance estimate changes similarly with respect to a set of additional feedback.

EVALUATION

We evaluated the system to find out if and how IntentStreams supports parallel browsing and branching behavior. IntentStreams was compared against a baseline system with an interface similar to a traditional Google search interface. Our hypothesis was that, compared to the baseline, IntentStreams generates (1.) more parallel streams, (2.) more revisits, and (3.) more branches. We used the following metrics: number of parallel streams, number of revisits, and number of branches. In the baseline, the number of parallel streams denotes the number of tabs opened, a revisit indicates returning to an already open tab, and a branch denotes a query updated after a revisit. In IntentStreams, a revisit occurs when a user performs certain activities (opening an article, weight change) on a previously created stream. A branch occurs when a new stream is created from an existing one. That includes both creating a new query by dragging a keyword or updating the existing stream by modifying the weights of its keywords.

Method

We evaluated the system with 13 volunteers (4 female). The participants' age ranged from 19 to 36 with mean of 28.4 ($SD = 4.05$). Their levels of education were: 8% PhD, 46% Master, 38% Bachelor, 8% High School. Each participant received two movie tickets for their participation. We used a within-subject design, where participants were asked to perform two tasks, one with IntentStreams and one with the baseline. We counterbalanced by changing the order in which the two tasks were performed and the order in which the two systems were used.

The task was set in an essay writing scenario and formulated as follows: *You have to write an essay on recent developments of X where you have to cover as many subtopics as possible. You have 20 minutes to collect the material that will provide inspiration for your essay. You have additional 5 minutes to write your essay.* The two tasks performed by the participants covered two topics: (1.) NASA, and (2.) China Mobile.

Experiments were run in a laboratory on a laptop with OS X operating system. Each participant signed a consent form. To determine the eligibility, we asked candidates how familiar they were with each chosen topic on a 1-5 scale, where 1 means "no knowledge" and 5 means "expert knowledge". Only those with a score lower than 3 were considered eligible. Before the experiment, participants received detailed instructions and performed a 5-minute training session.

To evaluate the system, we connected it to a news repository of English language editorial news articles crawled from publicly available news sources from September 2013 to March 2014. The database contains more than 25 million documents. The documents were originally collected for monitoring media presence of numerous interested parties, and hence the collection has wide topical coverage. All the documents were preprocessed by the Boilerpipe tool [19] and the keyphrases were extracted with the Maui toolkit [25].

The baseline system was connected to the same news repository. In the baseline system, users could type queries and receive a list of relevant news articles. To start a new parallel query, a new tab had to be opened.

FINDINGS

Table 1 shows the results of the log analysis. In the 20-minute long sessions, IntentStreams on average generated 7.84 more queries ($SD = 7.27$), 6.38 more parallel streams ($SD = 4.03$), 4.54 more revisits ($SD = 4.52$), and 3.62 more branches ($SD = 4.01$). A paired t-test indicates that all those differences are statistically significant ($p < 0.01$).

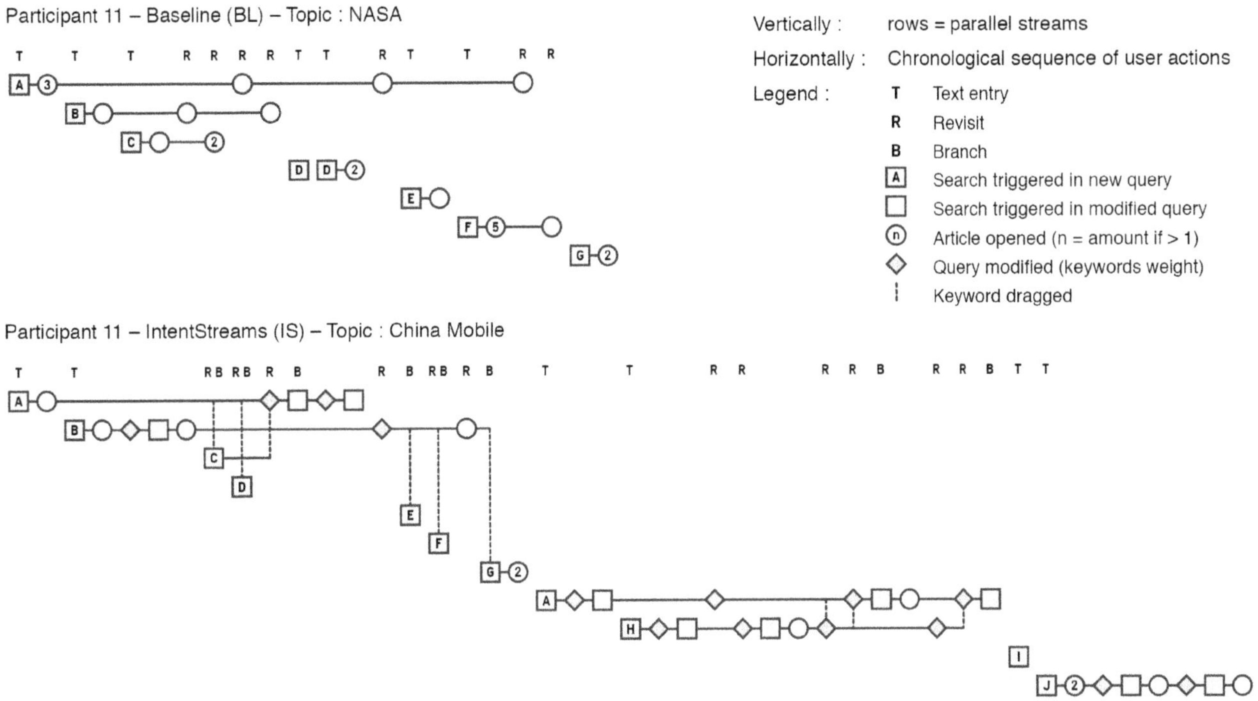

Figure 2. Example of branching behavior from the case study: top - Baseline; bottom - IntentStreams.

Parallel search supported in IntentStreams. Results show that users created more parallel streams than opened new tabs. While the system allows the creation of parallel streams, the users revisit earlier ones consistently, which denotes parallel search behavior. In fact, revisits are higher in the IS condition.

Branching supported in IntentStreams. In IntentStreams, more queries and parallel streams were created through branching. Figure 2 presents a visual representation of a participant's search behavior, showing the difference between the linear search behavior in the baseline and the more articulated search behavior in IntentStreams.

Further, IntentStreams supports more exploration. In IS, more exploration of the information space was done as can be seen from the higher number of queries.

CONCLUSIONS

We introduced the IntentStreams system for exploratory search of news based on parallel visualization of smart search streams. It models each search stream by an intent model, allows rapid tuning by feedback to keywords, and allows rapid initiation of new streams by keyword interaction without typing. Initial experiments show that users take advantage of the rich parallel search opportunities and engage in much stronger parallel browsing and branching behavior than in a traditional system.

This is an important finding as current browsing and searching behavior is already characterized by multitask search (in the same query field users alternate tasks [22, 21]), parallel browsing (users browse on parallel tabs or windows [14]), and branching (a new tab or window is created from a link or result of a previous window or tab [13]). Branching has been shown to be more important in informational browsing than navigational search [14]. The approach proposed in IntentStreams can be incorporated into other search interfaces to provide an effective way to branch search.

Table 1. Comparison between IntentStreams (IS) and the baseline (BL). The number of queries, parallel streams, revisits, and branches, for each participant P1,...,P13.

	queries		par. streams		revisits		branches	
	BL	IS	BL	IS	BL	IS	BL	IS
P1	5	5	2	5	0	7	0	1
P2	5	4	1	2	1	0	1	0
P3	7	17	1	12	1	6	1	4
P4	9	11	1	6	0	2	0	2
P5	14	18	1	12	0	9	0	7
P6	1	8	1	5	0	0	0	0
P7	12	18	7	14	5	7	2	3
P8	22	26	3	12	6	15	1	8
P9	6	18	6	12	4	4	0	0
P10	8	11	7	11	6	5	0	0
P11	8	21	7	11	7	12	0	8
P12	16	35	11	14	3	14	1	9
P13	3	26	3	18	0	11	0	11

ACKNOWLEDGMENTS

This work has been partially supported by TEKES (Re:Know and DIGILE programme D2I) and the Academy of Finland (decisions 251170, 252845, 266969, 278090, and 283311).

REFERENCES

1. Ahlberg, C., and Shneiderman, B. Visual information seeking: Tight coupling of dynamic query filters with

starfield displays. In *Proceedings of the SIGCHI Conference on Human Factors in Computing Systems*, ACM (New York, NY, USA, 1994), 313–317.

2. Ahn, J., and Brusilovsky, P. Adaptive visualization for exploratory information retrieval. *Information Processing & Management 49*, 5 (2013), 1139–1164.
3. Ahn, J.-w., and Brusilovsky, P. Adaptive visualization of search results: Bringing user models to visual analytics. *Information Visualization 8*, 3 (2009), 167–179.
4. Auer, P. Using confidence bounds for exploitation-exploration trade-offs. *Journal of Machine Learning Research 3* (2002), 397–422.
5. Bates, M. J. What is browsing–really? a model drawing from behavioural science research. *Inf. Res. 12*, 4 (2007).
6. Bilenko, M., and White, R. W. Mining the search trails of surfing crowds: identifying relevant websites from user activity. In *Proceedings of the 17th international conference on World Wide Web*, ACM (2008), 51–60.
7. Chau, D. H., Kittur, A., Hong, J. I., and Faloutsos, C. Apolo: Making sense of large network data by combining rich user interaction and machine learning. In *Proceedings of the SIGCHI Conference on Human Factors in Computing Systems*, ACM, ACM (New York, NY, USA, 2011), 167–176.
8. Chirita, P.-A., Firan, C. S., and Nejdl, W. Personalized query expansion for the web. In *Proceedings of the 30th annual international ACM SIGIR conference on Research and development in information retrieval*, ACM (2007), 7–14.
9. Głowacka, D., Ruotsalo, T., Konuyshkova, K., Kaski, S., Jacucci, G., et al. Directing exploratory search: Reinforcement learning from user interactions with keywords. In *Proceedings of the 2013 international conference on Intelligent user interfaces*, ACM (2013), 117–128.
10. Głowacka, D., and Shawe-Taylor, J. Content-based image retrieval with multinomial relevance feedback. In *Proc. of ACML* (2010), 111–125.
11. Havre, S., Hetzler, E., Perrine, K., Jurrus, E., and Miller, N. Interactive visualization of multiple query results. In *Proceedings of the IEEE Symposium on Information Visualization 2001*, IEEE Computer Society (Washington, DC, USA, 2001), 105.
12. Hearst, M. A. *Search User Interfaces*, 1st ed. Cambridge University Press, New York, NY, USA, 2009.
13. Huang, J., Lin, T., and White, R. W. No search result left behind: Branching behavior with browser tabs. In *Proceedings of the fifth ACM international conference on Web search and data mining*, ACM (2012), 203–212.
14. Huang, J., and White, R. W. Parallel browsing behavior on the web. In *Proceedings of the 21st ACM conference on Hypertext and hypermedia*, ACM (2010), 13–18.
15. Käki, M. Findex: Search result categories help users when document ranking fails. In *Proceedings of the SIGCHI Conference on Human Factors in Computing Systems*, ACM (New York, NY, USA, 2005), 131–140.
16. Kelly, D., and Fu, X. Elicitation of term relevance feedback: An investigation of term source and context. In *Proceedings of the 29th Annual International ACM SIGIR Conference on Research and Development in Information Retrieval*, ACM (New York, NY, USA, 2006), 453–460.
17. Kelly, D., Gyllstrom, K., and Bailey, E. W. A comparison of query and term suggestion features for interactive searching. In *Proceedings of the 32nd Annual International ACM SIGIR Conference on Research and Development in Information Retrieval*, ACM (New York, NY, USA, 2009), 371–378.
18. Klouche, K., Ruotsalo, T., Cabral, D., Andolina, S., Bellucci, A., and Jacucci, G. Designing for exploratory search on touch devices. In *Proceedings of the SIGCHI conference on Human factors in computing systems*, CHI 2015, ACM (2015).
19. Kohlschütter, C., Frankhauser, P., and Nejdl, W. Boilerplate detection using shallow text features. In *Proceedings of the Third ACM International Conference on Web Search and Data Mining*, ACM (2010).
20. Kules, W., Wilson, M. L., Schraefel, M. C., and Shneiderman, B. From keyword search to exploration: How result visualization aids discovery on the web. Tech. rep., University of Southampton, 2008.
21. Lucchese, C., Orlando, S., Perego, R., Silvestri, F., and Tolomei, G. Identifying task-based sessions in search engine query logs. In *Proceedings of the fourth ACM international conference on Web search and data mining*, ACM (2011), 277–286.
22. Lucchese, C., Orlando, S., Perego, R., Silvestri, F., and Tolomei, G. Discovering tasks from search engine query logs. *ACM Transactions on Information Systems (TOIS) 31*, 3 (2013), 14.
23. Marchionini, G. Exploratory search: From finding to understanding. *Communications of the ACM 49*, 4 (Apr. 2006), 41–46.
24. Matejka, J., Grossman, T., and Fitzmaurice, G. Citeology: Visualizing paper genealogy. In *CHI '12 Extended Abstracts on Human Factors in Computing Systems*, ACM (New York, NY, USA, 2012), 181–190.
25. Medelyan, O., Frank, E., and Witten, I. H. Human-competitive tagging using automatic keyphrase extraction. In *Proceedings of the 2009 Conference on Empirical Methods in Natural Language Processing* (2009), 1318–1327.
26. Micarelli, A., Gasparetti, F., Sciarrone, F., and Gauch, S. Personalized search on the world wide web. In *The Adaptive Eeb*. Springer, Berlin, Heidelberg, 2007, 195–230.

27. Pirolli, P., and Card, S. Information foraging in information access environments. In *Proceedings of the SIGCHI Conference on Human Factors in Computing Systems*, CHI '95, ACM Press/Addison-Wesley Publishing Co. (New York, NY, USA, 1995), 51–58.

28. Ruotsalo, T., Jacucci, G., Myllymäki, P., and Kaski, S. Interactive intent modeling: Information discovery beyond search. *Communications of the ACM 58*, 1 (Dec. 2014), 86–92.

29. Ruotsalo, T., Peltonen, J., Eugster, M., Głowacka, D., Konyushkova, K., Athukorala, K., Kosunen, I., Reijonen, A., Myllymäki, P., Jacucci, G., et al. Directing exploratory search with interactive intent modeling. In *Proceedings of the 22nd ACM international conference on Conference on information & knowledge management*, ACM (2013), 1759–1764.

30. Stasko, J., Görg, C., and Liu, Z. Jigsaw: supporting investigative analysis through interactive visualization. *Information visualization 7*, 2 (2008), 118–132.

31. Teevan, J., Dumais, S. T., and Liebling, D. J. To personalize or not to personalize: modeling queries with variation in user intent. In *Proceedings of the 31st annual international ACM SIGIR conference on Research and development in information retrieval*, ACM (2008), 163–170.

32. Terveen, L., Hill, W., and Amento, B. Constructing, organizing, and visualizing collections of topically related web resources. *ACM Transactions on Computer-Human Interaction 6*, 1 (1999), 67–94.

33. Venna, J., Peltonen, J., Nybo, K., Aidos, H., and Kaski, S. Information retrieval perspective to nonlinear dimensionality reduction for data visualization. *Journal of Machine Learning Research 11* (2010), 451–490.

34. Verbert, K., Parra, D., Brusilovsky, P., and Duval, E. Visualizing recommendations to support exploration, transparency and controllability. In *Proceedings of the 2013 International Conference on Intelligent User Interfaces*, ACM (2013), 351–362.

Building Image Sentiment Dataset with an Online Rating Game

Chanhee Yoon, Keumhee Kang and Eun Yi Kim
Visual Information Processing Lab., Dept. of Internet & Multimedia Engineering, Konkuk University
1 Hwayang-dong, Gwangjin-Gu, Seoul, Korea 143-701
{chanheeyoon0601, kh6563, eykim04}@gmail.com

ABSTRACT
In this paper, an online rating game called *Image-Battle* is developed to build the ground truth dataset for image sentiment analysis. Our goal is to provide more interesting and intuitive interface to users and to collect the images with more correct sentiment scores despite of less human intervention. For this, two schemes are designed: 1) a pair-wise competition and 2) a ranking algorithm based on visual link analysis. First, the system shows two images and asks the user which image is closer to a given sentiment. Thereafter, the ranking algorithm assigns the sentiment scores to the images based on all the competition results: the main idea is to give higher score to images that win more or to the images that beat images with high scores. To evaluate the proposed system, it was used to collect ground truth for 30,000 Photo.net images, each of which was labeled by six emotions. The ground truth was used to develop the sentiment recognition system, and its result was compared with that of other rating system. Then the result proved the excellence of the proposed method in terms of accuracy and user satisfaction.

Author Keywords
Image Sentiment Analysis; Visual Link Structure; Online Rating Game; Rank Algorithm; Pair-wise Competition.

ACM Classification Keywords
H.3.1. Information Storage and Retrieval: Content Analysis and Indexing.

INTRODUCTION
At present, many works are focusing on analyses of social media data to determine what people think about current topics of interest, for example, movies, products, companies, and/or political parties. These analyses are referred to as opinion mining, affective computing or sentiment analyses, and this area has many applications in economics and financial modeling.

Thus far, most existing sentiment analyses are based on textual information only, and relatively little attention has been focused on analyzing sentiments from visual images. However, along with textual information, images are important information through which a large number of interactions occur between the users of social media. For example, images constitute nearly 36% of all shared links on Twitter. In addition, sentiments expressed in image tweets are consistent with textual tweets [1].

Accordingly, sentiment analysis for social images remains an open issue in our understanding of users' opinions and sentiments. As representative sentiments to be captured from images, we can consider aesthetics [2], Ekman's emotions [3] and Kobayashi's affective words [4]. However, it is necessary initially to construct a dataset with which to develop the necessary techniques for analyzing such sentiments.

The only method currently available for obtaining a trustworthy dataset is manual labeling by human judgment, for which some available datasets exist. For example, the International Affective Picture System (IAPS) consists of 369 photos which are labeled according to emotions such as pleasure, arousal and dominance [5]. The Geneva Affective Picture Database (GAPED) comprises 730 pictures which are divided into three sentiments: negative, positive and natural [6]. Similarly, Shin et al. built a dataset based on Kobayashi's 15 affective groups (pretty, dynamic, chic, etc.), which provides 1,276 photographic images [7]. Such datasets were built by directly rating the individuals, which is tedious and thus extremely costly. Moreover, such a direct rating can often produce unstable and biased scores for the images.

In [8], a crowd median algorithm was proposed to identify more representative images in a dataset. The algorithm is based on the triplet task – a user select one irrelevant images among three shown images as outliers. Then, they select one image among the images selected with least numbers as outliers. The algorithm can reduce users' burden in selecting outliers, so that it can guarantee more representative centroids.

Accordingly, we present an online rating game known as Image Battle, which is based on pair-wise competition of images and ranking. In the pair-wise competition, the system shows two images and asks the user which image is closer to a given sentiment, e.g., which image is more beautiful. Thereafter, the ranking is performed based on the competition results.

IUI 2015, March 29–April 1, 2015, Atlanta, GA, USA.

http://dx.doi.org/10.1145/2678025.2701409

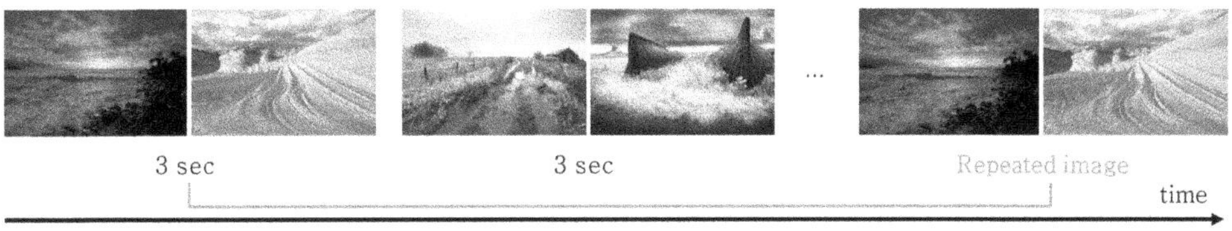

Figure 2. Consistency test: some pairs are repeated in one game stage to evaluate user's consistency.

For this, we propose a new ranking algorithm based on visual link analysis, which gives higher scores to the images that win more and to the images that beat the images with high scores. As the algorithm can effectively propagate one competition result to all of the images, it helps the proposed system assign more accurate sentiment scores to images with less competitions.

A PAIR-WISE COMPETITION

In order to measure an image's sentiment score more accurately, there is need for human judgment. However, to measure the sentiment score of images by simply asking people to rate individual images is tedious and can produce unstable results.

To prevent this, our rating system uses pair-wise competition, as shown in Figure 1. It involves comparing a pair of images at once. In the game, participants view a pair of images which are displayed for three seconds. Their task is to indicate the image that they think is preferred for the given query. Then, the pair of images is randomly selected from a database.

To evaluate the user consistency and attention, we use two rules: 1) for human consistency, we use repeated image pairs as shown in Figure 2. We put eight repeated pairs among total of 100 pairs per one game. Then, if a user chooses the different image at every competition, we think his consistency level is low, thereby discarding his answers. 2) If a user doesn't answer within 3 seconds, we regard he is not concentrating on the game, so we give a warning message to the user.

Using the pair-wise competition, participants can solve the problem intuitively, preventing biased ratings and confirming user consistency.

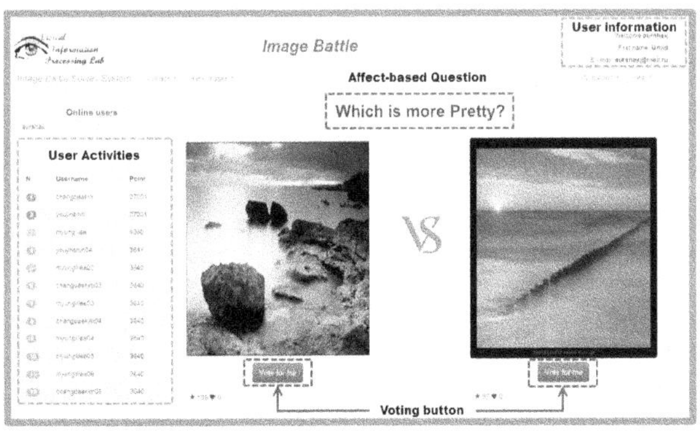

Figure 1. Image Battle: An online rating game where users see a pair of images and select which image is closer to a sentiment. (*http://vip.konkuk.ac.kr/ibattle*)

A RANKING ALGORITHM

Once all the pair-wise competitions are terminated, the sentiment scores are determined. For this, a new ranking algorithm is designed, which is inspired from PageRank [9]. The visual link structure based on the competition results is first established, and then the ranking is assigned.

Visual link structure

According to the competition results for the images, a graph is drawn, where the nodes correspond to the images and the links between them reflect the competition result. The node corresponding to the head of the link is the image that wins the pair-wise competition, whereas the node corresponding to its tail is the image that loses the competition. Fig. 3 shows one simple graph with three links, two real links and one inferred link. The real link describes the actual competition results between images (A, B) and (B, C). The dotted line describes the inferred results obtained from another competition. That is, from the result for (A, B) and (B, C), we can infer that image A will defeat image.

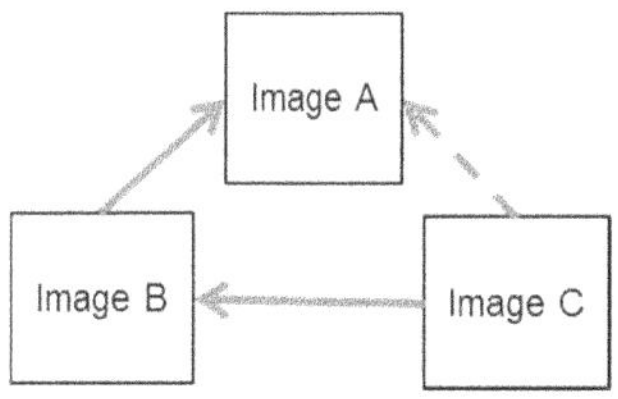

Figure 3. A simplified graph of the competition results.

Propagation of ranking through links

The main idea of the proposed ranking algorithm is to assign higher scores to images that win more and to assign higher scores to images that beat images with high scores.

Let u be an image. $u = \{u_1, u_2, \cdots, u_K\}$ Then, let F_u be a set of images which are defeated by u and $B_u = \{B_u(\rho) | \rho \leq 5\}$ be the set of images that u beats directly or indirectly. Then, $B_u(1)$ denotes images that u beats in the competition. $B_u(2)$ or $B_u(3)$ denotes images that u can beat after one or two deduction steps, which are inferred from other competitions. Then, $\mathbb{W}(u, v)$ is a weight matrix in which image u will obtain the score from image v.

The sentiment score of one image $R(u)$ is then defined as shown below.

$$R(u) = \frac{1-d}{N} + d \sum_{v \in B_u(\rho), \rho \leq 5} \mathbb{W}(u, v) * R(v) \quad (1)$$

That is, the score of one image $R(v)$ is divided to the images to which it loses. Thus, the images will receive the higher scores by acquiring the scores from images they win.

Unlike PageRank which assigns a uniform weight to all the images by which v is defeated (F_v), the $\mathbb{W}(u,v)$ is determined by the number of wins and the depth of inference. The weight matrix $\mathbb{W}$ is then composed of two terms $\mathbb{A}$ and $\mathbb{P}$ as follows:

$$\mathbb{W}(i,j) = \mathbb{A}(i,j) + \sum_{\rho \le depth} \mathbb{P}^{\rho}(i,j) * \alpha^{\rho} \qquad (2)$$

, where the adjacency matrix $\mathbb{A}$ represents the direct competition results among images, and the inferred adjacency matrix, $\mathbb{P}^{\rho}$ is the indirect competition results calculated from ρ_{th} inference. In addition, α is a penalizing term to reduce the impact of the weight as the depth increases.

The adjacency matrix $\mathbb{A}$ is built according to the competition results among images, which can be directly calculated from the competition result.

$$\mathbb{A} = \begin{bmatrix} l(1,1) & \cdots & l(1,K) \\ \vdots & \ddots & \vdots \\ l(K,1) & \cdots & l(K,K) \end{bmatrix}. \qquad (3)$$

In Eq. (3), the adjacency function $l(i,j)$ is defined by

$$l(i,j) = \begin{cases} 0 \quad , & if\ image\ j\ lost\ to\ image\ i \\ \mathrm{c(i,j)/c(j)}, & \mathrm{otherwise} \end{cases}$$

, where c(j) is the competition count for image j and c(i, j) is the number of defeats by image i. Thus, the element of each column in $\mathbb{A}$ sum up to 1, so the $\mathbb{A}$ is a stochastic matrix.

The inferred adjacency matrix $\mathbb{P}$ is identified by inferring the competition results of the images. The element of the matrix $\mathbb{P}^{\rho}(i,j)$ is calculated using the following equation:

$$\mathbb{P}^{\rho}(i,j) = \sum_{a \in B_u(\rho)} \sum_{j \le K} \mathbb{B}(a,j) * \mathbb{A}(a,j) \qquad (4)$$

, where $\mathbb{B}(a,j) = 1$, if the count that image a wins j is larger than $\mathrm{c}(a)/2$, and $\mathbb{B}(i,j) = 0$ if not.

The sentiment scores of all images are initialized to $1/K$ and iteratively evolved by Eq. (1), until convergence.

In the proposed system, the competition of one image can directly or indirectly affect more images, because we consider two adjacency matrixes $\mathbb{A}$ and $\mathbb{P}^{\rho}$ $(\rho \le 5)$. This mechanism makes competition results of images propagate more rapidly to others than just using pair-wise, thereby reducing the human intervention and improving the accuracy of their sentiment.

IMPROVING THE EFFICIENCY IN THE SPEED AND THE QUALITY OF RANKING

The rating game by pair-wise competition has the following advantages: 1) it provides more interesting and convenient interface to users; 2) it guarantees the unbiased rating scores.

However, it has one drawback: it requires too many human judgments. Let M be the number of users in participating in our Game and N be the number of images to be evaluated. When using the individual rating, the total number of users' evaluation is $M \times N$, whereas it is increasing to $M \times {}_N C_2$ in the pair-wise rating. Although we can reduce the number of evaluations by the propagation mechanism embedded in our ranking algorithm, we need another mechanism to reduce the burden of users.

For this, we divided the images into g subgroups, and processed the online rating game step-by-step while adding one subgroup at a time. The process is as follows:

- For the images of the first group (G_1), the competitions are fulfilled for all possible pairs of images, thereafter the sentiment score is ranked using Eq. (1). Thus, much more trustworthy ground truth is generated, which is used as seed dataset to evaluate the images of next subgroup.
- Then, the images of next subgroup (G_{t+1}, $t > 1$) are added to the current set of images (G_t), and the competition is done between images, each of which is randomly selected from G_{t+1} and G_t, respectively. Then, the number of competitions performed at each generation is gradually decreased as increasing the number of images. After finishing competitions, the ranking is performed. This process is iterated until all image subgroups are evaluated.

With this scheme, we can reduce the number of users' evaluations while preserving the quality of sentiment scores for the images.

EXPERIMENT

The proposed system was used to collect ground truth for 30,000 Photo.net images. Then six human affects from Kobayashi's sentiments were considered to label the images, such as colorful, dynamic, pretty, pure, romantic and wild.

For experiments, we recruited 20 peoples (10 males and 10 females). They are majored in computer engineering or media, and their average age was 26-years-old. They have no experience with the rating games. We gave a basic introduction of Image Battle to them and how to play the game. Each participant evaluates total 30,000 images during six months. We paid 10 dollars per one stage.

For objective evaluation, the performance of proposed system was compared with that of Shin et al.'s method [7]. For the same image sets, the individual rating was performed and the fuzzy rules were applied to remove some biased results between or within people.

Then, for the respective results, we chose 600 images with highest and lowest ranking scores. Figure 4 shows some examples of ground truth with positive and negative scores for a sentiment "pretty." Figs. 4(a) and (c) are the images with highest scores when using two systems, whereas Figs. 4(b) and (d) are ones with lowest scores.

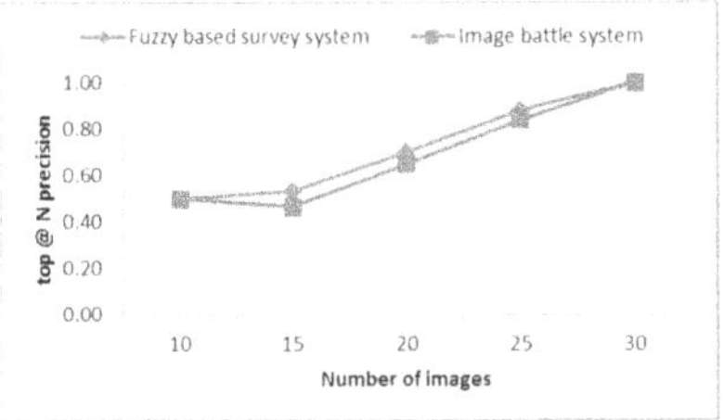

(a) Colorful

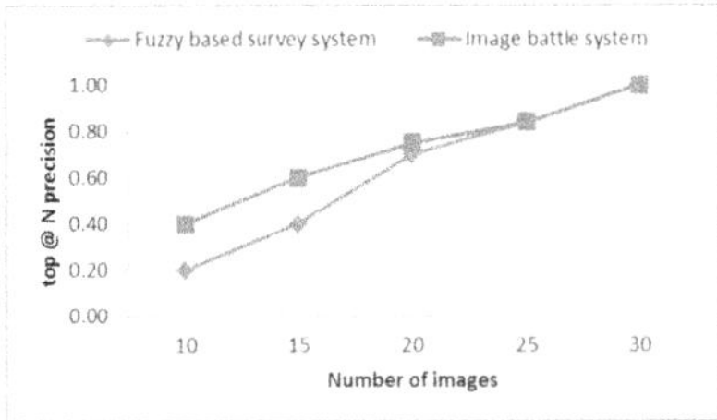

(d) Dynamic

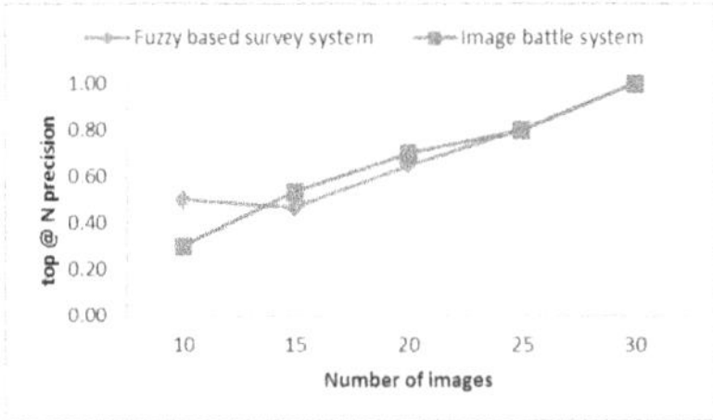

(c) Pretty

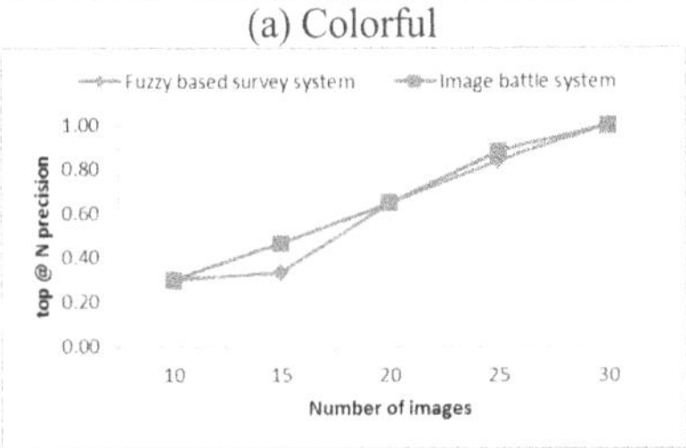

(d) Pure

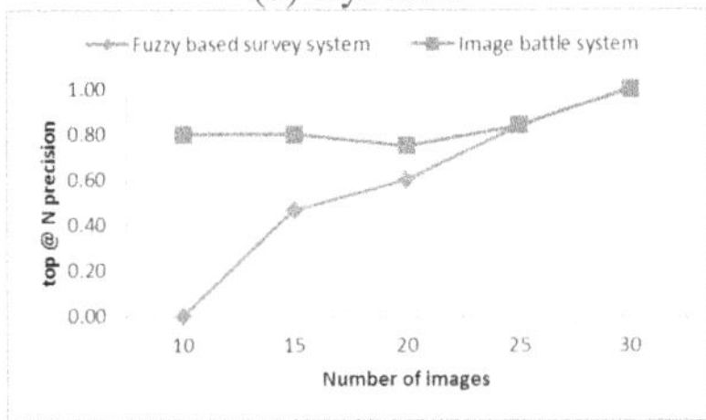

(e) Romantic

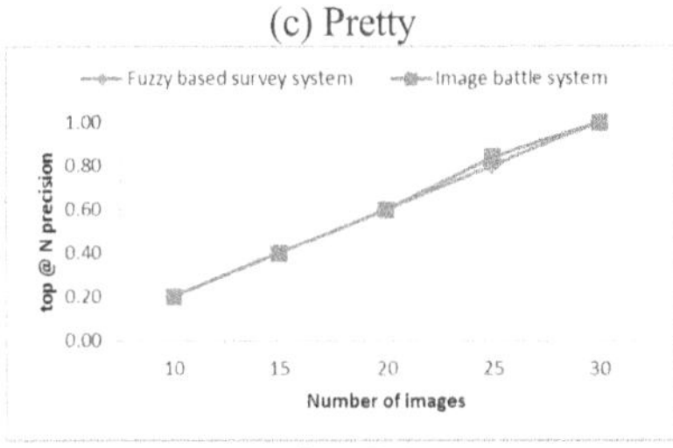

(f) Wild

Figure 5. The recognition accuracies.

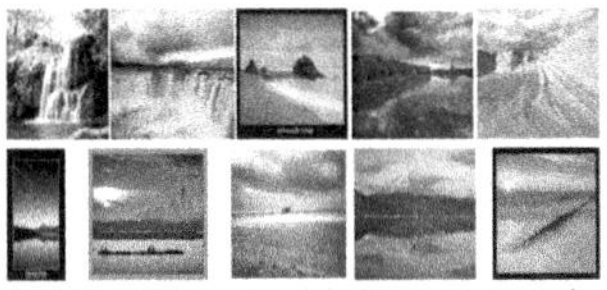

(a) images with highest scores in individual rating system

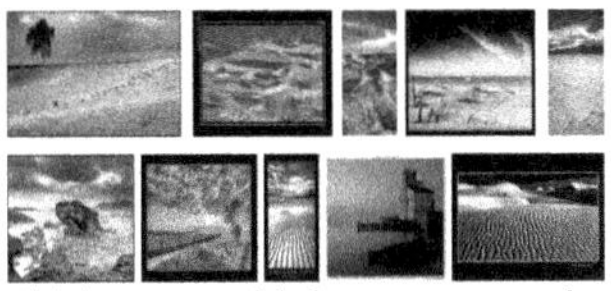

(b) images with lowest scores in individual rating system

(c) images with highest scores in the proposed system

(d) images with lowest scores in the proposed system

Figure 4. The images with highest and lowest scores for a sentiment "pretty".

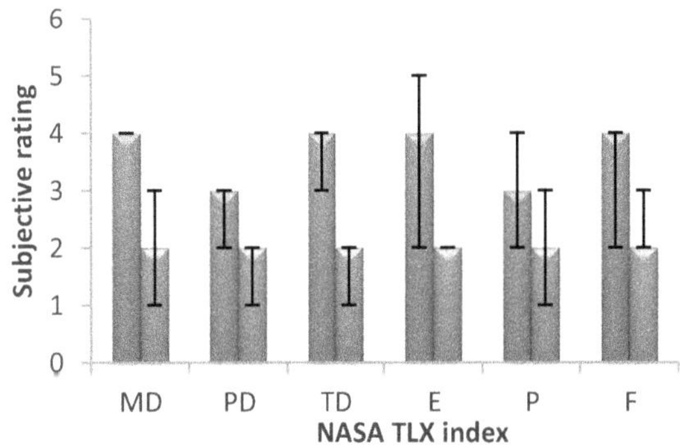

Figure 6. The NASA TLX subjective workload using individual rating system (red) and proposed system (blue).

Furthermore, to assess the validity of the proposed method, two image sets were used as ground truth to develop the recognition algorithm of six sentiments [7], and its result was compared with accuracy when using individual rating system. Then the half of 600 images was used for training and the others were used for testing.

As the metric to evaluate the performance of two systems, a top @ N precision was used. It is calculated as follows: 1) we made two affect-recognition systems using the ground truth that were generated by two systems, respectively; 2) using the respective recognition system, we labeled 300 test images with six affects and ranked them; 3) we selected top N images while changing the N value from 10 to 30. Then, the results were compared with real top N images labeled by human judgment, and the precision is calculated.

Figure 5 shows the performance comparison of two systems in terms of top @ N precision. As N is increasing, the precision is increasing. However, in most cases, the proposed system showed the higher precision in the smaller N. This means that the recognition system using the ground truth that generated by image battle is the superior the other in predicting the affects hidden in images.

User Satisfaction

To evaluate user's satisfaction, we measured the completion time and NASA TLX questionnaire [10-11], which contained six questions for which responses were obtained from a five point Likert scale. The abbreviations are {mental demand, physical demand, temporal demand, effort, performance, frustration}.

Figure 6 shows comparison of the workload results. We can confirm all the components using the proposed system were smaller than individual rating system. This means that the proposed system required less workload to participants and can provide convenient survey for the participants.

ACKNOWLEDGE

This research was supported by the MSIP(Ministry of Science, ICT and Future Planning), Korea, under the ITRC(Information Technology Research Center) support program (NIPA-2014-H0301-14-1001) and ITRC support program (NIPA-2014-H0301-14-1006) supervised by the NIPA(National IT Industry Promotion Agency)

REFERENCES

1. You, Quanzeng, and Jiebo Luo. "Towards social imagematics: sentiment analysis in social multimedia." Proceedings of the Thirteenth International Workshop on Multimedia Data Mining. ACM, 2013.
2. Murray, Naila, Luca Marchesotti, and Florent Perronnin. AVA: A large-scale database for aesthetic visual analysis. *Computer Vision and Pattern Recognition (CVPR), 2012 IEEE Conference on*. IEEE, 2012.
3. Ekman, Paul. An argument for basic emotions. *Cognition & Emotion* 6.3-4 (1992): 169-200.
4. Kobayashi, S. color image scale. *Publishing of Kodansha*, JAPAN, 1991.
5. Lang, Peter J., Margaret M. Bradley, and Bruce N. Cuthbert. "International affective picture system (IAPS): Technical manual and affective ratings." (1999).
6. Dan-Glauser, Elise S., and Klaus R. Scherer. "The Geneva affective picture database (GAPED): a new 730-picture database focusing on valence and normative significance." *Behavior research methods* 43.2 (2011): 468-477.
7. Shin, Y., Eun and Kim, E.Y. Probabilistic affective model with probabilistic latent semantic analysis for predicting human affect. In *Proc. ICPRAM* 2012, SCITEPRESS(2012).
8. Heikinheimo, Hannes, and Antti Ukkonen. "The Crowd-Median Algorithm." First AAAI Conference on Human Computation and Crowdsourcing. 2013.
9. Page, L., Brin, S., Motwani, R., & Winograd, T. (1999). The PageRank citation ranking: Bringing order to the web.
10. Hart, Sandra G., and Lowell E. Staveland. "Development of NASA-TLX (Task Load Index): Results of empirical and theoretical research." Advances in psychology 52 (1988): 139-183.
11. J.C. Byers, A.C. Bittner, S.G. Hill. Traditional and raw task load index (TLX) correlation: are paired comparison necessary? In Advances in Industrial Ergonomics and Safety. Taylor & Francis, 1989

Augmenting the Driver's View with Peripheral Information on a Windshield Display

Renate Häuslschmid[1], Sven Osterwald[2], Marcus Lang[3], Andreas Butz[4]
[1, 2, 3, 4] University of Munich (LMU), [1, 2, 3] IAV GmbH, Munich
[1]renate.haeuslschmid@iav.de, [2]osterwald@cip.ifi.lmu.de, [3]marcus@martinlang.com, [4]butz@ifi.lmu.de

ABSTRACT
Windshield displays (WSDs) are information displays covering the entire windshield. Current WSD test setups place information at different distances, but always within the driver's foveal field of view. We built two WSD test setups, which present information not only at various distances within the driver's visual focus, but also in the peripheral field of view. Then we evaluated the display of information in the periphery on both WSD setups in a user study. While making sure the participants would look at the peripheral information, we measured the display's impact on driving performance. Subjects were also asked about their driving experience with the windshield displays and their preference among the two setups.

Author Keywords
In-vehicle information system; visual focus; periphery; widget board; driving performance; user experience.

ACM Classification Keywords
H.1.2; H.5.2.

General Terms
Human Factors; Performance.

INTRODUCTION
Windshield displays (WSDs) are the big siblings of Head-Up Displays (HUDs). Both place information within the drivers' view through the windshield, which can provide a substantial safety benefit over so-called Head-Down Displays such as the instrument panel. While drivers need to move their head down to see information in those standard in-vehicle displays, WSDs and HUDs let them keep their heads up and the road situation in view. Drivers can stay aware of the road situation much easier and are less strained when changing focus between the virtual image and the road scene. The distant image enables a faster eye accommodation, and in turn a faster perception of the virtual image, resulting in shorter reaction times [7,8,10].

IUI'15, March 29 - April 01, 2015, Atlanta, GA, USA

ACM 978-1-4503-3306-1/15/03...$15.00
http://dx.doi.org/10.1145/2678025.2701393

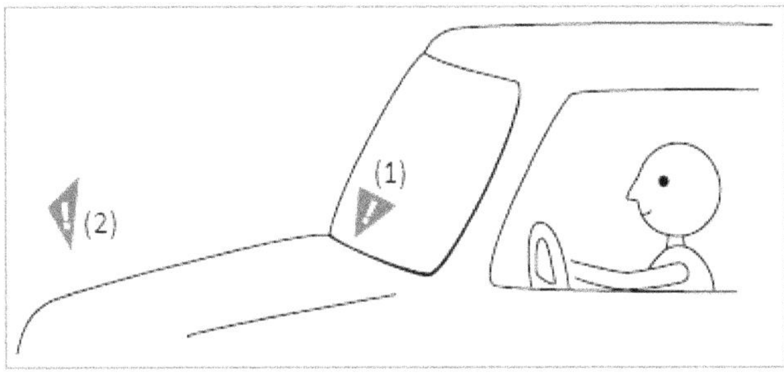

Figure 1: Information on a windshield display at different distances to the driver: (1) on the windshield, (2) in front of it

The term *windshield display* already implies the difference to HUDs: WSDs use large parts of the windshield area as a display pane. HUDs, on the contrary, usually cover only 3 to 6 inches [2]. The small display area strongly limits the content to driving- and safety-relevant information. Such displays could provide many opportunities as the dashboard area is increasingly crowded [22]. Functions currently located on the central information display could be relocated to the WSD, which offers a large space for information supporting the primary (driving) task, but also secondary and tertiary tasks. WSD applications could support safety (e.g., by displaying the distance to a leading vehicle, warnings or by highlighting hazards), navigation (e.g., through a route markup), or influence driver behavior (e.g., by an ambient display of fuel consumption).

Information could either be placed in the central region currently covered by HUDs, or in other parts of the driver's foveal and peripheral field of view (FoV). The foveal area is also the most relevant area for driving. Overlaying this space with a display can have disadvantages [6], as information in this area can occlude parts of the driving scene or even hazards. Using the space in the periphery has a much lower risk of occluding the driving scene. By periphery in this context we mean the area surrounding the foveal FoV, which corresponds to the borders of the WSD if the driver looks straight at the road scene. As the driving scene is spread out horizontally, the top and bottom areas of the windshield are good candidate areas for displaying information, which is not relevant to the driving task. On a flat road, the driver will normally only see the sky and engine hood in these areas. An often-proposed use case for WSDs [7,18] is the spatially registered (a.k.a. contact-analog) display of points of interest. These will also occupy the horizontally peripheral display areas, as POIs are mostly located in the horizontal plane around the car.

In the current literature, the peripheral area is mostly considered inappropriate for information display. The best region for HUDs was found to be within the foveal FoV, slightly below the driver's line of sight [9,24]. Positioning information outside of this field, (i.e., with an eccentricity >10°), is widely refused [9,22,26] and there are two main arguments against the display in the periphery:

(1) The driver would have to move his or her head in order to perceive the displayed information [4].

(2) Outside of the foveal FoV, human perception is very limited, but also highly sensitive to light changes and movements. To such changes in the periphery, people often react in a knee-jerk manner by visually focusing on the stimulus. This sudden shift of the locus of attention is very safety-critical [16].

The first argument actually also covers standard displays, such as the instrument cluster or the central information display (CID) in the center stack. To make things worse, these standard displays are even much smaller, making them more difficult to read.

The second argument is relativized by the zoom-lens model of attention [5]. This model suggests that the field of view a person attentively observes can be reduced to increase the resolution at the focus point. Several studies found strong evidence that this model holds in driving situations: The response of drivers to stimuli presented in the periphery was tested in independent studies [3,14]. They all found, that the participants' performance in detecting peripheral stimuli depended on the demand of the driving situation. When the driving situation is highly demanding, the driver performs worse in detecting changes in the environment. In consequence, this also means that a demanding driving situation will automatically reduce the risk of looking to the side as a reflex to visual changes in the periphery. Drivers will only respond to peripheral information when the driving situation allows shifting their attention.

To complete these arguments, it is also important to consider the content and amount of information typically displayed on a WSD. All aforementioned studies use very basic stimuli, while the typical information on a WSD will most probably be more diverse and of lower importance. Peripheral information is the type of additional information, which is not central to the execution of a primary task. Such information can be provided to help a person do a better job or to keep track of less important tasks [15], but it is not asking for attention. In contrast, highly dynamic and demanding information would be very distracting and should not be displayed in the visual periphery. Also safety-relevant information might be better placed in other areas, more central to the driver's locus of attention.

Finally, existing studies investigated the influence of the primary task on the peripheral task, but do not mention interactions. We could not find a study investigating the effect of visually attracting HUD/WSD content on driving.

In order to learn more about the potential risks and benefits of a peripheral display in the windshield area, we decided to perform a user study. 20 participants had to perceive and memorize information displayed in the middle area of the windshield (see figure 2) while performing lane changes. For this purpose, we built two experimental WSD setups, and since several focus distances have been suggested in the literature, we decided to investigate two alternative distances (see figure 1). We implemented two test setups, which can display information directly on the windshield as well as 1.7m in front of the windshield. With these setups, we evaluated peripheral information regarding its memorability, measured impacts on driving performance and compared both WSD setups regarding user experience.

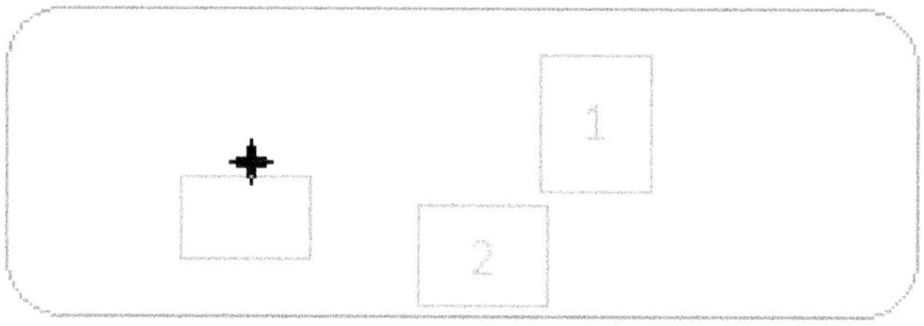

Figure 2: Area covered by a common HUD (blue) compared to the peripheral information areas in our user test (green) and the driver's average visual focus point (black cross)

RELATED WORK

Our work builds on existing studies of peripheral information display, as well as on other technical realizations of WSD test setups:

Information Display in the Periphery

Several studies found strong evidence that the zoom-lens model of attention holds in driving situations: Verwey presented digits for 750ms in the periphery to drivers and found that the detection performance depends on the demand of the driving situation [23]. This effect seems to be related to a shrinking of the functional field of view [3]. The functional field of view represents the area in which a human can acquire information without moving the head or the eye. The size of this area is limited by visual resolution, but also depends on processing demands and even anxiety. This is supported by the zoom-lens model of attention.

In another study, Crundall et al. [3] asked participants to search for hazards in video clips showing different driving situations. As a secondary task, subjects had to respond with button presses to target lights, which were displayed in the periphery. They confirmed that driving situations with increased processing demand lead to a lower success rate for the peripheral targets. Moreover, lower success rates were also found for increased eccentricity. Isomura, Kamiya and Hamatani [9,13] investigated a peripheral task at eccentricities between 10 and 40 degrees. A degradation of performance was found when the central task was either more demanding or the peripheral task was positioned more than 30 degrees off the central axis.

Iino, Otsuka and Suzuki [9,11] compared the reading times of information displayed on three HUDs positioned in the center, at 10° eccentricity, and at 20° eccentricity. For a speed below 70km/h, the reading times did not vary. If the participants drove at a higher speed, they could read faster in the central display area. Between the HUDs at 10° and 20° eccentricity, no differences in reading time were found. The difference between central and peripheral HUDs was more prominent with higher speeds.

In summary, not only the humans' state and the demand of the central task, but also the display's eccentricity and the driving speed have an influence on the peripheral task. A speed below 70km/h allowed for the same performance in the entire area up to 20° eccentricity. Independent of the speed, no difference was found between 10° and 20° eccentricity. However, more than 30° seem to degrade the performance in a peripheral task. We therefore used an eccentricity of 30° and a speed of 70km/h as the upper limits for our study design.

Technological Realization

A considerable number of HUD and WSD prototypes, test setups and concepts have been published by now. We reviewed the abilities, advantages and disadvantages of each approach in order to identify the ones, which could serve as a basis for our own test setup. In this review, we found the distance between the virtual image and the driver as a key differentiator. The proposed WSD systems provide information at various distances between 0m and 50m from the windshield [20,25]. We split the existing approaches according to their virtual image distance into the following three categories:

(1) Image presentation on the windshield

(2) Image presentation in front of the windshield

(3) Merging the virtual image and the real world

A large or even variable image distance, as needed for (3), is a desirable property of a WSD, but also increases its technical complexity. In order to keep the effort for our test setup manageable, we decided to focus on the categories (1) and (2) for this study. The following systems served as a basis for our own test setup:

Image Presentation on the Windshield

The display of information directly on the windshield constitutes the first step between standard in-vehicle displays, such as the instrument cluster or the central information display, and the classic Head-Up Display.

Image presentation on the windshield has been investigated by Volkswagen and General Motors [21,25]. Volkswagen already patented the integration of a transparent OLED into the windshield as well as the display of navigational hints on it. For this use case, they did neither try to cover the entire windshield area, nor to display the navigational arrows spatially close or adapted to the route. High-quality OLEDs, which would facilitate such information presentation, are still very cost-intensive and can only be produced in small sizes. A simpler and less expensive approach is to use the windshield as a projection surface. General Motors [25] used a uni-colored laser projector to mark up traffic signs on the windshield. In order to ensure correct highlighting, this requires a fixed head position.

Image Presentation in front of the Windshield

Most prototypes and test setups, which display the image in front of the windshield, are based on the same principle: The distant display of the virtual image to the driver is realized by the reflection of a display or a projector image.

Also HUDs are technically based on this principle. A display, positioned perpendicular below a combiner mirror, serves as the image source. The combiner is either realized by an additional glass pane in front of the windshield or integrated into the windshield itself. It serves as a transparent mirror and projects the image of the display 2m in front of the driver. Poitschke et al. [17] reflected the HUD image twice in order to reach a more distant image presentation. The proposed system is able to adapt to movements of the driver and thereby allows a correctly registered display of information.

Sato et al. [19] also used the described principle of reflection, but instead of positioning a display below the windshield, they attached a projector to the roof rack of a minivan and thereby created a street-ready prototype. A mirror and a retroreflector were used to project the image in front of the driver. The virtual image covers large parts of the windshield in front of the driver.

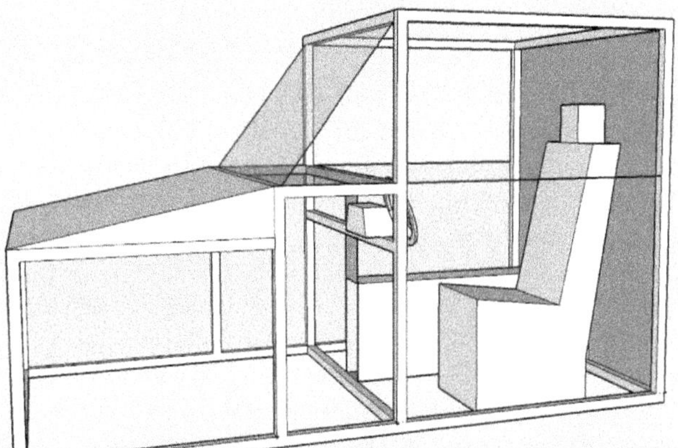

Figure 3: Basic construction of our test setup

CONSTRUCTION OF THE TEST SETUPS

The basic construction of the test setup is shown in figure 3. It consists of a wooden frame disguised by fabric and is equipped with a real windshield, a real car seat, and a gaming steering wheel to control the openDS[1] driving

[1] www.openDS.eu

simulator. The simulator scene is projected on the wall, approximately 4m in front of the test setup. The inside distances and angles are defined according to a BMW 1 series and, therefore, correspond to the dimensions of a real car. Our two test setups are implemented as follows:

Image presentation on the Windshield

As in the General Motors prototype, the first test setup is based on a high-end projector targeted onto a mirror, which is placed in the middle of the passenger compartment. The mirror forwards the image to the windshield, as visualized in figure 4. While direct projection leads to an irritating light refraction and glare and an insufficient imaging angle of the projector, the mirror enlarges the optical distance between the projector and the windshield and, therefore, scales the image to the windshield size. Depending on the driver's seat position, the distance between the driver and the image is approximately 0.7m.

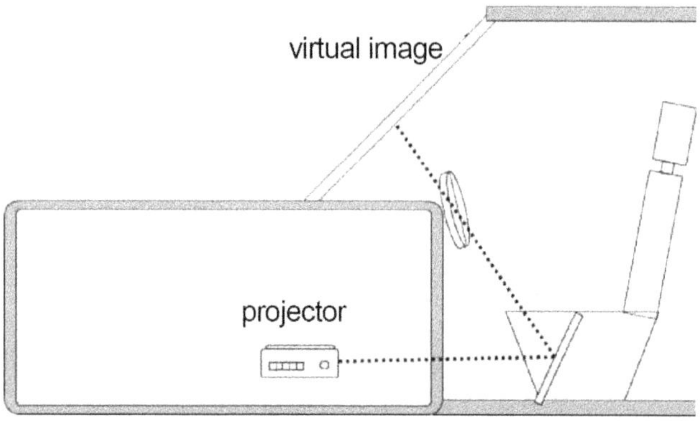

Figure 4: The projector image is forwarded to the windshield by a mirror.

As the windshield we used is highly transparent and does not diffuse enough light of the projector to provide a high-quality image, we laminated it with a foil. After testing various types of foils, we found a simple gift wrap foil to be the best compromise. It is cheap and highly transparent, but at the same time provides a surprisingly good light refraction. Covering the windshield on the outer side, we obtained a bright, sharp and colorful image without any double image effects. However, the fringe of the virtual image was slightly distorted due to the curvature of the windshield. An example image provided by this test setup is shown in figure 7. In the study, this setup will also be called the 'projector-based' approach.

Image presentation in front of the Windshield

In our second WSD test setup we lined up three displays below the windshield, which reflects the virtual image in front of the driver (see figure 5). We chose large displays (32 inch each) to create a virtual image that covers large parts of the view through the windshield. Even though we chose very bright displays, the room needed to be slightly darkened in order to obtain a crisp and colorful image.

The virtual image provided by this test setup is presented in figure 8. For the study, we will refer to this as the 'screen-based' approach.

The virtual image distance depends on the position of the displays. When they are close to the floor, the virtual image distance is 1.7m from the driver. At this distance, the image covers 60-70% of the driver's FoV. Lowering the distance between the display and the windshield decreases the virtual image distance, but also increases the subjective image size, as the closer image covers larger parts of the driver's field of view.

Currently, this WSD setup displays a slightly misaligned double image because both sides of the glass act as mirror surfaces. This double image cannot be corrected by adapting the image source. Instead, the windshield or combiner needs to be manipulated in form or material. One side of the combiner can be equipped with coatings which are anti-refractive or shaped like a wedge with increasing thickness [1]. As a first step, we decided to simply use a thinner acrylic pane to minimize the double image effect.

Compared with common HUDs, our distant image presentation does not require a fixed head position. The image is also visible to the driver when she or he moves or changes the seat position. Nevertheless, information, which is placed in relation and spatially close to environmental objects, has to be repositioned. Therefore, head-tracking will be needed in future iterations.

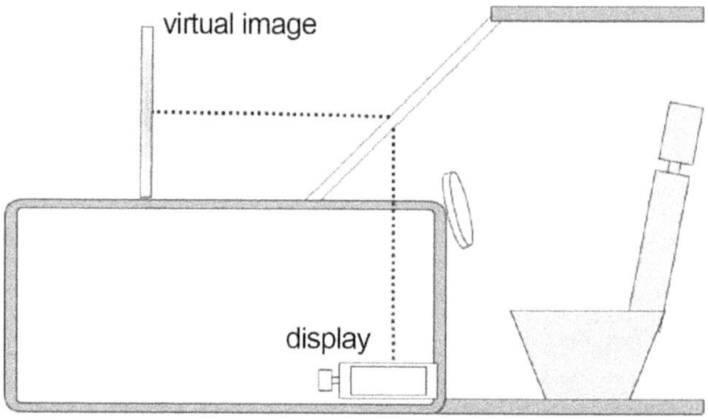

Figure 5: Three 32 inch displays are reflected in the windshield so that the virtual image appears in front of the driver.

For the study, we aimed to display one image in front of the car and the other one directly on the windshield, in order to compare these two viable and interesting approaches. Using the same hardware for both approaches would have been desirable, but was not possible due to the following reasons: It is not possible to use a projector for both images as a projected image can only be reflected to appear in front of the windshield if it first hits a projection surface on its way to the windshield. For this, it would need to be positioned at an angle or close to the windshield. The virtual image would then be of low contrast or positioned at a low image distance. This would decrease the difference between the two approaches. Neither was it possible to use a display for both approaches. For an image directly on the windshield, a transparent display, such as an OLED display would be needed. So far, no suitable display of this size is commercially available. Within the limits of the technologies we used, we made strong effort to provide comparable images in terms of brightness and resolution.

USER STUDY

In order to evaluate both windshield displays as well as the peripheral information displayed on them, we performed a user study with 20 participants. Subjects had to perceive and memorize information displayed on the WSD while performing lane changes. We investigated both systems regarding user experience and their impact on driving performance.

Study Design

In our study we aimed to investigate on the safety risk but also on the memorability of peripheral information, displayed on the two windshield display variants. Therefore, we decided to compare driving without an additional display (baseline) and driving with a windshield display (intervention). As we also wanted to compare both windshield display variants directly regarding user experience, we chose a within-subject study design. As each participant was supposed to test both WSD variants, for the memorability tests different peripheral information was provided. This resulted in a 2x2 study design.

Participants

We recruited 20 participants between 20 and 50 years of age (mean 28). Among them were six female and 14 male participants. All of them had a valid driver's license. For a counter-balanced study, we defined four test groups with different intervention configurations. We randomly assigned five out of 20 participants to the test groups B and C. Group A included six participants, group D four subjects. The defined groups A to D are depicted in table 1.

Table 1: Test groups with assigned intervention configuration

Test Group	Intervention Configuration	Windshield Display Variant	Widget Board Configuration
A	A	projector-based	1
	B	screen-based	2
B	A	screen-based	1
	B	projector-based	2
C	A	projector-based	2
	B	screen-based	1
D	A	screen-based	2
	B	projector-based	1

Lane Change Task

A widely accepted approach to evaluate the effects of in-vehicle systems and applications on driving performance is the Lane Chance Task (LCT). This method demands the alteration of baseline and intervention phases, starting with a baseline. The lane change task prompts the driver every 150m to change to a specified lane and provides measures and methods for analyzing the driving performance [12]. The within-subject design required two intervention phases. We decided to schedule three baseline phases, in order to compensate learning effects. The last baseline gave time to the participants to disengage their minds before filling a comparative questionnaire. The overall procedure of the user study is depicted in figure 6.

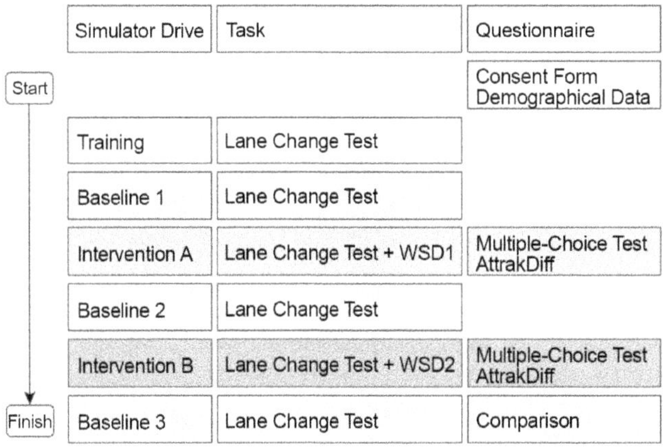

Figure 6: The procedure of the user study, including all tasks and questionnaires, took 35 to 45 minutes.

Each baseline and intervention phase was scheduled with three minutes, corresponding to three kilometers at a fixed speed of 60km/h. In each phase, subjects had to perform 18 lane changes, spread evenly throughout time and length. The directions of the lane changes were randomized but equal for all subjects. The lane change instructions are presented as green spots, placed on overhead gantries.

Memory Task

As a secondary task, we chose a memory task. It guaranteed that participants would pay attention to the peripheral information but did not require any interaction. Therefore, participants were able to shift attention to the display whenever they wanted.

As an application for the secondary task, we chose a widget board. The widget board corresponds to the user's desire of being always online and getting information everywhere on time. Therefore, usually smartphones are used. Since handling the phone while driving is illegal in many countries, the display of smartphone apps on an in-vehicle display is also an attractive use case.

We implemented two widget boards with different applications. Providing not only different content but also different widgets was supposed to help participants not to confuse the information of both tests. The content was supposed to be homologous, of comparable complexity and of equal value in order to provide a comparable basis for measuring distraction and memorability.

Figure 7: The first configuration of the widget board application displayed in front of the windshield.

The widget boards are located in the driver's peripheral field of view as recommended by Isomura [9,13]. We defined two regions for information presentation. Both regions were used in both widget boards. Information that is usually not accessible in vehicles, such as social media and weather information, was placed between the center and the right border of the WSD. This corresponds to an eccentricity of approximately 25-30°. The second cluster is positioned at the bottom in the middle of the windshield and presents information that is commonly visible on other displays. Apps such as the radio, clock or calendar are positioned at an eccentricity of approximately 15-20°. This arrangement was derived from common screen configurations and alignment of in-vehicle systems.

The position of the widgets was evaluated in pretests. It facilitated a good visual perception but also prevented the occlusion of important objects or parts of the driving scene. We also tested the amount of information displayed and the questions asked in the questionnaire before the actual user study started. Both were found to be manageable.

Widget Board Configurations

The first widget board configuration included the display of time, date, notifications, and friends nearby. In order to increase distraction and the amount of information to recall, both configurations included one widget which changed dynamically over time while driving. In this configuration it was the radar presenting friends nearby. The radar altered three times during one intervention: One friend appeared after 60 seconds, another one appeared after further 45 seconds and one disappeared after the next 45 seconds.

The second widget board configuration presented a radio, weather information, and Facebook status posts. In this widget board the Facebook post changed after 1.5 minutes, and a new post was displayed.

Both widget boards are depicted in the figures 7 and 8. For technical reasons, both photos were taken from the middle of the test setup, not from the driver's point of view. Therefore, the widgets appear more central than they have actually been in the study.

Figure 8: The second widget board configuration presented directly on the windshield.

Data Collection

We collected data about the users' experience and preference as well as the recall and driving performance:

Questionnaires

To test if the subjects paid attention to the peripheral information, we designed two recall questionnaires, one for each widget board configuration. Each questionnaire consisted of five questions about the content of the widgets. The question style was multiple-choice with four exact-value answers, spread evenly across the range of possible answers. If text was involved, four possible answers containing some similarity, such as identical key words, were provided. This approach ensured the recall of the headline by context and not by recognition of a key word.

We assessed the users' feelings about both windshield display systems by two AttrakDiff questionnaires. The major advantage of this questionnaire is that it produces quantitative and comparative data. It consists of 28 items, expressing properties whose poles are defined by opposite adjectives. Items are measured on a seven-step scale and can be automatically decoded and analyzed on the AttrakDiff Website[2].

Finally, participants had to provide their opinion about which system was more stunning or more readable. For this, we designed a questionnaire comparing the two WSD setups. Subjects were asked to fill out nine questions on a seven-step Likert-scale with the projector-based WSD on the one end and the screen-based WSD on the other. The position in the middle was neutral.

Driving Performance Measurement

To obtain objective data about the driving performance, the driving simulator logs the position of the vehicle. This allows the calculation of the mean deviation between optimal and driven line. The mean deviation is an indicator for driving quality and is sensitive to perception errors, reaction times, maneuvers, and lane keeping quality.

[2] www.attrakdiff.de

The reaction time is measured as the time between the appearance of the lane change command and the driver's steering reaction. As the driver can be in the act of performing a correction movement when a new command appears, we set a minimum threshold of 300ms for reliable recognition. As a last measure, we calculated the proportion of successfully performed lane changes. According to the LCT standard, the driver has to change to another lane (3500ms) and maintain stable control of the vehicle on this lane for at least 1500ms to perform a lane change successfully.

Procedure

In our initial explanation, we introduced our goal of comparing two windshield displays. To support the participants' understanding, we explained the concept of a windshield display and the goal of comparing two systems to the participants. To support the explanation, we showed an example widget board and described the task of memorizing the displayed information. We also emphasized the precedence of good driving performance. After this briefing, participants were asked to fill out a short demographical data sheet and respond to a few questions about applications and widgets they use on their phone.

The driving test started with a training session. During this phase, subjects were allowed to drive around freely, practice and get familiar with both the steering wheel and the overall system of the test. Afterwards, participants had to perform the first baseline drive.

The test continued with the intervention drive A. 10 of 20 participants started the test with the image presentation on the windshield. The remaining 10 participants drove with the image presentation in front of the windshield first. Also the widget board configurations were provided counter-balanced in the first intervention. Afterwards, participants had to fill the recall and the AttrakDiff questionnaire. Subsequently, participants had to drive another baseline to clear and disengage their minds. During the intervention B subjects drove with the other windshield display and widget board configuration. Also after this drive, participants hat to fulfill a recall and an AttrakDiff questionnaire. Finally, subjects were asked to perform a last baseline drive. This baseline gave time to the participants to take one step back from the recently tested windshield display version. This was important for the comparative questionnaire, which was handed over to the participants at the end of the study.

Results and Interpretation

In the following we present the results of our user study. We will also point at and interpret interesting findings.

Driving Performance

As a measure of driving performance, we measured the mean deviation from optimal line, the reaction time, and the successfully performed lane changes. To analyze the difference between baseline and driving with the windshield displays, we always compared the intervention with the two surrounding baselines. As both widget boards were designed to display homologous content (comparable in complexity and of equal value), they were not differentiated in the driving performance evaluation.

The average values for mean deviation are depicted in table 2. Participants showed a marginally better performance in baseline driving compared with the two different WSD concepts. The screen-based WSD yielded slightly better results than its counterpart.

The exact values for reaction time are listed in table 3 and depicted in figure 9. An ANOVA test revealed, that the reaction times were significantly deteriorated by both WSD variants ($F(3,19) = 10.73$, $p < .01$). Reaction times are increased but still very good. At the speed of 60km/h the increase corresponds to a line segment of only 0.6m and 0.8m respectively. In the case of an emergency braking, the car would be stopped not even one meter further.

Table 2: Mean deviation increased only marginally when driving with a WSD.

WSD Version	Baseline	Intervention	Effect
Screen-based	1.29 m^2	1.32 m^2	+1.9 %
Projector-based	1.31 m^2	1.33 m^2	+1.6 %

Table 3: Reaction time increased when driving with a WSD.

WSD Version	Baseline	Intervention	Effect
Screen-based	729 ms	763 ms	+4,72 %
Projector-based	737 ms	784 ms	+6,43 %

The rate of successfully completed lane changes is depicted in figure 9. The success rates dropped from 95.7% to 90.3% when using the screen-based WSD and from 95.1% to 86.9% when using the projector-based system. An ANOVA showed, that this decline is statistically significant for the projector-based system ($F(3,19) = 6.38$, $p < .01$).

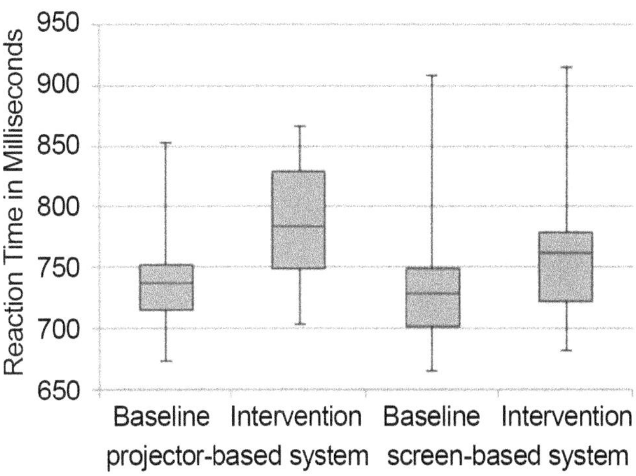

Figure 9: Reaction time increased when driving with a WSD, but especially when using the projector-based WSD

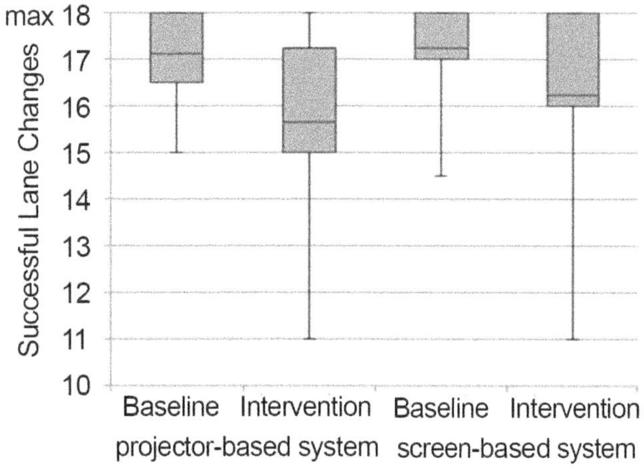

Figure 10: Lane change success rate was lowered when driving with both WSD variants.

Although we displayed the same information on both WSDs, we did not find the same effects on driving quality for the two versions. Both setups had only marginally different effects on the mean deviation, but looking at reaction time and success rate, the projector-based system had a considerably stronger effect than its counterpart.

Interpreting these results, the higher reaction times probably caused the drop in lane change success rate. The fact that success rate and reaction time are impaired, while mean deviation did not change noticeably, indicates that participants did not have problems to keep steady control of the vehicle but simply reacted more slowly.

Recall Performance

To verify whether subjects used the WSD application and were able to read and memorize the information displayed, multiple-choice questions were asked about the content that had been presented. In summary, participants performed very well on the recall questions (see figure 9). With 94% and 96% correct answers, both widget boards led to almost identical recall success rates. Eight correct answers were the minimum. Twelve of twenty users scored the maximum value of ten correct answers.

The high success rate in recalling the displayed information leads to the conclusion that participants used the windshield displays and looked at the peripheral information.

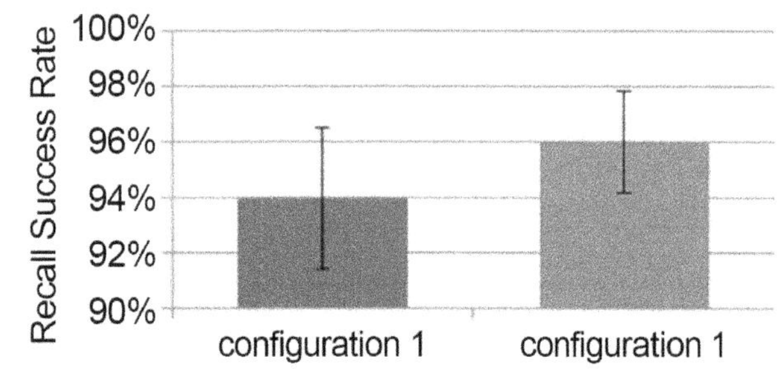

Figure 11: This chart shows the recall success rate and the error variances. The success rate of recalling the peripheral information was very high for both widget boards.

User Experience

The user experience questionnaire AttrakDiff was chosen to compare the two WSD types. In this questionnaire as well as in the additional, comparative questionnaire, we explicitly asked about the windshield displays, not about the widget board applications.

Figure 12 illustrates an overview of the user ratings. Both systems were rated as moderately attractive, but also show a clearly positive tendency. Both WSDs had good ratings for properties such as *clearly structured*, *presentable*, and *innovative*. These are all favorable aspects of a good user experience. They were also characterized as "good" and rated with equal values for this property.

For most properties, the screen-based setup received slightly better results. This system was valued as more presentable and manageable as well as clearer structured and less demanding. The projector-based system was rated remarkably better for the properties *innovative* and *novel*. This is most likely related to the prominence of HUDs and their distant image presentation. However, both systems need improvement, especially regarding professionalism and practicability. A system that is more human (natural) than technical in character and connects its users to the world rather than isolating them, would provide a more positive user experience.

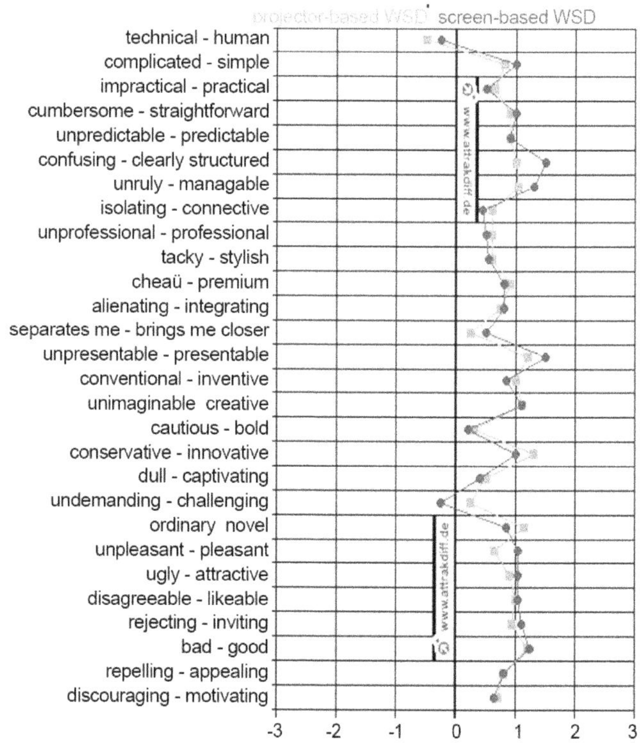

Figure 12: Both WSDs showed a good user experience.

The average ratings for pragmatic and hedonic quality of both systems correspond to a position within the neutral rectangle, but very close to the field 'desired' (see figure 13). The chart shows that the screen-based system has a slightly higher rating for pragmatic quality, corresponding to a rather task-oriented system. The projector-based system is rated with a marginally higher hedonic quality. This points to a rather self-orientated system. Though, both versions seem to provide a very good compromise of both orientations. The center points are surrounded by a small confidence rectangle, which indicates that subjects strongly agree in their evaluations.

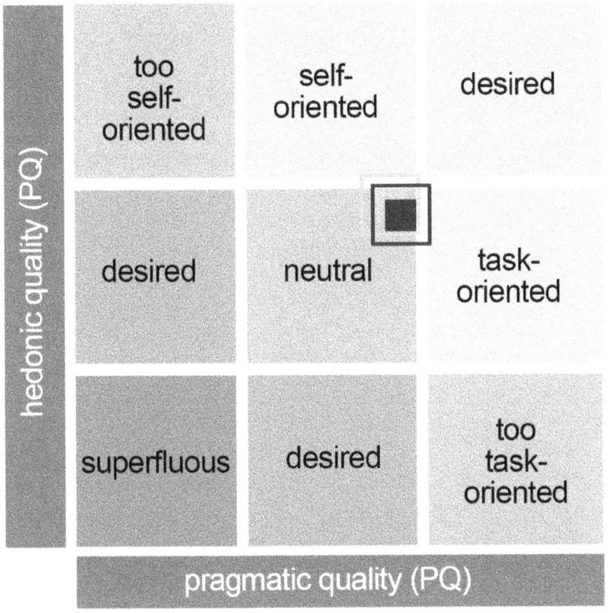

Figure 13: The pragmatic and hedonic quality of the screen-based (blue) and the projector-based (orange) WSDs are neutral but close to desired.

User Preferences

The last form of evaluation was a direct comparison of both WSD systems. Participants had to rate their preference on a scale from -3 to 3 with the projector-based system on the one end and the screen-based system on the other side. The value 0 represents a neutral attitude. A neutral rating means both systems are equal, but does not give an indication of how good or bad the systems are.

Figure 14 presents all user ratings. The average is presented by the group named 'complete' and the red line. Based on the ratings of the question about their favorite system, we differentiated three groups of users. Participants who valued this question with less than -1, were assigned to the group preferring the projector-based WSD (n = 4). Subjects who rated the first question above +1 were assigned to the group in favor of the screen-based WSD (n = 10). Participants who valued this question in the range of -1 to +1 were assigned to the group 'neutral' (n = 6). Three subjects assigned to the neutral group showed a tendency to the screen-based system and two tended to the projector-based system. One participant was completely neutral.

The preference for the screen-based system is not only demonstrated by the ratings of the first question. Looking at the overall ratings of the two groups favoring one system, it seems the group supporting the screen-based version was more enthusiastic. This group valued their preference with 1.42 on average. The group preferring the projector-based system only supported their preference with an average rating of 1.13, which is close to the threshold to the neutral group. Looking at the overall ratings for all questions of all participants, the average value is 0.55. All these values point at an overall preference for the image presentation in front of the display.

However, looking at the data in more detail, the screen-based system was not rated superior for all questions. Regarding distraction, both systems were rated equal (average = -0.15). Also the question which system made the subject feel safer was valued quite neutral (average = 0.45). Both questions of course only measure perceived safety. The results indicate that participants perceived both systems as equally safe. The readability of text was rated equally good for both systems, but in general, information seems to be better recognizable when presented in front of the windshield. Especially graphics are rated easier to perceive on this WSD version.

Participants in favor of one system did not answer the questions about the system they could imagine to use and their preferred system equally. This indicates that either the need for a WSD is not big enough or that the image quality of both systems is not convincing enough to actually buy such system.

DISCUSSION

The widget boards were placed at an eccentricity of 15-30° and the speed was fixed at 60km/h. These values are below the thresholds found by [11,13]. Higher values would probably have led to a worse driving performance.

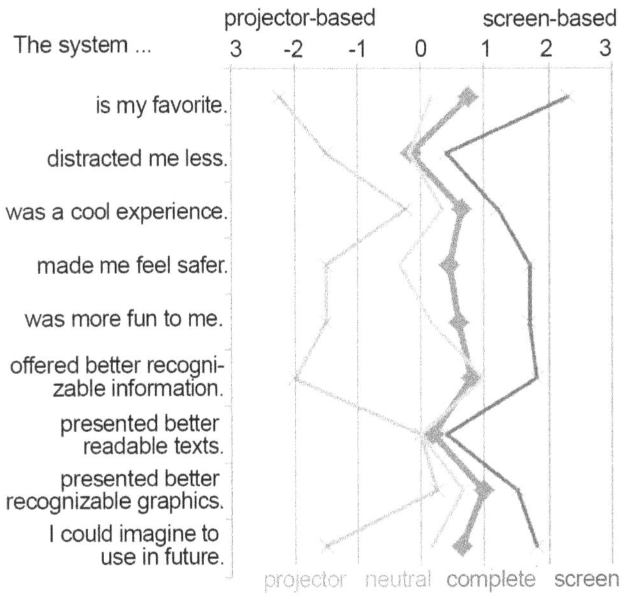

Figure 14: The comparison of both system shows that participants preferred the screen-based system (red line).

To perceive information that was displayed on the widget boards, participants had to look to the side and to remove their focus from the driving scene. The fact that they actually looked at the widget boards is documented by a high recall success rate. Reviewing the results of our driving performance measurements, the required looks to the side had no remarkable influence on the mean deviation. However, we did find deteriorations in lane change success rate and reaction time, compared to baseline driving. As success rate depends on reaction time, these measures can be related to the same problem. These results indicate that participants simply reacted slower but did not have problems in keeping the vehicle steady on the road, when peripheral information was displayed.

The effects on driving performance were more prominent for the projector-based system than for its screen-based counterpart. The main difference of these systems is the virtual image distance. Consequently, it is most likely that the increase in reaction time is related to the image distance. This relationship has been pointed out in other literature as well [8]. When the distance between driver and image is increased, the distance between the driving scene and the virtual image is decreased simultaneously. The more distant image enables a faster accommodation and eventually leads to a better reaction time, compared to a virtual image closer to the viewer. This was already mentioned in other studies, on information presented in HUDs.

The user experience evaluation exposed that participants liked both windshield display variants. The AttrakDiff evaluation in figure 13 shows that the rectangles representing both systems are close to the field 'desired'. While not directly visible in the results of the AttrakDiff evaluation, the analysis of the comparative questionnaire showed that users preferred the screen-based version. Although subjects stated to like the windshield displays, they seem not to be too enthusiastic about using a system which is comparable to one of our test setups in the future. This fact shows that both versions need improvement. A major weakness seems to be the recognizability of information.

As evident from the figures 7 and 8, both technologies provided homologous images. If at all, subjects may have had more problems to focus on and recognize the display-based image (due to double-image and reflection) compared to the projected one. They may have rated the screen-based WSD better, if it had been without its flaws. Therefore, if results have been influenced by technology, we would expect this to be in favor of the projector-based WSD due to its slightly better image quality. Nevertheless, the screen-based WSD was rated better. The difference may therefore even be bigger without this potential bias.

CONCLUSIONS AND FUTURE WORK

Motivated by the potential risks and benefits of a peripheral display in the windshield area, we performed a user study. We investigated the display of peripheral information at the height of the drivers' line of sight while driving. In related studies, the virtual image was either positioned within or close to the driver's central FoV or the displayed information was visually not demanding (only a simple stimulus) and investigated without observing its effects on driving performance. In our study, we set the lane change task as the primary, and a memory task as the secondary task. We investigated the peripheral information regarding its memorability as well as both WSD systems regarding user experience and preferences. Moreover, we measured impacts on driving performance. Interpreting the results of our study, we think that participants were able to look consciously at the peripheral information, presented on the screen-based windshield display, while keeping an acceptable level of driving performance.

For our user test, we built two windshield display test setups with different virtual image distances. The single test setups set themselves apart from the ones suggested in the literature by providing a large-scale image which also covers the outer parts of the windshield. This enables the evaluation of use cases, which refer not only to the road scene but also to the environment, such as the previously mentioned points of interest.

The distant image presentation is considered and was found to be the better approach but projection directly on the windshield is rather realizable. As follows, both visualization approaches should be further researched.

As a next step we want to enhance our test setups to reduce side effects related to image quality. Then we plan to test applications with a potential benefit for safety, and which rely on peripheral area. Such an application could for example be a hazard highlighting. People crossing from the sidewalk or wild animals in a rural environment could be marked up in the periphery using a windshield display.

Other future work, which we would like to encourage, would study peripheral information displayed more eccentric and also at larger distances. Moreover, we think that the human's response to a change of the peripheral information should be investigated more closely.

ACKNOWLEDGMENTS

This work was funded by IAV GmbH.

REFERENCES

[1] Betancur, J. A. (2011). Book chapter "Physical Variable Analysis Involved in Head-Up Display Systems Applied to Automobiles", Augmented Reality-Some Emerging Application Areas, edited by Dr. *Andrew Yeh Ching Nee.*

[2] BMW AG. BMW technology guide - BMW head-up display. http://www.bmw.com/com/en/insights/technology/technology_guide/articles/head_up_display.html, visited 28.11.2013.

[3] Crundall, D., Underwood, G., & Chapman, P. (1999). Driving experience and the functional field of view. *Perception-London, 28*(9), 1075-1088.

[4] Ecker, R. (2013). *Der verteilte Fahrerinteraktions-raum* (Doctoral dissertation, Ludwig-Maximilians-Universität München), 34.

[5] Eriksen, C. W., & Murphy, T. D. (1987). Movement of attentional focus across the visual field: A critical look at the evidence. *Attention, Perception, & Psychophysics, 42*(3), 299-305.

[6] Foyle, D.C., Sanford, B.D. and McCann, R.S. (1991). Attentional issues in superimposed flight symbology. In R.S. Jensen (Ed.), *Proceedings of the Sixth International Symposium on Aviation Psychology*, 577-582.

[7] Fujimura, K., Xu, L., Tran, C., Bhandari, R., & Ng-Thow-Hing, V. (2013, October). Driver queries using wheel-constrained finger pointing and 3-D head-up display visual feedback. In *Proceedings of the 5th International Conference on Automotive User Interfaces and Interactive Vehicular Applications* , 56-62.

[8] Gabbard, J. L., Fitch, G. M., & Kim, H. (2014). Behind the Glass: Driver Challenges and Opportunities for AR Automotive Applications. *Proceedings of the IEEE, 102*(2), 124-136.

[9] Gish, K. W., & Staplin, L. (1995). Human factors aspects of using head up displays in automobiles: A review of the literature.

[10] Horrey, W. J., Wickens, C. D., & Alexander, A. L. (2003, October). The effects of head-up display clutter and in-vehicle display separation on concurrent driving performance. In *Proceedings of the Human Factors and Ergonomics Society Annual Meeting*, 47(16), 1880-1884.

[11] Iino, T., Otsuka, T., & Suzuki, Y. (1988). *Development of Heads-Up Display for a Motor Vehicle*, 15-23.

[12] ISO, British Standards Institution. Road vehicles. Ergonomic aspects of transport information and control systems. Simulated lane change test to assess in-vehicle secondary task demand, 2010. ISO 26022.

[13] Isomura, A., Kamiya, K., & Hamatani, K. (1993). *Driver's Cognition in Peripheral Field of View.*

[14] Jahn, G., Oehme, A., Krems, J. F., & Gelau, C. (2005). Peripheral detection as a workload measure in driving: Effects of traffic complexity and route guidance system use in a driving study. *Transportation Research Part F: Traffic Psychology and Behaviour, 8*(3), 255-275.

[15] Maglio, P. P., & Campbell, C. S. (2000, April). Tradeoffs in displaying peripheral information. In *Proceedings of the SIGCHI conference on Human factors in computing systems* (pp. 241-248). ACM.

[16] Poitschke, T. M. (2011). *Blickbasierte Mensch-Maschine Interaktion im Automobil* (Doctoral dissertation, Technische Universität München).

[17] Poitschke, T. M., Ablaßmeier, M., Rigoll, G., Bardins, S., Kohlbecher, S., & Schneider, E. (2008, March). Contact-analog information representation in an automotive head-up display. In *Proceedings of the 2008 symposium on Eye tracking research & applications*, 119-122.

[18] Rümelin, S., Marouane, C., & Butz, A. (2013, October). Free-hand pointing for identification and interaction with distant objects. In *Proceedings of the 5th International Conference on Automotive User Interfaces and Interactive Vehicular Applications* (pp. 40-47). ACM.

[19] Sato, A., Kitahara, I., Kameda, Y., & Ohta, Y. (2006). Visual navigation system on windshield head-up display. In *Proc. 13th World Congress on Intelligent Transort Systems, CD-ROM.*

[20] Takaki, Y., Urano, Y., Kashiwada, S., Ando, H., & Nakamura, K. (2011). Super multi-view windshield display for long-distance image information presentation. *Optics express, 19*(2), 704-716.

[21] Transparente Anzeigevorrichtung für ein Kraftfahrzeug. Volkswagen AG, Patent, 2008.

[22] Tretten, P., Gärling, A., Nilsson, R., & Larsson, T. C. (2011, September). An On-Road Study of Head-Up Display Preferred Location and Acceptance Levels. In *Proceedings of the Human Factors and Ergonomics Society Annual Meeting*, 55(1), 1914-1918.

[23] Verwey, W. B. (2000). On-line driver workload estimation. Effects of road situation and age on secondary task measures. *Ergonomics, 43*(2), 187-209.

[24] Weihrauch, M., Meloeny, G. G., & Goesch, T. C. (1989). *The first head up display introduced by* general *motors* (No. 890288). SAE Technical Paper.

[25] Wu, W., Blaicher, F., Yang, J., Seder, T., & Cui, D. (2009, October). A prototype of landmark-based car navigation using a full-windshield head-up display system. In *Proceedings of the 2009 workshop on Ambient media computing*, 21-28.

[26] Yoo, H., Tsimhoni, O., Watanabe, H., Green, P., & Shah, R. (1999). *Display of HUD warnings to drivers: determining an optimal location* (No. UMTRI-99-9).

Attention Engagement and Cognitive State Analysis for Augmented Reality Text Display Functions

Takumi Toyama, Daniel Sonntag
German Reaserch Center for AI (DFKI)
Kaiserslautern, Germany
{takumi.toyama, daniel.sonntag}@dfki.de

Jason Orlosky, Kiyoshi Kiyokawa
Osaka University
Osaka, Japan
{orlosky@ist, kiyo@ime.cmc}.osaka-u.ac.jp

ABSTRACT
Human eye gaze has recently been used as an effective input interface for wearable displays. In this paper, we propose a gaze-based interaction framework for optical see-through displays. The proposed system can automatically judge whether a user is engaged with virtual content in the display or focused on the real environment and can determine his or her cognitive state. With these analytic capacities, we implement several proactive system functions including adaptive brightness, scrolling, messaging, notification, and highlighting, which would otherwise require manual interaction. The goal is to manage the relationship between virtual and real, creating a more cohesive and seamless experience for the user. We conduct user experiments including attention engagement and cognitive state analysis, such as reading detection and gaze position estimation in a wearable display towards the design of augmented reality text display applications. The results from the experiments show robustness of the attention engagement and cognitive state analysis methods. A majority of the experiment participants (8/12) stated the proactive system functions are beneficial.

Author Keywords
Attention engagement analysis; eye tracking; cognitive state analysis; augmented reality; gaze-based interface;

ACM Classification Keywords
H.5.2. User Interfaces: Input devices and strategies

General Terms
Human Factors; Design; Performance.

INTRODUCTION
In recent years, eye gaze input has become increasingly popular, and eye trackers are now available on the commercial market. With this type of input, the user usually does not need to move his or her hands for control since eye gaze can be used for interaction in many cases. Examples include text manipulation, activating commands, or application of drag-and-drop of virtual objects in the display by gaze alone [5, 12, 22]. Meanwhile, recent developments in optical see-through head-mounted display (HMD) technology have enabled augmented reality (AR), where virtual information is present in the same line of sight with the real environment, as shown in Figure 1. In augmented reality, virtual images are superimposed onto the environment directly in a user's field of view, which presents various challenges. Here we address two of these problems. The first is the fact that 1) traditional direction-based eye gaze input approaches cannot identify on which reality space (virtual or real) the user is focused and the second 2) is that the user may be involved in different cognitive tasks when he or she is interacting with augmented content, such as reading text, viewing pictures, or other activities [7, 8, 10].

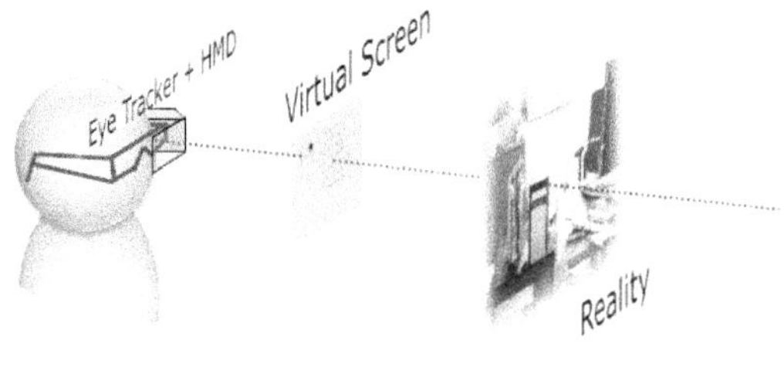

Figure 1. An image of the system. Wearing a see-through HMD, the user sees reality and virtual content on the screen in the same line of sight.

Though several eye gaze-based interactive AR systems have already been proposed [13, 26], there are still only a handful of interactions available through gaze, and many of them are limited to line of sight. Usually, line of sight-based techniques have an inevitable drawback when used with optical see-through displays in that they cannot distinguish on which interactive space (virtual or real) the user is focused. Thus, the system may mistakenly activate AR functionality in the HMD even if the user is not attending to the virtual space, which is often obstructive for the user. Furthermore, it was shown that recognition of user's cognitive state, such as reading, [17, 4] can effectively facilitate proactive, assistive functions [20, 5] with ordinary computer screen interactions but used in AR wearable displays. We also investigate advantages of cognitive state analysis for interactions with an AR see-through HMD.

In this paper, we have two primary goals. The first is to determine if we can extract a user's cognitive state based on eye-gaze alone (unlike previous classification or adaptive methods, we also use attention engagement estimation in a virtual

IUI 2015, March 29–April 1, 2015, Atlanta, GA, USA.
Copyright © 2015 ACM 978-1-4503-3306-1/15/03 ...$15.00.
http://dx.doi.org/10.1145/2678025.2701384

space, which gives us an additional dimension for analysis). Second, once we have determined a cognitive state, we want to use this knowledge to facilitate functions which would normally require manual or time consuming interaction to execute. When a user is reading text in a display, he or she should not have to manually scroll down to continue reading. Moreover, if he or she wants to glance at an environmental object, perhaps when at a crosswalk, virtual text should be dimmed for the duration of the glance, and immediately become visible again when the user looks back at the screen. Additionally, the user should be able to continue reading at the exact spot where he or she left off, without losing his or her place.

Though we focus on text display, related proactive user assistance that uses attention engagement and cognitive state analysis include the following practical examples. We focus on the implementation of several proactive system functions which intelligently control HMD screen interfaces using eye gaze input.

Automatic Dim

Automatic dim enables the system to control the brightness of the screen intelligently, by estimating the users attention engagement with the display. When the user is attending to the virtual screen, the system increases the brightness and vice versa when not attending. For attention engagement estimation, we propose two methods: gaze depth-based and vestibulo-ocular reflex (VOR)-based.

Automatic Scroll

Due to a narrow field of view, optical see-through displays typically cannot show full texts when the document is large. Therefore, only a portion of the text is present at once. The proposed function can scroll text automatically when the user is reading something in the display. This way, we can more effectively use display space and the user can read text seamlessly. In this paper, we propose a method to detect a user's reading state in the display.

Eye-Con

Eye-Cons are gaze-selectable icons in the HMD that are activated by attentional user gaze. Previous work shows that activation of commands using dwell-time-based approaches are useful, and can even detect fixations with noisy data [26]. We implement this function by detecting attention to icons on the display.

Last Read Word Highlighter (Identifier)

The user will also frequently need return his or her focus to reality, to shift attention to an emergency or other distractions for example. It is cumbersome for the user to come back to the place where he or she left off the screen, especially when he or she was reading text. To address this, the system highlights the last read word when the user comes back to the virtual screen, using the last word read prior to shifting gaze away from the display. This paper presents the algorithm for identification of the last word read.

Attentive Notification

When the user is engaged with a cognitively intensive task such as reading, notifications by the system such as email alert may be distracting. Based on active/passive cognitive state classification, the system predicts an appropriate moment for notification. The system then notifies the user attentively by presenting information only when the user is a passive cognitive state. We propose a method for prediction of a busy cognitive state during display interaction.

Our contribution in this work is to propose an intelligent interaction framework for augmented reality, taking user's attention and cognitive states into account. In experiments and user studies, we investigate robustness of the proposed attention engagement estimation and cognitive state classification approaches, and we evaluate usability of the proposed proactive system functions.

PRIOR WORK

Prior work includes a wide range of gaze based interaction approaches for virtual, physical and mixed environments. Early gaze-based interfaces presented by Jacob [11] and Bolt et al. [24] showed real potential of eye gaze input for human-computer interaction. Since then, a number of gaze-based interaction approaches have been proposed. Especially in virtual reality, users can control 3D objects and interact with content and menus using predefined gaze control [29, 12].

In [11], Jacob coined a term for a common challenge in gaze-based interface, called the *Midas-touch problem*, which accounts for unintentional function activation. This problem motivated researchers to develop intelligent methods for gaze-based interaction. For instance, the system presented by Qvarfordt and Zhai [18] analyzes user's eye gaze patterns to predict interested areas of the user in a city map.

To avoid unintentional interaction, it is useful to understand in which types of visual cognitive tasks eye gaze is involved. Many studies have contributed to understanding eye movements during individual cognitive tasks [21]. Eye movement analysis on reading and information processing is one of the main topics for such studies [19]. Based on these extensive studies, we can already develop a robust computational classifier of a user's reading state [7]. Recent work by Coco et al. [8] and Henderson et al. [10] also showed that further classification of cognitive state such as scene memorization and visual search is possible using eye gaze patterns. Such analysis on user's cognitive state could be used to enhance user experiences when he or she is interacting with a computer screen [20, 5] or with real document printouts [26], inferring in which type of cognitive state the user is involved.

Eye gaze input is also effectively used in augmented reality (AR) and mixed reality (MR). Using an optical see-through display, a user can interact with the real environment as well as virtual information overlay [13, 1]. Also, by measuring a user's eye gaze vectors in space, we can infer which plane he or she is interacting with out of multiple virtual planes [25, 2].

Such eye gaze-based interaction techniques have great potential for a wide variety of application areas. Augmentation and assistance of daily activities using eye gaze-based interfaces demonstrate benefits for those who suffer from handi-

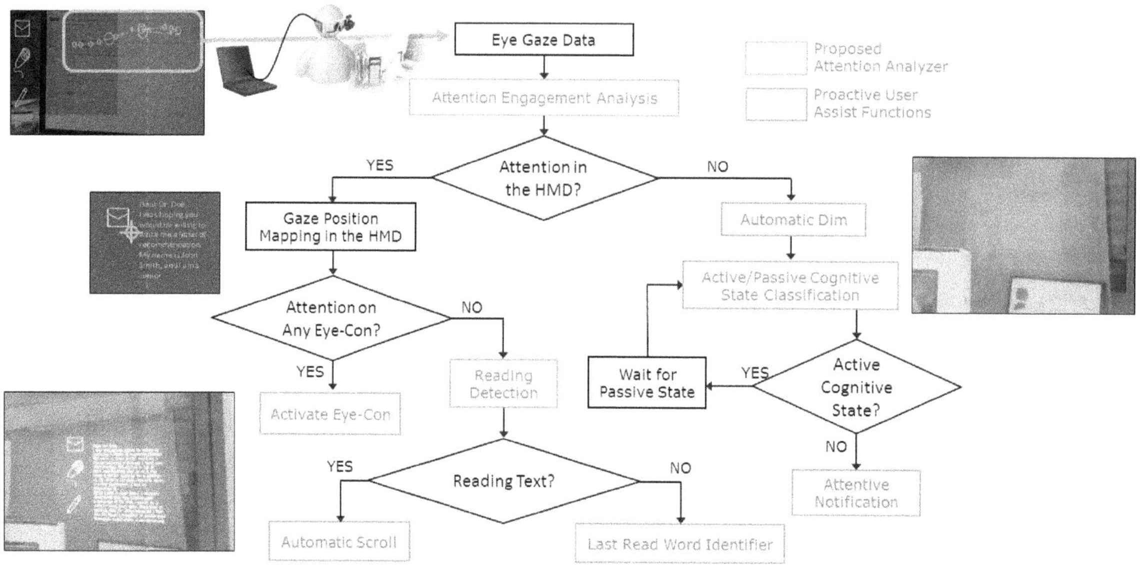

Figure 2. Flowchart of the proposed system. The entire interaction is driven by attention engagement analysis and cognitive state analysis. Blue boxes are the proposed attention analyzers and red boxes are the proposed proactive functions. From the user's eye, the HMD can be seen in the pictures (left-bottom: bright screen and right: dark screen (dimmed)).

caps such as SSPI [28] or dementia [16], for educational e-learning environments [3], and others.

APPROACH

Figure 2 illustrates a flowchart of the proposed architecture. The entire system is driven by eye gaze-based attention engagement and cognitive state analysis. Consequently, the proposed system interacts with the user intelligently and attentively. This paper presents methods for eye gaze-based attention analysis (blue boxes in the figure) and proactive user assist functions (red boxes). In this section, we present the approaches for respective analysis methods and how the proactive user assistive functions can be realized using the proposed attention analysis.

Hardware Setup

First, we build a prototypical eye-tracking see-through HMD. This apparatus consists of a pair of SMI Eye Tracking Glasses (ETG) and a Brother AirScouter, as shown in Figure 3. Using this apparatus, we can measure eye movements of the user both in the real environment and in the virtual screen. These two devices are connected by a 3D printed snap-on attachment.

From the user's view, the HMD virtual screen appears as shown in the bottom-left of Figure 2. Typical optical see-through HMDs that are currently available such as the Brother AirScouter has a quite limited range of field-of-view (22.4° diagonal). Thus, to develop an effective interface within a limited HMD screen is a challenging topic for augmented reality.

Attention Engagement Analysis

The first challenge is to estimate whether the user's attention is located in a virtual screen or in the reality space. We

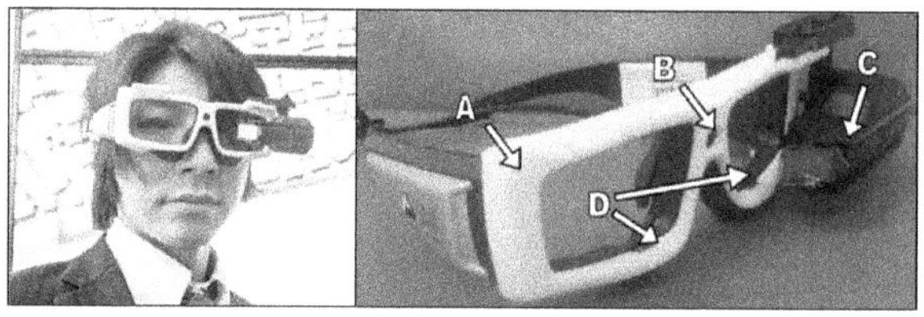

Figure 3. Left: a wearer of the glasses. Right: hardware setup showing A) 3D printed connector, B) outward facing scene camera, C) head mounted display, and D) inward facing eye cameras.

propose two approaches for attention engagement estimation: gaze depth-based method and VOR-based method.

Gaze Depth-based Method

Attentional focus is a function that primates innately possess, where visual acuity is best. By directing attention to a point of focus, humans can efficiently collect visual information in a scene. Thus, when the user's attention is engaged in a virtual display space, the 3D focal depth of eye gaze must be located near the virtual display plane in the space. Based on this observation, we estimate whether the user's attention is engaged with a virtual environment or reality. We calculate the user's gaze depth in the environment using online gaze data from the eye tracker. Since our eye tracker very reliably provides 2D gaze coordinates (horizontal and vertical) in a scene image (ETG accuracy 0.5°), we only implement the approach for gaze depth calculation.

Point of Convergence of Gaze Vectors. First, we extract gaze vectors of both eyes from the each eye camera. Using this data, we calculate the point of convergence of the two vectors in space as shown in Figure 4. Based on this convergent point, we estimate the focal depth of the user's eye gaze. Because scales of vectors from the eye tracker are different for

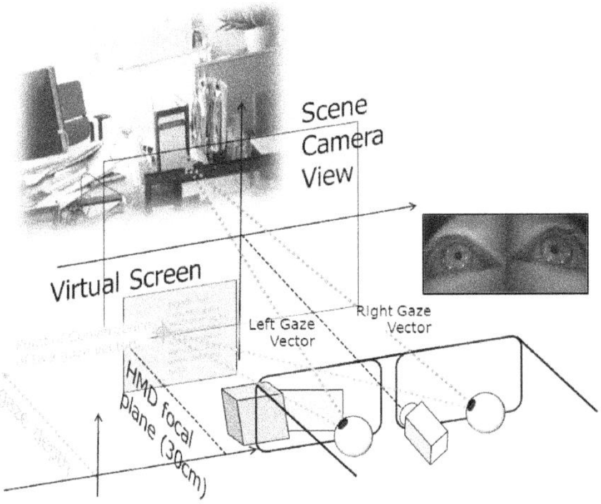

Figure 4. Setup of the virtual screen and real environment. We detect the user's attention engagement if gaze depth is near the plane.

individual users, the resulting depth value is relative for each user. Thus, we need to tune parameters for individual users. It has been shown that gaze vectors from an eye tracker do not always converge in 3D space [25]. If it is the case, we assume that gaze is in a far plane (thus, the user is focusing on a point in the real environment).

3D Gaze Focal Point for Attention Estimation. Using the depth value and 2D coordinates from the eye tracker, we find out whether user attention is located in the HMD or in reality. Figure 4 shows the model of our setup. We set the focal plane of the see-through HMD to a certain distance from the user's eye (30cm). As shown in this figure, the focal plane of the HMD is relatively near to the user's eye. Hence, if the user's gaze focal depth is near the plane, we can infer that the user is focusing on the display. We first collect gaze depth values when a user is focusing on the HMD for parameter validation. After parameter validation, we obtain the average depth d_{HMD} when the user is focusing on the HMD and the resulting standard deviation σ. We estimate the user is engaged with the virtual screen of the HMD if the calculated depth value d is:

$$-k\sigma + d_{HMD} \leq d \leq k\sigma + d_{HMD}.$$

In the experiment, we find an optimal k for the attention estimation (separating virtual and real).

A disadvantage of this gaze depth-based approach is that if the user focuses on objects near the virtual plane, the system cannot tell whether gaze is on the virtual screen or in the real world.

Vestibulo-Ocular Reflex Based Approach

When a human moves his/her head while fixating on an object in the environment, the eyeballs move opposite direction to the head movement. If such behavior occurs, a vestibulo-ocular reflex (VOR) is observed, which indicates that the human is actually attending to the object in the reality. Recent work by Vidal et al. [27] showed potential of attention engagement estimation using VOR. When a head movement occurs, eye gaze moves either to the same direction or to another direction, depending on the user's attention engagement with an HMD.

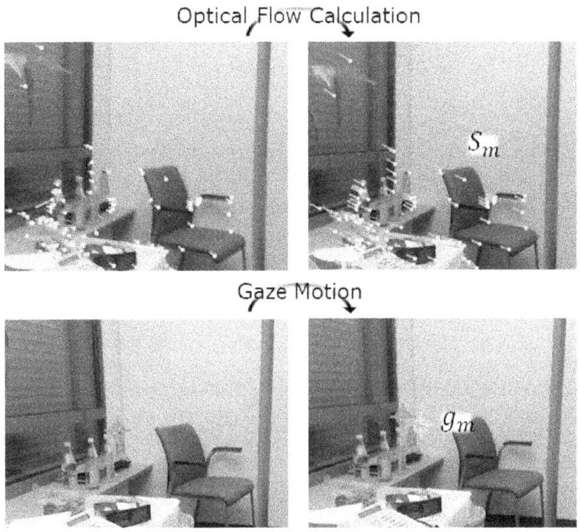

Figure 5. Optical flow and gaze motion vector from two consecutive video frames. When the user fixates on an object (a bottle cap), the gaze moves opposite direction to the head motion (the mean optical flow vector).

In this work, inspired by [27], we also implement an attention engagement estimation technique using head and eye gaze motion tracking. Instead of using an inertial measurement unit (IMU), we use optical-flow of scene images for head motion tracking.

We calculate optical flow between two consecutive scene images as shown in Figure 5. First, we extract local interest points using the Shi-Tomasi method [23]. Then, optical flow of each interest point is calculated by the Lucas-Kanade method [15]. We use the methods implemented in the OpenCV C++ library. Finally, we calculate the mean 2D vector S_m of optical flow from all the interest points. The mean vector shows motion of the scene camera (head).

On the other hand, we also extract the movement of gaze positions between two consecutive frames. By subtracting the previous gaze coordinate g_p from the current coordinate g_c, we obtain the gaze motion vector g_m. Hence, the difference between the head and gaze motion d_{abs} (which corresponds to the absolute gaze motion in space) is given by,

$$d_{abs} = \text{abs}(S_m - g_m).$$

If d_{abs} is small enough, we assume that the user is focusing on the display, and vice versa. In the experiment, we find an optimal value for the threshold value T_d.

Mapping Gaze Position in an HMD

Using the gaze coordinate in the scene image, we can also calculate the gaze position on the HMD when the user is attending to the virtual space. In this work, we employ a simple mapping method as shown in Figure 6. Using our own

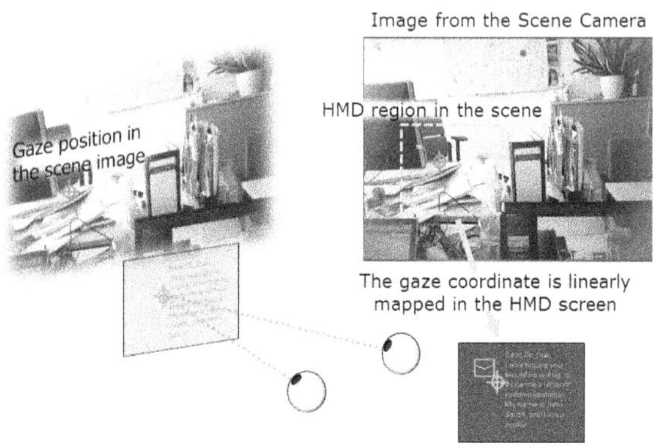

Figure 6. Gaze position mapping on an HMD screen. HMD screen positions in the same line of sight of the green rectangle in the right image. The HMD location must be calibrated in advance, by adjusting mapping parameters manually.

software, the user can adjust the HMD region in the scene image manually. Because the HMD is positioned in parallel to the scene image, the gaze coordinate in the image is linearly mapped to the position in the HMD ($(x_{hmd}, y_{hmd}) = (ax + \alpha, by + \beta)$, where (x, y) is the gaze coordinate in the scene image and (x_{hmd}, y_{hmd}) is the gaze position in the HMD). Once we get a gaze position in the HMD, we can activate interactive commands using user's eye input in the display. We implement a gaze-selectable user interface, called the *eye-con*, in the HMD.

Cognitive State Analysis

In our proposed framework, the system controls the graphical interfaces and proactive assistance functions according to user's cognitive state. The *automatic scroll* is activated when the system detects a reading state from the user in the virtual screen. And it also identifies the *last read word* when the user stops reading. Similarly, the *attentive notification* is driven based on results from an active/passive cognitive state classifier.

Reading State Detection

Reading is a very characteristic cognitive behavior of eye gaze. Usually a human moves his/her eyes alongside lines of text. With normal English text, they are aligned horizontally and the text begins from the left. Studies on eye movements during reading show that we often do not fixate on each word individually, but we often perceive three or four words at one fixation [19]. Up to now, a number of approaches have been proposed for reading detection based on eye gaze. In this work we use a basic approach for reading detection.

For reading detection, we extract fixations and saccades from gaze data using a dispersion approach [6]. Based on the fixations and saccades from a certain time window W, we compute dominant saccadic angular values in W. Suppose $S_a = \{s_{a1}, s_{a2}, ..., s_{ai}, ..., s_{an}\}$ $(0 < s_{ai} \leq 2\pi)$ is a set of angular values of the extracted saccades in W. Each angular value s_{ai} is quantized into one of 18 values (i.e., the range of each bin is $\pi/9$; 0 and π is horizontal angle). Consequently, we generate a histogram of angular values, which has 18 elements. The largest element of the histogram is the most dominant saccadic angular A_1 in W (1st-Sac) and the second largest one is the second most dominant angular A_2 (2nd-Sac). Because we focus on English text in this work, we analyze whether saccadic angular values are horizontal or not. Thus, a reading state of the user R is detected by,

$$R = \begin{cases} 1 & ((-\pi/9 < A_1 < \pi/9 \vee 8\pi/9 < A_1 < 10\pi/9) \\ & \wedge(-\pi/9 < A_2 < \pi/9 \vee 8\pi/9 < A_2 < 10\pi/9) \\ & \wedge(n > min_s)) \\ 0 & (otherwise), \end{cases}$$

where n is the number of extracted saccades and min_s is the minimum number of saccades for a reading state. In this work, we set $min_s = 5$ and $W = 2.0$ (sec.), which provide a good balance between latency and accuracy.

Last Read Word Identifier

In our proposed system, we aim for seamless interaction between the virtual environment and the real environment. Thus, it may often occur that the user suddenly switches his/her focus to reality while reading. In order to remind the user afterwards where he or she was reading, the system needs to identify the last word he or she read before leaving off the screen. The following is the algorithm (Algorithm 1) we propose for *last word identification*.

Algorithm 1 Last read word identification algorithm

procedure LASTWORDIDENTIFIER($GazeSequence$)
  $i \leftarrow 0$, $PrevGaze \leftarrow (0, 0)$, $readEnd \leftarrow 0$
  while $CurGaze \leftarrow GazeSequence[i]$ **do**
    if $CurGaze$ is in the Text Area **and** $PrevGaze.x - CurGaze.x > ReadForwardTh$ **and** $\text{abs}(PrevGaze.x - CurGaze.x) > LineTh$ **then**
      if $readEnd \neq i - 1$ **then**
        $LastReadGaze \leftarrow CurGaze$
      end if
      $readEnd \leftarrow i$
    else if $readEnd \neq i - 1$ **then**
      $LastReadGaze \leftarrow CurGaze$
    end if
    $i \leftarrow i + 1$, $PrevGaze \leftarrow CurGaze$
  end while
  return $GetNearestWord(LastReadGaze)$
end procedure

$ReadForwardTh$ and $LineTh$ are threshold values for the horizontal axis and the vertical axis, respectively. The proposed algorithm identifies the latest gaze sample located in the text area and moves towards the right. Similar to the reading detection, we validated the threshold parameters in a preliminary experiment: $ReadForwardTh = 50$ and $LineTh = 40$.

Classification of Active/Passive Cognitive State

During visual perception, eye movements may involve several different cognitive tasks. One typical type of these tasks is reading. Additionally, we can also assume that the user may be involved in scene memorization, visual search,...etc. Such visual cognitive tasks often require high mental workload and concentration. In this work, we classify the user cognitive state either passive or active in order to predict appropriate times to interact with the user, focusing on a system notification function. That is, the system proactively interacts with the user when he or she is in a cognitively relaxed state, i.e., a passive cognitive state.

In our preliminary experiment based on a classic study by Gaarder [9], we found that when people are involved in a non-visual task, such as listening to music or thinking about something, saccades occur less frequently. Thus, we classify the active/passive state using the frequency of saccades within W (the same as the reading detection). If the frequency of saccades f_s is less than T_f and the state is not *reading*, we classify the state as cognitively passive (We set $T_f = 10$).

As a prototypical application, we implement an interactive function that notifies the user when the user is in a passive state. Using this interaction technique, we present virtual information to the user at unobtrusive times. Note that this function may also be used while the user is interacting with an HMD, though we test the proposed method with a task only in the real world (in the experiment).

EXPERIMENTS

For evaluation of the proposed attention engagement and cognitive analysis methods and proactive assist functions, we conducted three different experiments. A total of 13 participants participated in the experiments. First, we conducted an experiment for evaluation of attention engagement estimation accuracy and the ability of users to focus on different planes (virtual and real). Second, we evaluated accuracy of reading detection and identification of the last read word with reading tasks in the HMD using actual emails. Finally, we conducted a user study for active/passive cognitive state classification with respect to attentive notification functions. In this experiment, we asked the participants to evaluate whether such cognitive state classification based attentive notification is actually beneficial or not.

Attention Engagement Analysis

First, we evaluate accuracy of the attention engagement estimation methods and the ability of users to switch focus between virtual and real.

In this experiment, we investigate the following three aspects:
1) attention engagement estimation accuracy of the proposed methods (both depth-based and VOR-based methods).
2) ability of users to switch focus between different focal planes (virtual and real, and different target distances in the reality)
3) ability of users to switch focus with varying display brightness and UI settings.

As stated above, we also examine whether users are able to focus on different planes when conditions are changed. In particular, we test the user's ability to focus on the virtual plane when the screen is dark (such as shown in Figure 2) since this is a crucial point for automatic dim function, and the user must eventually refocus on the darkened screen.

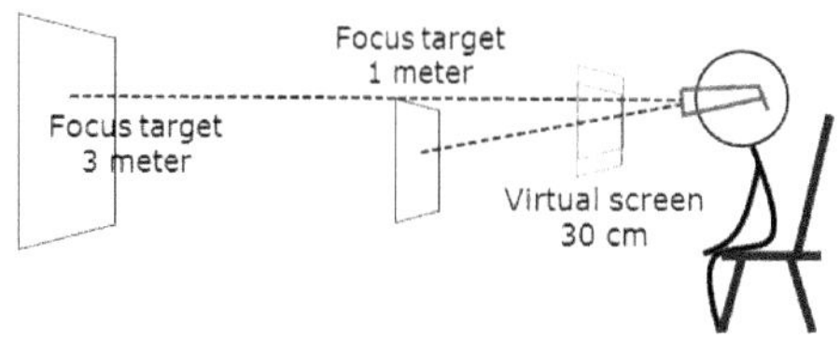

Figure 7. Experimental setup in the gaze depth-based attention estimation experiment.

Depth-based Method: Setup

First, we evaluate the depth-based method. The participant sits on a chair and wears the eye-tracking HMD. Facing the participant, a piece of paper (a focus target) is hung at 1 meter and 3 meter distances from the eyes as shown in Figure 7. We then record gaze data when he or she is focusing on the real (paper) or the virtual (HMD) target with multiple settings. We have three display settings – A: bright text and icon, B: dark text and icon, and C: icon only. For each setting, we have two distance options – a: physical far target (3m) and b: physical near target (1m). We repeat the following session three times for each distance option (a or b) and each display setting (A, B, or C). *The participant focuses on the virtual screen for 5 sec. (one recording).* → *After 5 sec., we request him or her to switch the focus to the real target.* → *He or she focuses on the real target for 5 sec.* → *We again request him or her to switch focus back to the virtual screen.*

When the participant finishes display setting A (A-a and A-b), we dim the display (change to B). After completing the same steps with the B setting (B-a and B-b), we also test with icon only UI setting (C-a and C-b), where only the *email* icon is shown in the HMD (see Figure 2). During the experiment, the participant keeps his or her head fixed and the HMD position is also kept fixed in the same line of sight as the real target from the eye. We recorded eye gaze data during the experiment and also measured time required to refocus on each plane. Consequently, we have gaze recordings from 3 different display settings (A, B, and C) $\times$ 2 distance options (a and b) $\times$ 3 sessions *focus virtual* and *focus real* (total 36 recordings) from one participant. We compare the icon only setting with the text and icon setting, to see whether the user has difficulty when focusing on the display when multiple items are present in the HMD.

Depth-based method: results

Using the recorded data, we calculated the depth value for each frame. On average, we have approximately 200 depth values for each recording (5 sec.).

First, in Figure 8 we show the averages and standard deviations (SDs) of estimated depth values for each condition (display setting, distance option, and virtual (HMD) or real (1m/3m)) on two representative participants. In this figure, we show the case with most easily separable values (P1: participant 1) and the case that was the most difficult to distinguish (P2: participant 2). With the easily separable values, we can clearly see that the averages are similar within each plane (HMD, 1m, and 3m). The focal plane is easily separable between HMD, 1m, and 3m in this case. However, with the data from P2, it is hard to separate between 1m and HMD

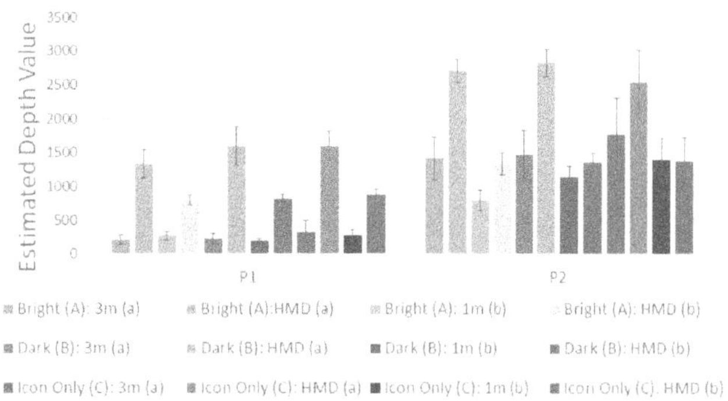

Figure 8. Average and SD (represented by an error bar) of estimated depth values for each recording from two representative participants (tidy and chaotic). Bars of odd columns are in virtual (HMD) whereas even ones are in the reality (3m and 1m). We can see that the estimated depths from P1 are easily separable between virtual and real. Note that the unit is supposed to be centimeters but actual calculated values do not necessarily match the units.

(b), though it seems possible between {HMD, 1m} vs. 3m. From this analysis, we found three things. First, the granularity of gaze depth estimation is dependent on the user. For some users, we can separate between 1m and HMD but for some other users we cannot. Second, however, separation between far (3m) and near (approx. until 1m) was still possible for all participants. Third, the value may not match to the actual distance. It is relative to the user.

Subsequently, we tested the proposed gaze depth-based attention engagement method using the recorded data. As the first test, we focused on the easiest case for the baseline. We divided one recording into two parts. One is used for parameter validation (to calculate d_{HMD} and σ). and the other part is used as test data. We computed accuracy of each engagement estimation: test with A-a (3m vs. HMD), test with A-b (1m vs. HMD), and so on, checking whether the system can correctly predict real or virtual. From several initial tests, we found that $k = 1$ (for $k\sigma$) yields the best accuracy for estimation. For most participants (9/13), the average accuracy of attention engagement estimation exceeds 90%. However, there are some participants who had difficulty estimating attention engagement (two of them had only 70%) because of noisy gaze data. It may be because the eye tracker accidentally moved or the participant had a problem focusing on the virtual screen. Two of the participants wore normal eyeglasses (with corrective lenses) and both of them had low accuracy. With our eye tracker (SMI ETG), such errors are inevitable since the accuracy with corrective lenses is not guaranteed. However, we may in general conclude that the proposed method can achieve quite high accuracy for many users.

To analyze the difference in different display settings, we compare the estimation accuracy between A, B, and C. In Figure 9 (left), we compare the averages and standard deviation (SD) of accuracy. The figure shows that the average accuracy decreases slightly when we use dark text and icon or an icon only setting. However, the result from a one-way ANOVA showed the p-value of these sets is 0.100, which

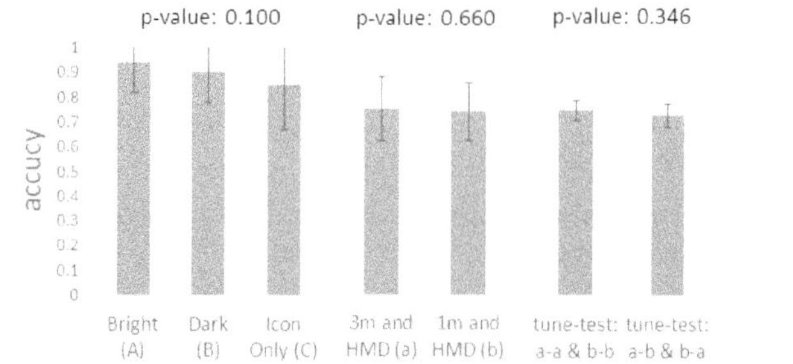

Figure 9. Comparison of estimation accuracy between different screen settings (left): A, B, and C, different distance options of real target (middle): a and b, and using different data for parameter tuning (right): tuned by a and b, and then vice versa. There is no significant difference between the middle and right. In the left, there are slight differences but they are not statistically significant (p-value is higher than 0.05).

shows that there may be slight difference, but we cannot conclude that there is a statistically significant difference. Also, the ANOVA on different distance options (3m-HMD (a) vs. 1m-HMD (b)) showed a large p-value (middle in Figure 9 $P = 0.66$). The above analysis showed that we can expect similar accuracy of attention engagement estimation, even if we use different display settings (bright, dark, and icon only) and different real target distances (3m or 1m). Furthermore, to investigate whether parameter tuning (validation) is feasible regardless of real target distance, we compare the following. On the right of the figure, we show the comparison of recordings from different distance options (a or b) for the validation (tuning) and test. The left bar is the baseline, where the same distance option was used for tuning and testing. The right shows the average accuracy when we use a for tuning and b for testing and vice versa. The result also shows that there is no significant difference. Thus, it is shown that the parameters are properly calculable whichever distance we have for the real background.

In order to test the focal ability of users, we also compare the time required for refocusing on each plane in Figure 10. Regarding the different types of display settings (A, B, or C), we see that there is no significant difference. A comparison between when the user focus switches from virtual to real and

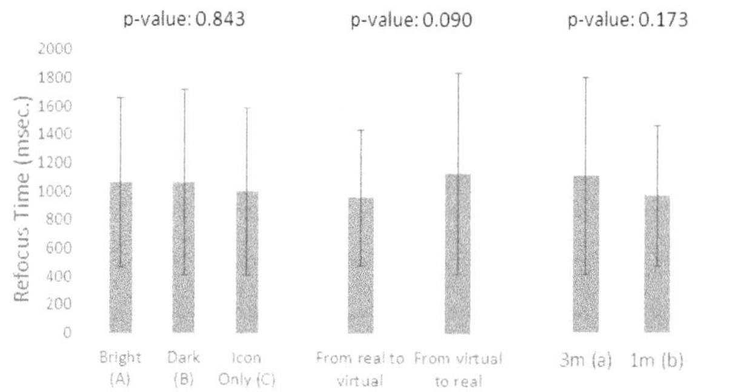

Figure 10. Measured time for refocusing on another plane. Overall, there is no significant difference. However, when the users switch the focus from virtual to real, refocusing time is slightly longer.

from real to virtual showed relatively low p-value, (0.090) but still not under 0.05. When the user returns focus to the physical environment, it may take longer than switching from physical to virtual. However, the difference was not significant. Also, there is no significant difference in refocusing time with different real target distances (a or b). Based on these results, we assume that users can focus on a dark virtual screen with text with less effort than a bright screen or icon only. These results also show the feasibility of the automatic dimming function, where the user needs to focus on a dark screen.

VOR-based Method

Next, we evaluate the VOR-based attention engagement estimation method. We record data while the participant moves his/her head with focusing on either the HMD or the 1m target, similar to the previous experiment. We again record 5 sec. of gaze data for both virtual and real and repeat this session three times. Then, based on gaze motion g_m and the calculated optical flow S_m, we compute d_{abs} for each frame. Using a separated validation data, we optimized $T_d = 25$ (pixels).

For the test of the VOR method, we calculated the accuracy of attention engagement estimation. If $d_{abs} < T_d$ and the participant was focusing on the HMD, the estimation was regarded as correct. For the overall average of all participants, we achieved accuracy of 89.8% ($SD = 8.0\%$). Compared the depth-based method, this method did not have such large differences between participants. This result shows the potential of the proposed method, though it can only be used when the user's head moves. However, we may combine the VOR-based approach with the depth-based approach for further improvement of the attention engagement analysis.

Reading Detection and Last Read Word Identification

In the second experiment, we evaluate accuracy of the reading state detection and the last read word identification method. We recorded gaze data while the participants read an email using the HMD. We also conducted a study where the participants tested the auto text scrolling function in comparison with static text.

Setup

The participant first puts on the eye-tracking HMD. We next ask the participants to read emails in the HMD. He or she is told to open an email by gazing at the email icon (using eye-con) and read to the end of the email. We have two emails: *A* and *B*). Since the entire emails cannot be displayed on the HMD screen, they are separated into several pages. *A* contains 5 pages (277 words) whereas *B* contains 4 pages (245 words). To go to the next page, the user gazes at a forward or backward eye-con.

Before starting the experiments, participants were given several minutes for testing and interacting with the interfaces, including eye-cons. All participants were able to grasp the functionality and could use them appropriately within approximately one minute of first use. The HMD position is calibrated accurately in advance to allow the eye-cons to work properly. For activating the eye-con, the user gazes at the icon approx. for 3 seconds[1].

We record the gaze data during reading of the email and test the reading detection and last read word identification. For the reading detection test, we have two types of gaze tasks: reading text or gazing at eye-cons. The proposed method must correctly identify when the user reads text in the HMD. For last word identification, the user verbally signals when he or she has reached the last word in the email. We then check if the gaze position identified as the last reading gaze is actually near the last word.

Result

Reading Detection. First, we discuss accuracy of reading detection. After recording the email reading data, we labeled the gaze classes in the recordings for test. When the participant is reading text, *read text* is used, and when gazing at eye-cons, *gaze at eye-cons* is used. Then first second in each class was dismissed since there is inherent latency during a transition of gaze state. On average, we have approximately 646 gaze samples for *read text* and 252 samples for *gaze at eye-cons*. We calculated the accuracy as the ratio of samples correctly classified to total samples.

On average over all participants, the accuracy of reading detection was 78.6% ($SD = 12.9\%$). This result is not perfect; however, as we can see with SD, there was again a large gap between the participants. For some participants, the accuracy was more than 90%, while one participant only had 51%. Similar to the depth analysis, this gap is mainly because of eye tracking error. We can improve the accuracy if we expand the window size $W = 2.0$. However, to keep the latency as short as possible, we think this value provides a good balance.

Last Read Word Identifier. Next, we evaluated the last read word identification method. We calculated the distance from the last read word predicted by the system to the actual last word in the email. The distance was 42.11 pixels on average ($SD = 32.60$), which is fairly good if we consider the HMD resolution (800x600). Since the field-of-view angle of the HMD is 22.4° (diagonal), the resulting offset angle is only approximately 1.0°. It is actually inevitable to have certain offset distance because eye tracking is also not perfectly accurate (accuracy is 0.5° with ETG). If we look at the recorded data, the predicted last word mostly matches the actual last word if we correct for eye tracking offset.

Figure 11 shows an example of the results where the system successfully identifies the last read word even though the last gaze sample in the recording sequence was moved away from the text area. The white dot is detected last gaze position in reading state, where the pink dot is the actual last gaze in the recorded sequence. The figure also shows the gaze positions (red dots) when the participant gazed at the eye-con. We can see the offset is not large. Thus, the eye-con activations were performed reasonably well.

[1]We set the dwell-time parameter to a slightly longer duration in order to avoid false positives as much as possible.

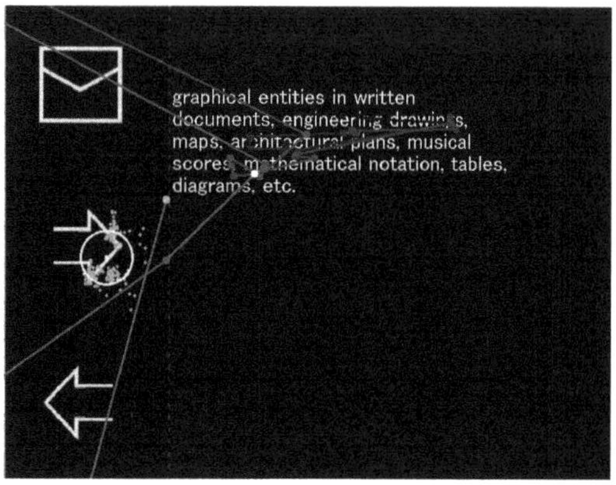

Figure 11. Example of last read word identification: The last gaze position (pink) and the detected last read position (white). Red dots are the gaze locations when the user gazed on the eye-con (next page) and blue dots (connected by blue lines) are the ones during reading. The gaze position moved after reading, (pink) but the system successfully detected a point near the last read word (white).

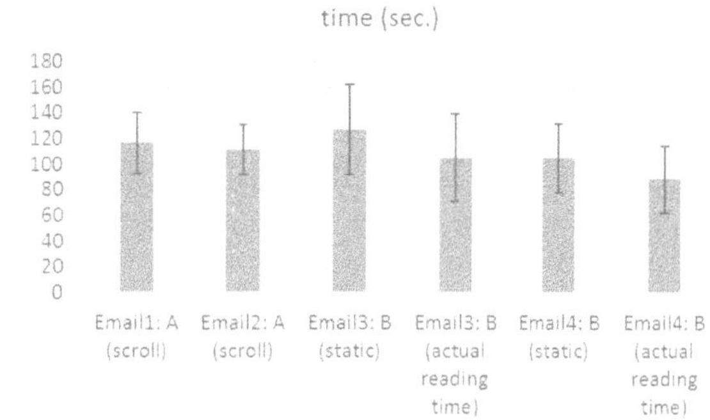

Figure 12. Average time required for complete reading text in each email. "Actual reading time" is calculated by subtracting the time for activating eye-cons from the time required in the interface B.

Evaluation of Automatic Scrolling Function. We also compare the proposed proactive scrolling function with static text from a reading efficiency point of view. The participants also read two other emails using the auto scroll function, which is activated when a reading state is detected. Using this function, the user does not need to gaze at eye-cons to switch the pages. Thus, he or she can keep reading text. Figure 12 shows the averages of time required for reading completion in each email. Having dwell-time for activation of each eye-con, the two interfaces (auto scroll and static text) had similar reading time. It becomes shorter when we subtract the time needed for eye-con activation. One of the reasons that auto-scroll required more time for reading is that the speed of the scroll is fixed in this experiment. Each user should have different reading speed. Some participants mentioned that the scroll speed was too fast whereas some other participants mentioned that it was too slow. Therefore, by adapting the scroll speed for each user, the reading process should become much more efficient.

Also, we have asked about preference regarding these two types of interfaces. A majority of the participants (8/12) commented that they preferred the automatic scroll to the eye-con page switch because they could read text continuously without having to pause. When users fixate on eye-cons, the process of reading and understanding text is interrupted. Because of this, users often feel stress. However, on the other hand, some participants disliked the automatic scroll function because it was hard for them to read moving text.

Figure 13. Alert in the attentive notification experiment.

Passive/Active Cognitive State Classification

In the third experiment, we conduct a user study to evaluate passive/active cognitive state classification with respect to the proposed attentive notification function. The proposed method infers an appropriate moment for a notification by analyzing eye gaze movements. Thus, the system notifies the user only when he or she is not involved in active cognitive tasks (i.e., passive cognitive state).

We run the system when the participant is performing office tasks (read an email with a normal computer screen and reply to it). After this, we ask the participants for subjective feedback. As mentioned previously, the tasks here are done on a physical device (a laptop) that is not in the virtual display, but the participant still receives notifications in the HMD (virtual).

Setup

The participant sits in front of a laptop computer wearing the apparatus. He or she reads an email with a web browser on a normal computer screen (of the laptop) and replies the email. During the task, four notifications (Figure 13 shows an example) are presented in the HMD. The participant performs the task two times with different notification timing inference methods: 1) predefined timing 2) attentive notification (notifies when the cognitive state is passive).

We do not explain the methods in advance. Instead, we only tell them that we would test two different inference techniques. After the task with two techniques, we ask the participants if they notice the difference and which they find more distractive.

Result

12 participants took part in this experiment. For half of the participants, the attentive method presented notifications after reading the emails and while typing a reply email. Three participants never received notifications because the system could not detect any passive cognitive states. The remaining three participants received notifications while reading an email. The method with predefined timing presented notifications both during reading and typing.

Those who did not receive notifications during reading noticed the difference between two techniques. Overall, seven participants preferred the attentive notifications, four participants had no preference, one participant preferred the predefined one. In summary, many participants found that receiving notifications while reading an email was very distracting. Some participants who never received the notifications also commented that it would have been distracting if they had received notifications when reading.

Although this study shows the potential of the proposed notification technique, when we design an actual system, we should take into account how urgent notification is for inferring the right timing for notification. Furthermore, the proposed method has the risk that a user may never receive any notification. However, the results from this study suggest that to notify the user when he or she is not in a cognitively busy state is beneficial.

DISCUSSION

The depth-based approach showed its robustness for attention engagement estimation. One drawback is as previously mentioned, this approach cannot distinguish if it is real or not when the user is switching focus to a near plane from the virtual one. Ideas to overcome this problem are to combine the depth-based approach with the VOR-based method or to analyze gaze positions with respect to visual content in the reality and in the virtual space. For example, if the user attentionally gazes at a particular location where an icon exists in the virtual screen, he or she is more likely engaged with the virtual space. Similar to the depth-based one, the VOR-based approach also showed its feasibility when user's head movements are detected. Our experimental results also showed that without using any physical measurement devices such as an IMU, we can track VOR based on optical flow calculation. Another important finding is that the users can actually focus on a dark screen successfully, even though it is less visible than the bright one. Some experiment participants mentioned that they found the dark screen was more practical when they needed to focus on the real, which shows a dimmed screen is actually useful for scene perception when wearing a see-through display.

Overall, the participants commented that they had very positive impressions regarding the system, including proposed proactive user assist functions. We asked the impressions on *automatic scroll*, *eye-cons*, and *attentive notifications*. Although adaptation of reading speed for each user is strongly required, many users enjoyed reading text with the automatic scrolling function. The biggest benefit for users is that they can seamlessly continue reading. This technique may also be used other mixed reality scenarios where text is overlaid onto real object planes such as walls or desktop surfaces. In order to maximize reading capabilities in a limited space, detection of reading state and proactive assistance such as scroll can be used effectively.

Participants also mentioned that it took a long time to activate eye-cons, but this is likely because we set a long duration for activation time in order to avoid false positives of eye-con activation in the experiment. We plan another experiment to evaluate accuracy and optimal duration for eye-con activation, and will take trade-offs between false-alarm rate and usability into account. HMD position can also be automatically calibrated by detecting the user's static fixations on a particular position, which often indicates a position of eye-con.

In the user study for active/passive cognitive state classification, we tested the proposed *attentive notification* function in an office work scenario. The principle idea of attentive notification is that a human might wait for the other person when he or she is involved in a busy task, such as reading an email. The proposed system can mimic such human behavior, by analyzing cognitive states of the user. In the future, we will conduct further analysis regarding different cognitive states that users may have during interaction with various AR systems. According to a state of the user, more proactive assistance functions could be added. For instance, we can guide users in a visual search task [14], if we detect a user's visual search activity.

CONCLUSION

We presented a novel eye gaze-based interactive system, which analyzes user's attention engagement and cognitive states to accordingly control interfaces in an HMD. Using such eye gaze analysis, the proposed system provides the user with various proactive assist functions such as automatic dim, automatic text scroll, eye-cons, last read word highlighter, and attentive notification.

Experimental results show that attention engagement can be estimated, and a reading state in the HMD can also be detected robustly. Lastly, we confirmed that users can actually focus on different planes in virtual and real regardless of screen UI settings. The feedback from participants showed the benefits of the proposed functions.

We think that the future of mixed and augmented reality must be well-blended with human attentional behaviors. Computer systems should consequently utilize attention-awareness to assist the users more attentively and intelligently.

REFERENCES

1. Ajanki, A., Billinghurst, M., Gamper, H., Järvenpää, T., Kandemir, M., Kaski, S., Koskela, M., Kurimo, M., Laaksonen, J., Puolamäki, K., Ruokolainen, T., and Tossavainen, T. An augmented reality interface to contextual information. *Virtual Reality 15* (2011), 161–173.

2. Alt, F., Schneegass, S., Auda, J., Rzayev, R., and Broy, N. Using eye-tracking to support interaction with layered 3D interfaces on stereoscopic displays. *Proceedings of the 19th international conference on Intelligent User Interfaces - IUI '14* (2014), 267–272.

3. Asteriadis, S., Tzouveli, P., Karpouzis, K., and Kollias, S. Estimation of behavioral user state based on eye gaze and head pose-application in an e-learning environment. *Multimedia Tools and Applications 41* (2009), 469–493.

4. Biedert, R., Buscher, G., and Dengel, A. The eyeBook Using Eye Tracking to Enhance the Reading Experience. *Informatik-Spektrum 33*, 3 (Sept. 2009), 272–281.
5. Biedert, R., Buscher, G., Schwarz, S., Hees, J., and Dengel, A. Text 2.0. *Proceedings of the 28th of the international conference extended abstracts on Human factors in computing systems - CHI EA '10* (2010), 4003.
6. Buscher, G., Dengel, A., and van Elst, L. Eye movements as implicit relevance feedback. *Proceeding of the twenty-sixth annual CHI conference extended abstracts on Human factors in computing systems - CHI '08* (2008), 2991.
7. Campbell, C. S., and Maglio, P. P. A robust algorithm for reading detection. *Proceedings of the 2001 workshop on Percetive user interfaces PUI 01 ACM Intern* (2001), 1–7.
8. Coco, M. I., and Keller, F. Classification of visual and linguistic tasks using eye-movement features. *Journal of Vision 14* (2014), 1–18.
9. Gaarder, K. Fine eye movements during inattention. *Nature* (1966), 83–84.
10. Henderson, J. M., Shinkareva, S. V., Wang, J., Luke, S. G., and Olejarczyk, J. Predicting Cognitive State from Eye Movements. *PLoS ONE 8* (2013).
11. Jacob, R. J. K. What you look at is what you get: eye movement-based interaction techniques. In *Proceedings of the SIGCHI conference on Human factors in computing systems Empowering people - CHI '90* (1990), 11–18.
12. Jimenez, J., Gutierrez, D., and Latorre, P. Gaze-based Interaction for Virtual Environments. *Journal Of Universal Computer Science 14* (2008), 3085–3098.
13. Lee, J.-Y., Park, H.-M., Lee, S.-H., Shin, S.-H., Kim, T.-E., and Choi, J.-S. Design and implementation of an augmented reality system using gaze interaction. *Multimedia Tools and Applications* (Dec. 2011).
14. Losing, V., Pfeiffer, T., Rottkamp, L., and Zeunert, M. Guiding visual search tasks using gaze-contingent auditory feedback. In *Proceedings of the 2014 ACM International Joint Conference on Pervasive and Ubiquitous Computing Adjunct Publication - UbiComp '14 Adjunct*, ACM Press (New York, New York, USA, 2014), 1093–1102.
15. Lucas, B. D., and Kanade, T. An iterative image registration technique with an application to stereo vision. *Proceedings of the 7th international joint conference on Artificial intelligence (IJCAI'81) Volume 2* (1981), 674–679.
16. Orlosky, J., Toyama, T., Sonntag, D., and Kiyokawa, K. Using Eye-Gaze and Visualization to Augment Memory. *Proceedings of the 16th International Conference on Human-Computer Interaction* (2014), 282–291.
17. Prendinger, H., Hyrskykari, A., Nakayama, M., Istance, H., Bee, N., and Takahasi, Y. Attentive interfaces for users with disabilities: eye gaze for intention and uncertainty estimation. *Universal Access in the Information Society 8*, 4 (Mar. 2009), 339–354.
18. Qvarfordt, P., and Zhai, S. Conversing with the user based on eye-gaze patterns. *Proceedings of the SIGCHI conference on Human factors in computing systems - CHI '05* (2005), 221.
19. Rayner, K. Eye movements in reading and information processing: 20 years of research. *Psychological bulletin 124*, 3 (Nov. 1998), 372–422.
20. Saloj, J., Puolam, K., and Kaski, S. Relevance feedback from eye movements for proactive information retrieval. In *Proceedings of the Workshop on Processing Sensory Information for Proactive Systems (PSIPS 2004)* (2004), 37–42.
21. Schütz, A. C., Braun, D. I., and Gegenfurtner, K. R. Eye movements and perception: A selective review. *Journal of vision 11* (2011).
22. Shi, F., Gale, A., and Purdy, K. A New Gaze-Based Interface for Environmental Control, 2007.
23. Shi, J. S. J., and Tomasi, C. Good features to track. *Computer Vision and Pattern Recognition, 1994. Proceedings CVPR '94., 1994 IEEE Computer Society Conference on* (1994), 593–600.
24. Starker, I., and Bolt, R. A. A gaze-responsive self-disclosing display. In *Proceedings of the SIGCHI conference on Human factors in computing systems* (1990), 3—-10.
25. Toyama, T., Orlosky, J., Sonntag, D., and Kiyokawa, K. A natural interface for multi-focal plane head mounted displays using 3D gaze. In *Proceedings of 12th International Working Conference on Advanced Visual Interfaces (AVI 2014)* (Como, Italy, 2014), 25–32.
26. Toyama, T., Suzuki, W., Dengel, A., and Kise, K. Wearable Reading Assist System : Augmented Reality Document Combining Document Retrieval and Eye Tracking. *Proceedings of the 12th International Conference on Document Analysis and Recognition (ICDAR)* (2013), 30–34.
27. Vidal, M., Nguyen, D. H., and Lyons, K. Looking At or Through ? Using Eye Tracking to Infer Attention Location for Wearable Transparent Displays. In *Proceedings of the 2014 ACM International Symposium on Wearable Computers* (2014), 87–90.
28. Vörös, G., Ver, A., Pintér, B., Miksztai-Réthey, B., Toyama, T., Lrincz, A., and Sonntag, D. Towards a Smart Wearable Tool to Enable People with SSPI to Communicate by Sentence Fragments. *Proceedings of the 4th International Symposium on Pervasive Computing Paradigms for Mental Health (MINDCARE2014)* (2014), 1–10.
29. Zeleznik, R. C., Forsberg, A. S., and Schulze, J. P. Look-That-There: Exploiting Gaze in Virtual Reality Interactions. *Technical Report CS-05-04*, March (2005).

Content-driven Multi-modal Techniques for Non-linear Video Navigation

Kuldeep Yadav, Kundan Shrivastava, S Mohana Prasad, Harish Arsikere, Sonal Patil, Ranjeet Kumar, Om Deshmukh
Xerox Research Centre, India
kuldeep.r@xerox.com, om.deshmukh@xerox.com

ABSTRACT
The growth of Massive Open Online Courses (MOOCs) has been remarkable in the last few years. A significant amount of MOOCs content is in the form of videos and participants often use non-linear navigation to browse through a video. This paper proposes the design of a system that provides non-linear navigation in educational videos using features derived from a combination of audio and visual content of a video. It provides multiple dimensions for quickly navigating to a given point of interest in a video i.e., customized dynamic *time-aware* word-cloud, video pages, and a 2-D timeline. In word-cloud, the relative placement of the words indicates their temporal ordering in the video whereas color codes are used to represent acoustic stress. The 2-D timeline is used to present multiple occurrences of a keyword/concept in the video in response to user click in the word-cloud. Additionally, visual content is analyzed to identify frames with "maximum written content", known as video pages. We conducted a user study with 20 users to evaluate the proposed system and compared it with transcription-based interfaces used by major MOOC providers. Our findings suggest that the proposed system leads to statistically significant navigation time savings especially on multimodal navigation tasks.

ACM Classification Keywords
H.5.1 Multimedia Information Systems: Video

Author Keywords
Video Navigation; MOOCs; Word-cloud; Acoustic Stress; Education; Video Analysis

INTRODUCTION
The growth of MOOCs is considered as one of the biggest revolutions in education in the last 200 years. MOOCs offer free online courses delivered by qualified professors from world-known universities and attended by millions of students remotely. For example, Coursera (one of the largest MOOC providers) enrolls nearly $7K$ participants every day across the globe [5]. However, nearly 90% of participants who register on MOOCs do not finish a course. This is primarily due to different learning goals of participants and in a traditional online setting, they often feel disengaged and lose interest very quickly. Various studies have found that most MOOC participants use non-linear navigation for the course content [8, 9]. On an average, certificate earners skip 22% of the content.

In an online course setting, participants spend most of their time watching videos in a MOOC course and use non-linear navigation in videos too [8] due to variety of reasons. One of the reasons being that they want to quickly get information about the key concepts discussed or gauge parameters such as teaching style. A study performed on the Edx platform found that certificate earning students spend only about 4.4 minutes on a 12 to 15 minute video. Further, participants keep referring to video content at different time intervals for specific information, which may be textual (i.e., keyword spotting), visual (i.e., a diagram/table), or combination of visual and textual. The part of the video that contains desired information is called a point of interest. A recent study shows that there is a point of interest every 2 minutes in a given educational video and found that students often want to go back to specific points of interest to get help for assignment problems [9]. Further, these points of interest could be different for different participants.

Online course providers assume that learners have access to high-bandwidth connection to support video streaming. Recent studies found that 40% of users stop watching a video if it takes more than 10 seconds to load [11]. Learners from many parts of the world especially developing countries have low bandwidth connections and streaming video could take significant time. Video navigation in such conditions is very difficult and often it creates poor watching experience, reduces student engagement, and increases drop-out rates [10]. Hence, there is a requirement of new techniques that can aid learners in quickly navigating through a video and reach their point of interest in the shortest possible time. Moreover, such techniques become a necessity to maintain student engagement in low-bandwidth scenarios.

This paper proposes a system to provide non-linear navigation in educational videos using features derived from the audio-visual content of the video. It provides multiple dimensions for quickly navigating to a given point of interest

IUI 2015, March 29–April 1, 2015, Atlanta, GA, USA.

http://dx.doi.org/10.1145/2678025.2701408

in a video i.e., customized dynamic *time-aware* word-cloud, visual frames, and a 2-D timeline. Specifically, customized dynamic word-cloud is created using audio transcription to provide handles for summarization/indexing and makes use of features such as location and color along with traditional font size to display key concepts in a given temporal context. The x-coordinate of the word location implies the mean temporal occurrence of the word in the video, the y-coordinate implies the spread of the word across the video, the color implies the acoustic emphasis the speaker puts on the word as captured by automatic stress analysis. The relative font size of the word retains the traditional indicator of frequency of occurrence of the word in the video. Accordingly, the user can select any word in the customized word-cloud and all the occurrences of the keyword appear on the 2-D timeline. Subsequently, she can navigate to a given point of interest by clicking on any of these occurrences.

Visual key frames are automatically extracted to create a visual summary of the video. These frames are captured when an instructor is about to erase the board or change the slide. These frames are called as *video-pages*, which is analogous to individual pages of a multi-page text document. Users can click on any of these video pages to navigate to a given point of interest in video. A localized *time-aware* word-cloud is also generated for each of these *video-pages*. The proposed system processes the video offline to create above described content-centric dimensions and a web-based customized video player is designed to display and help users in the navigation process. Furthermore, these dimensions are designed to provide quick, efficient, and content-based non-linear video navigation suited for low-bandwidth regions.

The contributions of this paper are as follows:

1. We design a system for enabling multimodal non-linear navigation and efficient summarization of educational videos with the help of various dimensions derived from audio and visual content of a given video.
2. The system provides a set of multimodal interaction techniques using customized word-cloud, video pages, and a 2-D timeline that help in quickly navigating to a point of interest in the video.
3. The end-to-end system is implemented and a user study is conducted on 20 different participants to evaluate the effectiveness of the system on five different categories of video navigation tasks.

RELATED WORK

We outline previous research in four broad categories i.e. word-cloud based navigation, techniques for non-linear video navigation, visual event detection in videos, and audio event detection.

Word-cloud based Navigation

Word-cloud based visualization techniques provide a concise and appealing way to create a summary of a document [4]. In recent years, there has been a growing interest in embedding semantic information and inter-word relationship in the word-cloud. Castella et al [12] present word storms to visually compare a set of documents. One of the novel features of word storms is that it puts the words appearing in multiple documents in the same color and orientation for all the word-clouds. Ada et. al. [13] uses cosine similarity measure to find relationship between two words and put them together in the word-cloud to improve readability. Authors in [22] present techniques for creating audio clouds from audio content to parallel the word clouds. None of the current approaches use different dimensions (i.e., X and Y axis) and color of a word-cloud to embed information similar to our approach.

Visual Event Detection

Visual content based video indexing and retrieval is an active area of research. Weiming et. al. [33] present a survey of various video content analysis techniques and their respective applications for various domains. Choudary et. al. [34] describe an approach to extract middle-level visual features for extracting the written text and figures from an educational video lecture. The TalkMiner system [36] analyzes educational videos to identify unique slide images, uses OCR techniques to automatically identify the text on the slides and subsequently, provides an index for easy search and retrieval of spoken as well as written words. Our approach combines various image cues to form a set of frames, which capture the entire written content of the lecture. Furthermore, the proposed system is robust to both slide-based videos (OCR-friendly) and videos involving free-flow writing (i.e., blackboard).

Video Navigation

Currently, there are two prominent navigation techniques being used in practice i.e., scrubber and transcription interface. Scrubber interface is used by YouTube and other related systems, where the user can move forward and backward using a video timeline. It provides a small visual snapshot in response to users' mouse roll-over event on a video timeline. Such a visual snapshot is not sufficient in majority of the cases due to reasons such as limited screen text and lack of localized context. The transcription interface is widely used by EdX [1] and other MOOC providers where a text transcript is placed alongside video to aid in the navigation process. Clicking on a text segment in the transcript navigates to the corresponding video segment. The transcription interface also includes functionalities of scrubbing-based interfaces. However, none of these techniques provides content-centric dimensions for non-linear navigation as proposed by our approach.

Recently, there has been research to use visual information for non-linear video navigation. NoteVideo [14] identifies conceptual objects and creates a summarized image using them. This image can be used for quickly navigating to the part of the video where the given object has first appeared. Swifter [17] is a generic system for locating a scene in the given video. It improves the traditional scrubbing technique by overlaying a grid of pre-cached thumbnails on the video interface for fast navigation. Panopticon [16] works in a similar way and displays video thumbnails on the screen without excluding any frames. One of the main limitations of these approaches is that they completely rely on visual information and ignore the voice/transcription content, which is an important attribute for the navigation. Therefore, these approaches are likely to take similar navigation time as YouTube player, when visual information is limited in the video [16].

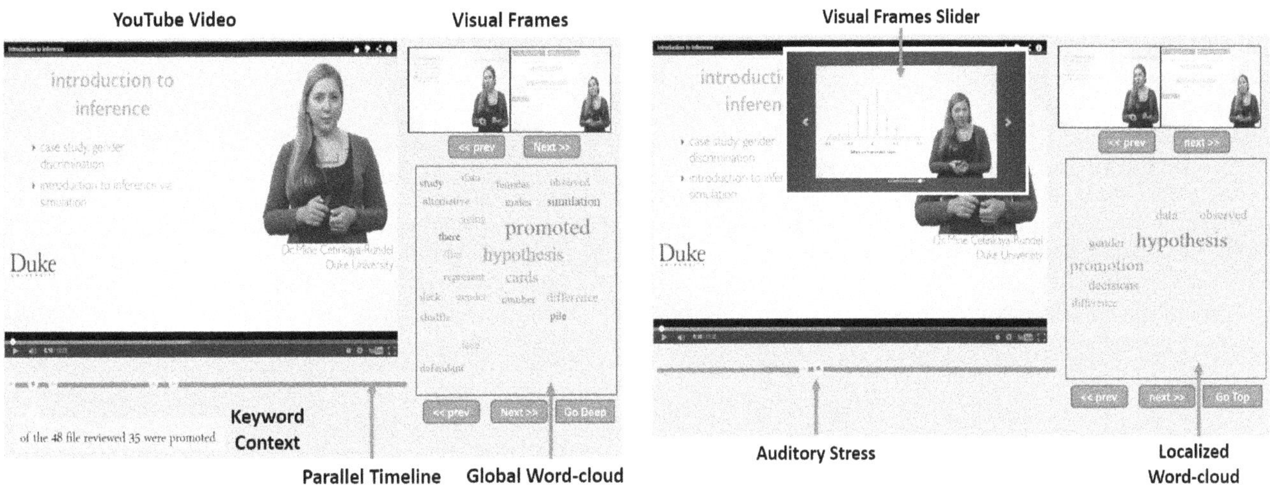

(a) Broad View (b) Localized View

Figure 1: Snapshots of the system prototype with different navigation components

LectureScape system [15] uses interaction data collected from previous usage logs to help in navigation. Along with interaction data, it uses data-enhanced transcript search and a visual summary representing points with high interaction activity. However, LectureScape requires availability of interaction data for bootstrapping and is helpful in videos which are watched many times.

Audio Event Detection

In speech and audio processing, key word spotting is an active area of research where the goal is to automatically identify occurrences of particular words in the video [18]. Potential applications are typically in a call center setting where the goal is to detect when a customer or agent is using one of the *hot* words. Other area of active research is in automatic evaluation of accuracy of spoken stress [20] with potential applications in second language learning. Speech analysis techniques are also heavily used for emotion detection in spoken dialogues [19]. Our main contribution is in establishing feasibility of acoustic-analysis based teaching style detection and providing ways to efficiently identify instances of acoustic stress in a video lecture.

DESIGN GOALS

In general, humans are efficient in non-linearly navigating through a text document or a book i.e., skimming through a multi-page document to estimate the temporal flow of concepts, skipping from the left top of the current page to the right bottom, and backing up to the middle of the page if needed, or judging the context of the occurrence of a particular keyword in a given paragraph. Multiple studies have shown that often MOOC participants also have similar requirements where they want to quickly navigate to a certain point of interest in the video based on prior information or their specific needs. In some cases, they also like to get a quick summary of the video content in a limited time.

We outline the following design goals for our system. These goals are the outcome of multiple field deployments of our system, interaction with the learners as well as instructors. For the ease of understanding, we describe these goals in the context of the above book example.

1. **Concept Timeline and their Prominence:** In current settings, learners use the scrubbing technique (i.e. clicking randomly) on the video timeline to learn about the different concepts discussed in a video. The learners have shown their desire to see a timeline of the concepts with their respective prominence (i.e. how frequently was it spoken), in roughly the same order in which they appeared in the video. Our system uses customized word-cloud to present the key concepts of the video where their relative placement on x-axis indicates the temporal ordering in the video and similarly, the placement on the y-axis shows the temporal spread, the font size shows their prominence and color indicates the level of acoustic stress.

2. **Visual and Textual Navigation:** Often, learners are interested in navigating to a point of interest in the video with the help of visual or textual clue or combination of both. A textual clue could be a keyword spoken by the instructor or a topic or a concept, whereas visual clue relates to the information presented on the blackboard, slides, etc. The proposed system uses a clickable and customized *time-aware* word-cloud with the *video-pages* i.e., frames with the maximum written content to help users in navigating to desired point of interest as quickly as possible. Additionally, we also provide mechanisms by which extra-lingual information is also conveyed to the learner such as acoustic stress on a given topic or keyword by the instructor.

3. **Video Summarization:** The new learning techniques such as flipped classrooms are emerging, where an instructor gives watching videos as homework and uses class time for clarifying doubts and assessments. An instructor has to go through multiple videos to select one or two of them, which are very relevant to his/her course material. It poses a requirement for creating a video summary, where most of

the important concepts discussed in the video are covered with appropriate detail. Our system provides time-ordered and localized word-clouds with their corresponding visual frames to achieve a quick yet fine-grained video summarization.

4. **Feasibility in low-bandwidth Regions:** Learners in many regions face problems while streaming a video due to low bandwidth. For example, whenever a learner goes forward in a scrubber interface, she has to wait a considerable amount of time before the video loads [17]. We design our navigation techniques in a way that video loading/buffering events can be minimized to a large extent, thus saving time for the learner and increasing engagement with the video.

SYSTEM DESIGN

There are mainly four different navigation components of the proposed system i.e., customized *time-aware* word-cloud, 2-D timeline, video pages, and a method for video summarization. In this section, we will focus on describing interaction techniques, which make use of the navigation components to enable non-linear navigation in the video.

Customized Word-cloud and 2-D Timeline

It is one of the key components that provides an aggregated view of various concepts discussed in the video as shown in Figure 1a. We design an algorithm to generate customized word-cloud using the audio transcript described in next section. The x-axis of the word-cloud represents the timeline w.r.t. the video and y-axis represents the spread of a keyword in the video. The font feature is used to depict the frequency similar to a traditional word-cloud. The color in the word-cloud represents the auditory stress, which is automatically detected by the proposed system as described in next section.

There are two categories of word-clouds used in the proposed system i.e., global word-cloud and localized word-cloud as shown in Figure 1. Global word-cloud is generated from the complete audio transcript of the video and it helps learners in identifying the time-ordered concepts or topics discussed with their relative prominence. The learner can click on any keyword in the word-cloud to navigate to the time where it was spoken in the video. The clicked keyword in the word-cloud turns green to inform the learner about her selection e.g., "promoted" word is clicked in Figure 1a. If there are multiple occurrences of a keyword in the video, instances within 20 seconds of each other are represented by a single instance to avoid clutter on the 2-D timeline as shown in Figure 1a. The learner can mouse-hover on each of these occurrences to learn about the context in which the keyword was spoken and accordingly select one of the options to navigate.

The localized word-cloud is specific to each *video-page* and it is created using the transcript of specific time window only. However, the process of creation of the word-cloud remains same for both global and localized word-cloud with a difference of the time window. If a learner clicks on a keyword in the localized word-cloud, all the occurrences of that keyword are highlighted on the 2-D timeline specific to the visual frame as shown in Figure 1b.

The customized word-cloud and parallel timeline also enable quick navigation to the concepts or topics, which were emphasized by the instructor. If a word has been emphasized majority of times in the given time window, it is displayed in dark red color in customized word-cloud (Red, one of the psychological primary colours, is associated with intensity and excitement [23]). For example, the word "hypothesis" has been emphasized by the instructor multiple times as shown in Figure 1a. Word occurrences associated with auditory stress are marked with red color on the 2-D timeline, whereas rest of them are shown in white color as shown in Figure 1.

Video Pages

This component is used for searching visual information in the given video. We design and implement automatic techniques to identify the frames with "maximum written content" and use them to extract all the key visual frames of the video. These frames, called *video pages*, are shown as image snapshots as shown in Figure 1a. Learner can use the "previous" and "next" buttons to navigate to a certain point of interest in the video. Some videos do not have rich visual information and it becomes difficult to spot a visual clue using the image snapshots. In such cases, learner can click on any of the image snapshot to launch the visual frames slider, which can be used to browse through all the frames with an enlarged view.

Video Summarization Method

This method works with the combination of customized word-cloud and video pages. As described earlier, global word-cloud presents an aggregated view of the concept discussed in the video. However, learner may need to go deep and learn about the content that was spoken inside the video. The proposed interface provides a functionality, where a learner can get a quick summary by taking a tour of all localized word-clouds and their associated video pages. This functionality can be accessed using the "Go Deep" button shown in Figure 1a. This feature is extremely useful in bandwidth constrained settings where a learner can get a fine-grained summary without playing the video.

MULTIMODAL NAVIGATION TECHNIQUES

As discussed earlier, the three main components of the proposed navigation system are: (a) identify the important keywords and place them in a *time-aware* word-cloud such that their relative placement indicates their temporal order and prominence in the lecture, (b) identify frames in the video that correspond to maximum written material (e.g., a full blackboard) or when the video transitions between talking-head and writing. These frames represent the different 'video-pages' of the lecture, and (c) identify instances of spoken words which are acoustically stressed and thus signify important acoustic events in the lecture.

The mechanism for each of these three components is described below in detail.

Customized Time-aware Word-cloud

The cloud generation method consists of four main steps: (a) speech-to-text conversion and time-stamp extraction, (b) text normalization, (c) content aggregation and cloud generation, and (d) optimal cloud display. Each of the steps is explained below.

Speech-to-Text and Time-Stamp Extraction: Several educational videos are accompanied with time-aligned subtitles for closed captioning purposes. There is no need of speech-to-text conversion in these videos. For others, the audio stream [3] is analyzed by an Automatic Speech Recognition (ASR) system which hypothesizes the spoken text and the time stamps of each word in the text. In the current setup, we used the HTK [24] ASR system for speech-to-text conversion and also to estimate the word and phone-level time stamps. The ASR system was trained on the WSJ database and is reported to operate at a word-error-rate of 6.91% [25]

Text Normalization: In this step, the text is normalized in following ways: (a) Stop words are removed because they carry little information about the topic being discussed. 'a', 'an', 'the','if', 'of' are some of the common examples of stop words. (b) Stemming [27] is the process of transforming a given word to its root form. For example, 'finding', 'find', 'finds' are mapped to 'find'. One of the main advantages of stemming is that it reduces the number of keywords to be processed. Often times, standard stemming tools do not always transform a given word to its correct root form, for example 'course', and 'courses' map to the stem 'cours'. In the context of our system, such nonsensical words can lead to reduced readability and poorer user experience. We describe a possible solution to overcome this problem in the next step.

Content Aggregation and Cloud Generation: As mentioned above, stemming can lead to some stems which may be nonsensical. To increase readability of the cloud the original word form has to be displayed. But, stemming is a many-to-one process and hence it is not invertible. To overcome this, we choose the most frequent original word form of the stemmed word in the lecture as the representative word (for e.g., if in the original transcript 'course' occurred 3 times and 'courses' occurred 4 times, we would choose 'courses' as the representative for the stem 'cours').

In word-cloud formation, the frequency of the words is typically used as the indicator of prominence and this is translated into a bigger font for cloud display. While, we use the frequency of the words as the initial prominence indicator, we also propose other novel aspects in determining their relative prominence and their relative placement in the word cloud as explained below.

- Temporal mean of occurrence: For every word in the lecture, we estimate the corresponding time of occurrence either through the ASR output or through the closed captions. These times are then used to estimate the temporal mean of occurrence of the word. We use the placement of the words on the x-axis of the word-cloud to indicate this relative time occurrence. Thus, words towards the left side of the cloud would have, on an average, occurred earlier in the video than the words towards the right side. The average values are normalized to be in the $[0-1]$ range.
- Temporal spread: Based on the time-stamps of the words, we also estimate how spread out the word is in the video. For example if the word occurs regularly throughout the video, it will have a much higher variance than a word which occurs, say, only in the beginning. We use the placement of the words on the y-axis of the word-cloud to indicate this relative temporal spread. Thus, words towards to the top would have occurred over a wider span of time in the lecture than words towards the bottom. The variance values are also normalized to be in the $[0-1]$ range.

Optimal Cloud Display: Even when the x- and y-coordinates of the words are identified in the above step, their placement in the word-cloud is a non-trivial task as we have to account for the likely event of multiple words with same x- and y-coordinates, variable character length of words, relative font sizes for these words and the dynamic resizing of the word-cloud display. The optimal cloud display strategy works as follows: The word-cloud is split into a grid of N_x rows and N_y columns leading to $N_x * N_y$ equi-sized boxes. The cloud area is normalized such that each box has an area of $1/(N_x * N_y)$. The x- and y-coordinates of the words are linearly quantized such that they take values in the $[0, 1/N_x, 2/N_x, \ldots, (N_x-1)/N_x]$ and $[0, 1/N_y, 2/N_y, \ldots, (N_y-1)/N_y]$ range, respectively. This ensures that the placement of the word is aligned with the left bottom corner of the box. The words are placed sequentially in the decreasing order of their font size (i.e., decreasing order of prominence). The actual font size of the first word is decided in such a way that the height of the word does not exceed one box and the breadth does not exceed two boxes. The font sizes of the subsequent words are reduced in proportion to their frequency of occurrence relative to the first placed (i.e., most frequent) word. If the ideal box for a word is already occupied, the nearest empty box is searched in an outward spiral fashion. Such a sequential ordering of placement ensures that more prominent words have a higher likelihood of being placed closest to their ideal x-, y-coordinates. In the current work, $N_x = N_y = 15$. Thus, the cloud can take at the most 225 most frequent words. We have seen that in most cases the number of words does not exceed 100.

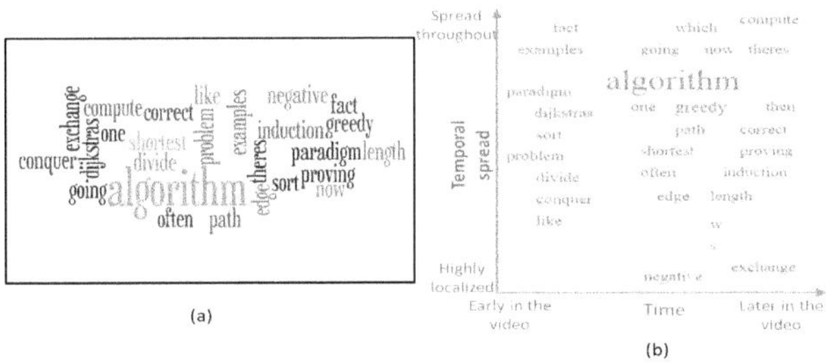

Figure 2: (a) Word-cloud generated by Wordle, (b) the proposed *time-aware* word-cloud

Figure 2 compares the word-cloud generated by the proposed *time-aware* word-cloud mechanism with the one that was generated by a standard service [4] for a 12 minute 34 second video lecture on *Algorithm Design*. A user study was conducted to evaluate the efficacy and usability of the proposed *time-aware* word-cloud. 5 users (3 males, 2 females) were shown the wordle-generated cloud and asked to summarize the temporal progression of the video in three lines such that the first line summarizes their impression of what may have been covered in the first one-third of video and similarly for the second and the third line. Similarly, 5 other users (4 males, 1 female) were shown the time-aware word-cloud and asked to perform the same task. All the 10 users had a Masters degree in engineering and had Algorithm Design as one of the courses in their formal engineering education. One of the authors, listened to the video multiple times to form the ground truth 3-line temporal progression summary. The ground truth had 18 key words from the displayed cloud: 6 each for the three sections of the video. If majority of the user's keywords in the i-th (i=1,2,3) line belonged to the j-th (j=1,2,3) line summary of the ground truth, the user is said to have estimated the j-th one-third of the video as i-th. For example, if the majority of the user's keywords in the 1-st line belonged to the 2-nd line of ground truth, the user is said to have confused the 2nd one-third of the summary as the 1st one-third. We thus get an ordered 3-dimensional summary from each user. For example, if the ordered summary of a user is $\{2, 1, 3\}$, it implies that the user's estimated 1-st one-third of the video is in reality the 2-nd one-third, the user's estimated 2-nd one-third of the video is in reality the 1-st one-third and the user estimated the last one-third correctly.

The comparison between users' ranked summary and the ground truth rank summary can now be thought of evaluating the efficacy of a retrieval algorithm. A popular measure in Information Retrieval community to evaluate user-estimated ranks with that of ground-truth ranks is the Discounted Cumulative Gain (DCG) [30]. DCG measure is given by:

$$DCG = \sum_{j=1}^{N} \frac{g(i)}{log(1+i)}$$

where N is the number of ranked sentences (N=3), i is the ground-truth rank of the sentence and $g(i)$ is the gain assigned with labeling that sentence. The gain values are 10, 5 and 0 for *exact match, missed-by-one,* and *missed-by-two*, respectively. *Exact match* implies that the user's rank matched the ground truth rank, *missed-by-one* implies that the user's rank and the ground truth rank were off by 1, and *missed-by-two* implies that the user's rank and the ground truth rank were off by 2. All the five users who were shown the proposed *time-aware* word-cloud had *exact match* with the ground truth for all the three sentences leading to a DCG score of 21.39. The ranks from the five users who were shown the wordle-generated cloud were $[\{2,1,3\}, \{2,3,1\}, \{2,1,3\}, \{1,3,2\}, \{2,3,1\}]$ and the average DCG score was 11.64. We thus show that the proposed time-aware word-cloud does indeed present a broad temporal progression of the video.

Acoustic analysis

The *time-aware* word-cloud described in the previous section can benefit immensely from acoustic-prosodic features that capture the lecturer's acosutic and linguistic stress patterns. Specifically, the color of a word in the 2-d cloud can be changed to reflect the average emphasis across all its instances. The motivation for doing this comes from the fact that the lecturers often employ acoustic stress to highlight the importance of a concept or to enhance the clarity of the message being communicated. Findings in experimental psychology also suggest that acoustic stress improves performance on recall tasks [26]. We now describe the proposed methodology for automatic stress detection along with empirical results that demonstrate its efficacy.

Data

Five lecture videos (all in American English accent) were used for this study. One male and two female lecturers featured in these videos and had different intonation patterns. Closed captions in SubRip Text (srt) format were available for all five videos. The captions provided time stamps on a segment-by-segment basis but not at the word level. The first step therefore was to estimate the word boundaries using the audio files and their corresponding closed captions.

Word-boundary estimation was achieved via a speech processing method called forced alignment. In forced alignment, the speech recognition system is 'forced' to recognize a given audio stream as a particular text (obtained from the caption). Given a set of phone acoustic models, a pronunciation dictionary, a speech signal and its corresponding word transcript, forced alignment provides word- and phoneme-level time stamps. In this study, we used the CMU pronunciation dictionary and Wall Street Journal (WSJ) acoustic models [25], both of which are well suited to American-English speech. By force aligning audio segments with their corresponding segment-level closed captions, word and phoneme boundaries were obtained for the five videos used.

The goal of this study is to be able to decide whether a given word is stressed or not: i.e., a binary decision. To this end, each word in our data set was labeled as either "stressed" (class +1) or "unstressed" (class -1). Words were labeled purely by listening to the audio files (i.e., the waveforms and spectrograms were not inspected visually). All the five audio files were annotated by a speech expert who had studied the stress patterns in spoken English. This led to 345 stressed and 5441 unstressed words.

The expected degree of acoustic emphasis required for a word to be labeled as stressed is subjective and varies widely even across experts. For example, authors in [20] report that for the task of labeling 4926 isolated words as 'correctly stressed' or 'incorrectly stressed' the inter human agreement across three annotators was 71.7%. To quantify the subjectivity in the present task, we had one other speech expert annotate one of these videos. Out of the 2872 words, 98 words were labelled as stressed by at least one labeler. Of these, 24 were labelled as stressed by both the labelers, 53 were labelled as stressed only by the first labeler and 21 were labelled as stressed only by the second labeller. If we assume the more conservative labeler's labels as the master ground truth, the inter human agreement for stressed labels is 53.3% $(= 24/(24 + 21))$, confirming that stress labeling is indeed a subjective especially in natural speech. The subjectivity was also reflected in our user studies as described later in the user study section. Of these five lectures, four were used to train the classifier and the performance was evaluated on the fifth one.

Prosodic Features

The three types of prosodic features used here to estimate stress are pitch-based, intensity-based and duration-based. Stressed words demonstrate a perceptual increase in pitch frequency and modulation as compared to unstressed words. To model this phenomenon, pitch contours were first obtained using the SNACK sound toolkit [21]. The contours provided pitch estimates at 10 ms intervals along with voiced/unvoiced classification (pitch is not defined for unvoiced sounds like /s/ and /f/). Using these contours, two pitch-based features were computed for any given word: (1) 95th percentile of the word's pitch estimates (capturing stress-induced increase in pitch frequency), and (2) standard deviation of the word's pitch estimates (capturing stress-induced increase in pitch modulation). Both these features were normalized with the median pitch of the corresponding segment.

Stressed words also demonstrate a perceptual increase in intensity as compared to unstressed words. To model this phenomenon, intensity contours were obtained using 30 ms frames separated by 10 ms intervals. The contours were smoothed using a 5-tap FIR filter (spanning 50 ms). Then, for a given word, the intensity-based feature was computed as the 95th percentile of the word's intensity estimates, normalized with respect to the median intensity of the corresponding segment. Phoneme elongation is also associated with stressed words. To capture this, our duration-based feature was simply taken to be the duration of the longest phoneme in the word under consideration. Note that the phoneme durations is directly computed using time stamps obtained via forced alignment. We thus compute four prosodic features for each word. Fig. 3 compares the distribution of these four features for stressed vs. unstressed instances.

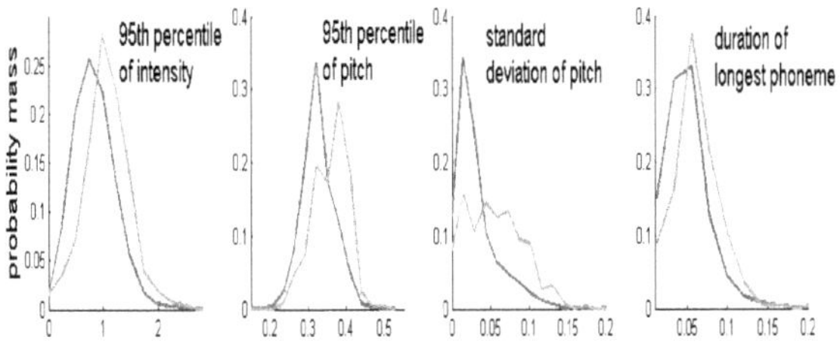

Figure 3: Comparison of the distribution of the four prosodic features for stressed (red-curve) and unstressed (blue-curve) instances.

Experimental Results

A SVM classifier was trained on the four video files using LIBSVM [28]. Since the number of stressed words is about 20 times smaller than the number of unstressed words, misclassification of positive samples was penalized more during the SVM training. The radial-basis-function kernel was used and the kernel parameter was set to 0.25.

The audio file used for evaluation had 50 stressed words and 2822 unstressed words. Figure 4 presents the ROC curve for this test set. A practical operating point would be the one

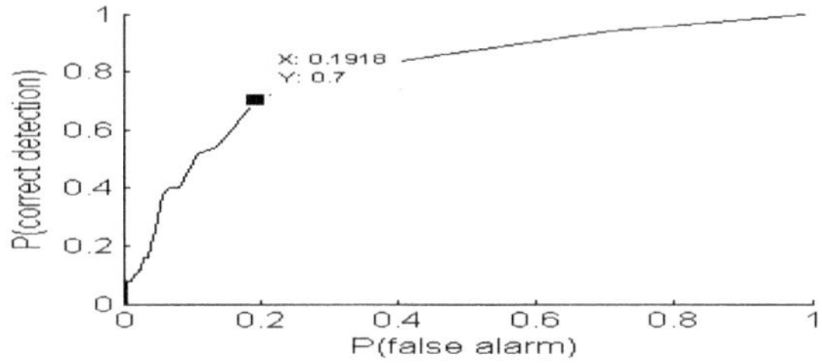

Figure 4: ROC curve for the proposed acoustic stress detector. The chosen operating point is highlighted.

shown in the Figure 4: 70% correct detection at a false-alarm rate of 19%. The detection accuracy is satisfactory considering the sparsity of stressed words and the relatively low inter-human agreement.

In the context of the proposed color coding scheme for display and navigation of stressed words in the *time aware word cloud*, there is one more navigation step: When a user clicks on a word in the global cloud, she is shown all the instances of the word along the video timeline. The instances that are stressed are highlighted in red (refer fig 1). Thus, while the global stress results displayed in the cloud were computed across all the words, there is a chance to refine the stress detection algorithm at this word-dependent level. Our proposed word-dependent refinement is as follows: Cumulative Euclidian distance of every instance of the word with the rest of the instances is computed on the 4-dimensional feature space. Instances that are more than M times the median cumulative distance are labelled as stressed. We empirically estimated M = 2 based on the four training files. The assumptions is that a given word has more unstressed instances than stressed, and unstressed instances would be relative closer to each other than they would be to the stressed instances.

Video-page detection

This section describes our technique to estimate the video-pages' in the video lecture. The goal is to detect the set of key frames that capture the entire *written content* of the lecture. We define *written content* as the text and figures written on the board (throughout the paper, we use 'written on board' to imply all the popular forms of writing in video lectures such as 'chalk on board', 'marker pen on board', 'pen on a sheet of paper', 'stylus pen on a computing device', 'animation to populate a powerpoint slide').

As the lecturer is explaining the material, she may also periodically write on the board till either the board is full or when she has to move on to a new concept. At this point, the board is erased clean (or a new slide is displayed) and the process repeats. Say, the time instance when the lecturer started writing on a clean board is X minute and erases the material at Y minute, the *written content* of the lecture between X and Y minutes is captured by a screen shot of the board at a few seconds before Y minutes. Thus, the goal is to detect instances where the *written content* has local maxima. We now explain our algorithm to detect and quantify *written content*. The main steps are: (a) identify frames containing the board, (b) segment the board region, and (c) quantify the *written content*.

1. Identify frames containing the board: A frame in the lecture can be categorized into one of the following four classes: (a) only board, (b) only lecturer, (c) lecturer plus the board, (d) other visual content. We further group these classes into 'board present' (i.e., (a) and (c)) and 'board not present' (i.e., (b) and (d)) classes. We restrict our analysis to the 'i-frames' in the video (as detected by ffmpeg) as these frames are most dissimilar from their adjacent frames. These frames are then parameterized using the Histogram of Oriented Gradients (HOG) feature. HOG features are motivated by the findings that shape and appearance of an object can be captured by the distribution of the local intensity gradients of the object. To compute HOG feature, the image is split into multiple uniform cells. The 1-d histogram of gradient directions is computed for all the pixels in the cell. The gradients are binned into orientation bins which are typically evenly spaced between 0 to 360 degrees. These gradient histograms are made robust to the variations in illumination and related ambient effects by computing histograms of local energies over multiple adjacent cells and normalizing the gradient histograms. The normalized gradient histograms form the HOG features [29].

   A linear SVM classifier is trained for the binary classification problem. Training data was obtained by manually labeling two videos of 30 minutes each from two different lecturers. The training data had 134 'board present' frames and 87 'board not present' frames. When evaluated on a third video of 50 minutes with 152 'board present' frames and 172 'board not present' frames, the classier was able to correctly identify 94.7% of the 'board present' frames while misclassifying only 1.2% (i.e., 2) of the 'board not present' frames.
2. Segment the board region: Given the 'board present' frames, the next step is to identify the board region. We would like this identification step to be robust to different board colors and also to imperfections in the erasures (such as chalk dust left by the erasures). We use the Mean Shift Segmentation (MSS) approach to segment the frames into multiple regions. MSS is a nonparametric clustering based segmentation technique that identifies the segments in a visual scene [31]. MSS returns labels for each pixel denoting the segment it belongs to. We assume that the maximum segment in the frame is the board region. This is a fair assumption as MSS is run only on the 'board present' frames. Also, note that the maximum segment need not be one big chunk: it can be a collection of regions, especially when the board is occluded by the lecturer. The boundary of the board is estimated using the hand-on-the-wall approach, where, once we find a boundary pixel of a maximum segment region, we traverse in clockwise direction, always turning to the right on the boundary, till we reach the originating pixel.
3. Quantify the *written content*: We define the *written content* as the proportion of the estimated number of chalk pixels in the board region. Note two important properties of writing on the board: (a) The chalk color is typically in contrast of the board color, and (b) the writing is sharp enough to be approximated as sharp transitions between the board and the written material (unlike a graded variation in artistic images). We thus use the Sobel operator [32] to estimate these sharp transitions. The Sobel operation invloves convolving a 3x3 pixel region around every pixel with a horizontal and a vertical second order difference approximation matricies. This results into a 2-d gradient map at each pixel. Combining these maps for all the pixels leads to a new image which has high values at the image edges. In our case, these edges are the writings on the board. Proportion of these edge pixels and the total board pixels gives the estimate of the *written content*. While we expect the *written content* to gradually and monotonically increase across successive frames as the lecturer writes and then drastically drop when the lecturer erases the board, in real situations board occlusion and errors in image processing estimations can lead to noise. In the proposed method, the temporal sequence of the *written content* is smoothed using the 7-point median smoothing technique. Frames corresponding to the local maxima in this smoothed temporal sequence are the estimated *video-pages* of the lecture.

   Seven video lectures,ranging between 20-50 minutes, were manually analyzed to identify ground truth *video pages* leading to 101 such pages. The proposed method was able to detect 83 of these *video pages*. In the other 19 instances the estimate was within 5 seconds of the ground truth label. The proposed method also led to three false alarms. Fig. 5 shows some of the detected *video-pages*.

(a) (b) (c) (d)

Figure 5: *video-pages* detected for different lecture videos.

For the sake of completeness, the 'video pages' list also includes representative frames of the lecturer if she is shown in close up for a certain duration in the video.

USER STUDY

We conduct a user study for the evaluation of the proposed system in real-world. Our user study is guided from following research questions.

1. How do learners navigate to specific point of interest in an video when there are different learning tasks presented to them?
2. How do learners make use of different navigation components of the proposed system?
3. How does the proposed system compare with baseline navigation interfaces in bandwidth-constrained settings?
4. What is the perception of learners about the proposed system after its usage?

Participants

We recruited 20 participants for the user study using convenience sampling. The only criteria used for participant recruiting was of basic exposure to video navigation system.

All the participants were fresh computer science and electronics graduates from different engineering colleges in India. Out of total 20 participants, five were female (mean age=25.2, stdev=1.3, max=27, min=24) and fifteen participants were male (mean age=26.3, SD=2.4, max=31, min=23). Seventeen participants had prior exposure to MOOC videos and they were enrolled in Coursera and EdX courses.

Study Design

Baseline: We use transcript interface as baseline for comparison purpose. An interactive transcript of the video was displayed alongside the video to emulate *transcript interface* of MOOC providers such as EdX and Khan Academy. Participants were also encouraged to use scrubber interface for visual clues.

Tasks: We created five different categories of navigation tasks. These tasks represent realistic video navigation scenarios from our observations and learning from related studies [8, 9].

1. Keyword Search: This task category was the simplest of all, where participants were required to navigate to the first spoken occurrence of a keyword in the given video.
2. Keyword Search with a Context: A keyword could have many occurrences in the video. In this task, participants had to spot the keyword with a given context. For example, participant had to spot the keyword "promotion" where the instructor discussed the relationship between promotion and gender.
3. Visual Search: Participants were required to navigate to a visual object in the video. For example, participants were asked to navigate to the part of the video, where the instructor shows how to divide the set of items into separate bins.
4. Multimodal Search: This task had the combination of visual and textual clue for the navigation. For example, participants had to navigate to a part of the video where the instructor computes the degree of freedom using a visual of the statistics table.
5. Emphasized Keyword Search: The participants were asked to navigate to the time at which instructor acoustically emphasizes on certain key words.

Using above task categories, we create 10 different navigation tasks where each category had two tasks.

Procedure: We divided the number of study participants in two equally sized groups. One group of the participants was given a baseline interface and other group was given the proposed system for video navigation. An interactive tutorial session on both the interfaces were given to the respective participants for nearly 15 minutes before the study. The tutorial was given on a demo video. Both the group of participants were given same video of approximately 13 minutes duration selected from a MOOC and asked to solve exactly same tasks on two different interfaces. Note that this video was also part of the test data used for the evaluation of the audio visual techniques mentioned in earlier sections. None of the participants have seen the selected video before the study. The tasks were attempted sequentially by all the participants. For example, tasks for multimodal search were given only when a participant finished the visual search. The participants were also asked not to discuss questions as well as the answers with their peers. After finishing of all the tasks, a post-study questionnaire containing 14 questions were given to all the participants to understand their overall experience of using the system and their feedback for improving the system.

Data Logging: We logged the fine-grained details about task performance (i.e. navigation time), interaction of the participants with the user interface (i.e. click, mouse-hover events, etc) with the misc events such as video buffering. The logs were collected for both baseline and proposed approaches. We analyze the logs in detail to answer research questions posed earlier.

Task Performance

Figure 6 compares the performance of the proposed system w.r.t. baseline in terms of time taken to complete each of the five different categories of tasks. The task time values are averaged across the 10 users for each of the two systems and the standard deviations are also presented. Subsequently, statistical significance of the time savings was also estimated using t-tests.

Among five different categories of task, the proposed system leads to significant time savings as compared to the baseline system for the last four tasks. The task time for both the systems is comparable for the first task. The proposed system does not lead to any significant ($t(17)=-1.71, p = 0.054$) time saving in the first task. This result is expected as the users can quickly navigate to a keyword occurrence by searching the transcript. We elaborate more on this in the next sub-section that describe our analysis of the user behaviour based on interaction usage logs. The proposed system helps search for a keyword term in a given context significantly quickly ($t(12)=-2.59, p < 0.05$) as compared to the the baseline. Because, the user only has to click on the desired word in the *time-aware* word-cloud to see all the time-aligned occurrences of the word in the 2-D timeline.

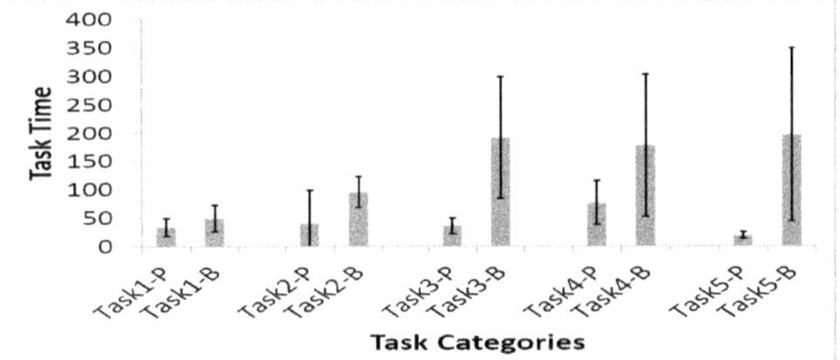

Figure 6: Comparison of task time across proposed (P) and baseline (B) approaches for different task categories

The time saving achieved by the proposed system in navigate to a particular visual event as compared to the baseline is very significant ($t(9)=-4.52, p < 0.01$). This is expected as the *video pages* provide a convenient way to flip through the visual commentary of the video as compared to random scrubbing or by searching the transcript for keywords. Similarly, the time saving achieved by the proposed system to navigate to a multimodal task (keyword associated with a visual cue) are significant (t(11)=-2.41,$p < 0.05$) as compared to the baseline but not as significant as for task 3. This is because the users can search for the keyword occurrences in the transcript and click through all of them till they reach the desired visual event.

We observed significant (t(9)=-3.01, $p < 0.01$) time savings by the proposed system in the task of navigating to a particular keyword with an associated audio cue (stress/emphasis). The color coding of the words in the *time-aware* word-cloud and then, the color coding of each instance of the word on the time-line help the user to visually perceive the audio cues. Interestingly, three users did not agree with the automatic stress assessment of the system in one instance each and spent time navigating to the keyword instance that they thought was stressed. As described earlier, it shows the inherent subjectivity in judging audio cues.

Navigation Patterns and Impact of Bandwidth

We analyzed the navigation patterns of the participants using the system usage logs. Nearly, all the participants in the proposed system tried to solve a task by clicking on a keyword first except task 3, which had only the visual clue. Interesting, in the multimodal search task, two participants (out of total 10) clicked and navigated using the video pages as opposed to eight other participants, who relied on navigation through keyword and subsequently, took help of visual information. *Our analysis also show that proposed system significantly minimizes the number of click events for nearly all the tasks.* Average number of clicks for task 1 to 5 in baseline approach were 2.7 (SD= 0.7), 7.2 (4.4), 5.0 (3.3), 11.0 (12.61), and 15.8 (9.7) respectively as compared to the proposed approach for different tasks 3.8 (SD= 1.2), 4.2 (0.6), 4.7 (1.4), 8.2 (2.1), 4.0 (0.0) respectively.

Even though, our user study was conducted in a workplace environment, the participants frequently experienced latency problems. As described earlier, latency or bandwidth constraints have a large impact on non-linear navigation of education videos. *Our analysis shows that our approach can minimize the number of buffering events as compared to baseline approach and thus, saving time for the users.* Average number of buffering events for the tasks $1-5$ in case of baseline were 3.0 (SD= 1.9), 3.5 (1.8), 8.8 (13.3), 6.8 (9.3), and 9.9 (9.7) respectively where as for the proposed approach for different tasks 3.9 (SD= 1.5), 3.0 (1.6), 2.3 (0.6), 5.4 (4.0), and 1.4 (0.9) respectively. In a scrubbing interface, participants clicked randomly to navigate to the point of interest where every click may lead to a buffering event, wasting significant time for the users. In the proposed system, the navigation is more targeted using *time-aware* word-cloud and video pages. Thus, the users can reach to a given point of interest with minimal buffering events.

Post Study Survey

We performed a post study survey with questions on usability, participant's perceptions about suitability of a given interface for different kind of navigation tasks, and feedback in improving the interfaces. On a 7-point Likert scale, participant rated the usability of the proposed system as 5.60 and transcript interface as 6. On asking about the distraction caused by additional navigation components, the participants rated it manageable (4.2 on a scale of 7). One of the participant also commented about the learning cycle of the interface. *"There is a small learning curve but after learning the process, video navigation becomes extremely easy."*

The two separate group of participants were asked about suitability of searching different information (i.e. keyword search, visual, multimodal, etc) on both the interfaces. The participants reported that textual interface is most suited for keyword search tasks (6.06/7) and least suited for finding visual object (3.19/7) and emphasized words (2.81/7). In case of the proposed system, the participants reported that it is suited for both visual and textual category tasks i.e. finding emphasized words (6.60/7), keyword search (6.30/7), visual search (5.50/7), and multimodal search (5.30/7). The participants indicated that they are very likely (5.90/7) to go though the word-cloud and video pages to get a summary of the video without playing it. Seven out of 10 participants said yes whenever they were asked whether the proposed interface is faster to navigate compared to other interfaces that they use regularly and rest were not sure. The participants indicated high inclination (5.90/7) for using the proposed interface in the day-to-day life. The t-test results on the post-study survey show preference for the proposed system for different tasks, visual search: t(17)=3.29, $p < 0.01$; multimodal search: t(15)=1.67, $p = 0.056$; and emphasized keyword search: t(10)=6.37, $p < 0.01$. We thus demonstrate that the proposed system not only leads to more efficient navigation but is also preferred by the users as compared to traditional navigation techniques used in current MOOC platforms. Finally, multiple participants have asked for a search option in the word-cloud in the next versions of the system.

DISCUSSION

A multimodal technique for non-linear navigation of educational videos, which mimics typical techniques used to navigate through textual documents is presented here. The audio discourse in the lecture is presented as a customized *time-aware* word-cloud. The word-cloud is populated in such a way that the placement of the words indicates their temporal ordering, relative frequency, and acoustic significance in the video. The intuitiveness of the proposed word-cloud was demonstrated on a set of users. The word-cloud is supplemented by a set of *video-pages*, which are the frames with "maximal written content". We also present techniques to tie the *video-pages* with localized *time-aware* word-clouds to get a quick summary of the video. User studies have shown that the proposed system leads to statistically significant time savings especially when the navigation tasks involve association across visual, textual, and audio cues. The proposed system also provides efficiency in minimizing the number of clicks and a reduced overhead for video streaming. Hence, it will help in increasing student engagement in bandwidth-constrained regions.

In future, we plan to deploy the system at large scale in different regions and study personal navigation preferences of the users. Further, the different content-centric dimensions of the proposed system can be customized based on the learning of navigation preferences.

REFERENCES

1. EdX MOOC Platform, https://www.edx.org/
2. Coursera MOOC Platform https://www.coursera.org/
3. FFMPEG Library, https://www.ffmpeg.org/
4. Wordle http://www.wordle.net/
5. Lindsay Ryan, MOOCs are on the Move: A Snapshot of the Rapid Growth of MOOCs, https://www.efmd.org/index.php/blog/view/250-white-paper-moocs-massive-open-online-courses
6. An Early Report Card on Massive Open Online Courses, http://goo.gl/jceRXA
7. Online viewers ditch slow-loading video after 2 seconds, http://edition.cnn.com/2012/11/12/tech/web/video-loading-study
8. Guo, P. J., & Reinecke, K. (2014, March). Demographic differences in how students navigate through MOOCs. In Proceedings of the first ACM conference on Learning@ scale conference (pp. 21-30). ACM. Chicago
9. Kim, J., Guo, P. J., Seaton, D. T., Mitros, P., Gajos, K. Z., & Miller, R. C. (2014, March). Understanding in-video dropouts and interaction peaks in online lecture videos. In Proceedings of the first ACM conference on Learning@ scale conference (pp. 31-40). ACM.
10. Cutrell, E., Bala, S., Bansal, C., Cross, A., Datha, N., John, A., ... & Thies, W. (2013). Massively Empowered Classroom: Enhancing Technical Education in India, MSR Technical Report.
11. Krishnan, S. S., & Sitaraman, R. K. (2013). Video stream quality impacts viewer behavior: inferring causality using quasi-experimental designs. IEEE/ACM Transactions on Networking (TON), 21(6), 2001-2014.
12. Castella, Q., & Sutton, C. (2014, April). Word storms: multiples of word clouds for visual comparison of documents. In Proceedings of the 23rd international conference on World wide web (pp. 665-676). International World Wide Web Conferences Steering Committee.
13. Ada, I., Thiel, K., & Berthold, M. R. (2010, October). Distance aware tag clouds. In Systems Man and Cybernetics (SMC), 2010 IEEE International Conference on (pp. 2316-2322). IEEE.
14. Monserrat, T. J. K. P., Zhao, S., McGee, K., & Pandey, A. V. (2013, April). NoteVideo: facilitating navigation of blackboard-style lecture videos. In Proceedings of the SIGCHI Conference on Human Factors in Computing Systems (pp. 1139-1148). ACM.
15. Kim, J., Guo, P. J., Cai, C. J., Li, S. W. D., Gajos, K. Z., & Miller, R. C. (2014, October). Data-driven interaction techniques for improving navigation of educational videos. In Proceedings of the 27th annual ACM symposium on User interface software and technology (pp. 563-572). ACM.
16. Nicholson, J., Huber, M., Jackson, D., & Olivier, P. (2014, April). Panopticon as an eLearning support search tool. In Proceedings of the 32nd annual ACM conference on Human factors in computing systems (pp. 1221-1224). ACM.
17. Matejka, J., Grossman, T., & Fitzmaurice, G. (2013, April). Swifter: improved online video scrubbing. In Proceedings of the SIGCHI Conference on Human Factors in Computing Systems (pp. 1159-1168). ACM.
18. Rohlicek, J. Robin, et al. "Continuous hidden Markov modeling for speaker-independent word spotting." Acoustics, Speech, and Signal Processing, 1989. ICASSP-89., 1989 International Conference on. IEEE, 1989.
19. Vidrascu, Laurence, and Laurence Devillers. "Detection of real-life emotions in call centers." INTERSPEECH. Vol. 2005. No. 10. 2005.
20. Deshmukh, Om D., and Ashish Verma. "Nucleus-level clustering for word-independent syllable stress classification." Speech Communication 51.12 (2009): 1224-1233.
21. SNACK sound toolkit http://www.speech.kth.se/snack/
22. Jitendra Ajmera, Om D. Deshmukh, Anupam Jain, Amit Anil Nanavati, Nitendra Rajput, Saurabh Srivastava: Audio cloud: creation and rendering. IUI 2012: 277-280
23. http://www.colour-affects.co.uk/psychological-properties-of-colours
24. Young, Steve, et al. "The HTK book (for HTK version 3.4)." Cambridge university engineering department 2.2 (2006): 2-3.
25. http://www.keithv.com/software/htk/us/
26. Reeves, Carolyn, A. Ren Schmauder, and Robin K. Morris. "Stress grouping improves performance on an immediate serial list recall task." Journal of Experimental Psychology: Learning, Memory, and Cognition 26.6 (2000): 1638.
27. C.J. van Rijsbergen, S.E. Robertson and M.F. Porter, 1980. New models in probabilistic information retrieval. London: British Library. (British Library Research and Development Report, no. 5587)
28. Chang, Chih-Chung, and Chih-Jen Lin. "LIBSVM: a library for support vector machines." ACM Transactions on Intelligent Systems and Technology (TIST) 2.3 (2011): 27.
29. Dalal, Navneet, and Bill Triggs. "Histograms of oriented gradients for human detection." Computer Vision and Pattern Recognition, 2005. CVPR 2005. IEEE Computer Society Conference on. Vol. 1. IEEE, 2005.

30. Jrvelin, Kalervo, and Jaana Keklinen. "IR evaluation methods for retrieving highly relevant documents." Proceedings of the 23rd annual international ACM SIGIR conference on Research and development in information retrieval. ACM, 2000.

31. Comaniciu, Dorin, and Peter Meer. "Mean shift: A robust approach toward feature space analysis." Pattern Analysis and Machine Intelligence, IEEE Transactions on 24.5 (2002): 603-619.

32. Ying-Dong, Qu, et al. "A fast subpixel edge detection method using¡ i¿ Sobel¡/i¿¡ i¿ Zernike moments¡/i¿ operator." Image and Vision Computing 23.1 (2005): 11-17.

33. Hu, Weiming, et al. "A survey on visual content-based video indexing and retrieval." Systems, Man, and Cybernetics, Part C: Applications and Reviews, IEEE Transactions on 41.6 (2011): 797-819.

34. Choudary, Chekuri, and Tiecheng Liu. "Summarization of visual content in instructional videos." Multimedia, IEEE Transactions on 9.7 (2007): 1443-1455.

35. Altman, Edward, Yu Chen, and Wai Chong Low. "Semantic exploration of lecture videos." Proceedings of the tenth ACM international conference on Multimedia. ACM, 2002.

36. Adcock, John, et al. "Talkminer: a lecture webcast search engine."Proceedings of the international conference on Multimedia. ACM, 2010.

Getting the Message? A Study of Explanation Interfaces for Microblog Data Analysis

James Schaffer
Dept. of Computer Science
University of California,
Santa Barbara, CA 93106
james_schaffer@cs.ucsb.edu

Prasanna Giridhar
Dept. of Computer Science
University of Illinois at Urbana
Champaign, Urbana, IL 61801
giridha2@illinois.edu

Debra Jones
SA Technologies Inc
751 Hebron Parkway Suite
310, Lewisville, Texas 75057
debra@satechnologies.com

Tobias Höllerer
Dept. of Computer Science
University of California,
Santa Barbara, CA 93106
holl@cs.ucsb.edu

Tarek Abdelzaher
Dept. of Computer Science
University of Illinois at Urbana
Champaign, Urbana, IL 61801
zaher@cs.uiuc.edu

John O'Donovan
Dept. of Computer Science
University of California,
Santa Barbara, CA 93106
jod@cs.ucsb.edu

ABSTRACT

In many of today's online applications that facilitate data exploration, results from information filters such as recommender systems are displayed alongside traditional search tools. However, the effect of prediction algorithms on users who are performing open-ended data exploration tasks through a search interface is not well understood. This paper describes a study of three interface variations of a tool for analyzing commuter traffic anomalies in the San Francisco Bay Area. The system supports novel interaction between a prediction algorithm and a human analyst, and is designed to explore the boundaries, limitations and synergies of both. The degree of explanation of underlying data and algorithmic process was varied experimentally across each interface. The experiment (N=197) was performed to assess the impact of algorithm transparency/explanation on data analysis tasks in terms of search success, general insight into the underlying data set and user experience. Results show that 1) presence of recommendations in the user interface produced a significant improvement in recall of anomalies, 2) participants were able to detect anomalies in the data that were missed by the algorithm, 3) participants who used the prediction algorithm performed significantly better when estimating quantities in the data, and 4) participants in the most explanatory condition were the least biased by the algorithm's predictions when estimating quantities.

Author Keywords

Anomaly Detection, Intelligent User Interfaces, Data Mining

ACM Classification Keywords

H.5.m. Information Interfaces and Presentation (e.g. HCI): Miscellaneous

IUI 2015, March 29–April 1, 2015, Atlanta, GA, USA.

http://dx.doi.org/10.1145/2678025.2701406

INTRODUCTION

Intelligent user interfaces have the goal of dynamically adapting to the needs of a user as they interact with an information system. Most people are familiar with personalized product recommendations (e.g. from Amazon) or movie recommendations (e.g. from Netflix). Google's search result lists are another popular example of dynamically adapted content, based on the search history of a target user. Across all of these examples, and most other adaptive information systems, users are typically kept at a distance from the the underlying mechanisms used to generate personalized content or predictions. In this work, we use the term 'recommender' to refer to complex prediction algorithms, data mining algorithms, intelligent systems, or any other algorithms which produce ranked lists of "interesting" data items, but are complex enough that they would not commonly have their mechanisms explained to the user. Note that recommendations from these systems are often presented through an otherwise static interface such as a list of search results or in a grid. Moreover, traditional browsing mechanisms such as text search, data overviews, and sorting mechanisms are often presented separately from, and operate independently of, recommendations (such as Amazon's product catalog).

During an exploratory search session with an interface, users perform iterated cycles of exploration, hypothesis, and discovery - a process often employed in scientific research, statistical analysis, and even catalog browsing. Users may start with very vague parameters, for example: "What are the most interesting movies in this genre?"; "What interesting things do Twitter users say about this topic?". Exploration can yield hypotheses that can then be answered with targeted search, for example, "is this Amazon product cheaper from another seller? Perhaps yes?"; "is this Twitter user familiar with this topic? Probably not."; "is there a higher-rated Netflix movie that is similar to this one? There has to be!". Each answer that the user finds may create new questions, prompt additional exploration, or cause the user to change his or her search strategy. Recommenders can be extremely valuable during these iterated cycles of exploration, but there is not yet a complete understanding of the interaction between recommender

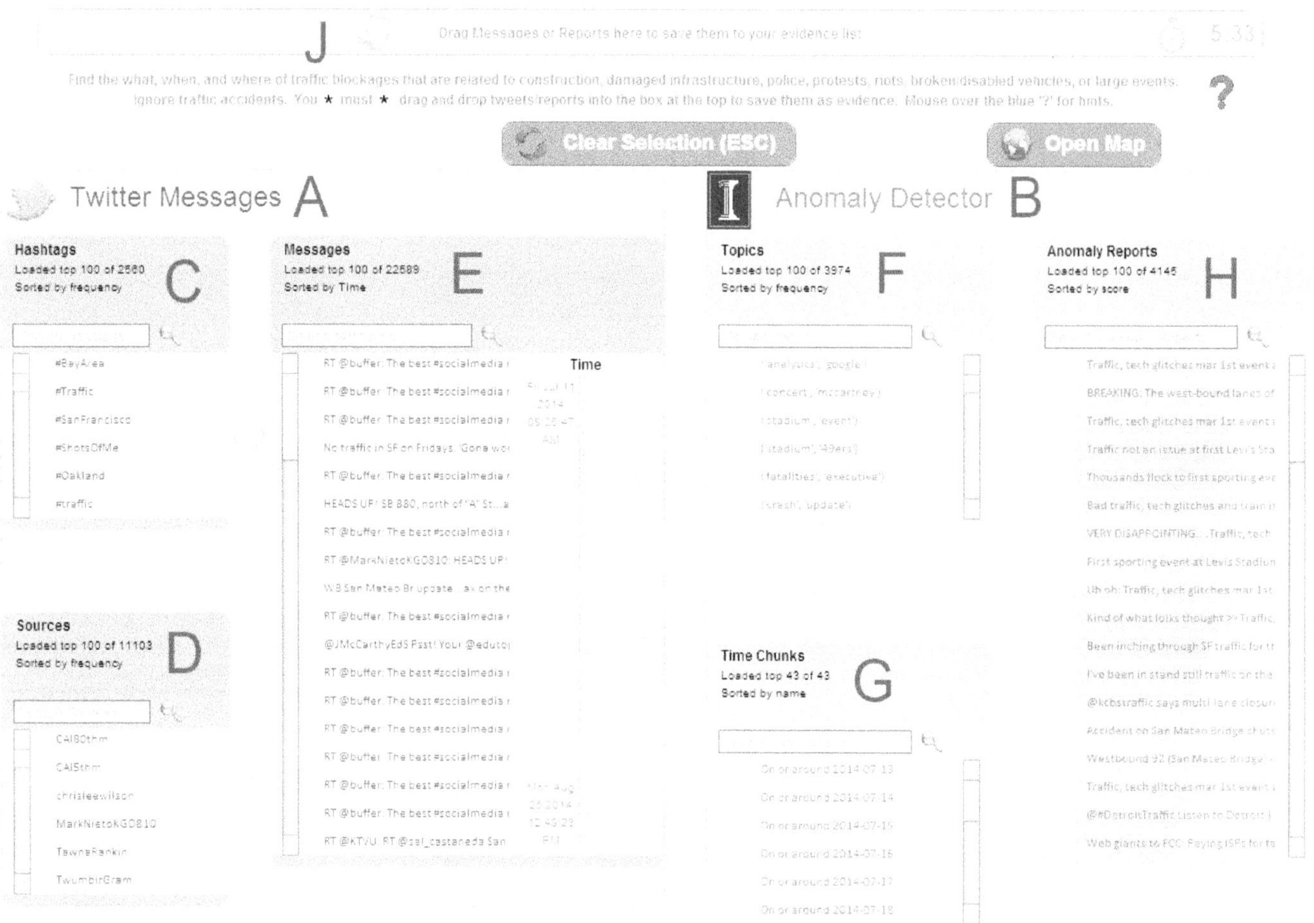

Figure 1. The provenance and data visualization tool, dubbed Fluo, showing A) the Tweet metadata, and B) metadata and results from Clarisense. Metadata from Twitter or Clarisense are organized into separate lists C) Twitter hashtags, D) Twitter sources, E) the tweets themselves, sorted by time, F) topics that Clarisense utilized for anomaly detection, G) intervals of time that Clarisense utilized for anomaly detection, and H) the final anomaly reports, ranked by Clarisense's anomaly score. At the top of the interface (J), the evidence box and remaining task time is displayed. The participant's task prompt (in green) is also shown during the duration of evidence collection as a reminder. When the user mouses over an item, additional details and explanation are displayed in a popup panel (not shown). In the experiment, participants saw a variation of the interface which omitted some metadata availability, see Table 2.

and user search strategies. Recent research in conversational or critiqued recommender systems [16, 29] go some way towards adapting to rapidly changing user needs. Research on explanation interfaces [13, 26, 25] shows that explanations can bias the user towards system predictions, but can also help the user understand why the system is predicting particular content, resulting in a better experience with the system and increased trust in its predictions. However, recommendation algorithms are not perfect as they struggle with noisy and unreliable user-provided content. We believe that providing more transparent and interactive recommenders to users performing exploratory search tasks can result in better consolidation of search strategies and thus improved performance.

Our research results that indicate that varying the degree of available information *about the underlying recommender* significantly affects the trade-offs between 1) information discovery (amount of interesting/useful information found), 2) general insight into the underlying data set, and 3) user experience with the system. By understanding these trade-offs, better interfaces that show the right content to the right user at the right time can be developed. We describe a user experiment ($N = 197$) designed to provide insight on three general research questions: 1) how can an interface be adapted to consolidate user and recommender search and exploration strategies? 2) how do recommendation algorithms change user perception of an underlying data set? 3) what are the positive and negative effects of explaining recommendation algorithms in this context?

As an example task for our experiment, we chose analysis of commuter traffic reports on Twitter in the San Francisco Bay area. This application scenario was chosen because of the large amount of potentially noisy user-provided content (Twitter postings) and associated metadata. The volume of data (22,580 messages) was large enough to make visual scanning of the messages inefficient, necessitating use of visualization and recommendation functionality within our interactive interface, Fluo [23]. An automated anomaly detector and recommendation algorithm [10], Clarisense, was used to generate recommendations of anomalous messages in the dataset. This system serves as an example of a prediction algorithm - the results from this experiment should reasonably apply to similar systems.

BACKGROUND

This research is about the boundaries, limitations and synergies that exist between a human information analyst and an automated algorithm. Visualization and recommender systems are both key components. While the example anomaly-detection algorithm used (Clarisense) is not a recommender system (RS) in the classic sense (e.g.: no personalization is used), we maintain that the study has particular relevance to recommender systems research because use of interactive interfaces [18, 5, 30], explanations [12, 14, 25] and control [15, 21] in recommenders is increasing, but there is still a limited amount of current research in this specific area. We are specifically interested in the interplay between the RS algorithm and the interactive interface using real world data. Other research in this specific area i includes Parra et al.'s SetFusion/ConferenceNavigator system [21], and Bostandjiev's TasteWeights experiments. [5, 15] We believe that this paper is a small but important step in this direction.

Recommender Systems and Explanations

Over the last 15 years, research has shown that explanation of a recommender system's reasoning can have a positive impact on trust and acceptance of recommendations. Early work by Herlocker [13] studied a variety of explanation mechanisms and their impact on trust, satisfaction and other subjective metrics, concluding that certain styles of explanation can convince a user to adopt recommendations. Bilgic et al. [4] furthered this work and explored explanation from the promotion vs. satisfaction perspective, finding that explanations can actually improve the user's impression of recommendation quality. Later work by Tintarev and Masthoff [25] surveyed literature on recommender explanations and noted several pitfalls to the explanation process, notably including the problem of confounding variables. This remains a difficult challenge for most interactive recommender systems [26], where factors such as user ability, mood and other propensities, experience with the interface, specific interaction pattern and generated recommendations can all impact on the user experience with the system. The importance of system transparency and explanation of recommendation algorithms has also been shown to increase user adoption of recommendations by Knijnenburg in [15].

The broader field of intelligent systems produced research relevant to our study. Gregor et al. [12] provide an excellent summary of the theory of crafting explanations for intelligent systems. User studies that test the effects of explanation typically vary explanation level and quantify concepts such as adherence or knowledge transfer. Key findings show that explanations will be more useful when the user has a goal of learning or when the user lacks knowledge to contribute to problem solving. Explanations have also been shown to improve learning overall and improve decision making. The impact of explanation on both novices and experts has also been extensively studied: novices are much more likely to adhere to the recommender/expert system due to a lack of domain knowledge, and expert users require a strong 'domain-oriented' argument before adhering to advice. Experts are also much more likely to request an explanation if an anomaly or contradiction is perceived. Most of these studies focus on decision making domains (financial analysis, auditing problems) and were conducted before the explosion of data which now characterize typical web databases. When browsing or analyzing data that is too large to be analyzed by hand, decision makers have no choice but to utilize automated filtering techniques as part of their search strategy - this creates new questions about what might change in the dynamics between humans and automated algorithms.

Evaluation of Interactive Interfaces

The visual analytics community has begun to favor open-ended protocols over benchmark tasks for the evaluation of interactive interfaces [7][17][28]. This is partly due to a realization that most visualization systems are overly-specific, and thus not agile or adaptive enough to handle non-deterministic, open-ended data exploration with a higher level goal of decision making or learning [2][1]. Though recent systems have become substantially more expressive [22][11], the question of how to effectively evaluate the usefulness of such systems is still open. Researchers recommend that participants in experimental visualization tasks should be allowed to explore the data in any way they choose, creating as many insights as possible, and then measuring their insight with a think-aloud protocol or qualitative measures, such as quantity estimation or distribution characterization. This contrasts starkly with typically well-defined benchmark tasks, which usually have users do things such as find minimum or maximum values, find an item that meets a specific criterion, etc. North [17] cautions that most benchmark tasks may only evaluate an interface or visualization along a very narrow axis of functionality. We believe that these recommendations on evaluation strategies go beyond the realm of visual analytics, and are applicable to the evaluation of interfaces such as Netflix or Amazon which users return to daily with new insights and understandings of what content or products are available.

Microblogs for Traffic Analysis

Daly et al. [8] also study the domain of commuter traffic, with a view to increasing user understanding of a large corpus of real time Twitter messages. The approach in this case contrasts with our research in that they evaluate a system using a novel combination of Linked Data and Twitter messages to inform users about anomalies, rather than studying how interfaces might best support explanation facilities in this context.

APPROACH

This section describes the the anomaly recommender, Clarisense, and the interactive interface, Fluo, in more detail. The Twitter tweets and related metadata shown to participants were collected between July 12, 2014 and August 24, 2014. Tweets were filtered by looking at the keyword 'traffic' near San Francisco, California, USA. These tweets were then fed to the content recommender for summary, and a provenance view of this operation was shown in the Fluo interface. In most treatments, participants were also given the original unfiltered dataset alongside the Clarisense recommendation.

Clarisense Architecture

Clarisense is a Twitter-targeted automated anomaly detection algorithm developed at UIUC. To rank microblog items, Clarisense employs a search strategy of examining the frequency of topics over time in the microblog collection. The first step in the Clarisense pipeline is the division of the input data into 24 hour time chunks followed by clustering within each chunk in order to retain only unique tweets and remove any redundant information if present. The 24 hour parameter was determined based on the percentage of delay between the retweets and the original tweet that was observed. In each cluster, only one tweet is chosen as relevant and passed to the next step in the pipeline. The next goal is to find the events within each cluster that stand out from the normal ongoing events during that period of time. We opted for an approach which uses keywords from each tweet as the primary purpose of identification. A pair of keywords, rather than single keywords or n-tuples, showed the highest correspondence between independent events and their keyword signatures. Discriminative keyword pairs were extracted from each time chunk by leveraging spatial and temporal data to determine which keywords were mundane. For each time chunk, the discriminative keyword pairs were used to rank the microblog entries in terms of their information gain. Finally, normalizing the information gain over all time chunks yields the data for the ranked list shown in Figure 1(H). A full description of Clarisense can be found in [10].

Fluo

This section introduces our interactive interface (and experimental platform), Fluo, and briefly describes its methodology.

Design

Fluo (Figure 1) is a provenance visualization that was designed for exploring the top-N results from a ranking algorithm. It is part of ongoing work in the inspectability and control of recommenders and data mining algorithms at UCSB [5]. In the interface, data items or intermediate calculations are represented as nodes and organized into columns, which can be placed serially (creating an upstream/downstream relationship) or in parallel (to represent that multiple sources are weighted together). Each node in the visualization may have a corresponding "score" which is shown as a gauge and can be mapped to any corresponding value in the underlying algorithm (e.g., Pearson Correlation for collaborative filtering). A mapping from interaction techniques to commonly recognized user intents [27] is shown in Table 1.

Fluo simplifies reconfiguration of metadata and visual relationships for each experimental treatment. A breakdown of which metadata is shown in which condition is provided in Table 2. During the experiment, users engaged in an interactive tutorial that explained the interface and all available metadata based on the treatment. The modular design of the interface and consistent interaction techniques across configurations for each treatment allowed for easy interpretation of results.

User Intent	User Action and Response
Select	User selects an item in a list, the system highlights the item and keeps it at the top its list. Details on demand and more explanation are shown on mouse-hover.
Explore	User scrolls a list, the system shows new items along a fixed parameter (time, frequency, relevance to search term)
Reconfigure	For the purpose of evaluation, the types of items represented and the sort parameters were fixed by the experimenters ahead of time.
Encode	For the purpose of evaluation, the color, size, and shape of items was fixed by the experimenters ahead of time.
Abstract /Elaborate	The user mouses over an item in a list, the system provides additional details about the item in a panel.
Filter	The user selects a time bin, only items from that time are shown. The user enters a search term, only items matching that term are shown.
Connect	The user selects an item, connected items (friends) are brought to the top of their respective list. The user can then expand the selection to show even more connected items (friends of friends).

Table 1. User intents supported by the interactive interface for this experiment.

Explanation of Clarisense

Clarisense's search strategy was simplified for participants and presented through the interface, as shown in Figure 1. Intermediate steps of the algorithm and their values (time chunks and topics or keyword pairs) were exposed as provenance metadata. During the training period, applicable participants were given a detailed explanation of each kind of metadata, how they relate, what constitutes a high or low anomaly score, and how to form queries that reveal relationships between the original dataset, the extracted keywords, and their frequency on various time chunks. Participants were also required to answer specific Clarisense-related questions during the training period before they could proceed, and all information about Clarisense remained available to participants even during the task phase.

Experiment Design

We examined how varying levels of explanation from the recommender affect the entire human-recommender system's ability to 1) find relevant, interesting data items and 2) generate an overall understanding or accurate perception of the data, especially when data items are too large to be browsed sequentially. We also measured the effects of various levels of explanation on the user's confidence, perception of the tool, and enjoyment of the task.

In our task protocol, we compromised between a truly open-ended task and a benchmark task by giving users a set of high-level search parameters relating to traffic blockages

Independent Variable	
Treatment	**Description**
Baseline - Tweet Metadata Only (Figure 1, A)	Twitter metadata (source, tweet, hashtags, time) shown. Text search over message body content, filter by time. Different selections of messages, sources, and hashtags unveil different relationships through edges on-demand.
Clarisense Only (Figure 1, H)	Clarisense's summarized reports with text search, filter by time. The 'what' of Clarisense's reports are summarized but not the 'how' (no provenance). Twitter metadata and messages are not present.
Clarisense in Context (Figure 1, A+H)	A combination of the two previous conditions. Additionally, users can see the relationship between the original tweets and the reports, making this a partial provenance view.
Clarisense in Context w/ Explanation (Figure 1, A+B)	Similar to the previous condition, but Clarisense's selected time intervals and topic modeling were exposed to the users, making this tool a full provenance view of Clarisense's anomaly calculation.

Table 2. In this experiment we manipulated the amount of explanation, control, and metadata availability. Above is a description of each experimental treatment.

and allowed them to explore the dataset in any way they chose. Additionally, we measured performance by comparing participant-reported events against a benchmark that was created post-hoc by examining all events discovered by participants. In agreement with [17], we believe that this methodology reduced evaluation biases that occur when users are assigned very specific search parameters. Additionally, this approach also sidestepped some of the major difficulties with longitudinal studies while still being a good representation of many real world exploratory search tasks.

The experimental toolkit was deployed as a web service and the link was made available on Amazon Mechanical Turk (AMT). The AMT web service is attractive for researchers who require large participant pools and low cost overhead for their experiments. However, there is valid concern that data collected online may be of low quality and require robust methods of validation. Numerous experiments have been conducted, notably [6] and [20], that have attempted to show the validity of using the service for the collection of data intended for academic and applied research. These studies have generally found that the quality of data collected from AMT is comparable to what would be collected from supervised laboratory experiments, if studies are carefully set up, explained, and controlled. Previous studies of recommender systems have also sucessfully leveraged AMT as a subject pool [5, 15], however, most AMT workers expect tasks between 60 seconds and 5 minutes on average. Longer tasks may catch users off guard, fatiguing them and increasing tendency for satisficing. While we took detailed timing metrics for all interactions, for some time windows it is difficult to tell if a user is merely thinking or, e.g., went to use the restroom. Additionally, if a participant suffers from a key misconception, we cannot correct or account for it. Fortunately, larger sample sizes and quicker uptake help mitigate some of this noise inherent in AMT experiments.

We carefully followed recommended best practices in our AMT experimental design and procedures [6] and [20]. For filtering AMT workers, we chose to require that participants had successfully completed at least 50 HITs on the system. Participants were paid an average of 4 dollars plus a 1 dollar performance-based incentive. The bonus payment was made to everyone who completed the study. Numerous satisficing checks [19] were placed throughout the pre-study (e.g. what is 4 + 8?), and the training phase (as outlined below) reasonably insured a minimum level of understanding before participants were allowed to proceed. We also collected some basic demographic information from each participant, including information about how frequently they drive a car and their familiarity (if any) with San Francisco's Bay Area.

Experiment Protocol

After accessing the experimental system through AMT, participants were presented with a pre-study questionnaire using the Qualtrics survey tool [1], collecting basic demographic and background information. Next, they were directed to one of the variations of our online tool for a training session. Once training was complete, the open-ended search task was described and participants used the interface to explore the tweets and Clarisense's reports into a list of evidence. Once time was up, the interface was removed and we asked them several questions related to key quantities in the dataset that were related to the exploration they performed. The training and evidence collection protocols are talked about in more detail below.

Training

Since the experimenters could not verbally direct the participants, a complex training module was created which walked the participant through key concepts before the evidence collection portion of the task. The participant was required to answer a series of targeted search questions, the answers to which could only be known once the participant identified which parts of the interface were providing what information. An unlimited number of attempts were given for each question. Easier questions were chosen as multiple choice with fewer than 4 options, while the hardest questions had blank response forms that required the entry of quantities. After informal pilot testing in the lab, it was decided that hints for every question were needed to alleviate participant fatigue during this portion of the study. During data collection, few participants reported difficulties completing the training in any condition. The average failure rate for targeted search questions related to the interface functions and Twitter metadata

[1] www.qualtrics.com

was 95% (which means that, on average, participants submitted a wrong answer for each question on the first attempt). For questions related to Clarisense and the anomaly detection strategy, the failure rate was only 27%.

Evidence Collection

Once training was completed, participants were prompted that the evidence collection phase was about to begin. They were told that the dataset contained numerous traffic blockages and that we were interested in studying blockages related to construction, infrastructure damage, broken or disabled vehicles, police activity (riots, protest), and planned public events. Participants were actively told to ignore traffic accidents, and distinctions were made between planned public events such as sports games or concerts and other events like riots. The active prompt for the task is shown in Figure 1 (J). Participants were told to look for these events and collect evidence in a list (by dragging and dropping either Tweets or anomaly reports), and that they would be paid a bonus for finding more interesting evidence related to blockages. Participants were restricted to 15 minutes for this portion of the task, and a ticking clock (Figure 1) indicated the time remaining.

Metrics

The independent variable in this experiment is detailed in Table 2 (see also Figure 1). An overview of the dependent variables in this experiment are are shown in Table 3.

Event Recall

Once all participant data was collected, an analysis of evidence yielded a list of events, which is shown in Table 4. Each event $e \in E$ was re-constructed by manual inspection from tweets chosen by participants. Non-descriptive tweets that mention traffic but do not mention at least the what or the where were not included in the final benchmark, nor were events that were reported by fewer than 3 participants. After identifying the where, what, and when of the events, we identified the complete set of tweets that described the event. For example, there were 17 tweets in the dataset that unambiguously identified the 'quake' event. During analysis, we said a participant discovered an event if they included at least one message in their evidence, $v \in V_p$, from that event's ground truth in the event benchmark, $g \in G_e$, with the rest of the submitted evidence being classified as noise $n \in N_p$, $N_p \subseteq V_p$. That is, noise is every message in the dataset not related to some event in the post-hoc benchmark. Recall is simply defined as the total number of events detected by a participant:

$$recall = \sum_{e \in E} \begin{cases} 1 & : |V_p \cap G_e| > 0 \\ 0 & : |V_p \cap G_e| = 0 \end{cases} \quad (1)$$

Note that recall is **not** normalized, and can fall between 0 and 22. Recall also indirectly gives us a rate of event discovery since all participants were limited to exactly 15 minutes for the evidence collection phase. However, there was one exception in our benchmark. Due to the large size of the 'Web Traffic' event (see Table 4) and because participants were not explicitly told that this event is interesting at the start of evidence collection, we assessed if participants made this insight using a multiple-choice question after the evidence collection phase.

Dependent Variable	Description
Event Recall	Total number of events the participant discovered through evidence submission during the fixed-time phase of the task.
Estimation Error	Participant's error in estimating the quantity of events related to specific types of blockages (disabled vehicles, damaged infrastructure, police/riot/protest,planned public events). Responses provided during the post-study.
Usability	Participant's confidence, enjoyment, and perceptions of the tool, taken on a Likert scale in the post-study.

Table 3. Description of dependent variables.

We also considered precision, which in this case measures the percentage of noise the participant included in their final evidence list N_p:

$$precision = \frac{|V_p| - |N_p|}{|V_p|} \quad (2)$$

Precision allows us to understand the quality of evidence the participant submitted (e.g., was the participant paying attention or merely grabbing as much evidence as possible?)

Estimation Error

After the evidence collection task ended, we requested that the participant estimate of the number of blockages that were actually represented in the dataset which pertained to a particular type of incident. Disabled vehicles, damaged infrastructure, police/riot/protest, and planned public events were chosen for these questions due to practical limitations on generating ground truth for events that are likely to have two instances occur simultaneously in time (construction, traffic accidents). Participants entered their answer in plain text boxes. These metrics gave us the participant's 'qualitative understanding' of the impact of each type of incident on traffic.

Usability

Participant perceptions of the tool were collected after the evidence collection and estimation tasks. Participants provided answers on a Likert scale (1-7) for each question on a web form. Participants were asked "How confident were you using the tool to complete the task?", "How much did you like the interface tool?", "How much did you like the training portion of the task?", and "How much did you enjoy the evidence collection portion of the task?"

Event	Description	Score	Size
gas leak	On 7/11, a gas leak caused a closure of 7th St and Broadway	0	4
drake/eliseo light	On 7/22, a traffic signal on Eliseo Dr malfunctioned	0.21	4
08/12 oil spill	Oil from a truck was spilled on the San Mateo bridge	0.82	10
08/21 oil spill	Oil from a truck was spilled on Magdalena Ave	0.34	6
cesar light	On 08/18, a traffic light malfunctioned on Cesar Chavez	0.29	4
quake	On 08/24, a major quake damaged multiple roads in Napa, Vallejo, and Sonoma	0.13	17
andy lopez	On 07/12, A protest demanding justice for Andy Lopez blocked highway 101	0.26	6
07/20 market st protest	A protest caused severe congestion on Market St	0	1
07/26 market st protest	A protest caused severe congestion on Market St	0.10	2
ferguson	On, 08/22, a protest of the Ferguson shooting caused traffic to stop near Civic Center Plaza	0.05	3
coliseum	On 07/25, a bomb threat at Coliseum Station caused highway 880 to become blocked	0.46	10
lombard	On 07/12 and 07/19, Lombard St was closed to the public by city officials	0.14	3
49ers	On 08/03, a 49ers game at Levi Stadium caused severe congestion	1.00	30
obama	On 07/23, an Obama visit caused multiple blockages/road closures near downtown	0.48	33
mccartney	On 08/14, a Paul McCartney concert caused severe congestion near Candlestick theater	0.48	30
soccer	On 07/26, a soccer game at UC Berkeley caused severe congestion	0.29	9
marathon	On 07/26, the San Francisco Marathon resulted in multiple road closures	0.18	13
japan	On 07/19, a J-Pop Festival in Japantown resulted in road closures and severe congestion	0.65	12
terminator	On 08/03, the Golden Gate Bridge was closed for the filming of Terminator 5	0.08	2
st francis constr	On 07/16, part of St Francis Dr was closed all day to traffic	0.03	2
slurry seal	on 08/07 and 08/08, construction caused delays and closures near Ralston Ave	0.08	6
web traffic	A significant percentage of the messages in the dataset related to web traffic	0.08	-

Table 4. The post-hoc benchmark - events discovered by participants during the task. 'Score' indicates Clarisense's recommendation for tweets associated with this event. 'Size' indicates the total number of distinct Tweets that identified the what, where, and when of the event.

Hypotheses

Evaluating features of each treatment separately, then in combination enabled systematic assessment of the value of each feature and additionally allows for the identification of synergistic value gained by the combinations. The following hypotheses were evaluated during this experiment:

- H_1: interface type impacts total number of events recalled
- H_2: interface type impacts which events are recalled
- H_3: interface type impacts evidence precision
- H_4: interface type affects estimation error
- H_5: interface type affects the user's confidence
- H_6: interface type affects the degree to which the user liked the tool
- H_7: interface type affects the degree to which the user liked the training session
- H_8: interface type affects the degree to which the user liked the open-ended search task

RESULTS

Participants

AMT participant age ranged from 18 to 65, with an average of 25 and a median of 27. 52% of participants were male while 48% were female. 563 workers completed the pre-study, but only 197 finished the study in its entirety. After visually inspecting the data and plotting the results, we found no strong outliers in the remaining 197.

Analysis

Table 5 shows precision and recall for participants across treatments for the post-hoc benchmark (Table 4). Note that we measure recall non-normalized as to best represent the magnitudes of the quantity of discoveries. A large increase in recall is seen between the Twitter Only' condition and the conditions where Clarisense was present. A slight drop in total discoveries seems to occur between the 'Clarisense Only' condition and the conditions with Clarisense AND the original Twitter data. Participants were grouped by whether the recommender was available (no=60,yes=137) and a single factor analysis of variance was run, showing a significant decrease of 60% when Clarisense was not present ($F = 92.87, p < 0.01$). When we compare the 'Clarisense Only' condition with the conditions that provided context and explanation facilities, we see a 25% drop in recall rate ($F = 19.54, p < 0.01$). Thus H_1 is supported.

We hypothesized that the presence of Clarisense and its presentation would have a significant impact on which events were discovered by participants. To test this, we considered only the events which we determined that Clarisense 'missed' or underrepresented due to its filtering and reporting mechanism (Figure 2). To qualitatively determine what Clarisense had 'missed', we decided that a lenient anomaly score threshold should be chosen that would give Clarisense a precision

Condition	Precision	Recall
Twitter Only	0.14	2.77
Clarisense Only	0.60	8.23
Clarisense with Context	0.44	6.44
Clarisense with Explanation	0.50	5.85

Table 5. Mean precision and recall for each interface configuration. Participants that only interacted with the anomaly recommender were able to incorporate more of its reported events in the same time period and take advantage of its precision.

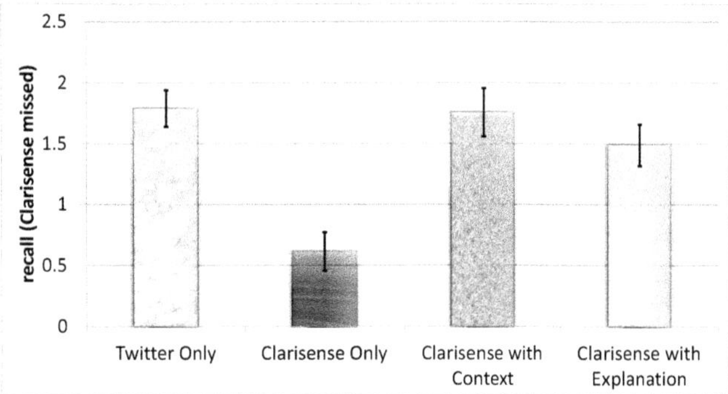

Figure 2. Participants that interacted with the original data were able to consistently find events that the anomaly recommender missed or classified as relatively less interesting

of at least that of the worst participant in the Twitter Metadata only condition (0.034). We settled on a score threshold of one standard deviation above the mean (0.15), which corresponded to a precision of 0.035. Referring to Table 4, this means that Clarisense reported 12 events total (slightly more than half) from 339 pieces of evidence total, which results in a list of 10 events that Clarisense missed. In the 'Clarisense Only' condition, participants only appear to be half as likely to discover one of these events. We again grouped the participants by whether they had the original Twitter data available (no=51,yes=146) and ran another single-factor ANOVA between conditions that contained the original Twitter dataset and the 'Clarisense Only' condition, finding a 63% decrease ($F = 33.65, p < 0.01$) in underrepresented events when only Clarisense was present. This supports H_2.

Looking at Table 5, it can be seen that the relative proportion of values within precision and recall was roughly the same, indicating that an increase in recall corresponded to a similar increase in precision, unfortunately reducing the usefulness of the precision metric when interpreting results. Still, an ANOVA revealed large differences between the conditions ($F = 57.44, p < 0.001$), with big differences between 'Twitter Only' and the other treatments ($p < 0.001$ for all), but also a difference was found between 'Clarisense Only' and 'Clarisense with Context' ($p < 0.001$), and another difference between 'Clarisense Only' and 'Clarisense with Explanation' ($p < 0.027$). Thus H_3 is supported.

Figure 3 shows the overall estimation error from our questionnaire which followed the evidence collection task. The vertical axis shows the average difference between actual and estimated distinct blockages for each treatment. Since the scales of the ground truth were similar (disabled vehicles: 29,

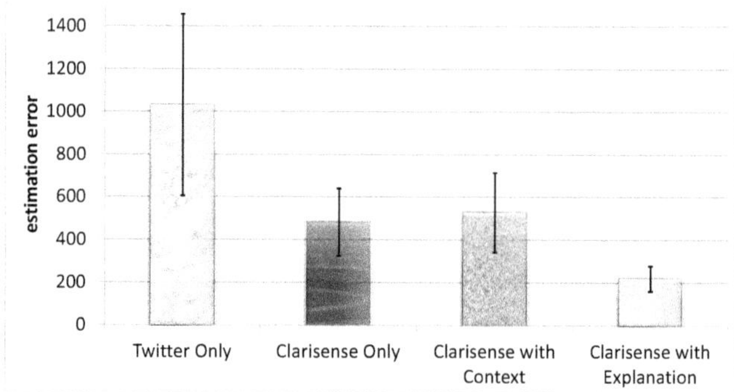

Figure 3. After the open-ended task, participants that interacted with the anomaly recommender consistently had a better understanding of the quantities in the data. The presence of explanation and provenance improved estimation further.

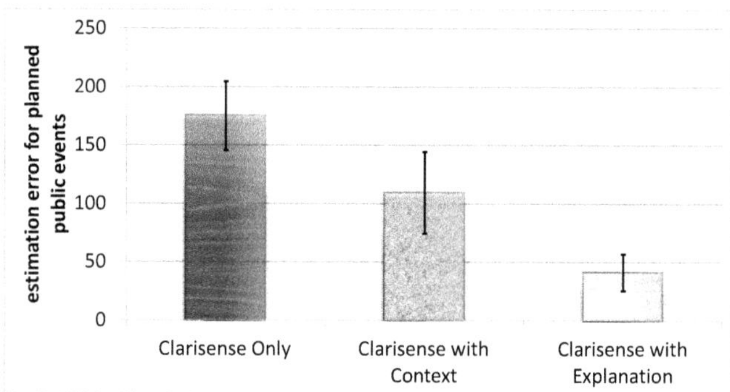

Figure 4. The anomaly recommender was much more likely to report major public events. The level of explanation greatly decreased the participant's error in perception for the frequency of these types of traffic blockages.

damage: 6, police/riot/protest: 9, planned public events: 12) we aggregated these results into one graph. A value of 0 indicates perfect accuracy. Participants were much more likely to overestimate than underestimate. A large increase in estimation accuracy can be seen between the condition where Clarisense was absent (Twitter Only) and the other three conditions. Another drop can be seen between the Clarisense explanation condition and the conditions where less explanation is given. We ran a single factor analysis of variance between the 'Twitter Only' condition and the conditions with the recommender, showing an estimation error decrease of 60% ($F = 4.8, p = 0.030$). We also tested the 56% drop in estimation error for 'Clarisense with Explanation' against the other two Clarisense conditions, finding it fell just short of the 0.05 significance level despite its notable effect size ($F = 2.99, p = 0.087$). To further investigate the decrease in estimation error for the full explanation condition, we plotted the estimation parameters for each type of blockage individually (Figure 4). The most notable of these was a large difference in planned public events - there was a 31% decrease in estimation error in the 'Clarisense with Context' condition and a 75% decrease in estimation error in the 'Clarisense with Explanation' condition. For the latter, we ran another single-factor ANOVA and found ($F = 4.10, p = 0.046$). These findings support H_4.

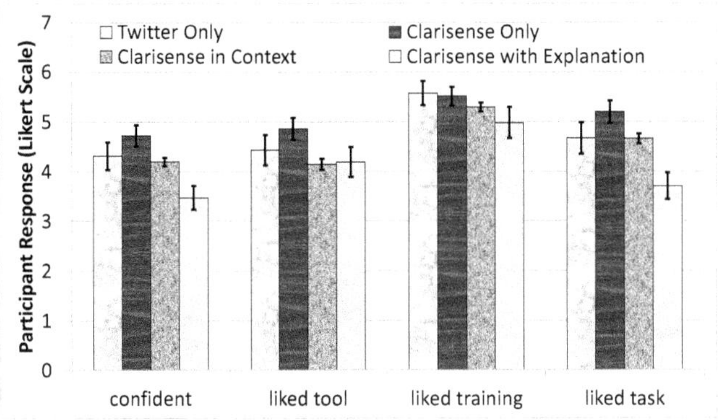

Figure 5. Presence of the original dataset and an increase in explanation corresponded to a decrease in confidence and enjoyment of the task.

Finally, we tested the impact of the increasingly complicated interface and explanation of Clarisense on the participant. Figure 5 shows the results from our post study questionnaire. The answers were provided on a Likert scale (1-7). From left to right, the questions were 'How confident were you using the tool to complete the task?' (confident), 'How much did you like the interface tool?' (like), 'How much did you enjoy the training portion of the task?' (training), 'How much did you enjoy the evidence collection portion of the task?' (task). Presence of the original Twitter data appeared to decrease both confidence and enjoyment of the task, with the largest drops (27% decrease in confidence, 29% decrease in task enjoyment) being between the 'Clarisense with Explanation' and the 'Clarisense Only' conditions. To test the differences between 'Clarisense Only' and 'Clarisense with Explanation', we ran two more single-factor ANOVAs yielding ($F = 15.28, p < 0.01$) for the 27% confidence drop and ($F = 7.074, p < 0.1$) for the 29% task enjoyment drop. More analysis was run for enjoyment of the training session and likeability of the tool, but nothing below the accepted significance level was found. Thus, H_5 and H_8 are supported, but we do not find enough evidence here to support H_6 and H_7.

DISCUSSION

The results uncovered numerous trade-offs related to diversity and quantity of reported events. H_1, H_2, and H_3 indicate that the recommender was useful overall when exploring the dataset, but strongly affected which events were reported. This result is not too surprising given that Clarisense presented several key events to participants even without any interaction. Participant records indicate that they drew their evidence from Clarisense with 50% likelihood in these conditions (remaining evidence came from the original Twitter data). Unfortunately, it seems that when participants spent time employing their own search strategy on the Twitter data, it detracted from the rate at which they considered and incorporated the recommender's discoveries. However, presenting the original Twitter data in the Fluo interface allowed the participants to develop search strategies that yielded different discoveries than Clarisense - note that two of the events discovered were not represented in the 'Clarisense Only' condition (gas leak, 07/26 market st protest), and the remaining 8 were classified as significantly less interesting by the recommender. Of particular note is the 'terminator' event, which saw remarkably higher probability of recall when both the Twitter data and Clarisense reports were present. Evidently, even our novice participants were able to develop search strategies that consistently contributed at least a few novel discoveries to the analysis process.

H_4 indicates that recommender presence had a positive impact on the ability to estimate quantities in the data. The dataset may have simply been too large to gain a good understanding in the limited time frame, but it seems as though the recommender was able to provide a better 'orientation' in the data in a much shorter time. We reason that when the participants scanned the informative tweets in the Clarisense column they formed a reasonable estimate of what was present in the dataset, since Clarisense's recall was comparatively high. The drop in estimation error when concerning planned public events becomes even more meaningful when we consider Clarisense's strategy for reporting interesting anomalies in the dataset. On Twitter, large public events usually have distinct key terms and usually hashtags associated with them that only appear in conjunction with the event. As such, Clarisense is more likely to view these as anomalous than other types of events in the dataset. From Table 4, it can be seen that planned public events dominate the top 5 most anomalous events from Clarisense's perspective. The 'Topics' column likely gave participants additional insight into the quantities and thus reduced estimation error, since it becomes obvious that Clarisense is very interested in large public events from scanning the top topics.

Our usability results (H_5, H_8) indicate that explanation facilities can potentially drop both a user's confidence and make the process of search more stressful. The drop in confidence with increased explanation may mean that participants were comparing the complexity of their own strategy against the one used by Clarisense, thus feeling like their contribution was not as significant. Across treatments, the participant's enjoyment of the training session and the likeability of the tool (H_6, H_7) did not appear to vary much, which was surprising due to the varying length of the session and complexity of the tool based on the treatment.

To get more insight on the training session and the likeability of the tool, we examined the qualitative feedback that was given at the end of the task. Though the free-text responses were too noisy to provide evidence for supporting H_6 and H_7, they still provided insight. By and large, participant comments indicated that the 'Clarisense Only' treatment was the easiest to use and the most "intuitive." Participants in the 'Clarisense with Explanation' condition often reported that the interface was too complicated or difficult to use, despite their competitive results (though, this feedback agrees with the 'confidence' scores). Participants across all conditions reported that the experiment was very interesting, e.g. "this certainly stretched my brain!" and that the training session was very helpful. Also recall that participants struggled much more on training questions related to the Twitter metadata and interface usage (seen by all participants) than training questions related to Clarisense, which helps explain the similar responses from participants about the training phase.

Key Takeaways

Recommend First, Search Second: Interfaces should highlight results from a recommender when a user begins the process of data exploration, but general search and exploration tools should always be available. The participants in our experiment benefited greatly from the recommender presence, consistently reporting better estimations of the quantities in the data over those that received no recommender. Participants that could search over the original dataset were still apt to do so, and through their own search strategy discovered events that the recommender missed. The recommendations themselves may also serve as catalysts for initial search strategies or improve learning [3][24], which can greatly help new users, novices, or those working with new datasets.

Contextualize and Explain Recommendations: Both the introduction of the original Twitter data and more explanation facilities appeared to help participants understand and contextualize Clarisense's search strategy, which greatly decreased their estimation error with respect to the events that Clarisense over-represented (public events). Explanation facilities should carefully explain the search strategy of a recommender to users when this is appropriate and put the recommendations in context to avoid these errors. Though not every recommendation system is the same, in domains where decisions are costly, perception biases could be disastrous. For example, analysts of epidemics might ask: what is the relative severity of illness x and hazard y at a specific location - which problem should more resources be allocated to? In other examples, web developers for digital storefronts may want to avoid creating misconceptions about the variety and quantity of items that his store has available, or a library might want to emphasize the impression of diversity among its titles. Ongoing research [9] is still trying to understand the effect of recommender systems on diversity of items delivered to users. It may be possible that users will abandon these services and others (e.g. Netflix, Amazon Prime, Hulu) if they misestimate the diversity of items in the catalog and develop a negative perception of the service.

Recommend to New Users, Explain to Returning Users: In this experiment, full explanation of the recommender decreased user confidence and enjoyment of the open-ended search task. Previous research has also shown the cost of digesting explanations from recommender systems [12]. However, in this case, the presence of the daunting Twitter dataset also appeared to contribute. While most of the participants in this task could be classified as novices in the field of information analysis, they were also new to the tool and some were new to the concept of Twitter. By creating and maintaining models of users, different configurations of the recommender and search tool might be shown at different times. For instance, a digital shop could minimalize their storefront and only initially show recommendations until the user requests a targeted search. When regular customers are established, the store can begin explaining/contextualizing recommendations so that the user can synthesize the recommendations with their own search strategy, potentially finding new products.

Limitations and Future Work

The evidence collection portion of the task was limited to 15 minutes and all users were essentially novices with the Fluo interface. Given more time and more comprehensive training, it is possible that users would have reached a 'saturation point,' where all useful information from the recommender would have been exhausted and more events from user-contributed search strategies would have emerged. To get more insight into the learning curves associated with the system, and therefore a better indication of performance, the authors plan a near-term follow up study to evaluate performance with the user interface without a time restriction.

The specific interaction methodology of Fluo was not varied between conditions, the only variation was in the amount of provenance and metadata shown. In future experiments, different interaction techniques to support different user intents (to better support a variety of user preferences) could be tested in tandem with different explanation facilities. It may be the case that different interaction techniques lend themselves to better presentation of contextualized explanation.

CONCLUSION

In this work, we sought to answer the questions: 1) how can an interface be designed to maximally leverage user and recommender search strategies for exploratory search? 2) how do recommendation algorithms change user perception of an underlying data set? and 3) what are the positive and negative effects of explaining recommendation algorithms in this context? An ($N = 197$) user experiment was run to determine the impact of explanation from a recommender during an exploratory search task. Results show that the presence of recommendations in the interface allowed participants to quickly find more interesting items and improved estimation ability. The presence of search tools allowed participants to develop their own search strategies and find items missed by the recommender, and participants in the most explanatory condition were able to avoid a perceptual bias that affected other participants (70% reduction in bias when estimating public events). We conclude that designers should carefully evaluate time costs and negative impact on user experience when providing explanations, but explanations remain an important design consideration due to their positive impact on a user's understanding of recommender search strategies.

ACKNOWLEDGMENT

The authors would like to thank Coty Gonzalez and Jason Harman at Carnegie Mellon University for their advice on this research. This work was partially funded by the U.S. Army Research Laboratory under Cooperative Agreement No. W911NF-09-2-0053. The views and conclusions contained in this document are those of the authors and should not be interpreted as representing the official policies, either expressed or implied, of the Army Research Laboratory or the U.S. Government. The U.S. Government is authorized to reproduce and distribute reprints for Government purposes notwithstanding any copyright notation here on.

REFERENCES

1. Ahn, J.-w., and Brusilovsky, P. Adaptive visualization for exploratory information retrieval. *Information Processing & Management 49*, 5 (2013), 1139–1164.
2. Amar, R. A., and Stasko, J. T. Knowledge precepts for design and evaluation of information visualizations. *Visualization and Computer Graphics, IEEE Transactions on 11*, 4 (2005), 432–442.
3. Arnold, V., Clark, N., Collier, P. A., Leech, S. A., and Sutton, S. G. The differential use and effect of knowledge-based system explanations in novice and expert judgment decisions. *Mis Quarterly* (2006), 79–97.
4. Bilgic, M., and Mooney, R. J. Explaining recommendations: Satisfaction vs. promotion. In *Beyond Personalization Workshop, IUI*, vol. 5 (2005).
5. Bostandjiev, S., O'Donovan, J., and Höllerer, T. Tasteweights: a visual interactive hybrid recommender system. In *RecSys*, P. Cunningham, N. J. Hurley, I. Guy, and S. S. Anand, Eds., ACM (2012), 35–42.
6. Buhrmester, M., Kwang, T., and Gosling, S. D. Amazon's mechanical turk: A new source of inexpensive, yet high-quality, data? *Perspectives on Psychological Science 6*, 1 (2011), 3–5.
7. Chang, R., Ziemkiewicz, C., Green, T. M., and Ribarsky, W. Defining insight for visual analytics. *Computer Graphics and Applications, IEEE 29*, 2 (2009), 14–17.
8. Daly, E. M., Lecue, F., and Bicer, V. Westland row why so slow?: fusing social media and linked data sources for understanding real-time traffic conditions. In *Proceedings of the 2013 international conference on Intelligent user interfaces*, ACM (2013), 203–212.
9. Fleder, D. M., and Hosanagar, K. Recommender systems and their impact on sales diversity. In *Proceedings of the 8th ACM conference on Electronic commerce*, ACM (2007), 192–199.
10. Giridhar, P., Amin, M. T. A., Abdelzaher, T. F., Kaplan, L. M., George, J., and Ganti, R. K. Clarisense: Clarifying sensor anomalies using social network feeds. In *2014 IEEE International Conference on Pervasive Computing and Communication Workshops, PerCom 2014 Workshops, Budapest, Hungary, March 24-28, 2014* (2014), 395–400.
11. Gratzl, S., Gehlenborg, N., Lex, A., Pfister, H., and Streit, M. Domino: Extracting, comparing, and manipulating subsets across multiple tabular datasets. *Visualization and Computer Graphics, IEEE Transactions on 20*, 12 (Dec 2014), 2023–2032.
12. Gregor, S., and Benbasat, I. Explanations from intelligent systems: Theoretical foundations and implications for practice. *MIS quarterly* (1999), 497–530.
13. Herlocker, J. L., Konstan, J. A., and Riedl, J. Explaining collaborative filtering recommendations. In *Proceedings of the 2000 ACM Conference on Computer Supported Cooperative Work*, CSCW '00, ACM (New York, NY, USA, 2000), 241–250.
14. Herlocker, J. L., Konstan, J. A., and Riedl, J. Explaining collaborative filtering recommendations. In *Proceedings of ACM CSCW'00 Conference on Computer-Supported Cooperative Work* (2000), 241–250.
15. Knijnenburg, B. P., Bostandjiev, S., O'Donovan, J., and Kobsa, A. Inspectability and control in social recommenders. In *Proceedings of the sixth ACM conference on Recommender systems*, ACM (2012), 43–50.
16. McCarthy, K., Reilly, J., McGinty, L., and Smyth, B. Experiments in dynamic critiquing. In *Proceedings of the 10th International Conference on Intelligent User Interfaces*, IUI '05, ACM (New York, NY, USA, 2005), 175–182.
17. North, C. Toward measuring visualization insight. *Computer Graphics and Applications, IEEE 26*, 3 (2006), 6–9.
18. O'Donovan, J., Smyth, B., Gretarsson, B., Bostandjiev, S., and Höllerer, T. Peerchooser: visual interactive recommendation. In *CHI '08: Proceeding of the twenty-sixth annual SIGCHI conference on Human factors in computing systems*, ACM (New York, NY, USA, 2008), 1085–1088.
19. Oppenheimer, D. M., Meyvis, T., and Davidenko, N. Instructional manipulation checks: Detecting satisficing to increase statistical power. *Journal of Experimental Social Psychology 45*, 4 (2009), 867–872.
20. Paolacci, G., Chandler, J., and Ipeirotis, P. G. Running experiments on amazon mechanical turk. *Judgment and Decision Making 5* (2010), 411–419.
21. Parra, D., Brusilovsky, P., and Trattner, C. See what you want to see: visual user-driven approach for hybrid recommendation. In *IUI'14 19th International Conference on Intelligent User Interfaces, IUI'14, Haifa, Israel, February 24-27, 2014* (2014), 235–240.
22. Ren, D., Hollerer, T., and Yuan, X. ivisdesigner: Expressive interactive design of information visualizations. *Visualization and Computer Graphics, IEEE Transactions on 20*, 12 (Dec 2014), 2092–2101.
23. Schaffer, J., Abdelzaher, T., Jones, D., Hollerer, T., Gonzalez, C., Harman, J., and O'Donovan, J. Truth, lies, and data: Credibility representation in data analysis. In *Cognitive Methods in Situation Awareness and Decision Support (CogSIMA), 2014 IEEE International Inter-Disciplinary Conference on*, IEEE (2014), 28–34.
24. Sinha, R., and Swearingen, K. The role of transparency in recommender systems. In *CHI'02 extended abstracts on Human factors in computing systems*, ACM (2002), 830–831.

25. Tintarev, N., and Masthoff, J. A survey of explanations in recommender systems. In *Data Engineering Workshop, 2007 IEEE 23rd International Conference on*, IEEE (2007), 801–810.

26. Tintarev, N., O'Donovan, J., Brusilovsky, P., Felfernig, A., Semeraro, G., and Lops, P. Recsys' 14 joint workshop on interfaces and human decision making for recommender systems. In *Proceedings of the 8th ACM Conference on Recommender systems*, ACM (2014), 383–384.

27. Yi, J. S., ah Kang, Y., Stasko, J. T., and Jacko, J. A. Toward a deeper understanding of the role of interaction in information visualization. *Visualization and Computer Graphics, IEEE Transactions on 13*, 6 (2007), 1224–1231.

28. Yi, J. S., Kang, Y.-a., Stasko, J. T., and Jacko, J. A. Understanding and characterizing insights: how do people gain insights using information visualization? In *Proceedings of the 2008 Workshop on BEyond time and errors: novel evaLuation methods for Information Visualization*, ACM (2008), 4.

29. Zhang, J., and Pu, P. A comparative study of compound critique generation in conversational recommender systems. In *In Proceedings of the 4th International Conference on Adaptive Hypermedia and Adaptive Web-Based Systems (AH2006*, Springer (2006), 234–243.

30. Zhang, J., Wang, Y., and Vassileva, J. Socconnect: A personalized social network aggregator and recommender. *Information Processing and Management 49*, 3 (2013), 721–737.

Prediction of Users' Learning Curves for Adaptation while Using an Information Visualization

Sébastien Lallé, Dereck Toker, Cristina Conati, Giuseppe Carenini
Department of Computer Science
University of British Columbia, Vancouver, Canada
{lalles, dtoker, conati, carenini}@cs.ubc.ca

ABSTRACT
User performance and satisfaction when working with an interface is influenced by how quickly the user can acquire the skills necessary to work with the interface through practice. Learning curves are mathematical models that can represent a user's skill acquisition ability through parameters that describe the user's initial expertise as well as her learning rate. This information could be used by an interface to provide adaptive support to users who may otherwise be slow in learning the necessary skills. In this paper, we investigate the feasibility of predicting in real time a user's learning curve when working with ValueChart, an interactive visualization for decision making. Our models leverage various data sources (a user's gaze behavior, pupil dilation, cognitive abilities), and we show that they outperform a baseline that leverages only knowledge on user task performance so far. We also show that the best performing model achieves good accuracies in predicting users' learning curves even after observing users' performance only on a few tasks. These results are promising toward the design of user-adaptive visualizations that can dynamically support a user in acquiring the necessary skills to complete visual tasks.

Author Keywords
Information visualization; learning curve; eye tracking; machine learning; user-adaptation

ACM Classification Keywords
H.5.m. Information interfaces and presentation (e.g., HCI): Miscellaneous.

INTRODUCTION
Information visualization (Infoviz) is gaining importance as a means for analyzing large and complex datasets. There is evidence that user performance and satisfaction in working with visualizations can be influenced by individual differences such as cognitive abilities (e.g., perceptual speed, visual working memory, and verbal working memory [13,17,41]), or personality traits (e.g., locus of control [23]). Thus, researches have started investigating how information visualization tools could be made more effective and usable by enabling them to adapt in real-time to some of these user characteristics. In this paper, we extend this line of work by focusing on another user characteristic that can influence the user's experience with a new visualization: the user's ability to acquire through practice the skills necessary to work with the visualization at best. In particular, we investigate whether a user's skill acquisition ability can be predicted in real-time while the user is working with a visualization. If accurate prediction is possible early on during interaction, adaptive interventions could be devised to support users who appear to be slow in learning the necessary skills.

Learning curves are mathematical models well-studied in cognitive psychology to model skill acquisition. They represent the relationship between practice and the associated changes in behaviour, such as the evolution of users' proficiency over time [e.g., 37]. For instance, in the context of Infoviz, a user's learning curve captures the user's initial level of expertise with a given visualization as well as how fast the user will learn the set of skills required to perform tasks with it. If we could predict and track these characteristics (initial expertise, learning speed) while users acquire a new set of visualization skills, individualized support could be provided in order to improve user performance and engagement. In this paper, we investigate the feasibility of predicting a user's learning curve while the user is performing tasks with ValueChart, a relatively complex, interactive visualization to support decision making.

In educational systems, modeling and tracking domain skill acquisition over time based on users' observed proficiency have been used to design real-time adaptive strategies to support learning. For instance, Intelligent Tutoring Systems (ITS) can provide visual, verbal or textual help, or suggest exercises of adapted difficulty depending on user/task features and the user's estimated mastery of domain skills [8,31]. To the best of our knowledge, the only work in Infoviz done on modeling learning skills is preliminary work presented in Toker et al. [42], where users performed visualization tasks with simple bar graphs. In that work, Toker et al. predict in real time the user's skill acquisition level in a coarse binary way (during learning vs. after

IUI' 2015, March 29–April 1, 2015, Atlanta, GA, USA.
Copyright is held by the owner/author(s). Publication rights licensed to ACM.
ACM 978-1-4503-3306-1/15/03...$15.00.
http://dx.doi.org/10.1145/2678025.2701376

learning). In contrast, in this paper, we intend to model the user's learning curve, i.e., a more detailed description of the user's learning experience with a visualization. We ultimately aim to design user-adaptive visualizations able to predict user's learning curves in real time and use this information to customize the visualization accordingly. For instance, we envision supporting users according to their predicted individualized learning curve in the following manner:

- If a user is predicted to have low initial expertise and low learning rate, support could be provided by simplifying the visualization in order to ensure that necessary basic skills are learned before the user becomes overwhelmed or confused.
- If a user is predicted to have high initial expertise and high learning rate, the system can engage the user with more advanced functionalities within the current visualization or possibly even offering more complex visualizations.

Predicting learning curves is particularly relevant at the beginning of the interaction with a novel visualization, as providing early adaptation can reduce disengagement and improve learning. In its most basic form, the simplest way to model learning curves is to observe past task performance. However, various data sources can also be leveraged to make these predictions in real-time. For example, Steichen et al. [41] highlighted the potential of using eye tracking to predict user's characteristics in Infoviz. Pupil dilation is also a data source worth investigating since it has been shown to be influenced by cognitive workload [27]. Other data sources that are plausible candidates for predicting user skill acquisition are long-term user characteristics, such as cognitive abilities and personality traits.

The goal of this paper is to compare the performance of models that leverage these various data sources, as well as basic information on past task performance, to predict users' skill acquisition in real-time. As a test-bed for our investigation, we use an interactive visualization for multiple-criteria decision making called ValueChart.

The rest of the paper is organized as follows: Section 2 gives an overview of the related work; Section 3 describes ValueChart and the study that generated the dataset used in our experiments; Section 4 describes how we build the learning curves that we aim to predict; Section 5 details the models we built to predict the curves; Section 6 discusses the performance of these models; and Section 7 concludes.

RELATED WORK

A typical method used in cognitive psychology for tracking how user performance improves with practice is by using a learning curve [40]. Learning curves are also frequently used in HCI for off-line comparison and evaluation of alternative interfaces, including information visualization systems, e.g., [35,39,45]. In contrast, in this paper we use the concept of a learning curve for building *predictive models* that can identify in real-time a user's evolving proficiency with an information visualization system.

Similar work has been extensively conducted in the field of Intelligent Tutoring Systems (ITS). In ITS, learning curves have been used to track and adapt help policies to a student's evolving skills in the target educational domain (e.g., performing one and two digit subtraction for a math tutor), based on her past interactions with the ITS tracked via action logs (e.g., [7,36,44]). In contrast, we aim to track and adapt to a user's evolving proficiency in using a visualization interface, leveraging gaze data as the main information source.

Some work exists in HCI on adapting to a user's level of familiarity with an interface. For example, [12] designed a mixed-initiative GUI-customization tool that provides suggestions on how to personalize the menus of a word processor based, among other factors, on the user's expertise with the word processor. However, the ability to track such expertise in real time was not implemented. Other work in HCI has focused on predicting user skills in a coarse binary way. For instance, Ghazarian et al. [21] built models to automatically classify a user's general skill in using different computer applications, based on mouse/keyboard logs and interface events such as menu selection, in order to adapt the complexity of the interfaces to novice/expert users. Hurst et al. [26] proposed a method to detect skilled vs. unskilled use of an image editing program by investigating menu usage and mouse logs, allowing them to design a user-adaptive menu based on the prediction of skilled behavior. In contrast in this paper, we look at user's learning with a visualization over time, by predicting continuous learning curves, rather than a binary categorization of users (i.e., skilled vs. unskilled).

Gaze data has been extensively used to detect different kinds of user states during interaction with an ITS, such as boredom, curiosity, disengagement [19,28], mind-wandering [10], as well as domain learning [11,29]. [9] has also used gaze data to predict users' problem-solving strategies as well as user performance while solving a visual puzzle. In addition, pupil dilation has been reliably shown to vary depending on changes in cognitive load [6,24]. In the context of building user-adaptive systems, [27] used pupil dilation measures to evaluate cognitive workload during route planning and document editing tasks in order to identify opportune moments for interrupting the user. Similarly, [37] monitored pupil dilation in order to predict user preferences when confronted with a choice of visually presented objects, and [33] tracked pupil dilation features in order to infer skills related to reading comprehension.

Within the Infovis community, eye tracking has been used off-line to understand how users with different domain expertise process relevant visualizations, e.g., [16,34]. Gaze data has also been investigated to predict long-term user traits (e.g., perceptual speed, visual working memory, verbal working memory, locus of control), as well as task type and task completion time [13,17,41]. Past studies have shown that user characteristics themselves (e.g., cognitive abilities, personality traits) can predict how well a user will perform on, or prefer, a given information visualization system [13,17,23,41].

The first attempt to predict interface skill acquisition in Infoviz is described in [42], where they evaluated users performing a series of low-level tasks using bar graphs. User performance on these tasks was categorized into two general phases of skill acquisition: *during* and *after*; indicating whether users were still in the process of acquiring, or had already acquired, the relevant visualization skills. These labels were derived based on performance across all users, as opposed to being customized to individual user performance. In contrast, in this paper, we extend that work not only by predicting actual continuous learning curves (as opposed to much coarser skill acquisition phases), but also by making predictions that are specific to each individual user (as opposed to being only based on pooled data). Furthermore, we look at skill acquisition within the context of a more complex and interactive visualization (ValueChart), as opposed to the simpler bar graphs used in [42].

VALUECHART AND USER STUDY

The dataset used in this paper was collected from a user study using ValueChart[1], an interactive visualization to support decision-makers in preferential choice, namely selecting the best option out of a set of alternatives characterized by a variety of attributes [14,15]. Figure 1 shows an example of ValueChart for selecting rental properties among ten available alternatives (listed in the leftmost column), based on a set of relevant attributes (e.g., location, bus distance, appliances, etc.). These attributes are arranged hierarchically in the top part of the ValueChart, forming the columns in the central part of the display. The width of each column indicates the relative weight assigned to the corresponding attribute (e.g., utilities is less important than rent). The available alternatives (i.e., rental homes) are represented as the rows in the display. Each cell specifies how the alternative in that row fares with respect to the attribute in that column, indicated by the amount of filled cell color. In the rightmost part of the ValueChart, all values for each alternative are accumulated and presented as horizontal stacked bars, displaying the overall value of each alternative (e.g., home4 is the best home in the example). Some of the interactive functionalities available to support the decision process include *inspecting* the specific domain value of each attribute (e.g., the rent of home1 being equal to $500), *sorting* the alternatives with respect to a specific attribute, *swapping* attribute columns, and *resizing* the width of an attribute's column to see how that would impact the decision outcome.

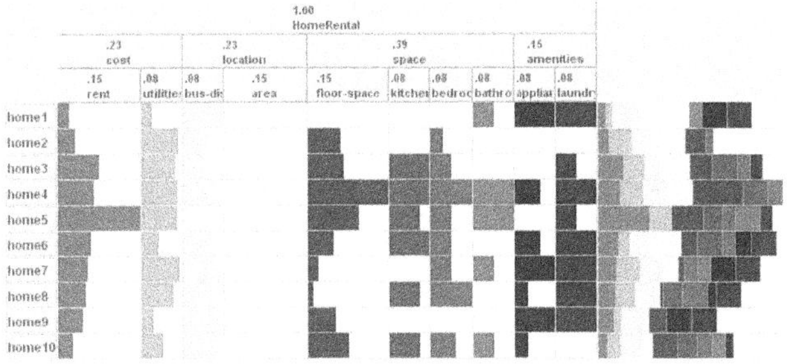

Figure 1: An example of the main elements of the ValueChart visualization, here displayed in a horizontal layout [17].

For the ValueChart user study (fully described in [17]), 95 participants were recruited (ages 16 to 40) to perform 5 different types of visualization tasks, chosen from a set of low-level data analysis tasks defined by Amar et al. [2]. These five tasks (shown in Table 1) require answering questions from different domains for preferential choice (i.e., rental homes, universities, cell phones, restaurants, and hotels) using functionalities of ValueChart (e.g., sorting, reordering, weighting attributes). For each of these tasks, Table 1 shows their definition from [2], a sample question from the study, and the conceptual operations involved in answering the question. These include both lower-level mathematical and cognitive actions (e.g. *generate aggregate value*, *compare values*) [2], as well as instances of the five Amar et al. tasks themselves (e.g., *compute derived value* typically requires multiple preceding *retrieve values*). The number of conceptual operations in Table 1 reflects this additional layer of actions per task type, and gives a conceptual measure of complexity (see [17] for more information). Thus, the quantities and types of conceptual operations in a task, in conjunction with the current level of skill a user has with these operations, will impact task performance. The specific operations shown in Table 1 are based on our study tasks, which always involved domains with 10 different alternatives and 10 attributes.

Participants repeated each task in Table 1 four times in a randomized fashion to account for within-user variability. For purposes outside the scope of this paper (described in [17]), two ValueChart layouts were evaluated: vertical vs. horizontal. The 20 study tasks were first performed with one of the two layouts for one domain, and then repeated with the second layout and a different domain, with order fully counterbalanced across users. Thus each participant performed a total of 40 tasks (5 task types x 4 repetitions x 2 layouts) equally divided in two sessions (one per layout). While performing these tasks, the use's gaze was tracked with a Tobii T120, a non-intrusive eye-tracker embedded in the study computer monitor. Each user also performed two decision making tasks in the study, but we will not consider

[1] Video demo: www.cs.ubc.ca/group/iui/VALUECHARTS

Task type	Task Definition from [2]	Sample task question from study	Conceptual operations	Mean response time (st.dev.)
Retrieve Value	Given a set of specific cases, find attributes of those cases.	Is the value of 'skytrain-distance' of home3 less than home6?	2 Retrieve values, 2 Compare values	15sec. (10)
Find Extremum	Find cases possessing an extreme valued attribute over its range within a data set.	What factor contributes the most towards the overall value of home4?	10 Retrieve values, 10 Compare values, 1 Retrieve labels	19sec. (14)
Sort	Given a set of cases, rank them according to some ordinal metric.	List the top 3 homes (in descending order) according to overall value.	10 Retrieve values, 10 Compare values, 1 Retrieve labels	17sec. (9)
Compute Derived Value 1	Given a set of data cases, compute an aggregate numeric representation of those data cases.	For how many homes is the 'rent' less than the 'rent' of home3?	10 Retrieve values, 10 Compare values, 1 Generate aggregate	20sec. (11)
Compute Derived Value 2		List the top 3 homes (in descending order) according to the aggregated value of 'cost' and 'space'.	20 Retrieve values, 10 Generate aggregates, 10 Compare aggregates, 3 Retrieve labels	42sec. (27)

Table 1: Descriptions of the five task types [17].

them in this paper because we don't have a sufficiently precise definition of users' performance for those tasks.

PREDICTION TARGET: LEARNING CURVES

Our goal is to predict a user's learning curve as they perform tasks with ValueChart, i.e., predict the curve parameters that model the acquisition of visualization skills relevant to work with this particular visualization.

A learning curve is a mathematical function that models changes in performance over time, as the amount of practice with a given activity increases. In psychology, a common approach to model learning curves is by fitting a *power law* function defined as follows [3,4,5]:

$$Y = a \times X^b \quad (1)$$

Where X is a variable ranging over the number of tasks performed by the user; Y is the observed performance of the user over X; a is the intercept denoting the initial expertise of the user; and b the slope representing the learning speed (a slope of zero indicates no apparent learning).

In Infoviz, two performance measures typically used for Y are: task accuracy (percentage of correctly/incorrectly performed tasks), and response time (i.e., time needed to complete a task). In this paper, we selected response time because there was a ceiling effect of accuracy over the study tasks.

In the next two subsections, we evaluate two alternative ways to define our target learning curves. The first assumes that the different types of tasks performed by the users are unknown when building the curve (*task-independent*), whereas the second requires this information to be available, and thus generates what we will call from now on *task-dependent* learning curves. Notice that both task–independent and task-dependent learning curves are models of the same data, i.e., the performance of the user on all the trials. The only difference between the two is in how the curves are fitted to the data. In the end, we chose the task-dependent model as our gold standard, because it yields a better fit of the data.

Task-independent learning curves

In order to get learning curve coefficients (i.e., the intercept a and the slope b in (1)), we simply fit a learning curve for each user using the power law function. A user's task-independent learning curve is fit by pooling together, with order maintained, the different types of tasks that were performed by that user. Due to the fact that users performed the same battery of tasks in each of the two study sessions (corresponding to using different ValueChart layouts, cf. supra), we average trials from the two sessions that were performed in the same order and use the resulting 20 data points per user to fit the learning curve for that user. Figure 2 shows an example of a learning curve for one user, where the red dots are the response times (in order of completion) for each of the 20 tasks performed by the user, and the black curve is the power law function fit over the red dots.

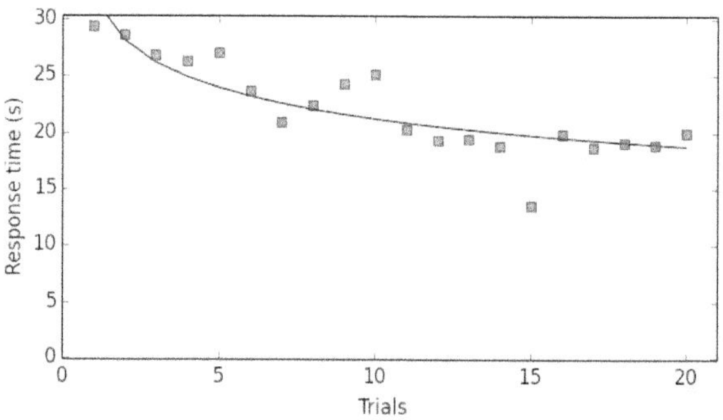

Figure 2: A sample learning curve for one user based on task response time in the ValueChart study.

The learning curves we obtained for the users in our study indicated that 88 users improved over time (negative slope), whereas 7 users showed no learning (zero or positive slope). The upper rows of Table 2 report the following summative statistics of the fitted task-independent learning curves: r^2 (a measure for how well a learning curve matches the underlying performance data); the fitted curve's intercept and slope (i.e., initial expertise and learning rate); and *final expertise*, i.e., the performance (here response time) expected to be achieved by the user at the end of the trial sequence. As Table 2 shows, for task-independent curves the fit is rather low (mean r^2=.33, std. dev= .25), indicating that the power law can only partially model a user's overall acquisition of visualization skills when information on user tasks is not taken into account. In our study, a plausible explanation for this low fit is that the complexity of the different task types varies considerably, as discussed in the previous section. Thus, different task types may generate different learning behaviors within users, which cannot be accurately captured by the task-independent approach described above. To address this problem, in cognitive psychology, learning curves are often fit for different activities, for instance based on the knowledge required to complete them [3,4], or using an additional parameter to model tasks difficulty [18]. In the next sub-section, we explore a similar approach by building individualized learning curves derived from fitting separate learning curves for each of the five different task types administered in the study (Table 1) and by then aggregating them.

Task-dependent learning curve

A task-dependent learning curve for a given user is computed by averaging the coefficient of her learning curves across all five task types as follows. First, we build five learning curves, one for each task type k:

$$Y = a_k \times X^{b_k} \quad k \in \{1..5\} \quad (2)$$

where, in each of the five learning curves, X is a variable ranging over the number of times the corresponding task type was performed by the user, Y is the observed response times, a_k is the intercept for task type k, and b_k the slope of task type k.

Next we compute: $a = avg(a_k)$ and $b = avg(b_k)$ with $k \in \{ 1..5\}$

Then, the task dependent learning curve can be again simply expressed as: $Y = a \times X^b$

The lower rows of Table 2 shows summary statistics for the learning curves obtained using this task-dependent approach. As expected (mean r^2 = .69, std. dev= .20) shows a better fit compared to the task-independent approach. We did find that the intercept coefficients for the task-independent and task-dependent curves are highly correlated (r^2 = .80), whereas slopes are not (r^2 = .45), confirming that learning speeds are different among tasks. Additionally, the correlation between values of final expected expertise (i.e., the predicted response time of the last trial) is high (r^2 = .75) indicating that the task-independent curves still provide an acceptable approximation for this measure despite the lower accuracy in predicting the learning trajectory that a user will follow to reach this expertise.

Given the overall better fit of the task-dependent curves, we use them as the target for our predictive models in the rest of the paper.[2]

		Min	Max	Mean	Std.dev
Task-independent	r^2	0.03	0.78	0.33	0.25
	Intercept	15	80	32.6	13.3
	Slope	-0.9	0.05	-0.18	0.15
	Final Expertise	3	40	18.6	5.8
Task-dependent	r^2	0.01	0.96	0.69	0.2
	Intercept	23	89	41.4	12.3
	Slope	-1.7	-0.02	-0.4	0.24
	Final Expertise	5	41	21.8	6.1

Table 2: Summary statistics of two approaches for defining individualized learning curve coefficients.

MACHINE LEARNING EXPERIMENTS

Our goal is to ascertain whether we can predict a user's skill acquisition process by predicting the intercept and the slope of that user's learning curve by using different data sources as predictors. This section describes these data sources, the machine learning models we built, and how they are evaluated.

Data Sources

Here we outline three feature sets that will be used as predictors for inferring learning curve parameters. One feature set consists of measures that summarize a user's gaze patterns, as tracked by the Tobii T 120 eye tracker during the study (*Gaze* feature set). A second set consists of measures that describe changes in a user's pupil size during tasks, also based on raw data provided by the eye-tracker (*Pupil* feature set). A third feature set models a variety of user's long-term characteristics that have been shown to impact visualization processing (*User Characteristics* feature set).

***Gaze* feature set.** Gaze data is captured by the Tobii eye-tracker in terms of fixations (gaze maintained at one point on the screen), and saccades (quick movement of gaze from one fixation point to another). We then processed this raw data using EMDAT, a gaze data analysis toolkit[3] to generate a battery of gaze-based features summarized in Table 3. Some of these features capture overall gaze activity on the screen (*Overall features*, top half of the table), while others do so for specific Areas of Interest (AOI) in the visualization (*AOI features*, middle part of Table 3). The seven AOIs defined for ValueChart in this study are shown in Figure 3. In total, we have 135 Gaze features.

[2] It should be noted, however, that we obtained results similar to those reported in the later sections of this paper when predicting task-independent learning curves.

[3] EMDAT: http://www.cs.ubc.ca/~skardan/EMDAT

Overall Gaze Features
Fixation rate
Mean & Std. deviation of fixation durations
Mean & Std. deviation of saccade length
Mean & Std. deviation of relative saccade angles
Mean & Std. deviation of absolute saccade angles
AOI Gaze Features (for each AOI)
Fixation rate in AOI
Longest fixation in AOI
Proportion of time, Proportion of fixations in AOI
Number & Prop. of transitions from this AOI to every AOI
Pupil Features
Mean, Std. deviation, Maximum, Minimum pupil width
Pupil width at the first and last fixation in a given trial

Table 3: List of Gaze, AOI, and pupil features.

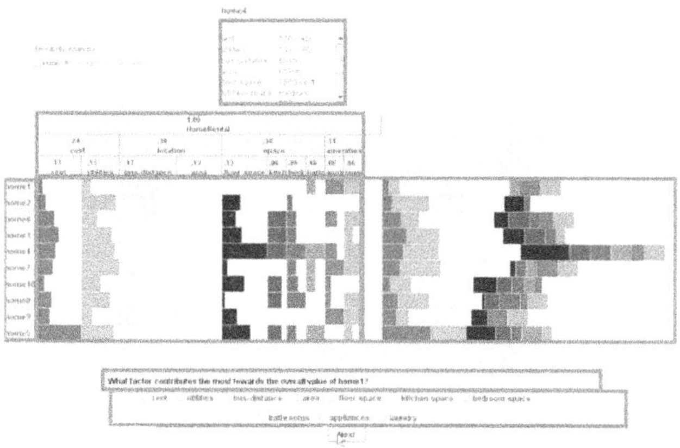

Figure 3: Areas of Interest (AOI) defined over the complete visualization interface for horizontal ValueChart.

***Pupil* feature set**. The Tobii eye-tracker records the user's pupil diameter (the horizontal width of each pupil) at each sample. We once more used EMDAT to compute a variety of features that describe the pupil diameter over the span of a task (bottom part of Table 3) for a total of 6 features. In order to avoid possible confounds on pupil size due to lighting changes, the study was administered in a windowless room with uniform lighting. To compensate for physiological differences in pupil size among individual users, we also collected pupil diameter baselines for each user by having them stare at a blank screen for ten seconds at the beginning of each session. Measured pupil dilation is adjusted using the *percentage change in pupil size* (PCPS), which is defined in [27] as:

$$\frac{\text{measured\_pupilsize} - \text{baseline\_pupilsize}}{\text{baseline\_pupilsize}} \quad (3)$$

***User characteristics* feature set**. Several long-term user traits were measured via standard tests administered to participants at the beginning of the study. We measured three cognitive abilities: *perceptual speed* (a measure of speed when performing simple perceptual tasks), *verbal working memory* (a measure of storage and manipulation capacity of verbal information), *visual working memory* (a measure of storage and manipulation capacity of visual and spatial information). We also measured the personality trait known as locus of control (a measure of the extent to which a person believes they are able to control events affecting them)[4]. We chose these particular user characteristics because other studies have shown that they impact the effectiveness of visualization processing [13,17,41], and thus they may likely also affect skills acquisition related to this processing.

Prediction models

In this subsection, we first present the method used to produce a baseline for predicting individualized learning curve coefficients (intercept and slope) based solely on task performance from previous tasks. Next, we describe the predictive models that leverage gaze data, pupil dilation data, and user characteristics as input data sources. It should be noted that all models in this section are built without considering information on which task type a user is performing, as this information may not always be available to a visualization system when a user is working with it.

Response-Time Baseline Model

A simple way to infer a user's learning curve is to track their task response times so far. To achieve this, as each task in our dataset is completed, we re-fit the learning curve function based on all the trials seen so far for that user. The result are two *temporary* learning curve coefficients which can be used as predictions of the actual final learning curve coefficients for that user. For instance at the end of trial 6, we fit a learning curve per user using only their 6 first completed trials. We use this approach as our baseline model since it requires only basic information regarding user task performance. At least two trials are required to fit a temporary learning curve this way.

Machine Learning Models

We want to ascertain whether we can achieve a better prediction of a user's learning curve than that afforded by the basic response-time baseline by using as predictors data sources not linked to task response time: gaze, pupil, and user characteristics. In particular, we evaluate each of the three feature sets (gaze, pupil, user char.) individually, along with a feature set with all three combined. Predictive models based on gaze and pupil features are built over increasing numbers of consecutive trials, from 1 trial to 20(all) in order to ascertain how model performance depends on the amount of evidence seen. This does not apply for the model based only on user-characteristics, because these features are static and do not change over trials. Thus, we built a total of 3 (feature sets) x 20 (trials) x 2 (learning curve coefficients) = 120 models utilizing gaze

[4] The standard tests are, for PS: Kit of Factor-Referenced Cognitive Tests-P3 [20]; for verbalWM: OSPAN test [43]; for visualWM: Luck & Vogel's test [32]; for Locus of Control: Rotter's test [38].

and pupil features, plus one model for user characteristics per coefficient, yielding a total of 122 models.

We used backward stepwise linear regression to build our models using Akaike information criterion (AIC) optimization [1] to fine-tune our models as well as handle the high number of gaze features. Models were trained and tested via 10-fold cross validation over users, namely for any given fold 90% of the users in the study are in the training set and 10% are in the test set. The model that generates predictions for learning curve coefficients after seeing n trails in the study trial sequence (where n varies from 1 to 20) is trained over features of these n trials pooled over all users in the training set. This model is then used to predict the coefficients of the individualized learning curve of each user in the test set. We used the R software environment for statistical computing to evaluate and compare models.

Model performance is measured via the root-mean-square error (RMSE) of the difference between the predicted learning curve coefficients and the actual ones. That is, the RMSE for each of our 122 models is computed as follows:

$$RMSE = \sqrt{\frac{\sum_{u=1}^{|U|}(\hat{y}_u - y_u)^2}{|U|}} \quad (4)$$

where U is the set of users in the study, $\hat{y}_u$ represents the predicted coefficient for a given user u, and y_u represents the actual target coefficient for that user.

RESULTS

In this section, we report and discuss the performance of our models in predicting individualized learning curve coefficients (intercept and slope), compared to the baseline derived solely from tracking users' response-times. We then discuss the ten features with highest predictive power for the best performing model. Finally, we report accuracy of this model in performing binary classification over the target coefficients (i.e., low/high intercept and slope) in order to give a more practical measure of model's reliability when used to guide adaptive interventions.

Predicting learning curves' coefficients

Figure 4 shows the RMSE for predicting learning curve *intercept* when the models described in the previous section are trained over different number of trials. Figure 5 shows the analogous results for *slope*.

To formally compare the effectiveness of the different models, we use each model *over-time performance*, i.e., RMSE averaged across the twenty trails. We then run pairwise comparisons between models using Bonferroni-adjusted t-tests with over-time performance as the dependent measure. Table 4 summarizes the results of these comparisons by ordering models according to their overtime RMSE, bold underlining indicates models for which there are no statistically significant differences (here statistical significance is reported at $p < .05$). For example, the comparisons for predicting Intercept coefficients shown in Table 4 indicate that All-features is better than Gaze which is better than UserChar. UserChar is better than Pupil but this difference is not significant, and Pupil is also not significantly better than the baseline model.

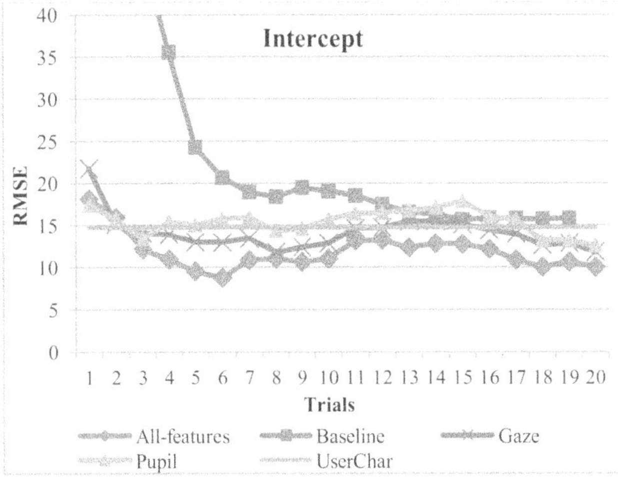

Figure 4: RMSE at each trial count for predicting learning curve intercept (lower values are better).

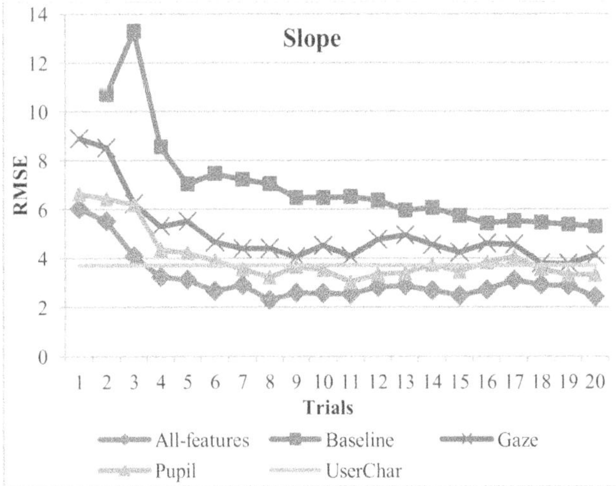

Figure 5: RMSE at each trial count for predicting learning curve slope.

Learning Curve	Comparison of models' performance
Intercept	All-features > Gaze > UserChar > Pupil > Baseline
Slope	All-features > Pupil > UserChar > Gaze > Baseline

Table 4: Effect of feature set on overall model performance across all trials.

The results for intercept and slope in Table 4 show that the *All-features* model has the best performance in both cases and is significantly better than the other models which consist of only one type of feature, including the baseline.

In fact all models statistically beat the baseline except for Pupil features for predicting intercept. These results indicate that eye tracking (gaze and pupil) as well as user characteristics are all valuable sources for the prediction of a user's learning curve and should all be considered together for optimal predictive performance. In terms of how early the prediction can be performed, the performance plots of the *All-features* model in Figure 4 and Figure 5 show that although the best performance (lowest RMSE) is achieved after 6 trials for intercept and 8 for slope, RMSE already drops considerably for both coefficients after seeing only 3 trials. These results indicate that eye tracking and user characteristics are valuable sources for early prediction of a user's learning curve. In practice early prediction of the slope can be used, for example, to support users who appear to be learning slowly in speeding up their learning process. Similarly, early prediction of the intercept can be used to support users with low initial expertise by, for instance, disabling advanced functionalities or recommending additional training examples.

If we look only at models built on one type of feature set, we can see that Gaze is better than both UserChar and Pupil for predicting intercept (i.e., initial expertise), whereas Pupil and UserChar are better than Gaze at predicting slope (i.e., learning rate). In other words, it seems that learning rate in visual tasks is better predicted by long-term cognitive abilities and pupil dilation features, whereas the initial expertise (intercept) can be captured best by gaze behavior. It is well established that pupil dilation is correlated to the level of a user's cognitive load [22], thus learning rate seems to be impacted by both long-term cognitive abilities (such as working memory or perceptual speed) as well as short-term cognitive load. In terms of adaptation, it means that customizing a visualization to reduce cognitive load could help slow learners.

Feature Selection: Exploring the Relative importance of features

As described in the previous section, we found that multiple data sources together can better infer a user's learning curve (i.e., *All-Features*), as opposed to any single source. In this section, we report the top selected features for this model in order to get a better sense of which features best predict the intercept and the slope of a user's learning curve, as well as the directionality of the relationships. To investigate the top 10 features, we averaged over all trials the relative importance of features at each individual trial. We applied the method described by Kruskal in [30] to get the relative importance of each feature, which consists in computing the R^2 contribution averaged over orderings among features for a regression model. Table 5 and Table 6 show the top ten selected features for intercept and slope respectively, where the relative importance is normalized so that the most important feature has a score of 100 and other scores express the relative importance proportionally to the top one. Additionally, a positive direction of the effect (D) indicates that initial expertise or learning rate is higher when the value of the feature increases. For the layout of the AOIs, refer to Figure 3.

Features predicting intercept	Set	D	Score
Fixation rate on 'data attributes'	Gaze/AOI	-	100
Perceptual speed	UserChar	+	71
Mean fixation duration	Gaze	-	68
Proportion of fixations on 'questions'	Gaze/AOI	-	41
Std.dev pupil size	Pupil	+	39
Proportion of time on 'questions'	Gaze/AOI	-	38
Fixations on 'items'	Gaze/AOI	-	32
Mean pupil size	Pupil	-	31
Std.dev saccade distance	Gaze	-	30
Transitions from 'data attributes' to 'data visualization'	Gaze/AOI	+	27

Table 5: Top 10 features for predicting intercept.

Features predicting slope	Set	D	Score
Perceptual Speed	UserChar	+	100
Std.dev pupil size	Pupil	+	84
Visual Working Memory	UserChar	+	74
Mean pupil size	Pupil	+	72
Std.dev fixation duration	Gaze	+	59
Transitions from the 'input' to the 'question'	Gaze/ AOI	-	49
Fixation rate	Gaze	+	29
Verbal Working Memory	UserChar	+	28
Proportion of fixations on the 'input'	Gaze/AOI	-	25
End pupil size	Pupil	-	18

Table 6: Top 10 features for predicting slope.

The preponderant features for predicting intercept are gaze related (7 out of 10) with five of these relating to AOIs, meaning that tracking gaze behavior on different parts of the interface is important to detect initial expertise. This result makes sense as users with different levels of initial expertise with ValueChart likely process the visual display differently up front. There are then two pupil-based features, mean and standard deviation of pupil size, both with positive directionality meaning that higher values for them correspond to higher initial expertise. Generally, increase in pupil size is correlated with higher cognitive load [22]. Thus the fact that higher mean pupil size relates to higher initial expertise may indicate that more advanced users are able to maintain an overall higher level of cognitive load, and higher std.dev pupil size indicates that more advanced users can more readily increase or reduce their mental processing depending on the tasks. Lastly, only one user characteristic, perceptual speed, appears in the top ten for intercept, although it has a prominent second place in the ranking.

In contrast, for slope three of the four user characteristics appear in the top 10 most predictive features: perceptual speed, visual working memory and verbal working memory. Since these are all cognitive abilities, it is not surprising that they are predictive of learning rate, and that they have positive directionality, namely that higher values of these abilities correspond to faster learning rate. These results suggest that measuring these user cognitive abilities prior to the interaction with a visualization is worthwhile if an adaptive system aims to predict learning rate. In particular, both perceptual speed and visual working memory are among the top three predictive features for learning rate, indicating that a big part of how quickly a user will learn depends on cognitive abilities relating to the capacity to process visual information. Given that these traits are typically considered fixed (i.e., a user has no control over them), we ought to design adaptive support which may 'ease' the visual load for users with low perceptual speed or visual working memory.

In general, the distribution of feature types in the top ten features for predicting learning rate is more balanced than for initial expertise: in addition to the 3 cognitive measures, there are 3 pupil-related features and 4 gaze-based features. Interestingly, only two of the four gaze features are AOI-related, suggesting that attention to specific areas of the visualization is not as predictive of learning rate as it is of initial expertise.

As far as pupil-related features are concerned, the two that appeared as top predictors for initial expertise also appear, with the same directionality, for learning rate suggesting that being able to maintain a high cognitive load, but have it vary with the demand of the task at hand, is predictive of faster learning rate. Interestingly, the third pupil-related feature in the top ten is one with a negative directionality with learning rate, namely end pupil size (i.e., size of pupil at the end of each trial). This finding suggests that this pupil measure provides an indication of excessive cognitive load that interferes with learning.

Binary classification

In this section we report the performance of the *All-Features* model in terms of binary classification accuracies for learning curves coefficients, to give a more practical measure of this model's predictive ability compared to RMSE. More specifically, we simulate the real-time classification of users into groups of fast/slow learners (slope) and high/low initial expertise (intercept).

Users are divided into two balanced groups for each coefficient using a median split: high/low intercept, and high/low slope. We compared different classifiers implemented in Weka [25] and selected the most promising one: Random forests tuned to 50 random trees. As we did for the prediction of the actual coefficients in a previous section, classification is carried out over incremental sequences of trials, from 1 to 20, using 10-fold cross validation. We report class accuracies and do not include a baseline accuracy since we have already shown in the previous section that the *All-features* model was always significantly better or equal to the baseline. Results for classification of intercepts are shown in Figure 6, those for slopes are shown in Figure 7.

T-tests between class accuracies across all trials shows no significant difference ($p > .05$) for either the intercept or the slope, indicating that both classifiers are well balanced (i.e., the random forest classifier can predict equally well high/low intercepts and high/low slopes). From a practical point of view, it means that adaptive strategies can be designed for each group of users.

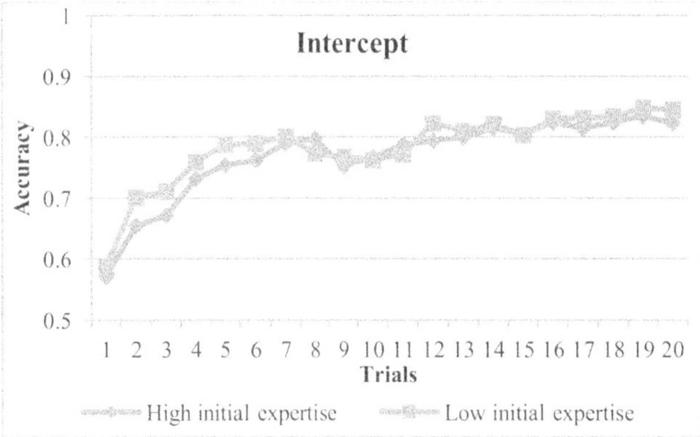

Figure 6: Class accuracies of binary predictions of intercepts using the *All-features* model.

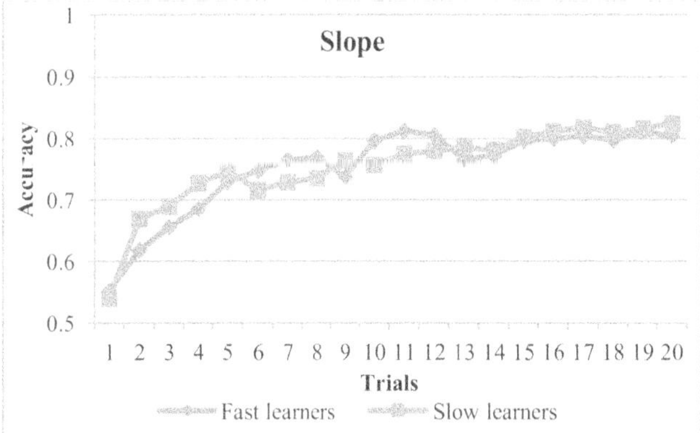

Figure 7: Class accuracies of binary predictions of slopes using the *All-features* model.

For the intercept, class accuracies range from 57% (after trial 1) to 83%, with an overtime accuracy of 77%. Regarding the slope, accuracies are slightly lower at the beginning (55% at trial 1) and reach as high as 82%, with overtime accuracy of 75%. We can notice that, for both coefficients, accuracies as high as 70% are reached after seeing only 4 trials. Very early predictions (i.e., trials 1-3) yield moderate accuracies ranging from 57% to 69% for the intercept, and from 55% to 67% for the slopes.

In terms of designing adaptive support for a visualization system, achieving accuracies of 70% after only 4 observed trials of data (which is on average 90 seconds of data) is promising in terms of inferring which users can benefit from tailored support.

CONCLUSION, DISCUSSION, AND FUTURE WORK

In this paper, we have studied the feasibility of predicting a user's learning curve while they perform a series of visual tasks using ValueChart, an interactive visualization for multiple-criteria decision making. Learning curves model a user's ability to learn new skills through practice, and in this paper we use them to model a user's initial expertise with a visualization, as well as their expected learning rate for the related skills. Our long-term goal is to leverage these predictions in user-adaptive visualizations that can tailor the interaction to a user's learning trajectory.

Whereas learning curves have been leveraged in the field of Intelligent Tutoring Systems to provide real-time adaptive support to learning a target educational domain, their usage in other areas of Intelligent User Interfaces has so far been limited. Toker et al. [42] have done preliminary work on using learning curves fit to population data to coarsely classify users as being either in the skill acquisition phase or having acquired necessary skills. We extended that work by predicting learning curves fit to individual users, thus achieving a finer-grained ability to track the user's skill acquisition process.

We showed that we can predict users' learning curve coefficients, i.e., the intercept (initial expertise) and the slope (learning rate) with substantial accuracy early on during the user's interaction with ValueChart. Our predictive models, which leverage different combinations of features including gaze behavior, pupil dilation, and cognitive abilities, significantly outperformed a simple but strong baseline model built on observed past performance. The best performing model overall leverages all of user gaze behavior, pupil dilation, and cognitive abilities to make its predictions. We described its performance both in terms of RMSE in predicting learning curve coefficients, as well as in terms of classifying users into binary groups (fast/slow learners; high/low initial expertise). On the latter measure, this model reached an accuracy of 70% after observing only 4 user tasks.

These results provide encouraging evidence that early prediction of user's skill acquisition is possible in information visualization, although it will of course be necessary to show the generality of these findings by replicating them with visualizations other than the ValueChart used in this study. Early prediction of skill acquisition, in turn, is important for our general goal of devising user-adaptive visualizations that can tailor information presentation to each user's individual needs. For instance, we plan to design and evaluate adaptation strategies for users predicted to have low initial expertise and low learning rate by either providing interventions that help these users identify and process the relevant elements of the visualization (for instance by highlighting relevant parts of the visualization), or by simplifying the visualization in order to ensure that necessary basic skills are learned before more advanced functionalities are available.

Another thread of future work relates to further improving our predictive models of skill acquisition. First, we expect that adding a measure of task performance to gaze, pupil, and user characteristics features can improve model accuracy. Second, we will study if stochastic models can reinforce predictions overtime. Lastly, we plan to investigate the addition of features based on interface actions, as ValueChart is an interactive visualization, and past work on combining gaze and action information has showed promising results [29].

ACKNOWLEDGEMENTS

This work was made possible thanks to funding from NSERC through the Grant: STPG381322-09.

REFERENCES

1. Akaike, H. A new look at the statistical model identification. *IEEE Transactions on Automatic Control 19*, 6 (1974), 716–723.
2. Amar, R., Eagan, J., and Stasko, J. Low-Level Components of Analytic Activity in Information Visualization. *Proceedings of the 2005 IEEE Symposium on Information Visualization*, IEEE Computer Society (2005), 15–21.
3. Anderson, J.R. *Cognitive Skills and Their Acquisition.* Psychology Press, 1981.
4. Anderson, J.R. *Rules of the Mind.* Psych. Press, 2014.
5. Bailey, C.D. and McIntyre, E.V. The relation between fit and prediction for alternative forms of learning curves and relearning curves. *IIE Transactions 29*, 6 (1997), 487–495.
6. Beatty, J. Task-evoked pupillary responses, processing load, and the structure of processing resources. *Psychological Bulletin 91*, 2 (1982), 276–292.
7. Beck, J.E. and Sison, J. Using knowledge tracing in a noisy environment to measure student reading proficiencies. *International Journal of Artificial Intelligence in Education 16*, 2 (2006), 129–143.
8. Beck, J.E., Woolf, B.P., and Beal, C.R. ADVISOR: a machine-learning architecture for intelligent tutor construction. University of Massachusetts (2000).
9. Bednarik, R., Eivazi, S., and Vrzakova, H. A Computational Approach for Prediction of Problem-Solving Behavior Using Support Vector Machines and Eye-Tracking Data. In *Eye Gaze in Intelligent User Interfaces*. Springer, 2013, 111–134.
10. Bixler, R., Kopp, K., and D'Mello, S. Evaluation of a Personalized Method for Proactive Mind Wandering Reduction. *Proc. of the 4th Workshop on Personalization Approaches for Learning Environments, UMAP* (2014), 33–41.

11. Bondareva, D., Conati, C., Feyzi-Behnagh, R., Harley, J.M., Azevedo, R., and Bouchet, F. Inferring Learning from Gaze Data during Interaction with an Environment to Support Self-Regulated Learning. *Proc. of the 16th Int. Conference on Artificial Intelligence in Education*, Springer (2013), 229–238.

12. Bunt, A., Conati, C., and McGrenere, J. Supporting Interface Customization Using a Mixed-initiative Approach. *Proc. of the 12th International Conference on Intelligent User Interfaces*, ACM (2007), 92–101.

13. Carenini, G., Conati, C., Hoque, E., Steichen, B., Toker, D., and Enns, J.T. Highlighting Interventions and User Differences: Informing Adaptive Information Visualization Support. *Proc. of the SIGCHI Conf. on Human Factors in Computing Systems*, ACM (2014).

14. Carenini, G. and Loyd, J. ValueCharts: analyzing linear models expressing preferences and evaluations. *Proceedings of the Working Conference on Advanced Visual Interfaces*, ACM (2004), 150–157.

15. Chamberlain, B.C., Carenini, G., Oberg, G., Poole, D., and Taheri, H. A Decision Support System for the Design and Evaluation of Sustainable Wastewater Solutions. *IEEE Trans. on Comp. 63*, (2014), 129–141.

16. Çöltekin, A., Fabrikant, S.I., and Lacayo, M. Exploring the efficiency of users' visual analytics strategies based on sequence analysis of eye movement recordings. *International Journal of Geographical Information Science 24*, 10 (2010), 1559–1575.

17. Conati, C., Carenini, G., Steichen, B., and Toker, D. Evaluating the Impact of User Characteristics and Different Layouts on an Interactive Visualization for Decision Making. *Proceedings of the 16th Eurographics Conf. on Visualization*, (2014), 371–380.

18. Desmarais, M. Performance comparison of item-to-item skills models with the IRT single latent trait model. *Proc. of UMAP*, (2011), 75–86.

19. D'Mello, S., Olney, A., Williams, C., and Hays, P. Gaze tutor: A gaze-reactive intelligent tutoring system. *Int. J. of Human-Comp. Studies 70*, 5 (2012), 377–398.

20. Ekstrom, R.B. and Harman, H.H. *Manual for Kit of Factor-referenced Cognitive Tests, 1976*. Educational Testing Service, 1976.

21. Ghazarian, A. and Noorhosseini, S.M. Automatic detection of users' skill levels using high-frequency user interface events. *User Modeling and User-Adapted Interaction 20*, 2 (2010), 109–146.

22. Granholm, E. and Steinhauer, S.R. Pupillometric measures of cognitive and emotional processes. *Int. Journal of Psychophysiology 52*, 1 (2004), 1–6.

23. Green, T.M. and Fisher, B. Towards the Personal Equation of Interaction: The impact of personality factors on visual analytics interface interaction. *Proc. of the 2010 IEEE Symposium on Visual Analytics Science and Technology*, IEEE (2010), 203–210.

24. Hess, E.H. and Polt, J.M. Pupil Size in Relation to Mental Activity during Simple Problem-Solving. *Science 143*, 3611 (1964), 1190–1192.

25. Holmes, G., Donkin, A., and Witten, I.H. Weka: A machine learning workbench. *Second Australian and New Zealand Conference on Intelligent Information Systems*, (1994), 357–361.

26. Hurst, A., Hudson, S.E., and Mankoff, J. Dynamic Detection of Novice vs. Skilled Use Without a Task Model. *Proc. of the SIGCHI Conference on Human Factors in Computing Systems*, ACM (2007), 271–280.

27. Iqbal, S.T., Adamczyk, P.D., Zheng, X.S., and Bailey, B.P. Towards an index of opportunity: understanding changes in mental workload during task execution. ACM Press (2005), 311.

28. Jaques, N., Conati, C., Harley, J.M., and Azevedo, R. Predicting Affect from Gaze Data during Interaction with an Intelligent Tutoring System. *Proceedings of ITS*, Springer (2014), 29–38.

29. Kardan, S. and Conati, C. Comparing and Combining Eye Gaze and Interface Actions for Determining User Learning with an Interactive Simulation. *Proceedings of UMAP*, (2013), 215–227.

30. Kruskal, W. Relative Importance by Averaging Over Orderings. *American Statistician 41*, 1 (1987), 6–10.

31. Lallé, S., Mostow, J., Luengo, V., and Guin, N. Comparing Student Models in Different Formalisms by Predicting their Impact on Help Success. *Proceesings of the 16th International Conference on Artificial Intelligence in Education*, (2013), 161–170.

32. Luck, S.J. and Vogel, E.K. The capacity of visual working memory for features and conjunctions. *Nature 390*, 6657 (1997), 279–281.

33. Martínez-Gómez, P. and Aizawa, A. Recognition of understanding level and language skill using measurements of reading behavior. *Proceedings of the 19th International Conference on Intelligent User Interfaces*, ACM (2014), 95–104.

34. Ooms, K., De Maeyer, P., and Fack, V. Study of the attentive behavior of novice and expert map users using eye tracking. *Cartography and Geographic Information Science 41*, 1 (2014), 37–54.

35. Pascual-Cid, V., Vigentini, L., and Quixal, M. Visualising Virtual Learning Environments: Case Studies of the Website Exploration Tool. *Proceedings of the 14th International Conference on Information Visualisation*, IEEE (2010), 149–155.

36. Pavlik, P.I., Cen, H., and Koedinger, K.R. Performance Factors Analysis–A New Alternative to Knowledge Tracing. *Proc. of the International Conf. on Artificial Intelligence in Education*, IOS Press (2009), 531–538.

37. Prendinger, H., Hyrskykari, A., Nakayama, M., Istance, H., Bee, N., and Takahasi, Y. Attentive interfaces for users with disabilities: eye gaze for intention and uncertainty estimation. *Universal Access in the Information Society 8*, 4 (2009), 339–354.

38. Rotter, J.B. Generalized expectancies for internal versus external control of reinforcement. *Psychological Monographs: General and Applied 80*, 1 (1966), 1–28.

39. Saraiya, P., North, C., and Duca, K. An Insight-Based Methodology for Evaluating Bioinformatics Visualizations. *IEEE Transactions on Visualization and Computer Graphics 11*, 4 (2005), 443–456.

40. Speelman, C.P. and Kirsner, K. *Beyond the Learning Curve: The Construction of Mind.* Oxford University Press, 2005.

41. Steichen, B., Conati, C., and Carenini, G. Inferring Visualization Task Properties, User Performance, and User Cognitive Abilities from Eye Gaze Data. *ACM Trans. on Interactive Intelligent Systems 4*, 2 (2014).

42. Toker, D., Steichen, B., Gingerich, M., Conati, C., and Carenini, G. Towards Facilitating User Skill Acquisition: Identifying Untrained Visualization Users Through Eye Tracking. *Proceedings of the 19th International Conference on Intelligent User Interfaces*, ACM (2014), 105–114.

43. Turner, M.L. and Engle, R.W. Is working memory capacity task dependent? *Journal of Memory and Language 28*, 2 (1989), 127–154.

44. Yudelson, M.V., Koedinger, K.R., and Gordon, G.J. Individualized Bayesian Knowledge Tracing Models. *Proceedings of AIED*, Springer (2013), 171–180.

45. Zhu, Y. Measuring Effective Data Visualization. *Proceedings of the 3rd International Symposium on Advances in Visual Computing*, Springer (2007), 652–661.

Halo Content: Context-aware View Management for Non-invasive Augmented Reality

Jason Orlosky, Kiyoshi Kiyokawa
Osaka University
Osaka, Japan
{orlosky@ist, kiyo@ime.cmc} .osaka-u.ac.jp

Takumi Toyama, Daniel Sonntag
German Research Center for Artificial Intelligence, Kaiserslautern, Germany
{takumi.toyama, daniel.sonntag} @dfki.de

ABSTRACT

In mobile augmented reality, text and content placed in a user's immediate field of view through a head worn display can interfere with day to day activities. In particular, messages, notifications, or navigation instructions overlaid in the central field of view can become a barrier to effective face-to-face meetings and everyday conversation. Many text and view management methods attempt to improve text viewability, but fail to provide a non-invasive personal experience for the user.

In this paper, we introduce Halo Content, a method that proactively manages movement of multiple elements such as e-mails, texts, and notifications to make sure they do not interfere with interpersonal interactions. Through a unique combination of face detection, integrated layouts, and automated content movement, virtual elements are actively moved so that they do not occlude conversation partners' faces or gestures. Unlike other methods that often require tracking or prior knowledge of the scene, our approach can deal with multiple conversation partners in unknown, dynamic situations. In a preliminary experiment with 14 participants, we show that the Halo Content algorithm results in a 54.8% reduction in the number of times content interfered with conversations compared to standard layouts.

Author Keywords

Augmented reality; view management; face detection; non-invasive; occlusion reduction; automation.

ACM Classification Keywords

H.5.2 User Interfaces: *Theory and methods;* H.5.2 User Interfaces: *User interface management systems (UIMS)*

INTRODUCTION

With the growing number of wearable, head worn, and head up displays, the need to manage content in a user's field of view is becoming increasingly important. Products like the Google Glass and Epson Moverio give users the ability to overlay virtual information directly onto their field of view, allowing for improved information display while mobile. There have accordingly been many attempts to address related view management problems, many of which focus on improving content readability and visibility [7]. Additionally, many algorithms have been designed to effectively manage labels on environmental objects and the resulting virtual clutter from those objects [2, 4, 6]. Other management schemes tend to focus on occlusion problems and making sure both content and labeled object are consistently visible [1, 14].

However, these methods typically focus on environment-centric text, which refers to labels that are previously registered to existing objects in the real world or in pre-defined content [7]. In contrast, user-centric items such as e-mails or personal notifications have only recently been targeted for mobile view management. Unlike labeling of known 3D objects or environments which may be stationary, view management of user-centric information must often rely on real time analysis of a more dynamic environment.

In this paper, we focus on content that can interfere with interpersonal interactions. For example, a pedestrian reading notifications or following navigation instructions in a head worn display (HWD) may stop to ask for directions. Our goal is to prevent virtual information from interfering with the following conversation or interpersonal interaction. To accomplish this, we detect faces in the scene and move content along a series of layout dependent vectors, pushing it up and away from its usual fixed screen location. This prevents text from occluding other people in the field of view (FOV), as shown in both images in Figure 1. This strategy can be applied to various social situations, chance outdoor meetings, and everyday conversations.

Figure 1. The Halo Content algorithm applied to billboard style text notifications in conversations with multiple participants in different environments.

IUI'15, March 29 - April 01 2015, Atlanta, GA, USA
Copyright 2015 ACM 978-1-4503-3306-1/15/03 \$15.00
http://dx.doi.org/10.1145/2678025.2701375

More specifically, we first utilize face detection to search for potential interaction targets in the environment. Faces are then constantly evaluated for persistence (whether or not the detected face is still in a user's field of view despite detection failures), and for conversation potential (the probability that a persistent face will engage in conversation at a certain distance). Once the face analysis portion of the system is complete, a layout management algorithm then actively moves content to ensure that other people in the user's field of view remain visible. In many cases, the algorithm forms what looks like a halo of content around other people in the environment, as can be seen in Figures 2 C and 3 B, hence the name Halo Content. In contrast with other similar algorithms, our system can deal with numerous environmental objects, handles multiple conversation partners and screen elements, and allows for temporary off-screen placement.

PREVIOUS WORK

Up to now, many view management algorithms have been proposed to manage virtual content. A majority of related algorithms attempt to minimize occlusion of virtual labels relative to a target object. For example, Tatzgern et al. define 2D and 3D labeling techniques to ensure that both labels and leader lines do not cross or occlude each other [10]. Similarly, Reitmayr et al. propose a method for semi-automatic annotation in combination with simultaneous localization and mapping algorithms [8]. Makita et al. affixed trackers to users in the real world, and developed a method for managing annotations around the users' bodies as they moved along in real time [6]. Most of these strategies are good for virtual immersion applications, gaming, when labels are fixed to a single, stationary location, or when 3D knowledge of the scene is already known. However, they are not necessarily ideal for mobile environments or face-to-face conversations. Several other strategies for managing mobile content include physical interaction strategies, for example pasting content on a nearby surface [3]. Other, more specific automation strategies have also been applied for managing content in vehicles, such as that of Tsai et al. [11]. The most recent and closest work to this one is the dynamic text management algorithm proposed by Orlosky et al. [7]. Dynamic text management uses background color and texture to maximize viewability of user-centric text for unknown environments. Object recognition is suggested as a potential way to deal with other environmental situations, which have implemented in this work.

In contrast to most of the work mentioned above, we focus on the user's interpersonal interactions, rather than readability or virtual clutter. Our strategy is to combine object recognition techniques with layout management to achieve augmented reality that is non-invasive. Additionally, no prior knowledge of the scene is necessary, both multiple conversation partners and virtual elements can be dealt with, and the approach can be applied with other object recognition algorithms for real-time use.

METHODOLOGY

Simply put, we want the user to be able to carry out everyday conversations and activities without having to worry about closing and/or managing text. To accomplish this, three primary steps are used to prevent text from entering the conversation/gesture area. These steps include defining layouts, face detection and processing, and managing direction and movement of screen items based on position, size, and number of detected faces.

Defining Layouts

Although environment centric layout management methods can usually manage multiple elements [2, 10], current user-centric text management systems often focus on the current window of content in the user's field of view [7]. Since users are often presented with a number of different user centric data items or notifications with limited screen size, we sought to manage multiple items in a constrained space. We chose layouts in which content can simultaneously move away from objects of concentration, and still have a minimal chance of occluding other content, regardless of the size and number of faces in the user's field of view. Although a number of different layouts are possible, we predefined layouts for anywhere between 1 and 6 blocks of content for demonstration and testing, as shown in A of Figure 2. Each of these layouts is designed in such a way that if any element is moved outward, it has a minimal chance of occluding an adjacent element. Additionally, order is always preserved during movement. This means content will always appear in the order the user last left it, preventing users from having to search for icons or widgets that have moved to a different screen location. Addition or removal of elements can also be accomplished without reordering. A simple example of how content would move within a layout is shown in B and C of Figure 2. Virtual elements lie on a number of vectors that run through the center of each piece of content. Each element is then checked to see if it occludes any faces in the scene, and moved away from its original location by a user-defined distance to prevent occlusion.

A)

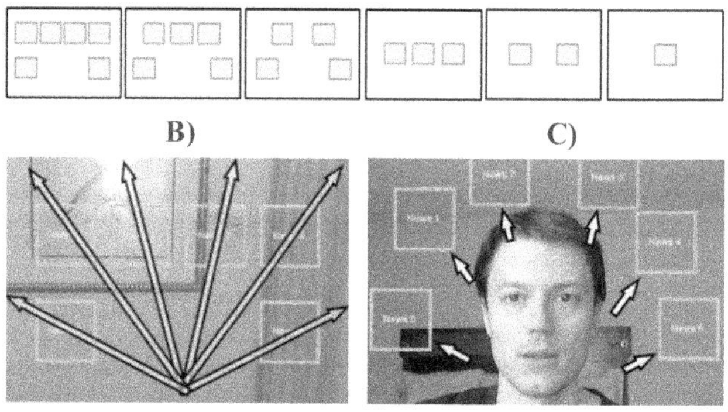

Figure 2. A) Diagram of content layouts allowing for between one and six virtual elements, B) example of movement vectors for a six element layout, and C) content that no longer occludes the conversation.

Face Detection and Persistence

The face processing library we used is from OpenCV, which implements a Haar classifier for face detection. Alone, this is not enough to guarantee consistent detection and subsequently smooth, consistent layout management. The problem of inconsistent detection, also referred to as a persistence problem, exists with many real time detection algorithms, including detection of markers for augmented reality and optical character recognition. In our case, regardless of several failed detection frames, content should still remain out of the path of the user's conversation.

In order to accomplish this, we first define a persistence variable (Pf) for each detected face, which functions like a threshold. Once a face is detected, it is loaded into a resizable array with a predefined Pf, the detected size, and x,y position. If multiple faces are detected, they are all inserted into the array within the same frame. After all detected faces have been processed, the persistence variable of any detected faces that had previously existed within the array is decremented by one. Any instance of a detection that has persistence of 0 or below is removed from the array. As a result, faces that have existed in at least one in the last Pf frames affect the content layout algorithms below. This means that even if face detection fails in several frames, content is still kept away from the person or people in the conversation. Pf regulates how long a face persists within the array, so a higher Pf (assuming more detection failures) will keep content away longer. One other benefit of this approach is that text movement exhibits a smoothing effect, since faces are more consistently present. Next, we had to figure out how to minimize occlusion of faces and content.

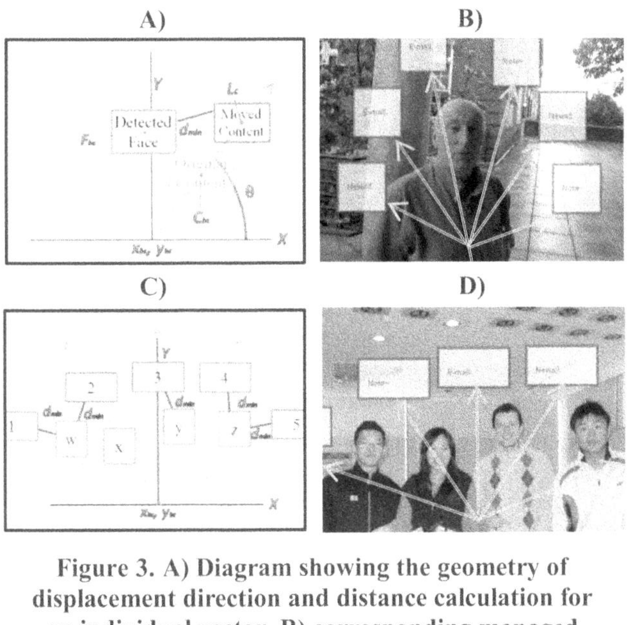

Figure 3. A) Diagram showing the geometry of displacement direction and distance calculation for an individual vector, B) corresponding managed content for one person and 6 virtual elements, C) geometry for a multi-face example with 4 people and 5 elements, and D) corresponding managed content. (Note that two elements in D are off-screen.)

Direction, Movement, and Dealing with Multiple Faces

In contrast with text readability, we are more concerned with the viewability of people in the conversation, so we designed a view management method that prioritizes visibility, is less invasive, and provides easy access to off-screen information.

Direction and Movement Algorithm

Using the previously mentioned layouts shown in Figure 2, vectors are first defined that start from a point at the bottom center of the screen (x_{bc}, y_{bc}) and run through the centroid of each virtual element at angle θ, as shown in images A and C of Figure 3. For multiple elements, the vectors run outwards towards the left, upper, and right borders of the screen as shown in C. Content can then move along each of these vectors whenever a face comes too close to a virtual element. Movement logic on the vector and distance (Lc) from (x_{bc}, y_{bc}) can be described by the following:

$$IF(Dv < thresh \;\&\&\; Fbc < Cbc), then{:}\; Lc = dmin + (Fbc - Cbc)$$

where Dv is the minimum distance from the detected face to the nearest vector, $dmin$ is the desired minimum distance from a detected face to moved content, and Fbc and Cbc are the Euclidean distances from each face to the origin and the content block under consideration to the origin, respectively. Each element is then moved along its respective vector so that there is a final distance of $dmin$ pixels between the element and the nearest face.

Multiple Faces

As seen in C and D of Figure 2, multiple faces are handled in a similar way to a single face. For every virtual element present, the distance to each face in the scene is first checked, and the element is then moved if necessary. For example, virtual elements in Figure 2 C (blue boxes) are moved $dmin$ away from detected faces (green boxes). When a virtual element occludes more than one detected face, the closer face is used in the calculation. Algorithmically, this means that we loop through the array containing persistent faces, and check for nearby virtual elements in every frame. This logic is also defined by the pseudo code shown below:

```
WHILE camera is on
  RUN face detection on current frame
    ADD any detected faces to persistence array with Pf
    DECREMENT Pf of any existing faces in array by 1
      FOR each virtual element
        FOR each face in persistence array
          IF distance between face and content vector (Dv)
             of nearest element < dmin
             AND face-origin distance (Fbc) <
             content-origin distance (Cbc)
          THEN use dmin to set new content distance (Lc)
          ENDFOR //incremented through all faces
      ENDFOR //incremented through all virtual elements
ENDWHILE
```

This idea was inspired by previous strategies that employ potential fields for content movement [4]. In the case of multiple faces occluding a single element, movement is based on the nearest face with respect to the origin (x_{bc}, y_{bc}). Since processing power is a concern for mobile devices, the distance is measured from a bounding box on both rendered content and nearby faces, thus simplifying the calculation, much like Minkowski Sums are used to detect collisions in gaming applications [12]. A running average is also taken for the position of each element, so content appears to smoothly move away from any faces coming into the user's field of view. A representative sample of resulting movement for different element layouts and number of conversation partners is shown in B and D of Figure 3.

Although less likely, the case of a user's face entering from the top of the screen must be dealt with differently since content blocks are never migrated downwards to avoid occluding bodies or hand gestures. In this case, as soon as a new face comes within *dmin* of the vector corresponding to the closest element, the element is migrated up and over the face and kept at *dmin* pixels away from the face from that time forward. Though we are still testing for other exceptions, the movement scheme we propose appears to generally solve occlusion problems in this context.

EVALUATION

When evaluating our system, we conducted a simple test to find out how well the Halo Content algorithm can prevent text from interfering with a number of different conversations. To do so, we asked participants to view a variety of frames taken from 3 different videos. Simulated content was then managed for each frame with the Halo Content algorithm, and compared to corresponding standard layouts as baselines. Participants evaluated content on each frame as "would interfere" or "would not interfere."

Setup

We started by taking three videos encompassing a variety of different conversational situations, including a chance outdoor meeting, a four-person research discussion, and an in-office consultation. These videos were taken from a first person perspective using a head worn display so that head movements and interactions would be recorded. 20 frames were extracted randomly from each of these videos, and frames without faces were rejected and replaced at random. We then applied the Halo Content algorithm to 3 different standard layouts, and for combinations of 2, 3, and 6 simulated blocks of content as shown in Figure 2 A, for a total of 60 processed frames at 640x480pixels (px). We also created a corresponding set of 60 frames with the same 3 layouts and block sizes, but did not apply the management algorithm to provide a baseline for comparison. The blocks of content were displayed as white, semi-transparent billboards containing a single randomly selected text notification. Sizes differed with respect to number of blocks present, with 200x180px, 150x200px, and 100x100px for the 2, 3, and 6 block layouts, respectively.

A total of 14 volunteers, 9 male and 5 female, with a mean age of 31.9, participated in the experiment. We employed a within subjects design, where each participant evaluated the management method on each of the 120 frames, for a total of 1680 evaluations. The order of conditions in each interface was randomized between participants to eliminate any ordering effects.

Results

Across all participants (group A), 86.5% of frames using layouts without management were evaluated as interfering, in comparison with 31.8% for those using Halo Content. A two-way analysis of variance shows a significant difference ($F_{(5,13)}$=26.42, P<.0001) between ratings of the two display methods across all sizes and numbers. Percentage of content rated as interfering with respect to management method and number of elements is shown in A of Figure 4.

We also noticed a clear division of ratings within the experiment. Out of the 14 participants, 5 rated a majority of content as interfering, regardless of whether it was managed by Halo Content or in a static layout. For the remaining 9 (group B), interference of the static layouts remained about the same, but resulting interference of Halo Content was significantly reduced. As shown in B of Figure 4, only 11.3% of frames managed by Halo Content were evaluated as interfering for these participants, resulting in a 73.3% reduction in interference compared to static layouts. A slight effect was found for number of elements ($F_{(2,8)}$=2.67, P<.05) for this group, which suggests that an increasing number of elements may result in increased interference.

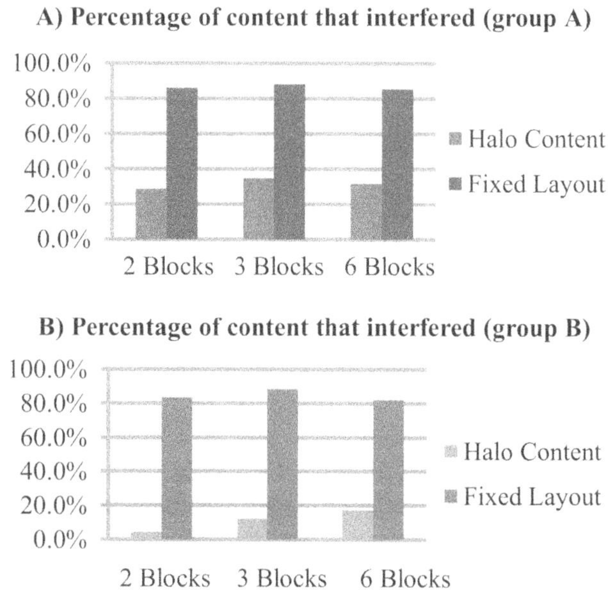

Figure 4. A) Table showing interference of the Halo Content algorithm compared to typical on-screen layouts for 2, 3, and 6 element layouts. B) The same as A, but excluding users who were unsatisfied when almost any virtual content was present in the scene.

DISCUSSION

The initial results of our experiments suggest that Halo Content may be a good way to prevent certain types of augmentative and virtual content from becoming invasive in conversational situations. As HWDs, AR applications, and virtual content increase, it will make sense to have a number of management algorithms in place for different situations. For example, Halo Content might be used for conversations, whereas 3D labeling techniques or visibility management might be used for industrial tasks. Of course, there are tradeoffs between using this vector based strategy versus other algorithms. For example, it may be difficult to mix environment relative labeling with user-centric e-mails. While vectors provide a very fast way for a user to manage mobile content, adaptations would also be necessary to view content with a shared view or perspective.

Although to some extent we provide robustness to failed face detections in our algorithm, it is important to note that this paper does not solve persistence problems completely. Face or object detection algorithms are out of the scope of this paper, but we plan to develop other methods to improve persistence as future work. Additionally, placement depth needs to be taken into account. While our strategy works well for monoscopic HWDs with a fixed focal plane, stereoscopic displays would benefit from content placed at the same depth as the user's gaze [9]. Eye tracking may be a potential solution to this problem. One other benefit of Halo Content is that it is applicable to devices other than see-through HWDs. There are many applications for immersive virtual reality, heads-up systems, and other static see-through displays. The algorithm and layout methods proposed here are easily adaptable to other virtual spaces. One good application example would be the migration of text or content away from vehicles for drivers when on the highway. The face recognition algorithm would be replaced with vehicle recognition, and layouts could be expanded for HUD sized displays.

Conclusion

In this paper, we introduce Halo Content, and find that it can reduce the invasiveness of virtual augmentations, while still providing easy access to content for the user. Since face and body detection algorithms are not perfectly robust, we also provide a way to account for facial persistence, which results in more consistent management and smoothed movement. Additionally, this framework can be used with other object or feature recognition algorithms, making it scalable and applicable to augmented reality applications in a wide variety of other fields.

REFERENCES

1. Ajanki, A., Billinghurst, M., Gamper, H., Järvenpää, T., Kandemir, M., Kaski, S., ... & Tossavainen, T. (2011). An augmented reality interface to contextual information. *Virtual reality, 15(2-3)*, (pp. 161-173).

2. Bell, B., Feiner, S., & Höllerer, T. (2001, November). View management for virtual and augmented reality. In *Proceedings of the 14th annual ACM symposium on User interface software and technology* (pp. 101-110).

3. Ens, B. M., Finnegan, R., & Irani, P. P. (2014, April). The personal cockpit: a spatial interface for effective task switching on head-worn displays. In *Proceedings of the 32nd annual ACM conference on Human factors in computing systems* (pp. 3171-3180).

4. Hartmann, K., Ali, K., & Strothotte, T. (2004, January). Floating labels: Applying dynamic potential fields for label layout. In *Smart Graphics* (pp. 101-113).

5. Ishiguro, Y., & Rekimoto, J. (2011, March). Peripheral vision annotation: noninterference information presentation method for mobile augmented reality. In *Proceedings of the 2nd Augmented Human International Conference* (p. 8).

6. Makita, K., Kanbara, M., & Yokoya, N. (2009, June). View management of annotations for wearable augmented reality. In *Multimedia and Expo, 2009. ICME 2009. IEEE International Conference on* (pp. 982-985).

7. Orlosky, J., Kiyokawa, K., & Takemura, H. (2013, March). Dynamic text management for see-through wearable and heads-up display systems. *In Proceedings of the 2013 international conference on Intelligent user interfaces* (pp. 363-370).

8. Reitmayr, G., Eade, E., & Drummond, T. W. (2007, November). Semi-automatic annotations in unknown environments. *In Mixed and Augmented Reality, 2007.* ISMAR 2007. 6th IEEE and ACM International Symposium on (pp. 67-70).

9. Tan, D. S., & Czerwinski, M. (2003). Effects of visual separation and physical discontinuities when distributing information across multiple displays. *In Proc. Interact* (Vol. 3, pp. 252-255).

10. Tatzgern, M., Kalkofen, D., Grasset, R., & Schmalstieg, D. (2014, March). Hedgehog labeling: View management techniques for external labels in 3D space. *In Virtual Reality (VR), 2014 iEEE* (pp. 27-32).

11. Tsai, H. C. (2013, November). Safety view management for augmented reality based on MapReduce strategy on multi-core processors. *In ITS Telecommunications (ITST), 2013 13th International Conference on* (pp. 151-156).

12. Van Den Bergen, G. (2001, March). Proximity queries and penetration depth computation on 3d game objects. *In Game developers conference* (Vol. 170).

13. Wierzbicki, R. J., Tschoeppe, C., Ruf, T., & Garbas, J. U. (2013). EDIS-Emotion-Driven Interactive Systems. *Other Publications of the AMEA Association*, (1).

14. Zhang, F., & Sun, H. (2005, December). Dynamic labeling management in virtual and augmented environments. *In Computer Aided Design and Computer Graphics, 2005. Ninth International Conference on* (pp. 6-pp).

Emotar: Communicating Feelings through Video Sharing

Tiffany C.K. Kwok[1] Michael Xuelin Huang[2] Wai Cheong Tam[3] Grace Ngai [4]

Department of Computing, Hong Kong Polytechnic University
Kowloon, Hong Kong
{tiffany.ck.kwok[1], grace.ngai[4]}@polyu.edu.hk,
{michael.xl.huang[2], andy.tam[3]}@connect.polyu.hk

ABSTRACT

Affect exchange is essential for healthy physical and social development [7], and friends and family communicate their emotions to each other instinctively. In particular, watching movies has always been a popular mode of socialization and video sharing is increasingly viewed as an effective way to facilitate communication of feelings and affects, even when the parties are not in the same location. We present an asynchronous video-sharing platform that uses *Emotars* to facilitate affect sharing in order to create and enhance the sense of togetherness through the experience of asynchronous movie watching. We investigate its potential impact and benefits, including a better viewing experience, supporting relationships, and strengthening engagement, connectedness and emotion awareness among individuals.

Author Keywords

Emotional communication; video sharing; social connectedness; social television

ACM Classification Keywords

H.5.3 Group and Organization Interfaces

INTRODUCTION

Research on Video Mediated Communication (VMC) shows that VMC can facilitate social bonding enhancement and increase the sense of togetherness between close friends and families [11,13,20]. In particular, asynchronous video communication is drawing increasing attention from the community, as it does not require both parties to be presented at the same time, but nevertheless can be as effective as synchronous communication [3].

Forms of VMC include video conversations [11] and vblogging [14], in which people share experiences and information via self-created videos rather than through text or static images. Other forms of VMC include video sharing [21] and social television [9,18,19], in which users share experience and information, facilitated by a video created *by a third party*. This is an intuitive and effective way to share ideas and experience, as it is natural for a viewer who is inspired or touched by a video to comment upon it, or to recommend it to friends, expecting them to have similar feelings. Such video sharing experiences are effective and popular means of sharing ideas and experiences [2], as evidenced by the many social media sites that are devoted to video sharing [24], or support video as one type of communication media [8,22].

Current state-of-the-art work in video sharing generally involves users explicitly and intentionally giving feedback on the video, either in the form of votes or comments. This allows for the sharing of very detailed and precise information, but it also requires user effort as well as a certain degree of comfortableness with the computer.

This work extends on previous work by investigating the potential of automated affect capture in facilitating *implicit* sharing of experiences. We use facial affect recognition techniques to detect the users' emotions, which are then used to label specific frame sequences in the video. This allows a spontaneous reaction that is precisely linked to point in the movie that triggered it. It also allows for users who may not be comfortable or literate with the computer.

In this sense, Cui et al.'s work [4] is similar to ours. They investigated emotional communication between close-knit individuals via photo-sharing by embedding viewer's facial response (an image) into the shared photo (*i.e.* the media). Their finding suggests that the shared response can help to convey feelings and create a sense of co-presence. However, conveying feelings through video involves more complicated issues.

To visualize human emotional states while encouraging people to share their emotional response, we introduce the *Emotar*, which is a combination of emoticon and avatar. Aoki et al. [1] pointed out that emoticons could express emotions that cannot be adequately communicated in words. Janssen et al. [12] suggested that emoticon used in communication increases the perceived intimacy. Derks et al. [5] considered emoticons as a visually salient representation of expression, which has the potential to be as rich as expressions in face-to-face interaction.

As an emotional avatar, Emotars allow viewers to share their affects and experience with others without disclosing their real facial expressions and/or features. This has

IUI'15, March 29 - April 01 2015, Atlanta, GA, USA
Copyright 2015 ACM 978-1-4503-3306-1/15/03...$15.00
http://dx.doi.org/10.1145/2678025.2701372

implications on user comfort and privacy, and we believe that using emoticons instead of photos of the user's facial response helps to increase the level of comfort and security, which encourages the users to be more willing to share with others. From the communication point of view, emoticons provide an efficient abstraction of viewers' emotional states. It takes less time to process, hence causing less distraction to receivers, which in turn results in higher overall efficiency in communication.

To the best of our knowledge, there is no prior research that investigates the communication of affects through automated affect capture. The findings of our work could begin to fill this gap and suggest development directions and possible guidelines for such intelligent user interfaces.

DESIGN

System Implementation

Figure 1 shows the system interface, which is implemented in HTML5 and can be accessed through the Internet as a web page. The movie plays in the center and Emotars are displayed on both sides of the movie window.

Each Emotar represents one person. To communicate the affect more effectively, we designed the Emotar with a background color that changes according to the emotion currently represented [6].

We experimented with two different types of Emotars. Figure 1 shows one implementation, which uses a texture model that allows customization of gender, hairstyle, and other characteristics. The other implementation uses a wireframe model that varies according to gender and affect, but is otherwise identical across users.

Automated Affect Capture and Emotar Generation

We investigate the efficacy of our system with two videos: one that is commonly regarded to be funny, and another that is commonly considered to be sad. The two movies are therefore designed to induce happiness and sadness, which are considered to be two primary, universal feelings. The viewers' affect was classified into seven types: *ecstatic, pleased, neutral, down, depressed, interested, and disgusted*. Each Emotar therefore has seven forms (or appearances) that correspond to these types.

To accurately represent the temporal change of viewers' facial expressions, we trained user-dependent facial affect models for individual subjects. For calibration, subjects were asked to simulate expressions that they felt would be representative of the target emotional states. 10 images were captured per subject for each state. We then used the Supervised Descent Method [23] to track 48 facial landmarks and Support Vector Machines (SVMs) to train a facial affect model on the calibration data for each user [17]. Our facial affect model therefore gives us the frame level affect sequence corresponding to the viewers' facial response, which then drives the Emotar.

Figure 1: Screenshot of System Interface

Since our objective is to explore the communication of affects and not to build a facial affect recognition system, we manually validated the automated facial affect recognition model and made necessary corrections to compensate for large head pose variance. This ensures that the Emotar correctly represents the viewers' emotions. In total, about 22% of the frames needed to be corrected.

Capturing and classifying the viewer's facial response on a per-frame level gives us a temporal sequence of Emotars. Aligning the Emotar sequence with the video generates a visualization of the viewer's emotional response.

EVALUATION

We are interested in the following issues:

Emotion awareness: do the subjects have a clear and correct awareness of other viewers' affects while they watch the video? How is such awareness influenced by the Emotar?

Engagement: how do the Emotars and emotion awareness influence the subjects' engagement during video watching?

Comfortableness: how comfortable are users with our interface? Are they willing to share their own feelings and responses if they are represented in such a manner?

Relationship: how do differences in factors such as relationship and gender between the viewer and the person represented by the Emotar impact the above issues?

Experiment Setup

To evaluate our system, we recruited 32 unpaid participants (21 female), aged between 19 to 47. They frequently watch videos and movies online (50% daily, others at least once a month) and are habitual users of social networking systems.

The functionality of the interface and the objective of the experiment were introduced to the subjects at the start of the experiment. A 5-minute practice session with a 2-minute test video allowed the subject to familiarize themselves with the interface. The formal experiment involved the subjects watching a happy video (~8 min) and a sad video (~20 min). The subjects were asked to behave spontaneously during the experiment. Post-experiment, we conducted a face-to-face focus interview with each subject.

All the experiments were performed on a 15-inch MacBook Pro using Google Chrome as the browser. The viewer's facial response was collected and processed offline to create their Emotar. (The system was "seeded" with 4 initial users who watched both movies without the Emotars; they are not included in the 32 participants.) To get a better sense of where the subjects were looking during the experiment, we used a Tobii EyeX Controller (visual angle error < 0.5°) to track the gaze points of the subjects. This allowed us to analyze the gaze behavior, including the moments when the subjects' gaze switches from the video to the Emotars.

The users were randomly divided into two groups to test the two different Emotar styles. During each experiment, the system displayed the Emotars of four people with different levels of closeness to the subject. The level of closeness was scored by the subject after the experiment. The subject's facial response was captured during the experiment and used to drive his/her Emotar for subsequent experiments for other subjects.

Findings

Emotion Awareness and Relationship

The eye tracker data revealed several interesting findings. The subjects that were presented with the cartoonish Emotars tended to look at it more frequently than those who were presented with the wire-frame Emotars. The former group spent 5% of the total time looking at the Emotars, compared with about 2% with the latter group. Since users tend to glance at the Emotars (as opposed to *watching* them), this 5% represents a large number of saccades -- on average, 50-60 times per video.

For most of the participants, the gaze position saccaded to the Emotars after they had experienced an emotion transition. Figure 3 shows an example portion of the data from one participant. The gaze saccades to the Emotars are superimposed as vertical lines over the normalized values of the changes in emotion intensity. The data suggest that a change in emotion intensity or a high level of emotion intensity often trigger gaze saccades to the Emotars.

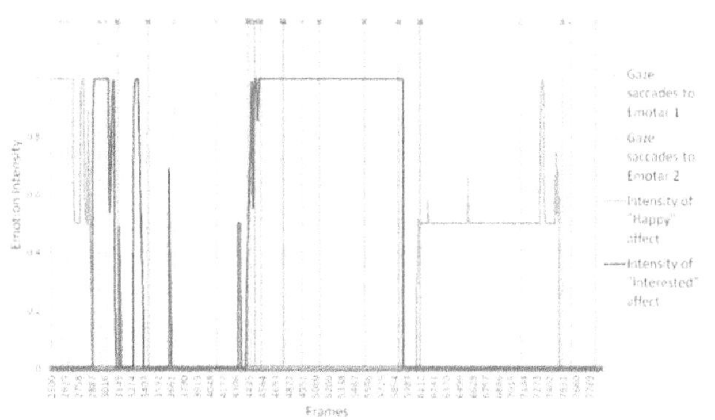

Figure 3: Relationship between viewer affect and Emotar attention for one subject. The gaze saccades to the Emotars are superimposed on the intensity values of two emotions.

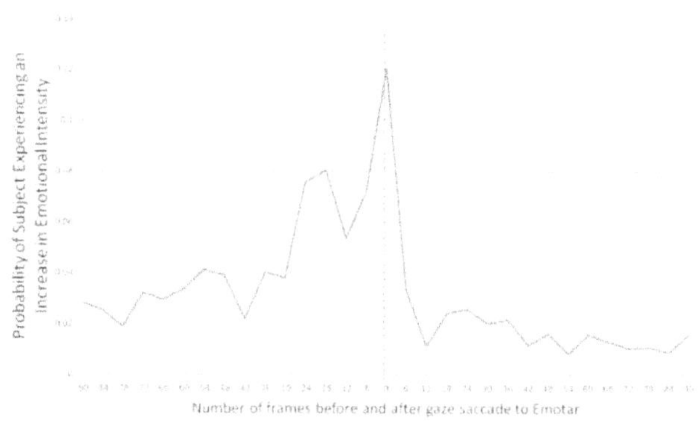

Figure 2: Relationship between emotional transition and Emotar attention. Subjects are more likely to have experienced an increase in emotional intensity before gaze saccades to the Emotar.

Figure 2 aggregates this information across all subjects. We calculate the probability of the user's emotion intensity reaching a peak within 3 seconds before and after a gaze saccade to the Emotars. The figure suggests that the user is more likely to have experienced an increase in emotional intensity before the gaze saccades occurs. In other words, users are more likely to look at the Emotar after something has triggered an intense emotion.

The nature of the video also appears to affect the interaction with the Emotars. In general, subjects tend to look at Emotars less often when they are watching a sad video, as opposed to a funny video. When interviewed, most of the subjects stated that they wanted more privacy when watching sad movies: (quotes unedited for grammar)

> *"Different from funny movie, I prefer to watch the sad movie on my own. I feel sad and I want to stay in my own world. That's why I rarely pay attention to the others."*

Figure 4Not surprisingly, subjects were more interested in the Emotar of a person that they knew. 70% of the Emotar glances were directed towards an Emotar of a close friend or family member (Figure 4). One subject put it thus:

> *"I think that the feelings of people, who are not close to me, are not important… I will pay more attention to these two (pointing to Emotars of her daughter and her best friend)."*

We observed that people were more likely to look at the female Emotars. 53% of the gaze saccades from female subjects were directed to female Emotars. This is even more pronounced with male subjects: 59% of their saccades were to female Emotars.

One of the female subjects reported that

> *"I will look at female first … likely to have same feelings."*

One of the male subjects even stated:

> *"I will look for girls and friends. It is normal for a boy to focus more on girls… Girls usually have more emotional changes while watching movies."*

To investigate the potential of the system for enhancing emotion awareness, subjects were asked to recall which parts their friends (the Emotars) felt happy or sad in the post-experiment interview. Most were able to recall two to three instances correctly.

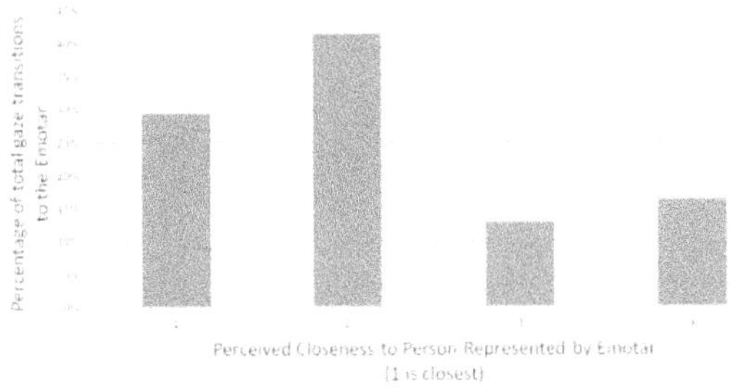

Figure 4: Relationship between perceived closeness and Emotar attention. Subjects were more likely to look at Emotars representing people they are close to.

Engagement

Encouragingly, the experiment results suggest that the increased emotional awareness may enhance the level of engagement. We replayed one part of the happy video, which is not commonly considered funny, to the interviewees, and asked whether they considered that part to be funny. Most of them answered "No" or "Not really". We then reviewed their facial features during that time period and found that some were actually smiling despite reporting that they did not find that part funny. When asked the follow-up question "Then why are you smiling?", some users pointed out that they smiled because they saw that their friends' Emotars were in the highest "happy" state.

> *"The video is so cracking me up. When I see my friends laughing with me, it makes me feel so high. This is great!"*

In contrast, some people reported that the Emotars actually helped them to *restrain* from getting too engaged:

> *"The clip was so striking my heart. I could not hold it and I felt tears rolling back and forth inside my eyes. I peeped at the others to see if they were exhibiting the same feeling. None of them was sad and so I told myself to hold the tears."*

This suggests that the social experience is valuable to watching videos, but it is not always possible for friends to watch movies together in the same place at the same time. Our experiment suggests that Emotars can be used to build an environment to create an atmosphere that is like watching videos together, which may help users to better resonate and engage with their friends.

Level of Comfort with the System

When people are engaged in a video sharing activity, privacy and security are extremely important. People may not object to communicating feelings with friends, but they are not comfortable posting actual videos of themselves (as a means of communicating emotions). Using an Emotar to represent a person could help to communicate one's facial expressions while still maintaining privacy and anonymity.

Among all 32 subjects, 21 (66%) stated that they would be willing to use our system to share their movie-watching experience with their friends. However, many of them were not willing to share a video of their face:

> *"I would prefer to watch the video with others' real facial expression. But ... I would not want to show mine to the others... sharing with these (pointing to Emotars) is ok."*

They also point out that a system that uses their actual images instead of Emotars would make them wary. Since people consider the risks and weigh them against the benefits when they decide to disclose information [16], and trust is the key to disclosure in online relationships, this may be due to a lack of trust in the social platform [10].

DESIGN GUIDELINES

Most of the participants agree that they are curious about how others feel when they themselves feel a certain emotion. However, facial expressions usually exhibit explicit emotions only for a small fraction of the time [15]. Since the Emotars represent the facial emotion of a person at a particular point in time, the Emotars display a "neutral" or low-intensity emotion most of the time.

Since we found that a user usually looks at the Emotars *after* an emotion change on their part, we suggest that the emotions of the Emotars could be extended slightly, such that when the user looks at the Emotars after they have finished laughing, for example, they find that their friends are feeling "happy" (a result lingering from the previous period of time) instead of "neutral".

Some of the users also suggested that if there had been some kinds of background sound, for example, a laugh track, for the Emotar, that would help them to better engage into the movie. This also suggests that Emotars with both sound effects as well as facial features may be useful.

The similarity between a person and his/her Emotar may also affect the level of engagement. Most of the users reported that if the Emotar more physically resembles their friends, the sense of "togetherness" is increased.

CONCLUSIONS & FUTURE WORK

We present a video experience sharing system that helps people to share the experience of watching a movie even when they are decoupled in time and space. Our system uses Emotars instead of real facial images to resolve concerns about user privacy and security. Results show that users tend to pay attention to their friends' reaction when they have intense emotional changes of their own. This suggests that our system has potential as a means for increasing emotion awareness as well as enhancing user engagement in the movie-watching experience.

In future work, we plan to further investigate different aspects of this mode of experience sharing, especially when used in the context of longer movies, as well as more emotionally complex Emotars and sound effects.

REFERENCES

[1] Aoki, S. and Uchida, O. A Method for automatically generating the emotional vectors for emoticons using weblog articles. *World Scientific and Engineering Academy and Society Press*, (2011).

[2] Butler, E.A., Egloff, B., Wilhelm, F.H., Smith, N.C., Erickson, E.A., and Gross, J.J. The social consequences of expressive suppression. *Emotion 3*, 1 (2003), 48–67.

[3] Cao, X., Sellen, A., Brush, A.J.B., Kirk, D., Edge, D., and Ding, X. Understanding Family Communication across Time Zones. *CSCW 2010*, (2010), 155–158.

[4] Cui, Y., Kangas, J., Holm, J., and Grassel, G. Front-Camera Video Recordings as Emotion Responses to Mobile Photos Shared Within Close-Knit Groups. *CHI'13*, (2013), 981–990.

[5] Derks, D., Fischer, A.H., and Bos, A.E.R. The role of emotion in computer-mediated communication: A review. *Computers in Human Behavior*, (2007).

[6] Do2Learn. Emotions Color Wheel. http://www.do2learn.com/organizationtools/EmotionsColorWheel/.

[7] Duprez, C., Christophe, V., Rime, B., Congard, A., and Antoine, P. Motives for the social sharing of an emotional experience. *Journal of Social and Personal Relationships*, (2014), 1–31.

[8] Facebook. Facebook. https://www.facebook.com/.

[9] Geerts, D. and Grooff, D.D. Supporting the Social Uses of Television: Sociability Heuristics for Social TV. *CHI'09*, (2009), 595–604.

[10] Hoffman, D.L., Novak, T.P., and Peralta, M. Building Consumer Trust Online. *Communications of the ACM 42*, 4 (1999), 80–85.

[11] Inkpen, K., Du, H., Roseway, A., Hoff, A., and Johns, P. Video Kids: Augmenting Close Friendships with Asynchronous Video Conversations in VideoPal. *CHI'12*, (2012), 2387–2396.

[12] Janssen, J.H., Ijsselsteijn, W.A., and Westerink, J.H.D.M. How affective technologies can influence intimate interactions and improve social connectedness. *International Journal of Human-Computer Studies 72*, (2014), 33–43.

[13] Judge, T.K., Neustaedter, C., and Kurtz, A.F. The Family Window: The Design and Evaluation of a Domestic Media Space. *CHI'10*, (2010), 2361–2370.

[14] Lui, L.S., Huh, J., NNeogi, Ti., Inkpen, K., and Pratt, W. Health Vlogger-Viewer Interaction in Chronic Illness Management. *CHI'13*, (2013), 49 – 58.

[15] Matsumoto, D. and Hwang, H.S. Reading facial expressions of emotion. *American Psychological Association Psychological Science Agenda*, 2011. http://www.apa.org/science/about/psa/2011/05/facial-expressions.aspx.

[16] Metzger, M.J. Privacy, Trust, and Disclosure: Exploring Barriers to Electronic Commerce. *Journal of Computer-Mediated Communication 9*, 4 (2004).

[17] Michel, P. and Kaliouby, R. El. Real Time Facial Expression Recognition in Video using Support Vector Machines. *ICMI'03*, (2003), 258–264.

[18] Nathan, M., Harrison, C., Yarosh, S., Terveen, L., Stead, L., and Amento, B. CollaboraTV: Making Television Viewing Social Again. *uxTV'08*, , 85–94.

[19] Palviainen, J., Kuusinen, K., and Väänänen-Vainio-Mattila, K. Designing for Presence in Social Television Interaction. *MUM'13*, (2013).

[20] Raffle, H., Revelle, G., Mori, K., et al. Hello, is Grandma there? Let's Read! StoryVisit: Family Video Chat and Connected E-Books. *CHI'11*, (2011).

[21] Shamma, D.A., Bastea-Forte, M., Joubert, N., and Liu, Y. Enhancing Online Personal Connections through the Synchronized Sharing of Online Video. *CHI'08*, (2008), 2931–2936.

[22] Twitter. Twitter. https://twitter.com/.

[23] Xiong, X. and Torre, F.D. la. Supervised Descent Method and Its Applications to Face Alignment. *2013 IEEE Conference on Computer Vision and Pattern Recognition*, (2013).

[24] YouTube. Youtube. https://www.youtube.com.

Automatic Detection of Learning-Centered Affective States in the Wild

Nigel Bosch, Sidney D'Mello
University of Notre Dame
384 Fitzpatrick Hall,
Notre Dame, IN 46556, USA
{pbosch1, sdmello}@nd.edu

Ryan Baker, Jaclyn Ocumpaugh
Teachers College,
Columbia University
525 W. 120th Street,
New York, NY 10027, USA
baker2@exchange.tc.columbia.edu, jocumpaugh@wpi.edu

Valerie Shute, Matthew Ventura, Lubin Wang, Weinan Zhao
Florida State University
3205G Stone Building,
1114 West Call Street,
Tallahassee, FL 32306-4453, USA
{vshute, mventura, lw10e}@fsu.edu,
weinan.zhao@gmail.com

ABSTRACT
Affect detection is a key component in developing intelligent educational interfaces that are capable of responding to the affective needs of students. In this paper, computer vision and machine learning techniques were used to detect students' affect as they used an educational game designed to teach fundamental principles of Newtonian physics. Data were collected in the real-world environment of a school computer lab, which provides unique challenges for detection of affect from facial expressions (primary channel) and gross body movements (secondary channel)—up to thirty students at a time participated in the class, moving around, gesturing, and talking to each other. Results were cross validated at the student level to ensure generalization to new students. Classification was successful at levels above chance for off-task behavior (area under receiver operating characteristic curve or AUC = .816) and each affective state including boredom (AUC =.610), confusion (.649), delight (.867), engagement (.679), and frustration (.631) as well as a five-way overall classification of affect (.655), despite the noisy nature of the data. Implications and prospects for affect-sensitive interfaces for educational software in classroom environments are discussed.

Author Keywords
Affect detection; naturalistic facial expressions; classroom data; in the wild.

ACM Classification Keywords
H.5.m. Information interfaces and presentation (e.g., HCI): Miscellaneous.

http://dx.doi.org/10.1145/2678025.2701397

INTRODUCTION
Learning from intelligent educational interfaces elicits frequent affective responses from students and wide variations in their behavior. A variety of affective states occur frequently in learning contexts, and can have both positive and negative effects on students' learning [12,38]. For example, students often encounter exercises that require information or techniques with which they are not familiar. Confusion, frustration, boredom, and other affective states are elicited in response to how these impasses are resolved [4,12,15]. These and other affective experiences are particularly important because they are inextricably bound to learning by coloring students' perceptions of a learning environment and changing how well they learn from it [9,19].

A human teacher can observe students' affect in a classroom or one-on-one tutoring situation (cf. [28]) and use that information to determine who needs help and to adjust the pace or content of learning materials. On the other hand, computerized learning environments used in school computer labs rarely incorporate such accommodations into their instructional strategies. One of the many challenges of creating intelligent educational interfaces is developing systems that can detect and respond to the affective states of students, though some initial progress has been made in laboratory settings (see [13] for a recent review). The goal of these interfaces is to provide a computerized learning environment that responds to the affective needs of students, whether by redirecting off-task behavior, providing encouragement, or altering learning materials to better suit the student. Much work remains to be done for effective affect-sensitivity in learning environments in the wild, however. At the core of such systems is the ability to detect or anticipate the affective state of students, a proposition considered in this paper.

Affect can be detected using various types of data. For example, interaction data (e.g., number of actions taken in an interface, speed of help requests) [3], facial expressions [5,26], posture [33], and other data sources have been used to detect the affective states of students (see [6,42] for recent reviews). Facial-feature based affect detection is particularly attractive because (a) there is a strong link between facial features and affective states [16], (b) it does not depend on learning environment or content, and (c) it does not require expensive hardware, as webcams are ubiquitous on laptops and mobile devices. For these reasons, we focus on vision-based techniques to detect affective states from facial features (primary channel) and body movements (secondary channel). Affect detection based on facial features has been the subject of considerable previous research (see [6,42] for reviews); albeit outside of learning contexts and mainly in laboratory settings (see exceptions discussed below). Laboratory environments have the advantage of relatively consistent lighting and freedom from distractions from other students, cell phones, walking around, and numerous other factors. Users of computer interfaces in the wild (e.g., students in a school computer lab) may be subject to such external distractions that make affective data far noisier than data collected in laboratory contexts. In many cases, motion, unusual head pose, and face-occluding gestures are so prevalent that facial feature detection is not possible and affect detection must be done using other modalities.

Much of the previous work in face-based affect detection has also focused on the so-called basic emotions of anger, fear, sadness, happiness, disgust, and surprise (see review in [6]). However, a recent review and meta-analysis of 24 studies indicated that these basic-emotions are quite infrequent in the context of learning with educational software [12]. Instead, students' affective experience mainly consists of learning-centered affective states (which we focus on in this study), such as engaged concentration, boredom, confusion, frustration, happiness, and anxiety. It is unclear if these states can be detected with similar fidelity as the basic emotions, where the links between emotion and expression have been carefully mapped out for decades [16,37]. Similar mappings for the learning-centered affective states are largely missing (see [30] for some initial work in this direction), and it is an entirely open question if such mappings even exist.

The present paper addresses these two challenges in an effort to detect naturalistic episodes of learning-centered affective states while students were using a computer interface in the setting of a school's computer lab. Students were in a context that was rich in interruptions, distractions, and conversations from fellow students. If successful, we will have shown that learning-centered affective states can be detected from facial expressions and body movements in the context most basic to education—a school.

RELATED WORK

There is a rich history on affect detection from facial features [6,42]. To keep scope manageable, we focus here on papers attempting to detect facial expressions in the wild and papers detecting learning-centered affective states from naturalistic facial expressions, as opposed to acted (posed) facial expressions. Furthermore, although we also consider gross body movements as an additional measure, the emphasis of the work and consequently the literature review is on facial features.

Facial Expression and Affect in the Lab

Kapoor et al. [25] developed the first system detecting affect in a learning environment. They used multimodal data channels including facial features (from video), a posture-sensing chair, a pressure-sensitive mouse, a skin conductance sensor, and interaction data to predict frustration in an automated learning companion. They were able to predict when a user would self-report frustration with 79% accuracy (chance being 58%). Furthermore, using similar multimodal sensor fusion techniques including facial features, Kapoor et al. [26] were able to classify interest/disinterest with 87% accuracy (chance being 52%).

Hoque et al. [23] used facial features and temporal information in videos to classify smiles as either frustrated or delighted – two states that are related to learning. They accurately distinguished between frustrated and delighted smiles correctly in 92% of cases. They also found differences between acted facial expressions and naturalistic facial expressions. In acted data only 10% of frustrated cases included a smile, whereas in naturally occurring frustration smiles were present in 90% of cases. These results illustrate the fact that there can be large differences between naturalistic and posed data.

In a more recent affect detection effort, Whitehill et al. [41] used Gabor features (appearance-based features capturing textures of various parts of the face) with a support vector machine (SVM) classifier to detect engagement as students interacted with cognitive skills training software. Labels used in their study were obtained from retrospective annotation of videos by human judges. Four levels of engagement were annotated, ranging from complete disengagement (not even looking at the material) to strong engagement. They were able to detect engagement with an Area Under the ROC Curve (AUC, averaged across all four levels of engagement) of .729 where AUC = .5 is chance level detection.

Gabor features have also been used for detection of Action Units (AUs). Action Units are labels for specific facial muscle activations (e.g., lowered brow) [17]. As noted in [39], detecting action units can be a useful intermediate step in the process of detecting affective states. AUs provide a small set of features for use in affect detection efforts. A large database of AU-labeled data can be used to train AU detectors, which can then be applied to new data to generate AU labels. This can be particularly useful for datasets that are difficult to collect (such as data in the wild) and may thus have few instances. The smaller set of features provided by the AU detector (compared to, for example, hundreds of Gabor features) can reduce overfitting.

The Computer Expression Recognition Toolbox (CERT) [29] is a computer vision tool used to automatically detect AUs as well as head pose and head position information. CERT uses features extracted from Gabor filters as inputs to SVMs to provide likelihood estimates for the presence of 19 different AUs in any given frame of a video stream. It also supplies measures of unilateral (one side of the face only) AUs for three action units, as well as "Fear Brow" and "Distress Brow," which indicate the presence of combinations of AU1 (Inner Brow Raiser), AU2 (Outer Brow Raiser), and AU4 (Brow Lowerer). CERT has been tested with databases of both posed facial expressions and spontaneous facial expressions, achieving accuracy of 90.1% and 79.9%, respectively, when discriminating between instances of the AU present vs. absent [29].

Grafsgaard et al. [20] used CERT to recognize the level of frustration (self-reported on a Likert scale) in a learning session and achieved modest results (R^2 = .24). Additionally, they achieved good agreement between the output of CERT AU recognition and human-coded ground truth measurements of AUs. After correcting for individual differences in facial feature movements they achieved Cohen's kappa = .68 and higher for several key AUs. They did not perform detection at a fine-grained level (i.e., specific affective episodes), instead detecting the presence of affect in the entire learning session. However, their work does provide evidence of the validity of CERT for automated AU detection.

In another study using CERT, Bosch and D'Mello [5] used machine learning to build fine-grained detectors for learning-centered affective states of novice programming students using the likelihoods of AUs provided by CERT. The students took part in the study in a laboratory setting. Students made retrospective judgments of their own affective states. Confusion and frustration were detected at levels above chance (22.1% and 23.2% better than chance, respectively), but performance was much lower for other states (11.2% above chance for engagement, 3.8% above chance for boredom).

Facial Expressions and Affect in the Wild

All of the aforementioned studies have been conducted during one-on-one interactions and with the high degree of control afforded by the laboratory, so generalizability to real-world contexts is uncertain. However, some relevant research has been done in real-world contexts including a classroom or school computer lab as reviewed below.

Facial expression data collected in the wild have been the subject of some research. The Affectiva-MIT Facial Expression Dataset (AM-FED) [31] contains videos of participants recorded on their own computers, in various settings while they watched Super Bowl commercials which were likely to elicit smiles. They provided baseline performance for smile detection (AUC = .90), AU2 (outer brow raise, AUC = .72), and AU4 (brow lower, AUC = .70). This dataset has been used for detection of whether viewers liked the commercials (AUC = .82) and wanted to view them again (AUC = .79) [32]. However, affect detectors have not been developed on this dataset to date.

Another study on smiles collected in the wild was conducted on a college campus using cameras set up in various university buildings. Hernandez et al. [21] used computer vision techniques to detect smiles and found expected patterns (e.g., more smiles on weekends and holidays). They demonstrated the feasibility of detecting smiles in the wild, but the question of whether data in the wild can be used for affect detection remains open.

The Emotion Recognition in the Wild Challenge [10] is an effort to unify detection of affect in the wild by creating a common benchmark for various state of the art audio and visual affect detection techniques. The data set used in this challenge was the *Acted Facial Expressions in the Wild* database, which was compiled by using clips from movies. This resulted in professionally acted affective expressions, rather than naturally experienced ones, which raises some concerns due to well-known differences between acted and naturalistic expressions (e,g., see [23]).

Perhaps the closest study to the current paper is one by Arroyo et al. [2]. They tracked emotions of high school and college mathematics students using self-reports and also recorded several modalities (interaction data from log-files, facial features, posture, skin conductance, and mouse movements). Their best models explained 52% of the variance (R^2) for confidence, 46% for frustration, 69% for excitement, and 29% for interest. Although this research suggests that it might be possible to perform automated affect detection in classroom, this conclusion should be interpreted with a modicum of caution. This is because the model was not validated with a separate testing set (i.e. no cross validation was performed), and the size of the data set was very small (20-36 instances depending on model) due to missing data. These issues raise concerns of overfitting to specific students and instances in the training data.

Current Study

The literature review revealed that there are studies that focus on detection of naturalistic affective states, many of which go beyond the basic emotions by considering learning-centered affect. However, this work has been done within controlled lab contexts, so it is unclear if the detectors will generalize to the wild. On the other hand, researchers have started to make great strides towards moving to the wild, but these studies are limited in that they either focus on more atomic facial expressions rather than affective state detection [21,31], are still in need of cross-validation [2], or study acted instead of naturalistic affect [10].

To address these challenges, the present study, for the first time, considers the detection of learning-centered affective states in the wild. Videos of students faces' and affect labels (for supervised learning) was collected while students interacted with a game-based physics education environment called Physics Playground (formerly Newton's Playground; [40]) in their school's computer lab, which was regularly used by students for academic purposes.

METHOD

Data Collection

Participants. The sample consisted of 137 8th and 9th grade students (57 male, 80 female) who were enrolled in a public school in a medium-sized city in the Southeastern U.S. They were tested in groups of about 20 students per class period for a total of four periods on different days (55 minutes per period). Students in the 8th and 9th grades were selected because of the alignment of the Physics Playground content and the State Standards (relating to Newtonian Physics) at those grade levels.

Interface. Physics Playground is a two-dimensional game that requires the player to apply principles of Newtonian Physics in an attempt to guide a green ball to a red balloon in many challenging configurations (key goal). The player can nudge the ball to the left and right (if the surface is flat) but the primary way to move the ball is by drawing/creating simple machines (which are called "agents of force and motion" in the game) on the screen that "come to life" once the object is drawn (example in Figure 1). Thus, the problems in Physics Playground require the player to draw/create four different agents (which are simple machine-like objects): inclined plane/ramps, pendulums, levers, and springboards. All solutions are drawn with colored lines using the mouse. Everything in the game obeys the basic laws of physics relating to gravity and Newton's three laws of motion.

Figure 1. Ramp solution for a simple Physics Playground problem

Procedure. The study took place in one of the school's computer-enabled classrooms, which was equipped with about 30 desktop computers for schoolwork. Each computer was equipped with a monitor, mouse, keyboard, webcam, and headphones. Inexpensive webcams ($30) were affixed at the top of the monitor on each computer. At the beginning of each session, the webcam software displayed an interface that allowed students to position their faces in the center of the camera's view by adjusting the camera angle up or down. This process was guided by on-screen instructions and verbal instructions given by the experimenters, who were also available to answer any additional questions and to troubleshoot any problems.

We administered a qualitative physics pretest during the first day and a posttest at the end of the fourth day (both online). In this study we consider data from the second and third days (roughly two hours total) when students were only playing the game and not being tested. Students' affective states and on-task vs. off-task behaviors were observed during their interactions with Physics Playground using the Baker-Rodrigo Observation Method Protocol (BROMP) field observation system as detailed below [35]. These observations served as the ground truth labels used in training automated detectors.

The affective states of interest were boredom, confusion, delight, engaged concentration, and frustration. This list of states was selected based on previous research [12] and from observing students during the first day of data collection (this data was not used in the current models). In addition to affect, some basic student behaviors were observed. Students were coded as *on task* when looking at their own computer, *on-task conversation* when conversing with other students about what was happening on their own or others' screens, and *off task* in other situations (e.g., task-unrelated conversation, watching other students without conversation, using a cellphone).

BROMP. BROMP is a field coding protocol. In BROMP trained observers perform live affect and behavior annotations by observing students one at a time using a round-robin technique (observing one student until visible affect is detected or 20 seconds have elapsed and moving on to the next student). Observers use side glances to make a holistic judgment of the students' affect based on facial expressions, speech, body posture, gestures, and student interaction with the computer program (e.g., whether a student is progressing or struggling). Observers record students in a pre-determined order to maintain a representative sampling of students' affect, rather than focusing on the most interesting (but not most prevalent) things occurring in the classroom. Every BROMP observer was trained and tested on the protocol and achieved sufficient agreement (kappa ≥ .6) with a certified BROMP observer before coding the data.

The coding process was implemented using the HART application for Android devices [35], which enforces the protocol while facilitating data collection. Observation-codes recorded in HART were synchronized with the videos recorded on the individual computers using Internet time servers.

It should be noted that there are many possible affect annotation schemes, each with their strengths and weaknesses, as recently reviewed in [36]. BROMP was selected for this study because it has been shown to achieve adequate reliability (among over 70 coders in over a dozen studies with a variety of learning environments [34]) in annotating affective states of a large number of students occurring in the "heat of the moment" and without interrupting or biasing students by asking them to self-report affect.

Instances of Affect Observed

It was not always possible to observe both affect and behavior in situations where students could not be easily observed (e.g., bathroom breaks, occlusions caused by hand to face gestures) or where the observer was not confident about an observation. Affect could not be observed in 8.1% of cases while on-task/off-task behavior could not be observed in 2.8% of cases. We obtained 1,767 successful observations of affective states and 1,899 observations of on-task/off-task behavior during the two days of data used in this study. The most common affective state observed was engaged concentration (77.6%), followed by frustrated (13.5%), bored (4.3%), delighted (2.3%), and confused (2.3%). On task behavior occurred 74.2% of the time, on-task conversation occurred 20.9% of the time, and off-task behavior occurred 4.9% of the time.

Model Building

Feature Engineering. We used FACET, a commercialized version of the CERT computer vision software, for facial feature extraction (http://www.emotient.com/products). Like CERT, FACET provides estimates of the likelihood estimates for the presence of nineteen AUs as well as head pose (orientation) and position information detected from video. Data from FACET was temporally aligned with affect observations in small windows. We tested five different window sizes (3, 6, 9, 12, and 20 seconds) for creation of features. Features were created by aggregating values obtained from FACET (AUs, orientation and position of the face) in a window of time leading up to each observation using maximum, median, and standard deviation. For example, with a six-second window we created three features from the AU4 channel (brow lower) by taking the maximum, median, and standard deviation of AU4 likelihood within the six seconds leading up to an affect observation. In all there were 78 facial features.

A quarter (25%) of the instances were discarded because FACET was not able to register the face and thus could not estimate the presence of AUs. Poor lighting, extreme head pose or position, occlusions from hand-to-face gestures, and rapid movements can all cause face registration errors; these issues were not uncommon due to the game-like nature of the software and the active behaviors of the young students in this study. We also removed 9% of instances because the window of time leading up to the observation contained less than one second (13 frames) of data in which the face could be detected.

We also used features computed from gross body movement present in the videos as well. Body movement was calculated by measuring the proportion of pixels in each video frame that differed from a continuously updated estimate of the background image generated from the four previous frames (illustration in Figure 2). Previous work has shown that features derived using this technique correlate with relevant affective states including boredom, confusion, and frustration [11]. We created three body movement features using the maximum, median, and standard deviation of the proportion of different pixels within the window of time leading up to an observation, similar to the method used to create FACET features.

Figure 2. Silhouette visualization of motion detected in a video.

Tolerance analysis was used to eliminate features with high multicollinearity (variance inflation factor > 5) [1]. Feature selection was used to obtain a sparser, more diagnostic set of features for classification. RELIEF-F [27] was run on the *training* data in order to rank features. A proportion of the highest ranked features were then used in the models (.1, .2, .3, .4, .5, and .75 proportions were tested). Feature selection was performed using nested cross-validation on training data only. Ten iterations of feature selection were run on the training data, using data from a randomly chosen 67% of students within the training set for each iteration.

Supervised Learning. We built a detector for the overall five-way affect discrimination (bored, confused, delighted, engaged, and frustrated). In addition to the five-way classification, we also built separate detectors for each state. Building individual detectors for each state allows the parameters (e.g., window size, features used) to be optimized for that particular affective state. A two-class approach was used for each affective state, where that affective state was discriminated from all others. For example, engaged was discriminated from all frustrated, bored, delighted, and confused instances combined (referred to as "all other"). Behaviors were grouped into two classes: 1) off task behaviors, and 2) both on task behaviors and on task conversation (i.e. not off task).

Classification	AUC	Accuracy	Classifier	No. Instances	No. Features	Window Size (secs)
Five-Way Affect	0.655	54%	Bayes Net	1209	38	9
Bored vs. Other	0.610	64%	Classification Via Clustering	1305	20	12
Confused vs. Other	0.649	74%	Bayes Net	1293	15	12
Delighted vs. Other	0.867	83%	Updateable Naïve Bayes	1003	24	3
Engaged vs. Other	0.679	64%	Bayes Net	1228	51	9
Frustrated vs. Other	0.631	62%	Bayes Net	1132	51	6
Off Task	0.816	81%	Logistic Regression	1381	15	12

Table 1. Details and results for classifiers.

The affective and behavior distributions lead to large class imbalances (e.g. .04 vs. .96 class priors in the bored vs. all other classification). Two different sampling techniques were used (on training data only) to compensate for class imbalance. These included downsampling (removal of random instances from the majority class) and synthetic oversampling (with SMOTE; [7]) to create equal class sizes. SMOTE creates synthetic training data by interpolating feature values between an instance and randomly chosen nearest neighbors. The distributions in the testing data were not changed, to preserve the validity of the results.

We built classification models for these seven discriminations (overall, five affective state models, and off task vs. on task), using 14 different classifiers including support vector machines, C4.5 trees, Bayesian classifiers, and others in the Waikato Environment for Knowledge Analysis (WEKA), a machine learning tool [22].

Models were cross-validated at the student level. Data from 66% of randomly-chosen students were used to train each classifier and the remaining students' data were used to test its performance. Each model was each trained and tested over 150 iterations with random students chosen each time, to help amortize random sampling errors. This helps models generalize to new learners since training and testing data sets are student-independent.

RESULTS

The best results for affect and off-task detection are presented in Table 1. The number of instances refers to the total number of instances that could be used to train the model, including negative examples. This number varies from model to model based on the window size because shorter windows have less data and are thus slightly less likely to contain at least one second of valid data (as stated earlier, windows with less than one second of valid data were not used).

Accuracy (recognition rate) for affect detectors varies widely in terms of percentage of instances correctly classified. However, accuracy is not a good performance metric for classification in situations where class distributions are highly skewed, as they are in this data. For example, delight occurs 2.3% of the time, which means a detector that simply guesses "Not delighted" for every single instance would have 97.7% accuracy. Other metrics such as Cohen's Kappa also provide unstable estimates when class distractions are widely skewed [24]. AUC is the recommended metric for skewed data and is used here as the primary measure of detection accuracy.

Area under the ROC curve (AUC) is only defined for binary classes, so we created an aggregate AUC by calculating AUC for each class versus all others within the five-way discrimination and averaging the results (see [18] for an overview of this and other methods of calculating AUC for multiple classes). The overall five-way discrimination between all affective states performed above chance with mean AUC = .655 (chance AUC = .500). For individual detectors, classification performed above chance for each affective state and off-task behavior.

Of particular note is the fact that classification was successful for infrequent states despite large class imbalances. Balanced classification performance is reflected in the confusion matrices for these states. For example, Table 2 shows the confusion matrix for delight, one of the most imbalanced affective states. Note that prior proportion of delighted is 2.9% rather than 2.3% as in the original observations because of instances removed due to face detection failures.

Actual	Classified		Priors
	Delighted	*All Other*	
Delighted	.685 (hit)	.315 (miss)	.029
All Other	.169 (false alarm)	.831 (correct rejection)	.971

Table 2. Confusion matrix for delighted affect.

The delight detector illustrated the effectiveness of using the SMOTE oversampling technique on the training data in order to improve model fit. In fact, SMOTE (as opposed to the alternatives, downsampling the training data or using no balancing techniques) improved the results for all of the individual models except engaged concentration, which was already a relatively balanced discrimination. It comprises 78% of the affect observations, so it is not surprising that oversampling the training set did not improve performance for that particular affective state.

Figure 3 further illustrates the effect of using SMOTE on the affect and off-task detection models. Note that the mean hit (true positive) rate improves noticeably for models built without SMOTE, though with a slightly lower correct rejection rate. This effect arises because the detectors trained without SMOTE are biased towards recognizing the majority class (i.e. "all other" for all affective states except engagement). On the other hand, detectors built with SMOTE have equal numbers of both the affective state and the "other" instances, so they are better trained to recognize the affective state of interest.

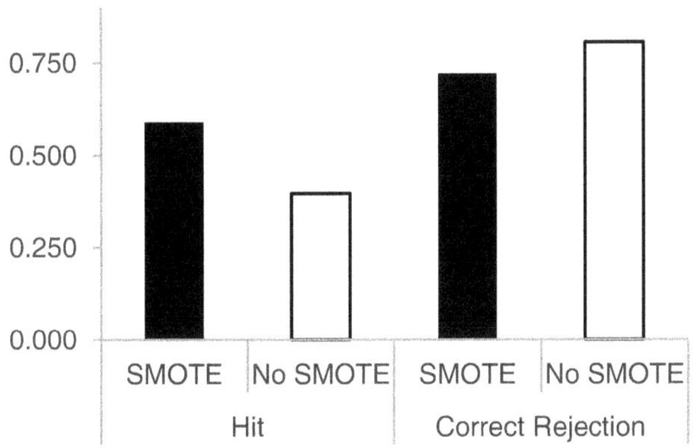

Figure 3. Comparison of mean hit rates and correct rejection rates for best models built with and without using SMOTE.

We also investigated the relationship between window size and classification performance in further detail. Figure 4 presents the performance of the best model for each affective state at different window sizes, which illustrates clear trends in the data.

Classification accuracy was not very dependent on the window size for boredom, engagement, and frustration (dotted lines in Figure 4), but it was clearly relevant for confusion, delight, and off task behavior (solid lines in Figure 4). The performance decrease for larger windows sizes in the detection of delight may be due to differences in the inherent temporal dynamics of expressive behavior for the different states [14]. For example, expressions of delight may last just a few seconds while confusion might be expressed for a longer period of time, though further research is needed to study this issue more thoroughly. Nevertheless, our results show that varying the window size between different detectors was an important consideration for some affective states. [1]

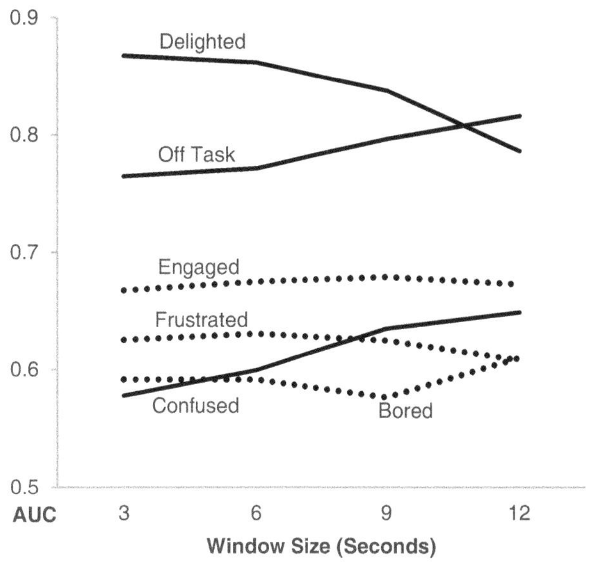

Figure 4. Detection results across window sizes.

DISCUSSION

Affect detection is a crucial component for affect-sensitive user interfaces, which aspire to improve students' engagement and learning by dynamically responding to affect. The inexpensive, ubiquitous nature of webcams on computers makes facial expression recognition an attractive modality to consider for affect detection. We expanded on the considerable body of vision-based affect detection research by building detectors for learning-centered affective states using data collected in the wild. Specifically, we have shown that affect detection is possible with data collected in a computer-enabled classroom environment in which students were subject to distractions, uncontrolled lighting conditions, and other factors which complicate affect detection. In this section, we discuss major findings, limitations of the present study, and implications of our affect detectors for future work with affect-sensitive interfaces.

Major Findings. Our key contribution was the development and validation of face-based detectors for learning-centered affect in a noisy school environment. We demonstrated that automatic detection of boredom, confusion, delight, engagement, frustration, and off-task behavior in the wild was possible for students using an educational game in a computer-enabled classroom environment—though many challenges exist for these classification tasks, such as classroom distractions and large imbalances in affective distributions.

[1] We also built models with a 20 second window. However, classification performance for those models was no better than other models so they were not further analyzed.

With respect to class distractions, students in the current study fidgeted, talked with one another, asked questions, left to go to the bathroom, and even occasionally used their cellphones (against classroom policy). In some situations multiple students crowded around the same screen to view something that another student had done. In short, students behaved as can be expected in a school computer lab. Furthermore, lighting conditions were inconsistent across students, in part due to placement of computers. Students' faces in some videos were well-illuminated, while they were barely visible in others. We were able to create detectors without excluding any of these difficult but realistic situations, except where faces could not be automatically detected at all in the video. In fact, we were unable to register the face in 34% of instances using modern computer vision techniques—an illustration of just how much uncontrolled lighting and the way students move, occlude, and pose their faces can make affect detection difficult in the wild.

Creating one set of parameters to use for all models is attractive for the sake of simplicity. However, we found differences in detection performance for some classifications with respect to window size. Confusion and off-task classifications worked better with larger window sizes, while delighted classification was better with a smaller window. Classifiers and feature selection parameters varied as well. This suggests that there are important differences in ideal parameters for different models, and that better performance can be achieved by tailoring models to their specific classification tasks.

Imbalance in affective state distributions is another challenge for affect detectors. This was a major concern with the present data, as three of the states occurred at rates less than 5%, while the most frequent state occurred at a rate nearing 80%. Despite this extreme skew, we were able to synthetically oversample the training data to create models that were not heavily biased against predicting the minority states. This is particularly important for future applications to affect-sensitive educational interfaces because detectors must be able to recognize relatively infrequent affective states that are important to learning (e.g., confusion) [12]. Infrequent does not mean inconsequential, however, since one or two episodes of intense frustration can disrupt an entire learning experience.

Limitations. This study is not without its limitations. First, the sample size is limited for some affective states, due in part to the difficulty of collecting data in the wild. This limitation was partially overcome by using SMOTE to create synthetic training data, but oversampling is not a perfect substitute for the diversity of genuine data. Second, though the students in this study varied widely across some demographic variables, they were all approximately the same age and in the same location. A further study testing detectors on data with more variability in age and geographic distribution would be useful for determining the level to which results might generalize to interfaces targeted at a different group of students, such as elementary school students. Third, the distribution of affective states experienced may be dependent on the interface used. The interface in this study was game-based, which may increase engagement and decrease the incidence of other affective states compared to some other types of interfaces. Similarly, the observation method used (BROMP) requires observers to be in the room, which could influence students displays of affect similar to the Hawthorne effect [8]. This could be addressed by an additional study comparing the incidence of affective states experienced by students in the wild using a variety of different educational interfaces and affect collection methodologies.

Towards Affect-Sensitive Intelligent Interfaces. The detectors we created will be used to create intelligent instructional strategies towards developing an affect-sensitive version of Physics Playground. Separate strategies will be used for each affective state and off-task behavior. For example, when the detectors determine that a student is engaged or delighted, Physics Playground may not intervene at all. Confusion and frustration offer intervention opportunities in the form of hints or revisiting introductory material related to the concepts in the current problem. If the student has recently been frustrated and unable to complete problems, an easier problem might be suggested. Conversely, a more difficult problem might be appropriate if the student has not been challenged by recently completed problems. Boredom might be addressed by suggesting that the student attempt a new problem or by calibrating difficulty.

These aforementioned strategies have the goal of improving learning, but much work remains to be done in determining what types of interventions should be used in this context and how frequently they should be applied. Special considerations must also be given to the probability of spurious detections (false alarms) when designing and implementing these strategies since incorrect interventions could cause confusion or annoyance. In particular, interventions must be fail-soft so that learning is not negatively impacted by the strategies. Subtle strategies, such as re-ordering the problems to display an easier problem after a frustrating experience, may prove more effective. Future work will be needed to test a variety of intervention strategies in order to determine the most effective way to respond to the sensed affect.

It is our hope that affect detection will one day lead to intelligent, adaptive educational interfaces for use in computer-enabled classrooms. The research presented in this paper represents an important initial step toward accomplishing this goal by demonstrating techniques that can be used to detect students' affect in a noisy real-world environment.

ACKNOWLEDGMENTS

This research was supported by the National Science Foundation (NSF) (DRL 1235958) and the Bill & Melinda Gates Foundation. Any opinions, findings and conclusions, or recommendations expressed in this paper are those of the authors and do not necessarily reflect the views of the NSF or the Bill & Melinda Gates Foundation.

REFERENCES

1. Allison, P.D. *Multiple regression: A primer.* Pine Forge Press, 1999.
2. Arroyo, I., Cooper, D.G., Burleson, W., Woolf, B.P., Muldner, K., and Christopherson, R. Emotion sensors go to school. *AIED*, (2009), 17–24.
3. Baker, R., Gowda, S.M., Wixon, M., et al. Towards sensor-free affect detection in cognitive tutor algebra. *Proceedings of the 5th International Conference on Educational Data Mining*, (2012), 126–133.
4. Baker, R., Rodrigo, M.M.T., and Xolocotzin, U.E. The dynamics of affective transitions in simulation problem-solving environments. In A.C.R. Paiva, R. Prada and R.W. Picard, eds., *Affective Computing and Intelligent Interaction.* Springer, Berlin Heidelberg, 2007, 666–677.
5. Bosch, N., Chen, Y., and D'Mello, S. It's written on your face: detecting affective states from facial expressions while learning computer programming. *Proceedings of the 12th International Conference on Intelligent Tutoring Systems (ITS 2014)*, Switzerland: Springer International Publishing (2014), 39–44.
6. Calvo, R.A. and D'Mello, S. Affect detection: An interdisciplinary review of models, methods, and their applications. *IEEE Transactions on Affective Computing 1*, 1 (2010), 18–37.
7. Chawla, N.V., Bowyer, K.W., Hall, L.O., and Kegelmeyer, W.P. SMOTE: synthetic minority over-sampling technique. *Journal of Artificial Intelligence Research 16*, (2011), 321–357.
8. Cook, D.L. The Hawthorne effect in educational research. *Phi Delta Kappan*, (1962), 116–122.
9. Craig, S., Graesser, A., Sullins, J., and Gholson, B. Affect and learning: An exploratory look into the role of affect in learning with AutoTutor. *Journal of Educational Media 29*, 3 (2004), 241–250.
10. Dhall, A., Goecke, R., Joshi, J., Wagner, M., and Gedeon, T. Emotion recognition in the wild challenge 2013. *Proceedings of the 15th ACM on International Conference on Multimodal Interaction*, ACM (2013), 509–516.
11. D'Mello, S. Dynamical emotions: bodily dynamics of affect during problem solving. *Proceedings of the 33rd Annual Conference of the Cognitive Science Society*, (2011).
12. D'Mello, S. A selective meta-analysis on the relative incidence of discrete affective states during learning with technology. *Journal of Educational Psychology 105*, 4 (2013), 1082–1099.
13. D'Mello, S., Blanchard, N., Baker, R., Ocumpaugh, J., and Brawner, K. I feel your pain: A selective review of affect-sensitive instructional strategies. In R. Sottilare, A. Graesser, X. Hu and B. Goldberg, eds., *Design Recommendations for Intelligent Tutoring Systems - Volume 2: Instructional Management.* 2014, 35–48.
14. D'Mello, S. and Graesser, A. The half-life of cognitive-affective states during complex learning. *Cognition & Emotion 25*, 7 (2011), 1299–1308.
15. D'Mello, S. and Graesser, A. Dynamics of affective states during complex learning. *Learning and Instruction 22*, 2 (2012), 145–157.
16. Ekman, P., Freisen, W.V., and Ancoli, S. Facial signs of emotional experience. *Journal of Personality and Social Psychology 39*, 6 (1980), 1125–1134.
17. Ekman, P. and Friesen, W.V. Facial action coding system. *Consulting Psychologist Press*, (1978), Palo Alto, CA.
18. Fawcett, T. An introduction to ROC analysis. *Pattern Recognition Letters 27*, 8 (2006), 861–874.
19. Frenzel, A.C., Pekrun, R., and Goetz, T. Perceived learning environment and students' emotional experiences: A multilevel analysis of mathematics classrooms. *Learning and Instruction 17*, 5 (2007), 478–493.
20. Grafsgaard, J.F., Wiggins, J.B., Boyer, K.E., Wiebe, E.N., and Lester, J.C. Automatically recognizing facial indicators of frustration: A learning-centric analysis. (2013).
21. Hernandez, J., Hoque, M. (Ehsan), Drevo, W., and Picard, R.W. Mood meter: Counting smiles in the wild. *Proceedings of the 2012 ACM Conference on Ubiquitous Computing*, ACM (2012), 301–310.
22. Holmes, G., Donkin, A., and Witten, I.H. WEKA: a machine learning workbench. *Proceedings of the Second Australian and New Zealand Conference on Intelligent Information Systems*, (1994), 357–361.
23. Hoque, M.E., McDuff, D., and Picard, R.W. Exploring temporal patterns in classifying frustrated and delighted smiles. *IEEE Transactions on Affective Computing 3*, 3 (2012), 323–334.
24. Jeni, L., Cohn, J.F., and de la Torre, F. Facing imbalanced data–Recommendations for the use of performance metrics. *2013 Humaine Association Conference on Affective Computing and Intelligent Interaction (ACII)*, (2013), 245–251.

25. Kapoor, A., Burleson, W., and Picard, R.W. Automatic prediction of frustration. *International Journal of Human-Computer Studies 65*, 8 (2007), 724–736.

26. Kapoor, A. and Picard, R.W. Multimodal affect recognition in learning environments. *Proceedings of the 13th Annual ACM International Conference on Multimedia*, ACM (2005), 677–682.

27. Kononenko, I. Estimating attributes: Analysis and extensions of RELIEF. In F. Bergadano and L.D. Raedt, eds., *Machine Learning: ECML-94*. Springer, Berlin Heidelberg, 1994, 171–182.

28. Lepper, M.R., Woolverton, M., Mumme, D.L., and Gurtner, J. Motivational techniques of expert human tutors: Lessons for the design of computer-based tutors. *Computers as cognitive tools 1993*, (1993), 75–105.

29. Littlewort, G., Whitehill, J., Wu, T., et al. The computer expression recognition toolbox (CERT). *2011 IEEE International Conference on Automatic Face Gesture Recognition and Workshops (FG 2011)*, (2011), 298–305.

30. McDaniel, B.T., D'Mello, S., King, B.G., Chipman, P., Tapp, K., and Graesser, A. Facial features for affective state detection in learning environments. *Proceedings of the 29th Annual Cognitive Science Society*, (2007), 467–472.

31. McDuff, D., El Kaliouby, R., Senechal, T., Amr, M., Cohn, J.F., and Picard, R. Affectiva-MIT facial expression dataset (AM-FED): Naturalistic and spontaneous facial expressions collected in-the-wild. *2013 IEEE Conference on Computer Vision and Pattern Recognition Workshops (CVPRW)*, (2013), 881–888.

32. McDuff, D., El Kaliouby, R., Senechal, T., Demirdjian, D., and Picard, R. Automatic measurement of ad preferences from facial responses gathered over the Internet. *Image and Vision Computing 32*, 10 (2014), 630–640.

33. Mota, S. and Picard, R.W. Automated posture analysis for detecting learner's interest level. *Conference on Computer Vision and Pattern Recognition Workshop (CVPRW '03)*, (2003), 49–56.

34. Ocumpaugh, J., Baker, R., Kamarainen, A., and Metcalf, S. Modifying field observation methods on the fly: Creative metanarrative and disgust in an environmental MUVE. *Proceedings of the 4th International Workshop on Personalization Approaches in Learning Environments (PALE), held in conjunction with the 22nd International Conference on User Modeling, Adaptation, and Personalization (UMAP 2014)*, (2014), 49–54.

35. Ocumpaugh, J., Baker, R., and Rodrigo, M.M.T. *Baker-Rodrigo observation method protocol (BROMP) 1.0. Training manual version 1.0.* Technical Report. New York, NY: EdLab. Manila, Philippines: Ateneo Laboratory for the Learning Sciences, 2012.

36. Porayska-Pomsta, K., Mavrikis, M., D'Mello, S., Conati, C., and Baker, R. Knowledge elicitation methods for affect modelling in education. *International Journal of Artificial Intelligence in Education 22*, 3 (2013), 107–140.

37. Reisenzein, R., Studtmann, M., and Horstmann, G. Coherence between emotion and facial expression: Evidence from laboratory experiments. *Emotion Review 5*, 1 (2013), 16–23.

38. Schutz, P. and Pekrun, R., eds. *Emotion in Education.* Academic Press, San Diego, CA, 2007.

39. Senechal, T., Bailly, K., and Prevost, L. Impact of action unit detection in automatic emotion recognition. *Pattern Analysis and Applications 17*, 1 (2014), 51–67.

40. Shute, V.J., Ventura, M., and Kim, Y.J. Assessment and learning of qualitative physics in Newton's Playground. *The Journal of Educational Research 106*, 6 (2013), 423–430.

41. Whitehill, J., Serpell, Z., Lin, Y.-C., Foster, A., and Movellan, J.R. The faces of engagement: Automatic recognition of student engagement from facial expressions. *IEEE Transactions on Affective Computing 5*, 1 (2014), 86–98.

42. Zeng, Z., Pantic, M., Roisman, G.I., and Huang, T.S. A survey of affect recognition methods: Audio, visual, and spontaneous expressions. *IEEE Transactions on Pattern Analysis and Machine Intelligence 31*, 1 (2009), 39–58.

Exploring Peripheral Physiology as a Predictor of Perceived Relevance in Information Retrieval

Oswald Barral[1], Manuel J. A. Eugster[2], Tuukka Ruotsalo[3], Michiel M. Spapé[3], Ilkka Kosunen[1], Niklas Ravaja[3,4], Samuel Kaski[1,2], Giulio Jacucci[1,3]
Helsinki Institute for Information Technology HIIT
[1]University of Helsinki, Department of Computer Science, PO Box 68, 00014, Finland
[2]Aalto University, Department of Computer Science, PO Box 15400, 00076, Finland
[3]Aalto University, PO Box 15600, 00076, Finland
[4]University of Helsinki, Department of Social Research, PO Box 54, 00014, Finland
first.last@hiit.fi

ABSTRACT
Peripheral physiological signals, as obtained using electrodermal activity and facial electromyography over the corrugator supercilii muscle, are explored as indicators of perceived relevance in information retrieval tasks. An experiment with 40 participants is reported, in which these physiological signals are recorded while participants perform information retrieval tasks. Appropriate feature engineering is defined, and the feature space is explored. The results indicate that features in the window of 4 to 6 seconds after the relevance judgment for electrodermal activity, and from 1 second before to 2 seconds after the relevance judgment for corrugator supercilii activity, are associated with the users' perceived relevance of information items. A classifier verified the predictive power of the features and showed up to 14% improvement predicting relevance. Our research can help the design of intelligent user interfaces for information retrieval that can detect the user's perceived relevance from physiological signals and complement or replace conventional relevance feedback.

Author Keywords
Electrodermal Activity; Corrugator Supercilii; Information Retrieval; Peripheral Physiology; Relevance Prediction; Implicit Relevance Feedback

ACM Classification Keywords
H.3.3. Information Search and Retrieval: Relevance feedback; H.1.2. User/Machine Systems: Human factors; H.5.2. User Interfaces: Evaluation/Methodology

INTRODUCTION
Information retrieval research relies on methods that are able to distinguish relevant from irrelevant information. These methods are based on obtaining relevance assessments from users when they are examining specific information items. The relevance assessments can then be utilized in feedback loops to specify the information need in subsequent iterations [13], direct a search using visual interfaces [24, 29], or simply gather relevance assessments from users for evaluation purposes.

IUI 2015, March 29–April 1, 2015, Atlanta, GA, USA.

http://dx.doi.org/10.1145/2678025.2701389

One way to obtain relevance assessments is implicit feedback by monitoring the user, that is, gathering user data in an unobtrusive way while users are engaged with an information retrieval system. Implicit monitoring has been found to be one of the most useful sources for acquiring relevance assessments from the user as it is does not require users to explicitly provide relevance judgments [18]. Previous research has found evidence for implicit behavioral measures, such as dwell-time (the time the user spends to examine an information item) and click-through activity, being useful predictors of perceived relevance [1, 14].

There is rising interest in implicit signals that could provide information about the user's perceived relevance without the requirement to rely on behavioral measures. Physiological signals that can capture users' emotions, attention, and focus could help information retrieval systems determine the relevance of the content for the user without the need to rely on behavioral measures that are dependent on the user interface and interaction design.

This paper reports on an experiment with 40 users, in which the use of two of the most applicable physiological signals, electrodermal activity (skin conductance) and corrugator supercilii activity (brow muscle) were studied as a potential source of implicit signals associated with perceived relevance. These peripheral physiological signals were chosen for this study because they are low cost, unobtrusive, and have been previously associated with psychophysiological functions that could be associated with perceived relevance [23, 30, 31, 33]. The signals were recorded in response to textual content shown during an information retrieval task, their association with perceived relevance was explored, and a classification experiment was conducted to predict relevance for unseen users and information items.

We analyzed the raw signals to study whether the physiological signals could be associated with perceived relevance. Then a set of features was engineered, and a set of important features was selected by exploratory data analysis. Finally, a classifier trained with the chosen features verified the power of the physiological signals for predicting relevance for unseen participants. The main findings of these experiments are the following:

1. The best-suited time windows for relevance prediction from electrodermal activity were found to be from 4 seconds to 6 seconds after the relevance judgment.
2. The best-suited time windows for relevance prediction from corrugator supercilii activity were found to be from 1 second before to 2 seconds after the relevance judgment.
3. A classifier verified the predictive power of the physiological signals with an improvement of 14% against a random baseline.

The rest of the paper is organized as follows. First, we review the background related to relevance feedback and to the use of peripheral physiology in information retrieval settings. Then we describe the experimental study, basic signal analysis, feature engineering, and the results of the exploratory feature analysis. Then we explain the classification setup and characterize the power of the signals for relevance predictions. Finally, we conclude with a discussion and future work. Figure 1 illustrates the analysis workflow, from the data collection to the predictive models.

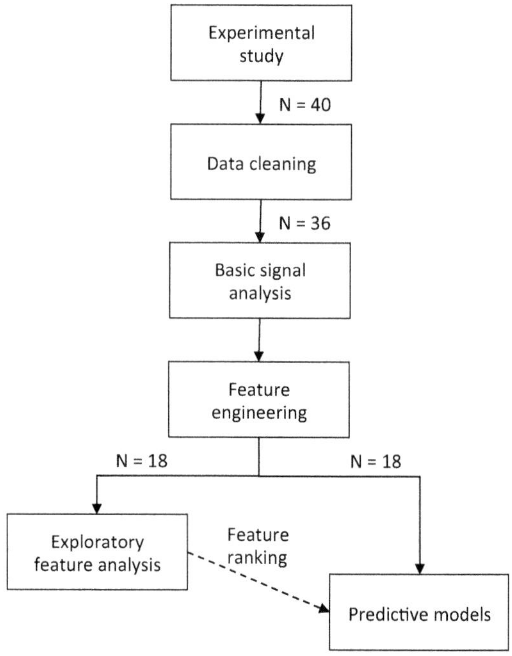

Figure 1. Workflow of the analysis. Physiological data of 40 participants was recorded during the experimental study. Data of four of the participants were rejected due to misplaced or loose sensors. Then, basic signal analysis was carried out in order to examine the association between the physiological signals and the perceived relevance of information items. Then, a set of 25 features was extracted from each of the signals, and the participants were split into two groups of the same size. The first group was used to explore the feature space and generate a feature ranking, which was used to train three predictive models. The models were then tested on the group of unseen participants.

BACKGROUND

Detecting perceived relevance of information presented for users is a central task of interactive information retrieval systems [22]. The perceived relevance can then be used to gather relevance assessments for evaluation purposes [16], direct a search in an interactive loop with the system [25], disambiguate the user's information need [27], or even to measure the user's satisfaction with the information retrieval system [9]. Relevance detection can be based on either explicit or implicit signals and is called explicit feedback and implicit feedback, respectively.

Explicit feedback is a robust method, as it selects relevant and irrelevant information based on direct user interaction [20]. Unfortunately, explicit feedback is operationalized at the expense of users' cognitive resources [16], as the user has to explicitly give commands for the information retrieval system to indicate which information is relevant or irrelevant. Explicit feedback techniques also suffer from a trade-off regarding the user's willingness to invest time to examine the returned information because the relevance feedback can only be targeted to contents that are explicitly judged by users. Eventually, as the task complexity increases the cognitive resources required from the users, the process of relevance assessment may turn into a non-trivial task [20].

Despite its robustness, explicit feedback is therefore often practically insufficient due to the cognitive burden that it causes for the user [17]. Implicit relevance feedback has been proposed to overcome this cognitive burden. The idea of implicit relevance feedback is that relevance of an information item is inferred from interactional data during the user's natural interaction with the search user interface [15].

Implicit feedback [18] has been proposed to obtain relevance assessments by passively observing searchers as they interact with the system. Implicit feedback has been implemented either through the use of surrogate measures based on interaction with documents (such as reading time, scrolling, or document retention) or using other interaction data. Implicit feedback has been shown to have mixed effectiveness because the measures that are good indicators of user interest are often affected by several factors, making the inferences drawn from user interaction not always valid [34].

Affective feedback is a specific type of implicit feedback, and has recently been under active research with a focus on using affective signals to detect the relevance of information [3]. Affective feedback is based on the idea that physiological signals are often associated with cognitive functions relevant to perceiving relevance [4]. Recently, preliminary evidence supporting a combination of basic implicit signals with physiological signals has been reported [21]. One of the main advantages of using physiological signals as implicit input, compared with traditional implicit monitoring, is that these signals can be detected within seconds or even milliseconds after the information items are shown to the user. Physiological signals have been shown to correlate with attention, focus, and semantic memory performance [6, 19], becoming a promising source for acquiring implicit user feedback.

Electrodermal activity (EDA), also known as galvanic skin response (GSR) or skin conductance response (SCR), among others, is a physiological signal that measures the changes in the electrical properties of the skin, due to the varying level of sweat-induced moisture. EDA has commonly been used to measure the activation of the sympathetic nervous system; therefore, it has proved to be a good indicator of the level of psychological, physiological and emotional arousal [2]. More recently, the short-term (phasic) EDA response has proved to be a useful indicator of stimulus novelty, intensity, emotional content, and significance [23]. Therefore, electrodermal activity has potential to be associated with relevance judgments while it is possible to be captured with very low cost and nonintrusive setup. For example, EDA sensors can be mounted in a computer mouse.

Facial Electromyography (fEMG) is the technique of measuring electrical activity associated with contractions of the facial muscle fibers. One of the muscle groups measured through facial electromyography is the corrugator supercilii muscle (brow muscle). The corrugator supercilii activity (CSA) is a physiological signal particularly promising for determining the relevance of information because it can be used to index negative valence, or frowning, mental workload, fatigue, and compensatory mental effort [30, 31, 33]. Corrugator supercilii activity also increases during tasks requiring heightened effortful attention [6]. As with EDA, it is possible to monitor CSA in a very low cost and nonintrusive setup, as it can be measured even via computer vision.

While some physiological signals have been found to be associated with cognitive functions related to perceived relevance, complete information retrieval systems that make use of physiological computing are still at an early stage. Recent work has addressed implicit inference of relevance using peripheral physiology [5], physiological and affective measures [21], or brain signals [8]. Nevertheless, it is still unclear which signals are the most useful and how they should be used (e.g., what are the best time windows for physiology-based relevance prediction). Our study seeks to address the abovementioned issues by focusing on two signals from the peripheral physiology and exploring their association with perceived relevance. Moreover, we study the predictive power of these signals for automatically detecting relevance.

EXPERIMENTAL STUDY

The present study was designed to 1) investigate how the perceived relevance of users of an information retrieval system is associated with peripheral physiology, 2) study whether perceived relevance can be predicted from features extracted from physiological signals, and 3) determine at what point in time the signals are best suited to indicate the perception of relevance. We recorded electrodermal activity (EDA) and corrugator supercilii activity (CSA) while participants were examining information items returned by a real information retrieval system.

Participants

Forty participants, 34 males and 6 females, participated in the study. We ensured that participants had previous experience in browsing scientific databases and that they were not under psychopharmacological medication. The age of the participants ranged from 21 years old to 47 years old (Mean = 28.17, Median = 26.5). Most of them were post-graduate (37) and the rest were undergraduate students. Only one of the participants reported being a native English speaker, and 17 different mother tongues were reported. Nevertheless, the overall English reading skills were self-reported as advanced. Participants reported themselves to be physically and mentally healthy.

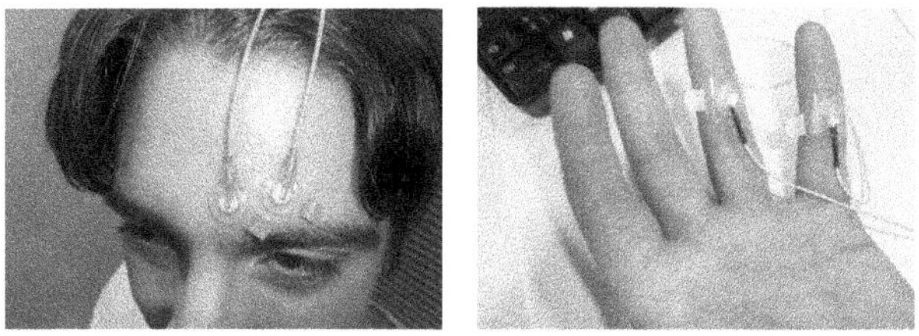

Figure 2. Physiological sensor setup. Sensors were placed in sites overlying the left corrugator supercilii muscle (left) and in the medial phalanges of the participant's left ring and little fingers to measure electrodermal activity (right).

Materials

The setup of the physiological sensors is illustrated in Figure 2. A QuickAmp (BrainProducts GmbH., Germany) amplifier recorded electrodermal activity (EDA) and corrugator supercilii activity (CSA) at a sample rate of 1000 Hz.

CSA sensors were filled with SYNAPSE conductive electrode cream (Kustomer Kinetics Inc., USA) and placed on sites overlying the left corrugator supercilii muscle regions as recommended by Fridlund and Cicoppo [10]. EDA electrodes were filled with TD-246 skin conductance electrode paste (Med Associates Inc., USA) and attached to the middle phalanges of the ring and little fingers of each participant's left hand after her hands were washed with soap and water [7].

The stimulus was presented in the Google Chrome browser. A custom JavaScript code was injected to record the exact time in milliseconds, in relation to the PC clock, when each event took place. To ascertain the synchrony between the browser timestamps and the physiological data, every second the experiment PC sent a synchronization pulse through the parallel port to the QuickAmp amplifier, and each of the browser events was synchronized to the closest pulse.

Task

The task was designed so that the participants could perform an actual search on a real topic of their interest, while still controlling for as many confounding variables as possible, by presenting only one search result at a time in the middle of the screen. The participants were presented with a search box and instructed to perform a query on a topic they were familiar with. They were furthermore informed that they were browsing a scientific database and consequently encouraged to select topics accordingly.

The system presented, in randomized order, six abstract snippets. Of these six snippets, three were always actual search results (relevant to the participant's query) and the other three were randomly generated (irrelevant to the participant's

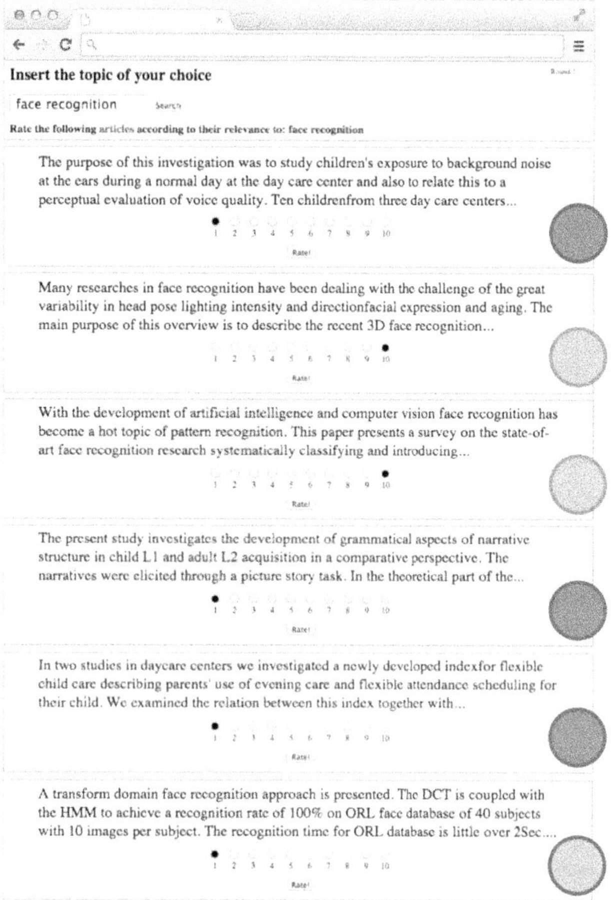

Figure 3. Experimental task and user interface. The participant submits a query, and the system retrieves six abstract snippets of which three are relevant and three are irrelevant. These are presented for the participant one at a time in a randomized order. The participant rates each result using a 1–10 scale. This is repeated for a total of six queries. The figure shows one specific query within a session where the participant searched for "face recognition." The rating scales show the participant judgments. The inner colors of the discs show the ground truth of the abstracts as returned by the search engine (green denotes *relevant*, red denotes *irrelevant*). The outer rings of the discs show the binarized participant judgments. For the first five abstracts, the participant rated according to the ground truth. The last relevant abstract was, according to the participant's judgment, irrelevant.

query). Each abstract was shown until the participant responded by rating the relevance on a scale from 1 to 10, which took ca. 8 seconds on average. Then, the snippet was replaced with the next snippet until all 6 were rated and the participant was asked to perform a search on the next topic. The experiment was completed after the participant rated 36 abstracts (6 topics x 6 abstract snippets).

Search Engine and Content Database

We built a custom search engine and user interface to have full control of the retrieval process, the presentation of results, and the content indexed by the retrieval system. We used a state-of-the-art unigram language modeling approach with Bayesian Dirichlet smoothing to rank the results [36]. The relevant results were retrieved based on the ranking provided by the ranking model directly. The irrelevant results were selected randomly with an additional boolean constraint to exclude results that contained words from the participant's query.

The content items were from a scientific article database consisting of over 50,000,000 articles from the Web of Science prepared by Thomson Reuters, Inc. and from the Digital Libraries of the ACM, the IEEE, and Springer. The first 40 words of the abstracts of the articles were used as result snippets, which we had found in pilot studies to be sufficient for the participants to decide whether the article is relevant.

Procedure

At the beginning of the session, the participants were briefed as to the procedure and purpose of the experiment, before signing informed consent. They were furthermore informed of their right to withdraw from the experiment at any time without any negative consequence. No training session was provided prior to the task, as the interaction with the system was particularly intuitive. Participants could first type a query, such as "face recognition" as shown in Figure 3. Then, the search engine returned six articles, three relevant and three irrelevant. The abstract snippets of the article were then shown for the participant one at the time in a randomized order. The participants then read the abstract snippet and was asked to rate the relevance of the article as soon as they made a decision on the relevance, without the need of reading the text until the end. After rating, the next article was shown. The procedure was repeated for a total of six user-selected topics. After the experiment, the participants were asked to fill in an online survey regarding their background information, and their participation was compensated with two movie tickets.

Data Cleaning

After visual inspection, data from four out of the 40 participants had to be rejected due to loosened or misplaced sensors. The data were binarized to irrelevant and relevant categories (illustrated in Figure 3 by the clicked radio buttons and colored outer rings of the discs). When the relevance judgment explicitly acquired from the participant was less than 4, it was categorized as an irrelevant judgment, and when the relevance judgment was higher than 7, it was categorized as a relevant judgment. Other trials were not categorized, as the judgments were interpreted as ambiguous and the psychophysiological responses associated to them were likely to be misleading.

The physiological signals were first filtered to reduce noise and artifacts. For electrodermal activity we used a low-pass filter with the cut-off at 5 Hz, and for corrugator supercilii activity, a high-pass filter with the cut-off at 10 Hz. To normalize the data, the signals for each participant were then divided by the standard deviation of the signal for that participant.

BASIC SIGNAL ANALYSIS

In order to get an idea on whether there was information about perceived relevance in the physiological signals, we started by analyzing the raw signals. We looked at an 8-second window time-locked to the moment when the participant gave the explicit judgment. The window spanned from 2 seconds before to 6 seconds after the explicit rating. For every second within this window, we computed the average signal value (i.e., average downsampling), resulting in eight values for each trial.

For both EDA and CSA signals, we executed the following analysis. Within each participant, we aggregated relevant and irrelevant trials with both the arithmetic mean and the more robust median. For a basic overview, we then computed the grand average, i.e., the mean or median of the participant-specific mean or median values for each second of the time window. For a more in-depth analysis, we computed repeated-measures analysis of variance (ANOVA) based on the mean or median values, with two-level factor "relevance" (relevant vs. irrelevant) and eight-level factor "time" (eight seconds of the window).

The results of the computed ANOVAs were corrected using the Greenhouse-Geisser correction on the degrees of freedom, as Mauchly's Test indicated that the assumption of sphericity had been violated.

Results

Figure 4 shows the grand average based on the mean values with 95% confidence intervals for both signals. In case of EDA, a difference was visible between relevant and irrelevant trials around 4 to 6 seconds after the explicit relevance judgment. In the case of CSA, a difference was visible around 1 second after the explicit relevance judgment. The confidence intervals mostly overlap, which is a first indication of the hardness of this prediction problem. The grand average based on the median values showed similar structure.

The ANOVA based on the mean EDA values showed a significant main effect of time, $F(1.46, 51.25) = 20.56, p < 0.0001$. The ANOVA based on median EDA values showed a significant main effect of relevance $F(1.00, 35.00) = 6.19, p < 0.02$ as well as time $F(1.13, 39.40) = 56.44, p < 0.0001$. The ANOVA based on the mean CSA values showed a significant main effect of time $F(4.26, 148.99) = 5.97, p < 0.0001$. In case of the median-based ANOVA, main effect of time on CSA activity was found as well, $F(3.83, 134.04) = 8.99, p < 0.0001$.

For both signals EDA and CSA, main effect of time was found, which indicates that the physiological signal changes reliably due to the relevance judgment. However, the direction of the judgment was only significant for electrodermal activity, as indicated by the significant main effect of the relevance. This means that decision-related physiological changes in corrugator supercilii activity are either not related to perceived relevance, too weakly related to become visible, or not stable enough across time as to cause an interactive effect.

FEATURE ENGINEERING

The results found in the previous section indicate the presence of information on perceived relevance in the psychophysiological responses. However, in order to capture this information, more sophisticated representations of the EDA and CSA

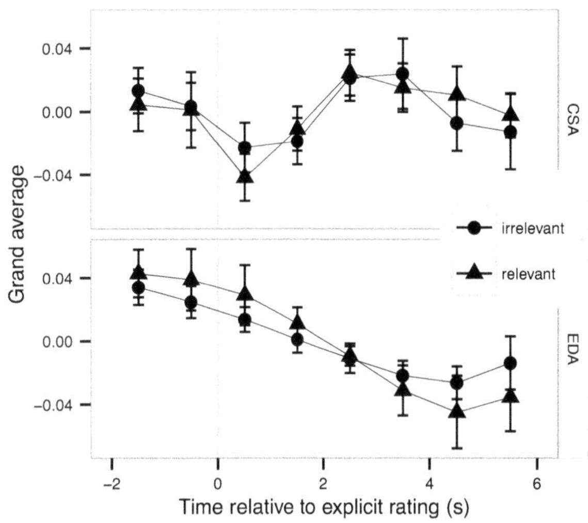

Figure 4. Grand average with 95% confidence interval within the 8-second window of the electrodermal activity (EDA, bottom) and corrugator supercilii activity (CSA, top) signals averaged over participants and trials. The vertical gray line at "0" indicates the explicit rating event. Differences in the signal can be observed around 1 second after the rating for corrugator supercilii activity and around 4 to 6 seconds after the rating for electrodermal activity.

signals are needed. The skin conductance response (SCR) elicited by a stimulus can take 1 to 3 or 4 seconds to manifest. After that, electrodermal SCR takes one to three seconds to reach its peak [7]. In contrast to electrodermal activity, electromyography response is fast, as corrugator supercilii activity is found to be elicited at most two seconds after processing a stimulus [35].

Feature window

Though it is very hard to know exactly when the implicit decision happened, there are two constraints that define the decision moment. First, it is clear that a person needs to read at least a few words to know what the text is about. The reading time required to assess the relevance of a text in our experiment is highly variable (Mean = 8.3s, SD = 4.5s), which is a large obstacle for stimulus-locked analyses (i.e. the window is locked to the moment when the text item appears on the screen). Second, as we instructed the participants to assess the relevance as soon as they had made any decision on it, even though relevance-related processing may start earlier, the final implicit decision on the relevance is expected to occur only shortly before the explicit rating (solid rectangle in Figure 5), which is best captured using response-locked analysis (i.e. the window is locked to the moment when the participant rates the information item). We therefore defined a time window that included a short time before the explicit decision (2s), which was considered to be sufficient to cover the 100s of milliseconds elapsed between the implicit decision and the explicit rating in relation to awareness, preparation of response and response execution (Sternberg stimulus-response model [28]); and a relatively long time following it (6s), as especially EDA changes very slowly (SCR can take up to 6 or 7 seconds to reach its peak [7]).

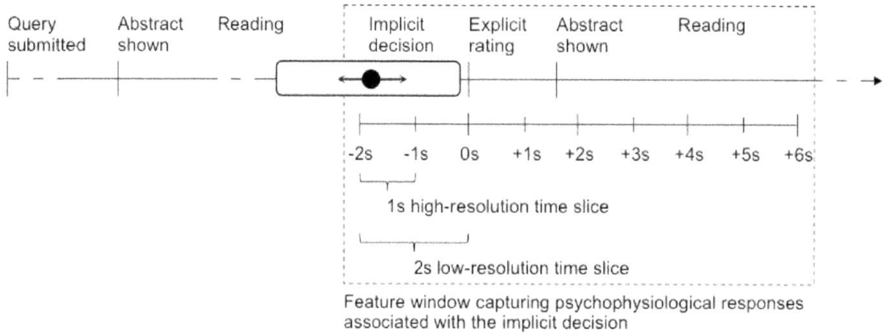

Figure 5. Feature window. The participant first submits the query; then a sequence of abstract snippets is presented, one snippet at a time. For each of those, the participant reads the text for an unfixed amount of time ($M = 8.3, SD = 4.5$, in seconds) and, after making a decision regarding its relevance to the query, rates accordingly. The time window selected to generate the features is outlined in the figure; it goes from 2 seconds before to 6 seconds after the rating. The decision on the relevance was assumed to happen at most 2 seconds before the rating, and the feature window was selected to capture the psychophysiological responses associated with it, which for corrugator supercilii activity takes around one to two seconds and in the case of electrodermal activity can take up to 6 or 7 seconds. Features were generated from eight 1-second (high-resolution) and four 2-second (low-resolution) time slices of the feature window.

Even though the selected time window overlaps with the next item presentation, the randomization of the presentation order of relevant and irrelevant text items together with the large number of participants should redress confounding noise and artifacts introduced by the next presented information item.

Feature generation

We generated features within this 8-second time window (dashed rectangle in Figure 5), time-locked to the moment when the participant gave the explicit rating ("0s" in Figure 5). Given the psychophysiolgical literature and the experimental procedure, it is now likely that this window contains the psychophysiological response associated with the point in time when the participant processed the stimuli and made a decision whether the information is relevant or irrelevant (i.e., implicit decision, black dot in Figure 5). Within the window, we generated high-resolution and low-resolution features; the first ones were based on nonoverlapping 1-second slices, the latter based on nonoverlapping 2-second slices.

Using this basic structure, we generated features describing four different characterizations of the signals within the time window of a trial. Let h indicate high-resolution features and l indicate low-resolution features. The set $I_h = \{-2, -1, 0, 1, 2, 3, 4, 5\}$ describes the start seconds of the 1-second slices, the set $I_l = \{-2, 0, 2, 4\}$ describes the start seconds of the 2-second slices, and the set $I_d = \{-1, 0, 1, 2, 3, 4, 5\}$ describes the middle second of adjacent 1-second slices. Furthermore, $s^{i,j}$ describes the values of the physiological signal $s \in \{\text{EDA}, \text{CSA}\}$ from i seconds to j seconds.

The *average signal features* quantify the mean signal per time slice. They are defined as follows:

$$h^i = \text{mean}(s^{i,i+1}) - \text{bl}_h, i \in I_h$$
$$l^j = \text{mean}(s^{j,j+1}) - \text{bl}_l, j \in I_l$$

These features are baseline-corrected, that is, centered by subtracting a trial-based baseline bl_h and bl_l.

The *difference features* quantify the amount of change of the signals between adjacent time slices. They are defined as followed:

$$d^k = (\text{mean}(s^{k,k+1}) - \text{mean}(s^{k-1,k})) - \text{bl}_d, k \in I_d$$

These are baseline-corrected, as they are centered by a trial-specific baseline bl_d describing the mean differences.

The *maximum signal features* quantify the maximum signal per window. They are defined as follows:

$$\text{max}_h = \max(h^i, i \in I_h)$$
$$\text{max}_l = \max(l^j, j \in I_l)$$
$$\text{max}_d = \max(d^k, k \in I_d)$$

The *latency features* quantify the latency to the maximum value. They are defined as follows:

$$\text{lat}_h = \text{argmax}_i(h^i, i \in I_h)$$
$$\text{lat}_l = \text{argmax}_j(l^j, j \in I_l)$$
$$\text{lat}_d = \text{argmax}_k(d^k, k \in I_d)$$

The defined characterizations describe a general feature engineering framework for physiological signals, where each signal is described by 25 features. Table 1 shows the final set of features generated for EDA and CSA using this procedure.

EXPLORATORY FEATURE ANALYSIS

In order to analyze the quality and importance of the individual features, we conducted an exploratory feature analysis. We wanted to identify specific features that are associated with perceived relevance using data of half of the valid participants ($N = 18$). We ranked the features according to their generalizability across participants utilizing a widely used feature-selection technique based on the filter principle [26]. Electrodermal activity and corrugator supercilii activity features were ranked separately using identical procedures.

Electrodermal activity (EDA)					Corrugator supercilii activity (CSA)				
Features	#Part.	$\bar{W}$	SD(W)	Rank	Features	#Part.	$\bar{W}$	SD(W)	Rank
lat_d	9	158	38	1	d^0	7	163	42	1
d^5	7	170	50	2	h^0	7	159	57	
d^3	7	151	38		max_h	7	141	36	
d^2	7	149	33		l^0	6	156	43	2
h^5	7	146	36		h^{-2}	5	153	29	3
l^4	7	146	24		max_d	5	137	48	
d^4	7	140	47		d^2	4	153	23	4
h^4	6	146	25	3	h^{-1}	4	136	16	
l^2	4	133	44	4	h^4	4	130	39	
max_d	4	122	29		d^{-1}	4	130	40	
h^3	3	156	2	5	lat_d	4	123	21	
h^{-2}	3	148	39		h^3	4	117	43	
max_l	3	140	33		l^{-2}	3	160	41	5
h^2	3	125	49		d^5	3	153	14	
l^{-2}	2	168	36	6	lat_l	3	150	20	
max_h	2	144	36		d^4	3	140	6	
d^1	2	123	44		l^2	3	133	38	
d^{-1}	2	110	23		max_l	3	123	53	
l^0	2	81	4		l^4	2	145	21	6
h^0	2	75	11		d^1	2	135	25	
lat_l	1	156	–	7	h^1	2	130	34	
lat_h	1	119	–		lat_h	2	126	30	
h^{-1}	1	111	–		h^2	2	122	52	
h^1	1	78	–		d^3	1	136	–	7
d^0	1	77	–		h^5	0	–	–	8

(Brackets beside the table: EDA — Model M_1: lat_d to d^4; Model M_2: lat_d to max_d; Model M_3: all features. CSA — Model M_1: d^0 to max_d; Model M_2: d^0 to h^3; Model M_3: all features.)

Table 1. The features were named as follows: h^i are the features generated in the high-resolution time window, from second i to second $i+1$, relative to the moment the participant gives explicit feedback. The l^i are the features generated in the low-resolution time window from second i to second $i+2$, relative to the moment the participant gives explicit feedback. The d^i are the features generated from the difference between i to $i+1$ and $i-1$ to i seconds relative to the moment the participant gives explicit feedback. $max_{h,l,d}$ and $lat_{h,l,d}$ are generated from the maximum value and latency to the maximum value in the high-resolution (h), low-resolution (l), and difference (d) features. Electrodermal activity-derived features are shown in the left part of the table and corrugator supercilii activity-derived features in the right. *#Part.* indicates the number of participants for whom the feature appears in the *top features*. The mean of the W statistic and the standard deviation for these participants are indicated in columns $\bar{W}$ and *SD* respectively. The features are ranked according to the number of times they are included in a participant's *top features*, which is indicated by *Rank*. Additionally, the set of features used for each of the three predictive models M_1, M_2, and M_3 is indicated as well.

For each participant, the Wilcoxon rank-sum statistic (W) was computed for every feature between relevant and irrelevant trials. The five features with highest W including draws were then selected for each participant (i.e., *top features*). Following, in order to analyze the features over participants, we ranked the features according to the number of times the features were included in a participant's *top features*.

Results

Table 1 contains the ranked features for electrodermal activity and corrugator supercilii activity, according to the number of participants' *top features* each feature belongs to. The mean W and standard deviation for these participants are included as well in the table.

Electrodermal activity was found to have the highest association with relevance via the lat_d feature, as half of the participants had this feature in their *top features*. This feature represents the latency to the maximal difference between two adjacent slices. Therefore, the point in time in which the maximum increase of EDA occurs appears to be a good indicator of the content of the relevance judgments. Interestingly, h^5, l^4, d^5, and d^4 are some of the top-ranked features and are all generated from the time window from 4 to 6 seconds after the relevance judgment. The h^5 and l^4 features refer to the amount of electrodermal activity between 5 to 6, and 4 to 6 seconds after the relevance judgment is made, respectively. The d^5 feature is a measure of how much the electrodermal activity changes five seconds after the relevance judgment, and d^4 measures the change of EDA around 4 seconds after the explicit judgment. As previously pointed out, the skin conductance response (SCR) elicited by a stimulus can take up to 6 or 7 seconds to reach its peak [7]. Thus, considering the implicit decision moment as the trigger for SCR, these features could well be related to the SCR peak, which in turn would be associated with relevance judgments. Moreover, the mean W for d^5 is very high compared with the other features. This is an indicator that for the participants for whom this feature is in the *top features*, there is a strong association between the increase of EDA around 5 seconds after the judgment, and the content of the judgment. Finally, it is worthy to recall the fact that many *difference features* appear in the top of the table for electrodermal activity, as five out of the seven first- and second-ranked features are *difference features*. This fact points in the direction that the association of EDA signal with perceived relevance relies on how the signal changes across time, more than in absolute values.

Corrugator supercilii activity was associated with relevance via the features generated from the signal around the moment when the participant made explicit the relevance judgment. The d^0 feature refers to the change in CSA between the slice before and the slice after the explicit relevance judgment is made. The h^0 and l^0 features refer to the first 1-second and 2-second slice after the relevance judgment, respectively. Based on the results of the ranking, it is likely that at least these three features, and therefore the time window from 1 second before to 2 seconds after the relevance judgment, are associated with users' perception of relevance of information items. As previously pointed out, corrugator supercilii activity is found to be elicited at most 2 seconds after processing a stimulus. Therefore, the finding that the highest ranked features are in this time window is coherent with the psychophysiological literature. Hence we can deduce that in the instants immediately before and after the relevance judgment is made, corrugator supercilii activity is potentially associated with perceived relevance. It is also interesting to point out that the maximum 1-second slice in the signal (i.e., max_h) belongs to the group of first-ranked features. Therefore, it appears that, contrarily to electrodermal activity where the association with perceived relevance seems to come from the changes in the signal (*difference features*), for corrugator supercilii activity, the peak value in the signal seems to be one of the properties more strongly associated with perceived relevance, together with the signal values around the moment of the explicit rating.

PREDICTIVE POWER

In order to verify that our generated features have predictive power, we built classifiers that predict relevance judgments for the 18 participants of our study not used in the exploratory feature analysis. This allowed us to test the generalizability of the features. We used a multiview learning method, a leave-one-participant-out strategy, and assumed the relevance judgments to be balanced [8, used the same scheme]. The latter assumption reassembles our original experimental design and allowed us to focus on the predictive power of the features rather then the problem of potentially imbalanced relevance judgments.

Prediction model

In detail, we used a multiple kernel learning (MKL) method to learn classification models of the following form:

$$y = f(\mathbf{v}_1, \ldots, \mathbf{v}_K) = \sum_{k=1}^{K} \beta_k \langle \mathbf{w}_k, \Phi_k(\mathbf{v}_k) \rangle + b.$$

Here, y denotes the binary relevance judgment, and $\mathbf{v}_k$ are the features generated from the different signals (called a view) that is, $\mathbf{v}_1$ is the view with the features for EDA and $\mathbf{v}_2$ is the view with the features for CSA. $\langle \cdot, \cdot \rangle$ denotes the scalar product, $\mathbf{w}_k$ the weight vector of the observations, $\Phi_k(\mathbf{v}_k)$ the feature map of the view $\mathbf{v}_k$, β_k the kernel weights, and b the bias. Given the selected features for each view $\mathbf{v}_k$, we normalized the data and computed a Gaussian kernel with the kernel width defined as the median distance between the observations [12]. For the concrete estimation of the classification models, we use a Bayesian MKL algorithm with an efficient inference based on variational approximation [11].

Prediction setup

We applied a leave-one-participant-out learning strategy as follows. For each participant we learned a classification model using the other participants' data (i.e., the remaining seventeen participants). The prediction accuracy was then computed on the participant's relevance observations. The number of relevance observations varies slightly for each participant because of the binarization. We established balanced data by randomly drawing the learning set and the test set from the set of relevant and the set of irrelevant observations, each with the number of observations defined by the smaller set. This reassembles our original experimental design and is a simple but well-established strategy to exclude possible problems of the classification method with imbalanced classes. To eliminate a possible observation sampling bias we repeated this procedure five times.

Model	Mean accuracy	SD accuracy	p-value	Mean improvement
M_3	0.5359	0.0814	0.0783	7.19%
M_1	0.5376	0.0787	0.0587	7.51%
M_2	0.5711	0.0997	**0.0076**	14.22%

Table 2. Classification results based on the unseen 18 participants for models based on different feature sets. The table lists the mean classification accuracy, the p-value indicating a significant different mean classification accuracy compared to the random baseline, and the corresponding mean improvement. Because of our experimental design, the random baseline prediction of whether an abstract is relevant or irrelevant is 0.5. Bold entries denote that improvements are statistically significant at a level of $\alpha = 0.05$, p-value $< \alpha$ with correction for multiple testing.

Model definition and feature sets

Based on the exploratory feature analysis, we defined three basic models, M_1, M_2, and M_3 with increasing sizes of feature sets, and computed classification models based on these feature sets. Model M_1 contained the top five features including draws, model M_2 the top ten features including draws, and model M_3 all features from both signals (see Table 1, column #Part.).

Results

Table 2 summarizes the classification accuracies for the models M_1, M_2, and M_3 based on the different feature sets. We report the mean classification accuracy, improvement over the random baseline, and the p-value of a t-test for significance corrected for multiple testing using the Bonferroni correction. The t-test was applicable because the Shapiro-Wilk test did not reject the null hypothesis that the samples come from a normal distribution.

The results verified that there is predictive power in the set of features generated for EDA and CSA and that the features generalize to new users. The M_2 (medium feature set) classification models predicted relevant and irrelevant abstracts for an unseen participant significantly better than the random baseline and achieved a mean improvement of 14%. In the cases of M_1 (smallest feature set) and M_3 (all features) classification models, no significant improvement could be found. Therefore, the M_1 feature set contained insufficient information to discriminate the relevant and irrelevant items. On the other hand, the M_3 feature set contained all possible information, but also introduced a significant amount of noise.

Figure 6 shows the individual classification performances using model M_2 for each of the 18 participants. Points indi-

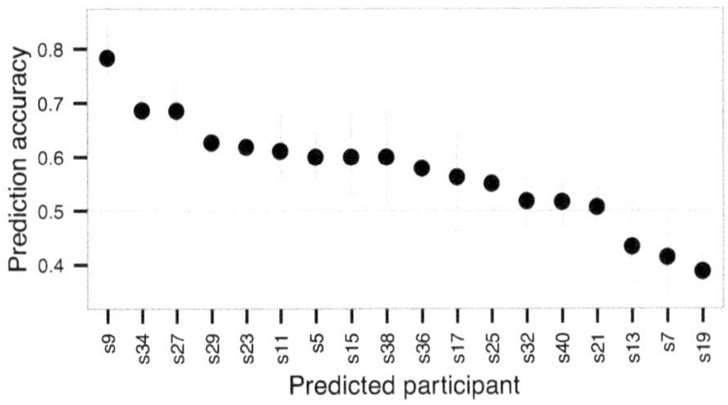

Figure 6. Individual classification accuracy using model M_2 for each of the 18 participants based on training on data of the remaining participants and ordered according to the accuracy. Points indicate the mean accuracy, the error bars show the bootstrap confidence intervals.

cate the mean predicting accuracy, and error bars show bootstrap confidence intervals. The horizontal line at 0.5 marks the random baseline. Fifteen participants are above, and 3 participants are below the random baseline. We also can observe that for some participants, the variation is very small (e.g., participants `s34`, `s29`, and `s23`), whereas for others it is substantial (e.g., participants `s15` and `s38`).

As a final observation, we want to point out participant `s34`, for whom the prediction worked well and with low variation. The exemplary "face recognition" search session in Figure 3 was part of his experiment. The classifier predicted the first five articles according to the participant's explicit ratings. The last article was predicted to be relevant, contrary to the participant's rating. However, the abstract can be seen as relevant. The participant perhaps made a mistake, and we could detect it using physiolgical signals. Even though this is only one specific case, it nicely illustrates the potential of this approach.

DISCUSSION

The results indicate that the EDA and CSA are associated with perceived relevance and the features extracted from the signals transfer to improved accuracy in a classification setup. However, our experimental setup leaves room for further research in three respects.

First, our models in general significantly outperform the random baseline, which indicates that psychophysiology alone can help predict relevance. However, the classification accuracy achieved using only the physiological signals hints that these signals alone are unlikely to serve as relevance predictors. Therefore, psychophysiology is envisioned to be used in combination with other implicit relevance feedback techniques, such as brain signals [8] or facial expressions [5], to strengthen current information retrieval systems.

Second, our experimental design is balanced between relevant and irrelevant abstracts in order to ensure that we measure signals and effects related to relevance judgments. In a real information retrieval setting, however, it is likely that the two classes are imbalanced with the majority of the information items being irrelevant. Experiments with more realistic data and larger amount of observations are needed to show how our results generalize to such scenarios.

Third, the prediction accuracy varies substantially across and within participants. As can be glanced from the left side of Figure 6, our approach achieves good accuracy for about 10 out of 18 unseen participants. Along with the specific observation regarding participant `s34`, this underlines the possibility that there may be substantial differences between users' physiological signals associated with perceived relevance. Other factors need to be taken into account as, for instance, it has been shown that there is a portion of users that are "EDA non-responders" [32]. Consequently, personalized models that are built for each user separately could further improve and stabilize the prediction accuracy.

CONCLUSIONS

Physiological sensors are becoming more ubiquitous and available for every day use. This has raised an interest in study of their usefulness for a wide spectrum of computing applications. We studied peripheral physiological signals for predicting users' perceived relevance when they are engaged in an information retrieval task. In the present work, we concentrated on two of the most promising physiological signals: electrodermal activity (EDA) and corrugator supercilii activity (CSA). Our results suggest that peripheral physiology can be used to predict relevance of information for a user when engaged in an information retrieval task, but that the prediction is sensitive to selecting correct features and time windows. Features in the window of 4 to 6 seconds after the relevance judgment for electrodermal activity (EDA) and from 1 second before to 2 seconds after the relevance judgment for corrugator supercilii activity (CSA) were found to be associated with the perceived relevance. Our findings can help to build systems that can detect relevance from physiology and open a horizon for adaptive intelligent systems that can proactively, with minimum user intervention, react to a user's information needs.

ACKNOWLEDGMENTS

This work has been partly supported by the Academy of Finland (278090, Multivire, 255725; and the Finnish Centre of Excellence in Computational Inference Research COIN, 251170), Re:Know funded by TEKES, and MindSee (FP7 – ICT; Grant Agreement # 611570). Certain data included herein are derived from the Web of Science prepared by THOMSON REUTERS, Inc., Philadelphia, Pennsylvania, USA: Copyright THOMSON REUTERS, 2011. All rights reserved. Data is also included from the Digital Libraries of the ACM, IEEE, and Springer.

REFERENCES

1. Agichtein, E., Brill, E., and Dumais, S. Improving web search ranking by incorporating user behavior information. In *Proceedings of the 29th Annual International ACM SIGIR Conference on Research and Development in Information Retrieval*, SIGIR '06, ACM (New York, NY, USA, 2006), 19–26.
2. Andreassi, J. L. *Psychophysiology: Human behavior & physiological response*. Psychology Press, 2000.

3. Arapakis, I. Affective feedback: An investigation into the role of emotions in the information seeking process. In *Proceedings of the 31st Annual International ACM SIGIR Conference on Research and Development in Information Retrieval*, SIGIR '08, ACM (New York, NY, USA, 2008), 891–891.
4. Arapakis, I., Athanasakos, K., and Jose, J. M. A comparison of general vs personalised affective models for the prediction of topical relevance. In *Proceedings of the 33rd international ACM SIGIR Conference on Research and Development in Information Retrieval*, SIGIR '10, ACM (New York, NY, USA, 2010), 371–378.
5. Arapakis, I., Konstas, I., and Jose, J. M. Using facial expressions and peripheral physiological signals as implicit indicators of topical relevance. In *Proceedings of the 17th ACM International Conference on Multimedia*, MM '09, ACM (New York, NY, USA, 2009), 461–470.
6. Cohen, B. H., Davidson, R. J., Senulis, J. A., Saron, C. D., and Weisman, D. R. Muscle tension patterns during auditory attention. *Biological Psychology 33*, 2-3 (1992), 133 – 156.
7. Dawson, M. E., Schell, A. M., Filion, D. L., and Berntson, G. G. The electrodermal system. In *Handbook of Psychophysiology*, J. T. Cacioppo, L. G. Tassinary, and G. Berntson, Eds., third ed. Cambridge University Press, 2007, 157–181. Cambridge Books Online.
8. Eugster, M. J., Ruotsalo, T., Spapé, M. M., Kosunen, I., Barral, O., Ravaja, N., Jacucci, G., and Kaski, S. Predicting term-relevance from brain signals. In *Proceedings of the 37th International ACM SIGIR Conference on Research and Development in Information Retrieval*, SIGIR '14, ACM (New York, NY, USA, 2014), 425–434.
9. Fox, S., Karnawat, K., Mydland, M., Dumais, S., and White, T. Evaluating implicit measures to improve web search. *ACM Transactions on Information Systems (TOIS) 23*, 2 (Apr. 2005), 147–168.
10. Fridlund, A. J., and Cacioppo, J. T. Guidelines for human electromyographic research. *Psychophysiology 23*, 5 (1986), 567–589.
11. Gönen, M. Bayesian efficient multiple kernel learning. In *Proceedings of the 29th International Conference on Machine Learning (ICML-12)*, J. Langford and J. Pineau, Eds., ACM (New York, NY, USA, 2012), 1–8.
12. Gretton, A., Borgwardt, K. M., Rasch, M. J., Schölkopf, B., and Smola, A. A kernel two-sample test. *The Journal of Machine Learning Research 13* (2012), 723–773.
13. Harman, D. Relevance feedback revisited. In *Proceedings of the 15th Annual International ACM SIGIR Conference on Research and Development in Information Retrieval*, SIGIR '92, ACM (New York, NY, USA, 1992), 1–10.
14. Joachims, T., Granka, L., Pan, B., Hembrooke, H., and Gay, G. Accurately interpreting clickthrough data as implicit feedback. In *Proceedings of the 28th Annual International ACM SIGIR Conference on Research and Development in Information Retrieval*, SIGIR '05, ACM (New York, NY, USA, 2005), 154–161.
15. Joachims, T., Granka, L., Pan, B., Hembrooke, H., Radlinski, F., and Gay, G. Evaluating the accuracy of implicit feedback from clicks and query reformulations in web search. *Transactions on Information Systems (TOIS) 25*, 2 (Apr. 2007).
16. Kelly, D. Methods for evaluating interactive information retrieval systems with users. *Foundations and Trends in Information Retrieval 3*, 1-2 (Jan. 2009), 1–224.
17. Kelly, D., and Fu, X. Elicitation of term relevance feedback: An investigation of term source and context. In *Proceedings of the 29th Annual International ACM SIGIR Conference on Research and Development in Information Retrieval*, SIGIR '06, ACM (New York, NY, USA, 2006), 453–460.
18. Kelly, D., and Teevan, J. Implicit feedback for inferring user preference: A bibliography. *SIGIR Forum 37*, 2 (Sept. 2003), 18–28.
19. Klimesch, W. Eeg alpha and theta oscillations reflect cognitive and memory performance: a review and analysis. *Brain research reviews 29*, 2 (1999), 169–195.
20. Koenemann, J., and Belkin, N. J. A case for interaction: A study of interactive information retrieval behavior and effectiveness. In *Proceedings of the SIGCHI Conference on Human Factors in Computing Systems*, CHI '96, ACM (New York, NY, USA, 1996), 205–212.
21. Moshfeghi, Y., and Jose, J. M. An effective implicit relevance feedback technique using affective, physiological and behavioural features. In *Proceedings of the 36th Annual International ACM SIGIR Conference on Research and Development in Information Retrieval*, SIGIR '13, ACM (New York, NY, USA, 2013), 133–142.
22. Moshfeghi, Y., Pinto, L., Pollick, F., and Jose, J. Understanding relevance: An fmri study. In *Advances in Information Retrieval*, P. Serdyukov, P. Braslavski, S. Kuznetsov, J. Kamps, S. Rger, E. Agichtein, I. Segalovich, and E. Yilmaz, Eds., vol. 7814 of *Lecture Notes in Computer Science*. Springer Berlin Heidelberg, 2013, 14–25.
23. Ravaja, N. Contributions of psychophysiology to media research: Review and recommendations. *Media Psychology 6*, 2 (2004), 193–235.
24. Ruotsalo, T., Jacucci, G., Myllymäki, P., and Kaski, S. Interactive intent modeling: Information discovery beyond search. *Commun. ACM 58*, 1 (Dec. 2014), 86–92.

25. Ruotsalo, T., Peltonen, J., Eugster, M. J., Glowacka, D., Konyushkova, K., Athukorala, K., Kosunen, I., Reijonen, A., Myllymäki, P., Jacucci, G., and Kaski, S. Directing exploratory search with interactive intent modeling. In *Proceedings of the 22nd ACM International Conference on Information and Knowledge Management*, CIKM '13, ACM (New York, NY, USA, 2013), 1759–1764.

26. Saeys, Y., Inza, I., and Larrañaga, P. A review of feature selection techniques in bioinformatics. *Bioinformatics 23*, 19 (2007), 2507–2517.

27. Shen, X., Tan, B., and Zhai, C. Implicit user modeling for personalized search. In *Proceedings of the 14th ACM International Conference on Information and Knowledge Management*, CIKM '05, ACM (New York, NY, USA, 2005), 824–831.

28. Sternberg, S. The discovery of processing stages: Extensions of donders' method. *Acta Psychologica 30*, 0 (1969), 276 – 315.

29. Teevan, J., Alvarado, C., Ackerman, M. S., and Karger, D. R. The perfect search engine is not enough: a study of orienteering behavior in directed search. In *Proceedings of the SIGCHI Conference on Human Factors in Computing Systems*, CHI '04, ACM (New York, NY, USA, 2004), 415–422.

30. Van Boxtel, A., and Jessurun, M. Amplitude and bilateral coherency of facial and jaw-elevator emg activity as an index of effort during a two-choice serial reaction task. *Psychophysiology 30*, 6 (1993), 589–604.

31. Veldhuizen, I., Gaillard, A., and De Vries, J. The influence of mental fatigue on facial emg activity during a simulated workday. *Biological Psychology 63*, 1 (2003), 59–78.

32. Venables, P., and Mitchell, D. The effects of age, sex and time of testing on skin conductance activity. *Biological Psychology 43*, 2 (1996), 87 – 101.

33. Waterink, W., and Van Boxtel, A. Facial and jaw-elevator emg activity in relation to changes in performance level during a sustained information processing task. *Biological Psychology 37*, 3 (1994), 183–198.

34. White, R. W., Ruthven, I., and Jose, J. M. A study of factors affecting the utility of implicit relevance feedback. In *Proceedings of the 28th Annual International ACM SIGIR Conference on Research and Development in Information Retrieval*, SIGIR '05, ACM (New York, NY, USA, 2005), 35–42.

35. Winkielman, P., and Cacioppo, J. T. Mind at ease puts a smile on the face: psychophysiological evidence that processing facilitation elicits positive affect. *Journal of Personality and Social Psychology 81*, 6 (2001), 989.

36. Zhai, C., and Lafferty, J. A study of smoothing methods for language models applied to information retrieval. *ACM Transactions on Information Systems (TOIS) 22*, 2 (Apr. 2004), 179–214.

Light-Bulb Moment? Towards Adaptive Presentation of Feedback based on Students' Affective State

Beate Grawemeyer
London Knowledge Lab
Birkbeck College
University of London, UK
beate@dcs.bbk.ac.uk

Wayne Holmes
London Knowledge Lab
UCL Institute of Education
University of London, UK
w.holmes@ioe.ac.uk

Sergio Gutiérrez-Santos
London Knowledge Lab
Birkbeck College
University of London, UK
sergut@dcs.bbk.ac.uk

Alice Hansen
London Knowledge Lab
UCL Institute of Education
University of London, UK
a.hansen@ioe.ac.uk

Katharina Loibl
Institute of Educational Research
Ruhr-Universität Bochum, Germany
katharina.loibl@rub.de

Manolis Mavrikis
London Knowledge Lab
UCL Institute of Education
University of London, UK
m.mavrikis@ioe.ac.uk

ABSTRACT

Affective states play a significant role in students' learning behaviour. Positive affective states can enhance learning, whilst negative affective states can inhibit it. This paper describes a Wizard-of-Oz study which investigates whether the way feedback is presented should change according to the affective state of a student, in order to encourage affect change if that state is negative. We presented high-interruptive feedback in the form of pop-up windows in which messages were immediately viewable; or low-interruptive feedback, a glowing light bulb which students needed to click in order to access the messages. Our results show that when students are confused or frustrated high-interruptive feedback is more effective, but when students are enjoying their activity, there is no difference. Based on the results, we present guidelines for adaptively tailoring the presentation of feedback based on students' affective states when interacting with learning environments.

Author Keywords

Affect; emotions; adaptive feedback presentation.

ACM Classification Keywords

H.5.m. Information Interfaces and Presentation (e.g. HCI): Miscellaneous

INTRODUCTION

This paper reports on a Wizard-of-Oz study which explores the effect of different presentations of feedback on students' affective states. Our aim is to provide guidelines for adaptive feedback presentation, which is tailored to the affective state of the student, in order to enhance the learning experience.

Affective states have physiological and behavioural manifestations, and prepare the body for actions [3, 7]. Further, as described in Kort et al. [8], affective states interact with and influence the learning process. While positive affective states such as awe, satisfaction or curiosity contribute towards constructive learning, negative ones including frustration or disillusionment at realising they have a misconceptions can inhibit learning. The learning process includes a range and combination of positive and negative affective states.

It is important then, to understand the role of affective states for learning, and to be able to move students out of states that inhibit learning. Pekrun [12] discusses achievement emotions or affective states, which arise in a learning situation. Achievement emotions are states that are linked to learning, instruction, and achievement. We focus on a subset of affective states identified by Pekrun: enjoyment, surprise, frustration, and boredom. We also add confusion, which has been identified elsewhere as an important affective state during learning (e.g. [13]).

As described in Woolf et al. [18] students can become overwhelmed (very confused or frustrated) during learning, which may increase cognitive load [17], especially for low-ability or novice students. However, appropriate feedback might help to overcome such problems. Carenini et al. [2] describe how effective support or feedback needs to answer three main questions: when, what, and how: (i) when the support should be provided during learning; (ii) what the support should contain; and (iii) how it should be presented.

In this paper we focus on *how* the support or feedback should be presented based on the student's affective state.

A limited number of researchers have looked at how the presentation of information or feedback could be adapted ac-

IUI 2015, March 29–April 1, 2015, Atlanta, GA, USA.

http://dx.doi.org/10.1145/2678025.2701377

cording to certain user characteristics. For example, in the area of information visualisation, Carenini et al. [2] describe a study that looks at tailoring visual prompts, based on task complexity, user characteristics (such as perceptual speed, visual working memory, and verbal working memory) and delivery times. Also, Grawemeyer & Cox [6] describe a system that is able to recommend a particular representation (bar chart, plot chart, pie chart, sector graph, eulers diagram, or table) based on the user expertise with representations as well as their preferences for particular representations, the task, the information to be presented and the representation's semantics. Additionally, Gotz & Wen [5] outline a system that is able to recommend alternative visualisations by inferring the user's intended visual task. Further, Ahn & Brusilovsky [1] describe a system which adapts the visualisation of search results dynamically, based on a user's emerging interests.

In contrast, in this project, we investigated the impact of students' affective state on the effectiveness of the presentation of feedback. We present guidelines for adaptively tailoring the presentation of feedback based on students' affective states when interacting with learning environments.

THE WIZARD-OF-OZ STUDY

Aims

One of our research aims is to design guidelines for adapting the presentation of feedback to a student's affective state in order to enhance their learning experience. We were specifically interested in the following questions:

- Is there an effect of different presentations of feedback on a student's affective state?
- Does a student's perception of the learning environment and the feedback differ, according to whether low or high-interruptive feedback is provided?

In order to address these questions we ran an ecologically valid Wizard-of-Oz study (e.g. [10, 4]) which investigated the effect of feedback presentation on students' affective states. Additional information about the study setup can be found in Mavrikis et al. [9].

Participants

In total, 17 Year-5 (9 to 10-year old) students took part in the Wizard-of-Oz study. The sessions were run in a typical classroom with multiple computers, where additional children were working with the learning platform (not wizarded) in order to support ecological validity.

Procedure

Participants were randomly assigned to two groups (8 participants in the high- and 9 participants in the low-interruptive feedback group). In both groups students were provided with a fixed sequence of tasks within an exploratory learning environment designed to learn fractions (Fractions Lab). Feedback was provided by the wizard based on student's speech and on their performance. Table 1 shows examples of the different feedback types provided during the study (additional information about the feedback can be found in Mavrikis et al. [9]).

Feedback type	Example
Affect boost	You're working really hard! Keep going!
Problem solving	You can't add fractions with different denominators.
Reflection	What do you notice about the two fractions?
Talk aloud	Remember to talk aloud, what are you thinking?
Talk mathematics	Can you explain that again using the terms denominator, numerator?

Table 1. Examples of feedback types.

Based on which group the student was assigned to, they either received this feedback in a 'high-interruptive' way as a pop-up window (see Figure 1) or in a 'low-interruptive' way through an indication that feedback was available which they could access through clicking on a highlighted light bulb button (see Figure 2).

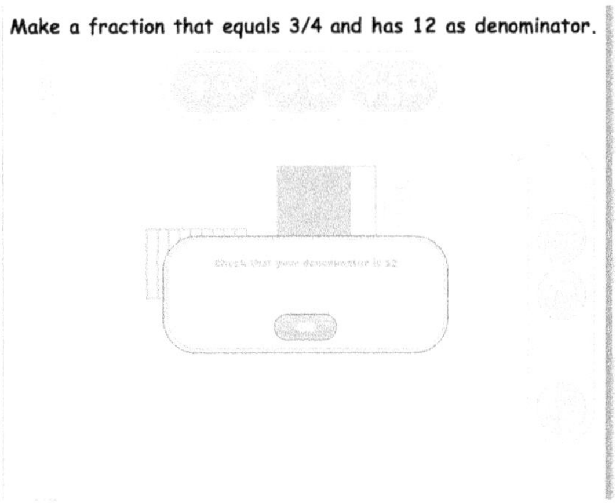

Figure 1. High-interruptive feedback - pop-up window that includes a feedback message.

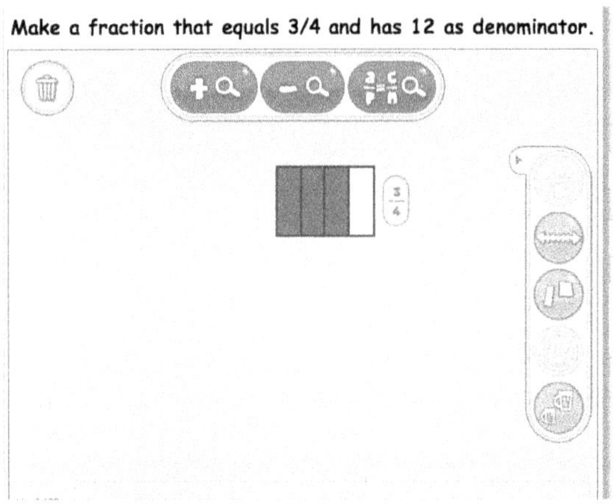

Figure 2. Low-interruptive feedback - light bulb glows (on the right hand side), indicating that feedback is available.

Participants in the low-interruptive group were able to ignore the feedback provided, by not clicking on the highlighted light bulb. In contrast, participants in the high-interruptive group had to dismiss the pop-up window before they could proceed with the task. Each session lasted on average 15 minutes.

Participants completed a post-session questionnaire about the learning environment, and in particular about what they thought of the feedback and whether they found it interruptive (7 questions). A smiley face scale [14] was used and scored 1 through 5 (see Figure 3).

Figure 3. Smiley scale used for post questionnaire

ANNOTATION OF AFFECTIVE STATES

From the Wizard-of-Oz study we recorded the students' screen display and their voices. From this data, we annotated affective states before and after feedback was provided.

As described earlier, for the affective state detection we discriminated between five different affective types: enjoyment, surprise, confusion, frustration, and boredom. For the annotation of those affective states we used a similar strategy to that described in [13], where a dialogue between a teacher and a student was annotated by categorising utterances in terms of different feedback types. We annotated the student's affective state before and after each piece of feedback was provided. In addition to the student's voice we also used the video of the screen capture to support the annotation process. Students' affective states were annotated as follows:

- **ENJOYMENT:** Engagement with the learning task. Statements like 'This is fun'.
- **SURPISE:** Gasping. Statements like 'Huh?' or 'Oh, no!'.
- **CONFUSION:** Failing to perform a particular task. Statements such as 'I'm confused!' or 'Why didn't it work?'.
- **FRUSTRATION:** Tendency to give up, repeatedly clicking on objects in the learning platform or repeatedly failing to perform a particular task, sighing, statements such as, 'What's going on?!'.
- **BOREDOM:** Statements such as 'Can we do something else?' or 'This is boring'.

RESULTS

Wizard-of-Oz session

In total 306 messages were sent to 17 students (153 high-interruptive and 153 low-interruptive messages). The feedback messages provided were based on students' speech as well as their interaction with the learning environment. On average students received 18 messages per session (min = 4; max = 35).

The video data combined with the sound files were analysed independently by two researchers who categorised the affective states of students. There was moderate agreement between the two researchers, Kappa=.52, p<.001. Where there was a mismatch, the categorisations were re-analysed and agreed upon between the researchers.

Figure 4 shows students' affective states that occurred before and after the feedback was given in respect to the different groups. Only three out of the five affective states were detected during this study (enjoyment, confusion, and frustration). This might be because the sessions only lasted 15 minutes and this may have been too short a time for students to get bored. Also, we might have missed the short-duration experience of surprise with our annotation strategy.

In order to investigate whether there was an effect of the presentation of the feedback on the learning experience, we looked at whether a student's affective state was enhanced, stayed the same or worsened. As the data is categorical [15],

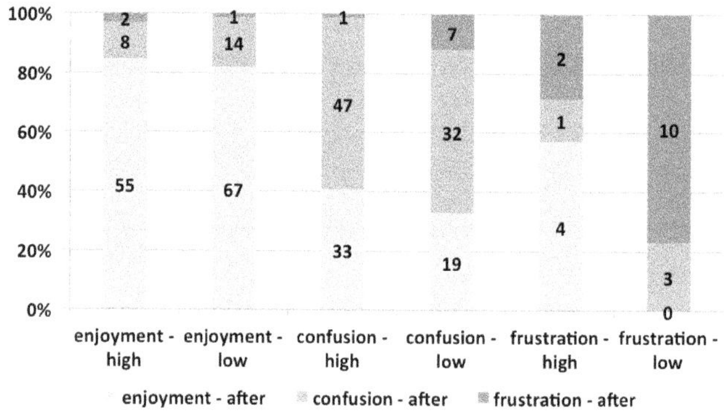

Figure 4. Students' affective states before and after feedback was given.

we applied chi-square tests to investigate whether there were statistically significant differences between the groups.

When students were enjoying their activity there was no significant difference between the groups on whether their affective state stayed the same or worsened after feedback was sent ($X^2(1, N=147) = .22, p>.05$). Students in the high-interruptive group mainly stayed within the same enjoyment state (85%). Their affective state worsened in 15% of cases. Similarly, the low-interruptive group stayed mainly in the same affective state (82%), and worsened in 18% of cases.

However, when students were confused there was a significant association of the group on the change of their affective states (improvement, same, worsened), $X^2(2, N=139) = 7.52$, $p<.05$. Here, within the high-interruptive group students' affective state was enhanced in 41% of cases, stayed the same in 58%, and worsened in only 1% of cases. In contrast, in the low-interruptive group, the affective state was enhanced in 33% of cases, stayed the same in 55%, and worsened in 12%.

When students were frustrated there was also a significant effect of the group on whether their affective state improved, or stayed the same, $X^2(1, N=20) = 4.43, p<.05$. Here, in the high-interruptive group, there was an enhancement of students' affective state in 71% of cases. For the other 29%, affective state remained the same. In contrast, in the low-interruptive group affective state was enhanced in only 23% of cases, and stayed the same for 77%.

	High	Low
Q1: Now that you have finished the session, how do you feel?	4.0 (3/4)	4.0 (3/5)
Q2: How much fun was it?	4.0 (3/5)	4.5 (3/5)
Q3: How helpful was the learning environment?	4.0 (2/5)	4.0 (2/5)
Q4: What did you think of the feedback?	4.0 (2/5)	4.0 (2/5)
Q5: Was the feedback easy to understand?	4.0 (2/5)	4.0 (2/5)
Q6: Was the feedback helpful?	3.0 (1/5)	4.0 (2/5)
Q7: How much did the feedback get in your way?	3.0 (2/4)	3.0 (2/4)

Table 2. Results of the post-assessment smiley questionnaire. Median (min/max).

Within the low-interruptive group there was a significant association between the different affective states and whether or not students clicked on the light bulb to view the feedback (X^2(2, N=153) = 13.12, p<.05). When students were enjoying their activity they clicked on the light bulb in 71% of cases, when confused in 81%, but when frustrated in only 31% of cases.

When students were confused within the low-interruptive group, there was a significant association between clicking on the light bulb and when the affective state was enhanced, stayed the same, or worsened (X^2(2, N=58) = 11.26, p<.05). Here, when students viewed the feedback, their affective state was enhanced in 41%, stayed the same in 53%, and worsened in 6% of cases. When students did not view the feedback, their affective state was unchanged in 64%, and became negative in 37% of cases.

When students were frustrated within the low-interruptive group, there was a significant association between message viewed and whether the student's affective state was enhanced or was unchanged (X^2(1, N=13) = 8.78, p<.05). When students viewed the feedback there was enhancement to their affective state in 75% of cases, and it stayed the same in 25% of cases. When students did not view the feedback the affective state stayed the same in 100% of cases.

Post-assessment questionnaire

Seven post-assessment questions were asked after each Wizard-of-Oz session. Table 2 shows medians (min/max) for each of the questions.

A Mann-Whitney test revealed no significant differences between the groups on any of the questions. A small non-statistically significant difference can be seen at Question 2 ('How much fun was it?') and Question 6 ('Was the feedback helpful?').

DISCUSSION

Effect of the presentation of feedback on a student's affective state

When students were enjoying their activity, both high- and low-interruptive feedback were effective. In both groups, students mainly stayed in the same positive affective state.

When students were confused, the results show that they welcomed feedback. However, when students in the low-interruptive group ignored the feedback available, this resulted in a significantly worsened affective state. Students may have ignored the feedback because their motivation at this point was low. In order to enhance the learning experience when students are confused, high-interruptive feedback should be provided.

Within the low-interruptive group, frustration was associated with not viewing the feedback, but when feedback was viewed it was associated with an enhanced affective state. This indicates that when students were frustrated they ignored the low-interruptive feedback. Frustration can increase cognitive load [16], which might explain why students did not react to the highlighted light bulb, as they might not have realised that help was available. Therefore, when students are frustrated, the presentation of the feedback should be highly visible and interruptive, as it is otherwise likely to be ignored.

Student's perception of the learning environment including feedback

Although there were no significant differences between the groups on the perception of the learning environment including the feedback provided, research from Mavrikis et al. [11] shows that students prefer to be able to decide themselves when to receive help (by e.g. clicking on a help button) rather than being interrupted by the learning environment.

This might also explain the slight increase in the low-interruptive feedback group (non-statistically significant) of how much fun the learning environment was and whether the feedback was helpful.

Therefore, the presentation of feedback should be tailored to the student's affective state. When students are enjoying their activity, low-interruptive feedback should be provided. However, as indicated by our results to the first research question, high-interruptive feedback should be provided when students are frustrated or confused.

CONCLUSION AND FUTURE WORK

This study reaffirms that the affective state of a student can be enhanced through feedback, and it demonstrates that when students are confused or frustrated, the way in which the feedback is presented is important. For these states, high-interruptive feedback is more effective: the cost of not viewing the feedback is likely to be a negative affective state.

Our next steps involve further development of intelligent feedback for a learning environment which is able to automatically tailor the presentation of the feedback (high- or low-interruptive) as well as the type of feedback (e.g. problem solving support, reflective prompts, affect boosts) according to the affective state of the student.

ACKNOWLEDGMENTS

This research has been funded by the European Union in the Seventh Framework Programme (FP7/2007-2013) in the iTalk2Learn project (318051).

REFERENCES

1. Ahn, J., and Brusilovsky, P. Adaptive visualization for exploratory information retrieval. *Information Processing and Management 49* (2013), 1139–1164.
2. Carenini, G., Conati, C., Hoque, E., Steichen, B., Toker, D., and Enns, J. Highlighting interventions and user differences: Informing adaptive information visualization support. In *CHI '14 Proceedings of the SIGCHI Conference on Human Factors in Computing Systems* (2014), 1835–1844.
3. Ekman, P. An argument for basic emotions. *Cognition & Emotion 6*, 3-4 (1992), 169–200.
4. Eynon, R., Davies, C., and Holmes, W. Supporting older adults in using technology for lifelong learning: the methodological and conceptual value of wizard of oz simulations. In *Proceedings of the 8th International Conference on Networked Learning 2012*, V. Hodgson, C. Jones, M. de Laat, D. McConnell, T. Ryberg, and P. Sloep, Eds. (2012), 66–73.
5. Gotz, D., and Wen, Z. Behaviour driven visualization recommendation. In *IUI '09 Proceedings of the 14th international conference on Intelligent user interfaces* (2009), 315–324.
6. Grawemeyer, B., and Cox, R. Graphical data displays and database queries: Helping users select the right display for the task. In *Smart Graphics, 5th International Symposium* (2005), 53–64.
7. Izard, C. The many meanings/aspects of emotion: Definitions, functions, activation, and regulation. *Emotion Review 2*, 4 (2010).
8. Kort, B., Reilly, R., and Picard, R. An affective model of the interplay between emotions and learning. In *IEEE International Conference on Advanced Learning Technologies*, no. 43-46 (2001).
9. Mavrikis, M., Grawemeyer, B., Hansen, A., and Gutiérrez-Santos, S. Exploring the potential of speech recognition to support problem solving and reflection - wizards go to school in the elementary maths classroom. In *Open Learning and Teaching in Educational Communities - 9th European Conference on Technology Enhanced Learning, EC-TEL 2014* (2014), 263–276.
10. Mavrikis, M., and Gutiérrez-Santos, S. Not all wizards are from Oz: Iterative design of intelligent learning environments by communication capacity tapering. *Computers & Education 54*, 3 (Apr. 2010), 641–651.
11. Mavrikis, M., Gutiérrez-Santos, S., Geraniou, E., and Noss, R. Design requirements, student perception indicators and validation metrics for intelligent exploratory learning environments. *Personal and Ubiquitous Computing 17*, 8 (May 2013), 1605–1620.
12. Pekrun, R. The control-value theory of achievement emotions: Assumptions, corollaries, and implications for educational research and practice. *J. Edu. Psych. Rev.* (2006), 315–341.
13. Porayska-Pomsta, K., Mavrikis, M., and Pain, H. Diagnosing and acting on student affect: the tutor's perspective. *User Modeling and User-Adapted Interaction 18*, 1 (Feb. 2008), 125–173.
14. Read, J., MacFarlane., S., and Casey, C. Endurability, engagement and expectations: Measuring children's fun. In *Interaction Design and Children* (2002).
15. Rosenthal, R., and Rosnow, R. *Essentials of Behavioral Research: Methods and data analysis*, 3rd ed. McGraw Hill, 2008.
16. Sweller, J. Cognitive load theory and the use of educational technology. *Educational Technology Magazine: The Magazine for Managers of Change in Education 48*, 1 (2008).
17. Sweller, J., van Merrienboer, J. G., and Paas, G. W. Cognitive Architecture and Instructional Design. *Educational Psychology Review 10* (1998), 251–296.
18. Woolf, B., Burleson, W., Arroyo, I., Dragon, T., Cooper, D., and Picard, R. Affect-aware tutors: recognising and responding to student affect. *Int. J. Learning Technology 4*, 3-4 (2009), 129–164.

BayesHeart: A Probabilistic Approach for Robust, Low-Latency Heart Rate Monitoring on Camera Phones

Xiangmin Fan[1,2], Jingtao Wang[1,2]
[1]Department of Computer Science
[2]Learning Research and Development Center (LRDC)
University of Pittsburgh, Pittsburgh, PA, USA
{xiangmin, jingtaow}@cs.pitt.edu

ABSTRACT
Recent technological advances have demonstrated the *feasibility* of measuring people's heart rates through commodity cameras by capturing users' skin transparency changes, color changes, or involuntary motion. However, such raw image data collected during everyday interactions (e.g. gaming, learning, and fitness training) is often noisy and intermittent, especially in mobile contexts. Such interference causes increased error rates, latency, and even detection failures for most existing algorithms. In this paper, we present BayesHeart, a probabilistic algorithm that extracts both heart rates and distinct phases of the cardiac cycle directly from raw fingertip transparency signals captured by camera phones. BayesHeart is based on an adaptive hidden Markov model, requires minimal training data and is user-independent. Through a comparative study of twelve state-of-the-art algorithms covering the design space of noise reduction and pulse counting, we found that BayesHeart outperforms existing algorithms in both accuracy and speed for noisy, intermittent signals.

Author Keywords
Heart rate; mobile phone; camera phone; hidden Markov model; healthcare

ACM Classification Keywords
H5.2. Information interfaces and presentation (e.g., HCI): User Interfaces

General Terms
Design, Experimentation, Human Factors

INTRODUCTION
Recent technological advances have demonstrated the *feasibility* of extracting people's heart rates through commodity cameras by capturing users' skin transparency changes [4, 25, 31], thermal changes [11], facial color changes [27], or involuntary motion [3]. As one crucial physiological signal, resting heart rate (RHR) is a key indicator of health condition [8, 10], fitness [9, 17], and expected life span [18, 32]. Heart rate and variations of heart rate have also been used to predict human emotion [26], cognitive workload [30], stress [6, 21], and attention. As a result, low cost, ubiquitous heart rate monitoring has enormous opportunities in healthcare, human-computer interaction [30], balancing physical exertion [23], and computer assisted tutoring [20, 36].

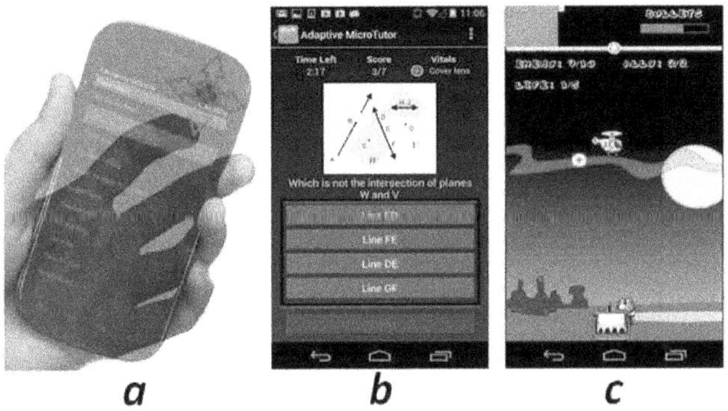

Figure 1: BayesHeart can detect heart rate *implicitly* from *intermittent* mobile interactions. (*a*) LensGesture [37] enhanced UI navigation; (*b*) mobile intelligent tutoring system; (*c*) LivePulse Games (LPG) [14].

Despite compelling advantages in cost, availability, portability, and ease-of-use [14, 28], commodity camera based heart rate monitoring techniques, when running on smartphones, also face three major challenges when compared with traditional approaches such as Electrocardiogram (ECG) and pulse oximetry. First, the indirectly captured Blood Volume Pulse (BVP) signals by cameras are noisier due to interference in background illumination, motion, and contact pressure. Second, the region of interests (ROI), be it human face, head, fingertip, or body, may not be always in the viewport of the camera. Brief but *intermittent* appearance of ROI (e.g. 2 – 20 seconds) will be the norm in many interaction scenarios. Such interference causes increased error rates, latency, and even detection failures when using certain existing algorithms. Last, the *sampling rate* of commodity camera based heart rate monitoring is bounded by the camera's frame rate (30 Hz), which is much lower when compared

IUI 2015, March 29–April 1, 2015, Atlanta, GA, USA.
Copyright 2015 © ACM 978-1-4503-3306-1/15/03...$15.00.
http://dx.doi.org/10.1145/2678025.2701364

with dedicated ECG (125-1500 Hz) devices and pulse oximeters (125-250 Hz). Such low sample rate prevents the adoption of state-of-the-art noise cancelation techniques in heart rate monitoring.

To address these challenges, we present BayesHeart, a probabilistic algorithm that extracts both heart rates and distinct phases of the cardiac cycle directly from noisy, intermittent ROI signals (e.g. fingertip transparency changes, facial color images) captured by camera phones. BayesHeart can extract heart rate from everyday mobile interactions *implicitly*. We use the term "*implicit*" to differentiate our envisioned scenarios with those that require users to mount sensing equipment, "explicitly" launch monitoring apps, and spend an uninterrupted amount of time in data collection. For example, Figure 1.a illustrates LensGesture [37] enhanced UI navigation. A user's heart rate can be inferred when scrolling menu item via back-of-device finger gestures on the camera lens; Figure 1.b shows a mobile intelligent tutoring system which adapts question difficulty based on both learners' stress inferred from heart rates and answer history; Figure 1.c are examples of LivePulse Games (LPG) [14]. LPG integrate users' camera lens covering actions as a control channel for game play and derive users' heart rates from lens-covering actions. In these scenarios, BayesHeart can infer users' heart rates as a *side effect* during everyday tasks.

BayesHeart uses an adaptive hidden Markov model, requiring no user-specific training. BayesHeart has four major advantages when compared with approaches in the existing literature: 1) lower latency and bootstrap time; 2) higher accuracy under noisy and incomplete data; 3) Easier integration with application scenarios that only capture ROI implicitly or intermittently [14, 37]; 4) Joint extraction of both heart rate and distinct phases of the cardiac cycles.

RELATED WORK

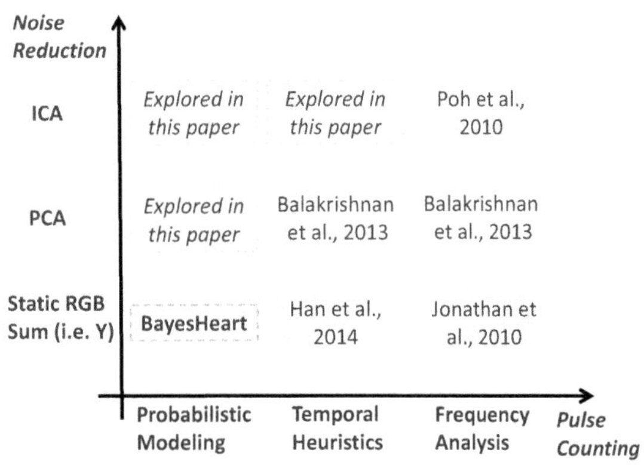

Figure 2. The design space of commodity camera based heart rate detection techniques.

Electrocardiography (ECG or EKG) and pulse oximetry (i.e. blood oxygen saturation or blood oxygenation) are the most widely adopted approaches for heart rate detection. ECG and pulse oximetry devices usually come in the form of chest bands, wrist bands, finger clips, or watches. Although the recent release of wearable computing devices such as Android Wear [1] and Apple Watch [2] opens new opportunities for continual heart rate sensing integrated with smartphones, the price and battery life may prevent their wide adoption in the near future.

Several commodity camera based heart rate detection techniques [3, 4, 5, 11. 14, 16, 19, 25, 27, 31] have arisen in recent years. These approaches are capable of extracting heart rate from consumer-grade webcams or smartphones, hence enabling enormous opportunities in health care, fitness training, and affective computing [26].

Along this line, researchers have shown the feasibility of extracting heart rate from finger transparency changes, i.e. photoplethysmography (PPG), captured by a smartphone camera [4, 19, 25]. Jonathan et al. [19] proposed to analyze fingertip video via Fast Fourier transform (FFT), however, the authors didn't conduct a formal evaluation of the accuracy. Poh et al. [27] successfully inferred heart rates by analyzing facial color changes captured by a webcam. Poh's algorithm first used Independent Component Analysis (ICA) to construct a less noisy signal channel from three R/B/G channels, then used FFT and thresholding in the frequency domain for pulse counting. Similarly, Balakrishnan [3] used PCA for noise reduction, frequency domain power analysis for channel selection, and a moving window in temporal domain for peak detection when analyzing involuntary head motions in video. It's also possible to measure heart rate by analyzing facial thermal changes [11]. With the popularization of camera phones, such camera based approaches have already become wildly popular when compared with solutions that rely on dedicated hardware. For example, Instant Heart Rate [16], a commercial camera based PPG app, attracted over 25 million users within two years.

Despite variations in underlying sensing mechanisms, most of today's algorithms adopt a two-step workflow, i.e. 1) noise reduction and 2) heart beat counting. The noise reduction step intends to diminish noise from digitizers, ambient light, body tissue, and motion. Commonly used noise reduction techniques include independent component analysis (ICA) [27], principle component analysis (PCA) [3], smoothing filters [4, 33], and heuristics [14]. The heart beat counting step leverages either temporal domain techniques (peak thresholding [3, 4, 33], heuristic based peak counting [14]) or frequency domain techniques (e.g., Fast Fourier Transform [3, 27]). Figure 2 shows the design space of commodity camera based cardiac pulse detection and the relationship of BayesHeart with existing techniques.

Unfortunately, although the two-step workflow works well on continual and relatively clean signals, it may break when dealing with *implicit* and *intermittent* mobile interaction scenarios (Figure 1). Figure 3 illustrates representative signals (i.e. (a) high quality signals, (b) noisy signals, and (c) intermittent signals) captured from such scenarios.

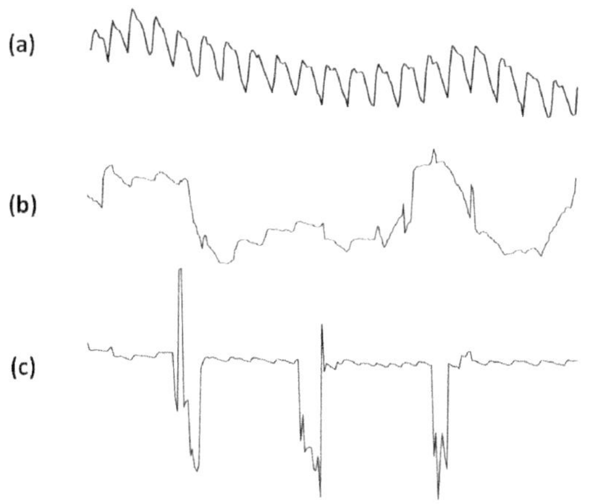

Figure 3. Sample PPG signals captured from a mobile camera (a: high quality signals; b: noisy signals; c: intermittent signals).

In the noise reduction step, component analysis techniques (ICA and PCA) require constructing and updating a linear transformation matrix from historical data. A 30-second window [27] will cause at least the same amount of bootstrap time and increased latency. The calculation of PCA or ICA transformation matrix becomes more challenging when dealing with intermittent signals that only last 5 - 20 seconds in each session.

In the heart beat counting step, an FFT based approach [27] requires *continual* signals meaning that it will break when handling intermittent signals. Meanwhile, temporal domain counting techniques only leverage the *amplitude* properties of pulse peaks and ignore the *temporal regularity* of pulse wave forms. As a result, both peak thresholding and peak counting techniques are sensitive to motion-induced noises, which are hard to eliminate during the noise reduction step.

BayesHeart uses probabilistic modeling to address challenges of existing algorithms in contexts of *noisy*, *implicit* and *intermittent* PPG signals captured by commodity cameras in everyday settings. Unique contributions of BayesHeart include: 1) The usage of an Adaptive Hidden Markov Model to extract both heart rates and distinct phases of the cardiac cycle directly from raw signals; 2) The usage of *discrete local trend* features to achieve both simplified model training and improved robustness; 3) Designing an effective 2/4-state model selection paradigm to exploit both the *temporal regularity* and the *intra-person diversity* in signals. We also advance the state-of-the-art by identifying the design space of commodity-camera based heart rate detection and presenting a comparative study of BayesHeart, existing algorithms, and their variants.

Hidden Markov models have been used in analyzing cardiac pulse signals (e.g., ECG and PPG) before, either for analyzing signal properties [7, 15], or for diagnosing disease [24]. BayesHeart is unique in that existing techniques focused on *continual clinical* signals captured from *medical-grade* devices collected by researchers or health-care providers. Thanks to the sampling rate (150–1500 Hz), form factors (wrist bands, chest bands, or finger clips), and usage scenarios (in-door, continual measurements in stationary postures), extrinsic noise and interruptions were not a major concerns in existing research. By comparison, BayesHeart explores the opportunities of *implicit* and *intermittent* heart rate monitoring for normal people in everyday environments. Existing techniques for analyzing medical grade ECG/PPG signals do not generalize directly to low frequency (below 30 Hz) and noisy signals captured by commodity cameras. We invented two novel techniques in BayesHeart to overcome new challenges encountered: 1) We defined four novel "local trend" features as the input to our learning algorithm. The absolute signal magnitude feature used by HMM models in ECG and PPG research do not work well on noisy and intermittent signals from commodity cameras; 2) We designed a simple but effective 2/4-state adaptive model to capture signal variances in the unique context of commodity camera based mobile interactions.

THE BAYESHEART ALGORITHM

Background

The underlying theory behind photoplethysmographic (PPG) imaging is as follows: the heart pumps fresh blood to the capillary vessels of a human body during systole in each cardiac cycle. Such blood volume changes lead to changes in fingertip transparency, which can be detected by the built-in camera of the mobile phone when the user covers the lens of the camera with her fingertip [12, 13, 19]. Therefore the changes of finger transparency can be viewed as a *generative process*, in which there are natural correlations between different regions of the PPG waveform and dedicated cardiac phase.

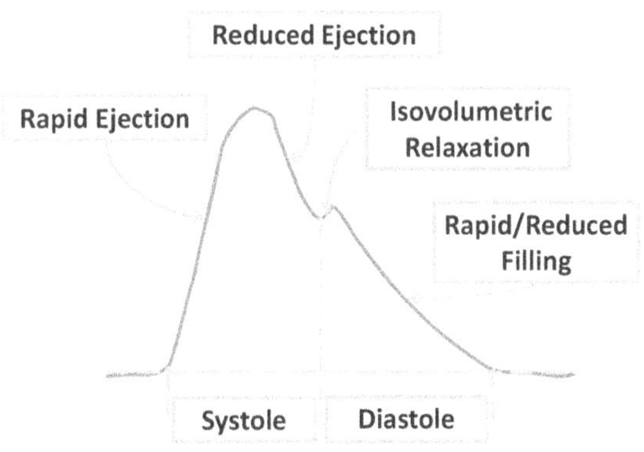

Figure 4. One-cycle waveform associated with the physical activities in one cardiac cycle.

Pulse Modeling

BayesHeart relies on a hidden Markov model to capture the temporal regularity of the different stages in cardiac cycles (hidden) and the finger transparency changes (observable). After training the model, given new observations, we can segment the observations into states by calculating an optimal alignment via Viterbi decoding [29]. Then heart rate can be estimated by extracting the duration of each cardiac cycle from the derived cardiac alignment.

Hidden States

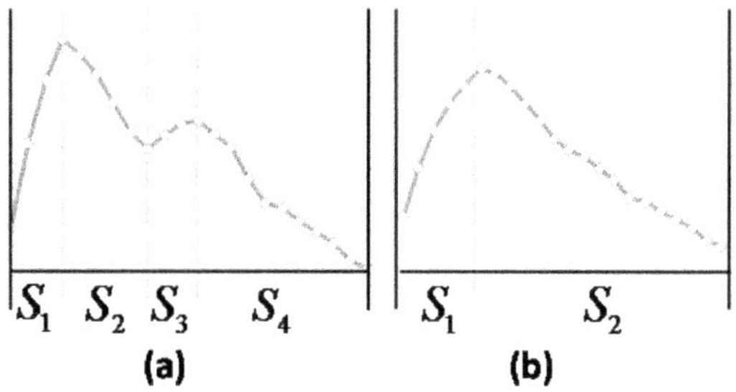

Figure 5. States selection based on the waveform shapes.

According to PPG imaging [22, 33], a typical cardiac cycle includes four distinct stages (Figure 4): 1) rapid ejection (i.e. systolic upstroke); 2) reduced ejection (i.e. systolic downstroke), 3) isovolumetric relaxation (i.e. a small upstroke caused by dicrotic notch); and 4) rapid/reduced filling (i.e. diastolic downstroke). Therefore it is a natural choice to use a 4-state hidden Markov model with each state corresponding to one cardiac stage (Figure 5.a). However, due to extrinsic noise and variations in tissue/skin reflections, the third cardiac stage (isovalumetric relaxation) can be hard to identify in the waveforms captured by commodity cameras. In such situations, the waveform of one cardiac cycle only shows two distinct phases (Figure 5.b): rapid ejection (i.e., systolic upstroke) and reduced ejection plus the whole diastole phase (i.e., a long downstroke). Hence we propose an adaptive 2/4 state model to capture both the subtlety and diversity of waveforms.

We do not consider models with more than 4 states for two reasons. 1) Although the model likelihood on training data improves as the number of states increases, it usually comes at the cost of data overfitting (i.e., more parameters) and more training samples. 2) Our main purpose is to estimate the *duration* of cardiac cycles rather than to analyze subtle changes within one cycle. For this purpose, fine grained segmentations, at the cost of more training data and increased algorithm complexity, won't bring us additional insight.

Observations

Unlike existing research on clinical ECG/PPG analysis [7, 15], we choose not to use the absolute observations (i.e. brightness of finger transparency) in our model because such absolute scales are sensitive to both the environmental illumination changes and motion-induced noise. Instead, we choose the "*local trend*" of each sample point as a more *robust* feature as our model observations. Interestingly, this feature is more *expressive* than the absolute scale in our context. For instance, the wave-form generates much more *increasing* observations in the rapid ejection stage than the filling stage. Such regularities encoded in the "*local trend*" feature are easier to capture by BayesHeart. We further define four types of discrete observations (o1 – o4) from the "*local trend*" feature (Figure 6, o1 represents increasing observations, o2 represents local minimum observations, o3 represents maximum observations, and o4 represents decreasing observations).

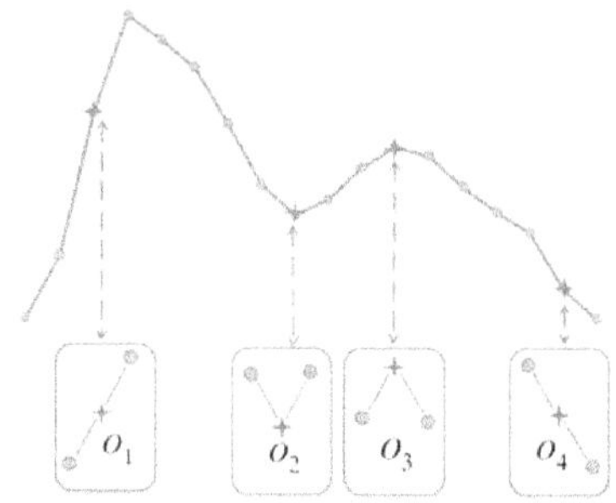

Figure 6. Four types of observations.

Mathematical formulation

BayesHeart is a discrete left-right HMM [29] defined as follows:

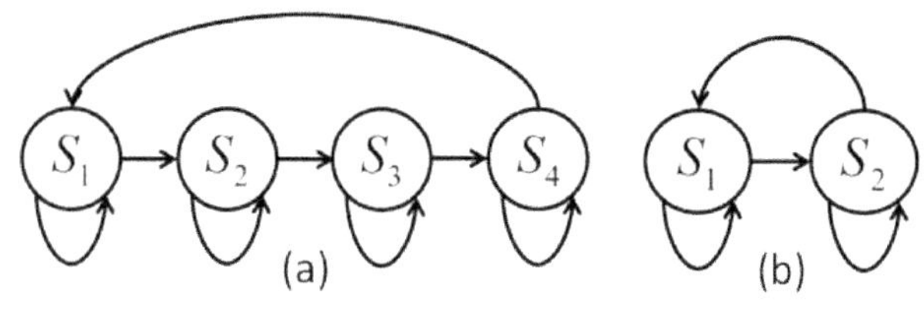

Figure 7. 4-state model (a) and 2-state model (b)

1) *N*, the number of states in the model

We denote the individual states as $S = S_1, \ldots, S_N$ and the state at time t as s_t. As mentioned above, there are two models (i.e., 4-state model and 2-state model, Figure 7) in our approach.

2) *M*, the number of distinct observation symbols per state,

In our case, *M*=4. We denote the individual symbols as $O = \{O_1, O_2, O_3, O_4\}$.

3) The initial state distribution $\pi = \{\pi_i\}$ where

$$\pi_i = P\{s_1 = S_i\}, 1 \le i \le N$$

4) The state transition probability distribution $A = \{a_{ij}\}$ where

$$a_{ij} = P\{s_{t+1} = S_j | s_t = S_i\}, \quad 1 \le i, j \le N$$

In BayesHeart, we add order constraints within each cardiac cycle by setting $a_{ij} = 0$ for the (i, j) pairs in which $i > j$. The only exception is $a_{N1} > 0$ which enables the model to start new cycles.

5) The observation symbol probability distribution in state j, $B = \{b_j(k)\}$, where

$$b_j(k) = P\{o_k \; at \; t \mid s_t = S_k\}, 1 \le j \le N, \quad 1 \le k \le M$$

The hidden Markov model in BayesHeart can be characterized in terms of three probability measures, A, B and π. For convenience, we denote the 4-state model as $\lambda_1 = (A_1, B_1, \pi_1)$ and the 2-state model as $\lambda_2 = (A_2, B_2, \pi_2)$ in a compact way.

Parameter estimation (model training)

To use the Baum-Welch method to estimate model parameters $\lambda = (A, B, \pi)$, we estimate initial distribution of π as the temporal duration of each cardiac state in the training data. For the state transition probability distribution A, we assign a high probability (i.e., 0.8) of remaining in the same state and low probabilities (i.e., 0.2) to transitioning between states. We set $a_{ij} = 0$ (except for a_{N1}) when $i > j$ because the cardiac stages appear sequentially and cannot be reversed.

We train the 4-state model λ_1 and the 2-state model λ_2 separately and use a model selection process detailed in the next section at runtime.

Heart Rate Estimation

After deriving the underlying model via offline training, the BayesHeart runtime includes four phases: 1) model selection; 2) state sequence generation; 3) cardiac pulse interval calculation; and 4) post-processing.

Model selection

BayesHeart uses the first 5 seconds[1] of observations for model selection. We leverage the Bayesian information criterion (BIC) [35] to find the better model λ^* from $\{\lambda_1, \lambda_2\}$ at the same time to prevent the 4-state model from overfitting the observations.

$$BIC_\lambda = -2 \cdot \ln \Pr(o^* | \lambda) + \mathrm{k} \cdot (\ln(n) - \ln(2\pi))$$

$$\lambda^* = \underset{\lambda \in \{\lambda_1, \lambda_2\}}{\operatorname{argmin}} BIC_\lambda$$

The model selection step does not introduce extra latency because it can be run in parallel with the state sequences generation step discussed later.

State sequences generation

In this step, we leverage the Viterbi algorithm to infer the optimal state sequence that is most likely to generate the observations by maximizing $Pr(o, s | \lambda)$.

Cardiac cycle/distinct phases extraction

We define the transition from the last state to the first state (i.e. $S_N \rightarrow S_1$) as the start of a new cardiac cycle and mark all of such transitions in the derived state sequence. Therefore, the duration d between two adjacent marks is the duration of one cycle (Figure 8). The instant heart rate estimate is:

$$Instant\ Heart\ Rate\ (bpm) = \frac{60000(ms)}{d\ (ms)}$$

Here bpm means beats per minutes. It is worth noticing that BayesHeart extracts distinct phases in each cardiac cycle in parallel with the heart rate estimation processing (Figure 8).

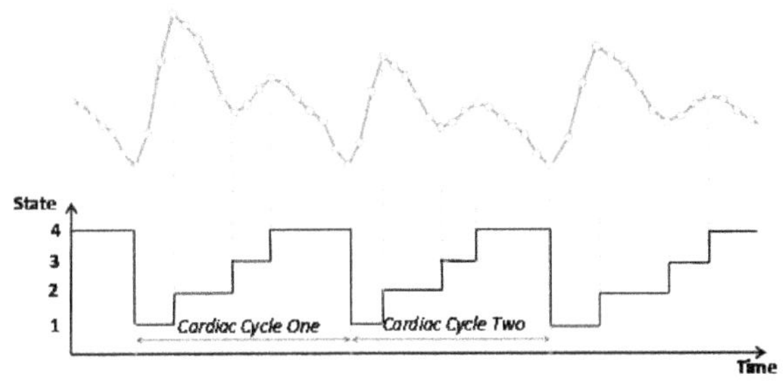

Figure 8. Cardiac cycle/ distinct phase extraction from the underlying state sequence.

Post-processing

Despite the robustness of our BayesHeart algorithm, we still impose two simple heuristics to reduce outliers in extreme situations. If either of the heuristics is violated, BayesHeart rejects the current estimation and outputs the first valid estimation in history.

Heuristic 1: Valid heart rates are within the range of [30, 300] bpm.

Heuristic 2: The maximal change between two adjacent bpm estimates should not be more than (k=5) bpm.

Intermittent signals

As highlighted in the introduction section, the intermittent appearance of ROI (e.g. 2 – 30 seconds) is the norm in many interaction scenarios (e.g., mobile gaming, mobile tutoring, etc.). Therefore we investigate how to extract heart rate via intermittent covering actions. There are three problems when dealing with intermittent covering: 1) how to detect users' covering actions (i.e., when users are covering the lens); 2) how to deal with the noise introduced by intermittent covering actions; 3) once users' covering actions can be detected, how to estimate heart rate based on several separate pieces of signals.

For the first problem, we leverage a fast and reliable linear classification model proposed in [37] to detect the lens covering gesture. The model uses the global mean and standard deviation of all the pixels in an image frame to infer whether the user is covering the lens or not with high accuracy (i.e., 97.9%). After this step, we get a set of data sequences (i.e., observation sequences), with each sequence corresponding to one covering action.

For the second problem, we find that most of the noise is generated by finger movements and pressure changes (e.g., at the beginning of each covering action). Therefore we

[1] We assume that owner change is rare for mobile devices and context (location, environment, etc.) change happens at the scale of minutes or hours rather than seconds. The model selection process can run more frequently when necessary.

apply two techniques to reduce the extreme noise that appears in intermittent signals: 1) Discard the observation sequences corresponding to the covering actions which last less than 2 seconds; 2) For the data sequences that are longer than 2 seconds, discard the first 1 second of data for each covering action (Figure 9, a).

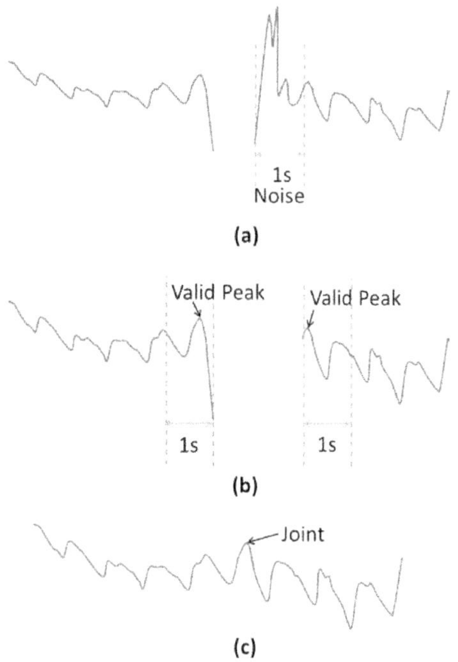

Figure 9. Additional steps with intermittent covering. a) Remove noise at the beginning of each covering action. b) Find two valid peaks. c) Connect the two valid peaks.

For the third problem, we have two strategies to extract heart rate through separate segments of signals: 1) Treat each sequence independently and apply HMM on each of them; 2) Concatenate the sequences to one whole sequence and then apply HMM on it. The first one may lead to lower utilization of the signal because we cannot make use of the front/back ends of each separate piece if the ends do not appear in a complete cycle in that piece. Therefore we try to concatenate them together to get a continuous and complete waveform.

One question emerges regarding how to concatenate separate pieces of signals. One brute force method is to directly connect the last sample of the previous piece with the first sample of the next piece. However, this cannot ensure that the concatenation of the two pieces can form one cycle and may introduce inaccurate estimations. Therefore we use a heuristic to concatenate two pieces trying to make use of the data at the very end/beginning of the signal pieces. The heuristic attempts to find the last valid peak of the previous piece and the first valid peak of the next piece and link them by joining the two peaks together. Since the normal resting heart rate for adults ranges from 60-100 bpm, valid peaks are close to 600ms-1000ms apart; therefore we assume that a valid peak can be found within a window with the size of 1000ms. So we apply a window at the end of the previous piece as well as the beginning of the next piece and localize the valid peak by choosing the local-maximum point (i.e., o3) with the largest amplitude within the windows (1000ms). (Figure 9, b). Then these two valid peaks are connected together to concatenate the two signals (Figure 9, c).

EVALUATION

We carried out two studies to evaluate the efficacy of BayesHeart. In the first study we investigated the impact of different design choices on BayesHeart, such as the inclusion of an adaptive model and the inclusion of the post processing step on both accuracy and latency. The second study was a comparison of the state-of-the-art algorithms in the design space (Figure 2) with BayesHeart. We report results on both accuracy and latency for both normal signals and intermittent signals.

Data Collection

We collected data from 20 subjects (7 female) from department mailing lists of a local university. The participants were between 23 and 45 years old (mean = 27.8, $\sigma = 4.9$). We collected two types of PPG data via the built-in camera of a smartphone: 1) 10 minutes static covering and 2) 10 minutes intermittent covering. For intermittent covering, participants were asked to cover the lens for 5-10 seconds and then move their finger away for 1-3 seconds, and to repeat this process for a total of 10 minutes. Participants used one hand to operate the mobile phone and we attached a pulse oximeter on their other hand to collect the ground truth heart rate data. Each participant was paid $5 for their time.

We used a Google Nexus smartphone running Android 4.1 for data collection. The Google Nexus has a 4.65 inch, 720*1280 pixels display, 1.2 GHz dual core ARM Cortex-A9 processor. It has a 5 mega-pixel back camera and an LED flash light. We set the built-in camera in preview mode, capturing color images of 144x176 pixel at 30 fps (frames per second). We sample 800 pixels evenly distributed in each frame and use the RGB/YUV sum of these 800 pixels to estimate the brightness of the frame. In this way we derive a set of time-stamped ROI signal vectors. We resample the data by linear interpolation to 30Hz to compensate for the jitter effect of the video stream.

The pulse oximeter in the experiment was a CMS 50D with USB port. CMS 50D is an FDA-approved, medical grade device. The accuracy of CMS 50D for pulse ratio was +/- 2 bpm.

Benchmarking Metrics

In the first part of the evaluation, we use 50% of the data (i.e., for each subject, we use 5-minute static covering data and 5-minute intermittent covering data) for training and the other 50% of the data for testing. For the second part, we use leave-one-out cross-validation (LOOCV) to test user-independent performance of BayesHeart compared with previous work.

We use ***mean error rate*** *(MER)* to measure algorithm accuracy. To derive the MER of a given algorithm/configuration, we compare the estimated heart rate with the gold standard *every second* and report the average. ***Estimation latency*** is defined as the time an algorithm needed to generate the first accurate heart rate estimation (+/- 5% when compared with the gold standard). We also define *utilization rate* to model the robustness of an algorithm. It is defined as the ratio between the quantity of samples from which BayesHeart derived valid cardiac cycles (i.e., cycles that are not eliminated in the post-processing step and are used in heart rate calculation) and the total quantity of samples in use.

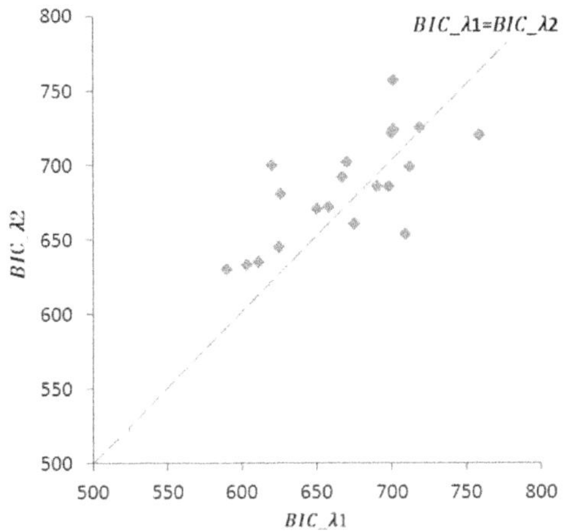

Figure 10. Plots of *BIC* values of 20 subjects. BayesHeart chooses a 4-state model for subjects above the decision boundary and a 2-state model for all others.

Understanding BayesHeart

Model Selection

Figure 10 shows the scatter plot of the Bayesian information criterion (BIC) for the two models. BayesHeart chose 6 subjects for the 2-state model and 14 subjects for the 4-state model.

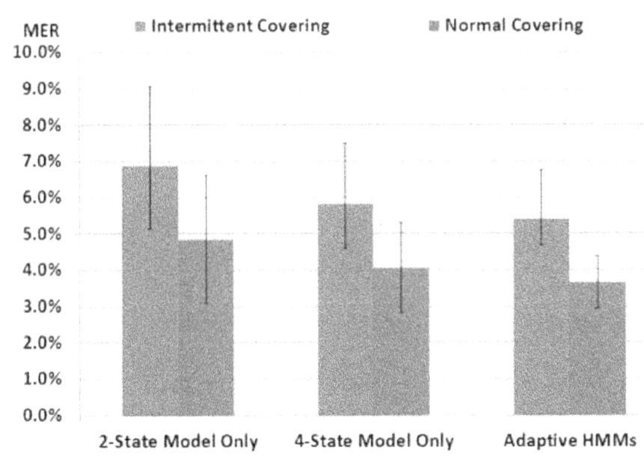

Figure 11. Mean error rates of BayesHeart with different types of models.

Figure 11 illustrates the impact of model selection on the accuracy for both the normal covering condition and intermittent covering condition. The three conditions shown are BayesHeart with 2-state model only, with 4-state model only and with adaptive HMMs.

Two-way within-subjects ANOVA shows that both signal types ($F_{1,19}$=75.36, $p<0.01$) and the model selection techniques ($F_{2,18}$=16.25, $p<0.01$) have a significant main effect on MER. Pairwise comparisons also show significant differences in MER between adaptive HMMs and 2-state model only. In summary, the model selection technique in BayesHeart leads to the lowest mean error rates in both normal (3.66% vs. 4.08% vs. 4.84%) and intermittent covering conditions (5.39% vs. 5.84% vs. 6.90%).

Post-Processing Heuristics

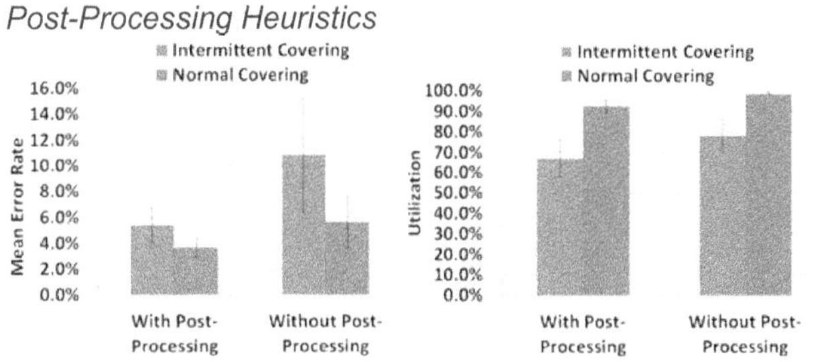

Figure 12: (left) Mean error rate (right) and utilization rate of BayesHeart with/without post-processing and with normal/intermittent covering data.

Figure 12 shows the impact of BayesHeart post-processing on MER and utilization rates. The post-processing step eliminates outliers of cardiac intervals. By eliminating unreasonable estimates, it leads to the reduction of utilization rate (Figure 12.b, 11.2% and 5.96% reductions in intermittent covering condition and normal covering condition, respectively). Accordingly, it improves the accuracy (Figure 12.a), especially for intermittent signals (5.39% vs. 10.86%). Two-way within-subject ANOVA shows that the MER can be significantly affected by the inclusion of post-processing ($F_{1,19}$=98.96, $p<0.01$).

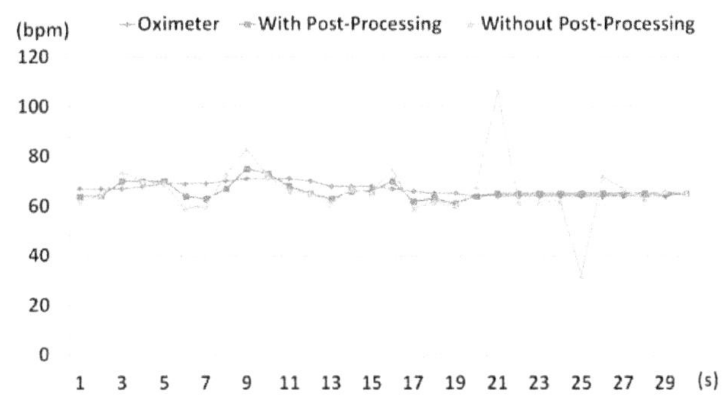

Figure 13. Heart rate estimates generated by the pulse oximeter and our algorithm during 30 seconds.

Figure 13 is a 30-second sample sequence, illustrating heart rate estimates from BayesHeart (both with and without post-processing) against the gold standard.

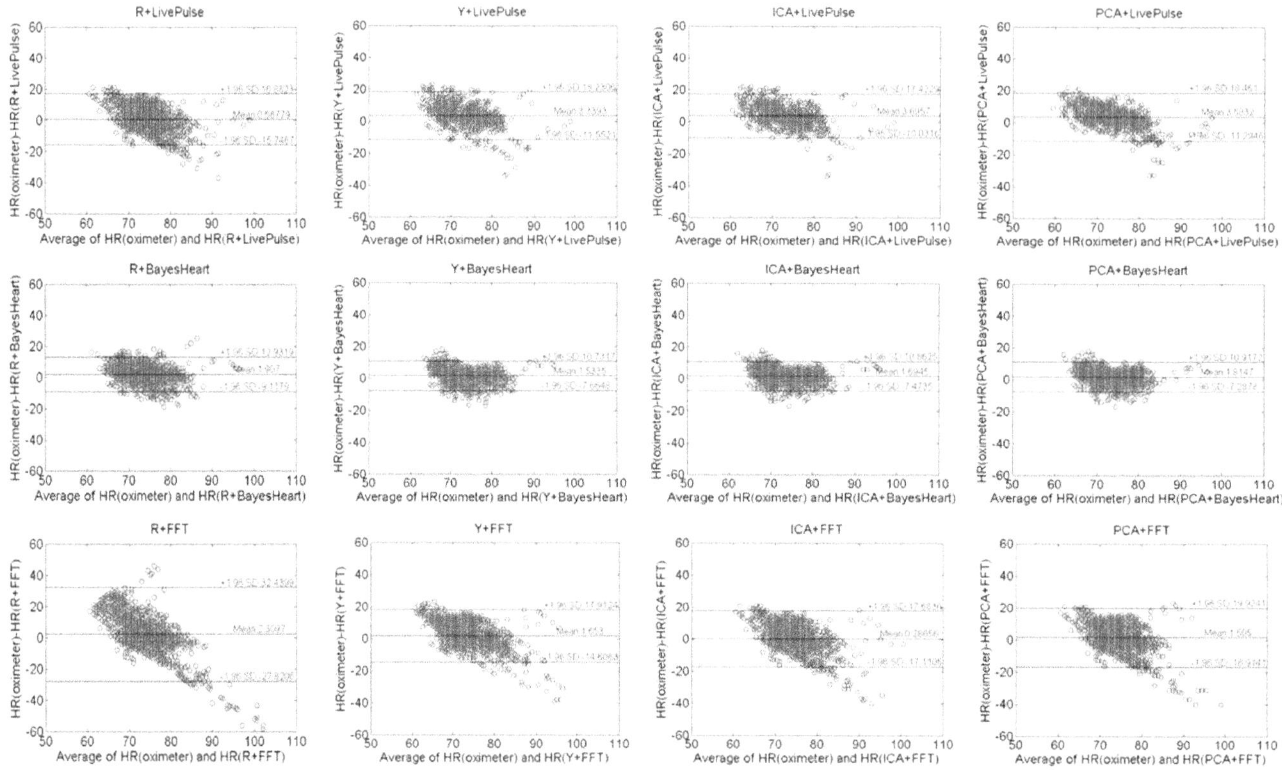

Figure 14. Bland-Altman plots demonstrating the agreement between heart rate measurements obtained from the nine state-of-the-art algorithms (with intermittent covering data) and the pulse oximeter. The lines represent the mean and 95% limits of agreement.

Design Space Exploration

We conducted a comparative study of twelve state-of-the-art algorithms (Figure 2) in the design space of extracting cardiac pulses from commodity cameras. Such a study is important because existing literature [3, 4, 14, 19, 27] focused primarily on the *feasibility* and *non-comparative evaluation* of proposed scenarios. With the popularization of wearable devices and affect/emotion-aware intelligent mobile apps, it is imperative for researchers to gain a deeper understanding of the state of the art. To the best of our knowledge, this is the first systematic study and exploration in commodity camera based heart rate monitoring.

We explore a space of 4 noise reduction techniques by 3 pulse counting techniques for a total of 12 algorithms.

Noise reduction methods we investigated include: **1**) Using the Red channel only (baseline condition [33]); **2**) Using the Y (brightness) channel (static-weighted sum of the R, G, B channels); **3**) Using the ICA technique (dynamic-weighted sum of the R, G, B channels by maximizing channel independence); **4**) Using the PCA technique[2] (dynamic-weighted sum of the R, G, B channels by maximizing channel variance).

Pulse counting techniques include: **A**) LivePulse (temporal domain, heuristic based counting)[3] [14]; **B**) FFT (frequency domain counting, window size = 6 sec[4]); **C**) BayesHeart (temporal domain, probabilistic model based alignment).

Ignoring subtle variations in signal preprocessing and post-processing, existing algorithms can be represented as combining one noise reduction technique and one pulse counting technique. For example, the facial color based method by Poh et al [27, 28] can be represented as **3B** (their baseline condition was **1B**). **The** facial motion based method by Balakrishnan et al [3] is **4A**[5]. LivePulse Games [14] used **2A** and the default BayesHeart algorithm is **2C.** Such a comparison will answer questions such as: Will the PCA/ICA based noise reduction technique be effective for detecting pulse amidst motion induced noise? Will adding a PCA/ICA based noise reduction technique improve the performance of BayesHeart even more? Quantitatively,

[2] We chose the most periodic channel by a method discussed in [3]. The periodicity of a signal is defined as the percentage of total spectral power accounted for by the frequency with maximal power.

[3] The LivePulse algorithm [14] is a heuristic based outlier removal and local peaks/valleys counting algorithm. LivePulse can be treated as a manually optimized, temporal domain adaptive thresholding algorithm.

[4] The choice of window size involves tradeoffs between frequency resolution, time accuracy, and latency.

[5] The original signal in [3] was head motion, but the same algorithm can be used to process PPG signals and vice-versa.

what's the impact of an algorithm chosen in each step on the overall performance?

We tested the 12 combinations of algorithms with both normal and intermittent covering signals and analyzed both the accuracy and latency for each method. Considering the importance of post-processing heuristics shown in previous sections, in order to minimize confounding factors in the study, we applied the same post-processing heuristics used in the default BayesHeart algorithm in all 12 algorithms.

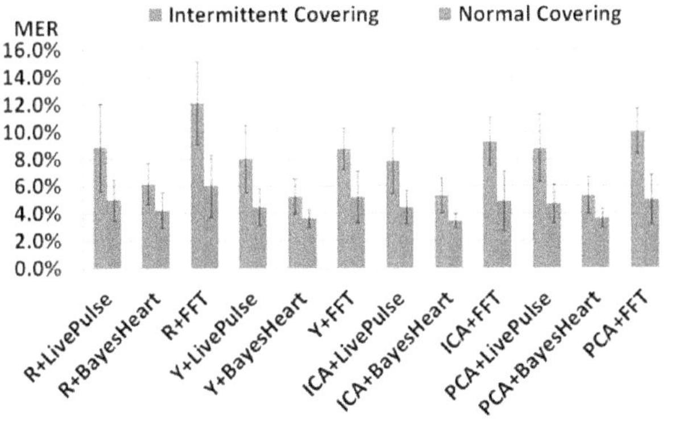

Figure 15. Mean error rates (MER) of algorithms.

Accuracy

Figure 14 shows the Bland-Altman plots demonstrating the agreement between heart rate estimates generated by the 12 algorithms and gold standard with intermittent covering data. The lines represent the mean and 95% limits of agreement. By comparing between different columns (i.e., different noise reduction techniques) we can see that using Y(**2**)/ICA(**3**)/PCA(**4**) could reduce the error compared to using R(**1**) directly. For example, when using BayesHeart on R channel, the mean bias was 1.91 bpm with 95% limits of agreement -9.12 to 12.93 bpm. The mean bias was reduced to 1.53 bpm with 95% limits of agreement -7.66 to 10.73 bpm when using Y(**2**). At the same time, by comparing different rows (i.e., different pulse counting methods) we can find that BayesHeart(**C**) can lower the errors compared to LivePulse(**A**)/FFT(**B**). For example, when applied on Y(**2**), LivePulse(**A**)'s mean bias was 3.34 bpm with 95% limits of agreement -11.55 to 18.23 bpm and FFT(**B**)'s mean bias was 1.61 bpm with 95% limits of agreement -14.61 to 17.91 bpm. In comparison, BayesHeart(**C**) reduced the mean bias to 1.53 bpm with 95% agreement -7.66 to 10.73 bpm.

Figure 15 shows the corresponding MERs. For intermittent covering, Y+BayesHeart(**2C**) has the lowest MER (5.23%), followed by PCA+BayesHeart(**4C**) (5.30%) and ICA+BayesHeart(**3C**) (5.31%). R+FFT(**1B**) has the highest MER (12.14%). For normal covering, ICA+BayesHeart(**3C**) has the lowest MER (3.44%), followed by PCA+BayesHeart(**4C**) (3.63%) and Y+BayesHeart(**2C**) (3.66%). A three-way (signal type vs. noise reduction method vs. pulse counting method) ANOVA shows that signal type has a significant main effect on MERs ($F_{1,19}$=620.94, p<0.01). Noise reduction techniques ($F_{3,17}$=38.29, p=0.02) and pulse counting methods ($F_{2,18}$=257.55, p<0.01) also have a significant main effect on MERs. Not surprisingly, all the 12 algorithms are significantly more accurate when dealing with normal signals.

Among noise reduction techniques, the mean error rates corresponding to Y(**2**), ICA(**3**), PCA(**4**) and R(**1**) (averaged in both signal types) are 5.87%, 5.86%, 6.23% and 7.06%, respectively. Pairwise comparisons show that both the static weighted sum approach in Y(**2**) and the dynamic weight sum approach in ICA(**3**)/PCA(**4**) are significantly better than R(**1**) despite signal quality (p<0.01). Such improvements may be caused by the increased equivalent pixel area in Y(**2**)/ ICA(**3**)/PCA(**4**). Although ICA(**3**) has a lower MER than Y(**2**), the difference is not significant (p=0.92). We attribute that to the non-linear nature of skin/tissue reflection and the latency involved in calculating the transformation matrix, which was in turn used to capture the dynamic nature of extrinsic noises.

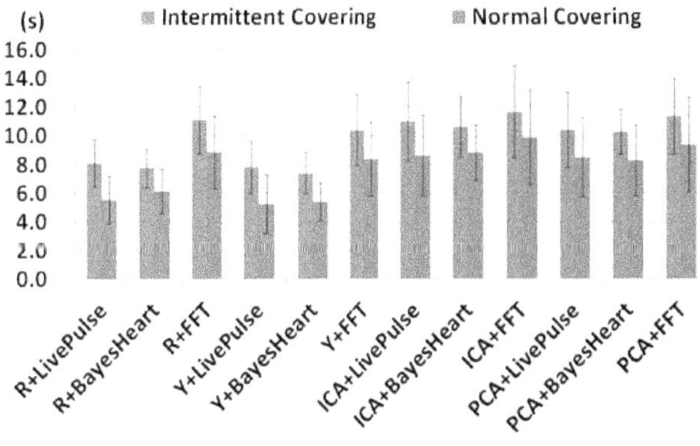

Figure 16. Average latency of algorithms.

Among pulse counting techniques, the mean error rates corresponding to LivePulse(**A**), FFT(**B**), and BayesHeart(**C**) (averaged in both signal types) are 6.50%, 7.65% and 4.62%, respectively. Pairwise comparisons show that BayesHeart can lower MERs significantly compared with LivePulse (p=0.01). And LivePulse can also significantly lower MERs compared with FFT (p<0.01). The reasons include: 1) the heuristic based method (e.g., LivePulse), although simple, could not capture both the diversity and regularity of signal with dealing with increased amount of signals; 2) FFT is the most sensitive technology to noise; the low-sampling rate (30HZ) could be one reason that led to the bad performance of FFT. Besides, the fixed-size window in FFT may also introduce increased noise when dealing with brief, highly intermittent signals; 3) BayesHeart exploits additional information in trellis structure, the state transition cost, and temporal regularity in signals through a simple yet robust probabilistic model; such increased "*signal/noise ratio*" becomes critical when dealing with increased extrinsic noise.

Estimation Latency

Figure 16 shows the average estimation latency of the 12 methods. For intermittent covering, Y+BayesHeart(**2C**) leads to the lowest latency (7.59s), followed by R+BayesHeart(**1C**) (8.02s) and Y+LivePulse(**2A**) (8.23s). ICA+FFT(**3B**) has the highest latency (12.21s). For normal covering, Y+LivePulse(**2A**) has the lowest latency (5.72s), followed by Y+BayesHeart(**2C**) (5.79s) and R+LivePulse(**1A**) (6.04s). PCA+FFT(**4B**) has the highest latency (9.88s).

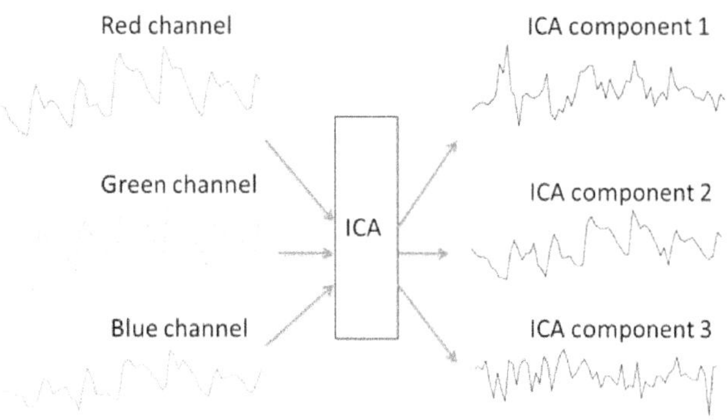

Figure 17. The components generated from ICA based noise reduction algorithm on 5-second R/G/B signal.

Three-way ANOVA shows that signal quality ($F_{1,19}$=411.44, p<0.01), noise reduction techniques ($F_{3,17}$=73.43, p<0.01) and pulse counting methods ($F_{2,18}$=55.51, p<0.01) all have a significant main effect on estimation latency. Pair-wise comparisons show that R(**1**) (8.42s) and Y(**2**) (7.84s) are significantly faster than ICA(**3**) (10.51s) and PCA(**4**) (10.12s) (p < 0.01). And there is no significant difference in latency between R(**1**) and Y(**2**), between ICA(**3**) and PCA(**4**). This is because ICA(**3**)/PCA(**4**) require additional time to construct and update the transformation matrix in use. In our experiments, ICA(**3**)/PCA(**4**) lead to 3-10 seconds of additional latency for normal signals or 5-12 seconds of additional latency for intermittent signals. Figure 17 shows an example of the components generated from ICA based on a 5-second normal covering R/G/B signal. We can see that when the transformation matrix in ICA(**3**) is outdated or out-of-sync, ICA could lead to *increased* noise

For pulse-counting methods, pairwise comparisons show that LivePulse and BayesHeart can significantly lower latencies when compared with FFT (p<0.01). This is because the relatively small number of signal samples and low sampling rate have a negative impact on the frequency domain resolution of FFT. Such low frequency domain resolution leads to less accurate estimates. Therefore the corresponding algorithms require more samples in order to derive accurate estimates.

CONCLUSION AND FUTURE WORK

We present BayesHeart, an accurate, low-latency probabilistic approach for heart rate monitoring via commodity cameras. Major contributions of the paper include: 1) we demonstrated both the feasibility and the quantitative performance of BayesHeart to measure heart rate via camera phone. 2) We reported and discussed the tradeoffs of BayesHeart in detail, especially *how* and *why* BayesHeart is robust to noisy and intermittent signals. 3) By decoupling existing camera based heart rate monitoring techniques into two steps, i.e. noisy reduction and cardiac pulse counting, we compared existing technologies side-by-side highlighting both their relationships and new opportunities. 4) In a 20-subject experiment, we systematically evaluated the state-of-the-art algorithms covering the design space regarding accuracy and latency performance.

BayesHeart is an initial step towards capturing, analyzing, and using physiological signals implicitly from everyday interactions. We believe there are tremendous opportunities if computer user interfaces could be aware of our physiological conditions [34], affect, and emotions. For example, when integrated with a Massive Open Online Courses (MOOC) mobile client, BayesHeart can be used infer the stress levels and cognitive workload of learners. Taking advantage of such information will be beneficial to both learners and instructors. Error correction algorithms in today's software touch keyboards (STK) can adapt to users' stress levels and cognitive workload in addition to holding postures [38] for better accuracy and less frustration. We hope the algorithmic design space we identified could inspire new ideas for the research community in the future.

In addition to accurately quantifying the average duration of each cardiac cycle, BayesHeart also provides opportunities to analyze different sub-phases within each cycle. The static prosperities, relative distributions, and temporal variations of sub-phases may be used as physiological makers of users' emotional states, health conditions, and even personal identities.

To encourage follow-up research and more creative usage of physiological signals in everyday interactions, we have released both the source code (written in Matlab and Java) of BayesHeart and data used in our comparative study to the public under a BSD license at URL http://mips.lrdc.pitt.edu/BayesHeart .

ACKNOWLEDGMENTS

We would like to thank Zitao Liu, Xiang Xiao, Qing Ma, Rui Wu, Brian Kocoloski, Wencan Luo, Andrew Head, Teng Han and Lanfei Shi for their suggestions and help. We also thank the anonymous reviewers for their constructive feedback.

REFERENCES

1. Android Wear Smart Watch OS, http://developer.android.com/wear
2. Apple Watch https://www.apple.com/watch/

3. Balakrishnan, G., Durand, F., & Guttag, J. Detecting Pulse from Head Motions in Video. In *Proc. CVPR 2013*, 3430-3437.
4. Banitsas, K., Pelegris, P., Orbach, T., Cavouras, D., Sidiropoulos, K., & Kostopoulos, S. A simple algorithm to monitor hr for real time treatment applications. In *Proc. ITAB 2009,* 1-5.
5. Cardiograph for iOS, https://itunes.apple.com/us/app/cardiograph/id441079429?ls=1&mt=8
6. Choi, J., & Gutierrez-Osuna, R. Using heart rate monitors to detect mental stress. In *BSN 2009. Sixth International Workshop,* 219-223.
7. Coast, D. A., Stern, R. M., Cano, G. G., & Briller, S. A. An approach to cardiac arrhythmia analysis using hidden Markov models. *Biomedical Engineering, IEEE Transactions on* 37.9 (1990): 826-836.
8. Cook, S., Togni, M., et al, High heart rate: a cardiovascular risk factor?, European heart journal, vol. 27(20), 2006.
9. Cooper, K., Pollock, M., et al, Physical Fitness Levels vs Selected Coronary Risk Factors A Cross-Sectional Study, The Journal of the American Medical Association (JAMA), vol. 236, No. 2, July, 1976.
10. Fox, K., Borer, J. S., Camm, A. J., Danchin, N., Ferrari, R., Sendon, J. L. L., ... & Tendera, M. (2007). Resting heart rate in cardiovascular disease. *Journal of the American College of Cardiology*, *50*(9), 823-830.
11. Garbey, M., Sun, N., Merla, A., & Pavlidis, I. Contact-free measurement of cardiac pulse based on the analysis of thermal imagery. Biomedical Engineering, IEEE Transactions on 54.8 (2007): 1418-1426.
12. Gregoski, M. J., Mueller, M., Vertegel, A., Shaporev, A., Jackson, B. B., Frenzel, R. M., ... & Treiber, F. A. Development and validation of a smartphone heart rate acquisition application for health promotion and wellness telehealth applications. *International journal of telemedicine and applications,2012*, 1.
13. Grimaldi, D., Kurylyak, Y., Lamonaca, F., & Nastro, A. Photoplethysmography detection by smartphone's videocamera. In *Proc. IDAACS 2011,* 488-491.
14. Han, T., Xiao, X., Shi, L., Canny, J., & Wang, J. Balancing Accuracy and Fun: Designing Engaging Camera Based Mobile Games for Implicit Heart Rate Monitoring. In *Proc. of CHI 2015*.
15. Hughes, N. P., Tarassenko L., and Roberts S.J. Markov Models for Automated ECG Interval Analysis. In *NIPS*. 2003.
16. Instant Heart Rate for iOS, https://itunes.apple.com/app/instant-heart-rate-measure/id395042892?mt=8
17. Janz, K., Dawson, J., Mahoney, L., Tracking physical fitness and physical activity from childhood to adolescence: the Muscatine study, Medicine and Science in Sports and Exercise, vol. 32(7), 2000.
18. Jensen, M. T., Suadicani, P., Hein, H. O., & Gyntelberg, F. (2013). Elevated resting heart rate, physical fitness and all-cause mortality: a 16-year follow-up in the Copenhagen Male Study. *Heart*, *99*(12), 882-887.
19. Jonathan, E., & Leahy, M. (2010). Investigating a smartphone imaging unit for photoplethysmography. *Physiological measurement*, *31*(11), N79.
20. Jraidi, I., Chaouachi, M., Frasson, C., A Dynamic Multimodal Approach for Assessing Learners' Interaction Experience, In Proc. ACM ICMI 2013.
21. Mark, G., et al, Stress and Multitasking in Everyday College Life: An Empirical Study of Online Activity, In Proc. CHI 2014.
22. McGhee, B. H., & Bridges, E. J. (2002). Monitoring arterial blood pressure: what you may not know. *Critical Care Nurse*, *22*(2), 60-79.
23. Mueller, F., Vetere, F., et al, Jogging over a Distance between Europe and Australia, In Proc. UIST 2010.
24. Pan, S. T., Hong, T. P., & Chen, H. C. Ecg signal analysis by using hidden markov model. In *Proc. iFUZZY 2012,* 288-293.
25. Pelegris, P., Banitsas, K., Orbach, T., & Marias, K. A novel method to detect heart beat rate using a mobile phone. In *Proc. EMBC 2010,* 5488-5491.
26. Picard, R.W., Vyzas, E., Healey, J.: Toward Machine Emotional Intelligence: Analysis of Affective Physiological State. IEEE Transactions on Pattern Analysis and Machine Intelligence 23(10), 2001.
27. Poh, M. Z., McDuff, D. J., & Picard, R. W. (2010). Non-contact, automated cardiac pulse measurements using video imaging and blind source separation. *Optics Express*, *18*(10), 10762-10774.
28. Poh, M. Z., McDuff, D., & Picard, R. A medical mirror for non-contact health monitoring. In *ACM SIGGRAPH 2011 Emerging Technologies*, 2.
29. Rabiner, Lawrence R. A tutorial on hidden Markov models and selected applications in speech recognition. Proceedings of the IEEE 77.2 (1989): 257-286.

30. Rowe, D.R., Sibert, J., and Irwin, D. Heart Rate Variability: Indicator of User State as an Aid to Human-Computer Interaction. In Proc. CHI 1998.

31. Scully, C., Lee, J., Meyer, J., Gorbach, A. M., Granquist-Fraser, D., Mendelson, Y., & Chon, K. H. (2012). Physiological parameter monitoring from optical recordings with a mobile phone. *Biomedical Engineering, IEEE Transactions on*, *59*(2), 303-306.

32. Seccareccia, F., Pannozzo, F., Dima, F., Minoprio, A., Menditto, A., Lo Noce, C., & Giampaoli, S. (2001). Heart rate as a predictor of mortality: the MATISS project. *American Journal of Public Health*, *91*(8), 1258-1263.

33. Singh, R. B., Nakade, P. K., & Bhosale, P. R. Heart Rate Measurement Through Photoplethysmography, In *Proc. BEATS 2010*, 170-174.

34. Sun, D., Canny, J., Paredes, P., MouStress: Detecting Stress from Mouse Motion, In Proc. CHI 2014.

35. Wit, Ernst, Edwin van den Heuvel, and Jan - Willem Romeijn. 'All models are wrong...': an introduction to model uncertainty. *Statistica Neerlandica* 66.3 (2012): 217-236.

36. Woolf, B., Burleson, W., Arroyo, I., Dragon, T., Cooper, D., and Picard, R., Affect-aware Tutors: Recognising and Responding to Student Affect. Intl J Learning Technology 4, 3 (2009).

37. Xiao, X., Han, T., & Wang, J. LensGesture: augmenting mobile interactions with back-of-device finger gestures. In *Proc. ICMI 2013*, 287-294.

38. Yin, Y., Ouyang, T., Partridge, K., Zhai, S., Making touchscreen keyboards adaptive to keys, hand postures, and individuals: a hierarchical spatial backoff model approach, In *Proc. CHI 2013*, 2775-2784.

Mixed-Initiative Real-Time Topic Modeling & Visualization for Crisis Counseling

Karthik Dinakar† Jackie Chen† Henry Lieberman† Rosalind Picard† Robert Filbin*
{karthik, jchen, lieber, picard}@media.mit.edu , bob@crisistextline.org
† Massachusetts Institute of Technology * Crisis Text Line

ABSTRACT

Text-based counseling and support systems have seen an increasing proliferation in the past decade. We present Fathom, a natural language interface to help crisis counselors on *Crisis Text Line*, a new 911-like crisis hotline that takes calls via text messaging rather than voice. Text messaging opens up the opportunity for software to read the messages as well as people, and to provide assistance for human counselors who give clients emotional and practical support. Crisis counseling is a tough job that requires dealing with emotionally stressed people in possibly life-critical situations, under time constraints. Fathom is a system that provides topic modeling of calls and graphical visualization of topic distributions, updated in real time. We develop a mixed-initiative paradigm to train coherent topic and word distributions and use them to power real-time visualizations aimed at reducing counselor cognitive overload. We believe Fathom to be the first real-time computational framework to assist in crisis counseling.

Author Keywords

Natural Language Interfaces, Topic Modeling, Visualizations, Mental Health Counseling

ACM Classification Keywords

H.5.2 User Interfaces: Natural Language; H.5.3 Group and Organization Interfaces: Web-based interaction

INTRODUCTION

Studies have estimated that more than one in four Americans aged eighteen and older are afflicted with a diagnostically determinable mental disorder in a given calendar year [26]. Though the distribution of mental disorders is widespread in the population, they manifest severely in a much smaller and concentrated proportion; six percent or one in seventeen Americans are thought to suffer grievously from such disorders [26]. Nearly a third of all practicing psychotherapists and counselors are expected to encounter grave crises of their clients at some point in their careers [23]. There has been a proliferation of hotlines to help people in crises within the last decade, where a distressed individual experiencing a crisis, or the ***caller***, is connected to a crisis ***counselor*** via telephone hotlines [12] and web-based chats [5] for crises ranging from suicide and self-harm to sexual assault. Yet there is evidence that for a distressed individual, communication via text can be preferable to voice phone calls. According a Pew report, there has been an increase of 45% in text communication since 2009 [24]. There is also growing evidence that distressed individuals are more comfortable sharing sensitive information using electronic-based media [1]. Text-based messaging provides opportunities for software to **(a)** read messages from distressed callers as they arrive, and **(b)** provide real-time assistance to the counselors who respond to crisis calls.

In this paper, we investigate the challenges of mental health crisis counselors on a national, 911-like hotline called *Crisis Text Line* and design analysis and visualization tools to help a counselor manage their cognitive load. We perform a contextual inquiry to identify key pain-points. We develop a mixed-initiative [17] probabilistic graphical topic model framework and a visualization framework to give real-time visual summaries to counselors of both ongoing and archived conversations. We evaluate our prototype on seven crisis counselors. An additional contribution is the integration of a mixed-initiative latent variable model like LDA with visualizations to analyze large scale call logs of crisis counseling that can potentially inform prevention science psychology.

BACKGROUND

Before going into the design of the Fathom prototype, it is worth situating it with an overview of Crisis Text Line (CTL). Crisis counseling [15] differs from conventional psychotherapy in its brevity - the short duration of counseling constrains extended interaction between a caller and a crisis counselor. While successful psychotherapy is conditioned on a more longitudinal and detailed understanding of an individual's plight, crisis counseling can help transition a caller to longitudinal psychotherapy [13].

CTL is a text-based platform supporting a network of organizations that offer crisis counseling and support, with a particular focus on adolescents. CTL is a platform that is used by crisis specialists or counselors from different crisis support centers across the United States. A distressed individual or caller undergoing a crisis may at any time send an SMS text message to the CTL help number. Upon receiving a message from a caller, she or he is connected to a trained specialist on one of the support centers that use the CTL platform. Figure 1 illustrates the CTL platform and the network of crisis support centers, each of which are organizations independent of

IUI 2015, March 29–April 1, 2015, Atlanta, GA, USA.

http://dx.doi.org/10.1145/2678025.2701395

each other and CTL. The crisis support centers are connected to the CTL platform via a web interface; each counselor that is part of one crisis center can see the load and status of every other support center as well as the queue of callers waiting to be served. For example, a counselor whose support center is in Boston can see the status of a counselor who might be a part of a crisis center in Chicago and vice-versa. Incoming callers are accepted regardless of where they are texting from geographically, as this information is not revealed to the counselors.

The counselors staffing a crisis support center are usually a mixture of paid staff and volunteers, who undergo a period of training prior to handling calls as counselors. The number of calls to crisis support centers have historically exceeds demand - callers who may not find an open counselor are made to wait in a queue.

Surveys have unearthed a high attrition rate among crisis counselors, with burnout and low morale as the top two contributing factors given the huge volume of messages they exchange with callers every day [18]. A stable, supportive work environment, with a concerted effort to reduce counselor cognitive workload and burnout are thought to help in retaining trained counselors [20]. In this work, we design a suite of tools to minimize counselor cognitive load and maximize counselor-caller interaction time by reducing the time and effort expended on cursory tasks other than communicating with the caller. While maximizing counselor-caller interaction time on its own cannot fully address problems of burn-out and better counselor, it was identified as significant contributor, which we focus on in this work.

CONTEXTUAL INQUIRY

Counselors using the CTL platform use chat-based web application to have counseling conversations with callers. The callers communicate with the counselors via SMS text messages. Each SMS message is limited to 160 characters. There are restrictions on how much information about a caller a counselor is allowed to access. Though callers are uniquely identified by their telephone numbers, these are not available to the counselor. Instead, each caller has a profile, with details and notes on the last three prior conversations; counselors handling new callers create their profiles. At any given time, a counselor handles two or more conversations in parallel, as these are asynchronous calls through text messages and not voice.

We performed a contextual inquiry (as shown in Fig 1) on two counselors for two hours each on three different days. Below, a work flow model involving the counselor, caller and a supervisor who manages each crisis support center. A typical work-flow of a counselor, along with the pain-points is explained below:

1. **Accept caller**: An alert is sounded when a new caller arrives, who is then placed in a waiting list. The counselor then examines the queue and chooses to accept a caller from the waiting list. Choosing a caller from the waiting list is conditioned on serving a mixture of new and repeat callers. Handling new callers involves more work than talking to repeat callers. On some occasions when the counselor was too overloaded, either because of the gravity of a particular conversation or handling more than three conversations in parallel, a conversation is **warm transferred** to another counselor, who has to pick up the conversation from where it was prior to being transferred.
2. **Check caller profile**: Upon accepting a caller, the counselor then glances through the caller profile if available. Details and notes from previous conversations that might have been handled by another counselor are examined. For new callers, the counselor elicits information from them to fill their profiles. Counselors are trained to treat each call, whether it is from a new or repeating caller, as a distinct and important call. Knowledge of prior conversations is not disclosed to the caller, even as it helps create a context in which the counselor begins the counseling session. Reading through prior notes was time consuming; in almost all cases, reading through the entire transcript of previous calls was even more time consuming.
3. **Counseling session**: The counselor then performs a counseling session with the caller, with three key elements for every conversation:
   - ***Risk assessment***: What is the crisis facing the caller? Is she or he a threat either to themselves or to others? For example, a caller with a history of *drug abuse* and *depression* and who is experiencing intense suicidal thoughts might be construed as being a *high risk* caller.
   - ***Issues & emotional state***: What are the main issues facing the caller? For example, a teen with *relationship difficulties* might be *depressed*.
   - ***Action plan***: What concrete steps can the caller to take to tide over the immediate crisis facing them? For example, a caller who has recently *divorced* might be asked to reach out to friends and family and possibly a therapist.
4. **Take notes**: For each conversation, counselors take real-time manual notes to indicate important aspects of the conversation based on the aforementioned key elements. While some counselors take notes at the end of a conversation, others choose to take notes as the conversation is progressing. Conversation notes for a given conversation are sharable across counselors and the time spent in taking manual notes is significant. During contextual inquiry, 38% of counselor's time went in taking notes, even as it delayed talking to other callers currently being served and the ones in the waiting list.
5. **Fill conversation report**: A report is filled at the end of each conversation based on a static template. This report has categories of issues and counselor responses, and is separate from the notes taken by the counselor. Again, filling the conversation report is a time consuming job that eats into time that could have been served in talking to another current caller or in accepting a new one from the waiting list.

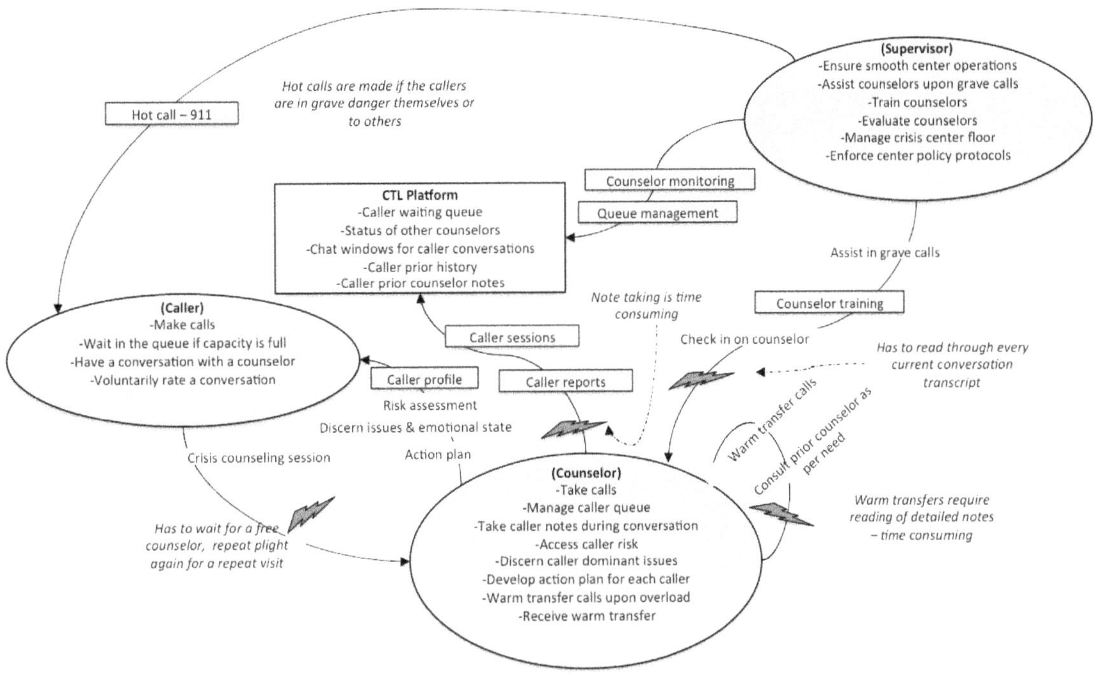

Figure 1. Contextual Inquiry:A work-flow model of a crisis support center using the CTL platform. Four key pain-points, depicted as lightning flashes are as follows: (1) Manual real-time note taking is time consuming; (2) Warm transfer of calls to a new counselor are time consuming because the new counselor has to read prior counselor notes; (3) COunselors notes, when not adequate to describe a conversation, forces repeat users to explain their plight again, and (4) There are no structured ways for a supervisor to examine a set of conversations.

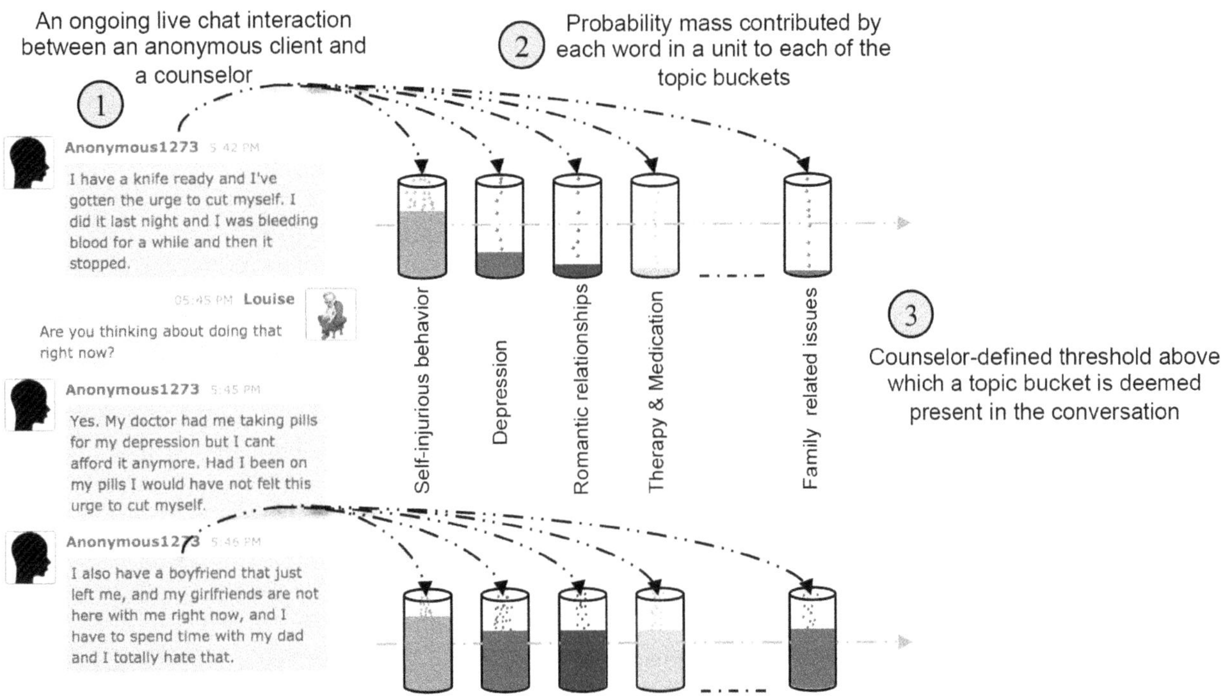

Figure 2. The relationship between the conversation text and the topic model. Words in the conversation each make a contribution to buckets representing topics. The set of topics were determined by an mixed-initiative process, involving annotation of a corpus of conversations by Prevention Science psychologists, in order to be appropriate for the crisis counseling application. A threshold is set for a bucket to be considered significant for that conversation. The conversation shown here is a canned example entered by a volunteer at the time of evaluation. Our IRB prevents us from showing any actual counselor-patient conversations.

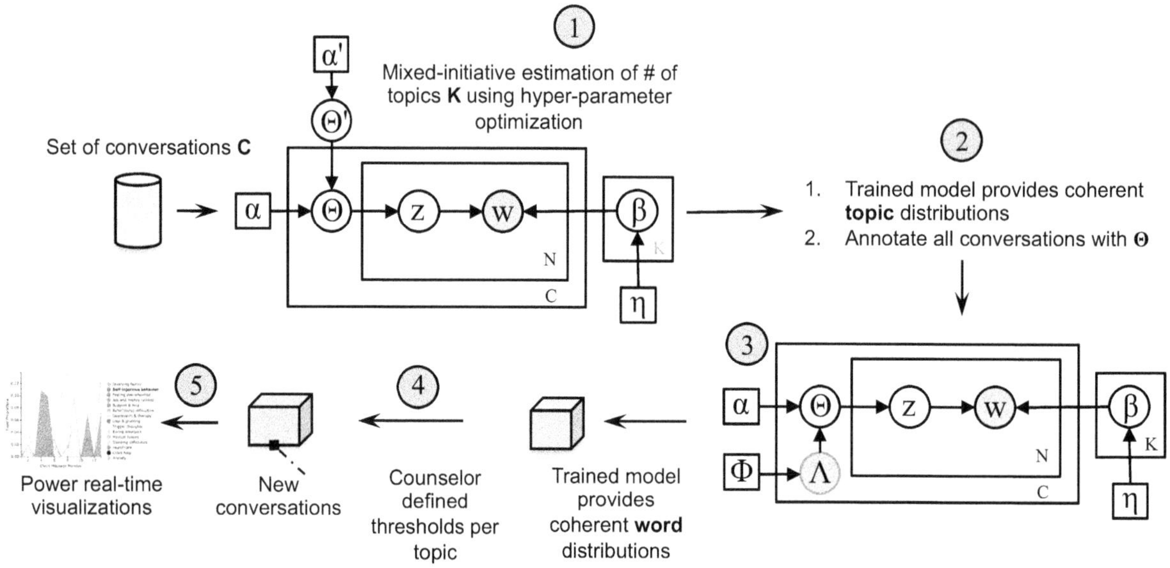

Figure 3. A two-stage mixed-initiative modeling process. (1) Run vanilla LDA with hyper-parameter optimization with prevention science psychologists in the loop using the mixed-initiative method to fetch coherent topics distributions; (2)Use the topic distributions to annotate all the conversations with psychologist-assigned topics; (3) Run a labeled LDA model using the annotated conversations and perform model selection over perplexity curves; (4) Use the word distributions from the model selected and assign user-defined thresholds for each topic; (5) Use the models real-time for each new conversation.

6. **Monitor waiting list**: Even as a counselor accepts calls and handles two or more calls at the same time, they also have to keep an eye on and monitor the waiting list. This is predicated on the belief that any of the callers in the waiting list might in a grave crisis, and minimizing wait time is a priority.

All three counselors that were interviewed during the contextual inquiry had similar pain-points. The task of having to take detailed notes while having conversations in parallel was deemed time consuming. For repeat callers, the manual task of going through prior conversation transcripts and notes was deemed very helpful, but was also time consuming. Filling in a report post-conversation was unanimously considered to be time consuming; the report itself was considered too simple to capture the complexity of issues faced by a caller. None of the three counselors read conversation reports of previous conversations and jumped right in to counselor notes and the conversation transcript. It was clear from contextual inquiry that there was a need to **(a)** visually summarize the content of a conversation for future use, **(b)** reduce the amount of note-taking by extracting clear themes and issues from a conversation in an automated manner, and finally **(c)** use salient issues extracted from a conversation to populate a report at the end of the counselor-caller interaction, that captures in better detail the complexity of issues faced by the caller.

TOPIC MODELS FOR CONVERSATION SUMMARIES

Traditional supervised learning is an analytic technique. Unsupervised techniques such as LDA are generative, but the problem is that the topics they generate may or may not be interesting and relevant to a particular application or purpose. Our methods provide a way to provide gentle guidance to an unsupervised learning process, while retaining the valuable ability to discover unanticipated salient topics. A visual summary of a conversation is predicated on an thematic understanding of the salient issues faced by a caller, her or his emotional state and reactions and the relationships between them. To train a computational model to summarize a conversation, we received a data set of through a licensing agreement with Crisis Text Line and after an IRB review.

We analyzed a total of 8106 conversations consisting of 469,849 (6,787,627 words) counselor messages and 412,050 caller messages. There were 214 counselors in total. The average length of a counselor message and a caller message were 14.4 and 10.5 words respectively.This data was received de-identified, devoid of any personally identifiable information.

In the machine learning literature, challenges in the computational modeling of interaction analysis are well known: sociolinguistic variation in interaction analysis, the presence of affect, of personality and ascription to community tend towards specificity and uniqueness, whereas much of machine learning and natural language processing tend towards abstraction and generalization [11]. Of the conventional supervised and unsupervised machine learning methods for natural language understanding and text classification, probabilistic graphical topic models have been successfully used in the context of

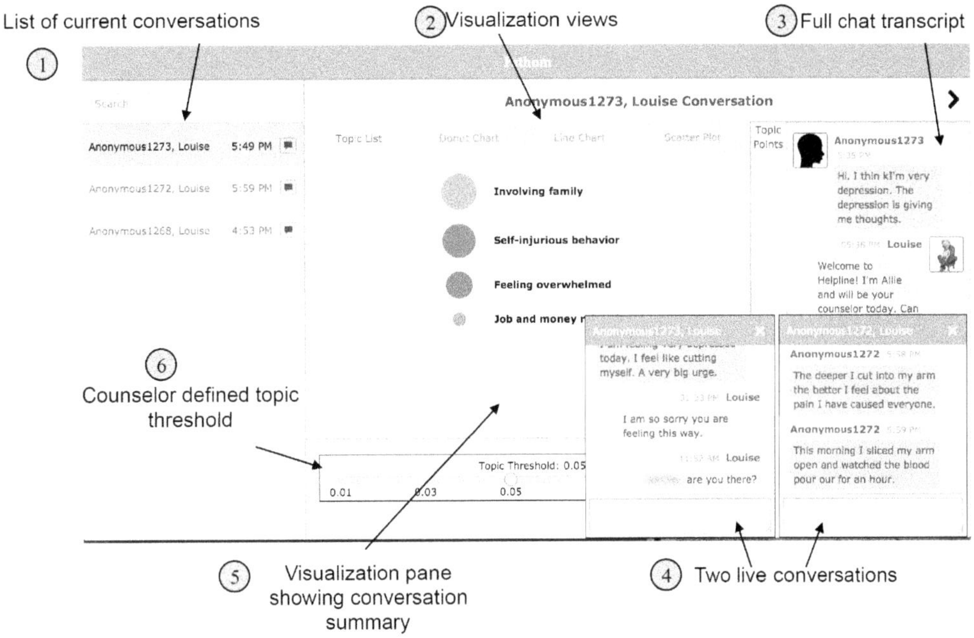

Figure 4. The Fathom interface shows a visualization pane that summarizes a conversation. The control interface omits the visualization engine. Note how a counselor is having more than one conversation in parallel at any given time.The interface here shows two live conversations in progress, with the full transcript of one of the conversations in the background. The visualization pane also has a counselor defined topic threshold setting, where a lower threshold generates more topics, explained in Fig 2. The conversations shown here are canned examples entered by volunteers during our experiment.

detecting teenage bullying and to help distressed teens find similar stories to theirs [8].

Mixed-initiative modeling

A key strength of topic models is their ability to generatively model corpora. They have been shown to work comparably with supervised learning models in their ability to model personal teenage stories of distress [8, 9] and in document classification [22]. We adopt a two-stage, mixed-initiative modeling process involving prevention science psychologists in the loop as shown in Fig 3.

In the first stage, we are interested in extracting meaningful topics (as validated by the prevention science psychologists), or in other words, a ***coherent topic distributions***. For this we use vanilla LDA with hyper-parameter optimization[25, 16] and use the mixed-initiative method of training LDA models with psychologists in the loop [8]. This is achieved by having a group of prevention science psychologists construct sentences from every intermediate topic distribution after a training loop (using as few other words as possible) and subsequently achieve agreement with other counselors to see if the particular distribution of words denotes a coherent topic. More details about this approach is fully described in our prior work [8]. Armed with a good topic distribution, we can then use such the topic distributions to annotate each conversation in the corpus.

Once we have we have an annotated set of conversations, we are then interested in generating a ***coherent word distributions*** for each topic. This is achieved by using a labeled LDA model [21] trained over the set of topics derived from stage 1. A model selected over the best perplexity curves over held-out data then gives us the best coherent word distribution for the corpus. The algorithmic details and its effectiveness as compared to more conventional approaches are detailed in an earlier paper presented to a more computational research venue [7] , but it is worth summarizing how our mixed-initiative LDA approach addresses the key requirements described above:

1. **Modeling the thematic distribution of issues and emotional reactions** -Topic models are mixture models [2]. Labeled latent Dirichlet allocation allows each story to be viewed as a mixture of various issues. The set of such issues and reactions across the corpus of stories provides an excellent overview of the corpus of conversations, allowing us to drill down into the constituent set of issues for each conversation and to view how these issues interact with one another at a corpus-wide level.

2. **Modeling the relationships between caller issues and emotional reactions** - By examining the most dominant issue in a conversation, we can examine the relationships between issues and see how they are related to each other. For example, issues related to loss of a job and loss of medical insurance may co-occur more with depression and relationships under duress.

3. **Modeling socio-linguistic variation** - Because topic models define each topic as a distribution over words, it captures relationships between words as pertaining to a topic. For example words denoting a therapist ranging from doc

to shrink were all clustered under the same issue of depression and therapy.

The trained model is used as follows to tag every ***unit*** or SMS message sent by a caller. Topics are distributions over corpus-wide vocabulary of words. For each word in a given unit, we see the probability mass contribution of that word to every topic bucket in the model. The topic bucket that cumulatively gives the most mass is the most dominant topic for that unit. The threshold for when a topic bucket is deemed dominant can be set by the counselor. This is depicted visually in Fig 2.

FATHOM INTERFACE

We use the suite of trained topic models to power a series of visualizations to visually summarize a conversation in real time.The same visualizations can also be used to see visual summaries of prior conversations and those that are warm transferred. We create a prototype interface, *Fathom*, that mimics the real CTL interface in its core functionality, with real-time conversations between a counselor using Fathom and a caller using SMS text messaging through a phone (shown in Fig 4). We design five visualizations using the *D3js* framework [1] to summarize a given conversation, with transitions updating real-time, with every unit spoken by the caller as follows:

1. **Quick summary**: In this visualization, topics extracted from the models are presented as a named topic list of colored nodes, with the radius of each node determined by the proportion of the respective topic in the conversation. The most most dominant topic extracted in the conversation appears first, and is the largest node in the list. Each subsequent node representing a topic is less and less dominant in the conversation (see figure 5).

2. **Conversation topic proportions**: A donut chart with the topic proportions determining the slice of the donut for the respective topic. The legend is a miniaturized version of the topic list summary discussed in the previous visualization. We see on hover that the topic 'involving family' constitutes 48% of the issues extracted from this conversation (see figure 6).

3. **Conversation topic evolution (non-cumulative)**: We design a line graph to show a chronological occurrence of topics in the conversation. We plot the unit number received from the caller on the x-axis and plot the topic proportions on the y-axis. We plot the topic proportion of each topic against the unit number. Selecting a topic in the legend highlights the positions in the graph where the respective topic occurred in the conversation as shown below (see figure 7).

4. **Conversation topic evolution (cumulative)**: We design a line graph to show a chronological occurrence of topics in the conversation. We plot the unit number received from the caller on the x-axis and plot the topic proportions on the y-axis. We plot the topic proportion of each topic against the unit number. Selecting a topic in the legend highlights the positions in the graph where the respective topic occurred in the conversation as shown below (see figure 8).

5. **Visual indexing via scatter plots**: In this visualization, each topic is a row. A topic when dominant (as set by the counselor threshold) is placed as a dot for the unit for which it was detected. The size of the dot is again determined by the proportion of the topic present. The main purpose of designing the scatter plot was to assist in visual indexing, which we explain in the next section.

[1] www.d3js.org

Figure 5. Quick Summary: An ordered list of topics extracted from a conversation. The node radius of a topic, arranged in descending order, is determined by the proportion of the respective topic in the conversation. In this example, the topic 'involving family' is the dominant topic in the conversation.

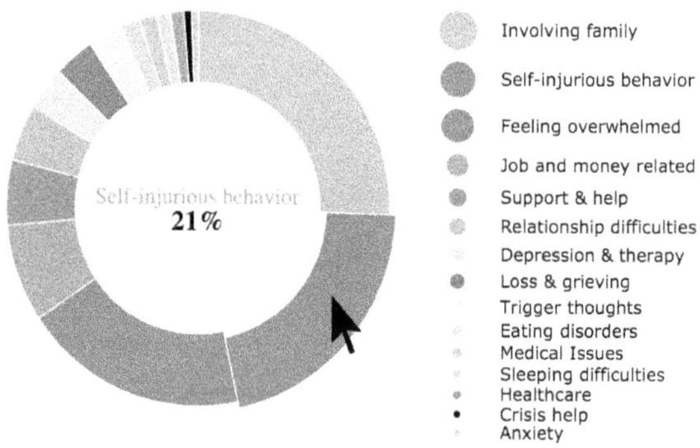

Figure 6. Conversation topic proportions: The slice of the donut is proportional to the dominance of the topic in the conversation. The topic 'involving family' is the most dominant topic in this example, constitutes 48% of the topics extracted from its conversation.

Visual indexing

The line graphs and scatter plots were designed to allow visual indexing of a conversation. Upon clicking on a point on the line graph or a dot on the scatter plot, the counselor is automatically taken to the part of the conversation transcript where the respective units were tagged with the topic. A visual summary of a conversation, both ongoing and historic, along with affordance for easy visual indexing was designed to give a counselor a quick and easy gist of the dominant topics in a conversation and spare them from having to read the entire chat transcript. Our contextual inquiry shows that visual summaries could potentially help a counselor to save time which might be better used in serving existing callers or those in the waiting lines. The figure below illustrates visual indexing via the scatter plot.

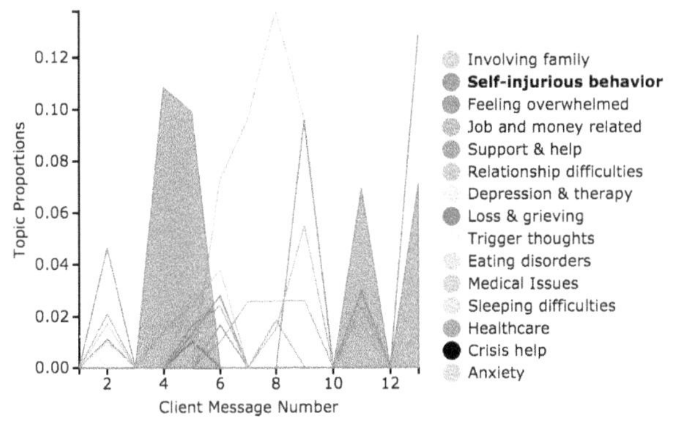

Figure 7. Conversation topic evolution (non-cumulative): The unit or message number, in the order they were received from the caller, is plotted against the topic proportions of topics extracted from those units. In this example, we select 'Self-injurious' behavior from the legend on the right. We see that it spikes at the beginning and at the end of the conversation. s

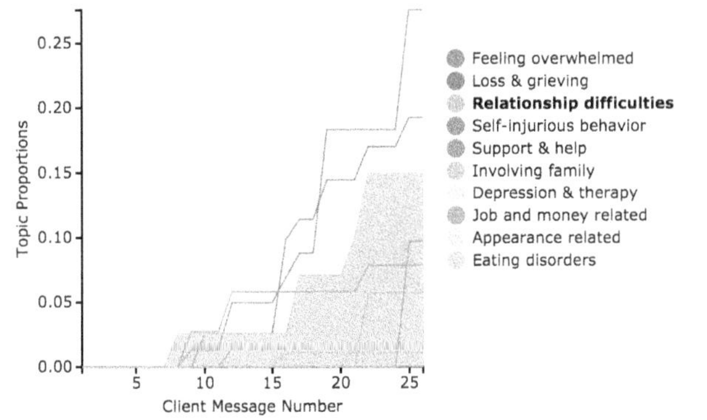

Figure 8. Conversation topic evolution (cumulative): This is a cumulative version of the previous visualization, where one can see if a given topic increases in dominance as the conversation progresses. The unit or message number, in the order they were received from the caller, is plotted against the topic proportions, cumulatively, of the topics extracted from each unit from the caller. In the example below, we select 'Relationship difficulties' in the legend and see how it grows in proportion as the conversation evolves. The topic 'Feeling overwhelmed' is the most dominant issue whose proportion increases as the conversation progresses.

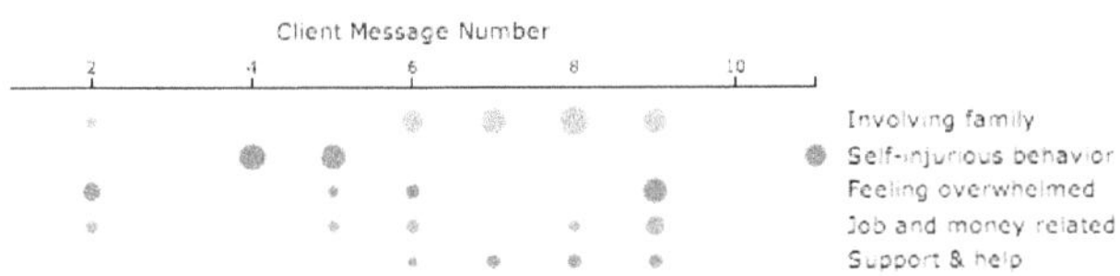

Figure 9. Scatter plot: In this example, we see that unit 9 was tagged for 4 topics, namely 'involving family', 'feeling overwhelmed', 'job and money related' and 'support and help'. The most recent unit was tagged for self-injurious behavior, but a counselor can quickly see at what other points in the conversation a particular topic was present.

EVALUATION

We evaluate the Fathom interface against a control interface (without the visualization engine as described in Figure 4) to discern if the visualization summaries of a conversation might be helpful to get a gist of dominant topics for repeat callers' conversation histories as well as warm-transferred conversations.

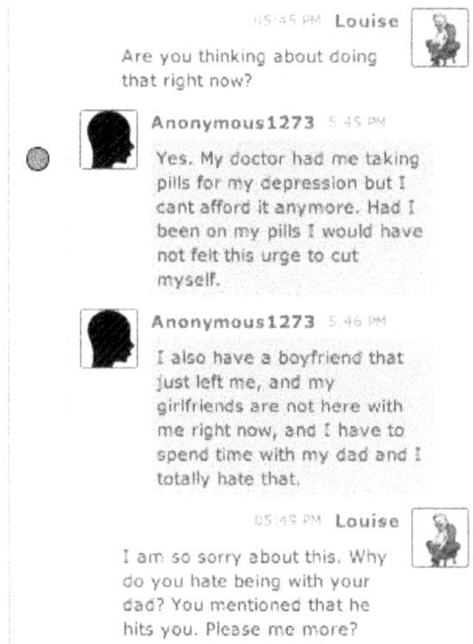

Figure 10. Visual indexing: Upon clicking the second red dot shown in the previous visualization (for self-injurious behavior), the chat transcript automatically scrolls to the corresponding unit in the conversation which was tagged for self-injurious behavior. This visual indexing allows for seamless and quick gist of conversations without having the read the entire chat transcript, saving time that might be better utilized in serving existing callers or the ones still waiting to be accepted by a counselor. The example shown here is a canned one entered by a participant at the time of evaluation.

Additionally, we also evaluate of the visualization framework could help in each of the key counseling foci of risk assessment, gist of topics and caller emotional state, and formulating an action plan for the caller.

Participant selection

We selected a total of 7 participants for evaluating Fathom. All 7 participants had undergone training as crisis counselors and three of them worked in a crisis support center currently using CTL as a platform to offer crisis counseling, with the other four actively engaged in the recruitment of counselors and who were well-versed with a plethora of crisis counseling software.

Experiment protocol

Each participant was shown two interfaces, Interface 1, and Interface 2, namely the control interface and Fathom respectively. The user evaluation instructions consisted of two parts. Six pre-selected and existing stories were shown per interface in part 1 to gauge how useful the visualization framework might be with respect to risk assessment, gist of topics and& emotional state of the caller and formulating an action plan for the caller. Participants were asked to imagine these conversations were warm-transferred to them, where they had to pick up these conversations at the point a previous counselor might have handed it to them.

In the second part of the experiment, participants were asked to engage in a live conversation with a member of the experiment team playing the role of a caller, and evaluating each of the visualizations in Fathom that updated dynamically with every unit from the test caller. The questions asked of the participants in both parts are as follows:

Part 1

- **Q1**: Which interface was useful for a risk assessment of a warm-transferred call (Interface 1 or Interface 2), and how useful was this interface? (1 not useful to 5-extremely useful)
- **Q2**: Which interface was useful for eliciting the list of issues and emotional state of a warm-transferred call (Interface 1 or interface 2), and how useful was this interface? (1 not useful to 5-extremely useful)
- **Q3**: Which interface was useful for developing an action plan for a warm-transferred call (Interface 1 or Interface 2), and how useful was this interface? (1 not useful to 5-extremely useful)
- **Q4**: Which interface was useful to get a conversation summary for repeat callers (Interface 1 or Interface 2), and how useful was this interface? (1 not useful to 5-extremely useful)

Part 2

- **Q5**: How useful was it to view the visualizations real-time for conversation note taking? (1 not useful to 5-extremely useful)
- **Q6**: Which visualization was the most useful for quick grasp of a conversation? (Quickly summary, topic proportions, topic evolution (non-cumulative), topic evolution (cumulative), visual indexing via scatter plots)

Participants were also allowed to add open-ended responses for each of the questions if they wished to elaborate on their votes.

Results

The results for each of the questions from Part 1 are tabulated below:

	Control		Fathom	
	Votes	Average Rating	Votes	Average Rating
Q1	71.38%	2.6	28.57%	3.5
Q2	14.28%	3	85.71%	3.9
Q3	57.14%	3	42.85%	3.3
Q4	0%	0	100%	4.42

Table 1. Results from Part 1 show that most of participants overwhelmingly preferred to read specific parts of the transcript at the beginning to discern callee risk. Fathom was rated by 85% and 100% of the participants for the most useful interface for eliciting callee emotional state and their issues, as well as the interface to help get a gist of prior conversations by repeat callees.

For part 2, question **Q5**, Fathom got an average rating of 4, denoting that our visualization framework was indeed useful in real-time conversations in terms of supplementing the manual taking of conversation notes. For **Q6**, 4 participants said that the scatter plot was the best visualization for visual indexing, while 2 preferred the topic list summary and only 1 preferred the non-cumulative line graph.

DISCUSSION

In their open-ended feedback, participants were very positive about the visualization framework of Fathom, but expressed a desire for even more functionality. Visualizing counselor notes along with conversation summaries, was a common feedback. Three participants also wanted certain topics such as suicide ideation and risk to be prominently displayed, no matter how dominant it might be in a conversation. Our evaluation shows that counselors preferred the control interface (where they see read the entire chat transcript) to Fathom for risk assessment (**Q1**) of a warm-transferred call. Verbatim feedback from them mentioned how risk assessment was counselor-specific - that it was a function of more than a set of topics and that the tone and intensity of the caller responses to risk-assessment questions was also a big factor. This shows the need for additional modeling of caller responses to sensitive risk-assessment questions from a counselor, which can happen at any point during a conversation. In terms of developing an action plan (**Q3**) however, opinion was divided. Two counselors thought that dispensing an action plan is closely is conditioned on risk assessment, suggesting that modeling risk-assessment better can also help in formulating action plans for warm-transferred calls.

The verdict for eliciting the emotional state of the caller (along with a list of topics underlying the conversation - **Q2**) and for viewing conversation summaries (**Q4**) for repeat callers was decisively in favor of Fathom. Counselors seemed particularly enthused by the possibility of using Fathom to augment the mandatory caller-report task at the end of conversations.

Overall, our evaluation suggests two takeaways: **(1)** A joint, generative topic modeling of counselor-caller interactions, with a specific focus on risk assessment, action plan formulation, eliciting emotional states and projection of empathy. Embedding counselor expertise in the approximate posterior inference while training is already an ongoing research direction we're pursuing. **(2)** Making risk assessment areas explicit and prominent in the visualizations, as they seem to bear an impact on formulating an action plan as well.

RELATED WORK

The workshop paper [7] described an earlier version of Fathom's interface. The present paper reports the Contextual Inquiry, details our mixed-initiative topic modeling, and presents the evaluation with the counselors.

The particular visualizations used by Fathom are described in the visualization toolkit D3JS [3]. The four visualizations, the quick summary, conversation topic proportions, topic evolution and visual indexing are all standard visualizations in D3JS's library. D3JS's emphasis on data-driven visual transformations makes it most suitable for Fathom's dynamic approach to topic modeling.

The most directly related work to Fathom is in the area of visualizing topic models. Several prior projects have provided different graphical views on topic models, and have also provided means for associating topic models or component words back to the original corpus, either in particular examples or in aggregate [4]. The major difference is that Fathom is intended for applying topic modeling to examples that unfold in real time conversations rather than on static documents or static corpora.

The Topic Browser [10] provides a variety of techniques for visualizing topic models, focusing on features that help users understand the context in which the model occurs, such as word clouds and keyword-in-context (KWIC) views. There is also an emphasis on helping the user to understand properties of weighted-word topic models, like document entropy, coherence, and model similarity, that help educate the user as to how the machine learning techniques achieve their summarization of the relationship of documents to corpora. Again, the documents and corpora are not expected to change during the user interaction with the visualization. In Fathom, each unit of a conversation is handled by a back-end suite of topic models to power a front-end visualization.

TextFlow [6] is a visually innovative visualization technique that does address the temporal element of evolution of topics in a document. As the authors state, it is less suited to associating topics with particular examples, and they advocate a hybrid approach. Certainly, in future work it would be worth experimenting with unconventional display methods such as this in our context, for highlighting dynamic evolution of topics.

Finally, another relevant area is software for call center management. Visualization is an important component of many call center management tools, of which Dundas [14] is a typical example. Many provide CRM (Customer Relationship Management) tools, and problem-solution databases to the responders. Some tools provide post-hoc monitoring of the performance of call center personnel and understanding in the aggregate the topics of the incoming calls [19]. We are not aware of any prior work that uses machine learning techniques such as topic models to provide real-time assistance to crisis counselors.

SUMMARY

Crisis counseling is a job that has a high cognitive load, and managing that load in real-time can make the difference between life and death for some people. Both graphical visualization and machine learning have been proven powerful computational tools for helping people deal with complex situations, and understand them quickly. But these fields have largely developed independently, and it is now time for them to work together to help solve this important problem.

We have presented Fathom, the first system that uses a variety of dynamic visualizations of topic models using the machine learning technique LDA, to help crisis counselors understand caller conversations in real time, and facilitate collaboration between counselors. When a mental health emergency strikes, both people and computers stand ready to lend a helping hand.

ACKNOWLEDGMENTS

This work was funded in part by the Reid Hoffman Fellowship and the Google Faculty grant. We thank the team at Crisis Text Line for their support and help. We thank Emma Kerry, Nate Baum and Ron White of Samaritans for their help and expertise.

REFERENCES

1. Alison Bryant, J., Sanders-Jackson, A., and Smallwood, A. M. Iming, text messaging, and adolescent social networks. *Journal of Computer-Mediated Communication 11*, 2 (2006), 577–592.
2. Blei, D. M. Probabilistic topic models. *Communications of the ACM 55*, 4 (2012), 77–84.
3. Bostock, M. D3. js. *Data Driven Documents* (2012).
4. Chaney, A. J.-B., and Blei, D. M. Visualizing topic models. In *ICWSM* (2012).
5. Christensen, H., Farrer, L., Batterham, P. J., Mackinnon, A., Griffiths, K. M., and Donker, T. The effect of a web-based depression intervention on suicide ideation: secondary outcome from a randomised controlled trial in a helpline. *BMJ open 3*, 6 (2013).
6. Cui, W., Liu, S., Tan, L., Shi, C., Song, Y., Gao, Z., Qu, H., and Tong, X. Textflow: Towards better understanding of evolving topics in text. *Visualization and Computer Graphics, IEEE Transactions on 17*, 12 (2011), 2412–2421.
7. Dinakar, K., Chaney, A. J., Lieberman, H., and Blei, D. M. Real-time topic models for crisis counseling. *Twentieth ACM Conference on Knowledge Discovery and Data Mining, Data Science for the Social Good Workshop* (2014).
8. Dinakar, K., Jones, B., Lieberman, H., Picard, R., Rose, C., Thoman, M., and Reichart, R. You too?! mixed-initiative lda story matching to help teens in distress, 2012.
9. Dinakar, K., Weinstein, E., Lieberman, H., and Selman, R. Stacked generalization learning to analyze teenage distress. *International AAAI Conference on Weblogs and Social Media* (2014).
10. Gardner, M. J., Lutes, J., Lund, J., Hansen, J., Walker, D., Ringger, E., and Seppi, K. The topic browser: An interactive tool for browsing topic models. In *NIPS Workshop on Challenges of Data Visualization* (2010).
11. Gianfortoni, P., Adamson, D., and Rosé, C. P. Modeling of stylistic variation in social media with stretchy patterns. In *Proceedings of the First Workshop on Algorithms and Resources for Modelling of Dialects and Language Varieties*, DIALECTS '11, Association for Computational Linguistics (Stroudsburg, PA, USA, 2011), 49–59.
12. Gould, M. S., Cross, W., Pisani, A. R., Munfakh, J. L., and Kleinman, M. Impact of applied suicide intervention skills training on the national suicide prevention lifeline. *Suicide and Life-Threatening Behavior 43*, 6 (2013), 676–691.

13. Gould, M. S., Munfakh, J. L., Kleinman, M., and Lake, A. M. National suicide prevention lifeline: enhancing mental health care for suicidal individuals and other people in crisis. *Suicide and Life-Threatening Behavior 42*, 1 (2012), 22–35.
14. Hedgebeth, D. Data-driven decision making for the enterprise: an overview of business intelligence applications. *VINE 37*, 4 (2007), 414–420.
15. Hoff, L. A., Hallisey, B. J., and Hoff, M. *People in crisis: Clinical and diversity perspectives*. Taylor & Francis, 2011.
16. Hoffman, M., Bach, F. R., and Blei, D. M. Online learning for latent dirichlet allocation. In *advances in neural information processing systems* (2010), 856–864.
17. Horvitz, E. Principles of mixed-initiative user interfaces. In *Proceedings of the SIGCHI conference on Human Factors in Computing Systems*, ACM (1999), 159–166.
18. Kinzel, A., and Nanson, J. Education and debriefing: Strategies for preventing crises in crisis-line volunteers. *Crisis: The Journal of Crisis Intervention and Suicide Prevention 21*, 3 (2000), 126–134.
19. Pallotta, V., Delmonte, R., Vrieling, L., and Walker, D. Interaction mining: the new frontier of call center analytics. *Proc. of DART* (2011).
20. Pratt, M. E. *The Future of Volunteers in Crisis Hotline Work*. PhD thesis, University of Pittsburgh, 2013.
21. Ramage, D., Hall, D., Nallapati, R., and Manning, C. D. Labeled lda: A supervised topic model for credit attribution in multi-labeled corpora. In *Proceedings of the 2009 Conference on Empirical Methods in Natural Language Processing: Volume 1-Volume 1*, Association for Computational Linguistics (2009), 248–256.
22. Rubin, T. N., Chambers, A., Smyth, P., and Steyvers, M. Statistical topic models for multi-label document classification. *Machine Learning 88*, 1-2 (2012), 157–208.
23. Schwartz, R. C., and Rogers, J. R. Suicide assessment and evaluation strategies: A primer for counselling psychologists. *Counselling Psychology Quarterly 17*, 1 (2004), 89–97.
24. Smith, A. 46% of american adults are smartphone owners. *Pew Internet & American Life Project* (2012).
25. Wallach, H. M., Mimno, D. M., and McCallum, A. Rethinking lda: Why priors matter. In *NIPS*, Y. Bengio, D. Schuurmans, J. D. Lafferty, C. K. I. Williams, and A. Culotta, Eds., Curran Associates, Inc. (2009), 1973–1981.
26. Wang, P. S., Lane, M., Olfson, M., Pincus, H. A., Wells, K. B., and Kessler, R. C. Twelve-month use of mental health services in the united states: results from the national comorbidity survey replication. *Archives of general psychiatry 62*, 6 (2005), 629–640.

Inferring Meal Eating Activities in Real World Settings from Ambient Sounds: A Feasibility Study

Edison Thomaz, Cheng Zhang, Irfan Essa, Gregory D. Abowd
{ethomaz, chengzhang, irfan, abowd}@gatech.edu
School of Interactive Computing
Georgia Institute of Technology
Atlanta, Georgia, USA

ABSTRACT
Dietary self-monitoring has been shown to be an effective method for weight-loss, but it remains an onerous task despite recent advances in food journaling systems. Semi-automated food journaling can reduce the effort of logging, but often requires that eating activities be detected automatically. In this work we describe results from a feasibility study conducted in-the-wild where eating activities were inferred from ambient sounds captured with a wrist-mounted device; twenty participants wore the device during one day for an average of 5 hours while performing normal everyday activities. Our system was able to identify meal eating with an F-score of 79.8% in a person-dependent evaluation, and with 86.6% accuracy in a person-independent evaluation. Our approach is intended to be practical, leveraging off-the-shelf devices with audio sensing capabilities in contrast to systems for automated dietary assessment based on specialized sensors.

Author Keywords
Activity recognition; Food journaling; Dietary intake; Automated dietary assessment; Ambient sound; Acoustic sensor; Sound classification; Machine learning

ACM Classification Keywords
H.5.m. Information Interfaces and Presentation (e.g. HCI): Miscellaneous

INTRODUCTION
Food journaling has been demonstrated to encourage individual to adopt healthier eating habits since the self-reflection that occurs when people keep track of what they eat plays an important role in behavior change [3]. Unfortunately, despite its benefits, food journaling remains a difficult undertaking; individuals must remember to log meals and snacks throughout the day, and then manually record eating activities on a food diary, a tedious and time-consuming task.

IUI'15, March 29–April 01, 2015, Atlanta, GA, USA
Copyright 2015 ACM 978-1-4503-3306-1/15/03$15.00
http://dx.doi.org/10.1145/2678025.2701405

Over the years researchers have suggested various approaches towards automatically recording eating activities. Although promising, they have often required individuals to wear specialized devices such as swallow-detecting neck collars and other sensors that have made many of these systems impractical for everyday use. Additionally, most approaches have focused on fully automating the food tracking process, a direction that is not only highly challenging from a technical perspective, but also misguided from a behavior one since it eliminates the self-reflective benefits brought forth by journaling.

An emerging form of behavior journaling called *semi-automated journaling* aims to minimize the effort associated with manual logging while still keeping individuals directly involved in the activity of interest. One of the keystones required for the implementation of semi-automated or automated food journaling systems is identifying *when* individuals are engaged in an eating activity. Inferring the moment or time window when individuals are consuming food supports a number of scenarios that ultimately help individuals reflect on their diet. For instance, the recognition that eating is taking place could automatically trigger a reminder to capture a relevant food photo. Moreover, if eating moments can be recognized in real time, adaptive systems supporting just-in-time dietary interventions can be realized.

To address the challenge of automatic eating activity detection, we present a system that identifies meal eating moments from ambient sounds using acoustic sensors. Our aim is to improve the practicality of current approaches associated with food journaling by leveraging devices available and in use by individuals. This approach, referred to as opportunistic sensing [11], contrasts to methods that require more specialized forms of sensing modalities (*e.g.,* electromyography for swallow detection). Microphones are simple sensors and virtually ubiquitous; they are guaranteed to be present in mobile handsets across the board, from top of the line smartphones to more basic feature phones. Additionally, audio data is contextually very rich, and has been successfully used in health-focused applications [9].

The two contributions of this work are (1) a practical system for the recognition of meal eating activities in the wild from ambient sounds and (2) a system evaluation using over 100 hours of audio collected *in-the-wild* from 20 participants.

RELATED WORK

Efforts focused on eating recognition date back to the 1980s when researchers tried to detect chews and swallows using oral sensors in order to measure the palatability and satiating value of foods [21]. Ongoing research work in this area ranges from the use of crowdsourcing techniques [15], wearables [8, 4], and instrumented objects [6]. Sound is a contextually-rich source of information that can be easily recorded using one of the simplest and most ubiquitous sensors; a microphone. Hence, a large body of work at the intersection of acoustic sensing and activity recognition has emerged over the last decade [22, 17, 10].

One of the most explored applications of sound-based activity recognition has been dietary intake tracking, realized through wearable devices. Sazonov *et al.* proposed a system for monitoring swallowing and chewing through the combination of a piezoelectric strain gauge positioned below the ear and a small microphone located over the laryngopharynx [18]. A promising and comprehensive approach to automated dietary monitoring was proposed by Amft *et al.* [1]. It involves having individuals wear sensors in the wrists, head and neck and automatically detect food intake gestures, chewing, and swallowing from accelerometer and acoustic sensor data.

More recently, Yatani and Truong presented BodyScope, a wearable acoustic sensor attached to the user's neck [24]. The system was able to recognize twelve activities at 79.5% F-measure accuracy in a lab study and four activities (eating, drinking, speaking, and laughing) in a in-the-wild study at 71.5% F-measure accuracy.

There are two elements that distinguish our work from previous initiatives around audio-based dietary monitoring. Firstly, our implementation is meant to be practical; our system recognizes eating moments from ambient sounds without the need for specialized sensors. Instead, our approach leverages devices such as smartphones, that individuals have already adopted into their lives. Secondly, the feasibility of our system was tested in-the-wild with twenty participants. Efforts like BodyScope [24] were also evaluated in real world conditions, but in smaller studies.

IMPLEMENTATION

Our system was designed to learn to recognize sounds that are associated with eating activities, such as the background noise in a restaurant environment, and the softer but highly distinguishable sounds generated by the mouth when chewing and biting. This sound identification task presents two technical challenges: the extraction of information-rich features from ambient audio collected with a microphone, and the design of a binary classifier with the ability to distinguish eating sounds from non-eating sounds from audio features.

Practicality was of utmost priority in the design of our system, therefore it does not rely on any specialized sensors. The implementation we propose could run on a smartphone device and was evaluated on the wrist in an effort to simulate a smart watch device or some other wearable piece of technology designed for everyday use.

Audio Frames and Features

Audio was recorded at a sample rate of 11,025Hz (16 bits per sample), and audio frames with size 50ms were extracted using a Hanning-filtered sliding window with an overlap of 50% (block size=552, step size=276). This audio frame size is larger than what is typically chosen for speech recognition applications but adequate to capture environmental sounds.

We extracted 50 features from each frame, using the Python-based Yaafe tool [13]. Based on previous work that also attempted to recognize human activities from audio [10, 17], we chose the following time and frequency domain features: Zero-Crossing Rate [19], Loudness [14], Energy, Envelope Shape Statistics, LPC [12], LSF [2, 20], Spectral Flatness, Spectral Flux, Spectral Rolloff [19], Spectral Shape Statistics [5], and Spectral Variation.

Clustering and Classification

Because many ambient sounds that characterize eating activities are often much longer than a single audio frame, we clustered 400 consecutive frames and calculated the mean and variance of each feature across these frames (Figure 1). This step also reduced feature "noise" that could be introduced if we had accounted for the acoustic characteristics of every single audio frame. For clustering, we applied a sliding window over the audio frame stream, also with 50% overlap. This resulted in a frame cluster vector of size 100 (mean and variance of 50 features). We chose 400 frames for each cluster because that is equivalent to a total of 10 seconds of audio, a duration that can encapsulate sounds of interest that are both short (e.g., the clicking sound of utensils hitting plates or bowls), and long (e.g., background noise in a restaurant). We performed classification with the Random Forest classifier available in the Scikit-learn Python package [16].

USER STUDY

To evaluate our system, we conducted an IRB-approved in-the-wild study, where we recruited participants and examined how our system performed when classifying ambient sounds collected in the real-world, as individuals performed their normal everyday activities. We recruited 21 participants (15 males and 6 females) between the ages of 21 and 55 through our social network, word-of-mouth, flyers and mailing lists. For joining the study, they received $20 as compensation. Participants included students, research scientists, designers, entrepreneurs and other professionals.

The study lasted between 4 and 7 hours on a single day; for 17 participants, the study began in the morning sometime between 8AM and 11AM and ended between 3PM and 4PM, while for 3 participants it began between 4PM and 7PM and ended before 10PM. This time period was enough to guarantee that all study participants had at least one meal (lunch or dinner).

Subjects wore an audio recording device on the wrist. We chose this placement for the collection of ambient sounds because we anticipate that smart watch-type devices will become popular in the near future. It is very likely that these devices will be capable of recording and even analyzing audio, despite their compact size.

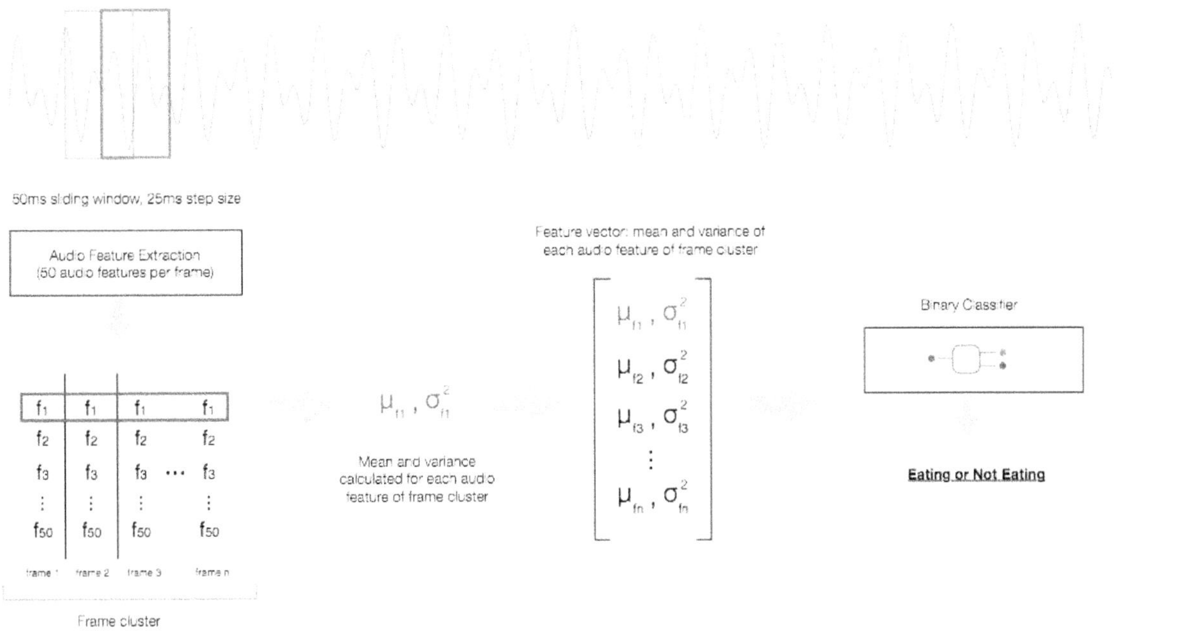

Figure 1. The audio processing pipeline consists of audio framing, audio feature extraction, frame clustering, frame clustering, and classification.

The audio recorder registered sounds continuously throughout the study. At the end of the study, participants were given the opportunity to review their audio file, and delete any audio segment that they did not want to share with us. After this initial step, we performed a walkthrough of the 4-7 hour study period with participants using the Day Reconstruction Method (DRM) [7]. At the end of this process, we were able to discover when individuals ate during the study interval and segmented and labeled their audio clips accordingly.

Ground Truth

To obtain ambient audio ground truth for the eating activities, we asked participants to recall their activities for the day and list them in order, indicating an estimated beginning and end time for each activity. This activity list in chronological order allowed us to discover if and when the participant had a meal. To make sure that time periods indicated by participants were in fact eating activities, two of the authors coded the audio files independently after agreeing on a guideline and then compared results. Disagreements beyond a range of 5 minutes at the beginning or end of an eating activity audio segment were discussed; there were 5 disagreements in total. The final set of ground truth data for each participant included the audio clip referring to the reported eating activity, and another clip with all the audio except for the eating activity segment. As expected, the eating activity audio clip was always much shorter in duration than the audio clip of non-eating activities.

RESULTS

To reiterate, our high-level goal is to develop and evaluate a *practical* approach to detect when meals are being consumed in the wild. In this work, the primary performance metric we wished to assess was whether the system could identify meal eating activities from ambient sounds. This assessment was driven by collecting data in real situations and learning models from the data to test our approach.

We evaluated our models using a person-dependent technique and reported results in terms of precision, recall and F-score metrics (Table 1); we performed 10-fold cross-validation on each study participant's data and then averaged the results across all participants to obtain an overall result. For comparison, we tested three different classifiers: Support Vector Machines (SVM), Nearest Neighbors (n=5), and Random Forest. The Random Forest classifier proved to be vastly superior to the other two classifiers, yielding an F-score of 79.8%. As a means of comparison, this result is equivalent to what Yatani et al. achieved with BodyScope [24]. On one hand, BodyScope was able to recognize multiple activities. On the other hand, our system does not require any specialized sensor, and can run in any off-the-shelf device that is capable of recording and processing audio, such as smartphones and smart watches.

A LOPO (leave-one-participant-out) cross-validation resulted in an F-score of 28.7%, suggesting that this approach would greatly benefit from personalization. It is important to note that F-measures below 50% are not uncommon in LOPO evaluations, particularly in the context of free-living studies [24].

DISCUSSION

Our ambient audio dataset included meal eating activities in a wide variety of contexts. Participants ate alone and with friends; they ate at home, at work, at school and in the classroom. Although desirable, this level of variety in the data made the classification task particularly challenging.

Classifier	Precision	Recall	F-score
SVM	47.5%	50.5%	48.9%
5-NN	53.3%	51.9%	51.4%
Random Forest	**89.6%**	**76.3%**	**79.8%**

Table 1. Person-dependent, 10-fold cross-validation results for each classified we evaluated. The Random Forest classifier performed significantly better that the SVM and Nearest Neighbors classifiers.

One factor that hampered the classifier's ability to identify meal eating was the short duration of meal events, which were shorter than 12 minutes in some cases. This resulted in a small number of frame clusters for the classifier to examine, and a misclassification proved very costly. Another difficulty was that some of the participants had their meals while performing other activities such as attending a class or working in the computer, which were not labeled as meal eating activities. It is likely that additional examples would help with activity class separation in this case. Finally, classifying meal-eating in quiet environments, such as one's office or home, has obvious challenges. This suggests a design rationale for training the classifier while emphasizing the specific characteristics of different sounds environments (e.g. home, school, restaurant).

Despite these difficulties, it is worth noting that it would have been impractical to evaluate our system in a controlled lab setting, since it would have been devoid of most of the natural environmental sounds that individuals are enveloped in when in real world settings and conditions.

Ground Truth

Estimating ground truth from the audio files proved to be a challenging undertaking. Individuals were asked to recall the exact time they had meals, but often could not do so accurately. In some cases, finding this segment proved particularly difficult, especially when the length of the meal was under 10 minutes. Moreover, while in some audio clips it was possible to hear that participants were eating or were in a restaurant environment, in other clips this was not clear at all. For instance, participants P9 and P14 ate in a classroom or classroom-like environment, whose sounds could not be easily identified as those that are characteristic of an eating activity. In these situations we had to rely on subtle cues, such as the sound of a food container coming out of a brown bag.

Another difficulty we faced in obtaining ground truth had to do with the characterization of an eating activity. Some participants had hour-long lunches, where they chatted with friends extensively before, during and after the meal. On the other hand, some participants had very short meals, eating uninterruptedly for 10 or 15 minutes. In the case of the long lunch, a question might be raised as to whether the whole meal event should be labelled as "eating" or only the period when individuals were actively eating.

Data Collection

Although our feasibility study represents a large ecologically-valid data collection effort, it is limited in two important ways. First of all, since participants joined the study for 4-6 hours in a single day, ambient audio data was recorded for only one meal of their day. For most participants the recorded meal was lunch. The system was evaluated on a per-participant basis through cross-validation, but having just one example of a meal eating activity per participant lowers the confidence that our results generalize over several days. In the future, we plan to address this weakness by collecting data for multiple days per participant. Additionally, the lack of multi-day audio data makes it unlikely that our system's capability to infer eating activities generalizes across individuals. Although we plan to evaluate our system using a person-independent metric in the future, we believe that most applications and interfaces built on top of our implementation will be personalized (e.g., a just-in-time intervention tailored to address an individual's specific challenges).

Secondly, snacking behavior was not the focus of this study. The duration of data collection per day combined with the times when the study began and ended precluded us from capturing ambient audio around snack-eating activities. However, there is no question that snacking is a highly relevant behavior, and we plan to improve our study design and techniques to account for it in the future. Having said this, a few of the meal eating activities logged in our feasibility study were shorter than 10 minutes, which more closely matches snack eating duration than a "traditional" meal eating duration. The truth is that there is a great deal of ambiguity when it comes to characterizing an eating activity as meal eating versus snack eating.

One of the key issues in audio-based activity recognition is privacy. Understandably, most people object to the recording and analysis of audio of their everyday lives, particularly if it is done completely autonomously and without human input. In our implementation we did not address this challenge, although techniques for protecting privacy in audio streams, and conversational speech in particular, have been proposed [23].

CONCLUSION

Based on our results, and despite the limitations of our study, it is clear that acoustic sensing represents a promising opportunity. Our system was able to identify meal eating with 89.6% precision and 76.3% recall in a person-dependent evaluation. Although our focus in this work is on the binary presence of eating moments in an audio stream, there are many other dimensions of eating that are relevant from a diet and behavior change perspective. With audio, it might be possible to determine whether individuals are eating alone or with friends, and whether they are eating while working (e.g. typing in a computer) or watching television. We hope to extend our audio-based activity classification platform in the future to capture these additional contextual parameters.

ACKNOWLEDGEMENTS

We would like to thank Thomas Ploetz for his feedback. This work was supported by the Intel Science and Technology Center for Pervasive Computing (ISTC-PC), and by the National Institutes of Health under award 1U54EB020404-01.

REFERENCES

1. Amft, O., and Tröster, G. Recognition of dietary activity events using on-body sensors. *Artificial Intelligence in Medicine 42*, 2 (Feb. 2008), 121–136.
2. Bäckström, T., and Magi, C. Properties of line spectrum pair polynomials—A review. *Signal Processing 86*, 11 (Nov. 2006), 3286–3298.
3. Burke, L. E., Wang, J., and Sevick, M. A. Self-Monitoring in Weight Loss: A Systematic Review of the Literature. *YJADA 111*, 1 (Jan. 2011), 92–102.
4. Dong, Y., Scisco, J., Wilson, M., Muth, E., and Hoover, A. Detecting periods of eating during free living by tracking wrist motion. *IEEE Journal of Biomedical Health Informatics* (Sept. 2013).
5. Gillet, O., and Richard, G. Automatic transcription of drum loops. In *2004 IEEE International Conference on Acoustics, Speech, and Signal Processing*, IEEE (2004), iv–269–iv–272.
6. Kadomura, A., Li, C.-Y., Tsukada, K., Chu, H.-H., and Siio, I. Persuasive technology to improve eating behavior using a sensor-embedded fork. In *the 2014 ACM International Joint Conference*, ACM Press (New York, New York, USA, 2014), 319–329.
7. Kahneman, D., Krueger, A. B., Schkade, D. A., and Schwarz, N. A Survey Method for Characterizing Daily Life Experience: The Day Reconstruction Method. *Science* (2004).
8. Kalantarian, H., Alshurafa, N., and Sarrafzadeh, M. A Wearable Nutrition Monitoring System. In *Wearable and Implantable Body Sensor Networks (BSN), 2014 11th International Conference on* (2014), 75–80.
9. Lu, H., Frauendorfer, D., Rabbi, M., Mast, M. S., Chittaranjan, G. T., Campbell, A. T., Gatica-Perez, D., and Choudhury, T. StressSense: detecting stress in unconstrained acoustic environments using smartphones. In *UbiComp '12: Proceedings of the 2012 ACM Conference on Ubiquitous Computing*, ACM Request Permissions (Sept. 2012).
10. Lu, H., Pan, W., Lane, N., Choudhury, T., and Campbell, A. SoundSense: scalable sound sensing for people-centric applications on mobile phones. *Proceedings of the 7th international conference on Mobile systems, applications, and services* (2009), 165–178.
11. Lukowicz, P., Pentland, A. S., and Ferscha, A. From Context Awareness to Socially Aware Computing. *IEEE pervasive computing 11*, 1 (2012), 32–40.
12. Makhoul, J. Linear prediction: A tutorial review. *Proceedings of the IEEE 63*, 4 (Apr. 1975), 561–580.
13. Mathieu, B., Essid, S., Fillon, T., Prado, J., and Richard, G. *YAAFE, an Easy to Use and Efficient Audio Feature Extraction Software*. In *proceedings of the 11th ISMIR conference, 2010* (Sept. 2010).
14. Moore, B. C. J., Glasberg, B. R., and Baer, T. A Model for the Prediction of Thresholds, Loudness, and Partial Loudness. *Journal of the Audio Engineering Society 45*, 4 (1997), 224–240.
15. Noronha, J., Hysen, E., Zhang, H., and Gajos, K. Z. Platemate: crowdsourcing nutritional analysis from food photographs. *Proceedings of the 24th annual ACM symposium on User interface software and technology* (2011), 1–12.
16. Pedregosa, F., Varoquaux, G., Gramfort, A., Michel, V., Thirion, B., Grisel, O., Blondel, M., Prettenhofer, P., Weiss, R., Dubourg, V., Vanderplas, J., Passos, A., Cournapeau, D., Brucher, M., Perrot, M., and Duchesnay, E. Scikit-learn: Machine learning in Python. *Journal of Machine Learning Research 12* (2011), 2825–2830.
17. Rossi, M., Feese, S., Amft, O., Braune, N., Martis, S., and Tröster, G. AmbientSense: A real-time ambient sound recognition system for smartphones. In *Pervasive Computing and Communications Workshops (PERCOM Workshops), 2013 IEEE International Conference on* (2013), 230–235.
18. Sazonov, E., Schuckers, S., Lopez-Meyer, P., Makeyev, O., Sazonova, N., Melanson, E. L., and Neuman, M. Non-invasive monitoring of chewing and swallowing for objective quantification of ingestive behavior. *Physiological Measurement 29*, 5 (Apr. 2008), 525–541.
19. Scheirer, E., and Slaney, M. Construction and evaluation of a robust multifeature speech/music discriminator. *IEEE Internation Conference on Acoustics, Speech and Signal Processing, p.1331-1334, 1997. 2* (1997), 1331–1334.
20. Schussler, H. A stability theorem for discrete systems. *IEEE Transactions on Acoustics, Speech, and Signal Processing 24*, 1 (Feb. 1976), 87–89.
21. Stellar, E., and Shrager, E. E. Chews and swallows and the microstructure of eating. *The American journal of clinical nutrition 42*, 5 (1985), 973–982.
22. Ward, J. A., Lukowicz, P., Tröster, G., and Starner, T. E. Activity Recognition of Assembly Tasks Using Body-Worn Microphones and Accelerometers. *Pattern Analysis and Machine Intelligence, IEEE Transactions on 28*, 10 (2006), 1553–1567.
23. Wyatt, D., Choudhury, T., and Bilmes, J. Conversation detection and speaker segmentation in privacy-sensitive situated speech data. *Proceedings of Interspeech* (2007), 586–589.
24. Yatani, K., and Truong, K. N. BodyScope: a wearable acoustic sensor for activity recognition. *UbiComp '12: Proceedings of the 2012 ACM Conference on Ubiquitous Computing* (2012), 341–350.

Learning Therapy Strategies from Demonstration Using Latent Dirichlet Allocation

Hee-Tae Jung[1] Richard G. Freedman[1] Tammie Foster[2]
Yu-Kyong Choe[3] Shlomo Zilberstein[1] Roderic A. Grupen[1]

[1] School of Computer Science, University of Massachusetts, Amherst, MA 01003
[2] Center for Human Motion, Cooley Dickinson Hospital, Northampton, MA 01061
[3] Department of Communication Disorders, University of Massachusetts, Amherst, MA 01003

ABSTRACT

The use of robots in stroke rehabilitation has become a popular trend in rehabilitation robotics. However, despite the acknowledged value of customized service for individual patients, research on programming adaptive therapy for individual patients has received little attention. The goal of the current study is to model teletherapy sessions in the form of a generative process for autonomous therapy that approximate the demonstrations of the therapist. The resulting autonomous programs for therapy may imitate the strategy that the therapist might have employed and reinforce therapeutic exercises between teletherapy sessions. We propose to encode the therapist's decision criteria in terms of the patient's motor performance features. Specifically, in this work, we apply Latent Dirichlet Allocation on the batch data collected during teletherapy sessions between a single stroke patient and a single therapist. Using the resulting models, the therapeutic exercise targets are generated and are verified with the same therapist who generated the data.

Author Keywords

Robot-Mediated Therapy; Customized Therapy; Learning from Demonstration; Latent Dirichlet Allocation.

ACM Classification Keywords

H.1.2. Models and Principles: User/Machine Systems; I.2.6. Artificial Intelligence: Learning; J.3 Life and Medical Sciences: Health

INTRODUCTION

Many countries are experiencing an increase in the elderly population, which may lead to spiraling healthcare costs and shortages of trained professionals to address the needs of the aging population [26]. Robots are often considered for healthcare applications including stroke rehabilitation which is the focus of the proposed work. To date, a common approach is to develop multiple special-purpose robots each of which is designed to serve a single particular rehabilitation goal. Good examples include the exoskeleton rehabilitation robots that are built to reconstruct upper or lower limb movements [4, 11]. Due to their size, cost, and special purpose nature, these robots are most affordable when they are shared by a large number of users in hospitals or rehabilitation centers [17]. This work takes a different approach by proposing that general-purpose personal robots–those that can reside with a patient and deliver various services–can be programmed by service providers to deliver some services autonomously, in a data-driven manner that adapts to changing client needs. In both cases, it is important to encourage patients to exercise with voluntary movements and therefore necessary to provide adpative exercise targets with appropriate difficulty levels.

Recently, researchers have started exploring ways to adapt the difficulty levels of exercise programs based on patient performance. For instance, Perry *et al.* increase the difficulty levels of exercise games when patients exceed predefined achievement thresholds [20]. Shirzad *et al.* explore various supervised learning methods to predict patients' intention to adjust the difficulty levels of games [22]. However, these approaches rely on generic games with predetermined exercise programs and difficulty levels. Also, they do not allow therapists to prescribe exercise targets or specify difficulty levels directly. Jung *et al.* allow therapists to select exercise targets to meet the specific needs of individual patients [16]. However, their approah encodes the targets in the Cartesian space and requires the frequent intervention of therapists to re-select the targets as the motor performance of patients change.

The goal of our research is to develop a new approach to create data-driven generative models that capture the decision making capacity of human therapists during therapy sessions with patients and verify that the new sessions generated by the resulting models can be vetted and endorsed by therapists. Specifically, we propose to use Latent Dirichlet Allocation (LDA) and learn the underlying features of therapist-selected targets. This may reveal the therapist's strategy as well as the motor characteristics that are specific to an individual patient. We test our approach using batch data of therapeutic exercise targets prescribed by an actual therapist for an actual stroke patient during teletherapy sessions. We contend that these technologies can be used to reinforce therapy delivered by remote service providers and may, thus, improve their productivity while it also improves client outcomes.

BACKGROUND

Robot-Mediated Therapy Using robots for stroke rehabili-

ACM 978-1-4503-3306-1/15/03 ...$15.00.
http://dx.doi.org/10.1145/2678025.2701403

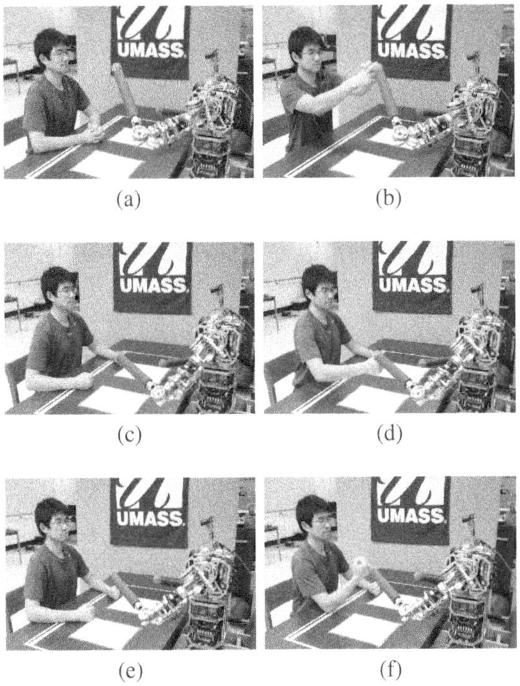

Figure 1: A research assistant demonstrating physical teletherapy sessions. The robot presents a reaching target position in 3D Cartesian space, which is determined by the therapist based on the individual client's motor performance. In task 1, the client is instructed to hold two hands together and reach the target (a, b). In task 2, the client is instructed to lift his impaired arm to reach the target (c, d). In task 3, the client lifts and rotates his impaired forearm to reach the target (e, f).

tation has received a lot of attention. Most effort has focused on developing new robot platforms and validating their feasibility [2, 19, 21]. The rehabilitation robots realize hands-on style therapy where stroke patients either hold onto or place their impaired arm on the end-point or the exoskeletal components of these robots. During therapy sessions, these robots provide assistance for low functioning patients to complete otherwise unattainable exercise targets in pre-programmed computer games with various exercise targets [5]. Since it is important that the patient makes voluntary movements with minimum support, the patient may benefit from carefully selected exercise targets tailored to his motor impairment.

Some explore the possibility of utilizing general purpose robots. Jung et al. explore the idea by Dijkers et al. [7] and induce voluntary exercise movements from post-stroke patients in both automated and tele-operated modes [13, 16]. In this approach, the challenge level of exercise is mostly regulated by the way the exercise targets are presented while the patient attains these targets through voluntary movements. If appropriate exercise targets are provided, empirical studies report that this can lead to larger range of motion [13–15]. Hence, it is apparent that the selection of the targets need to be tailored to the impairment and meet the needs of individual patients.

Latent Dirichlet Allocation LDA [1] is an unsupervised machine learning technique commonly used in text analysis. The underlying concept behind LDA is that an observed collection of D documents contains information about T topics, distributions $\phi_{t\in\{1,\ldots,T\}}$ over a list of words. However, these topics are not known *a-priori* and a single document may discuss more than one of these topics, represented by a distribution $\theta_{d\in\{1,\ldots,D\}}$. The topics are concepts which may be used as keywords to summarize the collection of documents, and a bag-of-words assumption (ordering does not matter) is applied to the collection of documents to emphasize this keywords notion. Thus identifying words such as "carrot" and "orange" anywhere in a document implies that it is likely to contain a topic about food, produce, or orange edible items; the unsupervised approach requires human experts to interpret the learned topics.

LDA finds these topics by clustering words in order to maximize underlying parameters that are part of a generative process explaining how the documents were created. In summary, the θ_d and ϕ_t distributions are each drawn from respective Dirichlet distributions, and then each word w_i in document d is generated by sampling topic $z_i \sim \theta_d$ so that $w_i \sim \phi_{z_i}$. This means that the likelihood of $\boldsymbol{\theta}$, $\boldsymbol{\phi}$, and the latent topic assignments $\mathbf{z}$ should be maximized for text $\mathbf{w}$:

$$P(\mathbf{z}, \boldsymbol{\theta}, \boldsymbol{\phi} \,|\mathbf{w}, \alpha, \beta) = \frac{P(\mathbf{w}|\mathbf{z}, \boldsymbol{\phi})P(\mathbf{z}|\boldsymbol{\theta})P(\boldsymbol{\theta}|\alpha)P(\boldsymbol{\phi}|\beta)}{P(\mathbf{w}|\alpha, \beta)}$$

where the denominator is a normalizing constant and α, β are hyperparameters describing the Dirichlet distributions. Once these parameters are learned using Gibbs sampling, we may use them to infer topics of newly observed documents assumed to be derived from the same generative process as well as find the likelihood that such documents were actually generated by the same model. LDA has also been widely used outside of text analysis by applying the bag-of-words assumption to other collections of objects including pixel regions [24] for semantic image analysis, streams of sensor data [8, 12, 18, 27] for activity recognition, and sequences of images [3, 25] for activity recognition and segmentation.

PROPOSED APPROACH

Learning Therapy Strategies The fundamental idea behind our approach is that the therapist's decision making criteria is reflected in the runtime performance of the patient during the prescription of therapeutic exercises. Given therapeutic tasks, exercise targets should be prescribed in a way that challenge an individual patient to an appropriate extent. In each therapy session, let us assume that the therapist determines N exercise targets. For each described exercise target p_n, the runtime motor performance of the patient $\mathbf{x}_n = [x_1, \cdots, x_M]^{\mathrm{T}}$ can be measured where M is the number of features describing the motor performance while the patient is attaining the target. We hypothesize that $(\mathbf{x}_1, \cdots, \mathbf{x}_N)$ can describe the dynamics of the challenges that the therapist wants to impose during the therapy sessions for the particular patient. In this work, each feature's measurement x_m is mapped to a representative symbol and $\mathbf{x}_n$ concatenates these M symbols to form word token w_n. Each therapy session then contains a vector of word tokens $\mathbf{w} = [w_1, \cdots, w_N]^T$ so that the session has a formalized document representation. This allows us to apply state-of-the-art topic modeling methods to capture the underlying structure of these words, i.e. the patient's performance features. We use LDA as it is a well-studied algorithm and we are uncertain which criteria best cluster reaching targets for physical therapy sessions. We consider two performance features in this work: the success of reaching movement and the duration taken while reaching. The difficulty of each given exercise target is modeled using these features.

Generating New Exercise Targets Using a teleoperation interface, the therapist can lay out therapeutic exercises in real time which requires constant intervention. However, we can use the learned parameters to generate new exercise targets according to the criteria learned from demonstrations. This will allow the therapist to see more patients per unit of time. Because each word in a session's document represents a single point in space, the bag-of-words assumption appears more applicable to our domain. Unlike text data in which word ordering is necessary for comprehensabilty, the set of points may be reordered and yield a similar therapeutic treatment. Hence we perform the generating process from which LDA derived our training data in order to create original documents that propose a set of points for new exercise targets in future training sessions. That is, for a new session containing N' points, we sample $z'_1, \ldots, z'_{N'} \sim \theta' \sim \text{Dirichlet}(\alpha)$ and then sample $w'_i \sim \phi_{z'_i}$ for each $i \in \{1, \ldots, N'\}$. For each w'_i, we can approximately invert the symbolic encoding to find Cartesian position $f^{-1}(w'_i) = p'_i$. Consequently, as the patient becomes tired or improves his motor performance, the exercise target p' is adjusted to yield similar motor performance features. Due to limited space, we simply note that we use the patient's performance database to compute f^{-1}.

EXPERIMENTS

Participants In order to validate the approach, we used a small dataset collected from five teletherapy sessions with a real patient and a real therapist. The patient was a 73-year-old male who experienced a stroke 10.5 years prior to the data collection. He scored 32 out of 66 points on the upper extremity portion of the Fugl-Meyer Assessments [6,9]. The therapist had 22 years of experience with expertise in neurological patients including stroke patients.

Data Collection In a single day, three tasks were performed using teleoperation. The therapist remotely controlled the robot and determined exercise targets for three different tasks following the method presented in Jung et al. [16]. See Figure 1 for a detailed description of the tasks. This was repeated five times yielding fifteen sets of data (3×5).

The exercise targets and the corresponding patient's performance were collected as batch data. For each reaching target in the Cartesian space $p \in \mathbb{R}^3$, two motor performance features were measured. The first was whether or not the patient successfully attained the target, and the second was the duration of time taken to reach the target from resting position. Note that the first feature $x_1 \in \{\text{success}, \text{failure}\}$ is discrete by nature while the second feature $x_2 \in \mathbb{R}$ is continuous and needs to be discretized. In this work, x_2 is discretized systematically using a specified constant interval, i.e. $i = 0.3$ for task 1 and $i = 0.5$ tasks 2 and 3. The intervals were determined empirically. These feature values were mapped to the corresponding symbols and concatenated.

Therapist's Evaluation It is important that therapists find the results useful. We investigated two criteria. First of all, the learned topics describing exercise targets should make sense, revealing some characteristics of the patient's performance and the pattern of exercise targets. The exercise targets were shown to the therapist in the form of plots and a list of the patient's corresponding motor performance. We asked if the therapist could identify any patterns and whether the learned topics made sense to her. Furthermore, we presented some newly generated therapy sessions and asked if she believed that they would be appropriate in terms of difficulty.

RESULTS & DISCUSSION

The model was trained using different values of T and the one providing the greatest log likelihood (LL) was chosen. For task 1, x_2 was discretized using $i = 0.3$ resulting in five intervals. $T = 2$ topics had the best LL where the first topic (red) included targets that were successfully attained in $0.6 \leq t < 1.2$ seconds by the patient. The second topic (blue) included targets successfully attained mostly within $t < 0.6$ seconds. There were a small number of targets that took $t \geq 1.2$ seconds to attain or that the patient failed to attain. When the results were presented to the therapist, she found this plausible and stated that:

> *He has flexor tone and it is easier [for him] to use his tone [to reach the targets]. For the external rotation, it's much more difficult to reach. It is easier to cross the middle line and reach because he can use his torso.*

For task 2, x_2 was discretized using $i = 0.5$ resulting in five intervals. The patient was instructed to make unassisted voluntary movements, taking more time in general. Based on the LL, $T = 3$ topics were learned. The first topic (red) includes targets attained in $0.5 \leq t < 1.0$ seconds, the second topic (blue) includes targets attainable in either $t < 0.5$ seconds or $1.5 \leq t < 2.5$ seconds, and the last topic (green) includes mostly targets the patient could not obtain (as well as a small number of targets attained in $1.0 \leq t < 1.5$ seconds). As seen in Figure 2b, topics were credited to the targets' heights.

For task 3, x_2 was discretized using $i = 0.5$ resulting in four intervals. Based on the LL, $T = 2$ topics were learned. The first topic (blue) includes attainable targets in $0.5 \leq t < 1.0$ seconds while the second topic (red) includes the remaining targets. This can be interpreted as one topic including the exercise targets that the patient can attain with *some* effort. The other topic includes targets that are attainable with minimum or significant effort in addition to those not attainable at all.

The therapist was given five suggested therapy sessions per task that were generated using the trained LDA models. Between thirty and fifty targets were randomly generated per session. For task 1, she felt that four out of five closely captured the therapy she would provide and would be willing to let the robot use all five suggested sets of execise targets. One

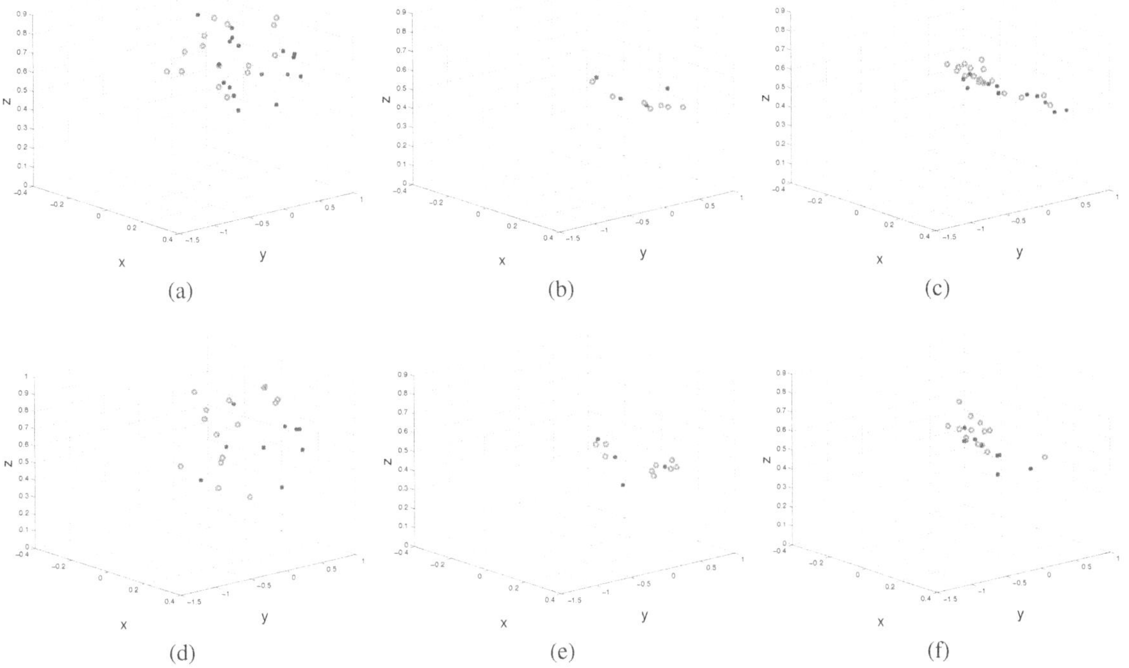

Figure 2: (a), (b), (c) are the target positions the therapist determined during her teletherapy sessions for tasks 1, 2, and 3 respectively. (d), (e), (f) are the target positions the trained model generated for autonomous therapy sessions for tasks 1, 2, and 3 respectively. A marker with cyan color at $(0, -1.05, 0)$ is the approximate sitting position of the patient. Units are in meters.

of the suggested sets of targets had *'less motions to the left (horizontal adduction) the way that was harder for the patient to reach.'* For task 2, the therapist thought all five suggested sets captured the therapy and would let the robot use them. However, for task 3, the therapist was satisfied with only one out of the five suggested sets due to the small number of targets in the four sets. She responded she would have endorsed them if the sufficient numbers were generated.

During the interview, the therapist thought the choice of features made sense because both play an important role in how she chooses exercise targets. However, she pointed out that it would be useful to separate cognitive and motor movement delay. In this work, they were encoded as a single duration feature. Additionally, she suggested that different spatial areas may challenge the patient differently because of the flexor tone specific to the patient. Lastly, she mentioned that it might be useful if temporal patterns can be captured.

It was encouraging that she found the presented plots useful for understanding the motor performance of the patient. This implies that topic modeling may be used to both provide visual feedback and model the therapist's strategy.

CONCLUSION

Through a single subject case study, we demonstrated that therapy strategies can be modeled in terms of the patient's motor performance and that the models can be automatically learned using LDA. We also showed that the learned parameters can be used to generate sets of new exercise targets that conform with the therapist's strategies. Using the proposed approach, the robot might be able to imitate the therapist's strategies and provide appropriately challenging targets even in his/her absence. This can increase the efficiency of the therapist's time in practice.

The proposed approach can be improved in multiple ways. For example, it is well known that LDA needs a large amount of training data. Here, the number of features and the available values were small which might have been the reason that LDA worked using the small data set. Further investigation needs to be done to determine whether simpler models with fewer parameters, such as the Bayesian mixture model, should be used. This is especially important because the size of the data we can collect in practice is small.

As the therapist implied, it is possible for her decision making process to evolve even within the same therapy session. Since LDA treats the data as a bag-of-words, it cannot capture this temporal distinction. It might be interesting to see if this can be learned using temporal extensions of LDA which integrate hidden Markov models or n-grams to acknowledge structure in the data [10, 23]. There are many variations of LDA that can address the new demands that are likely to arise as we continue to enrich the domain.

ACKNOWLEDGMENTS

This work was supported in part by an award from the American Heart Association (12CRP9010007) and the National Science Foundation (IIS-1116917).

REFERENCES

1. Blei, D. M., Ng, A. Y., and Jordan, M. I. Latent Dirichlet Allocation. *Journal of Machine Learning Research 3* (2003), 993–1022.
2. Brewer, B. R., McDowell, S. K., and Worthen-Chaudhari, L. C. Poststroke upper extremity rehabilitation: a review of robotic systems and clinical results. *Topics in stroke rehabilitation 14*, 6 (2007), 22–44.
3. Buchsbaum, D., Canini, K. R., and Griffiths. Segmenting and recognizing human action using low-level video features. In *Proceedings of the 33rd Annual Conference of the Cognitive Science Society* (2011).
4. Colombo, G., Wirz, M., and Dietz, V. Driven gait orthosis for improvement of locomotor training in paraplegic patients. *Spinal Cord 39*, 5 (2001), 252–255.
5. Colombo, R., Pisano, F., Mazzone, A., Delconte, C., Micera, S., Carrozza, M. C., Dario, P., and Minuco, G. Design strategies to improve patient motivation during robot-aided rehabilitation. *Journal of NeuroEngineering and Rehabilitation 4*, 3 (2007).
6. Deakin, A., Hill, H., and Pomeroy, V. M. Rough guide to the fugl-meyer assessment upper limb section. *Physiotherapy 89*, 12 (2003), 751–763.
7. Dijkers, M. P., deBear, P. C., Erlandson, R. F., Kristy, K., Geer, D. M., and Nichols, A. Patient and staff acceptance of robotic technology in occupational therapy: A pilot study. *Journal of Rehabilitation Research and Development 28*, 2 (1991), 33–44.
8. Freedman, R., Jung, H., and Zilberstein, S. Plan and activity recognition from a topic modeling perspective. In *Proceedings of the 24th International Conference on Automated Planning and Scheduling* (2014).
9. Fugl-Meyer, A., Jääskö, L., Leyman, I., Olsson, S., and Steglind, S. The post-stroke hemiplegic patient: a method for evaluation of physical performance. *Scandinavian journal of rehabilitation medicine 7*, 1 (1975), 13–31.
10. Griffiths, T. L., Steyvers, M., Blei, D. M., and Tenenbaum, J. B. Integrating topics and syntax. In *Proceedings of the 18th Annual Conference on Neural Information Processing Systems* (2004).
11. Hogan, N., Krebs, H. I., Charnnarong, J., Srikrishna, P., and Sharon, A. MIT-MANUS: A workstation for manual therapy and training I. In *Proceedings of the IEEE International Workshop on Robot and Human Communication* (1992).
12. Huỳnh, T., Fritz, M., and Schiele, B. Discovery of activity patterns using topic models. In *Proceedings of the 10th International Conference on Ubiquitous Computing* (2008).
13. Jung, H., Baird, J., Choe, Y., and Grupen, R. A. Upper extremity physical therapy for stroke patients using a general purpose robot. In *Proceedings of the 20th IEEE International Symposium on Robot and Human Interactive Communication* (2011).
14. Jung, H., Baird, J., Choe, Y., and Grupen, R. A. Upper-limb exercises for stroke patients through the direct engagement of an embodied agent. In *Proceedings of the 6th ACM/IEEE International Conference on Human-Robot Interaction* (2011).
15. Jung, H., Choe, Y., and Grupen, R. A. Extended virtual presence of therapists through home service robots. In *Proceedings of the 10th ACM/IEEE International Conference on Human-Robot Interaction* (2015).
16. Jung, H., Takahashi, T., Choe, Y., Baird, J., Foster, T., and Grupen, R. A. Towards extended virtual presence of the therapist in stroke rehabilitation. In *Proceedings of the IEEE International Conference on Rehabilitation Robotics* (2013).
17. Jung, H., and Yoo, D. Towards ethical research practice: Anticipating social consequences of robot-mediated rehabilitation. In *Proceedings of the IEEE International Symposium on Ethics in Engineering, Science, and Technology* (2014).
18. Koppula, H. S., and Saxena, A. Learning spatio-temporal structure from rgb-d videos for human activity detection and anticipation. In *Proceedings of the International Conference on Machine Learning* (2013).
19. Kwakkel, G., Kollen, B., and Krebs, H. Effects of robot-assisted therapy on upper limb recovery after stroke: a systematic review. *Neurorehabilitation and Neural Repair 22*, 2 (2008), 111–121.
20. Perry, J. C., Balasubramanian, S., de Pablo, C. R., and Keller, T. Improving the match between ability and challenge: toward a framework for automatic level adaptation in game-based assessment and training. In *Proceedings of the IEEE International Conference on Rehabilitation Robotics* (2013).
21. Prange, G., Jannink, M., Groothuis-Oudshoorn, C., Hermens, H., and IJzerman, M. Systematic review of the effect of robot-aided therapy on recovery of the hemiparetic arm after stroke. *Journal of Rehabilitation Research and Development 43*, 2 (2006), 171–184.
22. Shirzad, N., and der Loos, M. V. Adaptation of task difficulty in rehabilitation exercises based on the user's motor performance and physiological responses. In *Proceedings of the IEEE International Conference on Rehabilitation Robotics* (2013).
23. Wallach, H. M. Topic modeling: Beyond bag-of-words. In *Proceedings of the 23rd International Conference on Machine Learning* (2006).
24. Wang, G., Zhang, Y., and Li, F.-F. Using dependent regions for object categorization in a generative framework. In *Proceedings of the IEEE Computer Society Conference on Computer Vision and Pattern Recognition* (2006).
25. Wang, Y., and Mori, G. Human action recognition by semi-latent topic models. *IEEE Transactions on Pattern Analysis and Machine Intelligence Special Issue on Probabilistic Graphical Models in Computer Vision 31*, 10 (2009), 1762–1774.
26. Zarit, S. H., and Zarit, J. M. *Mental Disorders in Older Adults: Fundamentals of Assessment and Treatment*. The Guilford Press, New York, NY, 2011.
27. Zhang, H., and Parker, L. 4-dimensional local spatio-temporal features for human activity recognition. In *Procedings of the International Conference on Intelligent Robots and Systems* (2011).

Speech-based Interaction: Myths, Challenges, and Opportunities

Cosmin Munteanu
Institute of Communication, Culture, Information, and Technology,
University of Toronto Mississauga
cosmin.munteanu@utoronto.ca

Gerald Penn
Department of Computer Science
University of Toronto
gpenn@cs.toronto.edu

ABSTRACT
HCI research has for long been dedicated to better and more naturally facilitating information transfer between humans and machines. Unfortunately, humans' most natural form of communication, speech, is also one of the most difficult modalities to be understood by machines – despite, and perhaps, because it is the highest-bandwidth communication channel we possess. While significant research efforts, from engineering, to linguistic, and to cognitive sciences, have been spent on improving machines' ability to understand speech, the HCI community has been relatively timid in embracing this modality as a central focus of research. This can be attributed in part to the relatively discouraging levels of accuracy in understanding speech, in contrast with often-unfounded claims of success from industry, but also to the intrinsic difficulty of designing and especially evaluating speech and natural language interfaces.

The goal of this course is to inform the IUI community of the current state of speech and natural language research, to dispel some of the myths surrounding speech-based interaction, as well as to provide an opportunity for researchers and practitioners to learn more about how speech recognition and speech synthesis work, what are their limitations, and how they could be used to enhance current interaction paradigms. Through this, we hope that IUI researchers and general HCI, UI, and UX practitioners will learn how to combine recent advances in speech processing with user-centred principles in designing more usable and useful speech-based interactive systems.

Author Keywords
Speech-based Interaction; Automatic Speech Recognition; Text-to-Speech; Speech Synthesis; Multimodal Interfaces.

IUI'15, Mar 29 - Apr 01, 2015, Atlanta, GA, USA
ACM 978-1-4503-3306-1/15/03.
http://dx.doi.org/10.1145/2678025.2716263

ACM Classification Keywords
H.5.2 [User Interfaces]: Natural Language, Voice I/O; I.2.7 [Natural Language Processing]: Speech recognition and synthesis

MOTIVATION
The challenges in enabling speech-based interactions have often led to this modality being considered, at best, an error-prone alternative to "traditional" input or output mechanisms. However, this should not be a reason to abandon speech interaction – in fact, people are now exposed to many more situations in which they need to interact hands- and eyes-free with a computing device. Furthermore, achieving perfectly accurate speech processing is a lofty goal that is often nothing short of a fairy tale – a system that scores 100% in accuracy against an arbitrary standard such as a manual transcript is not guaranteed to be useful or usable for its users. There is significant research evidence pointing to the fact that proper interaction design can complement speech processing in ways that compensate for its less-than-perfect accuracy [4,7], or that in many tasks where users interact with spoken information, verbatim transcription of speech is not relevant at all [2].

Recent commercial applications (e.g. personal digital assistants) have brought renewed attention to speech-based interaction. However, as illustrated by the reviews and opinion pieces in popular media [2], such technologies are receiving mixed reviews, often due to unexpected low or inconsistent accuracy for some tasks – "voice recognition isn't that good", or due to perceived lack of usefulness – "more of a gimmick than a useful tool" [1]. This can be in part attributed to speech being marketed as an input/output modality, while in fact speech can assist with a wider range of tasks that are not limited to direct interactions.

If we are to pick just one example where such research is desperately needed, it would be the area of access to multimedia repositories. 72 hours of video are uploaded to Youtube each minute [9]. It is humanly impossible to consume the amount of data being generated, and it is increasingly difficult to search for information or navigate through such large and often multilingual collections. However, speech processing and human computer interaction have already been successfully combined in order to better address users' needs, as illustrated by the research conducted by this tutorial's presenters, such as speech and gestures to support realistic interactions with an immersive serious game environment [3], speech-enabled mobile language learning support [6], or human-in-the-loop approaches to reducing transcription error rates [5].

OUTLINE

In light of our demonstrated feasibility of combining HCI and ASR research to support user interactions, this tutorial addresses the following questions:

- How do Automatic Speech Recognition (ASR) and Speech Synthesis (or Text-To-Speech – TTS) work and why are these such computationally-difficult problems?
- Where are ASR and TTS used in current commercial interactive applications?
- What are the usability issues surrounding speech-based interaction systems, particularly in mobile computing?
- What are the challenges in enabling speech as a modality for mobile interaction?
- What is the current state-of-the-art in ASR and TTS?
- What are the differences between ASR systems' accuracies and the needs of interactive applications?
- What are the difficulties in evaluating the quality and usability of TTS systems?
- What opportunities exist to enhance systems' interactivity by enabling speech?

AUDIENCE, FORMAT, AND PROCEEDINGS

This interactive tutorial will be beneficial to all researchers or practitioners without a strong expertise in ASR or TTS, who still believe in fulfilling HCI's goal of developing methods and systems that allow humans to naturally interact with the increasingly ubiquitous mobile technology, but are disappointed with the lack of success in using speech and natural language to achieve this goal. This three-hour tutorial includes opportunities for classroom participation, discussion of recent uses of ASR and TTS in commercial hands-free products, and two interactive activities. The first activity will engage participants in proposing design alternatives for the error-handling interaction of a smartphone's voice-based intelligent search assistant, based on an empirical assessment of the type of ASR errors exhibited (e.g. acoustic, language, semantic). For the second activity, participants will conduct an evaluation of the quality of the synthetic speech output typically employed in mobile-based speech interfaces, and propose alternate evaluation methods that better reflect the mobile user experience.

AUTHORS' BIOGRAPHIES

Cosmin Munteanu (http://cosmin.taglab.ca) is an Assistant Professor at the Institute for Communication, Culture, Information, and Technology (University of Toronto at Mississauga), and Associate Director of the Technologies for Ageing Gracefully lab. His area of expertise is at the intersection of Human-Computer Interaction, Automatic Speech Recognition, Natural Language Processing, Mobile Computing, and Assistive Technologies. He has extensively studied the human factors of using imperfect speech recognition systems, and has designed and evaluated systems that improve humans' access to and interaction with information-rich media and technologies through natural language. Cosmin's multidisciplinary interests include speech and natural language interaction for mobile devices, mixed reality systems, learning technologies for marginalized users, assistive technologies for older adults, and ethics in human-computer interaction research.

Gerald Penn (http://www.cs.toronto.edu/~gpenn/) is a Professor of Computer Science at the University of Toronto. His area of expertise is in the study of human languages, both from a mathematical and computational perspective. Gerald is one of the leading scholars in Computational Linguistics, with significant contributions to the formal study of natural languages. His publications cover many areas, from Theoretical Linguistics, to Mathematics, and to Automatic Speech Recognition, as well as Human-Computer Interaction.

REFERENCES

1. Business Insider (2012). Frankly, It's Concerning that Apple is Still Advertising A Product as Flawed as Siri. http://www.businessinsider.com, 2012.
2. Gizmodo (2011). Siri is Apple's Broken Promise. http://www.gizmodo.com, 2011.
3. Fournier H., et al. (2011). A Multidisciplinary Approach to Enhancing Infantry Training through Immersive Technologies. Proc of I/ITSEC.
4. Munteanu, C. et al. (2006). Automatic speech recognition for webcasts: how good is good enough and what to do when it isn't. Proc. of ICMI.
5. Munteanu, C., Baecker, R., and Penn, G., (2008). Collaborative Editing for Improved Usefulness and Usability of Transcript-Enhanced Webcasts. Proc CHI.
6. Munteanu, C., et al. (2013). Hidden in plain sight: Low literacy adults in a developed country overcoming social and educational challenges through mobile learning support tools. In J of Pers and Ubiquitous Computing.
7. Oviatt, S. (2003). Advances in Robust Multimodal Interface Design. IEEE Comput. Graph. Appl. 23-5.
8. Penn, G. and Zhu, X. (2008). A critical reassessment of evaluation baselines for speech summarization. In Proc. of ACL-HLT.
9. Youtube (2012). Upload statistics. http://www.youtube.com/t/press_statistics

Tutorial on Personalization for Behaviour Change

Judith Masthoff
University of Aberdeen
Aberdeen, UK
j.masthoff@abdn.ac.uk

Julita Vassileva
University of Saskatchewan
Saskatoon, Canada
jiv@cs.usask.ca

ABSTRACT
Digital behaviour interventions aim to encourage and support people to change their behaviour, for their own or communal benefits. Personalization plays an important role in this, as the most effective persuasive and motivational strategies are likely to depend on user characteristics. This tutorial covers the role of personalization in behaviour change technology, and methods and techniques to design personalized behaviour change technology.

Author Keywords
Behaviour change; persuasive technology; personalization; gamification.

ACM Classification Keywords
H.5.2. [User Interfaces]: User-centered design; J.4 [Social and Behavioral Sciences]: Psychology; I2. Artificial Intelligence.

MOTIVATION
Digital behaviour intervention is a growing area of research which investigates how interactive systems can encourage and support people to change their behaviour, for their own or communal benefits. Personalization plays an important role in this, as the most effective persuasive and motivational strategies are likely to depend on user characteristics such as the user's personality, affective state, existing attitudes, behaviours, knowledge, and goals.

Example application areas include healthcare (e.g., encouraging people to eat more healthily and exercise more), education (e.g., motivating learners to study more), environment (e.g., encouraging people to use less energy and more public transport), and collaborative content development (e.g., incentivising people to annotate resources, participate online).

This tutorial covers the role of personalization in behaviour change technology, and methods and techniques to design personalized behaviour change technology. The tutorial includes both traditional and more recent approaches (such as gamification).

IUI'15, Mar 29 - Apr 01, 2015, Atlanta, GA, USA
ACM 978-1-4503-3306-1/15/03.
http://dx.doi.org/10.1145/2678025.2716264

TOPICS
This tutorial provides a structured overview of the relevant background (e.g. theories and techniques of behaviour change) as well as covering personalization in behaviour change. It provides learning opportunities through hands-on sessions.

Theories of Motivation
The tutorial covers two theoretical approaches to behavior change: (1) setting the environment so that it cues or triggers the desired behavior (Behavioural Economics), and (2) motivating people to do certain things (Social Psychology). It also covers Cialdini's persuasion principles.

Behaviour Change Techniques
The tutorial introduces determinants of behaviour, followed by behaviour change techniques that can be mapped onto these determinants. Eleven common behaviour change techniques are discussed: goal setting, (self) monitoring, feedback, review goals, reward (conditioning), (social)-comparison, punish, prompt (trigger, call to action), threaten (appeal to fear), verbal persuasion (argumentation), and motivational interviewing. Each technique is illustrated with examples of how it has been applied in existing digital behaviour interventions. It is also discussed which decisions needed to use the technique, showing opportunities for personalization.

Gamification and Incentives
The tutorial covers game-based approaches to behaviour change (persuasive games, serious games, reality games), and in particular gamification (embedding game mechanisms in non-game applications). It illustrates this with gamification used in existing applications, and provides examples of adaptive personalized incentives.

Personalized Persuasive Technology
The tutorial focuses on why persuasive technology needs personalization. It covers what can be personalized, to what user features (including aspects such as personality, interests, ability, context, attitudes, motivation, gamer types, and changes over time linked to transitional stage models). The tutorial covers both adaptation of persuasive technique parameters and messages, and the techniques, features and functions used by the application. This is illustrated with research examples, including the example of adapting the techniques used by a persuasive health game to user gamer types and the research on which it was based.

Evaluating Personalized Persuasive Technology

The tutorial introduces the need for a layered approach to evaluating personalized persuasive technology, including slicing and dicing. It illustrates this with empirical studies that have informed persuasive technology design.

The Ethics of Persuasive Technology

Finally, the tutorial encourages participants to consider the ethical aspects related to persuasive technology.

Hands-on sessions

Tutorial participants are provided with a case study and asked to design a persuasive component for an existing system (such as EasyChair). They work in groups. In a first session, they discuss which behaviour change techniques to apply and how to apply them. In a second session, they discuss what and how to personalize.

OBJECTIVES

By the end of this tutorial, given a scenario for a behaviour change intervention, attendees should be able to:

- describe which behaviour change theories are relevant
- decide or investigate which behaviour change strategies to apply, and how to apply them
- decide or investigate what personalization to use both within the chosen strategies, and to adapt the strategy choice
- plan an evaluation of the behaviour change intervention or strategy
- show an awareness of related ethical issues

BIBLIOGRAPHY

The tutorial includes an annotated bibliography, including literature on behavioural economics [1,2], motivating behaviours/participation [3-5], persuasion [6,7], determinants of behaviour [8-10], behaviour change techniques in general [11,12], goals setting, goals review and self-monitoring [13-15], feedback [15-18], rewards [14,19,20], (social) comparison [21,22], punish and threaten [23-26], prompt [27,28], suggest / argue [29-32], motivational interviewing [15,33], games for behaviour change [34,35], gamification [36,37], incentive mechanism design [38], reflection [39], source credibility and interface design [40-44], personalized persuasion [45-50], personalized feedback [51,52], personalized incentives and rewards [35,38,53], personalized prompts [28], personalized arguments [29,54-56], tailored choice of techniques [46, 57-60], adapting to culture [61,62], personalized / tailored persuasion for healthy eating [32, 63-65], ethics of persuasive technology [66], and evaluation methods [67,68].

REFERENCES

1. Ariely, D. *Predictably Irrational.* Harper-Collins. 2008.
2. Ariely D. TED http://www.ted.com/speakers/dan_ariely
3. Vassileva, J. Motivating Participation in Social Computing Applications: A User Modeling Perspective. *User Modeling and User Adapted Interaction, 22*:177-201. (2012)
4. Cameron, J. and Pierce, W.D. Reinforcement, Reward, and Intrinsic Motivation: A Meta-Analysis. *Review of Educational Research 64*, 3 (1994), 363.
5. Bandura, A. Self-efficacy: Toward a unifying theory of behavioral change. *Psychological Review 84*, 2 (1977), 191–215.
6. Cialdini, R.B. The Science of Persuasion. *Scientific American Mind 284*, 76–84. (2004)
7. Fogg, B.J. *Persuasive Technology: Using computers to change what we think and do.* Morgan Kaufmann. 2003.
8. Fishbein, M., Triandis, H.C., Kanfer, F.H., Becker, M., Middlestadt, S. E., Eichler, A. Factors influencing behaviour and behaviour change. In: Baum et al. (Eds.) *Handbook of health psychology.* Mahwah, NJ: Lawrence Erlbaum Associates, 3–17 (2001).
9. Fogg, B.J. A behavior model for persuasive design. *4th International Conference on Persuasive Technology*, Claremont, CA, 26–29 (2009).
10. Michie, S., Johnston, M., Abraham, C., Lawton, R., Parker D., Walker, A. Making psychological theory useful for implementing evidence based practice: a consensus approach. *Quality and Safety in Health Care, 14*, 26-33. (2005)
11. Michie, S., Johnston, M., Francis, J., Hardeman, W., Eccles, M. From theory to intervention: mapping theoretically derived behavioural determinants to behaviour change techniques. *Applied Psychology: An International Review*, 57(4), 660-680. (2008).
12. Webb, T.L. et al. Using the internet to promote health behaviour change: A systematic review and meta-analysis of the impact of theoretical basis, use of behaviour change techniques, and mode of delivery on efficacy. *Journal of Medical Internet Research* 12(1) (2010).
13. Munson, S. A., & Consolvo, S. Exploring goal-setting, rewards, self-monitoring, and sharing to motivate physical activity. *Int.Conf. on Pervasive Computing Technologies for Healthcare,* pp. 25-32. IEEE. (2012).
14. Gabrielli, S., Maimone, R., Forbes, P., Masthoff, J., Wells, S., Primerano, L., Haverinen, L., Bo, G., & Pompa, M. 2013. Designing motivational features for sustainable urban mobility. *CHI '13 Extended Abstracts on Human Factors in Computing Systems.* ACM, 1461-1466. (2013)
15. Nguyen, H., & Masthoff, J. Mary: A personalised virtual health trainer. *Adjunct Proceedings of UMAP*, 58-60. (2010)
16. Nakajima, T., & Lehdonvirta, V. Designing motivation using persuasive ambient mirrors. *Personal and Ubiquitous Computing, 17*, 1, 107-126. (2013)

17. Arroyo, E., Bonanni, L., & Selker, T. Waterbot: exploring feedback and persuasive techniques at the sink. *SIGCHI conference on Human factors in computing systems*, pp. 631-639. ACM. (2005)

18. Midden, C. and Ham, J. Using negative and positive social feedback from a robotic agent to save energy. In *Proceedings of the 4th International Conference on Persuasive Technology*. ACM (2009)

19. Consolvo, S., Klasnja, P., McDonald, D.W., Avrahami, D., Froehlich, J., LeGrand, L., Libby, R., Mosher, K., Landay, J.A. Flowers or a robot army? Encouraging awareness & activity with personal, mobile displays. *ACM Ubicomp* (2008)

20. Berkovsky, S., Freyne, J., & Coombe, M. 2012. Physical activity motivating games: Be active and get your own reward. *ACM Transactions in Computer-Human Interaction,* 19, 4, (2012)

21. Farzan, R., DiMicco, J. M., Millen, D. R., Dugan, C., Geyer, W., & Brownholtz, E. A. Results from deploying a participation incentive mechanism within the enterprise. In *SIGCHI Conference on Human Factors in Computing Systems*, pp. 563-572. ACM. (2008)

22. Gabrielli, S., Forbes, P., Jylhä, A., Wells, S., Sirén, M., Hemminki, S., Nurmi, P., Maimone, R., Masthoff, J., & Jacucci, G. Design challenges in motivating change for sustainable urban mobility. *Computers in Human Behavior* (2014).

23. Lin, J. J., Mamykina, L., Lindtner, S., Delajoux, G., & Strub, H. B. Fish'n'Steps: Encouraging physical activity with an interactive computer game. In *UbiComp 2006: Ubiquitous Computing* (pp. 261-278). Springer Berlin Heidelberg. (2006)

24. Nakajima, T., & Lehdonvirta, V. Designing motivation using persuasive ambient mirrors. *Personal and Ubiquitous Computing, 17*, 1, 107-126. (2013)

25. Kirman, B., Linehan, C., Lawson, S., Foster, D., & Doughty, M. There's a monster in my kitchen: using aversive feedback to motivate behaviour change. In *CHI '10 Extended Abstracts on Human Factors in Computing Systems*. ACM, 2685-2694. (2010)

26. Andrés del Valle, A.C. & Opalach, A. The persuasive mirror: Computerized persuasion for healthy living. *Proceedings of the 11th International Conference on Human-Computer Interaction*. (2005).

27. Fogg, B.J. A behavior model for persuasive design. *4th International Conference on Persuasive Technology*, Claremont, CA, 26–29 (2009).

28. Masthoff, J., Langrial, S., van Deemter, K. Personali-zing triggers for charity actions. *Persuasive Technology*, 125-136. (2013)

29. Carenini, G. & Moore, J. D. Generating and evaluating evaluative arguments. *Artificial Intelligence*, 170, 925-952 (2006).

30. Grasso, F., Cawsey, A., Jones, R. Dialectical argumentation to solve conflicts in advice giving: A case study in the promotion of healthy nutrition. International Journal of Human Computer Studies, 53, 1077-1115. (2000) doi: 10.1006/ijhc.2000.0429

31. Guerini, M., Stock, O., and Zancanaro, M. a Taxonomy of Strategies for Multimodal Persuasive Message Generation. *Applied Artificial Intelligence 21*, 2 (2007), 99–136.

32. Mazzotta, I., de Rosis, F., Carofiglio, V. Portia: A User-Adapted Persuasion System in the Healthy-Eating Domain. IEEE Intelligent Systems, 22, 42-51. (2007)

33. Nguyen, H., Masthoff, J. Designing persuasive dialogue systems: Using argumentation with care. *Persuasive technology* (2008)

34. Berkovsky, S., Coombe, M., Freyne, J., Bhandari, D., and Baghaei, N. Physical activity motivating games: virtual rewards for real activity. *Proceedings of the 28th international conference on Human factors in computing systems*, ACM (2010), 243–252.

35. Berkovsky, S., Freyne, J., Coombe, M., and Bhandari, D. Recommender algorithms in activity motivating games. *Proceedings of the fourth ACM conference on Recommender systems - RecSys '10*, ACM Press (2010), 175.

36. Deterding, S., Sicart, M., Nacke, L., O'Hara, K., and Dixon, D. Gamification. Using game-design elements in non-gaming contexts. *Extended abstracts on Human factors in computing systems - CHI EA '11*, ACM Press (2011), 2425.

37. McGonigal J.. *Reality is Broken*. Penguin .2011.

38. Cheng R., Vassileva J. Design and Evaluation of an Adaptive Incentive Mechanism for Sustained Educational Online Communities. *User Modelling and User-Adapted Interaction*, 16 (2/3), (2006), 321-348.

39. Colineau, N. and Paris, C. Can beneficial habits be induced through reflection? *Workshop on User Models and Motivational Systems: the affective and the rational routes to persuasion, with UMAP'2010.*

40. Cosley, D., Lam, S.K., Albert, I., Konstan, J.A., and Riedl, J. Is seeing believing?: How recommender system interfaces affect users' opinions. *CHI'03*, ACM Press, 585. (2003)

41. Cugelman, B., Thelwall, M., and Dawes, P. The dimensions of web site credibility and their relation to active trust and behavioural impact. *Communications of the Association for Information Systems 24*, 1 (2009)

42. Nguyen, H., & Masthoff, J. Is it me or is it what I say? Source image and persuasion. In *Persuasive Technology*, pp. 231-242, Springer (2007)

43. Nguyen, H., Masthoff, J. Using digital images to enhance the credibility of information. Persuasive Technology Symposium. (2008)

44. Baylor, A. L., & Kim, Y. Pedagogical agent design: The impact of agent realism, gender, ethnicity, and instructional role. In *Intelligent Tutoring Systems*, pp. 592-603, Springer (2004)

45. User Modeling and User-Adapted Interaction Journal Special Issue on Personalization for Behavior Change, 2014, edited by Masthoff, J., Grasso, F., and Ham, J.

46. Orji, R., Vassileva, J., Mandryk, R. Modeling the efficacy of persuasive strategies for different gamer types in serious games for health. *User Modeling and User-Adapted Interaction*. 24: 453-498 (2014)

47. Dijkstra, A. The persuasive effects of personalization through name mentioning in a smoking cessation message. *User Modeling and User-Adapted Interaction*. (2014).

48. Bouvier, P., Sehaba, K., Lavoue, E. A trace-based approach to identifying users' engagement and qualifying their engaged-behaviours in interactive systems: application to a social game. *User Modeling and User-Adapted Interaction 24:413-451*. (2014)

49. op den Akker, H., Jones, V.M., Hermens, H.J. Tailoring real-time physical activity coaching systems: a literature survey and model. *User Modeling and User-Adapted Interaction*. 24: 351-392 (2014)

50. Nguyen, H., and J. Masthoff. Developing personalised digital behaviour interventions: A multi stage process. *Workshop on user models for motivational systems*, with UMAP 2010, pp43-52. (2010)

51. Colineau, N., & Paris C. Motivating reflection about health within the family: the use of goal setting and tailored feedback. *User Modeling and User-Adapted Interaction*, 21, 341-376. (2011).

52. Dennis, M., Masthoff, J., Mellish C. Does Learner Conscientiousness Matter When Generating Emotional Support in Feedback? ACII, 209-214 (2013).

53. Dixon, D. Player Types and Gamification. *CHI 2011 Workshop on Gamification: Using Gane Design Elements in Non-Game Contexts*, (2011), 12–15.

54. Grasso, F., Cawsey, A., Jones, R. Dialectical argumentation to solve conflicts in advice giving: A case study in the promotion of healthy nutrition. *International Journal of Human Computer Studies*, 53, 1077-1115. (2000)

55. Mazzotta, I., de Rosis, F., Carofiglio, V. Portia: A User-Adapted Persuasion System in the Healthy-Eating Domain. *IEEE Intelligent Systems*, 22, 42-51. (2007)

56. Nguyen, H., Masthoff, J., Edwards, P. Modelling a Receiver's Position to Persuasive Arguments. Persuasive Technology, (2007), 271-282.

57. Halko, S. and Kientz, J. Personality and Persuasive Technology: An Exploratory Study on Health-Promoting Mobile Applications. *Persuasive Technology*, Springer (2010), 150–161.

58. Kaptein, M., Lacroix, J., and Saini, P. Individual differences in persuadability in the health promotion domain. *Persuasive technology*, (2010), 94–105.

59. Kaptein, M., De Ruyter, B., Markopoulos, P., and Aarts, E. Adaptive Persuasive Systems. *ACM Transactions on Interactive Intelligent Systems 2*, 2 (2012), 1–25.

60. Kaptein, M. Personalized persuasion in Ambient Intelligence. *Journal of Ambient Intelligence and Smart Environments 4*, 3 (2012), 279–280.

61. Khaled, R., Barr, P., and Fischer, R. Factoring culture into the design of a persuasive game. *Conference on Computer-Human Interaction: Design: Activities, Artefacts and Environments*, (2006), 213–220.

62. Khaled, R., Barr, P., and Biddle, R. Game design strategies for collectivist persuasion. *Proc. of the ACM SIGGRAPH Symposium on Video Games* (2009), 31–38.

63. Orji, R., Mandryk, R.L., Vassileva, J., and Gerling, K.M. Tailoring persuasive health games to gamer type. *CHI'13*, ACM Press (2013), 2467–2476.

64. Orji, R., Vassileva, J., and Mandryk, R. Towards an effective health interventions design: an extension of the health belief model. *Online journal of public health informatics 4*, 3 (2012).

65. Orji, R., Vassileva, J., and Mandryk, R.L. LunchTime: a slow-casual game for long-term dietary behavior change. *Personal and Ubiquitous Computing*, (2012)

66. Berdichevsky, D., & Neuenschwander, E. Toward an ethics of persuasive technology. *Communications of the ACM, 42*(5), 51-58 (1999).

67. Paramythis, A., Weibelzahl, S., & Masthoff, J. Layered evaluation of interactive adaptive systems: framework and formative methods. *User Modeling and User-Adapted Interaction, 20*(5), 383-453. (2010)

68. Masthoff, J. The user as wizard: A method for early involvement in the design and evaluation of adaptive systems. *Workshop on User-Centred Design and Evaluation of Adaptive Systems*, pp. 460-469.

Modelling User Affect and Sentiment in Intelligent User Interfaces

[A Tutorial Overview]

Björn W. Schuller[1,2]
[1]Department of Computing
Imperial College London
SW7 2AZ London, United Kingdom
+44-207-59-48357
bjoern.schuller@imperial.ac.uk
[2]Chair of Complex Systems Engineering
University of Passau
94032 Passau, Germany

ABSTRACT

The computer-based automatic analysis of human sentiment, and affect are broadly expected to play a major role that will likely make 'that difference' in future Intelligent User Interfaces, as they bear the promise to lend interactive systems emotional intelligence. Such comprise intelligent digital games, e. g., for empowerment and inclusion, tutoring systems, information systems or virtual companions, e. g., in the car to name but a few. This tutorial aims to give a good introduction into the related fields of user Sentiment Analysis and user Affect Modelling. Its intention is to show the general technology, and its current reliability, the ways for technical integration and efficient embedding of solutions in a user interface context, and the latest trends in this young and ever emerging field. Emphasis is laid on highlighting the range of toolkits available at this moment with the aim of empowering one to immediately craft own solutions. This description contains the general motivation, goals, objectives, and topics.

Author Keywords

Sentiment Analysis, Opinion Mining, Affective Computing, Intelligent Interaction

ACM Classification Keywords

H.1.2 User / Machine systems: Human information processing; H.5.5 Sound and Music Computing: Methodologies and techniques, Modeling, Signal analysis, synthesis, and processing; I.2.10 Vision and scene understanding: Video analysis; I.5.2 Design Methodology: Feature evaluation and selection, Classifier design and evaluation; I.5.4 Applications: Signal processing

General Terms

Human Factors, Signal processing, Feature evaluation and selection, Classifier design and evaluation, Experimentation

IUI'15, Mar 29 - Apr 01, 2015, Atlanta, GA, USA
ACM 978-1-4503-3306-1/15/03.
http://dx.doi.org/10.1145/2678025.2716265

INTRODUCTION

The computer-based automatic analysis of human sentiment [1, 12, 4], and affect [20, 10] are researched since more than a decade and a half by now, and are recently reaching increasing maturity. In fact, they are expected to play a major role that will likely make 'that difference' in future intelligent User Interfaces (IUIs), as they bear the promise to lend them emotional intelligence: Interfaces that 'know' and can react appropriately to, e. g., the satisfaction or anger of their users can lead us away from the often prevailing connotation of 'cold' and 'mechanical' that the interfaces of the current generation are still partially faced with. The information is thereby increasingly accessed from multiple modalities [15, 17] – both, in affect recognition and sentiment analysis – and 'in the wild' [33, 9], thanks to the availability of increasingly large and realistic resources [24] and improved algorithms [21] including deep learning [26] and long-short-term memory architectures [14] and weakly supervised learning methods [25]. Besides a certain focus on analysis in research to date, a system that emulates emotion is likely to be perceived as even more 'emotionally intelligent' given that it manages to overcome the uncanny valley.

In this light, this tutorial[1] aims to give a good introduction into the fields of user Sentiment Analysis and user Affect Modelling. Its intention is to show the general technology, and its current reliability, the ways for technical integration and efficient embedding of solutions in a user interface context, and the latest trends in this young and ever emerging field. Going one step further with a 'dash of tea leaf reading' it aims to distill likely future directions in and for this exciting

[1] cf. http://www.openaudio.eu for additional information.

and potentially game-changing discipline. In particular, emphasis is laid on highlighting the range of toolkits available at this moment to enable those interested in enriching current user interfaces by according social skills to immediately craft their own solutions.

In the following, the motivation, goals and objectives, and content related to a tutorial on modelling user affect and sentiment in the context of intelligent interfaces will be laid out.

GENERAL MOTIVATION

Socially aware and competent systems in general tend to be perceived as 'intelligent' and the connection and relevance to *intelligent* User Interfaces appears thus straightforward: Next generation IUIs will likely be increasingly expected to be able to understand factors such as user affect and exploit the automatic analysis of their users' sentiment for adaptation or related purposes.

The fields of Affective Computing and Sentiment Analysis both offer suitable approaches and methods to assess human states and are recently gaining much attention such as in workshops (even commonly, cf., e. g., [22]) or special issues (cf., e. g., [2, 3]) on the research level, but also more and more in real-world products.

GOALS AND OBJECTIVES

In detail, the goals and ambitions of this tutorial are threefold:

1. Introducing the existing efforts and major accomplishments in automatic, dimensional, and continuous analysis of emotions from multiple cues and user modalities;
2. Demonstrating and discussing the practical aspects, available frameworks, tools, databases, and automatic analysers, that can be easily used by user interface researchers around the world;
3. Encouraging the integration of the recent developments in the field into intelligent user interfaces.

The need for a tutorial arises thus from the demand to prepare the user interface community for an ongoing change of IUIs becoming more and more emotion-aware.

TOPICS

The topics to be touched upon can be roughly divided into theoretical and practical aspects besides aiming to distill future directions. They will be laid out in the following.

Theoretical Aspects

The theoretical aspects include in particular the 'savoir faire' when it comes to representation of affect and sentiment, different modalities, data, and the actual recognition framework including the feature extraction and classification.

Setting

The requirements needed are best derived from the specific *use cases* such as video gaming [16, 13] or other IUIs. In addition, *definitions* of the most relevant terms are required. The setting is complemented by benefits and limitations of sentiment and affect modelling per se.

Affect and Sentiment Representation

A number of different representation forms exist, predominantly those based on some type of *categories* – even in ordinal problems such as sentiment, e. g., by sentiment polarity or three classes ('low', 'middle', and 'high'), etc. [5], or with multiple categories per instance such as in *complex models*, and *tagging*. Further popular representations include the *circumplex model*, the value-continuous *Power-Arousal-Valence model*, and the *appraisal model* with varying *benefits and limitations*.

Modalities and Cues

The major modalities for the measurement and synthesis in the domain of IUIs are *speech and language*, *visual signals*, and *bio signals* – the latter, however, rather for analysis so far. In addition, haptic interaction analysis has ever since been considered with lower attention. Besides a range of different (dis-)advantages, these different modalities are known to be highly synergistic in terms of affect modelling.

User Data

Data is one of the major bottlenecks in this field. Major attention is thus given to efficient procedures of *data acquisition and annotation*, such as by weakly supervised [28] or even unsupervised [34] learning approaches. As it is mostly the labels that are sparse rather than the data, *crowd-sourcing and cooperative learning* [35] are further popular recent assets to lead quickly to rich resources of annotated affective usage data. Similarly, *transfer learning* [7] can be used to adapt 'similar' data to the current IUI case. In fact, a number of *benchmarks and important databases* exist today and are worth discussing with respect to the different types of user data and the challenges involved with them (cf. also in relation with the next subsection). Arguably there is a wide range of sentiment data for reviews, but less annotated video data or bio signals. A dominating problem is usually the amount of noise.

Automatic Analysis and Prediction

As outlined above, a number of information-bearing signals and methods exist to analyse users' affective state, including most notably *speech emotion recognition* [31], *opinion and sentiment analysis* from text or also multiple modalities, or the interpretation of *visual signals, motion capture, and thermal imaging signals* [11], and *bio signals* which are best (all) combined in a *synergistic modality fusion*. A number of different *classification schemes* are available to obtain best results depending on the application context and can be optimised in the loop with an according *performance evaluation*. More recently, *distribution* [36] of a recognition system's entities is becoming of interest, to provide also access on mobile IUIs. Further, to provide more information to the IUI than just the 'best guess' of a user's state, *confidence measurement* [6] can give an additional information on how reliable this 'guess' likely is.

Practical Aspects

To set up an 'affective' IUI, one has the option to go with existing toolkits and even to test it against a number of standardised benchmarks that will be touched upon next.

Frameworks and Tools

Today, luckily a number of *tools for user sentiment and affect modelling* exist [27]. To name but a very few, these include the *openSMILE* [8] audio/visual feature extractor, which has been and still is the official baseline feature extractor of the AVEC, INTERSPEECH ComParE, and MAPTRAITS comparative research competitions in the field of affect analysis (cf. also below). A further interesting piece of software particularly suited for IUI design can be the publicly available *Semaine system* [18] that offers a virtual agent sensing and synthesising affect and behaviour. In particular, for machine learning, deep and recurrent neural networks as provided by the *CURRENNT toolkit* [29] are at the state-of-the-art. However, a broad range of machine learning toolkits such as WEKA [32] offer a broad selection of alternative intelligence algorithms. A range of *suitable and necessary and needed tools* include, e. g., such for enhancement of the signal of interest as by blind source separation [30].

Competitions and Data Presentations

Interestingly, in addition to the increasing availability of data and tools, there has been an increasing number of competitions in the field. The majority of these have dealt with the analysis of sentiment and affect rather than their synthesis. This is likely due to the comparative ease with which analysis measures can be objectively compared. An *overview on competitions* includes the INTERSPEECH *ComParE 2009 – 2015* competition series, the *2011 – 2014 Audio/visual Emotion Challenges* (AVEC), the Emotion Recognition In The Wild challenges, a number of tasks within the MediaEval series, and those dealing also with traits such as the personality of users, e. g., the *MAPTRAITS 2014 Challenge*. In fact, most of these allow free access to the data that has been used, enabling one to *experiencing the selected data* in practice.

Future Directions

The future potential in this field is still huge owing to its comparably young age of roughly a decade and a half and the need for further improvements. Some of the current trends include more integration of user traits [23], also to better understand the user state, and gathering experience in 'the wild', best with integration of contextual knowledge. However, many further issues such as language and cultural independence are still far from being solved. Similarly, standardisation for the embedding in user interfaces is still needed in many ways, but is making good progress, such as by recent recommendations and discussion groups of the W3C [19].

ACKNOWLEDGMENTS

The research leading to these results has received funding from the European Communitys Seventh Framework Programme under grant agreements No. 338164 (ERC Starting Grant iHEARu) and No. 289021 (STREP ASC-Inclusion) and from its Horizon 2020 Framework Programme under grant agreement No. 645094 (Sentiment Analysis in the Wild – SEWA).

REFERENCES

1. Balahur-Dobrescu, A., Taboada, M., and Schuller, B. W. *Computational Methods for Affect Detection from Natural Language*. Computational Social Sciences. Springer, 2015. to appear.
2. Cambria, E., Schuller, B., Liu, B., Wang, H., and Havasi, C. Guest Editor's Introduction: Knowledge-based Approaches to Concept-Level Sentiment Analysis. *IEEE Intelligent Systems Magazine 28*, 2 (March/April 2013), 12–14.
3. Cambria, E., Schuller, B., Liu, B., Wang, H., and Havasi, C. Guest Editor's Introduction: Statistcial Approaches to Concept-Level Sentiment Analysis. *IEEE Intelligent Systems Magazine 28*, 3 (May/June 2013), 6–9.
4. Cambria, E., Schuller, B., Xia, Y., and Havasi, C. New Avenues in Opinion Mining and Sentiment Analysis. *IEEE Intelligent Systems Magazine 28*, 2 (March/April 2013), 15–21.
5. de Groot, R. *Data Mining for Tweet Sentiment Classification: Twitter Sentiment Analysis*. LAP LAMBERT Academic Publishing, November 2012.
6. Deng, J., and Schuller, B. Confidence Measures in Speech Emotion Recognition Based on Semi-supervised Learning. In *Proceedings INTERSPEECH 2012*, ISCA (Portland, OR, September 2012).
7. Deng, J., Zhang, Z., Eyben, F., and Schuller, B. Autoencoder-based Unsupervised Domain Adaptation for Speech Emotion Recognition. *IEEE Signal Processing Letters* (2014).
8. Eyben, F., Weninger, F., Groß, F., and Schuller, B. Recent Developments in openSMILE, the Munich Open-Source Multimedia Feature Extractor. In *Proceedings ACM Multimedia*, ACM (Barcelona, Spain, October 2013), 835–838.
9. Gunes, H., and Schuller, B. Dimensional and Continuous Analysis of Emotions for Multimedia Applications: a Tutorial Overview. In *Proceedings ACM Multimedia*, ACM, ACM (Nara, Japan, October 2012). 2 pages.
10. Gunes, H., and Schuller, B. Categorical and Dimensional Affect Analysis in Continuous Input: Current Trends and Future Directions. *Image and Vision Computing, Special Issue on Affect Analysis in Continuous Input 31*, 2 (February 2013), 120–136.
11. Gunes, H., Schuller, B., Pantic, M., and Cowie, R. Emotion Representation, Analysis and Synthesis in Continuous Space: A Survey. In *Proceedings International Workshop on Emotion Synthesis, rePresentation, and Analysis in Continuous spacE, EmoSPACE 2011 at FG 2011*, IEEE (Santa Barbara, CA, March 2011), 827–834.
12. Liu, B. *Sentiment Analysis: Mining Opinions, Sentiments, and Emotions*. Cambridge University Press, April 2015.
13. Marchi, E., Zhang, Y., Eyben, F., Ringeval, F., and Schuller, B. Autism and Speech, Language, and

Emotion - a Survey. In *Evaluating the Role of Speech Technology in Medical Case Management*, H. Patil and M. Kulshreshtha, Eds. De Gruyter, Berlin, 2015. to appear.

14. Metallinou, A., Wöllmer, M., Katsamanis, A., Eyben, F., Schuller, B., and Narayanan, S. Context-Sensitive Learning for Enhanced Audiovisual Emotion Classification. *IEEE Transactions on Affective Computing 3*, 2 (April – June 2012), 184–198.

15. Morency, L.-P., Mihalcea, R., and Doshi, P. Towards multimodal sentiment analysis: Harvesting opinions from the web. In *Proceeding of the 13th ACM International Conference on Multimodal Interfaces (ICMI)*, ACM (New York, USA, 2011), 169–176.

16. Paletta, L., Schuller, B. W., Robinson, P., and Sabouret, N. IDGEI 2015: 3rd international workshop on intelligent digital games for empowerment and inclusion. In *Proceedings IUI 2015*, ACM, ACM (Atlanta, GA, March 2015). 2 pages.

17. Raaijmakers, S., Truong, K., and Wilson, T. Multimodal subjectivity analysis of multiparty conversation. In *Proceedings of Conference on Empirical Methods in Natural Language Processing (EMNLP-2008)* (Edinburgh, UK, 2008), 466–474.

18. Schröder, M., Cowie, R., Heylen, D., Pantic, M., Pelachaud, C., and Schuller, B. Towards responsive Sensitive Artificial Listeners. In *Proceedings 4th International Workshop on Human-Computer Conversation* (Bellagio, Italy, October 2008). 6 pages.

19. Schröder, M., Devillers, L., Karpouzis, K., Martin, J.-C., Pelachaud, C., Peter, C., Pirker, H., Schuller, B., Tao, J., and Wilson, I. What should a generic emotion markup language be able to represent? In *Proceedings ACII 2007, Lisbon, Portugal*, A. Paiva, R. W. Picard, and R. Prada, Eds., vol. 4738/2007 of *LNCS*. Springer, Berlin/Heidelberg, 2007, 440–451.

20. Schuller, B., and Batliner, A. *Computational Paralinguistics: Emotion, Affect and Personality in Speech and Language Processing*. Wiley, 2013.

21. Schuller, B., Batliner, A., Steidl, S., and Seppi, D. Recognising Realistic Emotions and Affect in Speech: State of the Art and Lessons Learnt from the First Challenge. *Speech Communication 53*, 9/10 (November/December 2011), 1062–1087.

22. Schuller, B., Buitelaar, P., Devillers, L., Pelachaud, C., Declerck, T., Batliner, A., Rosso, P., and Gaines, S., Eds. *Proceedings of the 5th International Workshop on Emotion Social Signals, Sentiment & Linked Open Data (ES^3LOD 2014)*, ELRA, ELRA (Reykjavik, Iceland, May 2014). Satellite of LREC 2014.

23. Schuller, B., Steidl, S., Batliner, A., Nöth, E., Vinciarelli, A., Burkhardt, F., van Son, R., Weninger, F., Eyben, F., Bocklet, T., Mohammadi, G., and Weiss, B. A Survey on Perceived Speaker Traits: Personality, Likability, Pathology, and the First Challenge. *Computer Speech and Language 29*, 1 (January 2015), 100–131.

24. Schuller, B., and Vasileios, V. Sentiment Analysis and Opinion Mining: On Optimal Parameters and Performances. *WIREs Data Mining and Knowledge Discovery* (2015). 8 pages, to appear.

25. Schuller, B., and Weninger, F. Human Affect Recognition – Audio-Based Methods. In *Wiley Encyclopedia of Electrical and Electronics Engineering*, J. G. Webster, Ed. John Wiley & Sons, New York, 2015. to appear.

26. Stuhlsatz, A., Meyer, C., Eyben, F., Zielke, T., Meier, G., and Schuller, B. Deep Neural Networks for Acoustic Emotion Recognition: Raising the Benchmarks. In *Proceedings ICASSP 2011*, IEEE (Prague, Czech Republic, May 2011), 5688–5691.

27. Valentine, S. *Sentiment Analysis 19 Success Secrets - 19 Most Asked Questions On Sentiment Analysis - What You Need To Know*. Emereo Publishing, February 2014.

28. Wan, X. Co-training for cross-lingual sentiment classification. In *Proceedings of ACL* (2009), 235–243.

29. Weninger, F., Bergmann, J., and Schuller, B. Introducing CURRENNT – the Munich Open-Source CUDA RecurREnt Neural Network Toolkit. *Journal of Machine Learning Research 15* (2014). 5 pages.

30. Weninger, F., and Schuller, B. Optimization and Parallelization of Monaural Source Separation Algorithms in the openBliSSART Toolkit. *Journal of Signal Processing Systems 69*, 3 (2012), 267–277.

31. Weninger, F., Wöllmer, M., and Schuller, B. Emotion Recognition in Naturalistic Speech and Language - A Survey. In *Emotion Recognition: A Pattern Analysis Approach*, A. Konar and A. Chakraborty, Eds., 1st ed. Wiley-Blackwell, December 2014.

32. Witten, I., and Frank, E. *Data Mining: Practical Machine Learning Tools and Techniques*. Morgan Kaufmann, San Francisco, 2005.

33. Wöllmer, M., Weninger, F., Knaup, T., Schuller, B., Sun, C., Sagae, K., and Morency, L.-P. YouTube Movie Reviews: Sentiment Analysis in an Audiovisual Context. *IEEE Intelligent Systems Magazine 28*, 3 (May/June 2013), 46–53.

34. Zagibalov, T., and Carroll, J. Unsupervised classification of sentiment and objectivity in chinese text. In *Proceedings of the International Joint Conference on Natural Language Processing* (2008), 304–311.

35. Zhang, Z., Coutinho, E., Deng, J., and Schuller, B. Cooperative Learning and its Application to Emotion Recognition from Speech. *IEEE Transactions on Audio, Speech and Language Processing* (2014).

36. Zhang, Z., Coutinho, E., Deng, J., and Schuller, B. Distributing Recognition in Computational Paralinguistics. *IEEE Transactions on Affective Computing 21*, 9 (2014), 1068–1072.

PATCH 2015 - Personalized Access to Cultural Heritage

L. Ardissono and C. Gena
University of Torino
Computer Science Department
Italy
liliana.ardissono@unito.it,
cristina.gena@unito.it

Lora Aroyo
VU University Amsterdam
The Network Institute
The Netherlands
lora.aroyo@vu.nl

T. Kuflik and A.J. Wecker
University of Haifa
Department of Information Systems
Israel
tsvikak@is.haifa.ac.il,
ajwecker@gmail.com

Johan Oomen
Netherlands Institute
for Sound and Vision
The Netherlands
joomen@beeldengeluid.nl

Oliviero Stock
FBK-ICT IRST
Italy
stock@fbk.eu

ABSTRACT
Since 2007, the PATCH workshop series (https://patchworkshopseries.wordpress.com/) have been gathering successfully researchers and professionals from various countries and institutions to discuss the topics of digital access to cultural heritage and specifically the personalization aspects in this process. Due to this rich history, the reach of the PATCH workshop in various research communities is extensive.

Author Keywords
Cultural Heritage; Multimedia Interaction; Personalization

ACM Classification Keywords
J.5 [ARTS AND HUMANITIES]; H.5.3 [Group and Organization Interfaces]; H.5.4 [Hypertext/Hypermedia]; H.5.m. [Information interfaces and presentation (e.g., HCI)]

INTRODUCTION
The 2015 edition of the Personalized Access to Cultural Heritage (PATCH) workshop is the 8th edition of this workshop in conjunction with various research conferences, e.g. User Modeling 2007 (Greece), Adaptive Hypermedia 2008 (Germany), UMAP 2012 (Canada) and 2013 (Italy), ACM Multimedia 2012 (Japan) and Intelligent User Interfaces 2011 (USA) and 2014 (Israel). Having the workshop for the third time at the IUI conference is a timely and natural addition to the previous editions. The workshop papers deal specifically with mobile, personalized and context aware delivery of cultural heritage and the workshop topics were built upon lessons learned from past PATCH workshops and a number of research projects actively involved in the fields of intelligent user interfaces and personalization for cultural heritage for over seven years [1].

IUI 2015, March 29–April 1, 2015, Atlanta, GA, USA.
ACM 978-1-4503-3306-1/15/03.
http://dx.doi.org/10.1145/2678025.2716266

PATCH 2015 GOALS
The primary goal of this workshop is to gather researchers and practitioners from different fields, e.g., user interaction, arts and heritage curation, interface design, user modeling and personalization, in order to showcase novel applications and discuss opportunities that grow from the connections between users and multimedia systems in the cultural heritage domain [3, 6]. Special emphasis is placed on mobile, personalized and context-aware cultural heritage information delivery using a range of new and emerging types of devices.

The rapid development of information technologies and the vast growth of the Web has enabled memory organizations, such as museums, archives and libraries, to provide access to their collections online and ubiquitously, and thus attract wider audiences than those that visit the physical museums [5]. Various trends on the social web allow for users not only to be passive consumers, but also active participants. Additionally, personalization capitalizes on a user-centered intelligent interactive information exchange between websites or mobile guide systems and visitors [8, 9]. In this way the museum monologue turns into a dialogue, and personalization provides opportunities for a new communication strategy based on a continuous process of interaction, collaboration, learning and adaptation between the museum and its visitors [2].

Given these developments and trends, it is critical for the memory institutions to know their visitors (users), and provide personalized interactive methods and systems for accessing their collections and services, both online and in physical space [4]. Multimedia information systems (such as interactive tours, visualizations and search engines) are now positioned centrally in a shared information space consisting of (1) the digitized artifacts (2) the social web (3) and links between them. Personalization in multimedia information systems can improve the experience of visitors by assisting them in finding appropriate starting points, and in discovering new relevant information [7]. Critically, these systems must become intelligent, so that they are able to adaptively act, react, respond and learn intelligently from user interactions.

The PATCH2015 workshop investigates three timely and interrelated issues relevant to the domains of both intelligent user interaction and cultural heritage:

- Mobile, personalized and context-aware cultural heritage information delivery - using mobile devices, large displays, projectors embedded in the environment and new technologies including Google Glass.
- Grow existing knowledge with new knowledge - Explore methods and tools to capture knowledge resulting from interactions between users (collective intelligence), professionals and collection artifacts, and interaction between users and different (intelligent systems) collecting information about them
- Extend contexts of use - Appropriation of digitized artifacts from memory organizations outside the traditional museum and research context for both visitors and professionals

PATCH 2015 ORGANIZERS

The complementary expertise areas of the workshop organizers represent four domains, e.g. cultural heritage and museum studies, information science, user modeling and personalization and distributed computing. Together they cover the various perspectives relevant to explore this edition of PATCH at IUI2015.

Liliana Ardissono[1] is an associate professor at the Department of Computer Science, Università di Torino, Italy. Her research interests include user modeling & adaptive hypermedia, context-aware systems, and computer supported collaboration. She is a member of the Editorial Board of the international journal User Modeling and User-Adapted Interaction (Springer) and Secretary of the Board of Directors of User Modeling Inc.

Lora Aroyo[2] is an associate professor at the Web and Media group, part of the Network Institute, at the Department of Computer Science, VU University Amsterdam, the Netherlands. Her research interests are in using semantic web technologies for modeling user interests and context, recommendation systems and personalized access of online multimedia collections, e.g. cultural heritage collections, multimedia archives and interactive TV. She has co-edited special issue for IEEE Intelligent Systems on "AI and Cultural Heritage". She is also vice-president of the User Modeling, Inc.

Cristina Gena[3] is an assistant professor at the Department of Computer Science, Università di Torino where she teaches at the School of Multimedia and Arts. Her research interests include user modeling, adaptive user interfaces, intelligent user interfaces, interaction design, semantic and social web. She has been the scientific coordinator of a research project on the recommendations of cultural contents in an open data environment.

Tsvi Kuflik[4] is an associate professor and head of the Information Systems Department at the University of Haifa, Israel. His main areas of research are ubiquitous user modelling and intelligent user interfaces. For over ten years Tsvi is leading a research group at the University of Haifa, focusing on "Active Museum" – applying novel computing and communication technology for supporting museum visitors.

Johan Oomen[5] (Netherlands Institute for Sound and Vision) Drs. Johan Oomen is head of the R&D Department of the Netherlands Institute for Sound and Vision and researcher at the Web and Media group of the Vrije Universiteit Amsterdam. Since 2012, he is elected as Network Officer for Europeana and board member of CLICK-NL, The Dutch Creative Industries knowledge and innovation network. His PhD research focuses on how user engagement can help to establish a more open, smart and connected cultural heritage.

Alan J. Wecker[6] is Doctoral Candidate in a joint program both at University of Haifa and University of Trento. His research deals with lifelong user modeling to enhance the cultural heritage experience. His research interests include: technology for the cultural heritage environment, human-computer interaction, distributed computing, software engineering, XML, and information retrieval.

Oliviero Stock[7] is a senior fellow at FBK-ICT IRST, Italy. He has been at IRST since 1988 and has been its Director from 1997 to 2001. His activity is mainly in artificial intelligence, natural language processing, intelligent user interfaces, cognitive technologies, computational creativity.

---

[1] http://www.di.unito.it/~liliana/

[2] http://lora-aroyo.org

[3] http://www.di.unito.it/~cgena/

[4] http://mis.hevra.haifa.ac.il/~tsvikak/Home.htm

[5] http://nl.linkedin.com/in/johanoomen/

[6] http://www.linkedin.com/in/ajwecker

[7] http://ict.fbk.eu/people/profile/stock

ACKNOWLEDGMENTS

We would like to thank all the workshop program committee members for their help and quality reviewing:

Marco Streefkerk, DEN Foundation, The Netherlands; Julia Nordegraaf and Chris Dijkshoorn, VU University of Amsterdam, The Netherlands; Susan Hazan, Israel Museum Jerusalem, Israel; Geert-Jan Houben and Alessandro Bozzon, Delft University of Technology, The Netherlands; Richard Wright, BBC, UK; Massimo Zancanaro, FBK, Italy; Keith Cheverst, Lancaster University, UK; Vincenzo Lombardo, University of Torino, Italy; Otman Moritsch, Technisches Museum Wien, Austria; Christopher Lee, University of North Carolina – Chapel Hill, US, Raffaella Santucci, DigiLab, Centre for Research on Digital Humanities - Sapienza, University of Rome

REFERENCES

1. Ardissono, L., Petrelli, D. and Kuflik, T. Personalization in Cultural Heritage: The Road Travelled and the One Ahead. *USER MODELING AND USER-ADAPTED INTERACTION - The Journal of Personalization Research (Journal home), Special Issue on Coming of Age: Celebrating a Quarter Century of User Modeling and Personalization, 22*, 1-2 (2012), 73-99.
2. Aroyo, L., Brussee, R., Rutledge, L., Gorgels, P., Stash, N., Wang, Y. Personalized museum experience: The Rijksmuseum use case (2007). *Proceedings of Museums and the Web Conference 2007*, Archives & Museum Informatics
3. Dijkshoorn, C., Leyssen, M., Nottamkandath, A., Oosterman, J., Traub, M., Aroyo, L., Bozzon, A., Fokkink, W., Houben, GJ., Hovelmann, H. Personalized Nichesourcing: Acquisition of Qualitative Annotations from Niche Communities. *UMAP Workshops*. (2013).
4. Kuflik, T., Wecker, A. J., Lanir, J., Stock, O. An integrative framework for extending the boundaries of the museum visit experience: linking the pre, during and post visit phases. *Information Technology & Tourism*. (2014), 1-31, Springer Berlin Heidelberg
5. Oomen, J., Aroyo, L. Crowdsourcing in the cultural heritage domain: opportunities and challenges. *Proceedings of the 5th International Conference on Communities and Technologies* (2011), 138-149, ACM
6. Oomen, J., Tzouvaras, V., Hyyppa, K. Linking and visualizing television heritage: the EUscreen virtual exhibitions and the linked open data pilot. *Proceedings of the 22nd international conference on World Wide Web companion* (2013), 481-484
7. Stock, Oliviero; Kuflik, Tsvi; Zancanaro, Massimo; Goren-Bar, Dina; Gorfinkel, Ariel; Jbara, Sadek; Kats, Shahar; Sheidin, Julia; Kashtan, Nadav. Design and Evaluation of a Visitor Guide in an Active Museum. *Language, Culture, Computation. Computing of the Humanities, Law, and Narratives*. (2014), 47-71, Springer Berlin Heidelberg
8. Van Hage, W. Stash, N., Wang, Y., Aroyo, L. (2010). Finding your way through the Rijksmuseum with an adaptive mobile museum guide. *Proceedings of the International Semantic Web Conference: The Semantic Web: Research and Applications*, (2010), 46-59
9. Wang, Y., Stash, N., Sambeek, R., Schuurmans, Y., Aroyo, L., Schreiber, G., Gorgels, P. Cultivating personalized museum tours online and on-site. *Interdisciplinary Science Reviews*. (2009), 34, 2-3,139-153, Maney Publishing

IDGEI 2015 – 3rd International Workshop on Intelligent Digital Games for Empowerment and Inclusion

Lucas Paletta
Joanneum Research
Graz, Austria
lucas.paletta@joanneum.at

Björn W. Schuller
TU München
Munich, Germany
schuller@tum.de

Peter Robinson
Univ. of Cambridge
Cambridge, UK
pr10@cam.ac.uk

Nicolas Sabouret
University Paris Sud
Paris, France
nicolas.sabouret@lip6.fr

ABSTRACT

Digital Games for Empowerment and Inclusion have the potential to improve our society by preparing particular groups of people to meet social challenges in their everyday lives, and to do so in an enjoyable way through games. These games are developing rapidly to exploit new algorithms for computational intelligence supported by increasing availability of computing power to help analyze players' behavior, monitor their motivation and interest, and to adapt the progress of the games accordingly. The workshop on Intelligent Digital Games for Empowerment and Inclusion (IDGEI) explores the use of machine intelligence in serious digital games. In this context, we summarize the third international workshop on IDGEI held at the International Conference on Intelligent User Interfaces (IUI) 2015.

Author Keywords

Machine Intelligence; Digital Games for Empowerment and Inclusion; Serious Games; Affective Computing.

ACM Classification Keywords

H.5.m. Information interfaces and presentation (e.g., HCI): Miscellaneous.

INTRODUCTION

Digital Games for Empowerment and Inclusion possess the potential to change our society in a most positive way by preparing selected groups in a playful and fun way for their everyday life's social and special situations. Exemplary domains span as far as from children with Autism Spectrum Condition (ASC) to young adults preparing for their first job interviews, or migrants familiarizing with their new environment. The current generation of such games thereby increasingly demands for computational intelligence algorithms to help analyze players' behavior and monitor their motivation and interest to adapt game progress.

The development of such games not only requires expertise from the general gaming domain, but also particular understanding of a game's target domain, as well as technological savoir faire to provide intelligent analysis, interfaces and systems.

The first international workshop on Intelligent Digital Games for Empowerment and Inclusion, IDGEI 2013[1], was held at the Conference on Foundations of Digital Games 2013 (FDG 2013), Chania, Greece, May 14, 2013, and aimed at bridging these communities and disciplines by inviting researchers and experts to elaborate the latest perspectives and findings in the field of IDGEI together.

The second international workshop, IDGEI 2014[2], was held at the International Conference on Intelligent User Interfaces (IUI 2014), Haifa, Israel, February 24, 2014, and emphasized the focus of emotion recognition and human cognition in the frame of the IDGEI themes and the IUI community.

IDGEI's topics cover among others aspects of Machine Intelligence in Serious Games, Mobile and Real-World Serious Gaming, Emotion & Affect in Serious Games, Player Behavior and Attention Modeling, Player-Adaptation and Motivation, Novel Serious Games, and Human Factors & User Studies of Serious Games. In fact, it seems necessary to bring forth existing efforts and major accomplishments in the design of intelligent serious games, and to provide a forum for exchange in experience with intelligent serious games in practice, while encouraging the design of novel applications in context as diverse as health-oriented gaming, general learning and tutoring environments, or emergency preparation, and to focus on current trends and future directions in the field.

The international workshops on Intelligent Digital Games for Empowerment and Inclusion (IDGEI) [1,2] are aimed at bridging these communities and disciplines by inviting researchers and experts to elaborate the latest perspectives and findings in the field of IDGEI together.

The 3rd IDGEI 2015 was held at the ACM Conference on Intelligent User Interfaces, 29 March 2015, in Atlanta, GA, and targeted a broad audience of researchers and practioners interested in cognitive system aspects of game interfaces and their impact on human behavior, in the context of social inclusion. The workshop aimed (i) to bring forth existing efforts and major accomplishments in the

IUI'15, Mar 29 – Apr, 01, 2015, Atlanta, GA, USA.
ACM 978-1-4503-3306-1/15/03.
http://dx.doi.org/10.1145/2678025.2716268

1 http://idgei.fdg2013.org/
2 http://idgei2014.joanneum.at/

design of intelligent serious games, (ii) to provide a forum for exchange in experience with intelligent user interfaces and serious games in practice, (iii) while encouraging the design of novel applications in domains as diverse as health-oriented gaming, general learning and driving environments, or emergency preparation, and (iv) to focus on current trends and future directions in the field. It provided a specific focus on wearable miniaturized sensors that are becoming increasingly available for IDGEI applications.

Workshop setup

The IDGEI 2015 workshop included several keynote speeches by internationally acknowledged experts of various aspects of the field DGEI (Digital Games for Empowerment and Inclusion): The work of James C. Lester [6] (North Carolina State University, NC) on personalized learning ranges from game-based learning environments and intelligent tutoring systems to affective computing, computational models of narrative, and natural language tutorial dialogue. The research focus of James M. Rehg [7] (Georgia Institute of Technology, GA) is on developing methods for measuring, recognizing, and quantifying childrens' social and communicative behavior using video, audio, and wearable sensor data, as well as on computer vision aspects for future interfaces, such as egocentric video analysis using Google Glass. Alex Games [8] (Microsoft, WA; Michigan State University, MI) as leader in the Microsoft Learning and Engagement Program, manages the program of research and development of innovative learning and readiness UX using gaming mechanisms, including designs of social endorsement and learning incentive systems.

The keynote speeches were followed by the participants' oral presentations. The workshop hosted a technical demo-session that was particularly suited to convey advancement in the field of Digital Gaming. Finally, to foster discussion and actively involve attendees, a panel discussion involving the keynote speakers and selected experts was held.

CONTRIBUTIONS

The workshop presented the state-of-the-art in the field, focusing particularly on three main thematic aspects, as follows:

Novel Intelligent Game Frameworks

Novel game frameworks were investigated that focus on upcoming challenges. In the last decade, scenario-based serious-games have become a main tool for learning new skills and capabilities. The generation of scenarios can be facilitated and verified combining computer science techniques with the crowd. Recently, neuro- and psychophysiology based score measures were introduced, to measure actual value of demonstrated learning. Main effects related to biomarkers of vigilance and motivation enable to predict learning and support interpretation of on-task learning styles [9].

Emotion Recognition and Expression

Affective computing is a key component in intelligent games for its relevance to transfer social cues, such as, to extract and display motivation and intention for game users. The workshop identified novel aspects in emotion recognition and expression that have a strong impact on game play, such as (i) the analysis of emotion in body gestures as input for high level decision making, (ii) advanced facial emotion recognition for mapping and manipulating facial emotion appearance in real-time, to assist in communication processes, (iii) the usage of speech analysis for identifying atypical affective cues; and (iv) the expression of different social attitudes to train the user in different situations that can occur in real life [14,15,16].

Complex interaction frameworks for inclusion games were described and discussed: (i) Automated emotion recognition by agents plays a major role in job interview simulation; (ii) serious games that assist children with Autism Spectrum Conditions (ASC) allow them to learn how emotions can be expressed and recognized via playing games

Human Cognition and Context

Intelligent game interfaces must be capable of representing and reasoning about the user's mental state, in order to react appropriately, for example on social cues that inform the system about his/her social attitude. The workshop studied novel methodologies for user modeling in the context of serious games for empowerment and inclusion. Formal models of Theory of Mind [4,5] were introduced in the context of human-agent interaction.

Cultural Competency

Cultural competency as a challenging aspect of human cognition was recognized as objective for game based learning approaches [10,11], with critical views on the assessment of their reach and impact. Attention is a crucial aspect of cognition in the context of mobile games. Novel methodologies enable to track the focus of users in natural mobile interaction, such as, in mixed reality games. Language learning is often at the core of games to attend to cultural differences [12,13].

ACKNOWLEDGMENTS

The organizers would like to thank the members of the Technical Program Committee, namely: Elisabeth André (Univ. Augsburg, Germany), Timothy Bickmore (Northeastern Univ., MA), Ilona Buchem (Beuth Univ. Applied Sciences, Germany), Antonio Camurri (Univ. Genoa), Sara de Freitas (Murdoch Univ., Australia), Nick Degens (Hanze Univ., Netherlands), Ian Dunwell (Serious Games Institute, UK), Maria Garrido (Univ. Washington, WA), Mark Gaved (Open Univ., UK), Patrick Gebhard (DFKI, Germany), Wijnand Ijsselsteijn (Eindhoven UT,

Netherlands), Rilla Khaled (Univ. Malta), Kaska Porayska-Pomsta (Univ. of London, UK), Gabriela T. Richard (Univ. Pennsylvania, PA), Michael Schwarz (Joanneum Research, Austria), Stephanie Schwarz (AIT, Austria), and James Stewart (Univ. Edinburgh, UK).

The research leading to these results has received funding from the European Community's Seventh Framework Programme (FP7/2007-2013) under grant agreements Nos. 289021 (ASC-Inclusion[3]), 288587 (MASELTOV[4]), and 288578 (TARDIS[5]), three supporting projects that cooperate in a clustering activity, in collaboration with exploratory policy research led by JRC-IPTS, Spain, and the European Commission, to form a joint initiative on Digital Games for Empowerment and Inclusion [3].

The workshop website http://idgei2015.joanneum.at and the conference management system were managed by JOANNEUM RESEARCH Forschungsgesellschaft mbH.

Communication such as comments and feedback about the event can be tracked in Twitter via #IDGEI2015.

REFERENCES

1. Schuller, B., Paletta, L., and Sabouret, N., editors. *Proc. 1st International Workshop on Intelligent Digital Games for Empowerment and Inclusion*, IDGEI 2013, Chania, Greece, May 2013. SASDG.
2. Paletta, L., Schuller, B., Robinson, P., and Sabouret, N., editors. *Proc. 2nd International Workshop on Intelligent Digital Games for Empowerment and Inclusion*, IDGEI 2014, Haifa, Israel, February 2014, ACM.
3. Stewart, J., Bleumers, L., All, A., Mariën, I., Schurmans, D., Van Looy, J., Jacobs, A., Willaert, K., De Grove, F., Misuraca, G., and Centeno, C. *The Potential of Digital Games for Empowerment and Social Inclusion of Groups at Risk of Social and Economic Exclusion: Evidence and Opportunity for Policy*, JRC Scientific and Policy Report, Joint Research Centre, policy area 'Inclusion & Cultural Diversity', Sevilla, Spain, 2013.
4. Baron-Cohen, S. *Mindblindness: An essay on autism and theory of mind.* MIT press, 1997.
5. Bosse, T., Memon, Z. A. and Treur, J. *A recursive BDI agent model for Theory of Mind and its applications.* Applied Artificial Intelligence, 25(1), pp. 1-44, 2011.
6. Lester, J., Young Ha, E., Lee, S., Mott, B., Rowe, J. and Sabourin, J. Serious Games Get Smart: Intelligent Game-Based Learning Environments. *AI Magazine*, 34(4), pp. 31-45, 2013.
7. Rehg, J. M., Abowd, G. D., Rozga, A., Romero, M., Clements, M. A., Sclaroff, S., Essa, I., Ousley, O. Y., Li, Y., Kim, C., Rao, H., Kim, J. C., Presti, L. L., Zhang, J., Lantsman, D., Bidwell, J., and Yem Z. Decoding Children's Social Behavior. *Proceedings of IEEE Computer Vision and Pattern Recognition Conference*, CVPR'2013, Portland, OR.
8. Games, A.I. and Bauman, E.B. Virtual worlds: an environment for cultural sensitivity education in the health sciences. *International Journal of Web Based Communities*, 2(7), pp. 1741-8216, 2011.
9. Cowley, B.U. and Ravaja, N., Learning in balance: Using oscillatory EEG biomarkers of attention, motivation, and vigilance to interpret game-based learning. *Cogent Education*, 1(1): 962236, 2014.
10. Finkelstein, S., Yarzebinski, E., Vaughn, C., Ogan, A., & Cassell, J. The effects of culturally-congruent educational technologies on student achievement. *Proceedings of Artificial Intelligence in Education*, AIED 2013, July 9-13, 2013, Memphis, TN.
11. Gutiérrez, K. D., & Rogoff, B. Cultural ways of learning: Individual traits or repertoires of practice. *Educational Researcher*, 32(5), pp. 19-25, 2003.
12. von Ahn, L. Duolingo: learn a language for free while helping to translate the web. *Proceedings Intelligent User Interfaces*, IUI 2013, Santa Monica, CA, pp. 1-2, 2013.
13. Paletta, L., Dunwell, I., Gaved, M., Bobeth, J., Efremidis, S., Luley, P., Kukulska-Hulme, A., de Freitas, S., Lameras, P., Deutsch, S. Advances in the MASELTOV Game - Mobile Assistance for Social Inclusion and Empowerment of Immigrants with Persuasive Learning Technologies and Social Network Services, *Proceedings 10th International Conference on Advances in Computer Entertainment Technology*, ACE 2013, Twente, The Netherlands, November 13-15, 2013.
14. Schuller, B., Dunwell, I., Weninger, F., Paletta, L. Pervasive Serious Gaming for Behavior Change – The State of Play. *IEEE Pervasive Computing*, 3(12), Special Issue on Human Behavior Analysis for Inducing Behavior Change; Salah, A., Lepri, B., Pentland, A., Canny, J., Eds. pp. 48–55, July-Sept. 2013, IEEE Computer Society.
15. Chanel, G., Rebetez, C., Betrancourt, M., and Pun, T. Emotion Assessment From Physiological Signals for Adaptation of Game Difficulty. *IEEE Transactions on Systems, Man and Cybernetics, Part A: Systems and Humans*, vol. 41, no. 6, pp. 1052-1063, 2011.
16. Kobes, M., Oberijé, N. and Groenewegen- Ter Morsche, K., Serious Gaming for Behavioural Assessment and Research in Case of Emergency. An Evaluation of Experiments in Virtual Reality, *Proceedings of Simulation Conference and Exhibition*, SimTecT 2009, Adelaide, Australia, 2009.

[3] http://www.asc-inclusion.eu
[4] http://www.maseltov.eu
[5] http://www.tardis-project.eu

SmartObjects: Fourth Workshop on Interacting with Smart Objects

Dirk Schnelle-Walka
Max Mühlhäuser
Stefan Radomski
TU Darmstadt, Germany
{dirk,max,radomski}
@tk.informatik.tu-darmstadt.de

Oliver Brdiczka
Palo Alto Research Center
USA
brdiczka@parc.com

Jochen Huber
Singapore University of Technology and Design &
MIT Media Lab
jhuber@mit.edu

Kris Luyten
Hasselt University - tUL -
iMinds Expertise Centre for
Digital Media, Belgium
kris.luyten@uhasslet.be

Tobias Grosse-Puppendahl
Fraunhofer IGD, Germany
tobias.grosse-puppendahl
@igd.fraunhofer.de

ABSTRACT
The increasing number of smart objects in our everyday life shapes how we interact beyond the desktop. In this workshop we discussed how the interaction with these smart objects should be designed from various perspectives. This year's workshop put a special focus on affective computing with smart objects, as reflected by the keynote talk.

ACM Classification Keywords
H.5.m User Interfaces: Miscellaneous: .

WORKSHOP CONTENT
There is an ongoing trend to put computing capabilities into everyday objects, turning them into smart objects [5]. Well known examples range from smart kitchen appliances (smart coffee machines, smart knifes and cuttings boards) [1, 2] to smart (tangible) objects [3, 4] and even urban infrastructures [8]. While other venues have focused on the many technical challenges of implementing smart objects, far less research has been done on how the intelligence situated in these smart objects can be applied to improve their interaction with the users. This field of research poses unique challenges and opportunities for designing smart interaction. Smart objects typically have only very limited interaction capabilities. Yet, their behavior exhibits an amazing amount of intelligence. More information about the previous workshops can be found on our website at `http://www.smart-objects.org/`.

Extending the topics of our previous workshops, this year's workshop emphasized affective computing with smart objects with a keynote talk by Jean-Claude Martin[1]. Enabling objects to sense and react on human emotions broadens the acceptance and usefulness of such technologies. However, the physical restrictions in smart objects are very high, which sparked interesting discussions among all participants. Furthermore, the workshop focused on topics like user experience, sensing and actuation technologies, psychological aspects, and application scenarios with respect to smart objects.

PARTICIPANTS AND WORKSHOP PUBLICITY
The workshop had an interdisciplinary appeal. Our participants originated from the areas of IUI, HCI, UbiComp, IoT and related areas like psychology and product design. The program committee comprised researchers who are active in these research areas and who, moreover, encouraged researchers to submit to this workshop. Thereby, we ensured active participation in preparation and execution of the workshop. We especially encouraged young scientists and Ph.D. students to submit papers to explore their research topics with domain experts. The call for papers and participation was distributed through well-established mailing lists and websites in various research communities, including IUI, CHI, UIST, UbiComp, ITS and TEI. We also promoted the workshop through our website and OSNs. Always held in conjunction with IUI, the first workshop took place in 2011 (Palo Alto[2]) with following workshops in 2013 (Santa Monica[3]) and 2014 (Haifa[4]). These previous workshops were very successful, which helped us to attract other new participants to this workshop as well. The results of the workshop are made available on the workshop website as well as in the joint CEUR proceedings.

IUI'15, Mar 29 – Apr 01, 2015, Atlanta, GA, USA
ACM 978-1-4503-3306-1/15/03.
http://dx.doi.org/10.1145/2678025.2716269

[1] https://perso.limsi.fr/wiki/doku.php/martin/accueil
[2] http://www.smart-objects.org/2011/
[3] http://www.smart-objects.org/2013/
[4] http://www.smart-objects.org/2014/

FORMAT

Our full-day workshop accepted submissions in the following three categories:

(i) position papers and posters (2 pages) focusing on novel concepts or works in progress, (ii) demo submissions (2 pages) and (iii) full papers (4-6 pages) covering a finished piece of novel research.

Our goal was to attract high-quality submissions from several research disciplines to encourage and shape the discussion, thus, advancing the research of interacting with smart objects. To stimulate discussion between the workshop participants we conducted a poster and demo session to spark further in-depth discussions on selected topics. We also collected topics during the workshop whereby we focused on combining complementary topics. As in previous workshops, this strategy lead to a lively and productive discussion during the remainder of the conference. We also summarized the outcome and published it on the workshops website in addition to the joint CEUR proceedings. This publication strategy attracted higher quality submissions, and increased the exposure of the workshop before and after the event.

ORGANIZERS AND PROGRAM COMMITTEE

Most of the organizers were already members of the first three workshops on interacting with smart objects, held in conjunction with IUI 2011 [2], 2013 [6] and 2014 [7].

Dirk Schnelle-Walka leads the "Talk&Touch" group at the Telecooperation Lab at TU Darmstadt. His main research interest is on multimodal interaction in smart spaces.
Jochen Huber is an SUTD-MIT Postdoctoral Fellow at the MIT Media Lab, focusing oninteraction design for smart mobile projections and wearable technology.
Tobias Grosse-Puppendahl is a PhD candidate at Fraunhofer IGD in Darmstadt. His research focuses on new ways of perceiving the environment with unobtrusive modalities like capacitive sensing.
Stefan Radomski is a PhD candidate at the Telecooperation Lab at TU Darmstadt. His main research interest is about multimodal dialog managment in pervasive environments.
Oliver Brdiczka is the area manager of Contextual Intelligence at Palo Alto Research Center (PARC). His group focuses on constructing models for human activity and intent from various sensorsranging from PC desktop events to physical activity sensorsby employing machine learning methods.
Kris Luyten is associate professor at the Expertise Centre for Digital Media - iMinds, Hasselt University. His research focuses on engineering interactive systems, ubicomp, multi-touch interfaces and HCI in general.
Max Mühlhäuser is full professor and heads the Telecooperation Lab at TU Darmstadt. He has over 300 publications on ubicomp, HCI, IUI, e-learning and multimedia.

The list of program committee members is as follows:

Bo Begole (Samsung, USA), **Marco Blumendorf** (DAI Laboratory, Germany), **Aba-Sah Dadzie** (University of Birmingham, United Kingdom), **Fahim Kawsar** (Bell Labs, Belgium), **Alexander Kröner** (Technische Hochschule Nürnberg, Germany), **Germán Montoro** (UAM, Spain), **Patrick Reignier** (Inria, France), **Boris de Ruyter** (Philips, Netherlands), **Geert Vanderhulst** (Alcatel-Lucent Bell Laboratories, Belgium) and **Raphael Wimmer** (Universität Regensburg, Germany).

PC members helped the organizers to publicize the event in more scientific communities and allow for a competent peer-review process. All submissions were peer-reviewed by at least two reviewers.

REFERENCES

1. Filipponi, L., Vitaletti, A., Landi, G., Memeo, V., Laura, G., and Pucci, P. Smart city: An event driven architecture for monitoring public spaces with heterogeneous sensors. In *Sensor Technologies and Applications (SENSORCOMM), 2010 Fourth International Conference on*, IEEE (2010), 281–286.
2. Hartmann, M., Schreiber, D., Luyten, K., Brdiczka, O., and Mühlhäuser, M. Workshop on interacting with smart objects. In *Proceedings of the 16th international conference on Intelligent user interfaces*, ACM (2011), 481–482.
3. Kortuem, G., Kawsar, F., Fitton, D., and Sundramoorthy, V. Smart objects as building blocks for the internet of things. *Internet Computing, IEEE 14*, 1 (2010), 44–51.
4. Molyneaux, D., and Gellersen, H. Projected interfaces: enabling serendipitous interaction with smart tangible objects. In *Proceedings of the 3rd International Conference on Tangible and Embedded Interaction*, ACM (2009), 385–392.
5. Molyneaux, D., Izadi, S., Kim, D., Hilliges, O., Hodges, S., Cao, X., Butler, A., and Gellersen, H. Interactive environment-aware handheld projectors for pervasive computing spaces. In *Pervasive Computing*. Springer, 2012, 197–215.
6. Schnelle-Walka, D., Huber, J., Lissermann, R., Brdiczka, O., Luyten, K., and Mühlhäuser, M. SmartObjects: Second IUI Workshop on Interacting with Smart Objects. In *Proceedings of the 2013 ACM international conference on Intelligent User Interfaces*, ACM (Santa Monica, CA, USA, Mar. 2013).
7. Schnelle-Walka, D., Huber, J., Radomski, S., Brdiczka, O., Luyten, K., and Mühlhäuser, M. Smartobjects: third workshop on interacting with smart objects. In *Proceedings of the companion publication of the 19th international conference on Intelligent User Interfaces*, ACM (2014), 45–46.
8. Shepard, M. *Sentient City: Ubiquitous Computing, Architecture, and the Future of Urban Space*. The MIT Press, 2011.

IUI-TextVis 2015
Fourth Workshop on Interactive Visual Text Analytics

Jaegul Choo
Georgia Institute of Technology
jaegul.choo@cc.gatech.edu

Christopher Collins
University of Ontario Institute of Technology
christopher.collins@uoit.ca

Wenwen Dou
University of North Carolina at Charlotte
wdou1@uncc.edu

Alex Endert
Georgia Institute of Technology
endert@gatech.edu

ABSTRACT
Analyzing text documents has been a key research topic in many areas. Countless approaches has been proposed to tackle this problem, and they are largely categorized into fully automated approaches (via statistical techniques) or human-involved exploratory ones (via interactive visualization). The primary purpose of this workshop is to bring together researchers from both sides and provide them with opportunities to discuss ways to harmonize the power of these two complementary approaches. The combination will allow us to push the boundary of text analytics. The detailed workshop schedule, proceedings, and agenda will be available at `http://www.textvis.org`.

Author Keywords
text analysis; visual text analytics; heterogeneous text; exploratory text mining; interactive visual text mining

ACM Classification Keywords
H.1.2 Information Systems: Models and Principles—Human factors

MAIN OBJECTIVES
In the big data era we are entering, analyzing free-text documents is one of the biggest challenges. A myriad of automated approaches from machine learning, data mining, information retrieval, and natural language processing have been proposed so far, while the research fields such as human-computer interaction, information visualization, and visual analytics have also been developing their own interactive methods and systems.

IUI 2015, March 29–April 1, 2015, Atlanta, GA, USA.
ACM 978-1-4503-3306-1/15/03.
http://dx.doi.org/10.1145/2678025.2716270

The primary goal of the workshop[1] is to bridge the gap by bringing together researchers from both sides, which allows us to push the boundary of text analytics. The workshop should provide an opportunity to discuss and explore ways to harmonize the power of automated techniques and the exploratory nature of interactive visualization. Built on the theme of the previous workshops successfully held in 2011-2013 in conjunction with IEEE VIS, this workshop at ACM IUI'15 will foster ideas from a multi-disciplinary community of researchers to address the topics outlined below.

Specifically, the workshop will investigate the following challenges and discuss promising directions in text analytics.

Heterogeneous and ubiquitous text analytics. In many cases, text data are associated with other data types, such as authors, years, and locations. The workshop will collect various use cases about heterogeneous data and ubiquitous text analytics. From the use cases, one will be able to better understand the requirements of heterogeneous textual data analysis from a task-driven perspective. Although there is some previous work on visual analysis of heterogeneous textual data, there is not a clear understanding of the typical tasks that people would like to achieve in analyzing heterogeneous textual data.

Adaptive and intelligent analytics. The IUI conference offers a unique opportunity to consider how advanced machine learning and artifical intelligence techniques can be leveraged to improve visual text analytics. For example, how can an intelligent analytics interface suggest appropriate starting points for an investigation of a large document collection? Suggested views could be based on models of user knowledge and automated analysis of the dataset and contextual cues. Moving into the realm of IUI for visual text analytics we envision systems in which the interface is responsive to data and user characteristics.

Task-driven text analytics. How will different tasks influence the design and development of both text analytics and visualization technologies? The workshop will leverage the power of the crowd at the workshop to examine a number of

[1] `http://www.textvis.org`

use cases and draft a taxonomy that characterizes the design dimensions of the space and can also be used to guide the future design and development. Second, based on the use cases, the workshop will examine how to best leverage state-of-the-art text analytics and traditional data mining techniques in conjunction with novel interactive visual analytics to address the challenges manifested by the collected use cases.

Interactive visual text mining techniques. Most of the automated text mining and natural language processing algorithms cannot fully understand the semantics of textual data. The workshop will address how to improve them via human-in-the-loop interactive visualization techniques.

Real-time streaming text visual analytics. Nowadays, a lot of textual data from social media such as twitter has real-time aspects. The workshop will present the studies addressing these aspects through real-time text visual analytics systems and associated techniques.

Other than the above-mentioned topics, the workshop will broadly cover other related directions that can advance the state-of-the-art text analytics.

TOPICS OF INTEREST

The topics of interest for the workshop include (but are not limited to) the following:

- User-adaptive approaches to visual text analytics
- Coupling of machine learning- or artificial intelligence-based systems with visualization for text analytics
- Visualization to improve automated algorithms and models for text data
- Coordinated visualizations of textual and non-textual data
- Visual metaphors for textual data or ubiquitous text analytics
- Perception and cognition in visual text analytics
- Systems, languages, and architectures for visual textual analytics
- Collaborative analysis of textual and linked data
- Real-time visualization of streaming textual data
- Visual opinion analysis from textual data
- Visual event identification and prediction from textual data
- Uncertainty in interactive visual textual analytics
- Industry-specific applications of visual analysis of textual data, e.g., retail, healthcare, government, etc.
- Studies and evaluation of textual data visualization techniques, systems, metrics, and bench-marks
- Standardized datasets and tasks for visual text analytics

ORGANIZERS

The organizers and their qualifications are as follows:

Jaegul Choo

Dr. Jaegul Choo is a research scientist in the School of Computational Science and Engineering at Georgia Institute of Technology. He received a Ph.D in computational science ang engineering from Georgia Institute of Technology in 2013. He is broadly interested in integrating data mining techniques with visual analytics. He primarily focuses on dimension reduction and clustering techniques, which play essential roles in visualizing and interacting with large-scale high-dimensional data. Recently, he has mainly worked on text visual analytics research including an interactive topic modeling visual analytics system based on nonnegative matrix factorization published in IEEE Transactions on Visualization and Computer Graphics in 2013. He has published in SDM, WSDM, WWW, DMKD, VAST, IEEE TVCG, IEEE CG&A, etc. and has served as a program committee in various conferences and workshops including VDA, SDM, AISTATS.

Christopher Collins

Dr. Christopher Collins, Canada Research Chair in Linguistic Information Visualization, is an Assistant Professor of Computer Science at the University of Ontario Institute of Technology (UOIT). His research focus is interdisciplinary, combining information visualization and human-computer interaction with natural language processing to address the challenges of information management and the problems of information overload. His visual text analytics research has a focus on designing analytic interfaces for touch and gesture modalities. His publications have appeared in IEEE TVCG, IEEE VIS, EuroVis, ACM ITS, and other venues. Collins received his PhD in Computer Science from the University of Toronto in 2010. He collaborates with several universities, IBMs TJ Watson Research Laboratory, and a number of smaller software firms. He is a member of the IEEE Visualization and Graphics Technical Committee Executive.

Wenwen Dou

Dr. Wenwen Dou is a research assistant professor in the department of computer scientist at UNC Charlotte. Her research interests include Visual Analytics, Text Mining, and Human Computer Interaction. In particular, her research lies at the intersection of interactive visualization and text mining, with the specific area referred to as Visual Text Analytics. She has conducted extensive research on interactive visual analysis of large text corpora, in particular with focus on temporal analysis and event extraction. Dou has worked with various analytics domains in reducing information overload and providing interactive visual means to analyzing unstructured information. She has experience in turning cutting-edge research into technologies that have broad societal impacts, partially demonstrated by supports from both academic and industry partners, including PNNL, US Army Research Office, US Special Operations Command, NSF, US Army Engineering Research and Development Center, and Lowes company Inc.

Alex Endert

Dr. Alex Endert is an assistant professor in the School of Interactive Computing at Georgia Tech. His interests are primarily on visual data exploration, human-computer interaction, and information visualization. His research centers around exploring novel user interaction techniques for visual analytic systems to attempt to couple cognitive and computational processes for sensemaking. He is an active member of, and contributor to, premier venues for human-computer interaction and information visualization (ACM CHI, IEEE VIS, IEEE TVCG, IEEE CG&A). He received his Ph.D. in Computer Science at Virginia Tech in 2012, where he worked with Dr. Chris North. In 2013, his work on Semantic Interaction was awarded the IEEE VGTC VPG Pioneers Group Doctoral Dissertation Award, and the Virginia Tech Computer Science Best Dissertation Award.

PROGRAM COMMITTEE

The program committee of the workshop will include (not all of them are confirmed at the time of this proposal submission):

- Jason Chuang, University of Washington
- Nick Cramer, Pacific Northwest National Laboratory
- Weiwei Cui, Microsoft Research Asia
- Eser Kandogan, IBM Almaden Research Center
- Zhicheng Liu, Adobe Research
- Naren Ramakrishnan, Virginia Tech
- Christian Rohrdantz University of Konstanz
- John Stasko, Georgia Insitute of Technology

WORKSHOP PROGRAM

The workshop will be held for a full day on 2015/3/29. It will mainly have four sessions: two in the morning and the other two in the afternoon. We plan to organize them as a balanced mixture of one or two keynote talks, oral presentations of accepted papers, poster presentations, and panel discussions. Full details can be found at `http://www.textvis.org`.

ACKNOWLEDGMENTS

The organizers would like to thank all the authors for contributing to the workshop and all the members of the program committee for establishing the scientific quality of the workshop.

Privacy, Personalization, and Intelligent User Interfaces

Bart P. Knijnenburg
Department of Informatics
University of California, Irvine
bart.k@uci.edu

Shlomo Berkovsky
ICT Centre
CSIRO, Australia
shlomo.berkovsky@csiro.au

Pamela Wisniewski
College of Information Sciences and Technology
Pennsylvania State University
pam@pamspam.com

Eran Toch
Faculty of Engineering
Tel Aviv University
erant@post.tau.ac.il

Arik Friedman
Network Research Group
NICTA, Australia
arik.friedman@nicta.com.au

Norman Sadeh
School of Computer Science
Carnegie Mellon University
sadeh@cs.cmu.edu

ABSTRACT
Privacy can be a barrier to the adoption and growth of intelligent user interfaces (IUIs). This workshop considers architectural, algorithmic, and interactive solutions that can support privacy-preserving IUIs, focusing specifically on integrating existing solutions. Additionally, the workshop explores how users of information systems (not just intelligent systems) interact with privacy-setting interfaces and make decisions about privacy. Such behavioral analyses can be used to build intelligent privacy-setting user interfaces that simplify privacy decisions through personalized privacy recommendations. The workshop provides an outlook on the design, implementation, and evaluation of such intelligent user interfaces for privacy decision support.

Author Keywords
Privacy; personalization; intelligent user interfaces.

ACM Classification Keywords
H.5.2. Information Interfaces and Presentation (e.g. HCI): User Interfaces. I.2.1. Artificial Intelligence: Applications and Expert Systems.

INTRODUCTION
Privacy can be a potential barrier to the growth of e-commerce, social networks, location sharing services, and other ubiquitous computing systems. These concerns are arguably even more prominent in *intelligent systems*, which often use personal information or behavioral tracking to provide personalized user experiences [35]. As we move towards ubiquitous computing, adopt wearable devices, and let personalized algorithms make important decisions that affect our physical, social and financial well being, these issues will only increase in their relevance. This workshop explores the topics of privacy, personalization, and intelligent user interfaces. The goal of the workshop is twofold:

1. To investigate the privacy aspects of user-adaptive systems and intelligent user interfaces (i.e. "the privacy *of* intelligent systems").
2. To explore the idea of tailoring privacy (and/or the user interfaces for managing privacy) to the preferences of the user (i.e. "personalized privacy decision support *using* intelligent user interfaces").

To aid the positioning of these two topics within the fields of privacy, usability and intelligent user interfaces, this workshop description provides an overview of these topics and cites relevant existing work. More information about the workshop can be found at http://bit.ly/ppiui.

THE PRIVACY OF INTELLIGENT USER INTERFACES
Privacy can play a limiting role in users' adoption of intelligent systems [56]. Research has shown that personalization induces privacy concerns and subsequently limits the adoption of ubiquitous commerce services [51], personalized advertising [5], and recommender systems [8, 31, 36]. These findings have lead the FTC to highlight what Awad and Krishnan call the "personalization-privacy paradox" [5]: despite the benefits of personalization, users may not agree with the data collection required to make personalization work [22].

This is not to say that people outright reject all intelligent systems; indeed, they are willing to give up privacy for personalization [23, 44], as long as doing so gives them benefits [46], such as content relevance, time savings, more fluent interaction, enjoyment and novelty [24, 26]. Thus, researchers of Intelligent User Interfaces need to be aware of this delicate balance between privacy and intelligence [14, 63, 64].

One main focus of this workshop will be the *technical* means to maintaining this balance between privacy and personalization. For example, in the field of recommender systems there are both architectural and algorithmic solutions that anonymize the personalization process and/or restrict third-party access to personal information. On the architectural side, distributed architectures with client-side

IUI'15, Mar 29 - Apr 01, 2015, Atlanta, GA, USA
ACM 978-1-4503-3306-1/15/03.
http://dx.doi.org/10.1145/2678025.2716271

data storage limit the amount of information accessible by the provider of intelligent systems [9, 36, 57], and information access management protocols prevent unauthorized data access [16, 48]. On the algorithmic side, pseudonyms sever the link between a user's data and identity without giving up the ability to personalize interactions [37]; homomorphic encryption allows personalization algorithms to operate on encrypted data [12, 45]; differential privacy reduces an attacker's ability to infer personal information from the adaptive behavior of the system; and obfuscation of the collected information gives users the ability to deny the veracity of the information (plausible deniability) [10, 15].

Although architectural and algorithmic solutions to privacy problems are abound, these solutions typically address but a single specific privacy problem. A particular focus of the workshop will therefore be the challenge of integrating the diverse (and often conflicting) solutions from the architectural and algorithmic realms [20] to support "privacy-preserving intelligent user interfaces."

STUDYING USERS' PRIVACY BEHAVIORS

Although most users are willing to give up privacy for personalization [23, 44], the optimal balance between these two conflicting desires varies by user and even per situation [14, 63]. This is true even beyond intelligent systems; the large majority of Internet users are willing to trade off the anticipated benefits with the risks of disclosure (a decision process that has been dubbed *privacy calculus* [38]), but the balance between benefits and risks is highly dependent on the user and on the context [18, 27, 43].

Until recently, privacy has mainly been conceptualized as a rational (economic) decision [19, 21, 25, 47], but more recent work demonstrates that users' privacy-related behaviors are often erratic, if not irrational [2]. Work that describes users' actual privacy behaviors (cf. [3, 11, 30, 32, 34]) and integrates it with the traditional rational conceptualization (cf. [4, 7, 59]) can assist in further enhancing the adoption of information systems (intelligent and otherwise). Due to this heterogeneity of users' preference for privacy, many systems give users control over the amount of information they disclose [13, 65].

Another important focus of the workshop will therefore be to investigate how users of information systems (not just personalized systems) *behave* in regards to interacting with privacy-setting interfaces and making decisions about their privacy (cf. [33, 39, 60, 61]).

PERSONALIZED PRIVACY DECISION SUPPORT

As privacy decisions proliferate in our daily lives, privacy scholars increasingly realize that putting the burden of control on the user is not an effective solution [11, 42, 53]. For instance, research has found that people have great trouble effectively managing their privacy on social networks [40, 41], and that many users avoid managing their privacy at all [17].

As such, privacy researchers have moved towards "soft paternalistic" solutions to privacy, i.e. privacy *nudges* [1, 6, 58]. Carefully designed nudges can push users in the direction of more or less privacy, without completely removing their opportunity for manual control. But such nudges ignore the inherent population variability of privacy preferences because they assume that the same optimal cost-benefit trade-off holds across every user, piece of information, and situation. As this is obviously not the case, generalized nudges run the risk of reducing user autonomy [52, 53].

One proposed solution, then, is to *personalize* privacy decision support by means of IUIs [28]. For example, the field of location-sharing services has seen a number of papers proposing a prediction-based approach to supporting users in managing their privacy settings [50, 54, 62], and similar work has been conducted on privacy settings for social networking services [49, 55]. Early evaluations of IUIs that simplify privacy decision through privacy recommendations have been positive [29], and the idea has already found its way into commercial implementations, such as Facebook's "privacy dinosaur." Such interface agents can be enhanced to be *intelligent* user interfaces that provide personalized privacy support. This workshop will also examine the design and evaluation of such IUIs.

CONCLUSION

As information systems increasingly collect data for personalization purposes, privacy will become one of the most pertinent things to study in the field of intelligent user interfaces. This workshop explores the dichotomous nature of the link between privacy and intelligent user interfaces: On the one hand, intelligent user interfaces use personal data, creating privacy implications associated with such data collection practices. On the other hand, intelligent user interfaces can provide users with personalized privacy-setting interfaces that can provide intelligent decision support to preserve their privacy. With this workshop description we provide a useful vantage point for this upcoming research paradigm. We believe that the workshop itself can contribute to the reconciliation of privacy, personalization, and intelligent user interfaces, and thereby provide important contributions to the state-of-the-art.

REFERENCES

1. Acquisti, A. 2009. Nudging Privacy: The Behavioral Economics of Personal Information. *IEEE Security and Privacy*. 7, (Nov. 2009), 82–85. DOI= http://dx.doi.org/10.1109/MSP.2009.163.
2. Acquisti, A. and Grossklags, J. 2005. Privacy and Rationality in Individual Decision Making. *IEEE Security & Privacy*. 3, 1 (2005), 26–33. DOI= http://dx.doi.org/10.1109/MSP.2005.22.
3. Adjerid, I., Acquisti, A., Brandimarte, L. and Loewenstein, G. 2013. Sleights of Privacy: Framing, Disclosures, and the Limits of Transparency. *Proceedings of the Ninth Symposium on Usable Privacy and Security* (New York, NY, USA, 2013), 9:1–9:11. DOI= http://dx.doi.org/10.1145/2501604.2501613.
4. Angst, C.M. and Agarwal, R. 2009. Adoption of electronic health records in the presence of privacy concerns: the elaboration

likelihood model and individual persuasion. *MIS Q.* 33, 2 (Jun. 2009), 339–370.

5. Awad, N.F. and Krishnan, M.S. 2006. The Personalization Privacy Paradox: An Empirical Evaluation of Information Transparency and the Willingness to be Profiled Online for Personalization. *MIS Quarterly*. 30, 1 (Mar. 2006), 13–28.
6. Balebako, R., Leon, P.G., Mugan, J., Acquisti, A., Cranor, L.F. and Sadeh, N. 2011. Nudging users towards privacy on mobile devices. *CHI 2011 workshop on Persuasion, Influence, Nudge and Coercion Through Mobile Devices* (Vancouver, Canada, 2011), 23–26.
7. Bansal, G., Zahedi, F. and Gefen, D. 2008. The Moderating Influence of Privacy Concern on the Efficacy of Privacy Assurance Mechanisms for Building Trust: A Multiple-Context Investigation. *ICIS 2008 Proceedings* (Paris, France, 2008).
8. Berkovsky, S., Borisov, N., Eytani, Y., Kuflik, T. and Ricci, F. 2007. Examining Users' Attitude towards Privacy Preserving Collaborative Filtering. (2007).
9. Berkovsky, S., Eytani, Y., Kuflik, T. and Ricci, F. 2007. Enhancing privacy and preserving accuracy of a distributed collaborative filtering. *Proceedings of the 2007 ACM conference on Recommender systems* (Minneapolis, MN, 2007), 9–16. DOI= http://dx.doi.org/10.1145/1297231.1297234.
10. Berkovsky, S., Eytani, Y., Kuflik, T. and Ricci, F. 2006. Hierarchical Neighborhood Topology for Privacy Enhanced Collaborative Filtering. *Proceedings of PEP06, CHI 2006 Workshop on Privacy-Enhanced Personalization* (Montreal, Canada, 2006), 6–13.
11. Brandimarte, L., Acquisti, A. and Loewenstein, G. 2013. Misplaced Confidences: Privacy and the Control Paradox. *Social Psychological and Personality Science*. 4, 3 (2013), 340–347. DOI= http://dx.doi.org/10.1177/1948550612455931.
12. Canny, J. 2002. Collaborative Filtering with Privacy. *Proceedings of the 2002 IEEE Symposium on Security and Privacy* (Oakland, CA, May 2002), 45–57. DOI= http://dx.doi.org/10.1109/SECPRI.2002.1004361.
13. Cavusoglu, H., Phan, T. and Cavusoglu, H. 2013. Privacy Controls and Content Sharing Patterns of Online Social Network Users: A Natural Experiment. *ICIS 2013 Proceedings* (Milan, Italy, 2013).
14. Chellappa, R.K. and Sin, R. 2005. Personalization versus Privacy: An Empirical Examination of the Online Consumer's Dilemma. *Information Technology and Management*. 6, 2-3 (2005), 181–202. DOI= http://dx.doi.org/10.1007/s10799-005-5879-y.
15. Chow, R., Jin, H., Knijnenburg, B.P. and Saldamli, G. 2013. *Differential Data Analysis for Recommender Systems*. Technical Report #1310.0894.
16. Cissée, R. and Albayrak, S. 2007. An Agent-based Approach for Privacy-preserving Recommender Systems. *Proceedings of the 6th International Joint Conference on Autonomous Agents and Multiagent Systems* (New York, NY, USA, 2007), 182:1–182:8. DOI= http://dx.doi.org/10.1145/1329125.1329345.
17. Compañó, R. and Lusoli, W. 2010. The Policy Maker's Anguish: Regulating Personal Data Behavior Between Paradoxes and Dilemmas. *Economics of Information Security and Privacy*. T. Moore, D. Pym, and C. Ioannidis, eds. Springer US. 169–185.
18. Culnan, M.J. 1993. "How Did They Get My Name?": An Exploratory Investigation of Consumer Attitudes toward Secondary Information Use. *MIS Quarterly*. 17, 3 (1993), 341–363. DOI= http://dx.doi.org/10.2307/249775.
19. Danezis, G., Lewis, S. and Anderson, R. 2005. How Much is Location Privacy Worth? *Fourth Workshop on the Economics of Information Security* (Cambridge, MA, 2005).
20. Friedman, A., Knijnenburg, B.P., Vanhecke, K., Martens, L. and Berkovsky, S. 2015. Privacy Aspects of Recommender Systems. *Recommender Systems Handbook, 2nd edition*.
21. Friedman, A. and Wathieu, L. 2005. An Empirical Approach to Understanding Privacy Valuation. *Fourth Workshop on the Economics of Information Security (WEIS05)* (Cambridge, MA, 2005).
22. FTC 2010. *Protecting Consumer Privacy in an Era of Rapid Change: A Proposed Framework for Businesses and Policymakers*. Federal Trade Commission.
23. Hann, I.-H., Hui, K.-L., Lee, S.-Y. and Png, I. 2007. Overcoming Online Information Privacy Concerns: An Information-Processing Theory Approach. *Journal of Management Information Systems*. 24, 2 (Oct. 2007), 13–42. DOI= http://dx.doi.org/10.2753/MIS0742-1222240202.
24. Ho, S.Y. and Tam, K. 2006. Understanding the Impact of Web Personalization on User Information Processing and Decision Outcomes. *Management Information Systems Quarterly*. 30, 4 (Dec. 2006).
25. Hui, K.-L. and Png, I.P.L. 2006. The Economics of Privacy. *Handbook of Information Systems and Economics*. T. Hendershott, ed. Elsevier. Ch. 9.
26. Hui, K.-L., Tan, B.C.Y. and Goh, C.-Y. 2006. Online information disclosure: Motivators and measurements. *ACM Transactions on Internet Technology*. 6, 4 (Nov. 2006), 415–441. DOI= http://dx.doi.org/10.1145/1183463.1183467.
27. John, L.K., Acquisti, A. and Loewenstein, G. 2011. Strangers on a Plane: Context-Dependent Willingness to Divulge Sensitive Information. *Journal of consumer research*. 37, 5 (Feb. 2011), 858–873. DOI= http://dx.doi.org/10.1086/656423.
28. Knijnenburg, B.P. 2013. Simplifying Privacy Decisions: Towards Interactive and Adaptive Solutions. *Proceedings of the Recsys 2013 Workshop on Human Decision Making in Recommender Systems (Decisions@ RecSys'13)* (Hong Kong, China, 2013), 40–41.
29. Knijnenburg, B.P. and Jin, H. 2013. The Persuasive Effect of Privacy Recommendations. *Twelfth Annual Workshop on HCI Research in MIS* (Milan, Italy, 2013).
30. Knijnenburg, B.P. and Kobsa, A. 2014. Increasing Sharing Tendency Without Reducing Satisfaction: Finding the Best Privacy-Settings User Interface for Social Networks. *ICIS 2014 Proceedings* (Auckland, New Zealand, 2014).
31. Knijnenburg, B.P. and Kobsa, A. 2013. Making Decisions about Privacy: Information Disclosure in Context-Aware Recommender Systems. *ACM Transactions on Interactive Intelligent Systems*. 3, 3 (2013), 20:1–20:23. DOI= http://dx.doi.org/10.1145/2499670.
32. Knijnenburg, B.P., Kobsa, A. and Jin, H. 2013. Counteracting the Negative Effect of Form Auto-completion on the Privacy Calculus. *ICIS 2013 Proceedings* (Milan, Italy, 2013).
33. Knijnenburg, B.P., Kobsa, A. and Jin, H. 2013. Dimensionality of information disclosure behavior. *International Journal of Human-Computer Studies*. 71, 12 (2013), 1144–1162. DOI= http://dx.doi.org/10.1016/j.ijhcs.2013.06.003.
34. Knijnenburg, B.P., Kobsa, A. and Jin, H. 2013. Preference-based location sharing: are more privacy options really better? *Proceedings of the SIGCHI Conference on Human Factors in Computing Systems* (Paris, France, 2013), 2667–2676. DOI= http://dx.doi.org/10.1145/2470654.2481369.
35. Kobsa, A. 2001. Tailoring Privacy to Users' Needs (Invited Keynote). *User Modeling 2001*. M. Bauer, P.J. Gmytrasiewicz, and J. Vassileva, eds. Springer Verlag. 303–313.
36. Kobsa, A., Knijnenburg, B.P. and Livshits, B. 2014. Let's Do It at My Place Instead?: Attitudinal and Behavioral Study of Privacy in Client-side Personalization. *Proceedings of the SIGCHI*

Conference on Human Factors in Computing Systems (Toronto, Canada, 2014), 81–90. DOI= http://dx.doi.org/10.1145/2556288.2557102.

37. Kobsa, A. and Schreck, J. 2003. Privacy through pseudonymity in user-adaptive systems. *ACM Transactions on Internet Technology*. 3, (May 2003), 149–183. DOI= http://dx.doi.org/10.1145/767193.767196.
38. Laufer, R.S. and Wolfe, M. 1977. Privacy as a Concept and a Social Issue: A Multidimensional Developmental Theory. *Journal of Social Issues*. 33, 3 (1977), 22–42. DOI= http://dx.doi.org/10.1111/j.1540-4560.1977.tb01880.x.
39. Lipford, H.R., Wisniewski, P.J., Lampe, C., Kisselburgh, L. and Caine, K. 2012. Reconciling privacy with social media. *Proceedings of the ACM 2012 conference on Computer Supported Cooperative Work Companion* (New York, NY, USA, 2012), 19–20. DOI= http://dx.doi.org/10.1145/2141512.2141523.
40. Liu, Y., Gummadi, K.P., Krishnamurthy, B. and Mislove, A. 2011. Analyzing facebook privacy settings: user expectations vs. reality. *Proc. SIGCOMM 2011* (New York, NY, USA, 2011), 61–70. DOI= http://dx.doi.org/10.1145/2068816.2068823.
41. Madejski, M., Johnson, M. and Bellovin, S.M. 2012. A study of privacy settings errors in an online social network. *2012 IEEE International Conference on Pervasive Computing and Communications Workshops (PERCOM Workshops)* (Lugano, Switzerland, 2012), 340–345. DOI= http://dx.doi.org/10.1109/PerComW.2012.6197507.
42. Nissenbaum, H. 2011. A Contextual Approach to Privacy Online. *Daedalus*. 140, 4 (Oct. 2011), 32–48. DOI= http://dx.doi.org/10.1162/DAED_a_00113.
43. Nissenbaum, H. 2009. *Privacy in context: Technology, policy, and the integrity of social life*. Stanford University Press.
44. Olivero, N. and Lunt, P. 2004. Privacy versus willingness to disclose in e-commerce exchanges: The effect of risk awareness on the relative role of trust and control. *Journal of Economic Psychology*. 25, 2 (2004), 243–262. DOI= http://dx.doi.org/10.1016/S0167-4870(02)00172-1.
45. Paillier, P. 1999. Public-Key Cryptosystems Based on Composite Degree Residuosity Classes. *Advances in Cryptology — EUROCRYPT '99*. J. Stern, ed. Springer Berlin Heidelberg. 223–238.
46. Phelps, J., Nowak, G. and Ferrell, E. 2000. Privacy Concerns and Consumer Willingness to Provide Personal Information. *Journal of Public Policy & Marketing*. 19, 1 (2000), 27–41.
47. Posner, R.A. 1981. The Economics of Privacy. *The American Economic Review*. 71, 2 (May 1981), 405–409.
48. Put, A., Dacosta, I., Milutinovic, M., De Decker, B., Seys, S., Boukayoua, F., Naessens, V., Vanhecke, K., De Pessemier, T. and Martens, L. 2014. inShopnito: An Advanced yet Privacy-Friendly Mobile Shopping Application. *Proceedings of 2014 IEEE World Congress on Services* (Anchorage, Alaska, 2014).
49. Ravichandran, R., Benisch, M., Kelley, P. and Sadeh, N. 2009. Capturing Social Networking Privacy Preferences: *Privacy Enhancing Technologies*. I. Goldberg and M. Atallah, eds. Springer Berlin / Heidelberg. 1–18.
50. Sadeh, N., Hong, J., Cranor, L., Fette, I., Kelley, P., Prabaker, M. and Rao, J. 2009. Understanding and capturing people's privacy policies in a mobile social networking application. *Personal and Ubiquitous Computing*. 13, 6 (2009), 401–412. DOI= http://dx.doi.org/10.1007/s00779-008-0214-3.
51. Sheng, H., Nah, F.F.-H. and Siau, K. 2008. An Experimental Study on Ubiquitous commerce Adoption: Impact of Personalization and Privacy Concerns. *Journal of the Association for Information Systems*. 9, 6 (Jun. 2008).
52. Smith, N.C., Goldstein, D.G. and Johnson, E.J. 2013. Choice Without Awareness: Ethical and Policy Implications of Defaults. *Journal of Public Policy & Marketing*. 32, 2 (Fall 2013), 159–172. DOI= http://dx.doi.org/10.1509/jppm.10.114.
53. Solove, D.J. 2013. Privacy Self-Management and the Consent Dilemma. *Harvard Law Review*. 126, (2013), 1880–1903.
54. Toch, E., Cranshaw, J., Drielsma, P.H., Tsai, J.Y., Kelley, P.G., Springfield, J., Cranor, L., Hong, J. and Sadeh, N. 2010. Empirical models of privacy in location sharing. *Proc. of the 12th ACM intl. conference on Ubiquitous computing* (Copenhagen, Denmark, 2010), 129–138. DOI= http://dx.doi.org/10.1145/1864349.1864364.
55. Toch, E., Sadeh, N.M. and Hong, J. 2010. Generating default privacy policies for online social networks. *Ext. Abstracts CHI 2010* (Atlanta, Georgia, USA, 2010), 4243–4248. DOI= http://dx.doi.org/10.1145/1753846.1754133.
56. Toch, E., Wang, Y. and Cranor, L. 2012. Personalization and privacy: a survey of privacy risks and remedies in personalization-based systems. *User Modeling and User-Adapted Interaction*. 22, 1 (2012), 203–220. DOI= http://dx.doi.org/10.1007/s11257-011-9110-z.
57. Vallet, D., Friedman, A. and Berkovsky, S. 2014. Matrix Factorization without User Data Retention. *Advances in Knowledge Discovery and Data Mining*. V.S. Tseng, T.B. Ho, Z.-H. Zhou, A.L.P. Chen, and H.-Y. Kao, eds. Springer International Publishing. 569–580.
58. Wang, Y., Leon, P.G., Acquisti, A., Cranor, L.F., Forget, A. and Sadeh, N. 2014. A Field Trial of Privacy Nudges for Facebook. *Proceedings of the 32nd Annual ACM Conference on Human Factors in Computing Systems* (Toronto, Canada, 2014), 2367–2376. DOI= http://dx.doi.org/10.1145/2556288.2557413.
59. Wilson, D. and Valacich, J. 2012. Unpacking the Privacy Paradox: Irrational Decision-Making within the Privacy Calculus. *Proceedings of the International Conference on Information Systems* (Orlando, FL, Dec. 2012).
60. Wisniewski, P., Islam, A.K.M.N., Knijnenburg, B.P. and Patil, S. 2015. Give Social Network Users the Privacy They Want. *Proceedings of the 18th ACM Conference on Computer-Supported Collaborative Work and Social Computing* (Vancouver, Canada, 2015).
61. Wisniewski, P., Lipford, H. and Wilson, D. 2012. Fighting for my space: coping mechanisms for SNS boundary regulation. *Proceedings of the SIGCHI Conference on Human Factors in Computing Systems* (New York, NY, USA, 2012), 609–618. DOI= http://dx.doi.org/10.1145/2207676.2207761.
62. Xie, J., Knijnenburg, B.P. and Jin, H. 2014. Location Sharing Privacy Preference: Analysis and Personalized Recommendation. *Proceedings of the 19th International Conference on Intelligent User Interfaces* (Haifa, Israel, 2014), 189–198. DOI= http://dx.doi.org/10.1145/2557500.2557504.
63. Xu, H., Luo, X. (Robert), Carroll, J.M. and Rosson, M.B. 2011. The personalization privacy paradox: An exploratory study of decision making process for location-aware marketing. *Decision Support Systems*. 51, 1 (Apr. 2011), 42–52. DOI= http://dx.doi.org/10.1016/j.dss.2010.11.017.
64. Xu, H., Teo, H.-H., Tan, B.C.Y. and Agarwal, R. 2009. The Role of Push-Pull Technology in Privacy Calculus: The Case of Location-Based Services. *Journal of Management Information Systems*. 26, 3 (Dec. 2009), 135–174. DOI= http://dx.doi.org/10.2753/MIS0742-1222260305.
65. Xu, H., Wang, N. and Grossklags, J. 2012. Privacy-by-ReDesign: Alleviating Privacy Concerns for Third-Party Applications. *ICIS 2012 Proceedings* (Orlando, FL, 2012).

AUTHOR INDEX

www.ingramcontent.com/pod-product-compliance
Ingram Content Group UK Ltd.
Pitfield, Milton Keynes, MK11 3LW, UK
UKHW051413290926
15471UKWH00009B/1585

9 781450 337687